CONSTITUTIONAL LAW IN THE UNITED STATES

CONSTITUTIONAL LAW IN THE UNITED STATES

A Systematic Inquiry Into the Change and Relevance of Supreme Court Decisions

Third Edition

Randall Walton Bland
Joseph V. Brogan

Austin & Winfield Publishers
Lanham · New York · Oxford

Austin & Winfield Publishers
4720 Boston Way
Lanham, Maryland 20706

12 Hid's Copse Rd.
Cumnor Hill, Oxford OX2 9JJ

Printed in the United States of America
British Library Cataloging in Publication Information Available

Library of Congress Cataloging-in-Publication Data

Bland, Randall Walton
Constitutional law in the United States: a systematic inquiry into the Change and relevance of Supreme Court Decisions/ Randall Walton Bland and Joseph V. Brogan.—3rd ed.
p. cm.
Includes bibliographical references and index.
1. Constitutional law—United States—Cases. I. Brogan, Joseph V. II. Title.
KF4549.B55 1999 342.73—dc21 98-54992 CIP

ISBN 1-57292-090-4 (cloth: alk. ppr.)
ISBN 1-57292-091-2 (pbk: alk. ppr.)

™ The paper used in this publication meets the minimum requirements of American National Standard for Information Sciences—Permanence of Paper for Printed Library Materials, ANSI Z39.48—1984

DEDICATION

Dedicated to the memory of **Edward S. Corwin** (1878-1963) of Princeton University, this century's greatest legal mind, who influenced a generation of scholars including Clinton Rossiter, J.W. Peltason, Glendon Schubert, Louis Koenig, Harold Chase, Craig Ducat, Paul Bartholomew, Richard Loss, and myself

FOREWORD TO THE FIRST EDITION

This volume is aimed at a greater basic understanding of the government of the United States. An American can never really understand his government, its underlying principles, its purposes, its organization and functioning, and its care for the individual, until he knows the Constitution and the interpretations given its provisions by the Supreme Court. The very flexibility and adaptability of the instrument is a bit awe-inspiring especially when one considers the political, social, and economic crises it has endured with relatively so few amendments. This, of course, is a compliment to the Founding Fathers.

"The American Constitution is the most wonderful ever struck off at a given time by the brain and purpose of man." This very well-known observation, by one Mr. William Gladstone, of British fame, has had more of its share of critics, but none has had the temerity to question his use of the superlative in characterizing the Constitution as the greatest document ever produced by man. This being the situation, one might be justified in assuming that our supreme law would be the heritage of every American second only to his religion. Such should be, but such is not the case. Sometimes it seems that we have forgotten the Constitution and the blessings of liberty which it was to secure for us for all time.

Our fathers studied the Constitution and did not hesitate to inculcate its principles in the youth of the land. Lincoln urged this also, as he said: "Let it be taught in the schools, in seminaries and in colleges, let it be written in primers, in spelling books, and in almanacs; let it be preached from the pulpit, proclaimed in legislative halls, and enforced in the courts of justice. Let it become the political religion of the nation."

It is always a source of real satisfaction when one's former students succeed and especially satisfying when that success comes in the academic field. One rather basks in *reflected* glory.

Accordingly, may this volume, which serves as his contribution, play a proper role in bringing Americans to an appreciative understanding of our Constitution and of our government.

Paul C. Bartholomew
University of Notre Dame

INTRODUCTION TO THE SECOND EDITION

From the outset, I intended to make this casebook truly distinctive from other constitutional law textbooks. First, those texts entitled American Constitutional Law risk the legitimate criticism that the title is in error. What does the term "American" mean? Are the authors referring to North America inclusive of Canada and Mexico? Do they mean Latin or South America? Certainly our laws do not normally apply to other countries, although the Supreme Court has certainly made exceptions to this general prohibition; see *United States v. Alvarez-Machain* (1992). I employ the term United States simply because the constitution of the United States applies only to the fifty States of the Union and to this nation's territories including, for example, Puerto Rico and certain of the Virgin Islands.

Second, constitutional law texts today are both extremely *lengthy* (except for law school, perhaps) for undergraduate and graduate levels and thus, far too *expensive* for most students. A cursory review of the prices and lengths of the leading casebooks by well-known scholars – Louis Fisher, Gerald Gunther, Lockhart, and Lawrence Tribe – strongly reaffirms this point.

Third, and finally, a number of these sources are philosophically or politically *biased* particularly those advocating judicial activism on the part of the Supreme Court. In fact, some writers stake their professional and in some cases, national reputations in the *liberal, or "politically correct," crusade for students' minds*. This textbook advocates *no* cause except for a proper appreciation for American Constitutionalism and its legitimate role in our legal system and in our daily lives. The best safeguard of our liberty is a knowledge of our individual rights *and* responsibilities.

Please, address the attention of your class to the fact that this book is divided into three major parts, quite simply, apportioned to the major courses concerning the three principle areas of constitutional law: (1) The Structure and Authority of Government in the United States (p.33); (2) The Regulation of the Economy (P.109); (3) Individual Liberty and Civil Rights under the Constitution (p.171). These parallel the types of courses offered in most undergraduate and graduate programs.

Therefore, to reiterate, this casebook is primarily intended for use in undergraduate and graduate courses in constitutional law rather than for use in law school classrooms. While there are any number of texts presently on the market, I have made every possible attempt to make this study *distinctive* and, as such, an *improvement* on those employed for classroom use in most state and private universities. The material is presented in a clear forthright and objective manner. Hopefully, it is more interpretive than many texts *without* being excessively verbose. I have concentrated *only* on cases of "good" or *existing* law with regard to the study of major decisions. References to significant, but no longer ruling, cases are discussed in the introduction to the chapters. The analyses of the presidency and of the Congress are covered in two *separate* chapters since the students are often cheated when, for the sake of brevity, the two are treated collectively in a single chapter. I have included a glossary of legal concepts and terms for the convenience of the students. A *bibliography* of relevant primary and secondary sources is also included. Finally, I have compiled an *appendix* of supplementary materials to further assist the interested student in comprehending the more troublesome areas of constitutional law, particularly the Regulation of Commerce and the Doctrine of Incorporation.

A word should be mentioned with respect to the nature and salience of the opinions selected. While all students of the Court have their preferences, those contained in this edition were chosen carefully with the goal of painting the most accurate picture of constitutional interpretation as it is *presently* structured. The opinions are the creations of the justices who fathered them. Accordingly, the variation in style, the forcefulness of the argument (or the *lack* of it), the presentation of original conceptualizations and even the turning of a unique phrase should be appreciated by student and teacher alike, Accordingly, I have taken the liberty of giving emphasis, in the form of italics, to those portions of the opinion which give the decision its philosophical thrust or which make it historically noteworthy.

In conclusion, I would like to acknowledge, with deep gratitude, the many scholars who willingly offered their valuable advice and counsel. Many thanks to those who reviewed the manuscript and offered constructive criticisms, particularly the late Paul C. Bartholomew, Professor of Government and International Studies at the University of Notre Dame, Michael C. Dillion, Professors Alfred Sullivan, Kenneth Grasso and Theodore T. Hindson at Southwest Texas State University. Also, I am extremely indebted to my original research assistants and manuscript editors, Kathleen F. Houlahan and Mark J. Gimenez whose limitless energies and whose intellectual talents resulted in a tremendous contribution to this effort. Finally, I would like to express my gratitude to those who originally typed the manuscript, particularly Janet Overly and Terri Anderegg. I must also express my appreciation for the great assistance provided by my most recent student researchers, Zain Naboulsi (head assistant), Victor Saurs, and David McLane.

Randall Walton Bland
Professor of Constitutional Law
Southwest Texas State University
August 15, 1992

INTRODUCTION TO THE THIRD EDITION

A number of changes and additions have been made to this third edition of *Constitutional Law in the United States*. The most obvious is the addition of a co-author. Additional cases have been added, about doubling the size of the text. Among the new cases, we have decided to include several which are no longer "good law," thus breaking with the practice of previous editions. Our reason is that the increasing role the Court plays in American government, coupled with declining student interest in – and understanding of – history, necessitates inclusion of several historic cases, e.g. *Plessy v. Ferguson*. The structure of the text has only been slightly modified. The number of chapters remain the same, but they are now grouped under but two divisions: "The Structures and Powers of Government" and "Civil Rights and Liberties."

As the new co-author, I would like to take this opportunity to express my appreciation to Professor Bland. I have learned much from both his wisdom and his graciousness. I would also like to thank our mutual friend, Theodore Hindson of Southwest Texas State University, for suggesting to each of us that we might profitably collaborate with the other. My appreciation is extended to La Salle University for a semester's leave and a course reduction while I worked on this and related projects. I was also aided by a number of outstanding student assistants, including Joseph Hainthaler, Lynn Zikoski, Marci Pettay, Jon Sedlak, and Melissa Volin. Most importantly, I thank my family for the strength and support I draw from them.

Joseph V. Brogan
November 29, 1998

TABLE OF CONTENTS

CHAPTER I

LAW AND AMERICAN CONSTITUTIONAL DEVELOPMENT

Literally thousands of works have been written by scholars through the centuries, from Cicero to Friedman,[1] in attempts to define the nature of law and its significance. Perhaps Jerome Frank, one of this nation's more learned jurists, provided the most concise description:

> *Law is a complete body of rules ... from time immemorial and unchangeable except to the extent that legislatures have changed the rules by statutes.* Legislatures are ... empowered ... to change the law. But the judges are not to make or change the law but to apply it. The law, pre-exists ... judicial decisions.[2]

Of course, practical considerations may lead one to disagree with Judge Frank's dictum that judges "are not to make or change the law." To the extent that judges often subject varying interpretations and applications of the law to logical analysis, that their personal policy preferences may be an important consideration, and that they decide cases thereon, judges may or may not "make" law. As we shall see, the question as to whether judges merely interpret or make law continues to be the subject of legitimate debate. In any event, Frank's concept of the law provides a reasonable basis for a discussion of its significance and its application.

With few exceptions, most reasonable men embrace the theory that organized society is predicated on the *necessity* for laws or formal rules of conduct. Under law, civilized man is given both rights and responsibilities, an equal commitment must be given to both. Any society bound to one without the other is neither a "utopia" nor one based on law. A citizen is informed by law of his relationship with government *and* with his fellow man. Without the existence and the rule of law, it would be doubtful if society could exist, for it would not be able to govern itself effectively.

Our legal system in the United States is the resultant end-product of more than three centuries of an indigenous development of American culture, mores, and experience, intermingled with traditions and procedures inherited primarily from Great Britain. The late Roscoe Pound, noted American legalist and early twentieth century critic of "the rigidity in common law interpretation" by our federal and state judges, postulated that American law existed in three forms: (1) ***Legislation*** or laws enacted by authoritative statutory bodies, state and federal, which may be classified into three groups, (a) constitutions, (b) federal treaties and non-political state compacts, (c) statutes; (2) ***Judicial Decisions***, the decisions of federal and state courts which are inclusive of both criminal and civil interpretations, and (3) ***Books of Authority***, which are confined to specific applications of the law, e.g. the United States Code.[3] Pound criticized the common law tradition for its fixed mechanical philosophy of applying the strict letter of the law without regard to social and economic realities, for its adherence to outmoded inherited principles and the inertia of the judiciary – particularly locally elected judges – to needed reform which had brought it into conflict with the legislative departments of government.

Pound, an advocate of sociological jurisprudence who foresaw in the development of our legal system the necessity for the absorption of new theories closely related to the needs of society, pointed to *seven* main historical developments that directly contributed to the American spirit and system of law.[4] In chronological order, they were:

1. *Pre Feudal Germanic legal institutions and codes* which emphasized that the will of the Prince is law.
2. *Feudalism*, which introduced the concept of reciprocal relationship–in both rights and duties–between Medieval Lord and Serf.
3. *The legal struggle between the courts and the Crown in seventeenth century England* during which executive justice by administrative tribunals won out over judicial justice.
4. *Puritanism* which emphasized individual freedom and distrust of civil authority.
5. The concept of *the Rights of Englishmen and the Rights of Man in the eighteenth century.*
6. The conditions of the *pioneer communities and the rise of individualism accompanying Manifest Destiny in America between 1800 and 1850*, which had the effect of making American law provincial and of hindering the administration of justice.
7. *The Philosophy of Law formulated primarily by Immanuel Kant, Jeremy Bentham and Auguste Comte* in the nineteenth century, the ultimate result of which was the combination of economic interpretation and of positivism which gave rise to a kind of fatalist natural law.

It was Pound's contention that one common theme appeared to link most of these periods together: all of them, save one – *feudalism* – furthered the cause of "individualism," which made the American common law tradition so outdated that it was resented by popular feeling at the beginning of this century. On the other hand, feudal law introduced the concept of *reciprocal* relationship, in both rights and responsibilities, between medieval lord and serf. The old Germanic legal tradition, as expressed in the Institutes of Justinian – that the will of the Prince is law – was substituted by the recognition of rights and duties belonging *both* to the ruler and the ruled. The application of strict sovereign law was replaced by the use of will and relation, subjugation for protection.

Of particular importance to the development of constitutional law in the United States are the third and fourth stages of Pound's historical progression. Beginning with the enhancement of the rights of English lords and nobles under the terms of the Magna Carta in 1215, and the eventual acknowledgment of basic individual freedoms as contained in the Petition of Rights (1628); the Habeas Corpus Act (1679); and in the English Bill of Rights (1689); one may see, not only the fundamental liberties that, first the British, and later the American colonists had associated with the concept of "due process of law." It was in the seventeenth century struggle between the courts and the crown that the development of executive justice by "administrative" tribunals triumphed over judicial justice. Inevitably, the latter development was to lead to the doctrine of the *supremacy* of constitutional law. During this period of liberalization, religious or moral standards emphasized during the Puritan Revolution were infused into common law, equity and legal thought, in general. Referring to this evolution as viewed in the American legal experience, Pound wrote:

> ...the tendency to commit *everything* to boards and commissions, which proceed extra-judicially and are expected to be law unto themselves; the breakdown of our polity of individual initiative in the enforcement of law;... [the] substitution of administrative inspection and supervision; and the failure of the popular feeling for justice at all events which the common law postulates, appear to threaten a complete change in our attitude toward legal problems.[5] (emphasis added).

The Reformation's legacy of individual freedom, encouraged by the distrust of civil authority, was the essence of Puritanism. It intensified individualism with the attitude of protecting the individual against government and society, which the English common-law courts earlier had taken in the interests of the crown. Also, for which Charles I, given his adamant defense of the "Divine Right Of Kings" to rule as he – not the people – chose, lost his "divine" head by the executioners blade. At the start of the seventeenth century the spirit of constitutionalism had become latent in Great Britain; however, when the Puritans formed settlements in this country they brought with them the idea of the covenant or written *compact* in order to create governments and to define individual rights. The Puritans conceptualized "people" not as a mass but rather as an aggregation of individuals, each in possession of precise and ascribed rights. It should not be surprising that the United States Constitution, our supreme organic law, has as its most unique feature a *dual system* of both grants of authoritative power to the elected and appointed "rulers" and restraints on governmental authority for the protection of the rights of the "ruled."

The spirit of *individualism* – the substitution of individual policy preference for human realism – in judicial application of the law, which Pound criticized fifty years ago, remains, in lesser form, a question for continuing debate. Its seeds form the very basis of argumentation between judicial "restraintists" and judicial "activists," between judicial "conservatives" and judicial "liberals," and between strict-constructionists and broad-interpretationists. Most certainly the debate pre-dated Pound, for it is as old as the Constitutional Convention of 1787.

CONSTITUTIONAL DEVELOPMENT IN THE UNITED STATES 1776-1789

The first attempt at permanent self-government on the part of the colonies came about in July 1776, at the time the *Declaration of Independence* was adopted. Several members of the Continental Congress proposed the formation of a Confederation of States. Two years later, representatives from thirteen states along the eastern seaboard met in Philadelphia and after much debate submitted the *Articles of Confederation* for ratification. On March 1, 1781, eight months prior to the Battle of Yorktown, a reluctant Maryland finally agreed to become the thirteenth state to ratify, and the Articles became law.

From the outset, the operations of the national government under the Articles were a fiasco. The states, jealous of their power, had yielded precious little authority to the fledgling central government, and the inherent weaknesses of the Articles became glaringly apparent: the national government lacked control over individuals; it had a weak legislature and no real executive or judiciary; it had no power over interstate commerce; it was wanting in adequate financial and commercial power; it even lacked the authority to make treaties. The central problem was that the states simply refused to cooperate. After all, each state was sovereign and the national government had absolutely no coercive powers. As the Articles declared, "Each state retains its sovereignty, freedom and independence, and every power, jurisdiction and right, which is not expressly delegated to the United States, in Congress assembled." Although it was not expressly stated in the Articles, there was little doubt that a state could withdraw from this tenuous union at any time.

During this "critical period" of American history (1781-1789) the problems of self-government were compounded by the difficulties encountered by Americans as individuals. Inflation was running out of hand primarily because of the excessive powers of the states over currency. The rights of property, not expressly guaranteed, were insecure at best. There was an apparent lack of security on the national level. And far worse, the basic rights of individuals were placed in jeopardy by extreme judicial control exerted by the state legislatures, particularly since there existed *no* bill of rights restraining governmental authority.

Finally in 1787, fifty-five delegates from twelve states, not including Rhode Island, attended the Constitutional Convention in Philadelphia to rectify the defects of the Articles. The Founding Fathers were, for the most part, politically knowledgeable, middle-aged (the average age was forty-two years), and representative of a relatively homogeneous society of nearly four million whites of mostly British ancestry. In attendance were such luminaries as George Washington, James Madison, Alexander Hamilton, Oliver Ellsworth and James Wilson, all of whom advocated greater authority to the national government; and such champions of state sovereignty as George Mason, Luther Martin and Robert Yates. Contrary to opinion, Thomas Jefferson, who was representing The United States in Paris, did not take part in the convention. After weeks of debate and compromise the convention produced, not a basic revision of the Articles, but a wholly *new* constitution which incorporated aspects of both the Virginia Plan (or the "big" state plan) introduced by Edmund Randolph, and the New Jersey Plan (or the "small" state plan) proposed by William Paterson. The national legislature was to be bicameral, with the lower House based on representation of population (favoring the large states) and the Senate represented by two senators from each state (appeasing the small states). "The proposed constitution," wrote Madison of the Great Compromise in Federalist Paper #39, "is a strictness, neither a national nor a federal constitution, but is a composition of both."

Only after a long and bitter struggle by the friends of the proposed document were the requisite number of state ratifying conventions won over and the Constitution adopted in 1789. Basically, the Founders had been confined to a choice of one of *three* types of constitutional democracies in drawing up the Constitution. First, the *unitary system* under which sovereignty – the power to make, change or amend a nation's supreme law – is vested in the central government. Through a written constitution the central unit would determine the amount of governing power to be yielded, if any, to the subunits or states.

British government was eventually structured along the lines of the unitary system as were American state governments in relation to their political subdivisions (counties, municipal governments, etc.) under our constitution.

A second alternative was the *confederate system* which had been unsuccessfully attempted under the Articles of Confederation. This system vested all sovereignty in the states which, by way of a written constitution, would decide how much or how little power the central authority possessed.

The third possibility, and the one finally agreed upon by the Convention delegates, was the *federal system* under which sovereignty was held by the people. They would decide, through a written constitution, the amount of governing power to be given *both* to the central government and the states.

By definition, no requirement was placed on the people to distribute power *equally* among the governing units; however, because of our experiences during the "critical period" (1781-1789), Article VI of the Constitution did stipulate that "this Constitution, and the Laws of the United States which shall be made in Pursuance thereof and all Treaties made, or which shall be made, under the Authority of the United States, shall be the Supreme Law of the Land; and the Judges in every State shall be bound thereby, any Thing in the Constitution or Laws of any State to the contrary notwithstanding." Thus, in exercising its *delegated* powers, the national government is to be *supreme*.

Steps were taken at the Constitutional Convention to ensure that the American governmental system would not become tyrannical. In addition to incorporating the theories of limited government and popular sovereignty, the Forefathers also included the concepts of "separation of powers" and "checks and balances."

Stemming from the writings of Locke and Montesquieu, the thrust of separation of powers called for a basic *division* of governing authority into three branches: the power to make laws, to control foreign and interstate commerce, to tax and spend for the general welfare, and to declare war was to be vested in the national legislature (Article I); the "executive power of the United States" including the authority as commander in chief of the armed forces, as head of the executive department, and as chief of state was to be given to a single executive, the President (Article II); and finally, a non-political or non-elective judiciary was to be yielded the authority to interpret the law under its original and appellate jurisdictions (Article III). Under the guidelines of the Constitution, it was planned that the three branches would be equal and coordinate and that each would have sufficient powers and restraints to serve as a *check* and *balance* on the others; however, the vagueness and ambiguity of the language employed in the new Constitution resulting from political compromise at the Convention, coupled with the genius of the American experience, has dictated otherwise. True, the three departments of the national government are coordinate and a checks and balances system does exist, but the judicial branch, specifically the Supreme Court of the United States, has proved to be the *superior* branch. Appointed for a protective term of life or good behavior, the members of the Court interpret the constitutional "ground rules" by which the *other* branches of the government must play.

This is *not* to say that the Supreme Court is immune from the restraints of the checks and balances system. After all, the Court has "neither the power of the sword nor of the purse;" it must rely on popular support and the good faith compliance of the other branches of government for enforcement of its decisions. Even "democrats" including Andrew Jackson and Franklin D. Roosevelt have employed the power of the presidency to either defy or openly threaten an antagonistic Court. Moreover, the federal judiciary must depend on Congress for its appropriated funds and for the very structure of its organization. Finally, the Supreme Court is left open to direct controls: it is subject to "change of color" by the judicial appointments made by the president; it can have its appellate jurisdiction removed by Congress; and its decisions abrogated by the process of amendments.[6]

CHAPTER II

THE AMERICAN LEGAL SYSTEM

Today, the Constitution of the United States is the oldest, national, *written* Constitution still in force. Its longevity may be attributed to a number of factors but primarily the following: the Constitution was written as a "living document;" its general or vague phrases were to be interpreted by the federal judiciary; by future generations of Americans through the prism of existing political, social, and economic circumstances; and. finally, the people could end or change its terms by the process described in Article V. Although some parts articulate quite *specific rules,* (and the hotly debated clauses are *not* so many) the Constitution does call upon each generation to interpret and reinterpret its *broad principles*. While neither formless nor without real substance, the Constitution contains a "spirit," an essence, that embodies certain *rules* (specific) and *principles* (vague) which must be applied so as to be appropriate to the conditions of each period. The Constitution established a government of laws *and* men with the full realization that the latter make, define, and enforce laws.

Judges, particularly those in the federal court system, are responsible for giving interpretation to various types of law in the cases that come before them, In most instances, classifications of law overlap one another and some are even derivative of other forms. Basically there are *three* general classifications of law in the United States:

Constitutional Law – the interpretations and clarifications of our Constitution which have been countenanced by the Supreme Court of the United States. The Constitution, consisting of seven thousand words, contains numerous principles and rules that are written in such vague and ambiguous language that the federal courts are constantly being asked to shed new light on their exact meaning, e.g., the Due Process, Takings, and Equal Protection clauses. On appeal, the interpretation rendered by the lower federal courts may or may not be sanctioned by the Supreme Court. Under its appellate jurisdiction, the Court may review the decision of the lower court and uphold, moderate, or directly overrule it; or, the Court may indirectly sanction the decision by *not* taking the case at all.

Such terms as "essential fairness," "prior restraint," and "clear and present danger" are *not* found in the Constitution but are an integral part of the body of Constitutional Law.

Statutory Law – the area of law prescribed by *legislative* bodies. At the state and local levels of government one would include city ordinances enacted by municipal governments, as well as the statutes passed by the state legislature. At the federal level, statutory law would encompass not only laws enacted by Congress, but also treaties and "executive orders" issued by the president. Often the Supreme Court decides a case on matters of statutory rather than constitutional construction. On such occasions, the Court may not only determine the meaning of the words in the statute but also the *intent* of the legislators when the law was written. The Court will consult contemporary journals and the records of debates and hearings that took place at the time the law was formulated. All statutory law, whether state or national in origin, must conform to constitutional guidelines; any statute found in contravention of the Constitution cannot legally stand.

Common Law – the division of law formulated by the judges when constitutional and statutory law cannot be made to apply to a question raised in a case. It has as its antecedents the decisions rendered by the royal magistrates of twelfth century England who traveled from locality to locality adjudicating questions of law in compliance with local custom. The common law is enhanced by the principle of *stare decisis* ("let the decision stand") or, the rule of *precedent*. Put simply, it means that decisions of past courts will be adhered to by future courts and will be considered binding in all like cases. In the United States, common law is a product of the *state* court system, since there is no general federal common law. Even in "diversity of citizenship cases" involving disputes between two citizens of different states, the federal courts will decide the matter on the basis of the statutory, or in its absence, the common law of the designated state.

In addition, there are five specific types of law which in most cases are derivative from one or a combination of the above classifications:

Administrative Law – regulations, rules and decisions established by independent regulatory boards or commissions. In the late nineteenth century, as our economic system became increasingly complex, Congress began creating administrative agencies, composed of "experts" in various areas of the economy, to assist in regulation. Such agencies as the Securities and Exchange Commission, the Federal Trade Commission and National Labor Relations Board, to name but a few, possess quasi-legislative, quasi-judicial functions and their rulings greatly affect governmental operations. Their decisions may be reviewed by the United States Courts of Appeal and ultimately, the Supreme Court.

Admiralty and Maritime Law – subject to the jurisdiction of the federal courts this area of law is comprised of the regulations pertaining to navigation on both international waters and the inland waterways of the United States. All water-borne carriers, and the commerce carried therein, are affected by this very complicated set of regulations.

Civil Law – this form of law places greater emphasis on the codification of rules enacted by the legislature than on adjudication by the courts. Civil or private law governs the relations, transactions and disputes between individuals and between groups, and attempts to establish the legal rights of private parties. Its substantive features cover commercial law, torts, property, contracts, corporations and other private subjects.

Criminal Law – almost entirely statutory in nature, this division of law defines offenses against the community at large and assigns punishment. The bulk of criminal law in the United States has been formulated by *state and local* legislative bodies. The United States Constitution, specifically the Sixth Amendment, requires such laws to be written clearly and concisely; they cannot be vague, ambiguous or make irrational presumptions. Enforcement of criminal law comes under the jurisdiction of the executive department of government.

Equity – an area of "judge-made" law, applied by state and federal magistrates, which provides remedial justice in instances not adequately covered by civil, criminal or common law. Under this system of remedial law, a litigant who has suffered irreparable injury may seek from the court proportionate relief *not* provided by existing law. Recovery of monetary damages, restitution, the issuance of an injunction or the requirement of a specific performance may form the basis of the "equitable" relief sought.

Finally, all law, regardless of its classification, is both *substantive* and *procedural* in nature. The substantive area involves the "what" or the object of the law and includes governing powers, obligations, freedoms and basic rights, etc. On the other hand, the procedural area is concerned with the "how" of the law or the procedure under which law operates. It includes, among others, proper jurisdiction, the functions and operations of government bodies, courts and administrative agencies, pre-trial and trial procedure.

Of critical importance to an understanding of our judicial process is a recognition of the United States adversary system. An *adversary* proceeding is one in which the party seeking relief has given legal warning to the other party and afforded the latter an opportunity to contest it. In all cases involving "justiciable" questions – the Constitution, Congress, and most state constitutions have stated that some questions are more properly left to other divisions of government and are *not* subject to determination by the judiciary – the courts are presumed to be arenas of objectivity in which the lawyers representing both parties *advocate* their cause. The advocates touch upon every possible point that might lend support to their argument and are not responsible for establishing the truth. While they cannot use evidence which they know is false, advocates often selectively present the facts to support their point of view. The court is to impartially arbitrate the conflict and, having been exposed to the arguments of the parties involved, is entrusted with discerning the truth.

There are "dual" or two separate and distinct legal systems in the United States: *federal and state*. Each state constitution establishes a hierarchical network of common-law courts to handle criminal and civil cases. Invariably, most state systems include domestic courts, juvenile courts, corporation courts, justice of the peace courts (particularly in southern states), district courts, courts of appeal and the state supreme court. The judicial systems *vary* from state to state: unlike her sister states Louisiana places greater emphasis on civil law than common law; instead of investing equitable jurisdiction in the ordinary courts, Delaware, and a number of other states, maintain separate equity or Chancery courts; Texas has not one but *two* high courts – the Texas Supreme Court, which administers civil justice, and the Texas Court of Criminal Appeals. Despite such variances, all state judges possess the power of judicial review and, depending on the jurisdiction of the court, may be called upon to decide the validity of a law. They are entrusted with the responsibility of upholding not only their state constitution, but the laws, treaties and Constitution of the United States as well. All cases involving federal questions proceed from the state court of last resort, or the highest state court with proper jurisdiction, to the federal courts.

THE STRUCTURE AND ORGANIZATION OF THE FEDERAL COURTS

Article III of the Constitution invests the "judicial power of the United States" in the Supreme Court and "such inferior courts as the Congress may from time to time ordain and establish." Since 1789, Congress, in exercising this grant of authority, has enacted a number of "judiciary acts" creating an intricate network of inferior federal courts.[1] Courts thus established are called ***"Article III"*** or ***"Constitutional Courts."*** The federal district courts and the U.S. courts of appeal (see below) are "Article III Courts" of *general* jurisdiction, which means that their jurisdiction extends to *all* controversies "arising under the Constitution" that may be brought before them within the proper legal bounds of rights and remedies. Congress has also created constitutional courts of *special* or *limited* jurisdiction, which have jurisdiction *only* over a particular class of cases "arising under the Constitution." Judges on constitutional courts, whether general or special, are appointed by the President with the "advice and consent" of the Senate for a period of "good behavior." In effect, they are appointed *for life*.

Constitutional courts administering specific fields under the judicial power of Article III include:

The Court of Appeals for the Federal Circuit. This constitutional court of special jurisdiction was established by Congress in 1982. It replaced The United States Court of Customs and Patent Appeals, established in 1909, and the appellate division of the Court of Claims, established in 1855. It hears appeals from the United States Claims Court, the Court of International Trade, the Patent and Trademark Office, the Court of Veterans Appeals, the Merit Systems Protection Board, and in some contract and revenue cases from the district courts. There are twelve judges on the Court of Appeals for the Federal Circuit, and they normally hear cases in panels of three judges. Decisions may be appealed to the Supreme Court. The court is located in Washington, D.C.

The United States Court of International Trade was created by Congress in 1980 to replace the United States Customs Court. The Court is concerned with the decisions of customs collectors, the appraisals of imported goods, and cases arising from international trade. Its decisions can be appealed to the Court of Appeals for the Federal Circuit.

Legislative Courts are created by Congress under grants of authority in the Constitution other than Article III. Because they are created under Congress' delegated powers, they are usually referred to as "***Article I Courts.***" These courts have jurisdiction over "specialized" areas of, primarily, statutory law. As in the case of the other federal courts, the judges are appointed by the President with the approval of the Senate; however, they only serve a *set* term for a determined *number* of years. Among the "legislative courts" are the following:

The United States Claims Court was created in 1982 and replaced the United States Court of Claims, created by Congress in 1855. The Claims Court handles suits brought against the national government and settles claims referred by the executive and legislative departments. The court consists of sixteen judges appointed for fifteen years. Decisions of the Claims Court are appealed to the Court of Appeals for the Federal Circuit.

The United States Court of Military Appeals, created in 1950, is the highest court in the military tribunal system. For purposes of administrative expediency it serves as a part of the Department of Defense, but it is considered to be judicially *independent*. The Court administers military law which is formulated by Congress and is empowered to review cases on appeal from the lower military courts. In cases involving a "general or flag" officer; extending to death; on certification by the Judge Advocates General of the armed forces or by the General Counsel of the Treasury Department (acting for the Coast Guard); and petitions by the accused who received a sentence of at least a year's confinement or a disciplinary discharge, the decisions of the Court of Military Appeals are final and no further direct appeal is available. Only cases in which *constitutional issues* are *overriding* are subject to review by the United States Supreme Court. The Court of Military Appeals consists of three civilian judges who are appointed to serve a term of fifteen years.

The Court of Veterans Appeals was established by Congress in 1988. It hears appeals regarding veterans benefits. It consists of seven judges appointed for fifteen year terms. Decisions may be appealed to a Court of Appeals or to the Supreme Court.

Territorial courts, which are also "legislative" courts, are not created under Congress' powers in Article I of the Constitution. Rather, they are created by Congress under the authority of the United States in Article IV, section 3, clause 2 to govern the territorial possessions. The territorial courts in Guam, Puerto Rico, the Northern Mariana Islands and the Virgin Islands function as federal district courts, though they have a mixed jurisdiction over both federal questions and matters of local or domestic concern. The judges in these courts are appointed for a term of ten years. The exception is the district court in Puerto Rico which is classified a "court of the United States" like the other federal district courts. The judges there are appointed for life. Congress, of course, could place the "Constitutional" stamp on the other territorial district courts by simply changing the term of appointment to "good behavior" or life.

THE UNITED STATES DISTRICT COURTS

The district courts are the lowest of the three levels of federal courts of general jurisdiction. There are a total of ninety-four district courts – eighty-nine in the states, one in the District of Columbia, and the four territorial courts. Each state has at least one district court. California, New York, and Texas each have four. At the present time the number of judges in each district ranges from two to twenty-seven depending on docket load, population and the geographic size of the district.

The district courts possess original jurisdiction (jurisdiction to take cognizance of a cause at its inception) and are responsible for handling all cases involving federal questions except those few coming under the original jurisdiction of the Supreme Court. In most cases, only one federal judge adjudicates both civil and criminal matters. The district courts are the only federal courts to regularly employ the use of a jury – grand (indicting) and petit (trial).

In cases involving a constitutional challenge, the district court will be comprised of a "collegial" panel of three judges. On such occasions, the court is said to be sitting *en banc*, with all judges present. Ordinarily, the decisions of the district courts are reviewable by the courts of appeal; however, it is not uncommon for a decision of an en banc court to proceed directly to the Supreme Court.

There are a total of 645 district judgeships in the various states, 15 in the District of Columbia, 7 in Puerto Rico, 2 in the Virgin Islands and 1 each in Guam and the Northern Mariana Islands. In those districts with more than one judge, the person with the most seniority in judicial service and who has not exceeded sixty-nine years of age is chief judge. The staff of each district court includes a clerk, a United States attorney, a United States marshal, at least one United States commissioner, court reporters and other special court officers and their assistants.

In 1968, Congress created the Judicial Panel on Multi-District Litigation to expedite civil cases pending in various districts involving common questions of fact. The Panel consists of seven federal judges and is empowered to transfer such cases, for the purpose of coordinating and consolidating pretrial proceedings, to a single district.

THE UNITED STATES COURTS OF APPEAL

The courts of appeal, known as circuit courts of appeal until 1948, are the intermediate courts of appellate jurisdiction with the power to review and determine cases on appeal. They were created by Congress in 1891 to provide relief for the Supreme Court from reviewing all litigation on appeal from the district courts. They are authorized, with certain exceptions, to review all final and particular "interlocutory" (temporary or not final determinations) decisions of the district courts within their circuit. In addition, they have appellate jurisdiction with respect to the following: (1) the decisions and orders of many of the independent regulatory boards or commissions including the Federal Reserve Board, the Federal Trade Commission, the National Labor Relations Board, and the Securities and Exchange Commission, (2) the orders of certain executive agencies with quasi-judicial functions, e.g., Secretary of the Army with respect to regulation of navigable waters, and (3) the first, third, and ninth circuits are empowered to review the decisions of the district courts in the Territories.

There are eleven judicial circuits in the United States and two others located in the District of Columbia (the Court of Appeals for the District of Columbia, and the Court of Appeals for the Federal Circuit). For most cases, the Court of Appeals sits as a collegial panel of three judges and, depending on the docket load, the judge with seniority in judicial service, who has not exceeded sixty-nine years of age, will serve as chief judge. For cases involving a constitutional challenge, the collegial panel will usually expand its number to sit *en banc*, with all judges present.

Traditionally, each justice on the Supreme Court, who in years past was required to be a "circuit rider," is assigned at least one circuit for which he or she serves in a supervisory capacity. A litigant who wishes to seek equitable relief for an injury sustained at a time when his case is pending in the court of appeals will submit a plea to the justice assigned to that circuit.

THE UNITED STATES SUPREME COURT

In compliance with the command of Article III, the Supreme Court was created by act of Congress on September 24, 1789 and was formally organized some four months later. The Court first convened in 1790 in the city of Philadelphia. The Court is composed of one chief justice and a set number (eight) of associate justices to be established by Congress. For mostly political reasons, Congress has, from time to time, changed the number of judges from six (1789), to five (1801), back to six (1802), to seven (1807), to nine (1837), to ten (1863), to seven (1866), and finally to its present number of nine (1869).

The Supreme Court has both *original* and *appellate* jurisdiction over "all cases, in law and equity, arising under this Constitution, the laws of the United States, and treaties made, or which shall be made, under their authority." It has original jurisdiction over two types of cases: (1) those involving ambassadors, other public ministers and consuls; and (2) those in which a state is a party. In addition, the Court has appellate jurisdiction to review the decisions of the inferior courts in all other cases involving federal questions. Congress can, in no way, change or alter the *original* jurisdiction of the Court; however, it may make "exceptions and regulations" with respect to the Court's *appellate* jurisdiction.[2]

The Supreme Court is the Court of *last* resort for the federal system. Its decisions are binding on the inferior courts in that once the Court has reached a decision in a given case, the lower courts must decide in like manner in future cases involving the same issue and circumstances. This binding requirement is necessary to preserve the uniformity of constitutional law throughout the United States.

The United States Court System

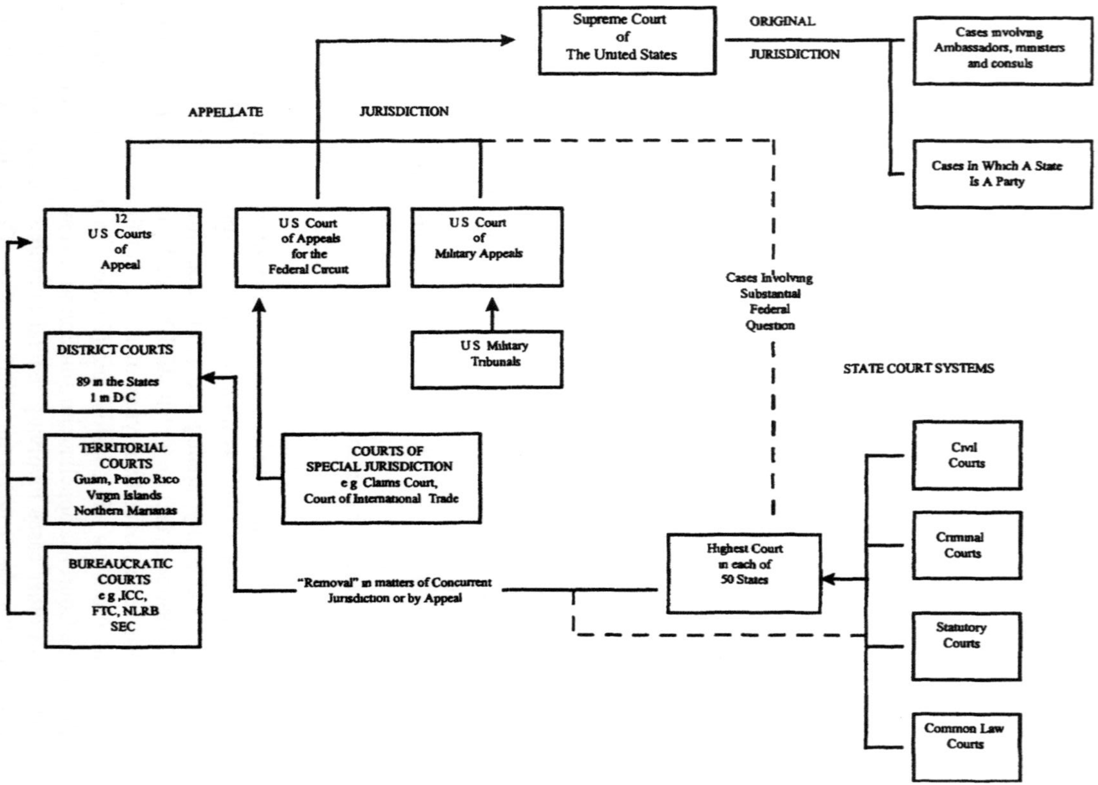

The annual term of the Court begins on the first Monday in October and, depending on the amount of business before the Court, continues until the second or third week of July. Usually on the first day of the term, the Court swears in the new members of the bar of the Court. Only members of this bar may practice before the Court. As required by law, six members must be present to constitute a quorum.

Although a very small percentage of the thousands of cases decided by the lower federal courts are ever brought before the Supreme Court, it still considers nearly 6,000 cases annually. Of these, only about 130 have written opinions accompanying them, the remainder take the form of *per curiam* or memorandum decisions, without substantial written comment. The work load of each justice is particularly heavy since nearly 1,500 applications of various types which call for individual action, are filed each year. To help assist it in the performance of its duties, the Court appoints its own officers including a magistrate, the *clerk*, the *reporter* of decisions, the *librarian*, and the *marshal*. In addition, each justice appoints his own staff including a clerk and other legal researchers.

Finally, the Supreme Court has been authorized by Congress to prescribe the rules of procedure – governing admiralty and maritime cases, appellate proceedings, criminal and civil cases in the district courts, copyright litigation and other cases – to be complied with by the lower federal courts. In 1967, the Federal Judicial Center was established by act of Congress to assist in this task by furthering the development and adoption of improved administration in the federal courts. The governing body for the administration of the entire federal judicial system is the *Judicial Conference of the United States*. It is composed of the chief judge of each circuit, a district judge elected for a three year term by the judicial council of federal judges in each circuit, the chief judge from the Court of Appeals for the Federal Circuit and the Chief Justice of the Supreme Court, who serves as chair. The Director of the Administrative Office of the United States Court, appointed by the Chief Justice, serves under the direction and supervision of this governing conference.

METHODS OF APPEAL

The courts of the United States at both federal and state levels are *passive* in nature. They do not "seek out" litigation, it must be properly brought before them for adjudication. Moreover, one must have *standing* or show qualifications as to why one is entitled to bring legal action. Depending on the jurisdiction of the court in question, the plaintiff must show that he has sustained, or is in immediate danger of sustaining some direct injury to his legal rights as the result of either private or public action. In short, one must prove a substantial interest, at least greater than that of others, in initiating the litigation.

There are three ways to appeal a case to the Supreme Court of the United States:

1. ***Certiorari*** – This procedure was created by Congress in the Judges' Bill of 1925. Its purpose was to allow the justices to control their docket with

respect to ordinary cases. Certiorari is a writ or an order to the lower court to send the complete proceedings and record of the case to the higher court for the purpose of reconsideration. The party adversely affected by the lower court's decision may petition the Supreme Court, stating the reasons why the Court should take the case. In judicial conference, the justices have the discretion to decide whether or not to review the case. If *four* favorable votes are cast, the writ will be issued and the case will be reviewed by the Court. Since 1988, almost all cases proceed to through the Supreme Court through certiorari.

2. ***Appeal*** – This type of procedure indicates the involvement of a matter of right on the part of one of the litigants, rather than privilege. Theoretically, when appeal is employed, the higher court must hear the case. However, the 1988 Act to Improve the Administration of Justice, gave the Supreme Court virtually complete discretion in deciding which cases to review. Mandatory appeals, which the Court must review, have been restricted to cases involving reapportionment, anti-trust laws, and the Civil Rights and Voting Rights acts.

3. ***Certification*** – This procedure, which is rarely used, is the only one initiated by the lower court rather than the litigants in the case. In essence, the lower court certifies to the Supreme Court particular legal questions raised in a case for clarification, so that the matter may be properly adjudicated.

THE CASE STUDY METHOD

The most commonly accepted approach to an examination of constitutional law is the case study method. The utility of this approach was aptly described by Harold J. Sapeth:

> In the first place, the case approach provides the student of the Court with the original document, the official record. He is not dependent for his knowledge upon a commentator's summary or interpretation, but can study the facts at firsthand.
>
> Second, the opinions of the Court constitute an intelligible and accessible record of the major political issues which have convulsed American society over the course of its history: federalism, separation of powers, the regulation of the economy, civil rights and liberties....
>
> Third, in considerations of major issues, the opinions of the Court frequently reveal a clash of views.... The justices are free to dissent, and the dissenting opinions present alternative ways of resolving the policy question at issue....
>
> Finally, the case approach is equally useful whether the focus of study is traditional or behavioral. Those of a traditional orientation have...long employed the case approach in their concern with legal argumentation, adherence to precedent, and the evolution of legal and constitutional principles.

> Behavioralists...have found the case approach germane to their focus upon the sociological, psychological and political aspects of judicial behavior and decision making.[3]

Thus, we study cases because these are the materials of the law, as plants are the material of botany. We examine the cases to view the arguments which show us the issues involved. This is particularly true for undergraduate courses, where part of the purpose is to gain a new perspective on the problems and issues of American politics by analyzing the arguments presented in the decisions.

Assigned cases are normally researched in either the original or secondary sources. The latter are case anthologies with extended analysis and which, for the most part, serve as college texts. The original materials include those publications of Supreme Court cases term by term. *The United States Reports* (U.S.) is the official United States government publication of Supreme Court decisions. *The Reports* began in 1790 and until 1882, the editions were in the name of the court reporter: 1789-1800 (Dallas), 1801-1815 (Cranch), 1816-1827 (Wheaton), 1828-1842 (Peters), 1843-1860 (Howard), 1861-1862 (Black), 1863-1874 (Wallace), 1875-1882 (Otto). Thereafter, the volumes were numbered and assigned the "U.S." citation beginning with Volume 108.

The remaining original materials which are also verbatim reports of the decisions, are published by private companies. *The United States Supreme Court Reports, Lawyers' Edition* (L.Ed.) is published by the Lawyers' Cooperative Publishing Company. Generally, the Lawyers' Edition is annotated and breaks down the various areas of law covered by the Court. In 1966, it began its second series (L.Ed.2d) starting once again with Volume 1. *The Supreme Court Reporter* (S.Ct.) covers only those terms of the Court since 1882 and is published by the West Publishing Company. The decisions of the inferior courts may be located in the following sources:

COURT	PERIOD	SOURCE
U.S. Courts of Appeal U.S. District Courts	Inception-1924	Federal Reporter (F.)
U.S. Courts of Appeal U.S. District Courts	1925-1931	Federal Reporter, second series (F. 2d.)
U.S. Courts of Appeal	1932-	Federal Reporter, second series (F. 2d.)
U. S. District Courts	1932-	Federal Supplement (F. Supp.)
Highest State Courts	Individually the volumes are produced by the state or by private publishing houses	Regionally-the North-eastern, Northwestern, Pacific, Southeastern, Southwestern Reports and the Atlantic and Southern Reporter

Aside from the annual bound volumes, advance sheets are also available when the Court is in session. *The United States Reports–Preliminary Prints* is published by the national government about two months after the decision has been rendered. During the term of the Court anywhere from ten to fifteen booklets are issued. Perhaps the quickest means of obtaining the complete text of Court decisions would be to subscribe to the services of the Commerce Clearing House which publishes the *Supreme Court Bulletin* or to the Bureau of National Affairs which furnishes *United States Law Week.* On a weekly basis both issue not only advanced sheets on the Court's decisions but also on the Court's docket, status table and rules.

Finally, if a student wishes to find a complete authoritative encyclopedic treatment of his subject based on all American cases, he should consult either *Corpus Juris Secundum* or *Shepard's Citations*. For succinct definitions of legal terminology it is suggested that he refer to *Black's Law Dictionary*.

UNDERSTANDING THE CASE TITLE AND CITATION

Realizing that very few cases originate with the Supreme Court–only those under its original jurisdiction–the student can usually determine the disposition of cases as they go to the Court. In two-party cases, the party on the left side of "versus" is known as the plaintiff or the litigant who initiated the legal action. Prior to a decision by the Supreme Court, one may assume that the plaintiff, as the party who asked the Court to review the case, had been adversely affected by the earlier decision of the lower court. The defendant, the party on the right side, was the apparent "winner" in the decision rendered by the lower court; however, there is no way to accurately predict how the Supreme Court will decide the case.

The terms given to the two parties change according to the means of appeal employed. Since the Court will rarely mention the proper names of the parties involved it is important that the student familiarize himself with the following terminology:

Plaintiff		V.		Defendant
or				or
Petitioner	←	(Certiorari)	→	Respondent
or				or
Appellant	←	(Appeal)	→	Appellee

Cases are cited by name; followed by the volume number, the appropriate Court Reporter, the page number on which the case begins, and the year of the decision. For example, ***United States v. Pink,* 315 U.S. 204 (1942)** means that the case of *United States v. Pink*, decided in 1942, may be found in Volume 315 of the *United States Reports* beginning on page 204. Depending on the year in which the case was decided, it may be included in the other original sources under a different citation. For example, *Leisy v. Hardin* decided in 1890, may be found in Volume 135, starting on page 100 of the *United States Reports*; in Volume 34, on page 128 in the *Lawyer's Edition*, first series; and in Volume 10, on page 681 of the *Supreme Court Reporter.*

Not infrequently, a Latin phrase may be used in the case title to describe the legal status of the suit or some other feature of the case, particularly where only one party is listed in the title, e.g. *Graves v. New York* ***ex rel.*** *O'Keefe;* ***In re.*** *Gault;* ***Ex parte*** *Leuitt, Brown* ***et al.*** *v. Board of Education of Topeka. Ex relatione (ex. rel.)* is a phrase meaning "on or by the relation of" and it denotes the person who has caused the government to act in his behalf. *In re.* means "in relation to or concerning." It is generally the phrase employed in single party controversies. *Ex parte*, on the other hand, indicates a statement originating from only one side in an examination or hearing and is less frequently used. *Et alii (et al.)* means "and another or others." It is used to show that a number of individuals, organizations or governmental agencies are jointly engaged in the case.

CHAPTER III

THE SUPREME COURT OF THE UNITED STATES

In disposing of its case load during the term, the Court is confined to those filed in each of three separate dockets: (1) the *original docket* contains those rare cases coming under the original jurisdiction of the Court; (2) the *appellate docket* consists of those cases brought up from the lower courts for review; and (3) the *miscellaneous docket* primarily includes petitions to overturn criminal convictions and to issue extraordinary writs.

Throughout the term, the Court alternates its activity: it hears oral argument for usually a two-week period, followed by a two-week recess during which it meets in judicial conference. At that time, the justices, meeting in private session, consider and decide not only the cases before them but also the future cases they will or will not take. In deciding a case, each member, beginning with the chief justice and continuing by way of decreasing seniority, announces his evaluation of the issues involved. Afterward, the justices give their decision in the case. For whatever reason, if there are justices who do not wish to join in the ***Opinion of the Court*** they may: (1) file an individual or joint ***concurring opinion*** which shows agreement with the Court's conclusion, but may have different reasons for reaching that result, or (2) file an individual or joint ***dissenting opinion*** in which one or more justices explicitly disagree with the decision passed by the majority and expound their views. If the chief justice is in the majority, he will assign the writing of the opinion to the colleague of his choice. In a particularly significant case, the chief justice may well take it upon himself to author the majority opinion. If the chief justice is not in the majority, the member of that group with the most seniority of service on the Court will make the assignment.

Serving primarily in the capacity of presiding judge, the influence of a chief justice on the decision-making process is almost *solely dependent* on the makeup of his own *personality*. John Marshall (1801-1835), Roger Brooke Taney

(1836-1864), Salmon P. Chase (1864-1873), and Charles Evans Hughes (1930-1941) were considered by most observers of the Court to be strong Chief Justices who by sheer force of logic and persuasion could "win over" a number of their colleagues to their legal point of view. On the other hand, Harlan Fiske Stone (1941-1946) and Fred M. Vinson (1946-1953) were generally felt to be much less effective.[1]

THE SELECTION AND MAKE UP OF THE MEMBERS OF THE COURT

Article II, section 2 of the Constitution provides that the President "shall have Power, by and with the Advice and Consent of the Senate to ... appoint ... Judges of the Supreme Court." Unlike the offices of the other branches of the government, the Constitution is silent as to the qualifications of those placed on the Court. Even though every justice who has served on the Court since its creation has been a lawyer, it is not constitutionally required. Precedent, tradition and the political influence of the American Bar Association have more or less dictated that vacancies on the Court be filled with recognized lawyers possessing some practical legal experience.

Most appointments to the Court are "political" in nature. The president is usually influenced by a number of factors in this regard: (1) the judicial philosophical leanings of the individual, (2) the nominee's standing in the legal community, (3) the professional and personal relationship of the nominee with the president, (4) the nominee's party affiliation and participation in partisan activities, (5) the age of the nominee is of importance since the President wishes the appointee to have time to make an impact on the Court's decision-making process, and (6) the nominee's religious preference, ethnic background or home state may be of prime importance in the politics of selection.

Until recently, it had generally been assumed that whomever the president selects, if at least nominally "qualified," the Senate would automatically confirm, even though controversial side issues have caused some nominees to have a rough sledding in the Senate – most notably Louis D. Brandeis in 1916 (his religion) and Hugo L. Black in 1937 (his earlier membership in the Ku Klux Klan). In the 75 years preceding 1968, only Judge John J. Parker in 1930 had been rejected by the Senate, primarily because of labor and black opposition to his prejudicial voting record.

In 1968 the Senate began to reassert its discretion to *withhold* consent. President Lyndon B. Johnson, in attempting to fill the vacancy created by the tentative resignation of Chief Justice Earl Warren, sought to elevate his old friend Associate Justice Abe Fortas to Chief Justice and to name Federal Judge Homer Thornberry of Texas to the Court. Upon disclosure of the financial indiscretions of Fortas and with increasing charges of "cronyism" in the selection by the President of his two associates, both withdrew their names from consideration before the Senate vote. Subsequently, Fortas resigned from the Court.

The Supreme Court itself became an issue in the Presidential election of 1968. Opponents of the Warren Court accused the liberal majority of, *inter alia*, bringing about a breakdown of "law and order" in the United States by its decisions expanding the rights of the accused in criminal cases "at the expense of the victims and the police." Prior to his election, Richard M. Nixon stated his position on future nominations to the Court; he would appoint,

> strict constructionists who saw their duty as interpreting law not making law. They would see themselves as caretakers of the Constitution and servants of the people, not super-legislators with a free hand to impose their social and political viewpoints upon the American people.[2]

Of course, Nixon's statement encompassed the view of one side of the age-old argument on the role of the Court in our constitutional framework; however, in the political context of the campaign the implication was clear – if elected, his nominees would preferably be conservative practitioners of judicial self-restraint, Southern, and Republican. The President had little trouble in winning Senate confirmation for his first nominee, Warren Earl Burger. The former judge of the United States Court of Appeals for the District of Columbia, known as a moderate on civil rights who opposed the direction of the Court in criminal cases, was confirmed by the Senate to succeed Earl Warren as Chief Justice. Thereafter, the President's troubles began.

When the next vacancy occurred with the resignation of Associate Justice Abe Fortas, President Nixon made two attempts at appointing Southerners to the Court and failed on each occasion. On November 22, 1969, the Senate rejected the nomination of Clement F, Haynsworth. Jr., a conservative federal judge on the Court of Appeals, Fourth Circuit, from South Carolina, by a vote of 55-45. Critics of Haynsworth cited conflict of interest because of his huge diversified financial holdings, as well as his supposed anti-labor, anti-civil rights voting record. The Haynsworth nomination was so politically unpalatable to the Senate that seventeen members of the President's own party voted against confirmation. The President's second choice, G. Harold Carswell, a conservative federal judge from Florida, suffered a similar fate. Carswell, his opponents charged, was racially biased and simply not qualified for the appointment. On April 9, 1970, the Senate by a vote of 51-45 defeated his bid for confirmation. Nixon, accusing the Senate of prejudice against the South, finally nominated Federal Judge Harry A. Blackmun of Minnesota, who was confirmed by the Senate with little difficulty shortly thereafter.

Although President Nixon's later selections of Louis Powell and William Rehnquist to fill the vacated seats of Associate Justices Hugo Black and John M. Harlan were approved by the Senate, confirmation came only after a close and detailed examination of their backgrounds. The Senate had served notice and henceforth, appointments to the High Court would be subject to public scrutiny and would not be *solely* within the Presidential prerogative.

The next several appointments, however, were relatively uneventful. The Senate confirmed President Ford's nomination of John Paul Stevens to replace Justice William O. Douglas by a vote of 98-0. Similarly, President Reagan's nomination of Sandra Day O'Connor to be the first female Justice of the Supreme Court met with virtually no opposition. Reagan's nomination of conservative Justice William Rehnquist to replace the retiring Warren E. Burger as Chief Justice occasioned spirited criticism by liberals, but was never in any real jeopardy. Rehnquist's replacement as Associate Justice, Antonin Scalia, was a highly respected, conservative Judge on the U.S. Court of Appeals for the D.C. Circuit. Somewhat surprisingly, Justice Scalia's nomination met little opposition in the Senate, which confirmed him by a vote of 98-0.

This was not the case with President Reagan's next nominee, Judge Robert Bork, also a member of the U.S. Court of Appeals for the D.C. Circuit. Judge Bork was a well-known judicial conservative who had served as Solicitor General during the Nixon Presidency and was a former professor at Yale Law School. Concerned that Bork's jurisprudence of original intent would solidify the conservative bloc on the Court, Democrats, who had regained control of the Senate in the 1986 elections, launched an all out effort to prevent his confirmation. Assisted by Harvard Law Professor Lawrence Tribe, himself a frequently named liberal Supreme Court hopeful, the Judiciary Committee of the Senate grilled Judge Bork regarding his views on abortion, affirmative action, civil rights, race relations and a host of other social issues. In addition, beginning with a demagogic press statement by Senator Edward Kennedy (D-Mass) on the very day Judge Bork was nominated, liberal politicians and interest groups mounted an unprecedented public attack which sought to depict the nominee as a right wing extremist.[3] Their tactics, both in and out of the Senate, were so successful that not only was Judge Bork not confirmed, but his surname became a verb. In Washington parlance, "to bork" someone means destroy their credibility (and job aspirations) by demagogic misrepresentations of their character and opinions.[4]

President Reagan's next nominee, Douglas H. Ginsburg, withdrew his name from consideration. In February, 1988, Anthony Kennedy finally replaced Justice Lewis Powell, Jr., who had retired from the Court in June, 1987. A Judge on the U.S. Court of Appeals for the Ninth Circuit, Justice Kennedy was confirmed 97-0 by the Senate. In 1990, David H. Souter, President George Bush's nominee to replace retiring Justice William J. Brennan, Jr., met with little Senate opposition.

A year later President Bush's nomination of Clarence Thomas touched off a firestorm of controversy and resulted in confirmation by the narrowest margin in history (52-48). Thomas was known as a conservative black Republican who advocated a position of "judicial restraint." He had been appointed Director of the Equal Employment Opportunity Commission (EEOC) by President Reagan in 1982. In 1990 President Bush appointed him to the U.S. Court of Appeals for the D.C. Circuit. When Justice Thurgood Marshall retired from the high Court, Bush nominated Thomas to replace him, a move which rankled many liberals. Justice

Marshall was a living legend. As counsel to the NAACP, Marshall had argued before the Court such landmark cases as *Brown v. Board of Education* (1954). In 1967, Marshall became the first black to serve on the Supreme Court. Along with Justice Brennan, Marshall was one of the Court's most outspoken liberal advocates of judicial activism. Thomas' nomination seem assured, however, until eleventh hour charges of sexual harassment were made by Anita Hill, a former subordinate of Thomas's at the EEOC. After days of additional testimony, which played like a soap opera on television, the Senate confirmed his appointment to the Court.

President Clinton's 1993 nomination of Ruth Bader Ginsburg to be the second woman to serve on the Supreme Court was the first by a Democratic President since Lyndon Johnson's nomination of Thurgood Marshall. Both Justice Ginsburg and Justice Stephen Breyer, who Clinton nominated in 1994 to replace Justice Blackmun, were easily confirmed by the Senate.

RELEVANCE OF JUDICIAL BEHAVIOR

Earnest students of the judicial process are required to know more about our system of constitutional law than just the interpretations of that basic document as expressed in the decisions of the Supreme Court. They must, by necessity, familiarize themselves with the statement of David Dudley Field that "judges are but men, and are swayed like other men by vehement prejudices." To put it less emphatically, the individuals who make up the Court are human beings, with differing backgrounds, motivations, experiences and beliefs, and these variables may often be used to explain the judicial behavior of a particular justice. Felix Frankfurter, one of the most eloquent advocates of judicial self-restraint, attempted to describe individual decision-making on the Court as follows:

> The decisions in the cases that really give trouble rest on judgment, and judgment derives from the totality of a man's nature and experience. Such judgment will be exercised by two types of men, broadly speaking, but of course with varying emphasis–those who express their private views of revelations, deeming them if not *vox dei*, at least *vox populi*; or those who feel strongly that they have no authority to promulgate law by their merely personal view and whose training and proved conclusions reflect understanding of, and due regard for, law as the expression of the views and feelings that may fairly be deemed representative of the community as a continuing society[5]

Accordingly, the late Associate Justice argued:

> Judges are men, not disembodied spirits. Of course a judge is not free from preferences or, if you will, biases. But he may

> deprive a bias of its meretricious authority by stripping it of the uncritical assumption that it is founded on compelling reason or the coercive power of a syllogism. He will be alert to detect that though a conclusion has a logical form it in fact represents a choice of competing considerations of policy, one of which for the time has won the day.

Therefore, as Frankfurter's description demonstrates, the importance that these "environmental" factors may have in the decision-making process must be subjected to closer analysis when viewed from the perspective of judicial reasoning and philosophy. The intervening variables which basically separate the justices are their views as to *what* is the common good and *how* that good may best be achieved. Two judges may indeed have similar backgrounds and experiences but may disagree strongly on their concept of the common good and its attainment. In fact, each may hold the other's position(s) to be illogical and thus, unacceptable. This interplay of views is suggested to counter notions held by students of the Court that background *alone* "determines" judicial behavior – a position that even much of the behavioralist literature has found untenable.

In the last twenty years, the examination and analysis of the judicial behavior of judges as individuals, groups, and blocs has become an integral part of the discipline at both the undergraduate and graduate levels. The seeds of this area of study were planted by C. Herman Pritchett in his classic examination of *The Roosevelt Court* published in 1948.[6] In scrutinizing the earlier background and the later performance of the justices who served on the Court during the transitional period between 1937-1947, Pritchett attempted to show a pattern of division between those appointed by Franklin Roosevelt and those appointed prior to his ascendancy to power. By the use of statistical data as employed in various charts and tables, he was able to demonstrate the critical division between the two groupings on such issues as regulation of the economy, welfare programs, civil liberties, labor-management relations and the practice of judicial self-restraint.

In later years, other studies were produced by scholars attempting to apply Pritchett's thesis in examining decision-making on the Court with usually more sophisticated methodological approaches. The behavioralists emphasize a "scientific" approach in evaluating the judicial behavior of judges. In analyzing such "inputs" as individual backgrounds, experiences and policy preferences, they tend to relegate the decisions of the Court as a secondary consideration ("outputs") to the study of interplaying variables in decision-making. They contend that by refining raw data on the voting behavior – past and present – of individuals and groups on the Court and that by applying accepted methodological techniques, a level of predictability can be achieved with respect to ultimate decisions. As mentioned, the causes of judicial behavior are hotly debated subjects: Are decisions of judges the result of accepting or rejecting arguments, for reasons of logic and consistency with principle, or are they the result of prior policy preferences or prejudices which are simply applied to the cases? Behavioralists tend to opt for the latter, while the bulk of traditionalist literature gives support to the former contention.[7]

Even those students employing an essentially traditional approach toward the study of constitutional law should be reminded that the philosophy of the Court on any given question is subject to *change*, as shifts in its membership occur. A judicial doctrine having the force of ruling law today, may well become a lone dissent tomorrow .

THE DUTY OF THE COURT: INTERPRETING OR LEGISLATING?

Although the Supreme Court has been generally held in reverence by the American people, that is not to say that during critical periods of our constitutional history it has not been subjected to rather extreme criticism. The Court under John Marshall (1801-1835) was attacked by the Jeffersonian Republicans for giving judicial life to a number of Federalist precepts on a strong central government. Even more vocal were the Unionists and Abolitionists whose rumblings rose to a furor when the Court under Marshall's successor, Roger Brooke Taney (1836-1864), attempted to mediate the slavery question by declaring the Missouri Compromise of 1850 unconstitutional in the Dred Scott Case. In modern times, the Court under Chief Justice Charles Evans Hughes was subjected to the abuse of New Deal supporters because of its intransigent opposition to the economic legislation proposed by Franklin D. Roosevelt. With an overwhelming electoral victory under his belt following the election of 1936, the President submitted his "court-packing" plan to Congress. Although the Congress failed to heed Roosevelt's plea, an intimidated Court got the message and began to uphold –usually by a one vote margin provided by the "switch" of Hughes and Justice Owen J. Roberts – New Deal legislation. The Court under Fred M. Vinson during the mid-40's and early 50's was accused by many legal scholars of retreating from the libertarian thrust in the area of civil liberties which had characterized Court decisions since 1937.

Perhaps no Court in history had to endure the wrath and scorn heaped upon it by opponents than the Court under Earl Warren (1953-1969). The liberal majority on the Court opened new vistas in such areas as the rights of the accused in criminal cases, basic racial equality, the reapportionment of Congressional and state legislative districts and the application of fundamental freedoms in the Bill of Rights to the states. The uproar in reaction to these decisions from Southern and rural politicians, conservatives, many law enforcement officers and other affected segments of American society seemed, at times, deafening. In its more intense forms, the protest against the Court ranged from defiance of federal court orders, to attempts at massive resistance and interposition on the part of state officials, to movements to impeach the Chief Justice himself. On a more rational basis, the tenor of the debate centered-and it still does-on the role and responsibility of the Supreme Court in our constitutional system. Even here, the Warren Court was the subject of a high degree of criticism from far more moderate members of the political spectrum concerning the Court's activism in plowing so much unbroken ground including Alexander Bickel, Paul Freund, Wallace Mendelson, Archibald Cox and Robert Bork.

For some time, legal scholars have debated the question of exactly which duties are confided to the judiciary, in general, and to the Court, in particular, and which are *not.* In a concise and perceptive way, Professor Craig Ducat argued that there are three modes of Constitutional interpretation: (1) ***Interpretivism*** (among whose advocates included Justice Hugo Black) holds that judges must give the words of the Constitution their simple and accepted meaning devoid of personal views. This contrasts with ***non-interpretivism***, which holds that judges must go beyond the text of the constitution and base their decisions on its broad principles; interpreting the text in light history, science, or natural law. Non-interpretivism includes those who espouse (2) ***judicial self-restraint*** (e.g., Felix Frankfurter) and (3) ***judicial activism*** (e.g., Justices Brennan and Marshall). The former is inclined to defer to the judgment of Congress and the States except in cases which "shock the conscience." The latter understands the role of the judge to adapt constitutional principles to the changing conditions and values of society.[8]

Whether the Constitution obliges judges to limit interpretation to specific non-political questions of law, or whether the realities of practical experience dictate that they assume an activist position has been debated since the Founding. The contemporary post-WWII dispute, however, dates from the period of the Warren Court's judicial activism in the 1950s and 1960s. The disagreement, as articulated at that time by Paul C. Bartholomew (University of Notre Dame) and August 0. Spain (Texas Christian University) is still worthy of closer examination.

Professor Bartholomew maintained that the courts were established to judge or to interpret and enforce the laws. Yet, beginning in 1954, the federal courts, he said, departed from this mandate. No longer satisfied to declare that a statute is invalid or even to insist that the legislature must act in a given situation, the courts declared themselves able to act if the legislature fails or refuses to act. It was his belief that the Supreme Court, in particular, had done more than declare relevant acts unconstitutional, it threatened direct judicial action, thus usurping legislative authority.[9] Bartholomew proceeded with the thrust of his critique:

> Among the fixed stars in our governmental constellation is the doctrine of separation of powers. No department is to exercise the functions of another, and this is true of both state and federal systems. But the courts have gone beyond this and have also violated the division of power as between federal and state govemments.[10]

He focused on two prime examples of law-making by the federal: (1) the actions of the federal courts, on the heels of the Segregation Cases of 1954, in ordering local boards of education to desegregate their schools or otherwise to be subjected to a specific court-ordered plan on integration; and (2) the mandate of the U.S. Supreme Court following *Baker v. Carr* (1962) that required both houses of bicameral state legislatures to reapportion their districts on the basis of population. Failure to comply would mean that district courts would present specific apportionment schemes that must be followed. This, said Bartholomew, was a clear cut violation of the doctrine of separated powers and the courts, as guardians of our legal system, should be the last governmental agencies to practice it. In conclusion, Bartholomew stated:

> There is no need for a judiciary to act out of character. This is pragmatism "run riot." The courts have not been "interpreting" the federal and state constitutions in these matters. The courts have been violating those constitutions .... This is dangerous precedent. We need our legislatures and we need our courts, but we do not need, and we should not have under our system, legislating courts.[11]

In his rejoinder to these views, Professor August 0. Spain contended that Bartholomew, along with other more temperate critics of the judiciary, had constructed "a theoretical model abstracted from phrases in the text of the Constitution and selected fragments of experience;" they "would establish a redoubt from which to denounce any action by the Court that runs contrary to any substantial body of political interest and opinion."[12] Admittedly, the doctrine of separation of powers is an important principle, but, he pointed out, it should not be glorified to the "extreme" at the expense of *other equally important* constitutional precepts, namely that of the checks and balances system. In upholding the supremacy of the Constitution, the Court is, at times, forced to deny to the "political" departments, the power to act. Referring to the specific examples provided by his colleague, Spain argued that to expect the courts to leave implementation of its decisions on reapportionment and racial equality *solely* and *permanently* in the hands of state and local political bodies is to ignore the lessons of recent experience. Only after local authorities have consistently resisted or delayed in compliance with a constitutional requirement, do the courts intervene:

> In the meantime "invidious" or "egregious" discrimination (denying constitutional right) is mitigated. A measure of justice is afforded, and right is not left to the delaying arts. Insistence upon such a transitional *modus operandi* expropriates no legislative power or authority to structure representation consistent with the Constitution ....
>
> As for the age-old cry of states rights, it is clear that these "rights" have been readjusted to "the exigencies of the union" throughout our national experience.[13]

He further pointed out that if the singular duty of the Supreme Court was to "find and declare law made by others" then this would reduce the Court to the level of "legal mechanics" which would probably be done more efficiently by computers. Spain concluded his defense of judicial "activism" by stating:

> Within a social order of such impressive size, complexity, diversity, and pluralism of interest and culture, the great deployment (decentralization) of constitutional powers (federalism, separation of powers, Bill of Rights, etc.) and occasional paralysis of political leadership exacted by the lack of a disciplined responsible two-party system now and then yield drift seriously negligent of vital spheres such as those of urban representation and racial justice in education.... In these doldrums the Supreme Court may well perform a most valuable service in getting us "dead center" by provoking response on the part of putative political leadership. Politics may thus be catalyzed into addressing challenges on the domestic scene sorely needing attention in the twentieth century world of international tensions, nuclear power, and the other wonders of protean science.[14]

LEGAL AND EXTRA-LEGAL PRESSURES ON JUDICIAL DECISION-MAKING

It is assumed that a decision of an individual justice on the Supreme Court is his or her own, but one should not ignore the fact that the decision is influenced by a number of factors. Quite naturally, the justice's judicial philosophy and, to a lesser extent, personal background are important factors in the interplay of inputs in the decision-making process. Among those considerations which are crucial to a judge's judicial philosophy are: (1) a conception of the common good; (2) of how this common good can best be achieved; and (3) of how active a role can and should the judiciary play in the American political process. Deciding the "solution" to these problems involves accepting some arguments and rejecting others at least in part on logical grounds. These are two types of things that judges argue about in their opinions, often accusing each other of not being logical, consistent or true to American constitutional principles. Judges' views as to what is or is not logical or acceptable may or may not be decisively influenced or determined by their personal opinions. Judges often say in their opinions that as a matter of policy preference they would rather decide a case in a particular manner, *but* that their reading of the Constitution or a statute won't allow that course. In this situation, background is of limited use in ferreting out the causes of judicial behavior. Naturally, a judge's experiences and background are important factors influencing judicial behavior; however, if the judge is conscientious, the vigorous logical analysis through which the arguments of both parties are put is equally influential. That analysis may or may not support a judge's policy preference. Also additional pressures are often brought to bear on the justice from both within and without the legal profession.

LEGAL INPUTS:

Other Lawyers. Each justice is a lawyer and usually has deep roots in the legal community. Many friends and associates are lawyers familiar with possible questions that confront the Court. Accordingly, the justice may be influenced by their views. ***Briefs***. The justice is most certainly affected by the quality of the briefs submitted by the lawyers in a case. Especially in more complicated litigation, a succinct, yet well-written, reasonably constructed brief which presents a distillation of detail and a logical sequence of legal argumentation may provide a "touchstone" for a judge already straining under the weight of a heavy docket load. So tremendous was the impact of the "Brandeis brief" on the legal community in the early twentieth century, that after 1937, sociological jurisprudence became the accepted doctrine of the Court. ***Oral Argument***. Some justices place more emphasis on the presentation of the oral argument than on the written brief. The late Associate Justice John M. Harlan once warned "that the lawyer who depreciates the oral argument as an effective instrument of appellate advocacy, and stakes all on his brief, is making a great mistake."[15] Harlan was convinced that every effective argument was possessive of four characteristics: (1) thoughtful selection of the issues to be presented; (2) simplicity of expression and presentation; (3) candor in facing up to the weak points which are usually present in every legal argument; and (4) resiliency in handling questions from the bench.[16] ***Lower Court Judges***. The justices are on occasion impressed with the opinions of judges on the lower federal courts as contained in decisions brought before them for review. A number of brilliant legal scholars have served with distinction on the district and appeals courts without being named to the High Court. The United States Court of Appeals for the Second Circuit in New York gained much of its reputation for having its majority opinions upheld on appeal because of the expertise of such judges as Learned Hand, Augustus Hand, Jerome Frank, Harold Medina and Thomas Swan. ***Law Review Articles***. Innovative legal concepts appearing in law reviews and journals may stimulate the thinking of individual justices which could result in the modification or the adjustment of a legal position. Also, serious and far-reaching criticism in law reviews has been known to have a decided effect on judges. The knowledge that a weak argument for a strongly held policy preference will be impaled over the pages of many law reviews may exercise a restraining influence on some judges. ***Congressional Authority***. Finally, the power of Congress to remove areas of appellate jurisdiction must exercise some influence on the decision-making process, at least at the parameters.

EXTRA-LEGAL INPUTS:

Aside from influences arising solely within the legal profession, significant pressure may develop in the community-at-large. ***Popular Opinion***. Although the justices are not subjected to the whims of the ballot box, they usually are attuned to the direction of public sentiment. The Court has no police force or army to enforce its decisions-outside of the occasional reliance on the good will of the President in those matters where civil rights are jeopardized by state action-and thus must ultimately depend on popular support. The decisions of the Warren Court to outlaw the required saying of prayers and of scripture-reading in public schools (*Engel v. Vitale*, 1962; *Abington School District v. Schempp*, 1963) caused such a national furor that the Court majority became unwilling to venture into the area thereafter.[17] ***The Other Branches***. In a number of instances, the actions of the President and the Congress have resulted in a shift in the direction of the Court's decisions, the obvious example being the reaction to Roosevelt's "court-packing" plan in 1937. Moreover, the justices may respect the opinion of particular administrative officials because of their personal stature or because of the importance of the office itself. In the School Desegregation Cases of the mid-1950's, the Court relied heavily on the position of the Department of Justice, as *amicus curiae*, as to the nature of implementation of its decree. ***Scholarly Publications.*** Newly advanced theories appearing in books, journals, and in other social science materials may provide members of the Court' with a modus operandi in deciding questions of social consequence. In its opinion in *Brown v. Board of Education* (1954), the Court cited, in footnote 10, the works of leading psychologists and sociologists to show the adverse psychological effects of segregation on young Negro children. The material provided a "back door" of sorts after the Court could not find sufficient justification in the legislative history of Congress to permit the striking down of the "separate but equal" concept in education. ***Organized Pressure Groups.*** Organizations representing various ethnic, religious, vocational and patriotic segments of American society have been rather successful in attempting to mold public policy as enunciated by the Court. Such groups freely provide legal talent in cases where the litigant is attempting to assert a matter of right closely connected to their special interests. The National Association for the Advancement of Colored People serves as a cogent example. Under the direction of Thurgood Marshall, before he was appointed an Associate Justice, the Legal Defense and Educational Fund of the NAACP was so effective in its attempt to seek legal parity for American Negroes in such areas as voting rights, equality in education and the rights of the accused, that between 1939-1958, it lost only six of forty-three cases brought before the Court.[18]

PART I

THE STRUCTURES AND POWERS OF GOVERNMENT

CHAPTER IV

THE FEDERAL COURTS AND THE DOCTRINE OF JUDICIAL REVIEW

Judicial review is the authority of the Supreme Court and inferior courts to declare actions of the other branches of government and state governments unconstitutional, null and void. This authority is the source of the judiciary's extraordinary power and significance in the American system of government. Its effects upon our everyday lives should never be underestimated. The Court's great contributions to the preservation of "ordered liberty" are justly celebrated, but its dark side cannot be ignored. For example, in the infamous Dred Scott case the Supreme Court overturned Congress' ban on slavery in the territories of the Union, and set the stage for the Civil War. It was also by virtue of judicial review that the Court prevented state and federal governments from enacting minimum wage laws and regulating working conditions. Exercising judicial review, the Court for many years sustained the legal supports for racial segregation in American society. Like all power, judicial review can be used for good or bad ends.

Despite its importance, judicial review is not explicitly granted to the Supreme Court. The closest the Constitution comes to an expressed grant of power occurs in the *supremacy clause* of Article VI which states: "This Constitution, and the laws of the United States which shall be made in pursuance thereof; and all treaties made, or which shall be made, under the Authority of the United States, shall be the supreme Law of the Land; and the Judges in every State shall be bound thereby, and any Thing in the Constitution or Laws of any State to the contrary notwithstanding."

This clause seems to grant judges the power of judicial review, but with some important qualifications. It *explicitly* empowers only *state* judges to review the constitutions and laws of their respective states for consistency with the Federal Constitution, laws and treaties. It says nothing about the *federal* it say anything explicit about the federal or state judiciary's authority to review and overturn acts *of Congress* or *of the President.*

For many of those who opposed a strong *national* union, the silence of the Constitution meant that the Supreme Court did not possess the power to review the constitutionality of state actions, or of the actions of the Congress or President. For example, in *Cohens v Virginia*, the State of Virginia denied that the Supreme Court could review a state court decision – even when the defendants in the case claimed that the state law violated the Constitution of the United States. "If it had been intended to give appellate jurisdiction over state courts,' Virginia argued, 'the proper expressions would have been used. There is not a word in the constitution that goes to set up the federal judiciary above the state judiciary.... [I]n no case can the federal courts revise the decisions of the state courts; no such power is expressly given by the constitution; and can it be believed that it was meant that the greatest, the most consolidating of all the powers of this government, should pass by an unnecessary implication?" *Cohens v Virginia* 6 Wheat. 318 (1821)

If the appellate jurisdiction of the Supreme Court did not extend to the states, however, the uniformity of constitutional law could *not* be maintained throughout the United States. State courts would be free to interpret the Constitution in many different ways, each valid only within their respective states. Contrary to Virginia's position, then, was a widespread understanding that the Supreme Court *necessarily* possessed the power of judicial review. Anticipation that the Supreme Court would exercise this power was voiced as early as the debates in the Constitutional Convention and the state ratifying conventions. It was clearly defended in the *Federalist* essays in defense of the Constitution written by Hamilton, Madison and Jay under the pen name "Publius."

Publius explained that all legitimate power rests with the people, who, through written constitutions, have delegated some of their authority to the state governments and some to the national government. These constitutions represent extraordinary legislative acts promulgated by the people themselves. They constitute *fundamental laws* which authorize the governments to exercise authority on behalf of the people, but only such authority as has been delegated and within the limits and restrictions imposed by the fundamental laws. If the governments violate the fundamental law by whose authority they act, their action is, by definition, unconstitutional and invalid. "No legislative act, therefore, contrary to the Constitution can be valid"

Since the Constitution has the *status of law*, it is the duty and responsibility of the judiciary to interpret and enforce it just as it would any other law. Whenever the legislative or executive representatives of the people violate the limits on their delegated authority, it is the responsibility of the judiciary to enforce the fundamental law. This power is *inherent in the function of the judiciary* – it is what judges do. *An explicit authorization* by the Constitution *is unnecessary.* The silence of the Constitution does not mean, as Virginia was to maintain, that the power of judicial review was not delegated. Rather, the

Constitution is silent because the power of judicial review is *inherent* in the Supreme Court of a limited, constitutional government.

The Federalist Papers were written to persuade the delegates to the New York ratifying convention to approve the Constitution. Similarly, the anti-federalist essays of the anonymous "Brutus" were published in New York newspapers with the intent of persuading the convention to *reject* the Constitution. One of the major reasons "Brutus" gave for repudiating the Constitution was precisely that it granted the Supreme Court the power of judicial review.

An advocate of the independence and sovereignty of the individual states, "Brutus" maintained that judicial review would enable the Court to extend the powers of the federal government "to the diminution, and finally to the destruction, of that of the respective States" The Court would use judicial review to create a national government supreme in *all* areas. Moreover, the Court itself would become the supreme power within this expanded national government, for, since "there is no power above them to set aside their judgement,... the judicial power under this system have a power which is above the legislature" The danger for "Brutus" was that of *judicial tyranny*. With power consolidated in the national government and the Court supreme within the national government, there would be no limits on its power short of revolution. Thus, both supporters and opponents of the new constitution assumed that the Supreme Court would have the power of judicial review. What they disagreed upon was whether that was a virtue or a vice of the proposed new union.

After the adoption of the Constitution, the Federal judiciary moved slowly toward exercising judicial review. In *Van Horne's Lessee v Dorrance* (1795), a Federal Circuit Court determined a Pennsylvania law to be unconstitutional. One year later, in *Hylton v. United States*, (1796), the Supreme Court reviewed the constitutionality of a national tax on carriages. However, since the Court found the tax to be constitutional, it postponed ruling on the question of "whether this court, constitutionally possesses the power to declare an act of Congress void, on the ground of its being made contrary to, and in violation of, the Constitution." In *Calder v Bull*, (1798), Justices Chase and Iredell took the opportunity to engage in a revealing debate regarding the limits of the Court's power of judicial review – a debate which foreshadowed much current. Justice Chase articulated an *expansive view* of judicial review which held that the courts were empowered to declare unconstitutional legislative actions which violated the principles of *natural justice*. Justice Iredell countered with a *narrower view* of the power which limited it to overruling laws *directly and clearly* in conflict with the Constitution.

Although cases like *Calder* and *Hylton* presumed the power to review the constitutionality of laws, the Supreme Court did not definitively justify its power until 1803. In the landmark case of *Marbury v. Madison*, Chief Justice John Marshall, following Hamilton,[1] articulated the constitutional basis for judicial review and, for the first time, declared an act of Congress unconstitutional.

In the election of 1800 Hamilton's Federalist Party – which supported a strong national government – lost both the Presidency and the Congress to

Jefferson and the state's rights oriented Democratic Party. Before leaving office, President John Adams and the Federalist controlled Congress rushed through a number of judicial appointments in order to maintain their party's presence in the national government. At this time John Marshall, recently appointed Chief Justice of the Supreme Court, was still serving as Adams' Secretary of State. It was his responsibility to deliver the letters of commission to the new judges. Marshall, however, was unable to complete this task before Adams' term expired, and he left several of the commissions to be delivered by Jefferson's incoming Secretary of State, James Madison. Among them was a commission appointing Marbury. Though signed and sealed, Marbury's commission was never delivered. Jefferson ordered Madison not to convey the commission. Marbury then requested the Supreme Court to issue Madison *a writ of mandamus*, which is a court order directing a public official to perform a required official act. This writ would have legally compelled Madison to deliver the commission to Marbury.

The Court was caught in a quandary. If it refused to issue the writ of mandamus, it would appear that it had caved in to pressure from the executive and this would severely affect the Court's prestige and independence. On the other hand, Jefferson had made it quite clear that his administration would ignore the Court's order if it issued the writ. This would reveal the Court's impotence, and, given the state's rights sympathies of the President and Congress, a weakened Court might have meant a permanently weakened union.

Marshall's decision in *Marbury* is testimony to his considerable political genius. Not only did he find a way out of the paradox with which the Court was faced, but he did it in a way that strengthened both the Court and the union. Marshall's decision agreed that Marbury had a legal right to the commission, that the administration's refusal to deliver it was wrong, and that a writ of mandamus was the proper legal remedy. Thus, he was able to chastise the Jefferson administration while maintaining the judiciary's authority to oversee ministers in the exercise of their duties. At the same time, however, Marshall was able to avoid displaying the Court's weakness by ruling that the Supreme Court lacked the authority to issue the writ of mandamus. Marshall's grounds for this was that the legislative act empowering the Court to issue mandamus was an unconstitutional expansion of the Court's original jurisdiction. In this way, Marshall avoided a disastrous confrontation with the Executive branch, and strengthened the power of the Court (and hence the national government). By refusing to grant the writ of mandamus, he had maneuvered the Democrats into silent approval of the Court's newly exercised power of judicial review.

Not everyone was convinced that Marshall had successfully defended the power of judicial review. Almost a quarter of a century after Marbury, Pennsylvania Supreme Court Justice John Gibson penned a dissenting opinion in *Eakin v. Raub* which many believe to be the best critical response to Marshall. Gibson did not take issue with the judiciary's power to review the constitutionality of acts of state governments. This, he noted, was granted by the supremacy clause of the Constitution. Gibson denied the power of the judicial branch to review the acts of coordinate branches of government. That is, Gibson denied that *state* courts could review the acts of *state* legislatures for violations of their *state* constitutions. Similarly, he denied that the *federal* courts could review the acts of *Congress* or the *President* for violations of the Federal Constitution.

Gibson argued that the legislature, even though limited, represents "the power of the people" and is, therefore, "sovereign as far as it extends." Its power is superior to the power of the judicial branch. In enacting statutes which might be contrary to the Constitution, Congress (or state legislatures with respect to state constitutions) "must necessarily first decide on the constitutionality of its own acts." Since the legislature represents the judgment of the representatives of the people, the Court does not have authority to substitute its interpretation of the meaning of the Constitution for that of the Congress. The remedy for an unconstitutional act by the government rests not with the Court, but "with the people, in whom full and absolute sovereign power resides...." It is the people who "correct abuses in legislation, by instructing their representatives to repeal the obnoxious act."

Although both "Brutus" and Justice Gibson expressed concern over the Court's power to nullify acts of Congress, the more pressing concern regarding judicial review in the early years of the Republic was the Court's oversight of state laws and constitutions. Indeed, much of the early controversy regarding judicial review was part of the larger debate between nationalists who wanted a strong centralized government and states' rights advocates who defended the sovereignty of the States. Brutus' major objection to judicial review, for example, was that it would inevitably lead to the total subordination of the States to the central government.

As significant as Marshall's decision in Marbury, then, are a series of cases which established the Court's power of judicial review over the state governments. In *Fletcher v. Peck, (1810)*, the Court asserted its authority to declare state legislative acts unconstitutional. In *Martin v. Hunter's Lessee, (1816)*, and in *Cohens v. Virginia, (1821)*, the Court insisted upon its authority to review the decisions of state courts whenever the Federal Constitution, laws or treaties were involved. A later and more pronounced expression of supremacy by the Court can be seen in *Cooper v. Aaron (1958)*.

LIMITATIONS ON JUDICIAL REVIEW

Very few Americans would today argue that the Supreme Court does not possess the power of judicial review. Rather, the continuing issue concerns the scope of the Court's power. Was "Brutus" correct when he argued that judicial review would inevitably lead to judicial tyranny? Are there limits on the Court's power? Can there be an unconstitutional exercise of judicial review? In recent years, concerns over judicial activism have grown so intense among even some mainstream critics as to lead them to begin to question the constitutional legitimacy of the Court itself.

There are, of course, a number of important limits upon the power of the Court. Among those which are *self-imposed* are:

1. *Adversity*. This means that the Court will not rule on the question of the constitutionality of an act except in a real "case" or "controversy" involving adverse parties, i.e., where there is a real conflict in the claims of the parties involved. Thus, the Court has declared that it will not give *advisory opinions*, judicial opinions upon the constitutionality of a law requested by a legislative body or a governmental agency, but not actually presented in a concrete case at law.
2. *Standing*. In order to challenge the validity of a governmental action, a person must have "standing." The plaintiff is required to demonstrate a substantial interest at stake in the controversy. In *Ex parte Levitt* (1937), the Court shed further light on the rule of standing by requiring persons challenging the constitutionality of a statute to show that they have sustained or are in immediate danger of sustaining a *direct* injury to their rights by the operation of the law. Consequently, the Court held in *Frothingham v. Mellon* (1923) that persons could not bring suit to enjoin the enforcement of federal appropriations statutes, including grants-in-aid, on the *sole* basis of being a taxpayer. Forty-five years later, in *Flast v. Cohen*, the Warren Court modified this ruling allowing "taxpayer suits" in controversies which involve a close nexus with a First Amendment right. Since then, the granting of standing to taxpayers or representatives of "public interest groups" has so waxed and waned that it is difficult to predict to whom the Court will grant standing, although the current Rehnquist Court has tended to tighten the rules of standing to make such suits more difficult to bring. See, for example, *Lujan v. Defenders of Wildlife*,(1992).
3. *Ripeness and mootness*. These represent flip sides of the same coin. The Court will dismiss a case for lack of ripeness when it believes the case has been prematurely brought. Mootness is used as the grounds to dismiss cases in which the controversy has been resolved by changing facts or laws. For example, when *Roe v. Wade* (1973) was appealed to the Supreme Court, Texas sought (unsuccessfully it turned out) to have the case dismissed because Roe had already given birth to the child she had been prevented by Texas law from aborting. That is, Texas claimed there was no longer any controversy; the issue was moot.
4. *Political Questions*. The Court has held for some time that it will not pass upon what it considers to be "political questions" or those which, because of the nature of the issues involved, should more properly be determined by the "political" or elective branches of the government – the president or the Congress. First in *Luther v. Borden* (1848), and later in *Pacific States Telephone & Telegraph Co. v. Oregon* (1912), the requirement of Article IV, Section 4, that each state have "a republican form of government" was held to be a "political question." The Court said that, under the doctrine of separated powers, Congress decides whether or not a state is "republican" in form when it seats a state's elected representatives in both houses of that body; it is not within the authority of the Court to do so. At first, the Court seemed to feel that the question of reapportionment of congressional and state legislative

districts was political in nature. In *Colegrove v. Green* (1946), by a 4-3 vote, the Court held that Article I, Section 4, designates that the federal responsibility of periodically redrawing Congressional districts is within the discretionary power of the state legislatures; if *malapportioned districts* are drawn, the matter is to be resolved either by act of Congress or through the political process of the ballot box, but not by the courts.[2] However, in the landmark case of *Baker v. Carr* (1962), this judicial policy was reversed.

The Court has continued to expand its supervision of elections and electoral districts since then. In *Powell v. McCormack* (1969), the Court held that a challenge to a congressman's qualifications to hold his seat was not completely political in nature even though each House of Congress is empowered by Article I to be the "judge" in such questions. In *Davis v. Bandemer* (1986) the Court extended its supervision of electoral districts to alleviate "*gerrymandered*" districts (districts whose boundaries are drawn to give a political party an advantage over its competitors) in addition to "malapportioned" districts. In *Shaw v. Reno* (1993) the Court extended this to include "*racial gerrymandering.*"

There are a number of *external* factors which limit the Court's effective exercise of the power of judicial review. The executive and/or state governments can refuse to implement a decision of the Court, or to "drag their feet" in doing so. The President can seek to influence the exercise of the power through whom he appoints to the Court. Congress can remove the Court's appellate jurisdiction thus preventing the Court from ruling on a case, or threaten the Court with budget cutbacks, or, in some cases, even pass a modified law to replace one the Court has determined to be unconstitutional. Congress could ultimately impeach members of the Court. As Hamilton noted, the Court possesses neither the purse nor the sword and can be forced to submit to either. However, the very recitation of the possible external limits also proves the point that the Constitution provided for an *independent* judiciary. Absent a constitutional crisis, limits on the Court's power of judicial review are essentially those which are self-imposed.

The Constitution provides one means for "correcting" decisions of the Supreme Court. A concomitant part of the "checks and balances system" is that Congress and the state legislatures are empowered to abrogate, in effect, decisions of the Supreme Court through the process of *amendment*. Since 1798, four amendments have been ratified which overruled "controversial" decisions of the Court: the Eleventh Amendment (*Chisholm v. Georgia*, 1793) the Fourteenth Amendment (*Dred Scott v. Sanford*, 1857), and the Sixteenth Amendment (*Pollock v. Farmer's Loan and Trust Co.*, 1895). The Twenty-sixth Amendment, which lowered the voting age to citizens of eighteen years of age in both federal and state elections, was ratified on July 5, 1971 on the heels of *Oregon v. Mitchell* (1970). The Court had held that while Congress could by statutory enactment, lower the voting age for citizens in national elections, it must rely on the amendment procedure to do so with respect to elections for state and local office. There have been a number of movements in recent years to pass amendments to overturn other Court decisions, including ones to repeal *Roe v. Wade* (1973), the right to an abortion, and *Engel v. Vitali* (1962), banning school prayer. The difficulty and infrequency of constitutional amendments emphasizes that the Court is indeed supreme.

FEDERALIST 78

To the People of the State of New York:

WE PROCEED now to an examination of the judiciary department of the proposed government.... According to the plan of the convention, all judges who may be appointed by the United States are to hold their offices DURING GOOD BEHAVIOR; which is conformable to the most approved of the State constitutions and among the rest, to that of this State. Its propriety having been drawn into question by the adversaries of that plan, is no light symptom of the rage for objection, which disorders their imaginations and judgments. The standard of good behavior for the continuance in office of the judicial magistracy, is certainly one of the most valuable of the modern improvements in the practice of government. In a monarchy it is an excellent barrier to the despotism of the prince; in a republic it is a no less excellent barrier to the encroachments and oppressions of the representative body. And it is the best expedient which can be devised in any government, to secure a steady, upright, and impartial administration of the laws.

Whoever attentively considers the different departments of power must perceive, that, in a government in which they are separated from each other, the judiciary, from the nature of its functions, will always be the least dangerous to the political rights of the Constitution; because it will be least in a capacity to annoy or injure them. The Executive not only dispenses the honors, but holds the sword of the community. The legislature not only commands the purse, but prescribes the rules by which the duties and rights of every citizen are to be regulated. The judiciary, on the contrary, has no influence over either the sword or the purse; no direction either of the strength or of the wealth of the society; and can take no active resolution whatever. It may truly be said to have neither FORCE nor WILL, but merely judgment; and must ultimately depend upon the aid of the executive arm even for the efficacy of its judgments.

This simple view of the matter suggests several important consequences. It proves incontestably, that the judiciary is beyond comparison the weakest of the three departments of power; that it can never attack with success either of the other two; and that all possible care is requisite to enable it to defend itself against their attacks. It equally proves, that though individual oppression may now and then proceed from the courts of justice, the general liberty of the people can never be endangered from that quarter; I mean so long as the judiciary remains truly distinct from both the legislature and the Executive. For I agree, that "there is no liberty, if the power of judging be not separated from the legislative and executive powers." And it proves, in the last place, that as liberty can have nothing to fear from the judiciary alone, but would have every thing to fear from its union with either of the other departments; that as all the effects of such a union must ensue from a dependence of the former on the latter, notwithstanding a nominal and apparent separation; that as, from the natural feebleness of the judiciary, it is in continual jeopardy of being overpowered, awed, or influenced by its coordinate branches; and that as nothing can contribute so much to its firmness and independence as permanency in office, this quality may therefore be justly regarded as an indispensable ingredient in its constitution, and, in a great measure, as the citadel of the public justice and the public security.

The complete independence of the courts of justice is peculiarly essential in a limited Constitution. By a limited Constitution, I understand one which contains certain specified exceptions to the legislative authority; such, for instance, as that it shall pass no bills of attainder, no ex-post-facto laws, and the like. Limitations of this kind can be preserved in practice no other way than through the medium of courts of justice, whose duty it must be to declare all acts contrary to the manifest tenor of the Constitution void. Without this, all the reservations of particular rights or privileges would amount to nothing.

Some perplexity respecting the rights of the courts to pronounce legislative acts void, because contrary to the Constitution, has arisen from an imagination that the doctrine would imply a superiority of the judiciary to the legislative power. It is urged that the authority which can declare the acts of another void, must necessarily be superior to the one whose acts may be declared void. As this doctrine is of great importance in all the American constitutions, a brief discussion of the ground on which it rests cannot be unacceptable.

There is no position which depends on clearer principles, than that every act of a delegated authority, contrary to the tenor of the commission under which it is exercised, is void. No legislative act, therefore, contrary to the Constitution, can be valid. To deny this, would be to affirm, that the deputy is greater than his principal; that the servant is above his master; that the representatives of the people are superior to the people themselves; that men acting by virtue of powers, may do not only what their powers do not authorize, but what they forbid.

If it be said that the legislative body are themselves the constitutional judges of their own powers, and that the construction they put upon them is conclusive upon the other departments, it may be answered, that this cannot be the natural presumption, where it is not to be collected from any particular provisions in the Constitution. It is not otherwise to be supposed that the Constitution could intend to enable the representatives of the people to substitute their WILL to that of their constituents. It is far more rational to suppose that the courts were designed to be an intermediate body between the people and the legislature, in order, among other things, to keep the latter within the limits assigned to their authority. The interpretation of the laws is the proper and peculiar province of the courts. A constitution is, in fact, and must be regarded by the judges, as a fundamental law. It therefore belongs to them to ascertain its meaning, as well as the meaning of any particular act proceeding from the legislative body. If there should happen to be an irreconcilable variance between the two, that which has the superior obligation and validity ought, of course, to be preferred; or, in other words, the Constitution ought to be preferred to the statute, the intention of the people to the intention of their agents.

Nor does this conclusion by any means suppose a superiority of the judicial to the legislative power. It only supposes that the power of the people is superior to both; and that where the will of the legislature, declared in its statutes, stands in opposition to that of the people, declared in the Constitution, the judges ought to be governed by the latter rather than the former. They ought to regulate their decisions by the fundamental laws, rather than by those which are not fundamental.... [N]ature and reason.... teach us that the prior act of a superior ought to be preferred to the subsequent act of an inferior and subordinate authority; and that accordingly, whenever a particular statute contravenes the Constitution, it will be the duty of the judicial tribunals to adhere to the latter and disregard the former. It can be of no weight to say that the courts, on the pretense of a repugnancy, may substitute their own pleasure to the constitutional intentions of the legislature. This might as well happen in the case of two contradictory statutes; or it might as well happen in every adjudication upon any single statute. The courts must declare the sense of the law; and if they should be disposed to exercise WILL instead of JUDGMENT, the consequence would equally be the substitution of their pleasure to that of the legislative body. The observation, if it prove any thing, would prove that there ought to be no judges distinct from that body.

If, then, the courts of justice are to be considered as the bulwarks of a limited Constitution against legislative encroachments, this consideration will afford a strong argument for the permanent tenure of judicial offices, since nothing will contribute so much as this to that independent spirit in the judges which must be essential to the faithful performance of so arduous a duty.

This independence of the judges is equally requisite to guard the Constitution and the rights of individuals from the effects of those ill humors, which the arts of designing men, or the influence of particular conjunctures, sometimes disseminate among the people themselves, and which, though they speedily give place to better information, and more deliberate reflection, have a tendency, in the meantime, to occasion dangerous innovations in the government, and serious oppressions of the minor party in the community. Though I trust the friends of the proposed Constitution will never concur with its enemies, in questioning that fundamental principle of republican government, which admits the right of the people to alter or abolish the established Constitution, whenever they find it inconsistent with their happiness, yet it is not to be inferred from this principle, that the representatives of the people, whenever a momentary inclination happens to lay hold of a majority of their constituents, incompatible with the provisions in the existing Constitution, would, on that account, be justifiable in a violation of those provisions; or that the courts would be under a greater obligation to connive at infractions in this shape, than when they had proceeded wholly from the cabals of the representative body. Until the people have, by some solemn and authoritative act, annulled or changed the established form, it is binding upon themselves collectively, as well as individually; and no presumption, or even knowledge, of their sentiments, can warrant their representatives in a departure from it, prior to such an act. But it is easy to see, that it would require an uncommon portion of fortitude in the judges to do their duty as faithful guardians of the Constitution, where legislative invasions of it had been instigated by the major voice of the community. But it is not with a view to infractions of the Constitution only, that the independence of the judges may be an essential safeguard against the effects of occasional ill humors in the society. These sometimes extend no farther than to the injury of the private rights of particular classes of citizens, by unjust and partial laws. Here also the firmness of the judicial magistracy is of vast importance in mitigating the severity and confining the operation of such laws. It not only serves to moderate the immediate mischiefs of those which may have been passed, but it operates as a check upon the legislative body in passing them; who, perceiving that obstacles to the success of iniquitous intention are to be expected from the scruples of the courts, are in a manner compelled, by the very motives of the injustice they meditate, to qualify their attempts. This is a circumstance calculated to have more influence upon the character of our governments, than but few may be aware of. The benefits of the integrity and moderation of the judiciary have already been felt in more States than one; and though they may have displeased those whose sinister expectations they may have disappointed, they must have commanded the esteem and applause of all the virtuous and disinterested. Considerate men, of every description, ought to prize whatever will tend to beget or fortify that temper in the courts: as no man can be sure that he may not be to-morrow the victim of a spirit of injustice, by which he may be a gainer to-day. And every man must now feel, that the inevitable tendency of such a spirit is to sap the foundations of public and private confidence, and to introduce in its stead universal distrust and distress.... PUBLIUS

FEDERALIST NO. 80

To the People of the State of New York:

To JUDGE with accuracy of the proper extent of the federal judicature, it will be necessary to consider, in the first place, what are its proper objects. It seems scarcely to admit of controversy, that the judicary authority of the Union ought to extend to these several descriptions of cases: 1st, to all those which arise out of the laws of the United States, passed in pursuance of their just and constitutional powers of legislation; 2d, to all those which concern the execution of the provisions expressly contained in the articles of Union; 3d, to all those in which the United States are a party; 4th, to all those which involve the PEACE of the CONFEDERACY, whether they relate to the intercourse between the United States and foreign nations, or to that between the States themselves; 5th, to all those which originate on the high seas, and are of admiralty or maritime jurisdiction; and, lastly, to all those in which the State tribunals cannot be supposed to be impartial and unbiased. The first point depends upon this obvious consideration, that there ought always to be a constitutional method of giving efficacy to constitutional provisions. What, for instance, would avail restrictions on the authority of the State legislatures, without some constitutional mode of enforcing the observance of them? The States, by the plan of the convention, are prohibited from doing a variety of things, some of which are incompatible with the interests of the Union, and others with the principles of good government. The imposition of duties on imported articles, and the emission of paper money, are specimens of each kind. No man of sense will believe, that such prohibitions would be scrupulously regarded, without some effectual power in the government to restrain or correct the infractions of them. This power must either be a direct negative on the State laws, or an authority in the federal courts to overrule such as might be in manifest contravention of the articles of Union. There is no third course that I can imagine. The latter appears to have been thought by the convention preferable to the former, and, I presume, will be most agreeable to the States. As to the second point, it is impossible, by any argument or comment, to make it clearer than it is in itself. If there are such things as political axioms, the propriety of the judicial power of a government being coextensive with its legislative, may be ranked among the number. The mere necessity of uniformity in the interpretation of the national laws, decides the question. Thirteen independent courts of final jurisdiction over the same causes, arising upon the same laws, is a hydra in government, from which nothing but contradiction and confusion can proceed. Still less need be said in regard to the third point. Controversies between the nation and its members or citizens, can only be properly referred to the national tribunals. Any other plan would be contrary to reason, to precedent, and to decorum. The fourth point rests on this plain proposition, that the peace of the WHOLE ought not to be left at the disposal of a PART. The Union will undoubtedly be answerable to foreign powers for the conduct of its members…. The fifth point will demand little animadversion. The most bigoted idolizers of State authority have not thus far shown a disposition to deny the national judiciary the cognizances of maritime causes. These so generally depend on the laws of nations, and so commonly affect the rights of foreigners, that they fall within the considerations which are relative to the public peace. The most important part of them are, by the present Confederation, submitted to federal jurisdiction. The reasonableness of the agency of the national courts in cases in which the State tribunals cannot be supposed to be impartial, speaks for itself. No man ought certainly to be a judge in his own cause, or in any cause in respect to which he has the least interest or bias. This principle has no inconsiderable weight in designating the federal courts as the proper tribunals for the determination of controversies between different States and their citizens. And it ought to have the same operation in regard to some cases between citizens of the same State. Claims to land under grants of different States, founded upon adverse pretensions of boundary, are of this description….

It has been asked, what is meant by "cases arising under the Constitution," in contradiction from those "arising under the laws of the United States"? The difference has been already explained. All the restrictions upon the authority of the State legislatures furnish examples of it. They are not, for instance, to emit paper money; but the interdiction results from the Constitution, and will have no connection with any law of the United States. Should paper money, notwithstanding, be emited, the controversies concerning it would be cases arising under the Constitution and not the laws of the United States, in the ordinary signification of the terms. This may serve as a sample of the whole....PUBLIUS.

THE ESSAYS OF BRUTUS

The nature and extent of the judicial power of the United States, proposed to be granted by this constitution, claims our particular attention.

...This government is a complete system, not only for making, but for executing laws. And the courts of law, which will be constituted by it, are not only to decide upon the constitution and the laws made in pursuance of it, but by officers subordinate to them to execute all their decisions. The real effect of this system of government, will therefore be brought home to the feelings of the people, through the medium of the judicial power. It is, moreover, of great importance, to examine with care the nature and extent of the judicial power, because those who are to be vested with it, are to be placed in a situation altogether unprecedented in a free country. They are to be rendered totally independent, both of the people and the legislature, both with respect to their offices and salaries. No errors they may commit can be corrected by any power above them, if any such power there be, nor can they be removed from office for making ever so many erroneous adjudications....

Though I am not competent to give a perfect explanation of the powers granted to this department of the government, I shall yet attempt to trace some of the leading features of it, from which I presume it will appear, that they will operate to a total subversion of the state judiciaries, if not, to the legislative authority of the states.

In article 3d, sect. 2d, it is said, "The judicial power shall extend to all cases in law and equity arising under this constitution, the laws of the United States, and treaties made, or which shall be made, under their authority, &c...."

This article, therefore, vests the judicial with a power to resolve all questions that may arise on any case on the construction of the constitution, either in law or in equity.

1st. They are authorised to determine all questions that may arise upon the meaning of the constitution in law. This article vests the courts with authority to give the constitution a legal construction, or to explain it according to the rules laid down for construing a law. These rules give a certain degree of latitude of explanation. According to this mode of construction, the courts are to give such meaning to the constitution as comports best with the common, and generally received acceptation of the words in which it is expressed, regarding their ordinary and popular use, rather than their grammatical propriety. Where words are dubious, they will be explained by the context. The end of the clause will be attended to, and the words will be understood, as having a view to it; and the words will not be so understood as to bear no meaning or a very absurd one.

2d. The judicial are not only to decide questions arising upon the meaning of the constitution in law, but also in equity.

By this they are empowered, to explain the constitution according to the reasoning spirit of it, without being confined to the words or letter.

"From this method of interpreting laws (says Blackstone) by the reason of them, arises what we call equity;" which is thus defined by Grotius, "the correction of that, wherein the law, by reason of its universality, is deficient; for since in laws all cases cannot be foreseen, or expressed, it is necessary, that when the decrees of the law cannot be applied to particular cases, there should some where be a power vested of defining those circumstances, which had they been foreseen the legislator would have expressed; ...

From these remarks, the authority and business of the courts of law, under this clause, may be understood.

They will give the sense of every article of the constitution, that may from time to time come before them. And in their decisions they will not confine themselves to any fixed or established rules, but will determine, according to what appears to them, the reason and spirit of the constitution. The opinions of the supreme court, whatever they may be, will have the force of law; because there is no power provided in the constitution, that can correct their errors, or controul their adjudications. From this court there is no appeal. And I conceive the legislature themselves, cannot set aside a judgment of this court, because they are authorised by the constitution to decide in the last resort. The legislature must be controuled by the constitution, and not the constitution by them....

The judicial power will operate to effect, in the most certain, but yet silent and imperceptible manner, what is evidently the tendency of the constitution: – I mean, an entire subversion of the legislative, executive and judicial powers of the individual states. Every adjudication of the supreme court, on any question that may arise upon the nature and extent of the general government, will affect the limits of the state jurisdiction. In proportion as the former enlarge the exercise of their powers, will that of the latter be restricted.

That the judicial power of the United States, will lean strongly in favour of the general government, and will give such an explanation to the constitution, as will favour an extension of its jurisdiction, is very evident from a variety of considerations.

1st. The constitution itself strongly countenances such a mode of construction. Most of the articles in this system, which convey powers of any considerable importance, are conceived in general and indefinite terms, which are either equivocal, ambiguous, or which require long definitions to unfold the extent of their meaning.... The clause which vests the power to pass all laws which are proper and necessary, to carry the powers given into execution, it has been shewn, leaves the legislature at liberty, to do every thing, which in their judgment is best....

2d. Not only will the constitution justify the courts in inclining to this mode of explaining it, but they will be interested in using this latitude of interpretation. Every body of men invested with office are tenacious of power; they feel interested, and hence it has become a kind of maxim, to hand down their offices, with all its rights and privileges, unimpared to their successors; the same principle will influence them to extend their power, and increase their rights; this of itself will operate strongly upon the courts to give such a meaning to the constitution in all cases where it can possibly be done, as will enlarge the sphere of their own authority. Every extension of the power of the general legislature, as well as of the judicial powers, will increase the powers of the courts; and the dignity and importance of the judges, will be in proportion to the extent and magnitude of the powers they exercise....

3d. Because they will have precedent to plead, to justify them in it. It is well known, that the courts in England, have by their own authority, extended their jurisdiction far beyond the limits set them in their original institution, and by the laws of the land....

When the courts will have a precedent before them of a court which extended its jurisdiction in opposition to an act of the legislature, is it not to be expected that they will extend theirs, especially when there is nothing in the constitution expressly against it? and they are authorised to construe its meaning, and are not under any controul?

This power in the judicial, will enable them to mould the government, into almost any shape they please. The manner in which this may be effected we will hereafter examine.

****

...First. Let us enquire how the judicial power will effect an extension of the legislative authority.

Perhaps the judicial power will not be able, by direct and positive decrees, ever to direct the legislature, because it is not easy to conceive how a question can be brought before them in a course of legal discussion, in which they can give a decision, declaring, that the legislature have certain powers which they have not exercised, and which, in consequence of the determination of the judges, they will be bound to exercise. But it is easy to see, that in their adjudications they may establish certain principles, which being received by the legislature, will enlarge the sphere of their power beyond all bounds.

It is to be observed, that the supreme court has the power, in the last resort, to determine all questions that may arise in the course of legal discussion, on the meaning and construction of the constitution. This power they will hold under the constitution, and independent of the legislature....

In determining these questions, the court must and will assume certain principles, from which they will reason, in forming their decisions. These principles, whatever they may be, when they become fixed, by a course of decisions, will be adopted by the legislature, and will be the rule by which they will explain their own powers. This appears evident from this consideration, that if the legislature pass laws, which, in the judgment of the court, they are not authorised to do by the constitution, the court will not take notice of them; for it will not be denied, that the constitution is the highest or supreme law. And the courts are vested with the supreme and uncontroulable power, to determine, in all cases that come before them, what the constitution means; they cannot, therefore, execute a law, which, in their judgment, opposes the constitution, unless we can suppose they can make a superior law give way to an inferior. The legislature, therefore, will not go over the limits by which the courts may adjudge they are confined. And there is little room to doubt but that they will come up to those bounds, as often as occasion and opportunity may offer, and they may judge it proper to do it. For as on the one hand, they will not readily pass laws which they know the courts will not execute, so on the other, we may be sure they will not scruple to pass such as they know they will give effect, as often as they may judge it proper.

From these observations it appears, that the judgment of the judicial, on the constitution, will become the rule to guide the legislature in their construction of their powers.

What the principles are, which the courts will adopt, it is impossible for us to say; but taking up the powers as I have explained them in my last number, which they will possess under this clause, it is not difficult to see, that they may, and probably will, be very liberal ones.

We have seen, that they will be authorized to give the constitution a construction according to its spirit and reason, and not to confine themselves to its letter....

The first object declared to be in view is, "To form a perfect union." It is to be observed, it is not an union of states or bodies corporate; had this been the case the existence of the state governments, might have been secured, But it is a union of the people of the United States considered as one body, who are to ratify this constitution, if it is adopted. Now to make a union of this kind perfect, it is necessary to abolish all inferior governments, and to give the general one compleat legislative, executive and judicial powers to every purpose. The courts therefore will establish it as a rule in explaining the constitution to give it such a construction as will best tend to perfect the union or take from the state governments every power of either making or executing laws....

As it sets out in the preamble with this declared intention, so it proceeds in the different parts with the same idea. Any person, who will peruse the 8th section with attention, in which most of the powers are enumerated, will perceive that they either expressly or by implication extend to almost every thing about which any legislative power can be employed. But if this equitable mode of construction is applied to this part of the constitution; nothing can stand before it.

This will certainly give the first clause in that article a construction which I confess I think the most natural and grammatical one, to authorise the Congress to do any thing which in their judgment will tend to provide for the general welfare, and this amounts to the same thing as general and unlimited powers of legislation in all cases.

******

I said in my last number, that the supreme court under this constitution would be exalted above all other power in the government, and subject to no controul. The business of this paper will be to illustrate this, and to shew the danger that will result from it. ...

The judges in England, it is true, hold their offices during their good behaviour, but then their determinations are subject to correction by the house of lords; and their power is by no means so extensive as that of the proposed supreme court of the union. I believe they in no instance assume the authority to set aside an act of parliament under the idea that it is inconsistent with their constitution. They consider themselves bound to decide according to the existing laws of the land, and never undertake to controul them by adjudging that they are inconsistent with the constitution – much less are they vested with the power of giving an *equitable* construction to the constitution.

The judges in England are under the controul of the legislature, for they are bound to determine according to the laws passed by them. But the judges under this constitution will controul the legislature, for the supreme court are authorised in the last resort, to determine what is the extent of the powers of the Congress; they are to give the constitution an explanation, and there is no power above them to set aside their judgment....

...There is no power above them, to controul any of their decisions. There is no authority that can remove them, and they cannot be controuled by the laws of the legislature. In short, they are independent of the people, of the legislature, and of every power under heaven. Men placed in this situation will generally soon feel themselves independent of heaven itself....

I have said that the judges under this system will be *independent* in the strict sense of the word: To prove this I will shew – That there is no power above them that can controul their decisions, or correct their errors....

1st. There is no power above them that can correct their errors or controul their decisions – The adjudications of this court are final and irreversible, for there is no court above them to which appeals can lie, either in error or on the merits....

2d. They cannot be removed from office or suffer a dimunition of their salaries, for any error in judgement or want of capacity....

3d. The power of this court is in many cases superior to that of the legislature. I have shewed, in a former paper, that this court will be authorised to decide upon the meaning of the constitution, and that, not only according to the natural and obvious meaning of the words, but also according to the spirit and intention of it. In the exercise of this power they will not be subordinate to, but above the legislature. For all the departments of this government will receive their powers, so far as they are expressed in the constitution, from the people immediately, who are the source of power. The legislature can only exercise such powers as are given them by the constitution, they cannot assume any of the rights annexed to the judicial, for this plain reason, that the same authority which vested the legislature with their powers, vested the judicial with theirs – both are derived from the same source, both therefore are equally valid, and the judicial hold their powers independently of the legislature, as the legislature do of the judicial. The supreme court then have a right, independent of the legislature, to give a construction to the constitution and every part of it, and there is no power provided in this system to correct their construction or do it away. If, therefore, the legislature pass any laws, inconsistent with the sense the judges put upon the constitution, they will declare it void; and therefore in this respect their power is superior to that of the legislature. In England the judges are not only subject to have their decisions set aside by the house of lords, for error, but in cases where they give an explanation to the laws or constitution of the country, contrary to the sense of the parliament, though the parliament will not set aside the judgement of the court, yet, they have authority, by a new law, to explain a former one, and by this means to prevent a reception of such decisions. But no such power is in the legislature. The judges are supreme – and no law, explanatory of the constitution, will be binding on them....

Perhaps nothing could have been better conceived to facilitate the abolition of the state governments than the constitution of the judicial. They will be able to extend the limits of the general government gradually, and by insensible degrees, and to accomodate themselves to the temper of the people. Their decisions on the meaning of the constitution will commonly take place in cases which arise between individuals, with which the public will not be generally acquainted; one adjudication will form a precedent to the next, and this to a following one. These cases will immediately affect individuals only; so that a series of determinations will probably take place before even the people will be informed of them. In the mean time all the art and address of those who wish for the change will be employed to make converts to their opinion.... In this situation, the general legislature, might pass one law after another, extending the general and abridging the state jurisdictions, and to sanction their proceedings would have a course of decisions of the judicial to whom the constitution has committed the power of explaining the constitution. If the states remonstrated, the constitutional mode of deciding upon the validity of the law, is with the supreme court, and neither people, nor state legislatures, nor the general legislature can remove them or reverse their decrees.

Had the construction of the constitution been left with the legislature, they would have explained it at their peril; if they exceed their powers, or sought to find, in the spirit of the constitution, more than was expressed in the letter, the people from whom they derived their power could remove them, and do themselves right; and indeed I can see no other remedy that the people can have against their rulers for encroachments of this nature. A constitution is a compact of a people with their rulers; if the rulers break the compact, the people have a right and ought to remove them and do themselves justice; but in order to enable them to do this with the greater facility, those whom the people chuse at stated periods, should have the power in the last resort to determine the sense of the compact; if they determine contrary to the understanding of the people, an appeal will lie to the people at the period when the rulers are to be elected, and they will have it in their power to remedy the evil; but when this power is lodged in the hands of men independent of the people, and of their representatives, and who are not, constitutionally, accountable for their opinions, no way is left to controul them but *with a high hand and an outstretched arm.*

CALDER V. BULL
3 Dallas 386; 1 L.Ed. 648 (1798)

In 1793, the Probate Court of Hartford rejected the will of N. Morrison under which Bull and his wife claimed property and gave its decision in favor of the claims of Calder and his wife. In 1795 the Connecticut legislature passed a law granting a new hearing in the case. In the new hearing, the Probate court upheld Morrison's will and the property was transferred to Bull. Calder appealed to the Supreme Court on the grounds that the Connecticut statute was an ex post facto law and therefore unconstitutional. The Supreme Court restricted the meaning of ex post facto to criminal laws, and upheld the Connecticut statute. The following excerpts from the case contain a famous exchange between Justices Chase and Iredell on the scope of judicial review.

CHASE, JUSTICE; ...

Whether the Legislature of any of the states can revise and correct by law, a decision of any of its courts of justice, although not prohibited by the constitution of the state, is a question of very great importance, and not necessary now to be determined; because the resolution or law in question does not go so far. I cannot subscribe to the omnipotence of a state Legislature, or that it is absolute and without control; although its authority should not be expressly restrained by the constitution, or fundamental law, of the state. The people of the United States erected their constitutions, or forms of government, to establish justice, to promote the general welfare, to secure the blessings of liberty, and to protect their persons and property from violence. The purposes for which men enter into society will determine the nature and terms of the social compact; and as they are the foundation of the legislative power, they will decide what are the proper objects of it: The nature, and ends of legislative power will limit the exercise of it. This fundamental principle flows from the very nature of our free Republican governments, that no man should be compelled to do what the laws do not require; nor to refrain from acts which the laws permit. There are acts which the federal, or state, Legislature cannot do, without exceeding their authority. There are certain vital principles in our free Republican governments, which will determine and overrule an apparent and flagrant abuse of legislative power; as to authorize manifest injustice by positive law; or to take away that security for personal liberty, or private property, for the protection whereof the government was established. An act of the Legislature (for I cannot call it a law) contrary to the great first principles of the social compact, cannot be considered a rightful exercise of legislative authority. The obligation of a law in governments established on express compact, and on republican principles, must be determined by the nature of the power, on which it is founded. A few instances will suffice to explain what I mean. A law that punished a citizen for an innocent action, or, in other words, for an act, which, when done, was in violation of no existing law; a law that destroys, or impairs, the lawful private contracts of citizens; a law that makes a man a judge in his own cause; or a law that takes property from A. and gives it to B. It is against all reason and justice, for a people to entrust a Legislature with such powers; and, therefore, it cannot be presumed that they have done it. The genius, the nature, and the spirit, of our state governments, amount to a prohibition of such acts of legislation; and the general principles of law and reason forbid them. The Legislature may enjoin, permit, forbid, and punish; they may declare new crimes; and establish rules of conduct for all its citizens in future cases; they may command what is right, and prohibit what is wrong; but they cannot change innocence into guilt; or punish innocence as a crime, or violate the right of an antecedent lawful private contract; or the right of private property. To maintain that our federal, or state, Legislature possesses such powers, if they had not been expressly restrained, would, in my opinion, be a political heresy, altogether inadmissible in our free republican governments....

IREDELL, JUSTICE; ...

If, then, a government, composed of legislative, executive and judicial departments, were established, by a Constitution, which imposed no limits on the legislative power, the consequence would inevitably be, that whatever the legislative power chose to enact, would be lawfully enacted, and the judicial power, could never interpose to pronounce it void. It is true, that some speculative jurists have held, that a legislative act against natural justice must, in itself, be void; but I cannot think that, under such a government, any court of justice would possess a power to declare it so. Sir William Blackstone, having put the strong case of an act of parliament, which should authorize a man to try his own cause, explicitly adds, that even in that case, "there is no court that has power to defeat the intent of the legislature, when couched in such evident and express words as leave no doubt whether it was the intent of the legislature, or no." 1 Bl. Com. 91.

In order, therefore, to guard against so great an evil, it has been the policy of all the American states, which have, individually, framed their state constitutions since the revolution, and of the people of the United States, when they framed the federal constitution, to define with precision the objects of the legislative power, and to restrain its exercise within marked and settled boundaries. If any act of Congress, or of the legislature of a state, violates those constitutional provisions, it is unquestionably void; though, I admit, that as the authority to declare it void is of a delicate and awful nature, the court will never resort to that authority, but in a clear and urgent case. If on the other hand, the legislature of the union, or the legislature of any member of the union, shall pass a law, within the general scope of their constitutional power, the court cannot pronounce it to be void merely because it is, in their judgment, contrary to the principles of natural justice. The ideas of natural justice are regulated by no fixed standard; the ablest and the purest men have differed upon the subject; and all that the court could properly say, in such an event, would be, that the legislature (possessed of an equal right of opinion) had passed an act which, in the opinion of the judges, was inconsistent with the abstract principles of natural justice. There are then but two lights, in which the subject can be viewed. 1st. If the legislature pursue the authority delegated to them, their acts are valid. 2d. If they transgress the boundaries of that authority, their acts are invalid. In the former case, they exercise the discretion vested in them by the people, to whom alone they are responsible for the faithful discharge of their trust; but in the latter case, they violate a fundamental law, which must be our guide, whenever we are called upon as judges to determine the validity of a legislative act....

MARBURY v. MADISON
1Cranch 137; 2 L.Ed. 60 (1803)

In the waning days of the Federalist administration of President John Adams, every effort was made "to stack" the federal courts with the party faithful before March 4, 1801, at which time Thomas Jefferson and the Republicans would assume power. In February, Congress enacted two statutes, including the Judiciary Act of 1801, which not only increased the number of federal judgeships but also permitted the President to appoint as many "justices of the peace" for the District of Columbia as he desired. In the latter category, one of the new judges appointed by Adams was William Marbury, whose commission was signed and sealed on March 3. Shortly thereafter, the new Secretary of State, James Madison, refused to grant Marbury his commission. The aggrieved appointee then filed suit with the Supreme Court to issue a writ of mandamus, *under its original jurisdiction, to compel Madison to take affirmative action. The authority of the Court to grant a writ in such cases was provided by the Judiciary Act of 1789. John Marshall, also the recipient of a "midnight appointment" by Adams, served as Chief Justice when the case came to the Court in 1803. Marbury v. Madison served as the first case in which the Court clearly declared an act of Congress unconstitutional.*

MR. CHIEF JUSTICE MARSHALL delivered the opinion of the Court:

In the order in which the Court has viewed this subject, the following questions have been considered and decided.

lst. Has the applicant a right to be commissioned as he demands?

2nd. If he has a right, and that right has been violated, do the laws of his country afford him a remedy? ... (The Court found in the affirmative-native on the 1st and 2nd questions.)

3rd. If they do afford him a remedy, is it a mandamus issuing from this court? ...

This, then, is a plain case for a mandamus, either to deliver the commission, or a copy of it from the record; and it only remains to be inquired whether it can issue from this court. The act to establish the judicial courts of the

United States authorizes the Supreme Court "to issue writs of mandamus in cases warranted by the principles and usages of law, to any courts appointed, or persons holding office, under the authority of the United States."

The Secretary of State, being a person holding an office tinder the authority of the United States, is precisely within the letter of the description, and if this court is not authorized to issue a writ of mandamus to such an officer, it must be because the law is unconstitutional, and therefore absolutely incapable of conferring the authority, and assigning the duties which its word purport to confer and assign.

The Constitution vests the whole judicial power of the United States in one Supreme Court, and such inferior courts as Congress shall, from time to time, ordain and establish ....

In the distribution of this power it is declared that "the Supreme Court shall have original jurisdiction in all cases affecting ambassadors, other public ministers and consuls, and those in which a state shall be a party. In all other cases, the Supreme Court shall have appellate jurisdiction…."

If it had been intended to leave it in the discretion of the legislature to apportion the judicial power between the supreme and inferior courts according to the will of that body, it would certainly have been useless to have proceeded further than to have defined the judicial power, and the tribunals in which it should be vested. The subsequent part of the section is mere surplusage, is entirely without meaning..., If Congress remains at liberty to give this court appellate jurisdiction, where the Constitution has declared their jurisdiction shall be original; and original where the Constitution has declared it shall be appellate, the distribution of jurisdiction, made in the Constitution, is form without substance ....

It cannot be presumed that any clause in the Constitution is intended to be without effect; and therefore, such a construction is inadmissible, unless the words require it ....

To enable this court, then, to issue a mandamus, it must be shown to be an exercise of appellate jurisdiction, or to be necessary to enable them to exercise appellate jurisdiction ....

It is the essential criterion of appellate jurisdiction, that it revises and corrects the proceedings in a cause already instituted, and does not create that cause. Although, therefore, a mandamus may be directed to courts, yet to issue such a writ to an officer for the delivery of a paper, is in effect the same as to sustain an original action for that paper, and therefore, seems not to belong to appellate, but to original jurisdiction. Neither is it necessary in such a case as this, to enable the court to exercise its appellate jurisdiction.

The authority, therefore, given to the Supreme Court, by the Act establishing the judicial courts of the United States, to issue writs of mandamus to public officers, appears not to be warranted by the Constitution; and it becomes necessary to inquire whether a jurisdiction so conferred can be exercised. The question, whether an Act, repugnant to the Constitution can become the law of the land, is a question deeply interesting to the United States; but, happily, not of an intricacy proportioned to its interest. It seems only necessary to recognize certain principles, supposed to have been long and well established, to decide it.

That the people have an original right to establish, for their future government, such principles as, in their opinion, shall most conduce to their own happiness, is the basis on which the whole American fabric has been erected. The exercise of this original right is a very great exertion; nor can it nor ought it to be frequently repeated. The principles, therefore, so established, are deemed fundamental. And as the authority from which they proceed is supreme, and can seldom act, they are designed to be permanent. This original and supreme will organizes the government, and assigns to different departments their respective powers. It may either stop here, or establish certain limits not to be transcended by those departments.

The government of the United States is of the later description. The powers of the legislature are defined and limited; and that those limits may not be mistaken, or forgotten, the Constitution is written. To what purpose are powers limited, and to what purpose is that limitation committed to writing, if these limits may, at any time, be passed by those intended to be restrained? The distinction between a government with limited and unlimited powers is abolished, if those limits do not confine the persons on whom they are imposed, and if acts prohibited and acts allowed are of equal obligation. It is a proposition too plain to be contested, that the Constitution controls any legislative Act repugnant to it; or, that the legislature may alter the Constitution by an ordinary Act.

Between those alternatives there is no middle ground. The Constitution is either a superior paramount law, unchangeable by ordinary means, or it is on a level with ordinary legislative Acts, and like other Acts, is alterable when the legislature shall please to alter it.

If the former part of the alternative be true, then a legislative Act contrary to the Constitution is not law; if the latter part be true, then written constitutions are absurd attempts, on the part of the people, to limit a power in its own nature illimitable.

Certainly all those who have framed written constitutions contemplate them as forming the fundamental and paramount law of the nation, and, consequently, the theory of every such government must be, that an Act of the Legislature, repugnant to the Constitution, is void.

This theory is essentially attached to a written Constitution, and, is consequently, to be considered, by this court, as one of the fundamental principles of our society. It is not therefore to be lost sight of in the further consideration of this subject.

If an Act of the Legislature, repugnant to the Constitution, is void, does it, notwithstanding its invalidity, bind the courts, and oblige them to give it effect? Or, in other words, though it be not law, does it constitute a rule as operative as if it was a law? This would be to overthrow in fact what was established in theory; and would seem, at first view, an absurdity too gross to be insisted on. It shall, however, receive a more attentive consideration.

It is emphatically the province and duty of the judicial department to say what the law is. Those who apply the rule to particular cases, must of necessity expound and interpret that rule. If two laws conflict with each other, the courts must decide on the operation of each.

So if a law be in opposition to the Constitution; if both the law and the Constitution apply to a particular case, so that the court must either decide that the case conformably to the law, disregarding the Constitution; or conformably to the Constitution, disregarding the law, the court must determine which of these conflicting rules govern the case. *This is of the very essence of judicial duty.*

The oath of office, too, imposed by the legislature, is completely demonstrative of the legislative opinion on this subject. It is in these words: "I do solemnly swear that I will administer justice without respect to persons, and do equal right to the poor and to the rich; and that I will faithfully and impartially discharge all the duties incumbent on me as ______________, according to the best of my abilities and understanding, agreeably to the Constitution and laws of the United States."

Why does a judge swear to discharge his duties agreeably to the Constitution of the United States, if that Constitution forms no rule for his government–if it is closed upon him, and cannot be inspected by him?

If such be the real state of things, this is worse than solemn mockery. To prescribe, or to take this oath, becomes equally a crime.

It is also not entirely unworthy of observation, that in declaring what shall be the supreme law of the land, the Constitution itself is first mentioned; and not the laws of the United States generally, but those only which shall be made in pursuance of the Constitution, have that rank.

Thus, the particular phraseology of the Constitution of the United States confirms and strengthens the principle, supposed to be essential to all written constitutions, that a law repugnant to the Constitution is void; and that courts, as well as other departments, are bound by that instrument.

The rule must be discharged.

EAKIN V. RAUB
12 Sergeant and Rawle 330 (PA, 1825)

The facts and decision of this Pennsylvania Supreme Court case are unimportant for present purposes. The excepts below are from Justice Gibson's dissent, which challenged Marshall's justification for judicial review in the Marbury *case.*

It seems to me there is a plain difference, hitherto unnoticed, between acts that are repugnant to the constitution of the particular state, and acts that are repugnant to the constitution of the United States; my opinion being, that the judiciary is bound to execute the former, but not the latter.... I am aware, that a right to declare all unconstitutional acts void, without distinction as to either constitution, is generally held as a professional dogma.... But ... no judge has ventured to discuss it, except Chief Justice Marshall ... and if the argument of a jurist so distinguished for the strength of his ratiocinative powers to be found inconclusive, it may be fairly set down to the weakness of the position which he attempts to defend....

...The constitution and the right of the legislature to pass the act, may be in collision. But is that a legitimate subject for judicial determination? If it be, the judiciary must be a peculiar organ, to revise the proceedings of the legislature, and to correct its mistakes; and in what part of the constitution are we to look for this proud pre-eminence? Viewing the matter in the opposite direction, what would be the thought of an act of assembly in which it should be declared that the Supreme Court had, in a particular case, put a wrong construction on the constitution of the United States, and that the judgment should therefore be reversed? It would doubtless be thought a usurpation of judicial power. But it is by no means clear, that to declare a law void which has been enacted according to the forms prescribed in the constitution, is not a usurpation of legislative power.... It is the business of the judiciary to interpret the laws, not scan the authority of the lawgiver; and without the latter, it cannot take cognizance of a collision between a law and the constitution. So that to affirm that the judiciary has a right to judge of the existence of such collision, is to take for granted the very thing to be proved....

...But it has been said to be emphatically the business of the judiciary, to ascertain and pronounce what the law is; and that this necessarily involves a consideration of the constitution. It does so: but how far? If the judiciary will inquire into any thing beside the form of the enactment, where shall it stop? There must be some point of limitation to such an inquiry; for no one will pretend, that a judge would be justifiable in calling for the election returns, or scrutinizing the qualifications of those who composed the legislature.

It is next supposed, that as the members of the legislature have no inherent right of legislation, but derive their authority from the people, no law can be valid where authority to pass it, is either simply not given or positively withheld: thus treating the members as the agents of the people, and the constitution as a letter of attorney containing their authority and bounding their sphere of action, and the consequence deduced being, that acts not warranted by the constitution are not the acts of the people, but of those that do them; and that they are therefore ipso facto void.... The legislature must acquiesce, although it may think the construction of the judiciary wrong. But why must it acquiesce? Only because it is bound to pay that respect to every other organ of the government, which it has a right to exact from each of them in turn. This is the argument.... But what I more immediately to press on the attention, is, the necessity of yielding to the acts of the legislature the same respect that is claimed for the acts of the judiciary. Repugnance to the constitution is not always self evident; for questions involving the consideration of its existence, require for their solution the most vigorous exertion of the higher faculties of mind, and conflicts will be inevitable, if any branch is to apply the constitution after its own fashion to the acts of all the others. I take it, then, the legislature is entitled to all the deference that is due to the judiciary; that its acts are in no case to be treated as ipso facto void, except where they would produce a revolution in the government; and that, to avoid them, requires the act of some tribunal competent under the constitution, (if any such there be,) to pass on their validity. All that remains, therefore, is to enquire whether the judiciary or the people are that tribunal.

Now, as the judiciary are not expressly constituted for that purpose, it must derive whatever authority of the sort it may possess, from the reasonableness and fitness of the thing. But, in theory, all the organs of the government are of equal capacity; or if not equal, each must be supposed to have superior capacity only for those things which peculiarly belong to it; and, as legislation peculiarly involves the consideration of those limitations which are put on the law-making power, and the interpretation of the laws when made, involves only the construction of the laws themselves, it follows that the construction of the constitution in this particular belongs to the legislature, which ought therefore to be taken to have superior capacity to judge of the constitutionality of its own acts. But suppose all to be of equal capacity in every respect, why should one exercise a controlling power over the rest? That the judiciary is of superior rank, has never been pretended, although it has been said to be co-ordinate. It is not easy, however, to comprehend how the power which gives law to all the rest, can be of no more than equal rank with the one which receives it, and is answerable to the former for the observance of its statutes. Legislation is essentially an act of sovereign power; but the execution of the laws by instruments that are governed by prescribed rules and exercise no power of volition, is essentially otherwise. The very definition of law, which is said to be "a rule of civil conduct prescribed by the supreme power in the state," shows the intrinsic superiority of the legislature. It may be said, the power of the legislature, also, is limited by prescribed rules. It is so. But it is, nevertheless, the power of the people, and sovereign as far as it extends. It cannot be said that the judiciary is co-ordinate merely because it is established by the constitution. If that were sufficient, sheriffs, registers of wills, and recorders of deeds, would be so too. Within the pale of their authority, the acts of these officers will have the power of the people for their support; but no one will pretend, they are of equal dignity with the acts of the legislature. Inequality of rank arises not from the manner in which the organ has been constituted, but from its essence and the nature of its functions; and the legislative organ is superior to every other, inasmuch as the power to will and to command, is essentially superior to the power to act and obey. It does not follow then, that every organ created by special provision in the constitution, is of equal rank. Both the executive, strictly as such, and the judiciary are subordinate; and an act of superior power exercised by an inferior ought, one would think, to rest on something more solid than implication....

Every one knows how seldom men think exactly alike on ordinary subjects; and a government constructed on the principle of assent by all its parts, would be inadequate to the most simple operations. The notion of a complication of counter checks has been carried to an extent in theory, of which the framers of the constitution never dreamt. When the entire sovereignty was separated into its elementary parts, and distributed to the appropriate branches, all things incident to the exercise of its powers were committed to each branch exclusively. The negative which each part of the legislature may exercise, in regards to the acts of the other, was thought sufficient to prevent material infractions of the restraints which were put on the power of the whole; for, had it been intended to interpose the judiciary as an additional barrier, the matter would surely not have been left in doubt. The judges would not have been left to stand on the insecure and ever shifting ground of public opinion as to constructive powers: they would have been placed on the impregnable ground of an express grant. They would not have been compelled to resort to the debates in the convention, or the opinion that was generally entertained at the time....

The power is said to be restricted to cases that are free from doubt or difficulty. But the abstract existence of a power cannot depend on the clearness or obscurity of the case in which it is to be exercised; for that is a consideration that cannot present itself, before the question of the existence of the power shall have been determined; and, if its existence be conceded, no considerations of policy arising from the obscurity of the particular case ought to influence the exercise of it....

But the judges are sworn to support the constitution, and are they not bound by it as the law of the land?... The oath to support the constitution ... must be understood in reference to supporting the constitution, only as far as that may be involved in his official duty; and, consequently, if his official duty does not comprehend an inquiry into the authority of the legislature, neither does his oath....

But do not the judges do a positive act in violation of the constitution, when they give effect to an unconstitutional law? Not if the law has been passed according to the forms established in the constitution. The fallacy of the question is, in supposing that the judiciary adopts the acts of the legislature as its own.... The fault is imputable to the legislature, and on it the responsibility exclusively rests. In this respect, the judges are in the predicament of jurors who are bound to serve in capital cases, although unable, under any circumstances, to reconcile it to their duty to deprive a human being of life. To one of those, who applied to be discharged from the panel, I once heard it remarked, by an eminent and humane judge, "You do not deprive a prisoner of his life by finding him guilty of a capital crime: you but pronounce his case to be within the law, and it is therefore those who declare the law, and not you, who deprive him of life."

...But it has been said, that this construction would deprive the citizen of the advantages which are peculiar to a written constitution, by at once declaring the power of the legislature, in practice, to be illimitable. I ask, what are those advantages? The principles of a written constitution are more fixed and certain, and more apparent to the apprehension of the people, than principles which depend on tradition and the vague comprehension of the individuals who compose the nation, and who cannot all be expected to receive the same impressions or entertain the same notions on any given subject. But there is no magic or inherent power in parchment and ink, to command respect and protect principles from violation.... Once let public opinion be so corrupt as to sanction every misconstruction of the constitution and abuse of power which the temptation of the moment may dictate, and the party which may happen to be predominant, will laugh at the puny efforts of a dependent power to arrest it in its course.

For these reasons, I am of the opinion that it rests with the people, in whom full and absolute sovereign power resides to correct abuses in legislation, by instructing their representatives to repeal the obnoxious act.... It might, perhaps, have been better to vest the power in the judiciary; as it might be expected that its habits of deliberation, and the aid derived from the arguments of counsel, would more frequently lead to accurate conclusions. On the other hand, the judiciary is not infallible; and an error by it would admit of no remedy but a more distinct expression of the public will, through the extraordinary medium of a convention; whereas, an error by the legislature admits of a remedy by an exertion of the same will, in the ordinary exercise of the right of suffrage, – a mode better calculated to end, without popular excitement....

But in regard to an act of [a state] assembly, which is found to be in collision with the constitution, laws, or treaties of the United States, I take the duty of the judiciary to be exactly the reverse. By becoming parties to the federal constitution, the states have agreed to several limitations of their individual sovereignty, to enforce which, it is necessary to prevent them from giving effect to laws in violation of those limitations, through the instrumentality of their own judges....

FLETCHER V. PECK
6 Cranch 87; 3 L.Ed. 162 (1810)

In 1795 the Georgia legislature passed a bill selling land, for 1.5 cents per acre, to four groups of land speculators collectively known as the Yazoo Land Companies. Widespread bribery and corruption was suspected, especially since all but one of the members of the legislature who had voted for the bill held shares in the land companies. In 1796, the new legislature rescinded the act of 1795 and took possession of the land. In the meantime, the land companies had sold the land to third parties, one of whom was Fletcher – who had bought the land from Peck. Fletcher sued Peck for the return of his purchase price in order to test the constitutionality of both the Georgia act of 1795 selling the land and the act of 1796 rescinding the sale.

MARSHALL, CH. J., delivered the opinion of the court as follows:...

That the legislature of Georgia, unless restrained by its own constitution, possesses the power of disposing of the unappropriated lands within its own limits, in such manner as its own judgment shall dictate, is a proposition not to be controverted. The only question,... for the consideration of the court, is this, did the then constitution of the state of Georgia prohibit the legislature to dispose of the lands, which were the subject of the contract, in the manner stipulated by the contract?

The question, whether a law be void for its repugnancy to the constitution, is, at all times, a question of much delicacy, which ought seldom, if ever, to be decided in the affirmative in a doubtful case. The court, when impelled by duty to render such a judgment, would be unworthy of its station, could it be unmindful of the solemn obligations which that station imposes. But it is not on slight implication and vague conjecture that the legislature is to be pronounced to have transcended its powers, and its acts to be considered as void. The opposition between the constitution and the law should be such that the judge feels a clear and strong conviction of their incompatibility with each other.

In this case the court can perceive no such opposition....

The second count assigns, in substance, as a breach of this covenant, that the original grantees from the state of Georgia promised and assured divers members of the legislature, then sitting in general assembly, that if the said members would assent to, and vote for, the passing of the act, and if the said bill should pass, such members should have a share of, and be interested in, all the lands purchased from the said state by virtue of such law....

That corruption should find its way into the governments of our infant republics, and contaminate the very source of legislation, or that impure motives should contribute to the passage of a law, or the formation of a legislative contract, are circumstances most deeply to be deplored. How far a court of justice would, in any case, be competent, on proceedings instituted by the state itself, to vacate a contract thus formed, and to annul rights acquired, under that contract, by third persons having no notice of the improper means by which it was obtained, is a question which the court would approach with much circumspection. It may well be doubted how far the validity of a law depends upon the motives of its framers, and how far the particular inducements, operating on members of the supreme sovereign power of a state, to the formation of a contract by that power, are examinable in a court of justice. If the principle be conceded, that an act of the supreme sovereign power might be declared null by the court, in consequence of the means which procured it, still would there be much difficulty in saying to what extent those means must be applied to produce this effect. Must it be direct corruption, or would interest or undue influence of any kind be sufficient? Must the vitiating cause operate on a majority, or on what number of the members? Would the act be null, whatever might be the wish of the nation, or would its obligation or nullity depend upon the public sentiment?

If the majority of the legislature be corrupted, it may well be doubted, whether it be within the province of the judiciary to control their conduct, and if less than a majority act from impure motives, the principle by which judicial interference would be regulated, is not clearly discerned....

This solemn question cannot be brought thus collaterally and incidentally before the court. It would be indecent in the extreme, upon a private contract between two individuals, to enter into an inquiry respecting the corruption of the sovereign power of a state. If the title be plainly deduced from a legislative act, which the legislature might constitutionally pass, if the act be clothed with all the requisite forms of a law, a court, sitting as a court of law, cannot sustain a suit brought by one individual against another founded on the allegation that the act is a nullity, in consequence of the impure motives which influenced certain members of the legislature which passed the law....

The lands in controversy vested absolutely in James Gunn and others, the original grantees, by the conveyance of the governor, made in pursuance of an act of assembly to which the legislature was fully competent. Being thus in full possession of the legal estate, they, for a valuable consideration, conveyed portions of the land to those who were willing to purchase.

If the original transaction was infected with fraud, these purchasers did not participate in it, and had no notice of it. They were innocent. Yet the legislature of Georgia has involved them in the fate of the first parties to the transaction, and, if the act [rescinding the sale] be valid, has annihilated their rights also.

The legislature of Georgia was a party to this transaction; and for a party to pronounce its own deed invalid, whatever cause may be assigned for its invalidity, must be considered as a mere act of power which must find its vindication in a train of reasoning not often heard in courts of justice....

If the agents be corrupt, others may be chosen, and, if their contracts be examinable, the common sentiment, as well as the common usage of mankind, points out a mode by which this examination may be made, and their validity determined.

If the legislature of Georgia was not bound to submit its pretensions to those tribunals which are established for the security of property, and to decide on human rights, if it might claim to itself the power of judging in its own case, yet there are certain great principles of justice, whose authority is universally acknowledged, that ought not to be entirely disregarded.

If the legislature be its own judge in its own case, it would seem equitable that its decision would be regulated by those rules which would have regulated the decision of a judicial tribunal. The question was, in its nature, a question of title, and the tribunal which decided it was either acting in the character of a court of justice, and performing a duty usually assigned to a court, or it was exerting a mere act of power in which it was controlled only by its own will.

If a suit be brought to set aside a conveyance obtained by fraud, and the fraud be clearly proved, the conveyance will be set aside, as between the parties; but the rights of third persons, who are purchasers without notice, for a valuable consideration, cannot be disregarded....

A court of chancery, therefore, had a bill been brought to set aside the conveyance made to James Gunn and others, as being obtained by improper practices with the legislature, whatever might have been its decision as respected the original grantees, would have been bound, by its own rules, and by the clearest principles of equity, to leave unmolested those who were purchasers, without notice, for a valuable consideration.

If the legislature felt itself absolved from those rules of property which are common to all the citizens of the United States, and from those principles of equity which are acknowledged in all our courts, its act is to be supported by its power alone, and the same power may devest any other individual of his lands, if it shall be the will of the legislature so to exert it.

It is not intended to speak with disrespect of the legislature of Georgia, or of its acts. Far from it. The question is a general question and is treated as one. For although such powerful objections to a legislative grant, as are alleged against this, may not again exist, yet the principle, on which alone this rescinding act is to be supported, may be applied to every case to which it shall be the will of any legislature to apply it. The principle is this: that a legislature may, by its own act, devest the vested estate of any man whatever, for reasons which shall, by itself, be deemed sufficient....

When, then, a law is in its nature a contract, when absolute rights have vested under that contract; a repeal of the law cannot devest those rights; and the act of annulling them, if legitimate, is rendered so by a power applicable to the case of every individual in the community.

It may well be doubted whether the nature of society and of government does not prescribe some limits to the legislative power; and, if any be prescribed, where are they to be found, if the property of an individual, fairly and honestly acquired, may be seized without compensation?...

The validity of this rescinding act, then, might well be doubted, were Georgia a single sovereign power. But Georgia cannot be viewed as a single, unconnected, sovereign power, on whose legislature no other restrictions are imposed than may be found in its own constitution. She is a part of a large empire; she is a member of the American Union; and that Union has a constitution the supremacy of which all acknowledge, and which imposes limits to the legislatures of the several states, which none claim a right to pass. The constitution of the United States declares that no state shall pass any bill of attainder, ex post facto law or law impairing the obligation of contracts.

Does the case now under consideration come within this prohibitory section of the constitution?

In considering this very interesting question, we immediately ask ourselves what is a contract? Is a grant a contract?

A contract is a compact between two or more parties, and is either executory or executed. An executory contract is one in which a party binds himself to do, or not to do, a particular thing; such was the law under which the conveyance was made by the governor. A contract executed is one in which the object of contract is performed; and this, says Blackstone, differs in nothing from a grant. The contract between Georgia and the purchasers was executed by the grant. A contract executed, as well as one which is executory, contains obligations binding on the parties. A grant, in its own nature, amounts to an extinguishment of the right of the grantor, and implies a contract not to re-assert that right. A party is, therefore, always estopped by his own grant.

Since, then, in fact, a grant is a contract executed, the obligation of which still continues, and since the constitution uses the general term contract, without distinguishing between those which are executory and those which are executed, it must be construed to comprehend the latter as well as the former. A law annulling conveyances between individuals, and declaring that the grantors should stand seized of their former estates, notwithstanding those grants, would be as repugnant to the constitution as a law discharging the vendors of property from the obligation of executing their contracts by conveyances. It would be strange if a contract to convey was secured by the constitution, while an absolute conveyance remained unprotected.

If, under a fair construction of the constitution, grants are comprehended under the term contracts, is a grant from the state excluded from the operation of the provision? Is the clause to be considered as inhibiting the state from impairing the obligation of contracts between two individuals, but as excluding from that inhibition contracts made with itself?

The words themselves contain no such distinction. They are general, and are applicable to contracts of every description....

Whatever respect might have been felt for the state sovereignties, it is not to be disguised that the framers of the constitution viewed, with some apprehension, the violent acts which might grow out of the feelings of the moment; and that the people of the United States, in adopting that instrument, have manifested a determination to shield themselves and their property from the effects of those sudden and strong passions to which men are exposed. The restrictions on the legislative power of the states are obviously founded in this sentiment; and the constitution of the United States contains what may be deemed a bill of rights for the people of each state.

No state shall pass any bill of attainder, ex post facto law, or law impairing the obligation of contracts.

A bill of attainder may affect the life of an individual, or may confiscate his property, or may do both.

In this form the power of the legislature over the lives and fortunes of individuals is expressly restrained. What motive, then, for implying in words which import a general prohibition to impair the obligation of those contracts into which the state may enter?...

It is, then, the unanimous opinion of the court, that, in this case, the estate having passed into the hands of a purchaser for a valuable consideration, without notice, the state of Georgia was restrained, either by general principles, which are common to our free institutions, or by the particular provisions of the constitution of the United States, from passing a law whereby the estate of the plaintiff in the premises so purchased could be constitutionally and legally impaired and rendered null and void....

JOHNSON, J. In this case I entertain, on two points, an opinion different from that which has been delivered by the court.

I do not hesitate to declare that a state does not possess the power of revoking its own grants. But I do it on a general principle, on the reason and nature of things: a principle which will impose laws even on the Deity....

As to the idea, that the grant of a legislature may be void because the legislature are corrupt, it appears to me to be subject to insuperable difficulties.

The acts of the supreme power of a country must be considered pure for the same reason that all sovereign acts must be considered just; because there is no power that can declare them otherwise. The absurdity in this case would have been strikingly perceived, could the party who passed the act of cession have got again into power, and declared themselves pure, and the intermediate legislature corrupt.

The security of a people against the misconduct of their rulers, must lie in the frequent recurrence to first principles, and the imposition of adequate constitutional restrictions....

I have thrown out these ideas that I may have it distinctly understood that my opinion on this point is not founded on the provision in the constitution of the United States, relative to laws impairing the obligation of contracts. It is much to be regretted that words of less equivocal signification had not been adopted in that article of the constitution....

I enter with great hesitation upon this question, because it involves a subject of the greatest delicacy and much difficulty. The states and the United States are continually legislating on the subject of contracts, prescribing the mode of authentication, the time within which suits shall be prosecuted for them, in many cases affecting existing contracts by the laws which they pass, and declaring them to cease or lose their effect for want of compliance, in the parties, with such statutory provisions. All these acts appear to be within the most correct limits of legislative powers, and most beneficially exercised, and certainly could not have been intended to be affected by this constitutional provision; yet where to draw the line, or how to define or limit the words, "obligation of contracts," will be found a subject of extreme difficulty.

To give it the general effect of a restriction of the state powers in favor of private rights, is certainly going very far beyond the obvious and necessary import of the words, and would operate to restrict the states in the exercise of that right which every community must exercise, of possessing itself of the property of the individual, when necessary for public uses; a right which a magnanimous and just government will never exercise without amply indemnifying the individual, and which perhaps amounts to nothing more than a power to oblige him to sell and convey, when the public necessity require it....

MARTIN V. HUNTER'S LESSEE
1 Wheaton 304; 4 L.Ed. 97 (1816)

Denny Martin, a British subject residing in England, claimed land in Virginia which he had inherited from Lord Fairfax. This land had not been confiscated prior to the 1783 Treaty of Peace with Great Britain. Hunter's lessee claimed title to the land under a Virginia grant of 1788. The Virginia Court of Appeals had ruled in favor of Hunter's lessee, but that decision had been overturned by the United States Supreme Court in Fairfax's Devisee v. Hunter's Lessee, 7 Cranch 603 (1813). *The Supreme Court mandated the Virginia Court of Appeals to carry its judgment into execution, but the state court refused to carry out the Supreme Court's ruling on the grounds "that the appellate power of the Supreme Court of the United States does not extend to this court, under a sound construction of the Constitution of the United States; [and] that so much of the 25th section of the act of Congress to establish the judicial courts of the United States, as extends the appellate jurisdiction of the Supreme Court to this court, is not in pursuance of the constitution of the United States." Martin then appealed once again to the Supreme Court.*

STORY, J., delivered the opinion of the court:...

Before proceeding to the principal questions, it may not be unfit to dispose of some preliminary considerations which have grown out of the arguments at the bar.

The constitution of the United States was ordained and established, not by the states in their sovereign capacities, but emphatically, as the preamble of the constitution declares, by "the people of the United States." There can be no doubt that it was competent to the people to invest the general government with all the powers which they might deem proper and necessary; to extend or restrain these powers according to their own good pleasure, and... to give them a paramount and supreme authority. As little doubt can there be that the people had a right to prohibit to the states the exercise of any powers which were, in their judgment, incompatible with the objects of the general compact; to make the powers of the state governments, in given cases, subordinate to those of the nation, or to reserve to themselves those sovereign authorities which they might not choose to delegate to either. The constitution was not, therefore, necessarily carved out of existing state sovereignties, nor a surrender of powers already existing in state institutions, for the powers of the states depend upon their own constitutions and the people of every state had the right to modify and restrain them, according to their own views of policy or principle. On the other hand, it is perfectly clear that the sovereign powers vested in the state governments, by their respective constitutions, remained unaltered and unimpaired, except so far as they were granted to the government of the United States.

These deductions do not rest upon general reasoning, plain and obvious as they seem to be. They have been positively recognized by one of the articles in amendment of the constitution, which declares, that "the powers not delegated to the United States by the constitution, nor prohibited by it to the states, are reserved to the states respectively, or to the people."

The government, then, of the United States, can claim no powers which are not granted to it by the constitution, and the powers actually granted, must be such as are expressly given, or given by necessary implication. On the other hand, this instrument, like every other grant, is to have a reasonable construction, according to the import of its terms; and where a power is expressly given in general terms, it is not to be restrained to particular cases, unless that construction grow out of the context expressly, or by necessary implication. The words are to be taken in their natural and obvious sense, and not in a sense unreasonably restricted or enlarged....

It did not suit the purposes of the people, in framing this great charter of our liberties, to provide for minute specifications of its powers, or to declare the means by which those powers should be carried into execution. It was foreseen that this would be a perilous and difficult, if not an impracticable, task. The instrument was not intended to provide merely for the exigencies of a few years, but was to endure through a long lapse of ages, the events of which were locked up in the inscrutable purposes of Providence.... Hence its powers are expressed in general terms, leaving to the legislature, from time to time, to adopt its own means to effectuate legitimate objects, and to mold and model the exercise of its powers, as its own wisdom and the public interests should require.

With these principles in view – principles in respect to which no difference of opinion ought to be indulged – let us now proceed to the interpretation of the constitution, so far as regards the great points in controversy....

The judicial power must, therefore, be vested in some court, by Congress; and to suppose that it was not an obligation binding on them, but might, at their pleasure, be omitted or declined, is to suppose that, under the sanction of the constitution they might defeat the constitution itself; a construction which would lead to such a result cannot be sound....

If, then, it is the duty of Congress to vest the judicial power of the United States, it is a duty to vest the whole judicial power.... It would seem, therefore, to follow that Congress are bound to create some inferior courts, in which to vest all that jurisdiction which, under the constitution, is exclusively vested in the United States, and of which the Supreme Court cannot take original cognizance. They might establish one or more inferior courts; they might parcel out the jurisdiction among such courts, from time to time, at their own pleasure. But the whole judicial power of the United States should be, at all times, vested either in an original or appellate form, in some courts created under its authority.

This leads us to the consideration of the great question as to the nature and extent of the appellate jurisdiction of the United States. We have already seen that appellate jurisdiction is given by the constitution to the Supreme Court in all cases, where it has not original jurisdiction; subject, however, to such exceptions and regulations as Congress may prescribe. It is, therefore, capable of embracing every case enumerated in the constitution, which is not exclusively to be decided by way of original jurisdiction. But the exercise of appellate jurisdiction is far from being limited by the terms of the constitution to the Supreme Court. There can be no doubt that Congress may create a succession of inferior tribunals, in each of which it may vest appellate as well as original jurisdiction. The judicial power is delegated by the constitution in the most general terms, and may, therefore, be exercised by Congress under every variety of form, of appellate or original jurisdiction. And as there is nothing in the constitution which restrains or limits this power, it must, therefore, in all other cases, subsist in the utmost latitude of which, in its own nature, it is susceptible.

As, then, by the terms of the constitution, the appellate jurisdiction is not limited as to the Supreme Court, and as to this court it may be exercised in all other cases than those of which it has original cognizance, what is there to restrain its exercise over state tribunals in the enumerated cases? The appellate power is not limited by the terms of the third article to any particular courts. The words are, "the judicial power (which includes appellate power) shall extend to all cases," etc., and "in all other cases before mentioned the Supreme Court shall have appellate jurisdiction." It is the case, then, and not the court, that gives the jurisdiction. If the judicial power extends to the case, it will be in vain to search in the letter of the constitution for any qualification as to the tribunal where it depends. It is incumbent, then, upon those who assert such a qualification to show its existence by necessary implication. If the text be clear and distinct, no restriction upon its plain and obvious import ought to be admitted, unless the inference be irresistible.

If the constitution meant to limit the appellate jurisdiction to cases pending in the courts of the United States, it would necessarily follow that the jurisdiction of these courts would, in all the cases enumerated in the constitution, be exclusive of state tribunals....

But it is plain that the framers of the constitution did contemplate that cases within the judicial cognizance of the United States not only might but would arise in the state courts, in the exercise of their ordinary jurisdiction. With this view the sixth article declares, that "this constitution, and the laws of the United States which shall be made in pursuance thereof, and all treaties made, or which shall be made, under the authority of the United States, shall be the supreme law of the land, and the judges in every state shall be bound thereby, anything in the constitution or laws of any state to the contrary notwithstanding." It is obvious that this obligation is imperative upon the state judges in their official, and not merely in their private, capacities. From the very nature of their judicial duties they would be called upon to pronounce the law applicable to the case in judgment. They were not to decide merely according to the laws or constitution of the state, but according to the constitution, laws and treaties of the United States – "the supreme law of the land...."

It must, therefore, be conceded that the constitution not only contemplated, but meant to provide for cases within the scope of the judicial power of the United States, which might yet depend before state tribunals. It was foreseen that in the exercise of their ordinary jurisdiction, state courts would incidentally take cognizance of cases arising under the constitution, the laws and treaties of the United States. Yet to all these cases the judicial power, by the very terms of the constitution, is to extend. It cannot extend by original jurisdiction if that was already rightfully and exclusively attached in the state courts, which (as has been already shown) may occur; it must, therefore, extend by appellate jurisdiction, or not at all. It would seem to follow that the appellate power of the United States must, in such cases, extend to state tribunals; and if in such cases, there is no reason why it should not equally attach upon all others within the purview of the constitution.

It has been argued that such an appellate jurisdiction over state courts is inconsistent wit the genius of our governments, and the spirit of the constitution. That the latter was never designed to act upon state sovereignties, but only upon the people, and that if the power exists, it will materially impair the sovereignty of the states, and the independence of their courts. We cannot yield to the force of this reasoning; it assumes principles which we cannot admit, and draws conclusions to which we do not yield our assent.

It is a mistake that the constitution was not designed to operate upon states, in their corporate capacities....

The courts of the United States can, without question, review the proceedings of the executive and legislative authorities of the states, and if they are found to be contrary to the constitution, may declare them to be of no legal validity. Surely the exercise of the same right over judicial tribunals is not a higher or more dangerous act of sovereign power.

Nor can such a right be deemed to impair the independence of state judges. It is assuming the very ground in controversy to assert that they possess an absolute independence of the United States. In respect to the powers granted to the United States, they are not independent; they are expressly bound to obedience by the letter of the constitution; and if they should unintentionally transcend their authority, or misconstrue the constitution, there is no more reason for giving their judgments an absolute and irresistible force than for giving it to the acts of the other co-ordinate departments of state sovereignty....

It is further argued that no great public mischief can result from a construction which shall limit the appellate power of the United States to cases in their own courts; first, because state judges are bound by an oath to support the constitution of the United States, and must be presumed to be men of learning and integrity; and, secondly, because Congress must have an unquestionable right to remove all cases within the scope of the judicial power from the state courts to the courts of the United States, at any time before final judgment, though not after final judgment. As to the first reason – admitting that the judges of the state courts are, and always will be, of as much learning, integrity, and wisdom, as those of the courts of the United States (which we very cheerfully admit), it does not aid the argument. It is manifest that the constitution has proceeded upon a theory of its own, and given or withheld powers according to the judgment of the American people, by whom it was adopted. We can only construe its powers, and cannot inquire into the policy or principles which induced the grant of them. The constitution has presumed (whether rightly or wrongly we do not inquire) that state attachments, state prejudices, state jealousies, and state interests, might sometimes obstruct, or control, or be supposed to obstruct or control, the regular administration of justice. Hence, in controversies between states; between citizens of different states; between citizens claiming grants under different states; between a state and its citizens, or foreigners, and between citizens and foreigners, it enables the parties, under the authority of Congress, to have the controversies heard, tried, and determined before the national tribunals. No other reason than that which has been stated can be assigned, why some, at least, of those cases should not have been left to the cognizance of the state courts....

This is not all. A motive of another kind, perfectly compatible with the most sincere respect for state tribunals, might induce the grant of appellate power over their decisions. That motive is the importance, and even necessity of uniformity of decisions throughout the whole United States, upon all subjects within the purview of the constitution. Judges of equal learning and integrity, in different states, might differently interpret a statute, or a treaty of the United States, or even the constitution itself. If there were no revising authority to control these jarring and discordant judgments, and harmonize them into uniformity, the laws, the treaties, and the constitution of the United States would be different in different states, and might, perhaps, never have precisely the same construction, obligation, or efficacy, in any two states. The public mischiefs that would attend such a state of things would be truly deplorable; and it cannot be believed that they could have escaped the enlightened convention which formed the constitution. What, indeed, might then have been only prophecy, has now become fact; and the appellate jurisdiction must continue to be the only adequate remedy for such evils....

On the whole, the court are of the opinion that the appellate power of the United States does extend to cases pending in the state courts; and that the 25th section of the judiciary act, which authorizes the exercise of this jurisdiction in the specified cases, by a writ of error, is supported by the letter and spirit of the constitution. We find no clause in that instrument which limits this power; and we dare not interpose a limitation where the people have not been disposed to create one....

JOHNSON, J. It will be observed in this case that the court disavows all intention to decide on the right to issue compulsory process to the state courts; thus leaving us, in my opinion, where the constitution and laws place us – supreme over persons and cases as far as our judicial powers extend, but not asserting any compulsory control over the state tribunals.

In this view I acquiesce in their opinion, but not altogether in the reasoning, or opinion, of my brother who delivered it. Few minds are accustomed to the same habit of thinking, and our conclusions are most satisfactory to ourselves when arrived at in our own way.

I have another reason for expressing my opinion on this occasion. I view this question as one of the most momentous importance; as one which may affect in its consequences, the permanence of the American Union. It presents an instance of collision between the judicial powers of the Union, and one of the greatest states in the Union, on a point the most delicate and difficult to be adjusted. On the one hand, the general government must cease to exist whenever it loses the power of protecting itself in the exercise of its constitutional powers. Force, which acts upon the physical powers of man, or judicial process, which addresses itself to his moral principles or his fears, are the only means to which governments can resort in the exercise of their authority. The former is happily unknown to the genius of our constitution, except as far as it shall be sanctioned by the latter; but let the latter be obstructed in its progress by an opposition which it cannot overcome or put by, and the resort must be to the former, or government is no more.

On the other hand, so firmly am I persuaded that the American people can no longer enjoy the blessings of a free government, whenever the state sovereignties shall be prostrated at the feet of the general government, nor the proud consciousness of equality and security, and longer than the independence of judicial power shall be maintained consecrated and intangible, that I could borrow the language of a celebrated orator, and exclaim: "I rejoice that Virginia has resisted."

Yet here I must claim the privilege of expressing my regret that the opposition of the high and truly respected tribunal of that state had not been marked with a little more moderation. The only point necessary to be decided in the case then before them was, *"whether they were bound to obey the mandate emanating from this court."* But in the judgment entered on their minutes, they have affirmed that the case was, in this court, *coram non judice*, or, in other words, that this court had not jurisdiction over it.

This is assuming a truly alarming latitude of judicial power. Where is it to end? It is an acknowledged principle of, I believe, every court in the world, that not only the decisions, but everything done under the judicial process of courts, not having jurisdiction, are, *ipso facto*, void. Are, then, the judgments of this court to be reviewed in every court of the Union? and is every recovery of money, every change of property, that has taken place under our process, to be considered as null, void, and tortuous?

We pretend not to more infallibility than other courts composed of the same frail materials which compose this. It would be the height of affectation to close our minds upon the recollection that we have been extracted from the same seminaries in which originated the learned men who preside over the state tribunals. But there is one claim which we can with confidence assert *in our own name* upon those tribunals – the profound, uniform, and unaffected respect which this court has always exhibited for state decisions, give us strong pretensions to judicial comity. And another claim I may assert, *in the name of the American people*; in this court, every state in the Union is represented; we are constituted by the voice of the Union, and when decisions take place, which nothing but a spirit to give ground and harmonize can reconcile, ours is the superior claim upon the comity of the state tribunals. It is the nature of the human mind to impress a favorite hypothesis too far, but magnanimity will always be ready to sacrifice the pride of opinion to public welfare.

COHENS v. VIRGINIA
6 Wheat. 264; 5 L.Ed. 257 (1821)

In order to raise additional revenue for Washington, D.C., to be used for municipal improvements, Congress enacted legislation permitting the District to conduct lotteries. Acting under this 1802 law, the city passed a lottery ordinance which provoked a legal controversy since Virginia law prohibited the sale of lottery tickets except for those sanctioned by the State. Subsequently, two persons named Cohen were arrested by Virginia agents for selling tickets for the

Washington lottery. After being convicted in a local court, the Cohens brought the matter to the Supreme Court (no intermediate appellate courts existed) on a writ of error. The case was significant. While upholding the convictions, the Court, in the forceful and persuasive words of Chief Justice John Marshall, reasserted *its authority to review decisions of the state courts.*

MR. CHIEF JUSTICE MARSHALL delivered the opinion of the Court:

... The first question to be considered is, whether the jurisdiction of this Court is excluded by the character of the parties, one of them being a State, and the other a citizen of that State?

The second section of the third article of the Constitution defines the extent of the judicial power of the United States. Jurisdiction is given to the Courts of the Union in two classes of cases. In the first, their jurisdiction depends on the character of the cause, whoever may be the parties. This class comprehends "all cases in law and equity arising under this Constitution, the laws of the United States, and treaties made, or which shall be made, under their authority." This clause extends the jurisdiction of the Court to all the cases described, without making in its terms any exception whatever, and without any regard to the condition of the party. If there be any exception, it is to be implied against the express words of the article....

If ... a case arising under the Constitution, or a law, must be one in which a party comes into Court to demand something conferred on him by the constitution or a law, we think the construction too narrow. A case in law or equity consists of the right of the one party, as well as of the other, and may truly be said to arise under the Constitution or a law of the United States, whenever its correct decision depends on the construction of either....

The jurisdiction of the Court, then, being extended by the letter of the Constitution to all cases arising under it, or under the laws of the United States, it follows that those who would withdraw any cases of this description from that jurisdiction, must sustain the exemption they claim on the spirit and true meaning must be so apparent as to overrule the words which its framers have employed ....

If jurisdiction depended entirely on the character of the parties, and was not given where the parties have not an original right to come into Court, that part of the second section of the third article, which extends the judicial power to all cases arising under the Constitution and laws of the United States, would be mere surplusage. It is to give jurisdiction where the character of the parties would not give it, that this very important part of the clause was inserted. It may be true, that the partiality of the State tribunals, in ordinary controversies between a State and its citizens, was not apprehended, and therefore the judicial power of the Union was not extended to such cases; but this was not the sole nor the greatest object for which this department was created. A more important, and much more interesting object, was the preservation of the Constitution and laws of the United States, so far as they can be preserved by judicial authority; and therefore the jurisdiction of the Courts of the Union was expressly extended to all cases arising under that Constitution and those laws....

It is the most true that this Court will not take jurisdiction if it should not: but it is equally true, that it must take jurisdiction if it should. The judiciary cannot, as the legislature may, avoid a measure because it approaches the confines of the Constitution. We cannot pass it by because it is doubtful. With whatever doubts, with whatever difficulties, a case may be attended, we must decide it, if it be brought before us. We have no more right to decline the exercise of jurisdiction which is given, than to usurp that which is not given. The one or the other would be treason to the Constitution. Questions may occur which we would gladly avoid; but we cannot avoid them. All we can do is, to exercise our best judgment, and conscientiously to perform our duty. In doing this, on the present occasion, we find this tribunal invested with appellate jurisdiction in all cases arising under the Constitution and laws of the United States. We find no exception to this grant and we cannot insert one....

It is, then, the opinion of the Court, that the defendant who removes a judgment rendered against him by a State Court into this Court, for the purpose of reexamining the question, whether that judgment be in violation of the Constitution or laws of the United States, does not commence or prosecute a suit against the States....

Second. The second objection to the jurisdiction of the Court is, that its appellate power cannot be exercised, in any case, over the judgment of a State Court.

This objection is sustained chiefly by arguments drawn from the supposed total separation of the judiciary of a State from that of the Union, and their entire independence of each other. The argument considers the federal judiciary as completely foreign to that of a State; and as being no more connected with it in any respect whatever, than the Court of a foreign State. If this hypothesis be just, the argument founded on it is equally so; but if the hypothesis be not supported by the Constitution, the argument fails with it ....

That the United States form, for many, and for most important purposes, a single nation, has not yet been defined. In war, we are one people. In making peace, we are one people. In all commercial regulations, we are one and the same people. In many other respects, the American people are one; and the government which is alone capable of controlling and managing their interests in all these respects, is the government of the Union. It is their government, and in that character they have no other. America has chosen to be, in many respects, and to many purposes, a nation; and for all these purposes, her government is complete; to all these objects, it is competent. The people have declared, that in the exercise of all powers given for these objects, it is supreme. It can, then, in effecting these objects, legitimately control all individuals or governments within the American territory. The constitution and laws of a State, so far as they are repugnant to the Constitution and laws of the United States, are absolutely void. These States are constituent parts of the United States. They are members of one great empire-for some purposes sovereign, for some purposes subordinate.

In a government so constituted, it is unreasonable that the judicial power should be competent to give efficacy to the constitutional laws of the legislature?

That department can decide on the validity of the constitution or law of a State, if it be repugnant to the Constitution or to a law of the United States. Is it unreasonable that it should also be empowered to decide on the judgment of a State tribunal enforcing such unconstitutional law? Is it so very unreasonable as to furnish a justification for controlling the words of the Constitution?

We think it is not. We think that in a government acknowledgedly supreme, with respect to objects of vital interest to the nation, there is nothing inconsistent with sound reason, nothing incompatible with the nature if government, in making all its departments supreme, so far as respects those objects, and so far as is necessary to their attainment. The exercise of the appellate power over those judgments of the State tribunals which may contravene the Constitution or laws of the United States, is, we believe, essential to the attainment of those objects....

This opinion has been already drawn out to too great a length to admit of entering into a particular consideration of the various forms in which the counsel who made this point has, with much ingenuity, presented his argument to the Court. The argument in all its forms is essentially the same. It is founded, not on the words of the Constitution, but on its spirit, a spirit extracted, not from the words of the instrument, but from his view of the nature of our Union, and of the great fundamental principles on which the fabric stands.

To this argument, in all its forms, the same answer may be given. Let the nature and objects of our Union be considered; let the great fundamental principles, on which the fabric stands, be examined; and we think the result must be, that there is nothing so extravagantly absurd in giving to the Court of the nation the power of revising the decisions of local tribunals on questions which affect the nation, as to require that words which import this power should be restricted by a forced construction....

COOPER V. AARON
358 U.S. 1; 78 S.Ct. 1401 (1958)

Shortly after it handed down its implementing decree in the Second School Desegregation Case [see Brown v. Board of Education, *(*1955*)], the* Supreme *Court found that the order was met with threats of "massive resistance" and "interposition" from political leaders in many southern states. Moreover, the nature of the decision itself - that* de jure *dual school systems should end with* "all deliberate speed" *and that actual implementation rested with the district courts within the districts affected - invited, if not enhanced, circumvention and delay. Perhaps the most blatant challenge to the Court's mandate occurred in Little Rock, Arkansas during the 1957-58 school year where the Governor and the state legislature acted forcefully to resist a plan to desegregate Central High School. The Governor had gone so far as to order units of the National Guard to prevent Negro students from entering the school. Given the explosiveness of the situation, members of the local school board, including Cooper, petitioned the federal district court to postpone the desegregation plan. The court granted the* *requested relief; however, the Negro litigants appealed and the Court of Appeals for the Eighth Circuit reversed. The Supreme Court issued a writ of certiorari and convened for a special summer term. The opinion of the court is particularly noteworthy because of its dramatic reassertion of "supremacy" in deciding constitutional controversies as witnessed by the fact that only rarely is an opinion signed by all nine justices.*

Opinion of the Court by THE CHIEF JUSTICE, MR. JUSTICE BLACK, MR. JUSTICE FRANKFURTER, MR. JUSTICE DOUGLAS, MR. JUSTICE BURTON, MR. JUSTICE CLARK, MR. JUSTICE HARLAN, MR. JUSTICE BRENNAN, and MR. JUSTICE WHITTAKER:

...As this case reaches us it raises questions of the highest importance to the maintenance of our federal system of government. It necessarily involves a claim the Governor and Legislature of a State that there is no duty on state officials to obey federal court orders resting on this Court's considered interpretation of the United States Constitution. Specifically it involves actions by the Governor and Legislature of Arkansas upon the premise that they are not bound by our holding in *Brown v. Board of Education*.... That holding was that the Fourteenth Amendment forbids States to use their governmental powers to bar children on racial grounds from attending schools where there is state participation through any arrangement, management, funds or property. We are urged to uphold a suspension of the Little Rock School Board's plan to do away with segregated public schools in Little Rock until state laws and efforts to upset and nullify our holding in *Brown v. Board of Education* have been further challenged and tested in the courts. We reject these contentions....

It was made plain that delay in any guise in order to deny the constitutional rights of Negro children could not be countenanced, and that only a prompt start, diligently and earnestly pursued, to eliminate racial segregation from the public schools could constitute good faith compliance. State authorities were thus bound to devote every effort toward initiating desegregation and bringing about the elimination of racial discrimination in the public school system....

While the School Board was thus going forward with its preparation for desegregating the Little Rock school system, other state authorities, in contrast, were actively pursuing a program designed to perpetuate in Arkansas the system of racial segregation which this Court had held violated the Fourteenth Amendment. First came, in November 1956, an amendment to the State Constitution flatly commanding the Arkansas General Assembly to oppose "in every Constitutional manner the Unconstitutional desegregation decisions of May 17, 1954, and May 31, 1955 of the United States Supreme Court...." Pursuant to this state constitution command, a law relieving school children from compulsory attendance at racially mixed schools ... and a law establishing a State Sovereignty Commission ... were enacted by the General Assembly in February 1957.

The School Board and the Superintendent of Schools nevertheless continued with preparations to carry out the first stage of the desegregation program. Nine Negro children were scheduled for admission in September 1957 to Central High School; which has more than 2000 students ....

On September 2, 1957, the day before these Negro students were to enter Central High School, the school authorities were met with drastic opposing action on the part of the Governor of Arkansas who dispatched units of the Arkansas National Guard to the Central High School grounds, and placed the school "off limits" to colored students. As found by the District Court in subsequent proceedings, the Governor's action had not been requested by the school authorities, and was entirely unheralded....

The Governor's action caused the School Board to request the Negro students on September 2 not to attend the high school "until the legal dilemma was solved." The next day, September 3, 1957, the Board petitioned the District Court for instructions, and the court, after a hearing, found that the Board's request of the Negro students to stay away from the high school had been made because of the stationing of the military guards by the state authorities....

On the morning of the next day, September 4, 1957, the Negro children attempted to enter the high school but, as the District Court later found, units of the Arkansas National Guard "acting pursuant to the Governor's order, stood shoulder to shoulder at the school grounds and thereby forcibly prevented the nine Negro students ... from entering," as they continued to do every school day during the following three weeks....

The next school day was Monday, September 23, 1957. The Negro children entered the high school that morning under the protection of the Little Rock Police Department and members of the Arkansas State Police. But the officers caused the children to be removed from the school during the morning because they had difficulty controlling a large and demonstrating crowd which had gathered at the high school.... On September 25, however, the President of the United States dispatched federal troops to Central High School and admission of the Negro students to the school was thereby effected. Regular army troops continued at the high school until November 27, 1957. They were then replaced by federalized National Guardsmen who remained throughout the balance of the school year. Eight of the Negro students remained in attendance at the school throughout the school year....

On February 20, 1958, the School Board and the Superintendent of Schools filed a petition in the District Court seeking a postponement of their program for desegregation. Their position in essence was that because of extreme public hostility, which they stated had been engendered largely by the official attitudes and actions of the Governor and the Legislature, the maintenance of a soured educational program at Central High School, with the Negro students in attendance, would be impossible....

After a hearing the District Court granted the relief requested by the Board. Among other things the court found that the past year at Central High School had been attended by conditions of "chaos, bedlam, and turmoil;" that there were "repeated incidents of more or less serious violence directed against the Negro students and their property...."

One may well sympathize with the position of the Board in the face of the frustrating conditions which have confronted it, but, regardless of the Board's good faith, the actions of the other state agencies responsible for those conditions compel us to reject the Board's legal position. Had Central High School been under the direct management of the State itself, it could hardly be suggested that those immediately in charge of the school should be heard to assert their own good faith as a legal excuse for delay in implementing the constitutional rights of these respondents, when vindication of those rights was rendered difficult or impossible by the actions of other state officials. The situation here is in no different posture because the members of the School Board and the Superintendent of Schools are local officials; from the point of view of the Fourteenth Amendment, they stand in this litigation as the agents of the State.

The constitutional rights of respondents are not to be sacrificed or yielded to the violence and disorder which have followed upon the actions of the Governor and Legislature....

Thus law and order are not here to be preserved by depriving the Negro children of their constitutional rights....

It is necessary only to recall some basic constitutional propositions which are settled doctrine....

Every state legislator and executive and judicial officer is solemnly committed by oath taken pursuant to Art. VI, Sec. 3 "to support this Constitution...."

No state legislator or executive or judicial officer can war against the Constitution without violating his undertaking to support it....

It is, of course, quite true that the responsibility for public education is primarily the concern of the States, but it is equally true that such responsibilities, like all other state activity, must be exercised consistently with federal constitutional requirements as they apply to state action. The Constitution created a government dedicated to equal justice under law. The Fourteenth Amendment embodied and emphasized that ideal. State support of segregated schools through an arrangement, management, funds, or property cannot be squared with the Amendment's command that no State shall deny to any person within its jurisdiction the equal protection of the laws. The right of a student not to be segregated on racial grounds in schools so maintained is indeed so fundamental and pervasive that it is embraced in the concept of due process of law. *Bolling v. Sharpe*.... The basic decision in *Brown* was unanimously reached by this Court only after the case had been briefed and twice argued and the issues had been given the most serious consideration. Since the first *Brown* opinion three new Justices have come to the Court. They are at one with the Justices still on the Court who participated in the basic decision as to its correctness, and that decision is now unanimously reaffirmed. The principles announced in that decision and the obedience of the States to them, according to the command of the Constitution, are indispensable for the protection of the freedoms guaranteed by our fundamental charter for all of us. Our constitutional ideal justice under law is thus made a living truth.

LUTHER v. BORDEN
7 HOW. 1; 12 L.Ed. 581 (1849)

In 1841, the established government of Rhode Island came under severe political attack from a growing number of citizens who resented the government's adherence to limited suffrage. The state constitution, which maintained the stringent limitations of the original colonial charter of 1663, made the ownership of property a prerequisite of the right to vote. In an attempt to challenge the existing regime and to establish adult manhood suffrage, a new constitution was drafted by the "rebels." Thomas W. Dorr, a leader of the revolt, was elected governor. The regular government appealed to President Tyler to send in federal troops, which he later did. Ultimately, the regular government succeeded in putting an end to the "Dorr Rebellion" and arrested its leaders on the charge of treason. Luther, one of Dorr's supporters, was arrested by Borden and other members of the state militia. Eventually, Luther was able to flee to Massachusetts where he sought to have the matter reach the Supreme Court on the basis of diversity of citizenship. Luther maintained that the Dorr government was the legitimate one, and sued Borden for illegal trespass. He rested his claim of legitimacy on the basis of popular support as consistent with the guarantee of Article IV, Section 4, that each State have "a republican form of government." Following a lower federal court's decision which sided with Borden, the case proceeded to the Supreme Court on a writ of error.

MR. CHIEF JUSTICE TANEY delivered the opinion of the Court:

Certainly, *the question which the plaintiff proposed to raise* by the testimony he offered *has not heretofore been recognized as a judicial one in any of the State courts....*

Moreover, the Constitution of the United States, as far as it has provided for an emergency of this kind, and authorized the general government to interfere in the domestic concerns of a State, has treated the subject as political in its nature, and placed the power in the hands of that department.

The fourth section of the fourth article of the Constitution of the United States provides that the United States shall guarantee to every state in the Union a republican form of government, and shall protect each of them against invasion; and on the application of the legislature or of the executive (when the legislature cannot be convened) against domestic violence.

Under this article of the Constitution it rests with Congress to decide what government is the established one in a state. For as the United States guarantee to each state a republican government, Congress must necessarily decide what government is established in the state before it can determine whether it is republican or not. And when the Senators and Representatives of a state are admitted into the councils of the Union, the authority of the government under which they are appointed, as well as its republican character, is recognized by the proper constitutional authority. And its decision is binding on every other department of the government, and could not be questioned in a judicial tribunal. It is true that the contest in this case did not last long enough to bring the matter to this issue; and as no Senators or Representatives were elected under the authority of the government of which Mr. Dorr was the head, Congress was not called upon to decide the controversy. Yet the right to decide is placed there, and not in the courts.

So, too, as relates to the clause in the above-mentioned article of the Constitution, providing for cases of domestic violence. It rested with Congress, too, to determine upon the means proper to be adopted to fulfill this guarantee. They might, if they had deemed it most advisable to do so, have placed it in the power of a court to decide when the contingency had happened which required the federal government to interfere. But Congress thought otherwise, and no doubt wisely; and by the act of February 28, 1975, provided that, "in case of any insurrection in any state against the government thereof, it shall be lawful for the President of the United States, on application of the legislature of such state or of the executive (when the legislature cannot be convened) to call forth such number of militia of any other state or states, as may be applied for, as he may judge sufficient to suppress such insurrection."

By this act, the power of deciding whether the exigency had arisen upon which the government of the United States is bound to interfere, is given to the President. He is to act upon the application of the legislature or of the executive, and consequently he must determine what body of men constitute the legislature, and who is the governor, before he can act. The fact that both parties claim the right to the government cannot alter the case, for both cannot be entitled to it. If there is an armed conflict, like the one of which we are speaking, it is a case of domestic violence, and one of the parties must be in insurrection against the lawful government. And the President must, of necessity, decide which is the government, and which party is unlawfully arrayed against it, before he can perform the duty imposed upon him by the act of Congress.

After the President has acted and called out the militia, is a circuit court of the United States authorized to inquire whether his decision was right? Could the court, while the parties were actually contending in arms for the possession of the government, call witnesses before it and inquire which party represented a majority of the people? If it could, then it would become the duty of the court (provided it came to the conclusion that the President had decided incorrectly to discharge those who were arrested or detained by the troops in the service of the United States or the government which the President was endeavoring to maintain. If the judicial power extends so far, the guarantee contained in the Constitution of the United States is a guarantee of anarchy, and not of order. Yet if this right does not reside in the courts when the conflict is raging, if the judicial power is, at that time, bound to follow the decision of the political, it must be equally bound when the contest is over. It cannot when peace is restored, punish as offenses and crimes the acts which it before recognized, and was bound to recognize, as lawful.

It is true that in this case the militia were not called out by the President. But upon the application of the governor under the charter government, the President recognized him as the executive power of the state, and took measures to call out the militia to support his, authority, if it should be found necessary for the general government to interfere; and it is admitted in the argument that it was the knowledge of this decision that put an end to the armed opposition to the charter government, and prevented any further efforts to establish by force the proposed constitution. The interference of the President, therefore, by announcing his determination, was as effectual as if the militia had been assembled under his orders. And it should be equally authoritative. For certainly no court of the United States, with a knowledge of this decision, would have been justified in recognizing of this decision, would have been justified in recognizing the opposing party as the lawful government, or in treating as wrong-doers or insurgents the officers of the government which the President had recognized, and was prepared to support by armed force. In the case of foreign nations, the government acknowledged by the President is always recognized in the courts of justice. And this principle has been applied by the act of Congress to the sovereign states of the Union.

It is said that this power in the President is dangerous to liberty, and may be abused. All power may be abused if placed in unworthy hands. But it would be difficult, we think, to point out any other hands in which this power would be more safe, and at the same time equally effectual. When citizens of the same state are in arms against each other, and the constituted authorities unable to execute the laws, the interposition of the United States must be prompt, or it is of little value. The ordinary course of proceedings in courts of justice would be utterly unfit for the crisis. And the elevated office of the President, chosen as he is by the people of the United States, and the high responsibility he could not fail to feel when acting in a case of so much moment, appear to furnish as strong safeguards against a willful abuse of power as human prudence and foresight could well provide. At all events, it is conferred upon him by the Constitution and laws of the United States, and must, therefore, be respected and enforced in its judicial tribunals.

...Undoubtedly, if the President, in exercising this power, shall fall into error, or invade the rights of the people of the state, it would be in the power of Congress to apply the proper remedy. But the courts must administer the law as they find it....

Much of the argument on the part of the plaintiff turned upon political rights and political questions, upon which the Court has been urged to express an opinion. We decline doing so. The high power has been conferred on this court of passing judgment upon the acts of the state sovereignties, and of the legislative and executive branches of the federal government, and of determining whether they are beyond the limits of power marked out for them respectively by the Constitution of the United States. This tribunal, therefore, should be the last to overstep the boundaries which limit its own jurisdiction. And while it should always be ready to meet any question confided to it by the Constitution, it is equally its duty not to pass beyond its appropriate sphere of action, and to take care not to involve itself in discussions which properly belong to other forums. No one, we believe, has ever doubted the proposition, that, according to the institutions of this country, the sovereignty in every state resides in the people of the state, and that they may alter and change their form of government at their own pleasure. But whether they have changed it or not by abolishing an old government, and establishing a new one in its place, is a question to be settled by the political power. And when that power has decided, the courts are bound to take notice of its decision, and to follow it.

The judgment of the Circuit Court must therefore be affirmed.

BAKER v. CARR
369 U.S. 186; 7 L.Ed. 2d. 663; 82 S.Ct. 691 (1962)

Baker, and other qualified voters in Tennessee, brought a class action suit in federal district court against the secretary of state and other state officials. They claimed that the apportionment of legislative districts, drawn under the authority of a 1901 statute which based apportionment on the number of qualified voters in each county, denied them "equal protection" in the voting process guaranteed by the Fourteenth Amendment. Not one proposal calling for reapportionment had passed either House of the Tennessee General Assembly in the 60 years since the enactment of the statute. As of the 1960 Federal Census, the percentage of population variance of some senatorial districts exceeded 300%. The federal district court dismissed the complaint in light of the Court's decision in Colegrove v. Green *(1946). The plaintiffs then appealed the case directly to the Supreme Court.*

MR. JUSTICE BRENNAN delivered the opinion of the Court:

I. The District Court's Opinion and Order for Dismissal.

...In light of the District Court's treatment of the case, we told today only (a) that the court possessed jurisdiction of the subject matter; (b) that a justiciable cause of action is stated upon which appellants would be entitled to appropriate relief; and (c) because appellees raise the issue before this Court, that the appellants have standing to challenge the Tennessee apportionment statutes. Beyond noting that we have no cause at this stage to doubt the District Court will be able to fashion relief if violations of constitutional rights are found, it is improper now to consider what remedy would be most appropriate if appellants prevail at the trial.

II. Jurisdiction of the Subject Matter

The District Court was uncertain whether our cases withholding federal judicial relief rested upon a lack of federal jurisdiction or upon the inappropriateness of the subject matter for judicial consideration – what we have designated "nonjusticiability." The distinction between the two grounds is significant. In the instance of nonjusticiability, consideration of the cause is not wholly and immediately foreclosed; rather, the Court's inquiry necessarily proceeds to the point of deciding whether the duty asserted can be judicially molded. In the instance of lack of jurisdiction the cause either does not "arise under" the Federal Constitution, laws or treaties (or fall within one of the other enumerated categories of Art. III §2), or is not a "case or controversy" within the meaning of that section; or the cause is not one described by any jurisdictional stature. Our conclusion that this cause presents no nonjusticiable "political question" settles the only possible doubt that it is a case or controversy. Under the present heading of "Jurisdiction of the Subject Matter," we hold only that the matter set forth in the complaint does arise under the Constitution....

Article III, §2 of the Federal Constitution provides that "The Judicial Power shall extend to all Cases, in Law and Equity, arising under this Constitution, the Laws of the United States, and Treaties made, or which shall be made, under their Authority..." It is clear that the cause of action is one which "arises under" the Federal Constitution. The complaint alleges that the 1901 statute effects an apportionment that deprives the appellants of the equal protection of the laws in violation of the Fourteenth Amendment. Dismissal of the complaint upon the ground only if that claim were "so attenuated and unsubstantial as to be absolutely devoid of merit...." Since the District Court obviously and correctly did not deem the asserted federal constitutional claim unsubstantial and frivolous, it should not have dismissed the complaint for want of jurisdiction of the subject matter. And of course no further consideration of the merits of the claim is relevant to a determination of the court's jurisdiction of the subject matter....

An unbroken line of our precedents sustains the federal courts' jurisdiction of the subject matter of federal constitutional claims of this nature. The first cases involved the redistricting of states for the purpose of electing Representatives to the Federal Congress. When the Ohio Supreme Court sustained Ohio legislation against an attack for repugnancy to Art. I § 4, of the Federal Constitution, we affirmed on merits and expressly refused to dismiss for want of jurisdiction "in view ... of the the subject-matter of the controversy and the Federal characteristics which inhere in it ..." *Ohio ex rel. Davis v. Hildebrant* (1916). When the Minnesota Supreme Court affirmed the dismissal of a suit to enjoin the Secretary of State of Minnesota from acting under Minnesota redistricting legislation, we reviewed the constitutional merits of the legislation and reversed the State Supreme Court. *Smiley v. Holm* (1932)....

The appellees refer to *Colegrove v. Green* (1946), as authority that the District Court lacked jurisdiction of the subject matter. Appellees misconceive the holding of that case. The holding was precisely contrary to their reading of it. Seven members of the Court participated in the decision. Unlike many other cases in this field which have assumed without discussion that there was jurisdiction, all three opinions filed in Colegrove discussed the question. Two of the opinions expressing the views of four of the Justices, a majority, flatly held that there was jurisdiction of the subject matter. MR. JUSTICE BLACK joined by MR. JUSTICE DOUGLAS and MR. JUSTICE MURPHY stated: "It is my judgment that the District Court had jurisdiction...." MR. JUSTICE RUTLEDGE, writing separately, expressed agreement with this conclusion....

We hold that the District Court has jurisdiction of the subject matter of the federal constitutional claim asserted in the complaint.

III. Standing

A federal court cannot "pronounce any statute, either of a State or of the United States, void, because irreconcilable with the Constitution, except as it is called upon to adjudge the legal rights of litigants in actual controversies...." Have the appellants alleged such a personal stake in the outcome of the controversy as to assure that concrete adverseness which sharpens the presentation of issues upon which the court so largely depends for illumination of difficult constitutional questions? This is the gist of the question of standing. It is, of course, a question of federal law....

We hold that the appellants do have standing to maintain this suit. Our decisions plainly support this conclusion. Many of the cases have assumed rather than articulated the premise in deciding the merits of similar claims. And *Colegrove v. Green* squarely held that voters who allege facts showing disadvantage to themselves as individuals have standing to sue....

These appellants seek relief in order to protect or vindicate an interest of their own, and of those similarly situated. Their constitutional claim is, in substance, that the 1901 statute constitutes arbitrary and capricious state action offensive to the Fourteenth Amendment in its irrational disregard of the standard of apportionment prescribed by the State's Constitution or of any standard, effecting a gross disproportion of, representation to voting population. The injury which appellants assert is that this classification disfavors the voters in the counties in which they reside, placing them in a position of constitutionally unjustifiable inequality vis-à-vis voters in irrationally favored counties. A citizen's right to vote free of arbitrary impairment by state action has been judicially recognized as a right secured by the Constitution when such impairment resulted from dilution by a false tally, cf. *United States v. Classic* (1941) or by a refusal to count votes from arbitrarily selected precincts,... or by a stuffing of the ballot box, cf. *Ex parte Siebold* (1880)....

It would not be necessary to decide whether appellant's allegations of impairment of their votes by the 1901 apportionment will, ultimately, entitle them to any relief, in order to hold that they have standing to seek it. If such impairment does produce a legally cognizable injury, they are among those who have sustained it. They are asserting "a plain, direct and adequate interest in maintaining the effectiveness of their votes,..." not merely a claim of "the right, possessed by every citizen, to require that the Government be administered according to law...." *Fairchild v. Hughes* (1922).... They are entitled to a hearing and to the District Court's decision on their claims. "The very essence of civil liberty certainly consists in the right of every individual to claim the protection of the laws, whenever he receives an injury."

IV. Justiciability

In holding that the subject matter of this suit was not justiciable, the District Court relied on *Colegrove v. Green*, and subsequent per curiam cases. The court stated: "From a review of these decisions there can be no doubt that the federal rule... is that the federal courts ... will not intervene in cases of this type to compel legislative reapportionment." We understand the District Court to have read, the cited cases as compelling the conclusion that since the appellants sought to have a legislative apportionment held unconstitutional, their suit presented a "political question" and was therefore nonjusticiable. We hold that this challenge to an apportionment presents no nonjusticiable "political question." The cited cases do not hold the contrary.

Of course the mere fact that the suit seeks protection of a political right does not mean it presents a political question. Such an objection "is little more than a play upon words...." Rather, it is argued that apportionment cases, whatever the actual wording of the complaint, can involve no federal constitutional right except one resting on the guaranty of a republican form of government, and that complaints based on that clause have been held to present political questions which are nonjusticiable.

We hold that the claim pleaded here neither rests upon nor implicates the Guaranty Clause and that its justiciability is therefore not foreclosed by our decisions of cases involving that clause. The District Court misinterpreted *Colegrove v. Green* and other decisions of this Court on which it relied. Appellants' claim that they are being denied equal protection is justiciable, and if "discrimination is sufficiently shown, the right to relief under the equal protection clause is not diminished by the fact that the discrimination relates to political rights...." To show why we reject the argument based on the Guaranty Clause, we must examine the authorities under it. But because there appears to be some uncertainty as to why those cases did present political questions, and specifically as to whether this apportionment case is like those cases, we deem it necessary first to consider the contours of the "political question" doctrine.

Our discussion, even at the price of extending this opinion, requires review of a number of political question cases, in order to expose the attributes of the doctrine-attributes which, in various settings, diverge, combine, appear, and disappear in seeming disorderliness. Since that review is undertaken solely to demonstrate that neither singly nor collectively do these cases support a conclusion that this apportionment case is nonjusticiable, we of course do not explore their implications in other contexts. That review reveals that in the Guaranty Clause cases and in the other "political question" cases, it is the relationship between the judiciary and the coordinate branches of the Federal Government, and not the federal judiciary's relationship to the States, which gives rise to the "political question."

We have said that "In determining whether a question falls within [the political question] category, the appropriateness under our system of government of attributing finality to the action of the political departments and also the lack of satisfactory criteria for a judicial determination are dominant considerations."

Coleman v. Miller. The nonjusticiability of a political question is primarily a function of the separation of powers. Much confusion results from the capacity of the "political question" label to obscure the need for case-by-case inquiry. Deciding whether a matter has in any measure been committed by the Constitution to another branch of government, or whether the action of that branch exceeds whatever authority has been committed, is itself a delicate exercise in constitutional interpretation, and is a responsibility of this Court as ultimate interpreter of the Constitution. To demonstrate this requires no less than to analyze representative cases and to infer from them the analytical threads that make up the political question doctrine....

We come, finally, to the ultimate inquiry whether our precedents as to what constitutes a nonjusticiable "political question" bring the case before us under the umbrella of that doctrine. A natural beginning is to note whether any of the common characteristics which we have been able to identify and label descriptively are present. We find none. The question here is the consistency of state action with the Federal Constitution. We have no question decided, or to be decided, by a political branch of government coequal with this Court. Nor do we risk embarrassment of our government abroad, grave disturbance at home if we take issue with Tennessee as to the constitutionality of her action here challenged. Nor need the appellants, in order to succeed in this action, ask the Court to enter upon policy determinations for which judicially manageable standards are lacking. Judicial standards under the Equal Protection Clause are well developed and familiar, and it has been open to courts since the enactment of the Fourteenth Amendment to determine, if on the particular facts they must, that a discrimination reflects no policy, but simply arbitrary and capricious action....

We conclude that the complaint's allegations of a denial of equal protection present a Justiciable constitutional cause of action upon which appellants are entitled to a trial and a decision. The right asserted is within the reach of judicial protection under the Fourteenth Amendment.

The judgment of the District Court is reversed and the cause is remanded for further proceedings consistent with this opinion.

Reversed and remanded,

MR. JUSTICE WHITTAKER did not participate in the decision of this case.

MR. JUSTICE DOUGLAS concurred:

While I join the opinion of the Court and, like the Court, do not reach the merits, a word of explanation is necessary. I put to one side the problems of "political" questions involving the distribution of power between this Court, the Congress, and the Chief Executive. We have here a phase of the recurring problem of the relation of the federal courts to state agencies. More particularly, the question is the extent to which a State may weight one person's vote more heavily than it does another's....

I agree with my Brother Clark that if the allegations in the complaint can be sustained a case for relief is established. We are told that a single vote in

Moore County, Tennessee, is worth 19 votes in Hamilton County, that one vote in Stewart or in Chester County is worth nearly eight times a single vote in Shelby or Knox County. The opportunity to prove that an "invidious discrimination" exists should therefore be given the appellants....

With the exceptions of *Colegrove v. Green*, *MacDougall v. Green*, *South v. Peters*, and the decisions they spawned, the Court has never thought that protection of voting rights was beyond judicial cognizance. Today's treatment of those cases removes the only impediment to judicial cognizance of the claims stated in the present complaint....

MR. JUSTICE CLARK concurred:

One emerging from the rash of opinions with their accompanying clashing of views may well find themselves suffering a mental blindness. The Court holds that the appellants have alleged a cause of action. However, it refuses to award relief here – although the facts are undisputed – and fails to give the District Court any guidance whatever. One dissenting opinion, bursting with words that go through so much and conclude with so little, condemns the majority action as "a massive repudiation of the experience of our whole past." Another describes the complaint as merely asserting conclusory allegations that Tennessee's apportionment is "incorrect," "arbitrary," "obsolete," and "unconstitutional." I believe it can be shown that this case is distinguishable from earlier cases dealing with the distribution of political power by a State, that a patent violation of the Equal Protection Clause of the United States Constitution has been shown, and that an appropriate remedy may be formulated.

...The widely heralded case of *Colegrove v. Green* was one not only in which the Court was bobtailed but in which there was no majority opinion. Indeed, even the "political question" point in Mr. Justice Frankfurter's opinion was no more than an alternative ground. Moreover, the appellants did not present an equal protection argument. While it has served as a Mother Hubbard to most of the subsequent cases, I feel it was in that respect ill-cast and for all of these reasons put it to one side....

MR. JUSTICE STEWART wrote a concurring opinion.

MR. JUSTICE FRANKFURTER, whom MR. JUSTICE HARLAN joined, dissented:

The Court today reverses a uniform course of decision established by a dozen cases, including one by which the very claim now sustained was unanimously rejected only five years ago. The impressive body of rulings thus cast aside reflected the equally uniform course of our political history regarding the relationship between population and legislative representations wholly different matter from denial of the franchise to individuals because of race, color, religion or sex. *Such a massive repudiation of the experience of our whole past in asserting destructively novel judicial power demands a detailed analysis of the role of this Court in our constitutional scheme.* Disregard of inherent limits in the effective exercise of the Court's "judicial power" not only presages the futility of judicial intervention in the essentially political conflict of forces by which the relation between population and representation has time out of mind been and now is determined. It may well impair the Court's position as the ultimate organ of "the supreme Law of the Land" in that vast range of legal problems, often strongly entangled in popular feeling, on which this Court must pronounce. *The Court's authority – possessed neither of the purse nor the sword – ultimately rests on sustained public confidence in its moral sanction. Such feeling must be nourished by the Court's complete detachment, in fact and in appearance, from political entanglements and by abstention from injecting itself into the clash of political forces in political settlements.... The Framers carefully and with deliberate forethought refused so to enthrone the judiciary.* In this situation, as in others of like nature, appeal for relief does not belong here. Appeal must be to an informed, civically militant electorate. In a democratic society like ours, relief must come through an aroused popular conscience that sears the conscience of the people's representatives. In any event there is nothing judicially more unseemly nor more self-defeating than for this Court to make *in terrorem* pronouncements, to indulge in merely empty rhetoric, sounding a word of promise to the ear, sure to be disappointing to the hope....

MR. JUSTICE HARLAN wrote a dissenting opinion in which MR. JUSTICE FRANKFURTER joined.

DAVIS v. BANDEMER
106 S.Ct. 2797; 478 U.S. 109; 92 L.Ed. 2d 85 (1986)

In cases subsequent to Baker v. Carr, *the Supreme Court has addressed the issue of malapportionment by insisting that electoral districts be compact, contiguous and approximately equal in population. Such guidelines do not, however, address the problems associated with gerrymandering – the artificial manipulation of electoral district boundaries for partisan advantage. Boundaries can be manipulated to advantage a particular political party even when meeting the requirements of one-person, one-vote. Here the Court rules that political gerrymendering violates the equal protection clause of the Constitution, and is therfore subject to constitutional challenge. The basic facts in this case are given in the decision below.*

Justice WHITE announced the judgment of the Court and delivered the opinion of the Court as to Part II and an opinion as to Parts I, III, and IV, in which Justice BRENNAN, Justice MARSHALL, and Justice BLACKMUN join.

In this case, we review a judgment from a three-judge District Court, which sustained an equal protection challenge to Indiana's 1981 state apportionment on the basis that the law unconstitutionally diluted the votes of Indiana Democrats.... Although we find such political gerrymandering to be justiciable, we conclude that the District Court applied an insufficiently demanding standard in finding unconstitutional vote dilution. Consequently, we reverse....

II

...The outlines of the political question doctrine were described and to a large extent defined in *Baker v. Carr.* The synthesis of that effort is found in the following passage in the Court's opinion:

> "It is apparent that several formulations which vary slightly according to the settings in which the questions arise may describe a political question, although each has one or more elements which identify it as essentially a function of the separation of powers. Prominent on the surface of any case held to involve a political question is found a textually demonstrable constitutional commitment of the issue to a coordinate political department; or a lack of judicially discoverable and manageable standards for resolving it; or the impossibility of deciding without an initial policy determination of a kind clearly for nonjudicial discretion; or the impossibility of a court's undertaking independent resolution without expressing lack of the respect due coordinate branches of government; or an unusual need for unquestioning adherence to a political decision already made; or the potentiality of embarrassment from multifarious pronouncements by various departments on one question...."

...In *Baker,* the Court applied this analysis to an equal protection claim based on a state legislative apportionment that allowed substantial disparities in the number of voters represented by each state representative.... In holding that claim to be justiciable, the Court concluded that none of the identifying characteristics of a political question were present:

> "The question here is the consistency of state action with the Federal Constitution. We have no question decided, or to be decided, by a political branch of government coequal with this Court. Nor do we risk embarrassment of our government abroad, or grave disturbance at home if we take issue with Tennessee as to the constitutionality of her action here challenged. Nor need the appellants, in order to succeed in this action, ask the Court to enter upon policy determinations for which judicially manageable standards are lacking. Judicial standards under the Equal Protection Clause are well developed and familiar, and it has been open to courts since the enactment of the Fourteenth Amendment to determine, if on the particular facts they must, that a discrimination reflects *no* policy, but simply arbitrary and capricious action."

This analysis applies equally to the question now before us. Disposition of this question does not involve us in a matter more properly decided by a coequal branch of our Government. There is no risk of foreign or domestic disturbance, and in light of our cases since *Baker* we are not persuaded that there are no judicially discernible and manageable standards by which political gerrymander cases are to be decided.

It is true that the type of claim that was presented in *Baker v. Carr* was subsequently resolved in this Court by the formulation of the "one person, one vote" rule. See, *e.g., Reynolds v. Sims....* The mere fact, however, that we may not now similarly perceive a likely arithmetic presumption in the instant context does not compel a conclusion that the claims presented here are nonjusticiable. The one person, one vote principle had not yet been developed when *Baker* was decided. At that time, the Court did not rely on the potential for such a rule in finding justiciability. Instead, as the language quoted above clearly indicates, the Court contemplated simply that legislative line drawing in the districting context would be susceptible of adjudication under the applicable constitutional criteria....

The issue here is of course different from that adjudicated in *Reynolds.* It does not concern districts of unequal size. Not only does everyone have the right to vote and to have his vote counted, but each elector may vote for and be represented by the same number of lawmakers. Rather, the claim is that each political group in a State should have the same chance to elect representatives of its choice as any other political group. Nevertheless, the issue is one of representation, and we decline to hold that such claims are never justiciable.

Our racial gerrymander cases such as *White v. Regester* and *Whitcomb v. Chavis* indicate as much. In those cases, there was no population variation among the districts, and no one was precluded from voting. The claim instead was that an identifiable racial or ethnic group had an insufficient chance to elect a representative of its choice and that district lines should be redrawn to remedy this alleged defect. In both cases, we adjudicated the merits of such claims, rejecting the claim in *Whitcomb* and sustaining it in *Regester.* Just as clearly, in *Gaffney v. Cummings,* where the districts also passed muster under the *Reynolds* formula, the claim was that the legislature had manipulated district lines to afford political groups in various districts an enhanced opportunity to elect legislators of their choice. Although advising caution, we said that "we *must* ... respond to [the] claims ... that even if acceptable population wise, the ... plan was invidiously discriminatory because a 'political fairness principle' was followed...." We went on to hold that the statute at issue did not violate the Equal Protection Clause.

These decisions support a conclusion that this case is justiciable. As *Gaffney* demonstrates, that the claim is submitted by a political group, rather than a racial group, does not distinguish it in terms of justiciability. That the characteristics of the complaining group are not immutable or that the group has not been subject to the same historical stigma may be relevant to the manner in which the case is adjudicated, but these differences do not justify a refusal to entertain such a case.

In fact, Justice O'CONNOR's attempt to distinguish this political gerrymandering claim from the racial gerrymandering claims that we have consistently adjudicated demonstrates the futility of such an effort. Her conclusion that the claim in this case is not justiciable seems to rest on a dual concern that no judicially manageable standards exist and that adjudication of such claims requires an initial policy decision that the judiciary should not make. Yet she does not point out how the standards that we set forth here for adjudicating this political gerrymandering claim are less manageable than the standards that have been developed for racial gerrymandering claims. Nor does she demonstrate what initial policy decision regarding, for example, the desirability of fair group representation, we have made here that we have not made in the race cases. She merely asserts that because race has historically been a suspect classification individual minority voters' rights are more immediately related to a racial minority group's voting strength. This, in combination with "the greater warrant the Equal Protection Clause gives the federal courts to intervene for protection against racial discrimination, suffice to render racial gerrymandering claims justiciable."

Reliance on these assertions to determine justiciability would transform the narrow categories of "political questions" that *Baker v. Carr* carefully defined into an ad hoc litmus test of this Court's reactions to the desirability of and need for judicial application of constitutional or statutory standards to a given type of claim. Justice O'CONNOR's own discussion seems to reflect such an approach: She concludes that because political gerrymandering may be a "self-limiting enterprise" there is no need for judicial intervention. She also expresses concern that our decision today will lead to "political instability and judicial malaise," because nothing will prevent members of other identifiable groups from bringing similar claims. To begin with, Justice O'CONNOR's factual assumptions are by no means obviously correct: It is not clear that political gerrymandering *is* a self-limiting enterprise or that other groups will have any great incentive to bring gerrymandering claims, given the requirement of a showing of discriminatory intent. At a more fundamental level, however, Justice O'CONNOR's analysis is flawed because it focuses on the perceived need for judicial review and on the potential practical problems with allowing such review. Validation of the consideration of such amorphous and wide-ranging factors in assessing justiciability would alter substantially the analysis the Court enunciated in *Baker v. Carr,* and we decline Justice O'CONNOR's implicit invitation to rethink that approach.

III

Having determined that the political gerrymandering claim in this case is justiciable, we turn to the question whether the District Court erred in holding that the appellees had alleged and proved a violation of the Equal Protection Clause.

Preliminarily, we agree with the District Court that the claim made by the appellees in this case is a claim that the 1981 apportionment discriminates against Democrats on a statewide basis. Both the appellees and the District Court have cited instances of individual districting within the State which they believe exemplify this discrimination, but the appellees' claim, as we understand it, is that Democratic voters over the State as a whole, not Democratic voters in particular districts, have been subjected to unconstitutional discrimination....

We also agree with the District Court that in order to succeed the Bandemer plaintiffs were required to prove both intentional discrimination against an identifiable political group and an actual discriminatory effect on that group. Further, we are confident that if the law challenged here had discriminatory effects on Democrats, this record would support a finding that the discrimination was intentional. Thus, we decline to overturn the District Court's finding of discriminatory intent as clearly erroneous.

Indeed, quite aside from the anecdotal evidence, the shape of the House and Senate Districts, and the alleged disregard for political boundaries, we think it most likely that whenever a legislature redistricts, those responsible for the legislation will know the likely political composition of the new districts and will have a prediction as to whether a particular district is a safe one for a Democratic or Republican candidate or is a competitive district that either candidate might win....

We do not accept, however, the District Court's legal and factual bases for concluding that the 1981 Act visited a sufficiently adverse effect on the appellees' constitutionally protected rights to make out a violation of the Equal Protection Clause. The District Court held that because any apportionment scheme that purposely prevents proportional representation is unconstitutional, Democratic voters need only show that their proportionate voting influence has been adversely affected. Our cases, however, clearly foreclose any claim that the Constitution requires proportional representation or that legislatures in reapportioning must draw district lines to come as near as possible to allocating seats to the contending parties in proportion to what their anticipated statewide vote will be....

The typical election for legislative seats in the United States is conducted in described geographical districts, with the candidate receiving the most votes in each district winning the seat allocated to that district. If all or most of the districts are competitive, defined by the District Court in this case as districts in which the anticipated split in the party vote is within the range of 45% to 55%, even a narrow statewide preference for either party would produce an overwhelming majority for the winning party in the state legislature. This consequence, however, is inherent in winner-take-all, district-based elections, and we cannot hold that such a reapportionment law would violate the Equal Protection Clause because the voters in the losing party do not have representation in the legislature in proportion to the statewide vote received by their party candidates....

To draw district lines to maximize the representation of each major party would require creating as many safe seats for each party as the demographic and predicted political characteristics of the State would permit. This in turn would leave the minority in each safe district without a representative of its choice. We upheld this "political fairness" approach in *Gaffney v. Cummings,* despite its tendency to deny safe district minorities any realistic chance to elect their own representatives. But *Gaffney* in no way suggested that the Constitution requires the approach that Connecticut had adopted in that case.

In cases involving individual multimember districts, we have required a substantially greater showing of adverse effects than a mere lack of proportional representation to support a finding of unconstitutional vote dilution. Only where there is evidence that excluded groups have "less opportunity to participate in the political processes and to elect candidates of their choice" have we refused to approve the use of multimember districts....

These holdings rest on a conviction that the mere fact that a particular apportionment scheme makes it more difficult for a particular group in a particular district to elect the representatives of its choice does not render that scheme constitutionally infirm. This conviction, in turn, stems from a perception that the power to influence the political process is not limited to winning elections. An individual or a group of individuals who votes for a losing candidate is usually deemed to be adequately represented by the winning candidate and to have as much opportunity to influence that candidate as other voters in the district. We cannot presume in such a situation, without actual proof to the contrary, that the candidate elected will entirely ignore the interests of those voters. This is true even in a safe district where the losing group loses election after election. Thus, a group's electoral power is not unconstitutionally diminished by the simple fact of an apportionment scheme that makes winning elections more difficult, and a failure of proportional representation alone does not constitute impermissible discrimination under the Equal Protection Clause....

As with individual districts, where unconstitutional vote dilution is alleged in the form of statewide political gerrymandering, the mere lack of proportional representation will not be sufficient to prove unconstitutional discrimination. Again, without specific supporting evidence, a court cannot presume in such a case that those who are elected will disregard the disproportionately underrepresented group. Rather, unconstitutional discrimination occurs only when the electoral system is arranged in a manner that will consistently degrade a voter's or a group of voters' influence on the political process as a whole.

Although this is a somewhat different formulation than we have previously used in describing unconstitutional vote dilution in an individual district, the focus of both of these inquiries is essentially the same. In both contexts, the question is whether a particular group has been unconstitutionally denied its chance to effectively influence the political process. In a challenge to an individual district, this inquiry focuses on the opportunity of members of the group to participate in party deliberations in the slating and nomination of candidates, their opportunity to register and vote, and hence their chance to directly influence the election returns and to secure the attention of the winning candidate. Statewide, however, the inquiry centers on the voters' direct or indirect influence on the elections of the state legislature as a whole. And, as in individual district cases, an equal protection violation may be found only where the electoral system substantially disadvantages certain voters in their opportunity to influence the political process effectively. In this context, such a finding of unconstitutionality must be supported by evidence of continued frustration of the will of a majority of the voters or effective denial to a minority of voters of a fair chance to influence the political process.

Based on these views, we would reject the District Court's apparent holding that *any* interference with an opportunity to elect a representative of one's choice would be sufficient to allege or make out an equal protection violation, unless justified by some acceptable state interest that the State would be required to demonstrate. In addition to being contrary to the above-described conception of an unconstitutional political gerrymander, such a low threshold for legal action would invite attack on all or almost all reapportionment statutes. District-based elections hardly ever produce a perfect fit between votes and representation. The one-person, one-vote imperative often mandates departure from this result as does the no-retrogression rule required by § 5 of the Voting Rights Act. Inviting attack on minor departures from some supposed norm would too much embroil the judiciary in second-guessing what has consistently been referred to as a political task for the legislature, a task that should not be monitored too closely unless the express or tacit goal is to effect its removal from legislative halls. We decline to take a major step toward that end, which would be so much at odds with our history and experience....

The District Court's findings do not satisfy this threshold condition to stating and proving a cause of action. In reaching its conclusion, the District Court relied primarily on the results of the 1982 elections: Democratic candidates for the State House of Representatives had received 51.9% of the votes cast statewide and Republican candidates 48.1%; yet, out of the 100 seats to be filled, Republican candidates won 57 and Democrats 43. In the Senate, 53.1% of the votes were cast for Democratic candidates and 46.9% for Republicans; of the 25 Senate seats to be filled, Republicans won 12 and Democrats 13. The court also relied upon the use of multimember districts in Marion and Allen Counties, where Democrats or those inclined to vote Democratic in 1982 amounted to 46.6% of the population of those counties but Republicans won 86%, 18 of 21, seats allocated to the districts in those counties. These disparities were enough to require a neutral justification by the State, which in the eyes of the District Court was not forthcoming.

Relying on a single election to prove unconstitutional discrimination is unsatisfactory. The District Court observed, and the parties do not disagree, that Indiana is a swing State. Voters sometimes prefer Democratic candidates, and sometimes Republican. The District Court did not find that because of the 1981 Act the Democrats could not in one of the next few elections secure a sufficient vote to take control of the assembly. Indeed, the District Court declined to hold that the 1982 election results were the predictable consequences of the 1981 Act and expressly refused to hold that those results were a reliable prediction of future ones. The District Court did not ask by what percentage the statewide Democratic vote would have had to increase to control either the House or the Senate. The appellants argue here, without a persuasive response from the appellees, that had the Democratic candidates received an additional few percentage points of the votes cast statewide, they would have obtained a majority of the seats in both houses. Nor was there any finding that the 1981 reapportionment would consign the Democrats to a minority status in the Assembly throughout the 1980's or that the Democrats would have no hope of doing any better in the reapportionment that would occur after the 1990 census. Without findings of this nature, the District Court erred in concluding that the 1981 Act violated the Equal Protection Clause.

The District Court's discussion of the multimember districts created by the 1981 Act does not undermine this conclusion. For the purposes of the statewide political gerrymandering claim, these districts appear indistinguishable from safe Republican and safe Democratic single-member districts. Simply showing that there are multimember districts in the State and that those districts are constructed so as to be safely Republican or Democratic in no way bolsters the contention that there has been *statewide* discrimination against Democratic voters. It could be, were the necessary threshold effect to be shown, that multimember districts could be demonstrated to be suspect on the ground that they are particularly useful in attaining impermissibly discriminatory ends; at this stage of the inquiry, however, the multi-member district evidence does not materially aid the appellees' case.

Furthermore, in determining the constitutionality of multi-member districts challenged as racial gerrymanders, we have rejected the view that "any group with distinctive interests must be represented in legislative halls if it is numerous enough to command at least one seat and represents a minority living in an area sufficiently compact to constitute a single-member district." Rather, we have required that there be proof that the complaining minority "had less opportunity ... to participate in the political processes and to elect legislators of their choice." In *Whitcomb,* we went on to observe that there was no proof that blacks were not allowed to register or vote, to choose the political party they desired to support, to participate in its affairs or to be equally represented on those occasions when candidates were chosen, or to be included among the candidates slated by the Democratic Party.

Against this background, we concluded that the failure of the minority "to have legislative seats in proportion to its population emerges more as a function of losing elections than of built-in bias against poor Negroes. The voting power of ghetto residents may have been 'cancelled out' as the District Court held, but this seems a mere euphemism for political defeat at the polls." *Whitcomb* accordingly rejected a challenge to multimember districts in Marion County, Indiana. A similar challenge was sustained in *White v. Regester,* but only by employing the same criterion, namely, that the plaintiffs must produce evidence to support a finding "that the political processes leading to nomination and election were not equally open to participation by the group in question, that its members had less opportunity than did other residents in the district to participate in the political processes and to elect legislators of their choice."

This participatory approach to the legality of individual multimember districts is not helpful where the claim is that such districts discriminate against Democrats, for it could hardly be said that Democrats, any more than Republicans, are excluded from participating in the affairs of their own party or from the processes by which candidates are nominated and elected. For constitutional purposes, the Democratic claim in this case, insofar as it challenges *vel non* the legality of the multimember districts in certain counties, is like that of the Negroes in *Whitcomb* who failed to prove a racial gerrymander, for it boils down to a complaint that they failed to attract a majority of the voters in the challenged multimember districts.

In response to our approach, Justice POWELL suggests an alternative method for evaluating equal protection claims of political gerrymandering....

[T]he crux of Justice POWELL's analysis seems to be that, at least in some cases, the intentional drawing of district boundaries for partisan ends and for no other reason violates the Equal Protection Clause in and of itself. We disagree, however, with this conception of a constitutional violation. Specifically, even if a state legislature redistricts with the specific intention of disadvantaging one political party's election prospects, we do not believe that there has been an unconstitutional discrimination against members of that party unless the redistricting does in fact disadvantage it at the polls.

Moreover, as we discussed above, a mere lack of proportionate results in one election cannot suffice in this regard. We have reached this conclusion in our cases involving challenges to individual multimember districts, and it applies equally here. In the individual multimember district cases, we have found equal protection violations only where a history of disproportionate results appeared in conjunction with strong indicia of lack of political power and the denial of fair representation....

This requirement of more than a showing of possibly transitory results is where we appear to depart from Justice POWELL. Stripped of its "factors" verbiage, Justice POWELL's analysis turns on a determination that a lack of proportionate election results can support a finding of an equal protection violation, at least in some circumstances. Here, the only concrete effect on the Democrats in Indiana in terms of election results that the District Court had before it was one election in which the percentage of Democrats elected was lower than the percentage of total Democratic votes cast. In Justice POWELL's view, this disproportionality, when combined with clearly discriminatory intent on the part of the 1981 General Assembly and the manipulation of district lines in the apportionment process, is sufficient to conclude that fair representation has been denied.

The factors other than disproportionate election results, however, do not contribute to a finding that Democratic voters have been disadvantaged in fact. They support a finding that an intention to discriminate was present and that districts were drawn in accordance with that intention, but they do not show any actual disadvantage beyond that shown by the election results. It surely cannot be an actual disadvantage in terms of fair representation on a group level just to be placed in a district with a supermajority of other Democratic voters or a district that departs from pre-existing political boundaries. Only when such placement affects election results and political power statewide has an actual disadvantage occurred.

Consequently, Justice POWELL's view would allow a constitutional violation to be found where the only proven effect on a political party's electoral power was disproportionate results in one (or possibly two) elections. This view, however, contains no explanation of why a lack of proportionate election results should suffice in these political gerrymandering cases while it does not in the cases involving racial gerrymandering. In fact, Justice POWELL's opinion is silent as to the relevance of the substantive standard developed in the multimember district cases to these political gerrymandering cases.

In rejecting Justice POWELL's approach, we do not mean to intimate that the factors he considers are entirely irrelevant. The election results obviously are relevant to a showing of the effects required to prove a political gerrymandering claim under our view. And the district configurations may be combined with vote projections to predict future election results, which are also relevant to the effects showing. The other factors, even if not relevant to the effects issue, might well be relevant to an equal protection claim. The equal protection argument would proceed along the following lines: If there were a discriminatory effect and a discriminatory intent, then the legislation would be examined for valid underpinnings. Thus, evidence of exclusive legislative process and deliberate drawing of district lines in accordance with accepted gerrymandering principles would be relevant to intent, and evidence of valid and invalid configuration would be relevant to whether the districting plan met legitimate state interests.

This course is consistent with our equal protection cases generally and is the course we follow here:...

IV

In sum, we hold that political gerrymandering cases are properly justiciable under the Equal Protection Clause. We also conclude, however, that a threshold showing of discriminatory vote dilution is required for a prima facie case of an equal protection violation. In this case, the findings made by the District Court of an adverse effect on the appellees do not surmount the threshold requirement. Consequently, the judgment of the District Court is

Reversed.

Chief Justice BURGER, concurring in the judgment....

Justice O'CONNOR, with whom THE CHIEF JUSTICE and Justice REHNQUIST join, concurring in the judgment.

Today the Court holds that claims of political gerrymandering lodged by members of one of the political parties that make up our two-party system are justiciable under the Equal Protection Clause of the Fourteenth Amendment. Nothing in our precedents compels us to take this step, and there is every reason not to do so. I would hold that the partisan gerrymandering claims of major political parties raise a nonjusticiable political question that the judiciary should leave to the legislative branch as the Framers of the Constitution unquestionably intended. Accordingly, I would reverse the District Court's judgment on the grounds that appellees' claim is nonjusticiable.

There can be little doubt that the emergence of a strong and stable two-party system in this country has contributed enormously to sound and effective government. The preservation and health of our political institutions, state and federal, depends to no small extent on the continued vitality of our two-party system, which permits both stability and measured change. The opportunity to control the drawing of electoral boundaries through the legislative process of apportionment is a critical and traditional part of politics in the United States, and one that plays no small role in fostering active participation in the political parties at every level. Thus, the legislative business of apportionment is fundamentally a political affair, and challenges to the manner in which an apportionment has been carried out, by the very parties that are responsible for this process, present a political question in the truest sense of the term.

To turn these matters over to the federal judiciary is to inject the courts into the most heated partisan issues. It is predictable that the courts will respond by moving away from the nebulous standard a plurality of the Court fashions today and toward some form of rough proportional representation for all political groups. The consequences of this shift will be as immense as they are unfortunate. I do not believe, and the Court offers not a shred of evidence to suggest, that the Framers of the Constitution intended the judicial power to encompass the making of such fundamental choices about how this Nation is to be governed. Nor do I believe that the proportional representation towards which the Court's expansion of equal protection doctrine will lead is consistent with our history, our traditions, or our political institutions.

The Court pays little heed to these considerations, which should inform any sensible jurisprudence of Article III and of the Equal Protection Clause... In cases such as this one, which may profoundly affect the governance of this Nation, it is not enough to cite precedent: we should examine it for possible limits, and if they are lacking, for possible flaws....

The step taken today is a momentous one, which if followed in the future can only lead to political instability and judicial malaise. If members of the major political parties are protected by the Equal Protection Clause from dilution of their voting strength, then members of every identifiable group that possesses distinctive interests and tends to vote on the basis of those interests should be able to bring similar claims. Federal courts will have no alternative but to attempt to recreate the complex process of legislative apportionment in the context of adversary litigation in order to reconcile the competing claims of political, religious, ethnic, racial, occupational, and socioeconomic groups. Even if there were some way of limiting such claims to organized political parties, the fact remains that the losing party or the losing group of legislators in every reapportionment will now be invited to fight the battle anew in federal court.

Apportionment is so important to legislators and political parties that the burden of proof the plurality places on political gerrymandering plaintiffs is unlikely to deter the routine lodging of such complaints. Notwithstanding the plurality's threshold requirement of discriminatory effects, the Court's holding that political gerrymandering claims are justiciable has opened the door to pervasive and unwarranted judicial superintendence of the legislative task of apportionment. There is simply no clear stopping point to prevent the gradual evolution of a requirement of roughly proportional representation for every cohesive political group.

In my view, this enterprise is flawed from its inception. The Equal Protection Clause does not supply judicially manageable standards for resolving purely political gerrymandering claims, and no group right to an equal share of political power was ever intended by the Framers of the Fourteenth Amendment. The Court rests its case on precedent, but the cases on which the Court relies do not require that we take this next and most far-reaching step into the "political thicket...."

Baker v. Carr itself involved just such an initial interpretation of the Equal Protection Clause: the Court in effect ruled that an arbitrary and capricious discrimination against individual voters with respect to the weight of their votes would state a cognizable claim under the Equal Protection Clause. That threshold determination about the reach and meaning of the Equal Protection Clause was the basis for the Court's holding that the complaint of the Tennessee voters was justiciable. Even this "arbitrary and capricious" standard threatened to prove unmanageable, but the difficulty was pretermitted when a relatively simple and judicially manageable requirement of population equality among districts was adopted the following term in *Reynolds v. Sims.*

Instead, the Court justifies the extension of vote dilution claims to mainstream political groups with the pronouncement that "*Reynolds* surely indicates the justiciability of claims going to the adequacy of representation in state legislatures...."

Where representation is apportioned substantially on a population basis, it is "obvious that nobody's vote has been 'diluted' in the sense in which that word was used in the *Reynolds* case." Thus, the individual's right to vote does not imply that political groups have a right to be free from discriminatory impairment of their group voting strength. Treating the vote dilution claims of political groups as cognizable would effectively collapse the "fundamental distinction between state action that inhibits an individual's right to vote and state action that affects the political strength of various groups that compete for leadership in a democratically governed community...."

... In order to gerrymander, the legislative majority must weaken some of its safe seats, thus exposing its own incumbents to greater risks of defeat – risks they may refuse to accept past a certain point. Similarly, an overambitious gerrymander can lead to disaster for the legislative majority: because it has created more seats in which it hopes to win relatively narrow victories, the same swing in overall voting strength will tend to cost the legislative majority more and more seats as the gerrymander becomes more ambitious. More generally, each major party presumably has ample weapons at its disposal to conduct the partisan struggle that often leads to a partisan apportionment, but also often leads to a bipartisan one. There is no proof before us that political gerrymandering is an evil that cannot be checked or cured by the people or by the parties themselves. Absent such proof, I see no basis for concluding that there is a need, let alone a constitutional basis, for judicial intervention.

The plurality agrees that it would be unwise to "embroil the judiciary in second-guessing what has consistently been referred to as a political task for the legislature." Moreover, the plurality is willing to presume that elected candidates will not ignore the interests of voters for the losing candidate, and it correctly observes that "the power to influence the political process is not limited to winning elections." But these propositions support my position – that the costs of judicial intervention will be severe and that political gerrymandering simply does not cause intolerable harm to the ability of major political groups to advance their interests.

Moreover, the new group right created by today's decision is particularly unjustifiable in the context of the claim here, which is founded on a supposed diminution of the *statewide* voting influence of a political group. None of the elections for the Indiana Legislature are statewide. Voters in each district elect their representatives from that district. To treat the loss of candidates nominated by the party of a voter's choice as a harm to the individual voter, when that voter cannot vote for such candidates and is not represented by them in any direct sense, clearly exceeds the limits of the Equal Protection Clause. On the Court's reasoning, members of a political party in one State should be able to challenge a congressional districting plan adopted in any other State, on the grounds that their party is unfairly represented in that State's congressional delegation, thus injuring them as members of the national party....

Furthermore, the Court fails to explain why a bipartisan gerrymander, which is what was approved in *Gaffney,* affects individuals any differently than a partisan gerrymander, which the Court makes vulnerable to constitutional challenge today. In *Gaffney,* Connecticut, as part of a bipartisan effort, had drawn up a plan intended to "provide a rough sort of proportional representation," for the two major political parties. The Court declined to invalidate this plan, which undertook "not to minimize or eliminate the political strength of any group or party, but to recognize it," and suggested that "judicial interest should be at its lowest ebb when a State purports fairly to allocate political power to the parties in accordance with their voting strength and, within quite tolerable limits, succeeds in doing so."

A bipartisan gerrymander employs the same technique, and has the same effect on individual voters, as does a partisan gerrymander. In each instance, groups of individuals are assigned to districts with an eye towards promoting the ends of a political party and its incumbent legislators. Some groups within each party will lose any chance to elect a representative who belongs to their party, because they have been assigned to a district in which the opposing party holds an overwhelming advantage. Independent voters may lose any chance to influence the outcome of elections in their district, if one party has a sufficiently strong majority. As the plurality acknowledges, the scheme upheld in *Gaffney* tended to "deny safe district minorities any realistic chance to elect their own representatives." If this bipartisan arrangement between two groups of self-interested legislators is constitutionally permissible, as I believe and as the Court held in *Gaffney,* then, in terms of the rights of individuals, it should be equally permissible for a legislative majority to employ the same means to pursue its own interests over the opposition of the other party.

The Court's determination to treat the claims of mainstream political parties as justiciable thus emerges as precisely the sort of "initial policy determination of a kind clearly for nonjudicial discretion" that *Baker v. Carr* recognized as characteristic of political questions. The Court has in effect decided that it is constitutionally acceptable for both parties to "waste" the votes of individuals through a bipartisan gerrymander, so long as the *parties* themselves are not deprived of their group voting strength to an extent that will exceed the plurality's threshold requirement. This choice confers greater rights on powerful political groups than on individuals; that cannot be the meaning of the Equal Protection Clause....

Moreover, any such intervention is likely to move in the direction of proportional representation for political parties. This is clear by analogy to the problem that arises in racial gerrymandering cases: "in order to decide whether an electoral system has made it harder for minority voters to elect the candidates they prefer, a court must have an idea in mind of how hard it 'should' be for minority voters to elect their preferred candidates under an acceptable system." Any such norm must make some reference, even if only a loose one, to the relation between the racial minority group's share of the electorate and its share of the elected representatives. In order to implement the plurality's standard, it will thus be necessary for courts to adopt an analogous norm, in order to assess whether the voting strength of a political party has been "degraded" by an apportionment, either on a statewide basis or in particular districts. Absent any such norm, the inquiry the plurality proposes would be so standardless as to make the adjudication of political gerrymandering claims impossible.

Implicit in the plurality's opinion today is at least some use of simple proportionality as the standard for measuring the normal representational entitlements of a political party. That is why the plurality can say that "a history (actual or projected) of disproportionate results," together with proof of "the denial of fair representation" and of "lack of political power," will constitute an equal protection violation. To be sure, the plurality has qualified its use of a *standard* of proportional representation in a variety of ways so as to avoid a *requirement* of proportional representation. The question is whether these qualifications are likely to be enduring in the face of the tremendous political pressures that courts will confront when called on to decide political gerrymandering claims. Because the most easily measured indicia of political power relate solely to winning and losing elections, there is a grave risk that the plurality's various attempts to qualify and condition the group right the Court has created will gradually pale in importance. What is likely to remain is a loose form of proportionality, under which *some* deviations from proportionality are permissible, but any significant, persistent deviations from proportionality are suspect. Courts will be forced to look for some form of "undue" disproportionality with respect to electoral success if political gerrymandering claims are justiciable, because otherwise they will find their decisions turning on imponderables such as whether the legislators of one party have fairly represented the voters of the other....

Unfortunately, a drift towards proportional representation is apparent even in the plurality opinion. Although at times the plurality seems to require that the political party be "essentially ... shut out of the political process" before a constitutional violation will be found, the plurality's explanation of the deficiencies in the District Court's approach focuses not on access to the political process as a whole, but entirely on statewide electoral success. Thus, the critical inquiry appears to be into whether the complaining political party could be expected to regain control of the state legislature in the next few elections if backed by a majority of voters. As an aid in this inquiry, courts must apparently also ask "by what percentage the statewide ... vote" for the complaining political party would have to increase to control the legislature or one of its Houses.

Under the plurality's approach, where it is shown that under a challenged apportionment plan one party will consistently fail to gain control of the legislature even if it wins a majority of the votes, a court would be justified in finding the "threshold showing" met, at which point "the legislation would be examined for valid underpinnings." It may fairly be doubted that this last step is anything more than a formality, except perhaps in the case of bipartisan gerrymanders that have proved unexpectedly favorable to one party. Consequently, although the plurality criticizes Justice POWELL for effectively concluding that "disproportionate election results alone are a sufficient effect to support a finding of a constitutional violation," the plurality itself arrives at the conclusion that foreseeable, disproportionate *long-term* election results suffice to prove a constitutional violation.

Thus, the plurality opinion ultimately rests on a political preference for proportionality – not an outright claim that proportional results are required, but a conviction that the greater the departure from proportionality, the more suspect an apportionment plan becomes. This preference for proportionality is in serious tension with essential features of state legislative elections. Districting itself represents a middle ground between winner-take-all statewide elections and proportional representation for political parties. If there is a constitutional preference for proportionality, the legitimacy of districting itself is called into question: the voting strength of less evenly distributed groups will invariably be diminished by districting as compared to at-large proportional systems for electing representatives. Moreover, one implication of the districting system is that voters cast votes for candidates in their districts, not for a statewide slate of legislative candidates put forward by the parties. Consequently, efforts to determine party voting strength presuppose a norm that does not exist – statewide elections for representatives along party lines.

The plurality's theory is also internally inconsistent. The plurality recognizes that, given a normal dispersion of party strength and winner-take-all, district-based elections, it is likely that even a narrow statewide preference for one party will give that party a disproportionately large majority in the legislature. The plurality is prepared to tolerate this effect, because not to do so would spell the end of district-based elections, or require reverse gerrymandering to ensure greater proportionality for the minority party. But this means that the plurality would extend greater protection to a party that can command a majority of the statewide vote than to a party that cannot; the explanation, once again, is that the plurality has made a political judgment, in this instance, that district-based elections must be taken as a given.

Because a statewide majority for a party's candidates will frequently result only if the "winning" party attracts independent voters and voters from the other party, under the plurality's approach a great deal will turn on whether the support of these voters is included as part of the party's voting strength. The plurality would reserve this question, but, however it is ultimately answered, anomalies will result. To measure a party's voting strength by including voters who only occasionally vote for that party's candidates is arbitrary; to ignore the role these voters play will be to further discriminate against parties that do not command a permanent majority of the electorate in a given State.

I would avoid the difficulties generated by the plurality's efforts to confine the effects of a generalized group right to equal representation by not recognizing such a right in the first instance. To allow district courts to strike down apportionment plans on the basis of their prognostications as to the outcome of future elections or future apportionments invites "findings" on matters as to which neither judges nor anyone else can have any confidence. Once it is conceded that "a group's electoral power is not unconstitutionally diminished by the simple fact of an apportionment scheme that makes winning elections more difficult," the virtual impossibility of reliably predicting how difficult it will be to win an election in 2, or 4, or 10 years should, in my view, weigh in favor of holding such challenges nonjusticiable. Racial gerrymandering should remain justiciable, for the harms it engenders run counter to the central thrust of the Fourteenth Amendment. But no such justification can be given for judicial intervention on behalf of mainstream political parties, and the risks such intervention poses to our political institutions are unacceptable. "Political affiliation is the keystone of the political trade. Race, ideally, is not."

Justice POWELL, with whom Justice STEVENS joins, concurring in part and dissenting in part.

This case presents the question whether a state legislature violates the Equal Protection Clause by adopting a redistricting plan designed solely to preserve the power of the dominant political party, when the plan follows the doctrine of "one person, one vote" but ignores all other neutral factors relevant to the fairness of redistricting.

In answering this question, the plurality expresses the view, with which I agree, that a partisan political gerrymander violates the Equal Protection Clause only on proof of "both intentional discrimination against an identifiable political group and an actual discriminatory effect on that group…." The plurality argues, however, that appellees failed to establish that their voting strength was diluted statewide despite uncontradicted proof that certain key districts were grotesquely gerrymandered to enhance the election prospects of Republican candidates. This argument appears to rest solely on the ground that the legislature accomplished its gerrymander consistent with "one person, one vote," in the sense that the legislature designed voting districts of approximately equal population and erected no direct barriers to Democratic voters' exercise of the franchise. Since the essence of a gerrymandering claim is that the members of a political party as a group have been denied their right to "fair and effective representation," I believe that the claim cannot be tested solely by reference to "one person, one vote." Rather, a number of other relevant neutral factors must be considered. Because the plurality ignores such factors and fails to enunciate standards by which to determine whether a legislature has enacted an unconstitutional gerrymander, I dissent….

Gerrymandering is "the deliberate and arbitrary distortion of district boundaries and populations for partisan or personal political purposes." As Justice STEVENS correctly observed, gerrymandering violates the Equal Protection Clause only when the redistricting plan serves "no purpose other than to favor one segment, whether racial, ethnic, religious, economic, or political, that may occupy a position of strength at a particular time, or to disadvantage a politically weak segment of the community…."

Because it is difficult to develop and apply standards that will identify the unconstitutional gerrymander, courts may seek to avoid their responsibility to enforce the Equal Protection Clause by finding that a claim of gerrymandering is nonjusticiable. I agree with the Court that such a course is mistaken, and that the allegations in this case raise a justiciable issue.

Moreover, I am convinced that appropriate judicial standards can and should be developed…. Under this definition, the merits of a gerrymandering claim must be determined by reference to the configurations of the districts, the observance of political subdivision lines, and other criteria that have independent relevance to the fairness of redistricting…. In this case, the District Court examined the redistricting in light of such factors and found, among other facts, that the boundaries of a number of districts were deliberately distorted to deprive Democratic voters of an equal opportunity to participate in the State's legislative processes. The plurality makes no reference to any of these findings of fact. It rejects the District Court's ultimate conclusion with no explanation of the respects in which appellees' proof fell short of establishing discriminatory effect….

The first cases in which this Court entertained equal protection challenges to redistricting involved allegations that state legislatures had refused to redesign

States' voting districts to eliminate gross population disparities among those districts; e.g., *Baker v. Carr, Reynolds v. Sims.* The Court's decision in *Reynolds v. Sims* illustrates two concepts that are vitally important in evaluating an equal protection challenge to redistricting. First, the Court recognized that equal protection encompasses a guarantee of equal *representation,* requiring a State to seek to achieve through redistricting "fair and effective representation for all citizens...." The concept of "representation" necessarily applies to groups: groups of voters elect representatives, individual voters do not. Gross population disparities violate the mandate of equal representation by denying voters residing in heavily populated districts, *as a group,* the opportunity to elect the number of representatives to which their voting strength otherwise would entitle them. While population disparities do dilute the weight of individual votes, their discriminatory effect is felt only when those individual votes are combined. Thus, the fact that individual voters in heavily populated districts are free to cast their ballot has no bearing on a claim of malapportionment.

Second, at the same time that it announced the principle of "one person, one vote" to compel States to eliminate gross disparities among district populations, the Court plainly recognized that redistricting should be based on a number of neutral criteria, of which districts of equal population was only one. *Reynolds v. Sims* identified several of the factors that should guide a legislature engaged in redistricting. For example, the Court observed that districts should be compact and cover contiguous territory, precisely because the alternative, "[i]ndiscriminate districting," would be "an open invitation to partisan gerrymandering." Similarly, a State properly could choose to give "independent representation" to established political subdivisions. Adherence to community boundaries, the Court reasoned, would both "deter the possibilities of gerrymandering," and allow communities to have a voice in the legislature that directly controls their local interests. Thus, *Reynolds v. Sims* contemplated that "one person, one vote" would be only one among several neutral factors that serve the constitutional mandate of fair and effective representation.... It was not itself to be the only goal of redistricting.

A standard that judges the constitutionality of a districting plan solely by reference to the doctrine of "one person, one vote" may cause two detrimental results. First, as a perceived way to avoid litigation, legislative bodies may place undue emphasis on mathematical exactitude, subordinating or ignoring entirely other criteria that bear directly on the fairness of redistricting.... Second, as this case illustrates, and as *Reynolds v. Sims* anticipated, exclusive or primary reliance on "one person, one vote" can betray the constitutional promise of fair and effective representation by enabling a legislature to engage intentionally in clearly discriminatory gerrymandering....

In light of the foregoing principles, I believe that the plurality's opinion is seriously flawed in several respects. First, apparently to avoid the forceful evidence that some district lines indisputably were designed to and did discriminate against Democrats, the plurality describes appellees' claim as alleging that "Democratic voters over the State as a whole, not Democratic voters in particular districts, have been subjected to unconstitutional discrimination." This characterization is not inconsistent with appellees' proof, and the District Court's finding, of statewide discriminatory effect resulting from "individual districting" that "exemplif[ies] this discrimination." If Democratic voters in a number of critical districts are the focus of unconstitutional discrimination, as the District Court found, the *effect* of that discrimination will be felt over the State as a whole.

The plurality also erroneously characterizes the harm members of the losing party suffer as a group when they are deprived, through deliberate and arbitrary distortion of district boundaries, of the opportunity to elect representatives of their choosing. It may be, as the plurality suggests, that representatives will not "entirely ignore the interests" of opposition voters. But it defies political reality to suppose that members of a losing party have as much political influence over state government as do members of the victorious party. Even the most conscientious state legislators do not disregard opportunities to reward persons or groups who were active supporters in their election campaigns. Similarly, no one doubts that partisan considerations play a major role in the passage of legislation and the appointment of state officers. Not surprisingly, therefore, the District Court expressly found that "[c]ontrol of the General Assembly is crucial" to members of the major political parties in Indiana. In light of those findings, I cannot accept the plurality's apparent conclusion that loss of this "crucial" position is constitutionally insignificant as long as the losers are not "entirely ignored" by the winners.

The plurality relies almost exclusively on the "one person, one vote" standard to reject appellees' convincing proof that the redistricting plan had a seriously discriminatory effect on their voting strength in particular districts. The plurality properly describes the claim in this case as a denial of fair and effective "representation," but it does not provide any explanation of how complying with "one person, one vote" deters or identifies a gerrymander that unconstitutionally discriminates against a cognizable group of voters. While that standard affords some protection to the voting rights of individuals, "it protects groups only indirectly at best," even when the group's identity is determined solely by reference to the fact that its members reside in a particular voting district. "One person, one vote" alone does not protect the voting rights of a group made up of persons affiliated with a particular political party who seek to achieve representation through their combined voting strength. Thus, the facts that the legislature permitted each Democratic voter to cast his or her one vote, erected no direct barriers to Democratic voters' exercise of the franchise, and drew districts of equal population, are irrelevant to a claim that district lines were drawn for the purpose and with the effect of substantially debasing the strength of votes cast by Democrats as a group.

The final and most basic flaw in the plurality's opinion is its failure to enunciate any standard that affords guidance to legislatures and courts. Legislators and judges are left to wonder whether compliance with "one person, one vote" completely insulates a partisan gerrymander from constitutional scrutiny, or whether a fairer but as yet undefined standard applies. The failure to articulate clear doctrine in this area places the plurality in the curious position of inviting further litigation even as it appears to signal the "constitutional green light" to would-be gerrymanderers.

In *Karcher v. Daggett,* Justice STEVENS, echoing the decision in *Reynolds v. Sims,* described factors that I believe properly should guide both legislators who redistrict and judges who test redistricting plans against constitutional challenges. The most important of these factors are the shapes of voting districts and adherence to established political subdivision boundaries. Other relevant considerations include the nature of the legislative procedures by which the apportionment law was adopted and legislative history reflecting contemporaneous legislative goals. To make out a case of unconstitutional partisan gerrymandering, the plaintiff should be required to offer proof concerning these factors, which bear directly on the fairness of a redistricting plan, as well as evidence concerning population disparities and statistics tending to show vote dilution. No one factor should be dispositive....

In conclusion, I want to make clear the limits of the standard that I believe the Equal Protection Clause imposes on legislators engaged in redistricting. Traditionally, the determination of electoral districts within a State has been a matter left to the legislative branch of the state government. Apart from the doctrine of separation of powers and the federal system prescribed by the Constitution, federal judges are ill equipped generally to review legislative decisions respecting redistricting. As the Court's opinion makes clear, however, our precedents hold that a colorable claim of discriminatory gerrymandering presents a justiciable controversy under the Equal Protection Clause. Federal courts in exercising their duty to adjudicate such claims should impose a heavy burden of proof on those who allege that a redistricting plan violates the Constitution. In light of *Baker v. Carr, Reynolds v. Sims,* and their progeny, including such comparatively recent decisions as *Gaffney v. Cummings,* this case presents a paradigm example of unconstitutional discrimination against the members of a political party that happened to be out of power. The well-grounded findings of the District Court to this effect have not been, and I believe cannot be, held clearly erroneous.

Accordingly, I would affirm the judgment of the District Court.

SHAW v. RENO
509 U.S. 630; 113 S.Ct. 2816; 125 L.Ed. 2d 511 (1993)

Gerrymandering does not always have to be in the service of favoring one party over another. The techniques can be used to favor any group over another. Here the implementation of the Voting Rights Act is challenged as creating an unconstitutional racial gerrymander.

Justice O'CONNOR delivered the opinion of the Court.

This case involves two of the most complex and sensitive issues this Court has faced in recent years: the meaning of the constitutional "right" to vote, and the propriety of race-based state legislation designed to benefit members of historically disadvantaged racial minority groups....

The voting age population of North Carolina is approximately 78% white, 20% black, and 1% Native American; the remaining 1% is predominantly Asian.... The black population is relatively dispersed; blacks constitute a majority of the general population in only 5 of the State's 100 counties.... The largest concentrations of black citizens live in the Coastal Plain, primarily in the northern part.... The General Assembly's first redistricting plan contained one majority-black district centered in that area of the State....

The Attorney General, acting through the Assistant Attorney General for the Civil Rights Division, interposed a formal objection to the General Assembly's plan. The Attorney General specifically objected to the configuration of boundary lines drawn in the south-central to southeastern region of the State. In the Attorney General's view, the General Assembly could have created a second majority-minority district "to give effect to black and Native American voting strength in this area" by using boundary lines "no more irregular than [those] found elsewhere in the proposed plan," but failed to do so for "pretextual reasons...."

[T]he General Assembly enacted a revised redistricting plan... that included a second majority-black district. The General Assembly located the second district not in the south-central to southeastern part of the State, but in the north-central region along Interstate 85....

The first of the two majority-black districts contained in the revised plan, District 1, is somewhat hook shaped. Centered in the northeast portion of the State, it moves southward until it tapers to a narrow band; then, with finger-like extensions, it reaches far into the southern-most part of the State near the South Carolina border. District 1 has been compared to a "Rorschach ink-blot test," ...

The second majority-black district, District 12, is even more unusually shaped. It is approximately 160 miles long and, for much of its length, no wider than the I-85 corridor. It winds in snake-like fashion through tobacco country, financial centers, and manufacturing areas "until it gobbles in enough enclaves of black neighborhoods...." Northbound and southbound drivers on I-85 sometimes find themselves in separate districts in one county, only to "trade" districts when they enter the next county. Of the 10 counties through which District 12 passes, five are cut into three different districts; even towns are divided. At one point the district remains contiguous only because it intersects at a single point with two other districts before crossing over them....

Appellants alleged not that the revised plan constituted a political gerrymander, nor that it violated the "one person, one vote" principle, but that the State had created an unconstitutional *racial* gerrymander. ...

Appellants contended that the General Assembly's revised reapportionment plan violated several provisions of the United States Constitution, including the Fourteenth Amendment. They alleged that the

General Assembly deliberately "create[d] two Congressional Districts in which a majority of black voters was concentrated arbitrarily, without regard to any other considerations, such as compactness, contiguousness, geographical boundaries, or political subdivisions" with the purpose "to create Congressional Districts along racial lines" and to assure the election of two black representatives to Congress.... Appellants sought declaratory and injunctive relief against the state appellees. They sought similar relief against the federal appellees, arguing, alternatively, that the federal appellees had misconstrued the Voting Rights Act or that the Act itself was unconstitutional.

The three-judge District Court granted the federal appellees' motion to dismiss....

By a 2-to-1 vote, the District Court also dismissed the complaint against the state appellees. ...

We noted probable jurisdiction....

"The right to vote freely for the candidate of one's choice is of the essence of a democratic society...." For much of our Nation's history, that right sadly has been denied to many because of race....

Ostensibly race-neutral devices such as literacy tests with "grandfather" clauses and "good character" provisos were devised to deprive black voters of the franchise. Another of the weapons in the States' arsenal was the racial gerrymander, "the deliberate and arbitrary distortion of district boundaries ... for [racial] purposes...." In the 1870's, for example, opponents of Reconstruction in Mississippi "concentrated the bulk of the black population in a 'shoestring' Congressional district running the length of the Mississippi River, leaving five others with white majorities...." Some 90 years later, Alabama redefined the boundaries of the city of Tuskegee "from a square to an uncouth twenty-eight-sided figure" in a manner that was alleged to exclude black voters, and only black voters, from the city limits....

Congress enacted the Voting Rights Act of 1965 as a dramatic and severe response to the situation. The Act proved immediately successful in ensuring racial minorities access to the voting booth; by the early 1970's, the spread between black and white registration in several of the targeted Southern States had fallen to well below 10%....

But it soon became apparent that guaranteeing equal access to the polls would not suffice to root out other racially discriminatory voting practices. Drawing on the "one person, one vote" principle, this Court recognized that "[t]he right to vote can be affected by a *dilution* of voting power as well as by an absolute prohibition on casting a ballot...." Where members of a racial minority group vote as a cohesive unit, practices such as multimember or at-large electoral systems can reduce or nullify minority voters' ability, as a group, "to elect the candidate of their choice." Accordingly, the Court held that such schemes violate the Fourteenth Amendment when they are adopted with a discriminatory purpose and have the effect of diluting minority voting strength.... Congress, too, responded to the problem of vote dilution. In 1982, it amended § 2 of the Voting

Rights Act to prohibit legislation that *results* in the dilution of a minority group's voting strength, regardless of the legislature's intent....

It is against this background that we confront the questions presented here. In our view, the District Court properly dismissed appellants' claims against the federal appellees. Our focus is on appellants' claim that the State engaged in unconstitutional racial gerrymandering. That argument strikes a powerful historical chord: It is unsettling how closely the North Carolina plan resembles the most egregious racial gerrymanders of the past.

An understanding of the nature of appellants' claim is critical to our resolution of the case. In their complaint, appellants did not claim that the General Assembly's reapportionment plan unconstitutionally "diluted" white voting strength. They did not even claim to be white. Rather, appellants' complaint alleged that the deliberate segregation of voters into separate districts on the basis of race violated their constitutional right to participate in a "color-blind" electoral process...

Despite their invocation of the ideal of a "color-blind" Constitution,... appellants appear to concede that race-conscious redistricting is not always unconstitutional.... That concession is wise: This Court never has held that race-conscious state decisionmaking is impermissible in *all* circumstances. What appellants object to is redistricting legislation that is so extremely irregular on its face that it rationally can be viewed only as an effort to segregate the races for purposes of voting, without regard for traditional districting principles and without sufficiently compelling justification. For the reasons that follow, we conclude that appellants have stated a claim upon which relief can be granted under the Equal Protection Clause....

The Equal Protection Clause provides that "[n]o State shall ... deny to any person within its jurisdiction the equal protection of the laws...." Its central purpose is to prevent the States from purposefully discriminating between individuals on the basis of race.... Laws that explicitly distinguish between individuals on racial grounds fall within the core of that prohibition.

No inquiry into legislative purpose is necessary when the racial classification appears on the face of the statute.... Express racial classifications are immediately suspect because, "[a]bsent searching judicial inquiry ..., there is simply no way of determining what classifications are 'benign' or 'remedial' and what classifications are in fact motivated by illegitimate notions of racial inferiority or simple racial politics...."

Classifications of citizens solely on the basis of race "are by their very nature odious to a free people whose institutions are founded upon the doctrine of equality...." They threaten to stigmatize individuals by reason of their membership in a racial group and to incite racial hostility.... Accordingly, we have held that the Fourteenth Amendment requires state legislation that expressly distinguishes among citizens because of their race to be narrowly tailored to further a compelling governmental interest....

These principles apply not only to legislation that contains explicit racial distinctions, but also to those "rare" statutes that, although race-neutral, are, on their face, "unexplainable on grounds other than race...."

Appellants contend that redistricting legislation that is so bizarre on its face that it is "unexplainable on grounds other than race,..." demands the same close scrutiny that we give other state laws that classify citizens by race. Our voting rights precedents support that conclusion.

In *Guinn v. United States,* the Court invalidated under the Fifteenth Amendment a statute that imposed a literacy requirement on voters but contained a "grandfather clause...." The determinative consideration for the Court was that the law, though ostensibly race-neutral, on its face "embod[ied] no exercise of judgment and rest[ed] upon no discernible reason" other than to circumvent the prohibitions of the Fifteenth Amendment. In other words, the statute was invalid because, on its face, it could not be explained on grounds other than race.

The Court applied the same reasoning to the "uncouth twenty-eight-sided" municipal boundary line at issue in *Gomillion.* Although the statute that redrew the city limits of Tuskegee was race-neutral on its face, plaintiffs alleged that its effect was impermissibly to remove from the city virtually all black voters and no white voters....

The Court extended the reasoning of *Gomillion* to congressional districting in *Wright v. Rockefeller....* At issue in *Wright* were four districts contained in a New York apportionment statute. The plaintiffs alleged that the statute excluded nonwhites from one district and concentrated them in the other three.... Every member of the Court assumed that the plaintiffs' allegation that the statute "segregate[d] eligible voters by race and place of origin" stated a constitutional claim.... The Justices disagreed only as to whether the plaintiffs had carried their burden of proof at trial....

Wright illustrates the difficulty of determining from the face of a single-member districting plan that it purposefully distinguishes between voters on the basis of race. A reapportionment statute typically does not classify persons at all; it classifies tracts of land, or addresses. Moreover, redistricting differs from other kinds of state decision making in that the legislature always is *aware* of race when it draws district lines, just as it is aware of age, economic status, religious and political persuasion, and a variety of other demographic factors. That sort of race consciousness does not lead inevitably to impermissible race discrimination. As *Wright* demonstrates, when members of a racial group live together in one community, a reapportionment plan that concentrates members of the group in one district and excludes them from others may reflect wholly legitimate purposes. The district lines may be drawn, for example, to provide for compact districts of contiguous territory, or to maintain the integrity of political subdivisions.

The difficulty of proof, of course, does not mean that a racial gerrymander, once established, should receive less scrutiny under the Equal Protection Clause than other state legislation classifying citizens by race. Moreover, it seems clear to us that proof sometimes will not be difficult at all. In some exceptional cases, a reapportionment plan may be so highly irregular that, on its face, it rationally cannot be understood as anything other than an effort to "segregat[e] ... voters" on the basis of race.... *Gomillion,* in which a tortured municipal boundary line was drawn to exclude black voters, was such a case. So, too, would be a case in which a State concentrated a dispersed minority population in a single district by disregarding traditional districting principles such as compactness, contiguity, and respect for political subdivisions. We emphasize that these criteria are important not because they are constitutionally required, they are not,... but because they are objective factors that may serve to defeat a claim that a district has been gerrymandered on racial lines....

Put differently, we believe that reapportionment is one area in which appearances do matter. A reapportionment plan that includes in one district individuals who belong to the same race, but who are otherwise widely separated by geographical and political boundaries, and who may have little in common with one another but the color of their skin, bears an uncomfortable resemblance to political apartheid. It reinforces the perception that members of the same racial group, regardless of their age, education, economic status, or the community in which the live, think alike, share the same political interests, and will prefer the same candidates at the polls. We have rejected such perceptions elsewhere as impermissible racial stereotypes.... By perpetuating such notions, a racial gerrymander may exacerbate the very patterns of racial bloc voting that majority-minority districting is sometimes said to counteract.

The message that such districting sends to elected representatives is equally pernicious. When a district obviously is created solely to effectuate the perceived common interests of one racial group, elected officials are more likely to believe that their primary obligation is to represent only the members of that group, rather than their constituency as a whole. This is altogether antithetical to our system of representative democracy. As Justice Douglas explained in his dissent in *Wright v. Rockefeller* nearly 30 years ago:

> Here the individual is important, not his race, his creed, or his color. The principle of equality is at war with the notion that District A must be represented by a Negro, as it is with the notion that District B must be represented by a Caucasian, District C by a Jew, District D by a Catholic, and so on.... That system, by whatever name it is called, is a divisive force in a community, emphasizing differences between candidates and voters that are irrelevant in the constitutional sense....

... For these reasons, we conclude that a plaintiff challenging a reapportionment statute under the Equal Protection Clause may state a claim by alleging that the legislation, though race-neutral on its face, rationally cannot be understood as anything other than an effort to separate voters into different districts on the basis of race, and that the separation lacks sufficient justification. It is unnecessary for us to decide whether or how a reapportionment plan that, on its face, can be explained in nonracial terms successfully could be challenged. Thus, we express no view as to whether "the intentional creation of majority-minority districts, without more" always gives rise to an equal protection claim....

Racial classifications of any sort pose the risk of lasting harm to our society. They reinforce the belief, held by too many for too much of our history, that individuals should be judged by the color of their skin. Racial classifications with respect to voting carry particular dangers. Racial gerrymandering, even for remedial purposes, may balkanize us into competing racial factions; it threatens to carry us further from the goal of a political system in which race no longer matters, a goal that the Fourteenth and Fifteenth Amendments embody, and to which the Nation continues to aspire. It is for these reasons that race-based districting by our state legislatures demands close judicial scrutiny.

In this case, the Attorney General suggested that North Carolina could have created a reasonably compact second majority-minority district in the south-central to southeastern part of the State. We express no view as to whether appellants successfully could have challenged such a district under the Fourteenth Amendment. We also do not decide whether appellants' complaint stated a claim under constitutional provisions other than the Fourteenth Amendment. Today we hold only that appellants have stated a claim under the Equal Protection Clause by alleging that the North Carolina General Assembly adopted a reapportionment scheme so irrational on its face that it can be understood only as an effort to segregate voters into separate voting districts because of their race, and that the separation lacks sufficient justification. If the allegation of racial gerrymandering remains uncontradicted, the District Court further must determine whether the North Carolina plan is narrowly tailored to further a compelling governmental interest. Accordingly, we reverse the judgment of the District Court and remand the case for further proceedings consistent with this opinion.

It is so ordered.

Justice WHITE, with whom Justice BLACKMUN and Justice STEVENS join, dissenting.

The facts of this case mirror those presented in *United Jewish Organizations of Williamsburgh, Inc. v. Carey, (UJO),* where the Court rejected a claim that creation of a majority-minority district violated the Constitution, either as a *per se* matter or in light of the circumstances leading to the creation of such a district. Of particular relevance, five of the Justices reasoned that members of the white majority could not plausibly argue that their influence over the political process had been unfairly cancelled. Accordingly, they held that plaintiffs were not entitled to relief under the Constitution's Equal Protection Clause. On the same reasoning, I would affirm the district court's dismissal of appellants' claim in this instance.

The Court today chooses not to overrule, but rather to sidestep, *UJO.* It does so by glossing over the striking similarities, focusing on surface differences, most notably the (admittedly unusual) shape of the newly created district, and imagining an entirely new cause of action. Because the holding is limited to such anomalous circumstances, it perhaps will not substantially hamper a State's legitimate efforts to redistrict in favor of racial minorities. Nonetheless, the notion that North Carolina's plan, under which whites remain a voting majority in a disproportionate number of congressional districts, and pursuant to which the State has sent its *first* black representatives since Reconstruction to the United States Congress, might have violated appellants' constitutional rights is both a fiction and a departure from settled equal protection principles. Seeing no good reason to engage in either, I dissent.

The grounds for my disagreement with the majority are simply stated: Appellants have not presented a cognizable claim, because they have not alleged a cognizable injury. To date, we have held that only two types of state voting practices could give rise to a constitutional claim. The first involves direct and outright deprivation of the right to vote, for example by means of a poll tax or literacy test.... Plainly, this variety is not implicated by appellants' allegations and need not detain us further. The second type of unconstitutional practice is that which "affects the political strength of various groups," ... As for this latter category, we have insisted that members of the political or racial group demonstrate that the challenged action have the intent and effect of unduly diminishing their influence on the political process. Although this severe burden has limited the number of successful suits, it was adopted for sound reasons.

Justice BLACKMUN, dissenting.

I join Justice WHITE's dissenting opinion.... I ... agree that the conscious use of race in redistricting does not violate the Equal Protection Clause unless the effect of the redistricting plan is to deny a particular group equal access to the political process or to minimize its voting strength unduly.... It is particularly ironic that the case in which today's majority chooses to abandon settled law and to recognize for the first time this "analytically distinct" constitutional claim ... is a challenge by white voters to the plan under which North Carolina has sent black representatives to Congress for the first time since Reconstruction. I dissent.

Justice STEVENS, dissenting.

For the reasons stated by Justice WHITE, the decision of the District Court should be affirmed. I add these comments to emphasize that the two critical facts in this case are undisputed: first, the shape of District 12 is so bizarre that it must have been drawn for the purpose of either advantaging or disadvantaging a cognizable group of voters; and, second, regardless of that shape, it *was* drawn for the purpose of facilitating the election of a second black representative from North Carolina.

These unarguable facts, which the Court devotes most of its opinion to proving, give rise to three constitutional questions: Does the Constitution impose a requirement of contiguity or compactness on how the States may draw their electoral districts? Does the Equal Protection Clause prevent a State from drawing district boundaries for the purpose of facilitating the election of a member of an identifiable group of voters? And, finally, if the answer to the second question is generally "No," should it be different when the favored group is defined by race? Since I have already written at length about these questions, my negative answer to each can be briefly explained.

The first question is easy. There is no independent constitutional requirement of compactness or contiguity.... In this case, however, we know what the legislators' purpose was: The North Carolina Legislature drew District 12 to include a majority of African-American voters....

As for the second question, I believe that the Equal Protection Clause is violated when the State creates the kind of uncouth district boundaries seen in ... this case, for the sole purpose of making it more difficult for members of a minority group to win an election. The duty to govern impartially is abused when a group with power over the electoral process defines electoral boundaries solely to enhance its own political strength at the expense of any weaker group. That duty, however, is not violated when the majority acts to facilitate the election of a member of a group that lacks such power because it remains underrepresented in the state legislature – whether that group is defined by political affiliation, by common economic interests, or by religious, ethnic, or racial characteristics. The difference between constitutional and unconstitutional gerrymanders has nothing to do with whether they are based on assumptions about the groups they affect, but whether their purpose is to enhance the power of the group in control of the districting process at the expense of any minority group, and thereby to strengthen the unequal distribution of electoral power. When an assumption that people in a particular minority group (whether they are defined by the political party, religion, ethnic group, or race to which they belong) will vote in a particular way is used to *benefit* that group, no constitutional violation occurs. Politicians have always relied on assumptions that people in particular groups are likely to vote in a particular way when they draw new district lines, and I cannot believe that anything in today's opinion will stop them from doing so in the future.

Finally, we must ask whether otherwise permissible redistricting to benefit an underrepresented minority group becomes impermissible when the minority group is defined by its race. The Court today answers this question in the affirmative, and its answer is wrong. If it is permissible to draw boundaries to provide adequate representation for rural voters, for union members, for Hasidic Jews, for Polish Americans, or for Republicans, it necessarily follows that it is permissible to do the same thing for members of the very minority group whose history in the United States gave birth to the Equal Protection Clause. A contrary conclusion could only be described as perverse.

Accordingly, I respectfully dissent.

Justice SOUTER, dissenting.

...Until today, the Court has analyzed equal protection claims involving race in electoral districting differently from equal protection claims involving other forms of governmental conduct, and before turning to the different regimes of analysis it will be useful to set out the relevant respects in which such districting differs from the characteristic circumstances in which a State might otherwise consciously consider race. Unlike other contexts in which we have addressed the State's conscious use of race,... electoral districting calls for decisions that nearly always require some consideration of race for legitimate reasons where there is a racially mixed population. As long as members of racial groups have the commonality of interest implicit in our ability to talk about concepts like "minority voting strength," and "dilution of minority votes,..." and as long as racial bloc voting takes place, legislators will have to take race into account in order to avoid dilution of minority voting strength in the districting plans they adopt. One need look no further than the Voting Rights Act to understand that this may be required, and we have held that race may constitutionally be taken into account in order to comply with that Act....

A second distinction between districting and most other governmental decisions in which race has figured is that those other decisions using racial criteria characteristically occur in circumstances in which the use of race to the advantage of one person is necessarily at the obvious expense of a member of a different race. Thus, for example, awarding government contracts on a racial basis excludes certain firms from competition on racial grounds....

In districting, by contrast, the mere placement of an individual in one district instead of another denies no one a right or benefit provided to others. All citizens may register, vote, and be represented. In whatever district, the individual voter has a right to vote in each election, and the election will result in the voter's representation. As we have held, one's constitutional rights are not violated merely because the candidate one supports loses the election or because a group (including a racial group) to which one belongs winds up with a representative from outside that group....

Our different approaches to equal protection in electoral districting and nondistricting cases reflect these differences. There is a characteristic coincidence of disadvantageous effect and illegitimate purpose associated with the State's use of race in those situations in which it has immediately triggered at-least heightened scrutiny (which every Member of the Court to address the issue has agreed must be applied even to race-based classifications designed to serve some permissible state interest). Presumably because the legitimate consideration of race in a districting decision is usually inevitable under the Voting Rights Act when communities are racially mixed, however, and because, without more, it does not result in diminished political effectiveness for anyone, we have not taken the approach of applying the usual standard of such heightened "scrutiny" to race-based districting decisions....

A consequence of this categorical approach is the absence of any need for further searching "scrutiny" once it has been shown that a given districting decision has a purpose and effect falling within one of those categories. If a cognizable harm like dilution or the abridgment of the right to participate in the electoral process is shown, the districting plan violates the Fourteenth Amendment. If not, it does not. Under this approach, in the absence of an allegation of such cognizable harm, there is no need for further scrutiny because a gerrymandering claim cannot be proven without the element of harm. Nor if dilution is proven is there any need for further constitutional scrutiny; there has never been a suggestion that such use of race could be justified under any type of scrutiny, since the dilution of the right to vote can not be said to serve any legitimate governmental purpose....

The Court offers no adequate justification for treating the narrow category of bizarrely shaped district claims differently from other districting claims. The only justification I can imagine would be the preservation of "sound districting principles," *UJO,* such as compactness and contiguity. But as Justice WHITE points out, and as the Court acknowledges, we have held that such principles are not constitutionally required, with the consequence that their absence cannot justify the distinct constitutional regime put in place by the Court today. Since there is no justification for the departure here from the principles that continue to govern electoral districting cases generally in accordance with our prior decisions, I would not respond to the seeming egregiousness of the redistricting now before us by untethering the concept of racial gerrymander in such a case from the concept of harm exemplified by dilution. In the absence of an allegation of such harm, I would affirm the judgment of the District Court. I respectfully dissent.

FLAST v. COHEN
392 U.S. 83; 88 S.Ct. 1942; 20 L.Ed. 2d 947 (1968)

Flast and other taxpayers of New York argued that federal funds had been disbursed by federal officials under the Elementary and Secondary Education Act of 1965 to finance instruction and the purchase of educational materials for use in religious and sectarian schools, in violation of the Establishment and Free Exercise Clauses of the First Amendment. Accordingly, they sought a declaration that the expenditures were not authorized by the Act or, in the alternative, that the Act was to that extent unconstitutional. An en banc federal district court ruled, on the authority of Frothingham v. Mellon, *262 U.S. 447 (1923), that appellants lacked standing to maintain the action. The case was then appealed to the Supreme Court.*

MR. CHIEF JUSTICE WARREN delivered the opinion of the Court:

In *Frothingham v. Mellon*, 262 U.S. 447 (1923), this Court ruled that a federal taxpayer is without standing to challenge the constitutionality of a federal statute. That ruling has stood for 45 years as an impenetrable barrier to suits against Acts of Congress brought by individuals who can assert only the interest of federal taxpayers. In this case, we must decide whether the *Frothingham* barrier should be lowered when a taxpayer attacks a federal statute on the ground that it violates the Establishment and Free Exercise Clauses of the First Amendment.

The gravamen of the appellants' complaint was that federal funds appropriated under the Act were being used to finance instruction in reading, arithmetic, and other subjects in religious schools, and to purchase textbooks and other instructional materials for use in such schools. Such expenditures were alleged to be in contravention of the Establishment and Free Exercise Clauses of the First Amendment. Appellants' constitutional attack focused on the statutory criteria which state and local authorities must meet to be eligible for federal grants under the Act. Title I of the Act establishes a program for financial assistance to local educational agencies for the education of low-income families. Federal payments are made to state educational agencies, which pass the payments on in the form of grants to local educational agencies.... While disclaiming any intent to challenge as unconstitutional all programs under Title I of the Act, the complaint alleges that federal funds have been disbursed under the Act, "with the consent and approval of the (appellees)," and that such funds have been used and will continue to be used to finance "instruction in reading, arithmetic and other subjects and for guidance in religious and sectarian schools" and "the purchase of textbooks and instructional and library materials for use in religions and sectarian schools." Such expenditures of federal tax funds, appellants alleged, violate the First Amendment because "they constitute a law respecting an establishment of religion" and because "they prohibit the free exercise of religion on the part of the (appellants) ... by reason of the fact that they constitute compulsory taxation for religious purposes." The complaint asked for a declaration that appellees' actions in approving the expenditure of federal funds for the alleged purposes were not authorized by the Act or, in the alternative, that if appellees' actions are deemed within the authority and intent of the Act, "the Act is to that extent unconstitutional and void." The complaint also prayed for an injunction to enjoin appellees from approving any expenditure of federal funds for the allegedly unconstitutional purposes. The complaint further requested that a three-judge court be convened....

I

We must deal first with the Government's contention that this Court lacks jurisdiction on direct appeal because a three-judge court was improperly convened below. Under 28 U.S.C. §1253, direct appeal to this Court from a district court lies only "from an order granting or denying ... an interlocutory or permanent injunction in any civil action, suit or proceeding required by an Act of Congress to be heard and determined by a district court of three judges." Thus, if the Government is correct, we lack jurisdiction over this direct appeal.

The Government's argument on this question is two-pronged. First, noting that appellants have conceded that the case should be deemed as one limited to the practices of the New York City Board of Education, the Government contends that appellants wish only to forbid specific local programs which they find objectionable and not to enjoin the operation of the broad range of programs under the statutory scheme. Only if the latter relief is sought, the Government argues, can a three-judge court properly be convened under 28 U.S.C. §2282. We cannot accept the Government's argument in the context of this case. It is true that the appellants' complaint makes specific reference to the

New York City Board of Education's programs which were funded under the challenged statute, and we can assume that appellants' proof at trial would focus on those New York City programs. However, we view these allegations of the complaint as imparting specificity and focus to the issues in the lawsuit and not as limiting the impact of the constitutional challenge made in this case.

Secondly, the Government argues that a three-judge court should not have been convened because appellants question not the constitutionality of the Elementary and Secondary Education Act of 1965 but its administration. The decision in *Zemel v. Rusk*, 381 U.S. 1 (1965), is dispositive on this issue. It is true that appellants' complaint states a nonconstitutional ground for relief, namely, that appellees' actions in approving the expenditure of federal funds for allegedly unconstitutional programs are in excess of their authority under the Act. However, the complaint also requests an alternative and constitutional ground for relief, namely, a declaration that, if appellees' actions "are within the authority and intent of the Act, the Act is to that extent unconstitutional and void." The Court noted in *Zemel v. Rusk*, supra "[W]e have often held that a litigant need not abandon his nonconstitutional arguments in order to obtain a three-judge court...." The complaint in this case falls within that rule.

Thus, since the three-judge court was properly convened below, direct appeal to this Court is proper. We turn now to the standing question presented by this case.

II

This Court first faced squarely the question whether a litigant asserting only his status as a taxpayer has standing to maintain a suit in a federal court in *Frothingham v. Mellon*, supra, and that decision must be the starting point for analysis in this case. The taxpayer in *Frothingham* attacked as unconstitutional the Maternity Act of 1921 ... which established a federal program of grants to those States which would undertake programs to reduce maternal and infant mortality. The taxpayer alleged that Congress, in enacting the challenged statute, had exceeded the powers delegated to it under Article I of the Constitution and had invaded the legislative province reserved to the several States by the Tenth Amendment. The taxpayer complained that the result of the allegedly unconstitutional enactment would be to increase her future federal tax liability and "thereby take her property without due process of law...." The Court noted that a federal taxpayer's "interest in the moneys of Treasury ... is comparatively minute and indeterminable" and that "the effect upon future taxation, of any payment out of the (Treasury's) funds,... (is) remote, fluctuating and uncertain...." As a result, the Court ruled that the taxpayer had failed to allege the type of "direct injury" necessary to confer standing....

Although the barrier *Frothingham* erected against federal taxpayer suits has never been breached, the decision has been the source of some confusion and the object of considerable criticism. The confusion has developed as commentators have tried to determine whether *Frothingham* establishes a constitutional bar to taxpayer suits or whether the Court was simply imposing a rule of self-restraint which was not constitutionally compelled. The conflicting viewpoints are reflected in the arguments made to this Court by the parties in this case. The Government has pressed upon us the view that *Frothingham* announced a constitutional rule, compelled by the Article III limitations on federal court jurisdiction and grounded in considerations of the doctrine of separation of powers. Appellants, however, insist that *Frothingham* expressed no more than a policy of judicial self-restraint which can be disregarded when compelling reasons for assuming jurisdiction over a taxpayer's suit exist. The opinion delivered in *Frothingham* can be read to support either position. The concluding sentence of the opinion states that, to take jurisdiction of the taxpayer's suit, "would be not to decide a judicial controversy, but to assume a position of authority over the governmental acts of another and co-equal department, an authority which plainly we do not possess." 262 U.S., at 489. Yet the concrete reasons given for denying standing to a federal taxpayer suggest that the Court's holding rests on something less than a constitutional foundation.

III

The jurisdiction of federal courts is defined and limited by Article III of the Constitution. In terms relevant to the question for decision in this case, the judicial power of federal courts is constitutionally restricted to "cases" and "controversies." As is so often the situation in constitutional adjudication, those two words have an iceberg quality, containing beneath their surface simplicity submerged complexities which go to the very heart of our constitutional form of government. Embodied in the words "cases" and "controversies" are two complementary but somewhat different limitations. In part those words limit the business of federal courts to questions presented in an adversary context and in a form historically viewed as capable of resolution through the judicial process. And in part those words define the role assigned to the judiciary in a tripartite allocation of power to assure that the federal courts will not intrude into areas committed to the other branches of government. Justiciability is the term of art employed to give expression to this dual limitation placed upon federal courts by the case-and-controversy doctrine. Justiciability is itself a concept of uncertain meaning and scope. Its reach is illustrated by the various grounds upon which questions sought to be adjudicated in federal courts have been held not to be justiciable. Thus, no justiciable controversy is presented when the parties seek adjudication of only a political question, when the parties are asking for an advisory opinion, when the question sought to be adjudicated has been mooted by subsequent developments, and when there is no standing to maintain the action. Yet it remains true that "[j]usticiability is ... not a legal concept with a fixed content or susceptible of scientific verification. Its utilization is the resultant of many subtle pressures...." *Poe v. Ullman*, 367 U.S. 49-i, 508 (1961).

Part of the difficulty in giving precise meaning and form to the concept of justiciability stems from the uncertain historical antecedents of the case-and-controversy doctrine.

It is in this context that the standing question presented by this case must be viewed and that the Government's argument on that question must be evaluated. As we understand it, the Government's position is that the constitutional scheme of separation of powers, and the deference owed by the federal judiciary to the other two branches of government within that scheme, presents an absolute bar to taxpayer suits challenging the validity of federal spending programs. The Government views such suits as involving no more than the mere disagreement by the taxpayer "with the uses to which tax money is put." According to the Government, the resolution of such disagreements is committed to other branches of the Federal Government and not to the judiciary. Consequently, the Government contends that, under no circumstances, should standing be conferred on federal taxpayers to challenge a federal taxing or spending program. An analysis of the function served by standing limitations compels a rejection of the Government's position.

Standing is an aspect of justiciability and, as such, the problem of standing is surrounded by the same complexities and vagaries that inhere in justiciability. Standing has been called one of "the most amorphous (concepts) in the entire domain of public law." Some of the complexities peculiar to standing problems result because standing "serves, on occasion, as a shorthand expression for all the various elements of justiciability." In addition, there are at work in the standing doctrine the many subtle pressures which tend to cause policy considerations to blend into constitutional limitations.

Despite the complexities and uncertainties, some meaningful form can be given to the jurisdictional limitations placed on federal court power by the concept of standing. The fundamental aspect of standing is that it focuses on the party seeking to get his complaint before a federal court and not on the issues he wishes to have adjudicated. The "gist of the question of standing" is whether the party seeking relief has "alleged such a personal stake in the outcome of the controversy as to assure that concrete adverseness which sharpens the presentation of issues upon which the court so largely depends for illumination of difficult constitutional questions." *Baker v. Carr*, 369 U.S. 186, 204 (1962). In other words, when standing is placed in issue in a case, the question is whether the person whose standing is challenged is a proper party to request and adjudication of a particular issue and not whether the issue itself is justiciable. Thus, a party may have standing in a particular case, but the federal court may nevertheless decline to pass on the merits of the case because, for example, it presents a political question.

When the emphasis in the standing problem is placed on whether the person invoking a federal court's jurisdiction is a proper party to maintain the action, the weakness of the Government's argument in this case becomes apparent. The question whether a particular person is a proper party to maintain the action does not, by its own force, raise separation of powers problems related to improper judicial interference in areas committed to other branches of the Federal Government. Such problems arise, if at all, only from the substantive issues the individual seeks to have adjudicated. Thus, in terms of Article III limitations on federal court jurisdiction, the question of standing is related only to whether the dispute sought to be adjudicated will be presented in an adversary context and in a form historically viewed as capable of judicial resolution. It is for that reason that the emphasis in standing problems is on whether the party invoking federal court jurisdiction has "a personal stake in the outcome of the controversy,"... and whether the dispute touches upon "the legal relations of parties having adverse legal interests...." A taxpayer may or may not have the requisite personal stake in the outcome, depending upon the circumstances of the particular case. Therefore, we find no absolute bar in Article III to suits by federal taxpayers challenging allegedly unconstitutional federal taxing and spending programs. There remains, however, the problem of determining the circumstances under which a federal taxpayer will be deemed to have the personal stake and interest that imparts the necessary concrete adverseness to such litigation so that standing can be conferred on the taxpayer qua taxpayer consistent with the constitutional limitations of Article III.

IV

The various rules of standing applied by federal courts have not been developed in the abstract. Rather, they have been fashioned with specific reference to the status asserted by the party whose standing is challenged and to the type of question he wishes to have adjudicated. We have noted that, in deciding the question of standing, it is not relevant that the substantive issues in the litigation might be nonjusticiable. However, our decisions establish that, in ruling on standing, it is both appropriate and necessary to look to the substantive issues for another purpose, namely, to determine whether there is a logical nexus between the status asserted and the claim sought to be adjudicated.... Such inquiries into the nexus between the status asserted by the litigant and the claim he presents are essential to assure that he is a proper and appropriate party to invoke federal judicial power. Thus, our point of reference in this case is the standing of individuals who assert only the status of federal taxpayers and who challenge the constitutionality of a federal spending program. Whether such individuals have standing to maintain that form of action turns on whether they can demonstrate the necessary stake as taxpayers in the outcome of the litigation to satisfy Article III requirements. The nexus demanded of federal taxpayers has two aspects to it. First, the taxpayer must establish a logical link between that status and the type of legislative enactment attacked. Thus, a taxpayer will be a proper party to allege the unconstitutionality only of exercises of congressional power under the taxing and spending clause of Art. I, §8, of the Constitution. It will not be sufficient to allege an incidental expenditure of tax funds in the administration of an essentially regulatory statute.... Secondly the taxpayer must establish a nexus between that status and the precise nature of the constitutional infringement alleged. Under this requirement, the taxpayer must show that the challenged enactment exceeds specific constitutional limitations imposed upon the exercise of the congressional taxing and spending power and not simply that the enactment is generally beyond the powers delegated to Congress by Art. 1, §8.

When both nexuses are established, the litigant will have shown a taxpayer's stake in the outcome of the controversy. and will be a proper and appropriate party to invoke a federal court's jurisdiction.

The taxpayer-appellants in this case have satisfied both nexuses to support their claim of standing under the test we announce today. Their constitutional challenge is made to an exercise by Congress of its power under Art. 1, §8, to spend for the general welfare, and the challenged program involves a substantial expenditure of federal tax funds. In addition, appellants have alleged that the challenged expenditures violate the Establishment and Free Exercise Clauses of the First Amendment. Our history vividly illustrates that one of the specific evils feared by those who drafted the Establishment Clause and fought for its adoption was that the taxing and spending power would be used to favor one religion over another or to support religion in general. The Establishment Clause was designed as a specific bulwark against such potential abuses of governmental power, and that clause of the First Amendment operates as a specific constitutional limitation upon the exercise by Congress of the taxing and spending power conferred by Art. 1, §8.

The allegations of the taxpayer in *Frothingham v. Mellon*, supra, were quite different from those made in this case, and the result in *Frothingham* is consistent with the test of taxpayer standing announced today. The taxpayer in *Frothingham* attacked a federal spending program and she, therefore, established the first nexus required. However, she lacked standing because her constitutional attack was not based on an allegation that Congress, in enacting the Maternity Act of 1921, had breached a specific limitation upon its taxing and. spending power. The taxpayer in *Frothingham* alleged essentially that Congress, by enacting the challenged statute, had exceeded the general powers delegated to it by Art. I §8, and that Congress had thereby invaded the legislative province reserved to the States by the Tenth Amendment. To be sure, Mrs. Frothingham made the additional allegation that her tax liability would be increased as a result of the allegedly unconstitutional enactment, and she framed that allegation in terms of deprivation of property without due process of law. However, the Due Process Clause of the Fifth Amendment does not protect taxpayers against increases in tax liability, and the taxpayer in *Frothingham* failed to make any additional claim that the harm she alleged resulted from a breach by Congress of the specific constitutional limitations imposed upon an exercise of the taxing and spending power. In essence, Mrs. Frothingham was attempting to assert the States' interest in their legislative prerogatives and not a federal taxpayer's interest in being free of taxing and spending in contravention of specific constitutional limitations imposed upon Congress' taxing and spending power.

We have noted that the Establishment Clause of the First Amendment does specifically limit the taxing and spending power conferred by Art. I, §8. Whether the Constitution contains other specific limitations can be determined only in the context of future cases. However, whenever such specific limitations are found, we believe a taxpayer will have a clear stake as a taxpayer in assuring that they are not breached by Congress. Consequently, we hold that a taxpayer will have standing consistent with Article III to invoke federal judicial power when he alleges that congressional action under the taxing and spending clause is in derogation of those constitutional provisions which operate to restrict the exercise of the taxing and spending power. The taxpayer's allegation in such cases would be that his tax money is being extracted and spent in violation of specific constitutional protections against such abuses of legislative power. Such an injury is appropriate for judicial redress, and the taxpayer has established the necessary nexus between his status and the nature of the allegedly unconstitutional action to support his claim of standing to secure judicial review. Under such circumstances, we feel confident that the questions will be framed with the necessary specificity, that the issues will be contested with the necessary adverseness and that the litigation will be pursued with the necessary vigor to assure that the constitutional challenge will be made in the form traditionally thought to be capable of judicial resolution. We lack that confidence in cases such as *Frothingham* where a taxpayer seeks to employ a federal court as a forum in which to air his generalized grievances about the conduct of government or the allocation of power in the Federal System.

While we express no view at all on the merits of appellants' claims in this case, their complaint contains sufficient allegations under the criteria we have outlined to give them standing to invoke a federal court's jurisdiction for an adjudication on the merits

Reversed.

MR. JUSTICE DOUGLAS joined by MR. JUSTICE STEWART and MR. JUSTICE FORTAS concurred....

MR., JUSTICE HARLAN dissented....

CHAPTER V

THE LEGISLATIVE SYSTEM

Under Article I, the Congress is vested with the "legislative powers" of the United States, or quite simply, the authority to enact national law in our federal system. In addition, other specific policy-making powers are delegated to either Congress as a whole or to one of the two houses separately.[1] These *nonlegislative* grants are specified not only in the first Article but by other sections of the Constitution as well. For example, Congress possesses the power of impeachment, the authority to formulate procedures in federal elections, to reapportion its membership, to coin money, and to create certain types of legislative courts (Article I). The Senate has the authority to "advise and consent" (two-thirds vote) in the matter of treaties negotiated by the President and in his nomination of certain offices of the government by a simple majority vote (Article II). Congress is empowered to create inferior federal courts (Article IV) and to initiate the process of amending the Constitution (Article V). Obviously, the Framers considered Congress the most essential element in the "checks and balances" system since, by its very nature, it was the branch of government most *representative* of majority popular will; not only in domestic matters but foreign policy as well.[2]

Scope and Supremacy of Legislative Powers: It is the legislative power which provides Congress with its central constitutional features. The *enumerated* or *expressed* powers are those listed specifically in the Constitution and include, primarily, the authority to control foreign and interstate commerce, to tax and spend for the general welfare, the war power, and the postal power. In addition, Congress has implied powers under which it may enact all laws which are "necessary and proper" to carry out its enumerated and other powers (Article 1, sec. 8, cl. 18). Regardless of the nature of the legislation, it must satisfy the *test of validity* as provided in the Supremacy Clause (Article VI), that it be made "*in pursuance* of the Constitution." In effect, Congress must provide some constitutional "hook" on which to hang or otherwise justify the law by relying on a *specific* legitimizing article, section or clause or by reasonably *inferring* ("necessary and proper") it therefrom. Treaties, on the other hand, need only be "made under the authority of the United States" which is a *loose* procedural test as verified in *Missouri v. Holland* (1920). Unlike treaties, there are *many* potential roadblocks to the validity of statutory law. Assuming that the "test" has been met and, unless the law is properly challenged in the courts as clearly violating the Constitution, it is the "supreme law of the land." As such, federal laws are superior to all existing state laws and policies. The broad scope and supremacy of implied legislation enacted by Congress were the focal points of John Marshall's classic opinion in *McCulloch v. Maryland* (1819). So broad is the Supremacy Clause (and the Court's interpretation of it) that in *Pennsylvania v. Nelson* (1955) it was held that by merely showing its interest to do so, Congress can supersede or pre-empt concurrent state participation from an entire policy-making area (e.g., subversive activities, certain oil pipeline regulation).

The Investigatory Power: An important implied power of Congress, which is inherent in the legislative process, is the authority to investigate in order to generate needed information leading to possible remedial legislation. Each house of Congress can establish an investigatory committee or assign existing ones to explore policy questions. Beginning with *Anderson v. Dunn* (1821), through the present time, the Supreme Court has held that Congress may properly utilize such common attributes of judicial power as the use of subpoena, contempt citations and grants of immunity in conducting investigations without violating the separation of powers doctrine; see *McGrain v. Daugherty* (1927), *Barry v. United States ex rel. Cunningham* (1929), *Barenblatt v. United States* (1959). Of course, there are legal parameters which Congress cannot constitutionally exceed. In *United States v. Rumely* (1953), for example, the Court held that a committee may not delve into areas which are not contained within the original mandate set by Congress. The most critical limitations placed upon the investigatory power, however, were detailed by the Court in *Watkins v. United States* (1957).

Under the Federal Immunity Act of 1954, Congress, operating through the district court, may grant full immunity to a witness to prevent the use of the testimony by either federal or state court. When extended such immunity, the witness is compelled to answer the questions since this protection fully displaces the relief provided by the "privilege" of the Fifth Amendment, see *Adams v. Maryland* (1954). While complete, such immunity need not be transactional and thus does not protect the witness from prosecution for offenses to which the compelled testimony relates; however, the prosecution would have the affirmative duty of proving that the evidence it proposes to use is derived from a legitimate source wholly independent from the statements made, see *Kastigar v. United States* (1972).

The Delegation of Legislative Power and the Legislative Veto: With respect to the exercise of its legislative powers, the Supreme Court has generally held that – because Congress exercises authority delegated to it by the People of the United States – it cannot delegate or give away its constitutional prerogatives to any other branch or to private parties. This stems from the legal maxim, *delegata potestas non potest delegari*, that delegated power cannot be delegated, see *J.W. Hampton, Jr. & Co. v. United States* (1928). In two 1935 cases, *Schechter Poultry Corporation v. United States and Panama Refining v. Ryan,* the Court ruled that Congress had unconstitutionally delegated legislative power to the Executive branch. However, from a pragmatic standpoint, the Court has made notable exceptions to this rule in realization of the fact that the nation could not function effectively if, at times, Congress could not yield a certain amount of "policy-making power" to the President, see *Brig Aurora v. United States* (1813), *Field v. Clark* (1892). In other instances, the Court has upheld similar distributions of discretion to other executive officers and independent agencies; see *Hood & Sons v. United States* (1939), *Opp Cotton Mills, Inc. v. Administrator* (1941). In his dissenting opinion in *Mistretta v. United States* (1989), however, Justice Scalia questions whether the Court has gone too far in permitting Congress to delegate power to "a sort of junior-varsity Congress."

In an age when it delegates extensive discretionary rule-making authority to executive and independent agencies, Congress has also devised the "legislative veto" as a means of maintaining control over those agencies. In what may prove to be one of its most far reaching decisions, the Court declared the "legislative veto" unconstitutional in *INS v. Chadha* (1983).

Congress and the Admission of New States: Congress has complete discretion as to whether a territory should be admitted as a State of the Union. This action is a grant of national sovereignty and therefore no territory has an arbitrary or automatic right to admission. Accordingly, since the admission of Ohio in 1802, Congress has regularly imposed conditions on incoming states in the form of enabling acts as the "price" of admission. There is, however, an intervening factor that may affect the nature of such agreements: Article IV assumes that all States of the Union are politically equal in the exercise of their powers. Since most of the enabling acts have been commercial in nature, (e.g., tax immunity on the sale of federal land in the state, the transfer of certain public lands to Congress), few constitutional problems have arisen; see *Stearns v. Minnesota* (1900), *Ervien v. United States* (1919). But if Congress imposes restrictions of a political or governmental nature, there may be some serious questions pertaining to the lasting effect of the agreement as seen in *Coyle v. Smith* (1911).

McCULLOCH v. MARYLAND
4 Wheat. 316; 4 L.Ed. 579 (1819)

In 1817, Congress established the Baltimore branch of the Second Bank of the United States. The Constitution gave Congress no enumerated or expressed power to do so. although Article I empowered Congress "to lay and collect taxes, to borrow money; to regulate commerce...." In 1819, Maryland enacted a commercial statute which imposed a tax on each issuance of bank notes or a yearly payment to the state of $15,000 on all banks not chartered by the state.

The cashier of the Baltimore branch, McCulloch, refused to comply; however, the highest state court sustained the tax. The cashier brought the case before the Supreme Court on a writ of error.

MR. CHIEF JUSTICE JOHN MARSHALL delivered the opinion of the Court:

... Among the enumerated powers, we do not find that of establishing a bank or creating a corporation. But there is no phrase in the instrument which, like the Articles of Confederation, excludes incidental or implied powers; and which requires that every thing granted shall be expressly and minutely described. Even the Tenth Amendment, which was framed for the purpose of quieting the excessive jealousies which had been excited, omits the word "expressly," and declares only that the powers "not delegated to the United States, nor prohibited to the States, are reserved to the States or to the people," thus leaving the question, whether the particular power which may become the subject of contest has been delegated to the one government, or prohibited to the other, to depend on a fair construction of the whole instrument. The men who drew and adopted this amendment had experienced the embarrassments resulting from the insertion of this word in the Articles of Confederation, and probably omitted it to avoid those embarrassments. A constitution, to contain an accurate detail of all the subdivisions of which its great powers will admit, and of all the means by which they may be carried into execution would partake of the prolixity of a legal code, and could scarcely be embraced by the human mind. It would probably never be understood by the public. Its nature, therefore, requires that only its great outlines should be marked, its important objects designated. and the minor ingredients which compose those objects be deduced from the nature of the objects themselves. That this idea was entertained by the framers of the American Constitution is not only to be inferred from the nature of the instrument, but from the language. Why else were some of the limitations, found in the ninth section of the first article, introduced? It is also, in some degree, warranted by their having omitted to use any restrictive term which might prevent its receiving a fair and just interpretation. In considering this question, then, we must never forget that it is a *constitution* we are expounding.

...But the Constitution of the United States has not left the right of Congress to employ the necessary means for the execution of the powers conferred on the government to general reasoning. To its enumeration of powers is added that of making "all laws which shall be necessary and proper, for carrying into execution the foregoing powers, and all other powers vested by this Constitution, in the government of the United States, or in any department thereof..."

Congress is not empowered by it to make all laws which may have relation to the powers conferred on the government, but such only as may be "*necessary and proper*" for carrying them into execution. The word "*necessary*," is considered as controlling the whole sentence, and as limiting the right to pass laws for the execution of the granted powers to such as are indispensable, and without which the power would be nugatory. That it excludes the choice of means, and leaves to Congress, in each case, that only which is most direct and simple....

We admit, as all must admit, that the powers of the government are limited, and that its limits are not to be transcended. But we think the sound construction of the Constitution must allow to the national legislature that discretion, with respect to the means by which the powers it confers are to be carried into execution, which will enable that body to perform the high duties assigned to it, in the manner most beneficial to the people. Let the end be legitimate, let it be within the scope of the Constitution, and all means which are appropriate, which are plainly adapted to that end, which are not prohibited, but consist with the letter and spirit of the Constitution, are constitutional ....

After the most deliberate consideration, it is the unanimous and decided opinion of this Court that the act to incorporate the Bank of the United States is a law made in pursuance of the Constitution, and is a part of the supreme law of the land.

That the power of taxation is one of vital importance; that it is retained by the States; that it is not abridged by the grant of a similar power to the government of the Union; that it is to be concurrently exercised by the two governments; are truths which have never been denied. But such is the paramount character of the Constitution that its capacity to withdraw any subject from the action of even this power is admitted. The States are expressly forbidden to lay any duties on imports or exports, except what may be absolutely necessary for executing their inspection laws. If the obligation of this prohibition must be conceded – if it may restrain a State from the exercise of its taxing power on imports and exports; the same paramount character would seem to restrain, as it certainly may restrain a State from such other exercise of this power as is in its nature incompatible with, and repugnant to, the constitutional laws of the Union.

... *That the power to tax involves the power to destroy*; that the power to destroy may defeat and render useless the power to create; that there is a plain repugnance in conferring on one government a power to control the constitutional measures of another, which other, with respect to those very measures, is declared to be supreme over that which exerts the control, are propositions not to be denied.

...If we apply the principle for which the State of Maryland contends to the Constitution generally, we shall find it capable of changing totally the character of that instrument. We shall find it capable of arresting all the measures of the government, and of prostrating it at the foot of the States. The American people have declared their Constitution, and the laws made in pursuance thereof, to be supreme; but this principle would transfer the supremacy, in fact, to the States.

... If the controlling power of the States be established; if their supremacy as to taxation be acknowledged; what is to restrain their exercising this control in any shape they may please to give it? Their sovereignty is not confined to taxation. That is not the only mode in which it might be displayed. The question. is, in truth, a question of supremacy; and, if the right of the States to tax the means employed by the general government be conceded, the declaration that the Constitution, and the laws made in pursuance thereof, shall be the supreme law of the land, is empty and unmeaning declamation.

...We are unanimously of opinion, that the law passed by the legislature of Maryland imposing a tax on the Bank of the United States is unconstitutional and void.

MISSOURI v. HOLLAND
252 U.S. 346; 40 S.Ct. 382; 64 L.Ed. 641 (1920)

In 1916, the United States signed a treaty with Great Britain, the Migratory Bird Treaty, and two years later Congress enacted legislation to enforce its terms. The law prohibited killing, capturing, or selling certain migratory birds in this country which were considered endangered species. Missouri challenged the enforcement of the act as an unconstitutional interference with States' rights under the Tenth Amendment. After the federal district court declined relief, Missouri appealed to the Supreme Court. The main questions presented were: (1) was the act of Congress considered a part of the treaty or was it ordinary legislation, and (2) to which test of validity under Article VI was the law subject – the more difficult substantive *test of being "made in pursuance of the Constitution" or the loose* procedural *requirement of being "made under the authority of the United States"'?*

MR. JUSTICE HOLMES delivered the opinion of the Court:

... *the question raised is the general one whether the treaty and statute are void as an interference with the rights reserved to the states.*

To answer this question, it is not enough to refer to the Tenth Amendment, reserving the powers not delegated to the United States, because by Article 11, § 2 the power to make treaties is delegated expressly, and by Article VI, treaties made under the authority of the United States, along with the Constitution and laws of the United States, made in pursuance thereof, are declared the supreme law of the land. If the treaty is valid, there can be no dispute about the validity of the statute under Article 1, § 8 as a necessary and proper means to execute the powers of the government. The language of the Constitution as to the supremacy of treaties being general, the question before us is narrowed to an inquiry into the ground upon which the present supposed exception is placed.

It is said that a treaty cannot be valid if it infringes the Constitution; that there are limits, therefore, to the treaty-making power; and that one such limit is that what an act of Congress could not do unaided, in derogation of the powers reserved to the states, a treaty cannot do.

...Acts of Congress are the supreme law of the land only when "*made in pursuance of the Constitution,*" while treaties are declared to be so when "*made under the authority of the United States.*" It is open to question whether the authority of the United States means more than the formal acts prescribed to make the convention. We do not mean to imply that there are no qualifications to the treaty-making power; but they must be ascertained in a different way. It is obvious that there may be matters of the sharpest exigency for the national well-being that an act of Congress could not deal with, but that a treaty followed by such an act could, and it is not lightly to be assumed that, in matters requiring national action, "a power which must belong to and somewhere reside in every civilized government" is not to be found .... The case before us must be considered in the light of our whole experience, and not merely in that of what was said a hundred years ago. The treaty in question does not contravene any prohibitory words to be found in the Constitution. The only question is whether it is forbidden by some invisible radiation from the general terms of the Tenth Amendment. We must consider what this country has become in deciding what that amendment has reserved .... If we are to be accurate, we cannot put the case of the state upon higher ground than that the treaty deals with creatures that for the moment are within the state borders, that it must be carried out by officers of the United States within the same territory, and that, but for the treaty, the state would be free to regulate this subject itself ... Here a national interest of very nearly the first magnitude is involved. It can be protected only by national action in concert with that of another power. The subject matter is only transitorily within the state, and has no permanent habitat therein. But for the treaty and the statute, there soon might be no birds for any powers to deal with. We see nothing in the Constitution that compels the government to sit by while a food supply is cut off and the protectors of our forests and of our crops are destroyed. It is not sufficient to rely upon the states. The reliance is vain, and were it otherwise, the question is whether the United States is forbidden to act. We are of opinion that the treaty and statute must be upheld...

MR. JUSTICE VAN DEVANTER and MR. JUSTICE PITNEY dissented.

PENNSYLVANIA v. NELSON
350 U.S. 497; 76 S.Ct. 477; 100 L.Ed. 640 (1956)

In 1940, when Congress enacted the Alien Registration Act (the Smith Act) it was apparently showing its intention, although not expressed in the law, to occupy the entire area of sedition against the United States. A number of states, including Pennsylvania, had similar statutes. Steve Nelson, who had been convicted and sentenced to a five-year term for his communist activities under the Smith Act, was later convicted for violating the Pennsylvania Sedition law. Upon challenge, the State Supreme Court overturned the State conviction on the ground that Pennsylvania had been preempted *from this area by the Smith Act. The case was then presented to the Supreme Court of the United States on a writ of certiorari.*

MR. CHIEF JUSTICE WARREN delivered the opinion of the Court:

It should be said at the outset that the decision in this case does not affect the right of States to enforce their sedition laws at times when the Federal Government has not occupied the field and is not protecting the entire country from seditious conduct....

Where, as in the instant case, Congress has not stated specifically whether a federal statute has occupied a field in which the States are otherwise free to legislate, different criteria have furnished touchstones for decision....

In this case, we think that each of several tests of supersession is met. First, "the scheme of federal regulation [is] so pervasive as to make reasonable the inference that Congress left no room for the States to supplement it...." The Congress determined in 1940 that it was necessary for it to re-enter the field of antisubversive legislation, which had been abandoned by it in 1921. In that year, it enacted the Smith Act, which proscribes advocacy of the overthrow of any government – federal, state, or local – by force and violence and organization of and knowing membership in a group which so advocates. Conspiracy to commit any of these acts is punishable under the general criminal conspiracy provisions.

... Second, the federal statutes "touch a field in which the federal interest is so dominant that the federal system (must) be assumed to preclude enforcement of State laws on the same subject...." Congress has devised an all-embracing program for resistance to the various forms of totalitarian aggression. Our external defenses have been strengthened, and a plan to protect against internal subversion has been made by it. It has appropriated vast sums, not only for our own protection, but also to strengthen freedom throughout the world. It has charged the Federal Bureau of Investigation and the Central Intelligence Agency with responsibility for intelligence concerning Communist seditious activities against our Government, and has denominated such activities as part of a world conspiracy. It accordingly proscribed sedition against all government in the nation... national, state, and local. Congress declared that these steps were taken "to provide for the common defense, to preserve the sovereignty of the United States as an independent nation, and to guarantee to each State a republican form of government...." Congress having thus treated seditious conduct as a matter of vital national concern, it is in no sense a local enforcement problem....

Third, enforcement of state sedition acts presents a serious danger of conflict with the administration of the federal program. Since 1939, in order to avoid a hampering of uniform enforcement of its program by sporadic local prosecutions, the Federal Government has urged local authorities not to intervene in such matters, but to turn over to the federal authorities immediately and unevaluated all information concerning subversive activities.

...Since we find that Congress has occupied the field to the exclusion of parallel state legislation, that the dominant interest of the Federal Government precludes state intervention, and that administration of state acts would conflict with the operation of the federal plan, we are convinced that the decision of the Supreme Court of Pennsylvania is unassailable....

The judgment of the Supreme Court of Pennsylvania is Affirmed.

MR. JUSTICE REED, with whom MR. JUSTICE BURTON and MR. JUSTICE MINTON joined, dissented.

WATKINS v. UNITED STATES
354 U.S. 178, 77 S.Ct. 1273, 1 L.Ed. 2d 1273 (1957)

During the "Red-baiting" heyday of the McCarthy Era (1949-1957) the House Committee on Un-American Activities and its subcommittees made continual media headlines because of its reckless investigations. In its attempts to expose communists in all walks of American life-education, labor unions, government service, entertainment-questions concerning the excess of constitutional authority were bound to be raised. In this case, John T. Watkins, a union leader, was called as a witness before one such committee in 1954. While he openly acknowledged his involvement with the Communist party during World War II, he refused to answer questions relating to his associates who might have been party members. Watkins argued that such inquiries were not "relevant" to the work of the committee and that it had no right to publicly "expose" persons because of their past activities. The House cited Watkins for contempt. He was convicted by a federal district court and was fined $100 and sentenced to a year in federal prison. After a court of appeals upheld his conviction, Watkins brought the matter to the Supreme Court on certiorari.

MR. CHIEF JUSTICE WARREN delivered the opinion of the Court:

...We start with several basic premises on which there is general agreement. The power of the Congress to conduct investigations is inherent in the legislative process. That power is broad. It encompasses inquiries concerning the administration of existing laws as well as proposed or possibly needed statutes. It includes surveys of defects in our social, economic, or political system for the purpose of enabling the Congress to remedy them. It comprehends probes into departments of the Federal Government to expose corruption, inefficiency, or waste. But broad as is this power of inquiry, it is not unlimited. There is no general authority to expose the private affairs of individuals without justification in terms of the functions of the Congress. This was freely conceded by the Solicitor General in his argument of this case. Nor is the Congress a law enforcement or trial agency. These are functions of the executive and judicial departments of government. No inquiry is an end in itself; it must be related to and in furtherance of a legitimate task of the Congress. Investigations conducted solely for the personal aggrandizement of the investigator or to "punish" those investigated are indefensible.

It is unquestionably the duty of all citizens to cooperate with the Congress in its efforts to obtain the facts needed for intelligent legislative action. It is their unremitting obligation to respond to subpoenas, to respect the dignity of the Congress and its committees, and to testify fully with respect to matters within the province of proper investigation. This, of course, assumes that the constitutional rights of witnesses will be respected by the Congress as they are in a court of justice. The Bill of Rights is applicable to investigations as to all forms of governmental action. Witnesses cannot be compelled to give evidence against themselves. They cannot be subjected to unreasonable search and seizure. Nor can the First Amendment freedoms of speech, press, religion, or political belief and association be abridged....

In the decade following World War II, there appeared a new kind of congressional inquiry unknown in prior periods of American history. Principally this was the result of the various investigations into the threat of subversion of the United States Government, but other subjects of congressional interest also contributed to the changed scene. This new phase of legislative inquiry involved a broad-scale intrusion into the lives and affairs of private citizens. It brought before the courts novel questions of the appropriate limits of congressional inquiry. Prior cases ... had defined the scope of investigative power in terms of the inherent limitations of the sources of that power. In the more recent cases, the emphasis shifted to problems of accommodating the interest of the Government with the rights and privileges of individuals. The central theme was the application of the Bill of Rights as a restraint upon the assertion of governmental power in this form....

...The theory of a committee inquiry is that the committee members are serving as the representatives of the parent assembly in collecting information for a legislative purpose. Their function is to act as the eyes and ears of the Congress in obtaining facts upon which the full legislature can act. To carry out this mission, committees and subcommittees, sometimes one Congressman, are endowed with the full power of the Congress to compel testimony....

An essential premise in this situation is that the House or Senate shall have instructed the committee members on what they are to do with the power delegated to them. It is the responsibility of the Congress, in the first instance, to insure that compulsory process is used only in furtherance of a legislative purpose. That requires that the instructions to an investigating committee spell out that group's jurisdiction and purpose with sufficient particularity. Those instructions are embodied in the authorizing resolution. That document is the committee's charter. Broadly drafted and loosely worded, however, such resolutions can leave tremendous latitude to the discretion of the investigators. The more vague the committee's charter is, the greater becomes the possibility that the committee's specific actions are not in conformity with the will of the parent House of Congress.

The authorizing resolution of the Un-American Activities Committee was adopted in 1938 when a select committee, under the chairmanship of Representative Dies, was created. Several years later, the Committee was made a standing organ of the House with the same mandate.

...It would be difficult to imagine a less explicit authorizing resolution. Who can define the meaning of "un-American"? What is that single, solitary "principle of the form of government as guaranteed by our Constitution"? There is no need to dwell upon the language, however. At one time, perhaps, the resolution might have been read narrowly to confine the Committee to the subject of propaganda. The events that have transpired in the fifteen years before the interrogation of petitioner make such a construction impossible at this date.

The members of the Committee have clearly demonstrated that they did not feel themselves restricted in any way to propaganda in the narrow sense of the word. Unquestionably the Committee conceived of its task in the grand view of its name. Un-American activities were its target, no matter how or where manifested. Notwithstanding the broad purview of the Committee's experience, the House of Representatives repeatedly approved its continuation. Five times it extended the life of the special committee. Then it made the group a standing committee of the House. A year later, the Committee's charter was embodied in the Legislative Reorganization Act. On five occasions, at the beginning of sessions of Congress, it has made the authorizing resolution part of the files of the House. On innumerable occasions, it has passed appropriation bills to allow the Committee to continue its efforts.

Combining the language of the resolution with the construction it has been given, it is evident that the preliminary control of the Committee exercised by the House of Representatives is slight or nonexistent. No one could reasonably deduce from the charter the kind of investigation that the Committee was directed to make. As a result, we are asked to engage in a process of retroactive rationalization. Looking backward from the events that transpired, we are asked to uphold the Committee's actions unless it appears that they were clearly not authorized by the charter. As a corollary to this inverse approach, the Government urges that we must view the matter hospitably to the power of the Congress – that if there is any legislative purpose which might have been furthered by the kind of disclosure sought, the witness must be punished for withholding it. No doubt every reasonable indulgence of legality must be accorded to the actions of a coordinate branch of our Government. But such deference cannot yield to an unnecessary and unreasonable dissipation of precious constitutional freedoms.

The Government contends that the public interest at the core of the investigations of the Un-American Activities Committee is the need by the Congress to be informed of efforts to overthrow the Government by force and violence so that adequate legislative safeguards can be erected. From this core, however, the Committee can radiate outward infinitely to any topic thought to be related in some way to armed insurrection. The outer reaches of this domain are known only by the content of "un-American activities." Remoteness of subject can be aggravated by a probe for a depth of detail even farther removed from any basis of legislative action. A third dimension is added when the investigators turn their attention to the past to collect minutiae on remote topics, on the hypothesis that the past may reflect upon the present.

The consequences that flow from this situation are manifold. In the first place, a reviewing court is unable to make the kind of judgment made by the Court in *United States v. Rumely*.... The Committee is allowed, in essence, to define its own authority, choose the direction and focus of its activities. In deciding what to do with the power that has been conferred upon them, members of the Committee may act pursuant to motives that seem to them to be the highest. Their decisions, nevertheless, can lead to ruthless exposure of private lives in order to gather data that is neither desired by the Congress nor useful to it. Yet it is impossible in this circumstance, with constitutional freedoms in jeopardy, to declare that the Committee has ranged beyond the area committed to it by its parent assembly because the boundaries are so nebulous.

More important and more fundamental than that, however, it insulates the House that has authorized the investigation from the witnesses who are subjected to the sanctions of compulsory process.

...The problem attains proportion when viewed from the standpoint of the witness who appears before a congressional committee. He must decide at the time the questions are propounded whether or not to answer.... He is "... bound rightly to construe the statute...." An erroneous determination on his part, even if made in the utmost good faith, does not exculpate him if the court should later rule that the questions were pertinent to the question under inquiry.

It is obvious that a person compelled to make this choice is entitled to have knowledge of the subject to which the interrogation is deemed pertinent. That knowledge must be available with the same degree of explicitness and clarity that the Due Process Clause requires in the expression of any element of a criminal offense. The "vice of vagueness" must be avoided here as in all other crimes. There are several sources that can outline the "question under inquiry" in such a way that the rules against vagueness are satisfied. The authorizing resolution, the remarks of the chairman or members of the committee, or even the nature of the proceedings themselves might sometimes make the topic clear. This case demonstrates, however, that these sources often leave the matter in grave doubt.

...[W]e remain unenlightened as to the subject to which the questions asked petitioner were pertinent. Certainly, if the point is that obscure after trial and appeal, it was not adequately revealed to petitioner when he had to decide at his peril whether or not to answer. Fundamental fairness demands that no witness be compelled to make such a determination with so little guidance. Unless the subject matter has been made to appear with indisputable clarity, it is the duty of the investigative body, upon objection of the witness on grounds of pertinency, to state for the record the subject under inquiry at that time and the manner in which the propounded questions are pertinent thereto. To be meaningful, the explanation must describe what the topic under inquiry is and the connective reasoning whereby the precise questions asked relate to it.

... Petitioner was thus not accorded a fair opportunity to determine whether he was within his rights in refusing to answer, and his conviction is necessarily invalid under the Due Process Clause of the Fifth Amendment.

...The legislature is free to determine the kinds of data that should be collected. It is only those investigations that are conducted by use of compulsory process that give rise to a need to protect the rights of individuals against illegal encroachment. That protection can be readily achieved through procedures which prevent the separation of power from responsibility and which provide the constitutional requisites of fairness for witnesses. A measure of added care on the part of the House and the Senate in authorizing the use of compulsory process and by their committees in exercising that power would suffice. That is a small price to pay if it serves to uphold the principles of limited, constitutional government without constricting the power of the Congress to inform itself.

The judgment of the Court of Appeals is reversed, and the case is remanded to the District Court with instructions to dismiss the indictment. It is so ordered.

MR. JUSTICE BURTON and MR. JUSTICE WHITTAKER took no part in the consideration or decision of this case. JUSTICE FRANKFURTER wrote a concurring opinion. MR. JUSTICE CLARK dissented.

A.L.A. SCHECHTER POULTRY CORP. et al. v. UNITED STATES
295 U.S. 495; 55 S.Ct. 837; 79 L.Ed. 1570 (1935)

During the first several months following his ascension to the Office of President in 1933, Franklin Delano Roosevelt and his advisors sent a mass of legislative proposals to the Congress in attempts to, at least, slow down the nation's deepening Depression. One of the most important of these proposals was entitled the National Industrial Recovery Act. It attempted to encourage cooperation within the business community by allowing them to have substantial input into the drawing up of "codes of fair competition." While viewed as a virtual suspension of governmental anti-trust activity, the law also provided for minimum wages, maximum work hours, the right of collective bargaining, and the prohibition of child labor, all of which had been controversial progressive proposals for some time. After the Court struck down the law in this case, Roosevelt lost whatever support he had had in the business community.

MR. CHIEF JUSTICE HUGHES delivered the opinion of the Court:

Petitioners ... were convicted in the District Court of the United States for the Eastern District of New York on eighteen counts of an indictment charging violations of what is known as the "Live Poultry Code," and on an additional count for conspiracy to commit such violations.... [T]he defendants contended (1) that the Code had been adopted pursuant to an unconstitutional delegation by Congress of legislative power; (2) that it attempted to regulate intrastate transactions which lay outside the authority of Congress; and (3) that in certain provisions it was repugnant to the due process clause of the Fifth Amendment....

...A.L.A. Schechter Poultry Corporation and Schechter Live Poultry Market are corporations conducting wholesale poultry slaughterhouse markets in Brooklyn, New York City.... They buy the poultry; it is trucked to their slaughterhouse markets in Brooklyn; it is there sold, usually within twenty-four hours, to retail poultry dealers and butchers who sell directly to consumers.... Defendants do not sell poultry in interstate commerce.

The "Live Poultry Code" was promulgated under §3 of the National Industrial Recovery Act. That section ... authorizes the President to approve "codes of fair competition."

...The Code fixes the number of hours for work-days. It provides that no employee, with certain exceptions, shall be permitted to work in excess of forty (40) hours in any one week, and that no employee, save as stated, "shall be paid in any pay period less than at the rate of fifty (50) cents per hour." The article containing "general labor provisions" prohibits the employment of any person under sixteen years of age, and declares that employees shall have the right of "collective bargaining," and freedom of choice with respect to labor organizations, in the terms of § 7(a) of the Act. The minimum number of employees who shall be employed by slaughterhouse operators is fixed, the number being graduated according to the average volume of weekly sales....

The seventh article, containing "trade practice provisions," prohibits various practices which are said to constitute "unfair methods of competition."

The President approved the Code by an executive order....

... First. Two preliminary points are stressed by the Government with respect to the appropriate approach to the important questions presented. We are told that the provision of the statute authorizing the adoption of codes must be viewed in the light of the grave national crisis with which Congress was confronted. Undoubtedly, the conditions to which power is addressed are always to be considered when the exercise of power is challenged. Extraordinary conditions may call for extraordinary remedies. But the argument necessarily stops short of an attempt to justify action which lies outside the sphere of constitutional authority. Extraordinary conditions do not create or enlarge constitutional power. The Constitution established a national government with powers deemed to be adequate, as they have proved to be both in war and peace, but these powers of the national government are limited by the constitutional grants. Those who act under these grants are not at liberty to transcend the imposed limits because they believe that more or different power is necessary. Such assertions of extraconstitutional authority were anticipated and precluded by the explicit terms of the Tenth Amendment.

... The Constitution provides that "All legislative powers herein granted shall be vested in a Congress of the United States, which shall consist of a Senate and House of Representatives." Art. 1, §1. And the Congress is authorized "To make all laws which shall be necessary and proper for carrying into execution" its general powers. Art. 1, §8, par. 18. The Congress is not permitted to abdicate or to transfer to others the essential legislative functions with which it is thus vested.

...What is meant by "fair competition" as the term is used in the Act? Does it refer to a category established in the law, and is the authority to make codes limited accordingly? Or is it used as a convenient designation for whatever set of laws the formulators of a code for a particular trade or industry may propose and the President may approve (subject to certain restrictions), or the President may himself prescribe, as being wise and beneficent provisions for the government of trade or industry in order to accomplish the broad purpose of rehabilitation, correction, and expansion which are stated in the first section of Title I?

The Act does not define "fair competition...."

...The answer is obvious. Such a delegation of legislative power is unknown to our law and is utterly inconsistent with the constitutional prerogatives and duties of Congress.

The question, then, turns upon the authority which section 83 of the Recovery Act vests in the President to approve or prescribe. If the codes have standing as penal statutes, this must be due to the effect of the executive action. But Congress cannot delegate legislative power to the President to exercise an unfettered discretion to make whatever laws he thinks may be needed or advisable for the rehabilitation and expansion of trade or industry....

...Section 3 of the Recovery Act is without precedent. It supplies no standards for any trade, industry, or activity. It does not undertake to prescribe rules of conduct to be applied to particular states of fact determined by appropriate administrative procedure. Instead of prescribing rules of conduct, it authorizes the making of codes to prescribe them.

...We think that the code-making authority thus conferred is an unconstitutional delegation of legislative power.

...The question of chief importance relates to the provisions of the Code as to the hours and wages of those employed in defendants' management of their local business. The persons employed in slaughtering and selling in local trade are not employed in interstate commerce. Their hours and wages have no direct relation to interstate commerce.

...The apparent implication is that the federal authority under the commerce clause should be deemed to extend to the establishment of rules to govern wages and hours in intrastate trade and industry generally throughout the country, thus overriding the authority of the States to deal with domestic problems arising from labor conditions in their internal commerce.

It is not the province of the Court to consider the economic advantages or disadvantages of such a centralized system. It is sufficient to say that the Federal Constitution does not provide for it.

...We are of the opinion that the attempt through the provisions of the Code to fix the hours and wages of employees of defendants in their intrastate business was not a valid exercise of federal power.

...In view of these conclusions, we find it unnecessary to discuss other questions which have been raised as to the validity of certain provisions of the Code under the due process clause of the Fifth Amendment.

...On both the grounds we have discussed, the attempted delegation of legislative power, and the attempted regulation of intrastate transactions which affect interstate commerce only indirectly, we hold the code provisions here in question to be invalid and that the judgment of conviction must be reversed....

MR. JUSTICE CARDOZO, joined by JUSTICE STONE, concurred.

MISTRETTA V. UNITED STATES
109 S.Ct. 647, 488 U.S. 361, 102 L.Ed. 2nd (1989)

In 1984, Congress passed the Sentencing Reform Act which created the United States Sentencing Commission. The Commission's function was to remedy the great disparities among the sentences federal judges across the country would give to individuals convicted of similar crimes by developing sentencing guidelines which federal judges would be bound to follow. Mistretta, sentenced under the new guidelines for selling cocaine, argued that the Commission violated the separation of powers and that Congress had unconstitutionally delegated legislative power to it. The District Court found the Commission and the guidelines constitutional. The case was appealed directly to the Supreme Court.

Justice BLACKMUN delivered the opinion of the Court.

In this litigation, we ... consider the constitutionality of the Sentencing Guidelines promulgated by the United States Sentencing Commission. The Commission is a body created under the Sentencing Reform Act of 1984 (Act), as amended. The United States District Court for the Western District of Missouri ruled that the Guidelines were constitutional.

For almost a century, the Federal Government employed in criminal cases a system of indeterminate sentencing. Statutes specified the penalties for crimes but nearly always gave the sentencing judge wide discretion to decide whether the offender should be incarcerated and for how long, whether he should be fined and how much, and whether some lesser restraint, such as probation, should be imposed instead of imprisonment or fine....

Both indeterminate sentencing and parole were based on concepts of the offender's possible, indeed probable, rehabilitation, a view that it was realistic to attempt to rehabilitate the inmate and thereby to minimize the risk that he would resume criminal activity upon his return to society. It obviously required the judge and the parole officer to make their respective sentencing and release decisions upon their own assessments of the offender's amenability to rehabilitation. As a result, the court and the officer were in positions to exercise, and usually did exercise, very broad discretion....

...Congress, of course, has the power to fix the sentence for a federal crime,...and the scope of judicial discretion with respect to a sentence is subject to congressional control.... Congress delegated almost unfettered discretion to the sentencing judge to determine what the sentence should be within the customarily wide range so selected. This broad discretion was further enhanced by the power later granted the judge to suspend the sentence and by the resulting growth of an elaborate probation system. Also, with the advent of parole, Congress moved toward a "three-way sharing" of sentencing responsibility by granting corrections personnel in the Executive Branch the discretion to release a prisoner before the expiration of the sentence imposed by the judge. Thus, under the indeterminate-sentence system, Congress defined the maximum, the judge imposed a sentence within the statutory range (which he usually could replace with probation), and the Executive Branch's parole official eventually determined the actual duration of imprisonment....

Serious disparities in sentences, however, were common. Rehabilitation as a sound penological theory came to be questioned and, in any event, was regarded by some as an unattainable goal for most cases. ...

... Fundamental and widespread dissatisfaction with the uncertainties and the disparities continued to be expressed. Congress had wrestled with the problem for more than a decade when, in 1984, it enacted the sweeping reforms that are at issue here....

The Act, as adopted, revises the old sentencing process in several ways:

1. It rejects imprisonment as a means of promoting rehabilitation,... and it states that punishment should serve retributive, educational, deterrent, and incapacitative goals,...

2. It consolidates the power that had been exercised by the sentencing judge and the Parole Commission to decide what punishment an offender should suffer. This is done by creating the United States Sentencing Commission, directing that Commission to devise guidelines to be used for sentencing, and prospectively abolishing the Parole Commission....

3. It makes all sentences basically determinate. A prisoner is to be released at the completion of his sentence reduced only by any credit earned by good behavior while in custody....

4. It makes the Sentencing Commission's guidelines binding on the courts, although it preserves for the judge the discretion to depart from the guideline applicable to a particular case if the judge finds an aggravating or mitigating factor present that the Commission did not adequately consider when formulating guidelines.... The Act also requires the court to state its reasons for the sentence imposed and to give "the specific reason" for imposing a sentence different from that described in the guideline....

5. It authorizes limited appellate review of the sentence. It permits a defendant to appeal a sentence that is above the defined range, and it permits the Government to appeal a sentence that is below that range. It also permits either side to appeal an incorrect application of the guideline....

The Commission is established "as an independent commission in the judicial branch of the United States...." It has seven voting members (one of whom is the Chairman) appointed by the President "by and with the advice and consent of the Senate." "At least three of the members shall be Federal judges selected after considering a list of six judges recommended to the President by the Judicial Conference of the United States...." No more than four members of the Commission shall be members of the same political party. The Attorney General, or his designee, is an ex officio non-voting member. The Chairman and other members of the Commission are subject to removal by the President "only for neglect of duty or malfeasance in office or for other good cause shown...." Except for initial staggering of terms, a voting member serves for six years and may not serve more than two full terms....

In addition to the duty the Commission has to promulgate determinative-sentence guidelines, it is under an obligation periodically to "review and revise" the guidelines. It is to "consult with authorities on, and individual and institutional representatives of, various aspects of the Federal criminal justice system." It must report to Congress "any amendments of the guidelines." It is to make recommendations to Congress whether the grades or maximum penalties should be modified. It must submit to Congress at least annually an analysis of the operation of the guidelines. It is to issue "general policy statements" regarding their application. And it has the power to "establish general policies … as are necessary to carry out the purposes" of the legislation, to "monitor the performance of probation officers" with respect to the guidelines, to "devise and conduct periodic training programs of instruction in sentencing techniques for judicial and probation personnel" and others, and to "perform such other functions as are required to permit Federal courts to meet their responsibilities" as to sentencing....

On December 10, 1987, John M. Mistretta (petitioner) and another were indicted in the United States District Court for the Western District of Missouri on three counts centering in a cocaine sale. Mistretta moved to have the promulgated Guidelines ruled unconstitutional on the grounds that the Sentencing Commission was constituted in violation of the established doctrine of separation of powers, and that Congress delegated excessive authority to the Commission to structure the Guidelines. As has been noted, the District Court was not persuaded by these contentions....

... The court also rejected petitioner's claim that the Act is unconstitutional because it requires Article III federal judges to serve on the Commission....

Petitioner argues that in delegating the power to promulgate sentencing guidelines for every federal criminal offense to an independent Sentencing Commission, Congress has granted the Commission excessive legislative discretion in violation of the constitutionally based nondelegation doctrine. We do not agree.

The nondelegation doctrine is rooted in the principle of separation of powers that underlies our tripartite system of Government. The Constitution provides that "[a]ll legislative Powers herein granted shall be vested in a Congress of the United States," U.S. Const., Art. I, § 1, and we long have insisted that "the integrity and maintenance of the system of government ordained by the Constitution" mandate that Congress generally cannot delegate its legislative power to another Branch.... We also have recognized, however, that the separation-of-powers principle, and the nondelegation doctrine in particular, do not prevent Congress from obtaining the assistance of its coordinate Branches.... So long as Congress "shall lay down by legislative act an intelligible principle to which the person or body authorized to [exercise the delegated authority] is directed to conform, such legislative action is not a forbidden delegation of legislative power...."

Applying this "intelligible principle" test to congressional delegations, our jurisprudence has been driven by a practical understanding that in our increasingly complex society, replete with ever changing and more technical problems, Congress simply cannot do its job absent an ability to delegate power under broad general directives....

Until 1935, this Court never struck down a challenged statute on delegation grounds. After invalidating in 1935 two statutes as excessive delegations, see *A.L.A. Schechter Poultry Corp. v. United States,* 295 U.S. 495, 55 S.Ct. 837, 79 L.Ed. 1570, and *Panama Refining Co. v. Ryan, supra,* we have upheld, again without deviation, Congress' ability to delegate power under broad standards....

In light of our approval of these broad delegations, we harbor no doubt that Congress' delegation of authority to the Sentencing Commission is sufficiently specific and detailed to meet constitutional requirements. Congress charged the Commission with three goals: to "assure the meeting of the purposes of sentencing as set forth" in the Act; to "provide certainty and fairness in meeting the purposes of sentencing, avoiding unwarranted sentencing disparities among defendants with similar records ... while maintaining sufficient flexibility to permit individualized sentences," where appropriate; and to "reflect, to the extent practicable, advancement in knowledge of human behavior as it relates to the criminal justice process." Congress further specified four "purposes" of sentencing that the Commission must pursue in carrying out its mandate: "to reflect the seriousness of the offense, to promote respect for the law, and to provide just punishment for the offense;" "to afford adequate deterrence to criminal conduct;" "to protect the public from further crimes of the defendant;" and "to provide the defendant with needed ... correctional treatment...."

In addition, Congress prescribed the specific tool – the guidelines system – for the Commission to use in regulating sentencing. More particularly, Congress directed the Commission to develop a system of "sentencing ranges" applicable "for each category of offense involving each category of defendant...."

To guide the Commission in its formulation of offense categories, Congress directed it to consider seven factors: the grade of the offense; the aggravating and mitigating circumstances of the crime; the nature and degree of the harm caused by the crime; the community view of the gravity of the offense; the public concern generated by the crime; the deterrent effect that a particular sentence may have on others; and the current incidence of the offense. Congress set forth 11 factors for the Commission to consider in establishing categories of defendants. These include the offender's age, education, vocational skills, mental and emotional condition, physical condition (including drug dependence), previous employment record, family ties and responsibilities, community ties, role in the offense, criminal history, and degree of dependence upon crime for a livelihood....

In addition to these overarching constraints, Congress provided even more detailed guidance to the Commission about categories of offenses and offender characteristics. Congress directed that guidelines require a term of confinement at or near the statutory maximum for certain crimes of violence and for drug offenses, particularly when committed by recidivists....

In other words, although Congress granted the Commission substantial discretion in formulating guidelines, in actuality it legislated a full hierarchy of punishment – from near maximum imprisonment, to substantial imprisonment, to some imprisonment, to alternatives – and stipulated the most important offense and offender characteristics to place defendants within these categories.

We cannot dispute petitioner's contention that the Commission enjoys significant discretion in formulating guidelines. The Commission does have discretionary authority to determine the relative severity of federal crimes and to assess the relative weight of the offender characteristics that Congress listed for the Commission to consider....

Congress has met that standard here. The Act sets forth more than merely an "intelligible principle" or minimal standards. One court has aptly put it: "The statute outlines the policies which prompted establishment of the Commission, explains what the Commission should do and how it should do it, and sets out specific directives to govern particular situations...."

Having determined that Congress has set forth sufficient standards for the exercise of the Commission's delegated authority, we turn to Mistretta's claim that the Act violates the constitutional principle of separation of powers....

Mistretta argues ... that Congress, in constituting the Commission as it did, effected an unconstitutional accumulation of power within the Judicial Branch while at the same time undermining the Judiciary's independence and integrity. Specifically, petitioner claims that in delegating to an independent agency within the Judicial Branch the power to promulgate sentencing guidelines, Congress unconstitutionally has required the Branch, and individual Article III judges, to exercise not only their judicial authority, but legislative authority, the making of sentencing policy, as well. Such rulemaking authority, petitioner contends, may be exercised by Congress, or delegated by Congress to the Executive, but may not be delegated to or exercised by the Judiciary....

At the same time, petitioner asserts, Congress unconstitutionally eroded the integrity and independence of the Judiciary by requiring Article III judges to sit on the Commission, by requiring that those judges share their rulemaking authority with nonjudges, and by subjecting the Commission's members to appointment and removal by the President. According to petitioner, Congress, consistent with the separation of powers, may not upset the balance among the Branches by co-opting federal judges into the quintessentially political work of establishing sentencing guidelines, by subjecting those judges to the political whims of the Chief Executive, and by forcing judges to share their power with nonjudges....

...Although the unique composition and responsibilities of the Sentencing Commission give rise to serious concerns about a disruption of the appropriate balance of governmental power among the coordinate Branches, we conclude, upon close inspection, that petitioner's fears for the fundamental structural protections of the Constitution prove, at least in this case, to be "more smoke than fire," and do not compel us to invalidate Congress' considered scheme for resolving the seemingly intractable dilemma of excessive disparity in criminal sentencing....

The Sentencing Commission unquestionably is a peculiar institution within the framework of our Government. Although placed by the Act in the Judicial Branch, it is not a court and does not exercise judicial power.... Our constitutional principles of separated powers are not violated, however, by mere anomaly or innovation. Setting to one side, for the moment, the question whether the composition of the Sentencing Commission violates the separation of powers, we observe that Congress' decision to create an independent rulemaking body to promulgate sentencing guidelines and to locate that body within the Judicial Branch is not unconstitutional unless Congress has vested in the Commission powers that are more appropriately performed by the other Branches or that undermine the integrity of the Judiciary....

As a general principle, we stated as recently as last Term that "'executive or administrative duties of a nonjudicial nature may not be imposed on judges holding office under Art. III of the Constitution.'..."

Nonetheless, we have recognized significant exceptions to this general rule and have approved the assumption of some nonadjudicatory activities by the Judicial Branch. In keeping with Justice Jackson's *Youngstown* admonition that the separation of powers contemplates the integration of dispersed powers into a workable Government, we have recognized the constitutionality of a "twilight area" in which the activities of the separate Branches merge. ...

That judicial rulemaking, at least with respect to some subjects, falls within this twilight area is no longer an issue for dispute. None of our cases indicate that rulemaking *per se* is a function that may not be performed by an entity within the Judicial Branch, either because rulemaking is inherently nonjudicial or because it is a function exclusively committed to the Executive Branch. On the contrary, we specifically have held that Congress, in some circumstances, may confer rulemaking authority on the Judicial Branch....

Pursuant to this power to delegate rulemaking authority to the Judicial Branch, Congress expressly has authorized this Court to establish rules for the conduct of its own business and to prescribe rules of procedure for lower federal courts in bankruptcy cases, in other civil cases, and in criminal cases, and to revise the Federal Rules of Evidence....

Our approach to other nonadjudicatory activities that Congress has vested either in federal courts or in auxiliary bodies within the Judicial Branch has been identical to our approach to judicial rulemaking: consistent with the separation of powers, Congress may delegate to the Judicial Branch nonadjudicatory functions that do not trench upon the prerogatives of another Branch and that are appropriate to the central mission of the Judiciary.... Though not the subject of constitutional challenge, by established practice we have recognized Congress' power to create the Judicial Conference of the United States, the Rules Advisory Committees that it oversees, and the Administrative Office of the United States Courts whose myriad responsibilities include the administration of the entire probation service. These entities, some of which are comprised of judges, others of judges and nonjudges, still others of nonjudges only, do not exercise judicial power in the constitutional sense of deciding cases and controversies, but they share the common purpose of providing for the fair and efficient fulfillment of responsibilities that are properly the province of the Judiciary. Thus, although the judicial power of the United States is limited by express provision of Article III to "Cases" and "Controversies," we have never held, and have clearly disavowed in practice, that the Constitution prohibits Congress from assigning to courts or auxiliary bodies within the Judicial Branch administrative or rulemaking duties that, in the words of Chief Justice Marshall, are "necessary and proper ... for carrying into execution all the judgments which the judicial department has power to pronounce...." Because of their close relation to the central mission of the Judicial Branch, such extrajudicial activities are consonant with the integrity of the Branch and are not more appropriate for another Branch.

In light of this precedent and practice, we can discern no separation-of-powers impediment to the placement of the Sentencing Commission within the Judicial Branch. As we described at the outset, the sentencing function long has been a peculiarly shared responsibility among the Branches of Government and has never been thought of as the exclusive constitutional province of any one Branch.... That Congress should vest such rulemaking in the Judicial Branch, far from being "incongruous" or vesting within the Judiciary responsibilities that more appropriately belong to another Branch, simply acknowledges the role that the Judiciary always has played, and continues to play, in sentencing.

Given the consistent responsibility of federal judges to pronounce sentence within the statutory range established by Congress, we find that the role of the Commission in promulgating guidelines for the exercise of that judicial function bears considerable similarity to the role of this Court in establishing rules of procedure under the various enabling Acts.... Just as the rules of procedure bind judges and courts in the proper management of the cases before them, so the Guidelines bind judges and courts in the exercise of their uncontested responsibility to pass sentence in criminal cases. In other words, the Commission's functions, like this Court's function in promulgating procedural rules, are clearly attendant to a central element of the historically acknowledged mission of the Judicial Branch.

Petitioner nonetheless objects that the analogy between the Guidelines and the rules of procedure is flawed: Although the Judicial Branch may participate in rulemaking and administrative work that is "procedural" in nature, it may not assume, it is said, the "substantive" authority over sentencing policy that Congress has delegated to the Commission. Such substantive decisionmaking, petitioner contends, entangles the Judicial Branch in essentially political work of the other Branches and unites both judicial and legislative power in the Judicial Branch.

We agree with petitioner that the nature of the Commission's rulemaking power is not strictly analogous to this Court's rulemaking power under the enabling Acts. Although we are loath to enter the logical morass of distinguishing between substantive and procedural rules, and although we have recognized that the Federal Rules of Civil Procedure regulate matters "falling within the uncertain area between substance and procedure, [and] are rationally capable of classification as either," we recognize that the task of promulgating rules regulating practice and pleading before federal courts does not involve the degree of political judgment integral to the Commission's formulation of sentencing guidelines. To be sure, all rulemaking is nonjudicial in the sense that rules impose standards of general application divorced from the individual fact situation which ordinarily forms the predicate for judicial action. Also, this Court's rulemaking under the enabling Acts has been substantive and political in the sense that the rules of procedure have important effects on the substantive rights of litigants. Nonetheless, the degree of political judgment about crime and criminality exercised by the Commission and the scope of the substantive effects of its work does to some extent set its rulemaking powers apart from prior judicial rulemaking....

We do not believe, however, that the significantly political nature of the Commission's work renders unconstitutional its placement within the Judicial Branch.... In this case, the "practical consequences" of locating the Commission within the Judicial Branch pose no threat of undermining the integrity of the Judicial Branch or of expanding the powers of the Judiciary beyond constitutional bounds by uniting within the Branch the political or quasi-legislative power of the Commission with the judicial power of the courts.

First, although the Commission is located in the Judicial Branch, its powers are not united with the powers of the Judiciary in a way that has meaning for separation-of-powers analysis. Whatever constitutional problems might arise if the powers of the Commission were vested in a court, the Commission is not a court, does not exercise judicial power, and is not controlled by or accountable to members of the Judicial Branch. The Commission, on which members of the Judiciary may be a minority, is an independent agency in every relevant sense. In contrast to a court's exercising judicial power, the Commission is fully accountable to Congress, which can revoke or amend any or all of the Guidelines as it sees fit either within the 180-day waiting period, or at any time....

Second, although the Commission wields rulemaking power and not the adjudicatory power exercised by individual judges when passing sentence, the placement of the Sentencing Commission in the Judicial Branch has not increased the Branch's authority. Prior to the passage of the Act, the Judicial Branch, as an aggregate, decided precisely the questions assigned to the Commission: what sentence is appropriate to what criminal conduct under what circumstances. ... Accordingly, in placing the Commission in the Judicial Branch, Congress cannot be said to have aggrandized the authority of that Branch or to have deprived the Executive Branch of a power it once possessed. ... And, since Congress did not unconstitutionally delegate its own authority, the Act does not unconstitutionally diminish Congress' authority. Thus, although Congress has authorized the Commission to exercise a greater degree of political judgment than has been exercised in the past by any one entity within the Judicial Branch, in the unique context of sentencing, this authorization does nothing to upset the balance of power among the Branches.

What Mistretta's argument comes down to, then, is not that the substantive responsibilities of the Commission aggrandize the Judicial Branch, but that that Branch is inevitably weakened by its participation in policymaking. We do not believe, however, that the placement within the Judicial Branch of an independent agency charged with the promulgation of sentencing guidelines can possibly be construed as preventing the Judicial Branch "from accomplishing its constitutionally assigned functions...."

Nor do the Guidelines, though substantive, involve a degree of political authority inappropriate for a nonpolitical Branch. Although the Guidelines are intended to have substantive effects on public behavior (as do the rules of procedure), they do not bind or regulate the primary conduct of the public or vest in the Judicial Branch the legislative responsibility for establishing minimum and maximum penalties for every crime. They do no more than fetter the discretion of sentencing judges to do what they have done for generations – impose sentences within the broad limits established by Congress. Given their limited reach, the special role of the Judicial Branch in the field of sentencing, and the fact that the Guidelines are promulgated by an independent agency and not a court, it follows that as a matter of "practical consequences" the location of the Sentencing Commission within the Judicial Branch simply leaves with the Judiciary what long has belonged to it....

We now turn to petitioner's claim that Congress' decision to require at least three federal judges to serve on the Commission and to require those judges to share their authority with nonjudges undermines the integrity of the Judicial Branch....

Our early history indicates that the Framers themselves did not read the Constitution as forbidding extrajudicial service by federal judges....

In light of the foregoing history and precedent, we conclude that the principle of separation of powers does not absolutely prohibit Article III judges from serving on commissions such as that created by the Act. The judges serve on the Sentencing Commission not pursuant to their status and authority as Article III judges, but solely because of their appointment by the President as the Act directs. Such power as these judges wield as Commissioners is not judicial power; it is administrative power derived from the enabling legislation. Just as the nonjudicial members of the Commission act as administrators, bringing their experience and wisdom to bear on the problems of sentencing disparity, so too the judges, uniquely qualified on the subject of sentencing, assume a wholly administrative role upon entering into the deliberations of the Commission. In other words, the Constitution, at least as a *per se* matter, does not forbid judges to wear two hats; it merely forbids them to wear both hats at the same time.

This is not to suggest, of course, that every kind of extrajudicial service under every circumstance necessarily accords with the Constitution. That the Constitution does not absolutely prohibit a federal judge from assuming extrajudicial duties does not mean that every extrajudicial service would be compatible with, or appropriate to, continuing service on the bench; nor does it mean that Congress may require a federal judge to assume extrajudicial duties as long as the judge is assigned those duties in an individual, not judicial, capacity. The ultimate inquiry remains whether a particular extrajudicial assignment undermines the integrity of the Judicial Branch.

With respect to the Sentencing Commission, we understand petitioner to argue that the service required of at least three judges presents two distinct threats to the integrity of the Judicial Branch. Regardless of constitutionality, this mandatory service, it is said, diminishes the independence of the Judiciary It is further claimed that the participation of judges on the Commission improperly lends judicial prestige and an aura of judicial impartiality to the Commission's political work. The involvement of Article III judges in the process of policymaking, petitioner asserts, "'[w]eakens confidence in the disinterestedness of the judicatory functions.'..."

In our view, petitioner significantly overstates the mandatory nature of Congress' directive that at least three members of the Commission shall be federal judges, as well as the effect of this service on the practical operation of the Judicial Branch....

We are somewhat more troubled by petitioner's argument that the Judiciary's entanglement in the political work of the Commission undermines public confidence in the disinterestedness of the Judicial Branch. While the problem of individual bias is usually cured through recusal, no such mechanism can overcome the appearance of institutional partiality that may arise from judiciary involvement in the making of policy. The legitimacy of the Judicial Branch ultimately depends on its reputation for impartiality and nonpartisanship. That reputation may not be borrowed by the political Branches to cloak their work in the neutral colors of judicial action.

Although it is a judgment that is not without difficulty, we conclude that the participation of federal judges on the Sentencing Commission does not threaten, either in fact or in appearance, the impartiality of the Judicial Branch. We are drawn to this conclusion by one paramount consideration: that the Sentencing Commission is devoted exclusively to the development of rules to rationalize a process that has been and will continue to be performed exclusively by the Judicial Branch. In our view, this is an essentially neutral endeavor and one in which judicial participation is peculiarly appropriate. Judicial contribution to the enterprise of creating rules to limit the discretion of sentencing judges does not enlist the resources or reputation of the Judicial Branch in either the legislative business of determining what conduct should be criminalized or the executive business of enforcing the law. Rather, judicial participation on the Commission ensures that judicial experience and expertise will inform the promulgation of rules for the exercise of the Judicial Branch's own business, that of passing sentence on every criminal defendant. To this end, Congress has provided, not inappropriately, for a significant judicial voice on the Commission....

Finally, we reject petitioner's argument that the mixed nature of the Commission violates the Constitution by requiring Article III judges to share judicial power with nonjudges. As noted earlier, the Commission is not a court and exercises no judicial power. Thus, the Act does not vest Article III power in nonjudges or require Article III judges to share their power with nonjudges....

Mistretta argues that this power of Presidential appointment and removal prevents the Judicial Branch from performing its constitutionally assigned functions. Although we agree with petitioner that the independence of the Judicial Branch must be "jealously guarded" against outside interference, and that, as Madison admonished at the founding, "neither of [the Branches] ought to possess directly or indirectly, an overruling influence over the others in the administration of their respective powers," we do not believe that the President's appointment and removal powers over the Commission afford him influence over the functions of the Judicial Branch or undue sway over its members.

The notion that the President's power to appoint federal judges to the Commission somehow gives him influence over the Judicial Branch or prevents, even potentially, the Judicial Branch from performing its constitutionally assigned functions is fanciful. We have never considered it incompatible with the functioning of the Judicial Branch that the President has the power to elevate federal judges from one level to another or to tempt judges away from the bench with Executive Branch positions. The mere fact that the President within his appointment portfolio has positions that may be attractive to federal judges does not, of itself, corrupt the integrity of the Judiciary. Were the impartiality of the Judicial Branch so easily subverted, our constitutional system of tripartite Government would have failed long ago. We simply cannot imagine that federal judges will comport their actions to the wishes of the President for the purpose of receiving an appointment to the Sentencing Commission.

The President's removal power over Commission members poses a similarly negligible threat to judicial independence. The Act does not, and could not under the Constitution, authorize the President to remove, or in any way diminish the status of Article III judges, as judges. Even if removed from the Commission, a federal judge appointed to the Commission would continue, absent impeachment, to enjoy tenure "during good Behaviour" and a full judicial salary....

In any event, we hold here no more than that Congress may vest in the President the power to remove for good cause an Article III judge from a nonadjudicatory independent agency placed within the Judicial Branch. Because an Article III judge serving on a nonadjudicatory commission is not exercising judicial power, and because such limited removal power gives the President no control over judicatory functions, interbranch removal authority under these limited circumstances poses no threat to the balance of power among the Branches. ...

We conclude that in creating the Sentencing Commission, an unusual hybrid in structure and authority, Congress neither delegated excessive legislative power nor upset the constitutionally mandated balance of powers among the coordinate Branches. The Constitution's structural protections do not prohibit Congress from delegating to an expert body located within the Judicial Branch the intricate task of formulating sentencing guidelines consistent with such significant statutory direction as is present here. Nor does our system of checked and balanced authority prohibit Congress from calling upon the accumulated wisdom and experience of the Judicial Branch in creating policy on a matter uniquely within the ken of judges. Accordingly, we hold that the Act is constitutional.

The judgment of United States District Court for the Western District of Missouri is affirmed.

It is so ordered.

Justice SCALIA, dissenting.

While the products of the Sentencing Commission's labors have been given the modest name "Guidelines," they have the force and effect of laws, prescribing the sentences criminal defendants are to receive. A judge who disregards them will be reversed. I dissent from today's decision because I can find no place within our constitutional system for an agency created by Congress to exercise no governmental power other than the making of laws.

There is no doubt that the Sentencing Commission has established significant, legally binding prescriptions governing application of governmental power against private individuals – indeed, application of the ultimate governmental power, short of capital punishment. Statutorily permissible sentences for particular crimes cover as broad a range as zero years to life,… Average prior sentences were to be a starting point for the Commission's inquiry, but it could and regularly did deviate from those averages as it thought appropriate. It chose, for example, to prescribe substantial increases over average prior sentences for white-collar crimes such as public corruption, antitrust violations, and tax evasion….

The Commission also determined when probation was permissible, imposing a strict system of controls because of its judgment that probation had been used for an "inappropriately high percentage of offenders guilty of certain economic crimes." Moreover, the Commission had free rein in determining whether statutorily authorized fines should be imposed in addition to imprisonment, and if so, in what amounts. It ultimately decided that every nonindigent offender should pay a fine according to a schedule devised by the Commission. Congress also gave the Commission discretion to determine whether 7 specified characteristics of offenses, and 11 specified characteristics of offenders, "have any relevance," and should be included among the factors varying the sentence. Of the latter, it included only three among the factors required to be considered, and declared the remainder not ordinarily relevant. …

It should be apparent from the above that the decisions made by the Commission are far from technical, but are heavily laden (or ought to be) with value judgments and policy assessments. This fact is sharply reflected in the Commission's product, as described by the dissenting Commissioner:

> "Under the guidelines, the judge could give the same sentence for abusive sexual contact that puts the child in fear as for unlawfully entering or remaining in the United States. Similarly,

> the guidelines permit equivalent sentences for the following pairs of offenses: drug trafficking and a violation of the Wild Free-Roaming Horses and Burros Act; arson with a destructive device and failure to surrender a cancelled naturalization certificate; operation of a common carrier under the influence of drugs that causes injury and alteration of one motor vehicle identification number; illegal trafficking in explosives and trespass; interference with a flight attendant and unlawful conduct relating to contraband cigarettes; aggravated assault and smuggling $11,000 worth of fish."

Petitioner's most fundamental and far-reaching challenge to the Commission is that Congress' commitment of such broad policy responsibility to any institution is an unconstitutional delegation of legislative power. It is difficult to imagine a principle more essential to democratic government than that upon which the doctrine of unconstitutional delegation is founded: Except in a few areas constitutionally committed to the Executive Branch, the basic policy decisions governing society are to be made by the Legislature....

But while the doctrine of unconstitutional delegation is unquestionably a fundamental element of our constitutional system, it is not an element readily enforceable by the courts. Once it is conceded, as it must be, that no statute can be entirely precise, and that some judgments, even some judgments involving policy considerations, must be left to the officers executing the law and to the judges applying it, the debate over unconstitutional delegation becomes a debate not over a point of principle but over a question of degree.... Since Congress is no less endowed with common sense than we are, and better equipped to inform itself of the "necessities" of government; and since the factors bearing upon those necessities are both multifarious and (in the nonpartisan sense) highly political – including, for example, whether the Nation is at war, or whether for other reasons "emergency is instinct in the situation," – it is small wonder that we have almost never felt qualified to second-guess Congress regarding the permissible degree of policy judgment that can be left to those executing or applying the law.... What legislated standard, one must wonder, can possibly be too vague to survive judicial scrutiny, when we have repeatedly upheld, in various contexts, a "public interest" standard?...

In short, I fully agree with the Court's rejection of petitioner's contention that the doctrine of unconstitutional delegation of legislative authority has been violated because of the lack of intelligible, congressionally prescribed standards to guide the Commission.

Precisely because the scope of delegation is largely uncontrollable by the courts, we must be particularly rigorous in preserving the Constitution's structural restrictions that deter excessive delegation. The major one, it seems to me, is that the power to make law cannot be exercised by anyone other than Congress, except in conjunction with the lawful exercise of executive or judicial power.

The whole theory of *lawful* congressional "delegation" is not that Congress is sometimes too busy or too divided and can therefore assign its responsibility of making law to someone else; but rather that a certain degree of discretion, and thus of lawmaking, *inheres* in most executive or judicial action, and it is up to Congress, by the relative specificity or generality of its statutory commands, to determine, up to a point, how small or how large that degree shall be....

The focus of controversy, in the long line of our so-called excessive delegation cases, has been whether the *degree* of generality contained in the authorization for exercise of executive or judicial powers in a particular field is so unacceptably high as to *amount* to a delegation of legislative powers. I say "so-called excessive delegation" because although that convenient terminology is often used, what is really at issue is whether there has been *any* delegation of legislative power, which occurs (rarely) when Congress authorizes the exercise of executive or judicial power without adequate standards. Strictly speaking, there is *no* acceptable delegation of legislative power. As John Locke put it almost 300 years ago, "[t]he power of the *legislative* being derived from the people by a positive voluntary grant and institution, can be no other, than what the positive grant conveyed, which being only to make *laws,* and not to make *legislators,* the legislative can have no power to transfer their authority of making laws, and place it in other hands...." In the present case, however, a pure delegation of legislative power is precisely what we have before us. It is irrelevant whether the standards are adequate, because they are not standards related to the exercise of executive or judicial powers; they are, plainly and simply, standards for further legislation.

The lawmaking function of the Sentencing Commission is completely divorced from any responsibility for execution of the law or adjudication of private rights under the law. It is divorced from responsibility for execution of the law not only because the Commission is not said to be "located in the Executive Branch" (as I shall discuss presently, I doubt whether Congress can "locate" an entity within one Branch or another for constitutional purposes by merely saying so); but, more importantly, because the Commission neither exercises any executive power on its own, nor is subject to the control of the President who does. The only functions it performs, apart from prescribing the law,... conducting the investigations useful and necessary for prescribing the law,... and clarifying the intended application of the law that it prescribes,... These latter activities, similar to functions performed by congressional agencies and even congressional staff, neither determine nor affect private rights, and do not constitute an exercise of governmental power.... And the Commission's lawmaking is completely divorced from the exercise of judicial powers since, not being a court, it has no judicial powers itself, nor is it subject to the control of any other body with judicial powers. The power to make law at issue here, in other words, is not ancillary but quite naked. The situation is no different in principle from what would exist if Congress gave the same power of writing sentencing laws to a congressional agency such as the General Accounting Office, or to members of its staff.

The delegation of lawmaking authority to the Commission is, in short, unsupported by any legitimating theory to explain why it is not a delegation of legislative power. To disregard structural legitimacy is wrong in itself, but since structure has purpose, the disregard also has adverse practical consequences. In this case, as suggested earlier, the consequence is to facilitate and encourage judicially uncontrollable delegation. Until our decision last Term in *Morrison v. Olson,* it could have been said that Congress could delegate lawmaking authority only at the expense of increasing the power of either the President or the courts. Most often, as a practical matter, it would be the President, since the judicial process is unable to conduct the investigations and make the political assessments essential for most policymaking. Thus, the need for delegation would have to be important enough to induce Congress to aggrandize its primary competitor for political power, and the recipient of the policymaking authority, while not Congress itself, would at least be politically accountable. But even after it has been accepted, pursuant to *Morrison,* that those exercising executive power need not be subject to the control of the President, Congress would still be more reluctant to augment the power of even an independent executive agency than to create an otherwise powerless repository for its delegation. Moreover, assembling the full-time senior personnel for an agency exercising executive powers is more difficult than borrowing other officials (or employing new officers on a short-term basis) to head an organization such as the Sentencing Commission.

By reason of today's decision, I anticipate that Congress will find delegation of its lawmaking powers much more attractive in the future. If rulemaking can be entirely unrelated to the exercise of judicial or executive powers, I foresee all manner of "expert" bodies, insulated from the political process, to which Congress will delegate various portions of its lawmaking responsibility. How tempting to create an expert Medical Commission (mostly M.D.'s, with perhaps a few Ph.D.'s in moral philosophy) to dispose of such thorny, "no-win" political issues as the withholding of life-support systems in federally funded hospitals, or the use of fetal tissue for research. This is an undemocratic precedent that we set, not because of the scope of the delegated power, but because its recipient is not one of the three Branches of Government. The only governmental power the Commission possesses is the power to make law; and it is not the Congress.

The strange character of the body that the Court today approves, and its incompatibility with our constitutional institutions, is apparent from that portion of the Court's opinion entitled "Location of the Commission." This accepts at the outset that the Commission is a "body within the Judicial Branch," and rests some of its analysis upon that asserted reality. Separation-of-powers problems are dismissed, however, on the ground that "[the Commission's] powers are not united with the powers of the Judiciary in a way that has meaning for separation-of-powers analysis," since the Commission "is not a court, does not exercise judicial power, and is not controlled by or accountable to members of the Judicial Branch." In light of the latter concession, I am at a loss to understand why the Commission is "within the Judicial Branch" in any sense that has relevance to today's discussion. I am sure that Congress can divide up the Government any way it wishes, and employ whatever terminology it desires, for *non* constitutional purposes, for example, perhaps the statutory designation that the Commission is "within the Judicial Branch" places it outside the coverage of certain laws which say they are inapplicable to that Branch, such as the Freedom of Information Act,...

It would seem logical to decide the question of which Branch an agency belongs to on the basis of who controls its actions: If Congress, the Legislative Branch; if the President, the Executive Branch; if the courts (or perhaps the judges), the Judicial Branch. In *Humphrey's Executor v. United States* we approved the concept of an agency that was controlled by (and thus within) none of the Branches. We seem to have assumed, however, that that agency (the old Federal Trade Commission, before it acquired many of its current functions) exercised no governmental power whatever, but merely assisted Congress and the courts in the performance of their functions. Where no governmental power is at issue, there is no strict constitutional impediment to a "branchless" agency, since it is only "[a]ll legislative Powers," Art. I, § 1, "[t]he executive Power," Art. II, § 1, and "[t]he judicial Power," Art. III, § 1, which the Constitution divides into three departments. (As an example of a "branchless" agency exercising no governmental powers, one can conceive of an Advisory Commission charged with reporting to all three Branches, whose members are removable only for cause and are thus subject to the control of none of the Branches.) Over the years, however, *Humphrey's Executor* has come in general contemplation to stand for something quite different, not an "independent agency" in the sense of an agency independent of all three Branches, but an "independent agency" in the sense of an agency *within* the Executive Branch (and thus authorized to exercise executive powers) independent of the control of the President.

We approved that concept last Term in *Morrison*. I dissented in that case, essentially because I thought that concept illogical and destructive of the structure of the Constitution. I must admit, however, that today's next step - recognition of an independent agency in the *Judicial* Branch - makes *Morrison* seem, by comparison, rigorously logical. "The Commission," we are told, "is an independent agency in every relevant sense." There are several problems with this. First, once it is acknowledged that an "independent agency" may be within *any* of the three Branches, and not merely within the Executive, then there really *is* no basis for determining what Branch such an agency belongs to, and thus what governmental powers it may constitutionally be given, except (what the Court today uses) Congress' say-so. More importantly, however, the concept of an "independent agency" simply does not translate into the legislative or judicial spheres. Although the Constitution says that "[t]he executive Power shall be vested in a President of the United States of America," Art. II, § 1, it was never thought that the President would have to exercise that power *personally*. He may generally authorize others to exercise executive powers, with full effect of law, in his place. It is already a leap from the proposition that a person who is not the President may exercise executive powers to the proposition we accepted in

Morrison that a person who is *neither* the President *nor* subject to the President's control may exercise executive powers. But with respect to the exercise of judicial powers (the business of the Judicial Branch) the platform for such a leap does not even exist. For unlike executive power, judicial and legislative powers have never been thought delegable. A judge may not leave the decision to his law clerk, or to a master. Senators and Members of the House may not send delegates to consider and vote upon bills in their place. Thus, however well established may be the "independent agencies" of the Executive Branch, here we have an anomaly beyond equal: an independent agency exercising governmental power on behalf of a Branch where all governmental power is supposed to be exercised personally by the judges of courts.

Today's decision may aptly be described as the *Humphrey's Executor* of the Judicial Branch, and I think we will live to regret it. Henceforth there may be agencies "within the Judicial Branch" (whatever that means), exercising governmental powers, that are neither courts nor controlled by courts, nor even controlled by judges. If an "independent agency" such as this can be given the power to fix sentences previously exercised by district courts, I must assume that a similar agency can be given the powers to adopt rules of procedure and rules of evidence previously exercised by this Court. The bases for distinction would be thin indeed.

Today's decision follows the regrettable tendency of our recent separation-of-powers jurisprudence, to treat the Constitution as though it were no more than a generalized prescription that the functions of the Branches should not be commingled too much; how much is too much to be determined, case-by-case, by this Court. The Constitution is not that. Rather, as its name suggests, it is a prescribed structure, a framework, for the conduct of government. In designing that structure, the Framers *themselves* considered how much commingling was, in the generality of things, acceptable, and set forth their conclusions in the document. That is the meaning of the statements concerning acceptable commingling made by Madison in defense of the proposed Constitution, and now routinely used as an excuse for disregarding it. When he said, as the Court correctly quotes, that separation of powers "'d[oes] not mean that these [three] departments ought to have no *partial agency* in, or no *controul* over the acts of each other,'" his point was that the commingling specifically provided for in the structure that he and his colleagues had designed – the Presidential veto over legislation, the Senate's confirmation of executive and judicial officers, the Senate's ratification of treaties, the Congress' power to impeach and remove executive and judicial officers – did not violate a proper understanding of separation of powers. He would be aghast, I think, to hear those words used as justification for ignoring that carefully designed structure so long as, in the changing view of the Supreme Court from time to time, "too much commingling" does not occur. Consideration of the degree of commingling that a particular disposition produces may be appropriate at the margins, where the outline of the framework itself is not clear; but it seems to me far from a marginal question whether our constitutional structure allows for a body which is not the Congress, and yet exercises no governmental powers except the making of rules that have the effect of laws.

I think the Court errs, in other words, not so much because it mistakes the degree of commingling, but because it fails to recognize that this case is not about commingling, but about the creation of a new Branch altogether, a sort of junior-varsity Congress. It may well be that in some circumstances such a Branch would be desirable; perhaps the agency before us here will prove to be so. But there are many desirable dispositions that do not accord with the constitutional structure we live under. And in the long run the improvisation of a constitutional structure on the basis of currently perceived utility will be disastrous.

I respectfully dissent from the Court's decision, and would reverse the judgment of the District Court.

IMMIGRATION AND NATURALIZATION SERVICE v. CHADHA
103 S.Ct. 2764; 462 U.S. 919; 77 L.Ed. 2d 317 (1983)

Chadha was admitted to the United States on a student visa, but remained after the visa had expired. The INS initiated deportation procedures. The Attorney General, acting under authority granted by the Immigration and Nationality Act, suspended the deportation. That same law permits either House of Congress to overrule the Attorney General's suspension of deportation by a simple resolution. The House of Representatives passed a resolution vetoing the Attorney General's action and deportation proceedings against Chadha were reinstituted. Chadha challenged the constitutionality of the Act and the Court of Appeals ruled that the Act violated the doctrine of the separation of powers.

Chief Justice BURGER delivered the opinion of the Court.

...We turn now to the question whether action of one House of Congress under § 244(c)(2) violates strictures of the Constitution. We begin, of course, with the presumption that the challenged statute is valid. Its wisdom is not the concern of the courts; if a challenged action does not violate the Constitution, it must be sustained:...

By the same token, the fact that a given law or procedure is efficient, convenient, and useful in facilitating functions of government, standing alone, will not save it if it is contrary to the Constitution. Convenience and efficiency are not the primary objectives or the hallmarks of democratic government and our inquiry is sharpened rather than blunted by the fact that Congressional veto provisions are appearing with increasing frequency in statutes which delegate authority to executive and independent agencies:...

Justice WHITE undertakes to make a case for the proposition that the one-House veto is a useful "political invention,"... and we need not challenge that assertion.... But policy arguments supporting even useful "political inventions" are subject to the demands of the Constitution which defines powers and, with respect to this subject, sets out just how those powers are to be exercised.

Explicit and unambiguous provisions of the Constitution prescribe and define the respective functions of the Congress and of the Executive in the legislative process. Since the precise terms of those familiar provisions are critical to the resolution of this case, we set them out verbatim. Art. I provides:

> "All legislative Powers herein granted shall be vested in a Congress of the United States, which shall consist of a Senate *and* a House of Representatives." Art. I, § 1. (Emphasis added).
> "Every Bill which shall have passed the House of Representatives *and* the Senate, *shall,* before it becomes a Law, be presented to the President of the United States;..." Art.I, §7, cl.2. (Emphasis added).
> "*Every* Order, Resolution, or Vote to which the Concurrence of the Senate and House of Representatives may be necessary (except on a question of Adjournment) *shall be* presented to the President of the United States; and before the Same shall take Effect, *shall be* approved by him, or being disapproved by him, *shall be* repassed by two thirds of the Senate and House of Representatives, according to the Rules and Limitations prescribed in the Case of a Bill." Art.I, §7, cl.3. (Emphasis added).

These provisions of Art. I are integral parts of the constitutional design for the separation of powers. We have recently noted that "[t]he principle of separation of powers was not simply an abstract generalization in the minds of the Framers: it was woven into the documents that they drafted in Philadelphia in the summer of 1787." The very structure of the articles delegating and separating powers under Arts. I, II, and III exemplify the concept of separation of powers and we now turn to Art. I.

The records of the Constitutional Convention reveal that the requirement that all legislation be presented to the President before becoming law was uniformly accepted by the Framers....

The decision to provide the President with a limited and qualified power to nullify proposed legislation by veto was based on the profound conviction of the Framers that the powers conferred on Congress were the powers to be most carefully circumscribed. It is beyond doubt that lawmaking was a power to be shared by both Houses and the President. In *The Federalist No. 73*, Hamilton focused on the President's role in making laws:

> "If even no propensity had ever discovered itself in the legislative body to invade the rights of the Executive, the rules of just reasoning and theoretic propriety would of themselves teach us that the one ought not to be left to the mercy of the other, but ought to possess a constitutional and effectual power of self-defense."

...The President's role in the lawmaking process also reflects the Framers' careful efforts to check whatever propensity a particular Congress might have to enact oppressive, improvident, or ill-considered measures....

The bicameral requirement of Art. I, §§ 1, 7 was of scarcely less concern to the Framers than was the Presidential veto and indeed the two concepts are interdependent. By providing that no law could take effect without the concurrence of the prescribed majority of the Members of both Houses, the Framers reemphasized their belief, already remarked upon in connection with the Presentment Clauses, that legislation should not be enacted unless it has been carefully and fully considered by the Nation's elected officials....

Hamilton argued that a Congress comprised of a single House was antithetical to the very purposes of the Constitution. Were the Nation to adopt a Constitution providing for only one legislative organ, he warned:

> "we shall finally accumulate, in a single body, all the most important prerogatives of sovereignty, and thus entail upon our posterity one of the most execrable forms of government that human infatuation ever contrived. Thus we should create in reality that very tyranny which the adversaries of the new Constitution either are, or affect to be, solicitous to avert."

...It emerges clearly that the prescription for legislative action in Art. I, §§1, 7 represents the Framers' decision that the legislative power of the Federal government be exercised in accord with a single, finely wrought and exhaustively considered, procedure.

The Constitution sought to divide the delegated powers of the new federal government into three defined categories, legislative, executive and judicial, to assure, as nearly as possible, that each Branch of government would confine itself to its assigned responsibility. The hydraulic pressure inherent within each of the separate Branches to exceed the outer limits of its power, even to accomplish desirable objectives, must be resisted.

Although not "hermetically" sealed from one another,... the powers delegated to the three Branches are functionally identifiable. When any Branch acts, it is presumptively exercising the power the Constitution has delegated to it.... When the Executive acts, it presumptively acts in an executive or administrative capacity as defined in Art. II. And when, as here, one House of Congress purports to act, it is presumptively acting within its assigned sphere.

Beginning with this presumption, we must nevertheless establish that the challenged action under § 244(c)(2) is of the kind to which the procedural requirements of Art. I, § 7 apply. Not every action taken by either House is subject to the bicameralism and presentment requirements of Art. I. Whether actions taken by either House are, in law and fact, an exercise of legislative power depends not on their form but upon "whether they contain matter which is properly to be regarded as legislative in its character and effect...."

Examination of the action taken here by one House pursuant to § 244(c)(2) reveals that it was essentially legislative in purpose and effect. In purporting to exercise power defined in Art. I, § 8, cl. 4 to "establish an uniform Rule of Naturalization," the House took action that had the purpose and effect of altering the legal rights, duties and relations of persons, including the Attorney General, Executive Branch officials and Chadha, all outside the legislative branch. Section 244(c)(2) purports to authorize one House of Congress to require the Attorney General to deport an individual alien whose deportation otherwise would be cancelled under § 244. The one-House veto operated in this case to overrule the Attorney General and mandate Chadha's deportation; absent the House action, Chadha would remain in the United States. Congress has *acted* and its action has altered Chadha's status.

The legislative character of the one-House veto in this case is confirmed by the character of the Congressional action it supplants. Neither the House of Representatives nor the Senate contends that, absent the veto provision in § 244(c)(2), either of them, or both of them acting together, could effectively require the Attorney General to deport an alien once the Attorney General, in the exercise of legislatively delegated authority, had determined the alien should remain in the United States. Without the challenged provision in § 244(c)(2), this could have been achieved, if at all, only by legislation requiring deportation. Similarly, a veto by one House of Congress under § 244(c)(2) cannot be justified as an attempt at amending the standards set out in § 244(a)(1), or as a repeal of § 244 as applied to Chadha. Amendment and repeal of statutes, no less than enactment, must conform with Art. I.

The nature of the decision implemented by the one-House veto in this case further manifests its legislative character. After long experience with the clumsy, time consuming private bill procedure, Congress made a deliberate choice to delegate to the Executive Branch, and specifically to the Attorney General, the authority to allow deportable aliens to remain in this country in certain specified circumstances. It is not disputed that this choice to delegate authority is precisely the kind of decision that can be implemented only in accordance with the procedures set out in Art. I. Disagreement with the Attorney General's decision on Chadha's deportation, that is, Congress' decision to deport Chadha, no less than Congress' original choice to delegate to the Attorney General the authority to make that decision, involves determinations of policy that Congress can implement in only one way; bicameral passage followed by presentment to the President. Congress must abide by its delegation of authority until that delegation is legislatively altered or revoked.

Finally, we see that when the Framers intended to authorize either House of Congress to act alone and outside of its prescribed bicameral legislative role, they narrowly and precisely defined the procedure for such action. There are but four provisions in the Constitution, explicit and unambiguous, by which one House may act alone with the unreviewable force of law, not subject to the President's veto:...

Clearly, when the Draftsmen sought to confer special powers on one House, independent of the other House, or of the President, they did so in explicit, unambiguous terms. These carefully defined exceptions from presentment and bicameralism underscore the difference between the legislative functions of Congress and other unilateral but important and binding one-House acts provided for in the Constitution. These exceptions are narrow, explicit, and separately justified; none of them authorize the action challenged here....

Since it is clear that the action by the House under § 244(c)(2) was not within any of the express constitutional exceptions authorizing one House to act alone, and equally clear that it was an exercise of legislative power, that action was subject to the standards prescribed in Article I. The bicameral requirement, the Presentment Clauses, the President's veto, and Congress' power to override a veto were intended to erect enduring checks on each Branch and to protect the people from the improvident exercise of power by mandating certain prescribed steps. To preserve those checks, and maintain the separation of powers, the carefully defined limits on the power of each Branch must not be eroded. To accomplish what has been attempted by one House of Congress in this case requires action in conformity with the express procedures of the Constitution's prescription for legislative action: passage by a majority of both Houses and presentment to the President.

The veto authorized by § 244(c)(2) doubtless has been in many respects a convenient shortcut; the "sharing" with the Executive by Congress of its authority over aliens in this manner is, on its face, an appealing compromise. In purely practical terms, it is obviously easier for action to be taken by one House without submission to the President; but it is crystal clear from the records of the Convention, contemporaneous writings and debates, that the Framers ranked other values higher than efficiency. The records of the Convention and debates in the States preceding ratification underscore the common desire to define and limit the exercise of the newly created federal powers affecting the states and the people. There is unmistakable expression of a determination that legislation by the national Congress be a step-by-step, deliberate and deliberative process.

The choices we discern having been made in the Constitutional Convention impose burdens on governmental processes that often seem clumsy, inefficient, even unworkable, but those hard choices were consciously made by men who had lived under a form of government that permitted arbitrary governmental acts to go unchecked. There is no support in the Constitution or decisions of this Court for the proposition that the cumbersomeness and delays often encountered in complying with explicit Constitutional standards may be avoided, either by the Congress or by the President. With all the obvious flaws of delay, untidiness, and potential for abuse, we have not yet found a better way to preserve freedom than by making the exercise of power subject to the carefully crafted restraints spelled out in the Constitution.

We hold that the Congressional veto provision in § 244(c)(2) is severable from the Act and that it is unconstitutional. Accordingly, the judgment of the Court of Appeals is

Affirmed.

Justice POWELL, concurring in the judgment.

The Court's decision, based on the Presentment Clauses, Art. I, § 7, cls. 2 and 3, apparently will invalidate every use of the legislative veto. The breadth of this holding gives one pause. Congress has included the veto in literally hundreds of statutes, dating back to the 1930s. Congress clearly views this procedure as essential to controlling the delegation of power to administrative agencies. One reasonably may disagree with Congress' assessment of the veto's utility, but the respect due its judgment as a coordinate branch of Government cautions that our holding should be no more extensive than necessary to decide this case. In my view, the case may be decided on a narrower ground. When Congress finds that a particular person does not satisfy the statutory criteria for permanent residence in this country it has assumed a judicial function in violation of the principle of separation of powers. Accordingly, I concur only in the judgment....

One abuse that was prevalent during the Confederation was the exercise of judicial power by the state legislatures. The Framers were well acquainted with the danger of subjecting the determination of the rights of one person to the "tyranny of shifting majorities...."

It was to prevent the recurrence of such abuses that the Framers vested the executive, legislative, and judicial powers in separate branches. Their concern that a legislature should not be able unilaterally to impose a substantial deprivation on one person was expressed not only in this general allocation of power, but also in more specific provisions, such as the Bill of Attainder Clause, Art. I, § 9, cl. 3....

The Constitution does not establish three branches with precisely defined boundaries.... Rather, as Justice Jackson wrote, "[w]hile the Constitution diffuses power the better to secure liberty, it also contemplates that practice will integrate the dispersed powers into a workable government. It enjoins upon its branches separateness but interdependence, autonomy but reciprocity...." The Court thus has been mindful that the boundaries between each branch should be fixed "according to common sense and the inherent necessities of the governmental coordination...." But where one branch has impaired or sought to assume a power central to another branch, the Court has not hesitated to enforce the doctrine....

Functionally, the doctrine may be violated in two ways. One branch may interfere impermissibly with the other's performance of its constitutionally assigned function.... Alternatively, the doctrine may be violated when one branch assumes a function that more properly is entrusted to another.... This case presents the latter situation....

On its face, the House's action appears clearly adjudicatory. The House did not enact a general rule; rather it made its own determination that six specific persons did not comply with certain statutory criteria. It thus undertook the type of decision that traditionally has been left to other branches. Even if the House did not make a *de novo* determination, but simply reviewed the Immigration and

Naturalization Service's findings, it still assumed a function ordinarily entrusted to the federal courts....

The impropriety of the House's assumption of this function is confirmed by the fact that its action raises the very danger the Framers sought to avoid – the exercise of unchecked power. In deciding whether Chadha deserves to be deported, Congress is not subject to any internal constraints that prevent it from arbitrarily depriving him of the right to remain in this country. Unlike the judiciary or an administrative agency, Congress is not bound by established substantive rules. Nor is it subject to the procedural safeguards, such as the right to counsel and a hearing before an impartial tribunal, that are present when a court or an agency adjudicates individual rights. The only effective constraint on Congress' power is political, but Congress is most accountable politically when it prescribes rules of general applicability. When it decides rights of specific persons, those rights are subject to "the tyranny of a shifting majority."

Chief Justice Marshall observed: "It is the peculiar province of the legislature to prescribe general rules for the government of society; the application of those rules would seem to be the duty of other departments...." In my view, when Congress undertook to apply its rules to Chadha, it exceeded the scope of its constitutionally prescribed authority. I would not reach the broader question whether legislative vetoes are invalid under the Presentment Clauses.

Justice WHITE, dissenting.

Today the Court not only invalidates § 244(c)(2) of the Immigration and Nationality Act, but also sounds the death knell for nearly 200 other statutory provisions in which Congress has reserved a "legislative veto." For this reason, the Court's decision is of surpassing importance. And it is for this reason that the Court would have been well-advised to decide the case, if possible, on the narrower grounds of separation of powers, leaving for full consideration the constitutionality of other congressional review statutes operating on such varied matters as war powers and agency rulemaking, some of which concern the independent regulatory agencies.

The prominence of the legislative veto mechanism in our contemporary political system and its importance to Congress can hardly be overstated. It has become a central means by which Congress secures the accountability of executive and independent agencies. Without the legislative veto, Congress is faced with a Hobson's choice: either to refrain from delegating the necessary authority, leaving itself with a hopeless task of writing laws with the requisite specificity to cover endless special circumstances across the entire policy landscape, or in the alternative, to abdicate its law-making function to the executive branch and independent agencies. To choose the former leaves major national problems unresolved; to opt for the latter risks unaccountable policymaking by those not elected to fill that role. Accordingly, over the past five decades, the legislative veto has been placed in nearly 200 statutes. The device is known in every field of governmental concern: reorganization, budgets, foreign affairs, war powers, and regulation of trade, safety, energy, the environment and the economy....

... [T]he legislative veto ... is an important if not indispensable political invention that allows the President and Congress to resolve major constitutional and policy differences, assures the accountability of independent regulatory agencies, and preserves Congress' control over lawmaking. Perhaps there are other means of accommodation and accountability, but the increasing reliance of Congress upon the legislative veto suggests that the alternatives to which Congress must now turn are not entirely satisfactory.

The history of the legislative veto also makes clear that it has not been a sword with which Congress has struck out to aggrandize itself at the expense of the other branches the concerns of Madison and Hamilton. Rather, the veto has been a means of defense, a reservation of ultimate authority necessary if Congress is to fulfill its designated role under Article I as the nation's lawmaker. While the President has often objected to particular legislative vetoes, generally those left in the hands of congressional committees, the Executive has more often agreed to legislative review as the price for a broad delegation of authority. To be sure, the President may have preferred unrestricted power, but that could be precisely why Congress thought it essential to retain a check on the exercise of delegated authority.

For all these reasons, the apparent sweep of the Court's decision today is regrettable. The Court's Article I analysis appears to invalidate all legislative vetoes irrespective of form or subject. Because the legislative veto is commonly found as a check upon rulemaking by administrative agencies and upon broad-based policy decisions of the Executive Branch, it is particularly unfortunate that the Court reaches its decision in a case involving the exercise of a veto over deportation decisions regarding particular individuals. Courts should always be wary of striking statutes as unconstitutional; to strike an entire class of statutes based on consideration of a somewhat atypical and more-readily indictable exemplar of the class is irresponsible. It was for cases such as this one that Justice Brandeis wrote:

> "The Court has frequently called attention to the 'great gravity and delicacy' of its function in passing upon the validity of an act of Congress.... The Court will not 'formulate a rule of constitutional law broader than is required by the precise facts to which it is to be applied.'..."

Unfortunately, today's holding is not so limited....

The Court holds that the disapproval of a suspension of deportation by the resolution of one House of Congress is an exercise of legislative power without compliance with the prerequisites for lawmaking set forth in Art. I of the Constitution. Specifically, the Court maintains that the provisions of § 244(c)(2) are inconsistent with the requirement of bicameral approval, implicit in Art. I, § 1, and the requirement that all bills and resolutions that require the concurrence of both Houses be presented to the President, Art. I, § 7, cl. 2 and 3.

I do not dispute the Court's truismatic exposition of these clauses. There is no question that a bill does not become a law until it is approved by both the House and the Senate, and presented to the President. Similarly, I would not hesitate to strike an action of Congress in the form of a concurrent resolution which constituted an exercise of original lawmaking authority. I agree with the Court that the President's qualified veto power is a critical element in the distribution of powers under the Constitution, widely endorsed among the Framers, and intended to serve the President as a defense against legislative encroachment and to check the "passing of bad laws through haste, inadvertence, or design." The records of the Convention reveal that it is the first purpose which figured most prominently but I acknowledge the vitality of the second. I also agree that the bicameral approval required by Art. I, §§ 1, 7 "was of scarcely less concern to the Framers than was the Presidential veto," and that the need to divide and disperse legislative power figures significantly in our scheme of Government. All of this, the Third Part of the Court's opinion, is entirely unexceptionable.

It does not, however, answer the constitutional question before us. The power to exercise a legislative veto is not the power to write new law without bicameral approval or presidential consideration. The veto must be authorized by statute and may only negative what an Executive department or independent agency has proposed. On its face, the legislative veto no more allows one House of Congress to make law than does the presidential veto confer such power upon the President. Accordingly, the Court properly recognizes that it "must establish that the challenged action under § 244(c)(2) is of the kind to which the procedural requirements of Art. I, § 7 apply" and admits that "not every action taken by either House is subject to the bicameralism and presentation requirements of Art. I....".

... The Court's holding today that all legislative type action must be enacted through the lawmaking process ignores that legislative authority is routinely delegated to the Executive branch, to the independent regulatory agencies, and to private individuals and groups....

This Court's decisions sanctioning such delegations make clear that Article I does not require all action with the effect of legislation to be passed as a law.

Theoretically, agencies and officials were asked only to "fill up the details," and the rule was that "Congress cannot delegate any part of its legislative power except under a limitation of a prescribed standard...." Chief Justice Taft elaborated the standard in *J.W. Hampton & Co. v. United States*. "If Congress shall lay down by legislative act an intelligible principle to which the person or body authorized to fix such rates is directed to conform, such legislative action is not a forbidden delegation of legislative power." In practice, however, restrictions on the scope of the power that could be delegated diminished and all but disappeared. In only two instances did the Court find an unconstitutional delegation. *Panama Refining Co. v. Ryan*, [and] *Schechter Poultry Corp. v.*

United States. In other cases, the "intelligible principle" through which agencies have attained enormous control over the economic affairs of the country was held to include such formulations as "just and reasonable," "public interest," "public convenience, interest, or necessity," and "unfair methods of competition."

The wisdom and the constitutionality of these broad delegations are matters that still have not been put to rest. But for present purposes, these cases establish that by virtue of congressional delegation, legislative power can be exercised by independent agencies and Executive departments without the passage of new legislation. For some time, the sheer amount of law, the substantive rules that regulate private conduct and direct the operation of government, made by the agencies has far outnumbered the lawmaking engaged in by Congress through the traditional process. There is no question but that agency rulemaking is lawmaking in any functional or realistic sense of the term. The Administrative Procedure Act, 5 U.S.C. § 551(4) provides that a "rule" is an agency statement "designed to implement, interpret, or prescribe law or policy." When agencies are authorized to prescribe law through substantive rulemaking, the administrator's regulation is not only due deference, but is accorded "legislative effect." These regulations bind courts and officers of the federal government, may preempt state law, and grant rights to and impose obligations on the public. In sum, they have the force of law.

If Congress may delegate lawmaking power to independent and executive agencies, it is most difficult to understand Article I as forbidding Congress from also reserving a check on legislative power for itself. Absent the veto, the agencies receiving delegations of legislative or quasi-legislative power may issue regulations having the force of law without bicameral approval and without the President's signature. It is thus not apparent why the reservation of a veto over the exercise of that legislative power must be subject to a more exacting test. In both cases, it is enough that the initial statutory authorizations comply with the Article I requirements.

Nor are there strict limits on the agents that may receive such delegations of legislative authority so that it might be said that the legislature can delegate authority to others but not to itself. While most authority to issue rules and regulations is given to the executive branch and the independent regulatory agencies, statutory delegations to private persons have also passed this Court's scrutiny. In *Currin v. Wallace,* the statute provided that restrictions upon the production or marketing of agricultural commodities was to become effective only upon the favorable vote by a prescribed majority of the affected farmers. *United States v. Rock Royal Cooperative,* upheld an act which gave producers of specified commodities the right to veto marketing orders issued by the Secretary of Agriculture. Assuming *Currin* and *Rock Royal Cooperative* remain sound law, the Court's decision today suggests that Congress may place a "veto" power over suspensions of deportation in private hands or in the hands of an independent agency, but is forbidden from reserving such authority for itself. Perhaps this odd result could be justified on other constitutional grounds, such as the separation of powers, but certainly it cannot be defended as consistent with the Court's view of the Article I presentment and bicameralism commands.

The Court's opinion in the present case comes closest to facing the reality of administrative lawmaking in considering the contention that the Attorney General's action in suspending deportation under § 244 is itself a legislative act. The Court posits that the Attorney General is acting in an Article II enforcement capacity under § 244. This characterization is at odds with *Mahler v. Eby,* where the power conferred on the Executive to deport aliens was considered a delegation of legislative power. The Court suggests, however, that the Attorney General acts in an Article II capacity because "[t]he courts when a case or controversy arises, can always 'ascertain whether the will of Congress has been obeyed,' and can enforce adherence to statutory standards." This assumption is simply wrong, as the Court itself points out: "We are aware of no decision ... where a federal court has reviewed a decision of the Attorney General suspending deportation of an alien pursuant to the standards set out in § 244(a)(1).... On the other hand, the Court's reasoning does persuasively explain why a resolution of disapproval under § 244(c)(2) need not again be subject to the bicameral process. Because it serves only to check the Attorney General's exercise of the suspension authority granted by § 244, the disapproval resolution unlike the Attorney General's action "cannot reach beyond the limits of the statute that created it a statute duly enacted pursuant to Article I...."

I do not suggest that all legislative vetoes are necessarily consistent with separation of powers principles. A legislative check on an inherently executive function, for example that of initiating prosecutions, poses an entirely different question. But the legislative veto device here, and in many other settings, is far from an instance of legislative tyranny over the Executive. It is a necessary check on the unavoidably expanding power of the agencies, both executive and independent, as they engage in exercising authority delegated by Congress.

I regret that I am in disagreement with my colleagues on the fundamental questions that this case presents. But even more I regret the destructive scope of the Court's holding. It reflects a profoundly different conception of the Constitution than that held by the Courts which sanctioned the modern administrative state. Today's decision strikes down in one fell swoop provisions in more laws enacted by Congress than the Court has cumulatively invalidated in its history. I fear it will now be more difficult "to insure that the fundamental policy decisions in our society will be made not by an appointed official but by the body immediately responsible to the people," I must dissent.

COYLE v. SMITH
221 U.S. 559; 31 S.Ct. 688; 55 L.Ed. 853 (1911)

In 1906, Congress passed an enabling act relating to the admission of Oklahoma as a State of the Union. The act, which took the form of an "irrevocable" agreement, stipulated that the state capital should be located at Guthrie, that the capital could not be relocated before 1913 and that the state should not appropriate any "unnecessary" money for public buildings. Four years later, however, the votes of Oklahoma initiated a bill that called for the immediate relocation of the capital to Oklahoma City in violation of the enabling act. The controversy was then brought to the Supreme Court.

MR. JUSTICE BURTON delivered the opinion of the Court, saying in part:

... The only question for review by us is whether the provision of the enabling act was a valid limitation upon the power of the State after its admission, which overrides any subsequent state legislation repugnant thereto.

The power to locate its own seat of government, and to determine when and how it shall be changed from one place to another, and to appropriate its own public funds for that purpose, are essentially and peculiarly state powers. That one of the original thirteen States could now go shorn of such powers by an act of Congress would not be for a moment entertained. The question, then, comes to this: Can a State be placed upon a plane of inequality with its sister States in the Union if the Congress chooses to impose conditions which so operate, at the time of its admission? The argument is, that while Congress may not deprive a State of any power which it possesses, it may, as a condition to the admission of a new State, constitutionally restrict its authority, to the extent, at least, of suspending its powers for a definite time in respect to the location of its seat of government. This contention is predicated upon the constitutional power of admitting new States to this Union, and the constitutional duty of guaranteeing to "every State in this Union" a republican form of government. The position of counsel for the plaintiff in error is substantially this: That the power of Congress to admit new states, and to determine whether or not its fundamental law is republican in form, are political powers, and as such, uncontrollable by the courts. That Congress may, in the exercise of such power, impose terms and conditions upon the admission of the proposed new state, which, if accepted, will be obligatory, although they operate to deprive the state of powers which it would otherwise possess, and, therefore, not admitted upon 'an equal footing with the original states.'

The power of Congress in respect to the admission of new States is found in the 3rd section of the 4th article of the Constitution. That provision is that, "new states may be admitted by the Congress into this Union." The only expressed restriction upon this power is that no new State shall be formed within the jurisdiction of any other State, nor by the junction of two or more States, or parts of States, without the consent of such States, as well as of the Congress.

But what is this power? It is not to admit political organizations which are less or greater, or different in dignity or power, from those political entities which constitute the Union. It is, as strongly put by counsel, a "power to admit States."

... "This Union" was and is a union of States, equal in power, dignity, and authority, each competent to exert that residuum of sovereignty not delegated to the United States by the Constitution itself. To maintain otherwise would be to say that the Union, through the power of Congress to admit new States, might come to be a union of States unequal in power, as including States whose powers were restricted only by the Constitution, with others whose powers had been further restricted by an act of Congress accepted as a condition of admission. Thus it would result, first, that the powers of Congress would not be defined by the Constitution alone, but in respect to new States, enlarged or restricted by the conditions imposed upon new States by its own legislation admitting them into the Union; and, second, that such new States might not exercise all of the powers which had not been delegated by the Constitution, but only such as had not been further bargained away as conditions of admission.

The argument that Congress derives from the duty of "guaranteeing to each State in this Union a republican form of government," power to impose restrictions upon a new State which deprive it of equality with other members of the Union, has no merit. It may imply the duty of such new State to provide itself with such state government, and impose upon Congress the duty of seeing that such form is not changed to one anti-republican,... but it obviously does not confer power to admit a new State which shall be any less a State than those which compose the Union.

We come now to the question as to whether there is anything in the decisions of this court which sanctions the claim that Congress may, by the imposition of conditions in an enabling act, deprive a new State of any of those attributes essential to his equality in dignity and power with other States. In considering the decisions of this court bearing upon the question, we must distinguish, first, between provisions which are fulfilled by the admission of the State; second, between compacts or affirmative legislation intended to operate in futuro, which are within the scope of the conceded powers of Congress over the subject; and third, compacts or affirmative legislation which operates to restrict the powers of such new States in respect of matters which would otherwise be exclusively within the sphere of state power.

As to requirements in such enabling acts as relate only to the contents of the constitution for the proposed new State, little needs to be said. The constitutional provision concerning the admission of new States is not a mandate, but a power to be exercised with discretion. From this alone it would follow that Congress may require, under penalty of denying admission, that the organic laws of a new State at the time of admission shall be such as to meet its approval. A constitution thus supervised by Congress, would, after all, be a constitution of a State, and as such subject to alteration and amendment by the State after admission. Its force would be that of a state constitution, and not that of an act of Congress....

So far as this court has found occasion to advert to the effect of enabling acts as affirmative legislation affecting the power of new states after admission, there is to be found no sanction for the contention that any state may be deprived of any of the power constitutionally possessed by other states, as states, by reason of the terms in which the acts admitting them to the Union have been framed.

... The plain deduction from this case is that when a new state is admitted into the Union, it is so admitted with all of the powers of sovereignty and jurisdiction which pertain to the original states, and that such powers may not be constitutionally diminished, impaired, or shorn away by any conditions, compacts, or stipulations embraced in the act under which the new state came into the Union, which would not be valid and effectual if the subject of congressional legislation after admission....

It may well happen that Congress should embrace in an enactment introducing a new state into the Union legislation intended as a regulation of commerce among the states, or with Indian tribes situated within the limits of such new state, or regulations touching the sole care and disposition of the public lands or reservations therein which might be upheld as legislation within the sphere of the plain power of Congress. But in every such case such legislation would derive its force not from any agreement or compact with the proposed new state, nor by reason of its acceptance of such enactment as a term of admission, but solely because the power of Congress extended to the subject, and therefore would not operate to restrict the state's legislative power in respect of any matter which was not plainly within the regulative power of Congress....

No such question is presented here. The legislation in the Oklahoma enabling act relating to the location of the capital of the state, if construed as forbidding a removal by the state after its admission as a state, is referable to no power granted to Congress over the subject, and if it is to be upheld at all, it must be implied from the power to admit new states.

... If anything was needed to complete the argument against the assertion that Oklahoma has not been admitted to the Union upon an equality of power, dignity, and sovereignty with Massachusetts or Virginia, it is afforded by the express provision of the act of admission, by which it is declared that when the people of the proposed new state have complied with the terms of the act, that it shall be the duty of the President to issue his proclamation, and that "thereupon the proposed state of Oklahoma shall be deemed admitted by Congress into the Union under and by virtue of this act, on an equal footing with the original states." The proclamation has been issued and the Senators and Representatives from the state admitted to their seats in the Congress.

Has Oklahoma been admitted upon an equal footing with the original states? If she has, she, by virtue of her jurisdictional sovereignty as such a state, may determine for her own people the proper location of the local seat of government. She is not equal in power to them if she cannot....

To this we may add that the constitutional equality of the states is essential to the harmonious operation of the scheme upon which the Republic was organized. When that equality disappears we may remain a free people, but the Union will not be the Union of the Constitution.

Judgment affirmed.

MR. JUSTICE McKENNA and MR. JUSTICE HOLMES dissented.

CHAPTER VI

THE PRESIDENT OF THE UNITED STATES

As in the case of Congress, the Framers of the Constitution gave somewhat limited power to the President in domestic affairs when contrasted with his rather broad discretionary authority in conducting foreign policy. "The executive power," proclaims Article II, "shall be vested in a President of the United States of America." In the domestic arena, one of the prime functions of the Chief Executive is to "take care that the laws be *faithfully* executed." This apparently means more than merely enforcing the laws enacted by Congress. A President who chooses to flagrantly ignore or to actively negate the expressed intention of Congress in the form of existing law may find himself in serious trouble. The article of impeachment which received the strongest support when recommended by the House Judiciary Committee in 1974 was that citing former President Richard M. Nixon for violating the Constitution by refusing to comply with Congressional subpoenas for his tapes and by impounding funds appropriated by Congress. Indirectly, at least, the Supreme Court in a number of subsequent decisions has given support to the view of Congress in this regard, see *Train v. New York* (1975). Of particular importance is *United States v. Nixon* (1974) in which the Court held, on narrow grounds, that the President cannot withhold tapes or other evidence essential to a criminal proceeding solely on the claim of "executive privilege." The question of how much privacy or confidentiality the President has in conducting affairs of state is a matter of conjecture not dealt with specifically in the Constitution.[1] The investigations by special prosecutor Kenneth Starr of the Clinton Administration, collectively and somewhat misleadingly referred to as the "Whitewater investigation," produced a number of privacy challenges by the White House. Among the issues considered by the federal courts were whether executive privilege extends to the President's personal counsel; whether Secret Service Agents can be compelled in criminal cases to reveal what they observe while guarding the President; and whether the confidentiality of the lawyer-client privilege can be abrogated in a criminal case after the client has died.

With respect to domestic relations, the Constitution has also accorded the President some policy-making authority which, particularly in times of crisis, the Congress has either enhanced or enlarged. (This grant of additional policy discretion or "sublegislation" must not be confused with "the legislative power of the United States" which Congress can never give away.) In *Mississippi v. Johnson* (1867), the Court made the very important distinction that only the President possesses the "executive" power, not his subordinate executive officials whose duties are "ministerial." They only carry out the policies the President sanctions. Because of the Doctrine of Separated Powers, the Court cannot restrain the President from executing his functions; it can, however, enjoin his subordinates from doing so.

The President is also empowered to recommend legislation to Congress and, in fact, the great bulk of significant legislation enacted in the last sixty years has been initiated by the executive branch. He is also required to lay before Congress the unfinished business of the nation in the form of the State of the Union address. In enacting legislation, Congress may call upon the chief executive not only to execute its terms, but also to use his discretion in doing so. However, Congress may not extend the President's discretionary authority to the point of granting the Chief Executive *a line item veto*; see *Clinton v. City of New York* (1998). An additional residuum of power rests in the President's authority to issue executive orders. Such directives, the Court held in *In re. Neagle* (1890), have the force of federal law and must be complied with by executive personnel. While the President may issue an executive order on any topic that is germane to his office and powers, he cannot usurp the powers of Congress as President Truman did in his attempt to seize the nation's steel mills in *Youngstown Sheet & Tube Company v. Sawyer* (1952).

The twentieth century expansion of the federal government has produced concern over the growing power of the President. One means by which Congress has limited the power of the Chief Executive is the "legislative veto" discussed in Chapter V. Another has been the creation of bureaucratic agencies independent of presidential control. Under Article II, the President has the power to appoint executive officers and personnel, as well as the power to remove. Although Congress cannot appoint the members of a regulatory commission it has created; see *Buckley v. Valeo*, 424 U.S. 1 (1976), it can limit the President's control over the agency by eliminating his power to remove board or commission members except for specific cause as approved by Congress: see *Myers v. United States* (1926), *Humphrey's Executor (Rathbun) v. United States* (1935), and *Wiener v. United States* (1958).

Congress also cannot vest executive authority in an officer accountable and removable (except by impeachment) by Congress; see *Bowsher v. Synar* (1986). It may, however, assign the appointment of "inferior officers," exercising executive authority to officers of other branches; see *Morrison v. Olson* (1988). *Morrison* concerned the constitutionality of the special prosecutor provisions of the Ethics in Government Act of 1978, which was passed in the aftermath of the Watergate scandal. There the court ruled that the appointment by a judicial commission of a special prosecutor to investigate high level executive branch officers (including the President) was constitutional. It is Justice Scalia's dissenting opinion in that case, however, which seems to best anticipate the constitutional problems which have arisen from the ever growing use of special prosecutors during the Reagan, Bush and Clinton presidencies.

To facilitate his role as Chief of State, the Framers gave the President the authority to make proclamations, such as a national holiday or a day of mourning, and to "grant reprieves and pardons" for all federal offenses except in cases of impeachment. The latter power of clemency by the "sovereign" is an evolutionary product derived from the ancient right of English monarchs. Despite the political controversy surrounding President Ford's full pardon of Richard Nixon, the President's power to do so is complete and unfettered whether the punishment is civil or criminal in nature; see *Michaelson. v. United States* (1924) and *Ex Parte Grossman* (1925). However, since a *pardon* is a deed under which its delivery is essential, the individual to whom it is extended may either accept or reject it; see *United States v. Wilson* (1833). Few pardons have ever been rejected, but the Court has held that if the grant is not accepted the pardon is not effective; see *Burdick v. United States* (1915). The same does not apply to the President's authority to grant reprieves or commutations of sentence. While a full pardon abolishes any punishment, present or future, for the offense committed, a *reprieve* serves as a commutation or change in the sentence imposed. Since the individual would have no choice but to fulfill the original sentence, he would likewise have no discretion but to accept the reprieve; see *Biddle v. Perovich* (1927).

In the conduct of foreign policy, both the Congress and the Supreme Court have acted to amplify the power and flexibility of the President. The Constitution designates the President as Commander in Chief of the armed forces. As such, all ultimate decisions including the use of thermonuclear weapons, disposition of forces, and the use of appropriations rest with him. In addition, he appoints all of our representatives to foreign countries and, while the senate must advise and consent, only the President *negotiates* the terms of a treaty. The President *alone* receives ambassadors and other emissaries thereby "recognizing" the country whom they represent.

Indeed, it is in the area of foreign affairs that the most significant battles between the President and Congress have taken place in recent times. For years, the Supreme Court had held that, despite their own distinctive constitutional functions, *both* political branches were to share in the formulation and execution of our policy abroad; see *Chae Chan Ping v. United Slates* (1889), *Fong Yue Ting v. United States* (1893). But do they jointly participate?[2]

Because of certain actions taken by the Supreme Court (and Congress itself) the question of authoritative jurisdiction over the policy-making process has become clouded. In *United States v. Curtiss-Wright Export Corporation* (1936), the Court upheld the authority of Congress to enact a joint resolution which, in fact, shifted legislative power to the President in a specified area of foreign policy. Admitting that such a delegation would, unquestionably be *invalid* in domestic affairs, the Court justified its decision by pointing out that the President serves "as the sole organ of the federal government in the field of international relations." For example, he has absolute discretion under the Administrative Procedure Act to establish the regulations and procedures on census and voting processes affecting military personnel residing in foreign countries; see *Franklin v. Massachusetts* (1992).

Unfortunately. the Court did not address itself to the question: if Congress, the branch most representative of popular opinion, is removed from policy-making, are not the *people* as well? Although the President has traditionally initiated the process, the Constitution specifies that Congress is to declare war, supposedly with his consent. James Madison reasoned that this mechanism was to prevent any President from conducting a war without the expressed approval of Congress in the form of a declaration. No such declarations were pronounced by Congress in the instances of Korea (1950-53) or Vietnam (1964-73). President Truman committed the United States to the "police action" in Korea through the United Nations Charter and by the vote of the Security Council. Congress, twenty-eight years after the *Curtiss-Wright* decision, enacted the Gulf of Tonkin Resolution which gave President Johnson the discretion to "Americanize" the war in Vietnam. In 1973 Congress, disillusioned with our involvement in Southeast Asia and frustrated by its inability to influence foreign policy, passed the War Powers Act over the veto of President Richard Nixon.[3] That Act specified that the president could send troops into battle in only three situations: 1. after Congress had formally declared war, 2. after Congress had specifically authorized, and 3. after an attack upon the United States. If the president does commit troops to battle absent Congressional authorization, they must be withdrawn within 60 days unless a 30 day extension is granted by Congress or war is declared. The constitutionality of the War Powers Act has not yet been tested in the courts, despite the fact that Presidents Reagan, Bush and Clinton have all ordered troops into combat situations without complying with it.

Finally, the Court provided the President with a convenient method to by-pass the treaty provision of the Constitution. In *United States v. Belmont* (1937), it held that an executive agreement negotiated by the President with other heads of state would not require the advice and consent of the senate. Although, if the agreement called for an appropriation of funds or other implementary legislation, Congress would have to approve such statutory measures; see *United States v. Pink* (1942).

Countless volumes have been churned out in efforts to analyze the expansion of the office and powers of the President in this century. Throughout the 1800's the activist Presidents – Jefferson, Jackson, and Lincoln – were the *exception* rather than the rule. However, since 1900, the American people have witnessed, at times uncomfortably, an extraordinary wielding of authority by a majority of the men who have held the office. Such diverse personalities as Theodore Roosevelt, Woodrow Wilson, Franklin D. Roosevelt, Harry Truman, John F. Kennedy, Lyndon Johnson, Richard Nixon, Ronald Reagan, and George Bush have all, at one time or another, been criticized for exceeding their constitutional mandate. For good or evil, the President today is not only the chief executive of the United States but holds the singularly most important position in the world. Considering the originally modest trappings of the office as envisioned by the Framers of the Constitution, the inevitable question is what factors led to this rapid growth.

Primarily of an extraconstitutional nature, there were at least *three* developments that have occurred during the last 150 years that directly affected the nature of the presidency. First, the *shift* in national affairs from domestic concerns in the nineteenth century to foreign policy in the twentieth. Following the adoption of the Federal Constitution, the United States was a relatively small agricultural country which was continually occupied with serious problems at home: the "critical period" (1781-1789) of political and economic turmoil that followed ratification; geographic expansion beginning with the purchase of the Louisiana Territory and culminating in the push to the West under Manifest Destiny; the political instability engendered by, first French, and then British intervention in our hemispheric relations resulting in the disastrous War of 1812; the critical question of the sovereignty of the states in Union coupled with the emotional and economic issue of slavery which led to the Civil War; the "industrial revolution" and the concomitant progress and poverty it bred; the assertions of white dominance as exemplified by the Indian Wars in the latter part of the century; and the national debates on currency, international trade and the tariff and immigration. In dealing with *domestic-related matters* such as these, the Presidents of the period were noticeably *restrained* by the boundaries set by the Constitution. Few formal powers were given and, consequently, few were exercised. However, by the time of our entry into World War I, the United States was becoming a major actor on the international scene. Thereafter, despite the period of isolationism in the Roaring Twenties and the Depression Thirties, the problems we faced as a nation were decidedly international in coloration. This dramatic shift in focus automatically acted to broaden the constitutional base of Presidential power.

A second consideration was the *change* in attitude and *perception* by the American people of the role of the national government, in general, and the President, in particular. Influenced by Jefferson's concept of limited government, eighteenth century Americans faced crucial, yet simplified, problems of everyday life – food, shelter, land, and survival – which the individual could handle sufficiently without the assistance of the national government. In the sparsely populated nation of that day, local government was both in theory and in fact closer to the people. After the period of industrial expansion and massive immigration during the late 1800's, the situation changed drastically. Americans living in a highly industrialized nation, in which the growth in population in the cities far outdistanced that of rural agricultural communities, were now faced with highly complex social and economic questions which begged for resolution. The individual alone would not suffice. These difficulties could only be resolved by collective action in the form of representative government. An individual can grow crops, build a home and defend himself, however, he would be hard pressed to regulate the economy, solve the problems of inflation or depression, cure unemployment, or to insure world peace, single-handedly. Most twentieth century Americans did not fully come to this realization until the Great Depression of the 1930's. They found to their dismay that the state governments, particularly the legislatures, had fallen into disrepute and misuse. Most legislatures were either grossly ineffective or corrupted by the control of business interests or, more often than not, both. A vacuum in power thus existed which was willingly filled by a pragmatic Franklin Roosevelt and his Democratic Congress. The social services once provided by the political machines of the big cities were thereafter transferred to Washington, D.C. Something had to be done, and the people, in desperation, instinctively seemed to turn to the single leader, the President of the United States. From a historical perspective, one could argue that the development of the "single-leader" theory, in this instance, was only a product of the international trend during this period as seen in such diverse countries as Germany, Italy, and the Soviet Union.

Third and finally, the introduction of highly advanced and sophisticated technology made its own unique contribution. Modern innovations in aeronautics and communications had the effect of reducing the size of the globe, which enhanced the President's position as a world leader. The development of nuclear weapons near the end of World War II (first by the United States and later by the Soviet Union) and the perfection of nearly instantaneous delivery systems, legitimized it.

Of course, there are other factors that could be discussed, such as the personality of the individual holding the office or the effects of the institutional or bureaucratic setting; however, the aforementioned considerations provide the more obvious explanations for the President's powers as they exist today. Perhaps, Congress will act in the future to reclaim some of the authority it had earlier abdicated. In order to do so, however, Congress will have to display an amount of determination and leadership that has been lacking in that body for some time. The enactment of the War Powers Resolution of 1973, without the will and determination of Congress to enforce it, has proved to be of little value in the delicate balance within the separated powers mechanism. More recently, the same Republican majorities that proclaimed the resurgence of Congressional leadership in the "Contract with America" voted to expand the president's domestic powers through the grant of the "line item veto." It was the Court, not Congress, that determined this was an infringement on Congress' legislative authority.

UNITED STATES v. NIXON
94 S. Ct. 3090; 418 U.S. 683 (1974)

In March 1974, President Richard M. Nixon was embroiled in a legal battle with the House Judiciary committee which was investigating the advisability of his possible impeachment and which had subpoenaed certain of his White House tapes. At the same time, the federal District Court for the District of

Columbia indicted seven of his former associates for numerous offenses, including conspiracy to defraud the United States and obstruction of justice. On April 18, the District Court issued a subpoena duces tecum to the President requiring the production of certain tapes, memoranda, papers, and transcripts relating to particular conversations which the special Prosecutor, Leon Jaworski, felt were essential to the criminal proceeding to come. The President's lawyer moved to have the motion quashed on the grounds that the materials were protected under the claim of "executive privilege." The Court denied the motion and the case was brought to the Supreme Court by writ of certiorari.

MR. CHIEF JUSTICE BURGER delivered the opinion of the Court: ...

JUSTICIABILITY

In the district court, the President's counsel argued that the court lacked jurisdiction to issue the subpoena because the matter was an intra-branch dispute between a subordinate and superior officer of the executive branch and hence not subject to judicial resolution. That argument has been renewed in this Court with emphasis on the contention that the dispute does not present a "case" or "controversy" which can be adjudicated in the federal courts. The President's counsel ... views the present dispute as essentially a "jurisdictional" dispute within the executive branch which he analogizes to a dispute between two Congressional committees. Since the executive branch has exclusive authority and absolute discretion to decide whether to prosecute a case,... it is contended that a President's decision is final in determining what evidence is to be used in a given criminal case. Although his counsel concedes the President has delegated certain specific powers to the special prosecutor, he has not "waived nor delegated to the special prosecutor the President's duty to claim privilege as to all materials... which fall within the President's inherent authority to refuse to disclose to any executive officer." The special prosecutor's demand for the items therefore presents, in the view of the President's counsel, a political question under *Baker v. Carr* since it involves a "textually demonstrable" grant of power under Article II.

The mere assertion of a claim of an "intra-branch dispute," without more, has never operated to defeat federal jurisdiction, justiciability does not depend on such a surface inquiry. In *United States v. ICC* (1949) the Court observed, "courts must look behind names that symbolize the parties to determine whether a justiciable case or controversy is presented."

Our starting point is the nature of the proceeding for which the evidence is sought – here a pending criminal prosecution. It is a judicial proceeding in a federal court alleging violation of federal laws and is brought in the name of the United States as sovereign. Under the authority of Article II, section 2, Congress has vested in the attorney general the power to conduct the criminal litigation of the United States government. It has also vested in him the power to appoint subordinate officers to assist him in the discharge of his duties. Acting pursuant to those statutes, the attorney general has delegated the authority to represent the United States in these particular matters to a special prosecutor with unique authority and tenure. The regulation gives the special prosecutor explicit power to contest the invocation of executive privilege deemed relevant to the performance of these specially delegated duties.

So long as this regulation is extant it has the force of law. In *Accardi v. Shaughnessy*, (1953), regulations of the attorney general delegated certain of his discretionary powers to the Board of Immigration Appeals and required that board to exercise its own discretion on appeals in deportation cases. The Court held that so long as the attorney general's regulations remained operative, he denied himself the authority to exercise the discretion delegated to the board even though the original authority was his and he could reassert it by amending the regulations.

Here, as in *Accardi,* it is theoretically possible for the attorney general to amend or revoke the regulation defining the special prosecutor's authority. But he has not done so. So long as this regulation remains in force the executive branch is bound by it, and indeed the United States as the sovereign composed of the three branches is bound to respect and to enforce it. Moreover, the delegation of authority to the special prosecutor in this case is not an ordinary delegation by the attorney general to a subordinate officer: with the authorization of the President, the acting attorney general provided in the regulation that the special prosecutor was not to be removed without the "consensus" of eight designated leaders of Congress.

The demands of and the resistance to the subpoena present an obvious controversy in the ordinary sense, but that alone is not sufficient to meet constitutional standards. In the constitutional sense, controversy means more than disagreement and conflict; rather it means the kind of controversy courts traditionally resolve. Here at issue is the production or nonproduction of specified evidence deemed by the special prosecutor to be relevant and admissible in a pending criminal case. It is sought by one official of the government within the scope of his express authority; it is resisted by the chief executive on the ground of his duty to preserve the confidentiality of the communications of the President. Whatever the correct answer on the merits, these issues are "of a type which are traditionally justiciable." *United States v. ICC.* The independent special prosecutor with his asserted need for the subpoenaed material in the underlying criminal prosecution is opposed by the President with his steadfast assertion of privilege against disclosure of the material. This setting assures there is "that concrete adverseness which sharpens the presentation of issues upon which the court so largely depends for illumination of difficult constitutional questions." *Baker v. Carr....*

In light of the uniqueness of the setting in which the conflict arises, the fact that both parties are officers of the executive branch cannot be viewed as a barrier to justiciability. It would be inconsistent with the applicable law and regulation, and the unique facts of this case to conclude other than that the special prosecutor has standing to bring this action and that a justiciable controversy is presented for decision....

THE CLAIM OF PRIVILEGE

(A) ...[W]e turn to the claim that the subpoena should be quashed because it demands "confidential conversations between a President and his close advisors that it would be inconsistent with the public interest to produce." The first contention is a broad claim that the separation of powers doctrine precludes judicial review of a president's claim of privilege. The second contention is that if he does not prevail on the claim of absolute privilege, the court should hold as a matter of constitutional law that the privilege prevails over the subpoena *duces tecum.*

In the performance of assigned constitutional duties each branch of the government must initially interpret the Constitution, and the interpretation of its powers by any branch is due great respect from the others. The President's counsel, as we have noted, reads the Constitution as providing absolute privilege of confidentiality for all Presidential communications. Many decisions of this Court, however, have unequivocally reaffirmed the holding of *Marbury v. Madison* that "it is emphatically the province and duty of the judicial department to say what the law is. " ...

Since this Court has consistently exercised the power to construe and delineate claims arising under express powers, it must follow that the Court has authority to interpret claims with respect to powers alleged to derive from enumerated powers.

Our system of government "requires that federal courts on occasion interpret the Constitution in a manner at variance with the construction given the document by another branch." *Powell v. McCormack,...*

Notwithstanding the deference each branch must accord the others, the "judicial power of the United States" vested in the federal courts by Article III, section 1 of the Constitution can no more be shared with the executive branch than the chief executive, for example, can share with the judiciary the veto power, or the Congress share with the judiciary the power to override a Presidential veto. Any other conclusion would be contrary to the basic concept of separation of powers and the checks and balances that flow from the scheme of a tripartite government. *The Federalist, No. 47.* We therefore reaffirm that it is "emphatically the province and the duty" of this Court "to say what the law is" with respect to the claim of privilege presented in this case. *Marbury v. Madison.*

(B) In support of his claim of absolute privilege, the President's counsel urges two grounds, one of which is common to all governments and one of which is peculiar to our system of separation of powers. The first ground is the valid need for protection of communications between high government officials and those who advise and assist them in the performance of their manifold duties; the importance of this confidentiality is too plain to require further discussion. Human experience teaches that those who expect public dissemination of their remarks may well temper candor with a concern for appearances and for their own interests to the detriment of the decision-making process. Whatever the nature of the privilege of confidentiality of Presidential communications in the exercise of Article II powers, the privilege can be said to derive from the supremacy of each branch within its own assigned area of constitutional duties. Certain powers and privileges flow from the nature of enumerated powers; the protection of the confidentiality of Presidential communications has similar constitutional underpinnings.

The second ground asserted by the President's counsel in support of the claim of absolute privilege rests on the doctrine of separation of powers. Here it is argued that the independence of the executive branch within its own sphere, *Humphrey's Executor v. United States; Kilbourn v. Thompson,* 103 U.S. 168 (1880), insulates a President from a judicial subpoena in an ongoing criminal prosecution, and thereby protects confidential Presidential communications. However, neither the doctrine of separation of powers, nor the need for confidentiality of high level communications, without more, can sustain an absolute, unqualified presidential privilege of immunity from judicial process under all circumstances. The President's need for complete candor and objectivity from advisers calls for great deference from the courts.

However, when the privilege depends solely on the broad, undifferentiated claim of public interest in the confidentiality of such conversations, a confrontation with other values arises. Absent a claim of need to protect military, diplomatic or sensitive national security secrets, we find it difficult to accept the argument that even the very important interest in confidentiality of presidential communications is significantly diminished by production of such material for *in camera* inspection with all the protection that a district court will be obliged to provide.

The impediment that an absolute, unqualified privilege would place in the way of the primary constitutional duty of the judicial branch to do justice in criminal prosecutions would plainly conflict with the function of the courts under Article III. In designing the structure of our government and dividing and allocating the sovereign power among three coequal branches, the framers of the Constitution sought to provide a comprehensive system, but the separate powers were not intended to operate with absolute independence....

To read the Article II powers of the president as providing an absolute privilege as against a subpoena essential to enforcement of criminal statutes on no more than a generalized claim of the public interest in confidentiality of nonmilitary and nondiplomatic discussions would upset the constitutional balance of "a workable government" and gravely impair the role the courts under Article III.

(C) Since we conclude that the legitimate needs of the judicial process may outweigh presidential privilege, it is necessary to resolve those competing interests in a manner that preserves the essential functions of each branch. The right and indeed the duty to resolve that question does not free the judiciary from according high respect to the representations made on behalf of the President. *United States v. Burr,* (1807)....

A President and those who assist him must be free to explore alternatives in the process of shaping policies and making decisions and to do so in a way many would be unwilling to express except privately. These are the considerations justifying a presumptive privilege for presidential communications. The privilege is fundamental to the operation of government and inextricably rooted in the separation of powers under the Constitution. In *Nixon v. Sirica*, 487 F. 2d 700 (1973), the Court of Appeals held that such Presidential communications are "presumptively privileged," and this position is accepted by both parties in the present litigation. We agree with Mr. Chief Justice Marshall's observation, therefore, that "in no case of this kind would a court be required to proceed against the President as against an ordinary individual." *United States v. Burr*.

But this presumptive privilege must be considered in light of our historic commitment to the rule of law. This is nowhere more profoundly manifest than in our view that "the twofold aim [of criminal justice] is that guilt shall not escape or innocence suffer." *Berger v. United States*, (1935). We have elected to employ an adversary system of criminal justice in which the parties contest all issues before a court of law. The need to develop all relevant facts in the adversary system is both fundamental and comprehensive. The ends of criminal justice would be defeated if judgments were to be founded on a partial or speculative presentation of the facts. The very integrity of the judicial system and public confidence in the system depend on full disclosure of all the facts, within the framework of the rules of evidence. To ensure that justice is done, it is imperative to the function of courts that compulsory process be available for the production of evidence needed either by the prosecution or by the defense....

In this case the President challenges a subpoena served on him as a third party requiring the production of materials for use in a criminal prosecution on the claim that he has a privilege against disclosure of confidential communications. He does not place his claim of privilege on the ground they are military or diplomatic secrets. As to these areas of Article II duties the courts have traditionally shown the utmost deference to presidential responsibilities....

No case of the Court, however, has extended this high degree of deference to a President's generalized interest in confidentiality. Nowhere in the Constitution, as we have noted earlier, is there any explicit reference to a privilege of confidentiality, yet to the extent this interest relates to the effective discharge of a president's powers, it is constitutionally based.

The right to the production of all evidence at a criminal trial similarly has constitutional dimensions. The Sixth Amendment explicitly confers upon every defendant in a criminal trial the right "to be confronted with the witnesses against him" and "to have compulsory process for obtaining witnesses in his favor." Moreover, the Fifth Amendment also guarantees that no person shall be deprived of liberty without due process of law. It is the manifest duty of the courts to vindicate those guarantees and to accomplish that it is essential that all relevant and admissible evidence be produced.

In this case we must weigh the importance of the general privilege of confidentiality of Presidential communications in performance of his responsibilities against the inroads of such a privilege on the fair administration of criminal justice. The interest in preserving confidentiality is weighty indeed and entitled to great respect. However, we cannot conclude that advisers will be moved to temper the candor of their remarks by the infrequent occasions of disclosure because of the possibility that such conversations will be called for in the context of a criminal prosecution.

On the other hand, the allowance of the privilege to withhold evidence that is demonstrably relevant in a criminal trial would cut deeply into the guarantee of due process of law and gravely impair the basic function of the courts. A President's acknowledged need for confidentiality in the communications of his office is general in nature, whereas the constitutional need for production of relevant evidence in a criminal proceeding is specific and central to the fair adjudication of a particular criminal case in the administration of justice. Without access to specific facts a criminal prosecution may be totally frustrated. The President's broad interest in confidentiality of communications will not be vitiated by disclosure of a limited number of conversations preliminarily shown to have some bearing on the pending criminal cases.

We conclude that when the ground for asserting privilege as to subpoenaed materials sought for use in a criminal trial is based only on the generalized interest in confidentiality, it cannot prevail over the fundamental demands of due process of law in the fair administration of criminal justice. The generalized assertion of privilege must yield to the demonstrated, specific need for evidence in a pending criminal trial.

(D) We have earlier determined that the district court did not err in authorizing the issuance of the subpoena. If a President concludes that compliance with a subpoena would be injurious to the public interest he may properly, as was done here, invoke a claim of privilege on the return of the subpoena. Upon receiving a claim of privilege from the chief executive, it became the further duty of the district court to treat the subpoenaed material as presumptively privileged and to require the special prosecutor to demonstrate that the Presidential material was "essential to the justice of the [pending criminal] case." *United States v. Burr*. Here the district court treated the material as presumptively privileged, proceeded to find that the special prosecutor had made a sufficient showing to rebut the presumption and ordered an *in camera* examination of the subpoenaed material. On the basis of our examination of the record we are unable to conclude that the district court erred in ordering the inspection. Accordingly we affirm the order of the district court that subpoenaed materials be transmitted to that court....

(E) Enforcement of the subpoena *duces tecum* was stayed pending this Court's resolution of the issues raised by the petitions for *certiorari*. Those issues now having been disposed of, the matter of implementation will rest with the district court. "[T]he guard, furnished to [the President] to protect him from being harassed by vexatious and unnecessary subpoenas, is to be looked for in the conduct of the [district] court after the subpoenas have issued; not in any circumstance which is to precede their being issued." *United States v. Burr*. Statements that meet the test of admissibility and relevance must be isolated; all other material must be excised....

It is obvious that the district court has a very heavy responsibility to see to it that Presidential conversations, which are either not relevant or not admissible, are accorded that high degree of respect due the President of the United States. Mr. Chief Justice Marshall, sitting as a trial judge in the Burr case, was extraordinarily careful to point out that:

> "[I]n no case of this kind would a court be required to proceed against the President as against an ordinary individual."

Marshall's statement cannot be read to mean in any sense that a president is above the law, but relates to the singularly unique role under Article II of a president's communications and activities, related to the performance of duties under that article. Moreover, a president's communications and activities encompass a vastly wider range of sensitive material than would be true of any "ordinary individual." It is therefore necessary in the public interest to afford Presidential confidentiality the greatest protection consistent with the fair administration of justice. The need for confidentiality even as to idle conversations with associates in which casual reference might be made concerning political leaders within the country or foreign statesmen is too obvious to call for further treatment. We have no doubt that the district judge will at all times accord to Presidential records that high degree of deference suggested in *United States v. Burr*.... Once the decision is made to excise, the material is restored to its privileged status and should be returned under seal to its lawful custodian.

Since this matter came before the Court during the pendency of a criminal prosecution, and on representations that time is of the essence, the mandate shall issue forthwith.

MR. JUSTICE REHNQUIST took no part in the consideration or decision of these cases.

MISSISSIPPI v. JOHNSON
4 Wall. 475; 18 L.Ed. 437 (1867)

In 1867, the State of Mississippi made a motion to file a bill of equity pleading the Supreme Court to enjoin and restrain President Andrew Johnson from executing the Reconstruction Acts enacted by Congress in March of that year, on the grounds that they were unconstitutional. The sole question for consideration: whether the Supreme Court could prevent the President of the United States from carrying out his constitutional duties.

CHIEF JUSTICE CHASE delivered the opinion of the Court:

It is assumed by the counsel for the State of Mississippi that the President, in the execution of the Reconstruction Acts, is required to perform a mere ministerial duty. In this assumption there is, we think, a confounding of the terms ministerial and *executive*, which are by no means equivalent in import.

A *ministerial* duty, the performance of which may, in proper cases, be required of the head of a department, by judicial process, is one in respect to which nothing is left to discretion. It is a simple, definite duty, arising under conditions admitted or proved to exist, and imposed by law....

Very different is the duty of the President in the exercise of the power to see that the laws are faithfully executed, and among these laws the acts named in the bill. By the first of these acts he is required to assign generals to command in the several military districts, and to detail sufficient military force to enable such officers to discharge their duties under the law. By the supplementary act, other duties are imposed on the several commanding generals and these duties must necessarily be performed under the supervision of the President as commander-in-chief. The duty thus imposed on the President is in no just sense ministerial. It is purely *executive* and political.

An attempt on the part of the judicial department of the government to enforce the performance of such duties by the President might be justly characterized, in the language of Chief Justice Marshall, as "an absurd and excessive extravagance."

It is true that in the instance before us the interposition of the court is not sought to enforce action by the Executive under constitutional legislation, but to restrain such action under legislation alleged to be unconstitutional. But we are unable to perceive that this circumstance takes the case out of the general principles which forbid judicial interference with the exercise of Executive discretion.

It was admitted in the argument that the application now made to us is without a precedent; and this is of much weight against it.

Had it been supposed at the bar that this court would, in any case, interpose by injunction to prevent the execution of an unconstitutional act of Congress, it can hardly be doubted that applications with that object would have been heretofore addressed to it....

It will hardly be contended that Congress (the Courts?) can interpose, in any case, to restrain the enactment of an unconstitutional law; and yet how can the right to judicial interposition to prevent such an enactment, when the purpose is evident and the execution of that purpose certain, be distinguished in principle from the right to such interposition against the execution of such a law by the President?

The Congress is the legislative department of the government; the President is the executive department. Neither can be restrained in its action by the judicial department; though the acts of both, when performed, are, in proper cases, subject to its cognizance....

It has been suggested that the bill contains a prayer that, if the relief sought cannot be had against Andrew Johnson as President, it may be granted against Andrew Johnson as a citizen of Tennessee. But it is plain that relief as against the execution of an act of Congress by Andrew Johnson, is relief against its execution by the President. A bill praying an injunction against the execution of an act of

Congress by the incumbent of the Presidential office cannot be received, whether it describes him as President or as a citizen of a State.

The motion for leave to file the bill is, therefore,
Denied.

WIENER v. UNITED STATES
357 U.S. 349; 78 S.Ct. 1275; 2 L.Ed. 2d 1377 (1958)

In 1948, Congress established the War Claims Commission to adjudicate claims relating to personal injury or damage of property suffered during World War II. The Commission was to be composed of three persons appointed by the President with the advice and consent of the Senate. No stipulation was made with respect to the removal of a commission member.

Two years later, President Truman nominated Myron Wiener, who with the consent of the Senate was named to the Commission. On December 10, 1953, with a new Republican administration in power, Wiener was removed by President Dwight Eisenhower. However, before the new commissioner was approved by the Senate, the Commission was abolished. Wiener then brought suit for back pay, but the U.S. Court of Claims dismissed the case. The Supreme Court granted certiorari.

MR. JUSTICE FRANKFURTER delivered the opinion of the Court, saying in part:

... This is another instance in which the most appropriate legal significance must be drawn from Congressional failure of explicitness. Necessarily this is a problem in probabilities. We start with one certainty. The problem of the President's power to remove members of agencies entrusted with duties of the kind with which the War Claims Commission was charged was within the lively knowledge of Congress. Few contests between Congress and the President have so recurringly had the attention of Congress as that pertaining to the power of removal. Not the least significant aspect of the *Myers* case (1926) is that on the Court's special invitation Senator George Wharton Pepper, of Pennsylvania, presented the position of Congress at the bar of this Court.

Humphrey's case (1935) was a cause célèbre – and not least in the halls of Congress. And what is the essence of the decision in *Humphrey's* case? It drew a sharp line of cleavage between officials who were part of the Executive establishment and were thus removable by virtue of the President's constitutional powers, and those who are members of a body "to exercise its judgment without the leave or hindrance of any other official or any department of the government," as to whom a power of removal exists only if Congress may fairly be said to have conferred it. This sharp differentiation derives from the difference in functions between those who are part of the Executive establishment and those whose tasks require absolute freedom from Executive interference. "For it is quite evident," again to quote *Humphrey's Executor*, "that one who holds his office only during the pleasure of another, cannot be depended upon to maintain an attitude of independence against the latter's will."

Thus, the most reliable factor for drawing an inference regarding the President's power of removal in our case is the nature of the function that Congress vested in the War Claims Commission. What were the duties that Congress confided to this Commission? And can the inference fairly be drawn from the failure of Congress to provide for removal that these Commissioners were to remain in office at the will of the President? For such is the assertion of power on which petitioner's removal must rest. The ground of President Eisenhower's removal of petitioner was precisely the same as President Roosevelt's removal of Humphrey. Both Presidents desired to have Commissioners, one on the Federal Trade Commission, the other on the War Claims Commission, "of my own selection." They wanted these Commissioners to be their men. The terms of removal in the two cases are identical and express the assumption that the agencies of which the two Commissioners were members were subject in the discharge of their duties to the control of the Executive. An analysis of the Federal Trade Commission Act left this Court in no doubt that such was not the conception of Congress in creating the Federal Trade Commission. The terms of the War Claims Act of 1948 leave no doubt that such was not the conception of Congress regarding the War Claims Commission.

The history of this legislation emphatically underlies this fact. The short of it is that the origin of the act was a bill... passed by the House that placed the administration of a very limited class of claims by Americans against Japan in the hands of the Federal Security Administrator and provided for a Commission to inquire into and report upon other types of claims.... The Federal Security Administrator was indubitably an arm of the President. When the House bill reached the Senate, it struck out all but the enacting clause, rewrote the bill, and established a Commission with "jurisdiction to receive and adjudicate according to law" three classes of claims, as defined by §§5, 6 and 7. The Commission was established as an adjudicating body with all the paraphernalia by which legal claims are put to the test of proof, with finality of determination "not subject to review by any other official of the United States or by any court, by mandamus or otherwise." Awards were to be paid out of a War Claims Fund in the hands of the Secretary of the Treasury, whereby such claims were given even more assured collectability than adheres to judgments rendered in the Court of Claims....

...Congress could, of course, have given jurisdiction over these claims to the District Courts and to the Court of Claims. The fact that it chose to establish a Commission to "adjudicate according to law" the classes of claims defined in the statute did not alter the intrinsic judicial character of the task with which the Commission was charged. The claims were to be "adjudicated according to law," that is, on the merits of each claim, supported by evidence and governing legal considerations, by a body that was "entirely free from the control of coercive influence, direct or indirect," *Humphrey's Exr. v. United States*, of either the Executive or the Congress. If, as one must take for granted, the War Claims Act precluded the President from influencing the Commission in passing on a particular claim, *a fortiori* must it be inferred that Congress did not wish to have hang over the Commission the Damocles' sword of removal by the President for no reason other than that he preferred to have on that Commission men of his own choosing.

For such is this case. We have not a removal for cause involving the rectitude of a member of an adjudicatory body, nor even a suspensory removal until the Senate could act upon it by confirming the appointment of a new Commissioner or otherwise dealing with the matter. Judging the matter in all the nakedness in which it is presented, namely, the claim that the President could remove a member of an adjudicatory body like the War Claims Commission merely because he wanted his own appointees on such a Commission, we are compelled to conclude that no such power is given to the President directly by the Constitution, and none is impliedly conferred upon him by statute simply because Congress said nothing about it. The philosophy of *Humphrey's Executor*, in its explicit language as well as its implications, precludes such a claim.

The judgment is
Reversed.

MORRISON v. OLSON
108 S.Ct. 2597; 487 U.S. 654; 101 L.Ed.2d 569 (1988)

Following the Watergate scandal, Congress passed the Ethics in Government Act of 1978 which provided for the appointment of an independent counsel to investigate allegations of wrongdoing by high-ranking members of the executive branch, including the president. The House Judiciary Committee issued a report suggesting that Olson and other officials of the Justice Department had given false testimony and withheld documents during an earlier House investigation of the Environmental Protection Agency and requested the Attorney General to request appointment of a special prosecutor to investigate the allegations. Subsequently, and at the request of the Attorney General, Morrison was appointed independent counsel by the Special Division (the special court created by the Ethics in Government Act) with authority to investigate Olson, but not others. Later, the Special Division ruled that the grant of authority was broad enough to cover investigation of others with whom Olson may have conspired, and Morrison then issued grand jury subpoenas to Olson and other officials of the Justice Department. The latter moved to quash the subpoenas on the grounds that the independent counsel provisions were unconstitutional. The District Court upheld the law, but the Court of Appeals reversed and found the Ethics in Government Act unconstitutional.

Chief Justice REHNQUIST delivered the opinion of the Court.

This case presents us with a challenge to the independent counsel provisions of the Ethics in Government Act of 1978, 28 U.S.C. §§ 49, 591 *et seq.* (1982 ed., Supp. V). We hold today that these provisions of the Act do not violate the Appointments Clause of the Constitution, Art. II, § 2, cl. 2, or the limitations of Article III, nor do they impermissibly interfere with the President's authority under Article II in violation of the constitutional principle of separation of powers....

III

The Appointments Clause of Article II reads as follows:

> "[The President] shall nominate, and by and with the Advice and Consent of the Senate, shall appoint Ambassadors, other public Ministers and Consuls, Judges of the Supreme Court, and all other Officers of the United States, whose Appointments are not herein otherwise provided for, and which shall be established by Law: but the Congress may by Law vest the Appointment of such inferior Officers, as they think proper, in the President alone, in the Courts of Law, or in the Heads of Departments." U.S. Const., Art. II, § 2, cl. 2."

The parties do not dispute that "[t]he Constitution for purposes of appointment ... divides all its officers into two classes...." "[P]rincipal officers are selected by the President with the advice and consent of the Senate. Inferior officers Congress may allow to be appointed by the President alone, by the heads of departments, or by the Judiciary." The initial question is, accordingly, whether appellant is an "inferior" or a "principal" officer. If she is the latter, as the Court of Appeals concluded, then the Act is in violation of the Appointments Clause.

The line between "inferior" and "principal" officers is one that is far from clear, and the Framers provided little guidance into where it should be drawn.... We need not attempt here to decide exactly where the line falls between the two types of officers, because in our view appellant clearly falls on the "inferior officer" side of that line. Several factors lead to this conclusion.

First, appellant is subject to removal by a higher Executive Branch official. Although appellant may not be "subordinate" to the Attorney General (and the President) insofar as she possesses a degree of independent discretion to exercise the powers delegated to her under the Act, the fact that she can be removed by the Attorney General indicates that she is to some degree "inferior" in rank and authority. Second, appellant is empowered by the Act to perform only certain, limited duties. An independent counsel's role is restricted primarily to investigation and, if appropriate, prosecution for certain federal crimes. Admittedly, the Act delegates to appellant "full power and independent authority to exercise all investigative and prosecutorial functions and powers of the Department of Justice," § 594(a), but this grant of authority does not include any authority to formulate policy for the Government or the Executive Branch, nor does it give appellant any administrative duties outside of those necessary to operate her office....

Third, appellant's office is limited in jurisdiction. Not only is the Act itself restricted in applicability to certain federal officials suspected of certain serious federal crimes, but an independent counsel can only act within the scope of the jurisdiction that has been granted by the Special Division pursuant to a request by the Attorney General. Finally, appellant's office is limited in tenure. There is concededly no time limit on the appointment of a particular counsel. Nonetheless, the office of independent counsel is "temporary" in the sense that an independent counsel is appointed essentially to accomplish a single task, and when that task is over the office is terminated, either by the counsel herself or by action of the Special Division...

This does not, however, end our inquiry under the Appointments Clause. Appellees argue that even if appellant is an "inferior" officer, the Clause does not empower Congress to place the power to appoint such an officer outside the Executive Branch. They contend that the Clause does not contemplate congressional authorization of "interbranch appointments," in which an officer of one branch is appointed by officers of another branch. The relevant language of the Appointments Clause is worth repeating. It reads: "... but the Congress may by Law vest the Appointment of such inferior Officers, as they think proper, in the President alone, in the courts of Law, or in the Heads of Departments." On its face, the language of this "excepting clause" admits of no limitation on interbranch appointments. Indeed, the inclusion of "as they think proper" seems clearly to give Congress significant discretion to determine whether it is "proper" to vest the appointment of, for example, executive officials in the "courts of Law...."

We do not mean to say that Congress' power to provide for interbranch appointments of "inferior officers" is unlimited. In addition to separation-of-powers concerns, which would arise if such provisions for appointment had the potential to impair the constitutional functions assigned to one of the branches, *Siebold* itself suggested that Congress' decision to vest the appointment power in the courts would be improper if there was some "incongruity" between the functions normally performed by the courts and the performance of their duty to appoint.... In this case, however, we do not think it impermissible for Congress to vest the power to appoint independent counsel in a specially created federal court. We thus disagree with the Court of Appeals' conclusion that there is an inherent incongruity about a court having the power to appoint prosecutorial officers.... Congress, of course, was concerned when it created the office of independent counsel with the conflicts of interest that could arise in situations when the Executive Branch is called upon to investigate its own high-ranking officers. If it were to remove the appointing authority from the Executive Branch, the most logical place to put it was in the Judicial Branch. In the light of the Act's provision making the judges of the Special Division ineligible to participate in any matters relating to an independent counsel they have appointed,... we do not think that appointment of the independent counsel by the court runs afoul of the constitutional limitation on "incongruous" interbranch appointments.

IV

Appellees next contend that the powers vested in the Special Division by the Act conflict with Article III of the Constitution. We have long recognized that by the express provision of Article III, the judicial power of the United States is limited to "Cases" and "Controversies...." As a general rule, we have broadly stated that "executive or administrative duties of a nonjudicial nature may not be imposed on judges holding office under Art. III of the Constitution...." The purpose of this limitation is to help ensure the independence of the Judicial Branch and to prevent the Judiciary from encroaching into areas reserved for the other branches....

Most importantly, the Act vests in the Special Division the power to choose who will serve as independent counsel and the power to define his or her jurisdiction. Clearly, once it is accepted that the Appointments Clause gives Congress the power to vest the appointment of officials such as the independent counsel in the "courts of Law," there can be no Article III objection to the Special Division's exercise of that power, as the power itself derives from the Appointments Clause, a source of authority for judicial action that is independent of Article III. Appellees contend, however, that the Division's Appointments Clause powers do not encompass the power to define the independent counsel's jurisdiction. We disagree. In our view, Congress' power under the Clause to vest the "Appointment" of inferior officers in the courts may, in certain circumstances, allow Congress to give the courts some discretion in defining the nature and scope of the appointed official's authority. Particularly when, as here, Congress creates a temporary "office" the nature and duties of which will by necessity vary with the factual circumstances giving rise to the need for an appointment in the first place, it may vest the power to define the scope of the office in the court as an incident to the appointment of the officer pursuant to the Appointments Clause. This said, we do not think that Congress may give the Division *unlimited* discretion to determine the independent counsel's jurisdiction. In order for the Division's definition of the counsel's jurisdiction to be truly "incidental" to its power to appoint, the jurisdiction that the court decides upon must be demonstrably related to the factual circumstances that gave rise to the Attorney General's investigation and request for the appointment of the independent counsel in the particular case.

The Act also vests in the Special Division various powers and duties in relation to the independent counsel that, because they do not involve appointing the counsel or defining his or her jurisdiction, cannot be said to derive from the Division's Appointments Clause authority. These duties include granting extensions for the Attorney General's preliminary investigation...; receiving the report of the Attorney General at the conclusion of his preliminary investigation...; referring matters to the counsel upon request...; receiving reports from the counsel regarding expenses incurred...; receiving a report from the Attorney General following the removal of an independent counsel...; granting attorney's fees upon request to individuals who were investigated but not indicted by an independent counsel; receiving a final report from the counsel...; deciding whether to release the counsel's final report to Congress or the public and determining whether any protective orders should be issued...; and terminating an independent counsel when his or her task is completed....

Leaving aside for the moment the Division's power to terminate an independent counsel, we do not think that Article III absolutely prevents Congress from vesting these other miscellaneous powers in the Special Division pursuant to the Act. As we observed above, one purpose of the broad prohibition upon the courts' exercise of "executive or administrative duties of a nonjudicial nature," ...is to maintain the separation between the Judiciary and the other branches of the Federal Government by ensuring that judges do not encroach upon executive or legislative authority or undertake tasks that are more properly accomplished by those branches. In this case, the miscellaneous powers described above do not impermissibly trespass upon the authority of the Executive Branch. Some of these allegedly "supervisory" powers conferred on the court are passive: the Division merely "receives" reports from the counsel or the Attorney General, it is not entitled to act on them or to specifically approve or disapprove of their contents. Other provisions of the Act do require the court to exercise some judgment and discretion, but the powers granted by these provisions are themselves essentially ministerial. The Act simply does not give the Division the power to "supervise" the independent counsel in the exercise of his or her investigative or prosecutorial authority....

We are more doubtful about the Special Division's power to terminate the office of the independent counsel.... As appellees suggest, the power to terminate, especially when exercised by the Division on its own motion, is "administrative" to the extent that it requires the Special Division to monitor the progress of proceedings of the independent counsel and come to a decision as to whether the counsel's job is "completed...." It also is not a power that could be considered typically "judicial," as it has few analogues among the court's more traditional powers. Nonetheless, we do not, as did the Court of Appeals, view this provision as a significant judicial encroachment upon executive power or upon the prosecutorial discretion of the independent counsel.

We think that the Court of Appeals overstated the matter when it described the power to terminate as a "broadsword and ... rapier" that enables the court to "control the pace and depth of the independent counsel's activities...." The termination provisions of the Act do not give the Special Division anything approaching the power to *remove* the counsel while an investigation or court proceeding is still underway; this power is vested solely in the Attorney General. As we see it, "termination" may occur only when the duties of the counsel are truly "completed" or "so substantially completed" that there remains no need for any continuing action by the independent counsel. It is basically a device for removing from the public payroll an independent counsel who has served his or her purpose, but is unwilling to acknowledge the fact. So construed, the Special Division's power to terminate does not pose a sufficient threat of judicial intrusion into matters that are more properly within the Executive's authority to require that the Act be invalidated as inconsistent with Article III.

Nor do we believe, as appellees contend, that the Special Division's exercise of the various powers specifically granted to it under the Act poses any threat to the "impartial and independent federal adjudication of claims within the judicial power of the United States...." We reach this conclusion for two reasons. First, the Act as it currently stands gives the Special Division itself no power to review any of the actions of the independent counsel or any of the actions of the Attorney General with regard to the counsel. Accordingly, there is no risk of partisan or biased adjudication of claims regarding the independent counsel by that court. Second, the Act prevents members of the Special Division from participating in "*any* judicial proceeding concerning a matter which involves such independent counsel while such independent counsel is serving in that office or which involves the exercise of such independent counsel's official duties, regardless of whether such independent counsel is still serving in that office...." We think both the special court and its judges are sufficiently isolated by these statutory provisions from the review of the activities of the independent counsel so as to avoid any taint of the independence of the Judiciary such as would render the Act invalid under Article III.

We emphasize, nevertheless, that the Special Division has *no* authority to take any action or undertake any duties that are not specifically authorized by the Act. The gradual expansion of the authority of the Special Division might in another context be a bureaucratic success story, but it would be one that would have serious constitutional ramifications. The record in other cases involving independent counsel indicate that the Special Division has at times given advisory opinions or issued orders that are not directly authorized by the Act. Two examples of this were cited by the Court of Appeals, which noted that the Special Division issued "orders" that ostensibly exempted the independent counsel from conflict-of-interest laws.... In another case, the Division reportedly ordered that a counsel postpone an investigation into certain allegations until the completion of related state criminal proceedings.... The propriety of the Special Division's actions in these instances is not before us as such, but we nonetheless think it appropriate to point out not only that there is no authorization for such actions in the Act itself, but that the Division's exercise of unauthorized powers risks the transgression of the constitutional limitations of Article III that we have just discussed.

V

We now turn to consider whether the Act is invalid under the constitutional principle of separation of powers. Two related issues must be addressed: The first is whether the provision of the Act restricting the Attorney General's power to remove the independent counsel to only those instances in which he can show "good cause," taken by itself, impermissibly interferes with the President's exercise of his constitutionally appointed functions. The second is whether, taken as a whole, the Act violates the separation of powers by reducing the President's ability to control the prosecutorial powers wielded by the independent counsel.

A

Two Terms ago we had occasion to consider whether it was consistent with the separation of powers for Congress to pass a statute that authorized a Government official who is removable only by Congress to participate in what we found to be "executive powers...." We held in *Bowsher* that "Congress cannot reserve for itself the power of removal of an officer charged with the execution of the laws except by impeachment...." A primary antecedent for this ruling was our 1926 decision in *Myers v. United States*.... *Myers* had considered the propriety of a federal statute by which certain postmasters of the United States could be removed by the President only "by and with the advice and consent of the Senate." There too, Congress' attempt to involve itself in the removal of an executive official was found to be sufficient grounds to render the statute invalid. As we observed in *Bowsher*, the essence of the decision in *Myers* was the judgment that the Constitution prevents Congress from "draw[ing] to itself ... the power to remove or the right to participate in the exercise of that power. To do this would be to go beyond the words and implications of the [Appointments Clause] and to infringe the constitutional principle of the separation of governmental powers...."

Unlike both *Bowsher* and *Myers*, this case does not involve an attempt by Congress itself to gain a role in the removal of executive officials other than its established powers of impeachment and conviction. The Act instead puts the removal power squarely in the hands of the Executive Branch; an independent counsel may be removed from office, "only by the personal action of the Attorney General, and only for good cause." There is no requirement of congressional approval of the Attorney General's removal decision, though the decision is subject to judicial review. In our view, the removal provisions of the Act make this case more analogous to *Humphrey's Executor v. United States*....

Appellees contend that *Humphrey's Executor* and *Wiener* are distinguishable from this case because they did not involve officials who performed a "core executive function." They argue that our decision in *Humphrey's Executor* rests on a distinction between "purely executive" officials and officials who exercise "quasi-legislative" and "quasi-judicial" powers. In their view, when a "purely executive" official is involved, the governing precedent is *Myers*, not *Humphrey's Executor*.... And, under *Myers*, the President must have absolute discretion to discharge "purely" executive officials at will....

We undoubtedly did rely on the terms "quasi-legislative" and "quasi-judicial" to distinguish the officials involved in *Humphrey's Executor* and *Wiener* from those in *Myers*, but our present considered view is that the determination of whether the Constitution allows Congress to impose a "good cause"-type restriction on the President's power to remove an official cannot be made to turn on whether or not that official is classified as "purely executive." The analysis contained in our removal cases is designed not to define rigid categories of those officials who may or may not be removed at will by the President, but to ensure that Congress does not interfere with the President's exercise of the "executive power" and his constitutionally appointed duty to "take care that the laws be faithfully executed" under Article II. *Myers* was undoubtedly correct in its holding, and in its broader suggestion that there are some "purely executive" officials who must be removable by the President at will if he is to be able to accomplish his constitutional role.... But as the Court noted in *Wiener:*

> "The assumption was short-lived that the *Myers* case recognized the President's inherent constitutional power to remove officials no matter what the relation of the executive to the discharge of their duties and no matter what restrictions Congress may have imposed regarding the nature of their tenure."

At the other end of the spectrum from *Myers,* the characterization of the agencies in *Humphrey's Executor* and *Wiener* as "quasi-legislative" or "quasi-judicial" in large part reflected our judgment that it was not essential to the President's proper execution of his Article II powers that these agencies be headed up by individuals who were removable at will. We do not mean to suggest that an analysis of the functions served by the officials at issue is irrelevant. But the real question is whether the removal restrictions are of such a nature that they impede the President's ability to perform his constitutional duty, and the functions of the officials in question must be analyzed in that light.

Considering for the moment the "good cause" removal provision in isolation from the other parts of the Act at issue in this case, we cannot say that the imposition of a "good cause" standard for removal by itself unduly trammels on executive authority. There is no real dispute that the functions performed by the independent counsel are "executive" in the sense that they are law enforcement functions that typically have been undertaken by officials within the Executive Branch. As we noted above, however, the independent counsel is an inferior officer under the Appointments Clause, with limited jurisdiction and tenure and lacking policy making or significant administrative authority. Although the counsel exercises no small amount of discretion and judgment in deciding how to carry out his or her duties under the Act, we simply do not see how the President's need to control the exercise of that discretion is so central to the functioning of the Executive Branch as to require as a matter of constitutional law that the counsel be terminable at will by the President.

Nor do we think that the "good cause" removal provision at issue here impermissibly burdens the President's power to control or supervise the independent counsel, as an executive official, in the execution of his or her duties under the Act. This is not a case in which the power to remove an executive official has been completely stripped from the President, thus providing no means for the President to ensure the "faithful execution" of the laws. Rather, because the independent counsel may be terminated for "good cause," the Executive, through the Attorney General, retains ample authority to assure that the counsel is competently performing his or her statutory responsibilities in a manner that comports with the provisions of the Act. Although we need not decide in this case exactly what is encompassed within the term "good cause" under the Act, the legislative history of the removal provision also makes clear that the Attorney General may remove an independent counsel for "misconduct...." Here, as with the provision of the Act conferring the appointment authority of the independent counsel on the special court, the congressional determination to limit the removal power of the Attorney General was essential, in the view of Congress, to establish the necessary independence of the office. We do not think that this limitation as it presently stands sufficiently deprives the President of control over the independent counsel to interfere impermissibly with his constitutional obligation to ensure the faithful execution of the laws.

B.

The final question to be addressed is whether the Act, taken as a whole, violates the principle of separation of powers by unduly interfering with the role of the Executive Branch. Time and again we have reaffirmed the importance in our constitutional scheme of the separation of governmental powers into the three coordinate branches.... As we stated in *Buckley v. Valeo,*... the system of separated powers and checks and balances established in the Constitution was regarded by the Framers as "a self-executing safeguard against the encroachment or aggrandizement of one branch at the expense of the other." We have not hesitated to invalidate provisions of law which violate this principle. On the other hand, we have never held that the Constitution requires that the three branches of Government "operate with absolute independence...."

We observe first that this case does not involve an attempt by Congress to increase its own powers at the expense of the Executive Branch.... Unlike some of our previous cases, most recently *Bowsher v. Synar,* this case simply does not pose a "dange[r] of congressional usurpation of Executive Branch functions.... Indeed, with the exception of the power of impeachment, which applies to all officers of the United States, Congress retained for itself no powers of control or supervision over an independent counsel. The Act does empower certain Members of Congress to request the Attorney General to apply for the appointment of an independent counsel, but the Attorney General has no duty to comply with the request, although he must respond within a certain time limit. Other than that, Congress' role under the Act is limited to receiving reports or other information and oversight of the independent counsel's activities, functions that we have recognized generally as being incidental to the legislative function of Congress....

Similarly, we do not think that the Act works any *judicial* usurpation of properly executive functions. As should be apparent from our discussion of the Appointments Clause above, the power to appoint inferior officers such as independent counsel is not in itself an "executive" function in the constitutional sense, at least when Congress has exercised its power to vest the appointment of an inferior office in the "courts of Law." We note nonetheless that under the Act the Special Division has no power to appoint an independent counsel *sua sponte;* it may only do so upon the specific request of the Attorney General, and the courts are specifically prevented from reviewing the Attorney General's decision not to seek appointment. In addition, once the court has appointed a counsel and defined his or her jurisdiction, it has no power to supervise or control the activities of the counsel. As we pointed out in our discussion of the Special Division in relation to

Article III, the various powers delegated by the statute to the Division are not supervisory or administrative, nor are they functions that the Constitution requires be performed by officials within the Executive Branch. The Act does give a federal court the power to review the Attorney General's decision to remove an independent counsel, but in our view this is a function that is well within the traditional power of the Judiciary.

Finally, we do not think that the Act "impermissibly undermine[s]" the powers of the Executive Branch, or "disrupts the proper balance between the coordinate branches [by] prevent[ing] the Executive Branch from accomplishing its constitutionally assigned functions," *Nixon v. Administrator of General Services*. It is undeniable that the Act reduces the amount of control or supervision that the Attorney General and, through him, the President exercises over the investigation and prosecution of a certain class of alleged criminal activity. The Attorney General is not allowed to appoint the individual of his choice; he does not determine the counsel's jurisdiction; and his power to remove a counsel is limited. Nonetheless, the Act does give the Attorney General several means of supervising or controlling the prosecutorial powers that may be wielded by an independent counsel. Most importantly, the Attorney General retains the power to remove the counsel for "good cause," a power that we have already concluded provides the Executive with substantial ability to ensure that the laws are "faithfully executed" by an independent counsel. No independent counsel may be appointed without a specific request by the Attorney General, and the Attorney General's decision not to request appointment if he finds "no reasonable grounds to believe that further investigation is warranted" is committed to his unreviewable discretion. The Act thus gives the Executive a degree of control over the power to initiate an investigation by the independent counsel. In addition, the jurisdiction of the independent counsel is defined with reference to the facts submitted by the Attorney General, and once a counsel is appointed, the Act requires that the counsel abide by Justice Department policy unless it is not "possible" to do so. Notwithstanding the fact that the counsel is to some degree "independent" and free from executive supervision to a greater extent than other federal prosecutors, in our view these features of the Act give the Executive Branch sufficient control over the independent counsel to ensure that the President is able to perform his constitutionally assigned duties.

VI

In sum, we conclude today that it does not violate the Appointments Clause for Congress to vest the appointment of independent counsel in the Special Division; that the powers exercised by the Special Division under the Act do not violate Article III; and that the Act does not violate the separation-of-powers principle by impermissibly interfering with the functions of the Executive Branch. The decision of the Court of Appeals is therefore

Reversed.

Justice KENNEDY took no part in the consideration or decision of this case.

Justice SCALIA, dissenting.

...The principle of separation of powers is expressed in our Constitution in the first section of each of the first three Articles. Article I, §1, provides that "[a]ll legislative Powers herein granted shall be vested in a Congress of the United States, which shall consist of a Senate and House of Representatives." Article III, § 1, provides that "[t]he judicial Power of the United States, shall be vested in one supreme Court, and in such inferior Courts as the Congress may from time to time ordain and establish." And the provision at issue here, Art. II, § 1, cl. 1, provides that "[t]he executive Power shall be vested in a President of the United States of America."

But just as the mere words of a Bill of Rights are not self-effectuating, the Framers recognized "[t]he insufficiency of a mere parchment delineation of the boundaries" to achieve the separation of powers. "[T]he great security," wrote Madison, "against a gradual concentration of the several powers in the same department consists in giving to those who administer each department the necessary constitutional means and personal motives to resist encroachments of the others. The provision for defense must in this, as in all other cases, be made commensurate to the danger of attack." ... Madison continued:

> "But it is not possible to give to each department an equal power of self-defense. In , republican government, the legislative authority necessarily predominates. The remedy for this inconveniency is to divide the legislature into different branches; and to render them, by different modes of election and different principles of action, as little connected with each other as the nature of their common functions and their common dependence on the society will admit.... As the weight of the legislative authority requires that it should be thus divided, the weakness of the executive may require, on the other hand, that it should be fortified...."

The major "fortification" provided, of course, was the veto power. But in addition to providing fortification, the Founders conspicuously and very consciously declined to sap the Executive's strength in the same way they had weakened the Legislature: by dividing the executive power. Proposals to have multiple executives, or a council of advisers with separate authority were rejected....

That is what this suit is about. Power. The allocation of power among Congress, the President, and the courts in such fashion as to preserve the equilibrium the Constitution sought to establish, so that "a gradual concentration of the several powers in the same department," can effectively be resisted. Frequently an issue of this sort will come before the Court clad, so to speak, in sheep's clothing: the potential of the asserted principle to effect important change in the equilibrium of power is not immediately evident, and must be discerned by a careful and perceptive analysis. But this wolf comes as a wolf.

I

The present case began when the Legislative and Executive Branches became "embroiled in a dispute concerning the scope of the congressional investigatory power, which, as is often the case with such interbranch conflicts, became quite acrimonious....

As a general matter, the Act before us here requires the Attorney General to apply for the appointment of an independent counsel within 90 days after receiving a request to do so, unless he determines within that period that "there are no reasonable grounds to believe that further investigation or prosecution is warranted." As a practical matter, it would be surprising if the Attorney General had any choice (assuming this statute is constitutional) but to seek appointment of an independent counsel to pursue the charges against the principal object of the congressional request, Mr. Olson. Merely the political consequences (to him and the President) of seeming to break the law by refusing to do so would have been substantial. How could it not be, the public would ask, that a 3,000-page indictment drawn by our representatives over 21/2 years does not even establish "reasonable grounds to believe" that further investigation or prosecution is warranted with respect to at least the principal alleged culprit? But the Act establishes more than just practical compulsion. Although the Court's opinion asserts that the Attorney General had "no duty to comply with the [congressional] request," that is not entirely accurate. He *had* a duty to comply unless he could conclude that there were "*no reasonable grounds to believe,*" not that prosecution was warranted, but merely that "*further investigation* " was warranted, (emphasis added), after a 90-day investigation in which he was prohibited from using such routine investigative techniques as grand juries, plea bargaining, grants of immunity, or even subpoenas. The Court also makes much of the fact that "the courts are specifically prevented from reviewing the Attorney General's decision not to seek appointment. Yes, but *Congress* is not prevented from reviewing it. The context of this statute is acrid with the smell of threatened impeachment. Where, as here, a request for appointment of an independent counsel has come from the Judiciary Committee of either House of Congress, the Attorney General must, if he decides not to seek appointment, explain to that Committee why....

Thus, by the application of this statute in the present case, Congress has effectively compelled a criminal investigation of a high-level appointee of the President in connection with his actions arising out of a bitter power dispute between the President and the Legislative Branch. Mr. Olson may or may not be guilty of a crime; we do not know. But we do know that the investigation of him has been commenced, not necessarily because the President or his authorized subordinates believe it is in the interest of the United States, in the sense that it warrants the diversion of resources from other efforts, and is worth the cost in money and in possible damage to other governmental interests; and not even, leaving aside those normally considered factors, because the President or his authorized subordinates necessarily believe that an investigation is likely to unearth a violation worth prosecuting; but only because the Attorney General cannot affirm, as Congress demands, that there are *no reasonable grounds to believe* that further investigation is warranted. The decisions regarding the scope of that further investigation, its duration, and, finally, whether or not prosecution should ensue, are likewise beyond the control of the President and his subordinates.

II

If to describe this case is not to decide it, the concept of a government of separate and coordinate powers no longer has meaning. The Court devotes most of its attention to such relatively technical details as the Appointments Clause and the removal power, addressing briefly and only at the end of its opinion the separation of powers. As my prologue suggests, I think that has it backwards. Our opinions are full of the recognition that it is the principle of separation of powers, and the inseparable corollary that each department's "defense must ... be made commensurate to the danger of attack,"... which gives comprehensible content to the Appointments Clause, and determines the appropriate scope of the removal power. Thus, while I will subsequently discuss why our appointments and removal jurisprudence does not support today's holding, I begin with a consideration of the fountainhead of that jurisprudence, the separation and equilibration of powers.

First, however, I think it well to call to mind an important and unusual premise that underlies our deliberations, a premise not expressly contradicted by the Court's opinion, but in my view not faithfully observed. It is rare in a case dealing, as this one does, with the constitutionality of a statute passed by the Congress of the United States, not to find anywhere in the Court's opinion the usual, almost formulary caution that we owe great deference to Congress' view that what it has done is constitutional,... and that we will decline to apply the statute only if the presumption of constitutionality can be overcome,...That caution is not recited by the Court in the present case *because it does not apply.* Where a private citizen challenges action of the Government on grounds unrelated to separation of powers, harmonious functioning of the system demands that we ordinarily give some deference, or a presumption of validity, to the actions of the political branches in what is agreed, between themselves at least, to be within their respective spheres. But where the issue pertains to separation of powers, and the political branches are (as here) in disagreement, neither can be presumed correct. The reason is stated concisely by Madison: "The several departments being perfectly co-ordinate by the terms of their common commission, neither of them, it is evident, can pretend to an exclusive or superior right of settling the boundaries between their respective powers...." The playing field for the present case, in other words, is a level one. As one of the interested and coordinate parties to the underlying constitutional dispute, Congress, no more than the President, is entitled to the benefit of the doubt.

To repeat, Article II, § 1, cl. 1, of the Constitution provides:

"The executive Power shall be vested in a President of the United States."

As I described at the outset of this opinion, this does not mean *some of* the executive power, but *all of* the executive power. It seems to me, therefore, that the decision of the Court of Appeals invalidating the present statute must be upheld on fundamental separation-of-powers principles if the following two questions are answered affirmatively: (1) Is the conduct of a criminal prosecution (and of an investigation to decide whether to prosecute) the exercise of purely executive power? (2) Does the statute deprive the President of the United States of exclusive control over the exercise of that power? Surprising to say, the Court appears to concede an affirmative answer to both questions, but seeks to avoid the inevitable conclusion that since the statute vests some purely executive power in a person who is not the President of the United States it is void.

The Court concedes that "[t]here is no real dispute that the functions performed by the independent counsel are 'executive'," though it qualifies that concession by adding "in the sense that they are law enforcement functions that typically have been undertaken by officials within the Executive Branch. The qualifier adds nothing but atmosphere. In what *other* sense can one identify "the executive Power" that is supposed to be vested in the President (unless it includes everything the Executive Branch is given to do) *except* by reference to what has always and everywhere, if conducted by government at all, been conducted never by the legislature, never by the courts, and always by the executive. There is no possible doubt that the independent counsel's functions fit this description. She is vested with the "full power and independent authority to exercise all *investigative and prosecutorial* functions and powers of the Department of Justice [and] the Attorney General." (emphasis added). Governmental investigation and prosecution of crimes is a quintessentially executive function....

As for the second question, whether the statute before us deprives the President of exclusive control over that quintessentially executive activity: The Court does not, and could not possibly, assert that it does not. That is indeed the whole object of the statute. Instead, the Court points out that the President, through his Attorney General, has at least *some* control. That concession is alone enough to invalidate the statute, but I cannot refrain from pointing out that the Court greatly exaggerates the extent of that "some" Presidential control. "Most importan[t]" among these controls, the Court asserts, is the Attorney General's "power to remove the counsel for 'good cause.' " This is somewhat like referring to shackles as an effective means of locomotion.... What we in *Humphrey's Executor* found to be a means of eliminating Presidential control, the Court today considers the "most importan[t]" means of assuring Presidential control. Congress, of course, operated under no such illusion when it enacted this statute, describing the "good cause" limitation as "protecting the independent counsel's ability to act independently of the President's direct control" since it permits removal only for "misconduct...."

Moving on to the presumably "less important" controls that the President retains, the Court notes that no independent counsel may be appointed without a specific request from the Attorney General. As I have discussed above, the condition that renders such a request mandatory (inability to find "no reasonable grounds to believe" that further investigation is warranted) is so insubstantial that the Attorney General's discretion is severely confined. And once the referral is made, it is for the Special Division to determine the scope and duration of the investigation. And in any event, the limited power over referral is irrelevant to the question whether, *once appointed,* the independent counsel exercises executive power free from the President's control. Finally, the Court points out that the Act directs the independent counsel to abide by general Justice Department policy, except when not "possible...." The exception alone shows this to be an empty promise. Even without that, however, one would be hard put to come up with many investigative or prosecutorial "policies" (other than those imposed by the Constitution or by Congress through law) that are absolute. Almost all investigative and prosecutorial decisions including the ultimate decision whether, after a technical violation of the law has been found, prosecution is warranted, involve the balancing of innumerable legal and practical considerations. Indeed, even political considerations (in the nonpartisan sense) must be considered, as exemplified by the recent decision of an independent counsel to subpoena the former Ambassador of Canada, producing considerable tension in our relations with that country.... Another pre-eminently political decision is whether getting a conviction in a particular case is worth the disclosure of national security information that would be necessary. The Justice Department and our intelligence agencies are often in disagreement on this point, and the Justice Department does not always win. The present Act even goes so far as specifically to take the resolution of that dispute away from the President and give it to the independent counsel.... In sum, the balancing of various legal, practical, and political considerations, none of which is absolute, is the very essence of prosecutorial discretion. To take this away is to remove the core of the prosecutorial function, and not merely "some" Presidential control....

It effects a revolution in our constitutional jurisprudence for the Court, once it has determined that (1) purely executive functions are at issue here, and (2) those functions have been given to a person whose actions are not fully within the supervision and control of the President, nonetheless to proceed further to sit in judgment of whether "the President's need to control the exercise of [the independent counsel's] discretion is *so central* to the functioning of the Executive Branch" as to require complete control, (emphasis added), whether the conferral of his powers upon someone else "*sufficiently* deprives the President of control over the independent counsel to interfere impermissibly with [his] constitutional obligation to ensure the faithful execution of the laws," (emphasis added), and whether "the Act give[s] the Executive Branch *sufficient* control over the independent counsel to ensure that the President is able to perform his constitutionally assigned duties," (emphasis added). It is not for us to determine, and we have never presumed to determine, how much of the purely executive powers of government must be within the full control of the President. The Constitution prescribes that they *all* are....

Is it unthinkable that the President should have such exclusive power, even when alleged crimes by him or his close associates are at issue? No more so than that Congress should have the exclusive power of legislation, even when what is at issue is its own exemption from the burdens of certain laws.... No more so than that this Court should have the exclusive power to pronounce the final decision on justiciable cases and controversies, even those pertaining to the constitutionality of a statute reducing the salaries of the Justices.... While the separation of powers may prevent us from righting every wrong, it does so in order to ensure that we do not lose liberty. The checks against any branch's abuse of its exclusive powers are twofold: First, retaliation by one of the other branch's use of *its* exclusive powers: Congress, for example, can impeach the executive who willfully fails to enforce the laws; the executive can decline to prosecute under unconstitutional statutes,...and the courts can dismiss malicious prosecutions. Second, and ultimately, there is the political check that the people will replace those in the political branches... who are guilty of abuse....

The Court has, nonetheless, replaced the clear constitutional prescription that the executive power belongs to the President with a "balancing test." What are the standards to determine how the balance is to be struck, that is, how much removal of Presidential power is too much? Many countries of the world get along with an executive that is much weaker than ours, in fact, entirely dependent upon the continued support of the legislature. Once we depart from the text of the Constitution, just where short of that do we stop? The most amazing feature of the Court's opinion is that it does not even purport to give an answer. It simply *announces,* with no analysis, that the ability to control the decision whether to investigate and prosecute the President's closest advisers, and indeed the President himself, is not "so central to the functioning of the Executive Branch" as to be constitutionally required to be within the President's control. Apparently that is so because we say it is so. Having abandoned as the basis for our decision-making the text of Article II that "the executive Power" must be vested in the President, the Court does not even attempt to craft a *substitute* criterion, a "justiciable standard," ...however remote from the Constitution, that today governs, and in the future will govern, the decision of such questions. Evidently, the governing standard is to be what might be called the unfettered wisdom of a majority of this Court, revealed to an obedient people on a case-by-case basis. This is not only not the government of laws that the Constitution established; it is not a government of laws at all....

Perhaps the boldness of the President himself will not be affected, though I am not even sure of that. (How much easier it is for Congress, instead of accepting the political damage attendant to the commencement of impeachment proceedings against the President on trivial grounds – or, for that matter, how easy it is for one of the President's political foes outside of Congress – simply to trigger a debilitating criminal investigation of the Chief Executive under this law.) But as for the President's high-level assistants, who typically have no political base of support, it is as utterly unrealistic to think that they will not be intimidated by this prospect, and that their advice to him and their advocacy of his interests before a hostile Congress will not be affected, as it would be to think that the Members of Congress and their staffs would be unaffected by replacing the

Speech or Debate Clause with a similar provision. It deeply wounds the President, by substantially reducing the President's ability to protect himself and his staff. That is the whole object of the law, of course, and I cannot imagine why the Court believes it does not succeed.

Besides weakening the Presidency by reducing the zeal of his staff, it must also be obvious that the institution of the independent counsel enfeebles him more directly in his constant confrontations with Congress, by eroding his public support. Nothing is so politically effective as the ability to charge that one's opponent and his associates are not merely wrongheaded, naive, ineffective, but, in all probability, "crooks." And nothing so effectively gives an appearance of validity to such charges as a Justice Department investigation and, even better, prosecution.... Thus, in the 10 years since the institution of the independent counsel was established by law, there have been nine highly publicized investigations, a source of constant political damage to two administrations....

III

As I indicated earlier, the basic separation-of-powers principles I have discussed are what give life and content to our jurisprudence concerning the President's power to appoint and remove officers. The same result of unconstitutionality is therefore plainly indicated by our case law in these areas....

Because appellant (who all parties and the Court agree is an officer of the United States,...) was not appointed by the President with the advice and consent of the Senate, but rather by the Special Division of the United States Court of Appeals, her appointment is constitutional only if (1) she is an "inferior" officer within the meaning of the above Clause, and (2) Congress may vest her appointment in a court of law.

As to the first of these inquiries, the Court does not attempt to "decide exactly" what establishes the line between principal and "inferior" officers, but is confident that, whatever the line may be, appellant "clearly falls on the 'inferior officer' side" of it.... The Court gives three reasons: *First,* she "is subject to removal by a higher Executive Branch official," namely, the Attorney General. *Second,* she is "empowered by the Act to perform only certain, limited duties...." *Third,* her office is "limited in jurisdiction" and "limited in tenure...."

The first of these lends no support to the view that appellant is an inferior officer.... I fail to see how the fact that appellant is more difficult to remove than most principal officers helps to establish that she is an inferior officer....

The second reason offered by the Court – that appellant performs only certain, limited duties – may be relevant to whether she is an inferior officer, but it mischaracterizes the extent of her powers. As the Court states: "Admittedly, the Act delegates to appellant [the] '*full power and independent authority to exercise all investigative and prosecutorial functions and powers of the Department of Justice.*'..." (emphasis added)

The Court seeks to brush this away by asserting that the independent counsel's power does not include any authority to "formulate policy for the Government or the Executive Branch." But the same could be said for all officers of the Government, with the single exception of the President. All of them only formulate policy within their respective spheres of responsibility – as does the independent counsel, who must comply with the policies of the Department of Justice only to the extent possible. ....

The final set of reasons given by the Court for why the independent counsel clearly is an inferior officer emphasizes the limited nature of her jurisdiction and tenure. Taking the latter first, I find nothing unusually limited about the independent counsel's tenure. To the contrary, unlike most high-ranking Executive Branch officials, she continues to serve until she (or the Special Division) decides that her work is substantially completed.... As to the scope of her jurisdiction, there can be no doubt that is small (though far from unimportant). But within it she exercises more than the full power of the Attorney General.... I think it preferable to look to the text of the Constitution and the division of power that it establishes. These demonstrate, I think, that the independent counsel is not an inferior officer because she is not *subordinate* to any officer in the Executive Branch (indeed, not even to the President). ...

That "inferior" means "subordinate" is also consistent with what little we know about the evolution of the Appointments Clause....

IV

Today, however, *Humphrey's Executor* is swept into the dustbin of repudiated constitutional principles. "[O]ur present considered view," the Court says, "is that the determination of whether the Constitution allows Congress to impose a 'good cause'-type restriction on the President's power to remove an official cannot be made to turn on whether or not that official is classified as 'purely executive.' " What *Humphrey's Executor* (and presumably *Myers*) really means, we are now told, is not that there are any "rigid categories of those officials who may or may not be removed at will by the President," but simply that Congress cannot "interefere with the President's exercise of the 'executive power' and his constitutionally appointed duty to 'take care that the laws be faithfully executed,'..."

One can hardly grieve for the shoddy treatment given today to *Humphrey's Executor,* which, after all, accorded the same indignity (with much less justification) to Chief Justice Taft's opinion 10 years earlier in *Myers v. United States*, – gutting, in six quick pages devoid of textual or historical precedent for the novel principle it set forth, a carefully researched and reasoned 70-page opinion. It is in fact comforting to witness the reality that he who lives by the *ipse dixit* dies by the *ipse dixit.* But one must grieve for the Constitution. *Humphrey's Executor* at least had the decency formally to observe the constitutional principle that the President had to be the repository of *all* executive power, which, as *Myers* carefully explained, necessarily means that he must be able to discharge those who do not perform executive functions according to his liking.... By contrast, "our present considered view" is simply that *any* executive officer's removal can be restricted, so long as the President remains "able to accomplish his constitutional role...." There are now no lines. If the removal of a prosecutor, the virtual embodiment of the power to "take care that the laws be faithfully executed," can be restricted, what officer's removal cannot? This is an open invitation for Congress to experiment. What about a special Assistant Secretary of State, with responsibility for one very narrow area of foreign policy, who would not only have to be confirmed by the Senate but could also be removed only pursuant to certain carefully designed restrictions? Could this possibly render the President "[un]able to accomplish his constitutional role"? Or a special Assistant Secretary of Defense for Procurement? The possibilities are endless, and the Court does not understand what the separation of powers, what "[a]mbition ... counteract[ing] ambition," is all about, if it does not expect Congress to try them. As far as I can discern from the Court's opinion, it is now open season upon the President's removal power for all executive officers, with not even the superficially principled restriction of *Humphrey's Executor* as cover. The Court essentially says to the President: "Trust us. We will make sure that you are able to accomplish your constitutional role." I think the Constitution gives the President, and the people, more protection than that....

V

Under our system of government, the primary check against prosecutorial abuse is a political one. The prosecutors who exercise this awesome discretion are selected and can be removed by a President, whom the people have trusted enough to elect. Moreover, when crimes are not investigated and prosecuted fairly, nonselectively, with a reasonable sense of proportion, the President pays the cost in political damage to his administration. If federal prosecutors "pick people that [they] thin[k] [they] should get, rather than cases that need to be prosecuted," if they amass many more resources against a particular prominent individual, or against a particular class of political protesters, or against members of a particular political party, than the gravity of the alleged offenses or the record of successful prosecutions seems to warrant, the unfairness will come home to roost in the Oval Office. I leave it to the reader to recall the examples of this in recent years. That result, of course, was precisely what the Founders had in mind when they provided that all executive powers would be exercised by a *single* Chief Executive. As Hamilton put it, "[t]he ingredients which constitute safety in the republican sense are a due dependence on the people, and a due responsibility." The President is directly dependent on the people, and since there is only *one* President, *he* is responsible. The people know whom to blame, whereas "one of the weightiest objections to a plurality in the executive ... is that it tends to conceal faults and destroy responsibility...."

That is the system of justice the rest of us are entitled to, but what of that select class consisting of present or former high-level Executive Branch officials?... An independent counsel is selected, and the scope of his or her authority prescribed, by a panel of judges. What if they are politically partisan, as judges have been known to be, and select a prosecutor antagonistic to the administration, or even to the particular individual who has been selected for this special treatment? There is no remedy for that, not even a political one. Judges, after all, have life tenure, and appointing a surefire enthusiastic prosecutor could hardly be considered an impeachable offense.... One thing is certain, however: it involves investigating and perhaps prosecuting a particular individual. Can one imagine a less equitable manner of fulfilling the executive responsibility to investigate and prosecute? What would be the reaction if, in an area not covered by this statute, the Justice Department posted a public notice inviting applicants to assist in an investigation and possible prosecution of a certain prominent person?... To be sure, the investigation must relate to the area of criminal offense specified by the life-tenured judges. But that has often been (and nothing prevents it from being) very broad – and should the independent counsel or his or her staff come up with something beyond that scope, nothing prevents him or her from asking the judges to expand his or her authority or, if that does not work, referring it to the Attorney General, whereupon the whole process would recommence and, if there was "reasonable basis to believe" that further investigation was warranted, that new offense would be referred to the Special Division, which would in all likelihood assign it to the same independent counsel. It seems to me not conducive to fairness. But even if it were entirely evident that unfairness was in fact the result – the judges hostile to the administration, the independent counsel an old foe of the President, the staff refugees from the recently defeated administration – *there would be no one accountable to the public to whom the blame could be assigned....*

...[A}n additional advantage of the unitary Executive that it can achieve a more uniform application of the law. Perhaps that is not always achieved, but the mechanism to achieve it is there. The mini-Executive that is the independent counsel, however, operating in an area where so little is law and so much is discretion, is intentionally cut off from the unifying influence of the Justice Department, and from the perspective that multiple responsibilities provide. What would normally be regarded as a technical violation (there are no rules defining such things), may in his or her small world assume the proportions of an indictable offense. What would normally be regarded as an investigation that has reached the level of pursuing such picayune matters that it should be concluded, may to him or her be an investigation that ought to go on for another year. How frightening it must be to have your own independent counsel and staff appointed, with nothing else to do but to investigate you until investigation is no longer worthwhile – with whether it is worthwhile not depending upon what such judgments usually hinge on, competing responsibilities. And to have that counsel and staff decide, with no basis for comparison, whether what you have done is bad enough, willful enough, and provable enough, to warrant an indictment. How admirable the constitutional system that provides the means to avoid such a distortion. And how unfortunate the judicial decision that has permitted it....

* * *

...By its shortsighted action today, I fear the Court has permanently encumbered the Republic with an institution that will do it great harm.

Worse than what it has done, however, is the manner in which it has done it. A government of laws means a government of rules. Today's decision on the basic issue of fragmentation of executive power is ungoverned by rule, and hence ungoverned by law. It extends into the very heart of our most significant constitutional function the "totality of the circumstances" mode of analysis that this Court has in recent years become fond of. Taking all things into account, we conclude that the power taken away from the President here is not really *too* much. The next time executive power is assigned to someone other than the President we may conclude, taking all things into account, that it *is* too much. That opinion, like this one, will not be confined by any rule. We will describe, as we have today (though I hope more accurately) the effects of the provision in question, and will authoritatively announce: "The President's need to control the exercise of the [subject officer's] discretion *is* so central to the functioning of the Executive Branch as to require complete control." This is not analysis; it is ad hoc judgment. And it fails to explain why it is not true that – as the text of the Constitution seems to require, as the Founders seemed to expect, and as our past cases have uniformly assumed – all purely executive power must be under the control of the President.

The ad hoc approach to constitutional adjudication has real attraction, even apart from its work-saving potential. It is guaranteed to produce a result, in every case, that will make a majority of the Court happy with the law. The law is, by definition, precisely what the majority thinks, taking all things into account, it *ought* to be. I prefer to rely upon the judgment of the wise men who constructed our system, and of the people who approved it, and of two centuries of history that have shown it to be sound. Like it or not, that judgment says, quite plainly, that "[t]he executive Power shall be vested in a President of the United States."

IN RE NEAGLE
135 U.S. 1; 10 S.Ct. 658; 34 L.Ed. 55 (1890)

Mr. Justice Field was serving as Circuit Justice in the Circuit Court in California when a disturbing incident occurred. After the determination of a particular case, one Mrs. Terry accused Field of "selling" justice and was immediately warned to remain quiet. Thereupon a fight took place and Mrs. Terry and her husband were cited for contempt. Sentenced to six months of confinement, Mrs. Terry swore to kill Justice Field if he should ever return to the state.

Sometime later Justice Field returned to California and, considering the threats made on his life, President Benjamin Harrison issued an executive order to provide him the protection of a United States Marshal. The bodyguard, Neagle, in carrying out his assignment shot and killed Mr. Terry after the latter threatened and assaulted Field in a railroad restaurant. Subsequently, Neagle was arrested by local authorities for murder; however, he was released by a writ of habeas corpus issued by the Circuit Court on the grounds that he was complying with an executive order and as such was pursuing the "law of the United States."

MR. JUSTICE MILLER delivered the opinion of the Court, saying in part:

...Without a more minute discussion of this testimony, it produces upon us the conviction of a settled purpose on the part of Terry and his wife, amounting to a conspiracy, to murder Justice Field. And we are quite sure that if Neagle had been merely a brother or a friend of Judge Field, traveling with him, and aware of all the previous relations of Terry to the judge – as he was – of his bitter animosity, his declared purpose to have revenge even to the point of killing him, he would have been justified in what he did in defense of Mr. Justice Field's life, and possibly of his own.

But such a justification would be a proper subject for consideration on a trial of the case for murder in the courts of the State of California, and there exists no authority in the courts of the United States to discharge the prisoner while held in custody by the state authorities for this offense, unless there be found in aid of the defense of the prisoner some element of power and authority asserted under the government of the United States.

This element is said to be found in the facts that Mr. Justice Field, when attacked, was in the immediate discharge of his duty as judge of the Circuit Courts of the United States within California; that the assault upon him grew out of the animosity of Terry and wife, arising out of the previous discharge of his duty as Circuit Justice in the case for which they were committed for contempt of court; and that the deputy marshal of the United States, who killed Terry in defense of Field's life, was charged with a duty under the law of the United States to protect Field from the violence which Terry was inflicting, and which was intended to lead to Field's death.

To the inquiry whether this proposition is sustained by law and the facts which we have recited, we now address ourselves....

We have no doubt that Mr. Justice Field when attacked by Terry was engaged in the discharge of his duties as Circuit Justice of the Ninth Circuit, and was entitled to all the protection under those circumstances which the law could give him.

It is urged, however, that there exists no statute authorizing any such protection as that which Neagle was instructed to give Judge Field in the present case, and indeed no protection whatever against a vindictive or malicious assault growing out of the faithful discharge of his official duties; and that the language of section 753 of the Revised Statutes, that the party seeking the benefit of the writ of habeas corpus must in this connection show that he is "in custody for an act done or committed in pursuance of a law of the United States," makes it necessary that upon this occasion it should be shown that the act for which Neagle is imprisoned was done by virtue of an Act of Congress. It is not supposed that any special Act of Congress exists which authorizes the marshals or deputy marshals of the United States in express terms to accompany the judges of the Supreme Court through their circuits, and act as a bodyguard to them, to defend them against malicious assaults against their persons. But we are of opinion that this view of the statute is an unwarranted restriction of the meaning of a law designed to extend in a liberal manner the benefit of the writ of habeas corpus to persons imprisoned for the performance of their duty. And we are satisfied that if it was the duty of Neagle, under the circumstances, a duty which could only arise under the laws of the United States, to defend Mr. Justice Field from a murderous attack upon him, he brings himself within the meaning of the section we have recited. This view of the subject is confirmed by the alternative provision, that he must be in custody "for an act done or committed in pursuance of a law of the United States or of an order, process, or decree of a court or judge thereof, or is in custody in violation of the Constitution or of a law or treaty of the United States."

In the view we take of the Constitution of the United States, any obligation fairly and properly inferable from that instrument, or any duty of the marshal to be derived from the general scope of his duties under the laws of the United States, is "a law" within the meaning of this phrase. It would be a great reproach to the system of government of the United States, declared to be within its sphere sovereign and supreme, if there is to be found within the domain of its powers no means of protecting the judges, in the conscientious and faithful discharge of their duties, from the malice and hatred of those upon whom their judgments may operate unfavorably....

Where, then, are we to look for the protection which we have shown Judge Field was entitled to when engaged in the discharge of his official duties? Not to the courts of the United States; because, as has been more than once said in this court, in the division of the powers of government between the three great departments, executive, legislative and judicial, the judicial is the weakest for the purposes of self-protection and for the enforcement of the powers which it exercises. The ministerial officers through whom its commands must be executed are marshals of the United States, and belong emphatically to the executive department of the government. They are appointed by the President, with the advice and consent of the Senate. They are removable from office at his pleasure. They are subjected by Act of Congress to the supervision and control of the Department of Justice, in the hands of one of the cabinet officers of the President, and their compensation is provided by Acts of Congress. The same may be said of the district attorneys of the United States, who prosecute and defend the claims of the government in the courts.

The legislative branch of the government can only protect the judicial officers by the enactment of laws for that purpose, and the argument we are now combating assumes that no such law has been passed by Congress.

If we turn to the Executive Department of the government, we find a very different condition of affairs. The Constitution, section 3, Article II, declares that the President "shall take care that the laws be faithfully executed," and he is provided with the means of fulfilling this obligation by his authority to commission all the officers of the United States, and, by and with the advice and consent of the Senate, to appoint the most important of them and to fill vacancies. He is declared to be commander-in-chief of the army and navy of the United States. The duties which are thus imposed upon him he is further enabled to perform by the recognition in the Constitution, and the creation by Acts of Congress, of executive departments, which have varied in number from four or five to seven or eight, the heads of which are familiarly called cabinet ministers.

These aid him in the performance of the great duties of his office, and represent him in a thousand acts to which it can hardly be supposed his personal attention is called, and thus he is enabled to fulfill the duty of his great department, expressed in the phrase that "he shall take care that the laws be faithfully executed."

Is this duty limited to the enforcement of Acts of Congress or of treaties of the United States according to their express terms, or does it include the rights, duties and obligations growing out of the Constitution itself, our international relations, and all the protection implied by the nature of the government under the Constitution?...

We cannot doubt the power of the President to take measures for the protection of a judge of one of the courts of the United States, who, while in the discharge of the duties of his office, is threatened with a personal attack which may probably result in his death, and we think it clear that where this protection is to be afforded through the civil power, the Department of Justice is the proper one to set in motion the necessary means of protection. The correspondence already recited in this opinion between the marshal of the Northern District of California, and the Attorney-General, and the district attorney of the United States for that district, although prescribing no very specific mode of affording this protection by the Attorney-General, is sufficient, we think, to warrant the marshal in taking the steps which he did take, in making the provisions which he did make, for the protection and defense of Mr. Justice Field.

But there is positive law investing the marshals and their deputies with powers which not only justify what Marshal Neagle did in this matter, but which imposed it upon him as a duty. In chapter fourteen of the Revised Statutes of the United States, which is devoted to the appointment and duties of the district attorneys, marshals and clerks of the courts of the United States, section 788 declares:

"The marshals and their deputies shall have, in each State, the same powers, in executing the laws of the United States, as the sheriffs and their deputies in such State may have, by law, in executing the laws thereof."

If, therefore, a sheriff of the State of California was authorized to do in regard to the laws of California what Neagle did, that is, if he was authorized to keep the peace, to protect a judge from assault and murder, then Neagle was authorized to do the same thing in reference to the laws of the United States....

That there is a peace of the United States; that a man assaulting a judge of the United States while in the discharge of his duties violates that peace; that in such case the marshal of the United States stands in the same relation to the peace of the United States which the sheriff of the county does to the peace of the State of California; are questions too clear to need argument to prove them. That it would be the duty of a sheriff, if one had been present at this assault by Terry upon Judge Field, to prevent this breach of the peace, to prevent this assault, to prevent the murder which was contemplated by it, cannot be doubted. And if, in performing this duty, it became necessary for the protection of Judge Field, or of himself, to kill Terry, in a case where, like this, it was evidently a question of the choice of who should be killed, the assailant and violator of the law and disturber of the peace, or the unoffending man who was in his power, there can be no question of the authority of the sheriff to have killed Terry. So the marshal of the United States, charged with the duty of protecting and guarding the judge of the United States court against this special assault upon his person and his life, being present at the critical moment, when prompt action was necessary, found it to be his duty, a duty which he had no liberty to refuse to perform, to take the steps which resulted in Terry's death. This duty was imposed on him by the section of the Revised Statutes which we have recited, in connection with the powers conferred by the State of California upon its peace officers, which become, by this statute, in proper cases, transferred as duties to the marshals of the United States....

The result at which we have arrived upon this examination is, that in the protection of the person and the life of Mr. Justice Field while in the discharge of his official duties, Neagle was authorized to resist the attack of Terry upon him; that Neagle was correct in the belief that without prompt action on his part the assault of Terry upon the judge would have ended in the death of the latter; that such being his well-founded belief, he was justified in taking the life of Terry, as the only means of preventing the death of the man who was intended to be his victim; that in taking the life of Terry, under the circumstances, he was acting under the authority of the law of the United States, and was justified in so doing; and that he is not liable to answer in the courts of California on account of his part in that transaction.

We therefore affirm the judgment of the Circuit Court authorizing his discharge from the custody of the sheriff of San Joaquin County.

MR. JUSTICE LAMAR delivered a dissenting opinion in which MR. CHIEF JUSTICE FULLER concurred. MR. JUSTICE FIELD did not sit in this case.

YOUNGSTOWN SHEET & TUBE CO., ET AL. v. SAWYER
343 U.S. 579; 72 S.Ct. 863; 96 L.Ed. 1153 (1952)

Commonly referred to as the Steel Seizure Case, this legal controversy arose during some of the heaviest fighting in the Korean War. Demanding new collective bargaining rights, the United Steelworkers of America entered negotiations with the major steel companies. Despite heavy behind-the-scenes activity on the part of the Truman Administration to bring about a settlement, the negotiations failed and the strike was set for April 9, 1952. Prior to the established deadline, the President issued an executive order directing the Secretary of Commerce, Sawyer, to seize and nationalize the major steel mills on the assumption that the vacant plants could be run by federal troops. Truman justified his action on the grounds that the stoppage of steel production would "seriously jeopardize national defense." Congress took no legislative action to endorse the Seizure. Although two earlier acts of Congress permitted the nationalization of private property under certain conditions, President Truman admitted that he was unwilling to take the steps necessary to do so because the existing legislation was too "cumbersome." On the request of mill owners, a district court issued an injunction restraining Sawyer from carrying out the order; however, the court of appeals stayed the injunction. The Supreme Court granted certiorari and handed down its decision within one month of the date the executive order was issued.

MR. JUSTICE BLACK delivered the opinion of the Court:

We are asked to decide whether the President was acting within his constitutional power when he issued an order directing the Secretary of Commerce to take possession of and operate most of the nation's steel mills. The mill owners argue that the President's order amounts to lawmaking, a legislative function which the Constitution has expressly confided to the Congress and not to the President. The Government's position is that the order was made on findings of the President that his action was necessary to avert a national catastrophe which would inevitably result from a stoppage of steel production, and that in meeting this grave emergency the President was acting within the aggregate of his constitutional powers as the nation's Chief Executive and the Commander-in-Chief of the Armed Forces of the United States....

The President's power, if any, to issue the order must stem either from an act of Congress or from the Constitution itself. There is no statute that expressly authorizes the President to take possession of property as he did here. Nor is there any act of Congress to which our attention has been directed from which such a power can fairly be implied. Indeed, we do not understand the Government to rely on statutory authorization for this seizure. There are two statutes which do authorize the President to take both personal and real property under certain conditions. (The Selective Service Act of 1948 and the Defense Production Act of 1950.) However, the Government admits that these conditions were not met and that the President's order was not rooted in either of the statutes. The Government refers to the seizure provisions of one of these statutes... as "much too cumbersome, involved, and time-consuming for the crisis which was at hand."

Moreover, the use of the seizure technique to solve labor disputes in order to prevent work stoppages was not only unauthorized by any Congressional enactment; prior to this controversy, Congress had refused to adopt that method of settling labor disputes. When the Taft-Hartley Act was under consideration in 1947, Congress rejected an amendment which would have authorized such governmental seizures in cases of emergency. Apparently it was thought that the technique of seizure, like that of compulsory arbitration, would interfere with the process of collective bargaining. Consequently, the plan Congress adopted in that Act did not provide for seizure under any circumstances. Instead, the plan sought to bring about settlements by use of the customary devices of mediation, conciliation, investigation by boards of inquiry, and public reports.

It is clear that if the President had authority to issue the order he did, it must be found in some provision of the Constitution. And it is not claimed that express constitutional language grants this power to the President. The contention is that Presidential power should be implied from the aggregate of his powers under the Constitution. Particular reliance is placed on provisions in Article II which say that "The executive Power shall be vested in a President...;" that "he shall take Care that the Laws be faithfully executed;" and that he "shall be Commander-in-Chief of the Army and Navy of the United States."

The order cannot properly be sustained as an exercise of the President's military power as Commander-in-Chief of the Armed Forces. The Government attempts to do so by citing a number of cases upholding broad powers in military commanders engaged in day-to-day fighting in a theater of war. Such cases need not concern us here. Even though "theater of war" be an expanding concept, we cannot with faithfulness to our constitutional system hold that the Commander-in-Chief of the Armed Forces has the ultimate power as such to take possession of private property in order to keep labor disputes from stopping production. This is a job for the nation's lawmakers, not for its military authorities.

Nor can the seizure order be sustained because of the several constitutional provisions that grant executive power to the President. In the framework of our Constitution, the President's power to see that the laws are faithfully executed refutes the idea that he is to be a lawmaker. The Constitution limits his functions in the lawmaking process to the recommending of laws he thinks wise and the vetoing of laws he thinks bad. And the Constitution is neither silent nor equivocal about who shall make laws which the President is to execute.

The President's order does not direct that a Congressional policy be executed in a manner prescribed by Congress – it directs that a Presidential policy be executed in a manner prescribed by the President. The preamble of the order itself, like that of many statutes, sets out reasons why the President believes certain policies should be adopted, proclaims these policies as rules of conduct to be followed, and again like a statute, authorizes a government official to promulgate additional rules and regulations consistent with the policy proclaimed and needed to carry that policy into execution. The power of Congress to adopt such public policies as those proclaimed by the order is beyond question. It can authorize the taking of private property for public use. It can make laws regulating the relationships between employers and employees, prescribing rules designed to settle labor disputes, and fixing wages and working conditions in certain fields of our economy. The Constitution does not subject this lawmaking power of Congress to Presidential or military supervision or control.

It is said that other Presidents without Congressional authority have taken possession of private business enterprises in order to settle labor disputes. But even if this be true, Congress has not thereby lost its exclusive constitutional authority to make laws necessary and proper to carry out the powers vested by the Constitution "in the Government of the United States, or any Department or Officer thereof."

The Founders of this nation entrusted the lawmaking power to the Congress alone in both good and bad times. It would do no good to recall the historical events, the fears of power and the hopes for freedom that lay behind their choice. Such a review would but confirm our holding that this seizure order cannot stand.

The judgment of the District Court is... Affirmed.

MR. JUSTICE FRANKFURTER concurred, saying in part:

Although the considerations relevant to the legal enforcement of the principle of separation of powers seem to me more complicated and flexible than may appear from what Mr. Justice Black has written, I join his opinion because I thoroughly agree with the application of the principle to the circumstances of this case....

The issue before us can be met, and therefore should be, without attempting to define the President's powers comprehensively. I shall not attempt to delineate what belongs to him by virtue of his office beyond the power even of Congress to contract; what authority belongs to him until Congress acts; what kind of problems may be dealt with either by the Congress or by the President or by both...; what power must be exercised by the Congress and cannot be delegated to the President. It is as unprofitable to lump together in an undiscriminating hotch-potch past Presidential actions claimed to be derived from occupancy of the office as it is to conjure up hypothetical future cases. The judiciary may, as this case proves, have to intervene in determining where authority lies as between the democratic forces in our scheme of government. But in doing so we should be wary and humble. Such is the teaching of this Court's role in the history of the country.

In any event, nothing can be plainer than that Congress made a conscious choice of policy in a field full of perplexity and peculiarly within legislative responsibility for choice. In formulating legislation for dealing with industrial conflicts, Congress could not more clearly and emphatically have withheld authority than it did in 1947...

By the Labor Management Relations Act of 1947, Congress said to the President, "You may not seize. Please report to us and ask for seizure power if you think it is needed in a specific situation...." But it is now claimed that the President has seizure power by virtue of the Defense Production Act of 1950 and its Amendments. And the claim is based on the occurrence of new events – Korea and the need for stabilization, etc. – although it was well known that seizure power was withheld by the Act of 1947, and although the President, whose specific requests for other authority were in the main granted by Congress, never suggested that in view of the new events he needed the power of seizure which Congress in its judgment had decided to withhold from him....

MR. JUSTICE CLARK concurred:

I conclude that where Congress has laid down specific procedures to deal with the *type of crisis* confronting the President, he must follow those procedures in meeting the crisis; but that *in the absence of such action by Congress, the President's independent power to act depends upon the gravity of the situation confronting the nation.* I cannot sustain the seizure in question because here... Congress had prescribed methods to be followed by the President in meeting the emergency at hand....

JUSTICES DOUGLAS, JACKSON and BURTON also wrote concurring opinions.

MR. CHIEF JUSTICE VINSON, with whom MR. JUSTICE REED and MR. JUSTICE MINTON joined, dissented:

Much of the argument in this case has been directed at straw men. We do not now have before us the case of a President acting solely on the basis of his own notions of the public welfare. Nor is there any question of unlimited executive power in this case. The President himself closed the door to any such claim when he sent his Message to Congress stating his purpose to abide by any action of Congress, whether approving or disapproving his seizure action. Here, the President immediately made sure that Congress was fully informed of the temporary action he had taken only to preserve the legislative programs from destruction until Congress could act.

The absence of a specific statute authorizing seizure of the steel mills as a mode of executing the laws – both the military procurement program and the anti-inflation program – has not until today been thought to prevent the President from executing the laws. Unlike an administrative commission confined to the enforcement of the statute under which it was created, or the head of a department when administering a particular statute, the President is a constitutional officer charged with taking care that a "mass of legislation" be executed. Flexibility as to mode of execution to meet critical situations is a matter of practical necessity....

As the District Judge stated, this is no time for "timorous" judicial action. But neither is this a time for timorous executive action. Faced with the duty of executing the defense programs which Congress had enacted and the disastrous effects that any stoppage in steel production would have on these programs, the President acted to preserve those programs by seizing the steel mills. There is no question that the possession was other than temporary in character and subject to Congressional direction – either approving, disapproving, or regulating the manner in which the mills were to be administered and returned to the owners. The President immediately informed Congress of his action and clearly stated his intention to abide by the legislative will. No basis for claims of arbitrary action, unlimited powers, or dictatorial usurpation of Congressional power appears from the facts of this case. On the contrary, judicial, legislative, and executive precedents throughout our history demonstrate that in this case the President acted in full conformity with his duties under the Constitution. Accordingly, we would reverse the order of the District Court.

UNITED STATES v. CURTISS-WRIGHT EXPORT CORPORATION
299 U.S. 304; 57 S.Ct. 216; 81 L.Ed. 255 (1936)

On May 28, 1934, President Franklin D. Roosevelt issued a proclamation forbidding any American company to sell armaments to the warring countries of Bolivia and Paraguay. The President's announcement was supported by a joint resolution of Congress which permitted him to take such action if, in his judgment, it might help to restore the peace in that area of the hemisphere. The Curtiss-Wright Export Corporation was charged with conspiracy to violate the proclamation; it argued that Congress had no authority to delegate its legislative power to the President. The Federal District Court in New York sustained the Corporation's claim, and the government appealed directly to the Supreme Court.

Mr. Justice SUTHERLAND delivered the opinion of the Court.

...It is contended that by the Joint Resolution, the going into effect and continued operation of the resolution was conditioned (a) upon the President's judgment as to its beneficial effect upon the re-establishment of peace between the countries engaged in armed conflict in the Chaco; (b) upon the making of a proclamation, which was left to his unfettered discretion, thus constituting an attempted substitution of the President's will for that of Congress; (c) upon the making of a proclamation putting an end to the operation of the resolution, which again was left to the President's unfettered discretion; and (d) further, that the extent of its operation in particular cases was subject to limitation and exception by the President, controlled by no standard. In each of these particulars, appellees urge that Congress abdicated its essential functions and delegated them to the Executive.

Whether, if the Joint Resolution had related solely to internal affairs it would be open to the challenge that it constituted an unlawful delegation of legislative power to the Executive, we find it unnecessary to determine. The whole aim of the resolution is to affect a situation entirely external to the United States, and falling within the category of foreign affairs. The determination which we are called to make, therefore, is whether the Joint Resolution, as applied to that situation, is vulnerable to attack under the rule that forbids a delegation of law-making power. In other words, assuming (but not deciding) that the challenged delegation, if it were confined to internal affairs, would be invalid, may it nevertheless be sustained on the ground that its exclusive aim was to afford a remedy for a hurtful condition within foreign territory?

It will contribute to the elucidation of the question if we first consider the differences between the powers of the federal government in respect of foreign or external affairs and those in respect of domestic or internal affairs. That there are differences between them, and that these differences are fundamental, may not be doubted.

The two classes of powers are different, both in respect of their origin and their nature. The broad statement that the federal government can exercise no powers except those specifically enumerated in the Constitution, and such implied powers as are necessary and proper to carry into effect the enumerated powers, is categorically true only in respect of our internal affairs. By the Declaration of Independence, "the Representatives of the United States of America" declared the United (not the several) Colonies to be free and independent states, and as such to have "full Power to levy War, conclude Peace, contract Alliances, establish Commerce and to do all other Acts and Things which Independent States may of right do."

As a result of the separation from Great Britain by the colonies acting as a unit, the powers of external sovereignty passed from the Crown not to the colonies severally, but to the colonies in their collective and corporate capacity as the United States of America. Even before the Declaration, the colonies were a unit in foreign affairs, acting through a common agency – namely the Continental Congress, composed of delegates from the thirteen colonies. That agency exercised the powers of war and peace, raised an army, created a navy, and finally adopted the Declaration of Independence. *Rulers come and go; governments end and forms of government change; but sovereignty survives.* A political society cannot endure without a supreme will somewhere. Sovereignty is never held in suspense.

The Union existed before the Constitution, which was ordained and established among other things to form "a more perfect Union...."

It results that the investment of the federal government with the powers of external sovereignty did not depend upon the affirmative grants of the Constitution. The powers to declare and wage war, to conclude peace, to make treaties, to maintain diplomatic relations with other sovereignties, if they had never been mentioned in the Constitution, would have vested in the federal government as necessary concomitants of nationality.... As a member of the family of nations, the right and power of the United States in that field are equal to the right and power of the other members of the international family. Otherwise, the United States is not completely sovereign....

Not only, as we have shown, is the federal power over external affairs in origin and essential character different from that over internal affairs, but participation in the exercise of the power is significantly limited. In this vast external realm, with its important, complicated, delicate and manifold problems, the President alone has the power to speak or listen as a representative of the nation. He *makes* treaties with the advice and consent of the Senate; but he alone negotiates. Into the field of negotiation the Senate cannot intrude; and Congress itself is powerless to invade it. As Marshall said..., "The President is the sole organ of the nation in its external relations, and its sole representative with foreign nations...."

It is important to bear in mind that we are here dealing not alone with an authority vested in the President by an exertion of legislative power, but with such an authority plus the very delicate, plenary and exclusive power of the President as the sole organ of the federal government in the field of international relations – a power which does not require as a basis for its exercise an act of Congress, but which, of course, like every other government power, must be exercised in subordination to the applicable provisions of the Constitution. It is quite apparent that if, in the maintenance of our international relations, embarrassment – perhaps serious embarrassment – is to be avoided and success for our aims achieved, Congressional legislation which is to be made effective through negotiation and inquiry within the international field must often accord to the President a degree of discretion and freedom from statutory restriction which would not be admissible were domestic affairs alone involved. Moreover, he, not Congress, has the better opportunity of knowing the conditions which prevail in foreign countries, and especially is this true in time of war. He has his confidential sources of information. He has his agents in the form of diplomatic, consular, and other officials. Secrecy in respect of information gathered by them may be highly necessary, and the premature disclosure of it productive of harmful results. Indeed, so clearly is this true that the first President refused to accede to a request to lay before the House of Representatives the instructions, correspondence, and documents relating to the negotiation of the Jay Treaty – a refusal the wisdom of which was recognized by the House itself and has never since been doubted....

Practically every volume of the United States contains one or more acts or joint resolutions of Congress authorizing action by the President in respect of subjects affecting foreign relations, which either leave the exercise of the power to his unrestricted judgment, or provide a standard far more general than that which has always been considered requisite with regard to domestic affairs....

...[B]oth upon principle and in accordance with precedent, we conclude there is sufficient warrant for the broad discretion vested in the President to determine whether the enforcement of the statute will have a beneficial effect upon the re-establishment of peace in the affected countries; whether he shall make proclamation to bring the resolution into operation; whether and when the resolution shall cease to operate and to make proclamation accordingly; and to prescribe limitations and exceptions to which the enforcement of the resolution shall be subject ...

MR. JUSTICE McREYNOLDS dissented.
MR. JUSTICE STONE took no part in this case.

UNITED STATES v. BELMONT
301 U.S. 324; 57 S.Ct. 758; 81 L.Ed. 1134 (1937)

After seizing power in Russia in 1917, the Bolsheviks initiated a policy of nationalizing private companies and confiscating their property and assets. One such company, the Petrograd Metal Works, had a portion of its assets on deposit at a New York bank owned by Belmont. In 1933, President Franklin D. Roosevelt extended diplomatic recognition to the government of the Soviet Union and, as part of the final agreement between the two countries, it was concluded the United States would lay claim to all monies owed by American nationals to the U.S.S.R.. The settlement, known as the Litvinov Assignments, was an executive agreement which had not been submitted to the Senate for ratification. On objection by Belmont, the district court did not grant title to the government on the grounds that the agreement was not a treaty and thus, not "the supreme law of the land." The case then proceeded to the Supreme Court.

MR. JUSTICE SUTHERLAND delivered the opinion of the Court, saying in part:

First. We do not pause to inquire whether in fact there was any policy of the State of New York to be infringed, since we are of opinion that no state policy can prevail against the international compact here involved.

This court has held, *Underhill v. Hernandez* [1897], that every sovereign state must recognize the independence of every other sovereign state; and that the courts of one will not sit in judgment upon the acts of the government of another, done within its own territory.

...This court held that the conduct of foreign relations was committed by the Constitution to the political departments of the government, and the propriety of what may be done in the exercise of this political power was not subject to judicial inquiry or decision; that who is the sovereign of a territory is not a judicial question, but one the determination of which by the political departments conclusively binds the courts; and that recognition by these departments is retroactive and validates all actions and conduct of the government of its existence....

We take judicial notice of the fact that coincident with the assignment set forth in the complaint, the President recognized the Soviet government, and normal diplomatic relations were established between that government and the government of the United States, followed by an exchange of ambassadors. The effect of this was to validate, so far as this country is concerned, all acts of the Soviet government here involved from the commencement of its existence. The recognition, establishment of diplomatic relations, the assignment, and agreements with respect thereto, were all parts of one transaction, resulting in an international compact between the two governments. That the negotiations, acceptance of the assignment and agreements and understandings in respect thereof were within the competence of the President may not be doubted. Governmental power over internal affairs is distributed between the national government and the several states. Governmental power over external affairs is not distributed, but is vested exclusively in the national government. And in respect of what was done here, the Executive had authority to speak as the sole organ of that government. The assignment and the agreements in connection therewith did not, as in the case of treaties, as that term is used in the treaty making clause of the Constitution (Article II, § 2), require the advice and consent of the Senate.

A treaty signifies "a compact made between two or more independent nations, with a view to the public welfare...." But an international compact, as this was, is not always a treaty which requires the participation of the Senate. There are many such compacts, of which a protocol, a *modus vivendi*, a postal convention, and agreements like that now under consideration are illustrations...

The distinction was pointed out by this court in the *Altman* case [1912], which arose under § 3 of the Tariff Act of 1897, authorizing the President to conclude commercial agreements with foreign countries in certain specified matters. We held that although this might not be a treaty requiring ratification by the Senate, it was a compact negotiated and proclaimed under the authority of the President, and as such was a "treaty" within the meaning of the Circuit Court of Appeals Act, the construction of which might be reviewed upon direct appeal to this court.

Plainly, the external powers of the United States are to be exercised without regard to state laws or policies. The supremacy of a treaty in this respect has been recognized from the beginning. Mr. Madison, in the Virginia Convention, said that if a treaty does not supersede existing state laws, as far as they contravene its operation, the treaty would be ineffective. "To counteract it by the supremacy of the state laws, would bring on the Union the just charge of national perfidy, and involve us in war"... And while this rule in respect of treaties is established by the express language of clause 2, Art. VI, of the Constitution, the same rule would result in the case of all international compacts and agreements from the very fact that complete power over international affairs is in the national government and is not and cannot be subject to any curtailment or interference on the part of the several states.... In respect of all international negotiations and compacts, and in respect of our foreign relations generally, state lines disappear. As to such purposes the state of New York does not exist. Within the field of its powers, whatever the United States rightfully undertakes, it necessarily has warrant to consummate. And when judicial authority is invoked in aid of such consummation, state constitutions, state laws, and state policies are irrelevant to the inquiry and decision. It is inconceivable that any of them can be interposed as an obstacle to the effective operation of a federal constitutional power....

Second. The public policy of the United States relied upon as a bar to the action is that declared by the Constitution, namely, that private property shall not be taken without just compensation. But the answer is that our Constitution, laws, and policies have no extraterritorial operation, unless in respect of our own citizens.... The substantive right to the moneys, as now disclosed, became vested in the Soviet Government as the successor to the corporation-, and this right that government has passed to the United States . It does not appear that respondents have any interest in the matter beyond that of a custodian. Thus far no question under the Fifth Amendment is involved....

Judgment reversed.

JUSTICES STONE, BRANDEIS, and CARDOZO concurred.

CHAPTER VII

THE CONTRACT CLAUSE

A *contract* is a deliberate agreement between two or more parties, with terms and conditions, obligating them to do or not to do a particular thing.[1] Article I, Section 10, forbids any state from enacting a law which would impair the obligation of such engagements.[2] The original intention of the Framers was to protect creditors engaged in *executory* or "private" contracts with other non-governmental parties from the whims of state legislatures. During periods of economic turmoil, the state legislature might be politically pressured into enacting laws which would release insolvent debtors from their economic obligations. Such laws were, in fact, frequently enacted during the "critical period" of fiscal chaos from the adoption of the Articles of Confederation to the ratification of the Constitution (1781-1789). However, in the first case involving the contract clause to come before the Supreme Court, Chief Justice John Marshall expanded its application by holding that an *executed* or "public" contract, in the form of a grant of land by the Georgia legislature to private purchasers, was also subject to the same protection; see *Fletcher v. Peck* (1810) in Chapter IV above.

Later, in a very important decision, *The Trustees of Dartmouth College v. Woodward* (1819), Marshall indicated his sense of strong nationalism and protectionism by holding that a corporate charter is a contract immune from state interference. Even though the charter in question related to an educational institution, the infant business community could now feel relatively safe that it could grow and expand without arbitrary restrictions imposed by state legislatures. In his subsequent attempt, however, to further expand the protection of the contract clause to include "all past and future" contracts, Marshall failed and, for the only time in his career as Chief Justice, dissented on a constitutional question; see *Ogden v. Saunders* (1827). Through the years, in the decisions that followed, Marshall's view of the contract clause, while not abandoned, was certainly modified. This process was enhanced by three developments: *first*, the more narrow, if not more reasoned, interpretation of the contract clause expounded by Marshall's successor, Chief Justice Roger Brooke Taney (1836-1864); *second*, the decline of the contract clause as a protection of private rights, and its replacement by the concept of "substantive" due process as utilized by the Supreme Court during the "laissez faire" period (1890-1937); and *third*, the impact of the Great Depression which, if only indirectly, brought about a more realistic attitude toward the legitimate exercise of the state police power for the benefit of creditor and debtor alike.

In *Charles River Bridge v. Warren Bridge* (1837) Taney held that, even though charter contracts were normally protected from state abridgment, the terms of such public grants were to be *strictly* construed; the state cannot give away its "paramount power" to private parties and nothing in a contract can be implied that it has done so. The application of this rule to a state franchise for a bridge company in this case, was later reaffirmed in *Larsen v. South Dakota* (1929). The term "paramount power" seemed to indicate those essential and fundamental attributes of governance, without which the state could not exist. While the Supreme Court in the past has allowed the states to yield a portion of the taxing power in the form of tax exemptions (see *New Jersey v. Wilson*, 1812), it has neither permitted the states to contract away their powers of eminent domain (see *West River Bridge Co. v. Dix,* 1848; *Pennsylvania Hospital v. Philadelphia*, 1917), nor their police power, such as the regulation of lotteries (see *Stone v. Mississippi,* 1880), nor, finally, the authority to create, maintain, and set the salary and qualifications for public officers; see *Newton v. Commissioners* (1880) and *Butler v. Pennsylvania* (1851). Accordingly, any contract in which the state, as a party, attempts to give away its "paramount power" is an *ultra vires* contract, or one in which the state exercised authority beyond its legitimate limits and is thus invalid.

The most important decision relating to the contract clause in the twentieth century is *Home Building and Loan Association v. Blaisdell* (1934). Here the Supreme Court, in the opinion of Chief Justice Charles Evans Hughes, upheld a state law which imposed a moratorium on the payment of home mortgages because of the then deepening Depression. Not only must existing state laws be read into the terms of every contract, Hughes said, but also "the reservation of essential attributes of sovereign power" to meet unforeseen emergencies including those brought about by physical and economic causes. In allowing the state impairment of a contract in this case, the Chief Justice argued:

> While emergency does not create power, emergency may furnish the occasion for the exercise of power ... The constitutional question presented in the light of an emergency is whether the power possessed embraces the particular exercise of it in response to particular conditions … But where constitutional grants and limitations of power are set forth in general clauses, which afford a broad outline, the process of construction is essential to *fill in the details*. That is true of the contract clause. (emphasis added)

For Hughes, this was an exceptionally broad recognition of governmental discretion in emergencies; one that he was unwilling to recognize on the part of the national government a short time later in *Schecter Poultry Corporation v. United States* (1935).

THE TRUSTEES OF DARTMOUTH COLLEGE v. WOODWARD
4 Wheat. 518; 4 L.Ed. 629 (1819)

In 1769, Dartmouth College was granted a charter by the English Crown with a board of trustees comprised of twelve members to govern its affairs. Ten years later, the founder and first president of the college died and his son, John Wheelock succeeded him. A number of serious conflicts which took place between Wheelock and the board of trustees thereafter led to his removal. The controversy had political ramifications and in 1816, the Republicans, in control of the New Hampshire legislature enacted several laws which amended the original charter to change the composition of the governing body. In addition, the name of the institution was changed to Dartmouth "University." So infuriated were the old trustees that they refused to comply with the new law and maintained that their authority to run the college was unaffected. The newly appointed trustees, however, replaced them and elected Wheelock president, claiming that the legislation abrogated the obligations of the original charter. The old board took the matter to the state courts and lost. The matter was then brought before the Supreme Court on a writ of error.

The opinion of the Court was delivered by MR. CHIEF JUSTICE MARSHALL:

...It can require no argument to prove that the circumstances of this case constitute a contract. An application is made to the Crown for a charter to incorporate a religious and literary institution. In the application, it is stated that large contributions have been made for the object, which will be conferred on the corporation, as soon as it shall be created. The charter is granted, and on its faith the property is conveyed. Surely in this transaction every ingredient of a complete and legitimate contract is to be found.

The points for consideration are,

1. Is this contract protected by the Constitution of the United States?
2. Is it impaired by the acts under which the defendant holds?

...On the first point it has been argued that the word "contract," in its broadest sense, would comprehend the political relations between the government and its citizens, would extend to offices held within a state for state purposes, and to many of those laws concerning civil institutions which must change with circumstances, and be modified by ordinary legislation; which deeply concern the public, and which, to preserve good government, the public judgment must control. That even marriage is a contract, and its obligations are affected by the laws respecting divorces. That the clause in the Constitution, if construed in its greatest latitude, would prohibit these laws. Taken in its broad unlimited sense, the clause would be an unprofitable and vexatious interference with the internal concerns of a state, would unnecessarily and unwisely embarrass its legislation, and render immutable those civil institutions which are established for purposes of internal government, and which, to subserve those purposes, ought to vary with varying circumstances. That as the framers of the Constitution could never have intended to insert in that instrument a provision so unnecessary, so mischievous, and so repugnant to its general spirit, the term "contract" must be understood in a more limited sense. That it must be understood as intended to guard against a power of at least doubtful utility, the abuse of which had been extensively felt; and to restrain the legislature in future from violating the right to property. That anterior to the formation of the Constitution, a course of legislation had prevailed in many, if not in all, of the states, which weakened the confidence of man in man, and embarrassed all transactions between individuals, by dispensing with a faithful performance of engagements. To correct this mischief, by restraining the power which produced it, the state legislatures were forbidden "to pass any law impairing the obligation of contracts," that is, of contracts respecting property, under which some individual could claim a right to something beneficial to himself; and that since the clause in the Constitution must in construction receive some limitation, it may be confined, and ought to be confined, to cases of this description; to cases within the mischief it was intended to remedy.

The general correctness of these observations cannot be controverted. That the framers of the Constitution did not intend to restrain the states in the regulation of their civil institutions, adopted for internal government, and that the instrument they have given us is not to be so construed, may be admitted . The provision of the Constitution never has been understood to embrace other contracts than those which respect property, or some object of value, and confer rights which may be asserted in a court of justice.

...The parties in this case differ less on general principles, less on the true construction of the Constitution in the abstract, than on the application of those principles to this case, and on the true construction of the charter of 1769. This is the point on which the case essentially depends. If the act of incorporation be a grant of political power, if it create a civil institution to be employed in the administration of the government, or if the funds of the college be public property, or if the state of New Hampshire, as a government, be alone interested in its transactions, the subject is one in which the legislature of the state may act according to its own judgment, unrestrained by any limitation of its power imposed by the Constitution of the United States.

...It becomes then the duty of the court most seriously to examine this charter, and to ascertain its true character... A corporation is an artificial being, invisible, intangible, and existing only in contemplation of law. Being the mere creature of law, it possesses only those properties which the charter of its creation confers upon it, either expressly, or as incidental to its very existence. These are such as are supposed best calculated to effect the object for which it was created. Among the most important are immortality, and, if the expression may be allowed, individuality; properties, by which a perpetual succession of many persons are considered as the same, and may act as a single individual. They enable a corporation to manage its own affairs, and to hold property without the perplexing intricacies, the hazardous and endless necessity, of perpetual conveyances for the purpose of transmitting it from hand to hand. It is chiefly for the purpose of clothing bodies of men, in succession, with these qualities and capacities, that corporations were invented, and are in use.

...The objects for which a corporation is created are universally such as the government wishes to promote. They are deemed beneficial to the country; and this benefit constitutes the consideration, and, in most cases, the sole consideration of the grant. In most eleemosynary institutions, the object would be difficult, perhaps unattainable, without the aid of a charter of incorporation. Charitable, or public-spirited individuals, desirous of making permanent appropriations for charitable or other useful purposes, find it impossible to effect their design securely, and certainly, without an incorporating act. They apply to the government, state their beneficent object, and offer to advance the money necessary for its accomplishment, provided the government will confer on the instrument which is to execute their designs the capacity to execute them ....

...This is plainly a contract to which the donors, the trustees, and the crown (to whose rights and obligations New Hampshire succeeds), were the original parties. It is a contract made on a valuable consideration. It is a contract for the security and disposition of property. It is a contract, on the faith of which, real and personal estate has been conveyed to the corporation. It is then a contract within the letter of the Constitution, and within its spirit also, unless the fact that the property is invested by the donors in trustees for the promotion of religion and education, for the benefit of persons who are perpetually changing, though the objects remain the same, shall create a particular exception, taking this case out of the prohibition contained in the Constitution.

It is more than possible that the preservation of rights of this description was not particularly in the view of the framers of the Constitution, when the clause under consideration was introduced into that instrument. It is probable that interferences of more frequent recurrence, to which the temptation was stronger, and of which the mischief was more extensive, constituted the great motive for imposing this restriction on the state legislatures. But although a particular and a rare case may not, in itself, be of sufficient magnitude to induce a rule, yet it must be governed by the rule, when established, unless some plain and strong reason for excluding it can be given. It is not enough to say that this particular case was not in the mind of the Convention when the article was framed, nor of the American people when it was adopted. It is necessary to go farther, and to say that, had this particular case been suggested, the language would have been so varied as to exclude it, or it would have been made a special exception. The case being within the words of the rule, must be within its operation likewise, unless there be something in the literal construction so obviously absurd, or mischievous, or repugnant to the general spirit of the instrument, as to justify those who expound the Constitution in making it an exception ....

The opinion of the court, after mature deliberation, is that this is a contract, the obligation of which cannot be impaired without violating the

Constitution of the United States. This opinion appears to us to be equally supported by reason, and by the former decisions of this court.

...A repeal of this charter at any time prior to the adoption of the present constitution of the United States would have been an extraordinary and unprecedented act of power, but one which could have been contested only by the restrictions upon the legislature to be found in the constitution of the State. But the Constitution of the United States has imposed this additional limitation, that the legislature of a state shall pass no act "impairing the obligation of contracts."

...The founders of the college contracted, not merely for the perpetual application of the funds which they gave, to the objects for which those funds were given; they contracted also, to secure that application by the constitution of the corporation. They contracted for a system which should, as far as human foresight can provide, retain forever the government of the literary institution they had formed, in the hands of persons approved by themselves. This system is totally changed. The charter of 1769 exists no longer. It is reorganized; and reorganized in such a manner as to convert a literary institution, moulded according to the will of its founders, and placed under the control of private literary men, into a machine entirely subservient to the will of government. This may be for the advantage of literature in general; but it is not according to the will of the donors, and is subversive of that contract, on the faith of which their property was given ....

It results from this opinion, that the acts of the legislature of New Hampshire which are stated in the special verdict found in this cause, are repugnant to the Constitution of the United States; and that the judgment on this special verdict ought to have been for the plaintiffs. The judgment of the State Court must, therefore, be
Reversed.

CHARLES RIVER BRIDGE CO. v. WARREN BRIDGE CO.
11 Pet. 420; 9 L.Ed. 773 (1837)

In 1785, the Massachusetts legislature granted a charter to the Charles River Bridge Company to construct a toll bridge to improve travel between the cities of Boston and Charleston. Up until that time the only means of passage was provided by ferries operated by Harvard College under an exclusive ferry franchise (1650), for which the college was compensated. While the completed bridge was a financial success, its management by the company became embroiled in local politics. In 1828, the state legislature, reacting to the tactics of the company, granted a public charter to the Warren Bridge Company to build a new structure close to the site of the old bridge. A temporary toll was charged for the use of the bridge only for a six year period until payment for the cost was completed. The Charles River Bridge Company sought relief on the grounds that the legislature had violated the Contract Clause. The state supreme court denied the motion and the case was brought to the Supreme Court on a writ of error.

MR. CHIEF JUSTICE TANEY delivered the opinion of the Court:

The questions involved in this case are of the gravest character, and the Court has given to them the most anxious and deliberate consideration. The value of the right claimed by the plaintiffs is large in amount; and many persons may no doubt be seriously affected in their pecuniary interests by any decision which the Court may pronounce; and the questions which have been raised as to the power of the several states, in relation to the corporations they have chartered, are pregnant with important consequences; not only to the individuals who are concerned in the corporate franchises, but to the communities in which they exist....

Much has been said in the argument of the principles of construction by which this law is to be expounded, and what undertakings, on the part of the state may be implied. The Court thinks there can be no serious difficulty on that head. It is the grant of certain franchises by the public to a private corporation, and in a matter where the public interest is concerned. The rule of construction in such cases is well settled, both in England, and by the decisions of our tribunals.... "The rule of construction in all such cases, is now fully established to be this – that any ambiguity in the terms of the contract, must operate against the adventurers, and in favor of the public, and the plaintiffs can claim nothing that is not clearly given them by the act...."

The object and end of all government is to promote the happiness and prosperity of the community by which it is established; and it can never be assumed that the government intended to diminish its power of accomplishing the end for which it was created. And in a country like ours, free, active, and enterprising, continually advancing in numbers and wealth, new channels of communication are daily found necessary, both for travel and trade; and are essential to the comfort, convenience, and prosperity of the people. A state ought never to be presumed to surrender this power, because, like the taxing power, the whole community have an interest in preserving it undiminished.... The continued existence of a government would be of no great value, if by implications and presumptions, it was disarmed of the powers necessary to accomplish the ends of its creation; and the functions it was designed to perform, transferred to the hands of privileged corporations.... While the rights of private property are sacredly guarded, we must not forget that the community also has rights, and that the happiness and well-being of every citizen depends on their faithful preservation.

Adopting the rule of construction above stated as the settled one, we proceed to apply it to the charter of 1785, to the proprietors of the Charles River Bridge. This act of incorporation is in the usual form, and the privileges such as are commonly given to corporations of that kind. It confers on them the ordinary faculties of a corporation, for the purpose of building the bridge; and establishes certain rates of toll, which the company are authorized to take. This is the whole grant. There is no exclusive privilege given to them over the waters of Charles River, above or below their bridge. No right to erect another bridge themselves, nor to prevent other persons from erecting one. No engagement from the state, that another shall not be erected; and no undertaking not to sanction competition, nor to make improvements that may diminish the amount of its income. Upon all these subjects the charter is silent; and nothing is said in it about a line of travel, so much insisted on in the argument, in which they are to have exclusive privileges. No words are used, from which an intention to grant any of these rights can be inferred; if the plaintiff is entitled to them, it must be implied, simply, from the nature of the grant; and cannot be inferred, from the words by which the grant is made....

Indeed, the practice and usage of almost every state in the Union, old enough to have commenced the work of internal improvement, is opposed to the doctrine contended for on the part of the plaintiffs in error. Turnpike roads have been made in succession, on the same line of travel; the later ones interfering materially with the profits of the first. These corporations have, in some instances, been utterly ruined by the introduction of newer and better modes of transportation and travelling. In some cases, railroads have rendered the turnpike roads on the same line of travel so entirely useless, that the franchise of the turnpike corporation is not worth preserving. Yet in none of these cases have the corporation supposed that their privileges were invaded, or any contract violated on the part of the state. Amid the multitude of cases which have occurred, and have been daily occurring, for the last forty or fifty years, this is the first instance in which such an implied contract has been contended for, and this court called upon to infer it, from an ordinary act of incorporation, containing nothing more than the usual stipulations and provisions to be found in every such law. The absence of any such controversy, when there must have been so many occasions to give rise to it, proves, that neither states, nor individuals, nor corporations, ever imagined that such a contract could be implied from such charters. It shows, that the men who voted for these laws, never imagined that they were forming such a contract; and if we maintain that they have made it, we must create it by a legal fiction, in opposition to the truth of the fact, and the obvious intention of the party. We cannot deal thus with the rights reserved to the states; and by legal intendments and mere technical reasoning, take away from them any portion of that power over their own internal police and improvement, which is so necessary to their well-being and prosperity....

The judgment of the supreme judicial court of the commonwealth of Massachusetts, dismissing the plaintiffs' bill, must, therefore, be affirmed, with costs.

Justice BALDWIN concurred.

Justice McLEAN wrote an opinion urging that the case be dismissed for lack of jurisdiction.

Justices STORY and THOMPSON dissented.

HOME BUILDING & LOAN ASSOCIATION v. BLAISDELL
290 U.S. 398; 54 S.Ct. 231; 78 L.Ed. 413 (1934)

In this case, the Home Building & Loan Association challenged the validity of the Minnesota Mortgage Moratorium Act of 1933 which provided procedures for temporary mortgage relief. The Association had foreclosed the mortgage on Blaisdell's property by reason of default. Upon Blaisdell's objection, the county court in Minneapolis granted him an extension of the period of redemption. The state supreme court affirmed the judgment and the Association, claiming that the act violated the Contract Clause, as well as the Due Process and Equal Protection Clauses of the Fourteenth Amendment, appealed to the Supreme Court.

Mr. Chief Justice Hughes delivered the opinion of the Court:

...The state court upheld the statute as an emergency measure. Although conceding that the obligations of the mortgage contract were impaired, the court decided that what it thus described as an impairment was, notwithstanding the contract clause of the Federal Constitution, within the police power of the state as that power was called into exercise by the public economic emergency which the legislature had found to exist....

In determining whether the provision for this temporary and conditional relief exceeds the power of the state by reason of the clause in the Federal Constitution prohibiting impairment of the obligations of contracts, we must consider the relation of emergency to constitutional power, the historical setting of the contract clause, the development of the jurisprudence of this Court in the construction of that clause, and the principles of construction which we may consider to be established.

Emergency does not create power. Emergency does not increase granted power or remove or diminish the restrictions imposed upon power granted or reserved. The Constitution was adopted in a period of grave emergency. Its grants of power to the Federal Government and its limitations of the power of the states were determined in the light of emergency and they are not altered by emergency. What power was thus granted and what limitations were thus imposed are questions which have always been, and always will be, the subject of close examination under our constitutional system.

While emergency does not create power, emergency may furnish the occasion for the exercise of power.... The constitutional question presented in the light of an emergency is whether the power possessed embraces the particular exercise of it in response to particular conditions. Thus, the war power of the Federal Government is not created by the emergency of war, but it is a power given to meet that emergency.... Thus, emergency would not permit a state to have more than two Senators in the Congress, or permit the election of President by a general popular vote without regard to the number of electors to which the states are respectively entitled, or permit the states to "coin money" or to "make anything but gold and silver coin a tender in payment of debts." But where constitutional grants and limitations of power are set forth in general clauses, which afford a broad outline, the process of construction is essential to fill in the details. That is true of the contract clause....

In the construction of the contract clause, the debates in the Constitutional Convention are of little aid. But the reasons which led to the adoption of that clause, and of the other prohibitions of Section 10 of Article I, are not left in doubt and have frequently been described with eloquent emphasis. The widespread distress following the Revolutionary period, and the plight of debtors, had called forth in the states an ignoble array of legislative schemes for the defeat of creditors and the invasion of contractual obligations. Legislative interferences had been so numerous and extreme that the confidence essential to prosperous trade had been undermined and the utter destruction of credit was threatened....

But full recognition of the occasion and general purpose of the clause does not suffice to fix its precise scope. Nor does an examination of the details of prior legislation in the states yield criteria which can be considered controlling. To ascertain the scope of the constitutional prohibition we examine the course of judicial decisions in its application. These put it beyond question that the prohibition is not an absolute one and is not to be read with literal exactness like a mathematical formula....

Not only is the constitutional provision qualified by the measure of control which the state retains over remedial processes, but the state also continues to possess authority to safeguard the vital interests of its people. It does not matter that legislation appropriate to that end "has the result of modifying or abrogating contracts already in effect...." Not only are existing laws read into contracts in order to fix obligations as between the parties, but the reservation of essential attributes of sovereign power is also read into contracts as a postulate of the legal order. The policy of protecting contracts against impairment presupposes the maintenance of a government by virtue of which contractual relations are worthwhile – a government which retains adequate authority to secure the peace and good order of society. This principle of harmonizing the constitutional prohibition with the necessary residuum of state power has had progressive recognition in the decisions of this Court....

The legislature cannot "bargain away the public health or the public morals." Thus, the constitutional provision against the impairment of contracts was held not to be violated by an amendment of the state constitution which put an end to a lottery theretofore authorized by the legislature.... The states retain adequate power to protect the public health against the maintenance of nuisances despite insistence upon existing contracts.... Legislation to protect the public safety comes within the same category of reserve power....

Undoubtedly, whatever is reserved of state power must be consistent with the fair intent of the constitutional limitation of that power. The reserved power cannot be construed so as to destroy the limitation, nor is the limitation to be construed in harmony with each other. This principle precludes a construction which would permit the state to adopt as its policy the repudiation of debts or the destruction of contracts or the denial of means to enforce them. But it does not follow that conditions may not arise in which a temporary restraint of enforcement may be consistent with the spirit and purpose of the constitutional provision and thus be found to be within the range of the reserved power of the states to protect the vital interests of the community. It cannot be maintained that the constitutional prohibition should be so construed as to prevent limited and temporary interpositions with respect to the enforcement of contracts if made necessary by a great public calamity such as fire, flood, or earthquake.... The reservation of state power appropriate to such extraordinary conditions may be deemed to be as much a part of all contracts, as is the reservation of state power to protect the public interest in the other situations to which we have referred. And if state power exists to give temporary relief from the enforcement of contracts in the presence of disasters due to physical causes such as fire, flood, or earthquake, that power cannot be said to be nonexistent when the urgent public need demanding such relief is produced by other and economic causes....

It is manifest ... that there has been a growing appreciation of public needs and of the necessity of finding ground for a rational compromise between individual rights and public welfare. The settlement and consequent contraction of the public domain, the pressure of a constantly increasing density of population, the interrelation of the activities of our people and the complexity of our economic interests, have inevitably led to an increased use of the organization of society in order to protect the very bases of individual opportunity. Where, in earlier days, it was thought that only the concerns of individuals or of classes were involved, and that those of the state itself were touched only remotely, it has later been found that the fundamental interests of the state are directly affected; and that the question is no longer merely that of one party to a contract as against another, but of the use of reasonable means to safeguard the economic structure upon which the good of all depends.

It is no answer to say that this public need was not apprehended a century ago, or to insist that what the provision of the Constitution meant to the vision of that day it must mean to the vision of our time. If by the statement that what the Constitution meant at the time of its adoption it means today, it is intended to say that the great clauses of the Constitution must be confined to the interpretation which the framers, with the conditions and outlook of their time, would have placed upon them, the statement carries its own refutation. It was to guard against such a narrow conception that Chief Justice Marshall uttered the memorable warning- "We must never forget that it is a constitution we are expounding" (*McCulloch v. Maryland...*) "a constitution intended to endure for ages to come, and consequently, to be adapted to the various crises of human affairs...."

With a growing recognition of public needs and the relation of individual right to public security, the court has sought to prevent the perversion of the states to protect their fundamental interests, This development is a growth from the seeds which the fathers planted....

We are of the opinion that the Minnesota statute as here applied does not violate the contract clause of the Federal Constitution. Whether the legislation is wise or unwise as a matter of policy is a question with which we are not concerned.

What has been said on that point is also applicable to the contention presented under the due process clause.

Nor do we think that the statute denies to the appellant the equal protection of the laws. The classification which the statute makes cannot be said to be an arbitrary one....

Judgment affirmed.

MR. JUSTICES SUTHERLAND, VAN DEVANTER, McREYNOLDS, and BUTLER dissented.

CHAPTER VIII

THE REGULATION OF INTERSTATE AND FOREIGN COMMERCE

Perhaps the most significant power that Congress lacked during the "critical period" under the Articles of Confederation (1781-1789) was the control of trade and commerce with foreign nations, and between the states. Tariff wars, embargoes, and other protective measures to benefit local businesses, which were characteristic of interstate relations, nearly resulted in political and economic catastrophe for the infant nation. Accordingly, at the Constitutional Convention in 1787 a compromise was reached to rest the power of *interstate* regulation in the Congress. Article I, section 8 states that Congress "shall have power ... to regulate commerce with foreign nations and among the several states...." It was assumed, but not specified, that *intrastate* commerce, taking place solely within the geographic boundaries of a state, would fall under the control of the state. Inevitably, the Supreme Court would be left with the power of arbitration over conflicting claims of jurisdiction between the national and state governments.

Early in the nineteenth century a number of states continued to engage in local protectionism by attempting to negate certain types of commerce. In the first case to involve an interpretation of the Commerce Clause, *Gibbons v. Ogden* (1824), Chief Justice John Marshall announced his leading decision: any state action which endeavors to regulate interstate commerce in conflict with a law of Congress is unconstitutional. In clear and unequivocal terms, the decision made the national government, not the states, supreme in the regulation of the nation's commerce. However, in no way could Marshall's opinion be interpreted as excluding the states completely from the regulatory scheme. Although Congress was to have the *last* word, there still may well be occasions when the states could reasonably exercise control over various aspects of interstate commerce. After all, the states not only possessed the concurrent power of taxation; they also retained the *police power* (or general welfare power) under which they had the affirmative obligation to promote and protect the health, safety, morals and general welfare of the community. In fact, Marshall himself acknowledged the exertion of the latter power by upholding the authority of Delaware to construct a dam across a navigable interstate waterway in order to drain certain marshes for the public health, an important consideration being that Congress had not shown its intention to act in this local matter; see *Willson v. Blackbird Creek Marsh Company* (1829).

The Court more directly confronted the question of state participation in the regulation of interstate commerce in *Cooley v. The Board of Wardens of the Port of Philadelphia* (1852). In this important decision, the Court established the general rule that *local* aspects of commerce, whether intrastate or interstate in origin, would fall under *state* regulation *if:* (1) some immediate governmental action was necessary; (2) Congress had not already acted on the matter; (3) such national uniform regulation would not be required; and (4) the controls subsequently established would not unduly burden or obstruct the flow of commerce from state to state. The effect of the decision was to make the Supreme Court the umpire in determining whether it was sufficiently local in nature to be subject to state control. The *Cooley* Doctrine has proven, over the years, to be a very complex and difficult rule to apply: for example, during the three decades which followed, the rate regulation of interstate carriers, particularly railroads, was placed in the hands of the states. However, in the 1880's this policy began to change. In 1886, the Court held that regulation of rates charged by all interstate railroads required national uniform treatment by Congress and therefore, all state controls were nullified; see *Wabash, St. L. & P. Ry. Co. v. Illinois.* Shortly thereafter, because of the outcries of Progressives, farmers and small businessmen over the excesses of the monopolies and trusts, Congress entered the field of national regulation by enacting the Interstate Commerce Act (1886) and the Sherman Anti-trust Act (1890).

The Cooley Doctrine also came into conflict with attempts by various states to regulate the intermingling of the races in public places following Reconstruction. With one notable exception, the Supreme Court during the period of 1878-1948, struck down every state law brought before it which either required or forbade racial segregation on interstate carriers, trains and buses.[1] The variance of such requirements from state to state, the Court held, imposed an undue burden on the flow of interstate commerce. Since national uniformity was required, the question of state racial policies affecting interstate carriers could only be resolved, if at all, by Congress; see *Hall v. DeCuir* (1877), and *Morgan v. Virginia* (1946). However, following the shock to our national conscience caused by the full realization of the Nazi atrocities in the name of racial supremacy, the disposition of the post-War Court, and a number of other important developments after the Second World War, the stage was set in American jurisprudence for the rise of the Civil Rights movement.[2] In what was apparently a policy decision, the Supreme Court in 1948 abandoned its adherence to the Cooley Doctrine. It upheld the application of the Michigan Civil Rights Act, which forbade segregation in all public places, to excursion steamers clearly plying foreign waters by crossing the international date line into Canada; see *Bob-Lo Excursion Company v. Michigan.* Certainly after *Brown v. Board of Education* (1954), the Court felt that the kinds of burdens imposed by such state regulations as viewed in *Hall* and *Morgan* no longer exist; see *Colorado Commission v. Continental Air Lines* (1963). Aside from the character of the commerce, the Court has traditionally been concerned with the "balancing test" between the proper exercise of the state's police power, on the one hand, and the sanctity of the free flow of interstate commerce, on the other. The general rules or guidelines of regulation formulated by the Court are applied separately to components of commerce – goods, articles, or persons – and, the carriers or vehicles employed to transport such interstate components. While extremely complex in its case to case application, the general formula created by the Court, simply stated, is as follows: While the states cannot use the police power to unreasonably interfere with the flow of interstate commerce, neither can the channels of such commerce be used to thwart the valid exercise of the states' power to regulate. Accordingly, it is assumed that goods or persons, while in the flow of interstate commerce, are immune from state taxation and regulation; see *the State Freight Tax Case* (1873). There are exceptions, of course, and the question as to what precisely constitutes the "flow" of interstate commerce is fraught with pitfalls.

Generally speaking, the flow of commerce is the period between the point of departure (where the items of commerce are loaded on their common carriers and are considered on their way) to the point of destination (where the goods are delivered to the company to whom they have been consigned). Before "departure" and after "destination," the goods are liable to reasonable, non-discriminatory state regulation and taxation; see *Coe v. Errol* (1886); *Henneford v. Silas Mason Co.* (1937); and *McGoldrick v. Berwind-White CoalMining Co.* (1940). While in the flow, the goods in their "original packages" are not subject to either state taxation or regulation. However, if the packages are broken, sold or if the goods are used for commercial purposes while in transit, they lose their interstate immunity; see *Leisy v. Hardin* (1890) and *Hoouen & Allison Co. v. Evatt* (1945). The "original package" doctrine was first formulated by the Court to protect goods in foreign commerce from intrastate regulation; see *Brown v. Maryland* (1827); *Woodruff v. Parham* (1869) and *Department of Revenue v. J.B. Beam Distilling Co.* (1964). While the Court has wavered in its application from time to time, the "original package" doctrine has maintained its vitality.

Keeping in mind the prerequisites of the Cooley rule, the vehicles or carriers transporting commerce are subject to reasonable safety regulations imposed by the state including laws imposing speed limitations, required license checks, and restrictions on the width, weight and length of certain trucks; see *South Carolina State Highway Dept. v. Barnwell Bros.* (1938), *Kassel v. Consolidated Freightways Corporation of Delaware* (1981). Vehicles not in compliance with such regulations can be subjected to fine, penalties, and may be prohibited from use of state highways if alternate routes are available; see *Bradley v. Public Utilities Committee* (1933). Accordingly, such required stops as truck weighing stations and highway license checks are validly applicable to the carriers; however, the goods are not subject to state taxation and maintain their interstate immunity. On the other hand, if the containers are voluntarily removed from the "flow" by agreement of the parties involved (e.g., the containers must be checked and weighed for leakage at the company warehouse) then the goods are subject to a reasonable, non-discriminatory "use" tax by the state; see *Bacon v. Illinois (1913).*

Finally, in employing the police power, if a state wishes to regulate the intrastate sale, manufacture or transportation of a particular commodity on the grounds of health, morals or general welfare, Congress has usually cooperated. In seeing that interstate immunity is not misused to circumvent a valid use of such power by the state, Congress, in the past, has enacted "divesting" statutes with respect to those states having prohibition laws. Such statutes divested or stripped liquor of its interstate immunity when in transit and allowed it to fall under state control; see *In re. Rahrer* (1891) *and Clark Distilling Co. v. Western Maryland Ry. Co.* (1917). In addition, the Supreme Court has also acted to protect such legitimate exercises of state regulation even if in their "original packages" with respect to the sale of oleomargarine colored like butter (*Plumley v. Massachusetts*, 1894), and the shipment of loose cigarettes within the state; see *Austin v. Tennessee* (1900) and *Cook v. Marshall County* (1905). However, as viewed in the cases of *Southern Pacific Co. v. Arizona* (1945); *Edwards v. California* (1941) and *Pike v. Church, Inc.* (1970), the Court struck down state restrictions on the grounds that either discrimination had resulted or a real contribution to safety had not been demonstrated. Moreover, states cannot use their police powers as a guise for economic protectionism, or favoring in-state companies against out-of-state competition; see *Dean Milk Company v. City of Madison* (1956), *Philadelphia, v. New Jersey* (1978), and *Wyoming v. Oklahoma* (1992).

GIBBONS v. OGDEN
9 Wheat 1; 6 L.Ed. 23 (1824)

In August 1807, steam navigation became a practical reality when Robert Fulton's steamboat made the first voyage from New York to Albany. Along with his partner, Robert R. Livingston, Fulton was granted exclusive operating rights and a five-year extension to his monopoly which was not to exceed thirty years. Accordingly, no one was permitted to navigate New York waters by steam without first receiving a license from Fulton and Livingston. The present controversy arose over the competition of steamboat services between Ogden, who had obtained such a license, and his former partner, Gibbons, who had obtained his license, not from Fulton and Livingston, but rather the United States government. Ogden petitioned the New York Court to enjoin Gibbons from continuing his coasting business in the state. The Court granted the injunction and Gibbons appealed to the Supreme Court.

MR. CHIEF JUSTICE MARSHALL delivered the opinion of the Court:

The appellant contends that this decree is erroneous, because the laws which purport to give the exclusive privilege it sustains, are repugnant to the Constitution and laws of the United States.

This instrument contains an enumeration of powers expressly granted by the people to their government. It has been said that these powers ought to be construed strictly. But why ought they to be so construed? Is there one sentence in the Constitution which gives countenance to this rule? In the last of the enumerated powers, that which grants, expressly, the means for carrying all others into execution, Congress is authorized "to make all laws which shall be necessary and proper" for the purpose. But this limitation on the means which may be used is not extended to the powers which are conferred; nor is there one sentence in the Constitution, which has been pointed out by the gentlemen of the bar, or which we have been able to discern that prescribes this rule. We do not, therefore, think ourselves justified in adopting it. What do gentlemen mean by a strict construction? If they contend only against that enlarged construction which would extend words beyond their natural and obvious import, we might question the application of the term, but should not controvert the principle. If they contend for that narrow construction which, in support of some theory not to be found in the Constitution, would deny to the government those powers which the words of the grant, as usually understood, import, and which are consistent with the general views and objects of the instrument; for that narrow construction, which would cripple the government, and render it unequal to the objects for which it is declared to be instituted, and to which the powers given, as fairly understood, render it competent; then we cannot perceive the propriety of this strict construction, nor adopt it as the rule by which the Constitution is to be expounded. As men whose intentions require no concealment generally employ the words which most directly and aptly express the ideas they intend to convey, the enlightened patriots who framed our Constitution, and the people who adopted it, must be understood to have employed words in their natural sense, and to have intended what they said. If, from the imperfection of human language, there should be serious doubts respecting the extent of any given power, it is a well-settled rule that the objects for which it was given, especially when those objects are expressed in the instrument itself, should have great influence in the construction. We know of no reason for excluding this rule from the present case. The grant does not convey power which might be beneficial to the grantor, if retained by himself, or which can enure solely to the benefit of the grantee; but is an investment of power for the general advantage, in the hands of agents selected for that purpose; which power can never be exercised by the people themselves, but must be placed in the hands of agents, or lie dormant. We know of no rule for construing the extent of such powers, other than is given by the language of the instrument which confers them, taken in connexion with the purposes for which they were conferred.

The words are, "Congress shall have power to regulate commerce with foreign nations, and among the several States, and with the Indian tribes."

The subject to be regulated is commerce; and our Constitution being, as was aptly said at the bar, one of enumeration and not of definition, to ascertain the extent of the power it becomes necessary to settle the meaning of the word. The counsel for the appellee would limit it to traffic, to buying and selling, or the interchange of commodities, and do not admit that it comprehends navigation. This would restrict a general term, applicable to many objects, to one of its significations. Commerce, undoubtedly, is traffic, but it is something more; it is intercourse. It describes the commercial intercourse between nations, and parts of nations, in all its branches, and is regulated by prescribing rules for carrying on that intercourse. The mind can scarcely conceive a system for regulating commerce between nations which shall exclude all laws concerning navigation, which shall be silent on the admission of the vessels of one nation into the ports of the other, and be confined to prescribing rules for the conduct of individuals in the actual employment of buying and selling, or of barter.

If commerce does not include navigation, the government of the Union has no direct power over that subject, and can make no law prescribing what shall constitute American vessels, or requiring that they shall be navigated by American seamen. Yet this power has been exercised from the commencement of the government, has been understood by all to be a commercial regulation. All America understands, and has uniformly understood, the word "commerce" to comprehend navigation. It was so understood, and must have been so understood, when the Constitution was framed. The power over commerce, including navigation, was one of the primary objects for which the people of America adopted their government, and must have been contemplated in forming it.

To what commerce does this power extend? The Constitution informs us, to commerce "with the foreign nations, and among the several States, and with the Indian tribes."

It has, we believe, been universally admitted that these words comprehend every species of commercial intercourse between the United States and foreign nations. No sort of trade can be carried on between this country and any other, to which this power does not extend. It has been truly said that commerce, as the word is used in the Constitution, is a unit, every part of which is indicated by the term.

If this be the admitted meaning of the word in its application to foreign nations, it must carry the same meaning throughout the sentence, and remain a unit, unless there be some plain intelligible cause which alters it.

The subject to which the power is next applied is to commerce "among the several States." The word "among" means intermingled with. A thing which is among others, is intermingled with them. Commerce among the States cannot stop at the external boundary line of each State, but may be introduced into the interior.

It is not intended to say that these words comprehend that commerce which is completely internal, which is carried on between man and man in a State, or between different parts of the same State, and which does not extend to or affect other States. Such a power would be inconvenient, and is certainly unnecessary.

Comprehensive as the word "among" is, it may very properly be restricted to that commerce which concerns more States than one.... The completely internal commerce of a State, then, may be considered as reserved for the State itself.

The power of Congress, then, whatever it may be, must be exercised within the territorial jurisdiction of the several States.

...We are now arrived at the inquiry – What is this power?

It is the power to regulate; that is, to prescribe the rule by which commerce is to be governed. This power, like all others vested in Congress, is complete in itself, may be exercised to its utmost extent, and acknowledges no limitations other than are prescribed in the Constitution. These are expressed in plain terms, and do not affect the questions which arise in this case, or which have been discussed at the bar. If, as has always been understood, the sovereignty of Congress, though limited to specified objects, is plenary as to those objects, the power over commerce with foreign nations, and among the several States, is vested in Congress as absolutely as it would be in a single government, having in its constitution the same restrictions on the exercise of the power as are found in the Constitution of the United States....

The power of Congress, then, comprehends navigation within the limits of every State in the Union; so far as that navigation may be, in any manner, connected with "commerce with foreign nations, or among the several States, or with the Indian tribes." It may, of consequence, pass the jurisdictional line of New York, and act upon the very waters to which the prohibition now under consideration applies.

But it has been urged with great earnestness that, although the power of Congress to regulate commerce with foreign nations, and among the several States, be co-extensive with the subject itself, and have no other limits than are prescribed in the Constitution, yet the States may severally exercise the same power within their respective jurisdictions. In support of this argument, it is said that they possessed it as an inseparable attribute of sovereignty before the formation of the Constitution, and still retain it, except so far as they have surrendered it by that instrument; that this principle results from the nature of the government, and is secured by the Tenth Amendment; that an affirmative grant of power is not exclusive, unless in its own nature it be such that the continued exercise of it by the former possessor is inconsistent with the grant, and that this is not of that description.

The appellant, conceding these postulates, except the last, contends that full power to regulate a particular subject implies the whole power, and leaves no residuum; that a grant of the whole is incompatible with the existence of a right in another to any part of it. This opinion has been frequently expressed in this Court, and is founded as well on the nature of the government as on the words of the Constitution. In argument, however, it has been contended that if a law passed by a State, in the exercise of its acknowledged sovereignty, comes into conflict with a law passed by Congress in pursuance of the Constitution, they affect the subject, and each other, like equal opposing powers.

But the framers of our Constitution foresaw this state of things, and provided for it by declaring the supremacy, not only of itself, but of the laws made in pursuance of it. The nullity of any act inconsistent with the Constitution is produced by the declaration that the Constitution is the supreme law. The appropriate application of that part of the clause which confers the same supremacy on laws and treaties, is to such acts of the State Legislatures as do not transcend their powers, but, though enacted in the execution of acknowledged State powers, interfere with or are contrary to the laws of Congress, made in pursuance of the Constitution, or some treaty made under the authority of the United States. In every such case, the act of Congress, or the treaty, is supreme; and the law of the State, though enacted in the exercise of powers not controverted, must yield to it.

This act authorizes a steamboat employed, or intended to be employed, only in a river or bay of the United States, owned wholly or in part by an alien, resident within the United States, to be enrolled and licensed as if the same belonged to a citizen of the United States.

This act demonstrates the opinion of Congress that steamboats may be enrolled and licensed in common with vessels using sails. They are, of course, entitled to the same privileges, and can no more be restrained from navigating waters, and entering ports which are free to such vessels, than if they were wafted on their voyage by winds instead of being propelled by the agency of fire. The one element may be as legitimately used as the other for every commercial purpose authorized by the law of the Union; and the act of a State inhibiting the use of either to any vessel having a license under the act of Congress comes, we think, in direct collision with that act. As this decides the cause, it is unnecessary to enter in an examination of that part of the Constitution which empowers Congress to promote the progress of science and the useful arts.
Reversed.

MR. JUSTICE JOHNSON concurred.

COOLEY v. THE BOARD OF WARDENS OF THE PORT OF PHILADELPHIA
12 How. 299; 13 L.Ed. 996 (1852)

This very important decision determined that Congress did not have exclusive or plenary control over interstate commerce. It involved the constitutionality of the Pennsylvania compulsory pilotage law which required that ships leaving the port of Philadelphia should pay a half fee if a pilot was not hired. Cooley refused to pay the fee claiming that Congress, not the states, had sole authority over all aspects of foreign and interstate commerce. The case was brought to the Supreme Court on a writ of error.

MR. JUSTICE CURTIS delivered the opinion of the Court:

We think this particular regulation concerning high-pilotage fees is an appropriate part of a general system of regulations of this subject. Testing it by the practice of commercial States and countries legislating on this subject, we find it has usually been deemed necessary to make similar provisions. Numerous laws of this kind are cited in the learned argument of the counsel for the defendant in error; and their fitness, as a part of a system of pilotage, in many places, may be inferred from their existence in so many different States and countries....

It remains to consider the objection that it is repugnant to the third clause of the eighth section of the first article. "The Congress shall have power to regulate commerce with foreign nations and among the several States, and with the Indian tribes."

That the power to regulate includes the regulation of navigation, we consider settled. And when we look to the nature of the service performed by pilots, to the relations which that service and its compensations bear to navigation between the several States, and between the ports of the United States and foreign countries, we are brought to the conclusion that the regulation of the qualifications of pilots, of the modes and times of offering and rendering their services, of the responsibilities which shall rest upon them, of the powers they shall possess, of the compensation they may demand, and of the penalties by which their rights and duties may be enforced, do constitute regulations of navigation, and consequently of commerce, within the just meaning of this clause of the Constitution.

The power to regulate navigation is the power to prescribe rules in conformity with which navigation must be carried on. It extends to the persons who conduct it, as well as to the instruments used. Accordingly, the first Congress assembled under the Constitution passed laws requiring the masters of ships and vessels of the United States to be citizens of the United States, and established many rules for the government and regulation of officers and seamen.... These have been from time to time added to and changed, and we are not aware that their validity has been questioned.

Now, a pilot, so far as respects the navigation of the vessel in that part of the voyage which is his pilotage-ground, is the temporary master charged with the safety of the vessel and cargo, and of the lives of those on board, and intrusted with the command of the crew. He is not only one of the persons engaged in navigation, but he occupies a most important and responsible place among those thus engaged. And if Congress has power to regulate the seamen who assist the pilot in the management of the vessel, a power never denied, we can perceive no valid reason why the pilot should be beyond the reach of the same power. It is true that, according to the usages of modern commerce on the ocean, the pilot is on board only during a part of the voyage between ports of different States, or between ports of the United States and foreign countries; but if he is on board for such a purpose and during so much of the voyage as to be engaged, as clearly as it would if he were to remain on board throughout the whole passage, from port to port. For it is a power which extends to every part of the voyage, and may regulate those who conduct or assist in conducting navigation in one part of a voyage as much as in another part, or during the whole voyage.

Nor should it be lost sight of that this subject of the regulation of pilots and pilotage has an intimate connection with, and an important relation to, the general subject of commerce with foreign nations and among the several States, over which it was one main object of the Constitution to create a national control. Conflicts between the laws of neighboring States and discriminations favorable or adverse to commerce with particular foreign nations might be created by State laws regulating pilotage, deeply affecting that equality of commercial rights, and that freedom from State interference, which those who formed the Constitution were so anxious to secure, and which the experience of more than half a century has taught us to value so highly.

...And a majority of the Court are of opinion, that a regulation of pilots is a regulation of commerce within the grant to Congress of the commercial power, contained in the third clause of the eighth section of the first article of the Constitution.

It becomes necessary, therefore, to consider whether this law of Pennsylvania, being a regulation of commerce, is valid.

...If the States were divested of the power to legislate on this subject by the grant of the commercial power to Congress, it is plain this act could not confer upon them the power thus to legislate. If the Constitution excluded the States from making any law regulating commerce, certainly Congress cannot regrant, or in any manner reconvey to the States that power.... [W]e are brought directly and unavoidably to the consideration of the question, whether the grant of the commercial power to Congress did *per se* deprive the States of all power to regulate pilots. This question has never been decided by this Court, nor in our judgment, has any case depending upon all the considerations which must govern this one come before this Court. The grant of commercial power to Congress does not contain any terms which expressly exclude the States from exercising an authority over its subject matter. If they are excluded, it must be because the nature of this power, like that to legislate for the District of Columbia, is absolutely and totally repugnant to the existence of similar power in the States. Probably no one would deny that the grant of the power to Congress as effectually and perfectly excludes the States from all future legislation on the subject as if express words had been used to exclude them. And on the other hand, if it were admitted that the existence of this power in Congress, like the power of taxation, is compatible with the existence of a similar power in the States, then it would be in conformity with the contemporary exposition of the Constitution (Federalist, No. 32) and with the judicial construction given from time to time by this Court, after the most deliberate consideration, to hold that the mere grant of such a power to Congress did not imply a prohibition on the States to exercise the same power; that it is not the mere existence of such a power, but its exercise by Congress, which may be incompatible with the exercise of the same power by the States, and that the States may legislate in the absence of congressional regulations....

The diversities of opinion, therefore, which have existed on this subject, have arisen from the different views taken of the nature of this power. But when the nature of a power like this is spoken of, when it is said that the nature of the power requires that it should be exercised exclusively by Congress, it must be intended to refer to the subjects of that power, and to say they are of such a nature as to require exclusive legislation by Congress. Now the power to regulate commerce embraces a vast field, containing not only many, but exceedingly various subjects, quite unlike in their nature; some imperatively demanding a single uniform rule, operating equally on the commerce of the United States in every port, and some, like the subject now in question, as imperatively demanding that diversity, which alone can meet the local necessities of navigation.

Either absolutely to affirm or deny that the nature of this power requires exclusive legislation by Congress is to lose sight of the nature of the subjects of this power, and to assert concerning all of them what is really applicable but to a part. Whatever subjects of this power are in their nature national, or admit only of one uniform system or plan of regulation, may justly be said to be of such a nature as to require exclusive legislation by Congress. That this cannot be affirmed of laws for the regulation of pilots and pilotage is plain. The Act of 1789 contains a clear and authoritative declaration by the first Congress, that the nature of this subject is such that, *until Congress should find it necessary to exert its power, it should be left to the legislation of the States; that it is local and not national;* that it is likely to be the best provided for, not by as many as the legislative discretion of the several States should deem applicable to the local peculiarities of the ports within their limits.

It manifests the understanding of Congress, at the outset of the government, that the nature of this subject is not such as to require its exclusive legislation. The practice of the States, and of the national government, has been in conformity with this declaration from the origin of the national government to this time; and the nature of the subject when examined is such as to leave no doubt of the superior fitness and propriety, not to say the absolute necessity, of different systems of regulation, drawn from local knowledge and experience, and conformed to local wants. How then can we say, that by the mere grant of power to regulate commerce, the States are deprived of all the power to legislate on this subject, because from the nature of the power the legislation of Congress must be exclusive. This would be to affirm that the nature of the power is in any case something different from the nature of the subject to which, in such case, the power extends, and that the nature of the power necessarily demands, in all cases, exclusive legislation by Congress, while the nature of one of the subjects of that power not only does not require such exclusive legislation, but may be best provided for by many different systems enacted by the States in conformity with the circumstances of the ports within their limits.

It is the opinion of a majority of the Court that the mere grant to Congress of the power to regulate commerce did not deprive the States of power to regulate pilots, and that although Congress has legislated on this subject, its legislation manifests an intention, with a single exception, not to regulate this subject, but to leave its regulation to the several States. To these precise questions, which are all we are called on to decide, this opinion must be understood to be confined. It does not extend to the question what other subjects, under the commercial power, are within the exclusive control of Congress, or may be regulated by the States in the absence of all congressional legislation; nor to the general question how far any regulation of a subject by Congress may be deemed to operate as an exclusion of all legislation by the States upon the same subject. We decide the precise questions before us, upon what we deem sound principles, applicable to this particular subject in the state in which the legislation of Congress has left it. We go no farther.

...We are of opinion that this State law ... is therefore valid, and the judgment of the Supreme Court of Pennsylvania in each case must be
Affirmed.

MR. JUSTICE McLEAN and MR. JUSTICE WAYNE dissented. MR. JUSTICE DANIEL wrote a concurring opinion.

SOUTHERN PACIFIC CO. v. ARIZONA
325 U.S. 761; 65 S.Ct. 1515; 89 L.Ed. 1915 (1945)

The Arizona legislature passed a law in 1912, which limited the length of passenger trains to fourteen cars and restricted those of freight carriers to seventy. In 1940, the state brought suit against Southern Pacific for violating the statute. The railroad claimed that the Arizona Train Limit Law was an unconstitutional regulation of interstate commerce in violation of the Cooley doctrine. After the state supreme court upheld the state suit, the company appealed to the Supreme Court of the United States.

MR. CHIEF JUSTICE STONE delivered the opinion of the Court:

...The questions for decision are whether Congress has, by legislative enactment, restricted the power of the states to regulate the length of interstate trains as a safety measure and, if not, whether the statute contravenes the commerce clause of the Federal Constitution....

Congress, in enacting legislation within its constitutional authority over interstate commerce, will not be deemed to have intended to strike down a state statute designed to protect the health and safety of the public unless its purpose to do so is clearly manifested... or unless the state law, in terms or in its practical administration, conflicts with the Act of Congress, or plainly and palpably infringes its policy....

Congress, although asked to do so, has declined to pass legislation specifically limiting trains to seventy cars. We are therefore brought to appellant's principal contention, that the state statute contravenes the commerce clause of the Federal Constitution.

Although the commerce clause conferred on the national government power to regulate commerce, its possession of the power does not exclude all state power of regulation. Ever since *Willson v. Blackbird Creek Marsh Co.*, 2 Pet, 245, and *Cooley v. Board of Wardens*, 12 How. 299, it has been recognized that, in the absence of conflicting legislation by Congress, there is a residuum of power in the state to make laws governing matters of local concern which nevertheless in some measure affect interstate commerce or even, to some extent, regulate it.... Thus the states may regulate matters which, because of their number and diversity, may never be adequately dealt with by Congress.... When the regulation of matters of local concern is local in character and effect, and its impact on the national commerce does not seriously interfere with its operation, and the consequent incentive to deal with them nationally is slight, such regulation has been generally held to be within state authority....

But ever since *Gibbons v. Ogden*... the states have not been deemed to have authority to impede substantially the free flow of commerce from state to state, or to regulate those phases of the national commerce which, because of the need of national uniformity, demand that their regulation, if any, be prescribed by a single authority.... Whether or not this long-recognized distribution of power between the national and the state governments is predicated upon the implications of the commerce clause itself... or upon the presumed intention of Congress, where Congress has not spoken... the result is the same.

In the application of these principles some enactments may be found to be without state power. But between these extremes lies the infinite variety of cases in which regulation of local matters may also operate as a regulation of commerce, in which reconciliation of the conflicting claims of state and national power is to be attained only by some appraisal and accommodation of the competing demands of the state and national interests involved....

For a hundred years it has been accepted constitutional doctrine that the commerce clause, without the aid of Congressional legislation, thus affords some protection from state legislation inimical to the national commerce, and that in such cases, where Congress has not acted, this Court, and not the state legislature, is under the commerce clause the final arbiter of the competing demands of state and national interests.

Hence the matters for ultimate determination here are the nature and extent of the burden which the state regulation of interstate trains, adopted as a safety measure, imposes on interstate commerce, and whether the relative weights of the state and national interests involved are such as to make inapplicable the rule, generally observed, that the free flow of interstate commerce and its freedom from local restraints in matters requiring uniformity of regulations are interests safeguarded by the commerce clause from state interference....

The findings show that the operation of long trains, that is, trains of more than fourteen passenger and more than seventy freight cars, is standard practice over the main lines of the railroads of the United States, and that, if the length of trains is to be regulated at all, national uniformity in the regulation adopted, such as only Congress can prescribe, is practically indispensable to the operation of an efficient and economical national railway system. On many railroads passenger trains of more than fourteen cars and freight trains of more than seventy cars are operated, and on some systems freight trains are run ranging from 125 to 160 cars in length. Outside of Arizona, where the length of trains is not restricted, appellant runs a substantial proportion of long trains....

The record shows a definite relationship between operating costs and the length of trains, the increase in length resulting in a reduction of operating costs per car. The additional cost of operation of trains complying with the Train Limit

Law in Arizona amounts for the two railroads traversing that state to about $1,000,000 a year. The reduction in train lengths also impedes efficient operation. More locomotives and more manpower are required; the necessary conversion and reconversion of train lengths at terminals, and the delay caused by breaking up and remaking long trains upon entering and leaving the state in order to comply with the law, delays the traffic and diminishes its volume moved in a given time, especially when traffic is heavy....

The unchallenged findings leave no doubt that the Arizona Train Limit Law imposes a serious burden on the interstate commerce conducted by appellant. It materially impedes the movement of appellant's interstate trains through the state and interposes a substantial obstruction to the national policy proclaimed by Congress, to promote adequate, economical, and efficient railway transportation service.... Enforcement of the law in Arizona, while train lengths remain unregulated or are regulated by varying standards in other states, must inevitably result in an impairment of uniformity of efficient railroad operation because the railroads are subjected to regulation which is not uniform in its application. Compliance with a state statute limiting train lengths requires interstate trains of a length lawful in other states to be broken up and reconstituted as they enter each state according as it may impose varying limitations upon train lengths. The alternative is for the carrier to conform to the lowest train limit restriction of any of the states through which its trains pass, whose laws thus control the carriers' operations both within and without the regulating state....

We think, as the trial court found, that the Arizona Train Limit Law, viewed as a safety measure, affords at most slight and dubious advantage, if any, over unregulated train lengths.... Its undoubted effect on the commerce is the regulation, without securing uniformity, of the length of trains operated in interstate commerce, which lack is itself a primary cause of preventing the free flow of commerce by delaying it and by substantially increasing its cost and impairing its efficiency. In these respects the case differs from those where a state, by regulatory measures affecting the commerce, has removed or reduced safety hazards without substantial interference with the interstate movement of trains....

The principle that, without controlling Congressional action, a state may not regulate interstate commerce so as substantially to affect its flow or deprive it of needed uniformity in its regulation is not to be avoided by "simply invoking the convenient apologetics of the police power."

...[W]e conclude that the state does go too far. Its regulation of train lengths, admittedly obstructive to interstate train operation, and having a seriously adverse effect on transportation efficiency and economy, passes beyond what is plainly essential for safety since it does not appear that it will lessen rather than increase the danger of accident. Its attempted regulations of the operation of interstate trains cannot establish nationwide control such as is essential to the maintenance of an efficient transportation system, which Congress alone can prescribe. The state interest cannot be preserved at the expense of the national interest by an enactment which regulates interstate train lengths without securing such control, which is a matter of national concern. To this the interest of the state here asserted is subordinate.

The state is responsible for their safe and economical administration. Regulations affecting the safety of their use must be applied alike to intrastate and interstate traffic. The fact that they affect alike shippers in interstate and intrastate commerce in great numbers, within as well as without the state, is a safeguard against regulatory abuses. Their regulation is akin to quarantine measures, game laws, and like local regulations of rivers, harbors, piers, and docks, with respect to which the state has exceptional scope for the exercise of its regulatory power, and which, Congress not acting, have been sustained even though they materially interfere with interstate commerce....

The contrast between the present regulation and the full train-crew laws in point of their effects on the commerce, and the like contrast with the highway safety regulations, in point of the nature of the subject of regulation, emphasize the considerations which enter into a determination of the relative weights of state and national interests where state regulation affecting interstate commerce is attempted. Here examination of all the relevant factors makes it plain that the state interest is outweighed by the interest of the nation in an adequate, economical, and efficient railway transportation service, which must prevail.

Reversed.

MR. JUSTICE RUTLEDGE concurred in the result.
MR. JUSTICES BLACK AND DOUGLAS dissented.

EDWARDS v. CALIFORNIA
314 U.S. 160; 62 S.Ct. 164; 86 L.Ed. 119 (1941)

The facts involved in this case were indisputable: Edwards, a citizen and resident of California, had traveled to Texas by car to pick up and bring back his indigent brother-in-law, Frank Duncan. A complaint was filed against Edwards for violating Section 2615 of the Welfare and Institutions Code of California which provided: "Every person ... that brings or assists in bringing into the State any indigent person who is not a resident of the State, knowing him to be an indigent person is guilty of a misdemeanor." Edwards was convicted and, arguing that this "anti-Okie" law was an invalid use of the police power, appealed to the Supreme Court.

MR. JUSTICE BYRNES delivered the opinion of the Court:

...Article I, section 8 of the Constitution delegates to the Congress the authority to regulate interstate commerce. And it is settled beyond question that the transportation of persons is "commerce," within the meaning of that provision. It is nevertheless true, that the States are not wholly precluded from exercising their police power in matters of local concern even though they may thereby affect interstate commerce.... The issue presented in this case, therefore, is whether the prohibition embodied in section 2615 against the "bringing" or transportation of indigent persons into California is within the police power of that State. We think that it is not, and hold that it is an unconstitutional barrier to interstate commerce.

The grave and perplexing social and economic dislocation which this statute reflects is a matter of common knowledge and concern. We are not unmindful of it. We appreciate that the spectacle of large segments of our population constantly on the move has given rise to urgent demands upon the ingenuity of government.... The State asserts that the huge influx of migrants into California in recent years has resulted in problems of health, morals, and especially finance, the proportions of which are staggering. It is not for us to say that this is not true. We have repeatedly and recently affirmed, and we now reaffirm, that we do not conceive it our function to pass upon "the wisdom, need, or appropriateness" of the legislative efforts of the States to solve such difficulties....

But this does not mean that there are no boundaries to the permissible area of State legislative activity. There are. And none is more certain than the prohibition against attempts on the part of any single State to isolate itself from difficulties common to all of them by restraining the transportation of persons and property across its borders. It is frequently the case that a State might gain a momentary respite from the pressure of events by the simple expedient of shutting its gates to the outside world. But, in the words of Mr. Justice Cardozo: "The Constitution was framed under the dominion of a political philosophy less parochial in range. It was framed upon the theory that the peoples of the several States must sink or swim together, and that in the long run prosperity and salvation are in union and not division." *Baldwin v. Seelig*, 294 U.S. 511, 523.

It is difficult to conceive of a statute more squarely in conflict with this theory than the section challenged here. Its express purpose and inevitable effect is to prohibit the transportation of indigent persons across the California border. The burden upon interstate commerce is intended and immediate; it is the plain and sole function of the statute. Moreover, the indigent nonresidents who are the real victims of the statute are deprived of the opportunity to exert political pressure upon the California legislature in order to obtain a change in policy.... We think this statute must fail under any known test of the validity of State interference with interstate commerce.

It is urged, however, that the concept which underlies section 2615 enjoys a firm basis in English and American history. This is the notion that each community should care for its own indigent, that relief is solely the responsibility of local government. Of this it must first be said that we are not now called upon to determine anything other than the propriety of an attempt by a State to prohibit the transportation of indigent nonresidents into its territory. The nature and extent of its obligation to afford relief to newcomers is not here involved. We do, however, suggest that the theory of the Elizabethan poor laws no longer fits the facts. Recent years, and particularly the past decade, have been marked by a growing recognition that in an industrial society the task of providing assistance to the needy has ceased to be local in character. The duty to share the burden, if not wholly to assume it, has been recognized not only by State governments, but by the Federal government as well. The changed attitude is reflected in the Social Security laws under which the Federal and State governments cooperate for the care of the aged, the blind, and dependent children.... It is reflected in the works programs under which work is furnished the unemployed, with the States supplying approximately 25 per cent and the Federal government approximately 75 per cent of the cost.... It is further reflected in the Farm Security laws, under which the entire cost of the relief provisions is borne by the Federal government....

Indeed, the record in this very case illustrates the inadequate basis in fact for the theory that relief is presently a local matter. Before leaving Texas, Duncan had received assistance from the Works Progress Administration. After arriving in California he was aided by the Farm Security Administration, which, as we have said, is wholly financed by the Federal government. This is not to say that our judgment would be different if Duncan had received relief from local agencies in Texas and California. Nor is it to suggest that the financial burden of assistance to indigent persons does not continue to fall heavily upon local and State governments. It is only to illustrate that in not inconsiderable measure the relief of the needy has become the common responsibility and concern of the whole nation.

...We are of the opinion that the transportation of indigent persons from State to State clearly falls within this class of subjects. The scope of Congressional power to deal with this problem we are not now called upon to decide.

There remains to be noticed only the contention that the limitation upon State power to interfere with the interstate transportation of persons is subject to an exception in the case of "paupers." It is true that support for this contention may be found in early decisions of this Court. In *City of New York v. Miln,* 11 Pet. 102, ... it was said that it is "as competent and as necessary for a State to provide precautionary measures against the moral pestilence of paupers, vagabonds, and possibly convicts, as it is to guard against the physical pestilence, which may arise from unsound and infectious articles imported...." This language has been casually repeated in numerous later cases up the turn of the century.... In none of these cases, however, was the power of a State to exclude "paupers" actually involved.

Whether an able-bodied but unemployed person like Duncan is a "pauper" within the historical meaning of the term is open to considerable doubt.... But assuming that the term is applicable to him and to persons similarly situated, we do not consider ourselves bound by the language referred to. *City of New York v. Miln* was decided in 1837. Whatever may have been the notion then prevailing, we do not think that it will now be seriously contended that because a person is without employment and without funds he constitutes a "moral pestilence." *Poverty and immorality are not synonymous.*

We are of the opinion that section 2615 is not a valid exercise of the police power of California; that it imposes an unconstitutional burden upon interstate commerce, and that the conviction under it cannot be sustained. In the view we have taken, it is necessary to decide whether the section is repugnant to other provisions of the Constitution.

Reversed.

MR. JUSTICE JACKSON concurred, saying in part:

The right of the citizen to migrate from state to state which, I agree with Mr. Justice Douglas, is shown by our precedents to be one of national citizenship, is not, however, an unlimited one. In addition to being subject to all constitutional limitations imposed by the federal government, such citizen is subject to some control by state governments. He may not, if a fugitive from justice, claim freedom to migrate unmolested, nor may he endanger others by carrying contagion about. These causes, and perhaps others that do not occur to me now, warrant any public authority in stopping a man where it finds him and arresting his progress across a state line quite as much as from place to place within the state.

It is here that we meet the real crux of this case. Does "indigence" as defined by the application of the California statute constitute a basis for restricting the freedom of a citizen, as crime or contagion warrants its restriction? We should say now, and in no uncertain terms, that a man's mere property status, without more, cannot be used by a state to test, qualify, or limit his rights as a citizen of the United States. "Indigence" in itself is neither a source of rights or a basis for denying them. The mere state of being without funds is a neutral fact – constitutionally an irrelevance, like race, creed, or color. I agree with what I understand to be the holding of the Court that cases which may indicate the contrary are overruled.

Any measure which would divide our citizenry on the basis of property into one class free to move from state to state and another class that is poverty-bound to the place where it has suffered misfortune is not only at war with the habit and custom by which our country has expanded, but is also a short-sighted blow at the security of property itself. Property can have no more dangerous, even if unwitting, enemy than one who would make its possession a pretext for unequal or exclusive civil rights. Where those rights are derived from national citizenship no state may impose such a test, and whether the Congress could do so we are not called upon to inquire.

I think California had no right to make the condition of Duncan's purse, with no evidence of violation by him of any law or social policy which caused it, the basis of excluding him or of punishing one who extended him aid.

Rich or penniless, Duncan's citizenship under the Constitution pledges his strength to the defense of California as a part of the United States, and his right to migrate to any part of the land he must defend is something she must respect under the same instrument. Unless this Court is willing to say that citizenship of the United States means at least this much to the citizen, then our heritage of constitutional privileges and immunities is only a promise to the ear to be broken to the hope, a teasing illusion like a munificent bequest in a pauper's will.

MR. JUSTICE DOUGLAS wrote a concurring opinion, in which MR. JUSTICE BLACK and MR. JUSTICE MURPHY joined.

PIKE v. BRUCE CHURCH, INC.
397 U.S. 137 (1970)

Bruce Church, Inc., grows cantaloupes in Parker, Arizona; however, since there are no packing sheds in Parker, the company sends its cantaloupes to packing facilities located nearby in Blythe, California. The packer then sorts, inspects, packs, and ships the fruit in containers bearing his name. Pike, a state official, issued an order forbidding Bruce Church from shipping the cantaloupes interstate unless they were packed in containers clearly identifying them as Arizona products as required under the state's Fruit and Vegetable Standardization Act. The company brought suit for injunctive relief which was issued by a federal district court. The case was then appealed to the Supreme Court.

MR. JUSTICE STEWART delivered the opinion of the Court:

The appellant's threshold contention here is that even though the challenged order expressly forbids the interstate bulk shipment of the company's cantaloupes, it imposes no burden upon interstate commerce. If the Arizona Act is complied with, he argues, all that will be regulated will be the intrastate packing of goods destined for interstate commerce. Articles being made ready for interstate movements are not necessarily yet in interstate commerce, which, he says, begins only when the articles are delivered to the interstate shipper.

If the appellant's theory were correct, then statutes expressly requiring that certain kinds of processing be done in the home State before shipment to a sister State would be immune from constitutional challenge. Yet such statutes have been consistently invalidated by this Court under the Commerce Clause. Thus it is clear that the appellant's order does affect and burden interstate commerce, and the question then becomes whether it does so unconstitutionally.

Although the criteria for determining the validity of state statutes affecting interstate commerce have been variously stated, the general rule that emerges can be phrased as follows: Where the statute regulates evenhandedly to effectuate a legitimate local public interest, and its effects on interstate commerce are only incidental, it will be upheld unless the burden imposed on such commerce is clearly excessive in relation to the putative local benefits. If a legitimate local purpose is found, then the question becomes one of degree. And the extent of the burden that will be tolerated will of course depend on the nature of the local interest involved, and on whether it could be promoted as well with a lesser impact on interstate activities. Occasionally the Court has candidly undertaken a balancing approach in resolving these issues, *Southern Pacific Co. v. Arizona*, 325 U.S. 761, but more frequently it has spoken in terms of "direct" and "indirect" effects and burdens. See, e.g., *Shafer v. Farmers Grain Co.*

At the core of the Arizona Fruit and Vegetable Standardization Act are the requirements that fruits and vegetables shipped from Arizona meet certain standards of wholesomeness and quality, and that they be packed in standard containers in such a way that the outer layer or exposed portion of the pack does not "materially misrepresent" the quality of the lot as a whole. The impetus for the Act was the fear that some growers were shipping inferior or deceptively packaged produce, with the result that the reputation of Arizona growers generally was being tarnished and their financial return concomitantly reduced. It was to prevent this that the Act was passed in 1929. The State has stipulated that its primary purpose is to promote and preserve the reputation of Arizona growers by prohibiting deceptive packaging.

We are not, then, dealing here with "state legislation in the field of safety where the propriety of local regulation has long been recognized," or with an Act designed to protect consumers in Arizona from contaminated or unfit goods. Its purpose and design are simply to protect and enhance the reputation of growers within the State. These are surely legitimate state interests. Therefore, as applied to Arizona growers who package their produce in Arizona, we may assume the constitutional validity of the Act. We may further assume that Arizona has full constitutional power to forbid the misleading use of its name on produce that was grown or packed elsewhere. And, to the extent the Act forbids the shipment of contaminated or unfit produce, it clearly rests on sure footing. For, as the Court has said, such produce is "not the legitimate subject of trade or commerce, nor within the protection of the commerce clause of the Constitution."

But application of the Act through the appellant's order to the appellee company has a far different impact, and quite a different purpose. The cantaloupes grown by the company at Parker are of exceptionally high quality. The company does not pack them in Arizona and cannot do so without making a capital expenditure of approximately $200,000. It transports them in bulk to nearby Bythe, California, where they are sorted, inspected, packed, and shipped in containers that do not identify them as Arizona cantaloupes, but bear the name of their California packer. The appellant's order would forbid the company to pack its cantaloupes outside Arizona, not for the purpose of keeping the reputation of its growers unsullied, but to enhance their reputation through the reflected good will of the company's superior produce. The appellant, in other words, is not complaining because the company is putting the good name of Arizona on an inferior or deceptively packaged product, but because it is not putting that name on a product that is superior and well packaged.

While the order issued under the Arizona statute does not impose such rigidity on an entire industry, it does impose just such a straitjacket on the appellee company with respect to the allocation of its interstate resources. Such an incidental consequence of a regulatory scheme could perhaps be tolerated if a more compelling state interest were involved. But here the State's interest is minimal at best – certainly less substantial than a State's interest in securing employment for its people, If the Commerce Clause forbids a State to require work to be done within its jurisdiction to promote local employment, then surely it cannot permit a State to require a person to go into a local packing business solely for the sake of enhancing the reputation of other producers within its borders. The judgment is Affirmed.

CHAPTER IX

THE GENERAL WELFARE: NATIONAL AND STATE

The Tenth Amendment was written with the hope of quieting the fears of those who were committed to the "sovereign rights" of states, and thus to assure the ratification of the Constitution. Many citizens were concerned that the national government might usurp the powers of the states "under the pressure of the supposed general welfare."[1] It was for this reason that Article I, section 8, grants Congress only the powers of taxing and spending for the "general welfare." As an additional precaution the Tenth Amendment stipulates: "The powers not delegated to the United States by the Constitution, nor prohibited by it to the States, are reserved to the States respectively, or to the people." It is of extreme importance that the word "*delegated*" and not "*enumerated*" was chosen by the writers of the Amendment. Since, by definition, the term "delegated" includes both the "enumerated" and "necessary and proper" (implied) powers, the overall authority of the national government was not weakened. Once the States joined the Union under the new Constitution they yielded the powers inherent in independent governments including the powers to declare war, to make treaties, to coin money, and to impose duties on imports and exports, which were thereafter "prohibited." As discussed earlier in the text, it was presumed that the broad concept of the general welfare or police power was reserved to the states. The legislatures could enact all laws (not in conflict with the "supreme law of the land") to protect and promote the health, safety, morals, and general welfare of the community. However, near the end of the nineteenth century the Supreme Court's interpretation of the Due Process Clause of the Fifth and Fourteenth Amendments came into conflict with state attempts to exercise this "paramount power."

During the period of Reconstruction, the Radical Republicans in control of Congress hoped that the Fourteenth Amendment would constitutionally justify the controversial Civil Rights Bill of 1866. The Amendment contained key provisions that guaranteed rights of Due Process, Equal Protection, and Privileges and Immunities for United States citizens and protected them from state interference. In the first litigation to reach the Supreme Court involving the provisions of the Fourteenth Amendment, it very narrowly interpreted their application; see *The Slaughterhouse Cases* (1873). It refused to uphold the claim of unemployed butchers that the Fourteenth Amendment was violated by a slaughterhouse monopoly established by Louisiana law. The Court's construction of the "privileges and immunities" clause (no state was to abridge the privileges and immunities of citizens of the United States) was so restricted that the clause remains of negligible importance today; for example, see *Madden v. Kentucky* (1940). However, the Court, in the words of Justice Miller, went on to also dismiss the importance of the "due process" and "equal protection" clauses:

> We doubt very much whether any action of a state not directed by way of discrimination against the Negroes as a class, or on account of their race, will ever be held to come within the preview of this provision. It is so clearly a provision for that race and that emergency, that a strong case would be necessary for its application to any other.

No predication could have further missed the mark. The "due process" clause alone has today become perhaps the singularly most important section of the Constitution. In any event, *The Slaughterhouse Cases* reflected the restraintist attitude of the Court of that day.

In a significant decision rendered four years later, the Court in *Munn v. Illinois* again showed its judicial restraint and general reluctance to interfere with state regulatory powers. The Court in this, the most important of the *Granger Cases*, upheld a state law which regulated the storage of grain in public elevators. Chief Justice Morrison R. Waite speaking for the Court pointed out that "when *private* property is devoted to a public use, it is subject to *public* regulation." The philosophical inclinations of the Court, however, were soon to change from judicial noninterference to judicial activism in defense of laissez faire economics.

The transition to a more active role of the Court began when it embraced the idea that "due process of law" protected not only procedural rights but substantive ones, including the private ownership of property, as well; see *Davidson v. New Orleans* (1878).[2] In 1890, the Court made the shift complete by abandoning its earlier narrow view for a much more sweeping concept of "due process," when it invalidated Minnesota's attempt to regulate railroad rates as a violation of the Fourteenth Amendment; see *Chicago, Milwaukee and St. Paul R.R. Co. v. Minnesota.* Coupled with its decision four years earlier that corporations were *persons* under law and thus entitled to Fourteenth Amendment protection, the Court was making clear its intention to restrict the general welfare power of the states to protect private enterprise; see *Santa Clara County v. Southern Pacific Railroad Co.* (1886).

The era of "substantive due process" or laissez faire lasted nearly a half century (1890-1937), during which the Court with alarming regularity struck down state and national attempts at economic regulation. The point could be legitimately made that the Court during these years was the strongest of the three branches even though its effect was negative in coloration. As the late Roscoe Pound described the period in his *Sources and Forms of Law*:

> The need of stability and certainty in the maturity of law and the importance of social interests in security of acquisitions and security of transactions in a commercial and industrial society called for an analytical rather than a philosophical method; the task of the jurist was to perfect what he found in the legal system rather than to build anew.[3]

In an important decision in 1905, the Court over the vigorous dissent of Justice Holmes declared that New York's Labor Law which limited the work-week for bakery employees to sixty hours and ten hours a day violated the Due Process Clause of the Fourteenth Amendment. In doing so, the Court invented the theory that the Clause protected "freedom or liberty of contract" between employer and employees; a contract with which government could never interfere without violating "due process of law;" see *Lochner v. New York* (1905). The Court later reiterated this concept when it voided a state minimum-wage law for women and children; see *Morehead v. New York ex rel. Tipaldo* (1936). Congress was by no means immune from the Lochner doctrine; the Court declared its minimum-wage for women and children in the District of Columbia unconstitutional in a controversial decision; see *Adkins v. Children's Hospital* (1923).[4] Moreover, the Court during the period was challenging the authority of Congress on a number of other fronts as well.

Beginning with the passage of the Interstate Commerce Act of 1887, the Congress attempted to expand its general welfare authority by creating an unofficial federal police power. It relied on the use of the Necessary and Proper Clause (Article 1, sect. 8, cl. 18) to imply additional discretion from its chief enumerated grants including the power to "tax and spend for the general welfare," the war and postal powers and, most importantly, the power to regulate interstate commerce. Eventually Congress implied sufficient powers to till such hitherto "unplowed" policy areas as law enforcement, regulation of the nation's economy, grants-in-aid funds to the states, civil rights, control of agricultural production and marketing, regulation of labor-management relations, etc. At first, the Court rarely restricted congressional exertions of an implied police power on the grounds that the Tenth Amendment reserved that power "exclusively" to the states; the Court's decision to exclude manufacturers from the terms of the Sherman Anti-Trust Act of 1890 (*United States v. EC. Knight Co.*, 1895) and its striking down of the federal Child Labor Law (*Hammer v. Dagenhart*, 1918) were chief among them. However, even before the New Deal of Franklin Roosevelt, the Court had upheld federal legislation banning the interstate shipment of lottery tickets (*Champion v. Ames*, 1903), the Mann Act which prohibited the "white slavery" trade (*Hoke v. United States*, 1913), the Selective Service Act (*Arver v.

United States, 1918), the federal tax on the sale of narcotics (*United States v. Doremus*, 1919); and the Packers and Stockyards Act *(Stafford v, Wallace*, 1922).

It also seemed to further expand Congress' power by holding that intrastate commerce which had a significant effect on interstate commerce, also fell under the federal regulations; see *The Shreveport Case (*1914). Moreover, in 1934 the Court handed down what was viewed as a very significant decision in *Nebbia v. New York*. For some time the Court had backtracked from its policy toward state regulatory measures as enunciated in *Munn*. Holding that businesses not "affected with a public interest" were not subject to government regulation of prices or services, the Court had nullified, as violative of "due process of law" provided by the Fourteenth Amendment, state laws pertaining to meat-packing houses (*Wolff Packing Co. v. Industrial Court*, 1929); to the business of selling theatre tickets (*Tyson and Brothers v. Banton*, 1927); employment agencies (*Ribnik v. McBride*, 1928); the price of gasoline (*Williams v. Standard Oil Co.*, 1929); and the sale of ice to private consumers (*New State Ice Co. v. Liebmann*, 1932), However, in *Nebbia*, the Court ruled that "a state is free to adopt whatever economic policy may reasonably be deemed to promote public welfare, and to enforce that policy by legislation adapted to its purpose." It was thought at the time that this decision provided a strong indication of a return to judicial restraint and that the Court would defer to the intent of Congress with respect to New Deal legislation. Such was not to be the case, as the Court usually by a 5-4 vote negated important social and economic legislation, particularly the National Industrial Recovery Act (1933) and the Agricultural Adjustment Act (1933); see *Panama Refining Co. v. Ryan* (1935), *Schechter Poultry Corp. v. United States* (1935); *United States v. Butler* (1936); and *Carter v. Carter Coal Co.* (1936).

On February 5, 1937, President Franklin Roosevelt reacted to the "nine old men" cutting the heart out of his New Deal program by submitting his court-packing scheme to Congress. While the plan was not approved, Justice Owen J. Roberts and Chief Justice Hughes began voting to sustain other social legislation ("the switch in time that *saved* nine") and the matter became moot. The change became evident when in *West Coast Hotel Co. v. Parrish* (1937) the Court overruled *Adkins* and upheld the state of Washington's minimum wage law for women and children. Four years later all but one of the justices (Harlan F. Stone) had been appointed by F.D.R.. Since that time, the judicial trend has been reversed. For the past sixty years the Court has taken a restraintist attitude toward congressional exercise of its general powers – interpreting the Tenth Amendment as imposing no real limits on federal action – while, for the most part, jealously protecting the constitutional liberties of individuals. In *NLRB v. Jones & Laughlin Steel Corporation* (1937), one of the most important decisions handed down in this century, the Court recognized for the first time the responsibility of the national government for the regulation of the nation's economy. Specifically, it upheld the validity of the National Labor Relations Act of 1935 (also known as the Wagner Act) which permitted the government broad power to regulate labor-management relations, particularly in all disputes which burdened or obstructed interstate commerce. The Court also allowed Congress to further enhance its police powers by upholding a number of significant laws implied from the commerce clause and the power to spend for the general welfare: the Social Security Act of 1935 (*Steward Machine Company v. Davis,* 1937); the Fair Labor Standards Act of 1938 (*United States v. Darby*, 1941), the second Agricultural Adjustment Act of 1938 first in *Mulford v. Smith* (1939) but more importantly in *Wickard v. Filburn* (1942); the Civil Rights Act of 1964 (*Heart of Atlanta Motel v. United States,* 1964); and upheld the power of Congress to reduce federal assistance for highway construction if a state failed to enact restrictive legislation limiting the alcohol drinking age to twenty-one year old persons and above. See *South Dakota v. Dole* (1987).

In recent years, however, the Court has indicated a willingness to once again consider (or, at least, debate) limits on the national government's powers. In *National League of Cities v. Usery* (1976), then Justice William Rehnquist wrote the 5-4 majority opinion which declared amendments making the minimum wage, maximum hour provisions of the Fair Labor Standards Act applicable to state and municipal employees to be unconstitutional violations of the Tenth Amendment. That decision, however, was overruled in *Garcia v. San Antonio Metropolitan Transit Authority* (1985). Again in a 5-4 majority opinion, Justice Blackmun (who had joined the majority in *Usery*) wrote that the political process was the proper means of protecting states' powers, not appeal to the Tenth Amendment. In a decision that is certain to generate additional challenges to federal "police powers," the Court overturned the Gun-Free School Zone Act of 1990 on the grounds that Congress did not have authority under the commerce clause to ban guns at schools; see *United States v. Lopez* (1995)

Congress traditionally has been less successful in extracting additional authority from its taxing power than it has from its other enumerated grants. This has been so because of two factors: *first,* Article I places certain expressed restrictions on the nature and types of taxes Congress may impose. *Duties, imposts, and excises* must be taxed uniformly throughout the fifty states (section 8, clause 1). On the other hand, direct taxes, which have rarely been used, must be apportioned among the states according to population. Prior to the ratification of the Sixteenth Amendment the Court had invalidated a federal income tax on the grounds that it was a non-apportioned direct tax (*Pollock v. Farmers' Loan and Trust Co*., 1895). *Second*, the Court has developed the doctrine that Congress may tax only to raise revenue and may not use the mechanism to penalize or destroy certain goods or activities otherwise beyond the reach of Congress. While on its face any penalty involved can only be incidental to the prime purpose of raising revenue, the Court has strongly indicated that it will not pry into the supposed motives of Congress; see *McCray v. United States* (1904); *Bailey v. Drexel Furniture Company* (1922); *Hill v. Wallace* (1922); *United States v. Constantine* (1935); and *Sonzinsky v. United States* (1937). In *Grosso v. United States* (1968), the Court invalidated the gambling tax provisions of the Revenue Act of 1951 which imposed a 10% excise tax on the total annual earnings of professional gamblers.

MUNN v. ILLINOIS
94 U.S. 113; 24 L.Ed. 77 (1877)

The Illinois state constitution of 1870 empowered the legislature to regulate the storage of grain. This was done to pacify, at least in part, the outcries of angry farmers and small businessmen against abuses brought about by the nation's powerful railroads. Munn, the operator of a grain warehouse, was convicted under a new state law of charging higher rates for storage than permitted and for not having an operator's permit. The case was brought to the Supreme Court on a writ of error.

MR. CHIEF JUSTICE WAITE delivered the opinion of the Court:

The question to be determined in this case is whether the general assembly of Illinois can, under the limitations upon the legislative power of the States imposed by the Constitution of the United States, fix by law the maximum of charges for the storage of grain in warehouses at Chicago and other places in the State having not less than 100,000 inhabitants, "in which grain of different owners is mixed together, or in which grain is stored in such a manner that the identity of different lots or parcels cannot be accurately preserved."

It is claimed that such a law is repugnant—

1. To that part of sect. 8, Art.I, of the Constitution of the United States which confers upon Congress the power "to regulate commerce with foreign nations and among the several States;"

2. To that part of sect. 9 of the same article which provides that "no preference shall be given by any regulation of commerce or revenue to the ports of one State over those of another;" and

3. To that part of Amendment Fourteen which ordains that no State shall "deprive any person of life, liberty, or property, without due process of law, nor deny to any person within its jurisdiction the equal protection of the laws."

We will consider the last of these objections first.

Every statute is presumed to be constitutional. The courts ought not to declare one to be unconstitutional, unless it is clearly so. If there is doubt, the expressed will of the legislature should be sustained.

The Constitution contains no definition of the word "deprive," as used in the Fourteenth Amendment. To determine its signification, therefore, it is necessary to ascertain the effect which usage has given it, when employed in the same or a like connection.

While this provision of the amendment is new in the Constitution of the United States, as a limitation upon the powers of the States, it is old as a principle of civilized government. It is found in Magna Carta, and, in substance if not in form, in nearly or quite all the constitutions that have been from time to time adopted by the several States of the Union. By the Fifth Amendment, it was introduced into the Constitution of the United States as a limitation upon the powers of the national government, and by the Fourteenth, as a guaranty against any encroachment upon an acknowledged right of citizenship by the legislatures of the States....

It is apparent that, down to the time of the adoption of the Fourteenth Amendment, it was not supposed that statutes regulating the use, or even the price of the use, of private property necessarily deprived an owner of his property without due process of law. Under some circumstances they may, but not under all. The amendment does not change the law in this particular: it simply prevents the States from doing that which will operate as such a deprivation.

This brings us to inquire as to the principles upon which this power of regulation rests, in order that we may determine what is within and what without its operative effect: Looking, then, to the common law, from whence came the right which the Constitution protects, we find that when private property is "affected with a public interest, it ceases to be *juris privati* only." This was said by Lord Chief Justice Hale more than 200 years ago..., and has been accepted without objection as an essential element in the law of property ever since. Property does become clothed with a public interest when used in a manner to make it of public consequence, and affect the community at large. When, therefore, one devotes his property to a use in which the public has an interest, he, in effect, grants to the public an interest in that use, and must submit to be controlled by the public for the common good, to the extent of the interest he has thus created. He may withdraw his grant by discontinuing the use; but, so long as he maintains the use, he must submit to the control....

Enough has already been said to show that, when private property is devoted to a public use, it is subject to public regulation. It remains only to ascertain whether the warehouses of these plaintiffs in error, and the business which is carried on there, come within the operation of this principle.

...The quantity [of grain] received in Chicago has made it the greatest grain market in the world. This business has created a demand for means by which the immense quantity of grain can be handled or stored, and these have been found in grain warehouses, which are commonly called elevators, because the grain is elevated from the boat or car, by machinery operated by steam, into bins prepared for its reception, and elevated from the bins, by a like process, into the vessel or car which is to carry it on .... In this way the largest traffic between the citizens of the country north and west of Chicago and the citizens of the country lying on the Atlantic coast north of Washington is in grain which passes through the elevators of Chicago. In this way the trade in grain is carried on by the inhabitants of seven or eight of the great States of the West with four or five of the States lying on the seashore, and forms the largest part of interstate commerce in these States. The grain warehouses or elevators in Chicago are immense structures, holding from 300,000 to 1,000,000 bushels at one time, according to size. They are divided into bins of large capacity and great strength.... They are located with the river harbor on one side and the railway tracks on the other; and the grain is run through them from car to vessel, or boat to car, as may be demanded in the course of business. It has been found impossible to preserve each owner's grain separate, and this has given rise to a system of inspection and grading, by which the grain of different owners is mixed, and receipts issued for the number of bushels which are negotiable, and redeemable in like kind, upon demand. This mode of conducting the business was inaugurated more than twenty years ago, and has grown to immense proportions. The railways have found it impracticable to own such elevators, and public policy forbids the transaction of such business by the carrier; the ownership has, therefore, been by private individuals, who have embarked their capital and devoted their industry to such business as a private pursuit.

In this connection it must also be borne in mind that, although in 1874 there were in Chicago fourteen warehouses adapted to this particular business, and owned by about thirty persons, nine business firms controlled them, and that the prices charged and received for storage were such "as have been from year to year agreed upon and established by the different elevators or warehouses in the city of Chicago, and which rates have been annually published in one or more newspapers printed in said city, in the month of January in each year, as the established rates for the year then next ensuing such publication." Thus it is apparent that all the elevating facilities through which these vast productions "of seven or eight great States of the West" must pass on the way "to four or five of the States on the sea-shore" may be a "virtual" monopoly.

Under such circumstances it is difficult to see why, if the common carrier, or the miller, or the ferryman, or the innkeeper, or the wharfinger, or the baker, or the cartman, or the hackney-coachman, pursues a public employment and exercises "a sort of public office," these plaintiffs in error do not. They stand, to use again the language of their counsel, in the very "gateway of commerce," and take toll from all who pass. Their business most certainly "tends to a common charge, and is become a thing of public interest and use." Every bushel of grain for its passage "pays a toll, which is a common charge," and, therefore, according to Lord Hale, every such warehouseman "ought to be under public regulation, viz., that he ... take but a reasonable toll." Certainly, if any business can be clothed "with a public interest, and cease to be *juris privati* only," this has been. It may not be made so by the operation of the Constitution of Illinois or this statute, but is by the facts.

We also are not permitted to overlook the fact that, for some reason, the people of Illinois, when they revised their Constitution in 1870, saw fit to make it the duty of the general assembly to pass laws "for the protection of producers, shippers, and receivers of grain and produce."

...Neither is it a matter of any moment that no precedent can be found for a statute precisely like this. It is conceded that the business is one of recent origin, that its growth has been rapid, and that it is already of great importance. And it must also be conceded that it is a business in which the whole public has a direct and positive interest. It presents, therefore, a case for the application of a long-known and well-established principle in social science, and this statute simply extends the law so as to meet this new development of commercial progress. There is no attempt to compel these owners to grant the public an interest in their property, but to declare their obligations, if they use it in this particular manner.

...The controlling fact is the power to regulate at all. If that exists, the right to establish the maximum of charge, as one of the means of regulation, is implied. In fact, the common-law rule, which requires the charge to be reasonable, is itself a regulation as to price. Without it the owner could make his rates at will, and compel the public to yield to his terms, or forego the use.

But a mere common-law regulation of trade or business may be changed by statute. A person has no property, no vested interest, in any rule of the common law which cannot be taken away without due process; but the law itself, as a rule of conduct, may be changed at the will, or even at the whim, of the legislature, unless prevented by constitutional limitations. Indeed, the great office of statutes is to remedy defects in the common law as they are developed, and to adapt it to the changes of time and circumstances. To limit the rate of charge for services rendered in a public employment, or for the use of property in which the public has an interest, is only changing a regulation which existed before. It establishes no new principle in the law, but only gives a new effect to an old one.

We know that this is a power which may be abused; but that is no argument against its existence. For protection against abuses by legislatures the people must resort to the polls, not to the courts.

...We come now to consider the effect upon this statute of the power of Congress to regulate commerce.

... "It is not everything that affects commerce that amounts to a regulation of it, within the meaning of the Constitution." The warehouses of these plaintiffs in error are situated and their business carried on exclusively within the limits of the State of Illinois. They are used as instruments by those engaged in State as well as those engaged in interstate commerce, but they are no more necessarily a part of commerce itself than the dray or the cart by which, but for them, grain would be transferred from one railroad station to another. Incidentally they may become connected with interstate commerce, but not necessarily so. Their regulation is a thing of domestic concern, and, certainly, until Congress acts in reference to their interstate relations, the State may exercise all the powers of government over them, even though in so doing it may indirectly operate upon commerce outside its immediate jurisdiction. We do not say that a case may not arise in which it will be found that a State, under the form of regulating its own affairs, has encroached upon the exclusive domain of Congress in respect to interstate commerce, but we do say that, upon the facts as they are represented to us in this record, that has not been done.

The remaining objection, to wit, that the statute in its present form is repugnant to sect. 9, Art I, of the Constitution of the United States, because it gives preference to the ports of one State over those of another, may be disposed of by the single remark that this provision operates only as a limitation of the powers of Congress, and in no respect affects the States in the regulation of their domestic affairs.

We conclude, therefore, that the statute in question is not repugnant to the Constitution of the United States…
Judgment Affirmed.

MR. JUSTICE FIELD, joined by MR. JUSTICE STRONG, dissented.

LOCHNER v. NEW YORK
25 S.Ct. 539; 198 U.S. 45; 49 L.Ed. 937 (1905)

Joseph Lochner was convicted of violating the New York Labor Law, which made it a crime to require or permit employees of a bakery to work more than sixty hours per week or ten hours in a single day. The state court of appeals upheld the conviction, and Lochner appealed to the Supreme Court.

MR JUSTICE PECKHAM, after making the foregoing statement of the facts, delivered the opinion of the court:

The indictment, it will be seen, charges that the plaintiff in error violated … the labor law of the state of New York, in that he wrongfully and unlawfully required and permitted an employee working for him to work more than sixty hours in one week.… The mandate of the statute, that "no employee shall be required or permitted to work," is the substantial equivalent of an enactment that "no employee shall contract or agree to work," more than ten hours per day; and, as there is no provision for special emergencies, the statute is mandatory in all cases. It is not an act merely fixing the number of hours which shall constitute a legal day's work, but an absolute prohibition upon the employer permitting, under any circumstances, more than ten hours' work to be done in his establishment. The employee may desire to earn the extra money which would arise from his working more than the prescribed time, but this statute forbids the employer from permitting the employee to earn it.

The statute necessarily interferes with the right of contract between the employer and employees, concerning the number of hours in which the latter may labor in the bakery of the employer. The general right to make a contract in relation to his business is part of the liberty of the individual protected by the 14th Amendment of the Federal Constitution. *Allgeyer v. Louisiana*.… Under that provision no state can deprive any person of life, liberty, or property without due process of law. The right to purchase or to sell labor is part of the liberty protected by this amendment, unless there are circumstances which exclude the right. There are, however, certain powers, existing in the sovereignty of each state in the Union, somewhat vaguely termed police powers, the exact description and limitation of which have not been attempted by the courts. Those powers, broadly stated, and without, at present, any attempt at a more specific limitation, relate to the safety, health, morals, and general welfare of the public. Both property and liberty are held on such reasonable conditions as may be imposed by the governing power of the state in the exercise of those powers, and with such conditions the 14th Amendment was not designed to interfere.

...The state, therefore, has power to prevent the individual from making certain kinds of contracts, and in regard to them the Federal Constitution offers no protection. If the contract be one which the state, in the legitimate exercise of its police power, has the right to prohibit, it is not prevented from prohibiting it by the 14th Amendment. Contracts in violation of a statute, either of the Federal or state government, or a contract to let one's property for immoral purposes, or to do any other unlawful act, could obtain no protection from the Federal Constitution, as coming under the liberty of person or of free contract. Therefore, when the state, by its legislature, in the assumed exercise of its police powers, has passed an act which seriously limits the right to labor or the right of contract in regard to their means of livelihood between persons who are *sui juris* (both employer and employee), it becomes of great importance to determine which shall prevail; the right of the individual to labor for such time as he may choose, or the right of the state to prevent the individual from laboring, or from entering into any contract to labor, beyond a certain time prescribed by the state.

This court has recognized the existence and upheld the exercise of the police powers of the states in many cases which might fairly be considered as border ones, and it has, in the course of its determination of questions regarding the asserted invalidity of such statutes, on the ground of their violation of the rights secured by the Federal Constitution, been guided by rules of a very liberal nature, the application of which has resulted, in numerous instances, in upholding the validity of state statutes thus assailed. Among the later cases where the state law has been upheld by this court is that of *Holden v. Hardy*.... A provision in the act of the legislature of Utah was there under consideration, the act limiting the employment of workmen in all the underground mines or workings, to eight hours per day, "except in cases of emergency, where life or property is in imminent danger." It also limited the hours of labor in smelting and other institutions for the reduction or refining of ores or metals to eight hours per day, except in like case of emergency. The act was held to be a valid exercise of the police powers of the state.

...There is nothing in *Holden v. Hardy* which covers the case now before us.

...It must, of course, be conceded that there is a limit to the valid exercise of the police power by the state. There is no dispute concerning this general proposition. Otherwise the 14th Amendment would have no efficacy and the legislatures of the states would have unbounded power, and it would be enough to say that any piece of legislation was enacted to conserve the morals, the health, or the safety of the people; such legislation would be valid, no matter how absolutely without foundation the claim might be. The claim of the police power would be a mere pretext; become another and delusive name for the supreme sovereignty of the state to be exercised free from constitutional restraint. This is not contended for. In every case that comes before this court, therefore, where legislation of this character is concerned, and where the protection of the Federal Constitution is sought, the question necessarily arises: Is this a fair, reasonable, and appropriate exercise of the police power of the state, or is it an unreasonable, unnecessary, and arbitrary interference with the right of the individual to his personal liberty, or to enter into those contracts in relation to labor which may seem to him appropriate or necessary for the support of himself and his family? Of course the liberty of contract relating to labor includes both parties to it. The one has as much right to purchase as the other to sell labor.

This is not a question of substituting the judgment of the court for that of the legislature. If the act be within the power of the state it is valid, although the judgment of the court might be totally opposed to the enactment of such a law. But the question would still remain: Is it within the police power of the state? and that question must be answered by the court.

The question whether this act is valid as a labor law, pure and simple, may be dismissed in a few words. There is no reasonable ground for interfering with the liberty of person or the right of free contract, by determining the hours of labor, in the occupation of a baker. There is no contention that bakers as a class are not equal in intelligence and capacity to men in other trades or manual occupations, or that they are not able to assert their rights and care for themselves without the protecting arm of the state, interfering with their independence of judgment and of action. They are in no sense wards of the state. Viewed in the light of a purely labor law, with no reference whatever to the question of health, we think that a law like the one before us involves neither the safety, the morals, nor the welfare, of the public, and that the interest of the public is not in the slightest degree affected by such an act. The law must be upheld, if at all, as a law pertaining to the health of the individual engaged in the occupation of a baker. It does not affect any other portion of the public than those who are engaged in that occupation. Clean and wholesome bread does not depend upon whether the baker works but ten hours per day or only sixty hours a week. The limitation of the hours of labor does not come within the police power on that ground.

It is a question of which of two powers or rights shall prevail; the power of the state to legislate or the right of the individual to liberty of person and freedom of contract. The mere assertion that the subject relates, though but in a remote degree, to the public health, does not necessarily render the enactment valid. The act must have a more direct relation, as a means to an end, and the end itself must be appropriate and legitimate, before an act can be held to be valid which interferes with the general right of an individual to be free in his person and in his power to contract in relation to his own labor.

...This case has caused much diversity of opinion in the state courts. In the supreme court two of the five judges composing the court dissented from the judgment affirming the validity of the act.

...We think the limit of the police power has been reached and passed in this case. There is, in our judgment, no reasonable foundation for holding this to be necessary or appropriate as a health law to safeguard the public health, or the health of the individuals who are following the trade of a baker. If this statute be valid, and if, therefore, a proper case is made out in which to deny the right of an individual, *sui juis*, as employer or employee, to make contracts for the labor of the latter under the protection of the provisions of the Federal Constitution, there would seem to be no length to which legislation of this nature might not go.

... We think that there can be no fair doubt that the trade of a baker, in and of itself, is not an unhealthy one to that degree which would authorize the legislature to interfere with the right to labor, and with the right of free contract on the part of the individual, either as employer or employee.... It might be safely affirmed that almost all occupations more or less affect the health. There must be more than the mere fact of the possible existence of some small amount of unhealthiness to warrant legislative interference with liberty. It is unfortunately true that labor, even in any department, may possibly carry with it the seeds of unhealthiness. But are we all, on that account, at the mercy of legislative majorities? A printer, a tinsmith, a locksmith, a carpenter, a cabinetmaker, a dry goods clerk, a bank's, a lawyer's, or a physician's clerk, or a clerk in almost any kind of business, would all come under the power of the legislature, on this assumption. No trade, no occupation, no mode of earning one's living, could escape this all-pervading power, and the acts of the legislature in limiting the hours of labor in all employments would be valid, although such limitation might seriously cripple the ability of the laborer to support himself and his family.... We do not believe in the soundness of the views which uphold this law. On the contrary, we think that such a law as this, although passed in the assumed exercise of the police power, and as relating to the public health, or the health of the employees named, is not within that power, and is invalid. The act is not, within any fair meaning of the term, a health law, but is an illegal interference with the rights of individuals, both employers and employees, to make contracts regarding labor upon such terms as they may think best, or which they may agree upon with the other parties to such contracts. Statutes of the nature of that under review, limiting the hours in which grown and intelligent men may labor to earn their living, are mere meddlesome interferences with the rights of the individual, and they are not saved from condemnation by the claim that they are passed in the exercise of the police power and upon the subject of the health of the individual whose rights are interfered with, unless there be some fair ground, reasonable in and of itself, to say that there is material danger to the public health, or to the health of the employees, if the hours of labor are not curtailed. If this be not clearly the case, the individuals whose rights are thus made the subject of legislative interference are under the protection of the Federal Constitution regarding their liberty of contract as well as of person; and the legislature of the state has no power to limit their right as proposed in the statute. All that it could properly do has been done by it with regard to the conduct of bakeries, as provided for in the other sections of the act, above set forth. These several sections provide for the inspection of the premises where the bakery is carried on, with regard to furnishing proper wash rooms and water-closets, apart from the bake room, also with regard to providing proper drainage, plumbing, and painting; the sections, in addition, provide for the height of the ceiling, the cementing or tiling of floors, where necessary in the opinion of the factory inspector, and for other things of that nature; alterations are also provided for, and are to be made where necessary in the opinion of the inspector, in order to comply with the provisions of the statute.

...This interference on the part of the legislatures of the several states with the ordinary trades and occupations of the people seems to be on the increase.

...It is impossible for us to shut our eyes to the fact that many of the laws of this character, while passed under what is claimed to be the police power for the purpose of protecting the public health or welfare, are, in reality, passed from other motives. We are justified in saying so when, from the character of the law and the subject upon which it legislates, it is apparent that the public health or welfare bears but the most remote relation to the law. The purpose of a statute must be determined from the natural and legal effect of the language employed; and whether it is or is not repugnant to the Constitution of the United States must be determined from the natural effect of such statutes when put into operation, and not from their proclaimed purpose.... The court looks beyond the mere letter of the law in such cases.

...It is manifest to us that the limitation of the hours of labor as provided for in this section of the statute under which the indictment was found, and the plaintiff in error convicted, has no such direct relation to, and no such substantial effect upon, the health of the employee, as to justify us in regarding the section as really a health law. It seems to us that the real object and purpose were simply to regulate the hours of labor between the master and his employees (all being men, *sui juris*), in a private business, not dangerous in any degree to morals, or in any real and substantial degree to the health of the employees. Under such circumstances the freedom of master and employee to contract with each other in relation to their employment, and in defining the same, cannot be prohibited or interfered with, without violating the Federal Constitution.

The judgment of the Court of Appeals of New York, as well as that of the Supreme Court and of the County Court of Oneida County, must be reversed and the case remanded to the County Court for further proceedings not inconsistent with this opinion.

MR. JUSTICE HOLMES dissenting:

I regret sincerely that I am unable to agree with the judgment in this case, and that I think it my duty to express my dissent.

This case is decided upon an economic theory which a large part of the country does not entertain. If it were a question whether I agreed with that theory, I should desire to study if further and long before making up my mind. But I do not conceive that to be my duty, because I strongly believe that my agreement or disagreement has nothing to do with the right of a majority to embody their opinions in law. It is settled by various decisions of this court that state constitutions and state laws may regulate life in many ways which we as legislators might think as injudicious, or if you like as tyrannical, as this, and which, equally with this, interfere with the liberty to contract. Sunday laws and usury laws are ancient examples. A more modern one is the prohibition of lotteries. The liberty of the citizen to do as he likes so long as he does not interfere with the liberty of others to do the same, which has been a shibboleth for some well-known writers, is interfered with by school laws, by the Postoffice, by every state or municipal institution which takes his money for purposes thought desirable, whether he likes it or not. The 14th Amendment does not enact Mr. Herbert Spencer's *Social Statics*. The other day we sustained the Massachusetts vaccination law. *Jacobson v. Massachusetts....* United States and state statutes and decisions cutting down the liberty to contract by way of combination are familiar to this court. *Northern Securities Co. v. United States....* Two Years ago we upheld the prohibition of sales of stock on margins, or for future delivery, in the Constitution of California. *Otis v. Parker.* The decision sustaining an eight-hour law for miners is still recent. *Holden v. Hardy....* Some of these laws embody convictions or prejudices which judges are likely to share. Some may not. But a Constitution is not intended to embody a particular economic theory, whether of paternalism and the organic relation of the citizen to the state or of *laissez faire*. It is made for people of fundamentally differing views, and the accident of our finding certain opinions natural and familiar, or novel, and even shocking, ought not to conclude our judgment upon the question whether statutes embodying them conflict with the *Constitution of the United States*.

General propositions do no decide concrete cases. The decision will depend on a judgment or intuition more subtle than any articulate major premise. But I think that the proposition just stated, if it is accepted, will carry us far toward the end. Every opinion tends to become a law. I think that the word "liberty," in the 14th Amendment, is perverted when it is held to prevent the natural outcome of a dominant opinion, unless it can be said that a rational and fair man necessarily would admit that the statute proposed would infringe fundamental principles as they have been understood by the traditions of our people and our law. It does not need research to show that no such sweeping condemnation can be passed upon the statute before us. A reasonable man might think it a proper measure on the score of health. Men whom I certainly could not pronounce unreasonable would uphold it as a first installment of a general regulation of the hours of work. Whether in the latter aspect it would be open to the charge of inequality I think it unnecessary to discuss.

MR. JUSTICE HARLAN (with whom MR. JUSTICE WHITE and MR. JUSTICE DAY concurred) dissenting:

While this court has not attempted to mark the precise boundaries of what is called the police power of the state, the existence of the power has been uniformly recognized, equally by the Federal and State courts.

All the cases agree that this power extends at least to the protection of the lives, the health, and the safety of the public against the injurious exercise by any citizen of his own rights.

...Speaking generally, the state, in the exercise of its powers, may not unduly interfere with the right of the citizen to enter into contracts that may be necessary and essential in the enjoyment of the inherent rights belonging to everyone, among which rights is the right "to be free in the enjoyment of all his faculties, to be free to use them in all lawful ways, to live and work where he will, to earn his livelihood by any lawful calling, to pursue any livelihood by any lawful calling, to pursue any livelihood or avocation." This was declared in *Allgeyer v. Louisiana*.... But in the same case it was conceded that the right to contract in relation to persons and property, or to do business, within a state, may be "regulated, and sometimes prohibited, when the contracts or business conflict with the policy of the state as contained in its statutes."

...While this court has held, notably in the cases *Davidson v. New Orleans*,... and *Yick Wo. v. Hopkins*,... that the police power cannot be put forward as an excuse for oppressive and unjust legislation, it may be lawfully resorted to for the purpose of preserving the public health, safety, or morals, or the abatement of public nuisances; and a large discretion 'is necessarily vested in the legislature to determine, not only what the interests of the public require, but what measures are necessary for the protection of such interests.' *Lawton v. Steele*

... Subsequently, in *Gundling v. Chicago* ... this court said: "Regulations respecting the pursuit of a lawful trade or business are of very frequent occurrence in the various cities of the country, and what such regulations shall be and to what particular trade, business, or occupation they shall apply, are questions for the state to determine, and their determination comes within the proper exercise of the police power by the state, and, unless the regulations are so utterly unreasonable and extravagant in their nature and purpose that the property and personal rights of the citizen are unnecessarily, and in a manner wholly arbitrary, interfered with or destroyed without due process of law, they do not extend beyond the power of the state to pass, and they form no subject for Federal interference."

... I take it to be firmly established that what is called the liberty of contract may, within certain limits, be subjected to regulations designed and calculated to promote the general welfare, or to guard the public health, the public morals, or the public safety. "The liberty secured by the Constitution of the United States to every person within its jurisdiction does not import," this court has recently said, "an absolute right in each person to be at all times and in all circumstances wholly freed from restraint. There are manifold restraints to which every person is necessarily subject for the common good." *Jacobson v. Massachusetts*....

Granting, then, that there is a liberty of contract which cannot be violated even under the sanction of direct legislative enactment, but assuming, as according to settled law we may assume, that such liberty of contract is subject to such regulations as the state may reasonably prescribe for the common good and well being of society, what are the conditions under which the judiciary may declare such regulations to be in excess of legislative authority and void? Upon this point there is no room for dispute; for the rule is universal that a legislative enactment, Federal or state, is never to be disregarded or held invalid unless it be, beyond question, plainly or palpably in excess of legislative power.... If there be doubt as to the validity of the statute, that doubt must therefore be resolved in favor of its validity, and the courts must keep their hands off, leaving the legislature to meet the responsibility for unwise legislation. If the end which the legislature seeks to accomplish be one to which its power extends, and if the means employed to that end, although not the wisest or best, are yet not plainly and palpably unauthorized by law, then the court cannot interfere. In other words, when the validity of a statute is questioned, the burden of proof, so to speak, is upon those who assert it to be unconstitutional. *McCulloch v. Maryland*....

...Be this as it may, the statute must be taken as expressing the belief of the people of New York that, as a general rule, and in the case of the average man, labor in the excess of sixty hours during a week in such establishments may endanger the health of those who thus labor. Whether or not this be wise legislation it is not the province of the court to inquire. Under our systems of government the courts are not concerned with the wisdom or policy of legislation. So that, in determining the question of power to interfere with liberty of contract, the court may inquire whether means devised by the state are germane to an end which may lawfully be accomplished and have a real or substantial relation to the protection of health, as involved in the daily work of the persons, male and female, engaged in bakery and confectionery establishments.

...It is enough for the determination of this case, and it is enough for this court to know, that the question is one about which there is room for debate and for an honest difference of opinion. There are many reasons of a weighty, substantial character, based upon the experience of mankind, in support of the theory that, all things considered, more than ten hours' steady work each day, from week to week, in a bakery or confectionery establishment, may endanger the health and shorten the lives of the workmen, thereby diminishing their physical and mental capacity to serve the state and to provide for those dependent upon them.

If such reasons exist that ought to be the end of this case, for the state is not amenable to the judiciary, in respect of its legislative enactments, unless such enactments are plainly, palpably, beyond all question, inconsistent with the Constitution of the United States. We are not to presume that the state of New York has acted in bad faith. Nor can we assume that its legislature acted without due deliberation, or that it did not determine this question upon the fullest attainable information and for the common good. We cannot say that the state has acted without reason, nor ought we to proceed upon the theory that its action is a mere sham. Our duty, I submit, is to sustain the statute as not being in conflict with the Federal Constitution, for the reason – and such is an all-sufficient reason – it is not shown to be plainly and palpably inconsistent with that instrument. Let the state alone in the management of its purely domestic affairs, so long as it does not appear beyond all question that it has violated the Federal Constitution. This view necessarily results from the principle that the health and safety of the people of a state are primarily for the state to guard and protect.

...No evils arising from such legislation could be more far reaching than those that might come to our system of government if the judiciary, abandoning the sphere assigned to it by the fundamental law, should enter the domain of legislation, and upon grounds merely of justice or reason or wisdom annul statutes that had received the sanction of the people's representatives. "We are reminded by counsel that it is the solemn duty of the courts in cases before them to guard the constitutional rights of the citizen against merely arbitrary power. That is unquestionably true. But it is equally true – indeed, the public interests imperatively demand – that legislative enactments should be recognized and enforced by the courts as embodying the will of the people, unless they are plainly and palpably beyond all question in violation of the fundamental law of the Constitution."

NEBBIA v. NEW YORK
291 U.S. 502; 54 S.Ct. 505; 78 L.Ed. 940 (1934)

The Depression of the 1930's adversely affected the milk industry in the State of New York. In 1933, the state legislature enacted a law to provide for the stabilization of milk prices. The law established a Milk Control Board to set minimum and maximum prices. A grocery store owner, Nebbia, was convicted of selling milk below the minimum price. After the state court of appeals sustained his conviction, Nebbia appealed to the Supreme Court.

MR. JUSTICE ROBERTS delivered the opinion of the Court:

...First. The appellant urges that the order of the Milk Control Board denies him the equal protection of the laws. It is shown that the order requires him, if he purchases his supply from a dealer, to pay eight cents per quart and five cents per pint, and to resell at not less than nine and six, whereas the same dealer may buy his supply from a farmer at lower prices and deliver milk to consumers at ten cents the quart and six cents the pint. We think the contention that the discrimination deprives the appellant of equal protection is not well founded. For aught that appears, the appellant purchased his supply of milk from a farmer as do distributors, or could have procured it from a farmer if he so desired. There is therefore no showing that the order placed him at a disadvantage, or in fact affected him adversely, and this alone is fatal to the claim of denial of equal protection. But if it were shown that the appellant is compelled to buy from a distributor, the difference in the retail price he is required to charge his customers, from that prescribed for sales by distributors, is not on its fact arbitrary or unreasonable, for there are obvious distinctions between the two sorts of merchants which may well justify a difference of treatment, if the legislature possess the power to control the prices to be charged for fluid milk.... Second. The more serious question is whether, in the light of the conditions disclosed, the enforcement of [the price regulation] denied the appellant the due process secured to him by the Fourteenth Amendment....

Under our form of government the use of property and the making of contracts are normally matters of private and not of public concern. The general rule is that both shall be free of governmental interference. But neither property rights nor contract rights are absolute; for government cannot exist if the citizen may at will use his property to the detriment of his fellows, or exercise his freedom of contract to work them harm. Equally fundamental with the private right is that of the public to regulate it in the common interest....

The milk industry in New York has been the subject of long-standing and drastic regulation in the public interest. The legislative investigation of 1932 was persuasive of the fact that for this and other reasons unrestricted competition aggravated existing evils, and the normal law of supply and demand was insufficient to correct maladjustments detrimental to the community. The inquiry disclosed destructive and demoralizing competitive conditions and unfair trade practices which resulted in retail price-cutting and reduced the income of the farmer below the cost of production. We do not understand the appellant to deny that in these circumstances the legislature might reasonably consider further regulation and control desirable for protection of the industry and the consuming public. That body believed economic conditions could be improved by preventing destructive price-cutting by stores which, due to the flood of surplus milk, were able to buy at much lower prices than the larger distributors and to sell without incurring the delivery costs of the latter. In the order of which complaint is made, the Milk Control Board fixed a price of ten cents per quart for sales by a distributor to a consumer, and nine cents by a store to a consumer, thus recognizing the lower costs of the store, and endeavoring to establish a differential which would be just to both. In the light of the facts, the order appears not to be unreasonable or arbitrary, or without relation to the purpose to prevent ruthless competition from destroying the wholesale price structure on which the farmer depends for his livelihood, and the community for an assured supply of milk.

But we are told that because the law essays to control prices it denies due process. Notwithstanding the admitted power to correct existing economic ills by appropriate regulation of business, even though an indirect result may be a restriction of the freedom of contract or a modification of charges for services or the price of commodities, the appellant urges that direct fixation of prices is a type of regulation absolutely forbidden. His position is that the Fourteenth Amendment requires us to hold the challenged statute void for this reason alone. The argument runs that the public control of rates or prices is *per se* unreasonable and unconstitutional, save as applied to business affected with a public interest; that a business so affected is one in which property is devoted to an enterprise of a sort which the public itself might appropriately undertake, or one whose owner relies on a public grant or franchise for the right to conduct the business, or in which he is bound to serve all who apply; in short, such as is commonly called utility; or a business in its nature a monopoly....

...We may as well say at once that the dairy industry is not, in the accepted sense of the phrase, a public utility. We think the appellant is also right in asserting that there is in this case no suggestion of any monopoly or monopolistic practice. It goes without saying that those engaged in the business are in no way dependent upon public grants or franchises for the privilege of conducting their activities. But if, as must be conceded, the industry is subject to regulation in the public interest, what constitutional principle bars the state from correcting existing maladjustments by legislation touching prices? We think there is no such principle. The due process clause makes no mention of sales or of prices any more than it speaks of business or contracts or buildings or other incidents of property. The thought seems nevertheless to have persisted that there is something peculiarly sacrosanct about the price one may charge for what he makes or sells, and that, however able to regulate other elements of manufacture or trade, with incidental effect upon price, the state is incapable of directly controlling the price itself. This view was negatived many years ago. *Munn v. Illinois*....

It is clear that there is no closed class or category of business affected with a public interest, and the function of courts in the application of the Fifth and Fourteenth Amendments is to determine in each case whether circumstances vindicate the challenged regulation as a reasonable exertion of governmental authority or condemn it as arbitrary or discriminatory.... The phrases "affected with a public interest," and "clothed with a public use," have been brought forward as the criteria of the validity of price control; it has been admitted that they are not susceptible of definition and form an unsatisfactory test of the constitutionality of legislation directed at business practices or prices. These decisions must rest, finally, upon the basis that the requirements of due process were not met because the laws were found arbitrary in their operation and effect. But there can be no doubt that upon proper occasion and by appropriate measures the state may regulate a business in any of its aspects, including the prices to be charged for the products or commodities it sells.

So far as the requirement of due process is concerned, and in the absence of other constitutional restriction, a state is free to adopt whatever economic policy may reasonably be deemed to promote public welfare, and to enforce that policy by legislation adapted to its purpose. The courts are without authority either to declare such policy, or, when it is declared by the legislature, to override it. *If the laws passed are seen to have a reasonable relation to a proper legislative purpose, and are neither arbitrary nor discriminatory, the requirements of due process are satisfied....*

Price control, like any form of regulation, is unconstitutional only if arbitrary, discriminatory, or demonstrably irrelevant to the policy the legislature is free to adopt, and hence an unnecessary and unwarranted interference with individual liberty...

The judgment is Affirmed.

MR. JUSTICE MC REYNOLDS, joined by MR. JUSTICES VAN DEVANTER, SUTHERLAND, and BUTLER, dissented.

WEST COAST HOTEL v. PARRISH
300 U.S. 379; 57 S.Ct. 578; 81 L.Ed. 703 (1937)

A Washington state law enacted in 1913 authorized the setting of a minimum wage for women and children by an administrative agency called the Industrial Welfare Commission. Elsie Parrish, a chambermaid for the West

Coast Hotel Company, took action under the law, on the grounds that she had not been paid the minimum wage set by the Commission ($14.50 for a 48 hour week). The trial court declined to uphold Parrish's contention; however, the state supreme court reversed. Brought to the Court on appeal, it set the stage for the judicial "revolution" of 1937.

MR. CHIEF JUSTICE HUGHES delivered the opinion of the Court:

...The appellant relies upon the decision of this Court in *Adkins v. Children's Hospital,* which held invalid the District of Columbia Minimum Wage Act, which was attacked under the due process clause of the Fifth Amendment. On the argument at bar, counsel for the appellees attempted to distinguish the *Adkins* case upon the ground that the appellee was employed in a hotel and that the business of an innkeeper was affected with a public interest. That effort at distinction is obviously futile, as it appears that in one of the cases ruled by the *Adkins* opinion the employee was a woman employed as an elevator operator in a hotel ....

The Supreme Court of Washington has upheld the minimum-wage statute of that State. It has decided that the statute is a reasonable exercise of the police power of the State. In reaching that conclusion the state court has invoked principles long established by this Court in the application of the Fourteenth Amendment. The state court has refused to regard the decision in the *Adkins* case as determinative and has pointed to our decisions both before and since that case as justifying its position. We are of the opinion that this ruling of the state court demands on our part a re-examination of the *Adkins* case. The importance of the question, in which many States having similar laws are concerned, the close division by which the decision in the *Adkins* case was reached, and the economic conditions which have supervened, and in the light of which the reasonableness of the exercise of the protective power of the State must be considered, make it not only appropriate, but we think imperative, that in deciding the present case the subject should receive fresh consideration....

The principle which must control our decision is not in doubt. The constitutional provision invoked is in the due process clause of the Fourteenth Amendment governing the States, as the due process clause invoked in the *Adkins* case governed Congress. In each case the violation alleged by those attacking minimum-wage regulation for women is deprivation of freedom of contract. What is this freedom? The Constitution does not speak of freedom of contract. It speaks of liberty and prohibits the deprivation of liberty without due process of law. In prohibiting that deprivation the Constitution does not recognize an absolute and uncontrollable liberty. Liberty in each of its phases has its history and connotation. But the liberty safeguarded is liberty in a social organization which requires the protection of law against the evils which menace the health, safety, morals, and welfare of the people. Liberty under the Constitution is thus necessarily subject to the restraints of due process, and regulation which is reasonable in relation to its subject and is adopted in the interests of the community is due process....

This power under the Constitution to restrict freedom of contract has had many illustrations. That it may be exercised in the public interest with respect to contracts between employer and employee is undeniable....

The point that has been strongly stressed that adult employees should be deemed competent to make their own contracts was decisively met nearly forty years ago in *Holden v. Hardy*, where we pointed out the inequality in the footing of the parties....

It is manifest that this established principle is peculiarly applicable in relation to the employment of women, in whose protection the State has a special interest. That phase of the subject received elaborate consideration in *Muller v. Oregon* (1908), 208 U.S. 412, where the constitutional authority of the State to limit the working hours of women was sustained....

This array of precedents and the principles they applied were thought by the dissenting Justices in the *Adkins* case to demand that the minimum-wage statute be sustained. The validity of the distinction made by the Court between a minimum wage and a maximum of hours in limiting liberty of contract was especially challenged.... That challenge persists and is without any satisfactory answer....

The minimum wage to be paid under the Washington statute is fixed after full consideration by representatives of employers, employees, and the public. It may be assumed that the minimum wage is fixed in consideration of the services that are performed in the particular occupations under normal conditions. Provision is made for special licenses at less wages in the case of women who are incapable of full service. The statement of Mr. Justice Holmes in the *Adkins* case is pertinent: "This statute does not compel anybody to pay anything. It simply forbids employment at rates below those fixed as the minimum requirement of health and right living. It is safe to assume that women will not be employed at even the lowest wages allowed unless they earn them, or unless the employer's business can sustain the burden. In short the law in its character and operation is like hundreds of so-called police laws that have been upheld...." And Chief Justice Taft forcibly pointed out the consideration which is basic in a statute of this character: "Legislatures which adopt a requirement of maximum hours or minimum wages may be presumed to believe that when sweating employers are prevented from paying unduly low wages by positive law they will continue their business, abating that part of their profits, which were wrung from the necessities of their employees, and will concede the better terms required by the law; and that while in individual cases hardships may result, the restriction will enure to the benefit of the general class of employees in whose interest the law is passed and so to that of the community at large....

We think that the views thus expressed are sound and that the decision in the *Adkins* case was a departure from the true application of the principles governing the regulation by the State of the relation of employer and employed....

With full recognition of the earnestness and vigor which characterize the prevailing opinion in the *Adkins* case, we find it impossible to reconcile that ruling with these well-considered declarations. What can be closer to the public interest than the health of women and their protection from unscrupulous and over-reaching employers? And if the protection of women is a legitimate end of the exercise of the state power, how can it be said that the requirement of the payment of a minimum wage fairly fixed in order to meet the very necessities of existence is not an admissible means to that end? The legislature of the State was clearly entitled to consider the situation of women in employment, the fact that they are in the class receiving the least pay, that their bargaining power is relatively weak, and that they are the ready victims of those who would take advantage of their necessitous circumstances. The legislature was entitled to adopt measures to reduce the evils of the "sweating system," the exploiting of workers at wages so low as to be insufficient to meet the bare cost of living, thus making their very helplessness the occasion of a most injurious competition. The legislature had the right to consider that its minimum-wage requirements would be an important aid in carrying out its policy of protection. The adoption of similar requirements by many States evidences a deep-seated conviction both as to the presence of the evil and as to the means adopted to check it. Legislative response to that conviction cannot be regarded as arbitrary or capricious, and that is all we have to decide. Even if the wisdom of the policy be regarded as debatable and its effects uncertain, still the legislature is entitled to its judgment.

There is an additional and compelling consideration which recent economic experience has brought into a strong light. The exploitation of a class of workers who are in an unequal position with respect to bargaining power and are thus relatively defenseless against the denial of a living wage is not only detrimental to their health and well-being but casts a direct burden for their support upon the community. What these workers lose in wages the taxpayers are called to pay. The bare cost of living must be met. We may take judicial notice of the unparalleled demands for relief which arose during the recent period of depression and still continue to an alarming extent despite the degree of economic recovery which has been achieved. It is unnecessary to cite official statistics to establish what is of common knowledge through the length and breadth of the land. While in the instant case no factual brief has been presented, there is no reason to doubt that the State of Washington has encountered the same social problem that is present elsewhere. The community is not bound to provide what is in effect a subsidy for unconscionable employers. The community may direct its lawmaking power to correct the abuse which springs from their selfish disregard of the public interest. The argument that the legislation in question constitutes an arbitrary discrimination, because it does not extend to men, is unavailing. This Court has frequently held that the legislative authority, acting within its proper field, is not bound to extend its regulation to all cases which it might possibly reach. The legislature "is free to recognize degrees of harm and it may confine its restrictions to those classes of cases where the need is deemed to be clearest." If "the law presumably hits the evil where it is most felt, it is not to be overthrown because there are other instances to which it might have been applied." There is no "doctrinaire requirement" that the legislation should be couched in all-embracing terms....

Our conclusion is that the case of *Adkins v. Children's Hospital*... should be, and it is, overruled. The judgment of the Supreme Court of the State of Washington is Affirmed.

MR. JUSTICE SUTHERLAND, joined by MR. JUSTICE VAN DEVANTER, MR. JUSTICE MC REYNOLDS, and MR. JUSTICE BUTLER, dissented.

NATIONAL LABOR RELATIONS BOARD v. JONES AND LAUGHLIN STEEL CORPORATION 301 U.S. 1; 57 S.Ct. 615; 81 L.Ed. 893 (1937)

The National Labor Relations (Wagner) Act of 1935 was enacted by Congress to protect the rights of workers and labor organizations and to reduce disputes which burdened interstate commerce. The Board (NLRB) had ordered Jones & Laughlin Steel, one of the larger corporations, to cease and desist from engaging in certain "unfair labor practices." The company refused to comply and the NLRB petitioned the circuit court of appeals to enforce the order. The court declined to do so, and the Supreme Court granted certiorari.

MR. CHIEF JUSTICE HUGHES delivered the opinion of the Court:

...The facts as to the nature and scope of the business of the Jones & Laughlin Steel Corporation have been found by the Labor Board.... The Labor Board has found: The corporation is organized under the laws of Pennsylvania and has its principal office at Pittsburgh. It is engaged in the business of manufacturing iron and steel in plants situated in Pittsburgh and nearby Aliquippa, Pennsylvania. It manufactures and distributes a widely diversified line of steel and pig iron, being the fourth largest producer of steel in the United States. With its subsidiaries – nineteen in number – it is a completely integrated enterprise, owning and operating ore, coal, and limestone properties, lake and river transportation facilities and terminal railroads located at its manufacturing plants. It owns or controls mines in Michigan and Minnesota. It operates four ore steamships on the Great Lakes used in the transportation of ore to its factories. It owns coal mines in Pennsylvania. It operates towboats and steam barges used in carrying coal to its factories. It owns limestone properties in various places in Pennsylvania and West Virginia. It owns the Monongahela connecting railroad, which connects the plants of the Pittsburgh works and forms an interconnection with the Pennsylvania, New York Central, and Baltimore and Ohio Railroad systems. It owns the Aliquippa and Southern Railroad Company, which connects the Aliquippa works with the Pittsburgh and Lake Erie, part of the New York Central system. Much of its product is shipped to its warehouses in Chicago, Detroit, Cincinnati, and Memphis – to the last two places by means of its own barges and transportation equipment. In Long Island City, New York, and in New Orleans it operates structural-steel fabricating shops in connection with the warehousing of semifinished materials sent from its works. Through one of its wholly-owned subsidiaries it owns, leases, and operates stores, warehouses, and yards for the distribution of equipment and supplies for drilling and operating oil and gas mills and for pipe lines, refineries, and pumping stations. It has sales offices in twenty cities in the United States and a wholly-owned subsidiary which is devoted exclusively to distributing its product in Canada. Approximately 75 per cent of its product is shipped out of Pennsylvania.

Summarizing these operations, the Labor Board concluded that the works in Pittsburgh and Aliquippa "might be likened to the heart of a self-contained, highly integrated body. They draw in the raw materials from Michigan, Minnesota, West Virginia, Pennsylvania in part through arteries and by means controlled by the respondent; they transform the materials and then pump them out of all parts of the nation through the vast mechanism which the respondent has elaborated...."

The Scope of the Act. The Act is challenged in its entirety as an attempt to regulate all industry, thus invading the reserved powers of the State over their local concerns. It is asserted that the references in the Act to interstate and foreign commerce are colorable at best; that the Act is not a true regulation of such commerce or of matters which directly affect it but on the contrary has the fundamental object of placing under the compulsory supervision of the Federal government all industrial labor relations within the nation. The argument seeks support in the broad words of the preamble (Section 1) and in the sweep of the provisions of the Act, and it is further insisted that its legislative history shows an essential universal purpose in the light of which its scope cannot be limited by either construction or by the application of the separability clause.

If this conception of terms, intent, and consequent inseparability were sound, the Act would necessarily fall by reason of the limitation upon the Federal power which inheres in the constitutional grant, as well as because of the explicit reservation of the Tenth Amendment. *A.L.A. Schechter Poultry Corp. v. United States....*

We think it clear that the National Labor Relations Act may be construed so as to operate within the sphere of constitutional authority. The jurisdiction conferred upon the Board, and invoked in this instance, is found in 810(a), which provides:

"Sec. 10(a), The Board is empowered, as hereinafter provided, to prevent any person from engaging in any unfair labor practice (listed in 88) affecting commerce." The critical words of this provision, prescribing the limits of the Board's authority in dealing with the labor practices, are "affecting commerce...."

There can be no question that the commerce thus contemplated by the Act (aside from that within a Territory or the District of Columbia) is interstate and foreign commerce in the constitutional sense. The Act also defines the term "affecting commerce" 82(7):

"The term 'affecting commerce' means in commerce, or burdening or obstructing commerce or the free flow of commerce, or having led or tending to lead to a labor dispute burdening or obstructing commerce or the free flow of commerce."

This definition is one of exclusion as well as inclusion. The grant of authority to the Board does not purport to extend to the relationship between all industrial employees and employers. Its terms do not impose collective bargaining upon all industry regardless of effects upon interstate or foreign commerce. It purports to reach only what may be deemed to burden or obstruct that commerce and, thus qualified, it must be construed as contemplating the exercise of control within constitutional bounds. It is a familiar principle that acts which directly burden or obstruct interstate or foreign commerce, or its free flow, are within the reach of the congressional power. Acts having that effect are not rendered immune because they grow out of labor disputes.... It is the effect upon commerce, not the source of the injury, which is the criterion.... Whether or not particular action does affect commerce in such a close and intimate fashion as to be subject to Federal control, and hence to lie within the authority conferred upon the Board, is left by the statute to be determined as individual cases arise....

The Application of the Act to Employees Engaged in Production – The Principle Involved. Respondent says that whatever may be said of employees engaged in interstate commerce, the industrial relations and activities in the manufacturing department of respondent's enterprise are not subject to Federal regulation. The argument rests upon the proposition that manufacturing in itself is not commerce....

The various parts of respondent's enterprise are described (by the government) as interdependent and as thus involving "a great movement of iron ore, coal, and limestone along well-defined paths to the steel mills, thence through them, and thence in the form of steel products into the consuming centers of the country – a definite and well-understood course of business." It is urged that these activities constitute a "stream" or "flow" of commerce, of which the Aliquippa manufacturing plant is the focal point, and that industrial strife at that point would cripple the entire movement....

We do not find it necessary to determine whether these features of defendant's business dispose of the asserted analogy to the "stream of commerce" cases. The instances in which that metaphor has been used are but particular, and not exclusive, illustrations of the protective power which the Government invokes in support of the present Act. The congressional authority to protect interstate commerce from burdens and obstructions is not limited to transactions which can be deemed to be an essential part of a "flow" of interstate or foreign commerce. Burdens and obstructions may be due to injurious action springing from other sources. The fundamental principle is that the power to regulate commerce is the power to enact "all appropriate legislation" for "its protection and advancement...;" to adopt measures "to promote its growth and insure its safety"...; "to foster, protect, control, and restrain...." That power is plenary and may be exerted to protect interstate commerce "no matter what the source of the dangers which threaten it...." Although activities may be intrastate in character when separately considered, if they have such a close and substantial relation to interstate commerce that their control is essential or appropriate to protect that commerce from burdens and obstructions. Congress cannot be denied the power to exercise that control.... Undoubtedly the scope of this power must be considered in the light of our dual system of government and may not be extended so as to embrace effects upon interstate commerce so indirect and remote that to embrace them, in view of our complex society, would effectually obliterate the distinction between what is national and what is local and create a completely centralized government.... The question is necessarily one of degree....

[T]he fact that the employees here concerned were engaged in production is not determinative. The question remains as to the effect upon interstate commerce of the labor practice involved. In the *A.L.A. Schechter Poultry Corp. Case*,... we found that the effect there was so remote as to be beyond the Federal power. To find "immediacy or directness" there was to find it "almost everywhere," a result inconsistent with the maintenance of our Federal system. In the *Carter Case*,... the Court was of the opinion that the provisions of the statute relating to production were invalid upon several grounds – that there was improper delegation of legislative power, and that the requirements not only went beyond any sustainable measure of protection of interstate commerce but were also inconsistent with due process. These cases are not controlling here....

Effects of the Unfair Labor Practice in Respondent's Enterprise. Giving full weight to respondent's contention with respect to a break in the complete continuity of the "stream of commerce" by reason of respondent's manufacturing operations, the fact remains that the stoppage of those operations by industrial strife would have a most serious effect upon interstate commerce. In view of respondent's far-flung activities, it is idle to say that the effect would be indirect or remote. It is obvious that it would be immediate and might be catastrophic. We are asked to shut our eyes to the plainest facts of our national life and to deal with the question of direct and indirect effects in an intellectual vacuum.

...When industries organize themselves on a national scale, making their relation to interstate commerce the dominant factor in their activities, how can it be maintained that their industrial labor relations constitute a forbidden field into which Congress may not enter when it is necessary to protect interstate commerce from the paralyzing consequences of industrial war? We have often said that interstate commerce itself is a practical conception. It is equally true that interferences with that commerce must be appraised by a judgment that does not ignore actual experience.

Experience has abundantly demonstrated that the recognition of the right of employees to self-organization and to have representatives of their own choosing for the purpose of collective bargaining is often an essential condition of industrial peace. Refusal to confer and negotiate has been one of the most prolific causes of strife....

It is not necessary again to detail the facts to respondent's enterprise. Instead of being beyond the pale, we think that it presents in a most striking way the close and intimate relation which a manufacturing industry may have to interstate commerce, and we have no doubt that Congress had constitutional authority to safeguard the right of respondent's employees to self-organization and freedom in the choice of representative for collective bargaining....

Our conclusion is that the order of the Board was within its competency and that the Act is valid as here applied. The judgment of the Circuit Court of Appeals is reversed and the cause is remanded for further proceedings in conformity with this opinion.

Reversed.

MR, JUSTICE MC REYNOLDS dissented, joined by MR. JUSTICES VAN DEVANTER, SUTHERLAND, and BUTLER.

STEWARD MACHINE CO. v. DAVIS
301 U.S. 548; 157 S.Ct. 883; 81 L.Ed. 1279 (1937)

This was the second decision (after NLRB) to be handed down by the Court which involved federal social or economic legislation after President Roosevelt's attempt to "pack" the Court. It concerned a challenge to the constitutionality of the Social Security Act of 1935, containing provisions which imposed a federal excise tax on employers of eight or more. The Steward Machine Company, an Alabama corporation. had paid the tax but then sued to recover the payment on the grounds that the Social Security Act was unconstitutional. Davis, an internal revenue official, won the case for the government in a district court decision which was later upheld by the court of appeals. The case was then brought to the Supreme Court by certiorari.

MR. JUSTICE CARDOZO delivered the opinion of the Court:

The validity of the tax imposed by the Social Security Act on employers of eight or more is here to be determined....

The Social Security Act ... is divided into eleven separate titles, of which only Titles IX and III are so related to this case as to stand in need of summary.

The caption of Title IX is "Tax on Employers of Eight or More." Every employer (with stated exceptions) is to pay for each calendar year "an excise tax, with respect to having individuals in his employ," the tax to be measured by prescribed percentages of the total wages payable by the employer during the calendar year with respect to such employment.... The proceeds, when collected, go into the Treasury of the United States like internal-revenue collections generally.... They are not earmarked in any way. In certain circumstances, however, credits are under a state law, he may credit such contributions against the federal tax, provided, however, that the total credit allowed to any taxpayer shall not exceed 90 per centum of the tax against which it is credited, and provided also that the state law shall have been certified to the Secretary of the Treasury by the Social Security Board as satisfying certain minimum criteria.... Some of the conditions thus attached to the allowance of a credit are designed to give assurance that the state unemployment compensation law shall be one in substance as well as name. Others are designed to give assurance that the contributions shall be protected against loss after payment to the state. To this last end there are provisions that before a state law shall have the approval of the

Board it must direct that the contributions to the state fund be paid over immediately to the Secretary of the Treasury to the credit of the "Unemployment Trust Fund...." [T]he Fund is to be held by the Secretary of the Treasury, who is to invest in government securities any portion not required in his judgment to meet current withdrawals. He is authorized and directed to pay out of the Fund to any competent state agency such sums as it may duly requisition from the amount standing to its credit....

Title III, which is also challenged as invalid, has the caption "Grants to States for Unemployment Compensation Administration." Under this title, certain sums of money are "authorized to be appropriated" for the purpose of assisting the states in the administration of their unemployment compensation laws.... No present appropriation is made to the extent of a single dollar. All that the title does is to authorize future appropriations ....

...The assault on the statute proceeds on an extended front. Its assailants take the ground that the tax is not an excise; that it is not uniform throughout the United States as excises are required to be; that its exceptions are so many and arbitrary as to violate the Fifth Amendment; that its purpose was not revenue, but an unlawful invasion of the reserved powers of the states; and that the states in submitting to it have yielded to coercion and have abandoned governmental functions which they are not permitted to surrender.

The objections will be considered seriatim with such further explanation as may be necessary to make their meaning clear.

First. The tax, which is described in the statute as an excise, is laid with uniformity throughout the United States as a duty, an impost, or an excise upon the relation of employment.

1. We are told that the relation of employment is one so essential to the pursuit of happiness that it may not be burdened with a tax. Appeal is made to history. From the precedents of colonial days we are supplied with illustrations of excises common in the colonies. They are said to have been bound up with the enjoyment of particular commodities. Appeal is also made to principle or the analysis of concepts. An excise, we are told, imports a tax upon a privilege; employment, it is said, is a right, not a privilege, from which it follows that employment is not subject to an excise. Neither the one appeal nor the other leads to the desired goal.

As to the argument from history: Doubtless there were many excises in the colonial days and later that were associated, more or less intimately, with the enjoyment or the use of property. This would not prove, even if no others were then known, that the forms then accepted were not subject to enlargement.... But in truth other excises were known, and known since early times.... Our colonial forbearers knew more about ways of taxing than some of their descendants seem to be willing to concede.

The historical prop failing, the prop or fancied prop of principle remains. We learn that employment for lawful gain is a "natural" or "inherent" or "inalienable" right, and not a "privilege" at all. But natural rights, so called, are as much subject to taxation as rights of less importance. An excise is not limited to vocations or activities that may be prohibited altogether. It is not limited to those who are the outcome of a franchise. It extends to vocations or activities pursued as of common right. What the individual does in the operation of a business is amenable to taxation just as much as what he owns, at all events if the classification is not tyrannical or arbitrary....

The subject matter of taxation open to the power of the Congress is as comprehensive as that open to the power of the states, though the method of apportionment may at times be different.... The statute books of the states are strewn with illustrations of taxes laid on occupations pursued of common right. We find no basis for a holding that the power in that regard which belongs by accepted practice to the legislatures of the states, has been denied by the Constitution to the Congress of the nation.

2. The tax being an excise, its imposition must conform to the canon of uniformity. There has been no departure from this requirement. According to the settled doctrine the uniformity exacted is geographical, not intrinsic.... .

Second. The excise is not invalid under the provisions of the Fifth Amendment by force of its exemptions.

The statute does not apply, as we have seen, to employers of less than eight. It does not apply to agricultural labor, or domestic service in a private home, or to some other classes of less importance. Petitioner contends that the effect of these restrictions is an arbitrary discrimination vitiating the tax.

The Fifth Amendment unlike the Fourteenth has no equal protection clause.... But even the states, though subject to such a clause, are not confined to a formula of rigid uniformity in framing measures of taxation.... They may tax some kinds of property at one rate, and others at another, and exempt others altogether.... They may lay an excise on the operations of a particular kind of business, and exempt some other kind of business closely akin thereto.... If this latitude of judgment is lawful for the states, it is lawful, *a fortiori*, in legislation by the Congress, which is subject to restraints less narrow and confining....

The classifications and exemptions directed by the statute now in controversy have support in considerations of policy and practical convenience that cannot be condemned as arbitrary. The classifications and exemptions would therefore be upheld if they had been adopted by a state and the provisions of the Fourteenth Amendment were invoked to annul them.... The act of Congress is therefore valid, so far at least as its system of exemptions is concerned, and this though we assume that discrimination, if gross enough, is equivalent to confiscation and subject under the Fifth Amendment to challenge and annulment.

Third. The excise is not void as involving the coercion of the States in contravention of the Tenth Amendment or of restrictions implicit in our Federal form of government.

The proceeds of the excise when collected are paid into the Treasury at Washington, and thereafter are subject to appropriation like public moneys generally.... No presumption can be indulged that they will be misapplied or wasted. Even if they were collected in the hope or expectation that some other and collateral good would be furthered as an incident, that, without more, would not make the act invalid.... This indeed is hardly questioned. The case for the petitioner is built on the contention that here an ulterior aim is wrought into the very structure of the act, and what is even more important, that the aim is not only ulterior but essentially unlawful. In particular, the 90 per cent credit is relied upon as supporting that conclusion. But before the statute succumbs to an assault upon these lines, two propositions must be made out by the assailant.... There must be a showing in the first place that separated from the credit the revenue provisions are incapable of standing by themselves. There must be a showing in the second place that the tax and the credit in combination are weapons of coercion, destroying or impairing the autonomy of the states. The truth of each proposition being essential to the success of the assault, we pass for convenience to a consideration of the second, without pausing to inquire whether there has been a demonstration of the first.

To draw the line intelligently between duress and inducement, there is need to remind ourselves of facts as to the problem of unemployment that are now matters of common knowledge.... During the years 1929 to 1936, when the country was passing through a cyclical depression, the number of the unemployed mounted to unprecedented heights. Often the average was more than 10 million; at times a peak was attained of 16 million or more. Disaster to the breadwinner meant disaster to dependents. Accordingly the roll of the unemployed, itself formidable enough, was only a partial roll of the destitute or needy. The fact developed quickly that the states were unable to give the requisite relief. The problem had become national in area and dimensions. There was need of help from the nation if the people were not to starve. It is late today for the argument to be heard with tolerance that in a crisis so extreme the use of the moneys of the nation to relieve the unemployed and their dependents is a use for any purpose narrower than the promotion of the general welfare....

In the presence of this urgent need for some remedial expedient, the question is to be answered whether the expedient adopted has overleapt the bounds of power. The assailants of the statute say that its dominant end and aim is to drive the state legislatures under the whip of economic pressure into the enactment of unemployment compensation laws at the bidding of the central government. Supporters of the statute say that its operation is not constraint, but the creation of a larger freedom, the states and the nation joining in a cooperative endeavor to avert a common evil. Before Congress acted, unemployment compensation insurance was still, for the most part, a project and no more....

Who then is coerced through the operation of this statute? Not the taxpayer. He pays in fulfillment of the mandate of the local legislature. Not the state. Even now she does not offer a suggestion that in passing the unemployment law she was affected by duress.... For all that appears she is satisfied with her choice, and would be sorely disappointed if it were now to be annulled. The difficulty with the petitioner's contention is that it confuses motive with coercion. "Every tax is in some measure regulatory. To some extent it interposes an economic impediment to the activity taxed as compared with others not taxed...." In like manner every rebate from a tax when conditioned upon conduct is in some measure a temptation. But to hold that motive or temptation is equivalent to coercion is to plunge the law in endless difficulties. The outcome of such a doctrine is the acceptance of a philosophical determinism by which choice becomes impossible. Till now the law has been guided by a robust common sense which assumes the freedom of the will as a working hypothesis in the solution of its problems. The wisdom of the hypothesis has illustration in this case. Nothing in the case suggests the exertion of a power akin to undue influence, if we assume that such a concept can ever be applied with fitness to the relations between state and nation. Even on that assumption the location of the point at which the pressure turns into compulsion, and ceases to be inducement, would be a question of degree – at times, perhaps, of fact. The point had not been reached when Alabama made her choice. We cannot say that she was acting, not of her unfettered will, but under the strain of a persuasion equivalent to undue influence, when she chose to have relief administered under laws of her own making, by agents of her own selection, instead of under federal laws, administered by federal officers, with all the ensuing evils, at least to many minds, of federal patronage and power. There would be a strange irony, indeed, if her choice were now to be annulled on the basis of an assumed duress in the enactment of a statute which, her courts have accepted as a true expression of her will.... We think the choice must stand....

United States v. Butler ... is cited by petitioner as a decision to the contrary. There a tax was imposed on processors of farm products, the proceeds to be paid to farmers who would reduce their acreage and crops under agreements with the Secretary of Agriculture, the plan of the act being to increase the prices of certain farm products by decreasing the quantities produced. The court held (1) that the so-called tax was not a true one,... the proceeds being earmarked for the benefit of farmers complying with the prescribed conditions, (2) that there was an attempt to regulate production without the consent of the state in which production was affected, and (3) that the payments to farmers were coupled with coercive contracts,... unlawful in their aim and oppressive in their consequences. The decision was by a divided court, a minority taking the view that the objections were untenable. "*None of them is applicable to the situation here developed.*"

(a) The proceeds of the tax in controversy are not earmarked for a special group.

(b) The unemployment compensation law which is a condition of the credit has had the approval of the state and could not be a law without it.

(c) The condition is not linked to an irrevocable agreement, for the state at its pleasure may repeal its unemployment law,... terminate the credit, and place itself where it was before the credit was accepted.

(d) The condition is not directed to the attainment of an unlawful end, but to an end, the relief of unemployment, for which nation and state may lawfully cooperate.

Fourth. The statute does not call for a surrender by the states of powers essential to their quasi-sovereign existence.

Finally and chiefly, abdication is supposed to follow from section 904 of the statute and the parts of section 903 that are complementary thereto.... By these the Secretary of the Treasury is authorized and directed to receive and hold in the Unemployment Trust Fund all moneys deposited therein by a state agency for a state unemployment fund and to invest in obligations of the United States such portion of the Fund as is not in his judgment required to meet current withdrawals. We are told that Alabama in consenting to that deposit has renounced the plenitude of power inherent in her statehood.

The same pervasive misconception is in evidence again. All that the state has done is to say in effect through the enactment of a statute that her agents shall be authorized to deposit the unemployment tax receipts in the Treasury at Washington.... The statute may be repealed.... The consent may be revoked. The deposits may be withdrawn. The moment the state commission gives notice to the depositary that it would like the moneys back, the Treasurer will return them. To find state destruction there is to find it almost anywhere. With nearly as much reason one might say that a state abdicates its functions when it places the state moneys on deposit in a national bank....

The inference of abdication thus dissolves in thinnest air when the deposit is conceived of as dependent upon a statutory consent, and not upon a contract effective to create a duty. By this we do not intimate that the conclusion would be different if a contract were discovered. Even sovereigns may contract without derogating from their sovereignty.... The states are at liberty, upon obtaining the consent of Congress, to make agreements with one another.... We find no room for doubt that they may do the like with Congress if the essence of their statehood is maintained without impairment. Alabama is seeking and obtaining a credit of many millions in favor of her citizens out of the Treasury of the nation. Nowhere in our scheme of government – in the limitations express or implied of our federal constitution – do we find that she is prohibited from assenting to conditions that will assure a fair and just requital for benefits received....

The judgment is Affirmed,

MR. JUSTICES McREYNOLDS, SUTHERLAND, VAN DEVANTER, and BUTLER dissented.

UNITED STATES v. DARBY
312 U.S. 100; 61 S.Ct. 451; 85 L.Ed. 609 (1941)

The Fair Labor Standards Act of 1938 was designed to set minimum wages and maximum work hours for employees engaged in producing goods for shipment in interstate commerce. Darby, who manufactured lumber for shipment in interstate commerce, allegedly violated the act by refusing to set proper wage standards. After a district court quashed the indictment against Darby, the government appealed to the Supreme Court. At the time, the Court's decision seemingly ended the constitutional concept of "dual federalism."

MR. JUSTICE STONE delivered the opinion of the Court:

The two principal questions raised by the record in this case are, first, whether Congress has constitutional power to prohibit the shipment in interstate commerce of lumber manufactured by employees whose wages are less than a prescribed minimum or whose weekly hours of labor at that wage are greater than a prescribed maximum, and, second, whether it has power to prohibit the employment of workmen in the production of goods "for interstate commerce" at other than prescribed wages and hours....

...The case comes here on assignments by the Government that the district court erred in so far as it held that Congress was without constitutional power to penalize the acts set forth in the indictment, and appellee seeks to sustain the decision below on the grounds that the prohibition by Congress of those Acts is unauthorized by the Commerce Clause and is prohibited by the Fifth Amendment.... [W]e ... confine our decision to the validity and construction of the statute....

While manufacture is not of itself interstate commerce, the shipment of manufactured goods interstate is such commerce and the prohibition of such shipment by Congress is indubitably a regulation of the commerce. The power to regulate commerce is the power "to prescribe the rule by which commerce is governed." *Gibbons v. Ogden*.... It extends not only to those regulations which aid, foster, and protect the commerce. but embraces those which prohibit it.... It is conceded that the power of Congress to prohibit transportation in interstate commerce includes noxious articles, *Lottery Case*,... stolen articles, *Brooks v. United States*,... kidnapped persons, *Gooch v. United States*,... and articles such as intoxicating liquor or convict-made goods, traffic in which is forbidden or restricted by the laws of the state of destination. *Kentucky Whip & Collar Co. v. Illinois Central R. Co*....

But it is said that the present prohibition falls within the scope of none of these categories; that while the prohibition is nominally a regulation of the commerce its motive or purpose is regulation of wages and hours of persons engaged in manufacture, the control of which has been reserved to the states and upon which Georgia and some of the states of destination have placed no restriction; that the effect of the present statute is not to exclude the prescribed articles from interstate commerce in aid of state regulation as in *Kentucky Whip & Collar Co. v. Illinois Central R. Co*.... but instead, under the guise of a regulation of interstate commerce, it undertakes to regulate wages and hours within the state contrary to the policy of the state which has elected to leave them unregulated....

The motive and purpose of the present regulation are plainly to make effective the Congressional conception of public policy that interstate commerce should not be made the instrument of competition in the distribution of goods produced under substandard labor conditions, which competition is injurious to the commerce and to the states from and to which the commerce flows. The motive and purpose of a regulation of interstate commerce are matters for the legislative judgment, upon the exercise of which the Constitution places no restriction and over which the courts are given no control.... Whatever their motive and purpose, regulations of commerce which do not infringe some constitutional prohibition are within the plenary power conferred on Congress by the Commerce Clause. Subject only to that limitation, presently to be considered, we conclude that the prohibition of the shipment interstate of goods produced under the forbidden substandard labor conditions is within the constitutional authority of Congress.

In the more than a century which has elapsed since the decision of *Gibbons v. Ogden*, these principles of constitutional interpretation have been so long and repeatedly recognized by this Court as applicable to the Commerce Clause, that there would be little occasion for repeating them now were it not for the decision of this Court twenty-two years ago in *Hammer v. Dagenhart*.... In that case it was held by a bare majority of the Court, over the powerful and now classic dissent of Mr. Justice Holmes setting forth the fundamental issues involved, that Congress was without power to exclude the products of child labor from interstate commerce. The reasoning and conclusion which we have reached, that the power of Congress under the Commerce Clause is plenary to exclude any article from interstate commerce subject only to the specific prohibitions of the Constitution.

Hammer v. Dagenhart has not been followed. The distinction on which the decision was rested that Congressional power to prohibit interstate commerce is limited to articles which in themselves have some harmful or deleterious property – a distinction which was novel when made and unsupported by any provision of the Constitution – has long since been abandoned....

The conclusion is inescapable that *Hammer v. Dagenhart* was a departure from the principles which have prevailed in the interpretation of the Commerce Clause both before and since the decision and that such vitality, as a precedent, as it then had has long since been exhausted. It should be and now is overruled.

Our conclusion is unaffected by the Tenth Amendment which provides: "The powers not delegated to the United States by the Constitution, nor prohibited by it to the States, are reserved to the States respectively, or to the people." The amendment states but a truism that all is retained which has not been surrendered. There is nothing in the history of its adoption to suggest that it was more than declaratory of the relationship between the national and state governments as it had been established by the Constitution before the amendment or that its purpose was other than to allay fears that the new national government might seek to exercise powers not granted, and that the states might not be able to exercise fully their reserved powers... .

Validity of the Wage and Hour Provisions Under the Fifth Amendment.

Both provisions are minimum-wage requirements compelling the payment of a minimum standard wage with a prescribed increased wage for overtime.... Since our decision in *West Coast Hotel Co. v. Parrish*,... it is no longer open to question that the fixing of a minimum wage is within the legislative power and that the bare fact of its exercise is not a denial of due process under the Fifth more than under the Fourteenth Amendment. Nor is it any longer open to question that it is within the legislative power to fix maximum hours....

The Act is sufficiently definite to meet constitutional demands. One who employs persons, without conforming to the prescribed wage and hour conditions, to work on goods which he ships or expects to ship across state lines, is warned that he may be subject to the criminal penalties of the Act. No more is required....

WICKARD v. FILBURN
317 U.S. 111; 63 S.Ct. 82; 87 L.Ed. 122 (1942)

The overriding purpose of the Agricultural Adjustment Act of 1938 was to stabilize agricultural production, and thus prices, through orderly marketing procedures, This case centered on an acreage allotment or quota established for wheat growers; any production in excess *of the quota was subject to penalty. Filburn, a wheat farmer in Ohio, exceeded his quota but claimed that the wheat was for his personal use and would not be sold or marketed. He refused to pay the penalty and obtained an injunction from a district court enjoining the Secretary of Agriculture, Wickard, from enforcing the AAA. Wickard appealed to the Supreme Court.*

MR. JUSTICE JACKSON delivered the opinion of the Court:

It is urged that under the commerce clause of the Constitution, Article 1. section 8, clause 3, Congress does not possess the power it has in this instance sought to exercise. The question would merit little consideration since our decision in *United States v. Darby* ... sustaining the federal power to regulate production of goods for commerce, except for the fact that this Act extends federal regulation to production not intended in any part for commerce but wholly for consumption on the farm. The Act includes a definition of "market" and its derivatives, so that as related to wheat, in addition to its conventional meaning, it also means to dispose of "by feeding (in any form) to poultry or livestock which, or the products of which, are sold, bartered, or exchanged, or to be so disposed of." Hence, marketing quotas not only embrace all that may be sold without penalty but also what may be consumed on the premises. Wheat produced on excess acreage is designated as "available for marketing" as so defined, and the penalty is imposed thereon. Penalties do not depend upon whether any part of the wheat, either within or without the quota, is sold or intended to be sold. The sum of this is that the Federal Government fixes a quota including all that the farmer may harvest for sale or for his own farm needs, and declares that wheat produced on excess acreage may neither be disposed of nor used except upon payment of the penalty, or except it is stored as required by the Act or delivered to the Secretary of Agriculture.

Appellee says that this is a regulation of production and consumption of wheat. Such activities are, he urges, beyond the reach of Congressional power under the commerce clause, since they are local in character, and their effects upon interstate commerce are at most "indirect." In answer the Government argues that the statute regulates neither production nor consumption, but only marketing, and, in the alternative, that if the Act does go beyond the regulation of marketing it is sustainable as a "necessary and proper" implementation of the power of Congress over interstate commerce.

The Government's concern lest the Act be held to be a regulation of production or consumption. rather than of marketing, is attributable to a few dicta and decisions of this Court which might be understood to lay it down that activities such as "production," "manufacturing," and "mining" are strictly "local" and, except in special circumstances which are not present here, cannot be regulated under the commerce power because their effects upon interstate commerce are, as matter of law, only "indirect." Even today, when this power has been held to have great latitude, there is no decision of this Court that such activities may be regulated where no part of the product is intended for interstate commerce or intermingled with the subjects thereof. We believe that a review of the course of decision under the commerce clause will make plain, however, that questions of the power of Congress are not to be decided by reference to any formula which would give controlling force to nomenclature such as "production" and "indirect" and foreclose consideration of the actual effects of the activity in question upon interstate commerce.

...Once an economic measure of the reach of the power granted to Congress in the commerce clause is accepted, questions of federal power cannot be decided simply by finding the activity in question to be "production," nor can consideration of its economic effects be foreclosed by calling them "indirect." The present Chief Justice has said in summary of the present state of the law: "The commerce power is not confined in its exercise to the regulation of commerce among the states. It extends to those activities intrastate which so affect interstate commerce, or the exertion of the power of Congress over it, as to make regulation of them appropriate means to the attainment of a legitimate end, the effective execution of the granted power to regulate interstate commerce.... The power of Congress over interstate commerce is plenary and complete in itself, may be exercised to its utmost extent, and acknowledges no limitations other than are prescribed in the Constitution.... It follows that no form of state activity can constitutionally thwart the regulatory power granted by the commerce clause to Congress. Hence the reach of that power extends to those intrastate activities which in a substantial way interfere with or obstruct the exercise of the granted power." *United States v. Wrightwood Dairy Co.*, 315 U.S. 110....

Whether the subject of the regulation in question was "production," "consumption," or "marketing" is, therefore, not material for purposes of deciding the question of federal power before us. That an activity is of a local character may help in a doubtful case to determine whether Congress intended to reach it. The same consideration might help in determining whether in the absence of congressional action it would be permissible for the state to exert its power on the subject matter, even though in so doing it to some degree affected interstate commerce. But even if appellee's activity be local and though it may not be regarded as commerce, it may still, whatever its nature, be reached by Congress if it exerts a substantial economic effect on interstate commerce, and this irrespective of whether such effect is what might at some earlier time have been defined as "direct" or "indirect."

...The maintenance by government regulation of a price for wheat undoubtedly can be accomplished as effectively by sustaining or increasing the demand as by limiting the supply. The effect of the statute before us is to restrict the amount which may be produced for market and the extent as well to which one may forestall resort to the market by producing to meet his own needs. The appellee's own contribution to the demand for wheat may be trivial by itself is not enough to remove him from the scope of federal regulation where, as here, his contribution, taken together with that of many others similarly situated, is far from trivial....

It is well established by decision of this Court that the power to regulate commerce includes the power to regulate the prices at which commodities in that commerce are dealt in and practices affecting such prices. One of the primary purposes of the Act in question was to increase the market price of wheat, and to that end to limit the volume thereof that could affect the market. It can hardly be denied that a factor of such volume and variability as home-consumed wheat would have a substantial influence on price and market conditions. This may arise because being in marketable condition such wheat overhangs the market and, if induced by rising prices, tends to flow into the market and check price increases. But if we assume that it is never marketed, it supplies a need of the man who grew it which would otherwise be reflected by purchases in the open market. Home-grown wheat in this sense competes with wheat in commerce. The stimulation of commerce is a use of the regulatory function quite as definitely as prohibitions or restrictions thereon. This record leaves us in no doubt that Congress may properly have considered that wheat consumed on the farm where grown, if wholly outside the scheme of regulation, would have a substantial effect in defeating and obstructing its purpose to stimulate trade therein at increased prices.

It is said, however, that this Act, forcing some farmers into the market to buy what they could provide for themselves, is an unfair promotion of the markets and prices of specializing wheat growers. It is of the essence of regulation that it lays a restraining hand on the self-interest of the regulated and that advantages from the regulation commonly fall to others. The conflicts of economic interest between the regulated and those who advantage by it are wisely left under our system to resolution by the Congress under its more flexible and responsible legislative process. Such conflicts rarely lend themselves to judicial determination. And with the wisdom, workability, or fairness of the plan of regulation we have nothing to do....

Reversed.

HEART OF ATLANTA MOTEL v. UNITED STATES
379 U.S. 241; 85 S.Ct. 348; 13 L.Ed. 2d 258 (1964)

In the Civil Rights Cases (1883), the Court had held that the Civil Rights Act of 1875, which forbade racial segregation and discrimination in public places, was invalid. Congress had based the law on the Thirteenth and Fourteenth Amendments, the enforcement of which can only be aimed at political discrimination at the hands of government, not social or private discrimination. Congress did not again attempt to deal with the problem of public accommodations and racism until the apex of the civil rights movement with the passage of the Civil Rights Act of 1964. The law closely resembled the 1875 act; however, the important sections of the statute, particularly Title II (the Public Accommodations section) were assertions of implied authority from the power of Congress over interstate and foreign commerce.

MR. JUSTICE CLARK delivered the opinion of the Court:

This is a declaratory judgment action attacking the constitutionality of Title II of the Civil Rights Act of 1964....

The Act as finally adopted was most comprehensive, undertaking to prevent through peaceful and voluntary settlement discrimination in voting, as well as in places of accommodation and public facilities, federally secured programs and in employment. Since Title II is the only portion under attack here, we confine our consideration to those public accommodation provisions.

Title II of the Act.

This is divided into seven sections beginning with section 201 (a) which provides that:

"All persons shall be entitled to the full and equal enjoyment of the goods, services, facilities, privileges, advantages, and accommodations of any place of public accommodation, as defined in this section, without discrimination or segregation on the ground of race, color, religion, or national origin."

There are listed in section 201 (b) four classes of business establishments, each of which "serves the public" and "is a place of public accommodation" within the meaning of section 201 (a) "if its operations affect commerce, or if discrimination or segregation by it is supported by State action." The covered establishments are:

"(1) any inn, hotel, motel, or other establishment which provides lodging to transient guests, other than an establishment located within a building which contains not more than five rooms for rent or hire and which is actually occupied by the proprietor of such establishment as his residence; (2) any restaurant, cafeteria ... (not here involved); (3) any motion picture house ... (not here involved); (4) any establishment ... which is physically located within the premises of any establishment otherwise covered by this subsection, or ... within the premises of which is physically located any such covered establishment ... (not here involved)."

Section 201 (c) defines the phrase "affect commerce" as applied to the above establishments. It first declares that "any inn, hotel, motel, or other establishment which provides lodging to transient guests" affects commerce per se....

Finally, section 203 prohibits the withholding or denial, etc., of any right or privilege secured by section 201 ... or the intimidation, threatening or coercion of any person with the purpose of interfering with any such right or the punishing, etc., of any person for exercising or attempting to exercise any such right.

The remaining sections of the Title are remedial ones for violations of any of the previous sections. Remedies are limited to civil actions for preventive relief. The Attorney General may bring suit where he has "reasonable cause to believe that any person or group of persons is engaged in a pattern or practice of resistance to the full enjoyment of any of the rights secured by this title, and that the pattern or practice is of such a nature and is intended to deny the full exercise of the rights herein described ...."

Application of Title II to Heart of Atlanta Motel.

It is admitted that the operation of the hotel brings it within the provisions of section 201 (a) of the Act and that appellant refused to provide lodging for transient Negroes because of their race or color and that it intends to continue that policy unless restrained.

The sole question posed is, therefore, the constitutionality of the Civil Rights Act of 1964 as applied to these facts. The legislative history of the Act indicates that Congress based the Act on section 5 and the Equal Protection Clause of the Fourteenth Amendment as well as its power to regulate interstate commerce under Art. 1, section 8, cl 3 of the Constitution.

The Senate Commerce Committee made it quite clear that the fundamental object of Title II was to vindicate "the deprivation of personal dignity that surely accompanies denials of equal access to public establishments." At the same time, however, it noted that such an objective has been and could be readily achieved "by congressional action based on the commerce power of the Constitution...." Our study of the legislative record, made in the light of prior cases, has brought us to the conclusion that Congress possessed ample power in this regard, and we have therefore not considered the other grounds relied upon. This is not to say that the remaining authority upon which it acted was not adequate, a question upon which we do not pass, but merely that since the commerce power is sufficient for our decision here we have considered it alone....

The Civil Rights Cases (1883), and their Application.

In light of our ground for decision, it might be well at the outset to discuss the *Civil Rights Cases*, which declared provisions of the Civil Rights Act of 1875 unconstitutional. We think that decision inapposite, and without precedential value in determining the constitutionality of the present Act. Unlike Title II of the present legislation, the 1875 Act broadly proscribed discrimination in "inns, public conveyances on land or water, theaters. and other public places of amusement," without limiting the categories of affected businesses to those impinging upon interstate commerce. In contrast, the applicability of Title II is carefully limited to enterprises having a direct and substantial reaction to the interstate flow of goods and people, except where state action is involved. Further, the fact that certain kinds of business may not in 1875 have been sufficiently involved in interstate commerce to warrant bringing them within the ambit of the commerce power is not necessarily dispositive of the same question today. Our populace had not reached its present mobility, nor were facilities, goods and services circulating as readily in interstate commerce as they are today. Although the principles which we apply today are those first formulated by Chief Justice Marshall in *Gibbons v. Ogden* [1824], the conditions of transportation and commerce have changed dramatically, and we must apply those principles to the present state of commerce. The sheer increase in volume of interstate traffic alone would give discriminatory practices which inhibit travel a far larger impact upon the Nation's commerce than such practices had on the economy of another day....

The Basis of Congressional Action.

While the Act as adopted carried no congressional findings the record of its passage through each house is replete with evidence of the burdens that discrimination by race or color places upon interstate commerce.... This testimony included the fact that our people of all races traveling from State to State; that Negroes in particular have been the subject of discrimination in transient accommodations, having to travel great distances to secure the same; that often they have been unable to obtain accommodations and have had to call upon friends to put them up overnight...; and that these conditions have become so acute as to require the listing of available lodging for Negroes in a special guidebook which was itself "dramatic testimony to the difficulties" Negroes encounter in travel.... These exclusionary practices were found to be nationwide, the Under Secretary of Commerce testifying that there is "no question that this discrimination in the North still exists to a large degree" and in the West and Midwest as well.... This testimony indicated a qualitative as well as quantitative effect on interstate travel by Negroes. The former was the obvious impairment of the Negro traveler's pleasure and convenience that resulted when he continually was uncertain of finding lodging. As for the latter, there was evidence that this uncertainty stemming from racial discrimination had the effect of discouraging travel on the part of a substantial portion of the Negro community.... This was the conclusion not only of the Under Secretary of Commerce but also of the Administrator of the Federal Aviation Agency who wrote the Chairman of the Senate Commerce Committee that it was his "belief that air commerce is adversely affected by the denial to a substantial segment of the traveling public of adequate and desegregated public accommodations...." We shall not burden this opinion with further details since the voluminous testimony presents overwhelming evidence that discrimination by hotels and motels impedes interstate travel.

The Power of Congress Over Interstate Travel.

The power of Congress to deal with these obstructions depends on the meaning of the Commerce Clause. Its meaning was first enunciated 140 years ago by the great Chief Justice John Marshall in *Gibbons v. Ogden*, in these words:

[The Court here quotes at length from the opinion concerning the nature of interstate commerce and congressional power over it.]

In short, the determinative test of the exercise of power by the Congress under the Commerce Clause is simply whether the activity sought to be regulated is "commerce which concerns more States than one" and has a real and substantial relation to the national interest. Let us now turn to this facet of the problem.

That the "intercourse" of which the Chief Justice spoke included the movement of persons through more States than one was settled as early as 1849, in the Passenger Cases where Mr. Justice McLean stated: "That the transportation of passengers is a part of commerce is not now an open question." Again in 1913 Mr. Justice McKenna, speaking for the Court, said: "Commerce among the States, we have said, consists of intercourse and traffic between their citizens, and includes the transportation of persons and property." *Hoke v. United States*. And only four years later in 1917 in *Caminetti v. United States*, Mr. Justice Day held for the Court:

"The transportation of passengers in interstate commerce, it has long been settled, is within the regulatory power of Congress, under the commerce clause of the Constitution, and the authority of Congress to keep the channels of interstate commerce free from immoral and injurious uses has been frequently sustained, and is no longer open to question."

...Thus the power of Congress to promote interstate commerce also includes the power to regulate the local incidents thereof, including local activities in both the States of origin and destination, which might have a substantial and harmful effect upon that commerce. One need only examine the evidence which we have discussed above to see that Congress may – as it has – prohibit racial discrimination by motels serving travelers, however "local" their operations may appear.

Nor does the Act deprive appellant of liberty or property under the Fifth Amendment. The commerce power invoked here by the Congress is a specific and plenary one authorized by the Constitution itself. The only questions are: (1) whether Congress had a rational basis for finding that racial discrimination by motels affected commerce, and (2) if it had such a basis, whether the means it selected to eliminate that evil are reasonable and appropriate. If they are, appellant has no "right" to select its guests as it sees fit, free from governmental regulation.

...We, therefore, conclude that the action of the Congress in the adoption of the Act as applied here to a motel which concededly serves interstate travelers is within the power granted it by the Commerce Clause of the Constitution, as interpreted by this Court for 140 years. It may be argued that Congress could have pursued other methods to eliminate the obstructions it found in interstate

commerce caused by racial discrimination. But this is a matter of policy that rests entirely with the Congress, not with the courts. How obstructions in commerce may be removed – what means are to be employed – is within the sound and exclusive discretion of the Congress. It is subject only to one caveat – that the means chosen by it must be reasonably adapted to the end permitted by the Constitution. We cannot say that its choice here was not so adapted. The Constitution requires no more.
Affirmed.

MR. JUSTICES BLACK, DOUGLAS and GOLDBERG concurred.

GROSSO v. UNITED STATES
390 U.S. 62 (1968)

Grosso was convicted in a district court for willful failure to pay the occupational tax on the earnings of professional gamblers and the excise tax required by the federal Wagering Act. Grosso claimed that not only was the tax a penalty but it also resulted in a violation of the Fifth Amendment's protection against compulsory self-incrimination. The case was decided by the Supreme Court as a companion with Marchetti v. United States.

MR. JUSTICE HARLAN delivered the opinion of the Court.

Petitioner did not assert below, and therefore has not urged here, that his privilege was violated by reason of his convictions for conspiracy and for failure to pay the special occupational tax. He has contended only that payment of the excise tax would have required him to incriminate himself, that he therefore may not properly be prosecuted for willful failure to pay the tax or for conspiracy to evade its payment, and that conduct of the trial court after submission of the case to the jury denied him a fair trial.

We turn first to petitioner's contention that payment of the wagering excise tax would have compelled him to incriminate himself We have summarized in *Marchetti, supra*, the various state and federal penalties which have been imposed upon wagering. It is enough now to reiterate that Pennsylvania, in which petitioner allegedly accepted wagers, has adopted a comprehensive statutory system for the punishment of gambling and ancillary activities. These penalties, in combination with the federal statutes place petitioner entirely within "an area permeated with criminal statutes," where he is "inherently suspect of criminal activities." *Albertson v. SACB*. The issues here are therefore whether payment of the excise tax would have provided information incriminating to petitioner, and, if it would have done so, whether petitioner is otherwise prevented from asserting the constitutional privilege.

Although failures to pay the excise tax and to file a return are separately punishable under 26 U.S.C. section 7203, the two obligations must be considered inseparable for purposes of measuring the hazards of self-incrimination which might stem from payment of the excise tax. Nothing in the pertinent statutes or regulations contemplates payment of the tax without submission of the return, and we are informed by the United States that if the return does not accompany the tax payment, "the money is not accepted." We must conclude that here the validity under the Constitution of criminal prosecutions for willful failure to pay the excise tax may properly be determined only after assessment of the hazards of incrimination which would result from "literal and full compliance" with all the statutory requirements.

Second, although there is no statutory instruction, as there is for the occupational tax, that state and local prosecuting officers be provided listings of those who have paid the excise tax, neither has Congress imposed explicit restrictions upon the use of information as a consequence of payment of the tax. Moreover, it appears that the Revenue Service, evidently acting under the authority of certain general statutory provisions, has undertaken to tender this information to interested prosecuting authorities. We can only conclude that those liable for payment of the excise tax reasonably may expect that information obtainable from its payment will ultimately be proffered to state and federal prosecuting officers.

In these circumstances, it would be impossible to say that the hazards of incrimination which stem from the obligation to pay the excise tax are "imaginary and unsubstantial." The criminal penalties for wagering with which petitioner is threatened are scarcely "remote possibilities out of the ordinary course of law," *Heike v. United States;* yet he is obliged, on pain of criminal prosecution, to provide information which would readily incriminate him, and which he may reasonably expect would be provided to prosecuting authorities. These hazards of incrimination can only be characterized as "real and appreciable." *Reg. v. Boyes; Brown v. Walker.* Moreover, unlike the income tax return at issue in *United States v. Sullivan*, petitioner's submission of an excise tax payment, and his replies to the questions on the attendant return, would directly and unavoidably have served to incriminate him; his claim of privilege as to the entire tax payment procedure was therefore neither "extreme" nor "extravagant."

We have concluded that the "required records" doctrine, *Shapiro v. United States,* 335 U.S. 1, cannot be appropriately applied to these circumstances. The premises of the doctrine, as it is described in *Shapiro*, are evidently three: first, the purposes of the United States' inquiry must be essentially regulatory; second, information is to be obtained by requiring the preservation of records of a kind which the regulated party has customarily kept; and third, the records themselves must have assumed "public aspects" which render them at least analogous to public documents. There is no need for present purposes to examine the relative significance of these three factors, or to undertake to define more specifically their incidents, for both the first and third factors are plainly absent from this case.

Here the statutory obligations are directed almost exclusively to individuals inherently suspect of criminal activities. The principal interest of the United States must be assumed to be the collection of revenue, and not the prosecution of gamblers, *United States v. Calamaro,* 354 U.S. 351, 358; but we cannot ignore either the characteristics of the activities about which information is sought, or the composition of the group to which the inquiries are made. These collateral circumstances, in combination with Congress' apparent wish that any information obtained as a consequence of the wagering taxes be made available to prosecuting authorities, readily suffice to distinguish these requirements from those at issue in *Shapiro*. Moreover, the information demanded here lacks every characteristic of a public document. No doubt it is desired by the United States, but we have concluded that this alone does not render information "public," and thus does not deprive it of constitutional protection.

Finally we have been urged by the United States to permit continued enforcement of wagering excise tax requirements by imposing restrictions upon the use by state and federal authorities of information obtained as a consequence of payment of the tax. We recognize that section 6107 is not by its terms applicable to the excise tax, and that there is no similar statutory obligation that the Commissioner provide prosecutors with listings of those who have paid the excise tax. Nonetheless, it would be inappropriate to impose such restrictions upon one portion of a statutory system, when we have concluded that it would be improper to do so upon "an integral part" of the same system. We therefore decline to impose the restrictions urged by the United States.

There remain for disposition the substantive counts for willful failure to pay the occupational tax, and the count for conspiracy to defraud. The latter was bottomed on allegations that petitioner had conspired to evade payment both of the excise tax and of the occupational tax. Petitioner has consistently contended that the constitutional privilege should have prevented his conviction on the conspiracy count, evidently on the basis that, insofar as it is founded on his failure to pay the excise tax, this count raises questions identical with those presented by the substantive counts for failure to pay that tax. We agree, and conclude that a taxpayer may not be convicted of conspiracy to evade payment of the tax, if the constitutional privilege would properly prevent his conviction for willful failure to pay it.

The judgment of the Court of Appeals is reversed in its entirety.

It is so ordered.

MR. JUSTICE MARSHALL took no part in the consideration or decision of this case.

MR. JUSTICES BRENNAN and STEWART concurred.

MR. CHIEF JUSTICE WARREN dissented.

UNITED STATES v. LOPEZ
115 S.Ct. 1624 (1995)

The facts in this case are contained in the opinion below.

Chief Justice REHNQUIST delivered the opinion of the Court....

On March 10, 1992, respondent, who was then a 12th-grade student, arrived at Edison High School in San Antonio, Texas, carrying a concealed .38

caliber handgun and five bullets.... He was arrested and charged under Texas law with firearm possession on school premises. The next day, the state charges were dismissed after federal agents charged respondent by complaint with violating the Gun-Free School Zones Act of 1990....

The District Court ... found him guilty of violating § 922(q), and sentenced him to six months imprisonment and two years supervised release.

On appeal, respondent challenged his conviction based on his claim that § 922(q) exceeded Congress' power to legislate under the Commerce Clause. The Court of Appeals for the Fifth Circuit agreed and reversed respondent's conviction.... Because of the importance of the issue, we granted certiorari....

We start with first principles. The Constitution creates a Federal Government of enumerated powers. As James Madison wrote, "[t]he powers delegated by the proposed Constitution to the federal government are few and defined. Those which are to remain in the State governments are numerous and indefinite...."

The Constitution delegates to Congress the power "[t]o regulate Commerce with foreign Nations, and among the several States, and with the Indian Tribes." The Court, through Chief Justice Marshall, first defined the nature of Congress' commerce power in *Gibbons v. Ogden*.

The commerce power "is the power to regulate; that is, to prescribe the rule by which commerce is to be governed. This power, like all others vested in Congress, is complete in itself, may be exercised to its utmost extent, and acknowledges no limitations, other than are prescribed in the constitution." The *Gibbons* Court, however, acknowledged that limitations on the commerce power are inherent in the very language of the Commerce Clause....

Jones & Laughlin Steel, Darby, and *Wickard* ushered in an era of Commerce Clause jurisprudence that greatly expanded the previously defined authority of Congress under that Clause....

But even these modern-era precedents which have expanded congressional power under the Commerce Clause confirm that this power is subject to outer limits....

[W]e have identified three broad categories of activity that Congress may regulate under its commerce power. First, Congress may regulate the use of the channels of interstate commerce.... Second, Congress is empowered to regulate and protect the instrumentalities of interstate commerce, or persons or things in interstate commerce, even though the threat may come only from intrastate activities.... Finally, Congress' commerce authority includes the power to regulate those activities having a substantial relation to interstate commerce....

Within this final category, admittedly, our case law has not been clear whether an activity must "affect" or "substantially affect" interstate commerce in order to be within Congress' power to regulate it under the Commerce Clause.... We conclude, consistent with the great weight of our case law, that the proper test requires an analysis of whether the regulated activity "substantially affects" interstate commerce.

We now turn to consider the power of Congress, in the light of this framework, to enact § 922(q). The first two categories of authority may be quickly disposed of.... Thus, if § 922(q) is to be sustained, it must be under the third category as a regulation of an activity that substantially affects interstate commerce....

Section 922(q) is a criminal statute that by its terms has nothing to do with "commerce" or any sort of economic enterprise, however broadly one might define those terms. Section 922(q) is not an essential part of a larger regulation of economic activity, in which the regulatory scheme could be undercut unless the intrastate activity were regulated. It cannot, therefore, be sustained under our cases upholding regulations of activities that arise out of or are connected with a commercial transaction, which viewed in the aggregate, substantially affects interstate commerce.

Second, § 922(q) contains no jurisdictional element which would ensure, through case-by-case inquiry, that the firearm possession in question affects interstate commerce.... § 922(q) has no express jurisdictional element which might limit its reach to a discrete set of firearm possessions that additionally have an explicit connection with or effect on interstate commerce....

The Government argues that possession of a firearm in a school zone may result in violent crime and that violent crime can be expected to affect the functioning of the national economy in two ways. First, the costs of violent crime are substantial, and, through the mechanism of insurance, those costs are spread throughout the population. Second, violent crime reduces the willingness of individuals to travel to areas within the country that are perceived to be unsafe. The Government also argues that the presence of guns in schools poses a substantial threat to the educational process by threatening the learning environment. A handicapped educational process, in turn, will result in a less productive citizenry. That, in turn, would have an adverse effect on the Nation's economic well-being. As a result, the Government argues that Congress could rationally have concluded that § 922(q) substantially affects interstate commerce.

We pause to consider the implications of the Government's arguments. The Government admits, under its "costs of crime" reasoning, that Congress could regulate not only all violent crime, but all activities that might lead to violent crime, regardless of how tenuously they relate to interstate commerce. Similarly, under the Government's "national productivity" reasoning, Congress could regulate any activity that it found was related to the economic productivity of individual citizens: family law (including marriage, divorce, and child custody), for example. Under the theories that the Government presents in support of § 922(q), it is difficult to perceive any limitation on federal power, even in areas such as criminal law enforcement or education where States historically have been sovereign. Thus, if we were to accept the Government's arguments, we are hard-pressed to posit any activity by an individual that Congress is without power to regulate.

Although Justice BREYER argues that acceptance of the Government's rationales would not authorize a general federal police power, he is unable to identify any activity that the States may regulate but Congress may not....

Justice BREYER rejects our reading of precedent and argues that "Congress ... could rationally conclude that schools fall on the commercial side of the line." Again, Justice BREYER's rationale lacks any real limits because, depending on the level of generality, any activity can be looked upon as commercial. Under the dissent's rationale, Congress could just as easily look at child rearing as "fall[ing] on the commercial side of the line" because it provides a "valuable service namely, to equip [children] with the skills they need to survive in life and, more specifically, in the workplace...."

To uphold the Government's contentions here, we would have to pile inference upon inference in a manner that would bid fair to convert congressional authority under the Commerce Clause to a general police power of the sort retained by the States. Admittedly, some of our prior cases have taken long steps down that road, giving great deference to congressional action. The broad language in these opinions has suggested the possibility of additional expansion, but we decline here to proceed any further. To do so would require us to conclude that the Constitution's enumeration of powers does not presuppose something not enumerated, and that there never will be a distinction between what is truly national and what is truly local. This we are unwilling to do.

For the foregoing reasons the judgment of the Court of Appeals is

Affirmed.

Justice KENNEDY, with whom Justice O'CONNOR joins, concurring.

... *Stare decisis* operates with great force in counseling us not to call in question the essential principles now in place respecting the congressional power to regulate transactions of a commercial nature. That fundamental restraint on our power forecloses us from reverting to an understanding of commerce that would serve only an 18th-century economy.... Congress can regulate in the commercial sphere on the assumption that we have a single market and a unified purpose to build a stable national economy....

It does not follow, however, that in every instance the Court lacks the authority and responsibility to review congressional attempts to alter the federal balance. This case requires us to consider our place in the design of the Government and to appreciate the significance of federalism in the whole structure of the Constitution....

The statute before us upsets the federal balance to a degree that renders it an unconstitutional assertion of the commerce power, and our intervention is required. As THE CHIEF JUSTICE explains, unlike the earlier cases to come before the Court here neither the actors nor their conduct have a commercial character, and neither the purposes nor the design of the statute have an evident commercial nexus.... The statute makes the simple possession of a gun within 1,000 feet of the grounds of the school a criminal offense. In a sense any conduct in this interdependent world of ours has an ultimate commercial origin or consequence, but we have not yet said the commerce power may reach so far. If Congress attempts that extension, then at the least we must inquire whether the exercise of national power seeks to intrude upon an area of traditional state concern....

The statute now before us forecloses the States from experimenting and exercising their own judgment in an area to which States lay claim by right of history and expertise, and it does so by regulating an activity beyond the realm of commerce in the ordinary and usual sense of that term....

Absent a stronger connection or identification with commercial concerns that are central to the Commerce Clause, that interference contradicts the federal balance the Framers designed and that this Court is obliged to enforce.

For these reasons, I join in the opinion and judgment of the Court.

Justice THOMAS, concurring.

...Although I join the majority, I write separately to observe that our case law has drifted far from the original understanding of the Commerce Clause. In a future case, we ought to temper our Commerce Clause jurisprudence in a manner that both makes sense of our more recent case law and is more faithful to the original understanding of that Clause....

In an appropriate case, I believe that we must further reconsider our "substantial effects" test with an eye toward constructing a standard that reflects the text and history of the Commerce Clause without totally rejecting our more recent Commerce Clause jurisprudence....

Today, however, I merely support the Court's conclusion with a discussion of the text, structure, and history of the Commerce Clause and an analysis of our early case law. My goal is simply to show how far we have departed from the original understanding and to demonstrate that the result we reach today is by no means "radical".... I also want to point out the necessity of refashioning a coherent test that does not tend to "obliterate the distinction between what is national and what is local and create a completely centralized government...."

...from the time of the ratification of the Constitution to the mid-1930's, it was widely understood that the Constitution granted Congress only limited powers, notwithstanding the Commerce Clause. Moreover, there was no question that activities wholly separated from business, such as gun possession, were beyond the reach of the commerce power. If anything, the "wrong turn" was the Court's dramatic departure in the 1930's from a century and a half of precedent....

...Apart from its recent vintage and its corresponding lack of any grounding in the original understanding of the Constitution, the substantial effects test suffers from the further flaw that it appears to grant Congress a police power over the Nation. When asked at oral argument if there were *any* limits to the Commerce Clause, the Government was at a loss for words.... The one advantage of the dissent's standard is certainty: it is certain that under its analysis everything may be regulated under the guise of the Commerce Clause.... .

...This extended discussion of the original understanding and our first century and a half of case law does not necessarily require a wholesale abandonment of our more recent opinions. It simply reveals that our substantial effects test is far removed from both the Constitution and from our early case law and that the Court's opinion should not be viewed as "radical" or another "wrong turn" that must be corrected in the future. The analysis also suggests that we ought to temper our Commerce Clause jurisprudence.

Unless the dissenting Justices are willing to repudiate our long-held understanding of the limited nature of federal power, I would think that they too must be willing to reconsider the substantial effects test in a future case. If we wish to be true to a Constitution that does not cede a police power to the Federal Government, our Commerce Clause's boundaries simply cannot be "defined" as being "'commensurate with the national needs'" or self-consciously intended to let the Federal Government "'defend itself against economic forces that Congress decrees inimical or destructive of the national economy.'..." Such a formulation of federal power is no test at all: it is a blank check....

Justice STEVENS, dissenting... .
Justice SOUTER, dissenting... .

Justice BREYER, with whom Justice STEVENS, Justice SOUTER, and Justice GINSBURG join, dissenting.

The issue in this case is whether the Commerce Clause authorizes Congress to enact a statute that makes it a crime to possess a gun in, or near, a school.... In my view, the statute falls well within the scope of the commerce power as this Court has understood that power over the last half-century.

...In reaching this conclusion, I apply three basic principles of Commerce Clause interpretation. First, the power to "regulate Commerce ... among the several States,"... encompasses the power to regulate local activities insofar as they significantly affect interstate commerce.... I use the word "significant" because the word "substantial" implies a somewhat narrower power than recent precedent suggests.... But, to speak of "substantial effect" rather than "significant effect" would make no difference in this case.

Second, in determining whether a local activity will likely have a significant effect upon interstate commerce, a court must consider, not the effect of an individual act (a single instance of gun possession), but rather the cumulative effect of all similar instances....

Third, the Constitution requires us to judge the connection between a regulated activity and interstate commerce, not directly, but at one remove. Courts must give Congress a degree of leeway in determining the existence of a significant factual connection between the regulated activity and interstate commerce – both because the Constitution delegates the commerce power directly to Congress and because the determination requires an empirical judgment of a kind that a legislature is more likely than a court to make with accuracy. The traditional words "rational basis" capture this leeway.... Thus, the specific question before us, as the Court recognizes, is not whether the "regulated activity sufficiently affected interstate commerce," but, rather, whether Congress could have had "*a rational basis*" for so concluding....

...To hold this statute constitutional is not to "obliterate" the "distinction of what is national and what is local,"... nor is it to hold that the Commerce Clause permits the Federal Government to "regulate any activity that it found was related to the economic productivity of individual citizens," to regulate "marriage, divorce, and child custody," or to regulate any and all aspects of education....

In sum, a holding that the particular statute before us falls within the commerce power would not expand the scope of that Clause. Rather, it simply would apply preexisting law to changing economic circumstances.... It would recognize that, in today's economic world, gun-related violence near the classroom makes a significant difference to our economic, as well as our social, well-being....

The majority's holding – that § 922 falls outside the scope of the Commerce Clause – creates three serious legal problems. First, the majority's holding runs contrary to modern Supreme Court cases that have upheld congressional actions despite connections to interstate or foreign commerce that are less significant than the effect of school violence....

The second legal problem the Court creates comes from its apparent belief that it can reconcile its holding with earlier cases by making a critical distinction between "commercial" and noncommercial "transaction[s]...."

And, if the majority instead means to distinguish generally among broad categories of activities, differentiating what is educational from what is commercial, then, as a practical matter, the line becomes almost impossible to draw. Schools that teach reading, writing, mathematics, and related basic skills serve *both* social and commercial purposes, and one cannot easily separate the one from the other....

Regardless, if there is a principled distinction that could work both here and in future cases, Congress (even in the absence of vocational classes, industry involvement, and private management) could rationally conclude that schools fall on the commercial side of the line....

The third legal problem created by the Court's holding is that it threatens legal uncertainty in an area of law that, until this case, seemed reasonably well settled....

PART II

CIVIL RIGHTS AND LIBERTIES

CHAPTER X

INDIVIDUAL LIBERTY: THE SUBSTANTIVE FREEDOMS OF THE FIRST AMENDMENT

Traditionally, *individual* or *personal* liberties encompass those *fundamental* rights which are guaranteed to all persons, citizen and non-citizen alike, under the United States Constitution. They primarily take the form of restraints on governmental authority and are found, for the most part, in the Bill of Rights. To be sure, certain individual rights are enumerated in the "main body" of the Constitution: suspension of the *writ of habeas corpus* is prohibited *except* in cases of rebellion, invasion, or if public safety is endangered (Article 1, Section 9); neither the national nor the state governments may enact *ex post facto* laws or *bills of attainder* (Article 1, sections 9, 10);[1] other than cases of impeachment, all crimes must be *tried by jury*; and the states must guarantee to non-residents the same *privileges* and *immunities* that it grants to its own citizens (Article IV, section 2); and no *religious* test can be required for holding any public office (Article VI, section 2). However, the most important and larger number of liberties are found in the first ten amendments.

This chapter examines the liberties guaranteed in the First Amendment which are *substantive* in nature, while the remaining guarantees are primarily *procedural*. By substantive, we mean that these rights are tangible, concrete and substantial. In essence, they are the "what" of the law, *without* which our procedural rights would be of little import: freedom of speech and press, the right to assemble peaceably and to associate, the "establishment" clause, freedom to exercise our religious beliefs, and the right to petition and to influence the governing process.

The Incorporation of the Bill of Rights

Contrary to what many people think, the limitations on government contained in the first ten amendments originally applied only to the national government and not to the governments of the states. As Chief Justice John

Marshall noted in his last landmark case, *Barron v. Baltimore* (1833), the Bill of Rights "contain no expression indicating an intention to apply them to the state governments." What this meant, for example, was that a state government could establish a state religion if it wanted, unless doing so was prohibited by the state's own constitution. The First Amendment to the Federal Constitution posed no barrier.

This began to change during the *Lochner* era. Just as the Justices had invalidated New York's law regulating working hours in bakeries because it interfered with employers and employees fundamental "right of contract" protected by the due process clause of the Fourteenth Amendment, they now began to invalidate state laws as violating "fundamental" rights found in the Bill of Rights. In *Gitlow v. New York* (1925), the Supreme Court of the United States rendered a landmark decision that directly effects state and local government to this very day. It held that the Fourteenth Amendment, which forbids a State from depriving a person of his "life, liberty or property without due process of law," could be used by the Court as a means to apply "fundamental" guarantees of the Bill of Rights to the States. Specifically, it *incorporated* the First Amendment's guarantee of "freedom of speech and press" into the term "*liberty*" so that henceforth, state and local governments would be subject to the same limitations as the Federal government. This process by which the Court identifies some of the individual liberties contained in the Bill of Rights as "fundamental" and applies them to the states through the "due process" clause of the Fourteenth Amendment is known as "*selective incorporation.*" Unlike the "right of contract" which the New Deal Court repudiated as unwarranted judicial activism, the incorporation of the Bill of Rights into the Fourteenth Amendment continued at an increasing pace during the New Deal and Warren Courts. Today nearly every one of the liberties listed in the Bill of Rights has been made *enforceable* against the States through incorporation into the Fourteenth Amendment.

FREEDOM OF SPEECH, PRESS AND ASSEMBLY

The First Amendment commands that "Congress shall make no law … abridging the freedom of speech or of the press; or the right of the people peaceably to assemble…." As strong as this restriction appears to be, it is by no means absolute. Only a few men who have served as a Justice on the Court – most notably Justices Black and Douglas – have ever adhered to an absolutist position. The overwhelming majority have recognized that these rights are limited and that, in fact, a person may abuse the rights of free speech, press, assembly and association to the point of committing illegal acts. No right, however fundamental, totally frees one from legitimate restraint by government. Otherwise, our limited democracy would collapse into anarchy.

CASES INCORPORATING LIBERTIES INTO THE 14th AMENDMENT

AMENDMENT I Congress shall make no law respecting an establishment of religion, or prohibiting the free exercise thereof; or abridging the freedom of speech, or of the press; or the right of the people peaceably to assemble, and to petition the Government for a redress of grievances.

Establishment:	*Everson v. Board of Education* (1947)
Free Exercise:	*Cantwell v. Connecticut* (1940)
Speech and Press:	*Gitlow v. New York* (1925)
	Near v Minnesota (1931)
Assembly and petition:	*De Jonge v. Oregon* (1937)

AMENDMENT IV The right of the people to be secure in their persons, houses, papers, and effects, against unreasonable searches and seizures, shall not be violated, and no Warrants shall issue, but upon probable cause, supported by Oath or affirmation, and particularly describing the place to be searched, and the persons or things to be seized.

Search and seizure:	*Wolf v. Colorado* (1949)

AMENDMENT V No person shall be held to answer for a capital, or otherwise infamous crime, unless on a presentment or indictment of a Grand Jury, except in cases arising in the land or naval forces, or in the Militia, when in actual service in time of War or public danger; nor shall any person be subject for the same offense to be twice put in jeopardy of life or limb; nor shall be compelled in any criminal case to be a witness against himself, nor be deprived of life, liberty, or property, without due process of law; nor shall private property be taken for public use, without just compensation.

Grand Jury Indictment:	NOT incorporated. *Hurtado v. California* (1884)
Double jeopardy:	*Benton v. Maryland* (1969)
Self-incrimination:	*Malloy v. Hogan* (1964)
Due Process:	Clause repeated in the 14th Amendment
Just compensation:	*Chicago, Milwaukee & St. Paul Ry v Minnesota* (1890)

AMENDMENT VI In all criminal prosecutions, the accused shall enjoy the right to a speedy and public trial, by an impartial jury of the State and district wherein the crime shall have been committed, which district shall have been previously ascertained by law, and to be informed of the nature and cause of the accusation; to be confronted with the witnesses against him; to have compulsory process for obtaining witnesses in his favor, and to have the Assistance of Counsel for his defense.

Speedy trial:	*Klopfer v. North Carolina* (1967)
Public trial:	*In re Oliver* (1948)
Impartial jury:	*Parker v. Gladden* (1966)
Jury trial in district:	*Duncan v. Louisiana* (1968)
Informed of charge:	Implied in: *Lanzetta v New Jersey* (1939) and *Pointer v. Texas* (1965)
Confront witnesses:	*Pointer v. Texas* (1965)
Compulsory process:	*Washington v. Texas* (1967)
Assistance of counsel:	*Powell v. Alabama* (1932) – capital cases; *Gideon v. Wainwright* (1963) – all felony cases; and *Angersinger v. Hamlin* (1972) all cases with possibility of imprisonment.

AMENDMENT VIII Excessive bail shall not be required, nor excessive fines imposed, nor cruel and unusual punishments inflicted.

Excessive bail:	NOT incorporated.
Excessive fines and cruel and unusual punishment:	*Robinson v. California* (1965)

What, however, are the limitations on the exercise of these rights? What can the government legitimately restrict? (The liberties of speech and press are normally covered together in Court cases. The major exception is the issue of "prior restraint;" see, *Near v. Minnesota* (1931)). These are especially problematic questions when it comes to subversive and politically unpopular speech. Much of the 20th century's jurisprudence regarding the First Amendment has revolved around them. Early in the century, the Court emphasized the "*bad tendency*" test, which stipulated that all speech which has a tendency, however remote, to bring about acts in violation of the law is punishable. This restrictive test on free speech was used by the Court when it sustained the conviction of Benjamin Gitlow for violating the New York Criminal Anarchy Act. In writing the majority opinion, Justice Sanford emphasized that the government did not have to wait until the speech had successfully incited lawless behavior before punishing the speaker. "It cannot,' he stated, 'reasonably be required to defer the adoption of measures for its own peace and safety until the revolutionary utterances lead to actual disturbances of the public peace or imminent and immediate danger of its own destruction; but it may, in the exercise of its judgment, suppress the threatened danger in its incipiency"

A less restrictive, and more famous, test was offered by Associate Justice Oliver Wendell Holmes in *Schenck v. United States* (1919). The "*clear and present danger*" test stipulates that speech becomes punishable only if there is a significant probability that the prohibited action the words seek to incite will soon be brought about. For much of the 20th century, the Court has vacillated between these two extremes – sometimes leaning toward the restrictive "bad tendency test," sometimes toward the less restrictive "clear and present danger" standard. The Court's position today is expressed in the *per curium* opinion of *Brandenburg v. Ohio* (1969). There the Court summarized the results of its speech and press cases as having "fashioned the principle that the constitutional guarantees of free speech and free press do not permit a State to forbid or proscribe advocacy of the use of force or of law violation except where such advocacy is directed to inciting or producing *imminent lawless action* and is *likely to incite or produce* such action" (Emphasis added).

Not all speech is constitutionally protected. *Libel* (and Slander) *obscenity* and "*fighting words*" are among the categories generally regarded as constitutionally unprotected. But, as the case law indicates, things are not quite that simple. Libel is not protected by the constitution, but, in the interest of open and free debate about political issues, the Court has made it very difficult to prove libel, at least against "public figures." In the landmark case *New York Times Co. v. Sullivan* (1964), the Court ruled that "actual malice" had to be shown and that publication of the statements had to be "with knowledge that it was false or with reckless disregard of whether it was false or not." Also see *Greenbelt Cooperative Publishing Assn. v. Bresier* (1943); *Philadelphia Newspapers, Inc. v. Hepps* (1986); and *Milkovich v. Lorain Journal (1990)*

Similarly, Court decisions since the 1950's have made it increasingly difficult to successfully prosecute obscenity and pornography. It is *not* that obscenity and pornography are constitutionally protected, it is just that they have become difficult to define. Prior to the post World War II period, the *Hicklin test* was used to determine whether something was obscene. This test judged a work obscene if any part of it had a *tendency* to corrupt those most susceptible. Thus, an entire book could be banned because one passage might be inappropriate for a child. The Court replaced this test during the late 50's and early 60's with what became known as the *Roth* test. Here a work could be deemed obscene only if the work as a whole appealed to the "prurient interest" of an average person (not the most susceptible) applying "contemporary community standards." This test solved little, for too many of its terms were ambiguous and difficult to operationalize. Are there "national" community standards? Or, are the standards for Des Moines different from New York? The result of the Roth test was that even "hard core" pornography was virtually impossible to censor. In 1973, the Court attempted to strengthen the ability of state and local governments to control and suppress pornography in *Miller v. California*, (1973) and *Paris Adult Theatre I v. Slaton* (1973). Local obscenity statutes are valid if they are framed along the following guidelines: (a) whether the average person, applying (local) contemporary community standards would find the work as a whole, appealing to the prurient (or lustful) interest, (b) whether the work depicts or describes in a patently offensive way sexual conduct specifically defined by the applicable state law, (c) whether the work as a whole lacks serious literary, artistic, political, or scientific value. The results of *Miller* remain mixed. The Court has agreed, however, to permit *strict* bans on child pornography; see *New York v. Ferber* (1982) and *Osborne v. Ohio* (1990). In *Reno v. ACLU* (1997) the Court addressed for the first time the issue of obscenity and pornography on what promises to be a revolutionary means of worldwide communication, the Internet.

Another category of speech which remains constitutionally unprotected is that of "fighting words" or "those which by their very utterance inflict injury or tend to incite an immediate breach of the peace." A person does not have the right to use abusive epithets, obscenity, or fighting words which disturb the peace, or to directly incite a crowd to riot. As the Court observed in *Chaplinsky v. New Hampshire* (1942): "It has been well observed that such utterances are no essential part of any exposition of ideas, and are of such slight social value as a step to truth that any benefit that may be derived from them is clearly outweighed by the social interest in order and morality."

Legitimate prohibitions on fighting words, however, cannot be the basis for prohibiting the expression of unpopular ideas. A city ordinance cannot forbid a speech which "stirs people to anger, invites public dispute, or brings about a condition of unrest" if the speech is given in a constitutionally protected area, e.g., a public park, courthouse grounds, city auditorium, etc. Generally speaking, a person making a symbolic controversial speech (e.g. burning the American flag) is protected even if the audience violently disagrees. *Terminiello v. Chicago* (1949); *Niemotho v. Maryland* (1951); *Poulos v. New Hampshire* (1953), *Texas v. Johnson,* (1989). The Court addressed the recent phenomena of "hate speech codes" in *R.A.V. v. St. Paul* (1992). Although the Court recognized that such codes might be constitutional as prohibitions on "fighting words," in declaring St. Paul's Bias Motivated Crime Ordinance unconstitutional it emphasized that such codes themselves can be neither content nor viewpoint biased.

Few would consider a protest march utilizing bullhorns on residential streets at 4:00 a.m. a reasonable expression of our First Amendment freedoms, and, in fact, governments do have the authority to impose *reasonable* regulations on the "*time, place and manner*" of our free expression. For example, a city ordinance may provide that no person shall make a public address in or upon any of the city's public grounds, except in accordance with a permit from the city, if there is uniformity and impartiality of treatment of those who so apply. *Davis v. Massachusetts* (1897). Such permit and fee requirements can be made to apply to public parades or processions as well. *Cox v. New Hampshire* (1941); *I.S.K.C. v. Lee* (1992). Moreover, a person does not have the right to give a speech in an constitutionally unprotected area such as a crowded street, military installation, or jailhouse grounds. *Feiner v. New York* (1951), *Greer v. Spock*, (1976); *Adderley v. Florida* (1967). Although the Court has indicated that the liberties of the First Amendment are in a "preferred position," that does not mean that the exercise of free speech does not have to give way to our constitutionally protected rights, e.g. private property. See, *Lloyd Corporation v. Tanner* (1972).

Regulations of "time, place and manner" cannot be used to prohibit the exercise of first Amendment rights, nor to discriminate against disfavored speakers. Thus, the right to distribute handbills on religious subjects on public streets cannot be prohibited at all times, at all places and under all circumstances. *Jamison v. Texas* (1943); *Texas Monthly v. Bullock*, (1989). A city cannot prohibit a person rightfully on a public street from handing literature to one willing to receive it, even though commercial soliciting can be regulated. *Schneider v. Irvington* (1939); *Pruneyard Shopping Center v. Robins*, (1980); *Frisby v. Schultz*, (1988). Nor can a city ordinance empower the mayor to grant or withhold a license for the sale of books as he deems "proper and advisable." *Largent v. Texas* (1943); *Lakewood v. Plain Dealer Publishing Co.*, (1988); *Young v. American Mini Theatres*, (1976). A local ordinance cannot prohibit loitering or picketing about a place of business for the purpose of influencing or inducing other persons not to trade with or work for the place of business if the picketing is related to the businesses' operations. *Thornhill v. Alabama* (1940); *Hudgens v. NLRB*, (1976).

FREEDOM OF RELIGION

From the outset the First Amendment specifically states that "Congress shall make no law respecting an establishment of religion, or prohibiting the free exercise thereof...." The very fact that this is the first guarantee listed in the first Amendment demonstrates the importance our forefathers attached to it. The first "edge" of this two-sided libertarian blade, the Establishment Clause, separates religion from government. It creates a "wall of separation" so that in its day-to-day operations, the government can neither hinder nor assist any or all churches, it must remain neutral in its activities, policies and laws. The other "edge" protects the freedom to exercise – to believe and to engage in – our religious beliefs or not to accept religion at all. The freedom to believe is absolute, but the freedom to act, as is the case with our other liberties, is not. The Court has repeatedly been called upon to draw the line of demarcation between which practices fall within the protected zone and which do not. It has also found that these two components – separation yet protection – are often at odds, if not in conflict.

In the first case to reach the Supreme Court concerning freedom of religion, it held that the "free exercise" provision does not protect criminal or illegal acts even if they are sanctioned by religious dogma and, accordingly, upheld the conviction of a Mormon for polygamy; see *Reynolds v. United States* (1879). In this century, the zeal and religious doctrine of the Jehovah's Witnesses has been responsible for bringing many significant cases to the Court regarding freedom of religion. In *Cantwell v. Connecticut* (1940) the Court *incorporated* the "free exercise" provision and made it applicable to state and local governments. It was not until seven years later that the Court, in *Everson v. Board of Education*, incorporated the Establishment Clause. Other important decisions covered in this chapter include the second "flag salute" case, *West Virginia State Board of Education v. Barnette* (1943), in which the late Justice Robert H. Jackson, not normally considered a strong libertarian, contributed one of the most beautiful opinions on First Amendment freedoms in the history of the Court to date.[2] Indicative of the intricate nature of the Court's interpretation of the concept of freedom of religion are the cited cases involving the "released time" program (*Zorach v. Clauson*, 1952); *the Sunday Closing Law Cases* (1961), in which the Court upheld such state statutes as providing a *civil*, not religious, *day of rest*; the striking down of a board of regents' policy which required recitation of prayers in public schools (*Engel v. Vitale*, 1962), and the nullification of state assistance to parochial *schools*, *teachers*, and to *parents* who send their children to them, *Lemon v. Kurtzman* (1971); *Committee for Public Education v. Nyquist*, (1973); *Meek v. Pittenger*, 421 U.S. 349 (1975); *Aguilar v. Felton* (1985), only aid which directly benefits the student is permissible, *Everson v. Board* (1947); *Hunt v. McNair* (1973); *Roemer v. Maryland Bd.* (1976); *Wolman v. Walter* (1977); *Mueller v. Allen* (1983).

BARRON v. BALTIMORE.
32 U.S. 243; 7 Pet. 243; 8 L.Ed. 672 (1833)

In paving streets, Baltimore diverted streams which then carried dirt and sand to Barron's wharf. The effect was that the water level became too shallow for the wharf to be used. Barron sued in the Maryland courts for compensation, but a favorable decision in the trial court was overturned by the court of appeals. Barron then appealed to the Supreme Court claiming his rights under the Fifth Amendment had been violated.

MARSHALL, Ch. J., delivered the opinion of the court.

...The question thus presented is, we think, of great importance, but not of much difficulty. The constitution was ordained and established by the people of the United States for themselves, for their own government, and not for the government of the individual states. Each state established a constitution for itself, and in that constitution, provided such limitations and restrictions on the powers of its particular government, as its judgment dictated. The people of the United States framed such a government for the United States as they supposed best adapted to their situation and best calculated to promote their interests. The powers they conferred on this government were to be exercised by itself; and the limitations on power, if expressed in general terms, are naturally, and, we think, necessarily, applicable to the government created by the instrument. They are limitations of power granted in the instrument itself; not of distinct governments, framed by different persons and for different purposes.

If these propositions be correct, the fifth amendment must be understood as restraining the power of the general government, not as applicable to the states. In their several constitutions, they have imposed such restrictions on their respective governments, as their own wisdom suggested; such as they deemed most proper for themselves. It is a subject on which they judge exclusively, and with which others interfere no further than they are supposed to have a common interest.

The counsel for the plaintiff in error insists, that the constitution was intended to secure the people of the several states against the undue exercise of power by their respective state governments; as well as against that which might be attempted by their general government. It support of this argument he relies on the inhibitions contained in the tenth section of the first article. We think, that section affords a strong, if not a conclusive, argument in support of the opinion already indicated by the court. The preceding section contains restrictions which are obviously intended for the exclusive purpose of restraining the exercise of power by the departments of the general government. Some of them use language applicable only to congress; others are expressed in general terms. The third clause, for example, declares, that "no bill of attainder or ex post facto law shall be passed." No language can be more general; yet the demonstration is complete, that it applies solely to the government of the United States. In addition to the general arguments furnished by the instrument itself, some of which have been already suggested, the succeeding section, the avowed purpose of which is to restrain state legislation, contains in terms the very prohibition. It declares, that "no state shall pass any bill of attainder or ex post facto law." This provision, then, of the ninth section, however comprehensive its language, contains no restriction on state legislation.

The ninth section having enumerated, in the nature of a bill of rights, the limitations intended to be imposed on the powers of the general government, the tenth proceeds to enumerate those which were to operate on the state legislatures. These restrictions are brought together in the same section, and are by express words applied to the states. 'No state shall enter into any treaty,' &c. Perceiving, that in a constitution framed by the people of the United States, for the government of all, no limitation of the action of government on the people would apply to the state government, unless expressed in terms, the restrictions contained in the tenth section are in direct words so applied to the states.

It is worthy of remark, too, that these inhibitions generally restrain state legislation on subjects intrusted to the general government, or in which the people of all the states feel an interest. A state is forbidden to enter into any treaty, alliance or confederation. If these compacts are with foreign nations, they interfere with the treaty-making power, which is conferred entirely on the general government; if with each other, for political purposes, they can scarcely fail to interfere with the general purpose and intent of the constitution. To grant letters of marque and reprisal, would lead directly to war; the power of declaring which is expressly given to congress. To coin money is also the exercise of a power conferred on congress. It would be tedious to recapitulate the several limitations on the powers of the states which are contained in this section. They will be found, generally, to restrain state legislation on subjects intrusted to the government of the Union, in which the citizens of all the states are interested. In these alone, were the whole people concerned. The question of their application to states is not left to construction. It is averred in positive words.

If the original constitution, in the ninth and tenth sections of the first article, draws this plain and marked line of discrimination between the limitations it imposes on the powers of the general government, and on those of the state; if, in every inhibition intended to act on state power, words are employed, which directly express that intent; some strong reason must be assigned for departing from this safe and judicious course, in framing the amendments, before that departure can be assumed. We search in vain for that reason.

Had the people of the several states, or any of them, required changes in their constitutions; had they required additional safe-guards to liberty from the apprehended encroachments of their particular governments; the remedy was in their own hands, and could have been applied by themselves. A convention could have been assembled by the discontented state, and the required improvements could have been made by itself. The unwieldy and cumbrous machinery of procuring a recommendation from two-thirds of congress, and the assent of three-fourths of their sister states, could never have occurred to any human being, as a mode of doing that which might be effected by the state itself. Had the framers of these amendments intended them to be limitations on the powers of the state governments, they would have imitated the framers of the original constitution, and have expressed that intention. Had congress engaged in the extraordinary occupation of improving the constitutions of the several states, by affording the people additional protection from the exercise of power by their own governments, in matters which concerned themselves alone, they would have declared this purpose in plain and intelligible language.

But it is universally understood, it is a part of the history of the day, that the great revolution which established the constitution of the United States, was not effected without immense opposition. Serious fears were extensively entertained, that those powers which the patriot statesmen, who then watched over the interests of our country, deemed essential to union, and to the attainment of those unvaluable objects for which union was sought, might be exercised in a manner dangerous to liberty. In almost every convention by which the constitution was adopted, amendments to guard against the abuse of power were recommended. These amendments demanded security against the apprehended encroachments of the general government-not against those of the local governments. In compliance with a sentiment thus generally expressed, to quiet fears thus extensively entertained, amendments were proposed by the required majority in congress, and adopted by the states. These amendments contain no expression indicating an intention to apply them to the state governments. This court cannot so apply them.

We are of opinion, that the provision in the fifth amendment to the constitution, declaring that private property shall not be taken for public use, without just compensation, is intended solely as a limitation on the exercise of power by the government of the United States, and is not applicable to the legislation of the states. We are, therefore, of opinion, that there is no repugnancy between the several acts of the general assembly of Maryland, given in evidence by the defendants at the trial of this cause, in the court of that state, and the constitution of the United States. This court, therefore, has no jurisdiction of the cause, and it is dismissed....

SCHENCK v. UNITED STATES.
39 S.Ct. 247; 249 U.S. 47; 63 L.Ed. 470 (1919)

Mr. Justice HOLMES delivered the opinion of the Court.

This is an indictment in three counts. The first charges a conspiracy to violate the Espionage Act of June 15, 1917,... by causing and attempting to cause insubordination, &c., in the military and naval forces of the United States, and to obstruct the recruiting and enlistment service of the United States, when the United States was at war with the German Empire, to-wit, that the defendant willfully conspired to have printed and circulated to men who had been called and accepted for military service ... a document set forth and alleged to be calculated to cause such insubordination and obstruction. The count alleges overt acts in pursuance of the conspiracy, ending in the distribution of the document set forth. The second count alleges a conspiracy to commit an offense against the United States, to-wit, to use the mails for the transmission of matter declared to be non-mailable.... The third count charges an unlawful use of the mails for the transmission of the same matter and otherwise as above. The defendants were found guilty on all the counts. They set up the First Amendment to the Constitution forbidding Congress to make any law abridging the freedom of speech, or of the press, and bringing the case here on that ground have argued some other points also of which we must dispose....

The document in question upon its first printed side recited the first section of the Thirteenth Amendment, said that the idea embodied in it was violated by the conscription act and that a conscript is little better than a convict. In impassioned language it intimated that conscription was despotism in its worst form and a monstrous wrong against humanity in the interest of Wall Street's chosen few. It said, 'Do not submit to intimidation,' but in form at least confined itself to peaceful measures such as a petition for the repeal of the act. The other and later printed side of the sheet was headed 'Assert Your Rights.' It stated reasons for alleging that any one violated the Constitution when he refused to recognize 'your right to assert your opposition to the draft,' and went on, 'If you do not assert and support your rights, you are helping to deny or disparage rights which it is the solemn duty of all citizens and residents of the United States to retain.' It described the arguments on the other side as coming from cunning politicians and a mercenary capitalist press, and even silent consent to the conscription law as helping to support an infamous conspiracy. It denied the power to send our citizens away to foreign shores to shoot up the people of other lands, and added that words could not express the condemnation such cold-blooded ruthlessness deserves , &c., &c., winding up, 'You must do your share to maintain, support and uphold the rights of the people of this country.' Of course the document would not have been sent unless it had been intended to have some effect, and we do not see what effect it could be expected to have upon persons subject to the draft except to influence them to obstruct the carrying of it out. The defendants do not deny that the jury might find against them on this point.

But it is said, suppose that that was the tendency of this circular, it is protected by the First Amendment to the Constitution. Two of the strongest expressions are said to be quoted respectively from well-known public men. It well may be that the prohibition of laws abridging the freedom of speech is not confined to previous restraints, although to prevent them may have been the main purpose, as intimated in *Patterson v. Colorado*.... We admit that in many places and in ordinary times the defendants in saying all that was said in the circular would have been within their constitutional rights. But the character of every act depends upon the circumstances in which it is done. *Aikens v. Wisconsin*.... The most stringent protection of free speech would not protect a man in falsely shouting fire in a theatre and causing a panic. It does not even protect a man from an injunction against uttering words that may have all the effect of force. *Gompers v. Buck's Stove & Range Co*.... The question in every case is whether the words used are used in such circumstances and are of such a nature as to create a clear and present danger that they will bring about the substantive evils that Congress has a right to prevent. It is a question of proximity and degree. When a nation is at war many things that might be said in time of peace are such a hindrance to its effort that their utterance will not be endured so long as men fight and that no Court could regard them as protected by any constitutional right. It seems to be admitted that if an actual obstruction of the recruiting service were proved, liability for words that produced that effect might be enforced. The statute of 1917 ... punishes conspiracies to obstruct as well as actual obstruction. If the act, (speaking, or circulating a paper,) its tendency and the intent with which it is done are the same, we perceive no ground for saying that success alone warrants making the act a crime. *Goldman v. United States*.... Indeed that case might be said to dispose of the present contention if the precedent covers all media *concludendi*. But as the right to free speech was not referred to specially, we have thought fit to add a few words.

It was not argued that a conspiracy to obstruct the draft was not within the words of the Act of 1917. The words are 'obstruct the recruiting or enlistment service,' and it might be suggested that they refer only to making it hard to get volunteers. Recruiting heretofore usually having been accomplished by getting volunteers the word is apt to call up that method only in our minds. But recruiting is gaining fresh supplies for the forces, as well by draft as otherwise. It is put as an alternative to enlistment or voluntary enrollment in this act. The fact that the Act of 1917 was enlarged by the amending Act of May 16, 1918,... of course, does not affect the present indictment and would not, even if the former act had been repealed....

Judgments affirmed.

GITLOW v. NEW YORK
268 U.S. 652; 45 S.Ct. 625; 69 L.Ed. 1138 (1925)

Under the New York Criminal Anarchy Act of 1902, a person, regardless of his intent, could be punished for certain kinds of publications and speech. Benjamin Gitlow was convicted in the Supreme Court of New York for having published and distributed materials advocating the overthrow of the government. Thereafter, he brought the case to the Supreme Court on writ of error to review the lower court decisions that had resulted in his conviction. This decision is important, not because of the facts of the case, but rather because of the fact that it was the beginning of the selective incorporation of the Bill of Rights.

MR. JUSTICE SANFORD delivered the opinion of the Court....

The contention here is that the statute, by its terms and as applied in this case, is repugnant to the due process clause of the Fourteenth Amendment....

The indictment was in two counts. The first charged that the defendant had advocated, advised and taught the duty, necessity and propriety of overthrowing and overturning organized government by force, violence and unlawful means, by certain writings therein set forth entitled "The Left Wing Manifesto;" the second that he had printed, published and knowingly circulated and distributed a certain paper called "The Revolutionary Age," containing the writings set forth in the first count, advocating, advising and teaching the doctrine that organized government should be overthrown by force, violence and unlawful means....

There was no evidence of any effect resulting from the publication and circulation of the Manifesto.

No witnesses were offered in behalf of the defendant.... Coupled with a review of the rise of Socialism, it [the Manifesto] condemned the dominant "moderate Socialism" for its recognition of the necessity of the "democratic parliamentary state" repudiated its policy of introducing Socialism by legislative measures; and advocated, in plain and unequivocal language, the necessity of accomplishing the "Communist Revolution" by a militant and "revolutionary Socialism," based on "the class struggle" and mobilizing the "power of the proletariat in action," through mass industrial revolts developing into mass political strikes and "revolutionary mass action," for the purpose of conquering and destroying the parliamentary state and establishing in its place, through a "revolutionary dictatorship of the proletariat," the system of Communist Socialism.

...The court, among other things, charged the jury, in substance, that they must define the meaning of Manifesto; that its words must be taken in their ordinary meaning, as they would be understood by people whom it might reach; that a mere statement or analysis of social and economic facts and historical incidents, in the nature of an essay, accompanied by prophecy as to the future course of events, but with no teaching, advice or advocacy of action would not constitute the advocacy, advice or teaching of a doctrine for the overthrow of government within the meaning of the statute; that a mere statement that unlawful acts might accomplish such a purpose would be insufficient, unless there was a teaching, advising and advocacy of employing such unlawful acts for the purpose of overthrowing government; and that if the jury had a reasonable doubt that the Manifesto did teach, advocate or advise the duty, necessity or propriety of using unlawful means for the overthrowing of organized government, the defendant was entitled to an acquittal....

The precise question presented, and the only question which we can consider under this writ of error, then is, whether the statute, as construed and applied in this case by the state courts, deprived the defendant of his liberty of expression in violation of the due process clause of the Fourteenth Amendment.

The statute does not penalize the utterance or publication of abstract "doctrine" or academic discussion having no quality of incitement to any concrete action. It is not aimed against mere historical or philosophical essays. It does not restrain the advocacy of changes in the form of government by constitutional and lawful means. What it prohibits is language advocating, advising or teaching the overthrow of organized government by unlawful means. These words imply urging to action. Advocacy is defined in the Century Dictionary as: "1. The act of pleading for, supporting, or recommending; active espousal." It is not the abstract "doctrine" of overthrowing organized government by unlawful means which is denounced by the statute, but the advocacy of action for the accomplishment of that purpose. It was so construed and applied by the trial judge, who specifically charged the jury that: "A mere grouping of historical events and a prophetic deduction from them would neither constitute advocacy, advice or teaching of a doctrine for the overthrow of government by force, violence or unlawful means. [And] if it were a mere essay on the subject, as suggested by counsel, based upon deductions from alleged historical events, with no teaching, advice or advocacy of action, it would not constitute a violation of the statute...."

The Manifesto, plainly, is neither the statement of abstract doctrine nor, as suggested by counsel, mere prediction that industrial disturbances and revolutionary mass strikes will result spontaneously in an inevitable process of evolution in the economic system. It advocates and urges in fervent language mass action which shall progressively foment industrial disturbances and through political mass strikes and revolutionary mass action overthrow and destroy organized parliamentary government. It concludes with a call to action in these words: "The proletariat revolution and the Communist reconstruction of society – *the struggle for these* – is now indispensable.... The Communist International calls the proletariat of the world to the final struggle!" This is not the expression of philosophical abstractions, the mere prediction of future events; it is the – language of direct incitement....

...That the jury were warranted in finding that the Manifesto advocated not merely the abstract doctrine of overthrowing organized government by force, violence and unlawful means, but action to that end is clear.

For present purposes we may and do assume that freedom of speech and of the press – which are protected by the First Amendment from abridgment by Congress – are among the fundamental personal rights and "liberties" protected by the due process clause of the Fourteenth Amendment from impairment by the states....

It is a fundamental principle, long established, that the freedom of speech and of the press which is secured by the Constitution, does not confer an absolute right to speak or publish, without responsibility, whatever one may choose, or an unrestricted and unbridled license that gives immunity for every possible use of language and prevents the punishment of those who abuse this freedom....

That a State in the exercise of its police power may punish those who abuse this freedom by utterances inimical to the public welfare, tending to corrupt public morals, incite to crime, or disturb the public peace, is not open to question....

...That utterances inciting to the overthrow of organized government by unlawful means, present a sufficient danger of substantive evil to bring their punishment within the range of legislative discretion, is clear. Such utterances, by their very nature, involve danger to the public peace and to the security of the State. They threaten breaches of the peace and ultimate revolution. And the immediate danger is none the less real and substantial, because the effect of a given utterance cannot be accurately foreseen. The State cannot reasonably be required to measure the danger from every such utterance in the nice balance of a jeweler's scale. A single revolutionary spark may kindle a fire that, smoldering for a time, may burst into a sweeping and destructive conflagration. It cannot be said that the State is acting arbitrarily or unreasonably when in the exercise of its judgment as to the measures necessary to protect the public peace and safety, it seeks to extinguish the spark without waiting until it has enkindled the flame or blazed into the conflagration. It cannot reasonably be required to defer the adoption of measures for its own peace and safety until the revolutionary utterances lead to actual disturbances of the public peace or imminent and immediate danger of its own destruction; but it may, in the exercise of its judgment, suppress the threatened danger in its incipiency....

We cannot hold that the present statute is an arbitrary or unreasonable exercise of the police power of the State unwarrantably infringing the freedom of speech or press; and we must and do sustain its constitutionality....

Affirmed.

MR. JUSTICE HOLMES, dissenting:

Mr. Justice Brandeis and I are of opinion that this judgment should be reversed. The general principle of free speech, it seems to me, must be taken to be included in the Fourteenth Amendment, in view of the scope that has been given to the word "liberty" as there used, although perhaps it may be accepted with a somewhat larger latitude of interpretation than is allowed to Congress by the sweeping language that governs or ought to govern the laws of the United States. If I am right, then I think that the criterion sanctioned by the full court in *Schenck v. United States*, *supra*, applies. "The question in every case is whether the words are used in such circumstances and are of such a nature as to create a clear and present danger that they will bring about the substantive evils that [the state] has a right to prevent."

BRANDENBURG v. OHIO.
89 S.Ct. 1827; 395 U.S. 444; 23 L.Ed.2d 430 (1969)

The facts in this case are given in the opinion below.

PER CURIAM.

The appellant, a leader of a Ku Klux Klan group, was convicted under the Ohio Criminal Syndicalism statute for 'advocat(ing) ... the duty, necessity, or propriety of crime, sabotage, violence, or unlawful methods of terrorism as a means of accomplishing industrial or political reform' and for 'voluntarily assembl(ing) with any society, group, or assemblage of persons formed to teach or advocate the doctrines of criminal syndicalism.'... He was fined $1,000 and sentenced to one to 10 years' imprisonment. The appellant challenged the constitutionality of the criminal syndicalism statute under the First and Fourteenth

Amendments to the United States Constitution, but the intermediate appellate court of Ohio affirmed his conviction without opinion. The Supreme Court of Ohio dismissed his appeal.... Appeal was taken to this Court, and we noted probable jurisdiction.... We reverse.

The record shows that a man, identified at trial as the appellant, telephoned an announcer-reporter on the staff of a Cincinnati television station and invited him to come to a Ku Klux Klan 'rally' to be held at a farm in Hamilton County. With the cooperation of the organizers, the reporter and a cameraman attended the meeting and filmed the events. Portions of the films were later broadcast on the local station and on a national network.

The prosecution's case rested on the films and on testimony identifying the appellant as the person who communicated with the reporter and who spoke at the rally. The State also introduced into evidence several articles appearing in the film, including a pistol, a rifle, a shotgun, ammunition, a Bible, and a red hood worn by the speaker in the films.

One film showed 12 hooded figures, some of whom carried firearms. They were gathered around a large wooden cross, which they burned. No one was present other than the participants and the newsmen who made the film. Most of the words uttered during the scene were incomprehensible when the film was projected, but scattered phrases could be understood that were derogatory of Negroes and, in one instance, of Jews. Another scene on the same film showed the appellant, in Klan regalia, making a speech. The speech, in full, was as follows:

> "This is an organizers' meeting. We have had quite a few members here today which are-we have hundreds, hundreds of members throughout the State of Ohio. I can quote from a newspaper clipping from the Columbus, Ohio Dispatch, five weeks ago Sunday morning. The Klan has more members in the State of Ohio than does any other organization. We're not a revengent organization, but if our President, our Congress, our Supreme Court, continues to suppress the white, Caucasian race, it's possible that there might have to be some revengeance taken.
>
> 'We are marching on Congress July the Fourth, four hundred thousand strong. From there we are dividing into two groups, one group to march on St. Augustine, Florida, the other group to march into Mississippi. Thank you."

The second film showed six hooded figures one of whom, later identified as the appellant, repeated a speech very similar to that recorded on the first film. The reference to the possibility of 'revengeance' was omitted, and one sentence was added: 'Personally, I believe the nigger should be returned to Africa, the Jew returned to Israel.' Though some of the figures in the films carried weapons, the speaker did not.

The Ohio Criminal Syndicalism Statute was enacted in 1919. From 1917 to 1920, identical or quite similar laws were adopted by 20 States and two territories.... In 1927, this Court sustained the constitutionality of California's Criminal Syndicalism Act,... the text of which is quite similar to that of the laws of Ohio. *Whitney v. California*,...(1927). The Court upheld the statute on the ground that, without more, 'advocating' violent means to effect political and economic change involves such danger to the security of the State that the State may outlaw it.... But *Whitney* has been thoroughly discredited by later decisions. See *Dennis v. United States*... (1951). These later decisions have fashioned the principle that the constitutional guarantees of free speech and free press do not permit a State to forbid or proscribe advocacy of the use of force or of law violation except where such advocacy is directed to inciting or producing imminent lawless action and is likely to incite or produce such action. As we said in *Noto v. United States*,... (1961), 'the mere abstract teaching ... of the moral propriety or even moral necessity for a resort to force and violence, is not the same as preparing a group for violent action and steeling it to such action.'... A statute which fails to draw this distinction impermissibly intrudes upon the freedoms guaranteed by the First and Fourteenth Amendments. It sweeps within its condemnation speech which our Constitution has immunized from governmental control....

Measured by this test, Ohio's Criminal Syndicalism Act cannot be sustained. The Act punishes persons who 'advocate or teach the duty, necessity, or propriety' of violence 'as a means of accomplishing industrial or political reform'; or who publish or circulate or display any book or paper containing such advocacy; or who 'justify' the commission of violent acts 'with intent to exemplify, spread or advocate the propriety of the doctrines of criminal syndicalism'; or who 'voluntarily assemble' with a group formed 'to teach or advocate the doctrines of criminal syndicalism.' Neither the indictment nor the trial judge's instructions to the jury in any way refined the statute's bald definition of the crime in terms of mere advocacy not distinguished from incitement to imminent lawless action.

Accordingly, we are here confronted with a statute which, by its own words and as applied, purports to punish mere advocacy and to forbid, on pain of criminal punishment, assembly with others merely to advocate the described type of action. Such a statute falls within the condemnation of the First and Fourteenth Amendments. The contrary teaching of *Whitney v. California* ... cannot be supported, and that decision is therefore overruled.

Mr. Justice BLACK, concurring.

I agree with the views expressed by Mr. Justice DOUGLAS in his concurring opinion in this case that the 'clear and present danger' doctrine should have no place in the interpretation of the First Amendment. I join the Court's opinion, which, as I understand it, simply cites *Dennis v. United States*,... (1951), but does not indicate any agreement on the Court's part with the 'clear and present danger' doctrine on which Dennis purported to rely.

Mr. Justice DOUGLAS, concurring.

While I join the opinion of the Court, I desire to enter a caveat.

The 'clear and present danger' test was adumbrated by Mr. Justice Holmes in a case arising during World War I – a war 'declared' by the Congress, not by the Chief Executive. The case was *Schenck v. United States*,... where the defendant was charged with attempts to cause insubordination in the military and obstruction of enlistment. The pamphlets that were distributed urged resistance to the draft, denounced conscription, and impugned the motives of those backing the war effort. The First Amendment was tendered as a defense. Mr. Justice Holmes in rejecting that defense said:

> 'The question in every case is whether the words used are used in such circumstances and are of such a nature as to create a clear and present danger that they will bring about the substantive evils that Congress has a right to prevent. It is a question of proximity and degree.'

...Though I doubt if the "clear and present danger" test is congenial to the First Amendment in time of a declared war, I am certain it is not reconcilable with the First Amendment in days of peace.

The Court quite properly overrules *Whitney v. California*,... which involved advocacy of ideas which the majority of the Court deemed unsound and dangerous.

Mr. Justice Holmes, though never formally abandoning the 'clear and present danger' test, moved closer to the First Amendment ideal when he said in dissent in Gitlow:

> 'Every idea is an incitement. It offers itself for belief and if believed it is acted on unless some other belief outweighs it or some failure of energy stifles the movement at its birth. The only difference between the expression of an opinion and an incitement in the narrower sense is the speaker's enthusiasm for the result. Eloquence may set fire to reason. But whatever may be thought of the redundant discourse before us it had no chance of starting a present conflagration. If in the long run the beliefs expressed in proletarian dictatorship are destined to be accepted by the dominant forces of the community, the only meaning of free speech is that they should be given their chance and have their way.'

We have never been faithful to the philosophy of that dissent....

My own view is quite different. I see no place in the regime of the First Amendment for any 'clear and present danger' test, whether strict and tight as some would make it, or free-wheeling as the Court in *Dennis* rephrased it.

When one reads the opinions closely and sees when and how the 'clear and present danger' test has been applied, great misgivings are aroused. First, the threats were often loud but always puny and made serious only by judges so wedded to the status quo that critical analysis made them nervous. Second, the test was so twisted and perverted in *Dennis* as to make the trial of those teachers of Marxism an all-out political trial which was part and parcel of the cold war that has eroded substantial parts of the First Amendment.

Action is often a method of expression and within the protection of the First Amendment.

Suppose one tears up his own copy of the Constitution in eloquent protest to a decision of this Court. May he be indicted?

Suppose one rips his own Bible to shreds to celebrate his departure from one 'faith' and his embrace of atheism. May he be indicted?

Last Term the Court held in *United States v. O'Brien*,... that a registrant under Selective Service who burned his draft card in protest of the war in Vietnam could be prosecuted. The First Amendment was tendered as a defense and rejected, the Court saying:

> 'The issuance of certificates indicating the registration and eligibility classification of individuals is a legitimate and substantial administrative aid in the functioning of this system. And legislation to insure the continuing availability of issued certificates serves a legitimate and substantial purpose in the system's administration.'

But O'Brien was not prosecuted for not having his draft card available when asked for by a federal agent. He was indicted, tried and convicted for burning the card. And this Court's affirmance of that conviction was not, with all respect, consistent with the First Amendment....

One's beliefs have long been thought to be sanctuaries which government could not invade. *Barenblatt* is one example of the ease with which that sanctuary can be violated. The lines drawn by the Court between the criminal act of being an 'active' Communist and the innocent act of being a nominal or inactive Communist mark the difference only between deep and abiding belief and casual or uncertain belief. But I think that all matters of belief are beyond the reach of subpoenas or the probings of investigators. That is why the invasions of privacy made by investigating committees were notoriously unconstitutional. That is the deep-seated fault in the infamous loyalty-security hearings which, since 1947 when President Truman launched them, have processed 20,000,000 men and women. Those hearings were primarily concerned with one's thoughts, ideas, beliefs, and convictions. They were the most blatant violations of the First Amendment we have ever known.

The line between what is permissible and not subject to control and what may be made impermissible and subject to regulation is the line between ideas and overt acts.

The example usually given by those who would punish speech is the case of one who falsely shouts fire in a crowded theatre.

This is, however, a classic case where speech is brigaded with action. See *Speiser v. Randall*, (Douglas, J., concurring.) They are indeed inseparable and a prosecution can be launched for the overt acts actually caused. Apart from rare instances of that kind, speech is, I think, immune from prosecution. Certainly there is no constitutional line between advocacy of abstract ideas as in *Yates* and advocacy of political action as in Scales. The quality of advocacy turns on the depth of the conviction; and government has no power to invade that sanctuary of belief and conscience.

CHAPLINSKY v. NEW HAMPSHIRE.
62 S.Ct. 766; 315 U.S. 568; 86 L.Ed. 1031 (1942)

The facts in this case are given in the opinion below.

Mr. Justice MURPHY delivered the opinion of the Court.

Appellant, a member of the sect known as Jehovah's Witnesses, was convicted in the municipal court of Rochester, New Hampshire, for violation of Chapter 378, Section 2, of the Public Laws of New Hampshire: "No person shall address any offensive, derisive or annoying word to any other person who is lawfully in any street or other public place, nor call him by any offensive or derisive name, nor make any noise or exclamation in his presence and hearing with intent to deride, offend or annoy him, or to prevent him from pursuing his lawful business or occupation."

The complaint charged that appellant "with force and arms, in a certain public place in said city of Rochester, to wit, on the public sidewalk on the easterly side of Wakefield Street, near unto the entrance of the City Hall, did unlawfully repeat, the words following, addressed to the complainant, that is to say, 'You are a God damned racketeer' and 'a damned Fascist and the whole government of Rochester are Fascists or agents of Fascists' the same being offensive, derisive and annoying words and names."

Upon appeal there was a trial *de novo* of appellant before a jury in the Superior Court. He was found guilty and the judgment of conviction was affirmed by the Supreme Court of the State....

By motions and exceptions, appellant raised the questions that the statute was invalid under the Fourteenth Amendment of the Constitution of the United States in that it placed an unreasonable restraint on freedom of speech, freedom of the press, and freedom of worship, and because it was vague and indefinite. These contentions were overruled and the case comes here on appeal.

There is no substantial dispute over the facts. Chaplinsky was distributing the literature of his sect on the streets of Rochester on a busy Saturday afternoon. Members of the local citizenry complained to the City Marshal, Bowering, that Chaplinsky was denouncing all religion as a 'racket'. Bowering told them that Chaplinsky was lawfully engaged, and then warned Chaplinsky that the crowd was getting restless. Some time later a disturbance occurred and the traffic officer on duty at the busy intersection started with Chaplinsky for the police station, but did not inform him that he was under arrest or that he was going to be arrested. On the way they encountered Marshal Bowering who had been advised that a riot was under way and was therefore hurrying to the scene. Bowering repeated his earlier warning to Chaplinsky who then addressed to Bowering the words set forth in the complaint.

Chaplinsky's version of the affair was slightly different. He testified that when he met Bowering, he asked him to arrest the ones responsible for the disturbance. In reply Bowering cursed him and told him to come along. Appellant admitted that he said the words charged in the complaint with the exception of the name of the Deity.

Over appellant's objection the trial court excluded as immaterial testimony relating to appellant's mission 'to preach the true facts of the Bible', his treatment at the hands of the crowd, and the alleged neglect of duty on the part of the police. This action was approved by the court below which held that neither provocation nor the truth of the utterance would constitute a defense to the charge.

It is now clear that 'Freedom of speech and freedom of the press, which are protected by the First Amendment from infringement by Congress, are among the fundamental personal rights and liberties which are protected by the Fourteenth Amendment from invasion by state action'....

Appellant assails the statute as a violation of all three freedoms, speech, press and worship, but only an attack on the basis of free speech is warranted. The spoken, not the written, word is involved. And we cannot conceive that cursing a public officer is the exercise of religion in any sense of the term. But even if the activities of the appellant which preceded the incident could be viewed as religious in character, and therefore entitled to the protection of the Fourteenth Amendment, they would not cloak him with immunity from the legal consequences for concomitant acts committed in violation of a valid criminal statute. We turn, therefore, to an examination of the statute itself.

Allowing the broadest scope to the language and purpose of the Fourteenth Amendment, it is well understood that the right of free speech is not absolute at all times and under all circumstances. There are certain well-defined and narrowly limited classes of speech, the prevention and punishment of which has never been thought to raise any Constitutional problem. These include the lewd and obscene, the profane, the libelous, and the insulting or 'fighting' words-those which by their very utterance inflict injury or tend to incite an immediate breach of the peace. It has been well observed that such utterances are no essential part of any exposition of ideas, and are of such slight social value as a step to truth that any benefit that may be derived from them is clearly outweighed by the social interest in order and morality. 'Resort to epithets or personal abuse is not in any proper sense communication of information or opinion safeguarded by the Constitution, and its punishment as a criminal act would raise no question under that instrument.'....

The state statute here challenged comes to us authoritatively construed by the highest court of New Hampshire. It has two provisions-the first relates to words or names addressed to another in a public place; the second refers to noises and exclamations. The court … said: 'The two provisions are distinct. One may stand separately from the other. Assuming, without holding, that the second were unconstitutional, the first could stand if constitutional.' We accept that construction of severability and limit our consideration to the first provision of the statute.

On the authority of its earlier decisions, the state court declared that the statute's purpose was to preserve the public peace, no words being 'forbidden except such as have a direct tendency to cause acts of violence by the person to whom, individually, the remark is addressed'. It was further said: "The word 'offensive' is not to be defined in terms of what a particular addressee thinks…. The test is what men of common intelligence would understand would be words likely to cause an average addressee to fight…. The English language has a number of words and expressions which by general consent and 'fighting words' when said without a disarming smile…. Such words, as ordinary men know, are likely to cause a fight. So are threatening, profane or obscene revilings. Derisive and annoying words can be taken as coming within the purview of the statute as heretofore interpreted only when they have this characteristic of plainly tending to excite the addressee to a breach of the peace…. The statute, as construed, does no more than prohibit the face-to-face words plainly likely to cause a breach of the peace by the addressee, words whose speaking constitute a breach of the peace by the speaker-including 'classical fighting words', words in current use less 'classical' but equally likely to cause violence, and other disorderly words, including profanity, obscenity and threats."

We are unable to say that the limited scope of the statute as thus construed contravenes the constitutional right of free expression. It is a statute narrowly drawn and limited to define and punish specific conduct lying within the domain of state power, the use in a public place of words likely to cause a breach of the peace….

Nor can we say that the application of the statute to the facts disclosed by the record substantially or unreasonably impinges upon the privilege of free speech. Argument is unnecessary to demonstrate that the appellations 'damn racketeer' and 'damn Fascist' are epithets likely to provoke the average person to retaliation, and thereby cause a breach of the peace.

The refusal of the state court to admit evidence of provocation and evidence bearing on the truth or falsity of the utterances is open to no Constitutional objection. Whether the facts sought to be proved by such evidence constitute a defense to the charge or may be shown in mitigation are questions for the state court to determine. Our function is fulfilled by a determination that the challenged statute, on its face and as applied, does not contravene the Fourteenth Amendment.

Affirmed.

TERMINIELLO v. CHICAGO
337 U.S. 11; 69 S.Ct. 894; 93 L.Ed. 1131 (1949)

Terminiello delivered an extremely provocative and brutal speech attacking certain minority groups to a primarily right-wing audience in the Chicago City Auditorium. Crowds of angry protesters outside the building became riotous in reacting to the diatribe and began throwing objects. The police, attempting to restore peace, asked Terminiello to stop speaking. He refused. Subsequently, he was arrested and convicted for breach of the peace in the state courts of Illinois. The case was brought to the Supreme Court on a writ of certiorari.

MR. JUSTICE DOUGLAS delivered the opinion of the Court.

Petitioner after jury trial was found guilty of disorderly conduct in violation of a city ordinance of Chicago and fined. The case grew out of an address he delivered in an auditorium in Chicago under the auspices of the Christian Veterans of America. The meeting commanded considerable public attention. The auditorium was filled to capacity with over 800 persons present. Others were turned away. Outside of the auditorium a crowd of about 1,000 persons gathered to protest against the meeting. A cordon of policemen was assigned to the meeting to maintain order, but they were not able to prevent several disturbances. The crowd outside was angry and turbulent.

Petitioner in his speech condemned the conduct of the crowd outside and vigorously, if not viciously, criticized various political and racial groups whose activities he denounced as inimical to the nation's welfare.

The trial court charged that "breach of the peace" consists of any "misbehavior which violates the public peace and decorum;" and that the "misbehavior may constitute a breach of peace if it stirs the public to anger, invites dispute, brings about a condition of unrest, or creates a disturbance, or if it molests the inhabitants in the enjoyment of peace and quiet by arousing alarm." Petitioner did not take exception to that instruction. But he maintained at all times that the ordinance as applied to his conduct violated his right of free speech under the Federal Constitution....

The argument here has been focused on the issue on whether the content of petitioner's speech was composed of derisive, fighting words, which carried it outside the scope of constitutional guaranties.... We do not reach that question, for there is a preliminary question that is dispositive of the case.

As we have noted, the statutory words "breach of the peace" were defined in instructions to the jury to include speech which "stirs the public to anger, invites dispute, brings about a condition of unrest, or creates a disturbance...."

...The vitality of civil and political institutions in our society depends on free discussion.... [I]t is only through free debate and free exchange of ideas that government remains responsive to the will of the people and peaceful change is effected. The right to speak freely and to promote diversity of ideas and programs is therefore one of the chief distinctions that sets us apart from totalitarian regimes.

Accordingly a function of free speech under our system of government is to invite dispute. It may indeed best serve its high purpose when it induces a condition of unrest, creates dissatisfaction with conditions as they are, or even stirs people to anger. Speech is often provocative and challenging. It may strike at prejudices and preconceptions and have profound unsettling effects as it presses for acceptance of an idea. That is why freedom of speech, though not absolute … is nevertheless protected against censorship or punishment, unless shown likely to produce a clear and present danger of a serious substantive evil that rises far above public inconvenience, annoyance, or unrest.… There is no room under our Constitution for a more restrictive view. For the alternative would lead to standardization of ideas either by legislatures, courts, or dominant political or community groups.

The ordinance as construed by the trial court seriously invaded this province. It permitted conviction of petitioner if his speech stirred people to anger, invited public dispute, or brought about a condition of unrest. A conviction resting on any of those grounds may not stand.

The fact that petitioner took no exception to the instruction is immaterial. No exception to the instructions was taken in *Stromberg v. California*, 283 U.S. 359. But a judgment of conviction based on a general verdict under a state statute was set aside in that case, because one part of the statute was unconstitutional.…

…[T]he gloss which Illinois placed on the ordinance gives it a meaning and application which are conclusive on us. We need not consider whether as construed it is defective in its entirety. As construed and applied it at least contains parts that are unconstitutional. The verdict was a general one; and we do not know on this record but what it may rest on the invalid clauses.

The statute as construed in the charge to the jury was passed on by the Illinois courts and sustained by them over the objection that as so read it violated the Fourteenth Amendment.

…But it is said that throughout the appellate proceedings the Illinois courts assumed that the only conduct punishable and punished under the ordinance was conduct constituting "fighting words." That emphasizes, however, the importance of the rule of the *Stromberg* case. Petitioner was not convicted under a statute so narrowly construed. For all anyone knows he was convicted under the parts of the ordinance (as construed) which, for example, make it an offense merely to invite dispute or to bring about a condition of unrest. We cannot avoid that issue by saying that all Illinois did was to measure petitioner's conduct, not the ordinance, against the Constitution. Petitioner raised both points – that his speech was protected by the Constitution; that the inclusion of his speech within the ordinance was a violation of the Constitution. We would, therefore, strain at technicalities to conclude that the constitutionality of the ordinance as construed and applied to petitioner was not before the Illinois courts. The record makes clear that petitioner at all times challenged the constitutionality of the ordinance as construed and applied to him.

Reversed.

MR. CHIEF JUSTICE VINSON and MR. JUSTICES FRANKFURTER and BURTON dissented.

MR. JUSTICE JACKSON dissented, saying in part:

...When the trial judge instructed the jury that it might find Terminiello guilty of inducing a breach of peace if his behavior stirred the public to anger, invited dispute, brought about unrest, created a disturbance or molested peace and quiet by arousing alarm, he was not speaking of these as harmless or abstract conditions. He was addressing his words to the concrete behavior and specific consequences disclosed by the evidence. He was saying to the jury, in effect, that if this particular speech added fuel to the situation already so inflamed as to threaten to get beyond police control, it could be punished as inducing a breach of peace....

Terminiello, advertised as a Catholic priest, but revealed at the trial to be under suspension by his Bishop, was brought to Chicago from Birmingham, Alabama, to address a gathering that assembled in response to a call signed by Gerald L.K. Smith....

...The court below, in addition to this recital, heard other evidence, that the crowd reached an estimated number of 1,500. Picket lines obstructed and interfered with access to the building. The crowd constituted "a surging howling mob hurling epithets" at those who would enter and "tried to tear their clothes off." One young woman's coat was torn off and she had to be assisted into the meeting by policemen. Those inside the hall could hear the loud noises and hear those on the outside yell, "Fascists," "Hitlers," and curse words like "damn Fascists." Bricks were thrown through the windowpanes before and during the speaking. About 28 windows were broken. The street was black with people on both sides for at least a block either way; bottles, stink bombs, and brickbats were thrown. Police were unable to control the mob, which kept breaking the windows at the meeting hall, drowning out the speaker's voice at times and breaking in through the back door of the auditorium. About seventeen of the group outside were arrested by the police.

Knowing of this environment, Terminiello made a long speech....

...Evidence showed that it stirred the audience not only to cheer and applaud but to expressions of immediate anger, unrest, and alarm. [The stenographic record of the speech, portions of which were quoted by Justice Jackson, were extremely provocative. Terminiello bitterly attacked the Jewish people and others, using abusive language.]

Terminiello, of course, disclaims being a Fascist. Doubtless many of the indoor audience were not consciously such. His speech, however, followed, with fidelity that is more than coincidental, the pattern of European fascist leaders....

I am unable to see that the local authorities have transgressed the Federal Constitution. Illinois imposed no prior censorship or suppression upon Terminiello. On the contrary, its sufferance and protection was all that enabled him to speak. It does not appear that the motive in punishing him is to silence the ideology he expressed as offensive to the State's policy or as untrue, or has any purpose of controlling his thought or its peaceful communication to others. There is no claim that the proceedings against Terminiello are designed to discriminate against him or the faction he represents or the ideas that he bespeaks. There is no indication that the charge against him is a mere pretext to give the semblance of legality to a covert effort to silence him or to prevent his followers or the public from hearing any truth that is in him.

A trial court and jury has found only that in the context of violence and disorder in which it was made, this speech was a provocation to immediate breach of peace and therefore cannot claim constitutional immunity from punishment. Under the Constitution as it has been understood and applied, at least until most recently, the State was within its powers in taking this action.

Rioting is a substantive evil, which I take it no one will deny that the State and the City have the right and the duty to prevent and punish. Where an offense is induced by speech, the Court has laid down and often reiterated a test of the power of the authorities to deal with the speaking as also an offense. "The question in every case is whether the words used are used in such circumstances and are of such a nature as to create a clear and present danger that they will bring about the substantive evils that Congress (or the State or City) has a right to prevent."

...[I]f we maintain a general policy of free speaking, we must recognize that its inevitable consequence will be sporadic local outbreaks of violence, for it is the nature of men to be intolerant of attacks upon institutions, personalities, and ideas for which they really care. In the long run, maintenance of free speech will be more endangered if the population can have no protection from the abuses which lead to violence. No liberty is made more secure by holding that its abuses are inseparable from its enjoyment....

This Court has gone far toward accepting the doctrine that civil liberty means the removal of all restraints from these crowds and that all local attempts to maintain order are impairments of the liberty of the citizen. The choice is not between order and liberty. It is between liberty with order and anarchy without either. There is danger that, if the Court does not temper its doctrinaire logic with a little practical wisdom, it will convert the constitutional Bill of Rights into a suicide pact.

I would affirm the conviction.

R.A.V. v. CITY OF ST. PAUL, MINNESOTA.
112 S.Ct. 2538; 505 U.S. 377; 120 L.Ed.2d 305 (1992)

The facts in this case are given in the opinion below.

Justice SCALIA delivered the opinion of the Court.

In the predawn hours of June 21, 1990, petitioner and several other teenagers allegedly assembled a crudely-made cross by taping together broken chair legs. They then allegedly burned the cross inside the fenced yard of a black family that lived across the street from the house where petitioner was staying. Although this conduct could have been punished under any of a number of laws, one of the two provisions under which respondent city of St. Paul chose to charge petitioner (then a juvenile) was the St. Paul Bias-Motivated Crime Ordinance,... (1990), which provides:

> "Whoever places on public or private property a symbol, object, appellation, characterization or graffiti, including, but not limited to, a burning cross or Nazi swastika, which one knows or has reasonable grounds to know arouses anger, alarm or resentment in others on the basis of race, color, creed, religion or gender commits disorderly conduct and shall be guilty of a misdemeanor."

Petitioner moved to dismiss this count on the ground that the St. Paul ordinance was substantially overbroad and impermissibly content-based and therefore facially invalid under the First Amendment. The trial court granted this motion, but the Minnesota Supreme Court reversed. That court rejected petitioner's overbreadth claim because, as construed in prior Minnesota cases,... the modifying phrase "arouses anger, alarm or resentment in others" limited the reach of the ordinance to conduct that amounts to " fighting words," i.e., "conduct that itself inflicts injury or tends to incite immediate violence ...," *In re Welfare of R.A.V...* (citing *Chaplinsky v. New Hampshire,...* (1942)), and therefore the ordinance reached only expression "that the first amendment does not protect...." The court also concluded that the ordinance was not impermissibly content-based because, in its view, "the ordinance is a narrowly tailored means toward accomplishing the compelling governmental interest in protecting the community against bias-motivated threats to public safety and order...."

I

In construing the St. Paul ordinance, we are bound by the construction given to it by the Minnesota court.... Accordingly, we accept the Minnesota Supreme Court's authoritative statement that the ordinance reaches only those expressions that constitute "fighting words" within the meaning of *Chaplinsky*.... Petitioner and his *amici* urge us to modify the scope of the *Chaplinsky* formulation, thereby invalidating the ordinance as " substantially overbroad,..." We find it unnecessary to consider this issue. Assuming, *arguendo*, that all of the expression reached by the ordinance is proscribable under the "fighting words" doctrine, we nonetheless conclude that the ordinance is facially unconstitutional in that it prohibits otherwise permitted speech solely on the basis of the subjects the speech addresses.

The First Amendment generally prevents government from proscribing speech,... or even expressive conduct,... because of disapproval of the ideas expressed. Content-based regulations are presumptively invalid.... From 1791 to the present, however, our society, like other free but civilized societies, has permitted restrictions upon the content of speech in a few limited areas, which are "of such slight social value as a step to truth that any benefit that may be derived from them is clearly outweighed by the social interest in order and morality...." We have recognized that "the freedom of speech" referred to by the First Amendment does not include a freedom to disregard these traditional limitations.... Our decisions since the 1960's have narrowed the scope of the traditional categorical exceptions for defamation, see *New York Times Co. v. Sullivan*,... (1964); *Gertz v. Robert Welch, Inc*,...(1974); see generally *Milkovich v. Lorain Journal Co*.,...(1990), and for obscenity, see *Miller v. California*, (1973), but a limited categorical approach has remained an important part of our First Amendment jurisprudence.

We have sometimes said that these categories of expression are "not within the area of constitutionally protected speech,..." or that the "protection of the First Amendment does not extend" to them.... Such statements must be taken in context, however, and are no more literally true than is the occasionally repeated shorthand characterizing obscenity "as not being speech at all,..." What they mean is that these areas of speech can, consistently with the First Amendment, be regulated because of their constitutionally proscribable content (obscenity, defamation, etc.)—not that they are categories of speech entirely invisible to the Constitution, so that they may be made the vehicles for content discrimination unrelated to their distinctively proscribable content. Thus, the government may proscribe libel; but it may not make the further content discrimination of proscribing only libel critical of the government. We recently acknowledged this distinction in *Ferber* where, in upholding New York's child pornography law, we expressly recognized that there was no "question here of censoring a particular literary theme...."

Our cases surely do not establish the proposition that the First Amendment imposes no obstacle whatsoever to regulation of particular instances of such proscribable expression, so that the government "may regulate [them] freely,..." (WHITE, J., concurring in judgment). That would mean that a city council could enact an ordinance prohibiting only those legally obscene works that contain criticism of the city government or, indeed, that do not include endorsement of the city government. Such a simplistic, all-or-nothing-at-all approach to First Amendment protection is at odds with common sense and with our jurisprudence as well. It is not true that "fighting words" have at most a "*de minimis*" expressive content, or that their content is in all respects "worthless and undeserving of constitutional protection,..." sometimes they are quite expressive indeed. We have not said that they constitute "*no* part of the expression of ideas," but only that they constitute "no *essential* part of any exposition of ideas." *Chaplinsky*... (emphasis added).

The proposition that a particular instance of speech can be proscribable on the basis of one feature (e.g., obscenity) but not on the basis of another (e.g., opposition to the city government) is commonplace, and has found application in many contexts. We have long held, for example, that nonverbal expressive activity can be banned because of the action it entails, but not because of the ideas it expresses – so that burning a flag in violation of an ordinance against outdoor fires could be punishable, whereas burning a flag in violation of an ordinance against dishonoring the flag is not.... Similarly, we have upheld reasonable "time, place, or manner" restrictions, but only if they are "justified without reference to the content of the regulated speech...." And just as the power to proscribe particular speech on the basis of a noncontent element (e.g., noise) does not entail the power to proscribe the same speech on the basis of a content element; so also, the power to proscribe it on the basis of one content element (e.g., obscenity) does not entail the power to proscribe it on the basis of other content elements.

In other words, the exclusion of "fighting words" from the scope of the First Amendment simply means that, for purposes of that Amendment, the unprotected features of the words are, despite their verbal character, essentially a "nonspeech" element of communication. Fighting words are thus analogous to a noisy sound truck: Each is, as Justice Frankfurter recognized, a "mode of speech;..." both can be used to convey an idea; but neither has, in and of itself, a claim upon the First Amendment. As with the sound truck, however, so also with fighting words: The government may not regulate use based on hostility – or favoritism – towards the underlying message expressed. Compare *Frisby v. Schultz*,... (1988) (upholding, against facial challenge, a content-neutral ban on targeted residential picketing) with *Carey v. Brown*,... (1980) (invalidating a ban on residential picketing that exempted labor picketing).

The concurrences describe us as setting forth a new First Amendment principle that prohibition of constitutionally proscribable speech cannot be "underinclusiv[e],..." (WHITE, J., concurring in judgment) – a First Amendment "absolutism" whereby "within a particular 'proscribable' category of expression,... a government must either proscribe all speech or no speech at all," ... (STEVENS, J., concurring in judgment). That easy target is of the concurrences' own invention. In our view, the First Amendment imposes not an "underinclusiveness" limitation but a "content discrimination" limitation upon a State's prohibition of proscribable speech. There is no problem whatever, for example, with a State's prohibiting obscenity (and other forms of proscribable expression) only in certain media or markets, for although that prohibition would be "underinclusive," it would not discriminate on the basis of content. See, e.g., *Sable Communications*,... (which prohibits obscene telephone communications).

Even the prohibition against content discrimination that we assert the First Amendment requires is not absolute. It applies differently in the context of proscribable speech than in the area of fully protected speech. The rationale of the general prohibition, after all, is that content discrimination "rais[es] the specter that the Government may effectively drive certain ideas or viewpoints from the marketplace...." But content discrimination among various instances of a class of proscribable speech often does not pose this threat.

When the basis for the content discrimination consists entirely of the very reason the entire class of speech at issue is proscribable, no significant danger of idea or viewpoint discrimination exists. Such a reason, having been adjudged neutral enough to support exclusion of the entire class of speech from First Amendment protection, is also neutral enough to form the basis of distinction within the class. To illustrate: A State might choose to prohibit only that obscenity which is the most patently offensive in its prurience-i.e., that which involves the most lascivious displays of sexual activity. But it may not prohibit, for example, only that obscenity which includes offensive political messages.... And the Federal Government can criminalize only those threats of violence that are directed against the President,... since the reasons why threats of violence are outside the First Amendment (protecting individuals from the fear of violence, from the disruption that fear engenders, and from the possibility that the threatened violence will occur) have special force when applied to the person of the President.... But the Federal Government may not criminalize only those threats against the President that mention his policy on aid to inner cities. And to take a final example (one mentioned by Justice STEVENS...), a State may choose to regulate price advertising in one industry but not in others, because the risk of fraud (one of the characteristics of commercial speech that justifies depriving it of full First Amendment protection...) is in its view greater there.... But a State may not prohibit only that commercial advertising that depicts men in a demeaning fashion....

Another valid basis for according differential treatment to even a content-defined subclass of proscribable speech is that the subclass happens to be associated with particular "secondary effects" of the speech, so that the regulation is "justified without reference to the content of the ...speech," *Renton v. Playtime Theatres, Inc.*, ... (1986).... A State could, for example, permit all obscene live performances except those involving minors. Moreover, since words can in some circumstances violate laws directed not against speech but against conduct (a law against treason, for example, is violated by telling the enemy the nation's defense secrets), a particular content-based subcategory of a proscribable class of speech can be swept up incidentally within the reach of a statute directed at conduct rather than speech.... Thus, for example, sexually derogatory "fighting words," among other words, may produce a violation of Title VII's general prohibition against sexual discrimination in employment practices.... Where the government does not target conduct on the basis of its expressive content, acts are not shielded from regulation merely because they express a discriminatory idea or philosophy.

These bases for distinction refute the proposition that the selectivity of the restriction is "even arguably 'conditioned upon the sovereign's agreement with what a speaker may intend to say.'" *Metromedia, Inc. v. San Diego*,... (1981) (STEVENS, J., dissenting in part) (citation omitted). There may be other such bases as well. Indeed, to validate such selectivity (where totally proscribable speech is at issue) it may not even be necessary to identify any particular "neutral" basis, so long as the nature of the content discrimination is such that there is no realistic possibility that official suppression of ideas is afoot. (We cannot think of any First Amendment interest that would stand in the way of a State's prohibiting only those obscene motion pictures with blue-eyed actresses.) Save for that limitation, the regulation of "fighting words," like the regulation of noisy speech, may address some offensive instances and leave other, equally offensive, instances alone.

II

Applying these principles to the St. Paul ordinance, we conclude that, even as narrowly construed by the Minnesota Supreme Court, the ordinance is facially unconstitutional. Although the phrase in the ordinance, "arouses anger, alarm or resentment in others," has been limited by the Minnesota Supreme Court's construction to reach only those symbols or displays that amount to "fighting words," the remaining, unmodified terms make clear that the ordinance applies only to "fighting words" that insult, or provoke violence, "on the basis of race, color, creed, religion or gender." Displays containing abusive invective, no matter how vicious or severe, are permissible unless they are addressed to one of the specified disfavored topics. Those who wish to use "fighting words" in connection with other ideas – to express hostility, for example, on the basis of political affiliation, union membership, or homosexuality – are not covered. The First Amendment does not permit St. Paul to impose special prohibitions on those speakers who express views on disfavored subjects....

In its practical operation, moreover, the ordinance goes even beyond mere content discrimination, to actual viewpoint discrimination. Displays containing some words – odious racial epithets, for example – would be prohibited to proponents of all views. But "fighting words" that do not themselves invoke race, color, creed, religion, or gender – aspersions upon a person's mother, for example – would seemingly be usable *ad libitum* in the placards of those arguing in favor of racial, color, etc. tolerance and equality, but could not be used by that speaker's opponents. One could hold up a sign saying, for example, that all "anti-Catholic bigots" are misbegotten; but not that all "papists" are, for that would insult and provoke violence "on the basis of religion." St. Paul has no such authority to license one side of a debate to fight freestyle, while requiring the other to follow Marquis of Queensbury Rules.

What we have here, it must be emphasized, is not a prohibition of fighting words that are directed at certain persons or groups (which would be facially valid if it met the requirements of the Equal Protection Clause); but rather, a prohibition of fighting words that contain (as the Minnesota Supreme Court repeatedly emphasized) messages of "bias-motivated" hatred and in particular, as applied to this case, messages "based on virulent notions of racial supremacy...." One must wholeheartedly agree with the Minnesota Supreme Court that "[i]t is the responsibility, even the obligation, of diverse communities to confront such notions in whatever form they appear," but the manner of that confrontation cannot consist of selective limitations upon speech. St. Paul's brief asserts that a general "fighting words" law would not meet the city's needs because only a content-specific measure can communicate to minority groups that the "group hatred" aspect of such speech "is not condoned by the majority." The point of the First Amendment is that majority preferences must be expressed in some fashion other than silencing speech on the basis of its content.

Despite the fact that the Minnesota Supreme Court and St. Paul acknowledge that the ordinance is directed at expression of group hatred, Justice STEVENS suggests that this "fundamentally misreads" the ordinance. It is directed, he claims, not to speech of a particular content, but to particular "injur[ies]" that are "qualitatively different" from other injuries. This is word-play. What makes the anger, fear, sense of dishonor, etc. produced by violation of this ordinance distinct from the anger, fear, sense of dishonor, etc. produced by other fighting words is nothing other than the fact that it is caused by a distinctive idea, conveyed by a distinctive message. The First Amendment cannot be evaded that easily. It is obvious that the symbols which will arouse "anger, alarm or resentment in others on the basis of race, color, creed, religion or gender" are those symbols that communicate a message of hostility based on one of these characteristics. St. Paul concedes in its brief that the ordinance applies only to "racial, religious, or gender-specific symbols" such as "a burning cross, Nazi swastika or other instrumentality of like import." Indeed, St. Paul argued in the Juvenile Court that "[t]he burning of a cross does express a message and it is, in fact, the content of that message which the St. Paul Ordinance attempts to legislate."

The content-based discrimination reflected in the St. Paul ordinance comes within neither any of the specific exceptions to the First Amendment prohibition we discussed earlier, nor within a more general exception for content discrimination that does not threaten censorship of ideas. It assuredly does not fall within the exception for content discrimination based on the very reasons why the particular class of speech at issue (here, fighting words) is proscribable. As explained earlier, the reason why fighting words are categorically excluded from the protection of the First Amendment is not that their content communicates any particular idea, but that their content embodies a particularly intolerable (and socially unnecessary) mode of expressing whatever idea the speaker wishes to convey. St. Paul has not singled out an especially offensive mode of expression – it has not, for example, selected for prohibition only those fighting words that communicate ideas in a threatening (as opposed to a merely obnoxious) manner. Rather, it has proscribed fighting words of whatever manner that communicate messages of racial, gender, or religious intolerance. Selectivity of this sort creates the possibility that the city is seeking to handicap the expression of particular ideas. That possibility would alone be enough to render the ordinance presumptively invalid, but St. Paul's comments and concessions in this case elevate the possibility to a certainty.

St. Paul argues that the ordinance comes within another of the specific exceptions we mentioned, the one that allows content discrimination aimed only at the "secondary effects" of the speech, see *Renton v. Playtime Theatres, Inc.*,... (1986). According to St. Paul, the ordinance is intended, "not to impact on [sic] the right of free expression of the accused," but rather to "protect against the victimization of a person or persons who are particularly vulnerable because of their membership in a group that historically has been discriminated against." Even assuming that an ordinance that completely proscribes, rather than merely regulates, a specified category of speech can ever be considered to be directed only to the secondary effects of such speech, it is clear that the St. Paul ordinance is not directed to secondary effects within the meaning of *Renton*. As we said in *Boos v. Barry*,... (1988), "[l]isteners' reactions to speech are not the type of 'secondary effects' we referred to in *Renton*.".... "The emotive impact of speech on its audience is not a 'secondary effect.'"

It hardly needs discussion that the ordinance does not fall within some more general exception permitting all selectivity that for any reason is beyond the suspicion of official suppression of ideas. The statements of St. Paul in this very case afford ample basis for, if not full confirmation of, that suspicion.

Finally, St. Paul and its *amici* defend the conclusion of the Minnesota Supreme Court that, even if the ordinance regulates expression based on hostility towards its protected ideological content, this discrimination is nonetheless justified because it is narrowly tailored to serve compelling state interests. Specifically, they assert that the ordinance helps to ensure the basic human rights of members of groups that have historically been subjected to discrimination, including the right of such group members to live in peace where they wish. We do not doubt that these interests are compelling, and that the ordinance can be said to promote them. But the "danger of censorship" presented by a facially content-based statute,... requires that that weapon be employed only where it is "necessary to serve the asserted [compelling] interest," ... The existence of adequate content-neutral alternatives thus "undercut[s] significantly" any defense of such a statute,...casting considerable doubt on the government's protestations that "the asserted justification is in fact an accurate description of the purpose and effect of the law...." The dispositive question in this case, therefore, is whether content discrimination is reasonably necessary to achieve St. Paul's compelling interests; it plainly is not. An ordinance not limited to the favored topics, for example, would have precisely the same beneficial effect. In fact the only interest distinctively served by the content limitation is that of displaying the city council's special hostility towards the particular biases thus singled out. That is precisely what the First Amendment forbids. The politicians of St. Paul are entitled to express that hostility – but not through the means of imposing unique limitations upon speakers who (however benightedly) disagree.

Let there be no mistake about our belief that burning a cross in someone's front yard is reprehensible. But St. Paul has sufficient means at its disposal to prevent such behavior without adding the First Amendment to the fire.

The judgment of the Minnesota Supreme Court is reversed, and the case is remanded for proceedings not inconsistent with this opinion.

It is so ordered.

Justice WHITE, with whom Justice BLACKMUN and Justice O'CONNOR join, and with whom Justice STEVENS joins except as to Part I(A), concurring in the judgment.

I agree with the majority that the judgment of the Minnesota Supreme Court should be reversed. However, our agreement ends there.

This case could easily be decided within the contours of established First Amendment law by holding, as petitioner argues, that the St. Paul ordinance is fatally overbroad because it criminalizes not only unprotected expression but expression protected by the First Amendment....

...[I]n the present case, the majority casts aside long-established First Amendment doctrine without the benefit of briefing and adopts an untried theory. This is hardly a judicious way of proceeding, and the Court's reasoning in reaching its result is transparently wrong.

I A

This Court's decisions have plainly stated that expression falling within certain limited categories so lacks the values the First Amendment was designed to protect that the Constitution affords no protection to that expression. *Chaplinsky v. New Hampshire,*... made the point in the clearest possible terms:

"There are certain well-defined and narrowly limited classes of speech, the prevention and punishment of which have never been thought to raise any Constitutional problem.... It has been well observed that such utterances are no essential part of any exposition of ideas, and are of such slight social value as a step to truth that any benefit that may be derived from them is clearly outweighed by the social interest in order and morality...."

Thus, as the majority concedes,... this Court has long held certain discrete categories of expression to be proscribable on the basis of their content. For instance, the Court has held that the individual who falsely shouts "fire" in a crowded theatre may not claim the protection of the First Amendment.... The Court has concluded that neither child pornography, nor obscenity, is protected by the First Amendment.... And the Court has observed that, "[l]eaving aside the special considerations when public officials [and public figures] are the target, a libelous publication is not protected by the Constitution." *Ferber*....

All of these categories are content based. But the Court has held that First Amendment does not apply to them because their expressive content is worthless or of *de minimis* value to society.... We have not departed from this principle, emphasizing repeatedly that, "within the confines of [these] given classification[s], the evil to be restricted so overwhelmingly outweighs the expressive interests, if any, at stake, that no process of case-by-case adjudication is required."... This categorical approach has provided a principled and narrowly focused means for distinguishing between expression that the government may regulate freely and that which it may regulate on the basis of content only upon a showing of compelling need.

Today, however, the Court announces that earlier Courts did not mean their repeated statements that certain categories of expression are "not within the area of constitutionally protected speech."... The present Court submits that such clear statements "must be taken in context" and are not "literally true."

To the contrary, those statements meant precisely what they said: The categorical approach is a firmly entrenched part of our First Amendment jurisprudence. Indeed, the Court in *Roth* reviewed the guarantees of freedom of expression in effect at the time of the ratification of the Constitution and concluded, "[i]n light of this history, it is apparent that the unconditional phrasing of the First Amendment was not intended to protect every utterance...."

In its decision today, the Court points to "[n]othing ... in this Court's precedents warrant[ing] disregard of this longstanding tradition." *Burson,...* (SCALIA, J., concurring in judgment).... Nevertheless, the majority holds that the First Amendment protects those narrow categories of expression long held to be undeserving of First Amendment protection-at least to the extent that lawmakers may not regulate some fighting words more strictly than others because of their content. The Court announces that such content-based distinctions violate the First Amendment because "the government may not regulate use based on hostility-or favoritism-towards the underlying message expressed." Should the government want to criminalize certain fighting words, the Court now requires it to criminalize all fighting words.

To borrow a phrase, "Such a simplistic, all-or-nothing-at-all approach to First Amendment protection is at odds with common sense and with our jurisprudence as well." It is inconsistent to hold that the government may proscribe an entire category of speech because the content of that speech is evil,... but that the government may not treat a subset of that category differently without violating the First Amendment; the content of the subset is by definition worthless and undeserving of constitutional protection.

The majority's observation that fighting words are "quite expressive indeed"... is no answer. Fighting words are not a means of exchanging views, rallying supporters, or registering a protest; they are directed against individuals to provoke violence or to inflict injury.... Therefore, a ban on all fighting words or on a subset of the fighting words category would restrict only the social evil of hate speech, without creating the danger of driving viewpoints from the marketplace.

Therefore, the Court's insistence on inventing its brand of First Amendment underinclusiveness puzzles me. The overbreadth doctrine has the redeeming virtue of attempting to avoid the chilling of protected expression,... but the Court's new "underbreadth" creation serves no desirable function. Instead, it permits, indeed invites, the continuation of expressive conduct that in this case is evil and worthless in First Amendment terms,... until the city of St. Paul cures the underbreadth by adding to its ordinance a catch-all phrase such as "and all other fighting words that may constitutionally be subject to this ordinance."

Any contribution of this holding to First Amendment jurisprudence is surely a negative one, since it necessarily signals that expressions of violence, such as the message of intimidation and racial hatred conveyed by burning a cross on someone's lawn, are of sufficient value to outweigh the social interest in order and morality that has traditionally placed such fighting words outside the First Amendment. Indeed, by characterizing fighting words as a form of "debate," the majority legitimates hate speech as a form of public discussion. Furthermore, the Court obscures the line between speech that could be regulated freely on the basis of content (i.e., the narrow categories of expression falling outside the First

Amendment) and that which could be regulated on the basis of content only upon a showing of a compelling state interest (i.e., all remaining expression). By placing fighting words, which the Court has long held to be valueless, on at least equal constitutional footing with political discourse and other forms of speech that we have deemed to have the greatest social value, the majority devalues the latter category....

B

In a second break with precedent, the Court refuses to sustain the ordinance even though it would survive under the strict scrutiny applicable to other protected expression. Assuming, *arguendo,* that the St. Paul ordinance is a content-based regulation of protected expression, it nevertheless would pass First Amendment review under settled law upon a showing that the regulation " 'is necessary to serve a compelling state interest and is narrowly drawn to achieve that end.'..."

Under the majority's view, a narrowly drawn, content-based ordinance could never pass constitutional muster if the object of that legislation could be accomplished by banning a wider category of speech. This appears to be a general renunciation of strict scrutiny review, a fundamental tool of First Amendment analysis....

Turning to the St. Paul ordinance and assuming *arguendo*, as the majority does, that the ordinance is not constitutionally overbroad, there is no question that it would pass equal protection review. The ordinance proscribes a subset of "fighting words," those that injure "on the basis of race, color, creed, religion or gender." This selective regulation reflects the City's judgment that harms based on race, color, creed, religion, or gender are more pressing public concerns than the harms caused by other fighting words. In light of our Nation's long and painful experience with discrimination, this determination is plainly reasonable. Indeed, as the majority concedes, the interest is compelling.

C

The Court has patched up its argument with an apparently nonexhaustive list of *ad hoc* exceptions, in what can be viewed either as an attempt to confine the effects of its decision to the facts of this case,...or as an effort to anticipate some of the questions that will arise from its radical revision of First Amendment law.

For instance, if the majority were to give general application to the rule on which it decides this case, today's decision would call into question the constitutionality of the statute making it illegal to threaten the life of the President.... Surely, this statute, by singling out certain threats, incorporates a content-based distinction; it indicates that the Government especially disfavors threats against the President as opposed to threats against all others.... But because the Government could prohibit all threats and not just those directed against the President, under the Court's theory, the compelling reasons justifying the enactment of special legislation to safeguard the President would be irrelevant, and the statute would fail First Amendment review.

To save the statute, the majority has engrafted the following exception onto its newly announced First Amendment rule: Content-based distinctions may be drawn within an unprotected category of speech if the basis for the distinctions is "the very reason the entire class of speech at issue is proscribable." Thus, the argument goes, the statute making it illegal to threaten the life of the President is constitutional, "since the reasons why threats of violence are outside the First Amendment (protecting individuals from the fear of violence, from the disruption that fear engenders, and from the possibility that the threatened violence will occur) have special force when applied to the person of the President."

The exception swallows the majority's rule. Certainly, it should apply to the St. Paul ordinance, since "the reasons why [fighting words] are outside the First Amendment ...have special force when applied to [groups that have historically been subjected to discrimination]."

To avoid the result of its own analysis, the Court suggests that fighting words are simply a mode of communication, rather than a content-based category, and that the St. Paul ordinance has not singled out a particularly objectionable mode of communication. Again, the majority confuses the issue. A prohibition on fighting words is not a time, place, or manner restriction; it is a ban on a class of speech that conveys an overriding message of personal injury and imminent violence,... a message that is at its ugliest when directed against groups that have long been the targets of discrimination. Accordingly, the ordinance falls within the first exception to the majority's theory.

As its second exception, the Court posits that certain content-based regulations will survive under the new regime if the regulated subclass "happens to be associated with particular 'secondary effects' of the speech...," which the majority treats as encompassing instances in which "words can ...violate laws directed not against speech but against conduct..." Again, there is a simple explanation for the Court's eagerness to craft an exception to its new First Amendment rule: Under the general rule the Court applies in this case, Title VII hostile work environment claims would suddenly be unconstitutional.

Title VII makes it unlawful to discriminate "because of [an] individual's race, color, religion, sex, or national origin,..." and the regulations covering hostile workplace claims forbid "sexual harassment," which includes "[u]nwelcome sexual advances, requests for sexual favors, and other verbal or physical conduct of a sexual nature" which creates "an intimidating, hostile, or offensive working environment."... The regulation does not prohibit workplace harassment generally; it focuses on what the majority would characterize as the "disfavored topi[c]" of sexual harassment. In this way, Title VII is similar to the St. Paul ordinance that the majority condemns because it "impose[s] special prohibitions on those speakers who express views on disfavored subjects." Under the broad principle the Court uses to decide the present case, hostile work environment claims based on sexual harassment should fail First Amendment review; because a general ban on harassment in the workplace would cover the problem of sexual harassment, any attempt to proscribe the subcategory of sexually harassing expression would violate the First Amendment.

Hence, the majority's second exception, which the Court indicates would insulate a Title VII hostile work environment claim from an underinclusiveness challenge because "sexually derogatory 'fighting words' ...may produce a violation of Title VII's general prohibition against sexual discrimination in employment practices." But application of this exception to a hostile work environment claim does not hold up under close examination.

First, the hostile work environment regulation is not keyed to the presence or absence of an economic quid pro quo,... but to the impact of the speech on the victimized worker. Consequently, the regulation would no more fall within a secondary effects exception than does the St. Paul ordinance. Second, the majority's focus on the statute's general prohibition on discrimination glosses over the language of the specific regulation governing hostile working environment, which reaches beyond any "incidental" effect on speech. *United States v. O'Brien*,... If the relationship between the broader statute and specific regulation is sufficient to bring the Title VII regulation within *O'Brien*, then all St. Paul need do to bring its ordinance within this exception is to add some prefatory language concerning discrimination generally.

As the third exception to the Court's theory for deciding this case, the majority concocts a catchall exclusion to protect against unforeseen problems, a concern that is heightened here given the lack of briefing on the majority's decisional theory. This final exception would apply in cases in which "there is no realistic possibility that official suppression of ideas is afoot." As I have demonstrated, this case does not concern the official suppression of ideas....

As I see it, the Court's theory does not work and will do nothing more than confuse the law. Its selection of this case to rewrite First Amendment law is particularly inexplicable, because the whole problem could have been avoided by deciding this case under settled First Amendment principles.

II

Although I disagree with the Court's analysis, I do agree with its conclusion: The St. Paul ordinance is unconstitutional. However, I would decide the case on overbreadth grounds....

I agree with petitioner that the ordinance is invalid on its face. Although the ordinance as construed reaches categories of speech that are constitutionally unprotected, it also criminalizes a substantial amount of expression that-however repugnant-is shielded by the First Amendment....

In construing the St. Paul ordinance, the Minnesota Supreme Court drew upon the definition of fighting words that appears in *Chaplinsky*- words "which by their very utterance inflict injury or tend to incite an immediate breach of the peace." However, the Minnesota court was far from clear in identifying the "injur[ies]" inflicted by the expression that St. Paul sought to regulate. Indeed, the Minnesota court emphasized (tracking the language of the ordinance) that " the ordinance censors only those displays that one knows or should know will create anger, alarm or resentment based on racial, ethnic, gender or religious bias...."

Our fighting words cases have made clear, however, that such generalized reactions are not sufficient to strip expression of its constitutional protection. The mere fact that expressive activity causes hurt feelings, offense, or resentment does not render the expression unprotected....

In the First Amendment context, "[c]riminal statutes must be scrutinized with particular care; those that make unlawful a substantial amount of constitutionally protected conduct may be held facially invalid even if they also have legitimate application...." The St. Paul antibias ordinance is such a law. Although the ordinance reaches conduct that is unprotected, it also makes criminal expressive conduct that causes only hurt feelings, offense, or resentment, and is protected by the First Amendment.... The ordinance is therefore fatally overbroad and invalid on its face.

III

Today, the Court has disregarded two established principles of First Amendment law without providing a coherent replacement theory. Its decision is an arid, doctrinaire interpretation, driven by the frequently irresistible impulse of judges to tinker with the First Amendment. The decision is mischievous at best and will surely confuse the lower courts. I join the judgment, but not the folly of the opinion.

Justice BLACKMUN, concurring in the judgment....

Justice STEVENS, with whom Justice WHITE and Justice BLACKMUN join as to Part I, concurring in the judgment.

... Because the regulated conduct has some communicative content-a message of racial, religious or gender hostility-the ordinance raises two quite different First Amendment questions. Is the ordinance "overbroad" because it prohibits too much speech? If not, is it "underbroad" because it does not prohibit enough speech?

In answering these questions, my colleagues today wrestle with two broad principles: first, that certain "categories of expression [including 'fighting words'] are 'not within the area of constitutionally protected speech,'" (WHITE, J., concurring in judgment); and second, that "[c]ontent-based regulations [of expression] are presumptively invalid." (Opinion of the Court). Although in past opinions the Court has repeated both of these maxims, it has-quite rightly-adhered to neither with the absolutism suggested by my colleagues. Thus, while I agree that the St. Paul ordinance is unconstitutionally overbroad for the reasons stated in Part II of Justice WHITE's opinion, I write separately to suggest how the allure of absolute principles has skewed the analysis of both the majority and concurring opinions.

I

Fifty years ago, the Court articulated a categorical approach to First Amendment jurisprudence.

"There are certain well-defined and narrowly limited classes of speech, the prevention and punishment of which have never been thought to raise any Constitutional problem...."

We have, as Justice WHITE observes, often described such categories of expression as "not within the area of constitutionally protected speech ." ...

The Court today revises this categorical approach. It is not, the Court rules, that certain "categories" of expression are "unprotected," but rather that certain "elements" of expression are wholly "proscribable." To the Court, an expressive act, like a chemical compound, consists of more than one element. Although the act may be regulated because it contains a proscribable element, it may not be regulated on the basis of another (nonproscribable) element it also contains. Thus, obscene antigovernment speech may be regulated because it is obscene, but not because it is antigovernment. It is this revision of the categorical approach that allows the Court to assume that the St. Paul ordinance proscribes only fighting words, while at the same time concluding that the ordinance is invalid because it imposes a content-based regulation on expressive activity....

I am, however, even more troubled by the second step of the Court's analysis-namely, its conclusion that the St. Paul ordinance is an unconstitutional content-based regulation of speech. Drawing on broadly worded dicta, the Court establishes a near-absolute ban on content-based regulations of expression and holds that the First Amendment prohibits the regulation of fighting words by subject matter. Thus, while the Court rejects the "all-or-nothing-at-all" nature of the categorical approach, it promptly embraces an absolutism of its own: within a particular "proscribable" category of expression, the Court holds, a government must either proscribe all speech or no speech at all. This aspect of the Court's ruling fundamentally misunderstands the role and constitutional status of content-based regulations on speech, conflicts with the very nature of First Amendment jurisprudence, and disrupts well-settled principles of First Amendment law.

Although the Court has, on occasion, declared that content-based regulations of speech are "never permitted,"... such claims are overstated.... Contrary to the broad dicta in *Mosley* and elsewhere, our decisions demonstrate that content-based distinctions, far from being presumptively invalid, are an inevitable and indispensable aspect of a coherent understanding of the First Amendment....

Likewise, whether speech falls within one of the categories of "unprotected" or "proscribable" expression is determined, in part, by its content. Whether a magazine is obscene, a gesture a fighting word, or a photograph[ed] child pornography is determined, in part, by its content. Even within categories of protected expression, the First Amendment status of speech is fixed by its content....

Consistent with this general premise, we have frequently upheld content-based regulations of speech. For example, in *Young v. American Mini Theatres*, the Court upheld zoning ordinances that regulated movie theaters based on the content of the films shown. In *FCC v. Pacifica Foundation*,... (1978) (plurality opinion), we upheld a restriction on the broadcast of specific indecent words. In *Lehman v. City of Shaker Heights*,... (plurality opinion), we upheld a city law that permitted commercial advertising, but prohibited political advertising, on city buses. In *Broadrick v. Oklahoma*,... we upheld a state law that restricted the speech of state employees, but only as concerned partisan political matters. We have long recognized the power of the Federal Trade Commission to regulate misleading advertising and labeling, see, e.g., *Jacob Siegel Co. v. FTC*,... (1946), and the National Labor Relations Board's power to regulate an employer's election-related speech on the basis of its content. See, e.g., *NLRB v. Gissel Packing Co.*,... (1969).

It is also beyond question that the Government may choose to limit advertisements for cigarettes,... but not for cigars; choose to regulate airline advertising, see *Morales v. Trans World Airlines*,... (1992), but not bus advertising; or choose to monitor solicitation by lawyers, see *Ohralik v. Ohio State Bar Assn*,... but not by doctors.

All of these cases involved the selective regulation of speech based on content-precisely the sort of regulation the Court invalidates today. Such selective regulations are unavoidably content based, but they are not, in my opinion, "presumptively invalid." As these many decisions and examples demonstrate, the prohibition on content-based regulations is not nearly as total as the *Mosley* dictum suggests.

Disregarding this vast body of case law, the Court today goes beyond even the overstatement in *Mosley* and applies the prohibition on content-based regulation to speech that the Court had until today considered wholly "unprotected" by the First Amendment-namely, fighting words. This new absolutism in the prohibition of content-based regulations severely contorts the fabric of settled First Amendment law.

Our First Amendment decisions have created a rough hierarchy in the constitutional protection of speech. Core political speech occupies the highest, most protected position; commercial speech and nonobscene, sexually explicit speech are regarded as a sort of second-class expression; obscenity and fighting words receive the least protection of all. Assuming that the Court is correct that this last class of speech is not wholly "unprotected," it certainly does not follow that fighting words and obscenity receive the same sort of protection afforded core political speech. Yet in ruling that proscribable speech cannot be regulated based on subject matter, the Court does just that. Perversely, this gives fighting words greater protection than is afforded commercial speech. If Congress can prohibit false advertising directed at airline passengers without also prohibiting false advertising directed at bus passengers and if a city can prohibit political advertisements in its buses while allowing other advertisements, it is ironic to hold that a city cannot regulate fighting words based on "race, color, creed, religion or gender" while leaving unregulated fighting words based on "union membership or homosexuality." The Court today turns First Amendment law on its head: Communication that was once entirely unprotected (and that still can be wholly proscribed) is now entitled to greater protection than commercial speech-and possibly greater protection than core political speech....

Similarly, it is impossible to reconcile the Court's analysis of the St. Paul ordinance with its recognition that "a prohibition of fighting words that are directed at certain persons or groups ...would be facially valid." (emphasis deleted). A selective proscription of unprotected expression designed to protect "certain persons or groups" (for example, a law proscribing threats directed at the elderly) would be constitutional if it were based on a legitimate determination that the harm created by the regulated expression differs from that created by the unregulated expression (that is, if the elderly are more severely injured by threats than are the nonelderly). Such selective protection is no different from a law prohibiting minors (and only minors) from obtaining obscene publications.... St. Paul has determined-reasonably in my judgment-that fighting-word injuries "based on race, color, creed, religion or gender" are qualitatively different and more severe than fighting-word injuries based on other characteristics. Whether the selective proscription of proscribable speech is defined by the protected target ("certain persons or groups") or the basis of the harm (injuries "based on race, color, creed, religion or gender") makes no constitutional difference: what matters is whether the legislature's selection is based on a legitimate, neutral, and reasonable distinction.

In sum, the central premise of the Court's ruling-that "[c]ontent-based regulations are presumptively invalid"-has simplistic appeal, but lacks support in our First Amendment jurisprudence. To make matters worse, the Court today extends this overstated claim to reach categories of hitherto unprotected speech and, in doing so, wreaks havoc in an area of settled law. Finally, although the Court recognizes exceptions to its new principle, those exceptions undermine its very conclusion that the St. Paul ordinance is unconstitutional. Stated directly, the majority's position cannot withstand scrutiny.

II

Although I agree with much of Justice WHITE's analysis, I do not join Part I-A of his opinion because I have reservations about the "categorical approach" to the First Amendment....

Admittedly, the categorical approach to the First Amendment has some appeal: either expression is protected or it is not-the categories create safe harbors for governments and speakers alike. But this approach sacrifices subtlety for clarity and is, I am convinced, ultimately unsound. As an initial matter, the concept of "categories" fits poorly with the complex reality of expression. Few dividing lines in First Amendment law are straight and unwavering, and efforts at categorization inevitably give rise only to fuzzy boundaries. Our definitions of "obscenity," ... and " public forum,"... illustrate this all too well. The quest for doctrinal certainty through the definition of categories and subcategories is, in my opinion, destined to fail.

Moreover, the categorical approach does not take seriously the importance of context. The meaning of any expression and the legitimacy of its regulation can only be determined in context. Whether, for example, a picture or a sentence is obscene cannot be judged in the abstract, but rather only in the context of its setting, its use, and its audience....

Perhaps sensing the limits of such an all-or-nothing approach, the Court has applied its analysis less categorically than its doctrinal statements suggest....

Similarly, we have consistently construed the "fighting words" exception set forth in *Chaplinsky* narrowly.... In short, the history of the categorical approach is largely the history of narrowing the categories of unprotected speech.

This evolution, I believe, indicates that the categorical approach is unworkable and the quest for absolute categories of "protected" and "unprotected" speech ultimately futile. My analysis of the faults and limits of this approach persuades me that the categorical approach presented in Part I-A of Justice WHITE's opinion is not an adequate response to the novel "underbreadth" analysis the Court sets forth today.

III

As the foregoing suggests, I disagree with both the Court's and part of Justice WHITE's analysis of the constitutionality of the St. Paul ordinance. Unlike the Court, I do not believe that all content-based regulations are equally infirm and presumptively invalid; unlike Justice WHITE, I do not believe that fighting words are wholly unprotected by the First Amendment. To the contrary, I believe our decisions establish a more complex and subtle analysis, one that considers the content and context of the regulated speech, and the nature and scope of the restriction on speech. Applying this analysis and assuming *arguendo* (as the Court does) that the St. Paul ordinance is not overbroad, I conclude that such a selective, subject-matter regulation on proscribable speech is constitutional....

In applying this analysis to the St. Paul ordinance, I assume *arguendo* – as the Court does – that the ordinance regulates only fighting words and therefore is not overbroad. Looking to the content and character of the regulated activity, two things are clear. First, by hypothesis the ordinance bars only low-value speech, namely, fighting words. By definition such expression constitutes "no essential part of any exposition of ideas, and [is] of such slight social value as a step to truth that any benefit that may be derived from [it] is clearly outweighed by the social interest in order and morality." *Chaplinsky*.... Second, the ordinance regulates "expressive conduct [rather] than ...the written or spoken word." *Texas v. Johnson*....

Looking to the context of the regulated activity, it is again significant that the statute (by hypothesis) regulates only fighting words . Whether words are fighting words is determined in part by their context . Fighting words are not words that merely cause offense; fighting words must be directed at individuals so as to "by their very utterance inflict injury." By hypothesis, then, the St. Paul ordinance restricts speech in confrontational and potentially violent situations. The case at hand is illustrative. The cross-burning in this case-directed as it was to a single African-American family trapped in their home-was nothing more than a crude form of physical intimidation. That this cross-burning sends a message of racial hostility does not automatically endow it with complete constitutional protection.

Significantly, the St. Paul ordinance regulates speech not on the basis of its subject matter or the viewpoint expressed, but rather on the basis of the harm the speech causes. In this regard, the Court fundamentally misreads the St. Paul ordinance. The Court describes the St. Paul ordinance as regulating expression "addressed to one of [several] specified disfavored topics,..." Contrary to the Court's suggestion, the ordinance regulates only a subcategory of expression that causes injuries based on "race, color, creed, religion or gender," not a subcategory that involves discussions that concern those characteristics....

Moreover, even if the St. Paul ordinance did regulate fighting words based on its subject matter, such a regulation would, in my opinion, be constitutional. As noted above, subject-matter based regulations on commercial speech are widespread and largely unproblematic. As we have long recognized, subject-matter regulations generally do not raise the same concerns of government censorship and the distortion of public discourse presented by viewpoint regulations. Thus, in upholding subject-matter regulations we have carefully noted that viewpoint-based discrimination was not implicated....

Contrary to the suggestion of the majority, the St. Paul ordinance does not regulate expression based on viewpoint. The Court contends that the ordinance requires proponents of racial intolerance to "follow the Marquis of Queensbury Rules" while allowing advocates of racial tolerance to "fight freestyle." The law does no such thing. The Court writes:

"One could hold up a sign saying, for example, that all 'anti- Catholic bigots' are misbegotten; but not that all 'papists' are, for that would insult and provoke violence 'on the basis of religion.'"

This may be true, but it hardly proves the Court's point. The Court's reasoning is asymmetrical. The response to a sign saying that "all [religious] bigots are misbegotten" is a sign saying that "all advocates of religious tolerance are misbegotten." Assuming such signs could be fighting words (which seems to me extremely unlikely), neither sign would be banned by the ordinance for the attacks were not "based on ... religion" but rather on one's beliefs about tolerance. Conversely (and again assuming such signs are fighting words), just as the ordinance would prohibit a Muslim from hoisting a sign claiming that all Catholics were misbegotten, so the ordinance would bar a Catholic from hoisting a similar sign attacking Muslims.

The St. Paul ordinance is evenhanded. In a battle between advocates of tolerance and advocates of intolerance, the ordinance does not prevent either side from hurling fighting words at the other on the basis of their conflicting ideas, but it does bar both sides from hurling such words on the basis of the target's "race, color, creed, religion or gender." To extend the Court's pugilistic metaphor, the St. Paul ordinance simply bans punches "below the belt" – by either party. It does not, therefore, favor one side of any debate.

Finally, it is noteworthy that the St. Paul ordinance is, as construed by the Court today, quite narrow. The St. Paul ordinance does not ban all "hate speech," nor does it ban, say, all cross-burnings or all swastika displays. Rather it only bans a subcategory of the already narrow category of fighting words. Such a limited ordinance leaves open and protected a vast range of expression on the subjects of racial, religious, and gender equality. As construed by the Court today, the ordinance certainly does not "'raise the specter that the Government may effectively drive certain ideas or viewpoints from the marketplace.'" Petitioner is free to burn a cross to announce a rally or to express his views about racial supremacy, he may do so on private property or public land, at day or at night, so long as the burning is not so threatening and so directed at an individual as to "by its very [execution] inflict injury." Such a limited proscription scarcely offends the First Amendment.

In sum, the St. Paul ordinance (as construed by the Court) regulates expressive activity that is wholly proscribable and does so not on the basis of viewpoint, but rather in recognition of the different harms caused by such activity. Taken together, these several considerations persuade me that the St. Paul ordinance is not an unconstitutional content-based regulation of speech. Thus, were the ordinance not overbroad, I would vote to uphold it.

MILLER v. CALIFORNIA
413 U.S. 15; 93 S.Ct. 2067; 37 L.Ed. 2d 419 (1973)

Miller was accused of sending brochures that advertised what he called "adult" material. These brochures, mailed at large, were sent to people who had not requested them. In Newport Beach, California, a restaurant manager and his mother opened an envelope containing Miller's "sexually explicit material" and called the police. Miller was convicted for violating a California statute that forbade the unsolicited mailing of obscene material.

MR. CHIEF JUSTICE BURGER delivered the opinion of the Court, saying in part:

This is one of a group of "obscenity-pornography" cases being reviewed by the Court in a re-examination of standards enunciated in earlier cases involving what Mr. Justice Harlan called "the intractable obscenity problem."

Appellant conducted a mass mailing campaign to advertise the sale of illustrated books, euphemistically called "adult" material. After a jury trial, he was convicted of violating California Penal Code section 311.2(a), a misdemeanor, by knowingly distributing obscene matter.... Appellant's conviction was specifically based on his conduct in causing five unsolicited advertising brochures to be sent through the mail in an envelope addressed to a restaurant in Newport Beach, California. The envelope was opened by the manager of the restaurant and his mother. They had not requested the brochures; they complained to the police.

The brochures advertise four books entitled "Intercourse," "Man-Woman," "Sex Orgies Illustrated," and "An Illustrated History of Pornography," and a film entitled "Marital Intercourse." While the brochures contain some descriptive printed material, primarily they consist of pictures and drawings very explicitly depicting men and women in groups of two or more engaging in a variety of sexual activities, with genitals often prominently displayed.

I

This case involves the application of a state's criminal obscenity statute to a situation in which sexually explicit materials have been thrust by aggressive sales action upon unwilling recipients who had in no way indicated any desire to receive such materials. This Court has recognized that the States have a legitimate interest in prohibiting dissemination or exhibition of obscene material when the mode of dissemination carries with it a significant danger of offending the sensibilities of unwilling recipients or of exposure to juveniles. *Stanley v. Georgia* (1969). *Ginsberg v. New York* (1968). *Interstate Circuit, Inc. v. Dallas* (1968). *Redrup v. New York* (1967). *Jacobellis v. Ohio* (1964).... It is in this context that we are called on to define the standards which must be used to identify obscene material that a State may regulate without infringing the First Amendment as applicable to the States through the Fourteenth Amendment.

The dissent of Mr. Justice Brennan reviews the background of the obscenity problem, but since the Court now undertakes to formulate standards more concrete than those in the past, it is useful for us to focus on two of the landmark cases in the somewhat tortured history of the Court's obscenity decisions. In *Roth v. United States* (1957), the Court sustained a conviction under a federal statute punishing the mailing of "obscene, lewd, lascivious or filthy..." materials. The key to that holding was the Court's rejection of the claim that obscene materials were protected by the First Amendment. Five Justices joined in the opinion stating:

> All ideas having even the slightest redeeming social importance – unorthodox ideas, controversial ideas, even ideas hateful to the prevailing climate of opinion – have full protection of the [First Amendment] guaranties, unless excludable because they encroach upon the limited area of more important interests. But implicit in the history of the First Amendment is the rejection of obscenity as utterly without redeeming social importance.... This is the same judgment expressed by this Court in *Chaplinsky v. New Hampshire* [19421.
>
> '...There are certain well-defined and narrowly limited classes of speech, the prevention and punishment of which have never been thought to raise any Constitutional problem. *These include the lewd and obscene.... It has been well observed that such utterances are no essential part of any exposition of ideas, and are of such slight social value as a step to truth that any benefit that may be derived from them is clearly outweighed by the social interest in order and morality....'*
>
> We hold that obscenity is not within the area of constitutionally protected speech or press.

Nine years later in *Memoirs v. Massachusetts* (1966), the Court veered sharply away from the *Roth* concept and, with only three Justices in the plurality opinion, articulated a new test of obscenity. The plurality held that under the *Roth* definition: "... as elaborated in subsequent cases, three elements must coalesce: it must be established that (a) the dominant theme of the material taken as a whole appeals to a prurient interest in sex; (b) the material is patently offensive because it affronts contemporary community standards relating to the description or representation of sexual matters; and (c) the material is utterly without redeeming social value." The sharpness of the break with *Roth*, represented by the third element of the *Memoirs* test and emphasized by Mr. Justice White's dissent, was further underscored when the *Memoirs* plurality went on to state: "The Supreme Judicial Court erred in holding that a book need not be 'unqualifiedly worthless before it can be deemed obscene.' A book cannot be proscribed unless it is found to be *utterly* without redeeming social value."

While *Roth* presumed "obscenity" to be "utterly without redeeming social value," *Memoirs* required that to prove obscenity it must be affirmatively established that the material is "*utterly* without redeeming social value." Thus, even as they repeated the words of *Roth*, the *Memoirs* plurality produced a drastically altered test that called on the prosecution to prove a negative, i.e., that the material was "*utterly* without redeeming social value" – a burden virtually impossible to discharge under our criminal standards of proof. Such considerations caused Mr. Justice Harlan to wonder if the "utterly without redeeming social value" test had any meaning at all....

Apart from the initial formulation in the *Roth* case, no majority of the Court has at any given time been able to agree on a standard to determine what constitutes obscene, pornographic material subject to regulation under the States' police power.... We have seen "a variety of views among the members of the Court unmatched in any other course of constitutional adjudication." *Interstate Circuit, Inc. v. Dallas* (Harlan, J., concurring and dissenting). This is not remarkable, for in the area of freedom of speech and press the courts must always remain sensitive to any infringement on genuinely serious literary, artistic, political, or scientific expression. This is an area in which there are few eternal verities.

The case we now review was tried on the theory that the California Penal Code section 311 approximately incorporates the three-stage *Memoirs* test. But now the *Memoirs* test has been abandoned as unworkable by its author and no member of the Court today supports the *Memoirs* formulation.

II

This much has been categorically settled by the Court, that obscene material is unprotected by the First Amendment.... We acknowledge, however, the inherent dangers of undertaking to regulate any form of expression. State statutes designed to regulate obscene materials must be carefully limited.... As a result, we now confine the permissible scope of such regulation to works which depict or describe sexual conduct. That conduct must be specifically defined by the applicable state law, as written or authoritatively construed. A state offense must also be limited to works which, taken as a whole, appeal to the prurient interest in sex, which portray sexual conduct in a patently offensive way, and which, taken as a whole, do not have serious literary, artistic, political, or scientific value.

The basic guidelines for the trier of fact must be: (a) whether "the average person, applying contemporary community standards" would find that the work, taken as a whole, appeals to the prurient interest.... (b) whether the work depicts or describes in a patently offensive way, sexual conduct specifically defined by the applicable state law, and (c) whether the work, taken as a whole, lacks serious literary, artistic, political, or scientific value. We do not adopt as a constitutional standard the "*utterly* without redeeming social value" test of *Memoirs v. Massachusetts*; that concept has never commanded the adherence of more than three Justices at one time. If a state law that regulates obscene material is thus limited, as written or construed, the First Amendment values applicable to the States through the Fourteenth Amendment are adequately protected by the ultimate power of appellate courts to conduct an independent review of constitutional claims when necessary....

We emphasize that it is not our function to propose regulatory schemes for the States. That must await their concrete legislative efforts. It is possible, however, to give a few plain examples of what a state statute could define for regulation under the second part (b) of the standard announced in this opinion, *supra*:

(a) Patently offensive representations or descriptions of ultimate sexual acts, normal or perverted, actual or simulated.

(b) Patently offensive representations or descriptions of masturbation, excretory functions, and lewd exhibition of the genitals.

Sex and nudity may not be exploited without limits by films or pictures exhibited or sold in places of public accommodation any more than live sex and nudity can be exhibited or sold without limit in such public places. At a minimum, prurient, patently offensive depiction or description of sexual conduct must have serious literary, artistic, political, or scientific value to merit First Amendment protection.... For example, medical books for the education of physicians and related personnel necessarily use graphic illustrations and descriptions of human anatomy. In resolving the inevitably sensitive questions of fact and law, we must continue to rely on the jury system accompanied by the safeguards that judges, rules of evidence, presumption of innocence, and other protective features provided, as we do with rape, murder, and a host of other offenses against society and its individual members.

Mr. Justice Brennan, author of the opinions of the Court, or the plurality opinions, in *Roth v. United States*, *Jacobellis v. Ohio*, *Ginzburg v. United States* (1966), *Mishkin v. New York* (1966), and *Memoirs v. Massachusetts*, has abandoned his former positions and now maintains that no formulation of this Court, the Congress, or the States can adequately distinguish obscene material unprotected by the First Amendment from protected expression, *Paris Adult Theatre v. Slaton* (1973) (Brennan, J., dissenting). Paradoxically, Mr. Justice Brennan indicates that suppression of unprotected obscene material is permissible to avoid exposure to unconsenting adults, as in this case, and to juveniles, although he gives no indication of how the materials may be drawn with greater precision for these purposes than for regulation of commercial exposure to consenting adults only. Nor does he indicate where in the Constitution he finds the authority to distinguish between a willing "adult" one month past the state law age of majority and a willing "juvenile" one month younger.

Under the holdings announced today, no one will be subject to prosecution for the sale or exposure of obscene materials unless these materials depict or describe patently offensive "hard core" sexual conduct specifically defined by the regulating state law, as written or construed. We are satisfied that these specific prerequisites will provide fair notice to a dealer in such materials that his public and commercial activities may bring prosecution.... If the inability to define regulated materials with ultimate, godlike precision altogether removes the power of the States or the Congress to regulate, then "hard core" pornography may be exposed without limit to the juvenile, the passerby, and the consenting adult alike, as, indeed, Mr. Justice Douglas contends.... In this belief, however, Mr. Justice Douglas now stands alone.

Mr. Justice Brennan also emphasizes "institutional stress" in justification of his change of view. Noting that "the number of obscenity cases on our docket gives ample testimony to the burden that has been placed upon this Court," he quite rightly remarks that the examination of contested materials "is hardly a source of edification to members of this Court." *Paris Adult Theatre v. Slaton* (Brennan, J., dissenting). He also notes, and we agree, that "uncertainty of the standards creates a continuing source of tension between state and federal courts...." "The problem is ... that one cannot say with certainty that material is obscene until at least five members of this Court, applying inevitably obscure standards, have pronounced it so."

It is certainly true that the absence, since *Roth,* of a single majority view of this Court as to proper standards for testing obscenity has placed a strain on both state and federal courts. But today, for the first time since *Roth* was decided in 1957, a majority of this Court has agreed on concrete guidelines to isolate "hard core" pornography from expression protected by the First Amendment. Now we may abandon the casual practice of *Redrup v. New York* and attempt to provide positive guidance to the federal and state courts alike.

This may not be an easy road, free from difficulty. But no amount of "fatigue" should lead us to adopt a convenient "institutional" rationale – an absolutist, "anything goes" view of the First Amendment – because it will lighten our burdens. "Such an abnegation of judicial supervision in this field would be inconsistent with our duty to uphold the constitutional guarantees."... Nor should we remedy "tension between state and federal courts" by arbitrarily depriving the States of a power reserved to them under the Constitution, a power which they have enjoyed and exercised continuously from before the adoption of the First Amendment to this day.... "Our duty admits of no 'substitute for facing up to the tough individual problem of constitutional judgment involved in every obscenity case.'..."

III

Under a national Constitution, fundamental First Amendment limitations on the powers of the States do not vary from community to community, but this does not mean that there are, or should or can be, fixed, uniform national standards of precisely what appeals to the "prurient interest" or is "patently offensive." These are essentially questions of fact, and our nation is simply too big and too diverse for this Court to reasonably expect that such standards could be articulated for all 50 States in a single formulation, even assuming the prerequisite consensus exists. When triers of fact are asked to decide whether "the average person, applying contemporary community standards" would consider certain materials "prurient," it would be unrealistic to require that the answer be based on some abstract formulation. The adversary system with lay jurors as the usual ultimate factfinders in criminal prosecutions, has historically permitted triers-of-fact to draw on the standards of their community, guided always by limiting instructions on the law. To require a State to structure obscenity proceedings around evidence of a *national* "community standard" would be an exercise in futility....

It is neither realistic nor constitutionally sound to read the First Amendment as requiring that the people of Maine or Mississippi accept public depiction of conduct found tolerable in Las Vegas, or New York City.... People in different States vary in their tastes and attitudes, and this diversity is not to be strangled by the absolutism of imposed uniformity. As the Court made clear in *Mishkin v. New York* (1966), the primary concern with requiring a jury to apply the standard of "the average person, applying contemporary community standards" is to be certain that, so far as material is not aimed at a deviant group, it will be judged by its impact on an average person, rather than a particularly susceptible or sensitive person-or indeed a totally insensitive one.... We hold the requirement that the jury evaluate the materials with reference to "contemporary standards of the State of California" serves this protective purpose and is constitutionally adequate.

IV

The dissenting justices sound the alarm of repression. But, in our view, to equate the free and robust exchange of ideas and political debate with commercial exploitation of obscene material demeans the grand conception of the First Amendment and its high purposes in the historic struggle for freedom. It is a "misuse of the great guarantees of free speech and free press...." The First Amendment protects works which, taken as a whole, have serious literary, artistic, political, or scientific value, regardless of whether the government or a majority of the people approve of the ideas these works represent. "The protection given speech and press was fashioned to assure unfettered interchange of *ideas* for the bringing about of political and social changes desired by the people."... But the public portrayal of hard core sexual conduct for its own sake, and for the ensuing commercial gain, is a different matter.

There is no evidence, empirical or historical, that the stern 19th century American censorship of public distribution and display of material relating to sex... in any way limited or affected expression of serious literary, artistic, political, or scientific ideas. On the contrary, it is beyond any question that the era following Thomas Jefferson to Theodore Roosevelt was an "extraordinarily vigorous period" not just in economics and politics, but in *belles lettres* and in "the outlying fields of social and political philosophies." We do not see the harsh hand of censorship of ideas – good or bad, sound or unsound – and "repression" of political liberty lurking in every state regulation of commercial exploitation of human interest in sex.

Mr. Justice Brennan finds "it is hard to see how state ordered regimentation of our minds can ever be forestalled." *Paris Adult Theatre I v. Slaton.* These doleful anticipations assume that courts cannot distinguish commerce in ideas, protected by the First Amendment, from commercial exploitation of obscene material. Moreover, state regulation of hard core pornography so as to make it unavailable to nonadults, a regulation which Mr. Justice Brennan finds constitutionally permissible, has all the elements of "censorship" for adults; indeed even more rigid enforcement techniques may be called for with such dichotomy of regulation.... One can concede that the "sexual revolution" of recent years may have had useful byproducts in striking layers of prudery from a subject long irrationally kept from needed ventilation. But it does not follow that no regulation of patently offensive "hard core" materials is needed or permissible; civilized people do not allow unregulated access to heroin because it is a derivative of medicinal morphine.

In sum we (a) reaffirm the *Roth* holding that obscene material is not protected by the First Amendment, (b) hold that such material can be regulated by the States, subject to the specific safeguards enunciated above, without a showing that the material is "utterly without redeeming social value," and (c) hold that obscenity is to be determined by applying "contemporary community standards," not "national standards."...

If there are to be restraints on what is obscene, then a constitutional amendment should be the way of achieving the end. There are societies where religion and mathematics are the only free segments. It would be a dark day for America if that were our destiny. But the people can make it such if they choose to write obscenity into the Constitution and define it.

We deal with highly emotional, not rational, questions. To many the Song of Solomon is obscene. I do not think we, the judges, were ever given the constitutional power to make definitions of obscenity. If it is to be defined, let the people debate and decide by a constitutional amendment what they want to ban as obscene and what standards they want the legislatures and the courts to apply. Perhaps the people will decide that the path towards a mature, integrated society requires that all ideas competing for acceptance must have no censor. Perhaps they will decide otherwise. Whatever the choice, the courts will have some guidelines. Now we have none except our own predilections.

MR. JUSTICE BRENNAN, with whom MR. JUSTICE STEWART and MR. JUSTICE MARSHALL joined, dissented.

PARIS ADULT THEATRE I v. SLATON
413 U.S. 49; 93 S.Ct. 2628; 37 L.Ed. 2d 446 (1973)

The Paris Adult Theatre was sued by Slaton, District Attorney, under Georgia civil law to prevent the showing of two allegedly obscene motion picture films. A trial court viewed the two movies and decided that they were "constitutionally permissible" when shown exclusively for consenting adults. The Georgia Supreme Court reversed the decision, holding that the First Amendment did not protect the two films. Handed down the same day as Miller, *this decision relates to the application of the Court's obscenity test.*

MR. CHIEF JUSTICE BURGER delivered the opinion of the Court, saying in part:

II

We categorically disapprove the theory, apparently adopted by the trial judge, that obscene, pornographic films acquire constitutional immunity from state regulation simply because they are exhibited for consenting adults only. This holding was properly rejected by the Georgia Supreme Court. Although we have often pointedly recognized the high importance of the state interest in regulating the exposure of obscene materials to juveniles and unconsenting adults, see *Miller v. California* (1973); *Stanley v. Georgia* (1969); *Redrup v. New York* (1967), this Court has never declared these to be the only legitimate state interests permitting regulation of obscene material. The states have a long-recognized legitimate interest in regulating the use of obscene material in local commerce and in all places of public accommodation, as long as these regulations do not run afoul of specific constitutional prohibitions....

In particular, we hold that there are legitimate state interests at stake in stemming the tide of commercialized obscenity, even assuming it is feasible to enforce effective safeguards against exposure to juveniles and to the passerby. Rights and interests "other than those of the advocates are involved."... These include the interest of the public in the quality of life and the total community environment, the tone of commerce in the great city centers, and, possibly, the public safety itself. The Hill-Link Minority Report of the Commission on Obscenity and Pornography indicates that there is at least an arguable correlation between obscene material and crime. Quite apart from sex crimes, however, there remains one problem of large proportions aptly described by Professor Bickel:

"It concerns the tone of the society, the mode, or to use terms that have perhaps greater currency, the style and quality of life, now and in the future. A man may be entitled to read an obscene book in his room, or expose himself indecently there.... We should protect his privacy. But if he demands a right to obtain the books and pictures he wants in the market, and to foregather in public places – discreet, if you will, but accessible to all – with others who share his tastes, *then to grant him his right is to affect the world about the rest of us, and to impinge on other privacies*. Even supposing that each of us can, if he wishes, effectively avert the eye and stop the ear (which, in truth, we cannot), what is commonly read and seen and heard and done intrudes upon us all, want it or not." 22 *The Public Interest* 25, 25-26 (Winter 1971). (Emphasis added.) As Mr. Chief Justice Warren stated there is a "right of the nation and of the states to maintain a decent society...." *Jacobellis v. Ohio* (1964) (Warren, C.J., dissenting)....

But, it is argued there is no scientific data which conclusively demonstrates that exposure to obscene materials adversely affects men and women or their society. It is urged on behalf of the petitioner that, absent such a demonstration, any kind of state regulation is "impermissible." We reject this argument. It is not for us to resolve empirical uncertainties underlying state legislation, save in the exceptional case where that legislation plainly impinges upon rights protected by the Constitution itself.... Although there is no conclusive proof of a connection between antisocial behavior and obscene material, the legislature of Georgia could quite reasonably determine that such a connection does or might exist. In deciding *Roth*, this Court implicitly accepted that a legislature could legitimately act on such a conclusion to protect "the social interest in order and morality." *Roth v. United States* quoting *Chaplinsky v. New Hampshire* (1942) (emphasis added in *Roth*).

From the beginning of civilized societies, legislators and judges have acted on various unprovable assumptions. Such assumptions underlie much lawful state regulation of commercial and business affairs.... On the basis of these assumptions both Congress and state legislatures have, for example, drastically restricted associational rights by adopting antitrust laws, and have strictly regulated public expression by issuers of and dealers in securities, profit sharing "coupons," and "trading stamps," commanding what they must and may not publish and an- nounce.... Understandably those who entertain an absolutist view of the First Amendment find it uncomfortable to explain why rights of association, speech, and press should be severely restrained in the marketplace of goods and money, but not in the marketplace of pornography....

If we accept the unprovable assumption that a complete education requires certain books, see *Bd. of Education v. Allen* (1968).... and the well nigh universal belief that good books, plays, and art lift the spirit, improve the mind, enrich the human personality and develop character, can we then say that a state legislature may not act on the corollary assumption that commerce in obscene books, or public exhibitions focused on obscene conduct, have a tendency to exert a corruption and debasing impact leading to antisocial behavior?...

It is argued that individual "free will" must govern, even in activities beyond the protection of the First Amendment and other constitutional guarantees of privacy, and that government cannot legitimately impede an individual's desire to see or acquire obscene plays, movies, and books. We do indeed base our society on certain assumptions that people have the capacity for free choice. Most exercises of individual free choice – those in politics, religion, and expression of ideas – are explicitly protected by the Constitution. Totally unlimited play for free will, however, is not allowed in ours or any other society. We have just noted, for example, that neither the First Amendment nor "free will" precludes States from having "blue sky" laws to regulate what sellers of securities may write or publish about their wares. Such laws are to protect the weak, the uninformed, the unsuspecting, and the gullible from the exercise of their own volition. Nor do modern societies leave disposal of garbage and sewage up to the individual "free will," but impose regulation to protect both public health and the appearance of public places....

...This Court, has, on numerous occasions, refused to hold that commercial ventures such as a motion-picture house are "private" for the purpose of civil rights litigation and civil rights statutes....

Our prior decisions recognizing a right to privacy guaranteed by the Fourteenth Amendment included "only those personal rights that can be deemed 'fundamental' or 'implicit in the concept of ordered liberty.' *Palko v. Connecticut. Roe v. Wade* (1973). This privacy right encompasses and protects the personal intimacies of the home, the family, marriage, motherhood, procreation, and child rearing.... Nothing, however, in this Court's decisions intimates that there is any "fundamental" privacy right "implicit in the concept of ordered liberty" to watch obscene movies in places of public accommodation....

...The idea of a "privacy" right and a place of public accommodation are, in the context, mutually exclusive. Conduct or depictions of conduct that the state police power can prohibit on a public street does not become automatically protected by the Constitution merely because the conduct is moved to a bar or a "live" theatre state, any more than a "live" performance of a man and woman locked in a sexual embrace at high noon in Times Square is protected by the Constitution because they simultaneously engage in a valid political dialogue.

It is also argued that the State has no legitimate interest in "control [of] the moral content of a person's thoughts," *Stanley v. Georgia* (1969), and we need not quarrel with this. But we reject the claim that the state of Georgia is here attempting to control the minds or thoughts of those who patronize theatres. Preventing unlimited display or distribution of obscene material, which by definition lacks any serious literary, artistic, political, or scientific value as communication.... The fantasies of a drug addict are his own and beyond the reach of government, but government regulation of drug sales is not prohibited by the Constitution.... Finally, petitioners argue that conduct which directly involves "consenting adults" only has, for that sole reason, a special claim to constitutional protection. Our Constitution establishes a broad range of conditions on the exercise of power by the states, but for us to say that our Constitution incorporates the proposition that conduct involving consenting adults only is always beyond state regulations, that is a step we are unable to take. Commercial exploitation of depictions, descriptions, or exhibitions of obscene conduct on commercial premises open to the adult public falls within a State's broad power to regulate commerce and protect the public environment. The issue in this context goes beyond whether someone, or even the majority, considers the conduct depicted as "wrong" or "sinful." The States have the power to make a morally neutral judgment that public exhibition of obscene material, or commerce in such material, has a tendency to injure the community as a whole, to endanger the public safety, or to jeopardize, in Mr. Chief Justice Warren's words, the States' "right ... to maintain a decent society." *Jacobellis v. Ohio* (1964) (dissenting opinion).

Vacated and remanded for further proceedings.

MR. JUSTICE BRENNAN, with whom MR. JUSTICE STEWART and MR. JUSTICE MARSHALL joined, dissenting, said in part:

III

Our expression with the *Roth* approach has certainly taught us that the outright suppression of obscenity cannot be reconciled with the fundamental principles of the First and Fourteenth Amendments. For we have failed to formulate a standard that sharply distinguishes protected from unprotected speech, and out of necessity, we have resorted to the Redrup approach, which resolves cases as between the parties, but offers only the most obscure guidance to legislation, adjudication by other courts, and primary conduct. By disposing of cases through summary reversal or denial certiorari we have deliberately and effectively obscured the rationale underlying the decision. It comes as no surprise that judicial attempts to follow our lead conscientiously have often ended in hopeless confusion.

Of course, the vagueness problem would be largely of our own creation if it stemmed primarily from our failure to reach a consensus on any one standard. But after 15 years of experimentation and debate I am reluctantly forced to the conclusion that none of the available formulas, including the one announced today, can reduce the vagueness to a tolerable level while at the same time striking an acceptable balance between the protections of the First and Fourteenth Amendments, on the one hand, and on the other the asserted state interest in regulating the dissemination of certain sexually-oriented materials. Any effort to draw a constitutionally acceptable boundary on state power must resort to such indefinite concepts as "prurient interest," "patent offensiveness," "serious literary value," and the like. The meaning of these concepts necessarily varies with the experience, outlook, and even idiosyncrasies of the person defining them. Although we have assumed that obscenity does exist and that we "know it when [we] see it," *Jacobellis v. Ohio* (1964) (Stewart, J., concurring), we are manifestly unable to describe it in advance except by reference to concepts so elusive that they fail to distinguish clearly between protected and unprotected speech....

In addition to problems that arise when any criminal statute fails to afford fair notice of what it forbids, a vague statute in the areas of speech and press creates a second level of difficulty. We have indicated that "stricter standards of permissible statutory vagueness may be applied to a statute having a potentially inhibiting effect on speech; a man may the less be required to act at his peril here, because the free dissemination of ideas may be the loser." *Smith v. California* (1959). That proposition draws its strength from our recognition that "[t]he fundamental freedoms of speech and press have contributed greatly to the development and well-being of our free society and are indispensable to its continued growth. Easeless vigilance is the watchword to prevent their erosion by Congress or by the states. The door barring federal and state intrusion into this area cannot be left ajar...."

The problems of fair notice and chilling protected speech are very grave standing alone. But it does not detract from their importance to recognize that a vague statute in this area creates a third, although admittedly more subtle, set of problems. These problems concern the institutional stress that inevitably results where the line separating protected from unprotected speech is excessively vague. In *Roth* we conceded that "there may be marginal cases in which it is difficult to determine the side of the line on which a particular fact situation falls...." Our subsequent experience demonstrates that almost every case is "marginal." And since the "margin" marks the point of separation between protected and unprotected speech, we are left with a system in which almost every obscenity case presents a constitutional question of exceptional difficulty. "The suppression of a particular writing or other tangible form of expression is ... an individual matter, and in the nature of things every such suppression raises an individual constitutional problem, in which a reviewing court must determine for itself whether the attacked expression is suppressible within constitutional standards." *Roth* (separate opinion of Harlan, J.)....

...The problem is, rather, that one cannot say with certainty that material is obscene until at least five members of this Court, applying inevitably obscure standards, have pronounced it so. The number of obscenity cases on our docket gives ample testimony to the burden that has been placed upon this Court.

But the sheer *number* of the cases does not define the full extent of the institutional problem. For quite apart from the number of cases involved and the need to make a fresh constitutional determination in each case, we are tied to the "absurd business of perusing and viewing the miserable stuff that pours into the Court." ...While the material may have varying degrees of social importance, it is hardly a source of edification to the members of this Court who are compelled to view it before passing on its obscenity....

...In addition, the uncertainty of the standards creates a continuing source of tension between the state and federal courts, since the need for an independent determination by this Court seems to render superfluous even the most conscientious analysis by state tribunals. And our inability to justify our decisions with a persuasive rationale – or indeed, any rationale at all-necessarily creates the impression that we are merely second – guessing state court judges.

The severe problems arising from the lack of fair notice, from the chill on protected expression, and from the stress imposed on the state and federal judicial machinery persuade me that a significant change in direction is urgently required. I turn, therefore, to the alternatives that are now open...

IV

...Although the Court concedes that "*Roth* presumed 'obscenity' to be 'utterly without redeeming social value,'" it argues that *Memoirs* produced "a drastically altered test that called on the prosecution to prove a negative, i.e., that the material was 'utterly without redeeming social value' – a burden virtually impossible to discharge under our criminal standards of proof." One should hardly need to point out that under the third component of the Court's test the prosecution is still required to "prove a negative" – i.e., that the material lacks serious literary, artistic, political, or scientific value. Whether it will be easier to prove that material lacks "serious" value than to prove that it lacks any value at all remains, of course, to be seen.

In any case, even if the Court's approach left undamaged the conceptual framework for *Roth*, and even if it clearly barred the suppression of works with at least some social value, I would nevertheless be compelled to reject it. For it is beyond dispute that the approach can have no ameliorative impact on the cluster of problems that grow out of the vagueness of our current standards....

V

Our experience since *Roth* requires us not only to abandon the effort to pick out obscene materials on a case-by-case basis, but also to reconsider a fundamental postulate of *Roth*: that there exists a definable class of sexually oriented expression that may be totally suppressed by the Federal and State governments. Assuming that such a class of expression does in fact exist, I am forced to conclude that the concept of "obscenity" cannot be defined with sufficient specificity and clarity to provide fair notice to persons who create and distribute sexually oriented materials, to prevent substantial erosions of protected speech as a by-product of the attempt to suppress unprotected speech, and to avoid very costly institutional harms. Given these inevitable side-effects of state efforts to suppress what is assumed to be unprotected speech, we must scrutinize with care the state interest that is asserted to justify the suppression. For in the absence of some very substantial interest in suppressing such speech, we can hardly condone the ill-effects that seem to flow inevitably from the effort....

Because we assumed – incorrectly, as experience has proven – that obscenity could be separated from other sexually oriented expression without significant costs either to the First Amendment or to the judicial machinery charged with the task of safeguarding First Amendment freedoms, we had no occasion in *Roth* to probe the asserted state interest in curtailing unprotected, sexually oriented speech. Yet as we have increasingly come to appreciate the vagueness of the concept of obscenity, we have begun to recognize and articulate the state interests at stake. Significantly, in *Redrup v. New York* where we set aside findings of obscenity with regard to three sets of material, we pointed out that "[i]n none of the cases was there a claim that the statute in question reflected a specific and limited state concern for juveniles. See *Prince v. Massachusetts* [1944]; cf. *Butler v. Michigan* [1957]. In none was there any suggestion of an assault upon individual privacy by publication in a manner so obtrusive as to make it impossible for an unwilling individual to avoid exposure to it.... And in none was there evidence of the sort of 'pandering' which the Court found significant in *Ginzburg v. United States* [19661...."

The opinions in *Redrup* and *Stanley v. Georgia* reflected our emerging views that the state interest in protecting children and in protecting unconsenting adults may stand on a different footing from the other asserted state interests. It may well be, as one commentator has argued, that "exposure to [erotic material] is for some persons an intense emotional experience. A communication of this nature, imposed upon a person contrary to his wishes, has all the characteristics of a physical assault.... [And it] constitutes an invasion of his privacy...." But cf. *Cohen v. California* (1971). Similarly, if children are "not possessed of that full capacity for individual choice which is the presupposition of the First Amendment guarantees," *Ginsberg v. New York* (1968) (Stewart, J., concurring), then the State may have a substantial interest in precluding the flow of obscene materials even to consenting juveniles....

...I would hold, therefore, that at least in the absence of distribution to juveniles or obtrusive exposure to unconsenting adults, the First and Fourteenth Amendments prohibit the state and federal governments from attempting wholly to suppress sexually oriented materials on the basis of their allegedly "obscene" contents. Nothing in this approach precludes those governments from taking action to serve what may be strong and legitimate interests through regulation of the manner of distribution of sexually oriented material....

MR. JUSTICE DOUGLAS dissented, saying in part:

My Brother Brennan is to be commended for seeking a new path through the thicket which the Court entered when it undertook to sustain the constitutionality of obscenity laws and to place limits on their application. I have expressed on numerous occasions my disagreement with the basic decision that held that "obscenity" was not protected by the First Amendment. I disagreed also with the definitions that evolved. Art and literature reflect tastes; and tastes, like musical appreciation, are hardly reducible to precise definitions. That is one reason I have always felt that "obscenity" was not an exception to the First Amendment. For matters of taste, like matters of belief, turn on the idiosyncrasies of individuals. They are too personal to define and too emotional and vague to apply, as witness the prison term for Ralph Ginzburg, *Ginzburg v. United States*, 380 U.S. 463, not for what he printed but for the sexy manner in which he advertised his creations.

The other reason I could not bring myself to conclude that "obscenity" was not covered by the First Amendment was that prior to the adoption of our Constitution and Bill of Rights the Colonies had no law excluding "obscenity" from the regime of freedom of expression and press that then existed. I could find no such laws.

People are, of course, offended by many offerings made by merchants in this area. They are also offended by political pronouncements, sociological themes, and by stories of official misconduct. The list of activities and publications and pronouncements that offend someone is endless. Some of it goes in private; some of it is inescapably public, as when a government official generates crime, becomes a blatant offender of the moral sensibilities of the people, engages in burglary, or breaches the privacy of the telephone, the conference room, or the home. Life in this crowded modern technological world creates many offensive statements and many offensive deeds. There is no protection against offensive ideas, only against offensive conduct.

I am sure I would find offensive most of the books and movies charged with being obscene. But in a life that has not been short, I have yet to be trapped into seeing or reading something that would offend me. I never read or see the materials coming to the Court under charges of "obscenity," because I have thought the First Amendment made it unconstitutional for me to act as a censor. I see ads in bookstores and neon lights over theaters that resemble bait for those who seek vicarious exhilaration. As a parent or a priest or as a teacher I would have no compunction in edging my children or wards away from the books and movies that did no more than excite man's base instincts. But I never supposed that government was permitted to sit in judgment on one's tastes or beliefs – save as they involved action within the reach of the police power of government.

I applaud the effort of my Brother Brennan to forsake the low road which the Court has followed in this field. The new regime he would inaugurate is much closer than the old, to the policy of abstention which the First Amendment proclaims. But since we do not have here the unique series of problems raised by government-imposed or government-approved captive audiences, cf. *Public Utilities Comm'n v. Pollak,* 343 U.S. 451, I see no constitutional basis for fashioning a rule that makes a publisher, producer, bookseller, librarian, or movie house criminally responsible, when he fails to take affirmative steps to protect the consumer against literature or books offensive to those who temporarily occupy the seats of the mighty.

When man was first in the jungle he took care of himself. When he entered a societal group, controls were necessarily imposed. But our society – unlike most in the world – presupposes that freedom and liberty are in a frame of reference that makes the individual, not government, the keeper of his tastes, beliefs, and ideas. That is the philosophy of the First Amendment; and it is the article of faith that sets us apart from most nations in the world.

MR. JUSTICE BRENNAN, with whom MR. JUSTICES STEWART and MARSHALL joined, dissented.

RENO v. AMERICAN CIVIL LIBERTIES UNION
117 S.Ct. 2329 (1997)

The Communications Decency Act of 1996 (CDA) made it a crime to knowingly send "obscene or indecent" messages to any recipient under 18 years of age, and also prohibited sending or displaying to a person under 18 of any message "that, in context, depicts or describes, in terms patently offensive as measured by contemporary community standards, sexual or excretory activities or organs." The District Court issued a preliminary injunction against enforcement. The Government appealed to the Supreme Court on the grounds that the District Court erred in holding that the CDA violated both the First and Fifth Amendments

Justice STEVENS delivered the opinion of the Court.

...At issue is the constitutionality of two statutory provisions enacted to protect minors from "indecent" and "patently offensive" communications on the Internet. Notwithstanding the legitimacy and importance of the congressional goal of protecting children from harmful materials, we agree with the three-judge District Court that the statute abridges "the freedom of speech" protected by the First Amendment.

II

The Telecommunications Act of 1996... was an unusually important legislative enactment. As stated on the first of its 103 pages, its primary purpose was to reduce regulation and encourage "the rapid deployment of new telecommunications technologies."... The Act includes seven Titles, six of which are the product of extensive committee hearings and the subject of discussion in Reports prepared by Committees of the Senate and the House of Representatives. By contrast, Title V known as the "Communications Decency Act of 1996" (CDA)-contains provisions that were either added in executive committee after the hearings were concluded or as amendments offered during floor debate on the legislation. An amendment offered in the Senate was the source of the two statutory provisions challenged in this case. They are informally described as the "indecent transmission" provision and the "patently offensive display" provision.

The first, 47 U.S.C.A. §223(a) (Supp.1997), prohibits the knowing transmission of obscene or indecent messages to any recipient under 18 years of age....

The second provision, §223(d), prohibits the knowing sending or displaying of patently offensive messages in a manner that is available to a person under 18 years of age....

The breadth of these prohibitions is qualified by two affirmative defenses. See §223(e)(5). One covers those who take "good faith, reasonable, effective, and appropriate actions" to restrict access by minors to the prohibited communications. §223(e)(5)(A). The other covers those who restrict access to covered material by requiring certain designated forms of age proof, such as a verified credit card or an adult identification number or code. §223(e)(5)(B).

III

...The judgment of the District Court enjoins the Government from enforcing the prohibitions in §223(a)(1)(B) insofar as they relate to "indecent" communications, but expressly preserves the Government's right to investigate and prosecute the obscenity or child pornography activities prohibited therein. The injunction against enforcement of §§223(d)(1) and (2) is unqualified because those provisions contain no separate reference to obscenity or child pornography.

The Government appealed under the Act's special review provisions, § 561, 110 Stat. 142-143, and we noted probable jurisdiction.... In its appeal, the Government argues that the District Court erred in holding that the CDA violated both the First Amendment because it is overbroad and the Fifth Amendment because it is vague. While we discuss the vagueness of the CDA because of its relevance to the First Amendment overbreadth inquiry, we conclude that the judgment should be affirmed without reaching the Fifth Amendment issue. We begin our analysis by reviewing the principal authorities on which the Government relies. Then, after describing the overbreadth of the CDA, we consider the Government's specific contentions, including its submission that we save portions of the statute either by severance or by fashioning judicial limitations on the scope of its coverage.

IV

In arguing for reversal, the Government contends that the CDA is plainly constitutional under three of our prior decisions: (1) *Ginsberg v. New York...* (1968); (2) *FCC v. Pacifica Foundation...* (1978); and (3) *Renton v. Playtime Theatres, Inc....* (1986). A close look at these cases, however, raises rather than relieves doubts concerning the constitutionality of the CDA.

In *Ginsberg*, we upheld the constitutionality of a New York statute that prohibited selling to minors under 17 years of age material that was considered obscene as to them even if not obscene as to adults. We rejected the defendant's broad submission that "the scope of the constitutional freedom of expression secured to a citizen to read or see material concerned with sex cannot be made to depend on whether the citizen is an adult or a minor."... In rejecting that contention, we relied not only on the State's independent interest in the well-being of its youth, but also on our consistent recognition of the principle that "the parents' claim to authority in their own household to direct the rearing of their children is basic in the structure of our society."

In four important respects, the statute upheld in *Ginsberg* was narrower than the CDA. First, we noted in *Ginsberg* that "the prohibition against sales to minors does not bar parents who so desire from purchasing the magazines for their children...." Under the CDA, by contrast, neither the parents' consent nor even their participation in the communication would avoid the application of the statute. Second, the New York statute applied only to commercial transactions,... whereas the CDA contains no such limitation. Third, the New York statute cabined its definition of material that is harmful to minors with the requirement that it be "utterly without redeeming social importance for minors."... The CDA fails to provide us with any definition of the term "indecent" as used in §223(a)(1) and, importantly, omits any requirement that the "patently offensive" material covered by §223(d) lack serious literary, artistic, political, or scientific value. Fourth, the New York statute defined a minor as a person under the age of 17, whereas the CDA, in applying to all those under 18 years, includes an additional year of those nearest majority.

In *Pacifica,* we upheld a declaratory order of the Federal Communications Commission, holding that the broadcast of a recording of a 12-minute monologue entitled "Filthy Words" that had previously been delivered to a live audience "could have been the subject of administrative sanctions."... The Commission had found that the repetitive use of certain words referring to excretory or sexual activities or organs "in an afternoon broadcast when children are in the audience was patently offensive" and concluded that the monologue was indecent "as broadcast."... The respondent did not quarrel with the finding that the afternoon broadcast was patently offensive, but contended that it was not "indecent" within the meaning of the relevant statutes because it contained no prurient appeal. After rejecting respondent's statutory arguments, we confronted its two constitutional arguments: (1) that the Commission's construction of its authority to ban indecent speech was so broad that its order had to be set aside even if the broadcast at issue was unprotected; and (2) that since the recording was not obscene, the First Amendment forbade any abridgment of the right to broadcast it on the radio.

In the portion of the lead opinion not joined by Justices Powell and Blackmun, the plurality stated that the First Amendment does not prohibit all governmental regulation that depends on the content of speech.... Accordingly, the availability of constitutional protection for a vulgar and offensive monologue that was not obscene depended on the context of the broadcast.... Relying on the premise that "of all forms of communication" broadcasting had received the most limited First Amendment protection,... the Court concluded that the ease with which children may obtain access to broadcasts, "coupled with the concerns recognized in *Ginsberg,*" justified special treatment of indecent broadcasting....

As with the New York statute at issue in *Ginsberg,* there are significant differences between the order upheld in *Pacifica* and the CDA. First, the order in *Pacifica*, issued by an agency that had been regulating radio stations for decades, targeted a specific broadcast that represented a rather dramatic departure from traditional program content in order to designate when rather than whether it would be permissible to air such a program in that particular medium. The CDA's broad categorical prohibitions are not limited to particular times and are not dependent on any evaluation by an agency familiar with the unique characteristics of the Internet. Second, unlike the CDA, the Commission's declaratory order was not punitive; we expressly refused to decide whether the indecent broadcast "would justify a criminal prosecution."... Finally, the Commission's order applied to a medium which as a matter of history had "received the most limited First Amendment protection," ... in large part because warnings could not adequately protect the listener from unexpected program content. The Internet, however, has no comparable history. Moreover, the District Court found that the risk of encountering indecent material by accident is remote because a series of affirmative steps is required to access specific material.

In *Renton*, we upheld a zoning ordinance that kept adult movie theatres out of residential neighborhoods. The ordinance was aimed, not at the content of the films shown in the theaters, but rather at the " secondary effects" such as crime and deteriorating property values that these theaters fostered: "It is th[e] secondary effect which these zoning ordinances attempt to avoid, not the dissemination of 'offensive' speech...." According to the Government, the CDA is constitutional because it constitutes a sort of "cyberzoning" on the Internet. But the CDA applies broadly to the entire universe of cyberspace. And the purpose of the CDA is to protect children from the primary effects of "indecent" and "patently offensive" speech, rather than any "secondary" effect of such speech. Thus, the CDA is a content-based blanket restriction on speech, and, as such, cannot be "properly analyzed as a form of time, place, and manner regulation."...

These precedents, then, surely do not require us to uphold the CDA and are fully consistent with the application of the most stringent review of its provisions....

VI

Regardless of whether the CDA is so vague that it violates the Fifth Amendment, the many ambiguities concerning the scope of its coverage render it problematic for purposes of the First Amendment. For instance, each of the two parts of the CDA uses a different linguistic form. The first uses the word "indecent," 47 U.S.C.A. §223(a) (Supp.1997), while the second speaks of material that "in context, depicts or describes, in terms patently offensive as measured by contemporary community standards, sexual or excretory activities or organs," §223(d). Given the absence of a definition of either term, this difference in language will provoke uncertainty among speakers about how the two standards relate to each other and just what they mean. Could a speaker confidently assume that a serious discussion about birth control practices, homosexuality, the First Amendment issues raised by the Appendix to our *Pacifica* opinion, or the consequences of prison rape would not violate the CDA? This uncertainty undermines the likelihood that the CDA has been carefully tailored to the congressional goal of protecting minors from potentially harmful materials.

The vagueness of the CDA is a matter of special concern for two reasons. First, the CDA is a content-based regulation of speech. The vagueness of such a regulation raises special First Amendment concerns because of its obvious chilling effect on free speech.... Second, the CDA is a criminal statute. In addition to the opprobrium and stigma of a criminal conviction, the CDA threatens violators with penalties including up to two years in prison for each act of violation. The severity of criminal sanctions may well cause speakers to remain silent rather than communicate even arguably unlawful words, ideas, and images.... As a practical matter, this increased deterrent effect, coupled with the "risk of discriminatory enforcement" of vague regulations, poses greater First

Amendment concerns than those implicated by the civil regulation reviewed in *Denver Area Ed. Telecommunications Consortium, Inc. v. FCC*... (1996).

The Government argues that the statute is no more vague than the obscenity standard this Court established in *Miller v. California*... (1973). But that is not so. In *Miller*, this Court reviewed a criminal conviction against a commercial vendor who mailed brochures containing pictures of sexually explicit activities to individuals who had not requested such materials.... Having struggled for some time to establish a definition of obscenity, we set forth in *Miller* the test for obscenity that controls to this day:

" (a) whether the average person, applying contemporary community standards would find that the work, taken as a whole, appeals to the prurient interest; (b) whether the work depicts or describes, in a patently offensive way, sexual conduct specifically defined by the applicable state law; and (c) whether the work, taken as a whole, lacks serious literary, artistic, political, or scientific value."...

Because the CDA's "patently offensive" standard (and, we assume *arguendo*, its synonymous "indecent" standard) is one part of the three-prong *Miller* test, the Government reasons, it cannot be unconstitutionally vague.

The Government's assertion is incorrect as a matter of fact. The second prong of the *Miller* test the purportedly analogous standard contains a critical requirement that is omitted from the CDA: that the proscribed material be "specifically defined by the applicable state law." This requirement reduces the vagueness inherent in the open-ended term "patently offensive" as used in the CDA. Moreover, the *Miller* definition is limited to "sexual conduct," whereas the CDA extends also to include (1) "excretory activities" as well as (2) "organs" of both a sexual and excretory nature.

The Government's reasoning is also flawed. Just because a definition including three limitations is not vague, it does not follow that one of those limitations, standing by itself, is not vague. Each of *Miller's* additional two prongs (1) that, taken as a whole, the material appeal to the "prurient" interest, and (2) that it "lac[k] serious literary, artistic, political, or scientific value" critically limits the uncertain sweep of the obscenity definition. The second requirement is particularly important because, unlike the "patently offensive" and "prurient interest" criteria, it is not judged by contemporary community standards.... This "societal value" requirement, absent in the CDA, allows appellate courts to impose some limitations and regularity on the definition by setting, as a matter of law, a national floor for socially redeeming value. The Government's contention that courts will be able to give such legal limitations to the CDA's standards is belied by *Miller's* own rationale for having juries determine whether material is "patently offensive" according to community standards: that such questions are essentially ones of fact.

In contrast to *Miller* and our other previous cases, the CDA thus presents a greater threat of censoring speech that, in fact, falls outside the statute's scope.

Given the vague contours of the coverage of the statute, it unquestionably silences some speakers whose messages would be entitled to constitutional protection. That danger provides further reason for insisting that the statute not be overly broad. The CDA's burden on protected speech cannot be justified if it could be avoided by a more carefully drafted statute.

VII

We are persuaded that the CDA lacks the precision that the First Amendment requires when a statute regulates the content of speech. In order to deny minors access to potentially harmful speech, the CDA effectively suppresses a large amount of speech that adults have a constitutional right to receive and to address to one another. That burden on adult speech is unacceptable if less restrictive alternatives would be at least as effective in achieving the legitimate purpose that the statute was enacted to serve.

In evaluating the free speech rights of adults, we have made it perfectly clear that "[s]exual expression which is indecent but not obscene is protected by the First Amendment...."

It is true that we have repeatedly recognized the governmental interest in protecting children from harmful materials.... But that interest does not justify an unnecessarily broad suppression of speech addressed to adults. As we have explained, the Government may not "reduc[e] the adult population ... to ... only what is fit for children...." "[R]egardless of the strength of the government's interest" in protecting children, " [t]he level of discourse reaching a mailbox simply cannot be limited to that which would be suitable for a sandbox."...

The District Court was correct to conclude that the CDA effectively resembles the ban on "dial-a-porn" invalidated in *Sable*.... In *Sable*,... this Court rejected the argument that we should defer to the congressional judgment that nothing less than a total ban would be effective in preventing enterprising youngsters from gaining access to indecent communications. *Sable* thus made clear that the mere fact that a statutory regulation of speech was enacted for the important purpose of protecting children from exposure to sexually explicit material does not foreclose inquiry into its validity. As we pointed out last Term, that inquiry embodies an "over-arching commitment" to make sure that Congress has designed its statute to accomplish its purpose "without imposing an unnecessarily great restriction on speech."...

In arguing that the CDA does not so diminish adult communication, the Government relies on the incorrect factual premise that prohibiting a transmission whenever it is known that one of its recipients is a minor would not interfere with adult-to-adult communication. The findings of the District Court make clear that this premise is untenable. Given the size of the potential audience for most messages, in the absence of a viable age verification process, the sender must be charged with knowing that one or more minors will likely view it. Knowledge that, for instance, one or more members of a 100-person chat group will be minor and therefore that it would be a crime to send the group an indecent message would surely burden communication among adults.

The District Court found that at the time of trial existing technology did not include any effective method for a sender to prevent minors from obtaining access to its communications on the Internet without also denying access to adults. The Court found no effective way to determine the age of a user who is accessing material through e-mail, mail exploders, newsgroups, or chat rooms.... As a practical matter, the Court also found that it would be prohibitively expensive for noncommercial as well as some commercial speakers who have Web sites to verify that their users are adults.... These limitations must inevitably curtail a significant amount of adult communication on the Internet. By contrast, the District Court found that "[d]espite its limitations, currently available user-based software suggests that a reasonably effective method by which parents can prevent their children from accessing sexually explicit and other material which parents may believe is inappropriate for their children will soon be widely available."...

The breadth of the CDA's coverage is wholly unprecedented. Unlike the regulations upheld in *Ginsberg* and *Pacifica,* the scope of the CDA is not limited to commercial speech or commercial entities. Its open-ended prohibitions embrace all nonprofit entities and individuals posting indecent messages or displaying them on their own computers in the presence of minors. The general, undefined terms "indecent" and "patently offensive" cover large amounts of nonpornographic material with serious educational or other value. Moreover, the "community standards" criterion as applied to the Internet means that any communication available to a nation-wide audience will be judged by the standards of the community most likely to be offended by the message. The regulated subject matter includes any of the seven "dirty words" used in the *Pacifica* monologue, the use of which the Government's expert acknowledged could constitute a felony. ... It may also extend to discussions about prison rape or safe sexual practices, artistic images that include nude subjects, and arguably the card catalogue of the Carnegie Library.

For the purposes of our decision, we need neither accept nor reject the Government's submission that the First Amendment does not forbid a blanket prohibition on all "indecent" and "patently offensive" messages communicated to a 17-year old no matter how much value the message may contain and regardless of parental approval. It is at least clear that the strength of the Government's interest in protecting minors is not equally strong throughout the coverage of this broad statute. Under the CDA, a parent allowing her 17-year-old to use the family computer to obtain information on the Internet that she, in her parental judgment, deems appropriate could face a lengthy prison term.... Similarly, a parent who sent his 17-year-old college freshman information on birth control via e-mail could be incarcerated even though neither he, his child, nor anyone in their home community, found the material "indecent" or "patently offensive," if the college town's community thought otherwise.

The breadth of this content-based restriction of speech imposes an especially heavy burden on the Government to explain why a less restrictive provision would not be as effective as the CDA. It has not done so. The arguments in this Court have referred to possible alternatives such as requiring that indecent material be "tagged" in a way that facilitates parental control of material coming into their homes, making exceptions for messages with artistic or educational value, providing some tolerance for parental choice, and regulating some portions of the Internet such as commercial web sites differently than others, such as chat rooms. Particularly in the light of the absence of any detailed findings by the Congress, or even hearings addressing the special problems of the CDA, we are persuaded that the CDA is not narrowly tailored if that requirement has any meaning at all.

VIII

In an attempt to curtail the CDA's facial overbreadth, the Government advances three additional arguments for sustaining the Act's affirmative prohibitions: (1) that the CDA is constitutional because it leaves open ample "alternative channels" of communication; (2) that the plain meaning of the Act's "knowledge" and "specific person" requirement significantly restricts its permissible applications; and (3) that the Act's prohibitions are "almost always" limited to material lacking redeeming social value.

The Government first contends that, even though the CDA effectively censors discourse on many of the Internet's modalities such as chat groups, newsgroups, and mail exploders it is nonetheless constitutional because it provides a "reasonable opportunity" for speakers to engage in the restricted speech on the World Wide Web.... This argument is unpersuasive because the CDA regulates speech on the basis of its content. A "time, place, and manner" analysis is therefore inapplicable.... It is thus immaterial whether such speech would be feasible on the Web (which, as the Government's own expert acknowledged, would cost up to $10,000 if the speaker's interests were not accommodated by an existing Web site, not including costs for database management and age verification). The Government's position is equivalent to arguing that a statute could ban leaflets on certain subjects as long as individuals are free to publish books. In invalidating a number of laws that banned leafletting on the streets regardless of their content we explained that "one is not to have the exercise of his liberty of expression in appropriate places abridged on the plea that it may be exercised in some other place."...

The Government also asserts that the "knowledge" requirement of both §§223(a) and (d), especially when coupled with the "specific child" element found in §223(d), saves the CDA from overbreadth. Because both sections prohibit the dissemination of indecent messages only to persons known to be under 18, the Government argues, it does not require transmitters to "refrain from communicating indecent material to adults; they need only refrain from disseminating such materials to persons they know to be under 18."...

This argument ignores the fact that most Internet fora including chat rooms, newsgroups, mail exploders, and the Web are open to all comers. The Government's assertion that the knowledge requirement somehow protects the communications of adults is therefore untenable. Even the strongest reading of the "specific person" requirement of §223(d) cannot save the statute. It would confer broad powers of censorship, in the form of a "heckler's veto," upon any opponent of indecent speech who might simply log on and inform the would-be discoursers that his 17-year-old child a "specific person ... under 18 years of age," 47 U.S.C.A. §223(d)(1)(A) (Supp.1997) would be present.

Finally, we find no textual support for the Government's submission that material having scientific, educational, or other redeeming social value will necessarily fall outside the CDA's "patently offensive" and " indecent" prohibitions.

IX

The Government's three remaining arguments focus on the defenses provided in §223(e)(5). First, relying on the "good faith, reasonable, effective, and appropriate actions" provision, the Government suggests that "tagging" provides a defense that saves the constitutionality of the Act. The suggestion assumes that transmitters may encode their indecent communications in a way that would indicate their contents, thus permitting recipients to block their reception with appropriate software. It is the requirement that the good faith action must be "effective" that makes this defense illusory. The Government recognizes that its proposed screening software does not currently exist. Even if it did, there is no way to know whether a potential recipient will actually block the encoded material. Without the impossible knowledge that every guardian in America is screening for the "tag," the transmitter could not reasonably rely on its action to be "effective."

For its second and third arguments concerning defenses which we can consider together the Government relies on the latter half of §223(e)(5), which applies when the transmitter has restricted access by requiring use of a verified credit card or adult identification. Such verification is not only technologically available but actually is used by commercial providers of sexually explicit material. These providers, therefore, would be protected by the defense. Under the findings of the District Court, however, it is not economically feasible for most noncommercial speakers to employ such verification. Accordingly, this defense would not significantly narrow the statute's burden on noncommercial speech. Even with respect to the commercial pornographers that would be protected by the defense, the Government failed to adduce any evidence that these verification techniques actually preclude minors from posing as adults. Given that the risk of criminal sanctions "hovers over each content provider, like the proverbial sword of Damocles," the District Court correctly refused to rely on unproven future technology to save the statute. The Government thus failed to prove that the proffered defense would significantly reduce the heavy burden on adult speech produced by the prohibition on offensive displays.

We agree with the District Court's conclusion that the CDA places an unacceptably heavy burden on protected speech, and that the defenses do not constitute the sort of "narrow tailoring" that will save an otherwise patently invalid unconstitutional provision. In *Sable*, we remarked that the speech restriction at issue there amounted to "'burn[ing] the house to roast the pig.'" The

CDA, casting a far darker shadow over free speech, threatens to torch a large segment of the Internet community.

X

At oral argument, the Government relied heavily on its ultimate fall-back position: If this Court should conclude that the CDA is insufficiently tailored, it urged, we should save the statute's constitutionality by honoring the severability clause,... and construing nonseverable terms narrowly. In only one respect is this argument acceptable.

A severability clause requires textual provisions that can be severed. We will follow §608's guidance by leaving constitutional textual elements of the statute intact in the one place where they are, in fact, severable. The "indecency" provision, 47 U.S.C.A. §223(a) (Supp.1997), applies to "any comment, request, suggestion, proposal, image, or other communication which is *obscene or indecent.* " (Emphasis added.) Appellees do not challenge the application of the statute to obscene speech, which, they acknowledge, can be banned totally because it enjoys no First Amendment protection.... As set forth by the statute, the restriction of "obscene" material enjoys a textual manifestation separate from that for "indecent" material, which we have held unconstitutional. Therefore, we will sever the term "or indecent" from the statute, leaving the rest of §223(a) standing. In no other respect, however, can §223(a) or §223(d) be saved by such a textual surgery.

The Government also draws on an additional, less traditional aspect of the CDA's severability clause, 47 U.S.C., §608, which asks any reviewing court that holds the statute facially unconstitutional not to invalidate the CDA in application to "other persons or circumstances" that might be constitutionally permissible. It further invokes this Court's admonition that, absent "countervailing considerations," a statute should "be declared invalid to the extent it reaches too far, but otherwise left intact."... There are two flaws in this argument.

First, the statute that grants our jurisdiction for this expedited review, 47 U.S.C.A. §561 (Supp.1997), limits that jurisdictional grant to actions challenging the CDA "on its face." Consistent with §561, the plaintiffs who brought this suit and the three-judge panel that decided it treated it as a facial challenge. We have no authority, in this particular posture, to convert this litigation into an "as-applied" challenge. Nor, given the vast array of plaintiffs, the range of their expressive activities, and the vagueness of the statute, would it be practicable to limit our holding to a judicially defined set of specific applications.

Second, one of the "countervailing considerations" mentioned in *Brockett* is present here. In considering a facial challenge, this Court may impose a limiting construction on a statute only if it is "readily susceptible" to such a construction.... The open-ended character of the CDA provides no guidance what ever for limiting its coverage.

This case is therefore unlike those in which we have construed a statute narrowly because the text or other source of congressional intent identified a clear line that this Court could draw.... Rather, our decision in *United States v. National Treasury Employees Union*...(1995), is applicable. In that case, we declined to "dra[w] one or more lines between categories of speech covered by an overly broad statute, when Congress has sent inconsistent signals as to where the new line or lines should be drawn" because doing so "involves a far more serious invasion of the legislative domain." This Court "will not rewrite a ... law to conform it to constitutional requirements...."

XI

In this Court, though not in the District Court, the Government asserts that in addition to its interest in protecting children its "[e]qually significant" interest in fostering the growth of the Internet provides an independent basis for upholding the constitutionality of the CDA.... The Government apparently assumes that the unregulated availability of "indecent" and "patently offensive" material on the Internet is driving countless citizens away from the medium because of the risk of exposing themselves or their children to harmful material.

We find this argument singularly unpersuasive. The dramatic expansion of this new marketplace of ideas contradicts the factual basis of this contention. The record demonstrates that the growth of the Internet has been and continues to be phenomenal. As a matter of constitutional tradition, in the absence of evidence to the contrary, we presume that governmental regulation of the content of speech is more likely to interfere with the free exchange of ideas than to encourage it. The interest in encouraging freedom of expression in a democratic society outweighs any theoretical but unproven benefit of censorship.

For the foregoing reasons, the judgment of the district court is affirmed....

Justice O'CONNOR, with whom THE CHIEF JUSTICE joins, concurring in the judgment in part and dissenting in part....

NEAR v. MINNESOTA
283 U.S. 697; 51 S.Ct. 625; 75 L.Ed. 1357 (1931)

In what amounted to an attempt to impose censorship in the form of a prior or previous restraint, the Minnesota legislature had enacted a law in 1925 prohibiting the publication of any "malicious, scandalous and defamatory newspaper, magazine or periodical." The Saturday Press, *published by Near, lashed out at numerous elected officials in highly anti-Semitic overtones. The responsible official sought to enjoin publication and the trial court granted the motion. The state court of last resort upheld the conviction and the publisher appealed to the Supreme Court.*

MR. CHIEF JUSTICE HUGHES delivered the opinion of the Court....

...The statute, for the suppression as a public nuisance of a newspaper or periodical, is unusual, if not unique, and raises questions of grave importance transcending the local interests involved in the particular action. It is no longer open to doubt that the liberty of the press and of speech is within the liberty safeguarded by the due process clause of the Fourteenth Amendment from invasion by state action. It was found impossible to conclude that this essential personal liberty of the citizen was left unprotected by the general guarantee of fundamental rights of person and property.... Liberty, in each of its phases, has its history and connotation and, in the present instance, the inquiry is as to the historic conception of the liberty of the press and whether the statute under review violates the essential attributes of that liberty....

First. The statute is not aimed at the redress of individual or private wrongs. Remedies for libel remain available and unaffected. The statute, said the state court, "is not directed at threatened libel but at an existing business which, generally speaking, involves more than libel." It is aimed at the distribution of scandalous matter as "detrimental to public morals and to the general welfare," tending "to disturb the peace of the community" and "to provoke assaults and commission of crime." In order to obtain an injunction to suppress the future publication of the newspaper or periodical, it is not necessary to prove the falsity of the charges that have been made in the publication condemned. In the present action there was no allegation that the matter published was not true. It is alleged, and the statute requires the allegation that the publication was "malicious." But, as in prosecutions for libel, there is no requirement of proof by the state of malice in fact as distinguished from malice inferred from the mere publication of the defamatory matter. The judgment in this case proceeded upon the mere proof of publication. The statute permits the defense, not of the truth alone, but only that the truth was published with good motives and for justifiable ends....

...Second. The statute is directed not simply at the circulation of scandalous and defamatory statements with regard to private citizens, but at the continued publication by newspapers and periodicals of charges against public officers of corruption, malfeasance in office, or serious neglect of duty. Such charges by their very nature create a public scandal.

...Third. The object of the statute is not punishment, in the ordinary sense, but suppression of the offending newspaper or periodical. The reason for the enactment, as the state court has said, is that prosecutions to enforce penal statutes for libel do not result in "efficient repression or suppression of the evils of scandal." Describing the business of publication as a public nuisance does not obscure the substance of the proceeding which the statute authorizes. It is the continued publication of scandalous and defamatory matter that constitutes the business and the declared nuisance. In the case of public officers, it is the reiteration of charges of official misconduct, and the fact that the newspaper or periodical is principally devoted to that purpose, that exposes it to suppression. In the present instance, the proof was that nine editions of the newspaper or periodical in question were published on successive dates, and that they were chiefly devoted to charges against public officers and in relation to the prevalence and protection of crime. In such a case, these officers are not left to their ordinary remedy in a suit for libel, or the authorities to a prosecution for criminal libel.

...This suppression is accomplished by enjoining publication, and that restraint is the object and effect of the statute.

Fourth. The statute not only operates to suppress the offending newspaper or periodical, but to put the publisher under an effective censorship....

If we cut through mere details of procedure, the operation and effect of the statute in substance is that public authorities may bring the owner or publisher of a newspaper or periodical before a judge upon a charge of conducting a business of publishing scandalous and defamatory matter – in particular that the matter consists of charges against public officers of official dereliction – and, unless the owner or publisher is able and disposed to bring competent evidence to satisfy the judge that the charges are true and are published with good motives and for justifiable ends, his newspaper or periodical is suppressed and further publication is made punishable as a contempt. This is of the essence of censorship. .

Equally unavailing is the insistence that the statute is designed to prevent the circulation of scandal which tends to disturb the public peace and to provoke assaults and the commission of crime. Charges of reprehensible conduct, and in particular of official malfeasance, unquestionably create a public scandal, but the theory of the constitutional guaranty is that even a more serious public evil would be caused by authority to prevent publication. "To prohibit the intent to excite those unfavorable sentiments against those who administer the Government, is. excitement of them; and to prohibit the actual excitement of them is equivalent to a prohibition of discussions having that tendency and effect; which, again, is equivalent to a protection of those who administer the Government, if they should at any time deserve the contempt or hatred of the people, against being exposed to it by free animadversions on their characters and conduct." There is nothing new in the fact that charges of reprehensible conduct may create resentment and the disposition to resort to violent means of redress, but this well-understood tendency did not alter the determination to protect the press against censorship and restraint upon publication....

Judgment reversed.

MR. JUSTICE BUTLER, joined by JUSTICES VAN DEVANTER, MC REYNOLDS, and SUTHERLAND, dissented.

LLOYD CORPORATION v. TANNER
407 U.S. 551 (1972)

Lloyd Center is a large modern shopping center in Portland, Oregon. Its principal shopping area is located in the "Mall," which is an enclosed multilevel complex of retail shops with no public streets although some stores face sidewalks and streets on the perimeter. In the fall of 1968, Donald Tanner and others entered the Mall and distributed handbills protesting the draft and the Vietnam War. The actions of the group were peaceful, nondisruptive and litter free. However, security guards employed by the Center informed the protesters that the corporation did not permit handbilling and warned them that if they continued they would be subject to arrest. The group departed but brought action for a declaratory judgment claiming that they had the right to so distribute handbills on private property when put to a public use. This decision cut deep into the hitherto broad protection afforded such activity in earlier cases, most notably the

Warren Court's decision in Amalgamated Food Employees v. Logan Valley Plaza *(1967).*

MR. JUSTICE POWELL delivered the opinion of the Court.

Although the stores close at customary hours, the malls are not physically closed, as pedestrian window shopping is encouraged within reasonable hours. Lloyd employs 12 security guards who are commissioned as such by the city of Portland. The guards have police authority within the Center, wear uniforms similar to those worn by city police, and are licensed to carry handguns. They are employed by and subject to the control of Lloyd. Their duties are the customary ones, including shoplifting surveillance and general security.

At a few places within the Center, small signs are embedded in the sidewalk, which state:

> "NOTICE – Areas In Lloyd Center Used By The Public Are Not Public Ways But Are For The Use Of Lloyd Center Tenants And The Public Transacting Business With Them. Permission To Use Said Areas May Be Revoked At Any Time. Lloyd Corporation, Ltd."

The Center is open generally to the public, with a considerable effort being made to attract shoppers and prospective shoppers, and to create "customer motivation" as well as customer good will in the community. In this respect the Center pursues policies comparable to those of major stores and shopping centers across the country, although the Center affords superior facilities for these purposes. Groups and organizations are permitted, by invitation and advance arrangement, to use the auditorium and other facilities. Rent is charged for the use of the auditorium except with respect to certain civic and charitable organizations, such as the Cancer Society, Boy and Girl Scouts. The Center also allows limited use of the malls by the American Legion to sell "Buddy Poppies" for disabled veterans, and by the Salvation Army and Volunteers of America to solicit Christmas contributions. It has denied similar use to other civic and charitable organizations. Political use is also forbidden, except that presidential candidates of both parties have been allowed to speak in the auditorium.

In *Logan Valley*, the Court extended the rationale of *Marsh* to peaceful picketing of a store located in a large shopping center, known as Logan Valley Mall, near Altoona, Pennsylvania. Weis Markets, Inc., an original tenant, had opened a supermarket in one of the larger stores and was employing a wholly nonunion staff. Within 10 days after Weis opened, members of the Amalgamated Food Employees Union Local 590 began picketing Weis, carrying signs stating that it was a nonunion market and that its employees were not receiving union wages or other union benefits. The picketing, conducted by nonemployees, was carried out almost entirely in the parcel pickup area immediately adjacent to the store and on portions of the adjoining parking lot. The picketing was peaceful, with the number of pickets varying from four to 13.

Weis and Logan Valley Plaza, Inc., sought and obtained an injunction against this picketing. The injunction required that all picketing be confined to public areas outside the shopping center. On appeal the Pennsylvania Supreme Court affirmed the issuance of the injunction, and this Court granted certiorari. In framing the question, this Court stated:

> "The case squarely presents...the question whether Pennsylvania's generally valid rules against trespass to private property can be applied in these circumstances to bar petitioners from the Weis and Logan premises." 392 U.S., at 315.

The Court noted that the answer would be clear "if the shopping center premises were not privately owned but instead constituted the business area of a municipality." In the latter situation, it has often been held that publicly owned streets, sidewalks and parks are so historically associated with the exercise of First Amendment rights that access to them for purposes of exercising such rights cannot be denied absolutely. *Lovell. v. Griffin*, 303 U.S. 444 (1938); *Hague v. CIO*, 307 U.S. 496 (1939); *Schnieder v. State,* 308 U.S. 147 (1939); *Jamison v. Texas, 318 U.S. 413 (1943).*

But the Court was careful not to go further and say that for all purposes and uses the privately owned streets, sidewalks and other areas of a shopping center are analogous to publicly owned facilities:

> "All we decide here is that because the shopping center serves as the community business block 'and is freely accessible and open to the people in the area and those passing through, *Marsh v. Alabama*, 326 U.S., at 508, the State may not delegate the power, through the use of its trespass laws, wholly to exclude those members of the public wishing to exercise their First Amendment rights on the premises in a manner and for a purpose generally consonant with the use to which the property is actually put."

The Court noted that the scope of its holding was limited, and expressly reserved judgment on the type of issue presented in this case:

> "The picketing carried on by petitioners was directed specifically at patrons of the Weis Market located within the shopping center and the message sought to be conveyed to the public concerned the manner in which that particular market was being operated. We are, therefore, not called upon to consider whether respondents' property rights could, consistently with the First Amendment, justify a bar on picketing which was not thus directly related in its purpose to the use to which the shopping center property was being put."

The Court also took specific note of the facts that the Union's picketing was "directed solely at one establishment within the shopping center," and that the public berms and sidewalks were "from 350 to 500 feet away from the Weis store." This distance made it difficult "to communicate [with] patrons of Weis" and "to limit [the] effect [of the picketing] to Weis only." *Logan Valley* was decided on the basis of this factual situation, and the facts in this case are significantly different.

II

The courts below considered the critical inquiry to be whether Lloyd Center was "the functional equivalent of a public business district." This phrase was first used in *Logan Valley*, but its genesis was in *Marsh*. It is well to consider what *Marsh* actually decided.

The Court simply held that where private interests were substituting for and performing the customary functions of government, First Amendment freedoms could not be denied where exercised in the customary manner on the town's sidewalks and streets. Indeed, as title to the entire town was held privately, there were no publicly owned streets, sidewalks or parks where such rights could be exercised.

Logan Valley extended *Marsh* to a shopping center situation in a different context from the company town setting, but it did so only in a context where the First Amendment activity was related to the shopping center's operations.

The holding in *Logan Valley* was not dependent upon the suggestion that the privately owned streets and sidewalks of a business district or a shopping center are the equivalent, for First Amendment purposes, of municipally owned streets and sidewalks. No such expansive reading of the opinion for the Court is necessary or appropriate. The opinion was carefully phrased to limit its holding to the picketing involved, where the picketing was "directly related in its purpose to the use to which the shopping center property was being put," and where the store was located in the center of a large private enclave with the consequence that no other reasonable opportunities for the pickets to convey their message to their intended audience were available. Neither of these elements is present in the case now before the Court.

A

The handbilling by respondents in the malls of Lloyd Center had no relation to any purpose for which the center was built and being used. It is nevertheless argued by respondents that since the Center is open to the public the private owner cannot enforce a restriction against handbilling on the premises. The thrust of this argument is considerably broader than the rationale of *Logan Valley*. It requires no relationship, direct or indirect, between the purpose of the expressive activity and the business of the shopping center. The message sought to be conveyed by respondents was directed to all members of the public, not solely to patrons of Lloyd Center or of any of its operations. Respondents could have distributed these handbills on any public street, on any public sidewalk, in any public park, or in any public building in the city of Portland.

Respondents' argument, even if otherwise meritorious, misapprehends the scope of the invitation extended to the public. The invitation is to come to the Center to do business with the tenants. It is true that facilities at the Center are used for certain meetings and for various promotional activities. The obvious purpose, recognized widely as legitimate and responsible business activity, is to bring potential shoppers to the Center, to create a favorable impression, and to generate goodwill. There is no open-ended invitation to the public to use the Center for any and all purposes, however incompatible with the interests of both the stores and the shoppers whom they serve.

It is noteworthy that respondents' argument based on the Center being "open to the public" would apply in varying degrees to most retail stores and service establishments across the country. They are all open to the public in the sense that customers and potential customers are invited and encouraged to enter. In terms of being open to the public, there are differences only of degree-not of principle-between a free standing store and one located in a shopping center, between a small store and a large one, between a single store with some malls and open areas designed to attract customers and Lloyd Center with its elaborate malls and interior landscaping.

B

A further fact, distinguishing the present case from *Logan Valley*, is that the Union picketers in that case would have been deprived of all reasonable opportunity to convey their message to patrons of the Weis store had they been denied access to the shopping center. The situation at Lloyd Center was notably different. The central building complex was surrounded by public sidewalks, totaling 66 linear blocks. All persons who enter or leave the private areas within the complex must cross public streets and sidewalks, either on foot or in automobiles. When moving to and from the privately owned parking lots, automobiles are required by law to come to a complete stop. Handbills may be distributed conveniently to pedestrians, and also to occupants of automobiles, from these public sidewalks and streets. Indeed, respondents moved to these public areas and continued distribution of their handbills after being requested to leave the interior malls. It would be an unwarranted infringement of property rights to require them to yield to the exercise of First Amendment rights under circumstances where adequate alternative avenues of communication exist. Such an accommodation would diminish property rights without significantly enhancing the asserted right of free speech. In ordering this accommodation the courts below erred in their interpretation of this Court's decisions in *Marsh* and *Logan Valley*.

III

The basic issue in this case is whether respondents, in the exercise of asserted First Amendment rights, may distribute handbills on Lloyd's private property contrary to its wishes and contrary to a policy enforced against all handbilling. In addressing this issue, it must be remembered that the First and Fourteenth Amendments safeguard the rights of free speech and assembly by limitations on state action, not on action by the owner of private property used nondiscriminatorily for private purposes only. The Due Process Clauses of the Fifth and Fourteenth Amendments are also relevant to this case. They provide that "no person shall ... be deprived of life, liberty or property, without due process of law." There is the further proscription in the Fifth Amendment against the taking of "private property ... for public use, without just compensation."

Although accommodations between the values protected by these three Amendments are sometimes necessary, and the courts properly have shown a special solicitude for the guarantees of the First Amendment, this Court has never held that a trespasser or an uninvited guest may exercise general rights of free speech on property privately owned and used nondiscriminatorily for private purposes only. Even where public property is involved, the Court has recognized that it is not necessarily available for speech, pickets or other communicative activities.

Respondents contend, however, that the property of a large shopping center is "open to the public," serves the same purposes as a "business district" of a municipality, and therefore has been dedicated to certain types of public use. The argument is that such a center has sidewalks, streets, and parking areas which are functionally similar to facilities customarily provided by municipalities. It is then asserted that all members of the public, whether invited as customers or not, have the same right of free speech as they would have on the similar public facilities in the streets of a city or town.

The argument reaches too far. The Constitution by no means requires such an attenuated doctrine of dedication of private property to public use. The closest decision in theory, *Marsh v. Alabama, supra*, involved the assumption by a private enterprise of all of the attributes of a state-created municipality and the exercise by that enterprise of semi-official municipal functions as a delegate of the State. In effect, the owner of the company town was performing the full spectrum of municipal powers and stood in the shoes of the State. In the instant case there is no comparable assumption or exercise of municipal functions or power.

Nor does property lose its private character merely because the public is generally invited to use it for designated purposes. Few would argue that a free standing store, with abutting parking space for customers, assumes significant public attributes merely because the public is invited to shop. Nor is size alone the controlling factor. The essentially private character of a store and its privately owned abutting property does not change by virtue of being large or clustered with other stores in a modern shopping center. This is not to say that no differences may exist with respect to government regulation or rights of citizens arising by virtue of the size and diversity of activities carried on within a privately owned facility serving the public. There will be, for example, problems with respect to public health and safety which vary in degree and in the appropriate government response, depending upon the size and character of a shopping center, an office building, a sports arena or other large facility serving the public for commercial purposes. We do say that the Fifth and Fourteenth Amendment rights of private property owners, as well as the First Amendment rights of all citizens, must be respected and protected. The Framers of the Constitution certainly did not think these fundamental rights of a free society are incompatible with each other. There may be situations where accommodations between them, and the drawing of lines to assure due protection of both, are not easy. But on the facts presented in this case, the answer is clear.

We hold that there has been no such dedication of Lloyd's privately owned and operated shopping center to public use as to entitle respondents to exercise therein the asserted First Amendment rights. Accordingly, we reverse the judgment and remand the case to the Court of Appeals with directions to vacate the injunction.

It is so ordered.

MR. JUSTICE MARSHALL, joined by MR. JUSTICES DOUGLAS, BRENNAN and STEWART, dissented.

CANTWELL v. CONNECTICUT
310 U.S. 296; 60 S.Ct. 900; 84 L.Ed. 1213 (1940)

Cantwell and his two sons, members of Jehovah's Witnesses, were convicted of two violations of a Connecticut law prohibiting the solicitation of money for alleged religious purposes without first obtaining a certificate of approval from the secretary of the Public Welfare Council. They were also convicted of inciting others to breach of the peace, by playing a phonograph record which attacked Roman Catholicism. The case came to the Supreme Court on appeal.

MR. JUSTICE ROBERTS delivered the opinion of the Court:

... *First.* We hold that the statute, as construed and applied to the appellants, deprives them of their liberty without due process of law in contravention of the Fourteenth Amendment. The fundamental concept of liberty embodied in that Amendment embraces the liberties guaranteed by the First Amendment. The First Amendment declares that Congress shall make no law respecting an establishment of religion or prohibiting the free exercise thereof. The Fourteenth Amendment has rendered the legislatures of the states as incompetent as Congress to enact such laws. The constitutional inhibition of legislation on the subject of religion has a double aspect. On the one hand, it forestalls compulsion by law of the acceptance of any creed or the practice of any form of worship. Freedom of conscience and freedom to adhere to such religious organization or form of worship as the individual may choose cannot be restricted by law. On the other hand, it safeguards the free exercise of the chosen form of religion. Thus the Amendment embraces two concepts – freedom to believe and freedom to act. The first is absolute but, in the nature of things, the second cannot be. Conduct remains subject to regulation for the protection of society. The freedom to act must have appropriate definition to preserve the enforcement of that protection. In every case the power to regulate must be so exercised as not, in attaining a permissible end, unduly to infringe the protected freedom. No one would contest the proposition that a State may not, by statute, wholly deny the right to preach or to disseminate religious views. Plainly such a previous and absolute restraint would violate the terms of the guaranty. It is equally clear that a State may by general and nondiscriminatory legislation regulate the times, the places, and the manner of soliciting upon its streets, and of holding meetings thereon; and may in other respects safeguard the peace, good order, and comfort of the community, without unconstitutionally invading the liberties protected by the Fourteenth Amendment. The appellants are right in their insistence that the Act in question is not such a regulation. If a certificate is procured, solicitation is permitted without restraint, but in the absence of a certificate solicitation is altogether prohibited....

It will be noted ... that the Act requires an application to the secretary of the public welfare council of the State; that he is empowered to determine whether the cause is a religious one, and that the issue of a certificate depends upon his affirmative action. If he finds that the cause is not that of religion, to solicit for it becomes a crime. He is not to issue a certificate as a matter of course. His decision to issue or refuse it involves appraisal of facts, the exercise of judgment, and the formation of an opinion. He is authorized to withhold his approval if he determines that the cause is not a religious one. Such a censorship of religion as the means of determining its right to survive is a denial of liberty protected by the First Amendment and included in the liberty which is within the protection of the Fourteenth.

The line between a discretionary and a ministerial act is not always easy to mark, and the statute has not been construed by the state court to impose a mere ministerial duty on the secretary of the welfare council. Upon his decision as to the nature of the cause, the right to solicit depends. Moreover, the availability of a judicial remedy for abuses in the system of licensing still leaves that system one of previous restraint which, in the field of free speech and press, we have held inadmissible. A statute authorizing previous restraint upon the exercise of the guaranteed freedom by judicial decision after trial is as obnoxious to the Constitution as one providing for like restraint by administrative action.

Nothing we have said is intended even remotely to imply that, under the cloak of religion, persons may, with impunity, commit frauds upon the public. Certainly penal laws are available to punish such conduct. Even the exercise of religion may be at some slight inconvenience in order that the State may protect its citizens from injury. Without doubt a State may protect its citizens from fraudulent solicitation by requiring a stranger in the community, before permitting him publicly to solicit funds for any purpose, to establish his identity and his authority to act for the cause which he purports to represent. The State is likewise free to regulate the time and manner of solicitation generally, in the interest of public safety, peace, comfort, or convenience. But to condition the solicitation of aid for the perpetuation of religious views or systems upon a license, the grant of which rests in the exercise of a determination by state authority as to what is a religious cause, is to lay a forbidden burden upon the exercise of liberty protected by the Constitution.

Second. The offense known as breach of the peace embraces a great variety of conduct destroying or menacing public order and tranquility. It includes not only violent acts but acts and words likely to produce violence in others. No one would have the hardihood to suggest that the principle of freedom of speech sanctions incitement to riot or that religious liberty connotes the privilege to exhort others to physical attack upon those belonging to another sect. When clear and present danger of riot, disorder, interference with traffic upon the public streets, or other immediate threat to public safety, peace, or order, appears, the power of the State to prevent or punish is obvious. Equally obvious is it that a State may not unduly suppress free communication of views, religious or other, under the guise of conserving desirable conditions. Here we have a situation analogous to a conviction under a statute sweeping in a great variety of conduct under a general and indefinite characterization, and leaving to the executive and judicial branches too wide a discretion in its application....

The record played by Cantwell embodies a general attack on all organized religious systems as instruments of Satan and injurious to man; it then singles out the Roman Catholic Church for strictures couched in terms which naturally would offend not only persons of that persuasion, but all others who respect the honestly-held religious faith of their fellows. The hearers were in fact highly offended.

We find in the instant case no assault or threatening of bodily harm, no truculent bearing, no intentional discourtesy, no personal abuse. On the contrary, we find only an effort to persuade a willing listener to buy a book or to contribute money in the interest of what Cantwell, however misguided others may think him, conceived to be true religion.

In the realm of religious faith, and in that of political belief, sharp differences arise. In both fields the tenets of one man may seem the rankest error to his neighbor. To persuade others to his own point of view, the pleader, as we know, at times, resorts to exaggeration, to vilification of men who have been, or are, prominent in church or state, and even to false statement. But the people of this nation have ordained in the light of history, that, in spite of the probability of excesses and abuses, these liberties are, in the long view, essential to enlightened opinion and right conduct on the part of the citizens of a democracy.

The essential characteristic of these liberties is, that under their shield many types of life, character, opinion, and belief can develop unmolested and unobstructed. Nowhere is this shield more necessary than in our own country for a people composed of many races and of many creeds. There are limits to the exercises of these liberties. The danger in these times from the coercive activities of those who in the delusion of racial or religious conceit would incite violence and breaches of the peace in order to deprive others of their equal right to the exercise of their liberties, is emphasized by events familiar to all. These and other transgressions of those limits the States appropriately may punish.

Although the contents of the record not unnaturally aroused animosity, we think that, in the absence of a statute narrowly drawn to define and punish specific conduct as constituting a clear and present danger to a substantial interest of the State, the petitioner's communication, considered in the light of the constitutional guaranties, raised no such clear and present menace to public peace and order as to render him liable to conviction of the common-law offense in question.

The judgment affirming the convictions on the third and fifth counts is reversed, and the cause is remanded for further proceedings not inconsistent with this opinion.

Reversed.

EVERSON v. BOARD OF EDUCATION
330 U.S. 1; 67 S.Ct. 504; 91 L.Ed. 711 (1947)

In 1941, a New Jersey statute authorized the school boards of the state to make regulations and contracts for the transportation of all children attending accredited schools including non-profit private and parochial school children. A taxpayer in the school district, Everson, challenged the right of the Board to such reimbursement. A state court upheld the challenge; however, the state court of errors and appeals overturned the decision. The case was then appealed to the Supreme Court.

MR. JUSTICE BLACK delivered the opinion of the Court:

... The only contention here is that the state statute and the resolution, in so far as they authorized reimbursement to parents of children attending parochial schools, violate the Federal Constitution in these two respects, which to some extent overlap. *First.* They authorize the State to take by taxation the private property of some and bestow it upon others, to be used for their own private purposes. This, it is alleged, violates the due process clause of the Fourteenth Amendment. *Second.* The statute and the resolution forced inhabitants to pay taxes to help support and maintain schools which are dedicated to, and which regularly teach, the Catholic Faith. This is alleged to be a use of state power to support church schools contrary to the prohibition of the First Amendment, which the Fourteenth Amendment made applicable to the states.

It is much too late to argue that legislation intended to facilitate the opportunity of children to get a secular education serves no public purpose.... The same thing is no less true of legislation to reimburse needy parents, or all parents, for payment of the fares of their children so that they can ride in public buses to and from schools rather than run the risk of traffic and other hazards incident to walking or "hitchhiking ."... Nor does it follow that a law has a private rather than a public purpose because it provides that tax-raised funds will be paid to reimburse individuals on account of money spent by them in a way which furthers a public program.... Subsidies and loans to individuals such as farmers and homeowners, and to privately-owned transportation systems, as well as many other kinds of businesses, have been commonplace practices in our state and national history....

The New Jersey statute is challenged as a "law respecting an establishment of religion." The First Amendment, as made applicable to the states by the Fourteenth ... commands that a state "shall make no law respecting an establishment of religion."

The "establishment of religion" clause of the First Amendment means at least this: Neither a state nor the Federal Government can set up a church. Neither can pass laws which aid one religion, aid all religions, or prefer one religion over another. Neither can force or influence a person to go to or remain away from church against his will or force him to profess a belief or disbelief in any religion. No person can be punished for entertaining or professing religious beliefs or disbeliefs, for church attendance or non-attendance. No tax in any amount, large or small, can be levied to support any religious activities or institutions, whatever they may be called, or whatever form they may adopt to teach or practice religion. Neither a state nor the Federal Government can, openly or secretly, participate in the affairs of any religious organizations or groups and vice versa. In the words of Jefferson, the clause against establishment of religion by law was intended to erect "a wall of separation between church and State...."

Measured by these standards, we cannot say that the First Amendment prohibits New Jersey from spending tax-raised funds to pay the bus fares of parochial-school pupils as a part of a general program under which it pays the fares of pupils attending public and other schools. It is undoubtedly true that children are helped to get to church schools. There is even a possibility that some of the children might not be sent to the church schools if the parents were compelled to pay their children's bus fares out of their own pockets when transportation to a public school would have been paid for by the State. The same possibility exists where the state requires a local transit company to provide reduced fares to school children, including those attending parochial schools, or where a municipally-owned transportation system undertakes to carry all school children free of charge. Moreover, state-paid policemen, detailed to protect children going to and from church schools from the very real hazards of traffic, would serve much the same purpose and accomplish much the same result as state provisions intended to guarantee free transportation of a kind which the state deems to be best for the school children's welfare. And parents might refuse to risk their children to the serious danger of traffic accidents going to and from parochial schools, the approaches to which were not protected by policemen. Similarly, parents might be reluctant to permit their children to attend schools which the state had cut off from such general government services as ordinary police and fire protection, connections for sewage disposal, public highways and sidewalks. The Amendment requires the state to be a neutral in its relations with groups of religious believers and nonbelievers; it does not require the state to be their adversary. State power is no more to be used so as to handicap religions than it is to favor them.

This Court has said that parents may, in the discharge of their duty under state compulsory education laws, send their children to religious rather than a public school if the school meets the secular educational requirements which the state has power to impose.... It appears that these parochial schools meet New Jersey's requirements. The State contributes no money to the schools. It does not support them. Its legislation, as applied, does no more than provide a general program to help parents get their children, regardless of their religion, safely and expeditiously to and from accredited schools.

The First Amendment has erected a wall between church and state. That wall must be kept high and impregnable. We could not approve the slightest breach. New Jersey has not breached it here.

Affirmed.

MR. JUSTICE JACKSON, dissented, saying in part:

...It is of no importance in this situation whether the beneficiary of this expenditure of tax-raised funds is primarily the parochial school and incidentally the pupil, or whether the aid is directly bestowed on the pupil with indirect benefits to the school. The state cannot maintain a Church and it can no more tax its citizens to furnish free carriage to those who attend a Church. The prohibition against establishment of religion cannot be circumvented by a subsidy, bonus, or reimbursement of expense to individuals for receiving religious instruction and indoctrination....

It seems to me that the basic fallacy in the Court's reasoning, which accounts for its failure to apply the principles it avows, is in ignoring the essentially religious test by which beneficiaries of this expenditure are selected. A policeman protects a Catholic, of course – but not because he is a Catholic; it is because he is a man and a member of our society. The fireman protects the Church school – but not because it is a Church school; it is because it is property, part of the assets of our society. Neither the fireman nor the policeman has to ask before he renders aid, "Is this man or building identified with the Catholic Church?" But before these school authorities draw a check to reimburse for a student's fare they must ask just that question, and if the school is a Catholic one they may render aid because it is such, while if it is of any other faith or is run for profit, the help must be withheld....

The Court's holding is that this taxpayer has no grievance because the state has decided to make the reimbursement a public purpose and therefore we are bound to regard it as such. I agree that this Court has left, and always should leave to each state, great latitude in deciding for itself, in the light of its own conditions, what shall be public purposes in its scheme of things. It may socialize utilities and economic enterprises and make taxpayers' business out of what conventionally had been private business. It may make public business of individual welfare, health, education, entertainment, or security. But it cannot make public business of religious worship or instruction, or of attendance at religious institutions of any character. There is no answer to the proposition, more fully expounded by Mr. Justice Rutledge, that the effect of the religious freedom Amendment to our Constitution was to take every form of propagation of religion out of the realm of things which could directly or indirectly be made public business and thereby be supported in whole or in part at taxpayers' expense. That is a difference which the Constitution sets up between religion and almost every other subject matter of legislation, a difference which goes to the very root of religious freedom and which the Court is overlooking today. This freedom was first in the Bill of Rights because it was first in the forefathers' minds; it was set forth in absolute terms, and its strength is in rigidity. It was intended not only to keep the states' hands out of religion, but to keep religion's hands off the state, and, above all, to keep bitter religious controversy out of public life by denying to every denomination any advantage from getting control of public policy or the public purse. Those great ends I cannot but think are immeasurably compromised by today's decision....

But we cannot have it both ways. Religious teaching cannot be a private affair when the state seeks to impose regulations which infringe on it indirectly, and a public affair when it comes to taxing citizens of one faith to aid another, or those of no faith to aid all. If these principles seem harsh in prohibiting aid to Catholic education, *it must not be forgotten that it is the same Constitution that alone assures Catholics the right to maintain these schools at all when predominant local sentiment would forbid them....* Nor should I think that those who have done so well without this aid would want to see this separation between Church and State broken down. If the state may aid these religious schools, it may therefore regulate them. Many groups have sought aid from tax funds only to find that it carried political controls with it. Indeed this Court has declared that "it is hardly lack of due process for the Government to regulate that which it subsidizes...."

But in any event, the great purposes of the Constitution do not depend on the approval or convenience of those they restrain. I cannot read the history of the struggle to separate political from ecclesiastical affairs ... without a conviction that the Court today is unconsciously giving the clock's hands a backward turn.

MR. JUSTICE FRANKFURTER joined in this opinion.

MR. JUSTICE RUTLEDGE, with whom MR JUSTICES FRANKFURTER, JACKSON, and BURTON agreed, dissented.

WEST VIRGINIA STATE BOARD OF EDUCATION v. BARNETTE
319 U.S. 624; 63 S.Ct. 1178; 87 L.Ed. 1628 (1943)

The West Virginia State Board of Education required all public school teachers and pupils to salute the flag. Any student who refused to do so and to recite the pledge of allegiance could be punished by expulsion from school. If expelled, the child could be considered unlawfully absent and thus, a delinquent. The only means of readmission to the school was for the child to comply with the ceremonial requirement. The children most affected were members of the Jehovah's Witnesses including Barnette and others. The Witnesses contended that the regulation violated their religious freedom and freedom of speech under the First and Fourteenth Amendments. The case came to the Supreme Court by direct appeal of the Board of Education. Ironically, the Court had earlier upheld a similar state statute in Minersville School District v. Gobitis, *310 U.S. 586 (1940).*

MR. JUSTICE JACKSON delivered the opinion of the Court:

...The freedom asserted by these appellees does not bring them into collision with rights asserted by any other individual. It is such conflicts which most frequently require intervention of the State to determine where the rights of one end and those of another begin. But the refusal of these persons to participate in the ceremony does not interfere with or deny rights of others to do so. Nor is there any question in this case that their behavior is peaceable and orderly. The sole conflict is between authority and the rights of the individual. The State asserts power to condition access to public education by punishing both parent and child. The latter stand on a right of self-determination in matters that touch individual opinion and personal attitude.

There is no doubt that, in connection with the pledges, the flag salute is a form of utterance. Symbolism is a primitive but effective way of communicating ideas. The use of an emblem or flag to symbolize some system, idea, institution, or personality, is a short cut from mind to mind. Causes and nations, political parties, lodges, and ecclesiastical groups seek to knit the loyalty of their followings to a flag or banner, a color or design. The State announces rank, function, and authority through crowns and maces, uniforms and black robes; the church speaks through the Cross, the Crucifix, the altar and shrine, and clerical raiment. Symbols of State often convey political ideas just as religious symbols come to convey theological ones. Associated with many of these symbols are appropriate gestures of acceptance or respect: a salute, a bowed or bared head, a bended knee. A person gets from a symbol the meaning he puts into it, and what is one man's comfort and inspiration is another's jest and scorn.

Over a decade ago Chief Justice Hughes led this Court in holding that the display of a red flag as a symbol of opposition by peaceful and legal means to organized government was protected by the free-speech guaranties of the Constitution. *Stromberg v. California*, 283 U.S. 359. Here it is the State that employs a flag as a symbol of adherence to government as presently organized. It requires the individual to communicate by word and sign his acceptance of the political ideas it thus bespeaks. Objection to this form of communication when coerced is an old one, well known to the framers of the Bill of Rights.

It is also to be noted that the compulsory flag salute and pledge requires affirmation of a belief and an attitude of mind. It is not clear whether the regulation contemplates that pupils forego any contrary convictions of their own and become unwilling converts to the prescribed ceremony, or whether it will be acceptable if they simulate assent by words without belief and by a gesture barren of meaning. It is now a commonplace that censorship or suppression of expression of opinion is tolerated by our Constitution only when the expression presents a clear and present danger of action of a kind the State is empowered to prevent and punish. It would seem that involuntary affirmation could be commanded only on even more immediate and urgent grounds than silence. But here the power of compulsion is invoked without any allegation that remaining passive during a flag-salute ritual creates a clear and present danger that would justify an effort even to muffle expression. To sustain the compulsory flag salute we are required to say that a Bill of Rights which guards the individual's right to speak his own mind, left it open to public authorities to compel him to utter what is not in his mind.

Whether the First Amendment to the Constitution will permit officials to order observance of ritual of this nature does not depend upon whether as a voluntary exercise we would think it to be good, bad, or merely innocuous. Any credo of nationalism is likely to include what some disapprove or to omit what others think essential, and to give off different overtones as it takes on different accents or interpretations. If official power exists to coerce acceptance of any patriotic creed, what it shall contain cannot be decided by courts, but must be largely discretionary with the ordaining authority, whose power it is to amend. Hence validity of the asserted power to force an American citizen publicly to profess any statement or belief or to engage in any ceremony of assent to one, presents questions of power that must be considered independently of any idea we may have as to the utility of the ceremony in question.

Nor does the issue as we see it turn on one's possession of particular religious views or the sincerity with which they are held. While religion supplies appellees' motive for enduring the discomforts of making the issue in this case, many citizens who do not share these religious views hold such a compulsory rite to infringe constitutional liberty of the individual. It is not necessary to inquire whether nonconformist beliefs will exempt from the duty to salute unless we first find power to make the salute a legal duty.

The *Gobitis* decision, however, *assumed*, as did the argument in that case and in this, that power exists in the State to impose the flag-salute discipline upon school children in general. The Court only examined and rejected a claim based on religious beliefs of immunity from an unquestioned general rule. The question which underlies the flag-salute controversy is whether such a ceremony so touching matters of opinion and political attitude may be imposed upon the individual by official authority under powers committed to any political organization under our Constitution. We examine rather than assume existence of this power and, against this broader definition of issues in this case, re-examine specific grounds assigned for the *Gobitis* decision.

1. It was said that the flag-salute controversy confronted the Court with "the problem which Lincoln cast in memorable dilemma: 'Must a government of necessity be too strong for the liberties of its people, or too *weak* to maintain its own existence?'" and that the answer must be in favor of strength....

We think these issues may be examined free of pressure or restraint growing out of such considerations.

It may be doubted whether Mr. Lincoln would have thought that the strength of government to maintain itself would be impressively vindicated by our confirming power of the State to expel a handful of children from school. Such over-simplification, so handy in political debate, often lacks the precision necessary to postulates of judicial reasoning. If validly applied to this problem, the utterance cited would resolve every issue of power in favor of those in authority and would require us to override every liberty thought to weaken or delay execution of their policies.

Government of limited power need not be anemic government. Assurance that rights are secure tends to diminish fear and jealousy of strong government, and by making us feel safe to live under it makes for its better support. Without promise of a limiting Bill of Rights it is doubtful if our Constitution could have mustered enough strength to enable its ratification. To enforce those rights today is not to choose weak government over strong government. It is only to adhere as a means of strength to individual freedom of mind in preference to officially disciplined uniformity, for which history indicates a disappointing and disastrous end.

The subject now before us exemplifies this principle. Free public education, if faithful to the ideal of secular instruction and political neutrality, will not be partisan or enemy of any class, creed, party, or faction. If it is to impose any ideological discipline, however, each party or denomination must seek to control, or failing that, to weaken the influence of the educational system. Observance of the limitations of the Constitution will not weaken government in the field appropriate for its exercise.

2. It was also considered in the *Gobitis* case that functions of educational officers in States, counties, and school districts were such that to interfere with their authority "would in effect make us the school board for the country."

The Fourteenth Amendment, as now applied to the States, protects the citizens against the State itself and all of its creatures – Boards of Education not excepted. These have, of course, important, delicate, and highly discretionary functions, but none that they may not perform within the limits of the Bill of Rights. They are educating the young for citizenship is reason for scrupulous protection of constitutional freedoms of the individual, if we are not to strangle the free mind at its source and teach youth to discount important principles of our government as mere platitudes....

3. The *Gobitis* opinion reasoned that this is a field "where courts possess no marked and certainly no controlling competence," that it is committed to the legislatures as well as the courts to guard cherished liberties and that it is constitutionally appropriate to "fight out the wise use of legislative authority in the forum of public opinion and before legislative assembles rather than to transfer such a contest to the judicial arena," since all the "effective means of inducing political changes are left free...."

The very purpose of a Bill of Rights was to withdraw certain subjects from the vicissitudes of political controversy, to place them beyond the reach of majorities and officials and to establish them as legal principles to be applied by the courts. One's right to life, liberty, and property, to free speech, a free press, freedom of worship and assembly, and other fundamental rights may not be submitted to vote; they depend on the outcome of no elections.

In weighing arguments of the parties it is important to distinguish between the due process clause of the Fourteenth Amendment as an instrument for transmitting the principles of the First Amendment and those cases in which it is applied for its own sake. The test of legislation which collides with the Fourteenth, because it also collides with the principles of the First, is much more definitive than the test when only the Fourteenth is involved. Much of the vagueness of the due process clause disappears when the specific prohibitions of the First become its standard. The right of a State to regulate, for example, a public utility may well include, so far as the due process test is concerned, power to impose all of the restrictions which a legislature may have a "rational basis" for adopting. But freedoms of speech and of press, of assembly, and of worship may not be infringed on such slender grounds. They are susceptible of restriction only to prevent grave and immediate danger to interests which the State may lawfully protect. It is important to note that while it is the Fourteenth Amendment which bears directly upon the State, it is the more specific limiting principles of the First Amendment that finally govern this case....

4. Lastly, and this is the very heart of the *Gobitis* opinion, it reasons that "National unity is the basis of national security," that the authorities have "the right to select appropriate means for its attainment," and hence reaches the conclusion that such compulsory measures toward "national unity" are constitutional.... Upon the verity of this assumption depends our answer in this case.

National unity as an end which officials may foster by persuasion and example is not in question. The problem is whether under our Constitution compulsion as here employed is a permissible means for its achievement.

Struggles to coerce uniformity of sentiment in support of some end thought essential to their time and country have been waged by many good as well as by evil men. Nationalism is a relatively recent phenomenon, but at other times and places the ends have been racial or territorial security, support of a dynasty or regime, and particular plans for saving souls. As first and moderate methods to attain unity have failed, those bent on its accomplishment must resort to an ever-increasing severity.

. . . Ultimate futility of such attempts to compel coherence is the lesson of every such effort from the Roman drive to stamp out Christianity as a disturber of its pagan unity, the Inquisition, as a means to religious and dynastic unity, the Siberian exiles as a means to Russian unity, down to the fast-failing efforts of our present totalitarian enemies. *Those who begin coercive elimination of dissent soon find themselves exterminating dissenters. Compulsory unification of opinion achieves only the unanimity of the graveyard.*

It seems trite but necessary to say that the First Amendment to our Constitution was designed to avoid these ends by avoiding these beginnings. There is no mysticism in the American concept of the State or of the nature or origin of its authority. We set up government by consent of the governed, and the Bill of Rights denies those in power any legal opportunity to coerce that consent. Authority here is to be controlled by public opinion, not public opinion by authority.

The case is made difficult not because the principles of its decision are obscure but because the flag involved is our own. Nevertheless, we apply the limitations of the Constitution with no fear that freedom to be intellectually and spiritually diverse or even contrary will disintegrate the social organization. To believe that patriotism will not flourish if patriotic ceremonies are voluntary and spontaneous instead of a compulsory routine is to make an unflattering estimate of the appeal of our institutions to free minds. We can have intellectual individualism and the rich cultural diversities that we owe to exceptional minds only at the price of occasional eccentricity and abnormal attitudes. When they are so harmless to others or to the State as those we deal with here, the price is not too great. But freedom to differ is not limited to things that do not matter much. That would be a mere shadow of freedom. The test of its substance is the right to differ as to things that touch the heart of the existing order.

If there is any fixed star in our constitutional constellation, it is that no official, high or petty, can prescribe what shall be orthodox in politics, nationalism, religion, or other matters of opinion or force citizens to confess by word or act their faith therein. If there are any circumstances which permit an exception, they do not now occur to us.

We think the action of the local authorities in compelling the flag salute and pledge transcends constitutional limitations on their power and invades the sphere of intellect and spirit which it is the purpose of the First Amendment to our Constitution to reserve from all official control.

The decision of this Court in *Minersville School District v. Gobitis* [is] overruled, and the judgment enjoining enforcement of the West Virginia Regulation is
Affirmed.

MR. JUSTICES BLACK, DOUGLAS, and MURPHY concurred.
MR. JUSTICE FRANKFURTER, dissenting:

One who belongs to the most vilified and persecuted minority in history is not likely to be insensible to the freedoms guaranteed by our Constitution. Were my purely personal attitudes relevant I should wholeheartedly associate myself with the general libertarian views in the Court's opinion, representing as they do the thought and action of a lifetime. But as judges we are neither Jew nor Gentile, neither Catholic nor agnostic. We owe equal attachment to the Constitution and are equally bound by our judicial obligations whether we derive our citizenship from the earliest or the latest immigrants to these shores. As a member of this Court I am not justified in writing my private notions of policy into the Constitution, no matter how deeply I may cherish them or how mischievous I may deem their disregard. The duty of a judge who must decide which of two claims before the Court shall prevail, that of a State to enact and enforce laws within its general competence or that of an individual to refuse obedience because of the demands of his conscience, is not that of the ordinary person. It can never be emphasized too much that one's own opinion about the wisdom or evil of a law should be excluded altogether when one is doing one's duty on the bench. The only opinion of our own even looking in that direction that is material is our opinion whether legislators could in reason have enacted such a law. In the light of all the circumstances, including the history of this question in this Court, it would require more daring than I possess to deny that reasonable legislators could have taken the action which is before us for review. Most unwillingly, therefore, I must differ from my brethren with regard to legislation like this. I cannot bring my mind to believe that the "liberty" secured by the Due Process Clause gives this Court authority to deny to the State of West Virginia the attainment of that which we all recognize as a legitimate legislative end, namely, the promotion of good citizenship, by employment of the means here chosen.

...The reason why from the beginning even the narrow judicial authority to nullify legislation has been viewed with a jealous eye is that it serves to prevent the full play of the democratic process. The fact that it may be an undemocratic aspect of our scheme of government does not call for its rejection or its disuse. But it is the best of reasons, as this Court has frequently recognized, for the greatest caution in its use.

... If the function of this Court is to be essentially no different from that of a legislature, if the considerations governing constitutional construction are to be substantially those that underlie legislation, then indeed judges should not have life tenure and they should be made directly responsible to the electorate....

MR. JUSTICES ROBERTS and REED also dissented.

ZORACH v. CLAUSON
343 U.S. 306; 72 S.Ct. 679; 96 L.Ed. 954 (1952)

In Illinois *ex. rel.* McCollum v. Board of Education *(1948), the Supreme Court had invalidated a "dismissed" time program which provided religious instruction for elementary and secondary school children taught in the public schools of Champaign. Thereafter, a public outcry occurred in reaction to the Court's supposed anti-religious stand. In this case Zorach and other residents of*

New York City brought suit against Clauson, a member of the Board of Education, to challenge the city's "released" time program which was similar to the Illinois plan, but under which the instruction took place off the tax-supported public school property. After the highest state court sustained the plan, the case was appealed to the Supreme Court.

MR. JUSTICE DOUGLAS delivered the opinion of the Court:

New York City has a program which permits its public schools to release students during the school day so that they may leave the school buildings and school grounds and go to religious centers for religious instruction or devotional exercises. A student is released on written request of his parents. Those not released stay in the classrooms. The churches make weekly reports to the schools, sending a list of children who have been released from public school but who have not reported for religious instruction.

This "released-time" program involves neither religious instruction in public-school classrooms nor the expenditure of public funds. All costs, including the application blanks, are paid by the religious organizations. The case is therefore unlike *McCollum v. Board of Education....* In that case the classrooms were turned over to religious instructors. We accordingly held that the program violated the First Amendment which (by reason of the Fourteenth Amendment) prohibits the states from establishing religion or prohibiting its free exercise....

[O]ur problem reduces itself to whether New York by this system has either prohibited the "free exercise" of religion or has made a law "respecting an establishment of religion" within the meaning of the First Amendment.

It takes obtuse reasoning to inject any issue of the "free exercises" of religion to the present case. No one is forced to go to the religious classroom and no religious exercise or instruction is brought to the classrooms of the public schools. A student need not take religious instruction. He is left to his own desires as to the manner or time of his religious devotions, if any.

There is suggestion that the system involves the use of coercion to get public-school students into religious classrooms. There is no evidence in the record before us that supports that conclusion. The present record indeed tells us that the school authorities are neutral in this regard and do no more than release students whose parents so request. If in fact coercion were used, if it were established that any one or more teachers were using their office to persuade or force students to take the religious instruction, a wholly different case would be presented. Hence we put aside that claim of coercion both as respects the "free exercise" of religion and "an establishment of religion" within the meaning of the First Amendment.

Moreover, apart from that claim of coercion, we do not see how New York by this type of "released-time" program has made a law respecting an establishment of religion within the meaning of the First Amendment. There is much talk of the separation of Church and State in the history of the Bill of Rights and in the decisions clustering around the First Amendment. See *Everson v. Board of Education....* There cannot be the slightest doubt that the First

Amendment reflects the philosophy that Church and State should be separated. And so far as interference with the "free exercise" of religion and an "establishment" of religion are concerned, the separation must be complete and unequivocal. The First Amendment within the scope of its coverage permits no exception; the prohibition is absolute. The First Amendment, however, does not say that in every and all respects there shall be a separation of Church and State. Rather, it studiously defines the manner, the specific ways, in which there shall be no concert or union or dependency one on the other. That is the common sense of the matter. Other-wise the state and religion would be aliens to each other – hostile, suspicious, and even unfriendly....

We are a religious people whose institutions presuppose a Supreme Being. We guarantee the freedom to worship as one chooses. We make room for as wide a variety of beliefs and creeds as the spiritual needs of man deem necessary. We sponsor an attitude on the part of government that shows no partiality to any one group and that lets each flourish according to the zeal of its adherents and the appeal of its dogma. When the state encourages religious instruction or cooperates with religious authorities by adjusting the schedule of public events to sectarian needs, it follows the best of our traditions. For it then respects the religious nature of our people and accommodates the public service to their spiritual need. To hold that it may not would be to find in the Constitution a requirement that the government show a callous indifference to religious groups. That would be preferring those who believe in no religion over those who do believe. Government may not finance religious groups nor undertake religious instruction nor blend secular and sectarian education nor use secular institutions to force one or some religion on any person. But we find no constitutional requirement which makes it necessary for government to be hostile to religion and to throw its weight against efforts to widen the effective scope of religious influence. The government must be neutral when it comes to competition between sects. It may not thrust any sect on any person. It may not make a religious observance compulsory. It may not coerce anyone to attend church, to observe a religious holiday, or to take religious instruction. But it can close its doors or suspend its operations as to those who want to repair to their religious sanctuary for worship or instruction. No more than that is undertaken here....

In the *McCollum* case the classrooms were used for religious instruction and the force of the public school was used to promote that instruction. Here, as we have said, the public schools do no more than accommodate their schedules to a program of outside religious instruction. We follow the *McCollum* case. But we cannot expand it to cover the present released-time program unless separation of Church and State means that public institutions can make no adjustments of their schedules to accommodate the religious needs of the people. We cannot read into the Bill of Rights such a philosophy of hostility to religion.
Affirmed.

MR. JUSTICE BLACK dissented, saying in part:

.... I see no significant difference between the invalid Illinois system and that of New York here sustained. Except for the use of the school buildings in Illinois, there is no difference between the systems which I consider even worthy of mention. In the New York program, as in that of Illinois, the school authorities release some of the children on the condition that they attend the religious classes, get reports on whether they attend, and hold the other children in the school building until the religious hour is over. As we attempted to make categorically clear, the *McCollum* decision would have been the same if the religious classes had not been held in the school building....

Under our system of religious freedom, people have gone to their religious sanctuaries not because they feared the law but because they loved their God. The choice of all has been as free as the choice of those who answered the call to worship moved only by the music of the old Sunday-morning church bells. The spiritual mind of man has thus been free to believe, disbelieve, or doubt, without repression, great or small, by the heavy hand of government. Statutes authorizing such repression have been stricken. Before today, our judicial opinions have refrained from drawing invidious distinctions between those who believe in no religion and those who do believe. The First Amendment has lost much if the religious follower and the atheist are no longer to be judicially regarded as entitled to equal justice under the law.

State help to religion injects political and party prejudices into a holy field. It too often substitutes force for prayer, hate for love, and persecution for persuasion. Government should not be allowed, under cover of the soft euphemism of "cooperation," to steal into the sacred area of religious choice.

MR. JUSTICES FRANKFURTER and JACKSON, also dissented.

SUNDAY CLOSING LAW CASES
366 U.S. 420; 81 S.Ct. 1101; 6 L.Ed. 2d 393 (1961)

The Sunday Closing Cases consist of four cases decided together by the Supreme Court. In all four, the laws were challenged on the ground that they violated the equal protection clause of the Fourteenth Amendment. In McGowan *and* Two Guys, *the petitioners also argued that on their face the statutes in question were laws respecting an "establishment of religion" and abridging free exercise of religion. In* Gallagher *and* Braunfeld, *the petitioners argued that, as orthodox Jews, their religious faith required the observance of Saturday as the Sabbath, and that the Sunday Closing laws penalized them for their religious beliefs. The case came to the Supreme Court on appeal from Maryland, Massachusetts and Pennsylvania. The opinion below is taken from* McGowan v. Maryland.

MR. CHIEF JUSTICE WARREN delivered the opinion of the Court: ....

First, appellants contend here that the statutes applicable to Anne Arundel County violate the constitutional guaranty of freedom of religion in that the statutes' effect is to prohibit the free exercise of religion in contravention of the First Amendment, made applicable to the States by the Fourteenth Amendment. But appellants allege only economic injury to themselves; they do not allege any infringement of their own religious freedoms due to Sunday closing. In fact, the record is silent as to what appellants' rule is that "a litigant may only assert his own constitutional rights or immunities," ... we hold that appellants have no standing to raise this contention....

Secondly, appellants contend that the statutes violate the guaranty of separation of church and state in that the statutes are laws respecting an establishment of religion contrary to the First Amendment, made applicable to the states by the Fourteenth Amendment. If the purpose of the "establishment" clause was only to insure protection for the "free exercise" of religion, then what we have said above concerning appellants' standing to raise the "free exercise" contention would appear to be true here. However, the writings of Madison, who was the First Amendment's architect, demonstrate that the establishment of a religion was equally feared because of its tendencies to political tyranny and subversion of civil authority.... Appellants here concededly have suffered direct economic injury, allegedly due to the imposition on them of the tenets of the Christian religion. We find that, in these circumstances, these appellants have standing to complain that the statutes are laws respecting an establishment of religion.

The essence of appellants' "establishment" argument is that Sunday is the Sabbath day of the predominant Christian sects; that the purpose of the enforced stoppage of labor on that day is to facilitate and encourage church attendance; that the purpose of setting Sunday as a day of universal rest is to induce people with no religion or people with marginal religious beliefs to join the predominant Christian sects; that the purpose of the atmosphere of tranquility created by Sunday closing is to aid the conduct of church services and religious observance of the sacred day.... There is no dispute that the original laws which dealt with Sunday labor were motivated by religious forces. But what we must decide is whether present Sunday legislation, having undergone extensive changes from the earliest forms, still retains its religious character.

Sunday Closing Laws go far back into American history, having been brought to the colonies with a background of English legislation dating to the thirteenth century.... [C]learly... the English Sunday legislation was in aid of the established church.

The American colonial Sunday restrictions arose soon after settlement. Starting in 1650, the Plymouth Colony proscribed servile work, unnecessary traveling, sports, and the sale of alcoholic beverages on the Lord's day and enacted laws concerning church attendance. The Massachusetts Bay Colony and the Connecticut and New Haven Colonies enacted similar prohibitions, some even earlier in the seventeenth century. The religious orientation of the colonial statutes was equally apparent....

But, despite the strongly religious origin of these laws, beginning before the eighteenth century, nonreligious arguments for Sunday closing began to be heard more distinctly and the statutes began to lose some of their totally religious flavor. In the middle 1700s, Blackstone wrote, "[T]he keeping one day in the seven holy, as a time of relaxation and refreshment as well as for public worship, is of admirable service to a state considered merely as a civil institution. It humanizes, by the help of conversation and society, the manners of the lower classes; which would otherwise degenerate into a sordid ferocity and savage selfishness of spirit; it enables the industrious workman to pursue his occupation in the ensuing week with health and cheerfulness."... The preamble to a 1679 Rhode Island enactment stated that the reason for the ban on Sunday employment was that "persons being evil minded, have presumed to employ in servile labor, more than necessity requireth, their servants...." With the advent of the First Amendment, the colonial provisions requiring church attendance were soon repealed....

More recently, further secular justifications have been advanced for making Sunday a day of rest, a day when people may recover from the labors of the week just passed and may physically and mentally prepare for the week's work to come....

The proponents of Sunday closing legislation are no longer exclusively representatives of religious interests. Recent New Jersey Sunday legislation was supported by labor groups and trade associations....

Almost every State in our country presently has some type of Sunday regulation and over forty possess a relatively comprehensive system.... Some of our States now enforce their Sunday legislation through Departments of Labor.... Thus have Sunday laws evolved from the wholly religious sanctions that originally were enacted....

The First Amendment, in its final form, did not simply bar a congressional enactment establishing a church; it forbade all laws respecting an establishment of religion. Thus, this Court has given the Amendment a "broad interpretation..." "in the light of its history and the evils it was designed forever to suppress...." It has found that the First and Fourteenth Amendments afford protection against religious establishment far more extensive than merely to forbid a national or state church....

However, it is equally true that the "Establishment" Clause does not ban federal or state regulation of conduct whose reason or effect merely happens to coincide or harmonize with the tenets of some or all religions. In many instances, the Congress or state legislatures conclude that the general welfare of society, wholly apart from any religious considerations, demands such regulation. Thus, for temporal purposes, murder is illegal. And the fact that this agrees with the dictates of the Judaeo-Christian religions while it may disagree with others does not invalidate the regulation. So too with the questions of adultery and polygamy....

In light of the evolution of our Sunday Closing Laws throughout the centuries, and of their more or less recent emphasis upon secular considerations, it is not difficult to discern that as presently written and administered, most of them, at least, are of a secular rather than of a religious character, and that presently they bear no relationship to establishment of religion as those words are used in the Constitution of the United States.

Throughout this century and longer, both the federal and state governments have oriented their activities very largely toward improvement of the health, safety, recreation and general well-being of our citizens. Numerous laws affecting public health, safety factors in industry, laws affecting hours and conditions of labor of women and children, week-end diversion at parks and beaches, and cultural activities of various kinds, now point the way toward the good life for all. Sunday Closing Laws, like those before us, have become part and parcel of this great governmental concern wholly apart from their original purposes or connotations. The present purpose and effect of most of them is to provide a uniform day of rest for all citizens; the fact that this day is Sunday, a day of particular significance for the dominant Christian sects, does not bar the State from achieving its secular goals. To say that the States cannot prescribe Sunday as a day of rest for these purposes solely because centuries ago such laws had their genesis in religion would give a constitutional interpretation of hostility to the public welfare rather than one of mere separation of church and State....

It is true that if the State's interest were simply to provide for its citizens a periodic respite from work, a regulation demanding that everyone rest one day in seven, leaving the choice of the day to the individual, would suffice.

However, the State's purpose is not merely to provide a one-day-in-seven work stoppage. In addition to this, the State seeks to set one day apart from all others as a day of rest, repose, recreation and tranquility – a day which all members of the family and community have the opportunity to spend and enjoy together, a day in which there exists relative quiet and disassociation from the everyday intensity of commercial activities, a day in which people may visit friends and relatives who are not available during working days.

Obviously, a state is empowered to determine that a rest-one-day-in-seven statute would not accomplish this purpose; that it would not provide for a general cessation of activity, a special atmosphere of tranquility, a day which all members of the family or friends and relatives might spend together. Furthermore, it seems plain that the problems involved in enforcing such a provision would be exceedingly more difficult than those in enforcing a common-day-of-rest provision.

Moreover, it is common knowledge that the first day of the week has come to have special significance as a rest day in this country. People of all religions and people with no religion regard Sunday as a time for family activity, for visiting friends and relatives, for late-sleeping, for passive and active entertainments, for dining out and the like.... Sunday is a day apart from all others. The cause is irrelevant; the fact exists. It would seem unrealistic for enforcement purposes and perhaps detrimental to the general welfare to require a state to choose a common-day-of-rest other than that which most persons would select of their own accord. For these reasons, we hold that the Maryland statutes are not laws respecting an establishment of religion....

Accordingly, the decision is

Affirmed.

MR. JUSTICES FRANKFURTER and HARLAN concurred.

ENGEL v. VITALE
370 U.S. 421; 82 S.Ct. 1261; 8 L.Ed. 2d 601 (1962)

In November, 1951, the New York Board of Regents composed the following prayer for use in the public schools: "Almighty God, we acknowledge our dependence upon Thee, and we beg Thy blessings upon us, our parents, our teachers and our Country." This prayer was not mandatory, but merely a recommendation which the local school boards were free to adopt or not as they wished. In a suburb of New York City, the school board of New Hyde Park adopted the Regents' prayer. The principal was to see to it that the prayer was said aloud by the class each morning. Steven Engel and other parents in the school district argued that the use of the official prayer "was contrary to the beliefs, religions and religious practices of both themselves and their children" and so was a violation of the First and Fourteenth Amendments. Engel et al., wanted a writ of mandamus *to compel the school board to discontinue the official prayer, but it was denied. The Supreme Court granted* certiorari.

MR. JUSTICE BLACK delivered the opinion of the Court:

...We think that by using its public school system to encourage recitation of the Regents' prayer, the State of New York has adopted a practice wholly inconsistent with the Establishment Clause. There can, of course, be no doubt that New York's program of daily classroom invocation of God's blessings as prescribed in the Regents' prayer is a religious activity. It is a solemn avowal of divine faith and supplication for the blessings of the Almighty. The nature of such a prayer has always been religious, none of the respondents has denied this and the trial court expressly so found:...

The petitioners contend among other things that the state laws requiring or permitting use of the Regents' prayer must be struck down as a violation of the Establishment Clause because that prayer was composed by governmental officials as a part of governmental program to further religious beliefs. For this reason, petitioners argue, the State's use of the Regents' prayer in its public school system breaches the constitutional wall of separation between Church and State. We agree with that contention since we think that the constitutional prohibition against laws respecting an establishment of religion must at least mean that in this country it is no part of the business of government to compose official prayers for any group of the American people to recite as a part of a religious program carried on by government.

It is a matter of history that this very practice of establishing governmentally composed prayers for religious services was one of the reasons which caused many of our early colonists to leave England and seek religious freedom in America. *The Book of Common Prayer*, which was created under governmental direction and which was approved by Acts of Parliament in 1548 and 1549, set out in minute detail the accepted form and content of prayer and other religious ceremonies to be used in the established, tax-supported Church of England. The controversies over the Book and what should be its content repeatedly threatened to disrupt the peace of that country as the accepted forms of prayer in the established church changed with the views of the particular ruler that happened to be in control at the time. Powerful groups representing some of the varying religious views of the people struggled among themselves to impress their particular views upon the Government and obtain amendments of the Book more suitable to their respective notions of how religious services should be conducted in order that the official religious establishment would advance their particular religious beliefs. Other groups, lacking the necessary political power to influence the Government on the matter, decided to leave England and its established church and seek freedom in America from England's governmentally ordained and supported religion.

It is an unfortunate fact of history that when some of the very groups which had most strenuously opposed the established Church of England found themselves sufficiently in control of colonial governments in this country to write their own prayers into law, they passed laws making their own religion the official religion of their respective colonies. Indeed, as late as the time of the Revolutionary War, there were established churches in at least eight of the thirteen former colonies and established religions in at least four of the other five. But the successful Revolution against English political domination was shortly followed by intense opposition to the practice of establishing religion by law....

There can be no doubt that New York's state prayer program officially establishes the religious beliefs embodied in the Regents' prayer. The respondents' argument to the contrary, which is largely based upon the contention that the Regents' prayer is "nondenominational" and the fact that the program, as modified and approved by state courts, does not require all pupils to recite the prayer but permits those who wish to do so to remain silent or be excused from the room, ignores the essential nature of the program's constitutional defects. Neither the fact that the prayer may be denominationally neutral, nor the fact that its observance on the part of the students is voluntary can serve to free it from the limitations of the Establishment Clause, as it might from the Free Exercise Clause, of the First Amendment, both of which are operative against the States by virtue of the Fourteenth Amendment. Although these two clauses may in certain instances overlap, they forbid two quite different kinds of governmental encroachment upon religious freedom. The Establishment Clause, unlike the Free Exercise Clause, does not depend upon any showing of direct governmental compulsion and is violated by the enactment of laws which establish an official religion whether those laws operate directly to coerce non-observing individuals or not. This is not to say, of course, that laws officially prescribing a particular form of religious worship do not involve coercion of such individuals. When the power, prestige and financial support of government is placed behind a particular religious belief, the indirect coercive pressure upon religious minorities to conform to the prevailing officially approved religion is plain. But the purposes underlying the Establishment Clause go much further than that. Its first and most immediate purpose rested on the belief that a union of government and religion tends to destroy government and to degrade religion.... The Establishment Clause thus stands as an expression of principle on the part of the Founders of our Constitution that religion is too personal, too sacred, too holy, to permit its "unhallowed perversion" by a civil magistrate. Another purpose of the Establishment Clause rested upon an awareness of the historical fact that governmentally established religions and religious persecutions go hand in hand. The Founders knew that only a few years after *The Book of Common Prayer* became the only accepted form of religious services in the established Church of England, an Act of Uniformity was passed to compel all Englishmen to attend those services and to make it a criminal offense to conduct or attend religious gatherings of any other kind.... It was in large part to get completely away from this sort of systematic religious persecution that the Founders brought into being our Nation, our Constitution, and our Bill of Rights with its prohibition against any governmental establishment of religion. The New York laws officially prescribing the Regents' prayer are inconsistent with both the purposes of the Establishment Clause and with the Establishment Clause itself.

It has been argued that to apply the Constitution in such a way as to prohibit state laws respecting an establishment of religious services in public schools is to indicate a hostility toward religion or toward prayer. Nothing, of course, could be more wrong. The history of man is inseparable from the history of religion. And perhaps it is not too much to say that since the beginning of that history many people have devoutly believed that "More things are wrought by prayer than this world dreams of." It was doubtless largely due to men who believed this that there grew up a sentiment that caused men to leave the cross-currents of officially established state religions and religious persecution in Europe and come to this country filled with the hope that they could find a place in which they could pray when they pleased to the God of their faith in the language they chose. And there were men of this same faith in the power of prayer who led the fight for adoption of our Constitution and also for our Bill of Rights with the very guaranties of religious freedom that forbid the sort of governmental activity which New York has attempted here. These men knew that the First Amendment, which tried to put an end to governmental control of religion and prayer, was not written to destroy either. They knew rather that it was written to quiet well-justified fears which nearly all of them felt arising out of an awareness that governments of the past had shackled men's tongues to make them speak only the religious thoughts that government wanted them to speak and to pray only to the God that government wanted them to pray to. It is neither sacrilegious nor antireligious to say that each separate government in this country should stay out of the business of writing or sanctioning official prayers and leave that purely religious function to the people themselves and to those the people choose to look to for religious guidance.

It is true that New York's establishment of its Regents' prayer as an officially approved religious doctrine of that State does not amount to a total establishment of one particular religious sect to the exclusion of all others – that, indeed, the governmental endorsement of that prayer seems relatively insignificant when compared to the governmental encroachments upon religion which were commonplace 200 years ago. To those who may subscribe to the view that because the Regents' official prayer is so brief and general there can be no danger to religious freedom in its governmental establishment, however, it may be appropriate to say in the words of James Madison, the author of the First Amendment:

> "[I]t is proper to take alarm at the first experiment on our liberties.... Who does not see that the same authority which can establish Christianity, in exclusion of all other Religions, may establish with the same ease any particular sect of Christians, in exclusion of all other Sects? That the same authority which can force a citizen to contribute three pence only of his property for the support of any one establishment, may force him to conform to any other establishment in all cases whatsoever?"

The judgment of the Court of Appeals of New York is reversed and the cause remanded for further proceedings not inconsistent with this opinion.
Reversed and remanded.

MR. JUSTICES FRANKFURTER and WHITE took no part in the decision of this case.
MR. JUSTICE DOUGLAS concurred.
MR. JUSTICE STEWART dissented, saying in part:

...The Court does not hold, nor could it, that New York has interfered with the free exercise of anybody's religion. For the state courts have made clear that those who object to reciting the prayer must be entirely free of any compulsion to do so, including any "embarrassments and pressures."... But the Court says that in permitting school children to say this simple prayer, the New York authorities have established "an official religion."

With all respect, I think the Court has misapplied a great constitutional principle. I cannot see how an "official religion" is established by letting those who want to say a prayer say it. On the contrary, I think that to deny the wish of these school children to join in reciting this prayer is to deny them the opportunity of sharing in the spiritual heritage of our Nation....

At the opening of each day's Session of this Court we stand, while one of our officials invokes the protection of God. Since the days of John Marshall our Crier has said, "God save the United States and this Honorable Court." Both the

Senate and the House of Representatives open their daily Sessions with prayer. Each of our Presidents, from George Washington to John F. Kennedy, has upon assuming his Office asked the protection and help of God.

The Court today says that the state and federal governments are without constitutional power to prescribe any particular form of words to be recited by any group of the American people on any subject touching religion.... In 1954, Congress added a phrase to the Pledge of Allegiance to the Flag so that it now contains the words "one Nation under God, indivisible, with liberty and justice for all." In 1952, Congress enacted legislation calling upon the President each year to proclaim a National Day of Prayer. Since 1865, the words "In God We Trust" have been impressed on our coins.

Countless similar examples could be listed, but there is no need to belabor the obvious....

I do not believe that this Court, or the Congress, or the President has by the actions and practices I have mentioned established an "official religion" in violation of the Constitution. And I do not believe the State of New York has done so in this case. What each has done has been to recognize and to follow the deeply entrenched and highly cherished spiritual traditions of our Nation-traditions which come down to us from those who almost two-hundred years ago avowed their "firm reliance on the Protection of Divine Providence" when they proclaimed the freedom and independence of this brave new world.

I dissent.

WISCONSIN v. YODER
406 U.S. 205; 92 S.Ct. 1526; 32 L. 2ed 15 (1972)

Wisconsin's compulsory school-attendance law requires every child in the state to attend school until the age of sixteen. Members of the Old Order Amish religion and the Conservative Amish Mennonite Church refused to send their children to public or private school after they had graduated from the eighth grade. The Amish, who have traditionally provided continuing informal vocational education to their children to prepare them for life in the rural community, sincerely believed that attendance beyond that level was contrary to their religious principles. More importantly, they believed that by complying with the law, they would endanger their own salvation and that of their children. After the state supreme court sustained the position of the Amish, the case was brought to the Supreme Court on a writ of certiorari.

MR. CHIEF JUSTICE BURGER delivered the opinion of the Court.

In support of their position, respondents presented as expert witnesses scholars on religion and education whose testimony is uncontradicted. They expressed their opinions on the relationship of the Amish belief concerning school attendance to the more general tenets of their religion, and described the impact that compulsory high school attendance could have on the continued survival of Amish communities as they exist in the United States today. The history of the

Amish sect was given in some detail, beginning with the Swiss Anabaptists of the 16th century who rejected institutionalized churches and sought to return to the early, simple, Christian life de-emphasizing material success, rejecting the competitive spirit, and seeking to insulate themselves from the modern world. As a result of the common heritage, Old Order Amish communities today are characterized by a fundamental belief that salvation requires life in a church community separate and apart from the world and worldly influence. This concept of life aloof from the world and its values is central to their faith.

A related feature of Old Order Amish communities is their devotion to a life in harmony with nature and the soil, as exemplified by the simple life of the early Christian era that continued in America during much of our early national life. Amish beliefs require members of the community to make their living by farming or closely related activities. Broadly speaking, the Old Order Amish religion pervades and determines the entire mode of life of its adherents. Their conduct is regulated in great detail by the *Ordnung*, or rules, of the church community. Adult baptism, which occurs in late adolescence, is the time at which Amish young people voluntarily undertake heavy obligations, not unlike the Bar Mitzvah of the Jews, to abide by the rules of the church community.

Amish objection to formal education beyond the eighth grade is firmly grounded in these central religious concepts. They object to the high school and higher education generally because the values it teaches are in marked variance with Amish values and the Amish way of life; they view secondary school education as an impermissible exposure of their children to a "worldly" influence in conflict with their beliefs. The high school tends to emphasize intellectual and scientific accomplishments, self-distinction, competitiveness, worldly success, and social life with other students. Amish society emphasizes informal learning-through-doing, a life of "goodness," rather than a life of intellect, wisdom, rather than technical knowledge, community welfare rather than competition, and separation, rather than integration with contemporary worldly society.

Formal high school education beyond the eighth grade is contrary to Amish beliefs not only because it places Amish children in an environment hostile to Amish beliefs with increasing emphasis on competition in class work and sports and with pressure to conform to the styles, manners, and ways of the peer group, but because it takes them away from their community, physically, and emotionally, during the crucial and formative adolescent period of life. During this period, the children must acquire Amish attitudes favoring manual work and self-reliance and the specific skills needed to perform the adult role of an Amish farmer or housewife. They must learn to enjoy physical labor. Once a child has learned basic reading, writing, and elementary mathematics, these traits, skills, and attitudes admittedly fall within the category of those best learned through example and "doing" rather than in a classroom. And, at this time in life, the Amish child must also grow in his faith and his relationship to the Amish Community if he is to be prepared to accept the heavy obligations imposed by adult baptism. In short, high school attendance with teachers who are not of the Amish faith - and may even be hostile to it - interposes a serious barrier to the integration of the Amish child into the Amish religious community. Dr. John Hostetler, one of the experts on Amish society, testified that the modern high school is not equipped, in curriculum or social environment, to impart the values promoted by Amish society.

The Amish do not object to elementary education through the first eight grades as a general proposition because they agree that their children must have basic skills in the "three R's" in order to read the Bible, to be good farmers and citizens, and to be able to deal with non-Amish people when necessary in the course of daily affairs. They view such basic education as acceptable because it does not significantly expose their children to worldly values or interfere with their development in the Amish community during the crucial adolescent period. While Amish accept compulsory elementary education generally, wherever possible they have established their own elementary schools in many respects like the small local schools of the past. In the Amish belief higher learning tends to develop values they reject as influences that alienate man from God.

On the basis of such considerations, Dr. Hostetler testified that compulsory high school attendance could not only result in great psychological harm to Amish children, because of the conflicts it would produce, but would also, in his opinion, ultimately result in the destruction of the Old Order Amish church community as it exists in the United States today. The testimony of Dr. Donald A. Erickson, an expert witness on education, also showed that the Amish succeed in preparing their high school age children to be productive members of the Amish community. He described their system of learning-through-doing the skills directly relevant to their adult roles in the Amish community as "ideal" and perhaps superior to ordinary high school education. The evidence also showed that the Amish have an excellent record as law-abiding and generally self-sufficient members of society.

Although the trial court in its careful findings determined that the Wisconsin compulsory school-attendance law "does interfere with the freedom of the Defendants to act in accordance with their sincere religious belief" it also concluded that the requirement of high school attendance until age 16 was a "reasonable and constitutional" exercise of governmental power, and therefore denied the motion to dismiss the charges. The Wisconsin Circuit Court affirmed the convictions. The Wisconsin Supreme Court, however, sustained respondents' claim under the Free Exercise Clause of the First Amendment and reversed the convictions. A majority of the court was of the opinion that the State had failed to make an adequate showing that its interest in "establishing and maintaining an educational system overrides the defendants' right to the free exercise of their religion."...

I

There is no doubt as to the power of a State, having a high responsibility for education of its citizens, to impose reasonable regulations for the control and duration of basic education. See, e.g., *Pierce v. Society of Sisters*, 268 U.S. 510, 534 (1925). Providing public schools ranks at the very apex of the function of a State. Yet even this paramount responsibility was, in *Pierce*, made to yield to the right of parents to provide an equivalent education in a privately operated system. There the Court held that Oregon's statute compelling attendance in a public school from age eight to age 16 unreasonably interfered with the interest of parents in directing the rearing of their offspring including their education in church-operated schools. As that case suggests, the values of parental direction of the religious upbringing and education of their children in their early and formative years have a high place in our society. See also *Ginsberg v. New York*, 390 U.S. 629, 639 (1968); *Meyer v. Nebraska*, 262 U.S. 390 (1923); cf. *Rowan v. Post Office Dept.*, 397 U.S. 728 (1970). Thus, a State's interest in universal education, however highly we rank it, is not totally free from a balancing process when it impinges on other fundamental rights and interests, such as those specifically protected by the Free Exercise Clause of the First Amendment and the traditional interest of parents with respect to the religious upbringing of their children so long as they, in the words of *Pierce*, "prepare them for additional obligations."...

It follows that in order for Wisconsin to compel school attendance beyond the eighth grade against a claim that such attendance interferes with the practice of a legitimate religious belief, it must appear either that the State does not deny the free exercise of religious belief by its requirement, or that there is a state interest of sufficient magnitude to override the interest claiming protection under the Free Exercise Clause. Long before there was general acknowledgment of the need for universal formal education, the Religious Clauses had specifically and firmly fixed the right to free exercise of religious beliefs, and buttressing this fundamental right was an equally firm, even if less explicit, prohibition against the establishment of any religion by government. The values underlying these two provisions relating to religion have been zealously protected, sometimes even at the expense of other interests of admittedly high social importance. The invalidation of financial aid to parochial schools by government grants for a salary subsidy for teachers is but one example of the extent to which courts have gone in this regard, notwithstanding that such aid programs were legislatively determined to be in the public interest and the service of sound educational policy by States and by Congress. *Lemon v. Kurtzman*, 403 U.S. 602 (1971); *Tilton v. Richardson*, 403 U.S. 672 (1971)....

The essence of all that has been said and written on the subject is that only those interests of the highest order and those not otherwise served can overbalance legitimate claims to the free exercise of religion. We can accept it as settled, therefore, that, however strong the State's interest in universal compulsory education, it is by no means absolute to the exclusion or subordination of all other interest....

II

We come then to the quality of the claims of the respondents concerning the alleged encroachment of Wisconsin's compulsory school-attendance statute on their rights and the rights of their children to the free exercise of the religious beliefs they and their forebears have adhered to for almost three centuries. In evaluating those claims we must be careful to determine whether the Amish religious faith and their mode of life are, as they claim, inseparable and interdependent. A way of life, however virtuous and admirable, may not be interposed as a barrier to reasonable state regulation of education if it is based on purely secular considerations; to have the protection of the Religion Clauses, the claims must be rooted in religious belief. Although a determination of what is a "religious" belief or practice entitled to constitutional protection may present a most delicate question, the very concept of ordered liberty precludes allowing every person to make his own standards on matters of conduct in which society as a whole has important interests. Thus, if the Amish asserted their claims because of their subjective evaluation and rejection of the contemporary secular values accepted by the majority, much as Thoreau rejected the social values of his time and isolated himself at Walden Pond, their claim would not rest on a religious basis, Thoreau's choice was philosophical and personal rather than religious, and such belief does not rise to the demands of the Religion Clauses.

Giving no weight to such secular considerations, however, we see that the record in this case abundantly supports the claim that the traditional way of life of the Amish is not merely a matter of personal preference, but one of deep religious conviction, shared by an organized group, and intimately related to daily living. That the Old Order Amish daily life and religious practice stem from their faith is shown by the fact that it is in response to their literal interpretation of the Biblical injunction from the Epistle of Paul to the Romans, "be not conformed to this world...." This command is fundamental to the Amish faith. Moreover, for the Old Order Amish, religion is not simply a matter of theocratic belief....

The record shows that the respondents' religious beliefs and attitude toward life, family, and home have remained constant – perhaps some would say static – in a period of unparalleled progress in human knowledge generally and great changes in education. The respondents freely concede, and indeed assert as an article of faith, that their religious beliefs and what we would today call "life style" have not altered in fundamentals for centuries. Their way of life in a church-oriented community, separated from the outside world and "worldly" influences, their attachment to nature and the soil, is a way inherently simple and uncomplicated, albeit difficult to preserve against the pressure to conform. Their rejection of telephones, automobiles, radios, and television, their mode of dress, of speech, their habits of manual work do indeed set them apart from much of contemporary society; these customs are both symbolic and practical.

As the society around the Amish has become more populous, urban, industrialized, and complex, particularly in this century, government regulation of human affairs has correspondingly become more detailed and pervasive. The Amish mode of life has thus come into conflict increasingly with requirements of contemporary society exerting a hydraulic insistence on conformity to majoritarian standards. So long as compulsory education laws were confined to eight grades of elementary basic education imparted in a nearby rural schoolhouse, with a large proportion of students of the Amish faith, the Old Order Amish had little basis to fear that school attendance would expose their children to the worldly influence they reject. But modem compulsory secondary education in rural areas is now largely carried on in a consolidated school, often remote from the student's home and alien to his daily home life.... The conclusion is inescapable that secondary schooling, by exposing Amish children to worldly influences in terms of attitudes, goals, and values contrary to beliefs, and by substantially interfering with the religious development of the Amish child and his integration into the way of life of the Amish faith community at the crucial adolescent stage of development, contravenes the basic religious tenets and practice of the Amish faith, both as to the parent and the child.

The impact of the compulsory-attendance law on respondents' practice of the Amish religion is not only severe, but inescapable, for the Wisconsin law affirmatively compels them, under threat of criminal sanction, to perform acts undeniably at odds with fundamental tenets of their religious beliefs.... Nor is the impact of the compulsory-attendance law confined to grave interference with important Amish religious tenets from a subjective point of view. It carries with it precisely the kind of objective danger to the free exercise of religion that the First Amendment was designed to prevent. As the record shows, compulsory school attendance to age 16 for Amish children carries with it a very real threat of undermining the Amish community and religious practice as they exist today; they must either abandon belief and be assimilated into society at large, or be forced to migrate to some other and more tolerant region.

In sum, the unchallenged testimony of acknowledged experts in education and religious history, almost 300 years of consistent practice, and strong evidence of a sustained faith pervading and regulating respondents' entire mode of life support the claim that enforcement of the State's requirement of compulsory formal education after the eighth grade would gravely endanger if not destroy the free exercise of respondents' religious beliefs.

III

Neither findings of the trial court nor the Amish claims as to the nature of their faith are challenged in this Court by the State of Wisconsin. Its position is that the State's interest in universal compulsory formal secondary education to age 16 is so great that it is paramount to the undisputed claims of respondents that their mode of preparing their youth for Amish life, after the traditional elementary education, is an essential part of their religious belief and practice. Nor does the State undertake to meet the claim that the Amish mode of life and education is inseparable from and a part of the basic tenets of their religion – indeed, as much a part of their religious belief and practices as baptism, the confessional, or a sabbath may be for others.

Wisconsin concedes that under the Religion Clauses religious beliefs are absolutely free from the State's control, but it argues that "actions," even though religiously grounded, are outside the protection of the First Amendment. But our decisions have rejected the idea that religiously grounded conduct is always outside the protection of the Free Exercise Clause....

The State advances two primary arguments in support of its system of compulsory education. It notes, as Thomas Jefferson pointed out early in our history, that some degree of education is necessary to prepare citizens to participate effectively and intelligently in our open political system if we are to preserve freedom and independence. Further, education prepares individuals to be self-reliant and self-sufficient participants in society. We accept these propositions.

However, the evidence adduced by the Amish in this case is persuasively to the effect that an additional one or two years of formal high school for Amish children in place of their long-established program of informal vocational education would do little to serve those interests. Respondents' experts testified at trial, without challenge, that the value of all education must be assessed in terms of its capacity to prepare the child for life. It is one thing to say that compulsory education for a year or two beyond the eighth grade may be necessary when its goal is the preparation of the child for life in modern society as the majority live, but it is quite another if the goal of education be viewed as the preparation of the child for life in the separated agrarian community that is the keystone of the Amish faith....

The State attacks respondents' position as one fostering "ignorance" from which the child must be protected by the State. No one can question the State's duty to protect children from ignorance but this argument does not square with the facts disclosed in the record. Whatever their idiosyncrasies as seen by the majority, this record strongly shows that the Amish community has been a highly successful social unit within our society even if apart from the conventional "mainstream." Its members are productive and very law-abiding members of society; they reject public welfare in any of its usual modern forms. The Congress itself recognized their self-sufficiency by authorizing exemptions of such groups as the Amish from the obligation to pay social security taxes....

We must not forget that in the Middle Ages important values of the civilization of the Western World were preserved by members of religious orders who isolated themselves from all worldly influences against great obstacles. There can be no assumption that today's majority is "right" and the Amish and others like them are "wrong." A way of life that is odd or even erratic but interferes with no rights or interests of others is not to be condemned because it is different....

There is nothing in this record to suggest that the Amish qualities of reliability, self-reliance, and dedication to work would fail to find ready markets in today's society. Absent some contrary evidence supporting the State's position, we are unwilling to assume that persons possessing such valuable vocational skills and habits are doomed to become burdens on society should they determine to leave the Amish faith, nor is there any basis in the record to warrant a finding that an additional one or two years of formal school education beyond the eighth grade would serve to eliminate any such problem that might exist....

The requirement of compulsory schooling to age 16 must therefore be viewed as aimed not merely at providing educational opportunities for children, but as an alternative to the equally undesirable consequence of unhealthful child labor displacing adult workers, or, on the other hand, forced idleness. The two kinds of statutes - compulsory school attendance and child labor laws - tend to keep children of certain ages off the labor market and in school; this in turn provides opportunity to prepare for livelihood of a higher order than that children could pursue without education and protects their health in adolescence.

In these terms, Wisconsin's interest in compelling the school attendance of Amish children to age 16 emerges as somewhat less substantial than requiring such attendance for children generally. For, while agricultural employment is not totally outside the legitimate concerns of the child labor laws, employment of children under parental guidance and on the family farm from age 14 to age 16 is an ancient tradition that lies at the periphery of the objectives of such laws. There is no intimation that the Amish employment of their children on family farms is in any way deleterious to their health or that Amish parents exploit children at tender years. Any such inference would be contrary to the record before us. Moreover, employment of Amish children on the family farm does not present the undesirable economic aspects of eliminating jobs that might otherwise be held by adults.

IV

Our holding in no way determines the proper resolution of possible competing interests of parents, children, and the State in an appropriate state court proceeding in which the power of the State is asserted on the theory that Amish parents are preventing their minor children from attending high school despite their expressed desires to the contrary. Recognition of the claim of the State in such a proceeding would, of course, call into question traditional concepts of parental control over the religious upbringing and education of their minor children recognized in this Court's past decisions. It is clear that such an intrusion by a State into family decisions in the area of religious training would give rise to grave questions of religious freedom comparable to those raised here and those presented in *Pierce v. Society of Sisters*, 268 U.S. 510 (1925). On this record we neither reach nor decide those issues.

The State's argument proceeds without reliance on any actual conflict between the wishes of parents and children. It appears to rest on the potential that exemption of Amish parents from the requirements of the compulsory-education law might allow some parents to act contrary to the best interests of their children by foreclosing their opportunity to make an intelligent choice between the Amish way of life and that of the outside world. The same argument could, of course, be made with respect to all church schools short of college. There is nothing in the record or in the ordinary course of human experience to suggest that non-Amish parents generally consult with children of ages 14-16 if they are placed in a church school of the parents' faith.

Indeed it seems clear that if the State is empowered, as *parens patriae*, to "save" a child from himself or his Amish parents by requiring an additional two years of compulsory formal high school education, the State will in large measure influence, if not determine, the religious future of the child. Even more markedly than in *Prince*, therefore, this case involves the fundamental interest of parents, as contrasted with that of the State, to guide the religious future and education of their children. The history and culture of Western civilization reflect a strong tradition of parental concern for the nurture and upbringing of their children. This primary role of the parents in the upbringing of their children is now established beyond debate as an enduring American tradition....

However read, the Court's holding in *Pierce* stands as a charter of the rights of parents to direct the religious upbringing of their children. And, when the interests of parenthood are combined with a free exercise claim of the nature revealed by this record, more than merely a "reasonable relation to some purpose within the competency of the State" is required to sustain the validity of the State's requirement under the First Amendment. To be sure, the power of the parent, even when linked to a free exercise claim, may be subject to limitation under *Prince* if it appears that parental decisions will jeopardize the health or safety of the child, or have a potential for significant social burdens. But in this case, the Amish have introduced persuasive evidence undermining the arguments the State has advanced to support its claims in terms of the welfare of the child and society as a whole. The record strongly indicates that accommodating the religious objections of the Amish by forgoing one, or at most two, additional years of compulsory education will not impair the physical or mental health of the child, or result in an inability to be self-supporting or to discharge the duties and responsibilities of citizenship, or in any other way materially detract from the welfare of society.

In the face of our consistent emphasis on the central values underlying the Religion Clauses in our constitutional scheme of government, we cannot accept a *parens patriae* claim of such all-encompassing scope and with such sweeping potential for broad and unforeseeable application as that urged by the State.

V

For the reasons stated we hold, with the supreme court of Wisconsin, that the First and Fourteenth Amendments prevent the State from compelling respondents to cause their children to attend formal high school to age 16. Our disposition of this case, however, in no way alters our recognition of the obvious fact that courts are not school boards or legislatures, and are ill-equipped to determine the "necessity" of discrete aspects of a State's program of compulsory education. This should suggest that courts must move with great circumspection in performing the sensitive and delicate task of weighing a State's legitimate social concern when faced with religious claims for exemption from generally applicable educational requirements. It cannot be overemphasized that we are not dealing with a way of life and mode of education by a group claiming to have recently discovered some "progressive" or more enlightened process for rearing children for modern life.

Aided by a history of three centuries as an identifiable religious sect and a long history as a successful and self-sufficient segment of American society, the Amish in this case have convincingly demonstrated the sincerity of their religious beliefs, the interrelationship of belief with their mode of life, the vital role that belief and daily conduct play in the continued survival of Old Order Amish communities and their religious organization, and the hazards presented by the State's enforcement of a statute generally valid as to others. Beyond this, they have carried the even more difficult burden of demonstrating the adequacy of their alternative mode of continuing informal vocational education in terms of precisely those overall interests that the State advances in support of its program of compulsory high school education. In light of this convincing showing, one that probably few other religious groups or sects could make, and weighing the minimal difference between what the State would require and what the Amish already accept, it was incumbent on the State to show with more particularity how its admittedly strong interest in compulsory education would be adversely affected by granting an exemption to the Amish. *Sherbert v. Verner.*

Nothing we hold is intended to undermine the general applicability of the State's compulsory school-attendance statutes or to limit the power of the State to promulgate reasonable standards that, while not impairing the free exercise of religion, provide for continuing agricultural vocational education under parental and church guidance by the Old Order Amish or others similarly situated. The States have had a long history of amicable and effective relationships with church-sponsored schools, and there is no basis for assuming that, in this related context, reasonable standards cannot be established concerning the content of the continuing vocational education of Amish children under parental guidance, provided always that state regulations are not inconsistent with what we have said in this opinion.

Affirmed.

MR. JUSTICES POWELL and REHNQUIST took no part in the consideration or decision of this case,

MR. JUSTICE STEWART, with whom MR. JUSTICE BRENNAN joined, concurred.

MR. JUSTICE WHITE, with whom MR. JUSTICES BRENNAN and STEWART joined, concurred.

MR. JUSTICE DOUGLAS dissented in part.

COMMITTEE FOR PUBLIC EDUCATION v. NYQUIST
413 U.S. 756; 93 S.Ct. 2955 (1974)

By the late 1960's, the national economic situation had deteriorated to such an extent that most parochial and private non-denominational educational institutions were facing financial ruin. A number of states enacted legislation to provide some form of relief, including New York which amended its Education and Tax Laws to create three financial aid programs for nonpublic elementary and secondary schools. One program provided for direct monetary grants to the schools for maintenance and repair of facilities and equipment, while the remaining two established a plan for tuition reimbursement and tax relief for "qualifying" parents of children attending such schools. A complaint was filed in a federal district court by the Committee for Public Education and Religious Liberty (Pearl), among others, challenging the programs as violative of the Establishment Clause. The Court held that only the tax relief provision was valid.

The case was then appealed to the Supreme Court. It was decided with a companion case from Pennsylvania, Sloan v. Lemon.

MR. JUSTICE POWELL delivered the opinion of the Court.

James Madison, in his Memorial and Remonstrance Against Religious Assessments, admonished that a "prudent jealousy" for religious freedoms required that they never become "entangled ...in precedents." His strongly held convictions, coupled with those of Thomas Jefferson and others among the Founders, are reflected in the first Clauses of the First Amendment of the Bill of Rights, which state that "Congress shall make no law respecting an establishment of religion, or prohibiting the free exercise thereof." Yet, despite Madison's admonition and the "sweep of the absolute prohibitions" of the Clauses, this Nation's history has not been one of entirely sanitized separation between Church and State. It has never been thought either possible or desirable to enforce a regime of total separation, and as a consequence cases arising under these Clauses have presented some of the most perplexing questions to come before this Court. Those cases have occasioned thorough and thoughtful scholarship by several of this Court's most respected former Justices, including Justices Black, Frankfurter, Harlan, Jackson, Rutledge, and Chief Justice Warren.

As a result of these decisions and opinions, it may no longer be said that the Religion Clauses are free of "entangling" precedents. Neither, however, may it be said that Jefferson's metaphoric "wall of separation" between Church and State has become "as winding as the famous serpentine wall" he designed for the University of Virginia. *McCollum v. Board of Education,*...(1948).... Indeed, the controlling constitutional standards have become firmly rooted and the broad contours of our inquiry are now well defined. Our task, therefore, is to assess New York's several forms of aid in the light of principles already delineated.

I

The first section of the challenged enactment, entitled "Health and Safety Grants for Nonpublic School Children," provides for direct money grants from the State to "qualifying" nonpublic schools to be used for the "maintenance and repair of ... school facilities and equipment to ensure health, welfare and safety of enrolled pupils." A "qualifying" school is any nonpublic, nonprofit elementary or secondary school which "has been designated during the immediately preceding year as serving a high concentration of pupils from low-income families for purposes of Title IV of the Federal Higher Education Act of nineteen hundred sixty-five...." Such schools are entitled to receive a grant of $30 per pupil per year, or $40 per pupil per year if the facilities are more than 25 years old. Each school is required to submit to the Commissioner of Education an audited statement of its expenditures for maintenance and repair during the preceding year, and its grant may not exceed the total of such expenses. The Commissioner is also required to ascertain the average per-pupil cost for equivalent maintenance and repair services in the public schools, and in no event may the grant to nonpublic qualifying schools exceed 50 % of that figure.

"Maintenance and repair" is defined by the statute to include "the provision of heat, light, water, ventilation and sanitary facilities; cleaning, janitorial and custodial services; snow removal; necessary upkeep and renovation of buildings, grounds and equipment; fire and accident protection; and such other items as the commissioner may deem necessary to ensure the health, welfare and safety of enrolled pupils." This section is prefaced by a series of legislative findings which shed light on the State's purpose in enacting the law. These findings conclude that the State "has a primary responsibility to ensure the health, welfare and safety of children attending ... nonpublic schools;" that the "fiscal crisis in nonpublic education ... has caused a diminution of proper maintenance and repair programs, threatening the health, welfare and safety of nonpublic school children" in low-income urban areas; and that "a healthy and safe school environment" contributes "to the stability of urban neighborhoods." For these reasons, the statute declares that "the state has the right to make grants for maintenance and repair expenditures which are clearly secular, neutral and non-ideological in nature."

The remainder of the challenged legislation ... is a single package captioned the "Elementary and Secondary Education Opportunity Program." It is composed, essentially, of two parts, a tuition grant program and a tax benefit program. Section 2 establishes a limited plan providing tuition reimbursements to parents of children attending elementary or secondary nonpublic schools. To qualify under this section a parent must have an annual taxable income of less than $5,000. The amount of reimbursement is limited to $50 for each grade school child and $100 for each high school child. Each parent is required, however, to submit to the Commissioner of Education a verified statement containing a receipted tuition bill, and the amount of state reimbursement may not exceed 50% of that figure. No restrictions are imposed on the use of the funds by the reimbursed parents....

Expressing a dedication to the "vitality of our pluralistic society," the findings state that a "healthy competitive and diverse alternative to public education is not only desirable but indeed vital to a state and nation that have continually reaffirmed the value of individual differences." The findings further emphasize that the right to select among alternative educational systems "is diminished or even denied to children of lower-income families, whose parents, of all groups, have the least options in determining where their children are to be educated."...

The remainder of the "Elementary and Secondary Education Opportunity Program" ... is designed to provide a form of tax relief to those who fail to qualify for tuition reimbursement. Under these sections parents may subtract from their adjusted gross income for state income tax purposes a designated amount for each dependent for whom they have paid at least $50 in nonpublic school tuition. If the taxpayer's adjusted gross income is less than $9,000 he may subtract $1,000 for each of as many as three dependents. As the taxpayer's income rises, the amount he may subtract diminishes. Thus, if a taxpayer has adjusted gross income of $15,000, he may subtract only $400 per dependent, and if his income is $25,000 or more, no deduction is allowed. The amount of the deduction is not dependent upon how much the taxpayer actually paid for nonpublic school tuition, and is given in addition to any deductions to which the taxpayer may be entitled for other religious or charitable contributions....

Of course, the characteristics of individual schools may vary widely.... Some 700,000 to 800,000 students, constituting almost 20% of the State's entire elementary and secondary school population, attend over 2,000 nonpublic schools approximately 85 % of which are church affiliated. And while "all or practically all" of the 280 schools entitled to receive "maintenance and repair" grants "are related to the Roman Catholic Church and teach Catholic religious doctrine to some degree," ...institutions qualifying under the remainder of the statute include a substantial number of Jewish, Lutheran, Episcopal, Seventh-Day Adventist, and other church-affiliated schools.

Plaintiffs argued below that because of the substantially religious character of the intended beneficiaries, each of the State's three enactments offended the Establishment Clause. The District Court, in an opinion carefully canvassing this Court's recent precedents, held unanimously that §1 (maintenance and repair grants) and §2 (tuition reimbursement grants) were valid. As to the income tax provisions of §§3, 4, and 5, however, a majority of the District Court, over the dissent of Circuit Judge Hays, held that the Establishment Clause had not been violated. Finding the provisions of the law severable, it enjoined permanently any further implementation of §§1 and 2 but, declared the remainder of the law independently enforceable.

II

The history of the Establishment Clause has been recounted frequently and need not be repeated here. See *Everson v. Board of Education*, 330 U.S. 1 (1947); ...*McCollum v. Board of Education*; ... *McGowan v. Maryland*, 366 U.S. 420 (1961); *Engel v. Vitale*, 370 U.S. 421 (1962). It is enough to note that it is now firmly established that a law may be one "respecting an establishment of religion" even though its consequence is not to promote a "state religion," *Lemon v. Kurtzman*, 403 U.S. 602 ...(1971), and even though it does not aid one religion more than another but merely benefits all religions alike. *Everson v. Board of Education*.... it is equally well established, however, that not every law that confers an "indirect," "remote," or "incidental" benefit upon religious institutions is, for that reason alone, constitutionally invalid. *Everson*, supra; *McGowan v. Maryland*, supra, at 450; *Walz v. Tax Comm'n*, 397 U.S. 664 ... (1970). What our cases require is careful examination of any law challenged on establishment grounds with a view to ascertaining whether it furthers any of the evils against which that Clause protects. Primary among those evils have been "sponsorship, financial support, and active involvement of the sovereign in religious activity." *Walz v. Tax Comm'n*; ... *Lemon v. Kurtzman*....

Most of the cases coming to this Court raising Establishment Clause questions have involved the relationship between religion and education. Among these religion-education precedents, two general categories of cases may be identified: those dealing with religious activities within the public schools, and those involving public aid in varying forms to sectarian educational institutions. While the New York legislation places this case in the latter category, its resolution requires consideration not only of the several aid-to-sectarian-education cases, but also of our other educational precedents and of several important noneducation cases. For the now well-defined three-part test that has emerged from our decisions is a product of considerations derived from the full sweep of the Establishment Clause cases. Taken together, these decisions dictate that to pass muster under the Establishment Clause the law in question, first, must reflect a clearly secular legislative purpose.... *Epperson v. Arkansas*, 393, U.S. 97 (1968), second, must have a primary effect that neither advances nor inhibits religion; ... *School District of Abington Township v. Schempp*, 374 U.S. 203 (1963), and, third, must avoid excessive government entanglement with religion; ...*Tilton v. Richardson*, 403 U.S. 672, 678 (1971).

In applying these criteria to the three distinct forms of aid involved in this case, we need touch only briefly on the requirement of a "secular legislative purpose." As the recitation of legislative purposes appended to New York's law indicates, each measure is adequately supported by legitimate, nonsectarian state interests. We do not question the propriety, and full secular content, of New York's interest in preserving a healthy and safe educational environment for all of its school children. And we do not doubt – indeed, we fully recognize – the validity of the State's interests in promoting pluralism and diversity among its public and nonpublic schools. Nor do we hesitate to acknowledge the reality of its concern for an already overburdened public school system that might suffer in the event that a significant percentage of children presently attending nonpublic schools should abandon those schools in favor of the public schools.

But the propriety of a legislature's purposes may not immunize from further scrutiny a law which either has a primary effect that advances religion, or which fosters excessive entanglements between Church and State. Accordingly, we must weigh each of the three aid provisions challenged here against these criteria of effect and entanglement....

What we have said demonstrates that New York's maintenance and repair provisions violate the Establishment Clause because their effect, inevitably, is to subsidize and advance the religious mission of sectarian schools. We have no occasion, therefore, to consider the further question whether those provisions as presently written would also fail to survive scrutiny under the administrative entanglement aspect of the three-part test because assuring the secular use of all funds requires too intrusive and continuing a relationship between Church and State, *Lemon v. Kurtzman*....

New York's tuition reimbursement program also fails the "effect" test, for much the same reasons that govern its maintenance and repair grants....

There can be no question that these grants could not, consistently with the Establishment Clause, be given directly to sectarian schools, since they would suffer from the same deficiency that renders invalid the grants for maintenance and repair. In the absence of an effective means of guaranteeing that the state aid derived from public funds will be used exclusively for secular, neutral, and nonideological purposes, it is clear from our cases that direct aid in whatever form is invalid. As Mr. Justice Black put it quite simply in Everson:

> "No tax in any amount, large or small, can be levied to support any religious activities or institutions, whatever they may be called, or whatever form they may adopt to teach or practice religion...."

The controlling question here, then, is whether the fact that the grants are delivered to parents rather than schools is of such significance as to compel a contrary result. The State ...[relies] on *Everson* and *Allen* for their claim that grants to parents, unlike grants to institutions, respect the "wall of separation" required by the Constitution. It is true that in those cases the Court upheld laws that provided benefits to children attending religious schools and to their parents. As noted above, in *Everson* parents were reimbursed for bus fares paid to send children to parochial schools, and in *Allen* textbooks were loaned directly to the children. But those decisions make clear that, far from providing a *per se* immunity from examination of the substance of the State's program, the fact that aid is disbursed to parents rather than to the schools is only one among many factors to be considered.

In *Everson*, the Court found the bus fare program analogous to the provision of services such as police and fire protection, sewage disposal, highways, and sidewalks for parochial schools.... Such services, provided in common to all citizens, are "so separate and so indisputably marked off from the religious function," ... that they may fairly be viewed as reflections of a neutral posture toward religious institutions. *Allen* is founded upon a similar principle. The Court there repeatedly emphasized that upon the record in that case there was no indication that textbooks would be provided for anything other than purely secular courses. "Of course books are different from buses. Most bus rides have no inherent religious significance, while religious books are common. However, the language of [the law under consideration] does not authorize the loan of religious books, and the State claims no right to distribute religious literature.... Absent evidence, we cannot assume that school authorities ... are unable to distinguish between secular and religious books or that they will not honestly discharge their duties under the law...."

The tuition grants here are subject to no such restrictions. There has been no endeavor "to guarantee the separation between secular and religious educational functions and to ensure that State financial aid supports only the former." *Lemon v. Kurtzman*.... Indeed, it is precisely the function of New York's law to provide assistance to private schools, the great majority of which are sectarian. By reimbursing parents for a portion of their tuition bill, the State seeks to relieve their financial burdens sufficiently to assure that they continue to have the option to send their children to religion-oriented schools. And while the other purposes for that aid – to perpetuate a pluralistic educational environment and to protect the fiscal integrity of overburdening public schools – are certainly unexceptionable, the effect of the aid is unmistakably to provide desired financial support for nonpublic, sectarian institutions....

Finally, the State argues that its program of tuition grants should survive scrutiny because it is designed to promote the free exercise of religion. The State notes that only "low-income parents" are aided by this law, and without state assistance their right to have their children educated in a religious environment "is diminished or even denied." It is true, of course, that this Court has long recognized and maintained the right to choose nonpublic over public education. *Pierce v. Society of Sisters*, 268 U.S. 510 (1925). It is also true that a state law interfering with a parent's right to have his child educated in a sectarian school would run afoul of the Free Exercise Clause. But this Court repeatedly has recognized that tension inevitably exists between the Free Exercise and the Establishment Clauses.... and that it may often not be possible to promote the former without offending the latter. As a result of this tension, our cases require the State to maintain an attitude of "neutrality," neither "advancing" nor "inhibiting" religion. In its attempt to enhance the opportunities of the poor to choose between public and nonpublic education, the State has taken a step which can only be regarded as one "advancing" religion. However great our sympathy ... for the burdens experienced by those who must pay public school taxes at the same time that they support other schools because of the constraints of "conscience and discipline," ...and notwithstanding the "high social importance" of the State's purposes, *Wisconsin v. Yoder*, 406 U.S. 205 ... (1972), neither may justify an eroding of the limitations of the Establishment Clause now firmly emplanted....

Sections 3, 4, and 5 establish a system for providing income tax benefits to parents of children attending New York's nonpublic schools.... Because of the peculiar nature of the benefit allowed, it is difficult to adopt any single traditional label lifted from the law of income taxation. It is, at least in its form, a tax deduction since it is an amount subtracted from adjusted gross income, prior to computation of the tax due....

In practical terms there would appear to be little difference, for purposes of determining whether such aid has the effect of advancing religion, between the tax benefit allowed here and the tuition grant allowed under §2. The qualifying parent under either program receives the same form of encouragement and reward for sending his children to nonpublic schools. The only difference is that one parent receives an actual cash payment while the other is allowed to reduce by an arbitrary amount the sum he would otherwise be obliged to pay over to the State....

Appellees place their strongest reliance on *Walz v. Tax Comm'n*, *supra*, in which New York's property tax exemption for religious organizations was upheld. We think that *Walz* provides no support for appellees' position. Indeed, its rationale plainly compels the conclusion that New York's tax package violates the Establishment Clause.

Tax exemptions for church property enjoyed an apparently universal approval in this country both before and after the adoption of the First

Amendment. The Court in *Walz* surveyed the history of tax exemptions and found that each of the 50 States has long provided for tax exemptions for places of worship, that Congress has exempted religious organizations from taxation for over three-quarters of a century, and that congressional enactments in 1802, 1813, and 1870 specifically exempted church property from taxation. In sum, the Court concluded that "[f]ew concepts are more deeply embedded in the fabric of our national life, beginning with pre-Revolutionary colonial times, than for the government to exercise at the very least this kind of benevolent neutrality toward churches and religious exercise generally...." We know of no historical precedent for New York's recently promulgated tax relief program....

Apart from its historical foundations, *Walz* is a product of the same dilemma and inherent tension found in most government-aid-to-religion controversies. To be sure, the exemption of church property from taxation conferred a benefit, albeit an indirect and incidental one. Yet that "aid" was a product not of any purpose to support or to subsidize, but of a fiscal relationship designed to minimize involvement and entanglement between Church and State.... The granting of the tax benefits under the New York statute, unlike the extension of an exemption, would tend to increase rather than limit the involvement between Church and State.

One further difference between tax exemptions for church property and tax benefits for parents should be noted. The exemption challenged in *Walz* was not restricted to a class composed exclusively or even predominantly of religious institutions. Instead, the exemption covered all property devoted to religious, educational, or charitable purposes. As the parties here must concede, tax reductions authorized by this law flow primarily to the parents of children attending sectarian, nonpublic schools. Without intimating whether this factor alone might have controlling significance in another context in some future case, it should be apparent that in terms of the potential divisiveness of any legislative measure the narrowness of the benefited class would be an important factor.

In conclusion, we find the *Walz* analogy unpersuasive, and in light of the practical similarity between New York's tax and tuition reimbursement programs, we hold that neither form of aid is sufficiently restricted to assure that it will not have the impermissible effect of advancing the sectarian activities of religious schools.

III

Because we have found that the challenged sections have the impermissible effect of advancing religion, we need not consider whether such aid would result in entanglement of the State with religion in the sense of "[a] comprehensive, discriminating, and continuing state surveillance." *Lemon v. Kurtzman*.... But the importance of the competing societal interests implicated here prompts us to make the further observation that, apart from any specific entanglement of the State in particular religious programs, assistance of the sort here involved carries grave potential for entanglement in the broader sense of continuing political strife over aid to religion.

Few would question most of the legislative findings supporting this statute. We recognized in *Board of Education v. Allen* ... that "private education has played and is playing a significant and valuable role in raising national levels of knowledge, competence, and experience," and certainly private parochial schools have contributed importantly to this role. Moreover, the tailoring of the New York statute to channel the aid provided primarily to afford low-income families the option of determining where their children are to be educated is most appealing. There is no doubt that the private schools are confronted with increasingly grave fiscal problems, that resolving these problems by increasing tuition charges forces parents to turn to the public schools, and that this in turn – as the present legislation recognizes – exacerbates the problems of public education at the same time that it weakens support for the parochial schools.

These, in briefest summary, are the underlying reasons for the New York legislation and for similar legislation in other States. They are substantial reasons. Yet they must be weighed against the relevant provisions and purposes of the First Amendment, which safeguard the separation of Church from State and which have been regarded from the beginning as among the most cherished features of our constitutional system....

All three of these programs start out at modest levels; the maintenance grant is not to exceed $40 per pupil per year in approved schools; the tuition grant provides parents not more than $50 a year for each child in the first eight grades and $100 for each child in the high school grades; and the tax benefit, though more difficult to compute, is equally modest. But we know from long experience with both Federal and State Governments that aid programs of any kind tend to become entrenched, to escalate in cost, and to generate their own aggressive constituencies. And the larger the class of recipients, the greater the pressure for accelerated increases. Moreover, the State itself, concededly anxious to avoid assuming the burden of educating children now in private and parochial schools, has a strong motivation for increasing this aid as public school costs rise and population increases. In this situation, where the underlying issue is the deeply emotional one of Church-State relationships, the potential for seriously divisive political consequences needs no elaboration. And while the prospect of such divisiveness may not alone warrant the invalidation of state laws that otherwise survive the careful scrutiny required by the decisions of this Court, it is certainly a "warning signal" not to be ignored....

Our examination of New York's aid provisions, in light of all relevant considerations, compels the judgment that each, as written, has a "primary effect that advances religion" and offends the constitutional prohibition against laws "respecting an establishment of religion." We therefore affirm the three-judge court's holding....

It is so ordered.

MR. CHIEF JUSTICE BURGER, joined in part by MR. JUSTICE WHITE, and joined by MR. JUSTICE REHNQUIST, concurred in part and dissented in part.

MR. JUSTICE WHITE, joined in part by THE CHIEF JUSTICE and MR. JUSTICE REHNQUIST, dissented, saying in part:

Each of the States regards the education of its young to be a critical matter – so much so that it compels school attendance and provides an educational system at public expense, Any otherwise qualified child is entitled to a free elementary and secondary school education, or at least an education that costs him very little as compared with its cost to the State.

This Court has held, however, that the Due Process Clause of the Constitution entitles parents to send their children to nonpublic schools, secular or sectarian, if those schools are sufficiently competent to educate the child in the necessary secular subjects. *Pierce v. Society of Sisters*, 268 U.S. 510 (1925). About 10% of the Nation's children, approximately 5.2 million students, now take this option and are not being educated in public schools at public expense. Under state law these children have a right to a free public education and it would not appear unreasonable if the State, relieved of the expense of educating a child in the public school, contributed to the expense of his education elsewhere. The parents of such children pay taxes, including school taxes. They could receive in return a free education in the public schools. They prefer to send their children, as they have the right to do, to nonpublic schools that furnish the satisfactory equivalent of a public school education but also offer subjects or other assumed advantages not available in public schools. Constitutional considerations aside, it would be understandable if a State gave such parents a call on the public treasury up to the amount it would have cost the State to educate the child in public school, or, to put it another way, up to the amount the parents save the State by not sending their children to public school.

In light of the Free Exercise Clause of the First Amendment, this would seem particularly the case where the parent desires his child to attend a school that offers not only secular subjects but religious training as well. A State should put no unnecessary obstacles in the way of religious training for the young. "When the state encourages religious instruction ...it follows the best of our traditions." *Zorach v. Clauson*, 343 U.S. 306 ... (1952); *Walz v. Tax Commn*, 397 U.S. 664 ... (1970). Positing an obligation on the State to educate its children, which every State acknowledges, it should be wholly acceptable for the State to contribute to the secular education of children going to sectarian schools rather than to insist that if parents want to provide their children with religious as well as secular education, the State will refuse to contribute anything to their secular training.

Historically, the States of the Union have not furnished public aid for education in private schools. But in the last few years, as private education, particularly the parochial school system, has encountered financial difficulties, with many schools being closed and many more apparently headed in that direction, there has developed a variety of programs seeking to extend at least some aid to private educational institutions. Some States have provided only fringe benefits or auxiliary services. Others attempted more extensive efforts to keep the private school system alive. Some made direct arrangements with private and parochial schools for the purchase of secular educational services furnished by those schools....

No one contends that he can discern from the sparse language of the Establishment Clause that a State is forbidden to aid religion in any manner whatsoever or, if it does not mean that, what kind of or how much aid is permissible. And one cannot seriously believe that the history of the First Amendment furnishes unequivocal answers to many of the fundamental issues of church-state relations. In the end, the courts have fashioned answers to these questions as best they can, language of the Constitution and its history having left them a wide range of choice among many alternatives. But decision has been unavoidable; and, in choosing, the courts necessarily have carved out what they deemed to be the most desirable national policy governing various aspects of church-state relationships.

The course of these decisions has made it clear that the First Amendment does not bar all state aid to religion, of whatever kind or extent....

The Court ... has *not* barred *all aid* to religion or *to religious institutions*. Rather, it has attempted to devise a formula that would help *identify* the kind and *degree of aid* that is permitted or *forbidden* by the Establishment Clause...

There is no doubt here that Pennsylvania and New York have sought in the challenged laws to keep their parochial schools system alive and capable of providing adequate secular education to substantial numbers of students. This purpose satisfies the Court, even though to rescue schools that would otherwise fail will inevitably enable those schools to continue whatever religious functions they perform, By the same token, it seems to me, preserving the secular functions of these schools is the overriding consequence of these laws and the resulting, but incidental, benefit to religion should not invalidate them.

At the very least, I would not strike down these statutes on their face. The Court's opinion emphasizes a particular kind of parochial school, one restricted to students of particular religious beliefs and conditioning attendance on religious study. Concededly, there are many parochial schools that do not impose such restrictions. Where they do not, it is even more difficult for me to understand why the primary effect of these statutes is to advance religion. I do not think it is and therefore dissent from the Court's judgment invalidating the challenged New York and Pennsylvania statutes.

CHAPTER XI

INDIVIDUAL LIBERTY: THE RIGHT OF PRIVACY

As seen in Chapter X, virtually every individual right found in the first eight amendments to the Constitution is now enforceable against state, as well as federal, action. Nonetheless, in what can be considered the Constitution's greatest archaism, John Marshall's decision in *Barron v. Baltimore* is still good law. The specific provisions of the Bill of Rights do not *directly* apply to the state governments. The reason for this lies in the means by which the Court applied the Bill of Rights to the states.

Although Justice Hugo Black, one of the greatest civil libertarians ever to sit on the Supreme Court, argued that the framers of the Fourteenth Amendment intended the entire Bill of Rights to be applicable to the states, the Supreme Court has never come close to adopting this view. Rather, the high court applied the Bill of Rights through the doctrine of substantive due process. Traditionally, and to common sense, the due process clauses of the Fifth and Fourteenth Amendments restrict only the *processes or procedures* by which the government deprives a person of his or her life, liberty or property. The purpose of *procedural due process* was understood to be to ensure fairness and to prevent arbitrary and capricious actions by the government. In this traditional sense, due process does not restrict the substance of what the government can do – so long as the proper procedures are followed. For example, the state can deprive a person of his or her life, but it cannot do so on the mere whim or arbitrary action of the governor or legislature. Rather, the government must follow the appropriate legislative and judicial procedures. In contrast, *substantive due process* refers to the Court's interpretation of the due process clauses as placing not simply procedural limits on government actions, but substantive limits as well. There are some things the government cannot do in the normal exercise of its powers – no matter how fair and correct are the procedures by which it does them. Such are laws infringing on "fundamental" rights. Through "selective incorporation" the Supreme Court defined just about all the liberties contained in the Bill of Rights to be "fundamental" and therefore contained in the due process clause of the Fourteenth Amendment and protected from infringement by the states.

The importance of this approach is that it means that the *substantive* rights protected by the due process clauses of the Fifth and Fourteenth Amendments are *not restricted to those expressed in the original Bill of Rights.* Indeed, this is why Justice Black rejected the substantive due process approach for applying the Bill of Rights to the States. In his view, substantive due process allows the Court to create a new right whenever a majority of the Court wants. This doctrine had been evoked twice before with disastrous results. In the *Dred Scott* case, Chief Justice Taney used the due process clause of the Fifth Amendment to grant slave owners a virtual absolute right to their human property. During the *Lochner* era, the Court created a "right of contract" protected by the Fourteenth Amendment's due process clause as the means of prohibiting state regulation of the economy.

During this period of "*economic due process*," the Court began the slow process of selective incorporation of the Bill of Rights, primarily with the application of the freedom of speech and press to the states. With respect to claims of other non-economic rights not found in the Bill of Rights, however, the Court tended to support government regulation by application of the *reasonableness test.* See, for example, *Jacobson v. Massachusetts* (1905) and *Buck v. Bell* (1927). As long as the government law or action had a "reasonable" relation to a legitimate government end, the Court upheld the limits imposed upon individual liberty. The reasonableness test is still used today. It generally means that the Court will presume that a challenged law or act is constitutional and that the burden of proof is on those challenging its validity to clearly demonstrate otherwise. Laws or actions restricting an individual's "fundamental" rights, however, are usually made subject to the "compelling" interest test. This means that the government must be able to show a "compelling" or commanding reason why it must infringe upon the personal liberty interest involved. In effect, this shifts the burden of proof from those challenging the government action to the government itself. The Court here presumes that the law is unconstitutional and the government must be able to persuade it to make, in essence, an exception to the general rule.

The New Deal Courts *repudiated* the notion that substantive due process provided the basis for *economic rights* which prevented or limited state regulation of the economy. It did *not*, however, repudiate the doctrine of substantive due process, but concentrated its focus upon the continued incorporation of the Bill of Rights. This emphasis tended to obscure the constitutional implications of substantive due process for several reasons. First, because many of the specific protections being defined as fundamental were themselves of a procedural nature, e.g., the right to trial by jury, the substantive aspects of their incorporation was not always noted. Secondly, those rights of a substantive nature, e.g., freedom of religion, were so much a part of American political culture that their application to the states was difficult (though not impossible) to argue against. Finally, the 35 years from Roosevelt's election in 1932 to Johnson's announcement in 1967 that he would not seek a second term as President marked a period of unparalleled trust in the efficacy and integrity of the national government. That the Court was expanding federal power was not a problem for most Americans.

Concern over the Court's continued use of substantive due process recurred as the selective incorporation of the Bill of Rights neared completion, and the Court once again turned to the creation of "fundamental" rights nowhere mentioned in the Constitution. As an earlier Court had created a "liberty of contract" in the *Lochner* case, the Warren Court enunciated *a fundamental right to privacy* in *Griswold v. Connecticut* (1965), striking down that state's anticontraceptive laws on the grounds that they interfered with the privacy of the marital relationship. Eight years later, in what is perhaps the most controversial decision since the *Dred Scott* case, the Court expanded the right of privacy to include a woman's right to an abortion. See below, *Roe v. Wade* (1973) and *Planned Parenthood of Southeastern Pennsylvania v. Casey* (1993). [1]

The privacy cases of today are not as far removed from the economic rights cases of the past as sometimes thought. Today's cases are really about personal autonomy – about how much control an individual has over his or her body. But, so too were cases like *Dred Scott*, where the question was how much autonomous control an individual had over real property, and *Lochner v. New York*, where the question was how much control an individual had over his or her own labor. All of these cases are concerned with the ownership of property (slaves or real property, one's labor as property, or one's own body as property) and the extent of control the individual autonomously exercises over his or her property. In reality, the line between economic and non-economic rights is very indistinct.

Precisely because modern privacy cases are about personal autonomy or control over the body, it has been almost a natural development (some would say "slippery slope") from contraception and abortion rights to sexuality and suicide. In *Bowers v. Hardwick* (1986) the Court confronted whether or not the due process clause included a fundamental right to engage in homosexual relations as part of a person's privacy control over his or her body. See also *Romer v. Evans* (1996) in Chapter XIII. In two cases, *Cruzon v. Director* (1990) and *Washington v. Glucksberg* (1997), the Court has faced the question of whether an individual's autonomous control of their body extends to a "right to die."

JACOBSON v. MASSACHUSETTS
197 U.S. 11; 25 S.Ct. 358; 49 L.Ed. 643 (1905)

A regulation requiring that all persons living in Cambridge, Massachusetts, be vaccinated against smallpox was adopted by the city's board of health. Jacobson, who flatly refused to be vaccinated, was arrested, tried and convicted for failing to comply with the requirement. The state supreme court sustained his conviction and Jacobson brought his case to the Supreme Court on a writ of error.

MR. JUSTICE HARLAN delivered the opinion of the Court, saying in part:

...The authority of the state to enact this statute is to be referred to what is commonly called the police power, a power which the state did not surrender when becoming a member of the Union under the Constitution. Although this court has refrained from any attempt to define the limits of that power, yet it has distinctly recognized the authority of a state to enact quarantine laws and "health laws of every description;" indeed, all laws that relate to matters completely within its territory and which do not by their necessary operation affect the people of other states. According to settled principles, the police power of a state must be held to embrace, at least, such reasonable regulations established directly by legislative enactment as will protect the public health and the public safety....

We come, then, to inquire whether any right given or secured by the Constitution is invaded by the statute as interpreted by the state court. The defendant insists that his liberty is invaded when the state subjects him to fine or imprisonment for neglecting or refusing to submit to vaccination; that a compulsory vaccination law is unreasonable, arbitrary, and oppressive, and, therefore, hostile to the inherent right of every freeman to care for his own body and health in such way as to him seems best; and that the execution of such a law against one who objects to vaccination, no matter for what reason, is nothing short of an assault upon his person. *But the liberty secured by the Constitution of the United States to every person within its jurisdiction does not import an absolute right in each person to be, at all times and in all circumstances, wholly freed from restraint.* There are manifold restraints to which every person is necessarily subject for the common good. On any other basis organized society could not exist with safety to its members. Society based on the rule that each one is a law unto himself would soon be confronted with disorder and anarchy. Real liberty for all could not exist under the operation of a principle which recognizes the right of each individual person to use his own, whether in respect of his person or his property, regardless of the injury that may be done to others. This court has more than once recognized it as a fundamental principle that "persons and property are subjected to all kinds of restraints and burdens in order to secure the general comfort, health, and prosperity of the state; of the perfect right of the legislature to do which no question ever was, or upon acknowledged general principles ever can be, made, so far as natural persons are concerned...."

Applying these principles to the present case, it is to be observed that the legislature of Massachusetts required the inhabitants of a city or town to be vaccinated only when, in the opinion of the board of health, that was necessary for the public health or the public safety. The authority to determine for all what ought to be done in such an emergency must have been lodged somewhere or in some body; and surely it was appropriate for the legislature to refer that question, in the first instance, to a board of health composed of persons residing in the locality affected, and appointed, presumably, because of their fitness to determine such questions. To invest such a body with authority over such matters was not unusual, nor an unreasonable or arbitrary, requirement. Upon the principle of self-defense, of paramount necessity, a community has the right to protect itself against an epidemic of disease which threatens the safety of its members.... There is, of course, a sphere within which the individual may assert the supremacy of his own will, and rightfully dispute the authority of any human government – especially of any free government existing under a written constitution – to interfere with the exercise of that will. But it is equally true that in every well-ordered society charged with the duty of conserving the safety of its members the rights of the individual in respect of his liberty may at times, under the pressure of great dangers, be subjected to such restraint, to be enforced by reasonable regulations, as the safety of the general public may demand....

Looking at the propositions embodied in the defendant's rejected offers of proof, it is clear that they are more formidable by their number than by their inherent value. Those offers in the main seem to have had no purpose except to state the general theory of those of the medical profession who attach little or no value to vaccination as a means of preventing the spread of smallpox, or who think that vaccination causes other diseases of the body. What everybody knows the court must know, and therefore the state court judicially knew, as this court knows, that an opposite theory accords with the common belief, and is maintained by high medical authority. We must assume that, when the statute in question was passed, the legislature of Massachusetts was not unaware of these opposing theories, and was compelled, of necessity, to choose between them. It was not compelled to commit a matter involving the public health and safety to the final decision of a court or jury. It is no part of the function of a court or a jury to determine which one of two modes was likely to be the most effective for the protection of the public against disease. That was for the legislative department to determine in the light of all the information it had or could obtain. It could not properly abdicate its function to guard the public health and safety. The state legislature proceeded upon the theory which recognized vaccination as at least an effective, if not the best-known, way in which to meet and suppress the evils of a smallpox epidemic that imperiled an entire population....

We are not prepared to hold that a minority, residing or remaining in any city or town where smallpox is prevalent, and enjoying the general protection afforded by an organized local government, may thus defy the will of its constituted authorities, acting in good faith for all, under the legislative sanction of the state. If such be the privilege of a minority, then a like privilege would belong to each individual of the community, and the spectacle would be presented of the welfare and safety of an entire population being subordinated to the notions of a single individual who chooses to remain a part of that population. We are unwilling to hold it to be an element in the liberty secured by the Constitution of the United States that one person, or a minority of persons, residing in any community and enjoying the benefits of its local government, should have the power thus to dominate the majority when supported in their action by the authority of the state. While this court should guard with firmness every right appertaining to life, liberty, or property as secured to the individual by the supreme law of the land, it is of the last importance that it should not invade the domain of local authority except when it is plainly necessary to do so in order to enforce that law. The safety and the health of the people of Massachusetts are, in the first instance, for that commonwealth to guard and protect. They are matters that do not ordinarily concern the national government. So far as they can be reached by any government, they depend, primarily, upon such action as the state, in its wisdom, may take; and we do not perceive that this legislation has invaded any right secured by the Federal Constitution....

We now decide only that the statute covers the present case, and that nothing clearly appears that would justify this court in holding it to be unconstitutional and inoperative in its application to the plaintiff in error. The judgment of the court below must be affirmed.

It is so ordered.

MR. JUSTICES BREWER and PECKHAM dissented.

BUCK v. BELL
274 U.S. 200; 47 S.Ct. 584; 71 L.Ed. 1000 (1927)

Acting under a state statute, the administrative board of the Virginia Colony for Epileptics and Feeble Minded, headed by superintendent Bell, issued an order calling for the sterilization of one of the inmates, Carrie Buck. The daughter of a feeble-minded mother in the same institution, and the mother of an illegitimate feeble-minded child of her own, Miss Buck challenged the decision. After the state court of appeals sustained the order, the case was brought to the Supreme Court on a writ of error.

MR. JUSTICE HOLMES delivered the opinion of the Court:

... An Act of Virginia approved March 20, 1924, recites that the health of the patient and the welfare of society may be promoted in certain cases by the sterilization of mental defectives, under careful safeguard, etc.; that the sterilization may be effected in males by vasectomy and in females by salpingectomy, without serious pain or substantial danger to life; that the Commonwealth is supporting in various institutions many defective persons who if now discharged would become a menace but if incapable of procreating might be discharged with safety and become self-supporting with benefit to themselves and to society; and that experience has shown that heredity plays an important part in the transmission of insanity, imbecility, etc. The statute then enacts that whenever the superintendent of certain institutions including the above-named State Colony shall be of opinion that it is for the best interests of the patients and of society that an inmate under his care should be sexually sterilized, he may have the operation performed upon any patient afflicted with hereditary forms of insanity, imbecility, etc., on complying with the very careful provisions by which the act protects the patients from possible abuse.

The superintendent first presents a petition to the special board of directors of his hospital or colony, stating the facts and the grounds for his opinion, verified by affidavit. Notice of the petition and of the time and place of the hearing in the institution is to be served upon the inmate, and also upon his guardian, and if there is no guardian the superintendent is to apply to the Circuit Court of the County to appoint one. If the inmate is a minor, notice also is to be given to his parents if any with a copy of the petition. The board is to see to it that the inmate may attend the hearings if desired by him or his guardian. The evidence is all to be reduced to writing, and after the board has made its order for or against the operation, the superintendent, or the inmate, or his guardian, may appeal to the Circuit Court of the County. The Circuit Court may consider the record of the board and the evidence before it and such other admissible evidence as may be offered, and may affirm, revise, or reverse the order of the board and enter such order as it deems just. Finally any party may apply to the Supreme Court of Appeals, which, if it grants the appeal, is to hear the case upon the record of the trial in the Circuit Court and may enter such order as it thinks the Circuit Court should have entered. There can be no doubt that so far as procedure is concerned the rights of the patient are most carefully considered, and as every step in this case was taken in scrupulous compliance with the statute and after months of observation, there is no doubt that in that respect the plaintiff in error has had due process of law.

The attack is not upon the procedure but upon the substantive law. It seems to be contended that in no circumstances could such an order be justified. It certainly is contended that the order cannot be justified upon the existing grounds. The judgment finds the facts that have been recited and that Carrie Buck "is the probable potential parent of socially inadequate offspring, likewise afflicted, that she may be sexually sterilized without detriment to her general health and that her welfare and that of society will be promoted by her sterilization," and thereupon makes the order. In view of the general declarations of the legislature and the specific findings of the court obviously we cannot say as matter of law that the grounds do not exist, and if they exist they justify the result. We have seen more than once that the public welfare may call upon the best citizens for their lives. It would be strange if it could not call upon those who already sap the strength of the State for these lesser sacrifices, often not felt to be such by those concerned, in order to prevent our being swamped with incompetence. It is better for all the world, if instead of waiting to execute degenerate offspring for crime, or to let them starve for their imbecility, society can prevent those who are manifestly unfit from continuing their kind. The principle that sustains compulsory vaccination is broad enough to cover cutting the Fallopian tubes. *Jacobson v. Massachusetts*....

But, it is said, however it might be if this reasoning were applied generally, it fails when it is confined to the small number who are in the institutions named and is not applied to the multitudes outside. It is the usual last resort of constitutional arguments to point out shortcomings of this sort. But the answer is that the law does all that is needed when it does all that it can, indicates a policy, applies it to all within the lines, and seeks to bring within the lines all similarly situated so far and so fast as its means allow. Of course so far as the operations enable those who otherwise must be kept confined to be returned to the world, and thus open the asylum to others, the equality aimed at will be more nearly reached.

Judgment affirmed.

MR. JUSTICE BUTLER dissented.

GRISWOLD v. CONNECTICUT
381 U.S. 479; 85 S.Ct. 1678; 14 L.Ed. 2d 510 (1965)

In violation of the General Statutes of Connecticut, Griswold, the Executive Director of the Planned Parenthood League, and Dr. Buxton, a licensed physician and professor at Yale Medical School, gave information, instruction and medical advice to married persons as to the means of preventing conception. They were convicted and fined $100 each as accessories to a criminal act. They appealed to the Supreme Court after the state appellate court upheld their conviction. Later in Eisenstadt v. Baird *(1972), the Court expanded the* Griswold *rule to include unmarried persons.*

MR. JUSTICE DOUGLAS delivered the opinion of the Court:

...The association of people is not mentioned in the Constitution nor in the Bill of Rights. The right to educate a child in a school of the parents' choice – whether public or private or parochial – is also not mentioned. Nor is the right to study any particular subject or any foreign language. Yet the First Amendment has been construed to include certain of those rights.

By *Pierce v. Society of Sisters* the right to educate one's children as one chooses is made applicable to the states by the force of the First and Fourteenth Amendments. By *Meyer v. Nebraska* the same dignity is given the right to study the German language in a private school. In other words, the state may not, consistently with the spirit of the First Amendment, contract the spectrum of available knowledge. The right of freedom of speech and press includes not only the right to utter or to print, but the right to distribute, the right to receive, the right to read ... and freedom of inquiry, freedom of thought, and freedom to teach.... Without those peripheral rights the specific rights would be less secure. And so we reaffirm the principle of the *Pierce* and *Meyer* cases.

In *NAACP v. Alabama* we protected the "freedom to associate and privacy in one's association," noting that freedom of association was a peripheral First Amendment right. Disclosure of membership lists of a constitutionally valid association, we held, was invalid "as entailing the likelihood of a substantial restraint upon the exercise by petitioner's members of their right to freedom of association." In other words, the First Amendment has a penumbra where privacy is protected from governmental intrusion. In like context, we have protected forms of "association" that are not political in the customary sense but pertain to the social, legal, and economic benefit of the members. *NAACP v. Button*.

The foregoing cases suggest that specific guarantees in the Bill of Rights have penumbras, formed by emanations from those guarantees that help give them life and substance.... Various guarantees create zones of privacy. The right of association contained in the penumbra of the First Amendment is one, as we have seen. The Third Amendment in its prohibition against the quartering of soldiers "in any house" in time of peace without the consent of the owner is another facet of that privacy. The Fourth Amendment explicitly affirms the "right of the people to be secure in their persons, houses, papers, and effects, against unreasonable searches and seizures." The Fifth Amendment in its self-incrimination clause enables the citizen to create a zone of privacy which government may not force him to surrender to his detriment. The Ninth Amendment provides: "The enumeration in the Constitution, of certain rights, shall not be construed to deny or disparage others retained by the people...."

The present case, then, concerns a relationship lying within the zone of privacy created by several fundamental constitutional guarantees. And it concerns a law which, in forbidding the use of contraceptives rather than regulating their manufacture or sale, seeks to achieve its goals by means having a maximum destructive impact upon the relationship. Such a law cannot stand in light of the familiar principle, so often applied by this Court, that a "governmental purpose to control or prevent activities constitutionally subject to state regulation may not be achieved by means which sweep unnecessarily broadly and thereby invade the area of protected freedoms." *NAACP v. Alabama.* Would we allow the police to search the sacred precincts of marital bedrooms for telltale signs of the use of contraceptives? The very idea is repulsive to the notions of privacy surrounding the marriage relationship.

We deal with a right of privacy older than the Bill of Rights – older than our political parties, older than our school system. Marriage is a coming together for better or for worse, hopefully enduring, and intimate to the degree of being sacred. It is an association that promotes a way of life, not causes; a harmony in living, not political faiths; a bilateral loyalty, not commercial or social projects. Yet it is an association for as noble a purpose as any involved in our prior decisions.

Reversed.

MR. JUSTICE GOLDBERG, whom THE CHIEF JUSTICE and MR. JUSTICE BRENNAN joined, concurred, saying in part:

I agree with the Court that Connecticut's birth control law unconstitutionally intrudes upon the right of marital privacy, and I join in its opinion and judgment. Although I have not accepted the view that " 'due process' as used in the Fourteenth Amendment incorporates all of the first eight Amendments,"... I do agree that the concept of liberty protects those personal rights that are fundamental, and is not confined to the specific terms of the Bill of Rights. My conclusion that the concept of liberty is not so restricted and that it embraces the right of marital privacy though that right is not mentioned explicitly in the Constitution is supported both by numerous decisions of this Court, referred to in the Court's opinion, and by the language and history of the Ninth Amendment. In reaching the conclusion that the right of marital privacy is protected, as being within the protected penumbra of specific guarantees of the Bill of Rights, the Court refers to the Ninth Amendment,... I add these words to emphasize the relevance of that amendment to the Court's holding....

A dissenting opinion suggests that my interpretation of the Ninth Amendment somehow "broaden[s] the powers of this Court...." With all due respect, I believe that it misses the import of what I am saying. I do not take the position of my Brother Black in his dissent in *Adamson* that the entire Bill of Rights is incorporated in the Fourteenth Amendment, and I do not mean to imply that the Ninth Amendment is applied against the states by the Fourteenth. Nor do I mean to state that the Ninth Amendment constitutes an independent source of rights protected from infringement by either the state or federal government. Rather, the Ninth Amendment shows a belief of the Constitution's authors that fundamental rights exist that are not expressly enumerated in the first eight amendments and an intent that the list of rights included there not be exhaustive. As any student of this Court's opinions knows, this Court has held, often unanimously, that the Fifth and Fourteenth Amendments protect certain fundamental personal liberties from abridgment by the federal government or the states.... The Ninth Amendment simply shows the intent of the Constitution's authors that other fundamental personal rights should not be denied such protection or disparaged in any other way simply because they are not specifically listed in the first eight constitutional amendments. I do not see how this broadens the authority of the Court; rather it serves to support what this Court has been doing in protecting fundamental, rights....

In sum, the Ninth Amendment simply lends strong support to the view that the "liberty" protected by the Fifth and Fourteenth Amendments from infringement by the federal government or the states is not restricted to rights specifically mentioned in the first eight amendments....

Although the Connecticut birth-control law obviously encroaches upon a fundamental personal liberty, the state does not show that the law serves any "subordinating [state] interest which is compelling" or that it is "necessary ... to the accomplishment of a permissible state policy." The state, at most, argues that there is some rational relation between this statute and what is admittedly a legitimate subject of state concern – the discouraging of extramarital relations. It says that preventing the use of birth control devices by married persons helps prevent the indulgence by some in such extramarital relations. The rationality of this justification is dubious, particularly in light of the admitted widespread availability to all persons in the state of Connecticut, unmarried as well as married, of birth control devices for the prevention of disease, as distinguished from the prevention of conception. But, in any event, it is clear that the state interest in safeguarding marital fidelity can be served by a more discriminately tailored statute, which does not, like the present one, sweep unnecessarily broadly, reaching far beyond the evil sought to be dealt with and intruding upon the privacy of all married couples....

In sum, I believe that the right of privacy in the marital relation is fundamental and basic – a personal right "retained by the people" within the meaning of the Ninth Amendment. Connecticut cannot constitutionally abridge this fundamental right, which is protected by the Fourteenth Amendment from infringement by the states. I agree with the Court that petitioners' convictions must therefore be
Reversed.

MR. JUSTICE HARLAN, concurred in the judgment.

MR. JUSTICE STEWART, whom MR. JUSTICE BLACK joined, dissented....

MR. JUSTICE BLACK, with whom MR. JUSTICE STEWART joined, dissented, saying in part;

The Court talks about a constitutional "right of privacy" as though there is some constitutional provision or provisions forbidding any law ever to be passed which might abridge the "privacy" of individuals. But there is not. There are, of course, guarantees in certain specific constitutional provisions which are designed in part to protect privacy at certain times and places with respect to certain activities. Such, for example, is the Fourth Amendment's guarantee against "unreasonable searches and seizures." But I think it belittles that amendment to talk about it as though it protects nothing but "privacy." To treat it that way is to give it a niggardly interpretation, not the kind of liberal reading I think any Bill of Rights provision should be given. The average man would very likely not have his feelings soothed any more by having his property seized privately and by stealth. He simply wants his property left alone. And a person can be just as much, if not more, irritated, annoyed and injured by an unceremonious public arrest by a policeman as he is by a seizure in the privacy of his office or home.

One of the most effective ways of diluting or expanding a constitutionally guaranteed right is to substitute for the crucial word or words of a constitutional guarantee another word, more or less flexible and more or less restricted in its meaning. This fact is well illustrated by the use of the term "right of privacy" as a comprehensive substitute for the Fourth Amendment's guarantee against "unreasonable searches and seizures." "Privacy" is a broad, abstract and ambiguous concept which can easily be shrunken in meaning but which can also, on the other hand, easily be interpreted as a constitutional ban against many things other than searches and seizures.... I like my privacy as well as the next one, but I am nevertheless compelled to admit that government has a right to invade it unless prohibited by some constitutional provision. For these reasons I cannot agree with the Court's judgment and the reasons it finds for holding this Connecticut law unconstitutional....

I realize that many good and able men have eloquently spoken and written, sometimes in rhapsodical strains, about the duty of this Court to keep the

Constitution in tune with the times. The idea is that the Constitution must be changed from time to time and that this Court is charged with a duty to make those changes. For myself, I must with all deference reject that philosophy. The Constitution makers knew the need for change and provided for it. Amendments suggested by the people's elected representatives can be submitted to the people or their selected agents for ratification. That method of change was good for our fathers, and being somewhat old-fashioned I must add it is good enough for me. And so, I cannot rely on the due process clause or the Ninth Amendment or any mysterious and uncertain natural law concept as a reason for striking down this state law. The due process clause with an "arbitrary and capricious" or "shocking to the conscience" formula was liberally used by this Court to strike down economic legislation in the early decades of this century, threatening, many people thought, the tranquility and stability of the nation. See, e.g., *Lochner v. New York*. That formula, based on subjective considerations of "natural justice," is no less dangerous when used to enforce this Court's views about personal rights than those about economic rights. I had thought that we had laid that formula, as a means for striking down state legislation, to rest once and for all in cases like *West Coast Hotel Co. v. Parrish*....

ROE v. WADE
410 U.S. 113; 93 S.Ct. 705; 35 L.Ed. 2d 147 (1973)

A pregnant, single woman living in Dallas, Texas, who for the purpose of anonymity is designated as Jane "Roe," wanted to obtain an abortion "performed by a competent, licensed physician, under safe, clinical conditions." Since Texas law forbade abortions unless the woman's life was threatened by the continuation of her pregnancy, she instituted legal action against Wade, the district attorney of the county. The case was brought to the Supreme Court by appeal and was decided along with a similar challenge from Georgia, Doe v. Bolton.

MR. JUSTICE BLACKMUN delivered the opinion of the Court:

Three reasons have been advanced to explain historically the enactment of criminal abortion laws in the nineteenth century and to justify their continued existence.

It has been argued occasionally that these laws were the product of a Victorian social concern to discourage illicit sexual conduct. Texas, however, does not advance this justification in the present case, and it appears that no court or commentator has taken the argument seriously....

A second reason is concerned with abortion as a medical procedure. When most criminal abortion laws were first enacted, the procedure was a hazardous one for the woman.... Consequently, any interest of the state in protecting the woman from an inherently hazardous procedure, except when it would be equally dangerous for her to forego it, has largely disappeared. Of course, important state interests in the area of health and medical standards do remain....

The prevalence of high mortality rates at illegal "abortion mills" strengthens, rather than weakens, the state's interest in regulating the conditions under which abortions are performed....

The third reason is the state's interest – some phrase it in terms of duty – in protecting prenatal life....

It is with these interests, and the weight to be attached to them, that this case is concerned.

The Constitution does not explicitly mention any right of privacy. In a line of decisions, however, the Court has recognized that a right of personal privacy, or a guarantee of certain areas or zones of privacy, does exist under the Constitution. In varying contexts the Court or individual justices have indeed found at least the roots of that right in the First Amendment, in the Fourth and Fifth Amendments, in the penumbras of the Bill of Rights, in the Ninth Amendment, or in the concept of liberty guaranteed by the first section of the Fourteenth Amendment. These decisions make it clear that only personal rights that can be deemed "fundamental" or "implicit in the concept of ordered liberty," *Palko v. Connecticut*, are included in this guarantee of personal privacy. They also make it clear that the right has some extensions to activities relating to marriage, *Loving v. Virginia*; procreation, *Skinner v. Oklahoma*; contraception, *Eisenstadt v. Baird*; family relationships, *Prince v. Massachusetts*; and child rearing and education, *Pierce v. Society of Sisters, Meyer v. Nebraska*....

The right of privacy ... is broad enough to encompass a woman's decision whether or not to terminate her pregnancy. The detriment that the state would impose upon the pregnant woman by denying this choice altogether is apparent. Specific and direct harm medically diagnosable even in early pregnancy may be involved. Maternity, or additional offspring, may force upon the woman a distressful life and future. Psychological harm may be imminent. Mental and physical health may be taxed by child care. There is also the distress, for all concerned, associated with the unwanted child, and there is the problem of bringing a child into a family already unable, psychologically and otherwise, to care for it. In other cases, as in this one, the additional difficulties and continuing stigma of unwed motherhood may be involved. All these are factors the woman and her responsible physician necessarily will consider in consultation.

On the basis of elements such as these, appellants and some *amici* argue that the woman's right is absolute and that she is entitled to terminate her pregnancy at whatever time, in whatever way, and for whatever reason she alone chooses. With this we do not agree.... As noted above, a state may properly assert important interests in safeguarding health, in maintaining medical standards, and in protecting potential life. At some point in pregnancy, these respective interests become sufficiently compelling to sustain regulation of the factors that govern the abortion decision....

Where certain "fundamental rights" are involved, the Court has held that regulation limiting these rights may be justified only by a "compelling state interest," ... and that legislative enactments must be narrowly drawn to express only the legitimate state interests at stake....

... Appellant, as has been indicated, claims an absolute right that bars any state imposition of criminal penalties in the area. Appellee argues that the state's determination to recognize and protect prenatal life from and after conception constitutes a compelling state interest. As noted above, we do not agree fully with either formulation.

A. The appellee and certain *amici* argue that the fetus is a "person" within the language and meaning of the Fourteenth Amendment. In support of this they outline at length and in detail the well-known facts of fetal development.

The Constitution does not define "person" in so many words. Section 1 of the Fourteenth Amendment contains three references to "person." The first, in defining "citizens," speaks of "persons born or naturalized in the United States." The word also appears both in the due process clause and in the equal protection clause. "Person" is used in other places in the Constitution.... But in nearly all these instances, the use of the word is such that it has application only postnatally. None indicate, with any assurance, that it has any possible pre-natal application.

All this, together with our observation that throughout the major portion of the 19th century prevailing legal abortion practices were far freer than they are today, persuades us that the word "person," as used in the Fourteenth Amendment, does not include the unborn....

This conclusion, however, does not of itself fully answer the contentions raised by Texas, and we pass on to other considerations.

B. The pregnant woman cannot be isolated in her privacy. She carries an embryo and, later, a fetus, if one accepts the medical definitions of the developing young in the human uterus.... The situation therefore is inherently different from marital intimacy, or bedroom possession of obscene material, or marriage, or procreation, or education, with which *Eisenstadt*, *Griswold*, *Stanley*, *Skinner*, *Pierce*, and *Meyer* were respectively concerned. As we have intimated above, it is reasonable and appropriate for a state to decide that at some point in time another interest, that of health of the mother or that of potential human life, becomes significantly involved. The woman's privacy is no longer sole and any right of privacy she possesses must be measured accordingly.

Texas urges that, apart from the Fourteenth Amendment, life begins at conception and is present throughout pregnancy, and that, therefore, the state has a compelling interest in protecting that life from and after conception. We need not resolve the difficult question of when life begins....

It should be sufficient to note briefly the wide divergence of thinking on this most sensitive and difficult question....

In areas other than criminal abortion the law has been reluctant to endorse any theory that life, as we recognize it, begins before live birth or to accord legal rights to the unborn except in narrowly defined situations and except when the rights are contingent upon live birth....

In view of all this, we do not agree that, by adopting one theory of life, Texas may override the rights of the pregnant woman that are at stake. We repeat, however, that the state does have an important and legitimate interest in preserving and protecting the health of the pregnant woman, whether she be a resident of the state or a non-resident who seeks medical consultation and treatment there, and that it has still another important and legitimate interest in protecting the potentiality of human life. These interests are separate and distinct. Each grows in substantiality as the woman approaches term and, at a point during pregnancy, each becomes "compelling."

With respect to the state's important and legitimate interest in the health of the mother, the "compelling" point, in the light of present medical knowledge, is at approximately the end of the first trimester. This is so because of the now established medical fact, referred to above, that until the end of the first trimester mortality in abortion is less than mortality in normal childbirth. It follows that, from and after this point, a state may regulate the abortion procedure to the extent that the regulation reasonably relates to the preservation and protection of maternal health. Examples of permissible state regulation in this area are requirements as to the qualifications of the person who is to perform the abortion; as to the licensure of that person; as to the facility in which the procedure is to be performed, that is, whether it must be a hospital or may be a clinic or some other place of less-than-hospital status; as to the licensing of the facility; and the like.

This means, on the other hand, that, for the period of pregnancy prior to this "compelling" point, the attending physician, in consultation with his patient, is free to determine, without regulation by the state, that in his medical judgment the patient's pregnancy should be terminated. If that decision is reached, the judgment may be effectuated by an abortion free of interference by the state.

With respect to the state's important and legitimate interest in potential life, the "compelling" point is at viability. This is so because the fetus then presumably has the capability of meaningful life outside the mother's womb. State regulation protective of fetal life after viability thus has both logical and biological justifications. If the state is interested in protecting fetal life after viability, it may go so far as to proscribe abortion during that period except when it is necessary to preserve the life or health of the mother.

Measured against these standards, the Texas Penal Code, in restricting legal abortions to those "procured or attempted by medical advice for the purpose of saving the life of the mother," sweeps too broadly....

Reversed.

MR. CHIEF JUSTICE BURGER and DOUGLAS concurred.
MR. JUSTICE WHITE dissented.

MR. JUSTICE REHNQUIST, dissented, saying in part:

...I have difficulty in concluding, as the Court does, that the right of "privacy" is involved in this case. Texas by the statute here challenged bars the performance of a medical abortion by a licensed physician on a plaintiff such as Roe. A transaction resulting in an operation such as this is not "private" in the ordinary usage of that word. Nor is the "privacy" which the Court finds here even a distant relative of the freedom from searches and seizures protected by the Fourth Amendment as embodying a right to privacy. *Katz v. United States*.

If the Court means by the term "privacy" no more than that the claim of a person to be free from unwanted state regulation of consensual transactions may be a form of "liberty" protected by the Fourteenth Amendment, there is no doubt that similar claims have been upheld in our earlier decisions on the basis of that liberty.... But that liberty is not guaranteed absolutely against deprivation, but only against deprivation without due process of law. The test traditionally applied in the area of social and economic legislation is whether or not a law such as that challenged has a rational relation to a valid state objective. *Williamson v. Lee Optical Co.*... The due process clause of the Fourteenth Amendment undoubtedly does place a limit on legislative power to enact laws such as this, albeit a broad one. If the Texas statute were to prohibit an abortion even where the mother's life is in jeopardy, I have little doubt that such a statute would lack a rational relation to a valid state objective under the test stated in *Williamson*.... But the Court's sweeping invalidation of any restrictions on abortion during the first trimester is impossible to justify under that standard, and the conscious weighing of competing factors which the Court's opinion apparently substitutes for the established test is far more appropriate to a legislative judgment than to a judicial one.

The Court eschews the history of the Fourteenth Amendment in its reliance on the "compelling state interest" test.... But the Court adds a new wrinkle to this test by transposing it from the legal considerations associated with the equal protection clauses of the Fourteenth Amendment to this case arising under the due process clause of the Fourteenth Amendment. Unless I misapprehend the consequences of this transplanting of the "compelling state interest test," the Court's opinion will accomplish the seemingly impossible feat of leaving this area of the law more confused than it found it.

While the Court's opinion quotes from the dissent of Mr. Justice Holmes in *Lochner v. New York*, the result it reaches is more closely attuned to the majority opinion of Mr. Justice Peckham in that case. As in *Lochner* and similar cases applying substantive due process standards to economic and social welfare legislation, the adoption of the compelling state interest standard will inevitably require this Court to examine the legislative policies and pass on the wisdom of these policies in the very process of deciding whether a particular state interest put forward may or may not be "compelling." The decision here is to break the term of pregnancy into three distinct terms and to outline the permissible restrictions the state may impose in each one, for example, partakes more of judicial legislation than it does of a determination of the intent of the drafters of the Fourteenth Amendment.

The fact that a majority of the states, reflecting after all the majority sentiment in those states, have had restrictions on abortions for at least a century seems to me as strong an indication there is that the asserted right to an abortion is not "so rooted in the traditions and conscience of our people as to be ranked as fundamental...." Even today, when society's views on abortion are changing, the very existence of the debate is evidence that the "right" to an abortion is not so universally accepted as the appellants would have us believe....

PLANNED PARENTHOOD OF SOUTHEASTERN PENNSYLVANIA v. CASEY
112 S.Ct. 2791; 120 L.Ed.2d 674 (1992).

The facts in this case are contained in the opinion below.

Justice O'CONNOR, Justice KENNEDY, and Justice SOUTER announced the judgment of the Court and delivered the opinion of the Court with respect to Parts I, II, III, V-A, V-C, and VI, an opinion with respect to Part V-E, in which Justice STEVENS joins, and an opinion with respect to Parts IV, V-B, and V-D.

I

Liberty finds no refuge in a jurisprudence of doubt. Yet 19 years after our holding that the Constitution protects a woman's right to terminate her pregnancy in its early stages,... that definition of liberty is still questioned. Joining the respondents as *amicus curiae*, the United States, as it has done in five other cases in the last decade, again asks us to overrule *Roe*....

At issue in these cases are five provisions of the Pennsylvania Abortion Control Act of 1982 as amended in 1988 and 1989.... The Act requires that a woman seeking an abortion give her informed consent prior to the abortion procedure, and specifies that she be provided with certain information at least 24 hours before the abortion is performed. § 3205. For a minor to obtain an abortion, the Act requires the informed consent of one of her parents, but provides for a judicial bypass option if the minor does not wish to or cannot obtain a parent's consent. § 3206. Another provision of the Act requires that, unless certain exceptions apply, a married woman seeking an abortion must sign a statement indicating that she has notified her husband of her intended abortion. § 3209. The Act exempts compliance with these three requirements in the event of a "medical emergency," which is defined in § 3203 of the Act.... In addition to the above provisions regulating the performance of abortions, the Act imposes certain reporting requirements on facilities that provide abortion services. §§ 3207(b), 3214(a), 3214(f).

Before any of these provisions took effect, the petitioners, who are five abortion clinics and one physician representing himself as well as a class of physicians who provide abortion services, brought this suit seeking declaratory and injunctive relief. Each provision was challenged as unconstitutional on its face. The District Court entered a preliminary injunction against the enforcement of the regulations, and, after a 3-day bench trial, held all the provisions at issue here unconstitutional, entering a permanent injunction against Pennsylvania's enforcement of them.... The Court of Appeals for the Third Circuit affirmed in part and reversed in part, upholding all of the regulations except for the husband notification requirement. 947 F.2d 682 (1991). We granted certiorari....

After considering the fundamental constitutional questions resolved by *Roe*, principles of institutional integrity, and the rule of *stare decisis*, we are led to conclude this: the essential holding of *Roe v. Wade* should be retained and once again reaffirmed.

It must be stated at the outset and with clarity that *Roe's* essential holding, the holding we reaffirm, has three parts. First is a recognition of the right of the woman to choose to have an abortion before viability and to obtain it without undue interference from the State. Before viability, the State's interests are not strong enough to support a prohibition of abortion or the imposition of a substantial obstacle to the woman's effective right to elect the procedure. Second is a confirmation of the State's power to restrict abortions after fetal viability, if the law contains exceptions for pregnancies which endanger a woman's life or health. And third is the principle that the State has legitimate interests from the outset of the pregnancy in protecting the health of the woman and the life of the fetus that may become a child. These principles do not contradict one another; and we adhere to each.

II

Constitutional protection of the woman's decision to terminate her pregnancy derives from the Due Process Clause of the Fourteenth Amendment. It declares that no State shall "deprive any person of life, liberty, or property, without due process of law." The controlling word in the case before us is "liberty." Although a literal reading of the Clause might suggest that it governs only the procedures by which a State may deprive persons of liberty, for at least 105 years, at least since *Mugler v. Kansas*,... (1887), the Clause has been understood to contain a substantive component as well, one " barring certain government actions regardless of the fairness of the procedures used to implement them." *Daniels v. Williams*,... (1986). As Justice Brandeis (joined by Justice Holmes) observed, "[d]espite arguments to the contrary which had seemed to me persuasive, it is settled that the due process clause of the Fourteenth Amendment applies to matters of substantive law as well as to matters of procedure. Thus all fundamental rights comprised within the term liberty are protected by the Federal Constitution from invasion by the States." *Whitney v. California*... (1927) (Brandeis, J., concurring)....

The most familiar of the substantive liberties protected by the Fourteenth Amendment are those recognized by the Bill of Rights. We have held that the Due Process Clause of the Fourteenth Amendment incorporates most of the Bill of Rights against the States. See, e.g., *Duncan v. Louisiana*... (1968). It is tempting, as a means of curbing the discretion of federal judges, to suppose that liberty encompasses no more than those rights already guaranteed to the individual against federal interference by the express provisions of the first eight amendments to the Constitution. See *Adamson v. California*... (1947) (Black, J., dissenting). But of course this Court has never accepted that view.

It is also tempting, for the same reason, to suppose that the Due Process Clause protects only those practices, defined at the most specific level, that were protected against government interference by other rules of law when the Fourteenth Amendment was ratified. See *Michael H. v. Gerald D.*,... (1989) (opinion of SCALIA, J.). But such a view would be inconsistent with our law. It is a promise of the Constitution that there is a realm of personal liberty which the government may not enter. We have vindicated this principle before. Marriage is mentioned nowhere in the Bill of Rights and interracial marriage was illegal in most States in the 19th century, but the Court was no doubt correct in finding it to be an aspect of liberty protected against state interference by the substantive component of the Due Process Clause in *Loving v. Virginia,...* (1967) (relying, in an opinion for eight Justices, on the Due Process Clause)....

Neither the Bill of Rights nor the specific practices of States at the time of the adoption of the Fourteenth Amendment marks the outer limits of the substantive sphere of liberty which the Fourteenth Amendment protects.... As the second Justice Harlan recognized:

"[T]he full scope of the liberty guaranteed by the Due Process Clause cannot be found in or limited by the precise terms of the specific guarantees elsewhere provided in the Constitution. This 'liberty' is not a series of isolated points pricked out in terms of the taking of property; the freedom of speech, press, and religion; the right to keep and bear arms; the freedom from unreasonable searches and seizures; and so on. It is a rational continuum which, broadly speaking, includes a freedom from all substantial arbitrary impositions and purposeless restraints,... and which also recognizes, what a reasonable and sensitive judgment must, that certain interests require particularly careful scrutiny of the state needs asserted to justify their abridgment." *Poe v. Ullman....*

The inescapable fact is that adjudication of substantive due process claims may call upon the Court in interpreting the Constitution to exercise that same capacity which by tradition courts always have exercised: reasoned judgment. Its boundaries are not susceptible of expression as a simple rule. That does not mean we are free to invalidate state policy choices with which we disagree; yet neither does it permit us to shrink from the duties of our office. As Justice Harlan observed:

"Due process has not been reduced to any formula; its content cannot be determined by reference to any code. The best that can be said is that through the course of this Court's decisions it has represented the balance which our Nation, built upon postulates of respect for the liberty of the individual, has struck between that liberty and the demands of organized society. If the supplying of content to this Constitutional concept has of necessity been a rational process, it certainly has not been one where judges have felt free to roam where unguided speculation might take them. The balance of which I speak is the balance struck by this country, having regard to what history teaches are the traditions from which it developed as well as the traditions from which it broke. That tradition is a living thing. A decision of this Court which radically departs from it could not long survive, while a decision which builds on what has survived is likely to be sound. No formula could serve as a substitute, in this area, for judgment and restraint." *Poe v. Ullman....*

Men and women of good conscience can disagree, and we suppose some always shall disagree, about the profound moral and spiritual implications of terminating a pregnancy, even in its earliest stage. Some of us as individuals find abortion offensive to our most basic principles of morality, but that cannot control our decision. Our obligation is to define the liberty of all, not to mandate our own moral code. The underlying constitutional issue is whether the State can resolve these philosophic questions in such a definitive way that a woman lacks all choice in the matter, except perhaps in those rare circumstances in which the pregnancy is itself a danger to her own life or health, or is the result of rape or incest.

It is conventional constitutional doctrine that where reasonable people disagree the government can adopt one position or the other. See, e.g., *Ferguson v. Skrupa*,...(1963); *Williamson v. Lee Optical of Oklahoma, Inc.*,... (1955). That theorem, however, assumes a state of affairs in which the choice does not intrude upon a protected liberty. Thus, while some people might disagree about whether or not the flag should be saluted, or disagree about the proposition that it may not be defiled, we have ruled that a State may not compel or enforce one view or the other. See *West Virginia State Bd. of Education v. Barnette*,... (1943); *Texas v. Johnson*,... (1989).

Our law affords constitutional protection to personal decisions relating to marriage, procreation, contraception, family relationships, child rearing, and education.... Our cases recognize "the right of the *individual*, married or single, to be free from unwarranted governmental intrusion into matters so fundamentally affecting a person as the decision whether to bear or beget a child." *Eisenstadt v. Baird*,... (emphasis in original). Our precedents "have respected the private realm of family life which the state cannot enter." *Prince v. Massachusetts*,... (1944). These matters, involving the most intimate and personal choices a person may make in a lifetime, choices central to personal dignity and autonomy, are central to the liberty protected by the Fourteenth Amendment. At the heart of liberty is the right to define one's own concept of existence, of meaning, of the universe, and of the mystery of human life. Beliefs about these matters could not define the attributes of personhood were they formed under compulsion of the State.

These considerations begin our analysis of the woman's interest in terminating her pregnancy but cannot end it, for this reason: though the abortion decision may originate within the zone of conscience and belief, it is more than a philosophic exercise. Abortion is a unique act. It is an act fraught with consequences for others: for the woman who must live with the implications of her decision; for the persons who perform and assist in the procedure; for the spouse, family, and society which must confront the knowledge that these procedures exist, procedures some deem nothing short of an act of violence against innocent human life; and, depending on one's beliefs, for the life or potential life that is aborted. Though abortion is conduct, it does not follow that the State is entitled to proscribe it in all instances. That is because the liberty of the woman is at stake in a sense unique to the human condition and so unique to the law. The mother who carries a child to full term is subject to anxieties, to physical constraints, to pain that only she must bear. That these sacrifices have from the beginning of the human race been endured by woman with a pride that ennobles her in the eyes of others and gives to the infant a bond of love cannot alone be grounds for the State to insist she make the sacrifice. Her suffering is too intimate and personal for the State to insist, without more, upon its own vision of the woman's role, however dominant that vision has been in the course of our history and our culture. The destiny of the woman must be shaped to a large extent on her own conception of her spiritual imperatives and her place in society.

It should be recognized, moreover, that in some critical respects the abortion decision is of the same character as the decision to use contraception, to which *Griswold v. Connecticut*, *Eisenstadt v.. Baird*, and *Carey v. Population Services International*, afford constitutional protection. We have no doubt as to the correctness of those decisions. They support the reasoning in *Roe* relating to the woman's liberty because they involve personal decisions concerning not only the meaning of procreation but also human responsibility and respect for it. As with abortion, reasonable people will have differences of opinion about these matters. One view is based on such reverence for the wonder of creation that any pregnancy ought to be welcomed and carried to full term no matter how difficult it will be to provide for the child and ensure its well-being. Another is that the inability to provide for the nurture and care of the infant is a cruelty to the child and an anguish to the parent. These are intimate views with infinite variations, and their deep, personal character underlay our decisions in *Griswold*, *Eisenstadt*, and *Carey*. The same concerns are present when the woman confronts the reality that, perhaps despite her attempts to avoid it, she has become pregnant.

It was this dimension of personal liberty that *Roe* sought to protect, and its holding invoked the reasoning and the tradition of the precedents we have discussed, granting protection to substantive liberties of the person. *Roe* was, of course, an extension of those cases and, as the decision itself indicated, the separate States could act in some degree to further their own legitimate interests in protecting pre-natal life. The extent to which the legislatures of the States might act to outweigh the interests of the woman in choosing to terminate her pregnancy was a subject of debate both in *Roe* itself and in decisions following it.

While we appreciate the weight of the arguments made on behalf of the State in the case before us, arguments which in their ultimate formulation conclude that *Roe* should be overruled, the reservations any of us may have in reaffirming the central holding of *Roe* are outweighed by the explication of individual liberty we have given combined with the force of *stare decisis*. We turn now to that doctrine.

III

A.

The obligation to follow precedent begins with necessity, and a contrary necessity marks its outer limit. With Cardozo, we recognize that no judicial system could do society's work if it eyed each issue afresh in every case that raised it. ... Indeed, the very concept of the rule of law underlying our own Constitution requires such continuity over time that a respect for precedent is, by definition, indispensable. ... At the other extreme, a different necessity would make itself felt if a prior judicial ruling should come to be seen so clearly as error that its enforcement was for that very reason doomed.

...[W]hen this Court reexamines a prior holding, its judgment is customarily informed by a series of prudential and pragmatic considerations designed to test the consistency of overruling a prior decision with the ideal of the rule of law, and to gauge the respective costs of reaffirming and overruling a prior case....

So in this case we may inquire whether *Roe's* central rule has been found unworkable; whether the rule's limitation on state power could be removed without serious inequity to those who have relied upon it or significant damage to the stability of the society governed by the rule in question; whether the law's growth in the intervening years has left *Roe* 's central rule a doctrinal anachronism discounted by society; and whether *Roe's* premises of fact have so far changed in the ensuing two decades as to render its central holding somehow irrelevant or unjustifiable in dealing with the issue it addressed.

1

Although *Roe* has engendered opposition, it has in no sense proven "unworkable," ... representing as it does a simple limitation beyond which a state law is unenforceable. While *Roe* has, of course, required judicial assessment of state laws affecting the exercise of the choice guaranteed against government infringement, and although the need for such review will remain as a consequence of today's decision, the required determinations fall within judicial competence.

2

The inquiry into reliance counts the cost of a rule's repudiation as it would fall on those who have relied reasonably on the rule's continued application. Since the classic case for weighing reliance heavily in favor of following the earlier rule occurs in the commercial context ... where advance planning of great precision is most obviously a necessity, it is no cause for surprise that some would find no reliance worthy of consideration in support of *Roe*.

...Abortion is customarily chosen as an unplanned response to the consequence of unplanned activity or to the failure of conventional birth control, and except on the assumption that no intercourse would have occurred but for *Roe's* holding, such behavior may appear to justify no reliance claim....

To eliminate the issue of reliance that easily, however, one would need to limit cognizable reliance to specific instances of sexual activity. But to do this would be simply to refuse to face the fact that for two decades of economic and social developments, people have organized intimate relationships and made choices that define their views of themselves and their places in society, in reliance on the availability of abortion in the event that contraception should fail. The ability of women to participate equally in the economic and social life of the Nation has been facilitated by their ability to control their reproductive lives.... The Constitution serves human values, and while the effect of reliance on *Roe* cannot be exactly measured, neither can the certain cost of overruling *Roe* for people who have ordered their thinking and living around that case be dismissed.

3

No evolution of legal principle has left *Roe*'s doctrinal footings weaker than they were in 1973. No development of constitutional law since the case was decided has implicitly or explicitly left *Roe* behind as a mere survivor of obsolete constitutional thinking.

It will be recognized, of course, that *Roe* stands at an intersection of two lines of decisions, but in whichever doctrinal category one reads the case, the result for present purposes will be the same. The *Roe* Court itself placed its holding in the succession of cases most prominently exemplified by *Griswold v. Connecticut*....When it is so seen, *Roe* is clearly in no jeopardy, since subsequent constitutional developments have neither disturbed, nor do they threaten to diminish, the scope of recognized protection accorded to the liberty relating to intimate relationships, the family, and decisions about whether or not to beget or bear a child....

Roe, however, may be seen not only as an exemplar of *Griswold* liberty but as a rule (whether or not mistaken) of personal autonomy and bodily integrity, with doctrinal affinity to cases recognizing limits on governmental power to mandate medical treatment or to bar its rejection. If so, our cases since *Roe* accord with *Roe's* view that a State's interest in the protection of life falls short of justifying any plenary override of individual liberty claims. *Cruzan v. Director, Missouri Dept. of Health*....

Finally, one could classify *Roe* as *sui generis*. If the case is so viewed, then there clearly has been no erosion of its central determination. The original holding resting on the concurrence of seven Members of the Court in 1973 was expressly affirmed by a majority of six in 1983, see *Akron v. Akron Center for Reproductive Health, Inc.*, (1983) (*Akron I*), and by a majority of five in 1986, see *Thornburgh v. American College of Obstetricians and Gynecologists*, (1986), expressing adherence to the constitutional ruling despite legislative efforts in some States to test its limits....

Nor will courts building upon *Roe* be likely to hand down erroneous decisions as a consequence. Even on the assumption that the central holding of *Roe* was in error, that error would go only to the strength of the state interest in fetal protection, not to the recognition afforded by the Constitution to the woman's liberty....

The soundness of this prong of the *Roe* analysis is apparent from a consideration of the alternative. If indeed the woman's interest in deciding whether to bear and beget a child had not been recognized as in *Roe*, the State might as readily restrict a woman's right to choose to carry a pregnancy to term as to terminate it, to further asserted state interests in population control, or eugenics, for example.... In any event, because *Roe*'s scope is confined by the fact of its concern with postconception potential life, a concern otherwise likely to be implicated only by some forms of contraception protected independently under *Griswold* and later cases, any error in *Roe* is unlikely to have serious ramifications in future cases.

4

We have seen how time has overtaken some of *Roe's* factual assumptions: advances in maternal health care allow for abortions safe to the mother later in pregnancy than was true in 1973,... and advances in neonatal care have advanced viability to a point somewhat earlier.... But these facts go only to the scheme of time limits on the realization of competing interests, and the divergences from the factual premises of 1973 have no bearing on the validity of *Roe*'s central holding, that viability marks the earliest point at which the State's interest in fetal life is constitutionally adequate to justify a legislative ban on nontherapeutic abortions. The soundness or unsoundness of that constitutional judgment in no sense turns on whether viability occurs at approximately 28 weeks, as was usual at the time of *Roe*, at 23 to 24 weeks, as it sometimes does today, or at some moment even slightly earlier in pregnancy, as it may if fetal respiratory capacity can somehow be enhanced in the future. Whenever it may occur, the attainment of viability may continue to serve as the critical fact, just as it has done since *Roe* was decided; which is to say that no change in *Roe*'s factual underpinning has left its central holding obsolete, and none supports an argument for overruling it.

5

The sum of the precedential inquiry to this point shows *Roe's* underpinnings unweakened in any way affecting its central holding. While it has engendered disapproval, it has not been unworkable. An entire generation has come of age free to assume *Roe*'s concept of liberty in defining the capacity of women to act in society, and to make reproductive decisions; no erosion of principle going to liberty or personal autonomy has left *Roe*'s central holding a doctrinal remnant; *Roe* portends no developments at odds with other precedent for the analysis of personal liberty; and no changes of fact have rendered viability more or less appropriate as the point at which the balance of interests tips. Within the bounds of normal *stare decisis* analysis, then, and subject to the considerations on which it customarily turns, the stronger argument is for affirming *Roe*'s central holding, with whatever degree of personal reluctance any of us may have, not for overruling it.

B

In a less significant case, *stare decisis* analysis could, and would, stop at the point we have reached. But the sustained and widespread debate *Roe* has provoked calls for some comparison between that case and others of comparable dimension that have responded to national controversies and taken on the impress of the controversies addressed. Only two such decisional lines from the past century present themselves for examination, and in each instance the result reached by the Court accorded with the principles we apply today.

The first example is that line of cases identified with *Lochner v. New York*,... (1905), which imposed substantive limitations on legislation limiting economic autonomy in favor of health and welfare regulation, adopting, in Justice Holmes' view, the theory of laissez-faire.... The *Lochner* decisions were exemplified by *Adkins v. Children's Hospital of D.C.*,... (1923), in which this Court held it to be an infringement of constitutionally protected liberty of contract to require the employers of adult women to satisfy minimum wage standards. Fourteen years later, *West Coast Hotel Co. v. Parrish*... (1937), signaled the demise of *Lochner* by overruling Adkins. In the meantime, the Depression had come and, with it, the lesson that seemed unmistakable to most people by 1937, that the interpretation of contractual freedom protected in *Adkins* rested on fundamentally false factual assumptions about the capacity of a relatively unregulated market to satisfy minimal levels of human welfare.... As Justice Jackson wrote of the constitutional crisis of 1937 shortly before he came on the bench, "The older world of laissez-faire was recognized everywhere outside the Court to be dead...." The facts upon which the earlier case had premised a constitutional resolution of social controversy had proved to be untrue, and history's demonstration of their untruth not only justified but required the new choice of constitutional principle that *West Coast Hotel* announced. Of course, it was true that the Court lost something by its misperception, or its lack of prescience, and the Court-packing crisis only magnified the loss; but the clear demonstration that the facts of economic life were different from those previously assumed warranted the repudiation of the old law.

The second comparison that 20th century history invites is with the cases employing the separate-but-equal rule for applying the Fourteenth Amendment's equal protection guarantee. They began with *Plessy v. Ferguson*,... (1896), holding that legislatively mandated racial segregation in public transportation works no denial of equal protection, rejecting the argument that racial separation enforced by the legal machinery of American society treats the black race as inferior. The *Plessy* Court considered "the underlying fallacy of the plaintiff's argument to consist in the assumption that the enforced separation of the two races stamps the colored race with a badge of inferiority. If this be so, it is not by reason of anything found in the act, but solely because the colored race chooses to put that construction upon it...." Whether, as a matter of historical fact, the Justices in the *Plessy* majority believed this or not,... this understanding of the implication of segregation was the stated justification for the Court's opinion. But this understanding of the facts and the rule it was stated to justify were repudiated in *Brown v. Board of Education*,... (1954). As one commentator observed, the question before the Court in *Brown* was "whether discrimination inheres in that segregation which is imposed by law in the twentieth century in certain specific states in the American Union. And that question has meaning and can find an answer only on the ground of history and of common knowledge about the facts of life in the times and places aforesaid...."

West Coast Hotel and *Brown* each rested on facts, or an understanding of facts, changed from those which furnished the claimed justifications for the earlier constitutional resolutions. Each case was comprehensible as the Court's response to facts that the country could understand, or had come to understand already, but which the Court of an earlier day, as its own declarations disclosed, had not been able to perceive. As the decisions were thus comprehensible they were also defensible, not merely as the victories of one doctrinal school over another by dint of numbers (victories though they were), but as applications of constitutional principle to facts as they had not been seen by the Court before. In constitutional adjudication as elsewhere in life, changed circumstances may impose new obligations, and the thoughtful part of the Nation could accept each decision to overrule a prior case as a response to the Court's constitutional duty.

Because the case before us presents no such occasion it could be seen as no such response. Because neither the factual underpinnings of *Roe*'s central holding nor our understanding of it has changed (and because no other indication of weakened precedent has been shown) the Court could not pretend to be reexamining the prior law with any justification beyond a present doctrinal disposition to come out differently from the Court of 1973. To overrule prior law for no other reason than that would run counter to the view repeated in our cases, that a decision to overrule should rest on some special reason over and above the belief that a prior case was wrongly decided....

C

The examination of the conditions justifying the repudiation of *Adkins* by *West Coast Hotel* and *Plessy* by *Brown* is enough to suggest the terrible price that would have been paid if the Court had not overruled as it did. In the present case, however, as our analysis to this point makes clear, the terrible price would be paid for overruling. Our analysis would not be complete, however, without explaining why overruling *Roe's* central holding would not only reach an unjustifiable result under principles of *stare decisis*, but would seriously weaken the Court's capacity to exercise the judicial power and to function as the Supreme Court of a Nation dedicated to the rule of law. To understand why this would be so it is necessary to understand the source of this Court's authority, the conditions necessary for its preservation, and its relationship to the country's understanding of itself as a constitutional Republic.

The root of American governmental power is revealed most clearly in the instance of the power conferred by the Constitution upon the Judiciary of the United States and specifically upon this Court. As Americans of each succeeding generation are rightly told, the Court cannot buy support for its decisions by spending money and, except to a minor degree, it cannot independently coerce obedience to its decrees. The Court's power lies, rather, in its legitimacy, a product of substance and perception that shows itself in the people's acceptance of the Judiciary as fit to determine what the Nation's law means and to declare what it demands.

The underlying substance of this legitimacy is of course the warrant for the Court's decisions in the Constitution and the lesser sources of legal principle on which the Court draws. That substance is expressed in the Court's opinions, and our contemporary understanding is such that a decision without principled justification would be no judicial act at all. But even when justification is furnished by apposite legal principle, something more is required. Because not every conscientious claim of principled justification will be accepted as such, the justification claimed must be beyond dispute. The Court must take care to speak and act in ways that allow people to accept its decisions on the terms the Court claims for them, as grounded truly in principle, not as compromises with social and political pressures having, as such, no bearing on the principled choices that the Court is obliged to make. Thus, the Court's legitimacy depends on making legally principled decisions under circumstances in which their principled character is sufficiently plausible to be accepted by the Nation.

The need for principled action to be perceived as such is implicated to some degree whenever this, or any other appellate court, overrules a prior case.

This is not to say, of course, that this Court cannot give a perfectly satisfactory explanation in most cases. People understand that some of the Constitution's language is hard to fathom and that the Court's Justices are sometimes able to perceive significant facts or to understand principles of law that eluded their predecessors and that justify departures from existing decisions. However upsetting it may be to those most directly affected when one judicially derived rule replaces another, the country can accept some correction of error without necessarily questioning the legitimacy of the Court.

In two circumstances, however, the Court would almost certainly fail to receive the benefit of the doubt in overruling prior cases. There is, first, a point beyond which frequent overruling would overtax the country's belief in the Court's good faith. Despite the variety of reasons that may inform and justify a decision to overrule, we cannot forget that such a decision is usually perceived (and perceived correctly) as, at the least, a statement that a prior decision was wrong. There is a limit to the amount of error that can plausibly be imputed to prior courts. If that limit should be exceeded, disturbance of prior rulings would be taken as evidence that justifiable reexamination of principle had given way to drives for particular results in the short term. The legitimacy of the Court would fade with the frequency of its vacillation.

That first circumstance can be described as hypothetical; the second is to the point here and now. Where, in the performance of its judicial duties, the Court decides a case in such a way as to resolve the sort of intensely divisive controversy reflected in *Roe* and those rare, comparable cases, its decision has a dimension that the resolution of the normal case does not carry. It is the dimension present whenever the Court's interpretation of the Constitution calls the contending sides of a national controversy to end their national division by accepting a common mandate rooted in the Constitution.

The Court is not asked to do this very often, having thus addressed the Nation only twice in our lifetime, in the decisions of *Brown* and *Roe*. But when the Court does act in this way, its decision requires an equally rare precedential force to counter the inevitable efforts to overturn it and to thwart its implementation. Some of those efforts may be mere unprincipled emotional reactions; others may proceed from principles worthy of profound respect. But whatever the premises of opposition may be, only the most convincing justification under accepted standards of precedent could suffice to demonstrate that a later decision overruling the first was anything but a surrender to political pressure, and an unjustified repudiation of the principle on which the Court staked its authority in the first instance. So to overrule under fire in the absence of the most compelling reason to reexamine a watershed decision would subvert the Court's legitimacy beyond any serious question....

The country's loss of confidence in the judiciary would be underscored by an equally certain and equally reasonable condemnation for another failing in overruling unnecessarily and under pressure. Some cost will be paid by anyone who approves or implements a constitutional decision where it is unpopular, or who refuses to work to undermine the decision or to force its reversal. The price may be criticism or ostracism, or it may be violence. An extra price will be paid by those who themselves disapprove of the decision's results when viewed outside of constitutional terms, but who nevertheless struggle to accept it, because they respect the rule of law. To all those who will be so tested by following, the Court implicitly undertakes to remain steadfast, lest in the end a price be paid for nothing. The promise of constancy, once given, binds its maker for as long as the power to stand by the decision survives and the understanding of the issue has not changed so fundamentally as to render the commitment obsolete. From the obligation of this promise this Court cannot and should not assume any exemption when duty requires it to decide a case in conformance with the Constitution. A willing breach of it would be nothing less than a breach of faith, and no Court that broke its faith with the people could sensibly expect credit for principle in the decision by which it did that.

It is true that diminished legitimacy may be restored, but only slowly. Unlike the political branches, a Court thus weakened could not seek to regain its position with a new mandate from the voters, and even if the Court could somehow go to the polls, the loss of its principled character could not be retrieved by the casting of so many votes. Like the character of an individual, the legitimacy of the Court must be earned over time. So, indeed, must be the character of a Nation of people who aspire to live according to the rule of law. Their belief in themselves as such a people is not readily separable from their understanding of the Court invested with the authority to decide their constitutional cases and speak before all others for their constitutional ideals. If the Court's legitimacy should be undermined, then, so would the country be in its very ability to see itself through its constitutional ideals. The Court's concern with legitimacy is not for the sake of the Court but for the sake of the Nation to which it is responsible.

The Court's duty in the present case is clear. In 1973, it confronted the already-divisive issue of governmental power to limit personal choice to undergo abortion, for which it provided a new resolution based on the due process guaranteed by the Fourteenth Amendment. Whether or not a new social consensus is developing on that issue, its divisiveness is no less today than in 1973, and pressure to overrule the decision, like pressure to retain it, has grown only more intense. A decision to overrule *Roe's* essential holding under the existing circumstances would address error, if error there was, at the cost of both profound and unnecessary damage to the Court's legitimacy, and to the Nation's commitment to the rule of law. It is therefore imperative to adhere to the essence of *Roe's* original decision, and we do so today.

IV

From what we have said so far it follows that it is a constitutional liberty of the woman to have some freedom to terminate her pregnancy. We conclude that the basic decision in *Roe* was based on a constitutional analysis which we cannot now repudiate. The woman's liberty is not so unlimited, however, that from the outset the State cannot show its concern for the life of the unborn, and at a later point in fetal development the State's interest in life has sufficient force so that the right of the woman to terminate the pregnancy can be restricted.

That brings us, of course, to the point where much criticism has been directed at *Roe*, a criticism that always inheres when the Court draws a specific rule from what in the Constitution is but a general standard. We conclude, however, that the urgent claims of the woman to retain the ultimate control over her destiny and her body, claims implicit in the meaning of liberty, require us to perform that function. Liberty must not be extinguished for want of a line that is clear. And it falls to us to give some real substance to the woman's liberty to determine whether to carry her pregnancy to full term.

We conclude the line should be drawn at viability, so that before that time the woman has a right to choose to terminate her pregnancy. We adhere to this principle for two reasons. First, as we have said, is the doctrine of *stare decisis*. Any judicial act of line-drawing may seem somewhat arbitrary, but *Roe* was a reasoned statement, elaborated with great care. We have twice reaffirmed it in the face of great opposition. See *Thornburgh v. American College of Obstetricians & Gynecologists*...; *Akron I*.... Although we must overrule those parts of *Thornburgh* and *Akron I* which, in our view, are inconsistent with *Roe's* statement that the State has a legitimate interest in promoting the life or potential life of the unborn... the central premise of those cases represents an unbroken commitment by this Court to the essential holding of *Roe*. It is that premise which we reaffirm today.

The second reason is that the concept of viability, as we noted in *Roe*, is the time at which there is a realistic possibility of maintaining and nourishing a life outside the womb, so that the independent existence of the second life can in reason and all fairness be the object of state protection that now overrides the rights of the woman.... Consistent with other constitutional norms, legislatures may draw lines which appear arbitrary without the necessity of offering a justification. But courts may not. We must justify the lines we draw. And there is no line other than viability which is more workable. To be sure, as we have said, there may be some medical developments that affect the precise point of viability,... but this is an imprecision within tolerable limits given that the medical community and all those who must apply its discoveries will continue to explore the matter. The viability line also has, as a practical matter, an element of fairness. In some broad sense it might be said that a woman who fails to act before viability has consented to the State's intervention on behalf of the developing child.

The woman's right to terminate her pregnancy before viability is the most central principle of *Roe v. Wade*. It is a rule of law and a component of liberty we cannot renounce.

On the other side of the equation is the interest of the State in the protection of potential life. The *Roe* Court recognized the State's " important and legitimate interest in protecting the potentiality of human life.... " The weight to be given this state interest, not the strength of the woman's interest, was the difficult question faced in *Roe*. We do not need to say whether each of us, had we been Members of the Court when the valuation of the State interest came before it as an original matter, would have concluded, as the *Roe* Court did, that its weight is insufficient to justify a ban on abortions prior to viability even when it is subject to certain exceptions. The matter is not before us in the first instance, and coming as it does after nearly 20 years of litigation in *Roe's* wake we are satisfied that the immediate question is not the soundness of *Roe's* resolution of the issue, but the precedential force that must be accorded to its holding. And we have concluded that the essential holding of *Roe* should be reaffirmed.

Yet it must be remembered that *Roe v. Wade* speaks with clarity in establishing not only the woman's liberty but also the State's "important and legitimate interest in potential life...." That portion of the decision in *Roe* has been given too little acknowledgment and implementation by the Court in its subsequent cases. Those cases decided that any regulation touching upon the abortion decision must survive strict scrutiny, to be sustained only if drawn in narrow terms to further a compelling state interest.... Not all of the cases decided under that formulation can be reconciled with the holding in *Roe* itself that the State has legitimate interests in the health of the woman and in protecting the potential life within her. In resolving this tension, we choose to rely upon *Roe*, as against the later cases.

Roe established a trimester framework to govern abortion regulations. Under this elaborate but rigid construct, almost no regulation at all is permitted during the first trimester of pregnancy; regulations designed to protect the woman's health, but not to further the State's interest in potential life, are permitted during the second trimester; and during the third trimester, when the fetus is viable, prohibitions are permitted provided the life or health of the mother is not at stake.... Most of our cases since *Roe* have involved the application of rules derived from the trimester framework....

The trimester framework no doubt was erected to ensure that the woman's right to choose not become so subordinate to the State's interest in promoting fetal life that her choice exists in theory but not in fact. We do not agree, however, that the trimester approach is necessary to accomplish this objective. A framework of this rigidity was unnecessary and in its later interpretation sometimes contradicted the State's permissible exercise of its powers.

Though the woman has a right to choose to terminate or continue her pregnancy before viability, it does not at all follow that the State is prohibited from taking steps to ensure that this choice is thoughtful and informed. Even in the earliest stages of pregnancy, the State may enact rules and regulations designed to encourage her to know that there are philosophic and social arguments of great weight that can be brought to bear in favor of continuing the pregnancy to full term and that there are procedures and institutions to allow adoption of unwanted children as well as a certain degree of state assistance if the mother chooses to raise the child herself.... It follows that States are free to enact laws to provide a reasonable framework for a woman to make a decision that has such profound and lasting meaning. This, too, we find consistent with *Roe's* central premises, and indeed the inevitable consequence of our holding that the State has an interest in protecting the life of the unborn.

We reject the trimester framework, which we do not consider to be part of the essential holding of *Roe*.... Measures aimed at ensuring that a woman's choice contemplates the consequences for the fetus do not necessarily interfere with the right recognized in *Roe*, although those measures have been found to be inconsistent with the rigid trimester framework announced in that case. A logical reading of the central holding in *Roe* itself, and a necessary reconciliation of the liberty of the woman and the interest of the State in promoting prenatal life, require, in our view, that we abandon the trimester framework as a rigid prohibition on all previability regulation aimed at the protection of fetal life. The trimester framework suffers from these basic flaws: in its formulation it misconceives the nature of the pregnant woman's interest; and in practice it undervalues the State's interest in potential life, as recognized in *Roe*....

Numerous forms of state regulation might have the incidental effect of increasing the cost or decreasing the availability of medical care, whether for abortion or any other medical procedure. The fact that a law which serves a valid purpose, one not designed to strike at the right itself, has the incidental effect of making it more difficult or more expensive to procure an abortion cannot be enough to invalidate it. Only where state regulation imposes an undue burden on a woman's ability to make this decision does the power of the State reach into the heart of the liberty protected by the Due Process Clause....

For the most part, the Court's early abortion cases adhered to this view....

These considerations of the nature of the abortion right illustrate that it is an overstatement to describe it as a right to decide whether to have an abortion "without interference from the State...." All abortion regulations interfere to some degree with a woman's ability to decide whether to terminate her pregnancy. It is, as a consequence, not surprising that despite the protestations contained in the original *Roe* opinion to the effect that the Court was not recognizing an absolute right,... the Court's experience applying the trimester framework has led to the striking down of some abortion regulations which in no real sense deprived women of the ultimate decision. Those decisions went too far because the right recognized by *Roe* is a right "to be free from unwarranted governmental intrusion into matters so fundamentally affecting a person as the decision whether to bear or beget a child...." Not all governmental intrusion is of necessity unwarranted; and that brings us to the other basic flaw in the trimester framework: even in *Roe's* terms, in practice it undervalues the State's interest in the potential life within the woman. *Roe v. Wade* was express in its recognition of the State's "important and legitimate interest[s] in preserving and protecting the health of the pregnant woman [and] in protecting the potentiality of human life...." The trimester framework, however, does not fulfill *Roe's* own promise that the State has an interest in protecting fetal life or potential life. *Roe* began the contradiction by using the trimester framework to forbid any regulation of abortion designed to advance that interest before viability.... Before viability, *Roe* and subsequent cases treat all governmental attempts to influence a woman's decision on behalf of the potential life within her as unwarranted. This treatment is, in our judgment, incompatible with the recognition that there is a substantial state interest in potential life throughout pregnancy....

The very notion that the State has a substantial interest in potential life leads to the conclusion that not all regulations must be deemed unwarranted. Not all burdens on the right to decide whether to terminate a pregnancy will be undue. In our view, the undue burden standard is the appropriate means of reconciling the State's interest with the woman's constitutionally protected liberty.

...Because we set forth a standard of general application to which we intend to adhere, it is important to clarify what is meant by an undue burden.

A finding of an undue burden is a shorthand for the conclusion that a state regulation has the purpose or effect of placing a substantial obstacle in the path of a woman seeking an abortion of a nonviable fetus. A statute with this purpose is invalid because the means chosen by the State to further the interest in potential life must be calculated to inform the woman's free choice, not hinder it. And a statute which, while furthering the interest in potential life or some other valid state interest, has the effect of placing a substantial obstacle in the path of a woman's choice cannot be considered a permissible means of serving its legitimate ends. To the extent that the opinions of the Court or of individual Justices use the undue burden standard in a manner that is inconsistent with this analysis, we set out what in our view should be the controlling standard.... Understood another way, we answer the question, left open in previous opinions discussing the undue burden formulation, whether a law designed to further the State's interest in fetal life which imposes an undue burden on the woman's decision before fetal viability could be constitutional.... The answer is no.

Some guiding principles should emerge. What is at stake is the woman's right to make the ultimate decision, not a right to be insulated from all others in doing so. Regulations which do no more than create a structural mechanism by which the State, or the parent or guardian of a minor, may express profound respect for the life of the unborn are permitted, if they are not a substantial obstacle to the woman's exercise of the right to choose.... Unless it has that effect on her right of choice, a state measure designed to persuade her to choose childbirth over abortion will be upheld if reasonably related to that goal. Regulations designed to foster the health of a woman seeking an abortion are valid if they do not constitute an undue burden.

Even when jurists reason from shared premises, some disagreement is inevitable.... That is to be expected in the application of any legal standard which must accommodate life's complexity. We do not expect it to be otherwise with respect to the undue burden standard. We give this summary:

(a) To protect the central right recognized by *Roe v. Wade* while at the same time accommodating the State's profound interest in potential life, we will employ the undue burden analysis as explained in this opinion. An undue burden exists, and therefore a provision of law is invalid, if its purpose or effect is to place a substantial obstacle in the path of a woman seeking an abortion before the fetus attains viability.

(b) We reject the rigid trimester framework of *Roe v. Wade*. To promote the State's profound interest in potential life, throughout pregnancy the State may take measures to ensure that the woman's choice is informed, and measures designed to advance this interest will not be invalidated as long as their purpose is to persuade the woman to choose childbirth over abortion. These measures must not be an undue burden on the right.

(c) As with any medical procedure, the State may enact regulations to further the health or safety of a woman seeking an abortion. Unnecessary health regulations that have the purpose or effect of presenting a substantial obstacle to a woman seeking an abortion impose an undue burden on the right.

(d) Our adoption of the undue burden analysis does not disturb the central holding of *Roe v. Wade*, and we reaffirm that holding. Regardless of whether exceptions are made for particular circumstances, a State may not prohibit any woman from making the ultimate decision to terminate her pregnancy before viability.

(e) We also reaffirm *Roe's* holding that "subsequent to viability, the State in promoting its interest in the potentiality of human life may, if it chooses, regulate, and even proscribe, abortion except where it is necessary, in appropriate medical judgment, for the preservation of the life or health of the mother." *Roe v. Wade*....

These principles control our assessment of the Pennsylvania statute, and we now turn to the issue of the validity of its challenged provisions.

V

The Court of Appeals applied what it believed to be the undue burden standard and upheld each of the provisions except for the husband notification requirement. We agree generally with this conclusion, but refine the undue burden analysis in accordance with the principles articulated above. We now consider the separate statutory sections at issue....

B

We next consider the informed consent requirement....

Our prior decisions establish that as with any medical procedure, the State may require a woman to give her written informed consent to an abortion.... Petitioners challenge the statute's definition of informed consent because it includes the provision of specific information by the doctor and the mandatory 24-hour waiting period. The conclusions reached by a majority of the Justices in the separate opinions filed today and the undue burden standard adopted in this opinion require us to overrule in part some of the Court's past decisions, decisions driven by the trimester framework's prohibition of all previability regulations designed to further the State's interest in fetal life....

To the extent *Akron I* and *Thornburgh* find a constitutional violation when the government requires, as it does here, the giving of truthful, nonmisleading information about the nature of the procedure, the attendant health risks and those of childbirth, and the "probable gestational age" of the fetus, those cases go too far, are inconsistent with *Roe's* acknowledgment of an important interest in potential life, and are overruled.... It cannot be questioned that psychological well-being is a facet of health. Nor can it be doubted that most women considering an abortion would deem the impact on the fetus relevant, if not dispositive, to the decision. In attempting to ensure that a woman apprehend the full consequences of her decision, the State furthers the legitimate purpose of reducing the risk that a woman may elect an abortion, only to discover later, with devastating psychological consequences, that her decision was not fully informed. If the information the State requires to be made available to the woman is truthful and not misleading, the requirement may be permissible.

We also see no reason why the State may not require doctors to inform a woman seeking an abortion of the availability of materials relating to the consequences to the fetus, even when those consequences have no direct relation to her health. An example illustrates the point. We would think it constitutional for the State to require that in order for there to be informed consent to a kidney transplant operation the recipient must be supplied with information about risks to the donor as well as risks to himself or herself.... This requirement cannot be considered a substantial obstacle to obtaining an abortion, and, it follows, there is no undue burden....

All that is left of petitioners' argument is an asserted First Amendment right of a physician not to provide information about the risks of abortion, and childbirth, in a manner mandated by the State.... We see no constitutional infirmity in the requirement that the physician provide the information mandated by the State here.

The Pennsylvania statute also requires us to reconsider the holding in *Akron I* that the State may not require that a physician, as opposed to a qualified assistant, provide information relevant to a woman's informed consent.... Since there is no evidence on this record that requiring a doctor to give the information as provided by the statute would amount in practical terms to a substantial obstacle to a woman seeking an abortion, we conclude that it is not an undue burden....

Our analysis of Pennsylvania's 24-hour waiting period between the provision of the information deemed necessary to informed consent and the performance of an abortion under the undue burden standard requires us to reconsider the premise behind the decision in *Akron I* invalidating a parallel requirement. In *Akron I* we said: "Nor are we convinced that the State's legitimate concern that the woman's decision be informed is reasonably served by requiring a 24-hour delay as a matter of course...." We consider that conclusion to be wrong. The idea that important decisions will be more informed and deliberate if they follow some period of reflection does not strike us as unreasonable, particularly where the statute directs that important information become part of the background of the decision. The statute, as construed by the Court of Appeals, permits avoidance of the waiting period in the event of a medical emergency and the record evidence shows that in the vast majority of cases, a 24-hour delay does not create any appreciable health risk. In theory, at least, the waiting period is a reasonable measure to implement the State's interest in protecting the life of the unborn, a measure that does not amount to an undue burden.

C

Section 3209 of Pennsylvania's abortion law provides, except in cases of medical emergency, that no physician shall perform an abortion on a married woman without receiving a signed statement from the woman that she has notified her spouse that she is about to undergo an abortion. The woman has the option of providing an alternative signed statement certifying that her husband is not the man who impregnated her; that her husband could not be located; that the pregnancy is the result of spousal sexual assault which she has reported; or that the woman believes that notifying her husband will cause him or someone else to inflict bodily injury upon her. A physician who performs an abortion on a married woman without receiving the appropriate signed statement will have his or her license revoked, and is liable to the husband for damages....

The spousal notification requirement is thus likely to prevent a significant number of women from obtaining an abortion. It does not merely make abortions a little more difficult or expensive to obtain; for many women, it will impose a substantial obstacle. We must not blind ourselves to the fact that the significant number of women who fear for their safety and the safety of their children are likely to be deterred from procuring an abortion as surely as if the Commonwealth had outlawed abortion in all cases....

This conclusion is in no way inconsistent with our decisions upholding parental notification or consent requirements.... Those enactments, and our judgment that they are constitutional, are based on the quite reasonable assumption that minors will benefit from consultation with their parents and that children will often not realize that their parents have their best interests at heart. We cannot adopt a parallel assumption about adult women....

D

We next consider the parental consent provision. Except in a medical emergency, an unemancipated young woman under 18 may not obtain an abortion unless she and one of her parents (or guardian) provides informed consent as defined above. If neither a parent nor a guardian provides consent, a court may authorize the performance of an abortion upon a determination that the young woman is mature and capable of giving informed consent and has in fact given her informed consent, or that an abortion would be in her best interests.

We have been over most of this ground before. Our cases establish, and we reaffirm today, that a State may require a minor seeking an abortion to obtain the consent of a parent or guardian, provided that there is an adequate judicial bypass procedure.... Under these precedents, in our view, the one-parent consent requirement and judicial bypass procedure are constitutional....

E

Under the recordkeeping and reporting requirements of the statute, every facility which performs abortions is required to file a report stating its name and address as well as the name and address of any related entity, such as a controlling or subsidiary organization. In the case of state-funded institutions, the information becomes public.

For each abortion performed, a report must be filed identifying: the physician (and the second physician where required); the facility; the referring physician or agency; the woman's age; the number of prior pregnancies and prior abortions she has had; gestational age; the type of abortion procedure; the date of the abortion; whether there were any pre-existing medical conditions which would complicate pregnancy; medical complications with the abortion; where applicable, the basis for the determination that the abortion was medically necessary; the weight of the aborted fetus; and whether the woman was married, and if so, whether notice was provided or the basis for the failure to give notice. Every abortion facility must also file quarterly reports showing the number of abortions performed broken down by trimester. See 18 Pa.Cons.Stat. §§ 3207, 3214 (1990). In all events, the identity of each woman who has had an abortion remains confidential.

In *Danforth*,... we held that recordkeeping and reporting provisions "that are reasonably directed to the preservation of maternal health and that properly respect a patient's confidentiality and privacy are permissible." We think that under this standard, all the provisions at issue here except that relating to spousal notice are constitutional. Although they do not relate to the State's interest in informing the woman's choice, they do relate to health. The collection of information with respect to actual patients is a vital element of medical research, and so it cannot be said that the requirements serve no purpose other than to make abortions more difficult. Nor do we find that the requirements impose a substantial obstacle to a woman's choice. At most they might increase the cost of some abortions by a slight amount. While at some point increased cost could become a substantial obstacle, there is no such showing on the record before us....

VI

Our Constitution is a covenant running from the first generation of Americans to us and then to future generations. It is a coherent succession. Each generation must learn anew that the Constitution's written terms embody ideas and aspirations that must survive more ages than one. We accept our responsibility not to retreat from interpreting the full meaning of the covenant in light of all of our precedents. We invoke it once again to define the freedom guaranteed by the Constitution's own promise, the promise of liberty.

The judgment in No. 91-902 is affirmed. The judgment in No. 91-744 is affirmed in part and reversed in part, and the case is remanded for proceedings consistent with this opinion, including consideration of the question of severability.

It is so ordered.

Justice STEVENS, concurring in part and dissenting in part.

The portions of the Court's opinion that I have joined are more important than those with which I disagree. I shall therefore first comment on significant areas of agreement, and then explain the limited character of my disagreement....

II

My disagreement with the joint opinion begins with its understanding of the trimester framework established in *Roe.* Contrary to the suggestion of the joint opinion, ante, at..., it is not a "contradiction" to recognize that the State may have a legitimate interest in potential human life and, at the same time, to conclude that that interest does not justify the regulation of abortion before viability (although other interests, such as maternal health, may). The fact that the State's interest is legitimate does not tell us when, if ever, that interest outweighs the pregnant woman's interest in personal liberty. It is appropriate, therefore, to consider more carefully the nature of the interests at stake.

First, it is clear that, in order to be legitimate, the State's interest must be secular; consistent with the First Amendment the State may not promote a theological or sectarian interest.... Moreover, as discussed above, the state interest in potential human life is not an interest in loco parentis, for the fetus is not a person.

Identifying the State's interests-which the States rarely articulate with any precision-makes clear that the interest in protecting potential life is not grounded in the Constitution. It is, instead, an indirect interest supported by both humanitarian and pragmatic concerns. Many of our citizens believe that any abortion reflects an unacceptable disrespect for potential human life and that the performance of more than a million abortions each year is intolerable; many find third-trimester abortions performed when the fetus is approaching personhood particularly offensive. The State has a legitimate interest in minimizing such offense. The State may also have a broader interest in expanding the population, believing society would benefit from the services of additional productive citizens – or that the potential human lives might include the occasional Mozart or Curie. These are the kinds of concerns that comprise the State's interest in potential human life.

In counterpoise is the woman's constitutional interest in liberty. One aspect of this liberty is a right to bodily integrity, a right to control one's person.... This right is neutral on the question of abortion: The Constitution would be equally offended by an absolute requirement that all women undergo abortions as by an absolute prohibition on abortions. "Our whole constitutional heritage rebels at the thought of giving government the power to control men's minds...." The same holds true for the power to control women's bodies.

The woman's constitutional liberty interest also involves her freedom to decide matters of the highest privacy and the most personal nature.... A woman considering abortion faces "a difficult choice having serious and personal consequences of major importance to her own future-perhaps to the salvation of her own immortal soul...." The authority to make such traumatic and yet empowering decisions is an element of basic human dignity. As the joint opinion so eloquently demonstrates, a woman's decision to terminate her pregnancy is nothing less than a matter of conscience.

Weighing the State's interest in potential life and the woman's liberty interest, I agree with the joint opinion that the State may "'expres[s] a preference for normal childbirth,'" that the State may take steps to ensure that a woman's choice "is thoughtful and informed," and that "States are free to enact laws to provide a reasonable framework for a woman to make a decision that has such profound and lasting meaning.... " Serious questions arise, however, when a State attempts to "persuade the woman to choose childbirth over abortion.... " Decisional autonomy must limit the State's power to inject into a woman's most personal deliberations its own views of what is best. The State may promote its preferences by funding childbirth, by creating and maintaining alternatives to abortion, and by espousing the virtues of family; but it must respect the individual's freedom to make such judgments....

Under these principles, §§ 3205(a)(2)(i)-(iii) of the Pennsylvania statute are unconstitutional. Those sections require a physician or counselor to provide the woman with a range of materials clearly designed to persuade her to choose not to undergo the abortion. While the State is free, pursuant to § 3208 of the Pennsylvania law, to produce and disseminate such material, the State may not inject such information into the woman's deliberations just as she is weighing such an important choice.

Under this same analysis, §§ 3205(a)(1)(i) and (iii) of the Pennsylvania statute are constitutional. Those sections, which require the physician to inform a woman of the nature and risks of the abortion procedure and the medical risks of carrying to term, are neutral requirements comparable to those imposed in other medical procedures. Those sections indicate no effort by the State to influence the woman's choice in any way. If anything, such requirements enhance, rather than skew, the woman's decisionmaking.

III

The 24-hour waiting period required by §§ 3205(a)(1)-(2) of the Pennsylvania statute raises even more serious concerns. Such a requirement arguably furthers the State's interests in two ways, neither of which is constitutionally permissible.

First, it may be argued that the 24-hour delay is justified by the mere fact that it is likely to reduce the number of abortions, thus furthering the State's interest in potential life. But such an argument would justify any form of coercion that placed an obstacle in the woman's path. The State cannot further its interests by simply wearing down the ability of the pregnant woman to exercise her constitutional right.

Second, it can more reasonably be argued that the 24-hour delay furthers the State's interest in ensuring that the woman's decision is informed and thoughtful. But there is no evidence that the mandated delay benefits women or that it is necessary to enable the physician to convey any relevant information to the patient. The mandatory delay thus appears to rest on outmoded and unacceptable assumptions about the decisionmaking capacity of women. While there are well-established and consistently maintained reasons for the State to view with skepticism the ability of minors to make decisions,... none of those reasons applies to an adult woman's decisionmaking ability....

In the alternative, the delay requirement may be premised on the belief that the decision to terminate a pregnancy is presumptively wrong. This premise is illegitimate. Those who disagree vehemently about the legality and morality of abortion agree about one thing: The decision to terminate a pregnancy is profound and difficult. No person undertakes such a decision lightly-and States may not presume that a woman has failed to reflect adequately merely because her conclusion differs from the State's preference. A woman who has, in the privacy of her thoughts and conscience, weighed the options and made her decision cannot be forced to reconsider all, simply because the State believes she has come to the wrong conclusion.

Part of the constitutional liberty to choose is the equal dignity to which each of us is entitled. A woman who decides to terminate her pregnancy is entitled to the same respect as a woman who decides to carry the fetus to term. The mandatory waiting period denies women that equal respect.

IV

In my opinion, a correct application of the "undue burden" standard leads to the same conclusion concerning the constitutionality of these requirements. A state-imposed burden on the exercise of a constitutional right is measured both by its effects and by its character: A burden may be "undue" either because the burden is too severe or because it lacks a legitimate, rational justification.

The 24-hour delay requirement fails both parts of this test. The findings of the District Court establish the severity of the burden that the 24-hour delay imposes on many pregnant women. Yet even in those cases in which the delay is not especially onerous, it is, in my opinion, "undue" because there is no evidence that such a delay serves a useful and legitimate purpose. As indicated above, there is no legitimate reason to require a woman who has agonized over her decision to leave the clinic or hospital and return again another day. While a general requirement that a physician notify her patients about the risks of a proposed medical procedure is appropriate, a rigid requirement that all patients wait 24 hours or (what is true in practice) much longer to evaluate the significance of information that is either common knowledge or irrelevant is an irrational and, therefore, "undue" burden.

The counseling provisions are similarly infirm. Whenever government commands private citizens to speak or to listen, careful review of the justification for that command is particularly appropriate. In this case, the Pennsylvania statute directs that counselors provide women seeking abortions with information concerning alternatives to abortion, the availability of medical assistance benefits, and the possibility of child- support payments. §§ 3205(a)(2)(i)-(iii). The statute requires that this information be given to all women seeking abortions, including those for whom such information is clearly useless, such as those who are married, those who have undergone the procedure in the past and are fully aware of the options, and those who are fully convinced that abortion is their only reasonable option. Moreover, the statute requires physicians to inform all of their patients of "the probable gestational age of the unborn child." §3205(a)(1)(ii). This information is of little decisional value in most cases, because 90% of all abortions are performed during the first trimester when fetal age has less relevance than when the fetus nears viability. Nor can the information required by the statute be justified as relevant to any "philosophic" or "social" argument,... either favoring or disfavoring the abortion decision in a particular case. In light of all of these facts, I conclude that the information requirements in § 3205(a)(1)(ii) and §§ 3205(a)(2)(i)-(iii) do not serve a useful purpose and thus constitute an unnecessary – and therefore undue – burden on the woman's constitutional liberty to decide to terminate her pregnancy.

Accordingly, while I disagree with Parts IV, V-B, and V-D of the joint opinion, I join the remainder of the Court's opinion.

Justice BLACKMUN, concurring in part, concurring in the judgment in part, and dissenting in part.

I join parts I, II, III, V-A, V-C, and VI of the joint opinion of Justices O'CONNOR, KENNEDY, and SOUTER,

Chief Justice REHNQUIST, with whom Justice WHITE, Justice SCALIA, and Justice THOMAS join, concurring in the judgment in part and dissenting in part.

The joint opinion, following its newly-minted variation on *stare decisis*, retains the outer shell of *Roe v. Wade*,... but beats a wholesale retreat from the substance of that case. We believe that *Roe* was wrongly decided, and that it can and should be overruled consistently with our traditional approach to *stare decisis* in constitutional cases. We would adopt the approach of the plurality in *Webster v. Reproductive Health Services*,... and uphold the challenged provisions of the Pennsylvania statute in their entirety.

I

...In arguing that this Court should invalidate each of the provisions at issue, petitioners insist that we reaffirm our decision in *Roe v. Wade*, supra, in which we held unconstitutional a Texas statute making it a crime to procure an abortion except to save the life of the mother. We agree with the Court of Appeals that our decision in *Roe* is not directly implicated by the Pennsylvania statute, which does not prohibit, but simply regulates, abortion. But, as the Court of Appeals found, the state of our post-*Roe* decisional law dealing with the regulation of abortion is confusing and uncertain, indicating that a reexamination of that line of cases is in order. Unfortunately for those who must apply this Court's decisions, the reexamination undertaken today leaves the Court no less divided than beforehand. Although they reject the trimester framework that formed the underpinning of *Roe*, Justices O'CONNOR, KENNEDY, and

SOUTER adopt a revised undue burden standard to analyze the challenged regulations. We conclude, however, that such an outcome is an unjustified constitutional compromise, one which leaves the Court in a position to closely scrutinize all types of abortion regulations despite the fact that it lacks the power to do so under the Constitution.

In *Roe*, the Court opined that the State "does have an important and legitimate interest in preserving and protecting the health of the pregnant woman,... and that it has still another important and legitimate interest in protecting the potentiality of human life...." In the companion case of *Doe v. Bolton*,... the Court referred to its conclusion in *Roe* "that a pregnant woman does not have an absolute constitutional right to an abortion on her demand...." But while the language and holdings of these cases appeared to leave States free to regulate abortion procedures in a variety of ways, later decisions based on them have found considerably less latitude for such regulations than might have been expected.

For example, after *Roe*, many States have sought to protect their young citizens by requiring that a minor seeking an abortion involve her parents in the decision. Some States have simply required notification of the parents, while others have required a minor to obtain the consent of her parents. In a number of decisions, however, the Court has substantially limited the States in their ability to impose such requirements. With regard to parental notice requirements, we initially held that a State could require a minor to notify her parents before proceeding with an abortion. *H. L. v. Matheson*... (1981). Recently, however, we indicated that a State's ability to impose a notice requirement actually depends on whether it requires notice of one or both parents. We concluded that although the Constitution might allow a State to demand that notice be given to one parent prior to an abortion, it may not require that similar notice be given to two parents, unless the State incorporates a judicial bypass procedure in that two-parent requirement. *Hodgson v. Minnesota*....

We have treated parental consent provisions even more harshly....

In *Roe*, the Court observed that certain States recognized the right of the father to participate in the abortion decision in certain circumstances. Because neither *Roe* nor *Doe* involved the assertion of any paternal right, the Court expressly stated that the case did not disturb the validity of regulations that protected such a right. *Roe v. Wade*.... But three years later, in *Danforth*, the Court extended its abortion jurisprudence and held that a State could not require that a woman obtain the consent of her spouse before proceeding with an abortion....

States have also regularly tried to ensure that a woman's decision to have an abortion is an informed and well-considered one....

We have not allowed States much leeway to regulate even the actual abortion procedure. Although a State can require that second-trimester abortions be performed in outpatient clinics, see *Simopoulos v. Virginia*... (1983), we concluded in *Akron* and *Ashcroft* that a State could not require that such abortions be performed only in hospitals.... Despite the fact that *Roe* expressly allowed regulation after the first trimester in furtherance of maternal health, "'present medical knowledge,'" in our view, could not justify such a hospitalization requirement under the trimester framework.... And in *Danforth*, the Court held that Missouri could not outlaw the saline amniocentesis method of abortion, concluding that the Missouri Legislature had "failed to appreciate and to consider several significant facts" in making its decision....

Although *Roe* allowed state regulation after the point of viability to protect the potential life of the fetus, the Court subsequently rejected attempts to regulate in this manner. In *Colautti v. Franklin*,... (1979), the Court struck down a statute that governed the determination of viability.... In the process, we made clear that the trimester framework incorporated only one definition of viability-ours-as we forbade States from deciding that a certain objective indicator-"be it weeks of gestation or fetal weight or any other single factor"-should govern the definition of viability.... In that same case, we also invalidated a regulation requiring a physician to use the abortion technique offering the best chance for fetal survival when performing postviability abortions.... In *Thornburgh*, the Court struck down Pennsylvania's requirement that a second physician be present at postviability abortions to help preserve the health of the unborn child, on the ground that it did not incorporate a sufficient medical emergency exception.... Regulations governing the treatment of aborted fetuses have met a similar fate. In *Akron*, we invalidated a provision requiring physicians performing abortions to " insure that the remains of the unborn child are disposed of in a humane and sanitary manner.... "

Dissents in these cases expressed the view that the Court was expanding upon *Roe* in imposing ever greater restrictions on the States. See *Thornburgh v. American College of Obstetricians and Gynecologists*,... (Burger, C. J., dissenting) ("The extent to which the Court has departed from the limitations expressed in *Roe* is readily apparent"); ... (WHITE, J., dissenting) ("[T]he majority indiscriminately strikes down statutory provisions that in no way contravene the right recognized in *Roe*"). And, when confronted with State regulations of this type in past years, the Court has become increasingly more divided: the three most recent abortion cases have not commanded a Court opinion....

The task of the Court of Appeals in the present case was obviously complicated by this confusion and uncertainty. Following *Marks v. United States*,... (1977), it concluded that in light of *Webster* and *Hodgson*, the strict scrutiny standard enunciated in *Roe* was no longer applicable, and that the "undue burden" standard adopted by Justice O'CONNOR was the governing principle. This state of confusion and disagreement warrants reexamination of the " fundamental right" accorded to a woman's decision to abort a fetus in *Roe*, with its concomitant requirement that any state regulation of abortion survive "strict scrutiny.... "

We have held that a liberty interest protected under the Due Process Clause of the Fourteenth Amendment will be deemed fundamental if it is " implicit in the concept of ordered liberty." *Palko v. Connecticut*,... (1937). Three years earlier, in *Snyder v. Massachusetts*... (1934), we referred to a "principle of justice so rooted in the traditions and conscience of our people as to be ranked as fundamental.... " These expressions are admittedly not precise, but our decisions implementing this notion of "fundamental" rights do not afford any more elaborate basis on which to base such a classification.

In construing the phrase "liberty" incorporated in the Due Process Clause of the Fourteenth Amendment, we have recognized that its meaning extends beyond freedom from physical restraint. In *Pierce v. Society of Sisters*,... (1925), we held that it included a parent's right to send a child to private school; *in Meyer v. Nebraska*, ... (1923), we held that it included a right to teach a foreign language in a parochial school. Building on these cases, we have held that the term "liberty" includes a right to marry, *Loving v. Virginia*,... (1967); a right to procreate, *Skinner v. Oklahoma ex rel. Williamson*,... (1942); and a right to use contraceptives. *Griswold v. Connecticut*,... (1965); *Eisenstadt v. Baird*,... (1972). But a reading of these opinions makes clear that they do not endorse any all-encompassing "right of privacy."

In *Roe v. Wade*, the Court recognized a "guarantee of personal privacy" which "is broad enough to encompass a woman's decision whether or not to terminate her pregnancy.... " We are now of the view that, in terming this right fundamental, the Court in *Roe* read the earlier opinions upon which it based its decision much too broadly. Unlike marriage, procreation and contraception, abortion "involves the purposeful termination of potential life." *Harris v. McRae*,... (1980). The abortion decision must therefore "be recognized as *sui generis*, different in kind from the others that the Court has protected under the rubric of personal or family privacy and autonomy." *Thornburgh v. American College of Obstetricians and Gynecologists*,... (WHITE, J., dissenting). One cannot ignore the fact that a woman is not isolated in her pregnancy, and that the decision to abort necessarily involves the destruction of a fetus. See *Michael H. v. Gerald D*.... (To look "at the act which is assertedly the subject of a liberty interest in isolation from its effect upon other people [is] like inquiring whether there is a liberty interest in firing a gun where the case at hand happens to involve its discharge into another person's body").

Nor do the historical traditions of the American people support the view that the right to terminate one's pregnancy is "fundamental." The common law which we inherited from England made abortion after "quickening" an offense. At the time of the adoption of the Fourteenth Amendment, statutory prohibitions or restrictions on abortion were commonplace; in 1868, at least 28 of the then-37 States and 8 Territories had statutes banning or limiting abortion.... On this record, it can scarcely be said that any deeply rooted tradition of relatively unrestricted abortion in our history supported the classification of the right to abortion as "fundamental" under the Due Process Clause of the Fourteenth Amendment.

We think, therefore, both in view of this history and of our decided cases dealing with substantive liberty under the Due Process Clause, that the Court was mistaken in *Roe* when it classified a woman's decision to terminate her pregnancy as a "fundamental right" that could be abridged only in a manner which withstood "strict scrutiny." In so concluding, we repeat the observation made in *Bowers v. Hardwick*,... (1986):

"Nor are we inclined to take a more expansive view of our authority to discover new fundamental rights imbedded in the Due Process Clause. The Court is most vulnerable and comes nearest to illegitimacy when it deals with judge-made constitutional law having little or no cognizable roots in the language or design of the Constitution...."

We believe that the sort of constitutionally imposed abortion code of the type illustrated by our decisions following *Roe* is inconsistent "with the notion of a Constitution cast in general terms, as ours is, and usually speaking in general principles, as ours does...." The Court in *Roe* reached too far when it analogized the right to abort a fetus to the rights involved in *Pierce*, *Meyer*, *Loving*, and *Griswold*, and thereby deemed the right to abortion fundamental.

II

The joint opinion of Justices O'CONNOR, KENNEDY, and SOUTER cannot bring itself to say that *Roe* was correct as an original matter, but the authors are of the view that "the immediate question is not the soundness of *Roe's* resolution of the issue, but the precedential force that must be accorded to its holding...." Instead of claiming that *Roe* was correct as a matter of original constitutional interpretation, the opinion therefore contains an elaborate discussion of *stare decisis*. This discussion of the principle of *stare decisis* appears to be almost entirely dicta, because the joint opinion does not apply that principle in dealing with *Roe*. *Roe* decided that a woman had a fundamental right to an abortion. The joint opinion rejects that view. *Roe* decided that abortion regulations were to be subjected to "strict scrutiny" and could be justified only in the light of "compelling state interests." The joint opinion rejects that view.... *Roe* analyzed abortion regulation under a rigid trimester framework, a framework which has guided this Court's decisionmaking for 19 years. The joint opinion rejects that framework....

Stare decisis is defined in *Black's Law Dictionary* as meaning "to abide by, or adhere to, decided cases...." Whatever the "central holding" of *Roe* that is left after the joint opinion finishes dissecting it is surely not the result of that principle. While purporting to adhere to precedent, the joint opinion instead revises it. *Roe* continues to exist, but only in the way a storefront on a western movie set exists: a mere facade to give the illusion of reality....

In our view, authentic principles of *stare decisis* do not require that any portion of the reasoning in *Roe* be kept intact. "*Stare decisis* is not ... a universal, inexorable command," especially in cases involving the interpretation of the Federal Constitution. *Burnet v. Coronado Oil & Gas Co.*,... (1932) (Brandeis, J., dissenting). Erroneous decisions in such constitutional cases are uniquely durable, because correction through legislative action, save for constitutional amendment, is impossible. It is therefore our duty to reconsider constitutional interpretations that " depar[t] from a proper understanding" of the Constitution.

Garcia v. San Antonio Metropolitan Transit Authority.... Our constitutional watch does not cease merely because we have spoken before on an issue; when it becomes clear that a prior constitutional interpretation is unsound we are obliged to reexamine the question....

The joint opinion discusses several *stare decisis* factors which, it asserts, point toward retaining a portion of *Roe*. Two of these factors are that the main "factual underpinning" of *Roe* has remained the same, and that its doctrinal foundation is no weaker now than it was in 1973.... Of course, what might be called the basic facts which gave rise to *Roe* have remained the same-women become pregnant, there is a point somewhere, depending on medical technology, where a fetus becomes viable, and women give birth to children . But this is only to say that the same facts which gave rise to *Roe* will continue to give rise to similar cases. It is not a reason, in and of itself, why those cases must be decided in the same incorrect manner as was the first case to deal with the question. And surely there is no requirement, in considering whether to depart from *stare decisis* in a constitutional case, that a decision be more wrong now than it was at the time it was rendered. If that were true, the most outlandish constitutional decision could survive forever, based simply on the fact that it was no more outlandish later than it was when originally rendered.

Nor does the joint opinion faithfully follow this alleged requirement. The opinion frankly concludes that *Roe* and its progeny were wrong in failing to recognize that the State's interests in maternal health and in the protection of unborn human life exist throughout pregnancy.... But there is no indication that these components of *Roe* are any more incorrect at this juncture than they were at its inception.

The joint opinion also points to the reliance interests involved in this context in its effort to explain why precedent must be followed for precedent's sake.... But, as the joint opinion apparently agrees,... any traditional notion of reliance is not applicable here....

The joint opinion thus turns to what can only be described as an unconventional-and unconvincing-notion of reliance, a view based on the surmise that the availability of abortion since *Roe* has led to "two decades of economic and social developments" that would be undercut if the error of *Roe* were recognized. The joint opinion's assertion of this fact is undeveloped and totally conclusory. In fact, one cannot be sure to what economic and social developments the opinion is referring. Surely it is dubious to suggest that women have reached their "places in society" in reliance upon *Roe*, rather than as a result of their determination to obtain higher education and compete with men in the job market, and of society's increasing recognition of their ability to fill positions that were previously thought to be reserved only for men.

In the end, having failed to put forth any evidence to prove any true reliance, the joint opinion's argument is based solely on generalized assertions about the national psyche, on a belief that the people of this country have grown accustomed to the *Roe* decision over the last 19 years and have "ordered their thinking and living around" it. As an initial matter, one might inquire how the joint opinion can view the "central holding" of *Roe* as so deeply rooted in our constitutional culture, when it so casually uproots and disposes of that same decision's trimester framework. Furthermore, at various points in the past, the same could have been said about this Court's erroneous decisions that the Constitution allowed "separate but equal" treatment of minorities.... The "separate but equal" doctrine lasted 58 years after *Plessy*, and *Lochner's* protection of contractual freedom lasted 32 years. However, the simple fact that a generation or more had grown used to these major decisions did not prevent the Court from correcting its errors in those cases, nor should it prevent us from correctly interpreting the Constitution here....

Apparently realizing that conventional *stare decisis* principles do not support its position, the joint opinion advances a belief that retaining a portion of *Roe* is necessary to protect the "legitimacy" of this Court.... Because the Court must take care to render decisions "grounded truly in principle," and not simply as political and social compromises,... the joint opinion properly declares it to be this Court's duty to ignore the public criticism and protest that may arise as a result of a decision. Few would quarrel with this statement, although it may be doubted that Members of this Court, holding their tenure as they do during constitutional "good behavior," are at all likely to be intimidated by such public protests.

But the joint opinion goes on to state that when the Court "resolve[s] the sort of intensely divisive controversy reflected in *Roe* and those rare, comparable cases," its decision is exempt from reconsideration under established principles of *stare decisis* in constitutional cases.... This is so, the joint opinion contends, because in those "intensely divisive" cases the Court has "call[ed] the contending sides of a national controversy to end their national division by accepting a common mandate rooted in the Constitution," and must therefore take special care not to be perceived as "surrender[ing] to political pressure" and continued opposition.... This is a truly novel principle, one which is contrary to both the Court's historical practice and to the Court's traditional willingness to tolerate criticism of its opinions. Under this principle, when the Court has ruled on a divisive issue, it is apparently prevented from overruling that decision for the sole reason that it was incorrect, unless opposition to the original decision has died away.

The first difficulty with this principle lies in its assumption that cases which are "intensely divisive" can be readily distinguished from those that are not. The question of whether a particular issue is "intensely divisive" enough to qualify for special protection is entirely subjective and dependent on the individual assumptions of the members of this Court. In addition, because the Court's duty is to ignore public opinion and criticism on issues that come before it, its members are in perhaps the worst position to judge whether a decision divides the Nation deeply enough to justify such uncommon protection. Although many of the Court's decisions divide the populace to a large degree, we have not previously on that account shied away from applying normal rules of *stare decisis* when urged to reconsider earlier decisions. Over the past 21 years, for example, the Court has overruled in whole or in part 34 of its previous constitutional decisions. See *Payne v. Tennessee*,...(listing cases).

The joint opinion picks out and discusses two prior Court rulings that it believes are of the "intensely divisive" variety, and concludes that they are of comparable dimension to *Roe*.... It appears to us very odd indeed that the joint opinion chooses as benchmarks two cases in which the Court chose not to adhere to erroneous constitutional precedent, but instead enhanced its stature by acknowledging and correcting its error, apparently in violation of the joint opinion's "legitimacy" principle.... One might also wonder how it is that the joint opinion puts these, and not others, in the "intensely divisive" category, and how it assumes that these are the only two lines of cases of comparable dimension to *Roe*. There is no reason to think that either *Plessy* or *Lochner* produced the sort of public protest when they were decided that *Roe* did. There were undoubtedly large segments of the bench and bar who agreed with the dissenting views in those cases, but surely that cannot be what the Court means when it uses the term "intensely divisive," or many other cases would have to be added to the list. In terms of public protest, however, *Roe*, so far as we know, was unique. But just as the Court should not respond to that sort of protest by retreating from the decision simply to allay the concerns of the protesters, it should likewise not respond by determining to adhere to the decision at all costs lest it seem to be retreating under fire. Public protests should not alter the normal application of *stare decisis*, lest perfectly lawful protest activity be penalized by the Court itself.

Taking the joint opinion on its own terms, we doubt that its distinction between *Roe*, on the one hand, and *Plessy* and *Lochner*, on the other, withstands analysis. The joint opinion acknowledges that the Court improved its stature by overruling *Plessy* in *Brown* on a deeply divisive issue. And our decision in *West Coast Hotel*, which overruled *Adkins v. Children's Hospital, supra*, and *Lochner*, was rendered at a time when Congress was considering President Franklin Roosevelt's proposal to "reorganize" this Court and enable him to name six additional Justices in the event that any member of the Court over the age of 70 did not elect to retire. It is difficult to imagine a situation in which the Court would face more intense opposition to a prior ruling than it did at that time, and, under the general principle proclaimed in the joint opinion, the Court seemingly should have responded to this opposition by stubbornly refusing to reexamine the *Lochner* rationale, lest it lose legitimacy by appearing to "overrule under fire."

The joint opinion agrees that the Court's stature would have been seriously damaged if in *Brown* and *West Coast Hotel* it had dug in its heels and refused to apply normal principles of *stare decisis* to the earlier decisions. But the opinion contends that the Court was entitled to overrule *Plessy* and *Lochner* in those cases, despite the existence of opposition to the original decisions, only because both the Nation and the Court had learned new lessons in the interim. This is at best a feebly supported, post hoc rationalization for those decisions.

For example, the opinion asserts that the Court could justifiably overrule its decision in *Lochner* only because the Depression had convinced "most people" that constitutional protection of contractual freedom contributed to an economy that failed to protect the welfare of all. Surely the joint opinion does not mean to suggest that people saw this Court's failure to uphold minimum wage statutes as the cause of the Great Depression! In any event, the *Lochner* Court did not base its rule upon the policy judgment that an unregulated market was fundamental to a stable economy; it simply believed, erroneously, that "liberty" under the Due Process Clause protected the "right to make a contract." *Lochner v. New York....* Nor is it the case that the people of this Nation only discovered the dangers of extreme laissez faire economics because of the Depression. State laws regulating maximum hours and minimum wages were in existence well before that time. A Utah statute of that sort enacted in 1896 was involved in our decision in *Holden v. Hardy,...* (1898), and other states followed suit shortly afterwards. See, e.g., *Muller v. Oregon,...* (1908); *Bunting v. Oregon,...* (1917). These statutes were indeed enacted because of a belief on the part of their sponsors that " freedom of contract" did not protect the welfare of workers, demonstrating that that belief manifested itself more than a generation before the Great Depression. Whether "most people" had come to share it in the hard times of the 1930's is, insofar as anything the joint opinion advances, entirely speculative. The crucial failing at that time was not that workers were not paid a fair wage, but that there was no work available at any wage.

When the Court finally recognized its error in *West Coast Hotel,* it did not engage in the post hoc rationalization that the joint opinion attributes to it today; it did not state that *Lochner* had been based on an economic view that had fallen into disfavor, and that it therefore should be overruled. Chief Justice Hughes in his opinion for the Court simply recognized what Justice Holmes had previously recognized in his *Lochner* dissent, that "[t]he Constitution does not speak of freedom of contract." *West Coast Hotel Co. v. Parrish,...*; *Lochner v. New York,...* (Holmes, J., dissenting) ("[A] Constitution is not intended to embody a particular economic theory, whether of paternalism and the organic relation of the citizen to the State or of laissez faire"). Although the Court did acknowledge in the last paragraph of its opinion the state of affairs during the then-current Depression, the theme of the opinion is that the Court had been mistaken as a matter of constitutional law when it embraced "freedom of contract" 32 years previously.

The joint opinion also agrees that the Court acted properly in rejecting the doctrine of "separate but equal" in *Brown.* In fact, the opinion lauds *Brown* in comparing it to *Roe.* This is strange, in that under the opinion's "legitimacy" principle the Court would seemingly have been forced to adhere to its erroneous decision in *Plessy* because of its "intensely divisive" character. To us, adherence to *Roe* today under the guise of "legitimacy" would seem to resemble more closely adherence to *Plessy* on the same ground. Fortunately, the Court did not choose that option in *Brown,* and instead frankly repudiated *Plessy.* The joint opinion concludes that such repudiation was justified only because of newly discovered evidence that segregation had the effect of treating one race as inferior to another. But it can hardly be argued that this was not urged upon those who decided *Plessy,* as Justice Harlan observed in his dissent that the law at issue "puts the brand of servitude and degradation upon a large class of our fellow-citizens, our equals before the law." *Plessy v. Ferguson*,... (Harlan, J., dissenting). It is clear that the same arguments made before the Court in *Brown* were made in *Plessy* as well. The Court in *Brown* simply recognized, as Justice Harlan had recognized beforehand, that the Fourteenth Amendment does not permit racial segregation. The rule of *Brown* is not tied to popular opinion about the evils of segregation; it is a judgment that the Equal Protection Clause does not permit racial segregation, no matter whether the public might come to believe that it is beneficial. On that ground it stands, and on that ground alone the Court was justified in properly concluding that the *Plessy* Court had erred.

There is also a suggestion in the joint opinion that the propriety of overruling a "divisive" decision depends in part on whether "most people" would now agree that it should be overruled. Either the demise of opposition or its progression to substantial popular agreement apparently is required to allow the Court to reconsider a divisive decision. How such agreement would be ascertained, short of a public opinion poll, the joint opinion does not say. But surely even the suggestion is totally at war with the idea of "legitimacy" in whose name it is invoked. The Judicial Branch derives its legitimacy, not from following public opinion, but from deciding by its best lights whether legislative enactments of the popular branches of Government comport with the Constitution. The doctrine of *stare decisis* is an adjunct of this duty, and should be no more subject to the vagaries of public opinion than is the basic judicial task.

There are other reasons why the joint opinion's discussion of legitimacy is unconvincing as well. In assuming that the Court is perceived as "surrender[ing] to political pressure" when it overrules a controversial decision, the joint opinion forgets that there are two sides to any controversy. The joint opinion asserts that, in order to protect its legitimacy, the Court must refrain from overruling a controversial decision lest it be viewed as favoring those who oppose the decision. But a decision to adhere to prior precedent is subject to the same criticism, for in such a case one can easily argue that the Court is responding to those who have demonstrated in favor of the original decision. The decision in *Roe* has engendered large demonstrations, including repeated marches on this Court and on Congress, both in opposition to and in support of that opinion. A decision either way on *Roe* can therefore be perceived as favoring one group or the other. But this perceived dilemma arises only if one assumes, as the joint opinion does, that the Court should make its decisions with a view toward speculative public perceptions. If one assumes instead, as the Court surely did in both *Brown* and *West Coast Hotel*, that the Court's legitimacy is enhanced by faithful interpretation of the Constitution irrespective of public opposition, such self-engendered difficulties may be put to one side.

Roe is not this Court's only decision to generate conflict. Our decisions in some recent capital cases, and in *Bowers v. Hardwick*,...(1986), have also engendered demonstrations in opposition. The joint opinion's message to such protesters appears to be that they must cease their activities in order to serve their cause, because their protests will only cement in place a decision which by normal standards of *stare decisis* should be reconsidered .... Strong and often misguided criticism of a decision should not render the decision immune from reconsideration, lest a fetish for legitimacy penalize freedom of expression.

The end result of the joint opinion's paeans of praise for legitimacy is the enunciation of a brand new standard for evaluating state regulation of a woman's right to abortion-the "undue burden" standard. As indicated above, *Roe v. Wade* adopted a "fundamental right" standard under which state regulations could survive only if they met the requirement of "strict scrutiny." While we disagree with that standard, it at least had a recognized basis in constitutional law at the time *Roe* was decided. The same cannot be said for the "undue burden" standard, which is created largely out of whole cloth by the authors of the joint opinion. It is a standard which even today does not command the support of a majority of this Court. And it will not, we believe, result in the sort of "simple limitation," easily applied, which the joint opinion anticipates. In sum, it is a standard which is not built to last.

In evaluating abortion regulations under that standard, judges will have to decide whether they place a "substantial obstacle" in the path of a woman seeking an abortion. In that this standard is based even more on a judge's subjective determinations than was the trimester framework, the standard will do nothing to prevent "judges from roaming at large in the constitutional field" guided only by their personal views. *Griswold v. Connecticut*,... (Harlan, J., concurring in judgment)....

Furthermore, while striking down the spousal notice regulation, the joint opinion would uphold a parental consent restriction that certainly places very substantial obstacles in the path of a minor's abortion choice . The joint opinion is forthright in admitting that it draws this distinction based on a policy judgment that parents will have the best interests of their children at heart, while the same is not necessarily true of husbands as to their wives. This may or may not be a correct judgment, but it is quintessentially a legislative one. The "undue burden" inquiry does not in any way supply the distinction between parental consent and spousal consent which the joint opinion adopts. Despite the efforts of the joint opinion, the undue burden standard presents nothing more workable than the trimester framework which it discards today. Under the guise of the Constitution, this Court will still impart its own preferences on the States in the form of a complex abortion code.

The sum of the joint opinion's labors in the name of *stare decisis* and "legitimacy" is this: *Roe v. Wade* stands as a sort of judicial Potemkin Village, which may be pointed out to passers by as a monument to the importance of adhering to precedent. But behind the facade, an entirely new method of analysis, without any roots in constitutional law, is imported to decide the constitutionality of state laws regulating abortion. Neither *stare decisis* nor "legitimacy" are truly served by such an effort.

We have stated above our belief that the Constitution does not subject state abortion regulations to heightened scrutiny. Accordingly, we think that the correct analysis is that set forth by the plurality opinion in *Webster*. A woman's interest in having an abortion is a form of liberty protected by the Due Process Clause, but States may regulate abortion procedures in ways rationally related to a legitimate state interest... With this rule in mind, we examine each of the challenged provisions....

IV

For the reasons stated, we therefore would hold that each of the challenged provisions of the Pennsylvania statute is consistent with the Constitution. It bears emphasis that our conclusion in this regard does not carry with it any necessary approval of these regulations. Our task is, as always, to decide only whether the challenged provisions of a law comport with the United States Constitution. If, as we believe, these do, their wisdom as a matter of public policy is for the people of Pennsylvania to decide.

Justice SCALIA, with whom THE CHIEF JUSTICE, Justice WHITE, and Justice THOMAS join, concurring in the judgment in part and dissenting in part.

My views on this matter are unchanged from those I set forth in my separate opinions in *Webster v. Reproductive Health Services*,... (1989) (SCALIA, J., concurring in part and concurring in judgment), and *Ohio v. Akron Center for Reproductive Health*,... (1990) (*Akron II*) (SCALIA, J., concurring). The States may, if they wish, permit abortion-on-demand, but the Constitution does not require them to do so. The permissibility of abortion, and the limitations upon it, are to be resolved like most important questions in our democracy: by citizens trying to persuade one another and then voting. As the Court acknowledges, "where reasonable people disagree the government can adopt one position or the other." The Court is correct in adding the qualification that this "assumes a state of affairs in which the choice does not intrude upon a protected liberty," but the crucial part of that qualification is the penultimate word. A State's choice between two positions on which reasonable people can disagree is constitutional even when (as is often the case) it intrudes upon a " liberty" in the absolute sense. Laws against bigamy, for example-which entire societies of reasonable people disagree with-intrude upon men and women's liberty to marry and live with one another. But bigamy happens not to be a liberty specially "protected" by the Constitution.

That is, quite simply, the issue in this case: not whether the power of a woman to abort her unborn child is a "liberty" in the absolute sense; or even whether it is a liberty of great importance to many women. Of course it is both. The issue is whether it is a liberty protected by the Constitution of the United States. I am sure it is not. I reach that conclusion not because of anything so exalted as my views concerning the "concept of existence, of meaning, of the universe, and of the mystery of human life." Rather, I reach it for the same reason I reach the conclusion that bigamy is not constitutionally protected-because of two simple facts: (1) the Constitution says absolutely nothing about it, and (2) the longstanding traditions of American society have permitted it to be legally proscribed. *Akron II*,... (SCALIA, J., concurring).

The Court destroys the proposition, evidently meant to represent my position, that "liberty" includes "only those practices, defined at the most specific level, that were protected against government interference by other rules of law when the Fourteenth Amendment was ratified," ... (citing *Michael H. v. Gerald D.*,... (1989) (opinion of SCALIA, J.). That is not, however, what *Michael H.* says; it merely observes that, in defining "liberty," we may not disregard a specific, "relevant tradition protecting, or denying protection to, the asserted right...." But the Court does not wish to be fettered by any such limitations on its preferences. The Court's statement that it is "tempting" to acknowledge the authoritativeness of tradition in order to "cur[b] the discretion of federal judges," is of course rhetoric rather than reality; no government official is "tempted" to place restraints upon his own freedom of action, which is why Lord Acton did not say "Power tends to purify." The Court's temptation is in the quite opposite and more natural direction-towards systematically eliminating checks upon its own power; and it succumbs.

Beyond that brief summary of the essence of my position, I will not swell the United States Reports with repetition of what I have said before; and applying the rational basis test, I would uphold the Pennsylvania statute in its entirety. I must, however, respond to a few of the more outrageous arguments in today's opinion, which it is beyond human nature to leave unanswered. I shall discuss each of them under a quotation from the Court's opinion to which they pertain.

"The inescapable fact is that adjudication of substantive due process claims may call upon the Court in interpreting the Constitution to exercise that same capacity which by tradition courts always have exercised: reasoned judgment."

Assuming that the question before us is to be resolved at such a level of philosophical abstraction, in such isolation from the traditions of American society, as by simply applying "reasoned judgment," I do not see how that could possibly have produced the answer the Court arrived at in *Roe v. Wade*... (1973). Today's opinion describes the methodology of *Roe*, quite accurately, as weighing against the woman's interest the State's "'important and legitimate interest in protecting the potentiality of human life. ...'" But "reasoned judgment" does not begin by begging the question, as *Roe* and subsequent cases unquestionably did by assuming that what the State is protecting is the mere "potentiality of human life...." The whole argument of abortion opponents is that what the Court calls the fetus and what others call the unborn child is a human life. Thus, whatever answer *Roe* came up with after conducting its "balancing" is bound to be wrong, unless it is correct that the human fetus is in some critical sense merely potentially human. There is of course no way to determine that as a legal matter; it is in fact a value judgment. Some societies have considered newborn children not yet human, or the incompetent elderly no longer so.

The authors of the joint opinion, of course, do not squarely contend that *Roe v. Wade* was a correct application of "reasoned judgment;" merely that it must be followed, because of *stare decisis*. But in their exhaustive discussion of all the factors that go into the determination of when *stare decisis* should be observed and when disregarded, they never mention "how wrong was the decision on its face?" Surely, if "[t]he Court's power lies ... in its legitimacy, a product of substance and perception," the "substance" part of the equation demands that plain error be acknowledged and eliminated. *Roe* was plainly wrong-even on the Court's methodology of "reasoned judgment," and even more so (of course) if the proper criteria of text and tradition are applied.

The emptiness of the "reasoned judgment" that produced *Roe* is displayed in plain view by the fact that, after more than 19 years of effort by some of the brightest (and most determined) legal minds in the country, after more than 10 cases upholding abortion rights in this Court, and after dozens upon dozens of *amicus* briefs submitted in this and other cases, the best the Court can do to explain how it is that the word "liberty" must be thought to include the right to destroy human fetuses is to rattle off a collection of adjectives that simply decorate a value judgment and conceal a political choice. The right to abort, we are told, inheres in "liberty" because it is among "a person's most basic decisions," it involves a "most intimate and personal choic[e]," it is "central to personal dignity and autonomy," it "originate[s] within the zone of conscience and belief," it is "too intimate and personal" for state interference, ante, it reflects "intimate views" of a "deep, personal character," it involves "intimate relationships," and notions of "personal autonomy and bodily integrity," and it concerns a particularly "'important decisio[n],'" But it is obvious to anyone applying "reasoned judgment" that the same adjectives can be applied to many forms of conduct that this Court (including one of the Justices in today's majority, see *Bowers v. Hardwick*,... (1986)) has held are not entitled to constitutional protection-because, like abortion, they are forms of conduct that have long been criminalized in American society. Those adjectives might be applied, for example, to homosexual sodomy, polygamy, adult incest, and suicide, all of which are equally "intimate" and "deep[ly] personal" decisions involving "personal autonomy and bodily integrity," and all of which can constitutionally be proscribed because it is our unquestionable constitutional tradition that they are proscribable. It is not reasoned judgment that supports the Court's decision; only personal predilection. Justice Curtis's warning is as timely today as it was 135 years ago:

"[W]hen a strict interpretation of the Constitution, according to the fixed rules which govern the interpretation of laws, is abandoned, and the theoretical opinions of individuals are allowed to control its meaning, we have no longer a Constitution; we are under the government of individual men, who for the time being have power to declare what the Constitution is, according to their own views of what it ought to mean." *Dred Scott v. Sandford*,... (1857) (Curtis, J., dissenting).

"Liberty finds no refuge in a jurisprudence of doubt."

One might have feared to encounter this august and sonorous phrase in an opinion defending the real *Roe v. Wade*, rather than the revised version fabricated today by the authors of the joint opinion. The shortcomings of *Roe* did not include lack of clarity: Virtually all regulation of abortion before the third trimester was invalid. But to come across this phrase in the joint opinion-which calls upon federal district judges to apply an "undue burden" standard as doubtful in application as it is unprincipled in origin-is really more than one should have to bear.

The joint opinion frankly concedes that the amorphous concept of "undue burden" has been inconsistently applied by the Members of this Court in the few brief years since that "test" was first explicitly propounded by Justice O'CONNOR in her dissent in *Akron I*.... Because the three Justices now wish to "set forth a standard of general application," the joint opinion announces that "it is important to clarify what is meant by an undue burden...." I certainly agree with that, but I do not agree that the joint opinion succeeds in the announced endeavor. To the contrary, its efforts at clarification make clear only that the standard is inherently manipulable and will prove hopelessly unworkable in practice.

The joint opinion explains that a state regulation imposes an "undue burden" if it "has the purpose or effect of placing a substantial obstacle in the path of a woman seeking an abortion of a nonviable fetus." An obstacle is "substantial," we are told, if it is "calculated[,] [not] to inform the woman's free choice, [but to] hinder it." This latter statement cannot possibly mean what it says. Any regulation of abortion that is intended to advance what the joint opinion concedes is the State's "substantial" interest in protecting unborn life will be "calculated [to] hinder" a decision to have an abortion. It thus seems more accurate to say that the joint opinion would uphold abortion regulations only if they do not unduly hinder the woman's decision. That, of course, brings us right back to square one: Defining an "undue burden" as an "undue hindrance" (or a "substantial obstacle") hardly "clarifies" the test. Consciously or not, the joint opinion's verbal shell game will conceal raw judicial policy choices concerning what is "appropriate" abortion legislation.

The ultimately standardless nature of the "undue burden" inquiry is a reflection of the underlying fact that the concept has no principled or coherent legal basis. As THE CHIEF JUSTICE points out, *Roe's* strict-scrutiny standard "at least had a recognized basis in constitutional law at the time *Roe* was decided," while "[t]he same cannot be said for the 'undue burden' standard, which is created largely out of whole cloth by the authors of the joint opinion..." The joint opinion is flatly wrong in asserting that "our jurisprudence relating to all liberties save perhaps abortion has recognized" the permissibility of laws that do not impose an "undue burden." It argues that the abortion right is similar to other rights in that a law "not designed to strike at the right itself, [but which] has the incidental effect of making it more difficult or more expensive to [exercise the right,]" is not invalid. I agree, indeed I have forcefully urged, that a law of general applicability which places only an incidental burden on a fundamental right does not infringe that right, see *R.A.V. v. St. Paul*,... (1992) ... *Employment*

Division, Dept. of Human Resources of Ore. v. Smith,... (1990), but that principle does not establish the quite different (and quite dangerous) proposition that a law which directly regulates a fundamental right will not be found to violate the Constitution unless it imposes an "undue burden." It is that, of course, which is at issue here: Pennsylvania has consciously and directly regulated conduct that our cases have held is constitutionally protected. The appropriate analogy, therefore, is that of a state law requiring purchasers of religious books to endure a 24-hour waiting period, or to pay a nominal additional tax of 1¢. The joint opinion cannot possibly be correct in suggesting that we would uphold such legislation on the ground that it does not impose a " substantial obstacle" to the exercise of First Amendment rights. The "undue burden" standard is not at all the generally applicable principle the joint opinion pretends it to be; rather, it is a unique concept created specially for this case, to preserve some judicial foothold in this ill-gotten territory. In claiming otherwise, the three Justices show their willingness to place all constitutional rights at risk in an effort to preserve what they deem the "central holding in *Roe*."

The rootless nature of the "undue burden" standard, a phrase plucked out of context from our earlier abortion decisions ...is further reflected in the fact that the joint opinion finds it necessary expressly to repudiate the more narrow formulations used in Justice O'CONNOR's earlier opinions. Those opinions stated that a statute imposes an "undue burden" if it imposes "*absolute* obstacles or *severe* limitations on the abortion decision," *Akron I*,... (O'CONNOR, J., dissenting) (emphasis added); see also *Thornburgh v. American College of Obstetricians and Gynecologists*,... (1986) (O'CONNOR, J., dissenting). Those strong adjectives are conspicuously missing from the joint opinion, whose authors have for some unexplained reason now determined that a burden is "undue" if it merely imposes a "substantial" obstacle to abortion decisions. Justice O'CONNOR has also abandoned (again without explanation) the view she expressed in *Planned Parenthood Assn. of Kansas City, Mo., Inc. v. Ashcroft*,... (1983) (dissenting opinion), that a medical regulation which imposes an "undue burden" could nevertheless be upheld if it "reasonably relate[s] to the preservation and protection of maternal health...." In today's version, even health measures will be upheld only "*if they do not constitute an undue burden*," (emphasis added). Gone too is Justice O'CONNOR's statement that "the State possesses *compelling* interests in the protection of potential human life ... throughout pregnancy," *Akron I*, (emphasis added); see also *Ashcroft*,... (O'CONNOR, J., concurring in judgment in part and dissenting in part); *Thornburgh*, (O'CONNOR, J., dissenting); instead, the State's interest in unborn human life is stealthily downgraded to a merely "substantial" or "profound" interest. (That had to be done, of course, since designating the interest as "compelling" throughout pregnancy would have been, shall we say, a "substantial obstacle" to the joint opinion's determined effort to reaffirm what it views as the "central holding" of *Roe*. See *Akron I*.... And "viability" is no longer the "arbitrary" dividing line previously decried by Justice O'CONNOR in *Akron I*...; the Court now announces that "the attainment of viability may continue to serve as the critical fact," It is difficult to maintain the illusion that we are interpreting a Constitution rather than inventing one, when we amend its provisions so breezily.

Because the portion of the joint opinion adopting and describing the undue-burden test provides no more useful guidance than the empty phrases discussed above, one must turn to [the] pages … applying that standard to the present facts for further guidance. In evaluating Pennsylvania's abortion law, the joint opinion relies extensively on the factual findings of the District Court, and repeatedly qualifies its conclusions by noting that they are contingent upon the record developed in this case. Thus, the joint opinion would uphold the 24-hour waiting period contained in the Pennsylvania statute's informed consent provision, 18 Pa.Cons.Stat. § 3205 (1990), because "the record evidence shows that in the vast majority of cases, a 24-hour delay does not create any appreciable health risk." The three Justices therefore conclude that "on the record before us,… we are not convinced that the 24-hour waiting period constitutes an undue burden." The requirement that a doctor provide the information pertinent to informed consent would also be upheld because "there is no evidence on this record that [this requirement] would amount in practical terms to a substantial obstacle to a woman seeking an abortion." Similarly, the joint opinion would uphold the reporting requirements of the Act, §§ 3207, 3214, because "there is no … showing on the record before us" that these requirements constitute a "substantial obstacle" to abortion decisions. But at the same time the opinion pointedly observes that these reporting requirements may increase the costs of abortions and that "at some point [that fact] could become a substantial obstacle." Most significantly, the joint opinion's conclusion that the spousal notice requirement of the Act, see § 3209, imposes an "undue burden" is based in large measure on the District Court's "detailed findings of fact," which the joint opinion sets out at great length.

I do not, of course, have any objection to the notion that, in applying legal principles, one should rely only upon the facts that are contained in the record or that are properly subject to judicial notice. But what is remarkable about the joint opinion's fact-intensive analysis is that it does not result in any measurable clarification of the "undue burden" standard. Rather, the approach of the joint opinion is, for the most part, simply to highlight certain facts in the record that apparently strike the three Justices as particularly significant in establishing (or refuting) the existence of an undue burden; after describing these facts, the opinion then simply announces that the provision either does or does not impose a "substantial obstacle" or an "undue burden." We do not know whether the same conclusions could have been reached on a different record, or in what respects the record would have had to differ before an opposite conclusion would have been appropriate. The inherently standardless nature of this inquiry invites the district judge to give effect to his personal preferences about abortion. By finding and relying upon the right facts, he can invalidate, it would seem, almost any abortion restriction that strikes him as "undue" – subject, of course, to the possibility of being reversed by a Circuit Court or Supreme Court that is as unconstrained in reviewing his decision as he was in making it.

To the extent I can discern any meaningful content in the "undue burden" standard as applied in the joint opinion, it appears to be that a State may not regulate abortion in such a way as to reduce significantly its incidence. The joint opinion repeatedly emphasizes that an important factor in the "undue burden" analysis is whether the regulation "prevent[s] a significant number of women from obtaining an abortion," whether a "significant number of women ... are likely to be deterred from procuring an abortion," and whether the regulation often "deters" women from seeking abortions. We are not told, however, what forms of "deterrence" are impermissible or what degree of success in deterrence is too much to be tolerated. If, for example, a State required a woman to read a pamphlet describing, with illustrations, the facts of fetal development before she could obtain an abortion, the effect of such legislation might be to "deter" a "significant number of women" from procuring abortions, thereby seemingly allowing a district judge to invalidate it as an undue burden. Thus, despite flowery rhetoric about the State's "substantial" and "profound" interest in "potential human life," and criticism of *Roe* for undervaluing that interest, the joint opinion permits the State to pursue that interest only so long as it is not too successful. As Justice BLACKMUN recognizes (with evident hope), the "undue burden" standard may ultimately require the invalidation of each provision upheld today if it can be shown, on a better record, that the State is too effectively "express[ing] a preference for childbirth over abortion." Reason finds no refuge in this jurisprudence of confusion.

"While we appreciate the weight of the arguments ... that *Roe* should be overruled, the reservations any of us may have in reaffirming the central holding of *Roe* are outweighed by the explication of individual liberty we have given combined with the force of *stare decisis*."

The Court's reliance upon *stare decisis* can best be described as contrived. It insists upon the necessity of adhering not to all of *Roe*, but only to what it calls the "central holding." It seems to me that *stare decisis* ought to be applied even to the doctrine of *stare decisis*, and I confess never to have heard of this new, keep-what-you-want-and-throw-away-the-rest version. I wonder whether, as applied to *Marbury v. Madison*,... (1803), for example, the new version of *stare decisis* would be satisfied if we allowed courts to review the constitutionality of only those statutes that (like the one in *Marbury*) pertain to the jurisdiction of the courts.

I am certainly not in a good position to dispute that the Court has saved the "central holding" of *Roe*, since to do that effectively I would have to know what the Court has saved, which in turn would require me to understand (as I do not) what the "undue burden" test means. I must confess, however, that I have always thought, and I think a lot of other people have always thought, that the arbitrary trimester framework, which the Court today discards, was quite as central to *Roe* as the arbitrary viability test, which the Court today retains. It seems particularly ungrateful to carve the trimester framework out of the core of

Roe, since its very rigidity (in sharp contrast to the utter indeterminability of the " undue burden" test) is probably the only reason the Court is able to say, in urging *stare decisis*, that *Roe* "has in no sense proven 'unworkable.'" I suppose the Court is entitled to call a "central holding" whatever it wants to call a "central holding"-which is, come to think of it, perhaps one of the difficulties with this modified version of *stare decisis*. I thought I might note, however, that the following portions of *Roe* have not been saved:

Under *Roe*, requiring that a woman seeking an abortion be provided truthful information about abortion before giving informed written consent is unconstitutional, if the information is designed to influence her choice, *Thornburgh*,... *Akron I*.... Under the joint opinion's "undue burden" regime (as applied today, at least) such a requirement is constitutional.

Under *Roe*, requiring that information be provided by a doctor, rather than by nonphysician counselors, is unconstitutional, *Akron I*.... Under the "undue burden" regime (as applied today, at least) it is not.

Under *Roe*, requiring a 24-hour waiting period between the time the woman gives her informed consent and the time of the abortion is unconstitutional, *Akron I*.... Under the "undue burden" regime (as applied today, at least) it is not.

Under *Roe*, requiring detailed reports that include demographic data about each woman who seeks an abortion and various information about each abortion is unconstitutional, *Thornburgh*.... Under the "undue burden" regime (as applied today, at least) it generally is not.

"Where, in the performance of its judicial duties, the Court decides a case in such a way as to resolve the sort of intensely divisive controversy reflected in *Roe* ..., its decision has a dimension that the resolution of the normal case does not carry. It is the dimension present whenever the Court's interpretation of the Constitution calls the contending sides of a national controversy to end their national division by accepting a common mandate rooted in the Constitution."

The Court's description of the place of *Roe* in the social history of the United States is unrecognizable. Not only did *Roe* not, as the Court suggests, resolve the deeply divisive issue of abortion; it did more than anything else to nourish it, by elevating it to the national level where it is infinitely more difficult to resolve. National politics were not plagued by abortion protests, national abortion lobbying, or abortion marches on Congress, before *Roe v. Wade* was decided. Profound disagreement existed among our citizens over the issue-as it does over other issues, such as the death penalty-but that disagreement was being worked out at the state level. As with many other issues, the division of sentiment within each State was not as closely balanced as it was among the population of the Nation as a whole, meaning not only that more people would be satisfied with the results of state-by-state resolution, but also that those results would be more stable. Pre-*Roe*, moreover, political compromise was possible.

Roe's mandate for abortion-on-demand destroyed the compromises of the past, rendered compromise impossible for the future, and required the entire issue to be resolved uniformly, at the national level. At the same time, *Roe* created a vast new class of abortion consumers and abortion proponents by eliminating the moral opprobrium that had attached to the act. ("If the Constitution *guarantees* abortion, how can it be bad?" – not an accurate line of thought, but a natural one.) Many favor all of those developments, and it is not for me to say that they are wrong. But to portray *Roe* as the statesmanlike "settlement" of a divisive issue, a jurisprudential Peace of Westphalia that is worth preserving, is nothing less than Orwellian. *Roe* fanned into life an issue that has inflamed our national politics in general, and has obscured with its smoke the selection of Justices to this Court in particular, ever since. And by keeping us in the abortion-umpiring business, it is the perpetuation of that disruption, rather than of any *pax Roeana*, that the Court's new majority decrees.

"[T]o overrule under fire ... would subvert the Court's legitimacy...."

"To all those who will be ... tested by following, the Court implicitly undertakes to remain steadfast.... The promise of constancy, once given, binds its maker for as long as the power to stand by the decision survives and ... the commitment [is not] obsolete...."

"[The American people's] belief in themselves as ... a people [who aspire to live according to the rule of law] is not readily separable from their understanding of the Court invested with the authority to decide their constitutional cases and speak before all others for their constitutional ideals. If the Court's legitimacy should be undermined, then, so would the country be in its very ability to see itself through its constitutional ideals."

The Imperial Judiciary lives. It is instructive to compare this Nietzschean vision of us unelected, life-tenured judges-leading a Volk who will be "tested by following," and whose very "belief in themselves" is mystically bound up in their "understanding" of a Court that "speak[s] before all others for their constitutional ideals" – with the somewhat more modest role envisioned for these lawyers by the Founders.

"The judiciary ... has ... no direction either of the strength or of the wealth of the society, and can take no active resolution whatever. It may truly be said to have neither Force nor Will but merely judgment...." *The Federalist No. 78*, pp. 393-394 (G. Wills ed. 1982).

Or, again, to compare this ecstasy of a Supreme Court in which there is, especially on controversial matters, no shadow of change or hint of alteration ("There is a limit to the amount of error that can plausibly be imputed to prior courts,"), with the more democratic views of a more humble man:

"[T]he candid citizen must confess that if the policy of the Government upon vital questions affecting the whole people is to be irrevocably fixed by decisions of the Supreme Court,... the people will have ceased to be their own rulers, having to that extent practically resigned their Government into the hands of that eminent tribunal." A. Lincoln, First Inaugural Address (Mar. 4, 1861), reprinted in Inaugural Addresses of the Presidents of the United States, S. Doc. No. 101-10, p. 139 (1989).

It is particularly difficult, in the circumstances of the present decision, to sit still for the Court's lengthy lecture upon the virtues of "constancy," of "remain[ing] steadfast," of adhering to "principle," Among the five Justices who purportedly adhere to *Roe*, at most three agree upon the principle that constitutes adherence (the joint opinion's "undue burden" standard)-and that principle is inconsistent with *Roe*. To make matters worse, two of the three, in order thus to remain steadfast, had to abandon previously stated positions. It is beyond me how the Court expects these accommodations to be accepted "as grounded truly in principle, not as compromises with social and political pressures having, as such, no bearing on the principled choices that the Court is obliged to make." The only principle the Court "adheres" to, it seems to me, is the principle that the Court must be seen as standing by *Roe*. That is not a principle of law (which is what I thought the Court was talking about), but a principle of *Realpolitik* – and a wrong one at that.

I cannot agree with, indeed I am appalled by, the Court's suggestion that the decision whether to stand by an erroneous constitutional decision must be strongly influenced-against overruling, no less-by the substantial and continuing public opposition the decision has generated. The Court's judgment that any other course would "subvert the Court's legitimacy" must be another consequence of reading the error-filled history book that described the deeply divided country brought together by *Roe*. In my history-book, the Court was covered with dishonor and deprived of legitimacy by *Dred Scott v. Sandford*,... (1857), an erroneous (and widely opposed) opinion that it did not abandon, rather than by *West Coast Hotel Co. v. Parrish*,... (1937), which produced the famous "switch in time" from the Court's erroneous (and widely opposed) constitutional opposition to the social measures of the New Deal. (Both *Dred Scott* and one line of the cases resisting the New Deal rested upon the concept of "substantive due process" that the Court praises and employs today. Indeed, *Dred Scott* was " very possibly the first application of substantive due process in the Supreme Court, the original precedent for *Lochner v. New York* and *Roe v. Wade....* "

But whether it would "subvert the Court's legitimacy" or not, the notion that we would decide a case differently from the way we otherwise would have in order to show that we can stand firm against public disapproval is frightening. It is a bad enough idea, even in the head of someone like me, who believes that the text of the Constitution, and our traditions, say what they say and there is no fiddling with them. But when it is in the mind of a Court that believes the

Constitution has an evolving meaning, that the Ninth Amendment's reference to "othe[r]" rights is not a disclaimer, but a charter for action, and that the function of this Court is to "speak before all others for [the people's] constitutional ideals" unrestrained by meaningful text or tradition-then the notion that the Court must adhere to a decision for as long as the decision faces "great opposition" and the Court is "under fire" acquires a character of almost czarist arrogance. We are offended by these marchers who descend upon us, every year on the anniversary of *Roe*, to protest our saying that the Constitution requires what our society has never thought the Constitution requires. These people who refuse to be "tested by following" must be taught a lesson. We have no Cossacks, but at least we can stubbornly refuse to abandon an erroneous opinion that we might otherwise change-to show how little they intimidate us.

Of course, as THE CHIEF JUSTICE points out, we have been subjected to what the Court calls "political pressure" by both sides of this issue. Maybe today's decision not to overrule *Roe* will be seen as buckling to pressure from that direction. Instead of engaging in the hopeless task of predicting public perception-a job not for lawyers but for political campaign managers-the Justices should do what is legally right by asking two questions: (1) Was *Roe* correctly decided? (2) Has *Roe* succeeded in producing a settled body of law? If the answer to both questions is no, *Roe* should undoubtedly be overruled.

In truth, I am as distressed as the Court is-and expressed my distress several years ago, see *Webster*,...-about the "political pressure" directed to the Court: the marches, the mail, the protests aimed at inducing us to change our opinions. How upsetting it is, that so many of our citizens (good people, not lawless ones, on both sides of this abortion issue, and on various sides of other issues as well) think that we Justices should properly take into account their views, as though we were engaged not in ascertaining an objective law but in determining some kind of social consensus. The Court would profit, I think, from giving less attention to the fact of this distressing phenomenon, and more attention to the cause of it. That cause permeates today's opinion: a new mode of constitutional adjudication that relies not upon text and traditional practice to determine the law, but upon what the Court calls "reasoned judgment," which turns out to be nothing but philosophical predilection and moral intuition. All manner of "liberties," the Court tells us, inhere in the Constitution and are enforceable by this Court-not just those mentioned in the text or established in the traditions of our society. Why even the Ninth Amendment-which says only that "[t]he enumeration in the Constitution of certain rights shall not be construed to deny or disparage others retained by the people"-is, despite our contrary understanding for almost 200 years, a literally boundless source of additional, unnamed, unhinted-at "rights," definable and enforceable by us, through "reasoned judgment."

What makes all this relevant to the bothersome application of "political pressure" against the Court are the twin facts that the American people love democracy and the American people are not fools. As long as this Court thought (and the people thought) that we Justices were doing essentially lawyers' work up here-reading text and discerning our society's traditional understanding of that text-the public pretty much left us alone. Texts and traditions are facts to study, not convictions to demonstrate about. But if in reality our process of constitutional adjudication consists primarily of making value judgments; if we can ignore a long and clear tradition clarifying an ambiguous text, as we did, for example, five days ago in declaring unconstitutional invocations and benedictions at public-high-school graduation ceremonies, *Lee v. Weisman*,... (1992); if, as I say, our pronouncement of constitutional law rests primarily on value judgments, then a free and intelligent people's attitude towards us can be expected to be (ought to be) quite different. The people know that their value judgments are quite as good as those taught in any law school-maybe better. If, indeed, the "liberties" protected by the Constitution are, as the Court says, undefined and unbounded, then the people should demonstrate, to protest that we do not implement their values instead of ours. Not only that, but confirmation hearings for new Justices should deteriorate into question-and-answer sessions in which Senators go through a list of their constituents' most favored and most disfavored alleged constitutional rights, and seek the nominee's commitment to support or oppose them. Value judgments, after all, should be voted on, not dictated; and if our Constitution has somehow accidentally committed them to the Supreme Court, at least we can have a sort of plebiscite each time a new nominee to that body is put forward. Justice BLACKMUN not only regards this prospect with equanimity, he solicits it.

There is a poignant aspect to today's opinion. Its length, and what might be called its epic tone, suggest that its authors believe they are bringing to an end a troublesome era in the history of our Nation and of our Court. "It is the dimension" of authority, they say, to "cal[l] the contending sides of national controversy to end their national division by accepting a common mandate rooted in the Constitution."

There comes vividly to mind a portrait by Emanuel Leutze that hangs in the Harvard Law School: Roger Brooke Taney, painted in 1859, the 82d year of his life, the 24th of his Chief Justiceship, the second after his opinion in *Dred Scott*. He is all in black, sitting in a shadowed red armchair, left hand resting upon a pad of paper in his lap, right hand hanging limply, almost lifelessly, beside the inner arm of the chair. He sits facing the viewer, and staring straight out. There seems to be on his face, and in his deep-set eyes, an expression of profound sadness and disillusionment. Perhaps he always looked that way, even when dwelling upon the happiest of thoughts. But those of us who know how the lustre of his great Chief Justiceship came to be eclipsed by *Dred Scott* cannot help believing that he had that case-its already apparent consequences for the Court, and its soon-to-be-played-out consequences for the Nation-burning on his mind. I expect that two years earlier he, too, had thought himself "call[ing] the contending sides of national controversy to end their national division by accepting a common mandate rooted in the Constitution."

It is no more realistic for us in this case, than it was for him in that, to think that an issue of the sort they both involved-an issue involving life and death, freedom and subjugation-can be "speedily and finally settled" by the Supreme Court, as President James Buchanan in his inaugural address said the issue of slavery in the territories would be. Quite to the contrary, by foreclosing all democratic outlet for the deep passions this issue arouses, by banishing the issue from the political forum that gives all participants, even the losers, the satisfaction of a fair hearing and an honest fight, by continuing the imposition of a rigid national rule instead of allowing for regional differences, the Court merely prolongs and intensifies the anguish.

We should get out of this area, where we have no right to be, and where we do neither ourselves nor the country any good by remaining.

BOWERS v. HARDWICK
106 S.Ct. 2841; 478 U.S. 186; 92 L.Ed.2d 140 (1986)

The facts in this case are contained in the opinion below.

Justice WHITE delivered the opinion of the Court.

In August 1982, respondent Hardwick ... was charged with violating the Georgia statute criminalizing sodomy by committing that act with another adult male in the bedroom of respondent's home. After a preliminary hearing, the District Attorney decided not to present the matter to the grand jury unless further evidence developed.

Respondent then brought suit in the Federal District Court, challenging the constitutionality of the statute insofar as it criminalized consensual sodomy. He asserted that he was a practicing homosexual, that the Georgia sodomy statute, as administered by the defendants, placed him in imminent danger of arrest, and that the statute for several reasons violates the Federal Constitution. The District Court granted the defendants' motion to dismiss for failure to state a claim, relying on *Doe v. Commonwealth's Attorney for the City of Richmond*,... which this Court summarily affirmed....

A divided panel of the Court of Appeals for the Eleventh Circuit reversed.... The court first held that, because *Doe* was distinguishable and in any event had been undermined by later decisions, our summary affirmance in that case did not require affirmance of the District Court. Relying on our decisions in *Griswold v. Connecticut*,... *Eisenstadt v. Baird*,... *Stanley v. Georgia*,... and *Roe v. Wade*,... the court went on to hold that the Georgia statute violated respondent's fundamental rights because his homosexual activity is a private and intimate association that is beyond the reach of state regulation by reason of the Ninth Amendment and the Due Process Clause of the Fourteenth Amendment. The case was remanded for trial, at which, to prevail, the State would have to prove that the statute is supported by a compelling interest and is the most narrowly drawn means of achieving that end.

Because other Courts of Appeals have arrived at judgments contrary to that of the Eleventh Circuit in this case, we granted the Attorney General's petition for certiorari questioning the holding that the sodomy statute violates the fundamental rights of homosexuals. We agree with petitioner that the Court of Appeals erred, and hence reverse its judgment.

This case does not require a judgment on whether laws against sodomy between consenting adults in general, or between homosexuals in particular, are wise or desirable. It raises no question about the right or propriety of state legislative decisions to repeal their laws that criminalize homosexual sodomy, or of state-court decisions invalidating those laws on state constitutional grounds. The issue presented is whether the Federal Constitution confers a fundamental right upon homosexuals to engage in sodomy and hence invalidates the laws of the many States that still make such conduct illegal and have done so for a very long time. The case also calls for some judgment about the limits of the Court's role in carrying out its constitutional mandate.

We first register our disagreement with the Court of Appeals and with respondent that the Court's prior cases have construed the Constitution to confer a right of privacy that extends to homosexual sodomy and for all intents and purposes have decided this case. The reach of this line of cases was sketched in *Carey v. Population Services International*.... *Pierce v. Society of Sisters* ... and *Meyer v. Nebraska* ... were described as dealing with child rearing and education; *Prince v. Massachusetts* ... with family relationships; *Skinner v. Oklahoma ex rel. Williamson* ... with procreation; *Loving v. Virginia* with marriage; *Griswold v. Connecticut* ... and *Eisenstadt v. Baird* ... with contraception; and *Roe v. Wade* ... with abortion. The latter three cases were interpreted as construing the Due Process Clause of the Fourteenth Amendment to confer a fundamental individual right to decide whether or not to beget or bear a child. *Carey v. Population Services International*....

Accepting the decisions in these cases and the above description of them, we think it evident that none of the rights announced in those cases bears any resemblance to the claimed constitutional right of homosexuals to engage in acts of sodomy that is asserted in this case. No connection between family, marriage, or procreation on the one hand and homosexual activity on the other has been demonstrated, either by the Court of Appeals or by respondent. Moreover, any claim that these cases nevertheless stand for the proposition that any kind of private sexual conduct between consenting adults is constitutionally insulated from state proscription is unsupportable. Indeed, the Court's opinion in *Carey* twice asserted that the privacy right, which the *Griswold* line of cases found to be one of the protections provided by the Due Process Clause, did not reach so far....

Precedent aside, however, respondent would have us announce, as the Court of Appeals did, a fundamental right to engage in homosexual sodomy. This we are quite unwilling to do. It is true that despite the language of the Due Process Clauses of the Fifth and Fourteenth Amendments, which appears to focus only on the processes by which life, liberty, or property is taken, the cases are legion in which those Clauses have been interpreted to have substantive content, subsuming rights that to a great extent are immune from federal or state regulation or proscription. Among such cases are those recognizing rights that have little or no textual support in the constitutional language. *Meyer*, *Prince*, and *Pierce* fall in this category, as do the privacy cases from *Griswold* to *Carey*.

Striving to assure itself and the public that announcing rights not readily identifiable in the Constitution's text involves much more than the imposition of the Justices' own choice of values on the States and the Federal Government, the Court has sought to identify the nature of the rights qualifying for heightened judicial protection. In *Palko v. Connecticut*,... it was said that this category includes those fundamental liberties that are "implicit in the concept of ordered liberty," such that "neither liberty nor justice would exist if [they] were sacrificed." A different description of fundamental liberties appeared in *Moore v. East Cleveland*,... (opinion of POWELL, J.), where they are characterized as those liberties that are " deeply rooted in this Nation's history and tradition...." See also *Griswold v. Connecticut*....

It is obvious to us that neither of these formulations would extend a fundamental right to homosexuals to engage in acts of consensual sodomy. Proscriptions against that conduct have ancient roots.... Sodomy was a criminal offense at common law and was forbidden by the laws of the original thirteen States when they ratified the Bill of Rights. In 1868, when the Fourteenth Amendment was ratified, all but 5 of the 37 States in the Union had criminal sodomy laws. In fact, until 1961, all 50 States outlawed sodomy, and today, 24 States and the District of Columbia continue to provide criminal penalties for sodomy performed in private and between consenting adults.... Against this background, to claim that a right to engage in such conduct is "deeply rooted in this Nation's history and tradition" or " implicit in the concept of ordered liberty" is, at best, facetious.

Nor are we inclined to take a more expansive view of our authority to discover new fundamental rights imbedded in the Due Process Clause. The Court is most vulnerable and comes nearest to illegitimacy when it deals with judge-made constitutional law having little or no cognizable roots in the language or design of the Constitution. That this is so was painfully demonstrated by the face-off between the Executive and the Court in the 1930's, which resulted in the repudiation of much of the substantive gloss that the Court had placed on the Due Process Clauses of the Fifth and Fourteenth Amendments. There should be, therefore, great resistance to expand the substantive reach of those Clauses, particularly if it requires redefining the category of rights deemed to be fundamental. Otherwise, the Judiciary necessarily takes to itself further authority to govern the country without express constitutional authority. The claimed right pressed on us today falls far short of overcoming this resistance.

Respondent, however, asserts that the result should be different where the homosexual conduct occurs in the privacy of the home. He relies on *Stanley v. Georgia*, where the Court held that the First Amendment prevents conviction for possessing and reading obscene material in the privacy of one's home: "If the First Amendment means anything, it means that a State has no business telling a man, sitting alone in his house, what books he may read or what films he may watch...."

Stanley did protect conduct that would not have been protected outside the home, and it partially prevented the enforcement of state obscenity laws; but the decision was firmly grounded in the First Amendment. The right pressed upon us here has no similar support in the text of the Constitution, and it does not qualify for recognition under the prevailing principles for construing the Fourteenth Amendment. Its limits are also difficult to discern. Plainly enough, otherwise illegal conduct is not always immunized whenever it occurs in the home. Victimless crimes, such as the possession and use of illegal drugs, do not escape the law where they are committed at home. *Stanley* itself recognized that its holding offered no protection for the possession in the home of drugs, firearms, or stolen goods.... And if respondent's submission is limited to the voluntary sexual conduct between consenting adults, it would be difficult, except by fiat, to limit the claimed right to homosexual conduct while leaving exposed to prosecution adultery, incest, and other sexual crimes even though they are committed in the home. We are unwilling to start down that road.

Even if the conduct at issue here is not a fundamental right, respondent asserts that there must be a rational basis for the law and that there is none in this case other than the presumed belief of a majority of the electorate in Georgia that homosexual sodomy is immoral and unacceptable. This is said to be an inadequate rationale to support the law. The law, however, is constantly based on notions of morality, and if all laws representing essentially moral choices are to be invalidated under the Due Process Clause, the courts will be very busy indeed. Even respondent makes no such claim, but insists that majority sentiments about the morality of homosexuality should be declared inadequate. We do not agree, and are unpersuaded that the sodomy laws of some 25 States should be invalidated on this basis.

Accordingly, the judgment of the Court of Appeals is
Reversed.

Chief Justice BURGER, concurring....

Justice POWELL, concurring....

Justice BLACKMUN, with whom Justice BRENNAN, Justice MARSHALL, and Justice STEVENS join, dissenting.

This case is no more about "a fundamental right to engage in homosexual sodomy," as the Court purports to declare ... than *Stanley v. Georgia* was about a fundamental right to watch obscene movies.... Rather, this case is about "the most comprehensive of rights and the right most valued by civilized men," namely, "the right to be let alone." *Olmstead v. United States*,... (Brandeis, J., dissenting).

The statute at issue ... denies individuals the right to decide for themselves whether to engage in particular forms of private, consensual sexual activity. The Court concludes that § 16-6-2 is valid essentially because "the laws of ... many

States ... still make such conduct illegal and have done so for a very long time...." I believe we must analyze Hardwick's claim in the light of the values that underlie the constitutional right to privacy. If that right means anything, it means that, before Georgia can prosecute its citizens for making choices about the most intimate aspects of their lives, it must do more than assert that the choice they have made is an "'abominable crime not fit to be named among Christians.'" *Herring v. State*, 119 Ga. 709, 721, 46 S.E. 876, 882 (1904).

I

In its haste to reverse the Court of Appeals and hold that the Constitution does not "confe[r] a fundamental right upon homosexuals to engage in sodomy," the Court relegates the actual statute being challenged to a footnote and ignores the procedural posture of the case before it. A fair reading of the statute and of the complaint clearly reveals that the majority has distorted the question this case presents.

First, the Court's almost obsessive focus on homosexual activity is particularly hard to justify in light of the broad language Georgia has used. Unlike the Court, the Georgia Legislature has not proceeded on the assumption that homosexuals are so different from other citizens that their lives may be controlled in a way that would not be tolerated if it limited the choices of those other citizens. Rather, Georgia has provided that "[a] person commits the offense of sodomy when he performs or submits to any sexual act involving the sex organs of one person and the mouth or anus of another...." The sex or status of the persons who engage in the act is irrelevant as a matter of state law....

Second, I disagree with the Court's refusal to consider whether § 16- 6-2 runs afoul of the Eighth or Ninth Amendments or the Equal Protection Clause of the Fourteenth Amendment....

II

"Our cases long have recognized that the Constitution embodies a promise that a certain private sphere of individual liberty will be kept largely beyond the reach of government." *Thornburgh v. American College of Obstetricians & Gynecologists*.... In construing the right to privacy, the Court has proceeded along two somewhat distinct, albeit complementary, lines. First, it has recognized a privacy interest with reference to certain decisions that are properly for the individual to make.... Second, it has recognized a privacy interest with reference to certain places without regard for the particular activities in which the individuals who occupy them are engaged.... The case before us implicates both the decisional and the spatial aspects of the right to privacy.

A.

...Only the most willful blindness could obscure the fact that sexual intimacy is "a sensitive, key relationship of human existence, central to family life, community welfare, and the development of human personality,"... The fact that individuals define themselves in a significant way through their intimate sexual relationships with others suggests, in a Nation as diverse as ours, that there may be many "right" ways of conducting those relationships, and that much of the richness of a relationship will come from the freedom an individual has to choose the form and nature of these intensely personal bonds....

In a variety of circumstances we have recognized that a necessary corollary of giving individuals freedom to choose how to conduct their lives is acceptance of the fact that different individuals will make different choices. For example, in holding that the clearly important state interest in public education should give way to a competing claim by the Amish to the effect that extended formal schooling threatened their way of life, the Court declared: "There can be no assumption that today's majority is 'right' and the Amish and others like them are 'wrong.' A way of life that is odd or even erratic but interferes with no rights or interests of others is not to be condemned because it is different." *Wisconsin v. Yoder*.... The Court claims that its decision today merely refuses to recognize a fundamental right to engage in homosexual sodomy; what the Court really has refused to recognize is the fundamental interest all individuals have in controlling the nature of their intimate associations with others.

B

The behavior for which Hardwick faces prosecution occurred in his own home, a place to which the Fourth Amendment attaches special significance. The Court's treatment of this aspect of the case is symptomatic of its overall refusal to consider the broad principles that have informed our treatment of privacy in specific cases. Just as the right to privacy is more than the mere aggregation of a number of entitlements to engage in specific behavior, so too, protecting the physical integrity of the home is more than merely a means of protecting specific activities that often take place there....

The Court's interpretation of the pivotal case of *Stanley v. Georgia*,... is entirely unconvincing. *Stanley* held that Georgia's undoubted power to punish the public distribution of constitutionally unprotected, obscene material did not permit the State to punish the private possession of such material. According to the majority here, *Stanley* relied entirely on the First Amendment, and thus, it is claimed, sheds no light on cases not involving printed materials.... But that is not what *Stanley* said. Rather, the *Stanley* Court anchored its holding in the Fourth Amendment's special protection for the individual in his home....

III

The Court's failure to comprehend the magnitude of the liberty interests at stake in this case leads it to slight the question whether petitioner, on behalf of the State, has justified Georgia's infringement on these interests....

The core of petitioner's defense ... is that respondent and others who engage in the conduct prohibited by § 16-6-2 interfere with Georgia's exercise of the "'right of the Nation and of the States to maintain a decent society,'"... Essentially, petitioner argues, and the Court agrees, that the fact that the acts described in § 16-6-2 "for hundreds of years, if not thousands, have been uniformly condemned as immoral" is a sufficient reason to permit a State to ban them today....

I cannot agree that either the length of time a majority has held its convictions or the passions with which it defends them can withdraw legislation from this Court's scrutiny. ... It is precisely because the issue raised by this case touches the heart of what makes individuals what they are that we should be especially sensitive to the rights of those whose choices upset the majority.

The assertion that "traditional Judeo-Christian values proscribe" the conduct involved ... cannot provide an adequate justification for § 16-6-2....

Nor can § 16-6-2 be justified as a "morally neutral" exercise of Georgia's power to "protect the public environment...." Certainly, some private behavior can affect the fabric of society as a whole. Reasonable people may differ about whether particular sexual acts are moral or immoral, but "we have ample evidence for believing that people will not abandon morality, will not think any better of murder, cruelty and dishonesty, merely because some private sexual practice which they abominate is not punished by the law...." Petitioner and the Court fail to see the difference between laws that protect public sensibilities and those that enforce private morality. Statutes banning public sexual activity are entirely consistent with protecting the individual's liberty interest in decisions concerning sexual relations: the same recognition that those decisions are intensely private which justifies protecting them from governmental interference can justify protecting individuals from unwilling exposure to the sexual activities of others. But the mere fact that intimate behavior may be punished when it takes place in public cannot dictate how States can regulate intimate behavior that occurs in intimate places....

This case involves no real interference with the rights of others, for the mere knowledge that other individuals do not adhere to one's value system cannot be a legally cognizable interest ... let alone an interest that can justify invading the houses, hearts, and minds of citizens who choose to live their lives differently.

IV

It took but three years for the Court to see the error in its analysis in *Minersville School District v. Gobitis* ... and to recognize that the threat to national cohesion posed by a refusal to salute the flag was vastly outweighed by the threat to those same values posed by compelling such a salute.... I can only hope that here, too, the Court soon will reconsider its analysis and conclude that depriving individuals of the right to choose for themselves how to conduct their intimate relationships poses a far greater threat to the values most deeply rooted in our Nation's history than tolerance of nonconformity could ever do. Because I think the Court today betrays those values, I dissent.

Justice STEVENS, with whom Justice BRENNAN and Justice MARSHALL join, dissenting....

CRUZAN by CRUZAN v. DIRECTOR, MISSOURI DEPT. of HEALTH
110 S.Ct. 2841; 497 U.S. 261; 111 L.Ed.2d 224 (1990)

The facts in this case are contained in the opinion below.

Chief Justice REHNQUIST delivered the opinion of the Court.

Petitioner Nancy Beth Cruzan was rendered incompetent as a result of severe injuries sustained during an automobile accident. Copetitioners Lester and Joyce Cruzan, Nancy's parents and coguardians, sought a court order directing the withdrawal of their daughter's artificial feeding and hydration equipment after it became apparent that she had virtually no chance of recovering her cognitive faculties. The Supreme Court of Missouri held that because there was no clear and convincing evidence of Nancy's desire to have life-sustaining treatment withdrawn under such circumstances, her parents lacked authority to effectuate such a request. We granted certiorari, and now affirm....

After it had become apparent that Nancy Cruzan had virtually no chance of regaining her mental faculties, her parents asked hospital employees to terminate the artificial nutrition and hydration procedures. All agree that such a removal would cause her death. The employees refused to honor the request without court approval. The parents then sought and received authorization from the state trial court for termination. The court found that a person in Nancy's condition had a fundamental right under the State and Federal Constitutions to refuse or direct the withdrawal of "death prolonging procedures." The court also found that Nancy's "expressed thoughts at age twenty-five in somewhat serious conversation with a housemate friend that if sick or injured she would not wish to continue her life unless she could live at least halfway normally suggests that given her present condition she would not wish to continue on with her nutrition and hydration."

The Supreme Court of Missouri reversed by a divided vote. The court recognized a right to refuse treatment embodied in the common-law doctrine of informed consent, but expressed skepticism about the application of that doctrine in the circumstances of this case.... The court also declined to read a broad right of privacy into the State Constitution which would "support the right of a person to refuse medical treatment in every circumstance," and expressed doubt as to whether such a right existed under the United States Constitution. It then decided that the Missouri Living Will statute... embodied a state policy strongly favoring the preservation of life. The court found that Cruzan's statements to her roommate regarding her desire to live or die under certain conditions were " unreliable for the purpose of determining her intent," "and thus insufficient to support the co-guardians['] claim to exercise substituted judgment on Nancy's behalf." It rejected the argument that Cruzan's parents were entitled to order the termination of her medical treatment, concluding that "no person can assume that choice for an incompetent in the absence of the formalities required under Missouri's Living Will statutes or the clear and convincing, inherently reliable evidence absent here." The court also expressed its view that "[b]road policy questions bearing on life and death are more properly addressed by representative assemblies" than judicial bodies.

We granted certiorari to consider the question whether Cruzan has a right under the United States Constitution which would require the hospital to withdraw life-sustaining treatment from her under these circumstances.

At common law, even the touching of one person by another without consent and without legal justification was a battery.... Before the turn of the century, this Court observed that "[n]o right is held more sacred, or is more carefully guarded, by the common law, than the right of every individual to the possession and control of his own person, free from all restraint or interference of others, unless by clear and unquestionable authority of law." *Union Pacific R. Co. v. Botsford*.... This notion of bodily integrity has been embodied in the requirement that informed consent is generally required for medical treatment.... The informed consent doctrine has become firmly entrenched in American tort law....

The logical corollary of the doctrine of informed consent is that the patient generally possesses the right not to consent, that is, to refuse treatment. Until about 15 years ago and the seminal decision in *In re Quinlan*, 70 N.J. 10, 355 A.2d 647,... the number of right-to-refuse-treatment decisions was relatively few. Most of the earlier cases involved patients who refused medical treatment forbidden by their religious beliefs, thus implicating First Amendment rights as well as common-law rights of self-determination. More recently, however, with the advance of medical technology capable of sustaining life well past the point where natural forces would have brought certain death in earlier times, cases involving the right to refuse life-sustaining treatment have burgeoned....

...In this Court, the question is simply and starkly whether the United States Constitution prohibits Missouri from choosing the rule of decision which it did. This is the first case in which we have been squarely presented with the issue whether the United States Constitution grants what is in common parlance referred to as a "right to die." We follow the judicious counsel of our decision in *Twin City Bank v. Nebeker* ... where we said that in deciding "a question of such magnitude and importance ... it is the [better] part of wisdom not to attempt, by any general statement, to cover every possible phase of the subject."

The Fourteenth Amendment provides that no State shall "deprive any person of life, liberty, or property, without due process of law." The principle that a competent person has a constitutionally protected liberty interest in refusing unwanted medical treatment may be inferred from our prior decisions. In *Jacobson v. Massachusetts*,... for instance, the Court balanced an individual's liberty interest in declining an unwanted smallpox vaccine against the State's interest in preventing disease. Decisions prior to the incorporation of the Fourth Amendment into the Fourteenth Amendment analyzed searches and seizures involving the body under the Due Process Clause and were thought to implicate substantial liberty interests. See, e.g., *Breithaupt v. Abram* .... ("As against the right of an individual that his person be held inviolable ...must be set the interests of society....")

Just this Term, in the course of holding that a State's procedures for administering antipsychotic medication to prisoners were sufficient to satisfy due process concerns, we recognized that prisoners possess "a significant liberty interest in avoiding the unwanted administration of antipsychotic drugs under the Due Process Clause of the Fourteenth Amendment." *Washington v. Harper* .... Still other cases support the recognition of a general liberty interest in refusing medical treatment. *Vitek v. Jones*,... (transfer to mental hospital coupled with mandatory behavior modification treatment implicated liberty interests); *Parham v. J.R.*,... ("[A] child, in common with adults, has a substantial liberty interest in not being confined unnecessarily for medical treatment").

But determining that a person has a "liberty interest" under the Due Process Clause does not end the inquiry; "whether respondent's constitutional rights have been violated must be determined by balancing his liberty interests against the relevant state interests." *Youngberg v. Romeo*.... See also *Mills v. Rogers*....

Petitioners insist that under the general holdings of our cases, the forced administration of life-sustaining medical treatment, and even of artificially delivered food and water essential to life, would implicate a competent person's liberty interest. Although we think the logic of the cases discussed above would embrace such a liberty interest, the dramatic consequences involved in refusal of such treatment would inform the inquiry as to whether the deprivation of that interest is constitutionally permissible. But for purposes of this case, we assume that the United States Constitution would grant a competent person a constitutionally protected right to refuse lifesaving hydration and nutrition.

Petitioners go on to assert that an incompetent person should possess the same right in this respect as is possessed by a competent person. They rely primarily on our decisions in *Parham v. J.R.* ... and *Youngberg v. Romeo*.... In *Parham*, we held that a mentally disturbed minor child had a liberty interest in "not being confined unnecessarily for medical treatment," ... but we certainly did not intimate that such a minor child, after commitment, would have a liberty interest in refusing treatment. In *Youngberg*, we held that a seriously retarded adult had a liberty interest in safety and freedom from bodily restraint.... *Youngberg*, however, did not deal with decisions to administer or withhold medical treatment.

The difficulty with petitioners' claim is that in a sense it begs the question: An incompetent person is not able to make an informed and voluntary choice to exercise a hypothetical right to refuse treatment or any other right. Such a "right" must be exercised for her, if at all, by some sort of surrogate. Here, Missouri has in effect recognized that under certain circumstances a surrogate may act for the patient in electing to have hydration and nutrition withdrawn in such a way as to cause death, but it has established a procedural safeguard to assure that the action of the surrogate conforms as best it may to the wishes expressed by the patient while competent. Missouri requires that evidence of the incompetent's wishes as to the withdrawal of treatment be proved by clear and convincing evidence. The question, then, is whether the United States Constitution forbids the establishment of this procedural requirement by the State. We hold that it does not.

Whether or not Missouri's clear and convincing evidence requirement comports with the United States Constitution depends in part on what interests the State may properly seek to protect in this situation. Missouri relies on its interest in the protection and preservation of human life, and there can be no gainsaying this interest. As a general matter, the States-indeed, all civilized nations-demonstrate their commitment to life by treating homicide as a serious crime. Moreover, the majority of States in this country have laws imposing criminal penalties on one who assists another to commit suicide. We do not think a State is required to remain neutral in the face of an informed and voluntary decision by a physically able adult to starve to death.

But in the context presented here, a State has more particular interests at stake. The choice between life and death is a deeply personal decision of obvious and overwhelming finality. We believe Missouri may legitimately seek to safeguard the personal element of this choice through the imposition of heightened evidentiary requirements. It cannot be disputed that the Due Process Clause protects an interest in life as well as an interest in refusing life-sustaining medical treatment. Not all incompetent patients will have loved ones available to serve as surrogate decisionmakers. And even where family members are present, "i[t] here will, of course, be some unfortunate situations in which family members will not act to protect a patient." *In re Jobes*.... A State is entitled to guard against potential abuses in such situations. Similarly, a State is entitled to consider that a judicial proceeding to make a determination regarding an incompetent's wishes may very well not be an adversarial one, with the added guarantee of accurate factfinding that the adversary process brings with it. See *Ohio v. Akron Center for Reproductive Health*.... Finally, we think a State may properly decline to make judgments about the "quality" of life that a particular individual may enjoy, and simply assert an unqualified interest in the preservation of human life to be weighed against the constitutionally protected interests of the individual.

In our view, Missouri has permissibly sought to advance these interests through the adoption of a "clear and convincing" standard of proof to govern such proceedings. "The function of a standard of proof, as that concept is embodied in the Due Process Clause and in the realm of factfinding, is to 'instruct the factfinder concerning the degree of confidence our society thinks he should have in the correctness of factual conclusions for a particular type of adjudication.'" *Addington v. Texas*.... "This Court has mandated an intermediate standard of proof-'clear and convincing evidence'-when the individual interests at stake in a state proceeding are both 'particularly important' and 'more substantial than mere loss of money.'" *Santosky v. Kramer*.... Thus, such a standard has been required in deportation proceedings, *Woodby v. INS*,... in denaturalization proceedings, *Schneiderman v. United States*,... in civil commitment proceedings, *Addington*... and in proceedings for the termination of parental rights, *Santosky*.... Further, this level of proof, "or an even higher one, has traditionally been imposed in cases involving allegations of civil fraud, and in a variety of other kinds of civil cases involving such issues as ...lost wills, oral contracts to make bequests, and the like." *Woodby....*

We think it self-evident that the interests at stake in the instant proceedings are more substantial, both on an individual and societal level, than those involved in a run-of-the-mill civil dispute. But not only does the standard of proof reflect the importance of a particular adjudication, it also serves as "a societal judgment about how the risk of error should be distributed between the litigants...." The more stringent the burden of proof a party must bear, the more that party bears the risk of an erroneous decision. We believe that Missouri may permissibly place an increased risk of an erroneous decision on those seeking to terminate an incompetent individual's life-sustaining treatment. An erroneous decision not to terminate results in a maintenance of the status quo; the possibility of subsequent developments such as advancements in medical science, the discovery of new evidence regarding the patient's intent, changes in the law, or simply the unexpected death of the patient despite the administration of life-sustaining treatment at least create the potential that a wrong decision will eventually be corrected or its impact mitigated. An erroneous decision to withdraw life-sustaining treatment, however, is not susceptible of correction. In *Santosky*, one of the factors which led the Court to require proof by clear and convincing evidence in a proceeding to terminate parental rights was that a decision in such a case was final and irrevocable.... The same must surely be said of the decision to discontinue hydration and nutrition of a patient such as Nancy Cruzan, which all agree will result in her death.

It is also worth noting that most, if not all, States simply forbid oral testimony entirely in determining the wishes of parties in transactions which, while important, simply do not have the consequences that a decision to terminate a person's life does. At common law and by statute in most States, the parol evidence rule prevents the variations of the terms of a written contract by oral testimony. The statute of frauds makes unenforceable oral contracts to leave property by will, and statutes regulating the making of wills universally require that those instruments be in writing.... There is no doubt that statutes requiring wills to be in writing, and statutes of frauds which require that a contract to make a will be in writing, on occasion frustrate the effectuation of the intent of a particular decedent, just as Missouri's requirement of proof in this case may have frustrated the effectuation of the not-fully-expressed desires of Nancy Cruzan. But the Constitution does not require general rules to work faultlessly; no general rule can.

In sum, we conclude that a State may apply a clear and convincing evidence standard in proceedings where a guardian seeks to discontinue nutrition and hydration of a person diagnosed to be in a persistent vegetative state. We note that many courts which have adopted some sort of substituted judgment procedure in situations like this, whether they limit consideration of evidence to the prior expressed wishes of the incompetent individual, or whether they allow more general proof of what the individual's decision would have been, require a clear and convincing standard of proof for such evidence....

The Supreme Court of Missouri held that in this case the testimony adduced at trial did not amount to clear and convincing proof of the patient's desire to have hydration and nutrition withdrawn. In so doing, it reversed a decision of the Missouri trial court which had found that the evidence "suggest[ed]" Nancy Cruzan would not have desired to continue such measures,... but which had not adopted the standard of "clear and convincing evidence" enunciated by the Supreme Court. The testimony adduced at trial consisted primarily of Nancy Cruzan's statements made to a housemate about a year before her accident that she would not want to live should she face life as a "vegetable," and other observations to the same effect. The observations did not deal in terms with withdrawal of medical treatment or of hydration and nutrition. We cannot say that the Supreme Court of Missouri committed constitutional error in reaching the conclusion that it did.

Petitioners alternatively contend that Missouri must accept the " substituted judgment" of close family members even in the absence of substantial proof that their views reflect the views of the patient. They rely primarily upon our decisions in *Michael H. v. Gerald D.*... and *Parham v. J.R.*... But we do not think these cases support their claim. In *Michael H.*, we upheld the constitutionality of California's favored treatment of traditional family relationships; such a holding may not be turned around into a constitutional requirement that a State must recognize the primacy of those relationships in a situation like this. And in *Parham*, where the patient was a minor, we also upheld the constitutionality of a state scheme in which parents made certain decisions for mentally ill minors. Here again petitioners would seek to turn a decision which allowed a State to rely on family decisionmaking into a constitutional requirement that the State recognize such decisionmaking. But constitutional law does not work that way.

No doubt is engendered by anything in this record but that Nancy Cruzan's mother and father are loving and caring parents. If the State were required by the United States Constitution to repose a right of "substituted judgment" with anyone, the Cruzans would surely qualify. But we do not think the Due Process Clause requires the State to repose judgment on these matters with anyone but the patient herself. Close family members may have a strong feeling – a feeling not at all ignoble or unworthy, but not entirely disinterested, either – that they do not wish to witness the continuation of the life of a loved one which they regard as hopeless, meaningless, and even degrading. But there is no automatic assurance that the view of close family members will necessarily be the same as the patient's would have been had she been confronted with the prospect of her situation while competent. All of the reasons previously discussed for allowing Missouri to require clear and convincing evidence of the patient's wishes lead us to conclude that the State may choose to defer only to those wishes, rather than confide the decision to close family members.

The judgment of the Supreme Court of Missouri is

Affirmed.

Justice O'CONNOR, concurring.

...Today's decision, holding only that the Constitution permits a State to require clear and convincing evidence of Nancy Cruzan's desire to have artificial hydration and nutrition withdrawn, does not preclude a future determination that the Constitution requires the States to implement the decisions of a patient's duly appointed surrogate. Nor does it prevent States from developing other approaches for protecting an incompetent individual's liberty interest in refusing medical treatment. As is evident from the Court's survey of state court decisions, no national consensus has yet emerged on the best solution for this difficult and sensitive problem. Today we decide only that one State's practice does not violate the Constitution; the more challenging task of crafting appropriate procedures for safeguarding incompetents' liberty interests is entrusted to the "laboratory" of the States....

Justice SCALIA, concurring.

The various opinions in this case portray quite clearly the difficult, indeed agonizing, questions that are presented by the constantly increasing power of science to keep the human body alive for longer than any reasonable person would want to inhabit it. The States have begun to grapple with these problems through legislation. I am concerned, from the tenor of today's opinions, that we are poised to confuse that enterprise as successfully as we have confused the enterprise of legislating concerning abortion – requiring it to be conducted against a background of federal constitutional imperatives that are unknown because they are being newly crafted from Term to Term. That would be a great misfortune.

While I agree with the Court's analysis today, and therefore join in its opinion, I would have preferred that we announce, clearly and promptly, that the federal courts have no business in this field; that American law has always accorded the State the power to prevent, by force if necessary, suicide – including suicide by refusing to take appropriate measures necessary to preserve one's life; that the point at which life becomes " worthless," and the point at which the means necessary to preserve it become "extraordinary" or "inappropriate," are neither set forth in the Constitution nor known to the nine Justices of this Court any better than they are known to nine people picked at random from the Kansas City telephone directory; and hence, that even when it is demonstrated by clear and convincing evidence that a patient no longer wishes certain measures to be taken to preserve his or her life, it is up to the citizens of Missouri to decide, through their elected representatives, whether that wish will be honored. It is quite impossible (because the Constitution says nothing about the matter) that those citizens will decide upon a line less lawful than the one we would choose; and it is unlikely (because we know no more about "life and death" than they do) that they will decide upon a line less reasonable.

The text of the Due Process Clause does not protect individuals against deprivations of liberty simpliciter. It protects them against deprivations of liberty "without due process of law." To determine that such a deprivation would not occur if Nancy Cruzan were forced to take nourishment against her will, it is unnecessary to reopen the historically recurrent debate over whether "due process" includes substantive restrictions.... It is at least true that no "substantive due process" claim can be maintained unless the claimant demonstrates that the State has deprived him of a right historically and traditionally protected against state interference. *Michael H. v. Gerald D....* (plurality opinion); *Bowers v. Hardwick...*; *Moore...* (plurality opinion). That cannot possibly be established here.

At common law in England, a suicide-defined as one who "deliberately puts an end to his own existence, or commits any unlawful malicious act, the consequence of which is his own death," ...was criminally liable. Although the States abolished the penalties imposed by the common law (i.e., forfeiture and ignominious burial), they did so to spare the innocent family and not to legitimize the act. Case law at the time of the adoption of the Fourteenth Amendment generally held that assisting suicide was a criminal offense.... And most States that did not explicitly prohibit assisted suicide in 1868 recognized, when the issue arose in the 50 years following the Fourteenth Amendment's ratification, that assisted and (in some cases) attempted suicide were unlawful.... Thus, "there is no significant support for the claim that a right to suicide is so rooted in our tradition that it may be deemed 'fundamental' or 'implicit in the concept of ordered liberty.'"...

Petitioners rely on three distinctions to separate Nancy Cruzan's case from ordinary suicide: (1) that she is permanently incapacitated and in pain; (2) that she would bring on her death not by any affirmative act but by merely declining treatment that provides nourishment; and (3) that preventing her from effectuating her presumed wish to die requires violation of her bodily integrity. None of these suffices. Suicide was not excused even when committed "to avoid those ills which [persons] had not the fortitude to endure...." "The life of those to whom life has become a burden-of those who are hopelessly diseased or fatally wounded-nay, even the lives of criminals condemned to death, are under the protection of the law, equally as the lives of those who are in the full tide of life's enjoyment, and anxious to continue to live...." Thus, a man who prepared a poison, and placed it within reach of his wife, "to put an end to her suffering" from a terminal illness was convicted of murder.... Nor would the imminence of the patient's death have affected liability. "The lives of all are equally under the protection of the law, and under that protection to their last moment.... [Assisted suicide] is declared by the law to be murder, irrespective of the wishes or the condition of the party to whom the poison is administered...."

The second asserted distinction – suggested by the recent cases canvassed by the Court concerning the right to refuse treatment – relies on the dichotomy between action and inaction. Suicide, it is said, consists of an affirmative act to end one's life; refusing treatment is not an affirmative act "causing" death, but merely a passive acceptance of the natural process of dying. I readily acknowledge that the distinction between action and inaction has some bearing upon the legislative judgment of what ought to be prevented as suicide – though even there it would seem to me unreasonable to draw the line precisely between action and inaction, rather than between various forms of inaction. It would not make much sense to say that one may not kill oneself by walking into the sea, but may sit on the beach until submerged by the incoming tide; or that one may not intentionally lock oneself into a cold storage locker, but may refrain from coming indoors when the temperature drops below freezing. Even as a legislative matter, in other words, the intelligent line does not fall between action and inaction but between those forms of inaction that consist of abstaining from "ordinary" care and those that consist of abstaining from "excessive" or "heroic" measures. Unlike action versus inaction, that is not a line to be discerned by logic or legal analysis, and we should not pretend that it is.

But to return to the principal point for present purposes: the irrelevance of the action-inaction distinction. Starving oneself to death is no different from putting a gun to one's temple as far as the common-law definition of suicide is concerned; the cause of death in both cases is the suicide's conscious decision to "pu[t] an end to his own existence...." Of course the common law rejected the action-inaction distinction in other contexts involving the taking of human life as well. In the prosecution of a parent for the starvation death of her infant, it was no defense that the infant's death was "caused" by no action of the parent but by the natural process of starvation, or by the infant's natural inability to provide for itself.... A physician, moreover, could be criminally liable for failure to provide care that could have extended the patient's life, even if death was immediately caused by the underlying disease that the physician failed to treat....

It is not surprising, therefore, that the early cases considering the claimed right to refuse medical treatment dismissed as specious the nice distinction between "passively submitting to death and actively seeking it. The distinction may be merely verbal, as it would be if an adult sought death by starvation instead of a drug. If the State may interrupt one mode of self-destruction, it may with equal authority interfere with the other...."

The third asserted basis of distinction – that frustrating Nancy Cruzan's wish to die in the present case requires interference with her bodily integrity – is likewise inadequate, because such interference is impermissible only if one begs the question whether her refusal to undergo the treatment on her own is suicide. It has always been lawful not only for the State, but even for private citizens, to interfere with bodily integrity to prevent a felony.... That general rule has of course been applied to suicide. At common law, even a private person's use of force to prevent suicide was privileged.... It is not even reasonable, much less required by the Constitution, to maintain that although the State has the right to prevent a person from slashing his wrists, it does not have the power to apply physical force to prevent him from doing so, nor the power, should he succeed, to apply, coercively if necessary, medical measures to stop the flow of blood. The state-run hospital, I am certain, is not liable under 42 U.S.C. § 1983 for violation of constitutional rights, nor the private hospital liable under general tort law, if, in a State where suicide is unlawful, it pumps out the stomach of a person who has intentionally taken an overdose of barbiturates, despite that person's wishes to the contrary.

The dissents of Justices BRENNAN and STEVENS make a plausible case for our intervention here only by embracing – the latter explicitly and the former by implication – a political principle that the States are free to adopt, but that is demonstrably not imposed by the Constitution. "[T]he State," says Justice BRENNAN, "has no legitimate general interest in someone's life, completely abstracted from the interest of the person living that life, that could outweigh the person's choice *to avoid medical treatment.*" ... (emphasis added). The italicized phrase sounds moderate enough and is all that is needed to cover the present case – but the proposition cannot logically be so limited. One who accepts it must also accept, I think, that the State has no such legitimate interest that could outweigh "the person's choice *to put an end to her life.*" Similarly, if one agrees with Justice BRENNAN that "the State's general interest in life must accede to Nancy Cruzan's particularized and intense interest in self-determination *in her choice of medical treatment*,"...(emphasis added), he must also believe that the State must accede to her "particularized and intense interest in self-determination *in her choice whether to continue living or to die.*" For insofar as balancing the relative interests of the State and the individual is concerned, there is nothing distinctive about accepting death through the refusal of "medical treatment," as opposed to accepting it through the refusal of food, or through the failure to shut off the engine and get out of the car after parking in one's garage after work. Suppose that Nancy Cruzan were in precisely the condition she is in today, except that she could be fed and digest food and water *without* artificial assistance. How is the State's "interest" in keeping her alive thereby increased, or her interest in deciding whether she wants to continue living reduced? It seems to me, in other words, that Justice BRENNAN's position ultimately rests upon the proposition that it is none of the State's business if a person wants to commit suicide. Justice STEVENS is explicit on the point: "Choices about death touch the core of liberty.... [N]ot much may be said with confidence about death unless it is said from faith, and that alone is reason enough to protect the freedom to conform choices about death to individual conscience." This is a view that some societies have held, and that our States are free to adopt if they wish. But it is not a view imposed by our constitutional traditions, in which the power of the State to prohibit suicide is unquestionable.

What I have said above is not meant to suggest that I would think it desirable, if we were sure that Nancy Cruzan wanted to die, to keep her alive by the means at issue here. I assert only that the Constitution has nothing to say about the subject. To raise up a constitutional right here we would have to create out of nothing (for it exists neither in text nor tradition) some constitutional principle whereby, although the State may insist that an individual come in out of the cold and eat food, it may not insist that he take medicine; and although it may pump his stomach empty of poison he has ingested, it may not fill his stomach with food he has failed to ingest. Are there, then, no reasonable and humane limits that ought not to be exceeded in requiring an individual to preserve his own life? There obviously are, but they are not set forth in the Due Process Clause. What assures us that those limits will not be exceeded is the same constitutional guarantee that is the source of most of our protection – what protects us, for example, from being assessed a tax of 100% of our income above the subsistence level, from being forbidden to drive cars, or from being required to send our children to school for 10 hours a day, none of which horribles are categorically prohibited by the Constitution. Our salvation is the Equal Protection Clause, which requires the democratic majority to accept for themselves and their loved ones what they impose on you and me. This Court need not, and has no authority to, inject itself into every field of human activity where irrationality and oppression may theoretically occur, and if it tries to do so it will destroy itself.

Justice BRENNAN, with whom Justice MARSHALL and Justice BLACKMUN join, dissenting.

Today the Court, while tentatively accepting that there is some degree of constitutionally protected liberty interest in avoiding unwanted medical treatment, including life-sustaining medical treatment such as artificial nutrition and hydration, affirms the decision of the Missouri Supreme Court. The majority opinion, as I read it, would affirm that decision on the ground that a State may require "clear and convincing" evidence of Nancy Cruzan's prior decision to forgo life-sustaining treatment under circumstances such as hers in order to ensure that her actual wishes are honored.... Because I believe that Nancy Cruzan has a fundamental right to be free of unwanted artificial nutrition and hydration, which right is not outweighed by any interests of the State, and because I find that the improperly biased procedural obstacles imposed by the Missouri Supreme Court impermissibly burden that right, I respectfully dissent. Nancy Cruzan is entitled to choose to die with dignity.

I

A

The question before this Court is a relatively narrow one: whether the Due Process Clause allows Missouri to require a now-incompetent patient in an irreversible persistent vegetative state to remain on life support absent rigorously clear and convincing evidence that avoiding the treatment represents the patient's prior, express choice. If a fundamental right is at issue, Missouri's rule of decision must be scrutinized under the standards this Court has always applied in such circumstances. As we said in *Zablocki v. Redhail*,... if a requirement imposed by a State "significantly interferes with the exercise of a fundamental right, it cannot be upheld unless it is supported by sufficiently important state interests and is closely tailored to effectuate only those interests."

B

The starting point for our legal analysis must be whether a competent person has a constitutional right to avoid unwanted medical care. Earlier this Term, this Court held that the Due Process Clause of the Fourteenth Amendment confers a significant liberty interest in avoiding unwanted medical treatment. *Washington v. Harper....* Today, the Court concedes that our prior decisions "support the recognition of a general liberty interest in refusing medical treatment." The Court, however, avoids discussing either the measure of that liberty interest or its application by assuming, for purposes of this case only, that a competent person has a constitutionally protected liberty interest in being free of unwanted artificial nutrition and hydration. Justice O'CONNOR's opinion is less parsimonious. She openly affirms that "the Court has often deemed state incursions into the body repugnant to the interests protected by the Due Process Clause," that there is a liberty interest in avoiding unwanted medical treatment, and that it encompasses the right to be free of "artificially delivered food and water."

But if a competent person has a liberty interest to be free of unwanted medical treatment, as both the majority and Justice O'CONNOR concede, it must be fundamental. "We are dealing here with [a decision] which involves one of the basic civil rights of man." *Skinner v. Oklahoma ex rel. Williamson*,...(invalidating a statute authorizing sterilization of certain felons). Whatever other liberties protected by the Due Process Clause are fundamental, "those liberties that are 'deeply rooted in this Nation's history and tradition'" are among them. *Bowers v. Hardwick....*

The right to be free from medical attention without consent, to determine what shall be done with one's own body, is deeply rooted in this Nation's traditions, as the majority acknowledges. This right has long been "firmly entrenched in American tort law" and is securely grounded in the earliest common law.... Thus, freedom from unwanted medical attention is unquestionably among those principles "so rooted in the traditions and conscience of our people as to be ranked as fundamental." *Snyder v. Massachusetts....*

That there may be serious consequences involved in refusal of the medical treatment at issue here does not vitiate the right under our common-law tradition of medical self-determination. It is "a well-established rule of general law ...that it is the patient, not the physician, who ultimately decides if treatment-any treatment-is to be given at all....

...Nor does the fact that Nancy Cruzan is now incompetent deprive her of her fundamental rights....

As the majority recognizes, the question is not whether an incompetent has constitutional rights, but how such rights may be exercised. As we explained in *Thompson v. Oklahoma...*: "[T]he law must often adjust the manner in which it affords rights to those whose status renders them unable to exercise choice freely and rationally. Children, the insane, and those who are irreversibly ill with loss of brain function, for instance, all retain 'rights,' to be sure, but often such rights are only meaningful as they are exercised by agents acting with the best interests of their principals in mind...."

II

A

The right to be free from unwanted medical attention is a right to evaluate the potential benefit of treatment and its possible consequences according to one's own values and to make a personal decision whether to subject oneself to the intrusion....

There are also affirmative reasons why someone like Nancy might choose to forgo artificial nutrition and hydration under these circumstances. Dying is personal. And it is profound. For many, the thought of an ignoble end, steeped in decay, is abhorrent. A quiet, proud death, bodily integrity intact, is a matter of extreme consequence...."

Such conditions are, for many, humiliating to contemplate, as is visiting a prolonged and anguished vigil on one's parents, spouse, and children. A long, drawn-out death can have a debilitating effect on family members.... For some, the idea of being remembered in their persistent vegetative states rather than as they were before their illness or accident may be very disturbing.

B

Although the right to be free of unwanted medical intervention, like other constitutionally protected interests, may not be absolute, no state interest could outweigh the rights of an individual in Nancy Cruzan's position. Whatever a State's possible interests in mandating life-support treatment under other circumstances, there is no good to be obtained here by Missouri's insistence that Nancy Cruzan remain on life-support systems if it is indeed her wish not to do so. Missouri does not claim, nor could it, that society as a whole will be benefited by Nancy's receiving medical treatment.

The only state interest asserted here is a general interest in the preservation of life. But the State has no legitimate general interest in someone's life, completely abstracted from the interest of the person living that life, that could outweigh the person's choice to avoid medical treatment. "[T]he regulation of constitutionally protected decisions ...must be predicated on legitimate state concerns *other than* disagreement with the choice the individual has made.... Otherwise, the interest in liberty protected by the Due Process Clause would be a nullity...." (emphasis added). Thus, the State's general interest in life must accede to Nancy Cruzan's particularized and intense interest in self-determination in her choice of medical treatment. There is simply nothing legitimately within the State's purview to be gained by superseding her decision.

Moreover, there may be considerable danger that Missouri's rule of decision would impair rather than serve any interest the State does have in sustaining life. Current medical practice recommends use of heroic measures if there is a scintilla of a chance that the patient will recover, on the assumption that the measures will be discontinued should the patient improve....

III

This is not to say that the State has no legitimate interests to assert here. As the majority recognizes, Missouri has a *parens patriae* interest in providing Nancy Cruzan, now incompetent, with as accurate as possible a determination of how she would exercise her rights under these circumstances. Second, if and when it is determined that Nancy Cruzan would want to continue treatment, the State may legitimately assert an interest in providing that treatment. But until Nancy's wishes have been determined, the only state interest that may be asserted is an interest in safe-guarding the accuracy of that determination.

Accuracy, therefore, must be our touchstone. Missouri may constitutionally impose only those procedural requirements that serve to enhance the accuracy of a determination of Nancy Cruzan's wishes or are at least consistent with an accurate determination. The Missouri "safeguard" that the Court upholds today does not meet that standard. The determination needed in this context is whether the incompetent person would choose to live in a persistent vegetative state on life support or to avoid this medical treatment. Missouri's rule of decision imposes a markedly asymmetrical evidentiary burden. Only evidence of specific statements of treatment choice made by the patient when competent is admissible to support a finding that the patient, now in a persistent vegetative state, would wish to avoid further medical treatment. Moreover, this evidence must be clear and convincing. No proof is required to support a finding that the incompetent person would wish to continue treatment.

A

The majority offers several justifications for Missouri's heightened evidentiary standard. First, the majority explains that the State may constitutionally adopt this rule to govern determinations of an incompetent's wishes in order to advance the State's substantive interests, including its unqualified interest in the preservation of human life. Missouri's evidentiary standard, however, cannot rest on the State's own interest in a particular substantive result. To be sure, courts have long erected clear and convincing evidence standards to place the greater risk of erroneous decisions on those bringing disfavored claims. In such cases, however, the choice to discourage certain claims was a legitimate, constitutional policy choice. In contrast, Missouri has no such power to disfavor a choice by Nancy Cruzan to avoid medical treatment, because Missouri has no legitimate interest in providing Nancy with treatment until it is established that this represents her choice. Just as a State may not override Nancy's choice directly, it may not do so indirectly through the imposition of a procedural rule.

Second, the majority offers two explanations for why Missouri's clear and convincing evidence standard is a means of enhancing accuracy, but neither is persuasive....

D

Finally, I cannot agree with the majority that where it is not possible to determine what choice an incompetent patient would make, a State's role as *parens patriae* permits the State automatically to make that choice itself. See *ante,* (explaining that the Due Process Clause does not require a State to confide the decision to "anyone but the patient herself"). Under fair rules of evidence, it is improbable that a court could not determine what the patient's choice would be. Under the rule of decision adopted by Missouri and upheld today by this Court, such occasions might be numerous. But in neither case does it follow that it is constitutionally acceptable for the State invariably to assume the role of deciding for the patient. A State's legitimate interest in safeguarding a patient's choice cannot be furthered by simply appropriating it....

I respectfully dissent.

Justice STEVENS, dissenting....

WASHINGTON v. GLUCKSBERG
117 S.Ct. 2258 (1997)

Several doctors and terminally ill patients challenged Washington State's ban on assisted-suicide, claiming it violated the right, protected by the due process clause, of a mentally competent, terminally ill adult to commit physician-assisted suicide. The District Court held that the State's ban was unconstitutional because it placed an "undue burden" on the exercise of a constitutional right. The appeals court affirmed the District Court's opinion. This case was decided with its companion case, Vacco v. Quill, *(see below, Chapter XIII) which presented an equal protection challenge to New York's ban on assisted suicide.*

Chief Justice REHNQUIST delivered the opinion of the Court.

The question presented in this case is whether Washington's prohibition against "caus[ing]" or "aid[ing]" a suicide offends the Fourteenth Amendment to the United States Constitution. We hold that it does not....

I

We begin, as we do in all due-process cases, by examining our Nation's history, legal traditions, and practices.... In almost every State indeed, in almost every western democracy it is a crime to assist a suicide. The States' assisted-suicide bans are not innovations. Rather, they are longstanding expressions of the States' commitment to the protection and preservation of all human life.... Indeed, opposition to and condemnation of suicide and, therefore, of assisting suicide are consistent and enduring themes of our philosophical, legal, and cultural heritages....

More specifically, for over 700 years, the Anglo-American common-law tradition has punished or otherwise disapproved of both suicide and assisting suicide....

For the most part, the early American colonies adopted the common-law approach. For example, the legislators of the Providence Plantations, which would later become Rhode Island, declared, in 1647, that " [s]elf-murder is by all agreed to be the most unnatural, and it is by this present Assembly declared, to be that, wherein he that doth it, kills himself out of a premeditated hatred against his own life or other humor :... his goods and chattels are the king's custom, but not his debts nor lands; but in case he be an infant, a lunatic, mad or distracted man, he forfeits nothing...."

Over time, however, the American colonies abolished these harsh common-law penalties. William Penn abandoned the criminal-forfeiture sanction in Pennsylvania in 1701, and the other colonies (and later, the other States) eventually followed this example....

...[T]he movement away from the common law's harsh sanctions did not represent an acceptance of suicide; rather, as Chief Justice Swift observed, this change reflected the growing consensus that it was unfair to punish the suicide's family for his wrongdoing....

That suicide remained a grievous, though nonfelonious, wrong is confirmed by the fact that colonial and early state legislatures and courts did not retreat from prohibiting assisting suicide. Swift, in his early 19th century treatise on the laws of Connecticut, stated that " [i]f one counsels another to commit suicide, and the other by reason of the advice kills himself, the advisor is guilty of murder as principal...." This was the well established common-law view,... as was the similar principle that the consent of a homicide victim is "wholly immaterial to the guilt of the person who cause[d] [his death],"... And the prohibitions against assisting suicide never contained exceptions for those who were near death. Rather, "[t]he life of those to whom life ha[d] become a burden of those who [were] hopelessly diseased or fatally wounded nay, even the lives of criminals condemned to death, [were] under the protection of law, equally as the lives of those who [were] in the full tide of life's enjoyment, and anxious to continue to live...."

The earliest American statute explicitly to outlaw assisting suicide was enacted in New York in 1828,... and many of the new States and Territories followed New York's example.... By the time the Fourteenth Amendment was ratified, it was a crime in most States to assist a suicide.... In this century, the Model Penal Code also prohibited "aiding" suicide, prompting many States to enact or revise their assisted-suicide bans. The Code's drafters observed that "the interests in the sanctity of life that are represented by the criminal homicide laws are threatened by one who expresses a willingness to participate in taking the life of another, even though the act may be accomplished with the consent, or at the request, of the suicide victim...."

Though deeply rooted, the States' assisted-suicide bans have in recent years been reexamined and, generally, reaffirmed. Because of advances in medicine and technology, Americans today are increasingly likely to die in institutions, from chronic illnesses.... Public concern and democratic action are therefore sharply focused on how best to protect dignity and independence at the end of life, with the result that there have been many significant changes in state laws and in the attitudes these laws reflect. Many States, for example, now permit " living wills," surrogate health-care decisionmaking, and the withdrawal or refusal of life-sustaining medical treatment.... At the same time, however, voters and legislators continue for the most part to reaffirm their States' prohibitions on assisting suicide.

The Washington statute at issue in this case,... was enacted in 1975 as part of a revision of that State's criminal code. Four years later, Washington passed its Natural Death Act, which specifically stated that the "withholding or withdrawal of life-sustaining treatment ... shall not, for any purpose, constitute a suicide" and that "[n]othing in this chapter shall be construed to condone, authorize, or approve mercy killing ...." In 1991, Washington voters rejected a ballot initiative which, had it passed, would have permitted a form of physician-assisted suicide. Washington then added a provision to the Natural Death Act expressly excluding physician-assisted suicide....

California voters rejected an assisted-suicide initiative similar to Washington's in 1993. On the other hand, in 1994, voters in Oregon enacted, also through ballot initiative, that State's "Death With Dignity Act," which legalized physician-assisted suicide for competent, terminally ill adults. Since the Oregon vote, many proposals to legalize assisted-suicide have been and continue to be introduced in the States' legislatures, but none has been enacted. And just last year, Iowa and Rhode Island joined the overwhelming majority of States explicitly prohibiting assisted suicide.... Also, on April 30, 1997, President Clinton signed the Federal Assisted Suicide Funding Restriction Act of 1997, which prohibits the use of federal funds in support of physician-assisted suicide....

Thus, the States are currently engaged in serious, thoughtful examinations of physician-assisted suicide and other similar issues....

Attitudes toward suicide itself have changed since Bracton, but our laws have consistently condemned, and continue to prohibit, assisting suicide. Despite changes in medical technology and notwithstanding an increased emphasis on the importance of end-of-life decisionmaking, we have not retreated from this prohibition. Against this backdrop of history, tradition, and practice, we now turn to respondents' constitutional claim.

II

The Due Process Clause guarantees more than fair process, and the "liberty" it protects includes more than the absence of physical restraint.... The Clause also provides heightened protection against government interference with certain fundamental rights and liberty interests.... In a long line of cases, we have held that, in addition to the specific freedoms protected by the Bill of Rights, the "liberty" specially protected by the Due Process Clause includes the rights to marry, *Loving v. Virginia*...; to have children, *Skinner v. Oklahoma ex rel. Williamson*...; to direct the education and upbringing of one's children, *Meyer v. Nebraska*...; *Pierce v. Society of Sisters*...; to marital privacy, *Griswold v. Connecticut*...; to use contraception, *ibid*; *Eisenstadt v. Baird*...; to bodily integrity, *Rochin v. California*...; and to abortion, *Casey*. We have also assumed, and strongly suggested, that the Due Process Clause protects the traditional right to refuse unwanted lifesaving medical treatment. *Cruzan*....

But we "ha[ve] always been reluctant to expand the concept of substantive due process because guideposts for responsible decisionmaking in this unchartered area are scarce and open-ended." *Collins*.... By extending constitutional protection to an asserted right or liberty interest, we, to a great extent, place the matter outside the arena of public debate and legislative action. We must therefore "exercise the utmost care whenever we are asked to break new ground in this field," lest the liberty protected by the Due Process Clause be subtly transformed into the policy preferences of the members of this Court....

Our established method of substantive-due-process analysis has two primary features: First, we have regularly observed that the Due Process Clause specially protects those fundamental rights and liberties which are, objectively, "deeply rooted in this Nation's history and tradition," ... ("so rooted in the traditions and conscience of our people as to be ranked as fundamental"), and "implicit in the concept of ordered liberty," such that "neither liberty nor justice would exist if they were sacrificed," *Palko v. Connecticut*.... Second, we have required in substantive-due-process cases a "careful description" of the asserted fundamental liberty interest. *Flores*...; *Collins*...; *Cruzan*.... Our Nation's history, legal traditions, and practices thus provide the crucial "guideposts for responsible decisionmaking," *Collins*,... that direct and restrain our exposition of the Due Process Clause. As we stated recently in *Flores*, the Fourteenth Amendment "forbids the government to infringe ... "'fundamental' liberty interests at all, no matter what process is provided, unless the infringement is narrowly tailored to serve a compelling state interest...."

Justice SOUTER, relying on Justice Harlan's dissenting opinion in *Poe v. Ullman*, would largely abandon this restrained methodology, and instead ask "whether [Washington's] statute sets up one of those 'arbitrary impositions' or 'purposeless restraints' at odds with the Due Process Clause of the Fourteenth Amendment...." In our view, however, the development of this Court's substantive-due-process jurisprudence, described briefly above, has been a process whereby the outlines of the "liberty" specially protected by the Fourteenth Amendment never fully clarified, to be sure, and perhaps not capable of being fully clarified have at least been carefully refined by concrete examples involving fundamental rights found to be deeply rooted in our legal tradition. This approach tends to rein in the subjective elements that are necessarily present in due-process judicial review. In addition, by establishing a threshold requirement that a challenged state action implicate a fundamental right before requiring more than a reasonable relation to a legitimate state interest to justify the action, it avoids the need for complex balancing of competing interests in every case.

Turning to the claim at issue here, the Court of Appeals stated that "[p]roperly analyzed, the first issue to be resolved is whether there is a liberty interest in determining the time and manner of one's death," or, in other words, "[i]s there a right to die?" Similarly, respondents assert a "liberty to choose how to die" and a right to "control of one's final days," and describe the asserted liberty as "the right to choose a humane, dignified death," and "the liberty to shape death." As noted above, we have a tradition of carefully formulating the interest at stake in substantive-due-process cases. For example, although *Cruzan* is often described as a "right to die" case,... we were, in fact, more precise: we assumed that the Constitution granted competent persons a "constitutionally protected right to refuse lifesaving hydration and nutrition...." The Washington statute at issue in this case prohibits "aid[ing] another person to attempt suicide," ... and, thus, the question before us is whether the "liberty" specially protected by the Due Process Clause includes a right to commit suicide which itself includes a right to assistance in doing so.

We now inquire whether this asserted right has any place in our Nation's traditions. Here, as discussed above,... we are confronted with a consistent and almost universal tradition that has long rejected the asserted right, and continues explicitly to reject it today, even for terminally ill, mentally competent adults. To hold for respondents, we would have to reverse centuries of legal doctrine and practice, and strike down the considered policy choice of almost every State. See *Jackman v. Rosenbaum Co.*,... ("If a thing has been practiced for two hundred years by common consent, it will need a strong case for the Fourteenth Amendment to affect it"); *Flores*,... ("The mere novelty of such a claim is reason enough to doubt that 'substantive due process' sustains it").

Respondents contend, however, that the liberty interest they assert is consistent with this Court's substantive-due-process line of cases, if not with this Nation's history and practice. Pointing to *Casey* and *Cruzan*, respondents read our jurisprudence in this area as reflecting a general tradition of "self-sovereignty,"... and as teaching that the "liberty" protected by the Due Process Clause includes "basic and intimate exercises of personal autonomy,"... ("It is a promise of the Constitution that there is a realm of personal liberty which the government may not enter"). According to respondents, our liberty jurisprudence, and the broad, individualistic principles it reflects, protects the "liberty of competent, terminally ill adults to make end-of-life decisions free of undue government interference...." The question presented in this case, however, is whether the protections of the Due Process Clause include a right to commit suicide with another's assistance. With this "careful description" of respondents' claim in mind, we turn to *Casey* and *Cruzan*.

In *Cruzan*, we considered whether Nancy Beth Cruzan, who had been severely injured in an automobile accident and was in a persistive vegetative state, "ha[d] a right under the United States Constitution which would require the hospital to withdraw life-sustaining treatment" at her parents' request.... We began with the observation that "[a]t common law, even the touching of one person by another without consent and without legal justification was a battery."

We then discussed the related rule that "informed consent is generally required for medical treatment." After reviewing a long line of relevant state cases, we concluded that "the common-law doctrine of informed consent is viewed as generally encompassing the right of a competent individual to refuse medical treatment." Next, we reviewed our own cases on the subject, and stated that "[t]he principle that a competent person has a constitutionally protected liberty interest in refusing unwanted medical treatment may be inferred from our prior decisions...." Therefore, "for purposes of [that] case, we assume[d] that the United States Constitution would grant a competent person a constitutionally protected right to refuse lifesaving hydration and nutrition...." We concluded that, notwithstanding this right, the Constitution permitted Missouri to require clear and convincing evidence of an incompetent patient's wishes concerning the withdrawal of life-sustaining treatment....

Respondents contend that in *Cruzan* we "acknowledged that competent, dying persons have the right to direct the removal of life-sustaining medical treatment and thus hasten death,"... and that "the constitutional principle behind recognizing the patient's liberty to direct the withdrawal of artificial life support applies at least as strongly to the choice to hasten impending death by consuming lethal medication...." Similarly, the Court of Appeals concluded that "*Cruzan*, by recognizing a liberty interest that includes the refusal of artificial provision of life-sustaining food and water, necessarily recognize[d] a liberty interest in hastening one's own death...."

The right assumed in *Cruzan*, however, was not simply deduced from abstract concepts of personal autonomy. Given the common-law rule that forced medication was a battery, and the long legal tradition protecting the decision to refuse unwanted medical treatment, our assumption was entirely consistent with this Nation's history and constitutional traditions. The decision to commit suicide with the assistance of another may be just as personal and profound as the decision to refuse unwanted medical treatment, but it has never enjoyed similar legal protection. Indeed, the two acts are widely and reasonably regarded as quite distinct.... In *Cruzan* itself, we recognized that most States outlawed assisted suicide and even more do today and we certainly gave no intimation that the right to refuse unwanted medical treatment could be somehow transmuted into a right to assistance in committing suicide....

Respondents also rely on *Casey*. There, the Court's opinion concluded that "the essential holding of *Roe v. Wade* should be retained and once again reaffirmed...." We held, first, that a woman has a right, before her fetus is viable, to an abortion "without undue interference from the State;" second, that States may restrict post-viability abortions, so long as exceptions are made to protect a woman's life and health; and third, that the State has legitimate interests throughout a pregnancy in protecting the health of the woman and the life of the unborn child. In reaching this conclusion, the opinion discussed in some detail this Court's substantive-due-process tradition of interpreting the Due Process Clause to protect certain fundamental rights and "personal decisions relating to marriage, procreation, contraception, family relationships, child rearing, and education," and noted that many of those rights and liberties "involv[e] the most intimate and personal choices a person may make in a lifetime...."

The Court of Appeals, like the District Court, found *Casey* "'highly instructive'" and "'almost prescriptive'" for determining "'what liberty interest may inhere in a terminally ill person's choice to commit suicide'":

> "Like the decision of whether or not to have an abortion, the decision how and when to die is one of 'the most intimate and personal choices a person may make in a lifetime,' a choice 'central to personal dignity and autonomy....'"

Similarly, respondents emphasize the statement in *Casey* that:

> "At the heart of liberty is the right to define one's own concept of existence, of meaning, of the universe, and of the mystery of human life. Beliefs about these matters could not define the attributes of personhood were they formed under compulsion of the State...."

By choosing this language, the Court's opinion in *Casey* described, in a general way and in light of our prior cases, those personal activities and decisions that this Court has identified as so deeply rooted in our history and traditions, or so fundamental to our concept of constitutionally ordered liberty, that they are protected by the Fourteenth Amendment. The opinion moved from the recognition that liberty necessarily includes freedom of conscience and belief about ultimate considerations to the observation that "though the abortion decision may originate within the zone of conscience and belief, it is *more than a philosophic exercise....*" (emphasis added). That many of the rights and liberties protected by the Due Process Clause sound in personal autonomy does not warrant the sweeping conclusion that any and all important, intimate, and personal decisions are so protected,... and *Casey* did not suggest otherwise.

The history of the law's treatment of assisted suicide in this country has been and continues to be one of the rejection of nearly all efforts to permit it. That being the case, our decisions lead us to conclude that the asserted "right" to assistance in committing suicide is not a fundamental liberty interest protected by the Due Process Clause. The Constitution also requires, however, that Washington's assisted-suicide ban be rationally related to legitimate government interests.... This requirement is unquestionably met here....

First, Washington has an "unqualified interest in the preservation of human life...." The State's prohibition on assisted suicide, like all homicide laws, both reflects and advances its commitment to this interest.... This interest is symbolic and aspirational as well as practical....

Relatedly, all admit that suicide is a serious public-health problem, especially among persons in otherwise vulnerable groups.... The State has an interest in preventing suicide, and in studying, identifying, and treating its causes....

Those who attempt suicide terminally ill or not often suffer from depression or other mental disorders.... Research indicates, however, that many people who request physician-assisted suicide withdraw that request if their depression and pain are treated.... The New York Task Force, however, expressed its concern that, because depression is difficult to diagnose, physicians and medical professionals often fail to respond adequately to seriously ill patients' needs. Thus, legal physician-assisted suicide could make it more difficult for the State to protect depressed or mentally ill persons, or those who are suffering from untreated pain, from suicidal impulses.

The State also has an interest in protecting the integrity and ethics of the medical profession.... And physician-assisted suicide could, it is argued, undermine the trust that is essential to the doctor-patient relationship by blurring the time-honored line between healing and harming....

Next, the State has an interest in protecting vulnerable groups including the poor, the elderly, and disabled persons from abuse, neglect, and mistakes. The Court of Appeals dismissed the State's concern that disadvantaged persons might be pressured into physician-assisted suicide as "ludicrous on its face." We have recognized, however, the real risk of subtle coercion and undue influence in end-of-life situations. *Cruzan*.... If physician-assisted suicide were permitted, many might resort to it to spare their families the substantial financial burden of end-of-life health-care costs.

The State's interest here goes beyond protecting the vulnerable from coercion; it extends to protecting disabled and terminally ill people from prejudice, negative and inaccurate stereotypes, and "societal indifference...." The State's assisted-suicide ban reflects and reinforces its policy that the lives of terminally ill, disabled, and elderly people must be no less valued than the lives of the young and healthy, and that a seriously disabled person's suicidal impulses should be interpreted and treated the same way as anyone else's....

Finally, the State may fear that permitting assisted suicide will start it down the path to voluntary and perhaps even involuntary euthanasia. The Court of Appeals struck down Washington's assisted-suicide ban only "as applied to competent, terminally ill adults who wish to hasten their deaths by obtaining medication prescribed by their doctors...." Washington insists, however, that the impact of the court's decision will not and cannot be so limited.... If suicide is protected as a matter of constitutional right, it is argued, "every man and woman in the United States must enjoy it...." The Court of Appeals' decision, and its expansive reasoning, provide ample support for the State's concerns. The court noted, for example, that the "decision of a duly appointed surrogate decision maker is for all legal purposes the decision of the patient himself,"... that "in some instances, the patient may be unable to self-administer the drugs and ... administration by the physician ... may be the only way the patient may be able to receive them," and that not only physicians, but also family members and loved ones, will inevitably participate in assisting suicide.... Thus, it turns out that what is couched as a limited right to "physician-assisted suicide" is likely, in effect, a much broader license, which could prove extremely difficult to police and contain. Washington's ban on assisting suicide prevents such erosion....

Throughout the Nation, Americans are engaged in an earnest and profound debate about the morality, legality, and practicality of physician-assisted suicide. Our holding permits this debate to continue, as it should in a democratic society. The decision of the en banc Court of Appeals is reversed, and the case is remanded for further proceedings consistent with this opinion.

It is so ordered.

Justice SOUTER, concurring in the judgment....

Justice O'CONNOR, concurring. Justice GINSBURG concurs in the Court's judgments substantially for the reasons stated in this opinion. Justice BREYER joins this opinion except insofar as it joins the opinions of the Court.

Death will be different for each of us. For many, the last days will be spent in physical pain and perhaps the despair that accompanies physical deterioration and a loss of control of basic bodily and mental functions. Some will seek medication to alleviate that pain and other symptoms.

The Court frames the issue in this case as whether the Due Process Clause of the Constitution protects a "right to commit suicide which itself includes a right to assistance in doing so," and concludes that our Nation's history, legal traditions, and practices do not support the existence of such a right. I join the Court's opinions because I agree that there is no generalized right to "commit suicide." But respondents urge us to address the narrower question whether a mentally competent person who is experiencing great suffering has a constitutionally cognizable interest in controlling the circumstances of his or her imminent death. I see no need to reach that question in the context of the facial challenges to the New York and Washington laws at issue here.... ("The Washington statute at issue in this case prohibits 'aid[ing] another person to attempt suicide,'... and, thus, the question before us is whether the 'liberty' specially protected by the Due Process Clause includes a right to commit suicide which itself includes a right to assistance in doing so"). The parties and *amici* agree that in these States a patient who is suffering from a terminal illness and who is experiencing great pain has no legal barriers to obtaining medication, from qualified physicians, to alleviate that suffering, even to the point of causing unconsciousness and hastening death.... In this light, even assuming that we would recognize such an interest, I agree that the State's interests in protecting those who are not truly competent or facing imminent death, or those whose decisions to hasten death would not truly be voluntary, are sufficiently weighty to justify a prohibition against physician-assisted suicide.... (STEVENS, J., concurring in judgments ... (SOUTER, J., concurring in judgment).

Every one of us at some point may be affected by our own or a family member's terminal illness. There is no reason to think the democratic process will not strike the proper balance between the interests of terminally ill, mentally competent individuals who would seek to end their suffering and the State's interests in protecting those who might seek to end life mistakenly or under pressure. As the Court recognizes, States are presently undertaking extensive and serious evaluation of physician-assisted suicide and other related issues.... (SOUTER, J., concurring in judgment). In such circumstances, "the ... challenging task of crafting appropriate procedures for safeguarding ... liberty interests is entrusted to the "laboratory' of the States ... in the first instance."...

In sum, there is no need to address the question whether suffering patients have a constitutionally cognizable interest in obtaining relief from the suffering that they may experience in the last days of their lives. There is no dispute that dying patients in Washington and New York can obtain palliative care, even when doing so would hasten their deaths. The difficulty in defining terminal illness and the risk that a dying patient's request for assistance in ending his or her life might not be truly voluntary justifies the prohibitions on assisted suicide we uphold here.

Justice STEVENS, concurring in the judgments.

The Court ends its opinion with the important observation that our holding today is fully consistent with a continuation of the vigorous debate about the "morality, legality, and practicality of physician-assisted suicide" in a democratic society.... I write separately to make it clear that there is also room for further debate about the limits that the Constitution places on the power of the States to punish the practice.

I

The morality, legality, and practicality of capital punishment have been the subject of debate for many years. In 1976, this Court upheld the constitutionality of the practice in cases coming to us from Georgia, Florida, and Texas. In those cases we concluded that a State does have the power to place a lesser value on some lives than on others; there is no absolute requirement that a State treat all human life as having an equal right to preservation. Because the state legislatures had sufficiently narrowed the category of lives that the State could terminate, and had enacted special procedures to ensure that the defendant belonged in that limited category, we concluded that the statutes were not unconstitutional on their face. In later cases coming to us from each of those States, however, we found that some applications of the statutes were unconstitutional.

Today, the Court decides that Washington's statute prohibiting assisted suicide is not invalid "on its face," that is to say, in all or most cases in which it might be applied. That holding, however, does not foreclose the possibility that some applications of the statute might well be invalid.

As originally filed, this case presented a challenge to the Washington statute on its face and as it applied to three terminally ill, mentally competent patients and to four physicians who treat terminally ill patients. After the District

Court issued its opinion holding that the statute placed an undue burden on the right to commit physician-assisted suicide,... the three patients died. Although the Court of Appeals considered the constitutionality of the statute "as applied to the prescription of life-ending medication for use by terminally ill, competent adult patients who wish to hasten their deaths,"... the court did not have before it any individual plaintiff seeking to hasten her death or any doctor who was threatened with prosecution for assisting in the suicide of a particular patient; its analysis and eventual holding that the statute was unconstitutional was not limited to a particular set of plaintiffs before it.

The appropriate standard to be applied in cases making facial challenges to state statutes has been the subject of debate within this Court.... Upholding the validity of the federal Bail Reform Act of 1984, the Court stated in *United States v. Salerno*,... (1987), that a "facial challenge to a legislative Act is, of course, the most difficult challenge to mount successfully, since the challenger must establish that no set of circumstances exists under which the Act would be valid."... I do not believe the Court has ever actually applied such a strict standard, even in *Salerno* itself, and the Court does not appear to apply *Salerno* here. Nevertheless, the Court does conceive of respondents' claim as a facial challenge addressing not the application of the statute to a particular set of plaintiffs before it, but the constitutionality of the statute's categorical prohibition against "aid[ing] another person to attempt suicide."... Accordingly, the Court requires the plaintiffs to show that the interest in liberty protected by the Fourteenth Amendment " includes a right to commit suicide which itself includes a right to assistance in doing so."...

History and tradition provide ample support for refusing to recognize an open-ended constitutional right to commit suicide. Much more than the State's paternalistic interest in protecting the individual from the irrevocable consequences of an ill-advised decision motivated by temporary concerns is at stake. There is truth in John Donne's observation that "No man is an island." The State has an interest in preserving and fostering the benefits that every human being may provide to the community a community that thrives on the exchange of ideas, expressions of affection, shared memories and humorous incidents as well as on the material contributions that its members create and support. The value to others of a person's life is far too precious to allow the individual to claim a constitutional entitlement to complete autonomy in making a decision to end that life. Thus, I fully agree with the Court that the "liberty" protected by the Due Process Clause does not include a categorical "right to commit suicide which itself includes a right to assistance in doing so."...

But just as our conclusion that capital punishment is not always unconstitutional did not preclude later decisions holding that it is sometimes impermissibly cruel, so is it equally clear that a decision upholding a general statutory prohibition of assisted suicide does not mean that every possible application of the statute would be valid. A State, like Washington, that has authorized the death penalty and thereby has concluded that the sanctity of human life does not require that it always be preserved, must acknowledge that there are situations in which an interest in hastening death is legitimate. Indeed, not only is that interest sometimes legitimate, I am also convinced that there are times when it is entitled to constitutional protection.

II

In *Cruzan v. Director, Mo. Dept. of Health*,... (1990), the Court assumed that the interest in liberty protected by the Fourteenth Amendment encompassed the right of a terminally ill patient to direct the withdrawal of life-sustaining treatment. As the Court correctly observes today, that assumption "was not simply deduced from abstract concepts of personal autonomy."... Instead, it was supported by the common-law tradition protecting the individual's general right to refuse unwanted medical treatment. We have recognized, however, that this common-law right to refuse treatment is neither absolute nor always sufficiently weighty to overcome valid countervailing state interests. As Justice Brennan pointed out in his *Cruzan* dissent, we have upheld legislation imposing punishment on persons refusing to be vaccinated,... citing *Jacobson v. Massachusetts*,... (1905), and as Justice SCALIA pointed out in his concurrence, the State ordinarily has the right to interfere with an attempt to commit suicide by, for example, forcibly placing a bandage on a self-inflicted wound to stop the flow of blood.... In most cases, the individual's constitutionally protected interest in his or her own physical autonomy, including the right to refuse unwanted medical treatment, will give way to the State's interest in preserving human life.

Cruzan, however, was not the normal case. Given the irreversible nature of her illness and the progressive character of her suffering, Nancy Cruzan's interest in refusing medical care was incidental to her more basic interest in controlling the manner and timing of her death. In finding that her best interests would be served by cutting off the nourishment that kept her alive, the trial court did more than simply vindicate Cruzan's interest in refusing medical treatment; the court, in essence, authorized affirmative conduct that would hasten her death. When this Court reviewed the case and upheld Missouri's requirement that there be clear and convincing evidence establishing Nancy Cruzan's intent to have life-sustaining nourishment withdrawn, it made two important assumptions: (1) that there was a "liberty interest" in refusing unwanted treatment protected by the Due Process Clause; and (2) that this liberty interest did not "end the inquiry" because it might be outweighed by relevant state interests.... I agree with both of those assumptions, but I insist that the source of Nancy Cruzan's right to refuse treatment was not just a common-law rule. Rather, this right is an aspect of a far broader and more basic concept of freedom that is even older than the common law. This freedom embraces, not merely a person's right to refuse a particular kind of unwanted treatment, but also her interest in dignity, and in determining the character of the memories that will survive long after her death. In recognizing that the State's interests did not outweigh Nancy Cruzan's liberty interest in refusing medical treatment, *Cruzan* rested not simply on the common-law right to refuse medical treatment, but at least implicitly on the even more fundamental right to make this "deeply personal decision...." (O'CONNOR, J., concurring).

Thus, the common-law right to protection from battery, which included the right to refuse medical treatment in most circumstances, did not mark "the outer limits of the substantive sphere of liberty" that supported the Cruzan family's decision to hasten Nancy's death. *Planned Parenthood of Southeastern Pa. v. Casey*,... (1992). Those limits have never been precisely defined. They are generally identified by the importance and character of the decision confronted by the individual, *Whalen v. Roe*,... (1977). Whatever the outer limits of the concept may be, it definitely includes protection for matters "central to personal dignity and autonomy." *Casey*.... It includes,

> "the individual's right to make certain unusually important decisions that will affect his own, or his family's, destiny. The Court has referred to such decisions as implicating 'basic values,' as being 'fundamental,' and as being dignified by history and tradition. The character of the Court's language in these cases brings to mind the origins of the American heritage of freedom the abiding interest in individual liberty that makes certain state intrusions on the citizen's right to decide how he will live his own life intolerable." *Fitzgerald v. Porter Memorial Hospital*....

The *Cruzan* case demonstrated that some state intrusions on the right to decide how death will be encountered are also intolerable. The now-deceased plaintiffs in this action may in fact have had a liberty interest even stronger than Nancy Cruzan's because, not only were they terminally ill, they were suffering constant and severe pain. Avoiding intolerable pain and the indignity of living one's final days incapacitated and in agony is certainly "[a]t the heart of [the] liberty ... to define one's own concept of existence, of meaning, of the universe, and of the mystery of human life." *Casey*,...

While I agree with the Court that *Cruzan* does not decide the issue presented by these cases, *Cruzan* did give recognition, not just to vague, unbridled notions of autonomy, but to the more specific interest in making decisions about how to confront an imminent death. Although there is no absolute right to physician-assisted suicide, *Cruzan* makes it clear that some individuals who no longer have the option of deciding whether to live or to die because they are already on the threshold of death have a constitutionally protected interest that may outweigh the State's interest in preserving life at all costs. The liberty interest at stake in a case like this differs from, and is stronger than, both the common-law right to refuse medical treatment and the unbridled interest in deciding whether to live or die. It is an interest in deciding how, rather than whether, a critical threshold shall be crossed.

III

The state interests supporting a general rule banning the practice of physician-assisted suicide do not have the same force in all cases. First and foremost of these interests is the "'unqualified interest in the preservation of human life,'"... That interest not only justifies it commands maximum protection of every individual's interest in remaining alive, which in turn commands the same protection for decisions about whether to commence or to terminate life-support systems or to administer pain medication that may hasten death. Properly viewed, however, this interest is not a collective interest that should always outweigh the interests of a person who because of pain, incapacity, or sedation finds her life intolerable, but rather, an aspect of individual freedom.

Many terminally ill people find their lives meaningful even if filled with pain or dependence on others. Some find value in living through suffering; some have an abiding desire to witness particular events in their families' lives; many believe it a sin to hasten death. Individuals of different religious faiths make different judgments and choices about whether to live on under such circumstances. There are those who will want to continue aggressive treatment; those who would prefer terminal sedation; and those who will seek withdrawal from life-support systems and death by gradual starvation and dehydration. Although as a general matter the State's interest in the contributions each person may make to society outweighs the person's interest in ending her life, this interest does not have the same force for a terminally ill patient faced not with the choice of whether to live, only of how to die. Allowing the individual, rather than the State, to make judgments "about the 'quality' of life that a particular individual may enjoy...." does not mean that the lives of terminally-ill, disabled people have less value than the lives of those who are healthy.... Rather, it gives proper recognition to the individual's interest in choosing a final chapter that accords with her life story, rather than one that demeans her values and poisons memories of her....

Similarly, the State's legitimate interests in preventing suicide, protecting the vulnerable from coercion and abuse, and preventing euthanasia are less significant in this context. I agree that the State has a compelling interest in preventing persons from committing suicide because of depression, or coercion by third parties. But the State's legitimate interest in preventing abuse does not apply to an individual who is not victimized by abuse, who is not suffering from depression, and who makes a rational and voluntary decision to seek assistance in dying. Although, as the New York Task Force report discusses, diagnosing depression and other mental illness is not always easy, mental health workers and other professionals expert in working with dying patients can help patients cope with depression and pain, and help patients assess their options....

Relatedly, the State and amici express the concern that patients whose physical pain is inadequately treated will be more likely to request assisted suicide. Encouraging the development and ensuring the availability of adequate pain treatment is of utmost importance; palliative care, however, cannot alleviate all pain and suffering.... An individual adequately informed of the care alternatives thus might make a rational choice for assisted suicide. For such an individual, the State's interest in preventing potential abuse and mistake is only minimally implicated.

The final major interest asserted by the State is its interest in preserving the traditional integrity of the medical profession. The fear is that a rule permitting physicians to assist in suicide is inconsistent with the perception that they serve their patients solely as healers. But for some patients, it would be a physician's refusal to dispense medication to ease their suffering and make their death tolerable and dignified that would be inconsistent with the healing role... For doctors who have long-standing relationships with their patients, who have given their patients advice on alternative treatments, who are attentive to their patient's individualized needs, and who are knowledgeable about pain symptom management and palliative care options,... heeding a patient's desire to assist in her suicide would not serve to harm the physician-patient relationship. Furthermore, because physicians are already involved in making decisions that hasten the death of terminally ill patients through termination of life support, withholding of medical treatment, and terminal sedation there is in fact significant tension between the traditional view of the physician's role and the actual practice in a growing number of cases.

As the New York State Task Force on Life and the Law recognized, a State's prohibition of assisted suicide is justified by the fact that the "ideal" case in which "patients would be screened for depression and offered treatment, effective pain medication would be available, and all patients would have a supportive committed family and doctor" is not the usual case.... Although, as the Court concludes today, these potential harms are sufficient to support the State's general public policy against assisted suicide, they will not always outweigh the individual liberty interest of a particular patient. Unlike the Court of Appeals, I would not say as a categorical matter that these state interests are invalid as to the entire class of terminally ill, mentally competent patients. I do not, however, foreclose the possibility that an individual plaintiff seeking to hasten her death, or a doctor whose assistance was sought, could prevail in a more particularized challenge. Future cases will determine whether such a challenge may succeed.

IV

In New York, a doctor must respect a competent person's decision to refuse or to discontinue medical treatment even though death will thereby ensue, but the same doctor would be guilty of a felony if she provided her patient assistance in committing suicide. Today we hold that the Equal Protection Clause is not violated by the resulting disparate treatment of two classes of terminally ill people who may have the same interest in hastening death. I agree that the distinction between permitting death to ensue from an underlying fatal disease and causing it to occur by the administration of medication or other means provides a constitutionally sufficient basis for the State's classification. Unlike the Court, however, I am not persuaded that in all cases there will in fact be a significant difference between the intent of the physicians, the patients or the families in the two situations.

There may be little distinction between the intent of a terminally-ill patient who decides to remove her life-support and one who seeks the assistance of a doctor in ending her life; in both situations, the patient is seeking to hasten a certain, impending death. The doctor's intent might also be the same in prescribing lethal medication as it is in terminating life support. A doctor who fails to administer medical treatment to one who is dying from a disease could be doing so with an intent to harm or kill that patient. Conversely, a doctor who prescribes lethal medication does not necessarily intend the patient's death rather that doctor may seek simply to ease the patient's suffering and to comply with her wishes. The illusory character of any differences in intent or causation is confirmed by the fact that the American Medical Association unequivocally endorses the practice of terminal sedation the administration of sufficient dosages of pain-killing medication to terminally ill patients to protect them from excruciating pain even when it is clear that the time of death will be advanced. The purpose of terminal sedation is to ease the suffering of the patient and comply with her wishes, and the actual cause of death is the administration of heavy doses of lethal sedatives. This same intent and causation may exist when a doctor complies with a patient's request for lethal medication to hasten her death.

Thus, although the differences the majority notes in causation and intent between terminating life-support and assisting in suicide support the Court's rejection of the respondents' facial challenge, these distinctions may be inapplicable to particular terminally ill patients and their doctors. Our holding today in *Vacco v. Quill* that the Equal Protection Clause is not violated by New York's classification, just like our holding in *Washington v. Glucksberg* that the Washington statute is not invalid on its face, does not foreclose the possibility that some applications of the New York statute may impose an intolerable intrusion on the patient's freedom.

There remains room for vigorous debate about the outcome of particular cases that are not necessarily resolved by the opinions announced today. How such cases may be decided will depend on their specific facts. In my judgment, however, it is clear that the so-called "unqualified interest in the preservation of human life," *Cruzan,... Glucksberg,...* is not itself sufficient to outweigh the interest in liberty that may justify the only possible means of preserving a dying patient's dignity and alleviating her intolerable suffering.

Justice GINSBURG, concurring in the judgments.

I concur in the Court's judgments in these cases substantially for the reasons stated by Justice O'CONNOR in her concurring opinion.

Justice BREYER, concurring in the judgments.

I believe that Justice O'CONNOR'S views, which I share, have greater legal significance than the Court's opinion suggests. I join her separate opinion, except insofar as it joins the majority. And I concur in the judgments. I shall briefly explain how I differ from the Court.

I agree with the Court in *Vacco v. Quill,* that the articulated state interests justify the distinction drawn between physician assisted suicide and withdrawal of life-support. I also agree with the Court that the critical question in both of the cases before us is whether "the 'liberty' specially protected by the Due Process Clause includes a right" of the sort that the respondents assert. *Washington v. Glucksberg....* I do not agree, however, with the Court's formulation of that claimed "liberty" interest. The Court describes it as a "right to commit suicide with another's assistance."... But I would not reject the respondents' claim without considering a different formulation, for which our legal tradition may provide greater support. That formulation would use words roughly like a "right to die with dignity." But irrespective of the exact words used, at its core would lie personal control over the manner of death, professional medical assistance, and the avoidance of unnecessary and severe physical suffering combined.

As Justice SOUTER points out,... Justice Harlan's dissenting opinion in *Poe v. Ullman,...* (1961), offers some support for such a claim. In that opinion, Justice Harlan referred to the "liberty" that the Fourteenth Amendment protects as including "a freedom from all substantial arbitrary impositions and purposeless restraints" and also as recognizing that "certain interests require particularly careful scrutiny of the state needs asserted to justify their abridgment...." The "certain interests" to which Justice Harlan referred may well be similar (perhaps identical) to the rights, liberties, or interests that the Court today, as in the past, regards as "fundamental."...

Justice Harlan concluded that marital privacy was such a "special interest." He found in the Constitution a right of "privacy of the home" with the home, the bedroom, and "intimate details of the marital relation" at its heart by examining the protection that the law had earlier provided for related, but not identical, interests described by such words as "privacy," "home," and "family."... The respondents here essentially ask us to do the same. They argue that one can find a "right to die with dignity" by examining the protection the law has provided for related, but not identical, interests relating to personal dignity, medical treatment, and freedom from state-inflicted pain . See *Ingraham v. Wright,...* (1977*); Cruzan v. Director, Mo. Dept. of Health,...* (1990); *Casey....*

I do not believe, however, that this Court need or now should decide whether or a not such a right is "fundamental." That is because, in my view, the avoidance of severe physical pain (connected with death) would have to comprise an essential part of any successful claim and because, as Justice O'CONNOR points out, the laws before us do not force a dying person to undergo that kind of pain.... Rather, the laws of New York and of Washington do not prohibit doctors from providing patients with drugs sufficient to control pain despite the risk that those drugs themselves will kill.... And under these circumstances the laws of New York and Washington would overcome any remaining significant interests and would be justified, regardless.

Medical technology, we are repeatedly told, makes the administration of pain-relieving drugs sufficient, except for a very few individuals for whom the ineffectiveness of pain control medicines can mean, not pain, but the need for sedation which can end in a coma.... We are also told that there are many instances in which patients do not receive the palliative care that, in principle, is available,..., but that is so for institutional reasons or inadequacies or obstacles, which would seem possible to overcome, and which do not include a prohibitive set of laws....

This legal circumstance means that the state laws before us do not infringe directly upon the (assumed) central interest (what I have called the core of the interest in dying with dignity) as, by way of contrast, the state anticontraceptive laws at issue in *Poe* did interfere with the central interest there at stake by bringing the State's police powers to bear upon the marital bedroom.

Were the legal circumstances different for example, were state law to prevent the provision of palliative care, including the administration of drugs as needed to avoid pain at the end of life then the law's impact upon serious and otherwise unavoidable physical pain (accompanying death) would be more directly at issue. And as Justice O'CONNOR suggests, the Court might have to revisit its conclusions in these cases.

CHAPTER XII

INDIVIDUAL LIBERTY: THE PROCEDURAL RIGHTS OF THE ACCUSED

In addition to *substantive* rights such as those found in the First Amendment, the Constitution also guarantees *procedural* rights. These include those related to the following stages of the criminal process: pretrial rights (Fourth and Fifth Amendments); trial rights (Sixth Amendment); and certain, albeit *not* all, post-trial rights (Eighth Amendment). These rights of procedure (or if you will, the "how" of the law) protect all persons – not simply citizens – with respect to the national government's conduct of law enforcement. More importantly, since most criminal laws are produced by the state governments, the Court has used the process of "selective incorporation" to apply most procedural rights to the states through the Due Process Clause of the Fourteenth Amendment.

THE CRIMINAL PROCESS & INDIVIDUAL RIGHTS

The Investigatory Process

Although there are variations in procedures and institutions from state to state, the basic stages of criminal procedure are the same: (1) investigatory and accusatory, (2) trial, and (3) custody and corrections. Despite the fact that a great number of crimes go unreported, the investigatory process begins only with reliable input – a report or "tip" – that a crime has been, or is being, committed as conveyed to a law enforcement agency. Most commonly the agencies involved are the municipal police and the county sheriff, deputies and constables; however, depending on the nature of the crime and the jurisdiction involved, the investigation may be carried out by the state's department of public safety.

In any event, the investigation may lead to the issuance of a search warrant in order to ascertain evidence relating to the crime. The officer must swear or affirm in support of his "probable cause" before a magistrate, usually a district judge. The most important element in determining the "reasonableness" of a search is the sufficiency of "probable cause." While a mere *hunch* or *suspicion* on the part of the officer does *not* constitute "probable cause," the officer need *not* have the kind of proof necessary to convict. To experienced law enforcement personnel, "probable cause" consists of "the practical considerations of everyday life on which reasonable and prudent individuals, not legal technicians, act;" see *Draper* v. *United States* (1959). If the judge decides that sufficient "probable cause" exists, he or she will issue the warrant and the person(s) named in the warrant may well be involved in the commission of an offense. The search warrant must "particularly describe" the *persons* to be searched and the *things* to be seized. Since *Mapp* v. *Ohio* (1961) state and local officers have become aware that the products or evidence resulting from an *unreasonable* search are inadmissible in court, *unless* the officers "believe" that they are acting in "good faith;" see *Massachusetts* v. *Sheppard*, 468 U.S. 981 (1984). All searches and seizures are *not* prohibited; only "unreasonable" or excessive searches are barred. As spelled out in the Fourteenth Amendment, *reasonable* or permissible searches include those conducted with a proper search warrant. In addition, the following searches are also permissible in the *absence* of a warrant:

1. *In connection with a valid arrest.* Based on the common law right of an officer to search for concealed weapons for self protection, and any evidence which might be destroyed, an officer may search the individual at the time of arrest. However, the extent of the search is *limited* to that area which falls under the "immediate control" of the accused usually "within arm's reach." Accordingly, a person arrested on the street is subject to a search, but the officer may *not* go farther and search his office, home, or automobile *without* a search warrant. In the case of an individual arrested in his office, home or automobile, the officer may search his person and that area within his reach, such as opened closets and drawers *excluding* locked containers, *e.g.*, glove compartments, trunks, safes, desk drawers; see *Chimel* v. *California* 395 U.S. 752 (1969); *Delaware* v. *Prouse*, 440 U.S. 648 (1979); *United States* v. *Ross*, 456 U.S. 798 (1982); *Colorado* v. *Bertine* (1987); and *Florida* v. *Wells*, 495 U.S. 1 (1990); *Maryland* v. *Buie*, 494 U.S. 325 (1990).
2. *The officer lacks sufficient time to obtain a warrant.* If the officer has probable cause that a crime is being committed and the evidence is too easily disposable (e.g., narcotics) to permit time for the warrant procedure, he may conduct a search. Most commonly such "limited-time" searches occur in cases involving moving vehicles where it is assumed that "time is of the essence;" see *Carroll* v. *United States* 267 U.S. 132 (1925), *Welsh* v. *Wisconsin*, 466 U.S. 740 (1984), *New York* v. *Class*, 475 U.S. 106 (1986).

3. *Voluntary consent*. Upon request, if the individual agrees to a search without a warrant, the officer may feel constitutionally free to do so, and in some instances, they may do so; see *Coolidge* v. *New Hampshire*, 403 U.S. 443 (1971); *Arizona* v. *Youngblood* (1989).

It may be assumed as a postulate of judicial reasoning that *any* evidence found during the course of a reasonable or proper search is admissible, even though not related to the crime under investigation, see *Washington* v. *Chrismon*, 455 U.S. 1 (1982).

Finally, while the rule of *Mapp* remains intact even with respect to evidence unreasonably seized by the use of electronic eavesdropping devices (*Katz* v. *United States*, 1967), there is some indication that the trend may be for a majority on the Supreme Court to back away somewhat from the exclusionary rule. The court has held that under certain conditions a witness can be forced to give testimony relating to illegally-seized evidence in federal grand jury proceedings in *United States* v. *Calandra* 414 U.S. 338 (1973).[1]

A great deal of the confusion centering on the Fourth Amendment and the "exclusionary rule" as its enforcement "mechanism," lies in the constitutional delineation among the three major decisions of *Weeks, Wolf* and, of course, *Mapp*. The first case of importance was *Weeks* v. *United States,* 232 U.S. 383 (1914). To prevent official lawlessness at the federal level, the Supreme Court *created* the exclusionary rule in this case. In order to give the ban on "unreasonable" searches and seizures by federal law enforcement personnel - members of the Federal Bureau of Investigation, the Department of Justice and federal marshals, the U.S. Treasury Department, the U.S. Secret Service, U.S. Customs agents, etc. - real, effective "teeth," the Supreme Court tied together the Fourth Amendment ban *and* the Fifth Amendment's guarantee of the right of silence, to provide that the admission of illegally-seized evidence is *prohibited* from being used in a federal criminal trial; any conviction based on such evidence at the federal level of courts, primarily district courts, cannot stand and will be thrown-out on proper appeal! However, as we have seen, at the turn of the century, the Supreme Court was unready to apply federal criminal standards to state courts by way of incorporation. Consequently, the exclusionary or "Weeks" rule was limited to federal courts.

Thirty-five years later, in what must be one of the most misunderstood decisions in the arena of individual procedural rights, the court handed down its decision in *Wolf* v. *Colorado* (1979). Associate Justice Felix Frankfurter, who wrote the opinion for a narrow decision, was aware that most states (30) did *not* follow the exclusionary rule, while less than 20 afforded this procedural protection. A judicial "restraintist" to the core, Justice Frankfurter wrote that while it is unconstitutional for state officers to conduct "fishing expeditions" until some evidence *finally* shows up, just so far the Supreme Court's jurisdiction can be stretched to prevent state officials from doing so:

> The knock at the door, whether by day or by night, as a prelude to a search without the authority of the law but solely on the distention of police ... [is] inconsistent with the conception of human rights enshrined in ... history....
>
> Accordingly, we have no hesitation in saying that were a state affirmatively to sanction such police incursion into privacy it would run counter to the guaranty of the Fourteenth Amendment. But the ways of enforcing such a basic right raise questions of a *different* order.
>
> ...[W]e cannot brush aside the experience of states which deem the incidence of such conduct by the police too *slight* to call for a determent remedy, not by way of disciplinary measures, but by overriding the relevant rules of evidence....

In other words, Frankfurter was saying that while it is unconstitutional conduct on the part of state officers to engage in illegal searches, it is *unenforceable*! Saying that the guarantee of a right, close and personal, of the individual is *mandatory* but that such illegal evidence is not barred in state convictions, is to not require its fulfillment. The result of *Wolf* was negligible at best and almost completely *ignored* by most state law enforcement officials.

For years after *Wolf*, both federal and state police engaged in what was called the "silver platter" doctrine: federal and state enforcement agencies would "swap" or exchange unreasonably-seized evidence for admission primarily in state criminal proceedings. Finally, in 1963, the Supreme Court put an end to this procedural ruse on the part of law enforcement. Two years earlier, the Supreme Court eliminated the "loop hole" left by Associate Justice Frankfurter in *Wolf*, by incorporating the "exclusionary rule" and making it *applicable* to state law enforcement officers by virtue of the Due Process Clause of the Fourteenth Amendment in *Mapp* v. *Ohio*, 367 U.S. 643 (1961). In a 6-3 decision delivered by Associate Justice Tom Clark - in what many consider his *finest* state paper - argued forcefully:

> Today, we once again examine *Wolf's* constitutional documentation of the right to privacy free from unreasonable state intrusion, and, after its dozen years on our books, are led by it to close the *only* courtroom *door* remaining open to evidence secured by *official Lawlessness* in flagrant abuse of that basic right, reserved to *all persons* as a specific guarantee against that very same unlawful conduct. (emphases added)

Justice Clark, thereafter, destroyed the rationale for *Wolf's* philosophical underpinnings and concluded:

> The ignoble shortcut to conviction left open to the state tends to

> *destroy* the entire system of constitutional restraints on which the liberties of the *people* rest.... Our decision, founded on reason and truth, gives to the individual no *more* than that which the constitution guarantees him, to the police officer no *less* than that to which honest law enforcement is entitled, and, to the courts, that judicial integrity so *necessary* in the timely administration of justice. (emphases added).

Eventually, however, the Supreme Court's Chief Justices, as well as most of its membership, were to become more and more conservative and, therefore, become more "charitable" to federal and state law enforcement officers, and much less so toward the defendants in criminal cases. Warren Burger was named to replace Earl Warren as Chief Justice by President Richard Nixon in 1969. By 1976, Nixon had, after some "rough and tumble" with the Senate named Associate Justices Lewis Powell, and William Rehinquist. In *Stone* v. *Powell*, 428 U.S. 465, the Court ruled that unlimited appeals to the federal courts were to be curtailed at the state court of last resort. If the state highest court ruled that the evidence in a case was *not* unreasonably seized, the defendant could *not*, thereafter, use the appellate process to "remove" the case to the federal courts, see *Stone* v. *Powell*, 428 U.S. 465 (1976). Nonetheless, the Court was to emasculate the exclusionary rule to a much greater extent in the 1980s.

The rationale for the exclusionary rule was not only to protect the right of the accused to be *free* of illegal searches but, more importantly, to deter unreasonable police conduct. This two-pronged purpose was made abundantly clear in both *Weeks* and *Mapp*; however, in 1984, the Supreme Court in *United States* v. *Leon*, 468 U.S. 897, down-played the first element and all but *rejected* the second. Associate Justice Byron White, a long-time foe of the exclusionary rule, spoke for a 6-3 majority in upholding a conviction for drug trafficking on the basis of evidence seized during an otherwise illegal search by officers who possessed an unlawful search warrant. The officers had *no* knowledge that the warrant was *defective* and had acted "in good faith." Said White:

> As we observed in *Michigan* v. *Tucker*, 417 U.S. 433 (1974) and reiterated in *United States* v. *Peltier*, 422 U.S. 539 (1975) ... where the officers' conduct is objectively reasonable, "excluding the evidence will not further the ends of the exclusionary rule in any appreciable way; for it is painfully apparent that ... the officer is acting as a reasonable officer would and should act under the circumstances. Excluding the evidence can *in no way* affect his *future* conduct unless it is to make him less willing to do his duty. (emphasis added)

In other words, the exclusionary rule was not meant to protect an individual right to privacy nor any other kind of right; it was meant to have only a deterrent effect on the officer. Thus, since it did *not* do so in this case, the further application of exclusion is useless.

On the same day, the Court decided that this "good faith" rule should also be employed at the state level. See, *Massachusetts* v. *Sheppard*, 468 U.S. 981 (1984). The high wall of exclusion that the Warren Court had so carefully constructed in *Mapp* to prohibit unreasonably-seized evidence from state, as well as federal, courts was now *permanently* breached; Justice Frankfurter's opinion in *Wolf* was, in effect, resurrected by the *Sheppard* decision.

THE ACCUSATORY PROCESS

After the investigation has been completed and sufficient evidence has been gathered, the accusatory process is usually initiated by the issuance of an arrest warrant. Of course, if the officer is *present* during the commission of a crime, a warrant is not necessary. In most instances the proper magistrate, upon a submission of the sworn statement of the officer, issues an arrest warrant to be presented to the accused; at that point, the accused has the right of counsel. The Supreme Court has held that the right of counsel, including court-appointed attorneys for indigents, must be extended to *all* offenses – petty, misdemeanor, or felony – which involve *any* form of imprisonment; see *Angersinger* v. *Hamlin* 407U.S.25 (1972). Under *Miranda* v. *Arizona*, 384U.S.436 (1966), in cases of serious misdemeanors, as well as felonies, the arresting officer must inform the alleged offender of the so-called *Miranda* "litany" – that he or she has a right to remain silent; that anything he or she says can be used in court; that one is entitled to the presence of an attorney, and further, that if counsel cannot be afforded, one will be provided by the court *prior* to any questioning if he or she so desires. If the accused wishes to waive these rights and make a statement, they are required to sign an affidavit to that effect; however, anything the accused may say *voluntarily*, at their *own* discretion, with or without the Miranda warnings having been read, is *admissible* as evidence in the trial. See *Rhode Island* v. *Innis*, 446 U.S.291(1980); *Nix* v. *Williams*, 467U.S.431(1984); *Arizona* v. *Robeson*, 486U.S.675(1988). The accused is then confined, for a reasonable period, until he or she can be brought before a magistrate. At this time, the magistrate presents the charges and again informs the accused of his or her constitutional and statutory rights. If the accused wishes to waive these rights, he or she again must sign a statement so stating. Hereafter, if at any time he or she wishes to claim his or her procedural rights, he or she may do so; *any* incriminating statements made prior to that claim cannot be *used* by the prosecution *unless* the accused commits perjury on the witness stand; see *Harris* v. *New York* (1971).[2] Depending on the seriousness of the offense and the evidence presented, the magistrate will either issue a warning or complaint; call for an examining trial, if requested; and, thereafter, commit or release the individual. If the accused is subject to a grand jury trial for a felony, the judge has the discretion to set bail bond.

Under criminal statutes, in a substantial number of states, alleged felons are then bound over for the grand jury; although, they may choose to waive this guaranty. The role of the grand jury is to assure that no person shall be brought to trial on *serious* criminal charges unless an impartial group of citizens has good reason to *believe* that the accused may be guilty; however, since *Hurtado* remains "good" on ruling law, the states are not compelled by the Fourteenth Amendment to guarantee this right. Therefore, it depends on the state constitution as to whether grand juries are required at all. If sufficient evidence establishing a causal relationship between the alleged offender and the crime is lacking, the grand jury will present a "no bill" or "pass." However, it is more likely that the grand jury will indict the individual, if the performance of grand juries in recent years is a reliable indicator. The district clerk, upon receiving the indictment returned by the grand jury, issues the writ of attachment or *capias* (A Latin term meaning "That you take." It is a general name for several types of writs which require the officer to take the "body" of the defendant into custody.) and sets a new bond. The case is then placed on the docket to await trial. In those states, where the grand jury is *not* employed, the power to initiate trial proceedings is usually placed in the hands of the district attorney.

THE TRIAL

To many Americans, our system of justice seems to break down altogether at this stage of the criminal process. The acquittal of O.J. Simpson, the early release of connected murderers, drug traffickers and child molesters, plus the fact that "technicalities" are used to overturn numerous convictions on appeal has been most disturbing to many. There are a growing number of judicial scholars who have criticized the Court under Chief Justices Warren and Burger for its *over* emphasis on the importance of the Bill of Rights and individual liberties at the direct expense of *equally* important provisions of the Constitution which emphasize individual *responsibility* and civic *obligations* to other persons and to the government in fulfilling its legitimate functions. They argue, rather strongly, that such well-crafted principles as the "separation of powers" and the "checks and balances" system were primarily designed also to protect individual liberty; even though these mechanisms are found in the "main body," rather the first ten amendments to, the Constitution. (For example, see Raoul Berger's classic work, *Government by Judiciary* (1977) and, more specifically, to "Activism and Restraint: A Cloak for the Justices' Policy Preferences" by Harold J. Spaeth and Stuart H. Teger in Halpen and Lamb, *Supreme Court: Activism and Restraint* (Lexington Books, 1982) pp. 277-302; and, James V. Calvi and Susan Coleman, *Cases in Constitutional Law: Summaries and Critiques* (Englewood Cliffs, NJ: Prentice Hall, 1994) pp. 3-5.)

The trial process begins in court, when the judge presents the defendant with several important questions: Is counsel desired? Can the defendent afford an attorney? Is a jury or bench trial desired? If the accused is an indigent, the judge will designate an attorney to plead his or her defense. After consulting with the lawyer, the defendant chooses which plea to enter. There is, of course, the much-used option of "plea bargaining" through which the defendant agrees to plead guilty in *exchange* for a concession on the part of the prosecution, *e.g.*, a "lesser" charge preferred, recommendation of a lighter sentence or even probation.

Because of the overcrowded dockets of trial courts, judges will regularly agree to such a "bargain." Once the plea has been entered, the actual trial begins. If a *petit* (trial) jury is to be used, the selection of *veniremen* (jury members) is one of the most important elements in the adversary system. Experienced prosecution and defense lawyers will carefully pick, choose, and eliminate veniremen because of "prejudices which may adversely affect their cause," socioeconomic background, race or ethnic origin, political views or any number of other factors.

During the trial, the judge is the constitutional "officer" responsible for safeguarding the "fairness" of the procedure. The defendant may claim the Fifth Amendment privilege by *not* taking the stand in his or her *own* defense or waive it verbally, by testifying as verified by the Supreme Court in *Malloy* v. *Hogan*, 378 U.S. 1(1964). In any event, the burden of proof of guilt rests with the government; the accused does *not* have the legal obligation to prove his or her innocence. Neither the trial judge, nor the prosecutor, can make "adverse" comments on the defendant's decision to claim the right of silence; see *Griffin* v. *California*, 381 U.S. 957 (1965). If the fairness of the trial is adversely affected by the obtrusiveness of the press or, if the coverage is so prejudicial as to influence the jury, the judge may conduct a *closed* proceeding or even sequester the jury; see *Sheppard* v. *Maxwell*, 384 U.S. 333 (1966). On the other hand, the Supreme Court held in *Illinois* v. *Allen* (1970), if the *defendant* conducts his behavior in such a way as to *antagonize* the jury, or otherwise *disturb* the proceedings and thus endanger his cause, the judge has broad discretion at his disposal to preserve the "fairness of the trial."

If the defendant is not acquitted and found guilty, the next step of course is consultation with a probation officer. Based on the interview with the offender, the probation officer submits a *pre*-sentence report to the judge. Some state courts are without probation officers and may omit this function in the process. In most cases, other than capital or death penalty the trial judge passes sentence; however, if a jury trial was used, the defendant may choose sentencing by the *petit* jury. If it is a capital punishment case then the jury sits *twice*: trial (conviction) and penalty (life/death penalty) phases. The state may permissibly opt for two types of trial juries for *non*-capital cases; either a jury of six members under which the decision must be unanimous; see, *Williams* v. *Florida*, 399 U.S. 78 (1970); and a twelve-member jury with a *less* than unanimous verdict, (*e.g.*, 9-3); see *Apodaca* v. *Oregon*, 406 U.S. 404 (1972).

The Eighth Amendment provides: "Excessive bail shall not be required, nor excessive fines imposed." Specific levels of bails and fines have been established by statute at the federal level; however, since the Supreme Court has *not* incorporated this limitation, there exist great variances in the setting of "bail and fines" from state to state. More importantly, the Amendment prohibits the imposition of "cruel and unusual punishments," which the Court has made enforceable against the states; see *Robinson* v. *California*, 370 U.S. 660 (1962). In *Furman* v. *Georgia*, 408 U.S. 238 (1972), it held that existing state laws providing for capital punishment were unconstitutional and, as enforced, the statutes constituted a "cruel and unusual punishment." The decision left the question of the death penalty in doubt, although seven of the Justices indicated that capital punishment, as such, was not conclusively rejected; they suggested that a properly-drawn and administered statute could survive a challenge in the Court as it later *did* in *Gregg* v. *Georgia*, 428 U.S. 153 (1976); *McCleskey* v. *Kemp*, 481 U.S. 279.

In most cases, commitment to a penal institution begins the third stage of criminal justice-correction and rehabilitation. Municipal and county jails are temporary custodial facilities for those taken into custody following arrest and those convicted of misdemeanors. Many are paid by the United States government to serve as "holding pens" until space is available in federal penitentiaries. The overwhelming number of prisoners and the smaller number of jails are substandard by using virtually *any* criteria. In many states, they are operated without any state guidelines or control; they lack any professionally trained corrections personnel; they're run by municipal and county law enforcement officers, and, in the main they are "filthy honeycombs of confinement characterized by inadequate facilities, sexual assaults, poor food, official neglect and public indifference." The rate of recidivism among convicted persons having served their sentences in county and municipal jails is extremely high-about four times higher than those who have served sentences in the state prison system. The probation picture is somewhat brighter. Although most county probation departments are understaffed and underfunded, they have done fairly well. Convicted felons who are sentenced to confinement are sent to one of a number of state penitentiaries. Nevertheless, inmates have few, if any, individual rights and the state has sweeping powers over them; see, *Block* v. *Rutherford*, *Judson* v. *Palmer*, and *U.S.* v. *Gouvera* (1984).

JUVENILE JUSTICE

The subject of juvenile offenders – usually those between the ages of seven and seventeen – is somewhat an ambiguous one. Most state laws accept the theory that juveniles cannot commit "crimes" and they are, therefore, subject to *civil* proceedings. However, several decisions by the Supreme Court of the United States have had the effect of casting great doubt on this theory. Specifically, the Court has held that in juvenile court proceedings which determine delinquency and which may result in possible commitment to an institution, the child and/or his parents or guardian must be: (1) provided with sufficient notice to permit preparation of defense to charges, (2) informed of the juvenile's right to counsel including a court appointed attorney if necessary, and (3) extended the privilege against compulsory self incrimination and the guarantees of confrontation and cross-examination; see *In re. Gault* (1967). In addition, the Court has held that "proof beyond a reasonable doubt is among 'essentials of due process and fair treatment' required during the adjudicatory stage when a juvenile is charged with an act that would constitute a crime if committed by an adult;" see *In re. Winship* (1970). In 1967, the President's Commission on Law Enforcement and Administration of Justice reported that an astonishing number of juveniles were placed in correctional institutions for offenses that would not be considered crimes if committed by adults, e.g., smoking, drinking, using vulgar language, violating curfew laws, patronizing bars. Accordingly, the Commission recommended for every state the organization of local Youth Services Bureaus to facilitate those youthful offenders whom, the juvenile courts felt, could best be handled *outside* the regular justice system.

The juvenile judge, who has always had extensive powers in attempting to strike a balance between the "general welfare" of the youthful offenders and the interests of the supervision by the child's parents, may require the child's participation in a local rehabilitation program if one is available. If necessary, the court could place the child under the jurisdiction of an adult state court; even mentally-retarded juveniles are *not* exempt from adult criminal trials; see *Stanford* v. *Kentucky* , 492 U.S. 361 (1989).

THE WAR POWER AND INDIVIDUAL LIBERTY

As in the case of any other sovereign nation, the United States is possessive of certain *inherent* powers which are derived, not necessarily from constitutional grants, but rather from the very *existence* of the nation state. It could be argued that if, in fact, the most basic motivation in individuals is *self-preservation*, the same could be said for a nation, which represents the individual in the collective sense.[3] Although there are notable exceptions, the broad sweep of history supports the contention that a country will take *whatever* actions are necessary under the concept of "inherent" powers when it perceives a threat to its *security*, whether from without or within. Not surprisingly, such instances pose serious problems for those democratic governments that have guaranteed certain rights to the people. For in time of war or other serious exigency, governments may be forced to curtail or even deprive individual rights which had previously been recognized. Two prime examples in the history of the United States are provided in the last two decisions of this chapter.

During the Civil War, Abraham Lincoln often took drastic measures to achieve military success for the Union. Probably the most extreme of these was a presidential order to suspend the *writ of habeas corpus* even in those northern and broader states where no fighting was taking place. Literally meaning "You may have the body," such writs are important elements of the criminal process. A *writ of habeas corpus* is a court order directing a person be brought before the court to determine the validity of the reasons for the detention. Article I, section 9, C1. 2 prohibits *Congress* from suspending the writ except in cases of "Rebellion, Invasion or for the public safety." Lincoln's suspension of this procedural grant, therefore usurped congressional powers. His intention was to facilitate the apprehension of suspected southern agents in the northern states, and it was challenged successfully in *Ex Parte Milligan* (1866). However, it is interesting to note that the Civil War had been *concluded* for one year and Lincoln was buried in his grave by the time the Supreme Court was *willing* to adjudicate the controversy.

Perhaps, more shocking from the standpoints of law and history was the "Japanese Exclusion" case, *Korematsu* v. *United States* (1944) which centered on the "emergency powers" of the President and the "war powers" of Congress. The Court sustained President Franklin D. Roosevelt's executive order to his military commanders to remove all Japanese and Japanese-Americans from the West Coast and place them in War Relocation Centers. Obviously, in the eyes of the Court, the gravity of the Second World War permitted Roosevelt much broader discretion to act on his *own*, than the Korean War did later for President Truman in attempting to seize the nation's major steel industries in the *Steel Seizure Case* (1952).

MAPP v. OHIO
367 U.S. 643; 81 S.Ct. 1684; 6 L.Ed. 2d 1081 (1961)

In 1957, three police officers in Cleveland arrived at a two-story house the second floor of which was occupied by Miss Dollree Mapp and her daughter. The officers were acting on information that someone who was wanted for questioning concerning a recent bombing was hiding in the house and that there was "a large amount of policy paraphernalia being hidden in the home." That material was not found; however, after the exhaustive search described below, obscene literature was found, for which Miss Map was arrested and convicted. After the state supreme court upheld the conviction, the case was appealed to the Supreme Court.

MR. JUSTICE CLARK delivered the opinion of the Court:

...Upon their arrival at the house, the officers knocked on the door and demanded entrance but appellant, after telephoning her attorney, refused to admit them without a search warrant. They advised their headquarters of the situation and undertook a surveillance of the house.

The officers again sought entrance some three hours later when four or more additional officers arrived on the scene. When Miss Mapp did not come to the door immediately, at least one of the several doors to the house was forcibly opened and the policemen gained admittance. Meanwhile Miss Mapp's attorney arrived, but the officers, having secured their own entry, and continuing in their defiance of the law, would permit him neither to see Miss Mapp nor to enter the house. It appears that Miss Mapp was halfway down the stairs from the upper floor to the front door when the officers, in this highhanded manner, broke into the hall. She demanded to see the search warrant. A paper, claimed to be a warrant, was held up by one of the officers. She grabbed the "warrant" and placed it in her bosom. A struggle ensued in which the officers recovered the piece of paper and as a result of which they handcuffed appellant because she had been "belligerent" in resisting their official rescue of the "warrant" from her person.... Appellant, in handcuffs, was then forcibly taken upstairs to her bedroom where the officers searched a dresser, a chest of drawers, a closet and some suitcases. They also looked into a photo album and through personal papers belonging to the appellant. The search spread to the rest of the second floor including the child's bedroom, the living room, the kitchen and a dinette. The basement of the building and a trunk found therein were also searched. The obscene materials for possession of which she was ultimately convicted were discovered in the course of that widespread search.

At the trial no search warrant was produced by the prosecution, nor was the failure to produce one explained or accounted for. At best, "there is, in the record, considerable doubt as to whether there ever was any warrant for the search of defendant's home...."

The State says that even if the search were made without authority, or otherwise unreasonably, it is not prevented from using the unconstitutionally seized evidence at trial, citing *Wolf v. Colorado* in which this Court did indeed hold "that in a prosecution in a State court for a State crime the Fourteenth Amendment does not forbid the admission of evidence obtained by an unreasonable search and seizure...."

I

Seventy-five years ago, in *Boyd v. United States*, 116 U.S. 616 (1886), considering the Fourth and Fifth Amendments as running "almost into each other," on the facts before it, this Court held the doctrines of those Amendments

> "apply to all invasions on the part of the government and its employees of the sanctity of a man's home and the privacies of life. It is not the breaking or his doors, and the rummaging of his drawers, that constitutes the essence of the offense, but it is the invasion of his indivisible right of personal security, personal liberty and private property...."

...Less than thirty years after *Boyd*, this Court, in *Weeks v. United States*, 232 U.S. 383 (1914), stated that

> "the Fourth Amendment ...put the courts of the United States and Federal officials, in the exercise of their power and authority, under limitations and restraints [and] ...forever secure[d] the people, their person, houses, papers and effects against all unreasonable searches and seizures under the guise of law ...and the duty of giving to it force and effect is obligatory upon all entrusted under our Federal system with the enforce- ment of the laws...."

...Finally, the Court in that case clearly stated that use of the seized evidence involved "a denial of the constitutional rights of the accused...." Thus, in the year 1914, in the Weeks case, this Court "for the first time" held that "in a federal prosecution the Fourth Amendment barred the use of evidence secured through an illegal search and seizure...." This Court has ever since required of federal law officers a strict adherence to that command which this Court has held to be a clear, specific, and constitutionally required-even if judicially implied-deterrent safeguard without insistence upon which the Fourth Amendment would have been reduced to "a form of words...." It meant, quite simply, that "conviction by means of unlawful seizures and enforced confessions ...should find no sanction in the judgments of the courts...."

There are in the cases of this Court some passing references to the *Weeks* rule as being one of evidence. But the plain and unequivocal language of *Weeks* – and its later paraphrase in *Wolf* – to the effect that the *Weeks* rule is of constitutional origin, remains entirely undisturbed....

II

In 1949, thirty-five years after *Weeks* was announced, this Court, in *Wolf v. Colorado, supra*, again for the first time, discussed the effect of the Fourth Amendment upon the States through the operation of the Due Process Clause of the Fourteenth Amendment....

...Nevertheless, after declaring that the "security of one's privacy against arbitrary intrusion by the police" is "implicit in the 'concept of ordered liberty' and as such enforceable against the States through the Due Process Clause," ...and announcing that it "stoutly adhere[d]" to the *Weeks* decision, the Court decided that the *Weeks* exclusionary rule would not then be imposed upon the States as "an essential ingredient of the right...."

III

Some five years after *Wolf*, in answer to a plea made here term after term that we overturn its doctrine on applicability of the *Weeks* exclusionary rule, this Court indicated that such should not be done until the States had "adequate opportunity to adapt or reject the [*Weeks*] rule...."

Today we once again examine *Wolf's* constitutional documentation of the right to privacy free from unreasonable state intrusion, and, after its dozen years on our books, are led by it to close the only courtroom door remaining open to evidence secured by official lawlessness in flagrant abuse of that basic right, reserved to all persons as a specific guaranty against that very same unlawful conduct. We hold that all evidence obtained by searches and seizures in violation of the Constitution is, by that same authority, inadmissible in a state court.

IV

Since the Fourth Amendment's right of privacy has been declared enforceable against the States through the Due Process Clause of the Fourteenth, it is enforceable against them by the same sanction of exclusion as is used against the Federal Government. Were it otherwise, then just as without the *Weeks* rule the assurance against unreasonable federal searches and seizures would be "a form of words," valueless and undeserving of mention in a perpetual character of inestimable human liberties, so too, without that rule the freedom from state invasions of privacy would be so ephemeral and so neatly severed from its conceptual nexus with the freedom from all brutish means of coercing evidence as not to merit this Court's high regard as a freedom "implicit in the concept of ordered liberty...."

...We find that, as to the Federal Government, the Fourth and Fifth Amendments and, as to the States, the freedom from unconscionable invasions of privacy and the freedom from convictions based upon coerced confessions do enjoy an "intimate relation" in their perpetuation of "principles of humanity and civil liberty [secured] ...only after years of struggle...."

V

Moreover, our holding that the exclusionary rule is an essential part of both the Fourth and Fourteenth Amendments is not only the logical dictate of prior cases, but it also makes very good sense. There is no war between the Constitution and common sense. Presently, a federal prosecutor may make no use of evidence illegally seized, but a State's attorney across the street may, although he supposedly is operating under the enforceable prohibitions of the same Amendment. Thus the State, by admitting evidence unlawfully seized, serves to encourage disobedience to the Federal Constitution which it is bound to uphold.... In nonexclusionary States, federal officers, being human, were by it invited to and did, as our cases indicate, step across the street to the State's attorney with their unconstitutionally seized evidence. Prosecution on the basis of that evidence was then had in a state court in utter disregard of the enforceable Fourth Amendment. If the fruits of an unconstitutional search had been inadmissible in both state and federal courts, this inducement to evasion would have been sooner eliminated....

...The ignoble shortcut to conviction left open to the State tends to destroy the entire system of constitutional restraints on which the liberties of the people rest. Having once recognized that the right to privacy embodied in the Fourth Amendment is enforceable against the States, and that the right to be secure against rude invasions of privacy by state officers is, therefore, constitutional in origin, we can no longer permit that right to remain an empty promise. Because it is enforceable in the same manner and to like effect as other basic rights secured by the Due Process Clause, we can no longer permit it to be revocable at the whim of any police officer who, in the name of law enforcement itself, chooses to suspend its enjoyment. Our decision, founded on reason and truth, gives to the individual no more than that which the Constitution guarantees him, to the police officer no less than that to which honest law enforcement is entitled, and to the courts, that judicial integrity so necessary in the true administration of justice.

The judgment of the Supreme Court of Ohio is reversed and the case remanded for further proceedings not inconsistent with this opinion.

Reversed and remanded.

MR. JUSTICES BLACK and DOUGLAS concurred.

MR. JUSTICE HARLAN, whom MR. JUSTICE FRANKFURTER and MR. JUSTICE WHITTAKER joined, dissented.

CHIMEL v. CALIFORNIA
395 U.S. 752; 89 S.Ct. 2034; 23 L.Ed. 2d 685 (1969)

The search involved in this case took place in a home in Santa Ana, California, in the fall of 1965. The officers carried with them a warrant authorizing Chimel's arrest for the burglary of a coin shop. During the search described below evidence was found and subsequently used to convict Chimel of the crime. The case was brought to the Supreme Court on a writ of certiorari.

MR. JUSTICE STEWART delivered the opinion of the Court:

This case raises basic questions concerning the permissible scope under the Fourth Amendment of a search incident to a lawful arrest.

...The officers knocked on the door, identified themselves to the petitioner's wife, and asked if they might come inside. She ushered them into the house, where they waited 10 or 15 minutes until the petitioner returned home from work. When the petitioner entered the house, one of the officers handed him the arrest warrant and asked for permission to "look around." The petitioner objected, but was advised that "on the basis of the lawful arrest," the officers would nonetheless conduct a search. No search warrant had been issued.

Accompanied by the petitioner's wife, the officers then looked through the entire three-bedroom house, including the attic, the garage, and a small workshop. In some rooms the search was relatively cursory. In the master bedroom and sewing room, however, the officers directed the petitioner's wife to open drawers and "to physically move contents of the drawers from side to side so that [they] might view any items that would have come from [the] burglary." After completing the search, they seized numerous items – primarily coins, but also several medals, tokens, and a few other objects. The entire search took between 45 minutes and an hour.

At the petitioner's subsequent state trial on two charges of burglary, the items taken from his house were admitted into evidence against him, over his objection that they had been unconstitutionally seized....

...the Court in 1914 as dictum in *Weeks v. United States* ... in which the Court stated:

> "What then is the present case? Before answering that inquiry specifically, it may be well by a process of exclusion to state what it is not. It is not an assertion of the right on the part of the Government, always recognized under English and American law, to search the person of the accused when legally arrested to discover and seize the fruits or evidences of crime...."

That statement made no reference to any right to search the *place* where an arrest occurs, but was limited to a right to search the "person." Eleven years later the case of *Carroll v. United States*, brought the following embellishment of the Weeks statement:

> "When a man is legally arrested for an offense, whatever is found upon his person or in his control which it is unlawful for him to have and which may be used to prove the offense, may be seized and held as evidence in the prosecution."

Still, that assertion too was far from a claim that the "place" where one is arrested may be searched so long as the arrest is valid. Without explanation, however, the principle emerged in expanded form a few months later in *Agnello v. United States* ... although still by way of dictum:

> "The right without a search warrant contemporaneously to search persons lawfully arrested while committing crime and to search the place where the arrest is made in order to find and seize things connected with the crime as its fruits or as the means by which it was committed, as well as weapons and other things to effect an escape from custody, is not to be doubted."

... in *Marron v. United States* ...two years later, the dictum of *Agnello* appeared to be the foundation of the Court's decision. In that case federal agents had secured a search warrant authorizing the seizure of liquor and certain articles used in its manufacture. When they arrived at the premises to be searched, they saw "that the place was used for retailing and drinking intoxicating liquors...." They proceeded to arrest the person in charge and to execute the warrant. In searching a closet for the items listed in the warrant they came across an incriminating ledger, concededly not covered by the warrant, which they also seized. The Court upheld the seizure of the ledger by holding that since the agents had made a lawful arrest, "[t]hey had a right without a warrant contemporaneously to search the place in order to find and seize the things used to carry on the criminal enterprise...."

That the *Marron* opinion did not mean all that it seemed to say became evident, however, a few years later in *Go-Bart Importing Co. v. United States*,...and *United States v. Lefkowitz*.... In *Go-Bart*, agents had searched the office of persons whom they had lawfully arrested, and had taken several papers from a desk, a safe, and other parts of the office. The Court noted that no crime had been committed in the agent's presence, and that although the agent in charge "had an abundance of information and time to swear out a valid [search] warrant, he failed to do so...."

The limited views expressed in *Go-Bart* and *Lefkowitz* were thrown to the winds, however, in *Harris v. United States*, decided in 1947. In that case, officers had obtained a warrant for Harris' arrest on the basis of his alleged involvement with the cashing and interstate transportation of a forged check. He was arrested in the living room of his four-room apartment, and in an attempt to recover two canceled checks thought to have been used in effecting the forgery, the officers undertook a thorough search of the entire apartment. Inside a desk drawer they found a sealed envelope marked "George Harris, personal papers." The envelope, which was then torn open, was found to contain altered selective service documents, and those documents were used to secure Harris's conviction for violating the Selective Training and Service Act of 1940. The Court rejected Harris' Fourth Amendment claim, sustaining the search as "incident to arrest...."

Only a year after *Harris*, however, the pendulum swung again. In *Trupiano v. United States* ...agents raided the site of an illicit distillery, saw one of several conspirators operating the still, and arrested him, contemporaneously "seiz[ing] the illicit distillery." The Court held that the arrest and others made subsequently had been valid, but that the unexplained failure of the agents to procure a search warrant – in spite of the fact that they had had more than enough time before the mid to do so – rendered the search unlawful....

In 1950, two years after *Trupiano,* came *United States v. Rabinowitz*, the decision upon which California primarily relies in the case now before us. In *Rabinowitz*, federal authorities had been informed that the defendant was dealing in stamps bearing forged overprints. On the basis of that information they secured a warrant for his arrest, which they executed at his one-room business office. At the time of the arrest, the officers "searched the desk, safe, and file cabinets in the office for about an hour and a half,..." and seized 573 stamps with forged overprints. The stamps were admitted into evidence at the defendant's trial, and this Court affirmed his conviction, rejecting the contention that the warrantless search had been unlawful. The Court held that the search in its entirety fell within the principle giving law enforcement authorities "[t]he right 'to search the place where the arrest is made in order to find and seize things connected with the crime....'" *Harris* was regarded as "ample authority" for that conclusion.... The opinion rejected the rule of *Trupiano* that "in seizing goods and articles, law enforcement agents must secure and use search warrants wherever reasonably practicable." The test, said the Court, "is not whether it is reasonable to procure a search warrant, but whether the search was reasonable."

Rabinowitz has come to stand for the proposition, *inter alia*, that a warrantless search "incident to a lawful arrest" may generally extend to the area that is considered to be in the "possession" or under the "control" of the person arrested. And it was on the basis of that proposition that the California courts upheld the search of the petitioner's entire house in this case. That doctrine, however, at least in the broad sense in which it was applied by the California courts in this case, can withstand neither historical nor rational analysis.

Even limited to its own facts, the *Rabinowitz* decision was, as we have seen, hardly founded on an unimpeachable line of authority....

Only last Term in *Terry v. Ohio* ...we emphasized that "the police must, whenever practicable, obtain advance judicial approval of searches and seizures through the warrant procedure," ...and that "[t]he scope of [a] search must be 'strictly tied to and justified by' the circumstances which rendered its initiation permissible...." The search undertaken by the officer in that "stop and frisk" case was sustained under that test, because it was no more than a "protective ...search for weapons...." But in a companion case, *Sibron v. New York* ... we applied the same standard to another set of facts and reached a contrary result, holding that a policeman's action in thrusting his hand into a suspect's pocket had been neither motivated by nor limited to the objective of protection. Rather, the search had been made in order to find narcotics, which were in fact found.

A similar analysis underlies the "search incident to arrest" principle, and marks its proper extent. When an arrest is made, it is reasonable for the arresting officer to search the person arrested in order to remove any weapons that the latter might seek to use in order to resist arrest or effect his escape. Otherwise, the officer's safety might well be endangered, and the arrest itself frustrated. In addition, it is entirely reasonable for the arresting officer to search for and seize any evidence on the arrestee's person in order to prevent its concealment or destruction. And the area into which an arrestee might reach in order to grab a weapon or evidentiary items must, of course, be governed by a like rule. A gun on a table or in a drawer in front of one who is arrested can be as dangerous to the arresting officer as one concealed in the clothing of the person arrested. There is ample justification, therefore, for a search of the arrestee's person and the area "within his immediate control" – construing that phrase to mean the area from within which he might gain possession of a weapon or destructible evidence.

There is no comparable justification, however, for routinely searching rooms other than that in which an arrest occurs – or, for that matter, for searching through all the desk drawers or other closed or concealed areas in that room itself. Such searches, in the absence of well-recognized exceptions, may be made only under the authority of a search warrant. The "adherence to judicial processes" mandated by the Fourth Amendment requires no less.

This is the principle that underlay our decision in *Preston v. United States*. In that case three men had been arrested in a parked car, which had later been towed to a garage and searched by police. We held the search to have been unlawful under the Fourth Amendment, despite the contention that it had been incidental to a valid arrest….

It would be possible, of course, to draw a line between *Rabinowitz* and *Harris* on the one hand, and this case on the other. For *Rabinowitz* involved a single room, and *Harris* a four-room apartment, while in the case before us an entire house was searched. But such a distinction would be highly artificial. The rationale that allowed the searches and seizures in *Rabinowitz* and *Harris* would allow the searches and seizures in this case. No consideration relevant to the Fourth Amendment suggests any point of rational limitation, once the search is allowed to go beyond the area from which the person arrested might obtain weapons or evidentiary items. The only reasoned distinction is one between a search of the person arrested and the area within his reach on the one hand, and more extensive searches on the other.

The petitioner correctly points out that one result of decisions such as *Rabinowitz* and *Harris* is to give law enforcement officials the opportunity to engage in searches not justified by probable cause, by the simple expedient of arranging to arrest suspects at home rather than elsewhere. We do not suggest that the petitioner is necessarily correct in his assertion that such a strategy was utilized here, but the fact remains that had he been arrested earlier in the day, at his place of employment rather than at home, no search of his house could have been made without a search warrant....

Rabinowitz and *Harris* have been the subject of critical commentary for many years, and have been relied upon less and less in our own decisions. It is time, for the reasons we have stated, to hold that on their own facts, and insofar as the principles they stand for are inconsistent with those that we have endorsed today, they are no longer to be followed.

Application of sound Fourth Amendment principles to the facts of this case produces a clear result. The search here went far beyond the petitioner's person and the area from within which he might have obtained either a weapon or something that could have been used as evidence against him. There was no constitutional justification, in the absence of a search warrant, for extending the search beyond that area. The scope of the search was, therefore, "unreasonable" under the Fourth Amendment, and the petitioner's conviction cannot stand.

MR. JUSTICE HARLAN concurred.

MR. JUSTICE WHITE, with whom MR. JUSTICE BLACK joined, dissented.

KATZ v. UNITED STATES
389 U.S. 347; 88 S.Ct. 507; 19 L.Ed. 2d 576 (1967)

Katz was convicted under an indictment charging him with transmitting wagering information by telephone across state lines in violation of federal law. The evidence used to convict was obtained by FBI agents who had attached an electronic listening and recording device to the outside of the telephone booth from which the calls were made. After the court of appeals affirmed the conviction, Katz brought the case to the Supreme Court by a writ of certiorari.

MR. JUSTICE STEWART delivered the opinion of the Court:

The petitioner was convicted in the District Court for the Southern District of California under an eight-count indictment charging him with transmitting wagering information by telephone from Los Angeles to Miami and Boston in violation of a federal statute. At trial the Government was permitted, over the petitioner's objection, to introduce evidence of the petitioner's end of telephone conversations, overheard by FBI agents who had attached an electronic listening and recording device to the outside of the public telephone booth from which he had placed his calls. In affirming his conviction, the Court of Appeals rejected the contention that the recordings had been obtained in violation of the Fourth Amendment, because "[t]here was no physical entrance into the area occupied by [the petitioner]." The correct solution of Fourth Amendment problems is not necessarily promoted by incantation of the phrase "constitutionally protected area." Secondly, the Fourth Amendment cannot be translated into a general constitutional "right to privacy." That Amendment protects individual privacy against certain kinds of governmental intrusion, but its protections go further, and often have nothing to do with privacy at all. Other provisions of the Constitution protect personal privacy from other forms of governmental invasion. But the protection of a person's *general* right to privacy – his right to be let alone by other people – is, like the protection of his property and of his very life, left largely to the law of the individual States.... The petitioner has strenuously argued that the booth was a "constitutionally protected area." The Government has maintained with equal vigor that it was not. But this effort to decide whether or not a given "area," viewed in the abstract, is "constitutionally protected" deflects attention from the problem presented by this case. *For the Fourth Amendment protects people not places.* What a person knowingly exposes to the public, even in his own home or office, is not a subject of Fourth Amendment protection.... But what he seeks to preserve as private, even in an area accessible to the public, may be constitutionally protected.... No less than an individual in a business office, in a friend's apartment, or in a taxicab, a person in a telephone booth may rely upon the protection of the Fourth Amendment. One who occupies it, shuts the door behind him, and pays the toll that permits him to place a call, is surely entitled to assume that the words he utters into the mouthpiece will not be broadcast to the world. To read the Constitution more narrowly is to ignore the vital role that the public telephone has come to play in private communication.

The Government contends, however, that the activities of its agents in this case should not be tested by Fourth Amendment requirements, for the surveillance technique they employed involved no physical penetration of the telephone booth from which the petitioner placed his calls. It is true that the absence of such penetration was at one time thought to foreclose further Fourth Amendment inquiry, *Olmstead v. United States*...; *Goldman v. United States*, for that Amendment was thought to limit only searches and seizures of tangible property. But "[t]he premise that property interests control the right of the Government to search and seize has been discredited." *Warden, Md. Penitentiary v. Hayden*.... Thus, although a closely divided Court supposed in *Olmstead* that surveillance without any trespass and without the seizure of any material object fell outside the ambit of the Constitution, we have since departed from the narrow view on which that decision rested. Indeed, we have expressly held that the Fourth Amendment governs not only the seizure of tangible items, but extends as well to the recording of oral statements overheard without any "technical trespass under ... local property law." *Silverman v. United States*.... Once this much is acknowledged, and once it is recognized that the Fourth Amendment protects people – and not simply "areas" – against unreasonable searches and seizures it becomes clear that the reach of that Amendment cannot turn upon the presence or absence of a physical intrusion into any given enclosure.

We conclude that the underpinnings of *Olmstead* and *Goldman* have been so eroded by our subsequent decisions that the "trespass" doctrine there enunciated can no longer be regarded as controlling. The Government's activities in electronically listening to and recording the petitioner's words violated the privacy upon which he justifiably relied while using the telephone booth and thus constituted a "search and seizure" within the meaning of the Fourth Amendment.

The fact that the electronic device employed to achieve that end did not happen to penetrate the wall of the booth can have no constitutional significance.... It is clear that this surveillance was so narrowly circumscribed that a duly authorized magistrate, properly notified of the need for such investigation, specifically informed of the basis on which it was to proceed, and clearly apprised of the precise intrusion it would entail, could constitutionally have authorized, with appropriate safeguards, the very limited search and seizure that the Government asserts in fact took place. Only last Term we sustained the validity of such an authorization, holding that, under sufficiently "precise and discriminate circumstances," a federal court may empower government agents to employ a concealed electronic device "for the narrow and particularized purpose of ascertaining the truth of the ... allegations" of a "detailed factual affidavit alleging the commission of a specific criminal offense." *Osborn v. United States....* Discussing that holding, the Court, in *Berger v. State of New York,*...said that "the order authorizing the use of the electronic device" in *Osborn* "afforded similar protections to those ... of conventional warrants authorizing the seizure of tangible evidence." Through those protections, "no greater invasion of privacy was permitted than was necessary under the circumstances...." Here, too, a similar judicial order could have accommodated "the legitimate needs of law enforcement" by authorizing the carefully limited use of electronic surveillance.

In the absence of such safeguards, this Court has never sustained a search upon the sole ground that officers reasonably expected to find evidence of a particular crime and voluntarily confined their activities to the least intrusive means consistent with that end.... The Government ...urges the creation of a new exception to cover this case. It argues that surveillance of a telephone booth should be exempted from the usual requirement of advance authorization by a magistrate upon a showing of probable cause. We cannot agree. Omission of such authorization "bypasses the safeguards provided by an objective predetermination of probable cause, and substitutes instead the far less reliable procedure of an after-the-event justification for the ... search, too likely to be subtly influenced by the familiar shortcomings of hindsight judgment." *Beck v. State of Ohio*, 379 U.S. 89, 96.... The government agents here ignored "the procedure of antecedent justification...that is central to the Fourth Amendment," a procedure that we hold to be a constitutional precondition of the kind of electronic surveillance involved in this case. Because the surveillance here failed to meet that condition, and because it led to the petitioner's conviction, the judgment must be reversed.

MR. JUSTICE MARSHALL took no part in this case.

MR. JUSTICES DOUGLAS, BRENNAN, HARLAN, and WHITE concurred.
MR. JUSTICE BLACK dissented.

UNITED STATES v. CALANDRA
414 U.S. 338; 94 S.Ct. 613; 38 L.Ed. 2d 561 (1974)

When John Calandra's place of business, the Royal Machine & Tool Co. in Cleveland, Ohio, was being searched for bookmaking records and wagering paraphernalia one of the agents, knowing of a pending federal investigation of loansharking activities, discovered and seized some related materials. Subsequently, a grand jury investigating loansharking activity subpoenaed Calandra to question him on the seized evidence but he refused to testify on Fifth Amendment grounds. The district court sustained his contention that the evidence had been illegally seized and that he could not be forced to testify even though the government would extend transactional immunity. The case proceeded to the Supreme Court on a writ of certiorari.

MR. JUSTICE POWELL delivered the opinion of the Court:

...On March 1, 1971, a special grand jury was convened in the Northern District of Ohio to investigate possible loansharking activities in violation of federal laws. The grand jury subpoenaed Calandra in order to ask him questions based on the evidence seized during the search of his place of business on December 15, 1970. Calandra appeared before the grand jury on August 17, 1971, but refused to testify, invoking his Fifth Amendment privilege against self-incrimination. The Government then requested the District Court to grant Calandra transactional immunity pursuant to 18 U.S. C §2514. Calandra requested and received a postponement of the hearing on the Government's application for the immunity order so that he could prepare a motion to suppress the evidence seized in the search.

Calandra later moved ... for suppression and return of the seized evidence on the grounds that the affidavit supporting the warrant was insufficient and that the search exceeded the scope of the warrant. On August 27, the District Court held a hearing at which Calandra stipulated that he would refuse to answer questions based on the seized materials. On October 1, the District Court entered its judgment ordering the evidence suppressed and returned to Calandra and further ordering that Calandra need not answer any of the grand jury's questions based on the suppressed evidence.... The court held that "due process ... allows a witness to litigate the question of whether the evidence which constitutes the basis for the questions asked of him before the grand jury has been obtained in a way which violates the constitutional protection against unlawful search and seizure...." The court found that the search warrant had been issued without probable cause and that the search had exceeded the scope of the warrant.

The Court of Appeals for the Sixth Circuit affirmed, holding that the District Court had properly entertained the suppression motion and that the exclusionary rule may be invoked by a witness before the grand jury to bar questioning based on evidence obtained in an unlawful search and seizure.... The offer to grant Calandra immunity was deemed irrelevant....

We granted the Government's petition for certiorari.... We now reverse.

II

The institution of the grand jury is deeply rooted in Anglo-American history. In England, the grand jury served for centuries both as a body of accusers sworn to discover and present for trial persons suspected of criminal wrongdoing and as a protector of citizens against arbitrary and oppressive governmental action. In this country the Founders thought the grand jury so essential to basic liberties that they provided in the Fifth Amendment that federal prosecution for serious crimes can only be instituted by "a presentment or indictment of a Grand Jury...." The grand jury's historic functions survive to this day. Its responsibilities continue to include both the determination whether there is probable cause to believe a crime has been committed and the protection of citizens against unfounded criminal prosecutions. *Branzburg v. Hayes*, 408 U.S. 665 ...(1972).

Traditionally the grand jury has been accorded wide latitude to inquire into violations of criminal law. No judge presides to monitor its proceedings. It deliberates in secret and may determine alone the course of its inquiry. The grand jury may compel the production of evidence or the testimony of witnesses as it considers appropriate, and its operation generally is unrestrained by the technical procedural and evidentiary rules governing the conduct of criminal trials. "It is a grand inquest, a body with powers of investigation and inquisition, the scope of whose inquiries is not to be limited narrowly by questions of propriety or forecasts of the probable result of the investigation, or by doubts whether any particular individual will be found properly subject to an accusation of crime." *Blair v. United States*, 250 U.S. 273 ...(1919).

The scope of the grand jury's powers reflects its special role in insuring fair and effective law enforcement. A grand jury proceeding is not an adversary hearing in which the guilt or innocence of the accused is adjudicated. Rather, it is an *ex parte* investigation to determine whether a crime has been committed and whether criminal proceedings should be instituted against any person. The grand jury's investigative power must be broad if its public responsibility is adequately to be discharged....

The power of a federal court to compel persons to appear and testify before a grand jury is also firmly established. *Kastigar v. United States*, 406 U.S. 441 (1972). The duty to testify has long been recognized as a basic obligation that every citizen owes his Government.... In *Branzburg v. Hayes* ...the Court noted that "[c]itizens generally are not constitutionally immune from grand jury subpoenas..." and that "the longstanding principle that 'the public ... has a right to every man's evidence' ... is particularly applicable to grand jury proceedings." The duty to testify may on occasion be burdensome and even embarrassing. It may cause injury to a witness' social and economic status. Yet the duty to testify has been regarded as "so necessary to the administration of justice" that the witness' personal interest in privacy must yield to the public's overriding interest in full disclosure.... Furthermore, a witness may not interfere with the course of the grand jury's inquiry. He "is not entitled to urge objections of incompetency or irrelevancy, such as a party might raise, for this is no concern of his...." Nor is he entitled "to challenge the authority of the court or of the grand jury" or "to set limits to the investigation that the grand jury may conduct...."

Of course, the grand jury's subpoena power is not unlimited. It may consider incompetent evidence, but it may not itself violate a valid privilege, whether established by the Constitution, statutes, or the common law.... Although, for example, an indictment based on evidence obtained in violation of a defendant's Fifth Amendment privilege is nevertheless valid,... the grand jury may not force a witness to answer questions in violation of that constitutional guarantee. Rather, the grand jury may override a Fifth Amendment claim only if the witness is granted immunity co-extensive with the privilege against self-incrimination. *Kastigar v. United States, supra.* Similarly, a grand jury may not compel a person to produce books and papers that would incriminate him. *Boyd v. United States*, 116 U.S. 616 ... (1886).... The grand jury is also without power to invade a legitimate privacy interest protected by the Fourth Amendment. A grand jury's subpoena *duces tecum* will be disallowed if it is "far too sweeping in its terms to be regarded as reasonable" under the Fourth Amendment.... Judicial supervision is properly exercised in such cases to prevent the wrong before it occurs.

III

In the instant case, the Court of Appeals held that the exclusionary rule of the Fourth Amendment limits the grand jury's power to compel a witness to answer questions based on evidence obtained from a prior unlawful search and seizure. The exclusionary rule was adopted to effectuate the Fourth Amendment right of all citizens "to be secure in their persons, houses, papers, and effects, against unreasonable searches and seizures...." Under this rule, evidence obtained in violation of the Fourth Amendment cannot be used in a criminal proceeding against the victim of the illegal search and seizure. *Weeks v. United States*, 232 U.S. 383 (1914); *Mapp v. Ohio*, 367 U.S. 643 (1961). This prohibition applies as well to the fruits of the illegally seized evidence. *Wong Sun v. United States*, 371 U.S. 471 (1963); *Siluerthorne Lumber Co. v. United States*, 251 U.S. 385 (1920).

The purpose of the exclusionary rule is not to redress the injury to the privacy of the search victim:

> "[T]he ruptured privacy of the victims' homes and effects cannot be restored. Reparation comes too late." *Linkletter v. Walker*, 381 U.S. 618 ...(1965).

Instead, the rule's prime purpose is to deter future unlawful police conduct and thereby effectuate the guarantee of the Fourth Amendment against unreasonable search and seizures:

> "The rule is calculated to prevent, not to repair. Its purpose is to deter – to compel respect for the constitutional guaranty in the only effectively available way-by removing the incentive to

disregard it." *Elkins v. United States*, 364 U.S. 206 ...(1960)....

In sum, the rule is a judicially created remedy designed to safeguard Fourth Amendment rights generally through its deterrent effect, rather than a personal constitutional right of the party aggrieved.

Despite its broad deterrent purpose, the exclusionary rule has never been interpreted to proscribe the use of illegally seized evidence in all proceedings or against all persons. As with any remedial device, the application of the rule has been restricted to those areas where its remedial objectives are thought most efficaciously served. The balancing process implicit in this approach is expressed in the contours of the standing requirement. Thus, standing to invoke the exclusionary rule has been confined to situations where the Government seeks to use such evidence to incriminate the victim of the unlawful search.... This standing rule is premised on a recognition that the need for deterrence and hence the rationale for excluding the evidence are strongest where the Government's unlawful conduct would result in imposition of a criminal sanction on the victim of the search.

IV

In deciding whether to extend the exclusionary rule to grand jury proceedings, we must weigh the potential injury to the historic role and functions of the grand jury against the potential benefits of the rule as applied in this context. It is evident that this extension of the exclusionary rule would seriously impede the grand jury. Because the grand jury does not finally adjudicate guilt or innocence, it has traditionally been allowed to pursue its investigative and accusatorial functions unimpeded by the evidentiary and procedural restrictions applicable to a criminal trial. Permitting witnesses to invoke the exclusionary rule before a grand jury would precipitate adjudication of issues hitherto reserved for the trial on the merits and would delay and disrupt grand jury proceedings. Suppression hearings would halt the orderly progress of an investigation and might necessitate extended litigation of issues only tangentially related to the grand jury's primary objective. The probable result would be "protracted interruption of grand jury proceedings,..." effectively transforming them into preliminary trials on the merits. In some cases the delay might be fatal to the enforcement of the criminal law.... In sum, we believe that allowing the grand jury witness to invoke the exclusionary rule would unduly interfere with the effective and expeditious discharge of the grand jury's duties.

Against this potential damage to the role and functions of the grand jury, we must weigh the benefits to be derived from this proposed extension of the exclusionary rule. Suppression of the use of illegally seized evidence against the search victim in a criminal trial is thought to be an important method of effectuating the Fourth Amendment. But it does not follow that the Fourth Amendment requires adoption of every proposal that might deter police misconduct.

...Any incremental deterrent effect which might be achieved by extending the rule to grand jury proceedings is uncertain at best. Whatever deterrence of police misconduct may result from the exclusion of illegally seized evidence from criminal trials, it is unrealistic to assume that application of the rule to grand jury proceedings would significantly further that goal. Such an extension would deter only police investigation consciously directed toward the discovery of evidence solely for use in a grand jury investigation. The incentive to disregard the requirement of the Fourth Amendment solely to obtain an indictment from a grand jury is substantially negated by the inadmissibility of the illegally seized evidence in a subsequent criminal prosecution of the search victim. For the most part, a prosecutor would be unlikely to request an indictment where a conviction could not be obtained. We therefore decline to embrace a view that would achieve a speculative and undoubtedly minimal advance in the deterrence of police misconduct at the expense of substantially impeding the role of the grand jury.

V

Respondent also argues that each and every question based on evidence obtained from an illegal search and seizure constitutes a fresh and independent violation of the witness' constitutional rights. Ordinarily, of course, a witness has no right of privacy before the grand jury. Absent some recognized privilege of confidentiality, every man owes his testimony. He may invoke his Fifth Amendment privilege against compulsory self-incrimination, but he may not decline to answer on the grounds that his responses might prove embarrassing or result in an unwelcome disclosure of his personal affairs. *Blair v. United States* ...(1919). Respondent's claim must be, therefore, not merely that the grand jury's questions invade his privacy but that, because those questions are based on illegally obtained evidence, they somehow constitute distinct violations of his Fourth Amendment rights. We disagree.

The purpose of the Fourth Amendment is to prevent unreasonable governmental intrusions into the privacy of one's person, house, papers, or effects. The wrong condemned is the unjustified governmental invasion of these areas of an individual's life. That wrong, committed in this case, is fully accomplished by the original search without probable cause. Grand jury questions based on evidence obtained thereby involve no independent governmental invasion of one's person, house, papers, or effects, but rather the usual abridgment of personal privacy common to all grand jury questioning. Questions based on illegally obtained evidence are only a derivative use of the product of a past unlawful search and seizure. They work no new Fourth Amendment wrong. Whether such derivative use of illegally obtained evidence by a grand jury should be proscribed presents a question, not of rights, but of remedies.

In the usual context of a criminal trial, the defendant is entitled to the suppression of, not only the evidence obtained through an unlawful search and seizure, but also any derivative use of that evidence. The prohibition of the exclusionary rule must reach such derivative use if it is to fulfill its function of deterring police misconduct. In the context of a grand jury proceeding, we believe that the damage to that institution from the unprecedented extension of the exclusionary rule urged by respondent outweighs the benefit of any possible incremental deterrent effect. Our conclusion necessarily controls both the evidence seized during the course of an unlawful search and seizure and any question or evidence derived therefrom (the fruits of the unlawful search). The same considerations of logic and policy apply to both the fruits of an unlawful search and seizure and derivative use of that evidence, and we do not distinguish between them.

The judgment of the Court of Appeals is
Reversed.

MR. JUSTICE BRENNAN, with whom MR. JUSTICES DOUGLAS and MARSHALL joined, dissented, saying in part,

The Court holds that the exclusionary rule in search-and-seizure cases does not apply to grand jury proceedings because the principal objective of the rule is "to deter future unlawful police conduct,..." and "it is unrealistic to assume that application of the rule to grand jury proceedings would significantly further that goal...." This downgrading of the exclusionary rule to a determination whether its application in a particular type of proceeding furthers deterrence of future police misconduct reflects a startling misconception, unless it is a purposeful rejection, of the historical objective and purpose of the rule.

The commands of the Fourth Amendment are, of course, directed solely to public officials. Necessarily, therefore, only official violations of those commands could have created the evil that threatened to make the Amendment a dead letter. But curtailment of the evil, if a consideration at all, was at best only a hoped-for effect of the exclusionary rule, not its ultimate objective. Indeed, there is no evidence that the possible deterrent effect of the rule was given any attention by the judges chiefly responsible for its formulation. Their concern as guardians of the Bill of Rights was to fashion an enforcement tool to give content and meaning to the Fourth Amendment's guarantees....

It is true that deterrence was a prominent consideration in the determination whether *Mapp v. Ohio*...(1961), which applied the exclusionary rule to the States, should be given retrospective effect. *Linkletter v. Walker*, 381 U.S. 618 (1965). But that lends no support to today's holding that the application of the exclusionary rule depends solely upon whether its invocation in a particular type of proceeding will significantly further the goal of deterrence....

The Court seriously errs in describing the exclusionary rule as merely "a judicially created remedy designed to safeguard Fourth Amendment rights generally through its deterrent effect.... Rather, the exclusionary rule is "part and parcel of the Fourth Amendment's limitation upon [governmental] encroachment of individual privacy," *Mapp v. Ohio*,... and "an essential part of both the Fourth and Fourteenth Amendments,..." that "gives to the individual no more than that which the Constitution guarantees him, to the police officer no less than that to which honest law enforcement is entitled, and, to the courts, that judicial integrity so necessary in the true administration of justice...." This *Mapp* summation crystallizes the series of decisions that developed the rule and with which today's holding is plainly at war. For the first time, the Court today discounts to the point of extinction the vital function of the rule to insure that the judiciary avoid even the slightest appearance of sanctioning illegal government conduct....

The judges who developed the exclusionary rule were well aware that it embodied a judgment that it is better for some guilty persons to go free than for the police to behave in forbidden fashion. A similar judgment led the Court to decide in *Silverthorne Lumber Co. v. United States*, 251 U.S. 385 (1920), that a grand jury must be denied access to plainly relevant but illegally seized papers. In that case, after federal agents unlawfully seized papers belonging to the Silverthornes and their corporation, and presented the documents to a grand jury which had previously indicted the Silverthornes, a district court ordered the documents returned and copies that had been prepared in the interim impounded. After returning the originals, the grand jury attempted to recoup them by issuance of a subpoena *duces tecum*. Compliance with the subpoena was refused, and contempt convictions, the Court, speaking through Mr. Justice Holmes, held that the Government was barred from utilizing any fruits of its forbidden act, stating that "[t]he essence of a provision forbidding the acquisition of evidence in a certain way is that not merely evidence so acquired shall not be used before the Court but that it shall not be used at all...."

Silverthome plainly controls this case. Respondent, like plaintiffs in error in *Silverthome*, seeks to avoid furnishing the grand jury with evidence that he would not have been called upon to supply but for the unlawful search and seizure....

It is no answer, to suggest as the Court does, that the grand jury witnesses' Fourth Amendment rights will be sufficiently protected "by the inadmissibility of the illegally seized evidence in a subsequent criminal prosecution of the search victim." This, of course, is no alternative for Calandra, since he was granted transactional immunity and cannot be criminally prosecuted. But the fundamental flaw of the alternative is that to compel Calandra to testify in the first place under penalty of contempt necessarily "thwarts" his Fourth Amendment protection and "entangle[s] the courts in the illegal acts of Government agents"-consequences that *Silverthome* condemned as intolerable....

In *Mapp*, the Court thought it had "close[d] the only courtroom door remaining open to evidence secured by official lawlessness" in violation of Fourth Amendment rights.... The door is again ajar. As a consequence, I am left with the uneasy feeling that today's decision may signal that a majority of my colleagues have positioned themselves to reopen the door still further and abandon altogether the exclusionary rule in search-and-seizure cases; for surely they cannot believe that application of the exclusionary rule at trial furthers the goal of deterrence, but that its application in grand jury proceedings will not "significantly" do so. Unless we are to shut our eyes to the evidence that crosses our desks every day, we must concede that official lawlessness has not abated and that no empirical data distinguishes trials from grand jury proceedings. I thus fear that when next we confront a case of conviction rested on illegally seized evidence, today's decision will be invoked to sustain the conclusion in that case also that "it is unrealistic to assume" that application of the rule at trial would "significantly further" the goal of deterrence – though, if the police are presently undeterred, it is difficult to see how removal of the sanction of exclusion will induce more lawful official conduct.

The exclusionary rule gave life to Madison's prediction that "independent tribunals of justice ... will be naturally led to resist every encroachment upon rights expressly stipulated for in the Constitution by the declaration of rights." 1 Annals of Cong. 439 (1789). We betray the trust upon which that prediction rested by today's long step toward abandonment of the exclusionary rule....

I dissent and would affirm the judgment of the Court of Appeals.

MIRANDA v. ARIZONA
384 U.S. 436; 86 S.Ct. 1602; 16 L.Ed. 2d 694 (1966)

This case, which was decided along with three others, is probably the most important, yet controversial, one in the area of criminal procedure in this century. In 1963, Ernesto Miranda was arrested for rape after being identified by his victim in a police lineup. He later confessed to the crime without being informed of his right to remain silent by the police and in the absence of counsel. On the basis of this confession Miranda was convicted. Later, Miranda appealed his case to the Supreme Court arguing that on the precedent of the Court's decision in Escobedo v. Illinois *(1964), his conviction was invalid. After the Court's decision in this case, Miranda was retried and sentenced to a maximum of thirty years in Arizona State Prison.*

MR. CHIEF JUSTICE WARREN delivered the opinion of the Court:

... We start here, as we did in *Escobedo*, with the premise that our holding is not an innovation in our jurisprudence, but is an application of principles long recognized and applied in other settings. We have undertaken a thorough reexamination of the *Escobedo* decision and the principles it announced, and we reaffirm it. That case was but an explication of basic rights that are enshrined in our Constitution – that "No person ...shall be compelled in any criminal case to be a witness against himself," and that "the accused shall ...have the Assistance of Counsel" – rights which were put in jeopardy in that case through official overbearing. These precious rights were fixed in our Constitution only after centuries of persecution and struggle. And in the words of Chief Justice Marshall, they were secured "for ages to come and ...designed to approach immortality as nearly as human institutions can approach it," *Cohens v. Virginia*, 6 Wheat. 264, 387 (1821)....

Our holding ... briefly stated ... is this: the prosecution may not use statements, whether exculpatory or inculpatory, stemming from custodial interrogation of the defendant unless it demonstrates the use of procedural safeguards effective to secure the privilege against self-incrimination. By custodial interrogation, we mean questioning initiated by law enforcement officers after a person has been taken into custody or otherwise deprived of his freedom of action in any significant way. As for the procedural safeguards to be employed, unless other fully effective means are devised to inform accused persons of their right of silence and to assure a continuous opportunity to exercise it, the following measures are required. Prior to any questioning, the person must be warned that he has a right to remain silent, that any statement he does make may be used as evidence against him, and that he has a right to the presence of an attorney, either retained or appointed. The defendant may waive effectuation of these rights, provided the waiver is made voluntarily, knowingly, and intelligently. If, however, he indicates in any manner and at any stage of the process that he wishes to consult with an attorney before speaking there can be no questioning. Likewise, if the individual is alone and indicates in any manner that he does not wish to be interrogated, the police may not question him. The mere fact that he may have answered some questions or volunteered some statements on his own does not deprive him of the right to refrain from answering any further inquiries until he has consulted with an attorney and thereafter consents to be questioned.

The constitutional issue we decide in each of these cases is the admissibility of statements obtained from a defendant questioned while in custody and deprived of – his freedom of action. In each, the defendant was questioned by police officers, detectives, or a prosecuting attorney in a room in which he was cut off from the outside world. In none of these cases was the defendant given a full and effective warning of his rights at the outset of the interrogation process. In all the cases, the questioning elicited oral admissions, and in three of them, signed statements as well which were admitted at their trials. They all thus share salient features – incommunicado interrogation of individuals in a police-dominated atmosphere, resulting in self-incriminating statements without full warnings of constitutional rights.

An understanding of the nature and setting of this in-custody interrogation is essential to our decisions today. The difficulty in depicting what transpires at such interrogations stems from the fact that in this country they have largely taken place incommunicado. From extensive factual studies undertaken in the early 1930's, including the famous Wickersham Report to Congress by a Presidential Commission, it is clear that police violence and the "third degree" flourished at that time. In a series of cases decided by this Court long after these studies, the police resorted to physical brutality – beatings, hanging, whipping – and to sustained and protracted questioning incommunicado in order to extort confessions. The 1961 Commission on Civil Rights found much evidence to indicate that "some policemen still resort to physical force to obtain confessions...." The use of physical brutality and violence is not, unfortunately, relegated to the past or to any part of the country.

Again we stress that the modern practice of in-custody interrogation is psychologically rather than physically oriented. As we have stated before, "Since *Chambers v. Florida*,...this Court has recognized that coercion can be mental as well as physical, and that the blood of the accused is not the only hallmark of an unconstitutional inquisition." *Blackburn v. Alabama*, 361U.S.199.... Interrogation still takes place in privacy. Privacy results in secrecy and this in turn results in a gap in our knowledge as to what in fact goes on in the interrogation rooms. A valuable source of information about present police practices, however, may be found in various police manuals and texts which document procedures employed with success in the past, and which recommend various other effective tactics. [The opinion surveys manuals and texts.]

From these representative samples of interrogation techniques, the setting prescribed by the manuals and observed in practice becomes clear. In essence, it is this: To be alone with the subject is essential to prevent distraction and to deprive him of any outside support. The aura of confidence in his guilt undermines his will to resist. He merely confirms the preconceived story the police seek to have him describe. Patience and persistence, at times relentless, questioning, are employed. To obtain a confession, the interrogator must "patiently maneuver himself or his quarry into a position from which the desired object may be obtained." When normal procedures fail to produce the needed result, the police may resort to deceptive stratagems such as giving false legal advice. It is important to keep the subject off balance, for example, by trading on his insecurity about himself or his surroundings. The police then persuade, trick, or cajole him out of exercising his constitutional rights.

Even without employing brutality, the "third degree" or the specific stratagems described above, the very fact of custodial interrogation exacts a heavy toll on individual liberty and trades on the weakness of individuals.

In these cases, we might not find the defendants' statements to have been involuntary in traditional terms. Our concern for adequate safeguards to protect precious Fifth Amendment rights is, of course, not lessened in the slightest. To be sure, the records do not evince overt physical coercion or patent psychological ploys. The fact remains that in none of these cases did the officers undertake to afford appropriate safeguards at the outset of the interrogation to insure that the statements were truly the product of free choice.

It is obvious that such an interrogation environment is created for no purpose other than to subjugate the individual to the will of his examiner. This atmosphere carries its own badge of intimidation. To be sure, this is not physical intimidation, but is equally destructive of human dignity. The current practice of incommunicado interrogation is at odds with one of our Nation's most cherished principles – that the individual may not be compelled to incriminate himself. Unless adequate protective devices are employed to dispel the compulsion inherent in custodial surroundings, no statement obtained from the defendant can truly be the product of his free choice....

Today ... there can be no doubt that the Fifth Amendment privilege is available outside of criminal court proceedings and serves to protect persons in all settings in which their freedom of action is curtailed from being compelled to incriminate themselves. We have concluded that without proper safeguards the process of in-custody interrogation of persons suspected or accused of crime contains inherently compelling pressures which work to undermine the individual's will to resist and to compel him to speak where he would not otherwise do so freely. In order to combat these pressures and to permit a full opportunity to exercise the privilege against self-incrimination, the accused must be adequately and effectively appraised of his rights and the exercise of those rights must be fully honored....

The circumstances surrounding in-custody interrogation can operate very quickly to overbear the will of one merely made aware of his privilege by his interrogators. Therefore, the right to have counsel present at the interrogation is indispensable to the protection of the Fifth Amendment privilege under the system we delineate today. Our aim is to assure that the individual's right to choose between silence and speech remains unfettered throughout the interrogation process....

Our decision is not intended to hamper the traditional function of police officers in investigating crime. See *Escobedo v. Illinois*.... When an individual is in custody on probable cause, the police may, of course, seek out evidence in the field to be used at trial against him. Such investigation may include inquiry of persons not under restraint. General on-the-scene questioning as to facts surrounding a crime or other general questioning of citizens in the fact-finding process is not affected by our holding. It is an act of responsible citizenship for individuals to give whatever information they may have to aid in law enforcement. In such situations the compelling atmosphere inherent in the process of in-custody interrogation is not necessarily present.

In dealing with statements obtained through interrogation, we do not purport to find all confessions inadmissible. Confessions remain a proper element in law enforcement. Any statement given freely and voluntarily without any compelling influences is, of course, admissible in evidence. The fundamental import of the privilege while an individual is in custody is not whether he is allowed to talk to the police without the benefit of warnings and counsel, but whether he can be interrogated. There is no requirement that police stop a person who enters a police station and states that he wishes to confess to a crime, or to a person who calls the police to offer a confession or any other statement he desires to make. Volunteered statements of any kind are not barred by the Fifth Amendment and their admissibility is not affected by our holding today....

In announcing these principles, we are not unmindful of the burdens which law enforcement officials must bear, often under trying circumstances. We also fully recognize the obligation of all citizens to aid in enforcing the criminal laws. This court, while protecting individual rights, has always given ample latitude to law enforcement agencies in the legitimate exercise of their duties. The limits we have placed on the interrogation process should not constitute an undue interference with a proper system of law enforcement. As we have noted, our decision does not in any way preclude police from carrying out their traditional investigatory functions....

MR. JUSTICE HARLAN, whom MR. JUSTICES STEWART and WHITE joined, dissented, saying in part:

I believe the decision of the Court represents poor constitutional law and entails harmful consequences for the country at large. How serious these consequences may prove to be only time can tell.... The new rules are not designed to guard against police brutality or other unmistakably banned forms of coercion. Those who use third-degree tactics and deny them in court are equally able and destined to lie as skillfully about warnings and waivers. Rather, the thrust of the new rules is to negate all pressures, to reinforce the nervous or ignorant suspect, and ultimately to discourage any confession at all. The aim in short is toward "voluntariness" in a utopian sense, or to view it from a different angle, voluntariness with a vengeance.

To incorporate this notion into the Constitution requires a strained reading of history and precedent and a disregard of the very pragmatic concerns that alone may on occasion justify such strains. I believe that reasoned examination will show that the Due Process Clauses provide an adequate tool for coping with confessions and that, even if the Fifth Amendment privilege against self-incrimination be invoked, its precedents taken as a whole do not sustain the present rules. Viewed as a choice based on pure policy, these new rules prove to be a highly debatable if not one-sided appraisal of the competing interests, imposed over widespread objection, at the very time when judicial restraint is most called for by the circumstances.

...The Court's opinion in my view reveals no adequate basis for extending the Fifth Amendment's privilege against self-incrimination to the police station. Far more important, it fails to show that the Court's new rules are well supported, let alone compelled, by Fifth Amendment precedents. Instead, the new rules actually derive from quotation and analogy drawn from precedents under the Sixth Amendment, which should properly have no bearing on police interrogation....

The more important premise is that pressure on the suspect must be eliminated though it be only the subtle influence of the atmosphere and surroundings. The Fifth Amendment, however, has never been thought to forbid all pressure to incriminate oneself in the situations covered by it.... However, the Court's unspoken assumption that any pressure violates the privilege is not supported by the precedents and it has failed to show why the Fifth Amendment prohibits that relatively mild pressure the Due Process Clause permits....

The Court's new rules aim to offset these minor pressures and disadvantages intrinsic to any kind of police interrogation. The rules do not serve due process interests in preventing blatant coercion since, as I noted earlier, they do nothing to contain the policeman who is prepared to lie from the start. The rules work for reliability in confessions almost only in the Pickwickian sense that they can prevent some from being given at all.

It is no secret that concern has been expressed lest long-range and lasting reforms be frustrated by this Court's too-rapid departure from existing constitutional standards. Despite the Court's disclaimer, the practical effect of the decision made today must inevitably be to handicap seriously sound efforts at reform, not least by removing options necessary to a just compromise of competing interests. Of course, legislative reform is rarely speedy or unanimous, though this Court has been more patient in the past. But the legislative reforms when they came would have the vast advantage of empirical data and comprehensive study, they would allow experimentation and use of solutions not open to the courts, and they would restore initiative in criminal law reform to those forums where it truly belongs.

MR. JUSTICE CLARK dissented.

MALLOY v. HOGAN
378 U.S. 1; 84 S.Ct. 1489; 12 L.Ed. 2d 653 (1964)

In 1959, Malloy was arrested during a gambling raid in Hartford, Connecticut. After pleading guilty to pool selling, a misdemeanor, he was given a suspended sentence. Some time later he was ordered to testify before a referee, appointed by the superior court of the county, who was to conduct an inquiry into alleged gambling and other criminal activities. When asked questions, Malloy refused to answer "on the grounds it may tend to incriminate me." The court adjudged him in contempt and committed him to prison until such time as he would be willing to cooperate. Malloy's application for a writ of habeas corpus was denied and later affirmed by the Connecticut Supreme Court of Errors. The Supreme Court of the United States granted certiorari.

MR. JUSTICE BRENNAN delivered the opinion of the Court:

In this case we are asked to reconsider prior decisions holding that the privilege against self-incrimination is not safe-guarded against state action by the Fourteenth Amendment. *Twining v. New Jersey, Adamson v. California.*

The petitioner was arrested during a gambling raid in 1959 by Hartford, Connecticut, police. He pleaded guilty to the crime of pool selling, a misdemeanor, and was sentenced to one year in jail and fined $500. The sentence was ordered to be suspended after ninety days, at which time he was to be placed on probation for two years. About sixteen months after his guilty plea, petitioner was ordered to testify before a referee appointed by the Superior Court of Hartford County to conduct an inquiry into alleged gambling and other criminal activities in the county. The petitioner was asked a number of questions related to events surrounding his arrest and conviction. He refused to answer any question "on the grounds it may tend to incriminate me." The Superior Court adjudged him in contempt, and committed him to prison until he was willing to answer the questions. Petitioner's application for a writ of habeas corpus was denied by the Superior Court, and the Connecticut Supreme Court of Errors affirmed.... The latter court held that the Fifth Amendment extended no privilege to him, and that the petitioner had not properly invoked the privilege available under the Connecticut Constitution....

The Court has not hesitated to re-examine past decisions according the Fourteenth Amendment a less central role in the preservation of basic liberties than that which was contemplated by its Framers when they added the Amendment to our constitutional scheme. Thus, although the Court as late as 1922 said that "neither the Fourteenth Amendment nor any other provisions of the

Constitution of the United States imposes upon the States any restrictions about 'freedom of speech'..." three years later *Gitlow v. New York* ... initiated a series of decisions which today hold immune from state invasion every First Amendment protection for the cherished rights of mind and spirit – the freedoms of speech, press, religion, assembly, association, and petition for redress of grievances.

Similarly, *Palko v. Connecticut* ...decided in 1937, suggested that the rights secured by the Fourth Amendment were not protected against state action, citing the statement of the Court in 1914 in *Weeks v. United States*, that "the 4th Amendment is not directed to individual misconduct of state officials." In 1961, however, the Court held that in the light of later decisions, it was taken as settled that "...the Fourth Amendment's right of privacy has been declared enforceable against the States through the Due Process Clause of the Fourteenth.... " *Mapp v. Ohio*.... Again, although the Court held in 1942 that in a state prosecution for a noncapital offense, "appointment of counsel is not a fundamental right," *Betts v. Brady*; cf. *Powell v. Alabama*...only last Term this decision was re-examined and it was held that provision of counsel in all criminal cases was "a fundamental right, essential to a fair trial," and thus was made obligatory on the States by the Fourteenth Amendment. *Gideon v. Wainwright*....

We hold today that the Fifth Amendment's exception from compulsory self-incrimination is also protected by the Fourteenth Amendment against abridgment by the States. Decisions of the Court since *Twining* and *Adamson* have departed from the contrary view expressed in those cases. We discuss first the decisions which forbid the use of coerced confessions in state criminal prosecutions.

Brown v. Mississippi ...was the first case in which the Court held that the Due Process Clause prohibited the States from using the accused's coerced confessions against him. The Court in *Brown* felt impelled, in light of *Twining,* to say that its conclusion did not involve the privilege against self-incrimination. "Compulsion by torture to extort a confession is a different matter...." But this distinction was soon abandoned, and today the admissibility of a confession in a state criminal prosecution is tested by the same standard applied in federal prosecutions since 1897, when, in *Bram v. United States*,... the Court held that "[i]n criminal trials, in the courts of the United States, wherever a question arises whether a confession is incompetent because not voluntary, the issue is controlled by that portion of the Fifth Amendment to the constitution of the United States commanding that no person 'shall be compelled in any criminal case to be a witness against himself.'..."

The marked shift to the federal standard in state cases began with *Lisenba v. California*,...where the Court spoke of the accused's "free choice to admit, to deny, or to refuse to answer...." See *Ashcraft v. Tennessee*; *Malinski v. New York*; *Spano v. New York*; *Lynumn v. Illinois*; *Haynes v. Washington*.... The shift reflects recognition that the American system of criminal prosecution is accusatorial, not inquisitorial, and that the Fifth Amendment privilege is its essential mainstay. *Rogers v. Richmond*....

Governments, state and federal, are thus constitutionally compelled to establish guilt by evidence independently and freely secured, and may not by coercion prove a charge against an accused out of his own mouth. Since the Fourteenth Amendment prohibits the States from inducing a person to confess through "sympathy falsely aroused," *Spano v. New York*,...or other like inducement far short of "compulsion by torture," *Haynes v. Washington*, it follows *a fortiori* that it also forbids the States to resort to imprisonment, as here, to compel him to answer questions that might incriminate him. The Fourteenth Amendment secures against state invasion the same privilege that the Fifth Amendment guarantees against federal infringement – the right of a person to remain silent unless he chooses to speak in the unfettered exercise of his own will, and to suffer no penalty, as held in *Twining*, for such silence.

This conclusion is fortified by our recent decision in *Mapp v. Ohio*; ... overruling *Wolf v. Colorado*,...which had held "that in a prosecution in a State court for a State crime the Fourteenth Amendment does not forbid the admission of evidence obtained by an unreasonable search and seizure...." *Mapp* held that the Fifth Amendment privilege against self-incrimination implemented the Fourth Amendment in such cases, and that the two guarantees of personal security conjoined in the Fourteenth Amendment to make the exclusionary rule obligatory upon the States. We relied upon the great case of *Boyd v. United States*,...decided in 1886, which, considering the Fourth and Fifth Amendments as running "almost into each other," ...held that "Breaking into a house and opening boxes and drawers are circumstances of aggravation; but any forcible and compulsory extortion of a man's own testimony, or of his private papers to be used as evidence to convict him of crime, or to forfeit his goods, is within the condemnation of [those Amendments]...." We said in *Mapp*:

> "We find that, as to the Federal Government the Fourth and Fifth Amendments and, as to the States, the freedom from unconscionable invasions of privacy and the freedom from convictions based upon coerced confessions do enjoy an 'intimate relation' in their perpetuation of 'principles of humanity and civil liberty [secured] ...only after years of struggle....' The philosophy of each Amendment and of each freedom is complementary to, although not dependent upon, that of the other in its sphere of influence – the very least that together they assure in either sphere is that no man is to be convicted on unconstitutional evidence...."

In thus returning to the *Boyd* view that the privilege is one of the "principles of a free government,..." *Mapp* necessarily repudiated the *Twining* concept of the privilege as a mere rule of evidence "best defended not as an unchangeable principle of universal justice, but as a law proved by experience to be expedient...."

The State urges, however, that the availability of the federal privilege to a witness in a state inquiry is to be determined according to a less stringent standard than is applicable in a federal proceeding. We disagree. We have held that the guarantees of the First Amendment, *Gitlow v. New York*; *Cantwell v. Connecticut*,... the prohibition of unreasonable searches and seizures of the Fourth Amendment, *Kerr v. California*,... and the right to counsel guaranteed by the Sixth Amendment, *Gideon v. Wainwright*, are all to be enforced against the States under the Fourteenth Amendment according to the same standards that protect those personal rights against federal encroachment.... The Court thus has rejected the notion that the Fourteenth Amendment applies to the States only a "watered-down, subjective version of the individual guarantees of the Bill of Rights...." If *Cohen v. Hurley* ... and *Adamson v. California*, suggest such an application of the privilege against self-incrimination, that suggestion cannot survive recognition of the degree to which the *Twining* view of the privilege has been eroded. What is accorded is a privilege of refusing to incriminate one's self, and the feared prosecution may be by either federal or state authorities. *Murphy v. Waterfront Commission*.... It would be incongruous to have different standards determine the validity of a claim of privilege based on the same feared prosecution, depending on whether the claim was asserted in a state or federal court. Therefore, the same standards must determine whether an accused's silence in either a federal or state proceeding is justified....

It was admitted on behalf of the State at oral argument – and indeed it is obvious from the questions themselves – that the State desired to elicit from the petitioner the identity of the person who ran the pool-selling operation in connection with which he had been arrested in 1959. It was apparent that petitioner might apprehend that if this person were still engaged in unlawful activity, disclosure of his name might furnish a link in a chain of evidence sufficient to connect the petitioner with a more recent crime for which he might still be prosecuted....

We conclude, therefore, that as to each of the questions, it was "evident from the implications of the question, in the setting in which it [was] asked, that a responsive answer to the question or an explanation of why it [could not] be answered might be dangerous because injurious disclosure could result," *Hoffman v. United States*....

Reversed.

MR. JUSTICE DOUGLAS concurred.

MR. JUSTICE HARLAN, whom MR. JUSTICE CLARK joined, dissented.

MR. JUSTICES WHITE and STEWART dissented.

ILLINOIS v. ALLEN
397 U.S. 337; 90 S.Ct. 1057; 25 L.Ed. 2d 353 (1970)

Allen, who was on trial for robbery, was removed from the courtroom for repeated disruptive behavior and the use of vile and abusive language directed at the trial judge. Allen had been warned by the judge that he would be removed if he engaged in another outburst. Thereafter he was convicted and this judgment was affirmed by the State Supreme Court. Allen filed a petition for a writ of habeas corpus in a federal district court contending that his forced removal from the courtroom had denied him the guarantee of "confrontation of witnesses" under the Sixth and Fourteenth Amendments. The district court denied the writ and the court of appeals reversed. The case then was brought to the Supreme Court by writ of certiorari.

MR. JUSTICE BLACK delivered the opinion of the Court.

The Confrontation Clause of the Sixth Amendment to the United States Constitution provides that: "In all criminal prosecutions, the accused shall enjoy the right ... to be confronted with the witnesses against him...." We have held that the Fourteenth Amendment makes the guarantees of this clause obligatory upon the States. *Pointer v. Texas*, 380 U.S. 400 (1965). One of the most basic of the rights guaranteed by the Confrontation Clause is the accused's right to be present in the courtroom at every stage of his trial. *Lewis v. United States*, 146 U.S. 370 (1892). The question presented in this case is whether an accused can claim the benefit of this constitutional right to remain in the courtroom while at the same time he engages in speech and conduct which is so noisy, disorderly, and disruptive that it is exceedingly difficult or wholly impossible to carry on the trial.

The issue arose in the following way. The respondent, Allen, was convicted by an Illinois jury of armed robbery and was sentenced to serve 10 to 30 years in the Illinois State Penitentiary. The evidence against him showed that on August 12, 1956, he entered a tavern in Illinois and, after ordering a drink, took $200 from the bartender at gunpoint. The Supreme Court of Illinois affirmed his conviction.... Later Allen filed a petition for a writ of habeas corpus in federal court alleging that he had been wrongfully deprived by the Illinois trial judge of his constitutional right to remain present throughout his trial....

The facts surrounding Allen's expulsion from the courtroom are set out in the Court of Appeals' opinion sustaining Allen's contention:...

> The trial began on September 9, 1957. After the State's Attorney had accepted the first four jurors following their voir dire examination, the petitioner began examining the first juror and continued at great length. Finally, the trial judge interrupted the petitioner, requesting him to confine his questions solely to matters relating to the prospective juror's qualifications. At that point, the petitioner started to argue with the judge in a most abusive and disrespectful manner. At last, and seemingly in

> desperation, the judge asked appointed counsel to proceed with the examination of the jurors. The petitioner continued to talk, proclaiming that the appointed attorney was not going to act as his lawyer. He terminated his remarks by saying, 'When I go out for lunchtime, you're [the judge] going to be a corpse here.' At that point he tore the file which his attorney had and threw the papers on the floor. The trial judge thereupon stated to the petitioner, 'One more outbreak of that sort and I'll remove you from the courtroom.' This warning had no effect on the petitioner. He continued to talk back to the judge, saying, 'There's not going to be no trial, either. I'm going to sit here and you're going to talk and you can bring your shackles out and strait jacket and put them on me and tape my mouth, but it will do no good because there's not going to be no trial.' After more abusive remarks by the petitioner, the trial judge ordered the trial to proceed in the petitioner's absence. The petitioner was removed from the courtroom. The voir dire examination then continued and the jury was selected in the absence of the petitioner. After a noon recess and before the jury was brought into the courtroom, the petitioner, appearing before the judge, complained about the fairness of the trial and his appointed counsel. He also said he wanted to be present in the court during his trial. In reply, the judge said that the petitioner would be permitted to remain in the courtroom if he "behaved [himself] and [did] not interfere with the introduction of the case." The jury was brought in and seated. Counsel for the petitioner then moved to exclude the witnesses from the courtroom. The defendant protested this effort on the part of his attorney, saying: 'There is going to be no proceeding. I'm going to start talking and I'm going to keep on talking all through the trial. There's not going to be no trial like this. I want my sister and my friends here in court to testify for me.' The trial judge thereupon ordered the petitioner removed from the courtroom....

After this second removal, Allen remained out of the courtroom during the presentation of the State's case-in-chief, except that he was brought in on several occasions for purposes of identification. During one of these latter appearances, Allen responded to one of the judge's questions with vile and abusive language. After the prosecution's case had been presented, the trial judge reiterated his promise to Allen that he could return to the courtroom whenever he agreed to conduct himself properly. Allen gave some assurances of proper conduct and was permitted to be present through the remainder of the trial, principally his defense, which conducted by his appointed counsel....

The Court of Appeals felt that the defendant's Sixth Amendment right to be present at his own trial was so "absolute" that, no matter how unruly or disruptive the defendant's conduct might be, he could never be held to have lost that right so long as he continued to insist upon it, as Allen clearly did. Therefore the Court of Appeals concluded that a trial judge could never expel a defendant from his own trial and that the judge's Sultanate remedy when faced with an obstreperous defendant like Allen who determines to make his trial impossible is to bind and gag him. We cannot agree that the Sixth Amendment, the cases upon which the Court of Appeals relied, or any other cases of this Court so handicap a trial judge in conducting a criminal trial. The broad dicta in *Hopt v. Utah*, 110 U.S. 574 (1884), and *Lewis v. United States*, 146 U.S. 370 (1892), that a trial can never continue in the defendant's absence, have been expressly rejected. *Diaz v. United States*, 223 U.S. 442 (1912). We accept instead the statement of Mr. Justice Cardozo who, speaking for the Court in *Snyder v. Massachusetts*, 291 U.S. 97 ... (1934), said, "No doubt the privilege [of personally confronting witnesses] may be lost by consent or at times even by misconduct." Although mindful that courts must indulge every reasonable presumption against the loss of constitutional rights,... we explicitly hold today that a defendant can lose his right to be present at trial if, after he has been warned by the judge that he will be removed if he continues his disruptive behavior, he nevertheless insists on conducting himself in a manner so disorderly, disruptive, and disrespectful of the court that his trial cannot be carried on with him in the courtroom. Once lost, the right to be present can, of course, be reclaimed as soon as the defendant is willing to conduct himself consistently with the decorum and respect inherent in the concept of courts and judicial proceedings.

It is essential to the proper administration of criminal justice that dignity, order, and decorum be the hallmarks of all court proceedings in our country. The flagrant disregard in the courtroom of elementary standards of proper conduct should not and cannot be tolerated. We believe trial judges confronted with disruptive, contumacious, stubbornly defiant defendants must be given sufficient discretion to meet the circumstances of each case. No one formula for maintaining the appropriate courtroom atmosphere will be best in all situations. *We think there are at least three constitutionally permissible ways for a trial judge to handle an obstreperous defendant like Allen: (1) bind and gag him, thereby keeping him present; (2) cite him for contempt; (3) take him out of the courtroom until he promises to conduct himself properly.*

I

Trying a defendant for a crime while he sits bound and gagged before the judge and jury would to an extent comply with that part of the Sixth Amendment's purposes that accords the defendant an opportunity to confront the witnesses at the trial. But even to contemplate such a technique, much less to see it, arouses a feeling that no person should be tried while shackled and gagged except as a last resort. Not only is it possible that the sight of shackles and gags might have a significant effect on the jury's feelings about the defendant, but the use of this technique is itself something of an affront to the very dignity and decorum of the judicial proceedings that the judge is seeking to uphold.

Moreover, one of the defendant's primary advantages of being present at the trial, his ability to communicate with his counsel, is greatly reduced when the defendant is in a condition of total physical restraint. It is in part because of these inherent disadvantages and limitations in this method of dealing with disorderly defendants that we decline to hold with the Court of Appeals that a defendant cannot under any possible circumstances be deprived of his right to be present at trial. However, in some situations which we need not attempt to foresee, binding and gagging might possibly be the fairest and most reasonable way to handle a defendant who acts as Allen did here.

II

In a footnote the Court of Appeals suggested the possible availability of contempt of court as a remedy to make Allen behave in his robbery trial, and it is true that citing or threatening to cite a contumacious defendant for criminal contempt might in itself be sufficient to make a defendant stop interrupting a trial. If so, the problem would be solved easily, and the defendant could remain in the courtroom. Of course, if the defendant is determined to prevent any trial, then a court in attempting to try the defendant for contempt is still confronted with the identical dilemma that the Illinois court faced in this case. And criminal contempt has obvious limitations as a sanction when the defendant is charged with a crime so serious that a very severe sentence such as death or life imprisonment is likely to be imposed. In such a case the defendant might not be affected by a mere contempt sentence when he ultimately faces a far more serious sanction. Nevertheless, the contempt remedy should be borne in mind by a judge in the circumstances of this case.

Another aspect of the contempt remedy is the judge's power, when exercised consistently with state and federal law, to imprison an unruly defendant such as Allen for civil contempt and discontinue the trial until such time as the defendant promises to behave himself. This procedure is consistent with the defendant's right to be present at trial, and yet it avoids the serious shortcomings of the use of shackles and gags. It must be recognized, however, that a defendant might conceivably, as a matter of calculated strategy, elect to spend a prolonged period in confinement for contempt in the hope that adverse witnesses might be unavailable after a lapse of time. A court must guard against allowing a defendant to profit from his own wrong in this way.

III

The trial court in this case decided under the circumstances to remove the defendant from the courtroom and to continue his trial in his absence until and unless he promised to conduct himself in a manner befitting an American courtroom. As we said earlier, we find nothing unconstitutional about this procedure. Allen's behavior was clearly of such an extreme and aggravated nature as to justify either his removal from the courtroom or his total physical restraint. Prior to his removal he was repeatedly warned by the trial judge that he would be removed from the courtroom if he persisted in his unruly conduct, and, as Judge Hastings observed in his dissenting opinion, the record demonstrates that

Allen would not have been at all dissuaded by the trial judge's use of his criminal contempt powers. Allen was constantly informed that he could return to the trial when he would agree to conduct himself in an orderly manner. Under these circumstances we hold that Allen lost his right guaranteed by the Sixth and Fourteenth Amendments to be present throughout his trial.

IV

It is not pleasant to hold that the respondent Allen was properly banished from the court for a part of his own trial. But our courts, palladiums of liberty as they are, cannot be treated disrespectfully with impunity. Nor can the accused be permitted by his disruptive conduct indefinitely to avoid being tried on the charges brought against him. It would degrade our country and our judicial system to permit our courts to be bullied, insulted, and humiliated and their orderly progress thwarted and obstructed by defendants brought before them charged with crimes. As guardians of the public welfare, our state and federal judicial systems strive to administer equal justice to the rich and the poor, the good and the bad, the native and foreign born of every race, nationality, and religion. Being manned by humans, the courts are not perfect and are bound to make some errors. But, if our courts are to remain what the Founders intended, the citadels of justice, their proceedings cannot and must not be infected with the sort of scurrilous, abusive language and conduct paraded before the Illinois trial judge in this case. The record shows that the Illinois judge at all times conducted himself with that dignity, decorum, and patience that befit a judge. Even in holding that the trial judge had erred, the Court of Appeals praised his "commendable patience under severe provocation."

We do not hold that removing this defendant from his own trial was the only way the Illinois judge could have constitutionally solved the problem. We do hold, however, that there is nothing whatever in this record to show that the judge did not act completely within his discretion. Deplorable as it is to remove a man from his own trial, even for a short time, we hold that the judge did not commit legal error in doing what he did.

The judgment of the Court of Appeals is
Reversed.

MR. JUSTICE BRENNAN concurred.

MR. JUSTICE DOUGLAS concurred, saying in part:

I agree with the Court that a criminal trial, in the constitutional sense, cannot take place where the courtroom is a bedlam and either the accused or the judge is hurling epithets at the other. A courtroom is a hallowed place where trials must proceed with dignity and not become occasions for entertainment by the participants, by extraneous persons, by modern mass media, or otherwise.

My difficulty is not with the basic hypothesis of this decision, but with the use of this case to establish the appropriate guidelines for judicial control....

We should not reach the merits but should reverse the case for staleness of the record and affirm the denial of relief by the District Court. After all, behind the issuance of a writ of habeas corpus is the exercise of an informed discretion. The question, how to proceed in a criminal case against a defendant who is a mental case, should be resolved only on a full and adequate record.

Our real problems of this type lie not with this case but with other kinds of trials. First are the political trials. They frequently recur in our history and insofar as they take place in federal courts we have broad supervisory powers over them. That is one setting where the question arises whether the accused has rights of confrontation that the law invades at its peril.

In Anglo-American law, great injustices have at times been done to unpopular minorities by judges, as well as by prosecutors. I refer to London in 1670 when William Penn, the gentle Quaker, was tried for causing a riot when all that he did was to preach a sermon on Grace Church Street, his church having been closed under the Conventicle Act....

The panel of judges who tried William Penn were sincere, law-and-order men of their day. Though Penn was acquitted by the jury, he was jailed by the court for his contemptuous conduct. Would we tolerate removal of a defendant from the courtroom during a trial because he was insisting on his constitutional rights, albeit vociferously, no matter how obnoxious his philosophy might have been to the bench that tried him? Would we uphold contempt in that situation?

Problems of political indictments and of political judges raise profound questions going to the heart of the social compact. For that compact is two-sided: majorities undertake to press their grievances within limits of the Constitution and in accord with its procedures; minorities agree to abide by constitutional procedures in resisting those claims.

Does the answer to that problem involve defining the procedure for conducting political trials or does it involve the designing of constitutional methods for putting an end to them? This record is singularly inadequate to answer those questions. It will be time enough to resolve those weighty problems when a political trial reaches this Court for review.

Second are trials used by minorities to destroy the existing constitutional system and bring on repressive measures. Radicals on the left historically have used those tactics to incite the extreme right with the calculated design of fostering a regime of repression from which the radicals on the left hope to emerge as the ultimate victor. The left in that role is the provocateur. The Constitution was not designed as an instrument for that form of rough-and-tumble contest. The social compact has room for tolerance, patience, and restraint, but not for sabotage and violence. Trials involving that spectacle strike at the very heart of constitutional government.

I would not try to provide in this case the guidelines for those two strikingly different types of cases. The case presented here is the classical criminal case without any political or subversive overtones. It involves a defendant who was a sick person and who may or may not have been insane in the classical sense but who apparently had a diseased mind. And, as I have said, the record is so stale that it is now much too late to find out what the true facts really were.

EX PARTE MILLIGAN
4 Wall. 2; 18 L.Ed. 281 (1866)

On March 3, 1863, Congress enacted a law which authorized President Abraham Lincoln to suspend the writ of habeas corpus and directed federal courts to discharge prisoners in instances where the grand jury had failed to take action. In 1864, Lambdin P. Milligan, an admitted "copperhead" and citizen of Indiana, was arrested by the military for conspiracy against the United States, for giving aid and comfort to the Confederacy and other charges. Brought before a military commission he was tried, convicted and sentenced to death by hanging. Thereafter Milligan petitioned a circuit court for a writ of habeas corpus arguing that as a civilian he could not be tried by the military since the civilian courts were still open in Indiana. The court certified the questions before them to the Supreme Court.

MR. JUSTICE DAVIS delivered the opinion of the Court:

The controlling question in the case is this: Upon the facts stated in Milligan's petition, and the exhibits filed, had the military commission mentioned in its jurisdiction, legally, to try and sentence him? Milligan, not a resident of one of the rebellious states, or a prisoner of war, but a citizen of Indiana for twenty years past, and never in the military or naval service, is, while at his home, arrested by the military power of the United States, imprisoned, and, on certain criminal charges preferred against him, tried, convicted, and sentenced to be hanged by a military commission, organized under the direction of the military commander of the military district of Indiana. Had this tribunal the *legal* power and authority to try and punish this man?

...The Constitution of the United States is a law for rulers and people, equally in war and in peace, and covers with the shield of its protection an classes of men, at all times, and under all circumstances. No doctrine involving more pernicious consequences was ever invented by the wit of man than that any of its provisions can be suspended during any of the great exigencies of government. Such a doctrine leads directly to anarchy or despotism, but the theory of necessity on which it is based is false; for the government, within the Constitution, has all the powers granted to it which are necessary to preserve its existence; as has been happily proved by the result of the great effort to throw off its just authority.

Have any of the rights guaranteed by the Constitution been violated in the case of Milligan? and if so, what are they?

Every trial involves the exercise of judicial power; and from what source did the military commission that tried him derive their authority? Certainly no part of the judicial power of the country was conferred on them; because the Constitution expressly vests it "in our supreme court and such inferior courts as the Congress may from time to time ordain and establish," and it is not pretended that the commission was a court ordained and established by Congress. They cannot justify on the mandate of the President; because he is controlled by law, and has his appropriate sphere of duty, which is to execute, not to make, the laws; and there is no unwritten criminal code to which resort can be had as a source of jurisdiction....

It can serve no useful purpose to inquire what those laws and usages are, whence they originated, where found and on whom they operate; they can never be applied to citizens in states which have upheld the authority of the government, and where the courts are open and their process unobstructed. This court has judicial knowledge that in Indiana the Federal authority was always unopposed, and its courts always open to hear criminal accusations and redress grievances; and no usage of war could sanction a military trial there for any offense whatever of a citizen in civil life, in nowise connected with the military service. *Congress could grant no such power*; and to the honor of our national legislature be it said, it has never been provoked by the state of the country even to attempt its exercise. One of the plainest constitutional provisions was, therefore, infringed when Milligan was tried by a court not ordained and established by Congress, and not composed of judges appointed during good behavior.

Why was he not delivered to the Circuit Court of Indiana to be proceeded against according to law? No reason of necessity could be urged against it; because Congress had declared penalties against the offenses charged, provided for their punishment, and directed that court to hear and determine them. And soon after this military tribunal was ended, the Circuit Court met, peacefully transacted its business, and adjourned. It needed no bayonets to protect it, and required no military aid to execute its judgments. It was held in a state, eminently distinguished for patriotism, by judges commissioned during the Rebellion, who were provided with juries, upright, intelligent, and selected by a marshal appointed by the President. The government had no right to conclude that Milligan, if guilty, would not receive in that court merited punishment; for its records disclose that it was constantly engaged in the trial of similar offenses, and was never interrupted in its administration of criminal justice. If it was dangerous, in the distracted condition of affairs, to leave Milligan unrestrained of his liberty, because he "conspired against the government, afforded aid and comfort to rebels, and incited the people to insurrection," the law said arrest him, confine him closely, render him powerless to do further mischief; and then present his case to the grand jury of the district, with proofs of his guilt, and, if indicted, try him according to the course of the common law....

Another guaranty of freedom was broken when Milligan was denied a trial by jury.... The Sixth Amendment affirms that "in all criminal prosecutions the accused shall enjoy the right to a speedy and public trial by an impartial jury," language broad enough to embrace all persons and cases; but the Fifth recognizes the necessity of an indictment, or presentment, before any one can be held to answer for high crimes, "except cases arising in the land or naval forces, or in the militia, when in actual service, in time of war or public danger;" and the framers of the Constitution, doubtless, meant to limit the right of trial by jury, in the Sixth

Amendment, to those persons who were subject to indictment or presentment in the Fifth....

It is claimed that martial law covers with its broad mantle the proceedings of this military commission. The proposition is this: that in a time of war the commander of an armed force (if in his opinion the exigencies of the country demand it, and of which he is to judge), has the power, within the lines of his military district, to suspend all civil rights and their remedies, and subject citizens as well as soldiers to the rule of his will; and in the exercise of his lawful authority cannot be restrained, except by his superior officer or the President of the United States.

If this position is sound to the extent claimed, then when war exists, foreign or domestic, and the country is sub-divided into military departments for mere convenience, the commander of one of them can, if he chooses, within his limits, on the plea of necessity, with the approval of the Executive, substitute military force for and to the exclusion of the laws, and punish all persons as he thinks right and proper without fixed or certain rules.

The statement of this proposition shows its importance; for, if true, republican government is a failure, and there is an end of liberty regulated by law. Martial law, established on such a basis, destroys every guaranty of the Constitution, and effectually renders the "military independent of and superior to the civil power" – the attempt to do which by the King of Great Britain was deemed by our fathers such an offense, that they assigned it to the world as one of the causes which impelled them to declare their independence. Civil liberty and this kind of martial law cannot endure together; the antagonism is irreconcilable; and, in the conflict, one or the other must perish.

...But, it is insisted that the safety of the country in time of war demands that this broad claim for martial law shall be sustained. If this were true, it could be well said that a country preserved at the sacrifice of all the cardinal principles of liberty, is not worth the cost of preservation. Happily, it is not so.

It will be borne in mind that this is not a question of the power to proclaim martial law, when war exists in a community and the courts and civil authorities are overthrown. Nor is it a question what rule a military commander, at the head of his army, can impose on states in rebellion to cripple their resources and quell the insurrection. The jurisdiction claimed is much more extensive. The necessities of the service, during the late Rebellion, required that the loyal states should be placed within the limits of certain military districts and commanders appointed in them; and, it is urged, that this, in a military sense, constituted them the theater of military operations; and, as in this case, Indiana had been and was again threatened with invasion by the enemy, the occasion was furnished to establish martial law. The conclusion does not follow from the premises. If armies were collected in Indiana, they were to be employed in another locality, where the laws were obstructed and the national authority disputed. On her soil there was no hostile foot; if once invaded, that invasion was at an end, and with it all pretext for martial law. Martial law cannot arise from a threatened invasion.

The necessity must be actual and present; the invasion real, such as effectually closes the courts and deposes the civil administration.

It is difficult to see how the safety of the country required martial law in Indiana. If any of her citizens were plotting treason, the power of arrest could secure them until the government was prepared for their trial, when the courts were open and ready to try them. It was as easy to protect witnesses before a civil as a military tribunal; and as there could be no wish to convict, except on sufficient legal evidence surely an ordained and established court was better able to judge of this than a military tribunal composed of gentlemen not trained to the profession of the law.

It follows, from what has been said on this subject, that there are occasions when martial rule can be properly applied. If, in foreign invasions or civil war, the courts are actually closed, and it is impossible to administer criminal justice according to law, then, in the theater of active military operations, where war really prevails, there is a necessity to furnish a substitute for the civil authority, thus overthrown, to preserve the safety of the army and society; and as no power is left but the military, it is allowed to govern by martial rule until the laws can have their free course. *As necessity creates the rule, so it limits its duration, for, if this government is continued after the courts are reinstated, it is a gross usurpation of power.* Martial rule can never exist where the courts are open, and in the proper and unobstructed exercise of their jurisdiction. It is also confined to the locality of actual war....

But it is insisted that Milligan was a prisoner of war, and, therefore, excluded from the privileges of the statute. It is not easy to see how he can be treated as a prisoner of war, when he lived in Indiana for the past twenty years, was arrested there, and had not been, during the late troubles, a resident of any of the states in rebellion. If in Indiana he conspired with bad men to assist the enemy, he is punishable for it in the courts of Indiana; but, when tried for the offense, he cannot plead the rights of war; for he was not engaged in legal acts of hostility against the government, and only such persons, when captured, are prisoners of war. If he cannot enjoy the immunities attaching to the character of a prisoner of war, how can he be subject to their pains and penalties?...

MR. CHIEF JUSTICE CHASE, joined by MR. JUSTICES WAYNE, SWAYNE and MILLER, dissented.

KOREMATSU v. UNITED STATES
323 U.S. 214; 65 S.Ct. 193; 89 L.Ed. 194 (1944)

On February 20, 1942, President Franklin D. Roosevelt issued an executive order authorizing the establishment of military areas in the United States from which certain individuals could not be allowed to either leave, enter, remain or be removed in order to prevent espionage and sabotage. Acting under the War power, Congress supported the President and enacted a law providing penalties for violations of the military regulations. The general responsible for the Western Defense Command began by imposing certain restrictions, such as curfew, on all Japanese residents of the area including Americans of Japanese ancestry.

Thereafter, the decision was made to relocate or compulsorily remove all persons of Japanese heritage from the West Coast to War Relocation Centers in the interior of the country. One of the American citizens affected was Korematsu, who refused to leave his home in California. A federal district court convicted him for knowingly violating the exclusion order and a circuit court affirmed. The case was then brought to the Supreme Court on a writ of certiorari. A number of evacuees, including some who had also had their property seized by the State of California, renounced their citizenship. On May 20, 1959, the Congress fully restored the citizenship of those who had done so; nearly thirty years later Congress finally agreed to pay compensation to the survivors of the camps.

MR. JUSTICE BLACK delivered the opinion of the Court:

In the light of the principles we announced in [*Hirabayashi v. United States*, 320 U.S. 81 (1943)], we are unable to conclude that it was beyond the war power of Congress and the Executive to exclude those of Japanese ancestry from the West Coast war area at the time they did. True, exclusion from the area in which one's home is located is far greater deprivation than constant confinement to the home from 8 P.M. to 6 A.M. Nothing short of apprehension by the proper military authorities of the gravest imminent danger to the public safety can constitutionally justify either. But exclusion from a threatened area, no less than curfew, has a definite and close relationship to the prevention of espionage and sabotage. The military authorities, charged with the primary responsibility of defending our shores, concluded that curfew provided inadequate protection and ordered exclusion. They did so, as pointed out in our *Hirabayashi* opinion, in accordance with Congressional authority to the military to say who should, and who should not, remain in the threatened areas....

Like curfew, exclusion of those of Japanese origin was deemed necessary because of the presence of an unascertained number of disloyal members of the group, most of whom we have no doubt were loyal to this country. It was because we could not reject the finding of the military authorities that it was impossible to bring about an immediate segregation of the disloyal from the loyal that we sustained the validity of the curfew order as applying to the whole group. In the instant case, temporary exclusion of the entire group was rested by the military on the same ground. The judgment that exclusion of the whole group was for the same reason a military imperative answers the contention that the exclusion was in the nature of group punishment based on antagonism to those of Japanese origin.... Approximately 5000 American citizens of Japanese ancestry refused to swear unqualified allegiance to the United States and to renounce all allegiance to the Japanese Emperor, and several thousand evacuees requested repatriation to Japan.

We uphold the exclusion order as of the time it was made and when the petitioner violated it.... In doing so, we are not unmindful of the hardships imposed by it upon a large group of American citizens.... But hardships are part of war, and war is an aggregation of hardships. All citizens alike, both in and out of uniform, feel the impact of war in greater or lesser measure. Citizenship has its responsibilities as well as its privileges, and in time of war the burden is always heavier. Compulsory exclusion of large groups of citizens from their homes, except under circumstances of direst emergency and peril, is inconsistent with our basic governmental institutions. But when under conditions of modern warfare our shores are threatened by hostile forces, the power to protect must be commensurate with the threatened danger.

It is said that we are dealing here with the case of imprisonment of a citizen in a concentration camp solely because of his ancestry, without evidence or inquiry concerning his loyalty and good disposition towards the United States. Our task would be simple, our duty clear, were this a case involving the imprisonment of a loyal citizen in a concentration camp because of racial prejudice. Regardless of the true nature of the assembly and relocation centers – and we deem it unjustifiable to call them concentration camps with all the ugly connotations that term implies – we are dealing specifically with nothing but an exclusion order. To cast this case into outlines of racial prejudice, without reference to the real military dangers which were presented, merely confuses the issue. Korematsu was not excluded from the military area because of hostility to him or to his race. He was excluded because we are at war with the Japanese Empire, because the properly constituted military authorities feared an invasion of our West Coast and felt constrained to take proper security measures, because they decided that the military urgency of the situation demanded that all citizens of Japanese ancestry be segregated from the West Coast temporarily, and finally, because Congress, reposing its confidence in this time of war in our military leaders – as inevitably it must – determined that they should have the power to do just this. There was evidence of disloyalty on the part of some, the military authorities considered that the need for action was great, and time was short. We cannot – by availing ourselves of the calm perspective of hindsight – now say that at that time these actions were unjustified.
Affirmed.

MR. JUSTICE FRANKFURTER wrote a concurring opinion.

MR. JUSTICE ROBERTS dissented, saying in part:

I dissent, because I think the indisputable facts exhibit a clear violation of constitutional rights.

This is not a case of keeping people off the streets at night as was *Hirabayashi v. United States*... nor a case of temporary exclusion of a citizen from an area for his own safety or that of the community, nor a case of offering him an opportunity to go temporarily out of an area where his presence might cause danger to himself or to his fellows. On the contrary, it is the case of convicting a citizen as a punishment for not submitting to imprisonment in a concentration camp, based on his ancestry, and solely because of his ancestry, without evidence or inquiry concerning his loyalty and good disposition towards the United States....

MR. JUSTICE MURPHY dissented, saying in part,

This exclusion of "all persons of Japanese ancestry, both alien and nonalien," from the Pacific Coast area on a plea of military necessity in the absence of martial law ought not to be approved. *Such exclusion goes over "the very brink of constitutional power" and falls into the ugly abyss of racism....*

The military necessity which is essential to the validity of the evacuation order ... resolves itself into a few intimations that certain individuals actively aided the enemy, from which it is inferred that the entire group of Japanese-Americans could not be trusted to be or remain loyal to the United States. No one denies, of course, that there were some disloyal persons of Japanese descent on the Pacific Coast who did all in their power to aid their ancestral land. Similar disloyal activities have been engaged in by many persons of German, Italian, and even more pioneer stock in our country. *But to infer that examples of individual disloyalty can justify discriminatory action against the entire group is to deny that under our system of law individual guilt is the sole basis for deprivation of rights.* Moreover, this inference, which is at the very heart of the evacuation orders, has been used in support of the abhorrent and despicable treatment of minority groups by the dictatorial tyrannies which this nation is now pledged to destroy. To give constitutional sanction to that inference in this case, however well-intentioned may have been the military command on the Pacific Coast, is to adopt one of the cruelest of the rationales used by our enemies to destroy the dignity of the individual and to encourage and open the door to discriminatory actions against other minority groups in the passions of tomorrow.

No adequate reason is given for the failure to treat these Japanese-Americans on an individual basis by holding investigations and hearings to separate the loyal from the disloyal, as was done in the case of persons of German and Italian ancestry.... It is asserted merely that the loyalties of this group "were unknown and time was of the essence." Yet nearly four months elapsed after Pearl Harbor before the first exclusion order was issued; nearly eight months went by until the last order was issued; and the last of these "subversive" persons was not actually removed until almost eleven months had elapsed. Leisure and deliberation seem to have been more of the essence than speed....

I dissent, therefore, from this legalization of racism. Racial discrimination in any form and in any degree has no justifiable part whatever in our democratic way of life. It is unattractive in any setting but it is utterly revolting among a free people who have embraced the principles set forth in the Constitution of the United States. All residents of this nation are kin in some way by blood or culture to a foreign land. Yet they are primarily and necessarily a part of the new and distinct civilization of the United States. They must accordingly be treated at all times as the heirs of the American experiment and as entitled to all the rights and freedoms guaranteed by the Constitution.

MR. JUSTICE JACKSON dissented.

CHAPTER XIII

EQUAL PROTECTION OF THE LAWS

The Fourteenth Amendment provides that "No State shall ... deny to any person within its jurisdiction the equal protection of the laws." This means that all persons are to be treated equally under law. The state and local governments, in their laws and policies, cannot capriciously classify or otherwise discriminate on the basis of race, color, sex, religion, ethnic origin or social status. Although the term "persons' is used in the Constitution, the rights which have been created and protected by the amending process, laws enacted by Congress, decisions of the Supreme Court, and executive orders are *positive* guarantees which extend almost *exclusively* to American *citizens*. In 1866, the framers and drafters of the Amendment fully intended to make newly freed slaves citizens of the United States and to protect their rights form invasion by state and local governments; to, in effect, overrule the *Dred Scott* decision (1857). All citizens of this nation, *without* discrimination or classification, have a right to vote, to run for public office, to serve on juries, to purchase and own property according to their means, to travel freely, and to have the privilege of an education. The Amendments, other than the Fourteenth, that embrace the concept of civil rights lend support to these propositions, particularly with respect to political rights: the *Thirteenth* abolished slavery and involuntary servitude; the *Fifteenth* guaranteed the right to vote in federal elections to all citizens regardless of race or color; the *Nineteenth* extended the right to vote in federal elections to all citizens regardless of sex; the *Twenty-third* permitted the District of Columbia to participate in presidential elections; the *Twenty-fourth* eliminated the State-imposed poll tax or any other tax as a requisite for exercising the franchise in federal elections; the *Twenty-sixth* lowered the voting age to citizens eighteen years or older in state and federal elections.

While other groups, (e.g., Hispanics, Native-Americans, women, and the elderly) have been instrumental in probing the frontiers of contemporary civil rights, all have built upon the experiences and struggles of black Americans. An understanding of the development of modern civil rights thus requires an understanding of the injustices black Americans have had to overcome.

POLITICAL AND SOCIAL DISCRIMINATION: RACE, COLOR, ETHNIC ORIGIN

Among the most controversial issues debated by the Founders was the legal disposition of Negroes under the Constitution. The Framers wanted to *avoid* the slavery question at that time because of the overriding concern of national survival; the unity of North and South was of the utmost importance if a stable Union was to be created. The delegates agreed to establish a deadline of twenty years of continued importation of slaves, after which, it would be *illegal* (Article 1, Section 9, Paragraph 1). Another aspect of the "slavery problem" was related to representation of states in Congress. The southern slave owners wanted slaves to be counted when determining the number of representatives in the House; while the northern representatives objected, claiming they should be able to include their livestock, if the South could include their "property." The result of this debate was the infamous "Three-Fifths Compromise": it allowed Negroes to be considered *three-fifths* of a person for proportional representation purposes (Article 1, Section 2, Paragraph 3).

Almost immediately following the Civil War and President Lincoln's assassination in 1865, the Radical Republicans in control of Congress embarked on a harsh policy of political and social Reconstruction of the South. Such a program was engendered by three factors: *First*, the Civil War itself. The very fact that the eleven Confederate states had rebelled against the just authority of the Union and, by doing so, had cost the lives of millions of innocent Americans; *second*, many Republicans demanded military occupation of the Southern states for the protection of the newly-freed slave; and finally, Republican leaders, especially Thaddeus Stevens and Charles Sumner, realized that the party's national position was precarious. It had only *regional* power in the Midwestern and New England States, and Pennsylvania. Only the Democrats had a national, albeit factionalized, following. Accordingly, it was only realistic that a policy of making the Negro a citizen, with political and civil rights protected from state interference, was inevitable. Given Negroes' *allegiance* to the Republican party whose government had freed them, coupled with the fact that Southern Democrats who participated in the "rebellion" would lose the franchise, the Republicans could expect a healthy southern power base in the future.

To achieve these objectives, Congress created a virtual sea of legislative and constitutional proposals. The Civil Rights Acts of 1866, 1870, and 1871, called for broad protection of Negro political rights and permitted the filing of civil suits for damages in cases of possible violations. The Thirteenth, Fifteenth, and particularly the Fourteenth Amendments were proposed and ratified to constitutionally justify these sweeping legislative measures. The Reconstruction Era was to last only a decade.

The end of Reconstruction came with the disputed presidential election of 1876. Tilden, the Democratic candidate, received 4,300,590 popular and 184 electoral votes; the Republican, Rutherford B. Hayes was able to muster only 4,036,298 popular and 163 electoral votes. Tilden needed only *one* of twenty-two contested electoral votes from Louisiana. Hayes had to gain *all* of the contested votes to become President. On January 29, 1877, an Electoral Commission of eight Republicans and seven Democrats was created to settle the matter. During the proceedings Republican and Democratic representatives negotiated a "deal:" *end* military occupation and Reconstruction of the South, and all twenty-two votes would go to Hayes. On March 2, at 4:10 A.M. the leader of the Senate announced to both houses of Congress the election of Rutherford B. Hayes as President of the United States. Within the next year, state legislatures throughout the South, now back in the hands of white southern conservatives, enacted "Jim Crow" laws which established segregation and eliminated the political and economic power of Negroes.

EQUAL JUSTICE UNDER LAW

The Equal Protection Clause of the Fourteenth Amendment to the Constitution has been the legal foundation upon which the struggle to regain legal and political equality developed. Almost all cases advanced against racial discrimination were based on the contention that such discriminatory practices violated this Constitutional requirement. In the *Civil Rights Cases* of 1883, the Supreme Court let it be known that this was a Constitutional mandate applied directly to the state and local governments and available to Congress only as a basis for corrective legislation designed to counteract injuries incurred due to state action. It was *not* available as an injunction against wrongful acts committed by *individuals*, for such action "is simply a private wrong" and cannot impair the civil rights of another individual unless supported by state law. Therefore, non-governmental discrimination against blacks or private groups, no matter how wrongful, does not violate the Reconstruction Amendments.

Accordingly, an obvious target of litigation were state restrictions on the right to vote since the Fifteenth Amendment had even more specifically guaranteed the exercise of the franchise. In a number of decisions, the Supreme Court struck down such devices as the "grandfather" clause and membership restrictions in political parties; see *Guinn v. United States* (1915); *Nixon v. Herndon* (1929); *Nixon v. Condon* (1932). In *Smith v. Allwright* (1944), the Court invalidated the Texas "white primary" which had allowed only white citizens to participate in the Democratic primary in that one-party state as a violation of the Fifteenth Amendment. The last vestiges of disenfranchisement were erased by the ratification of the Twenty-fourth Amendment, which prohibited the poll tax and the passage of the Voting Rights Acts of 1965 and 1970 eliminated the administering of "literacy" tests.

On the other hand, the distinction between civil or political discrimination and social discrimination opened the door for sophisticated efforts of racism, such as the use of restrictive covenants, by which private landowners contracted not to sell their property to Negroes. This practice necessitated even more rulings from the Court, in which very fine Constitutional distinctions were drawn.

Whites resorted to restrictive covenants after 1917, when the Court handed down an opinion which invalidated a city ordinance segregating the races in residential areas as a violation of the Fourteenth Amendment; see *Buchanan v.*

Warley. Since the city could not legally segregate residential areas, private citizens took it upon themselves "to save" their communities. When asked to void private covenants, the Court unanimously refused, saying that such agreements were not unconstitutional. Since *Corrigan v. Buckley* (1926) involved a controversy in Washington, D.C., the decision held that the Fifth Amendment Due Process Clause was prohibitive only against the federal government, not individuals. If the action had been initiated in the states, the Fourteenth Amendment would have been the obvious basis of the ruling.

Restrictive covenants became widespread until 1948 when the Court spelled the end for state enforcement of this discriminative practice. In *Shelley v. Kraemer* (1948), the Court drew the line between private and state discrimination, when it held that, although the Fourteenth Amendment could not be used to enjoin individuals involved in racial discrimination, it still prevented state support of such agreements. So, though not rejecting *Corrigan*, the Court said that to allow enforcement of covenants in the state courts would be allowing the states to participate in discrimination and thus violate the Fourteenth Amendment. At the same time, the Justices avoided the constitutional issues involved in federal enforcement of restrictive covenants, since such discrimination was forbidden by the Civil Rights Act of 1866; see *Hurd v. Hodge* (1948). Also, the Court rejected the enforcement of damage suits against violators of covenant restrictions, for to allow such recourse would be inviting the employment of state judicial power to enforce segregation; see *Burrows v. Jackson* (1953).

This was *not* to stifle the imagination and determination of various white communities, as Californians were successful in passing a state constitutional amendment which would effectively prevent interference with covenants by state governments. However, the California State Supreme Court voided the amendment as repugnant to the Fourteenth Amendment and the Supreme Court affirmed; see *Eitman v. Mulkey* (1967).

White citizens of Akron, Ohio, came up with a new twist in a futile attempt to maintain racial segregation by amending their city charter to provide for popular approval of all fair housing projects that were designed to end housing discrimination based on race, color, religion, national origin or ancestry, with race carrying a much greater burden of proof than the other factors for approval. The Court, pursuant to the federal Open Housing Act of 1968, necessarily rejected this provision; see *Hunter v. Erickson* (1969).

DISCRIMINATION IN EDUCATION

The Court, in a landmark case in 1896, held that "the enforced separation of the races, as applied to the internal commerce of the states, neither abridges the privileges or the immunities of the colored man, deprives him of his property without due process nor deprives him the equal protection of the laws;" see *Plessy v. Ferguson*. In its view, if the *separate* facilities provided for whites and blacks were *intrinsically* or tangibly *equal*, the requirements of the Equal Protection Clause has been satisfied, i.e., "*separate but equal*." The Court's callous opinion, written by Justice *Brown*, further stated philosophically that segregation of the races does not mark Negroes inferior to whites. "If this be so, it is not because of anything found in the act, but solely because the colored race chooses to put that construction upon it." The Court went on to say that it was only concerned with the civil and political rights of citizens and "if one race be inferior to the other socially, the Constitution of the United States *cannot* put them on the same plane." Although his colleagues could not see any direct linkage between required segregation and inferior social status, Justice Harlan, in his most quoted opinion, asserted that "our Constitution is *color-blind*, and neither knows nor tolerates classes among citizens.... We boast of a freedom enjoyed by our people above all other peoples, but it is difficult to reconcile that boast with a state of the law which, practically, puts the brand of servitude and degradation upon a large class of our fellow citizens.... the judgment this day rendered will, in time, prove to be quite as pernicious as the decision made by this tribunal in the *Dred Scott* case."

This decision made "separate but equal" a nearly unbearable fact of life for African-Americans for the next sixty years. However, the "equality" of the separate facilities, particularly the schools, was an easily attained myth, as accommodations for the races were never even *comparable*. The Court never demanded absolute equality, and sometimes not even a reasonable facsimile. Three years after *Plessy*, the Court accepted financial inability as a valid reason for a county not to provide high school education facilities for some sixty Negroes, even though it was capable of maintaining such a school for whites. The most ironic aspect of the case was that Negro residents were paying taxes for their children's education, which the Court dismissed by saying that "it is impracticable to distribute taxes equally;" see *Cummings v. County Board of Education* (1899).

Even when an educational institution, on its own, attempted to disregard race as the basis for admission and substitute knowledge for all children instead, the Court sided with the state; see *Berea College v. Kentucky* (1908). Berea College admitted blacks into its classrooms along with whites, in violation of state laws forbidding integration. When the case came to the Supreme Court, the state law was upheld on the ground that the College was a corporation from which the "state may withhold powers which may be exercised by and cannot be denied to an individual...." The corporate grant to the College was not impaired by an amendment providing for separate instruction of the races.

By 1938, the attitude of the Court was gradually changing its view point and insisted upon stricter standards of equality in separate facilities. This shift was evidenced in a case in which a Negro had been denied admission to the University of Missouri Law School because of his racial background; see *Missouri ex rel. Gaines v. Canada* (1938). By all other standards, Gaines was eligible. Since Missouri had *no* Negro Law School for Gaines to attend, the University curators, in accordance with state law, offered to pay his tuition to any willing law school of any *adjacent* state. The Court felt that this arrangement did not constitute "equal facilities" because the "separate but equal doctrine" was applicable to *each* state in isolation from the others: "The admissibility of laws separating the races in the enjoyment of privileges afforded by the state rests wholly upon the quality of the privileges which the laws give to the separate groups within the State." Thus, the Court ordered Gaines to be enrolled at the University of Missouri Law School.

A decade later, the Court, in a *per curiam* opinion, reaffirmed *Gaines*, when a Negro woman was not allowed to attend the University of Oklahoma Law School. It held that for "equal protection of the laws" to be satisfied, the state must provide a legal education for Negroes and "to do so as soon as it does for whites;" see *Sipuel v. University of Oklahoma* (1950).

After these decisions, it became increasingly clear to all institutions of higher learning that it would no longer be *possible* to deny admission to Negroes solely because they were Negroes. Nonetheless, this did not stop them from making last-ditch attempts at imposing restrictions upon the Negro students once they were *admitted*. One such case involved a Negro graduate student at the University of Oklahoma who was required to occupy a single chair placed *outside* of the classroom, a *separate* table in the library, and in the cafeteria. In an unanimous opinion, the Court said that under the Equal Protection Clause of the Fourteenth Amendment, once admitted, Negro students *must* receive the same treatment as whites at the hands of the state; see *McLaurin v. Oklahoma State Regents* (1950).

Throughout these cases, the Court was upholding "separate-equality" standard, but was insisting on *more* significant equality than it had earlier. In *Sweatt v. Painter* (1950), the Court took the final steps in the area of higher education when it ruled that a Negro must be admitted to the University of Texas Law School, the best in the state, even though a separate Negro law school was in existence. Although the Court reserved judgment on whether the "separate but equal" doctrine had a constitutional place in the field of education, it did base its decision on grounds that rendered it virtually impossible for states to create a "make-shift" Negro law school which provided "equal facilities," by emphasizing intangible factors over mere intrinsic disparities. The unanimous opinion spelled out that where such intangibles as the reputation of the faculty, the standing of the alumni, and the tradition and prestige of the school afford it a superior status, equality is not achieved by admitting qualified blacks to a school of lesser esteem.

This decree removed all doubt as to the constitutional invalidity of "separate but equal" in the post graduate institutes and raised much doubt as to the application of that doctrine to *lower* levels of education. The Warren Court attempted to settle this issue four years later, when it unanimously held in four state cases under the title of *Brown v. Board of Education* (1954), that "separate but equal" had *no* place in the field of *education*: "Separate educational facilities are *inherently* unequal."

After the Allied conquest of Nazi Germany and the discovery of the atrocious results of racism carried out in Nazi concentration camps during World War II, America found itself increasingly pressed to justify its *own* particular brand of racial discrimination. At the same time, Thurgood Marshall and other civil rights lawyers in the NAACP were bombarding the Court with extensive briefs illustrating the detrimental sociological and psychological effects of segregation upon Negro children. This undoubtedly affected Chief Justice Earl Warren, who, in turn, greatly influenced his associates. This view was verified in Warren's opinion, when he wrote that "to separate them [Negro children] from others of similar age and qualifications solely because of their race generates a feeling of inferiority as to their status in the community that may affect their *hearts* and *minds* in a way unlikely ever to be undone." Unfortunately, the Court failed to rely on Justice Harlan's dissent in *Plessy*. The failure to do so not only blunted the thrust of the decision, but it has also led to the complicated issues of "color blind" vs. "color conscious" and outcries of "reverse discrimination" on the part of whites, see *De Funis v. Odegaard* (1974), *McDaniel v. Barres* (1991), *Regents v. Bakke* (1978); *Fullilove v. Klutznick* (1980).

The Court also ruled on the companion case of *Brown* in *Bolling v. Sharpe* (1954) which dealt with segregation in the District of Columbia. For the first time in the history of the United States, the Due Process Clause of the Fifth Amendment was so interpreted as to prohibit the federal government from engaging in racial segregation.

It must be understood that *Brown* did *not* overrule *Plessy*, per se, since the latter dealt with separate railroad facilities involved in interstate transportation services. The Court's nullification was limited in application *solely* to *education*. After 1954, *Plessy* was still technically *ruling* law except for education and interstate commerce. Accordingly, the Court decided on a piecemeal approach to nullify *Plessy's* application in other areas, case by case.

The most unusual aspect of the *Brown* case was that, after the Court handed down its verdict, it then decided to *delay* implementation of corrective action for one year. The Court asked for arguments to be presented at a later date on the best methods by which to carry-out integration. This decision for delay was applauded at the time as a *brilliant* maneuver in that it allowed for a cooling-off period in the Southern states affected; however, in effect, the Court which ruled that civil rights were being denied, allowed this unconstitutional practice to continue and the flames of racial prejudice to be fueled. Moreover, this Highest Court of law, for whatever reasons, relied more on sociological jurisprudence dealing with the harmful effects of segregation, than on sound *legal* and *historical* argumentation centered on the Equal Protection Clause of the Fourteenth Amendment. With the erosion of time, this factor has left *Brown I* open to logical and legitimate criticisms.

A year later, in *Brown v. Board of Education* (1955), the Justices deliberated on the question of the proper means of desegregation. The Court once again failed to set definite standards or deadlines for relief, requiring only a "prompt, and reasonable start toward compliance," to be pursued "with all *deliberate speed*." The Court then remanded all cases to the district courts which would consider the adequacy of the desegregation plans and determine if the "good faith compliance" command was satisfied. This ruling only served to bring *more* litigation to the Court because of varying connotations of "good faith" by obstructionist federal judges sitting on southern district courts. Nevertheless,

Thurgood Marshall and his NAACP lawyers were satisfied, at the time, with the Supreme Court's decisions in *Brown I* and *II*.

As can be imagined, the age-old practice of segregation was not put asunder overnight. After the *Brown II* was handed down, there were varied reactions. In a few schools, integration came swiftly with little opposition, in most others, desegregation was bitterly fought, to the point of outright refusals to comply with the Court's dicta, and even leading to the closing of *all* public schools in some states. In one such action, the public schools of Prince Edward County in Virginia were closed in 1959 when the school board refused to appropriate funds for their maintenance but did so for "private" all-white schools.

When confronted with a court decree requiring admission of blacks, the board said that, "Knowing the people of this county as we do, we know that it is not possible to operate the schools of this county with the terms of that principle, and, at the same time, maintain an atmosphere conducive to the educational benefit of our people." Obviously, the board did not feel that Negroes were equal citizens, with personal and immediate rights, since they sought not to educate them at all *if* force was to be used against them. Private schools were operated for whites only who received state and county tuition grants to help defray costs.

The Court ruled that the Equal Protection Clause had been violated by the closure because the Prince Edward pupils were receiving different treatment from students of other counties since they had *no* public schools. Most importantly, since the state provided funds for these so-called "private" schools, it established an unconstitutional precedent which allowed the state to participate, if not encourage, this discriminatory activity; see *Griffin v. County School Board of Prince Edward County* (1964).

Other school boards, instead of flagrantly opposing integration, formulated plans that pronounced "compliance," but which, in reality, offered no such thing. In 1965, New Kent County of Virginia employed a "freedom-of-choice" program by which students could choose between the two county schools, one previously all-white, the other Negro. Three years later, it was discovered that 85% of the Negroes still attended one school, with whites going to the other. The Court decided that the New Kent plan was unacceptable because other speedier and more effective means of desegregation were "reasonably" available;" *Green v. County School Board of New Kent County* (1968).

After this case, it was apparent that a deadline for full desegregation was necessary, so the U.S. Court of Appeals for the Fifth Circuit ordered complete unitary school systems by the fall of 1969 for the five southern states under its jurisdiction. In midsummer of 1969 it was obvious that some schools would not be properly prepared to meet the deadline, so the national government requested a postponement. However, on appeal to the Supreme Court, the government's plea was denied and the Court held, in a *per curiam* opinion, that "continued operation of racially segregated schools under the standard of 'all deliberate speed' is no longer *constitutionally* permissible." *Alexander v. Holmes County Board of Education* (1968).[1]

A later case introduced another type of discrimination in education for the Court to consider; this plan being based on monetary value of the school district. In *San Antonio School District v. Rodriguez* (1973), the Court, in a 5 - 4 decision, held that "education, of course, is *not* among the rights afforded explicit protection under our Federal Constitution." This statement was brought about when the Texas system of school financing was challenged as being discriminatory to poor residents, in that each school district in the state supplements state aid with an *ad valorem* tax on property *within* its jurisdiction, and if the land is low in value, as it is in most minority group areas, the per child expenditure is also low. Other more wealthy districts had much higher expenditures because of the higher land value within its jurisdiction. The Court said that although such a system is imperfect, it does offer each child a basic education, and does *not* violate the Equal Protection Clause of the Fourteenth Amendment. Justice Marshall, dissenting, said that "the right of every American to an equal start in life, so far as the provision of state service as important as education is concerned, is far too vital to permit discrimination."[2]

Addressing itself to *de jure* segregation, the Supreme Court has generally upheld the use of court-ordered busing to achieve racial balance within each school district; see *Swann v. Charlotte-Mecklenburg Board of Education* (1971); *Wright v. Council of Emporia* (1972), *United States v. Scotland Neck Board of Education* (1972). Moreover, a year later the Court reaffirmed its holding that in racial segregation suits, the burden of proof is on the accused to show that invidious discrimination is *not* being enforced; see *Keyes v. School District No. 1., Denver, Colorado* (1973). In this case, the school board had effectuated segregation by manipulating student attendance zones, school site selections, and by implementation of neighborhood school policies. The Court held this to be *de jure* segregation and allowed the court-ordered busing plan to take effect, even though there was no Colorado law *requiring* or allowing a dual school system. After *Brown*, each state assumed "an affirmative duty to effectuate a transition to a racially nondiscriminatory school system." See *Untied States v. Fordice* (1992).

However, in cases involving *more* than two school districts where discrimination cannot be shown, the court has shown its unwillingness to uphold complicated busing remedies created by federal district courts as plainly evidenced in *Milliken v. Bradley* (1974), *Pasadena Bd. v. Spangler* (1976); *Crawford v. Bd. of Los Angeles* (1982); *Howlett v. Rose* (1990).

Finally, with respect to equal access to public accommodations, the Court upheld the validity of the Civil Rights Act of 1964 which prohibits discrimination on the basis of color, race, religion, or sex in public accommodations engaged in interstate commerce, *e.g.*, hotels, motels, service stations, restaurants, theaters and other places of public entertainment; see *Heart of Atlanta Motel v. United States* (1964); *Katzenbach v. McClung* (1964). However, the court made a fine distinction when it ruled that a state could validly grant a liquor license to a private fraternal organization which practiced racial discrimination. In *Moose Lodge v. Irvis* (1972), the Court said that "individious discriminations" by the state were prerequisites to hold that state as a partner in racial discrimination under the Fourteenth Amendment. Liquor licenses and other state-provided minimal services such as police and fire protection afforded organizations that practiced racial discrimination, were not to be considered as constituting invidious discrimination on the state's behalf. With respect to discrimination on the basis of sex, the Court has constantly applied the Public Facilities Section (Title II) to end it in private organizations and public service groups; *Roberts v. Jaycees* (1984); *California Savings & Loan v. Guerra* (1987); *Johnson v. Transportation Agency* (1987).

CRIMINAL COURTS
MORE EQUAL JUSTICE FOR SOME, THAN FOR OTHERS

Racial discrimination in the spectrum of criminal procedure is another era to which the Equal Protection Clause has been effectively invoked in an effort to provide fair and equal justice for Negroes. However, in so doing, it was necessary once again for the Court to articulate narrow guidelines, as in 1880, when the Court upheld a Congressional statute that prohibited any manner of racial discrimination during the selection of petit and grand juries (*Ex parte Virginia*), while concurrently ruling that Negroes were not *entitled* to have members of their race on their indicting and trial juries; see *Virginia v. Rives*. In these cases, the Court was defining "an impartial jury" as one whose jurors are chosen in a non-discriminatory manner, but not one with a specified racial composition. This was later elaborated upon when the Court reviewed the case of *Akins v. Texas* (1944) and held that no group of persons merited a proportional representation of their peers on their grand and petit juries; *Batson v. Kentucky*, 476 U.S. 79 (1986); *Powers v. Ohio*, 111 S. Ct. 1364 (1991).

In 1900, the Court laid down a definite policy concerning service by Negroes on grand juries. "Whenever by any action of a State, whether through its legislature, through its courts, or through its executive or administrative officers, all persons of the African race are excluded, solely because of their race or color, from serving as grand jurors in the criminal prosecution of a person of the African race, the equal protection of the laws is denied to him, contrary to the Fourteenth Amendment.... ;" see *Carter v. Texas* (1900). This was also applicable to other racial groups, such as Mexican-Americans, *Hernandez v. Texas* (1954), and in an ironic turn of events, to whites, as the Court ruled that a white man was denied "equal protection" if Negroes were barred from his juries; see *Peters v. Kiff* (1972).

Although the defendant is usually innocent until proven guilty, in discrimination cases the Court has assumed that the *state* is guilty until proven innocent; see *Hill v. Texas* (1942). The Court ruled that the state must prove to the Court's satisfaction that it did not *intentionally* discriminate in jury selection when alleged to have done so. This rule was applied in the case of *Avery v. Georgia* (1953), when the Court was not appeased by the state's defense for printing potential jurors' names on different colored cards based on their race. "Equal protection of the laws" had been denied to those Negroes whose names were printed on cards distinguishable from those upon which white applicants were printed.

Another example of invidious discrimination arose in a system under which jury commissioners selected jurors for the lists through personal friendships even though some Negroes were among the chosen few; see *Cassell v. Texas* (1950). The commissioners were constitutionally bound to familiarize themselves with Negroes qualified for jury service.

In two decisions that seemingly contradicted its previous rulings, the Court, when confronted with the legality of two different, yet questionable, methods of jury selection, affirmed on both counts. In one case, which concerned the employment of the "struck jury" method of juror selection in Alabama resulted in a diversion from the peremptory challenge process; see *Swain v. Alabama* (1965). This procedure involved the "striking" of prospective jurors one-per-turn by the prosecutor and two-per-turn by the defense, until the final twelve remained. In the county under investigation, not one Negro chosen had ever been a member of the twelve. Nevertheless, the Court still held the system valid and free of discrimination, despite evidence to the contrary that it permitted the state to strike all Negroes, a commonplace practice in Southern court. However, in 1992, the Court overturned its earlier rule in *Swain* and prohibited the use of peremptory challenges to eliminate certain groups of persons from serving on the jury; see, *Edmonson v. Lecoille Concrete* and *Georgia v. McCollum*, 111 S. Ct. 2077 (1992).

Finally, a particular point of concern among civil rights advocates is the long-standing observation that some "color-neutral" criminal statutes are often applied with a heavier hand on blacks and other minorities than on whites. From May 1996 to February 1997, the Court made the following rulings on traffic stops and road blocks: (1) the validity of a traffic stop that is based on "probable cause" is not dependent upon the intent of the officer; see *Whren v. United States*, 116 S.Ct. 1769 (1996); (2) a vehicle stop to determine the "standard of review" for findings relevant to the existence of probable cause *or* "reasonable suspicion," a somewhat *less* demanding standard for searches. See *Omelas v. United States*, 116 S.Ct. 1657 (1996); (3) the validity of a state officer conducting a traffic stop to seek permission to search the automobile *without* first making it clear to the driver that he is neither being legally detained nor that he is free to drive on; and (4) finally, that police may order passengers *and* the driver out of the vehicle with first being placed under arrest.

BEYOND RACE

All laws discriminate. Of necessity, they make distinctions among types of actions, groups of people and varieties of behavior. For example, a law which requires individuals to pay a 5% tax on income earned as wages is not taxing income earned from investments. The law, therefore, classifies individuals as either wage earners or non-wage earners. It also discriminates against wage earners compared, to say, investment earners, for the former would pay $5 of every hundred dollars earned in taxes; the latter would pay nothing. Such discrimination, however, would almost certainly pass constitutional muster. The Court would subject the law to a *"rational basis test."* That is, the Court would ask whether the discrimination between wage earners and non-wage earners was a reasonable one, or one that had *a rational basis in some legitimate government activity*. As in due process cases, this rational basis test essentially means that the benefit of the doubt will go to the government, and the law will be deemed constitutional as long as the government can show *any* reasonable justification. The burden is on the plaintiff to prove the law's unconstitutionality by demonstrating that there is no possible reasonable explanation for the government's actions.

Other criteria for discriminating among persons, however, are considered by the Court to be *suspect classifications* – race and ethnic origin are examples. Laws or government actions which are directed against a suspect classification are subject to much more stringent review by the Court than those not involving a suspect classification. This more searching review is referred to as *"strict scrutiny."* Laws and actions subject to "strict scrutiny" must pass the *"compelling interest test,"* i.e. a law which is based on a suspect classification must be shown to be *a necessary means of advancing a compelling state interest.* Suspect classifications, therefore, are presumed unconstitutional and the burden of proof is on the government to show why they are necessary to achieve an overwhelmingly significant government end.

Whether a classification is constitutional, therefore, depends upon whether or not it is defined as "suspect," and subject to strict scrutiny and the compelling interest test. Laws involving "suspect" classification are almost always found unconstitutional. Laws assuming a classification that has not been deemed "suspect" almost always are found constitutional.

A problem for the Court, therefore, is determining the principle for identifying some classifications as "suspect" and not others. Why, for example, is race a "suspect classification" and not income level? One suggestion is that suspect classifications are those, like race and ethnicity, over which the individual has no control, but even this common sense rule of thumb is not without its problems. In the first place, classifications such as race and ethnicity are at least partially socially constructed, i.e., who is black, who white; who Irish, who Chinese is *partially* determined by social convention, not nature. Likewise, not all classifications which are rooted in nature would seem to be suspect, e.g., age, or mental health, such that laws discriminating along them would be presumed unconstitutional.

The difficulties involved with strict scrutiny and suspect classifications are quite evident in cases involving gender-based discrimination. (Indeed, the problems are suggested by reference to the classification as gender-based rather than sex-based. For many, gender-based discrimination means bias rooted in the social construction of gender roles; whereas sex based would refer to differences, if any, rooted in nature.) In *Reed v. Reed* (1971) the Supreme Court overturned an Idaho law which gave preference to males over females seeking to be appointed administrator of an estate. The case marks one of the few times the

Court has declared a law unconstitutional on the basis of the rational basis test, and inaugurated the debate over whether gender discrimination should be subject to strict scrutiny. Two years later, Justice Brennan argued in the affirmative. His opinion in *Frontiero v. Richardson* (1973) held that "classifications based upon sex, like classifications based upon race, alienage, and national origin, are inherently suspect and must therefore be subjected to close judicial scrutiny." However, Justice Brennan, joined only by Justices Douglas, White and Marshall, was unable to persuade a majority of the Court to endorse this view. (Current Justice Ruth Bader Ginsberg represented the ACLU as amicus curiae in this case.)

Three years later, in *Craig v. Boren* (1976), Justice Brennan introduced a third test; one between the "compelling interest test" for suspect classifications and the rational basis test for all other classifications. Gender classifications were *quasi-suspect* and subject to *intermediate scrutiny* – more than most classifications identified in laws, but less than strict scrutiny classifications. Whereas routine scrutiny requires classifications to be *reasonably related* to a legitimate government interest and strict scrutiny requires *a necessary relationship* to a compelling government interest; intermediate scrutiny requires that a quasi-suspect classifications, such as gender, "must serve *important governmental objectives and must be substantially related* to achievement of those objectives." (emphasis added)

Of course, the introduction of intermediate scrutiny did not solve the problems faced by the Court in non-racial equal protection cases. If it is difficult to identify the criteria by which some classifications are "suspect," it is even more trying to determine a principle which identifies those that are "quasi-suspect." Similarly, what is the difference between an "important" government interest and a "compelling" government interest? Indeed, the intermediate test would seem to have made an ambiguous field even more unclear. For all their lack of precision, the rational basis test and the compelling interest test could achieve a degree of clarity in operation. When the Court announces that a classification is not suspect and needs only meet the requirements of the rational basis test, it is basically holding that laws discriminating on the basis of that classification are constitutional. When it announces that a classification is suspect and subject to the compelling interest test, it is basically holding that laws discriminating on the basis of that classification are unconstitutional. In holding some classifications as "quasi-suspect" and subject to "intermediate scrutiny," however, the Court communicates no operational principle. Laws discriminating on such bases may or may not be constitutional. Short of a ruling by the Supreme Court, there is no way to determine whether specific uses of the classification will or will not be held constitutional. Some will, some will not be constitutional. Just as the "*Roth*" test once forced the Court to review what was and was not pornographic on a case by case basis, so too the intermediate scrutiny classification seems to indicate that the Court will be forced to review any and all laws involving quasi-suspect classifications. Their opinions in these cases, moreover, will be open to the criticism that the ultimate decision relies solely on who happens to be serving on the Court at the time the case is decided. See, *United States v. Virginia* (1996).

In recent years, the equal protection clause has increasingly emerged as a second battleground (along with the due process clause) for establishing constitutional protection for substantive rights. In *Romer v. Evans* (1996) the Court extended the defenses of the equal protection clause to laws based on classifications according to sexual orientation. cf. *Bowers v. Hardwick* (1986). In *Vacco v. Quill* (1997), the companion case to *Glucksberg,* the Court considered the question of whether laws banning physician-assisted suicide violated the equal protection clause. In this case the High Court *overturned* a circuit court opinion that held laws banning assisted suicide treated the terminally ill who wished to commit suicide by taking prescribed drugs differently than those who direct the removal of life-support systems to hasten their deaths, and that there was no "rational basis" related to a legitimate state end for the distinction.

THE CIVIL RIGHTS CASES
109 U.S. 3; 3 S.Ct. 18; 27 L.Ed. 835 (1883)

In the waning days of the Reconstruction Period, Southern whites were regaining their positions of power in state and local offices. In order to strengthen the protection already offered Negroes in the South, Congress enacted the Civil Rights Act of 1875. The law aimed at social discrimination by private individuals in public places and made it a misdemeanor to deny any person equal rights and privileges in theatres, inns, restaurants, and transportation facilities on account of race, color or previous condition of servitude. The act was based on the enforcement power of Congress under the Thirteenth and Fourteenth Amendments (Section 2).

MR. JUSTICE BRADLEY delivered the opinion of the Court:

...It is obvious that the primary and important question in all the cases is the constitutionality of the law: for if the law is unconstitutional none of the prosecutions can stand...

The essence of the law is, not to declare broadly that all persons shall be entitled to the full and equal enjoyment of the accommodations, advantages, facilities, and privileges of inns, public conveyances, and theaters; but that such enjoyment shall not be subject to any conditions applicable only to citizens of a particular race or color, or who had been in a previous condition of servitude....

Has Congress constitutional power to make such a law? Of course, no one will contend that the power to pass it was contained in the Constitution before the adoption of the last three amendments. The power is sought, first, in the Fourteenth Amendment, and the views and arguments of distinguished Senators, advanced whilst the law was under consideration, claiming authority to pass it by virtue of that amendment, are the principal arguments adduced in favor of the power....

The first section of the Fourteenth Amendment (which is the one relied on), after declaring who shall be citizens of the United States, and of the several

States, is prohibitory in its character, and prohibitory upon the States. It declares that:

> "No State shall make or enforce any law which shall abridge the privileges or immunities of citizens of the United States; nor shall any State deprive any person of life, liberty, or property without due process of law; nor deny to any person within its jurisdiction the equal protection of the laws."

It is State action of a particular character that is prohibited. Individual invasion of individual rights is not the subject-matter of the amendment. It has a deeper and broader scope. It nullifies and makes void all State legislation, and State action of every kind, which impairs the privileges and immunities of citizens of the United States, or which injures them in life, liberty or property without due process of law, or which denies to any of them the equal protection of the laws.... It does not authorize Congress to create a code of municipal law for the regulation of private rights; but to provide modes of redress against the operation of State laws, and the action of State officers executive or judicial, when these are subversive of the fundamental rights specified in the amendment. Positive rights and privileges are undoubtedly secured by the Fourteenth Amendment; but they are secured by way of prohibition against State laws and State proceedings affecting those rights and privileges, and by power given to Congress to legislate for the purpose of carrying such prohibition into effect: and such legislation must necessarily be predicated upon such supposed State laws or State proceedings, and be directed to the correction of their operation and effect....

[U]ntil some State law has been passed, or some State action through its officers or agents has been taken, adverse to the rights of citizens sought to be protected by the Fourteenth Amendment, no legislation of the United States under said amendment, nor any proceeding under such legislation, can be called into activity; for the prohibitions of the amendment are against State laws and acts done under State authority. Of course, legislation may, and should be, provided in advance to meet the exigency when it arises; but it should be adapted to the mischief and wrong which the amendment was intended to provide against; and this is, State laws, or State action of some kind, adverse to the rights of the citizen secured by the amendment. Such legislation cannot properly cover the whole domain of rights appertaining to life, liberty and property, defining them and providing for their vindication.... In fine, the legislation which Congress is authorized to adopt in this behalf is not general legislation upon the rights of the citizen, but corrective legislation, that is, such as may be necessary and proper for counteracting such laws as the States may adopt or enforce, and which, by the amendment, they are prohibited from making or enforcing, or such acts and proceedings as the States may commit or take, and which, by the amendment, they are prohibited from committing or taking. It is not necessary for us to state, if we could, what legislation would be proper for Congress to adopt. It is sufficient for us to examine whether the law in question is of that character.

An inspection of the law shows that it makes no reference whatever to any supposed or apprehended violation of the Fourteenth Amendment on the part of the States. It is not predicated on any such view. It proceeds *ex directo* to declare that certain acts committed by individuals shall be deemed offenses, and shall be prosecuted and punished by proceedings in the courts of the United States. It does not profess to be corrective of any constitutional wrong committed by the States; it does not make its operation to depend upon any such wrong committed....

If this legislation is appropriate for enforcing the prohibitions of the amendment, it is difficult to see where it is to stop. Why may not Congress with equal show of authority enact a code of laws for the enforcement and vindication of all rights of life, liberty, and property? If it is supposable that the States may deprive persons of life, liberty, and property without due process of law (and the amendment itself does suppose this), why should not Congress proceed at once to prescribe due process of law for the protection of every one of these fundamental rights, in every possible case, as well as to prescribe equal privileges in inns, public conveyances, and theaters? The truth is, that the implication of a power to legislate in this manner is based upon the assumption that if the States are forbidden to legislate or act in a particular way on a particular subject, and power is conferred upon Congress to enforce the prohibition, this gives Congress power to legislate generally upon that subject, and not merely power to provide modes of redress against such State legislation or action. The assumption is certainly unsound. It is repugnant to the Tenth Amendment of the Constitution, which declares that powers not delegated to the United States by the Constitution, nor prohibited by it to the States, are reserved to the States respectively or to the people....

In this connection it is proper to state that civil rights, such as are guaranteed by the Constitution against State aggression, cannot be impaired by the wrongful acts of individuals, unsupported by State authority in the shape of laws, customs, or judicial or executive proceedings. The wrongful act of an individual, unsupported by any such authority, is simply a private wrong, or a crime of that individual; an invasion of the rights of the injured party, it is true, whether they affect his person, his property, or his reputation; but if not sanctioned in some way by the State, or not done under State authority, his rights remain in full force, and may presumably be vindicated by resort to the laws of the State for redress. An individual cannot deprive a man of his right to vote, to hold property, to buy and sell, to sue in the courts, or to be a witness or a juror; he may, by force or fraud, interfere with the enjoyment of the right in a particular case; he may commit an assault against the person, or commit murder, or use ruffian violence at the polls, or slander the good name of a fellow citizen; but, unless protected in these wrongful acts by some shield of State law or State authority, he cannot destroy or injure the right; he will only render himself amenable to satisfaction or punishment; and amenable therefore to the laws of the State where the wrongful acts are committed. Hence, in all those cases where the Constitution seeks to protect the rights of the citizen against discriminative and unjust laws of the State by prohibiting such laws, it is not individual offenses, but abrogation and denial of rights, which it denounces, and for which it clothes the Congress with power to provide a remedy....

We have discussed the question presented by the law on the assumption that a right to enjoy equal accommodation and privileges in all inns, public conveyances, and places of public amusement, is one of the essential rights of the citizen which no State can abridge or interfere with. Whether it is such a right, or not, is a different question which, in the view we have taken of the validity of the law on the ground already stated, it is not necessary to examine....

But the power of Congress to adopt direct and primary, as distinguished from corrective legislation, on the subject in hand, is sought, in the second place, from the Thirteenth Amendment, which abolishes slavery.... This amendment, as well as the Fourteenth, is undoubtedly self-executing without any ancillary legislation, so far as its terms are applicable to any existing state of circumstances. By its own unaided force and effect it abolished slavery, and established universal freedom....

The only question under the present head, therefore, is whether the refusal to any persons of the accommodations of an inn, or a public conveyance, or a place of public amusement, by an individual, and without any sanction or support from any State law or regulation, does inflict upon such persons any manner of servitude, or form of slavery, as those terms are understood in this country? ...

It would be running the slavery argument into the ground to make it apply to every act of discrimination which a person may see fit to make as to the guests he will entertain, or as to the people he will take into his coach or cab or car, or admit to his concert or theater, or deal with in other matters of intercourse or business.... On the whole we are of opinion, that no countenance of authority for the passage of the law in question can be found in either the Thirteenth or Fourteenth Amendment of the Constitution; and no other ground of authority for its passage being suggested, it must necessarily be declared void, at least so far as its operation in the several States is concerned....

MR. JUSTICE HARLAN dissented, saying in part:

The opinion in these cases proceeds, it seems to me, upon grounds entirely too narrow and artificial. I cannot resist the conclusion that the substance and spirit of the recent amendments of the Constitution have been sacrificed by a subtle and ingenious verbal criticism....

The court adjudges, I think erroneously, that Congress is without power, under either the Thirteenth or Fourteenth Amendment, to establish such regulations and that the first and second sections of the statute are, in all their parts, unconstitutional and void....

Congress has not, in these matters, entered the domain of State control and supervision. It does not ... assume to prescribe the general conditions and limitations under which inns, public conveyances, and places of public amusement, shall be conducted or managed. It simply declares, in effect, that since the nation has established universal freedom in this country, for all time, there shall be no discrimination, based merely upon race or color, in respect of the accommodations and advantages of public conveyances, inns, and places of public amusement.

I am of the opinion that such discrimination practiced by corporations and individuals in the exercise of their public or quasi-public functions is a badge of servitude the imposition of which Congress may prevent under its power, by appropriate legislation, to enforce the Thirteenth Amendment; and, consequently, without reference to its enlarged power under the Fourteenth Amendment, the act of March 1, 1875, is not, in my judgment, repugnant to the Constitution....

The Supreme law of the land has decreed that no authority shall be exercised in this country upon the basis of discrimination, in respect of civil rights, against free men and citizens because of their race, color, or previous condition of servitude. To that decree – for the due enforcement of which, by appropriate legislation, Congress has been invested with express power – every one must bow, whatever may have been, or whatever now are, his individual views as to the wisdom or policy, either of the recent changes in the fundamental law, or of the legislation which has been enacted to give them effect.

For the reasons stated I feel constrained to withhold my assent to the opinion of the Court.

PLESSY v. FERGUSON.
16 S.Ct. 1138; 163 U.S. 537; 41 L.Ed. 256 (1896)

The facts in this case are contained in the opinion below.

Mr. Justice BROWN ... delivered the opinion of the court.

This case turns upon the constitutionality of an act of the general assembly of the state of Louisiana, passed in 1890, providing for separate railway carriages for the white and colored races....

The first section of the statute enacts "that all railway companies carrying passengers in their coaches in this state, shall provide equal but separate accommodations for the white, and colored races, by providing two or more passenger coaches for each passenger train, or by dividing the passenger coaches by a partition so as to secure separate accommodations: provided, that this section shall not be construed to apply to street railroads. No person or persons shall be permitted to occupy seats in coaches, other than the ones assigned to them, on account of the race they belong to."

By the second section it was enacted "that the officers of such passenger trains shall have power and are hereby required to assign each passenger to the coach or compartment used for the race to which such passenger belongs; any passenger insisting on going into a coach or compartment to which by race he does not belong, shall be liable to a fine of twenty-five dollars, or in lieu thereof to imprisonment for a period of not more than twenty days in the parish prison, and any officer of any railroad insisting on assigning a passenger to a coach or compartment other than the one set aside for the race to which said passenger belongs, shall be liable to a fine of twenty-five dollars, or in lieu thereof to imprisonment for a period of not more than twenty days in the parish prison; and should any passenger refuse to occupy the coach or compartment to which he or she is assigned by the officer of such railway, said officer shall have power to refuse to carry such passenger on his train, and for such refusal neither he nor the railway company which he represents shall be liable for damages in any of the courts of this state."

...The information filed in the criminal district court charged, in substance, that Plessy, being a passenger between two stations within the state of Louisiana, was assigned by officers of the company to the coach used for the race to which he belonged, but he insisted upon going into a coach used by the race to which he did not belong. Neither in the information nor plea was his particular race or color averred.

The petition for the writ of prohibition averred that petitioner was seven-eighths Caucasian and one-eighth African blood; that the mixture of colored blood was not discernible in him; and that he was entitled to every right, privilege, and immunity secured to citizens of the United States of the white race; and that, upon such theory, he took possession of a vacant seat in a coach where passengers of the white race were accommodated, and was ordered by the conductor to vacate said coach, and take a seat in another, assigned to persons of the colored race, and, having refused to comply with such demand, he was forcibly ejected, with the aid of a police officer, and imprisoned in the parish jail to answer a charge of having violated the above act.

The constitutionality of this act is attacked upon the ground that it conflicts both with the thirteenth amendment of the constitution, abolishing slavery, and the fourteenth amendment, which prohibits certain restrictive legislation on the part of the states.

1. That it does not conflict with the thirteenth amendment, which abolished slavery and involuntary servitude, except as a punishment for crime, is too clear for argument. Slavery implies involuntary servitude, a state of bondage; the ownership of mankind as a chattel, or, at least, the control of the labor and services of one man for the benefit of another, and the absence of a legal right to the disposal of his own person, property, and services. This amendment was said in the Slaughter-House Cases, 16 Wall. 36, to have been intended primarily to abolish slavery, as it had been previously known in this country, and that it equally forbade Mexican peonage or the Chinese coolie trade, when they amounted to slavery or involuntary servitude, and that the use of the word "servitude" was intended to prohibit the use of all forms of involuntary slavery, of whatever class or name. It was intimated, however, in that case, that this amendment was regarded by the statesmen of that day as insufficient to protect the colored race from certain laws which had been enacted in the Southern states, imposing upon the colored race onerous disabilities and burdens, and curtailing their rights in the pursuit of life, liberty, and property to such an extent that their freedom was of little value; and that the fourteenth amendment was devised to meet this exigency.

So, too, in the Civil Rights Cases ... it was said that the act of a mere individual, the owner of an inn, a public conveyance or place of amusement, refusing accommodations to colored people, cannot be justly regarded as imposing any badge of slavery or servitude upon the applicant, but only as involving an ordinary civil injury, properly cognizable by the laws of the state, and presumably subject to redress by those laws until the contrary appears. "It would be running the slavery question into the ground,' said Mr. Justice Bradley, 'to make it apply to every act of discrimination which a person may see fit to make as to the guests he will entertain, or as to the people he will take into his coach or cab or car, or admit to his concert or theater, or deal with in other matters of intercourse or business."

A statute which implies merely a legal distinction between the white and colored races – a distinction which is founded in the color of the two races, and which must always exist so long as white men are distinguished from the other race by color – has no tendency to destroy the legal equality of the two races, or re-establish a state of involuntary servitude. Indeed, we do not understand that the thirteenth amendment is strenuously relied upon by the plaintiff in error in this connection.

2. By the fourteenth amendment, all persons born or naturalized in the United States, and subject to the jurisdiction thereof, are made citizens of the United States and of the state wherein they reside; and the states are forbidden from making or enforcing any law which shall abridge the privileges or immunities of citizens of the United States, or shall deprive any person of life, liberty, or property without due process of law, or deny to any person within their jurisdiction the equal protection of the laws.

The proper construction of this amendment was first called to the attention of this court in the Slaughter-House Cases, 16 Wall. 36, which involved, however, not a question of race, but one of exclusive privileges. The case did not call for any expression of opinion as to the exact rights it was intended to secure to the colored race, but it was said generally that its main purpose was to establish the citizenship of the negro, to give definitions of citizenship of the United States and of the states, and to protect from the hostile legislation of the states the privileges and immunities of citizens of the United States, as distinguished from those of citizens of the states.

The object of the amendment was undoubtedly to enforce the absolute equality of the two races before the law, but, in the nature of things, it could not have been intended to abolish distinctions based upon color, or to enforce social, as distinguished from political, equality, or a commingling of the two races upon terms unsatisfactory to either. Laws permitting, and even requiring, their separation, in places where they are liable to be brought into contact, do not necessarily imply the inferiority of either race to the other, and have been generally, if not universally, recognized as within the competency of the state legislatures in the exercise of their police power. The most common instance of this is connected with the establishment of separate schools for white and colored children, which have been held to be a valid exercise of the legislative power even by courts of states where the political rights of the colored race have been longest and most earnestly enforced.

One of the earliest of these cases is that of *Roberts v. City of Boston*, 5 Cush. 198, in which the supreme judicial court of Massachusetts held that the general school committee of Boston had power to make provision for the instruction of colored children in separate schools established exclusively for them, and to prohibit their attendance upon the other schools. "The great principle,' said Chief Justice Shaw, 'advanced by the learned and eloquent advocate for the plaintiff [Mr. Charles Sumner], is that, by the constitution and laws of Massachusetts, all persons, without distinction of age or sex, birth or color, origin or condition, are equal before the law.... But, when this great principle comes to be applied to the actual and various conditions of persons in society, it will not warrant the assertion that men and women are legally clothed with the same civil and political powers, and that children and adults are legally to have the same functions and be subject to the same treatment; but only that the rights of all, as they are settled and regulated by law, are equally entitled to the paternal consideration and protection of the law for their maintenance and security." It was held that the powers of the committee extended to the establishment of separate schools for children of different ages, sexes and colors, and that they might also establish special schools for poor and neglected children, who have become too old to attend the primary school, and yet have not acquired the rudiments of learning, to enable them to enter the ordinary schools. Similar laws have been enacted by congress under its general power of legislation over the District of Columbia ... as well as by the legislatures of many of the states, and have been generally, if not uniformly, sustained by the courts....

Laws forbidding the intermarriage of the two races may be said in a technical sense to interfere with the freedom of contract, and yet have been universally recognized as within the police power of the state. *State v. Gibson*....

The distinction between laws interfering with the political equality of the negro and those requiring the separation of the two races in schools, theaters, and railway carriages has been frequently drawn by this court. Thus, in *Strauder v. West Virginia* ... it was held that a law of West Virginia limiting to white male persons 21 years of age, and citizens of the state, the right to sit upon juries, was a discrimination which implied a legal inferiority in civil society, which lessened the security of the right of the colored race, and was a step towards reducing them to a condition of servility. Indeed, the right of a colored man that, in the selection of jurors to pass upon his life, liberty, and property, there shall be no exclusion of his race, and no discrimination against them because of color, has been asserted in a number of cases.... So, where the laws of a particular locality or the charter of a particular railway corporation has provided that no person shall be excluded from the cars on account of color, we have held that this meant that persons of color should travel in the same car as white ones, and that the enactment was not satisfied by the company providing cars assigned exclusively to people of color, though they were as good as those which they assigned exclusively to white persons. *Railroad Co. v. Brown*....

Upon the other hand, where a statute of Louisiana required those engaged in the transportation of passengers among the states to give to all persons traveling within that state, upon vessels employed in that business, equal rights and privileges in all parts of the vessel, without distinction on account of race or color, and subjected to an action for damages the owner of such a vessel who excluded colored passengers on account of their color from the cabin set aside by him for the use of whites, it was held to be, so far as it applied to interstate commerce, unconstitutional and void. *Hall v. De Cuir.* The court in this case, however, expressly disclaimed that it had anything whatever to do with the statute as a regulation of internal commerce, or affecting anything else than commerce among the states.

In the Civil Rights Cases ... it was held that an act of congress entitling all persons within the jurisdiction of the United States to the full and equal enjoyment of the accommodations, advantages, facilities, and privileges of inns, public conveyances, on land or water, theaters, and other places of public amusement, and made applicable to citizens of every race and color, regardless of any previous condition of servitude, was unconstitutional and void, upon the ground that the fourteenth amendment was prohibitory upon the states only, and the legislation authorized to be adopted by congress for enforcing it was not direct legislation on matters respecting which the states were prohibited from making or enforcing certain laws, or doing certain acts, but was corrective legislation, such as might be necessary or proper for counter-acting and redressing the effect of such laws or acts. In delivering the opinion of the court, Mr. Justice Bradley observed that the fourteenth amendment "does not invest congress with power to legislate upon subjects that are within the domain of state legislation, but to provide modes of relief against state legislation or state action of the kind referred to. It does not authorize congress to create a code of municipal law for the regulation of private rights, but to provide modes of redress against the operation of state laws, and the action of state officers, executive or judicial, when these are subversive of the fundamental rights specified in the amendment. Positive rights and privileges are undoubtedly secured by the fourteenth amendment; but they are secured by way of prohibition against state laws and state proceedings affecting those rights and privileges, and by power given to congress to legislate for the purpose of carrying such prohibition into effect; and such legislation must necessarily be predicated upon such supposed state laws or state proceedings, and be directed to the correction of their operation and effect."

Much nearer, and, indeed, almost directly in point, is the case of the *Louisville N. O. & T. Ry. Co. v. State,...* wherein the railway company was indicted for a violation of a statute of Mississippi, enacting that all railroads carrying passengers should provide equal, but separate, accommodations for the white and colored races, by providing two or more passenger cars for each passenger train, or by dividing the passenger cars by a partition, so as to secure separate accommodations. The case was presented in a different aspect from the one under consideration, inasmuch as it was an indictment against the railway company for failing to provide the separate accommodations, but the question considered was the constitutionality of the law. In that case, the supreme court of Mississippi ... had held that the statute applied solely to commerce within the state, and, that being the construction of the state statute by its highest court, was accepted as conclusive. "If it be a matter' said the court,... 'respecting commerce wholly within a state, and not interfering with commerce between the states, then, obviously, there is no violation of the commerce clause of the federal constitution.... No question arises under this section as to the power of the state to separate in different compartments interstate passengers, or affect, in any manner, the privileges and rights of such passengers. All that we can consider is whether the state has the power to require that railroad trains within her limits shall have separate accommodations for the two races. That affecting only commerce within the state is no invasion of the power given to congress by the commerce clause."

...While we think the enforced separation of the races, as applied to the internal commerce of the state, neither abridges the privileges or immunities of the colored man, deprives him of his property without due process of law, nor denies him the equal protection of the laws, within the meaning of the fourteenth amendment, we are not prepared to say that the conductor, in assigning passengers to the coaches according to their race, does not act at his peril, or that the provision of the second section of the act that denies to the passenger compensation in damages for a refusal to receive him into the coach in which he properly belongs is a valid exercise of the legislative power. Indeed, we understand it to be conceded by the state's attorney that such part of the act as exempts from liability the railway company and its officers is unconstitutional. The power to assign to a particular coach obviously implies the power to determine to which race the passenger belongs, as well as the power to determine who, under the laws of the particular state, is to be deemed a white, and who a colored, person. This question, though indicated in the brief of the plaintiff in error, does not properly arise upon the record in this case, since the only issue made is as to the unconstitutionality of the act, so far as it requires the railway to provide separate accommodations, and the conductor to assign passengers according to their race.

It is claimed by the plaintiff in error that, in a mixed community, the reputation of belonging to the dominant race, in this instance the white race, is "property," in the same sense that a right of action or of inheritance is property. Conceding this to be so, for the purposes of this case, we are unable to see how this statute deprives him of, or in any way affects his right to, such property. If he be a white man, and assigned to a colored coach, he may have his action for damages against the company for being deprived of his so-called "property." Upon the other hand, if he be a colored man, and be so assigned, he has been deprived of no property, since he is not lawfully entitled to the reputation of being a white man.

In this connection, it is also suggested by the learned counsel for the plaintiff in error that the same argument that will justify the state legislature in requiring railways to provide separate accommodations for the two races will also authorize them to require separate cars to be provided for people whose hair is of a certain color, or who are aliens, or who belong to certain nationalities, or to enact laws requiring colored people to walk upon one side of the street, and white people upon the other, or requiring white men's houses to be painted white, and colored men's black, or their vehicles or business signs to be of different colors, upon the theory that one side of the street is as good as the other, or that a house or vehicle of one color is as good as one of another color. The reply to all this is that every exercise of the police power must be reasonable, and extend only to such laws as are enacted in good faith for the promotion of the public good, and not for the annoyance or oppression of a particular class. Thus, in *Yick Wo v. Hopkins*, it was held by this court that a municipal ordinance of the city of San Francisco, to regulate the carrying on of public laundries within the limits of the municipality, violated the provisions of the constitution of the United States, if it conferred upon the municipal authorities arbitrary power, at their own will, and without regard to discretion, in the legal sense of the term, to give or withhold consent as to persons or places, without regard to the competency of the persons applying or the propriety of the places selected for the carrying on of the business. It was held to be a covert attempt on the part of the municipality to make an arbitrary and unjust discrimination against the Chinese race....

So far, then, as a conflict with the fourteenth amendment is concerned, the case reduces itself to the question whether the statute of Louisiana is a reasonable regulation, and with respect to this there must necessarily be a large discretion on the part of the legislature. In determining the question of reasonableness, it is at liberty to act with reference to the established usages, customs, and traditions of the people, and with a view to the promotion of their comfort, and the preservation of the public peace and good order. Gauged by this standard, we cannot say that a law which authorizes or even requires the separation of the two races in public conveyances is unreasonable, or more obnoxious to the fourteenth amendment than the acts of congress requiring separate schools for colored children in the District of Columbia, the constitutionality of which does not seem to have been questioned, or the corresponding acts of state legislatures.

We consider the underlying fallacy of the plaintiff's argument to consist in the assumption that the enforced separation of the two races stamps the colored race with a badge of inferiority. If this be so, it is not by reason of anything found in the act, but solely because the colored race chooses to put that construction upon it. The argument necessarily assumes that if, as has been more than once the case, and is not unlikely to be so again, the colored race should become the dominant power in the state legislature, and should enact a law in precisely similar terms, it would thereby relegate the white race to an inferior position. We imagine that the white race, at least, would not acquiesce in this assumption. The argument also assumes that social prejudices may be overcome by legislation, and that equal rights cannot be secured to the negro except by an enforced commingling of the two races. We cannot accept this proposition. If the two races are to meet upon terms of social equality, it must be the result of natural affinities, a mutual appreciation of each other's merits, and a voluntary consent of individuals. As was said by the court of appeals of New York in *People v. Gallagher*...: "This end can neither be accomplished nor promoted by laws which conflict with the general sentiment of the community upon whom they are designed to operate. When the government, therefore, has secured to each of its citizens equal rights before the law, and equal opportunities for improvement and progress, it has accomplished the end for which it was organized, and performed all of the functions respecting social advantages with which it is endowed." Legislation is powerless to eradicate racial instincts, or to abolish distinctions based upon physical differences, and the attempt to do so can only result in accentuating the difficulties of the present situation. If the civil and political rights of both races be equal, one cannot be inferior to the other civilly or politically. If one race be inferior to the other socially, the constitution of the United States cannot put them upon the same plane.

It is true that the question of the proportion of colored blood necessary to constitute a colored person, as distinguished from a white person, is one upon which there is a difference of opinion in the different states; some holding that any visible admixture of black blood stamps the person as belonging to the colored race ... others, that it depends upon the preponderance of blood and still others, that the predominance of white blood must only be in the proportion of three-fourths. But these are questions to be determined under the laws of each state, and are not properly put in issue in this case. Under the allegations of his petition, it may undoubtedly become a question of importance whether, under the laws of Louisiana, the petitioner belongs to the white or colored race.

The judgment of the court below is therefore affirmed.

Mr. Justice BREWER did not hear the argument or participate in the decision of this case.

Mr. Justice HARLAN dissenting.

...However apparent the injustice of such legislation may be, we have only to consider whether it is consistent with the constitution of the United States.

In respect of civil rights, common to all citizens, the constitution of the United States does not, I think, permit any public authority to know the race of those entitled to be protected in the enjoyment of such rights. Every true man has pride of race, and under appropriate circumstances, when the rights of others, his equals before the law, are not to be affected, it is his privilege to express such pride and to take such action based upon it as to him seems proper. But I deny that any legislative body or judicial tribunal may have regard to the race of citizens when the civil rights of those citizens are involved. Indeed, such legislation as that here in question is inconsistent not only with that equality of rights which pertains to citizenship, national and state, but with the personal liberty enjoyed by every one within the United States.

The thirteenth amendment does not permit the withholding or the deprivation of any right necessarily inhering in freedom. It not only struck down the institution of slavery as previously existing in the United States, but it prevents the imposition of any burdens or disabilities that constitute badges of slavery or servitude. It decreed universal civil freedom in this country. This court has so adjudged. But, that amendment having been found inadequate to the protection of the rights of those who had been in slavery, it was followed by the fourteenth amendment, which added greatly to the dignity and glory of American citizenship, and to the security of personal liberty, by declaring that "all persons born or naturalized in the United States, and subject to the jurisdiction thereof, are citizens of the United States and of the state wherein they reside," and that "no state shall make or enforce any law which shall abridge the privileges or immunities of citizens of the United States; nor shall any state deprive any person of life, liberty or property without due process of law, nor deny to any person within its jurisdiction the equal protection of the laws." These two amendments, if enforced according to their true intent and meaning, will protect all the civil rights that pertain to freedom and citizenship. Finally, and to the end that no citizen should be denied, on account of his race, the privilege of participating in the political control of his country, it was declared by the fifteenth amendment that "the right of citizens of the United States to vote shall not be denied or abridged by the United States or by any state on account of race, color or previous condition of servitude."

These notable additions to the fundamental law were welcomed by the friends of liberty throughout the world. They removed the race line from our governmental systems. They had, as this court has said, a common purpose, namely, to secure "to a race recently emancipated, a race that through many generations have been held in slavery, all the civil rights that the superior race enjoy." They declared, in legal effect, this court has further said, "that the law in the states shall be the same for the black as for the white; that all persons, whether colored or white, shall stand equal before the laws of the states; and in regard to the colored race, for whose protection the amendment was primarily designed, that no discrimination shall be made against them by law because of their color." We also said: "The words of the amendment, it is true, are prohibitory, but they contain a necessary implication of a positive immunity or right, most valuable to the colored race; the right to exemption from unfriendly legislation against them distinctively as colored; exemption from legal discriminations, implying inferiority in civil society, lessening the security of their enjoyment of the rights which others enjoy; and discriminations which are steps towards reducing them to the condition of a subject race." It was, consequently, adjudged that a state law that excluded citizens of the colored race from juries, because of their race, however well qualified in other respects to discharge the duties of jurymen, was repugnant to the fourteenth amendment.... At the present term, referring to the previous adjudications, this court declared that "underlying all of those decisions is the principle that the constitution of the United States, in its present form, forbids, so far as civil and political rights are concerned, discrimination by the general government or the states against any citizen because of his race. All citizens are equal before the law...."

It was said in argument that the statute of Louisiana does not discriminate against either race, but prescribes a rule applicable alike to white and colored citizens. But this argument does not meet the difficulty. Every one knows that the statute in question had its origin in the purpose, not so much to exclude white persons from railroad cars occupied by blacks, as to exclude colored people from coaches occupied by or assigned to white persons. Railroad corporations of Louisiana did not make discrimination among whites in the matter of [ac]commodation for travelers. The thing to accomplish was, under the guise of giving equal accommodation for whites and blacks, to compel the latter to keep to themselves while traveling in railroad passenger coaches. No one would be so wanting in candor as to assert the contrary. The fundamental objection, therefore, to the statute, is that it interferes with the personal freedom of citizens. "Personal liberty," it has been well said, "consists in the power of locomotion, of changing situation, or removing one's person to whatsoever places one's own inclination may direct, without imprisonment or restraint, unless by due course of law...." If a white man and a black man choose to occupy the same public conveyance on a public highway, it is their right to do so; and no government, proceeding alone on grounds of race, can prevent it without infringing the personal liberty of each.

It is one thing for railroad carriers to furnish, or to be required by law to furnish, equal accommodations for all whom they are under a legal duty to carry. It is quite another thing for government to forbid citizens of the white and black races from traveling in the same public conveyance, and to punish officers of railroad companies for permitting persons of the two races to occupy the same passenger coach. If a state can prescribe, as a rule of civil conduct, that whites and blacks shall not travel as passengers in the same railroad coach, why may it not so regulate the use of the streets of its cities and towns as to compel white citizens to keep on one side of a street, and black citizens to keep on the other? Why may it not, upon like grounds, punish whites and blacks who ride together in street cars or in open vehicles on a public road or street? Why may it not require sheriffs to assign whites to one side of a court room, and blacks to the other? And why may it not also prohibit the commingling of the two races in the galleries of legislative halls or in public assemblages convened for the consideration of the political questions of the day? Further, if this statute of Louisiana is consistent with the personal liberty of citizens, why may not the state require the separation in railroad coaches of native and naturalized citizens of the United States, or of Protestants and Roman Catholics?

The answer given at the argument to these questions was that regulations of the kind they suggest would be unreasonable, and could not, therefore, stand before the law. Is it meant that the determination of questions of legislative power depends upon the inquiry whether the statute whose validity is questioned is, in the judgment of the courts, a reasonable one, taking all the circumstances into consideration? A statute may be unreasonable merely because a sound public policy forbade its enactment. But I do not understand that the courts have anything to do with the policy or expediency of legislation. A statute may be valid, and yet, upon grounds of public policy, may well be characterized as unreasonable. Mr. Sedgwick correctly states the rule when he says that, the legislative intention being clearly ascertained, "the courts have no other duty to perform than to execute the legislative will, without any regard to their views as to the wisdom or justice of the particular enactment...." There is a dangerous tendency in these latter days to enlarge the functions of the courts, by means of judicial interference with the will of the people as expressed by the legislature. Our institutions have the distinguishing characteristic that the three departments of government are co-ordinate and separate. Each much keep within the limits defined by the constitution. And the courts best discharge their duty by executing the will of the law-making power, constitutionally expressed, leaving the results of legislation to be dealt with by the people through their representatives. Statutes must always have a reasonable construction. Sometimes they are to be construed strictly, sometimes literally, in order to carry out the legislative will. But, however construed, the intent of the legislature is to be respected if the particular statute in question is valid, although the courts, looking at the public interests, may conceive the statute to be both unreasonable and impolitic. If the power exists to enact a statute, that ends the matter so far as the courts are concerned. The adjudged cases in which statutes have been held to be void, because unreasonable, are those in which the means employed by the legislature were not at all germane to the end to which the legislature was competent.

The white race deems itself to be the dominant race in this country. And so it is, in prestige, in achievements, in education, in wealth, and in power. So, I doubt not, it will continue to be for all time, if it remains true to its great heritage, and holds fast to the principles of constitutional liberty. But in view of the constitution, in the eye of the law, there is in this country no superior, dominant, ruling class of citizens. There is no caste here. Our constitution is color-blind, and neither knows nor tolerates classes among citizens. In respect of civil rights, all citizens are equal before the law. The humblest is the peer of the most powerful. The law regards man as man, and takes no account of his surroundings or of his color when his civil rights as guarantied by the supreme law of the land are involved. It is therefore to be regretted that this high tribunal, the final expositor of the fundamental law of the land, has reached the conclusion that it is competent for a state to regulate the enjoyment by citizens of their civil rights solely upon the basis of race.

In my opinion, the judgment this day rendered will, in time, prove to be quite as pernicious as the decision made by this tribunal in the Dred Scott Case.

...The present decision, it may well be apprehended, will not only stimulate aggressions, more or less brutal and irritating, upon the admitted rights of colored citizens, but will encourage the belief that it is possible, by means of state enactments, to defeat the beneficent purposes which the people of the United States had in view when they adopted the recent amendments of the constitution, by one of which the blacks of this country were made citizens of the United States and of the states in which they respectively reside, and whose privileges and immunities, as citizens, the states are forbidden to abridge. Sixty millions of whites are in no danger from the presence here of eight millions of blacks. The destinies of the two races, in this country, are indissolubly linked together, and the interests of both require that the common government of all shall not permit the seeds of race hate to be planted under the sanction of law. What can more certainly arouse race hate, what more certainly create and perpetuate a feeling of distrust between these races, than state enactments which, in fact, proceed on the ground that colored citizens are so inferior and degraded that they cannot be allowed to sit in public coaches occupied by white citizens? That, as all will admit, is the real meaning of such legislation as was enacted in Louisiana.

The sure guaranty of the peace and security of each race is the clear, distinct, unconditional recognition by our governments, national and state, of every right that inheres in civil freedom, and of the equality before the law of all citizens of the United States, without regard to race. State enactments regulating the enjoyment of civil rights upon the basis of race, and cunningly devised to defeat legitimate results of the war, under the pretense of recognizing equality of rights, can have no other result than to render permanent peace impossible, and to keep alive a conflict of races, the continuance of which must do harm to all concerned. This question is not met by the suggestion that social equality cannot exist between the white and black races in this country. That argument, if it can be properly regarded as one, is scarcely worthy of consideration; for social equality no more exists between two races when traveling in a passenger coach or a public highway than when members of the same races sit by each other in a street car or in the jury box, or stand or sit with each other in a political assembly, or when they use in common the streets of a city or town, or when they are in the same room for the purpose of having their names placed on the registry of voters, or when they approach the ballot box in order to exercise the high privilege of voting.

There is a race so different from our own that we do not permit those belonging to it to become citizens of the United States. Persons belonging to it are, with few exceptions, absolutely excluded from our country. I allude to the Chinese race. But, by the statute in question, a Chinaman can ride in the same passenger coach with white citizens of the United States, while citizens of the black race in Louisiana, many of whom, perhaps, risked their lives for the preservation of the Union, who are entitled, by law, to participate in the political control of the state and nation, who are not excluded, by law or by reason of their race, from public stations of any kind, and who have all the legal rights that belong to white citizens, are yet declared to be criminals, liable to imprisonment, if they ride in a public coach occupied by citizens of the white race. It is scarcely just to say that a colored citizen should not object to occupying a public coach assigned to his own race. He does not object, nor, perhaps, would he object to separate coaches for his race if his rights under the law were recognized. But he does object, and he ought never to cease objecting, that citizens of the white and black races can be adjudged criminals because they sit, or claim the right to sit, in the same public coach on a public highway.

The arbitrary separation of citizens, on the basis of race, while they are on a public highway, is a badge of servitude wholly inconsistent with the civil freedom and the equality before the law established by the constitution. It cannot be justified upon any legal grounds.

If evils will result from the commingling of the two races upon public highways established for the benefit of all, they will be infinitely less than those that will surely come from state legislation regulating the enjoyment of civil rights upon the basis of race. We boast of the freedom enjoyed by our people above all other peoples. But it is difficult to reconcile that boast with a state of the law which, practically, puts the brand of servitude and degradation upon a large class of our fellow citizens, our equals before the law. The thin disguise of "equal" accommodations for passengers in railroad coaches will not mislead any one, nor atone for the wrong this day done.

The result of the whole matter is that while this court has frequently adjudged, and at the present term has recognized the doctrine, that a state cannot, consistently with the constitution of the United States, prevent white and black citizens, having the required qualifications for jury service, from sitting in the same jury box, it is now solemnly held that a state may prohibit white and black citizens from sitting in the same passenger coach on a public highway, or may require that they be separated by a "partition" when in the same passenger coach. May it not now be reasonably expected that astute men of the dominant race, who affect to be disturbed at the possibility that the integrity of the white race may be corrupted, or that its supremacy will be imperiled, by contact on public highways with black people, will endeavor to procure statutes requiring white and black jurors to be separated in the jury box by a "partition," and that, upon retiring from the court room to consult as to their verdict, such partition, if it be a movable one, shall be taken to their consultation room, and set up in such way as to prevent black jurors from coming too close to their brother jurors of the white race. If the "partition" used in the court room happens to be stationary, provision could be made for screens with openings through which jurors of the two races could confer as to their verdict without coming into personal contact with each other. I cannot see but that, according to the principles this day announced, such state legislation, although conceived in hostility to, and enacted for the purpose of humiliating, citizens of the United States of a particular race, would be held to be consistent with the constitution.

I do not deem it necessary to review the decisions of state courts to which reference was made in argument. Some, and the most important, of them, are wholly inapplicable, because rendered prior to the adoption of the last amendments of the constitution, when colored people had very few rights which the dominant race felt obliged to respect. Others were made at a time when public opinion, in many localities, was dominated by the institution of slavery; when it would not have been safe to do justice to the black man; and when, so far as the rights of blacks were concerned, race prejudice was, practically, the supreme law of the land. Those decisions cannot be guides in the era introduced by the recent amendments of the supreme law, which established universal civil freedom, gave citizenship to all born or naturalized in the United States, and residing here, obliterated the race line from our systems of governments, national and state, and placed our free institutions upon the broad and sure foundation of the equality of all men before the law.

I am of opinion that the state of Louisiana is inconsistent with the personal liberty of citizens, white and black, in that state, and hostile to both the spirit and letter of the constitution of the United States. If laws of like character should be enacted in the several states of the Union, the effect would be in the highest degree mischievous. Slavery, as an institution tolerated by law, would, it is true, have disappeared from our country; but there would remain a power in the states, by sinister legislation, to interfere with the full enjoyment of the blessings of freedom, to regulate civil rights, common to all citizens, upon the basis of race, and to place in a condition of legal inferiority a large body of American citizens, now constituting a part of the political community, called the "People of the United States," for whom, and by whom through representatives, our government is administered. Such a system is inconsistent with the guaranty given by the constitution to each state of a republican form of government, and may be stricken down by congressional action, or by the courts in the discharge of their solemn duty to maintain the supreme law of the land, anything in the constitution or laws of any state to the contrary notwithstanding.

For the reason stated, I am constrained to withhold my assent from the opinion and judgment of the majority.

SMITH *v.* ALLWRIGHT
321 U.S. 649; 64 S.Ct. 757; 88 L.Ed. 987 (1944)

In 1923, the Texas legislature passed a law providing that "in no event shall a Negro be eligible to participate in a Democratic party primary election held in the state of Texas, and should a Negro vote in a Democratic primary election, such ballot shall be void and election officials are herein directed to throw out such ballot, and not count the same." Lonnie Smith, a black citizen of Houston, sought to obtain a ballot in the Democratic party primary election of 1940 and was denied by the precinct election judge, S.E. Allwright. Smith sued for damages. The federal district court, relying on the rationale of Grovey v. Townsend, *204 U.S. 45 (1935), that political parties are private clubs, dismissed the complaint. The case was then brought to the Supreme Court by certiorari.*

MR. JUSTICE REED delivered the opinion of the Court:

Texas is free to conduct her elections and limit her electorate as she may deem wise, save only as her action may be affected by the prohibitions of the United States Constitution or in conflict with powers delegated to be exercised by the National Government. The Fourteenth Amendment forbids a State from making or enforcing any law which abridges the privileges or immunities of citizens of the United States, and the Fifteenth Amendment specifically interdicts any denial or abridgment by a State of the right of citizens to vote on account of color. Respondents appeared in the District Court and the Circuit Court of Appeals and defended on the ground that the Democratic party of Texas is a voluntary organization with members banded together for the purpose of selecting individuals of the group representing the common political beliefs as candidates in the general election. As such a voluntary organization, it was claimed, the Democratic party is free to select its own membership and limit to whites participation in the party primary. Such action, the answer asserted, does not violate the Fourteenth, Fifteenth, or Seventeenth Amendment, as officers of government cannot be chosen at primaries and the Amendments are applicable only to general elections where governmental officers are actually elected. Primaries, it is said, are political party affairs, handled by party, not governmental, officers....

The right of a Negro to vote in the Texas primary has been considered heretofore by this Court. The first case was *Nixon v. Herndon*, 273 U.S. 536. At that time, 1924, the Texas statute ... declared, "in no event shall a Negro be eligible to participate in a Democratic Party primary election in the State of Texas." Nixon was refused the right to vote in a Democratic primary and brought a suit for damages against the election officers.... It was urged to this Court that the denial of the franchise to Nixon violated his Constitutional rights under the Fourteenth and Fifteenth Amendments. Without consideration of the Fifth, this Court held that the action of Texas in denying the ballot to Negroes by statute was in violation of the equal protection clause of the Fourteenth Amendment and reversed the dismissal of the suit.

The legislature of Texas re-enacted the article but gave the State Executive Committee of a party the power to prescribe the qualifications of its members for voting or other participation. This article remains in the statutes. The State Executive Committee of the Democratic party adopted a resolution that white Democrats and none other might participate in the primaries of that party. Nixon as refused again the privilege of voting in a primary and again brought suit for damages.... This Court again reversed the dismissal of the suit for the reason that the Committee action was deemed to be state action and invalid as discriminatory under the Fourteenth Amendment. The test was said to be whether the Committee operated as representative of the State in the discharge of the State's authority, *Nixon v. Condon*, 286 U.S. 73. The question of the inherent power of a political party in Texas "without restraint by any law to determine its own membership" was left open....

In *Grovey v. Townsend*, 295 U.S. 45, this Court had before it suit for damages for the refusal in a primary of a county clerk, a Texas officer with only public functions to perform, to furnish petitioner, a Negro, an absentee ballot. The refusal was solely on the ground of race. This case differed from *Nixon v. Condon*... in that a state convention of the Democratic party had passed the resolution of May 24, 1932, herein before quoted. It was decided that the determination by the state convention of the membership of the Democratic party made a significant change from a determination by the Executive Committee. The former was party action, voluntary in character. The latter, as had been held in the *Condon* case, was action by authority of the State. The managers of the primary election were therefore declared not to be state officials in such sense that their action was state action. A state convention of a party was said not to be an organ of the State....

Since *Grovey v. Townsend* and prior to the present suit, no case from Texas involving primary elections has been before this Court. We did decide, however, *United States v. Classic*, 313 U.S. 299. We there held that §4 of Article I of the Constitution authorized Congress to regulate primary as well as general elections ... "where the primary is by law made an integral part of the election machinery."

The fusing by the *Classic* case of the primary and general elections into a single instrumentality for choice of officers has a definite bearing on the permissibility under the Constitution of excluding Negroes from primaries. This is not to say that the *Classic* case cuts directly into the rationale of *Grovey v. Townsend*. This latter case was not mentioned in the opinion. *Classic* bears upon *Grovey v. Townsend* not because exclusion of Negroes from primaries is any more or less state action by reason of the unitary character of the electoral process but because the recognition of the place of the primary in the electoral scheme makes clear that state delegation to a party of the power to fix the qualifications of primary elections is delegation of a state function that may make the party's action the action of the State. When *Grovey v. Townsend* was written, the Court looked upon the denial of a vote in a primary as a mere refusal by a party of party membership.... As the Louisiana statutes for holding primaries are similar to those of Texas, our ruling in *Classic* as to the unitary character of the electoral process calls for re-examination as to whether or not the exclusion of Negroes from a Texas party primary was state action....

It may now be taken as a postulate that the right to vote in such a primary for the nomination of candidates without discrimination by the State, like the right to vote in a general election, is a right secured by the Constitution.... By the terms of the Fifteenth Amendment that right may not be abridged by any State on account of race. Under our Constitution the great privilege of the ballot may not be denied a man by the State because of his color....

We think that this statutory system for the selection of party nominees for inclusion on the general election ballot makes the party which is required to follow these legislative directions an agency of the State in so far as it determines the participants in a primary election. The party takes its character as a state agency from the duties imposed upon it by state statutes; the duties do not become matters of private law because they are performed by a political party. The plan of the Texas primary follows substantially that of Louisiana, with the exception that in Louisiana the State pays the cost of the primary while Texas assesses the cost against candidates. In numerous instances, the Texas statutes fix or limit the fees to be charged. Whether paid directly by the State or through state requirements, it is state action which compels. When primaries become a part of the machinery for choosing officials, state and national, as they have here, the same tests to determine the character of discrimination or abridgment should be applied to the primary as are applied to the general election. If the State requires a certain electoral procedure, prescribes a general election ballot made up of party nominees so chosen, and limits the choice of the electorate in general elections for state offices, practically speaking, to those whose names appear on such a ballot, it endorses, adopts, and enforces the discrimination against Negroes practiced by a party entrusted by Texas law with the determination of the qualifications of the participants in the primary. This is state action within the meaning of the Fifteenth Amendment....

The United States is a constitutional democracy. Its organic law grants to all citizens a right to participate in the choice of elected officials without restriction by any State because of race. This grant to the people of the opportunity for choice is not to be nullified by a State through casting its electoral process in a form which permits a private organization to practice racial discrimination in the election. Constitutional rights would be of little value if they could be thus indirectly denied....

The privilege of membership in a party may be, as this Court said in *Grovey v. Townsend* ... no concern of a State. But when, as here, that privilege is also the essential qualification for voting in a primary to select nominees for a general election, the State makes the action of the party the action of the State. In reaching this conclusion we are not unmindful of the desirability of continuity of decision in constitutional questions. However, when convinced of former error, this Court has never felt constrained to follow precedent. In constitutional questions, where correction depends upon amendment and not upon legislative action, this Court throughout its history has freely exercised its power to re-examine the basis of its constitutional decisions. This has long been accepted practice, and this practice has continued to this day. This is particularly true when the decision believed erroneous is the application of a constitutional principle rather than an interpretation of the Constitution to extract the principle itself. Here we are applying, contrary to the recent decision in *Grovey v. Townsend*, the well-established principle of the Fifteenth Amendment, forbidding the abridgment by a State of a citizen's right to vote. *Grovey v. Townsend* is overruled.
Judgment reversed.

MR. JUSTICE FRANKFURTER concurred in the result.
MR. JUSTICE ROBERTS dissented.

SHELLEY v. KRAEMER
334 U.S. 1; 68 S.Ct. 836, 92 L.Ed. 1161 (1948)

Restrictive covenants are contracts entered into by private individuals respecting the control and disposition of their property. Commonly, these agreements restricted the sale and ownership of property to white Caucasians and prohibited the transfer of said property to Negroes, Latinos, Orientals, and Jews. In this case, the Court dealt with two such covenants from St. Louis and Detroit which were quite similar in nature.

MR. CHIEF JUSTICE VINSON delivered the opinion of the Court:

These cases present for our consideration questions relating to the validity of court enforcement of private agreements, generally described as restrictive covenants, which have as their purpose the exclusion of persons of designated race or color from the ownership or occupancy of real property. Basic constitutional issues of obvious importance have been raised.

The first of these cases comes to this Court on certiorari to the Supreme Court of Missouri. On February 16, 1911, thirty out of a total of thirty-nine owners of property fronting both sides; of Labadie Avenue between Taylor and Cora Avenue in the city of St. Louis, signed an agreement, which was subsequently recorded, providing in part:

> "...the said property is hereby restricted to the use and occupancy for the term of Fifty (50) years from this date, so that it shall be a condition all the time and whether recited and referred to as (sic) not in subsequent conveyances and shall attach the land as a condition precedent to the sale of the same, that hereafter no part of said property or any portion thereof shall be, for said term of Fifty years, occupied by any person not of the Caucasian race, it being intended hereby to restrict the use of said property for said period of time against the occupancy as owners or tenants of any portion of said property for resident or other purpose by people of the Negro or Mongolian Race."

...On August 11, 1945, pursuant to a contract for sale, petitioners Shelley, who are Negroes, for valuable consideration received from one Fitzgerald a warranty deed to the parcel in question. The trial court found that petitioners had no actual knowledge of the restrictive agreement at the time of purchase....

Respondents, as owners of other property subject to the terms of the restrictive covenant, brought suit in the Circuit Court of the city of St. Louis praying that petitioners Shelley be restrained from taking possession of the property and that judgment be entered divesting title out of petitioners Shelley and revesting title in the immediate grantor or in such other person as the court should direct. The trial court denied the requested relief on the ground that the restrictive agreement, upon which respondents based their action, had never become final and complete because it was the intention of the parties to that agreement that it was not to become effective until signed by all property owners in the district, and signatures of all the owners had never been obtained. The Supreme Court of Missouri sitting en banc reversed and directed the trial court to grant relief for which the respondents had prayed....

Specifically, petitioners urge that they have been denied the equal protection of the laws, deprived of property without due process of law, and have been denied privileges and immunities of citizens of the United States. We pass to a consideration of those issues.

I

Whether the equal protection clause of the Fourteenth Amendment inhibits judicial enforcement by state courts of restrictive covenants based on race or color is a question which this Court has not heretofore been called upon to consider....

It is well, at the outset, to scrutinize the terms of the restrictive agreements involved in these cases. In the Missouri case, the covenant declares that no part of the affected property shall be "occupied by any person not of the Caucasian race, it being intended hereby to restrict the use of said property ... against the occupancy as owners or tenants of any portion of said property for resident or other purpose by people of the Negro or Mongoloid Race." Not only does the restriction seek to proscribe the use and occupancy of the affected properties by members of the excluded class, but as construed by the Missouri court, the agreement requires that title of any person who uses his property in violation of the restriction shall be divested....

It cannot be doubted that among the civil rights intended to be protected from discriminatory state action by the Fourteenth Amendment are the rights to acquire, enjoy, own, and dispose of property. Equality in the enjoyment of property rights was regarded by the framers of that Amendment as an essential precondition to the realization of other basic civil rights and liberties which the Amendment was intended to guarantee....

It is likewise clear that restrictions on the right of occupancy of the sort sought to be created by the private agreements in these cases could not be squared with the requirements of the Fourteenth Amendment if imposed by state statute or local ordinance....

But the present cases ... do not involve action by state legislatures or city councils. Here the particular patterns of discrimination and the areas in which the restrictions are to operate, are determined, in the first instance, by the terms of agreements among private individuals. Participation of the State consists in the enforcement of the restrictions so defined. The crucial issue with which we are here confronted is whether this distinction removes these cases from the operation of the prohibitory provisions of the Fourteenth Amendment.

Since the decision of this Court in the Civil Rights Cases, 109 U.S. 3 (1883), the principle has become firmly embedded in our constitutional law that the action inhibited by the first section of the Fourteenth Amendment is only such action as may fairly be said to be that of the States. That Amendment erects no shield against merely private conduct, however discriminatory or wrongful.

We conclude, therefore, that the restrictive agreements standing alone cannot be regarded as violative of any rights guaranteed to petitioners by the Fourteenth Amendment. So long as the purposes of those agreements are effectuated by voluntary adherence to their terms, it would appear clear that there has been no action by the State and the provisions of the Amendment have not been violated....

But here there was more. These are cases in which the purposes of the agreements were secured only by judicial enforcement by state courts of the restrictive terms of the agreements. The respondents urge that judicial enforcement of private agreements does not amount to state action; or, in any event, the participation of the State is so attenuated in character as not to amount to state action within the meaning of the Fourteenth Amendment. Finally, it is suggested, even if the States in these cases may be deemed to have acted in the constitutional sense, their action did not deprive petitioners of rights guaranteed by the Fourteenth Amendment. We move to a consideration of these matters.

II

That the action of state courts and judicial officers in their official capacities is to be regarded as action of the State within the meaning of the Fourteenth Amendment, is a proposition which has long been established by decisions of this Court. That principle was given expression in the earliest cases involving the construction of the terms of the Fourteenth Amendment....

The short of the matter is that from the time of the adoption of the Fourteenth Amendment until the present, it has been the consistent ruling of this Court that the action of the States to which the Amendment has reference includes action of state courts and state judicial officials....

III

... We have no doubt that there has been state action in these cases in the full and complete sense of the phrase. The undisputed facts disclose that petitioners were willing purchasers of properties upon which they desired to establish homes. The owners of the properties were willing sellers; and contracts of sale were accordingly consummated. It is clear that but for the active intervention of the state courts, supported by the full panoply of state power, petitioners would have been free to occupy the properties in question without restraint.

These are not cases, as has been suggested, in which the States have merely abstained from action, leaving private individuals free to impose such discriminations as they see fit. Rather, these are cases in which the States have made available to such individuals the full coercive power of government to deny to petitioners, on the grounds of race or color, the enjoyment of property rights in premises which petitioners are willing and financially able to acquire and which the grantors are willing to sell. The difference between judicial enforcement and nonenforcement of the restrictive covenants is the difference to petitioners between being denied rights of property available to other members of the community and being accorded full enjoyment of those rights on an equal footing....

We hold that in granting judicial enforcement of the restrictive agreements in these cases, the States have denied petitioners the equal protection of the laws and that, therefore, the action of the state courts cannot stand. We have noted that freedom from discrimination by the States in the enjoyment of property rights was among the basic objectives sought to be effectuated by the framers of the Fourteenth Amendment. That such discrimination has occurred in these cases is clear. Because of the race or color of these petitioners they have been denied rights of ownership or occupancy enjoyed as a matter of course by other citizens of different race or color...

The rights created by the first section of the Fourteenth Amendment are, by its own terms, guaranteed to the individual. The rights established are personal rights. It is, therefore, no answer to these petitioners to say that the courts may also be induced to deny white persons rights of ownership and occupancy on grounds of race or color. Equal protection of the laws is not achieved through indiscriminate imposition of inequalities....

The historical context in which the Fourteenth Amendment became a part of the Constitution should not be forgotten. Whatever else the framers sought to achieve, it is clear that the matter of primary concern was the establishment of equality in the enjoyment of basic civil and political rights and the preservation of those rights from discriminatory action on the part of the States based on considerations of race or color. Seventy-five years ago this Court announced that the provisions of the Amendment are to be construed with this fundamental purpose in mind. Upon full consideration, we have concluded that in these cases the States have acted to deny petitioners the equal protection of the laws guaranteed by the Fourteenth Amendment. Having so decided, we find it unnecessary to consider whether petitioners have also been deprived of property without due process of law or denied privileges and immunities of citizens of the United States....

Reversed.

MR. JUSTICES REED, JACKSON, and RUTLEDGE took no part in the consideration or decision of these cases.

SWEATT v. PAINTER
339 U.S. 629; 70 S.Ct. 848; 94 L.Ed. 1114 (1950)

Herman Marion Sweatt, a Negro postal clerk, filed an application for admission to the University of Texas Law School for the 1946 term. Although state law prohibited admission of blacks to the institution, Texas had no separate law school for Negroes. After being refused admission, Sweatt sought a writ of mandamus to compel Painter and other officials at the school to admit him. The state court postponed the trial and granted the regents of the university a six-month period to create a law school for Negroes "substantially equal to the one at the University of Texas." Eight months later, the Negro school opened; however, Sweatt refused to enter and maintained his original legal action. The state courts denied the mandamus on the grounds that the "separate but equal" doctrine had been satisfied. The case was then brought to the Supreme Court on certiorari.

MR. CHIEF JUSTICE VINSON delivered the opinion of the Court:

This case and *McLaurin v. Oklahoma State Regents* ... present different aspects of this general question: To what extent does the Equal Protection Clause of the Fourteenth Amendment limit the power of a state to distinguish between students of different races in professional and graduate education in a state university? Broader issues have been urged for our consideration, but we adhere to the principle of deciding constitutional questions only in the context of the particular case before the Court. We have frequently reiterated that this Court will decide constitutional questions only when necessary to the disposition of the case at hand, and that such decisions will be drawn as narrowly as possible....

The University of Texas Law School, from which petitioner was excluded, was staffed by a faculty of sixteen full-time and three part-time professors, some of whom are nationally recognized authorities in their field. Its student body numbered 850. The library contained over 65,000 volumes. Among the other facilities available to the students were a law review, moot-court facilities, scholarship funds, and Order of the Coif affiliation. The school's alumni occupy the most distinguished positions in the private practice of the law and in the public life of the State. It may properly be considered one of the nation's ranking law schools.

The law school for Negroes which was to have opened in February 1947, would have had no independent faculty or library. The teaching was to be carried on by four members of the University of Texas Law School faculty, who were to maintain their offices at the University of Texas while teaching at both institutions. Few of the 10,000 volumes ordered for the library had arrived; nor was there any full-time librarian. The school lacked accreditation.

Since the trial of this case, respondents report the opening of a law school at the Texas State University for Negroes. It is apparently on the road to full accreditation. It has a faculty of five full-time professors; a student body of twenty-three; a library of some 16,500 volumes serviced by a full-time staff; a practice court and legal aid association; and one alumnus who has become a member of the Texas bar.

Whether the University of Texas Law School is compared with the original or the new law school for Negroes, we cannot find substantial equality in the educational opportunities offered white and Negro law students by the State. In terms of number of the faculty, variety of courses and opportunity for specialization, size of the student body, scope of the library, availability of law review and similar activities, the University of Texas Law School is superior. What is more important, the University of Texas Law School possesses to a far greater degree those qualities which are incapable of objective measurement but which make for greatness in a law school. Such qualities, to name but a few, include reputation of the faculty, experience of the administration, position and influence of the alumni, standing in the community, traditions and prestige. It is difficult to believe that one who had a free choice between these law schools would consider the question close.

Moreover, although the law is a highly learned profession, we are well aware that it is an intensely practical one. The law school, the proving ground for legal learning and practice, cannot be effective in isolation from the individuals and institutions with which the law interacts. Few students and no one who has practiced law would choose to study in an academic vacuum, removed from the interplay of ideas and exchange of views with which the law is concerned. The law school to which Texas is willing to admit petitioner excludes from its student body members of the racial groups which number 85 per cent of the population of the State and include most of the lawyers, witnesses, jurors, judges, and other officials with whom petitioner will inevitably be dealing when he becomes a member of the Texas bar. With such a substantial and significant segment of society excluded, we cannot conclude that the education offered petitioner is substantially equal to that which he would receive if admitted to the University of Texas Law School.

It may be argued that excluding petitioner from that school is no different from excluding white students from the new law school. This contention overlooks realities. It is unlikely that a member of a group so decisively in the majority, attending a school with rich traditions and prestige which only a history of consistently maintained excellence could command, would claim that the opportunities afforded him for legal education were unequal to those held open to petitioner. That such a claim, if made, would be dishonored by the State, is no answer. "Equal protection of the laws is not achieved through indiscriminate imposition of inequalities."

...Petitioner may claim his full constitutional right: legal education equivalent to that offered by the State to students of other races. Such education is not available to him in a separate law school as offered by the State. We cannot, therefore, agree with respondents that the doctrine of *Plessy v. Ferguson*... requires affirmance of the judgment below. Nor need we reach petitioner's contention that *Plessy v. Ferguson* should be re-examined in the light of contemporary knowledge respecting the purposes of the Fourteenth Amendment and the effects of racial segregation.... We hold that the Equal Protection Clause of the Fourteenth Amendment requires that petitioner be admitted to the University of Texas Law School. The judgment is reversed and the case is remanded for proceedings not inconsistent with this opinion.
Reversed.

BROWN v. BOARD OF EDUCATION OF TOPEKA
347 U.S. 483; 74 S.Ct. 693; 98 L.Ed. 591 (1954)

Fifty-four years after the "separate but equal" doctrine, formulated in Plessy v. Ferguson *(1896), seventeen states and the District of Columbia required segregation in public schools while four states left the decision of segregation to the local communities. The segregation of black and white children in dual school systems was challenged in four cases from the States of Kansas, South Carolina, Virginia and Delaware as violating the Equal Protection Clause of the Fourteenth Amendment. The litigation reached the Supreme Court first in 1952. All four cases were decided together under the title of the litigation from Topeka, Kansas.*

MR. CHIEF JUSTICE WARREN delivered the opinion of the Court:

... In each of the cases, minors of the Negro race, through their legal representatives, seek the aid of the courts in obtaining admission to the public schools of their community on a nonsegregated basis. In each instance, they had been denied admission to schools attended by white children under laws requiring or permitting segregation according to race. This segregation was alleged to deprive the plaintiffs of the equal protection of the laws under the Fourteenth Amendment. In each of the cases other than the Delaware case, a three-judge federal district court denied relief to the plaintiffs on the so-called "separate but equal" doctrine announced by this Court in *Plessy v. Ferguson*....

The plaintiffs contend that segregated public schools are not "equal" and cannot be made "equal," and that hence they are deprived of the equal protection of the laws. Because of the obvious importance of the question presented, the Court took jurisdiction. Argument was heard in the 1952 Term, and reargument was heard this Term on certain questions propounded by the Court.

Reargument was largely devoted to the circumstances surrounding the adoption of the Fourteenth Amendment in 1868. It covered exhaustively consideration of the Amendment in Congress, ratification by the states, then existing practices in racial segregation, and the view of the proponents and opponents of the Amendment. This discussion and our own investigation convince us that, although these sources cast some light, it is not enough to resolve the problem with which we are faced. At best, they are inconclusive. The most avid proponents of the postwar Amendments undoubtedly intended them to remove all legal distinctions among "all persons born or naturalized in the United States." Their opponents, just as certainly, were antagonistic to both the letter and the spirit of the Amendments and wished them to have the most limited effect. What others in Congress and the state legislatures had in mind cannot be determined with any degree of certainty.

An additional reason for the inclusive nature of the Amendment's history, with respect to segregated schools, is the status of public education at that time. In the South, the movement toward free common schools, supported by general taxation, had not yet taken hold. Education of white children was largely in the hands of private groups. Education of Negroes was almost nonexistent, and practically all of the race were illiterate. In fact, any education of Negroes was forbidden by law in some states. Today, in contrast, many Negroes have achieved outstanding success in the arts and sciences as well as in the business and professional world. It is true that public education had already advanced further in the North, but the effect of the Amendment on northern states was generally ignored in the congressional debates. Even in the North, the conditions of public education did not approximate those existing today. The curriculum was usually rudimentary; ungraded schools were common in rural areas; the school term was but three months a year in many states; and compulsory school attendance was virtually unknown. As a consequence, it is not surprising that there should be so little in the history of the Fourteenth Amendment relating to its intended effect on public education.

In the first cases in this Court construing the Fourteenth Amendment, decided shortly after its adoption, the Court interpreted it as proscribing all state-imposed discriminations against the Negro race. The doctrine of "separate but equal" did not make its appearance in this Court until 1896 in the case of *Plessy v. Ferguson*, involving not education but transportation. American courts have since labored with the doctrine for over half a century. In this Court, there have been six cases involving the "separate but equal" doctrine in the field of public education. In *Cumming v. County Board of Education*, 175 U.S. 528, and *Gong Lum v. Rice*, 275 U.S. 78, the validity of the doctrine itself was not challenged. In more recent cases, all on the graduate-school level, inequality was found in that specific benefits enjoyed by white students were denied to Negro students of the same educational qualifications. *Missouri ex rel. Gaines v. Canada*, 305 U.S. 337; *Sipuel v. Oklahoma*, 332 U.S. 631; *Sweatt v. Painter*, 33.9 U.S. 629; *McLaurin v. Oklahoma State Regents*, 339 U.S. 637. In none of these cases was it necessary to re-examine the doctrine to grant relief to the Negro plaintiff. And in *Sweatt v. Painter* ... the Court expressly reversed the decision on the question whether *Plessy v. Ferguson* should be held inapplicable to public education.

In the instant cases, that question is directly presented. Here, unlike *Sweatt v. Painter*, there are findings below that the Negro and white schools involved have been equalized, or are being equalized, with respect to buildings, curricula, qualifications and salaries of teachers, and other "tangible" factors. Our decision, therefore, cannot turn on merely a comparison of these tangible factors in the Negro and white schools involved in each of the cases. We must look instead to the effect of segregation itself on public education.

In approaching this problem, we cannot turn the clock back to 1868 when the Amendment was adopted, or even to 1896 when *Plessy v. Ferguson* was written. We must consider public education in the light of its full development and its present place in American life throughout the Nation. Only in this way can it be determined if segregation in public schools deprives these plaintiffs of the equal protection of the laws.

Today, education is perhaps the most important function of state and local governments. Compulsory school-attendance laws and the great expenditures for education both demonstrate our recognition of the importance of education to our democratic society. It is required in the performance of our most basic public responsibilities, even service in the armed forces. It is the very foundation of good citizenship. Today it is a principal instrument in awakening the child to cultural values, in preparing him for later professional training, and in helping him to adjust normally to his environment. In these days, it is doubtful any child may reasonably be expected to succeed in life if he is denied the opportunity of an education. Such an opportunity, where the state has undertaken to provide it, is a right which must be made available to all on equal terms.

We come then to the question presented: Does segregation of children in public schools solely on the basis of race, even though the physical facilities and other "tangible" factors may be equal, deprive the children of the minority group of equal educational opportunities? We believe that it does.

In *Sweatt v. Painter*,... in finding that a segregated law school for Negroes could not provide them equal educational opportunities, this Court relied in large part on "those qualities which are incapable of objective measurement but which make for greatness in a law school. " In *McLdurin v. Oklahoma State Regents*,... the Court, in requiring that a Negro admitted to a white graduate school be treated like all other students, again resorted to intangible consideration: "... his ability to study, to engage in discussions and exchange views with other students, and, in general, to learn his profession." Such considerations apply with added force to children in grade and high schools. To separate them from others of similar age and qualifications solely because of their race generates a feeling of inferiority as to their status in the community that may affect their hearts and minds in a way unlikely ever to be undone. The effect of this separation of their educational opportunities was well stated by a finding in the Kansas case by a court which nevertheless felt compelled to rule against the Negro plaintiffs:

> Segregation of white and colored children in public schools has a detrimental effect upon the colored children. The impact is greater when it has the sanction of the law; for the policy of separating the races is usually interpreted as denoting the inferiority of the Negro group. A sense of inferiority affects the motivation of a child to learn. Segregation with the sanction of law, therefore, has a tendency to retard the educational and mental development of Negro children and to deprive them of some of the benefits they would receive in a racially integrated school system.

Whatever may have been the extent of psychological knowledge at the time of *Plessy v. Ferguson*, this finding is amply supported by modern authority. Any language in *Plessy v. Ferguson* contrary to this finding is rejected.

We conclude that in the field of public education the doctrine of "separate but equal" has no place. Separate educational facilities are inherently unequal. Therefore, we hold that the plaintiffs and others similarly situated for whom the actions have been brought are, by reason of the segregation complained of, deprived of the equal protection of the laws guaranteed by the Fourteenth Amendment. This disposition makes unnecessary any discussion whether such segregation also violates the Due Process Clause of the Fourteenth Amendment,.,

Because these are class actions, because of the wide applicability of this decision, and because of the great variety of local conditions, the formulation of decrees in these cases presents problems of considerable complexity. On reargument, the consideration of appropriate relief was necessarily subordinated to the primary question-the constitutionality of segregation in public education. We have now announced that such segregation is a denial of the equal protection of the laws. In order that we may have the full assistance of the parties in formulating decrees, the cases will be restored to the docket, and the parties are requested to present further argument on questions ... previously propounded by

the Court for the reargument this term. The Attorney General of the United States is again invited to participate. The Attorneys General of the states requiring or permitting segregation in public education will also be permitted to appear as amici curiae ... upon request to do so by September 15, 1954, and submission of briefs by October 1, 1954.
It is so ordered.

BOLLING *v.* SHARPE
347 U.S. 497; 74 S.Ct. 686; 98 L.Ed. 583 (1954)

The existence of segregated schools in the District of Columbia, the jurisdiction of which rests in the hands of Congress, posed a peculiar problem to the Supreme Court, since the limitations of the Fourteenth Amendment do not restrict federal action. Moreover, until this case, the Court had refused to hold that racial discrimination on the part of the national government violated the Due Process Clause of the Fifth Amendment. Specifically, in Hurd *v.* Hodge, *334 U.S. 24 (1948), the Court had held that judicial enforcement of restrictive covenants violated the Civil Rights Act of 1866 and thus avoided the question of constitutional application.*

MR. CHIEF JUSTICE WARREN delivered the opinion of the Court:

This case challenges the validity of segregation in the public schools of the District of Columbia. The petitioners, minors of the Negro race, allege that such segregation deprives them of due process of law under the Fifth Amendment. They were refused admission to a public school attended by white children solely because of their race. They sought the aid of the District Court for the District of Columbia in obtaining admission. That court dismissed their complaint. We granted a writ of certiorari before judgment in the Court of Appeals because of the importance of the constitutional question presented....

We have this day held that the Equal Protection Clause of the Fourteenth Amendment prohibits the states from maintaining racially segregated public schools. The legal problem in the District of Columbia is somewhat different, however. The Fifth Amendment, which is applicable in the District of Columbia, does not contain an equal protection clause as does the Fourteenth Amendment, which applies only to the states. But the concepts of equal protection and due process, both stemming from our American ideal of fairness, are not mutually exclusive. The "equal protection of the laws" is a more implicit safeguard of prohibited unfairness than "due process of law," and, therefore, we do not imply that the two are always interchangeable phrases. But, as this Court has recognized, discrimination may be so unjustifiable as to be violative of due process.

Classifications based solely upon race must be scrutinized with particular care, since they are contrary to our traditions and hence constitutionally suspect. As long ago as 1896, this Court declared the principle "that the Constitution of the United States, in its present form, forbids, so far as civil and political rights are concerned, discrimination by the General Government, or by the States, against any citizen because of his race." And in *Buchanan v. Warley*, 245 U.S. 60, the Court held that a statute which limited the right of a property owner to convey his property to a person of another race was, as an unreasonable discrimination, a denial of due process of law.

Although the Court has not assumed to define "liberty" with any great precision, that term is not confined to mere freedom from bodily restraint. Liberty under law extends to the full range of conduct which the individual is free to pursue, and it cannot be restricted except for a proper governmental objective. Segregation in public education is not reasonably related to any proper governmental objective, and thus it imposes on Negro children of the District of Columbia a burden that constitutes an arbitrary deprivation of their liberty in violation of the Due Process Clause.

In view of our decision that the Constitution prohibits the states from maintaining racially segregated public schools, it would be unthinkable that the same Constitution would impose a lesser duty on the Federal Government. We hold that racial segregation in the public schools of the District of Columbia is a denial of the due process of law guaranteed by the Fifth Amendment to the Constitution.

For the reasons set out in *Brown v. Board of Education*, this case will be restored to the docket for reargument on questions ... previously propounded by the Court.

It is so ordered.

BROWN v. BOARD OF EDUCATION (BROWN II)
349 U.S. 294; 74 S.Ct. 753; 99 L.Ed. 1083 (1955)

From the time this decision was handed down, it has been subjected to attack from students of the Court. The most telling criticism was that by allowing the States to have additional time to end the dual school system with "all deliberate speed," instead of setting a reasonable date for its accomplishment, the Supreme Court created a reprieve which permitted Southern politicians to fan the flames of public passion to resist the decree. By 1969, recognizing that the dual school system had yet to be completely dismantled, the Court abandoned the "all deliberate speed" rule and ordered designation "immediately" in Alexander v. Holmes County Board of Education.

MR. CHIEF JUSTICE WARREN delivered the opinion of the Court:

These cases were decided on May 17, 1954. The opinions of that date, declaring the fundamental principle that racial discrimination in public education is unconstitutional, are incorporated herein by reference. All provisions of federal, state, or local law requiring or permitting such discrimination must yield to this principle. There remains for consideration the manner in which relief is to be accorded....

Full implementation of these constitutional principles may require solution of varied local school problems. School authorities have the primary responsibility for elucidating, assessing, and solving these problems; courts will have to consider whether the action of school authorities constitutes good faith implementation of the governing constitutional principles. Because of their proximity to local conditions and the possible need for further hearings, the courts which originally heard these cases can best perform this judicial appraisal. Accordingly, we believe it appropriate to remand the cases to those courts.

In fashioning and effectuating the decrees, the courts will be guided by equitable principles. Traditionally, equity has been characterized by a practical flexibility in shaping its remedies and by a facility for adjusting and reconciling public and private needs. These cases call for the exercise of these traditional attributes of equity power. At stake is the personal interest of the plaintiffs in admission to public schools as soon as practicable on a nondiscriminatory basis. To effectuate this interest may call for elimination of a variety of obstacles in making the transition to school systems operated in accordance with the constitutional principles set forth in our May 17, 1954, decision. Courts of equity may properly take into account the public interest in the elimination of such obstacles in a systematic and effective manner. But it should go without saying that the vitality of these constitutional principles cannot be allowed to yield simply because of disagreement with them.

While giving weight to these public and private considerations, the courts will require that the defendants make a prompt and reasonable start toward full compliance with our May 17, 1954, ruling. Once such a start has been made, the courts may find that additional time is necessary to carry out the ruling in an effective manner. The burden rests upon the defendants to establish that such time is necessary in the public interest and is consistent with good faith compliance at the earliest practicable date. To that end, the courts may consider problems related to administration, arising from the physical condition of the school plant, the school transportation system, personnel, revision of school districts and attendance areas into compact units to achieve a system of determining admission to the public schools on a nonracial basis, and revision of local laws and regulations which may be necessary in solving the foregoing problems. They will also consider the adequacy of any plans the defendants may propose to meet these problems and to effectuate a transition to a racially nondiscriminatory school system. During this period of transition, the courts will retain jurisdiction of these cases....

The cases are remanded to the District Courts to take such proceedings and enter such orders and decrees consistent with this opinion as are necessary and proper to admit to public schools, on a racially nondiscriminatory basis with all deliberate speed, the parties to these cases.

It is so ordered.

MOOSE LODGE *v.* IRVIS
407 U.S. 163; 92 S.Ct. 1965; 32 L.Ed. 2d 627 (1972)

A member of Moose Lodge, a private club, brought Irvis, a Negro, to the establishment as his guest. Irvis was refused the services of the club's dining room and bar solely on the basis of his race. Because the Pennsylvania liquor board had issued Moose Lodge a private club liquor license, Irvis contended that the discrimination was state action and therefore a violation of the Fourteenth Amendment. The District Court found the club's membership and guest practices discriminatory and declared the liquor license invalid as long as the discrimination was practiced. The case came to the Supreme Court on appeal.

MR. JUSTICE REHNQUIST delivered the opinion of the Court.

...Irvis, a Negro,... was refused service by appellant Moose Lodge, a local branch of the national fraternal organization located in Harrisburg, Pennsylvania... He claimed that because the Pennsylvania liquor board had issued appellant Moose Lodge a private club license that authorized the sale of alcoholic beverages on its premises, the refusal of service to him was "state action" for the purposes of the Equal Protection Clause of the Fourteenth Amendment. He named both Moose Lodge and the Pennsylvania Liquor Authority as defendants, seeking injunctive relief that would have required the defendant liquor board to revoke Moose Lodge's license so long as it continued its discriminatory practices. Appellee sought no damages....

Appellant urges, in the alternative, that we either vacate the judgment below because there is not presently a case or controversy between the parties, or that we reverse on the merits....

II

Moose Lodge is a private club in the ordinary meaning of that term. It is a local chapter of a national fraternal organization having well-defined requirements for membership. It conducts all of its activities in a building that is owned by it. It is not publicly funded. Only members and guests are permitted in any lodge of the order; one may become a guest only by invitation of a member or upon invitation of the house committee.

Appellee, while conceding the right of private clubs to choose members upon a discriminatory basis, asserts that the licensing of Moose Lodge to serve liquor by the Pennsylvania Liquor Control Board amounts to such state involvement with the club's activities as to make its discriminatory practices forbidden by the Equal Protection Clause of the Fourteenth Amendment. The relief sought and obtained by appellee in the District Court was an injunction forbidding the licensing by the liquor authority of Moose Lodge until it ceased its discriminatory practices. We conclude that Moose Lodge's refusal to serve food and beverages to a guest by reason of the fact that he was a Negro does not, under the circumstances here presented, violate the Fourteenth Amendment.

In 1883, this Court in The Civil Rights Cases, 109 U.S. 3, set forth the essential dichotomy between discriminatory action by the State, which is prohibited by the Equal Protection Clause, and private conduct, "however discriminatory or wrongful," against which that clause "erects no shield," *Shelley v. Kraemer*, 334 U.S. 1, 13 (1948).... And in *Burton v. Wilmington Parking Authority*, 365 U.S. 715 (1961).

While the principle is easily stated, the question of whether particular discriminatory conduct is private, on the one hand, or amounts to "state action," on the other hand, frequently admits of no easy answer. "Only by sifting facts and weighing circumstances can the nonobvious involvement of the State in private conduct be attributed its true significance." *Burton v. Wilmington Parking Authority*....

Our cases make clear that the impetus for the forbidden discrimination need not originate with the State if it is state action that enforces privately originated discrimination. *Shelley v. Kraemer*.... The Court held in *Burton v. Wilmington Parking Authority* ... that a private restaurant owner who refused service because of a customer's race violated the Fourteenth Amendment, where the restaurant was located in a building owned by a state-created parking authority and leased from the authority. The Court, after a comprehensive review of the relationship between the lessee and the parking authority concluded that the latter had "so far insinuated itself into a position of interdependence with Eagle [the restaurant owner] that it must be recognized as a joint participant in the challenged activity, which, on that account, cannot be considered to have been so 'purely private' as to fall without the scope of the Fourteenth Amendment...."

The Court has never held, of course, that discrimination by an otherwise private entity would be violative of the Equal Protection Clause if the private entity receives any sort of benefit or service at all from the State, or if it is subject to state regulation in any degree whatever. Since state-furnished services include such necessities of life as electricity, water, and police and fire protection, such a holding would utterly emasculate the distinction between private as distinguished from state conduct set forth in The Civil Rights Cases ... and adhered to in subsequent decisions. Our holdings indicate that where the impetus for the discrimination is private, the State must have "significantly involved itself with invidious discriminations," *Reitman v. Mulkey* 387 U.S. 369, 380 (1967), in order for the discriminatory action to fall within the ambit of the constitutional prohibition.

Here there is nothing approaching the symbiotic relationship between lessor and lessee that was present in *Burton*, where the private lessees obtained the benefit of locating in a building owned by the state-created parking authority, and the parking authority was enabled to carry out its primary public purpose of furnishing parking space by advantageously leasing portions of the building constructed for that purpose to commercial lessees such as the owner of the Eagle Restaurant. Unlike *Burton*, the Moose Lodge building is located on land owned by it, not by any public authority. Far from apparently holding itself out as a place of public accommodation, Moose Lodge quite ostentatiously proclaims the fact that it is not open to the public at large, nor is it located and operated in such surroundings that, although private in name, it discharges a function or performs a service that would otherwise in all likelihood be performed by the State. In short, while Eagle was a public restaurant in a public building, Moose Lodge is a private social club in a private building.

With the exception hereafter noted, the Pennsylvania Liquor Control Board plays absolutely no part in establishing or enforcing the membership or guest policies of the club that it licenses to serve liquor. There is no suggestion in this record that Pennsylvania law, either as written or as applied, discriminates against minority groups either in their right to apply for club licenses themselves or in their right to purchase and be served liquor in places of public accommodation. The only effect that the state licensing of Moose Lodge to serve liquor can be said to have, on the right of any other Pennsylvanian to buy or be served liquor on premises other than those of Moose Lodge, is that for some purposes club licenses are counted in the maximum number of licenses that may be issued in a given municipality. Basically each municipality has a quota of one retail license for each 1,500 inhabitants. Licenses issued to hotels, municipal golf courses, and airport restaurants are not counted in this quota, nor are club licenses until the maximum number of retail licenses is reached. Beyond that point, neither additional retail licenses nor additional club licenses may be issued so long as the number of issued and outstanding retail licenses remains at or above the statutory maximum....

However detailed this type of regulation may be in some particulars, it cannot be said to foster or encourage racial discrimination. Nor can it be said to make the State in any realistic sense a partner or even a joint venturer in the club's enterprise. The limited effect of the prohibition against obtaining additional club licenses when the maximum number of retail licenses allotted to a municipality has been issued, when considered together with the availability of liquor from hotel, restaurant, and retail licensees, falls far short of conferring upon club licensees a monopoly in the dispensing of liquor in any given municipality or in the State as a whole. We therefore hold that, with the exception hereafter noted, the operation of the regulatory scheme enforced by the Pennsylvania Liquor Control Board does not sufficiently implicate the State in the discriminatory guest policies of Moose Lodge so as to make the latter "state action" within the ambit of the Equal Protection Clause of the Fourteenth Amendment....

There can be no doubt that the label "private club" can be and has been used to evade both regulations of state and local liquor authorities, and statutes requiring places of public accommodation to serve all persons without regard to race, color, religion, or national origin....

Even though the Liquor Control Board regulation in question is neutral in its terms, the result of its application in a case where the constitution and bylaws of a club required discrimination would be to invoke the sanctions of the State to enforce a concededly discriminatory private rule. State action, for purposes of the Equal Protection Clause, may emanate from rulings of administrative and regulatory agencies as well as from legislative or judicial action.... Although the record before us is not as clear as one would like, appellant has not persuaded us that the District Court should have denied any and all relief.

Appellee was entitled to a decree enjoining the enforcement of §113.09 of the regulations promulgated by the Pennsylvania Liquor Control Board insofar as that regulation requires compliance by Moose Lodge with prodiscriminatory provisions. He was entitled to no more. The judgment of the District Court is reversed, and the case remanded with instructions to enter a decree in conformity with this opinion.

Reversed and remanded.

MR. JUSTICE DOUGLAS, with whom MR. JUSTICE MARSHALL joined, dissented.

MR. JUSTICE BRENNAN, with whom MR. JUSTICE MARSHALL joined, dissented, saying in part:

When Moose Lodge obtained its liquor license, the State of Pennsylvania became an active participant in the operation of the lodge bar. Liquor licensing laws are only incidentally revenue measures; they are primarily pervasive regulatory schemes under which the State dictates and continually supervises virtually every detail of the operation of the licensee's business. Very few, if any, other licensed businesses experience such complete state involvement. Yet the Court holds that such involvement does not constitute "state action" making the lodge's refusal to serve a guest liquor, solely because of his race, a violation of the Fourteenth Amendment. The vital flaw in the Court's reasoning is its complete disregard of the fundamental value underlying the "state action" concept. That value is discussed in my separate opinion in *Adickes v. Kress & Co.*, 398 U.S. 144 ... (1970):

> The state-action doctrine reflects the profound judgment that denials of equal treatment, and particularly denials on account of race or color, are singularly grave when government has or shares responsibility for them. Government is the social organ to which all in our society look for the promotion of liberty, justice, fair and equal treatment, and the setting of worthy norms and goals for social conduct. Therefore something is uniquely amiss in a society where the government, the authoritative oracle of community values, involves itself in racial discrimination. Accordingly,... the cases that have come before us [in which] this Court has condemned significant state involvement in racial discrimination, however subtle and indirect it may have been and whatever form it may have taken[,] ... represent vigilant fidelity to the constitutional principle that no State shall in any significant way lend its authority to the sordid business of racial discrimination.

Plainly, the State of Pennsylvania's liquor regulations intertwine the State with the operation of the lodge bar in a "significant way [and] lend [the State's] authority to the sordid business of racial discrimination...."

This is thus a case requiring application of the principle that until today has governed our determinations of the existence of "state action": "Our prior decisions leave no doubt that the mere existence of efforts by the State, through legislation or otherwise, to authorize, encourage, or otherwise support racial discrimination in a particular facet of life constitutes illegal state involvement in those pertinent private acts of discrimination that subsequently occur...."

I therefore dissent and would affirm the final decree entered by the District Court.

SAN ANTONIO INDEPENDENT SCHOOL DISTRICT *v.* RODRIGUEZ 411 U.S. 1; 93 S.Ct. 1278; 36 L.Ed. 2d 16 (1973)

The state and local communities participate in the financing of public elementary and secondary schools in Texas. Each district has an ad valorem *tax on property within its jurisdiction to aid the state in the finance. Accordingly, in a number of higher-income white districts, the state was spending as much as $815 per student annually. In several lower income minority districts, as little as $305 was being spent on each student per year. Rodriguez and other parents brought class action on behalf of school children who came from poor families who reside in school districts having a low property tax base. Rodriguez felt that this system violated equal protection requirements. The case proceeded to the Supreme Court on appeal.*

MR. JUSTICE POWELL delivered the opinion of the Court.

This suit attacking the Texas system of financing public education was initiated by Mexican-American parents whose children attend the elementary and secondary schools in the Edgewood Independent School District, an urban school district in San Antonio, Texas. They brought a class action on behalf of school children throughout the State who are members of minority groups or who are poor and reside in school districts having a low property tax base. Named as defendants were the State Board of Education, the Commissioner of Education, the State Attorney General, and the Bexar County (San Antonio) Board of Trustees. The complaint was filed in the summer of 1968, and a three-judge court was impaneled in January, 1969. In December, 1971, the panel rendered its judgment in a per curiam opinion holding the Texas school finance system unconstitutional under the Equal Protection Clause of the Fourteenth Amendment. The State appealed, and we noted probable jurisdiction to consider the far-reaching constitutional questions presented.... For the reasons stated in this opinion, we reverse the decision of the District Court.

I

The first Texas State Constitution, promulgated upon Texas' entry into the Union in 1845, provided for the establishment of a system of free schools. Early in its history, Texas adopted a dual approach to the financing of its schools, relying on mutual participation by the local school districts and the State. As early as 1883, the state constitution was amended to provide for the creation of local school districts empowered to levy *ad valorem* taxes with the consent of local taxpayers for the "erection ... of school buildings" and for the "further maintenance of public free schools." Such local funds as were raised were supplemented by funds distributed to each district from the State's Permanent and Available School Funds. The Permanent School Fund, its predecessor established in 1854 with $2,000,000 realized from an annexation settlement, was thereafter endowed with millions of acres of public land set aside to assure a continued source of income for school support. The Available School Fund, which received income from the Permanent School Fund as well as from a state *ad valorem* property tax and other designated taxes, served as the disbursing arm for most state educational funds throughout the late 1800's and first half of this century. Additionally, in 1918 an increase in state property taxes was used to finance a program providing free textbooks throughout the State.

Until recent times, Texas was a predominantly rural State and its population and property wealth were spread relatively evenly across the State. Sizable differences in the value of assessable property between local school districts became increasingly evident as the State became more industrialized and as rural-to-urban population shifts became more pronounced. The location of commercial and industrial property began to play a significant role in determining the amount of tax resources available to each school district. These growing disparities in population and taxable property between districts were responsible in part for increasingly notable differences in levels of local expenditure for education....

Recognizing the need for increased state funding to help offset disparities in local spending and to meet Texas' changing educational requirements, the state legislature in the late 1940's undertook a thorough evaluation of public education with an eye toward major reform. In 1947, an 18-member committee, composed of educators and legislators, was appointed to explore alternative systems in other States and to propose a funding scheme that would guarantee a minimum or basic educational offering to each child and that would help overcome interdistrict disparities in taxable resources. The Committee's efforts led to the passage of the Gilmer-Aikin bills, named for the Committee's cochairman, establishing the Texas Minimum Foundation School Program. Today, this Program accounts for approximately half of the total educational expenditures in Texas.

The Program calls for state and local contributions to a fund earmarked specifically for teacher salaries, operating expenses, and transportation costs. The State, supplying funds from its general revenues, finances approximately 80% of the Program, and the school districts are responsible – as a unit – for providing the remaining 20%. The districts' share, known as the Local Fund Assignment, is apportioned among the school districts under a formula designed to reflect each district's relative taxpaying ability. The Assignment is first divided among Texas' 254 counties pursuant to a complicated economic index that takes into account the relative value of each county's contribution to the State's total income from manufacturing, mining, and agricultural activities. It also considers each county's relative share of all payrolls paid within the State and, to a lesser extent, considers each county's share of all property in the State. Each county's assignment is then divided among its school districts on the basis of each district's share of assessable property within the county. The district, in turn, finances its share of the Assignment out of revenues from local property taxation.

The design of this complex system was twofold. First, it was an attempt to assure that the Foundation Program would have an equalizing influence on expenditure levels between school districts by placing the heaviest burden on the school district most capable of paying. Second, the Program's architects sought to establish a Local Fund Assignment that would force every school district to contribute to the education of its children but that would not by itself exhaust any district's resources. Today every school district does impose a property tax from which it derives locally expendable funds in excess of the amount necessary to satisfy its Local Fund Assignment under the Foundation Program....

The school district in which appellees reside, the Edgewood Independent School District, has been compared throughout this litigation with the Alamo Heights Independent School District. This comparison between the least and most affluent districts in the San Antonio area serves to illustrate the manner in which the dual system of finance operates and to indicate the extent to which substantial disparities exist despite the State's impressive progress in recent years. Edgewood is one of seven public school districts in the metropolitan area. Approximately 22,000 students are enrolled in these 25 elementary and secondary schools. The district is situated in the core-city sector of San Antonio in a residential neighborhood that has little commercial or industrial property. The residents are predominantly of Mexican-American descent: approximately 90% of the student population is Mexican-American and over 6% is Negro. The average assessed property value per pupil is $5,960-the lowest in the metropolitan area-and the median family income ($4,686) is also the lowest. At an equalized tax rate of $1.05 per $100 of assessed property-the highest in the metropolitan area-the district contributed $26 to the education of each child for the 1967-1968 school year above its Local Fund Assignment for the Minimum Foundation Program. The Foundation Program contributed $222 per pupil for a state-local total of $248. Federal funds added another $108 for a total of $356 per pupil.

Alamo Heights is the most affluent school district in San Antonio. Its six schools, housing approximately 5,000 students, are situated in a residential community quite unlike the Edgewood District. The school population is predominantly "Anglo," having only 18% Mexican-Americans and less than 1% Negroes. The assessed property value per pupil exceeds $49,000, and the median family income is $8,001. In 1967-1968, the local tax rate of $.85 per $100 of valuation yielded $333 per pupil over and above its contribution to the Foundation Program. Coupled with the $225 provided from that Program, the district was able to supply $558 per student. Supplemented by a $36 per-pupil grant from federal sources, Alamo Heights spent .$594 per pupil....

Texas virtually concedes that its historically rooted dual system of financing education could not withstand the strict judicial scrutiny that this Court has found appropriate in reviewing legislative judgments that interfere with fundamental constitutional rights or that involve suspect classifications. If, as previous decisions have indicated, strict scrutiny means that the State's system is not entitled to the usual presumption of validity, that the State rather than the complainants must carry a "heavy burden of justification," that the State must demonstrate that its educational system has been structured with "precision," and is "tailored" narrowly to serve legitimate objectives, and that it has selected the "less drastic means" for effectuating its objectives, the Texas financing system and its counterpart in virtually every other State will not pass muster. The State candidly admits that "[n]o one familiar with the Texas system would contend that it has yet achieved perfection." Apart from its concession that educational financing in Texas has "defects" and "imperfections," the State defends the system's rationality with vigor and disputes the District Court's finding that it lacks a "reasonable basis."

This, then, establishes the framework for our analysis. We must decide, first, whether the Texas system of financing public education operates to the disadvantage of some suspect class or impinges upon a fundamental right explicitly or implicitly protected by the Constitution, thereby requiring strict judicial scrutiny. If so, the judgment of the District Court should be affirmed. If not, the Texas scheme must still be examined to determine whether it rationally furthers some legitimate, articulated state purpose and therefore does not constitute an invidious discrimination in violation of the Equal Protection Clause of the Fourteenth Amendment.

II

The District Court's opinion does not reflect the novelty and complexity of the constitutional questions posed by appellees' challenge to Texas' system of school financing. In concluding that strict judicial scrutiny was required, that court relied on decisions dealing with the rights of indigents to equal treatment in the criminal trial and appellate processes, and on cases disapproving wealth restrictions on the right to vote. Those cases, the District Court concluded, established wealth as a suspect classification. Finding that the local property tax system discriminated on the basis of wealth, it regarded those precedents as controlling. It then reasoned, based on decisions of this Court affirming the undeniable importance of education, that there is a fundamental right to education and that, absent some compelling state justification, the Texas system could not stand.

We are unable to agree that this case, which in significant aspects is *sui generis*, may be so neatly fitted into the conventional mosaic of constitutional analysis under the Equal Protection Clause. Indeed, for the several reasons that follow, we find neither the suspect-classification nor the fundamental-interest analysis persuasive.

A

The wealth discrimination discovered by the District Court in this case, and by several other courts that have recently struck down school-financing laws in other States, is quite unlike any of the forms of wealth discrimination heretofore reviewed by this Court. Rather than focusing on the unique features of the alleged discrimination, the courts in these cases have virtually assumed their findings of a suspect classification through a simplistic process of analysis: since, under the traditional systems of financing public schools, some poorer people receive less expensive educations than other more affluent people, these systems discriminate on the basis of wealth. This approach largely ignores the hard threshold questions, including whether it makes a difference for purposes of consideration under the Constitution that the class of disadvantaged "poor" cannot be identified or defined in customary equal protection terms, and whether the relative-rather than absolute-nature of the asserted deprivation is of significant consequence. Before a State's laws and the justifications for the classifications they create are subjected to strict judicial scrutiny, we think these threshold considerations must be analyzed more closely than they were in the court below.

The case comes to us with no definitive description of the classifying facts or delineation of the disfavored class. Examination of the District Court's opinion and of appellees' complaint, briefs, and contentions at oral argument suggests, however, at least three ways in which the discrimination claimed here might be described. The Texas system of school financing might be regarded as discriminating (1) against "poor" persons whose incomes fall below some identifiable level of poverty or who might be characterized as functionally "indigent," or (2) against those who are relatively poorer than others, or (3) against all those who, irrespective of their personal incomes, happen to reside in relatively poorer school districts. Our task must be to ascertain whether, in fact, the Texas system has been shown to discriminate on any of these possible bases and, if so, whether the resulting classification may be regarded as suspect.

The precedents of this Court provide the proper starting point. The individuals, or groups of individuals, who constituted the class discriminated against in our prior cases shared two distinguishing characteristics: because of their impecunity they were completely unable to pay for some desired benefit, and as a consequence, they sustained an absolute deprivation of a meaningful opportunity to enjoy that benefit. In *Griffin v. Illinois*, 351 U.S. 12 (1956), and its progeny, the Court invalidated state laws that prevented an indigent criminal defendant from acquiring a transcript, or an adequate substitute for a transcript, for use at several stages of the trial and appeal process. The payment requirements in each case were found to occasion *de facto* discrimination against those who, because of their indigency, were totally unable to pay for transcripts. And the Court in each case emphasized that no constitutional violation would have been shown if the State had provided some "adequate substitute" for a full stenographic transcript.

...In *Bullock v. Carter*, 405 U.S. 134 (1972), the Court invalidated the Texas filing-fee requirement for primary elections. Both of the relevant classifying facts found in the previous cases were present there. The size of the fee, often running into the thousands of dollars and, in at least one case, as high as $8,900, effectively barred all potential candidates who were unable to pay the required fee. As the system provided "no reasonable alternative means of access to the ballot" ... inability to pay occasioned an absolute denial of a position on the primary ballot.

Only appellees' first possible basis for describing the class disadvantaged by the Texas school-financing system-discrimination against a class of definably "poor" persons-might arguably meet the criteria established in these prior cases. Even a cursory examination, however, demonstrates that neither of the two distinguishing characteristics of wealth classifications can be found here....

We thus conclude that the Texas system does not operate to the peculiar disadvantage of any suspect class. But in recognition of the fact that this Court has never heretofore held that wealth discrimination alone provides an adequate basis for invoking strict scrutiny, appellees have not relied solely on this contention. They also assert that the State's system impermissibly interferes with the exercise of a "fundamental" right and that accordingly the prior decisions of this Court require the application of the strict standard of judicial review.... It is this question-whether education is a fundamental right, in the sense that it is among the rights and liberties protected by the Constitution-which has so consumed the attention of courts and commentators in recent years.

B

In *Brown v. Board of Education*, 347 U.S. 483 (1954), a unanimous Court recognized that "education is perhaps the most important function of state and local governments."

Nothing this Court holds today in any way detracts from our historic dedication to public education. We are in complete agreement with the conclusion of the three-judge panel below that "the grave significance of education both to the individual and to our society" cannot be doubted. But the importance of a service performed by the State does not determine whether it must be regarded as fundamental for purposes of examination under the Equal Protection Clause....

It is not the province of this Court to create substantive constitutional rights in the name of guaranteeing equal protection of the laws. Thus, the key to discovering whether education is "fundamental" is not to be found in comparisons of the relative societal significance of education as opposed to subsistence or housing. Nor is it to be found by weighing whether the answer lies in assessing whether there is a right to education explicitly or implicitly guaranteed by the Constitution. *Eisenstadt v. Baird*, 405 U.S. 438 (1972); *Dunn v. Blumstein*, 405 U.S. 330 (1972); *Police Dept. of Chicago v. Mosely*, 408 U.S. 92 (1972); *Skinner v. Oklahoma*, 316 U.8. 535 (1942).

Education, of course, is not among the rights afforded explicit protection under our Federal Constitution. Nor do we find any basis for saying it is implicitly so protected. As we have said, the undisputed importance of education will not alone cause this Court to depart from the usual standard for reviewing a

State's social and economic legislation. It is appellees' contention, however, that education is distinguishable from other services and benefits provided by the State because it bears a peculiarly close relationship to other rights and liberties accorded protection under the Constitution. Specifically, they insist that education is itself a fundamental personal right because it is essential to the effective exercise of First Amendment freedoms and to intelligent utilization of the right to vote. In asserting a nexus between speech and education, appellees urge that the right to speak is meaningless unless the speaker is capable of articulating his thoughts intelligently and persuasively. The "marketplace of ideas" is an empty forum for those lacking basic communicative tools. Likewise, they argue that the corollary right to receive information becomes little more than a hollow privilege when the recipient has not been taught to read, assimilate, and utilize available knowledge....

We have carefully considered each of the arguments supportive of the District Court's finding that education is a fundamental right or liberty and have found those arguments unpersuasive. In one further respect we find this a particularly inappropriate case in which to subject state action to strict judicial scrutiny. The present case, in another basic sense, is significantly different from any of the cases in which the Court has applied strict scrutiny to state or federal legislation touching upon constitutionally protected rights. Each of our prior cases involved legislation which "deprived," "infringed," or "interfered" with the free exercise of some fundamental personal right or liberty.

...Every step leading to the establishment of the system Texas utilizes today – including the decisions permitting localities to tax and expend locally, and creating a continuously expanding state aid-was implemented in an effort to extend public education and to improve its quality. Of course, every reform that benefits some more than others may be criticized for what it fails to accomplish. But we think it plain that, in substance, the thrust of the Texas system is affirmative and reformatory and, therefore, should be scrutinized under judicial principles sensitive to the nature of the State's efforts and to the rights reserved to the States under the Constitution.

C

It should be clear, for the reasons stated above and in accord with the prior decisions of this Court, that this is not a case in which the challenged state action must be subjected to the searching judicial scrutiny reserved for laws that create suspect classifications or impinge upon constitutionally protected rights.

We need not rest our decision, however, solely on the inappropriateness of the strict-scrutiny test. A century of Supreme Court adjudication under the Equal Protection Clause affirmatively supports the application of the traditional standard of review, which requires only that the State's system be shown to bear some rational relationship to legitimate state purposes. This case represents far more than a challenge to the manner in which Texas provides for the education of its children. We have here nothing less than a direct attack on the way in which Texas has chosen to raise and disburse state and local tax revenues. We are asked to condemn the State's judgment in conferring on political subdivisions the power to tax local property to supply revenues for local interests.

...We stand on familiar ground when we continue to acknowledge that the Justices of this Court lack both the expertise and the familiarity with local problems so necessary to the making of wise decisions with respect to the raising and disposition of public revenues. Yet, we are urged to direct the States either to alter drastically the present system or to throw out the property tax altogether in favor of some other form of taxation. No scheme of taxation, whether the tax is imposed on property, income, or purchases of goods and services, has yet been devised which is free of all discriminatory impact. In such a complex arena in which no perfect alternatives exist, the Court does well not to impose too rigorous a standard of scrutiny lest all local fiscal schemes become subjects of criticism under the Equal Protection Clause....

It must be remembered, also, that every claim arising under the Equal Protection Clause has implications for the relationship between national and state power under our federal system. Questions of federalism are always inherent in the process of determining whether a State's laws are to be accorded the traditional presumption of Constitutionality, or are to be subjected instead to rigorous judicial scrutiny. While "[t]he maintenance of the principles of federalism is a foremost consideration in interpreting any of the pertinent constitutional provisions under which this Court examines state action," it would be difficult to imagine a case having a greater potential impact on our federal system than the one now before us, in which we are urged to abrogate systems of financing public education presently in existence in virtually every State.

The foregoing considerations buttress our conclusion that Texas' system of public school finance is an inappropriate candidate for strict judicial scrutiny. These same considerations are relevant to the determination whether that system, with its conceded imperfections, nevertheless bears some rational relationship to a legitimate state purpose. It is to this question that we next turn our attention.

III

The basic contours of the Texas school finance system have been traced at the outset of this opinion. We will now describe in more detail that system and how it operates, as these facts bear directly upon the demands of the Equal Protection Clause.

Apart from federal assistance, each Texas school receives its funds from the State and from its local school district. On a statewide average, a roughly comparable amount of funds is derived from each source....

In its reliance on state as well as local resources, the Texas system is comparable to the systems employed in virtually every other State. The power to tax local property for educational purposes has been recognized in Texas at least since 1883. When the growth of commercial and industrial centers and accompanying shifts in population began to create disparities in local resources, Texas undertook a program calling for a considerable investment of state funds.

...While assuring a basic education for every child in the State, it permits and encourages a large measure of participation in and control of each district's schools at the local level. In an era that has witnessed a consistent trend toward centralization of the functions of government, local sharing of responsibility for public education has survived....

The persistence of attachment to government at the lowest level where education is concerned reflects the depth of commitment of its supporters. In part, local control means ... the freedom to devote more money to the education of one's children. Equally important, however, is the opportunity it offers for participation in the decision-making process that determines how those local tax dollars will be spent. Each locality is free to tailor local programs to local needs. Pluralism also affords some opportunity for experimentation, innovation, and a healthy competition for educational excellence. An analogy to the Nation-State relationship in our federal system seems uniquely appropriate. Mr. Justice Brandeis identified as one of the peculiar strengths of our form of government each State's freedom to "serve as a laboratory; and try novel social and economic experiments." No area of social concern stands to profit more from a multiplicity of viewpoints and from a diversity of approaches than does public education....

Moreover, if local taxation for local expenditures were an unconstitutional method of providing for education then it might be an equally impermissible means of providing other necessary services customarily financed largely from local property taxes, including local police and fire protection, public health and hospitals, and public utility facilities of various kinds. We perceive no justification for such a severe denigration of local property taxation and control as would follow from appellees' contentions. It has simply never been within the constitutional prerogative of this Court to nullify statewide measures for financing public services merely because the burdens or benefits thereof fall unevenly depending upon the relative wealth of the political subdivisions in which citizens live.

In sum, to the extent that the Texas system of school financing results in unequal expenditures between children who happen to reside in different districts, we cannot say that such disparities are the product of a system that is so irrational as to be invidiously discriminatory. Texas has acknowledged its shortcomings and has persistently endeavored - not without some success - to ameliorate the differences in levels of expenditures without sacrificing the benefits of local participation. The Texas plan is not the result of hurried, ill-conceived legislation. It certainly is not the product of purposeful discrimination against any group or class. On the contrary, it is rooted in decades of experience in Texas and elsewhere, and in major part is the product of responsible studies by qualified people.... One also must remember that the system here challenged is not peculiar to Texas or to any other State. In its essential characteristics, the Texas plan for financing public education reflects what many educators for a half century have thought was an enlightened approach to a problem for which there is no perfect solution. We are unwilling to assume for ourselves a level of wisdom superior to that of legislators, scholars, and educational authorities in 50 States, especially where the alternatives proposed are only recently conceived and nowhere yet tested. The constitutional standard under the Equal Protection Clause is whether the challenged state action rationally furthers a legitimate state purpose or interest. *McGinnis v. Royster*, 410 U.S. 263 (1973). We hold that the Texas plan abundantly satisfies this standard.

IV

In light of the considerable attention that has focused on the District Court opinion in this case ... a cautionary postcript seems appropriate. It cannot be questioned that the constitutional judgment reached by the District Court and approved by our dissenting Brothers today would occasion in Texas and elsewhere an unprecedented upheaval in public education. Some commentators have concluded that, whatever the contours of the alternative financing programs that might be devised and approved, the result could not avoid being a beneficial one. But, just as there is nothing simple about the constitutional issues involved in these cases, there is nothing simple or certain about predicting the consequences of massive change in the financing and control of public education. Those who have devoted the most thoughtful attention to the practical ramifications of these cases have found no clear or dependable answers and their scholarship reflects no such unqualified confidence in the desirability of completely uprooting the existing system....

The consideration and initiation of fundamental reforms with respect to state taxation and education are matters reserved for the legislative processes of the various States, and we do no violence to the values of federalism and separation of powers by staying our hand. We hardly need add that this Court's action today is not to be viewed as placing its judicial imprimatur on the status quo. The need is apparent for reform in tax systems which may well have relied too long and too heavily on the local property tax. And certainly innovative thinking as to public education, its methods, and its funding is necessary to assure both a higher level of quality and greater uniformity of opportunity. These matters merit the continued attention of the scholars who already have contributed much by their challenges. But the ultimate solutions must come from the lawmakers and from the democratic pressures of those who elect them.

Reversed.

MR. JUSTICE STEWART, concurring:

The method of financing public schools in Texas, as in almost every other State, has resulted in a system of public education that can fairly be described as chaotic and unjust. It does not follow, however, and I cannot find, that this system violates the Constitution of the United States. I join the opinion and judgment of the Court because I am convinced that any other course would mark an extraordinary departure from principled adjudication under the Equal Protection Clause of the Fourteenth Amendment....

Unlike other provisions of the Constitution, the Equal Protection Clause confers no substantive rights and creates no substantive liberties. The function of the Equal Protection Clause, rather, is simply to measure the validity of classifications created by state laws.

There is hardly a law on the books that does not affect some people differently from others. But the basic concern of the Equal Protection Clause is with state legislation whose purpose or effect is to create discrete and objectively identifiable classes. And with respect to such legislation, it has long been settled that the Equal Protection Clause is offended only by laws that are invidiously discriminatory – only by classifications that are wholly arbitrary or capricious....

In refusing to invalidate the Texas system of financing its public schools, the Court today applies with thoughtfulness and understanding the basic principles I have so sketchily summarized. First, as the Court points out, the Texas system has hardly created the kind of objectively identifiable classes that are cognizable under the Equal Protection Clause. Second, even assuming the existence of such discernible categories, the classifications are in no sense based upon constitutionally "suspect" criteria. Third, the Texas system does not rest "on grounds wholly irrelevant to the achievement of the State's objective." Finally, the Texas system impinges upon no substantive constitutional rights or liberties....

MR. JUSTICE WHITE, with whom MR. JUSTICES DOUGLAS and BRENNAN joined, dissented.

MR. JUSTICE MARSHALL with whom MR. JUSTICE DOUGLAS concurred, dissented, saying in part,

The Court today decides, in effect, that a State may constitutionally vary the quality of education which it offers its children in accordance with the amount of taxable wealth located in the school districts within which they reside. The majority's decision represents an abrupt departure from the mainstream of recent state and federal court decisions concerning the unconstitutionality of state educational financing schemes dependent upon taxable local wealth. More unfortunately, though, the majority's holding can only be seen as a retreat from our historic commitment to equality of educational opportunity and as unsupportable acquiescence in a system which deprives children in their earliest years of the chance to reach their full potential as citizens. The Court does this despite the absence of any substantial justification for a scheme which arbitrarily channels educational resources in accordance with the fortuity of the amount of taxable wealth within each district.

In my judgment, the right of every American to an equal start in life so far as the provision of a state service as important as education is concerned, is far too vital to permit state discrimination on grounds as tenuous as those presented by this record. Nor can I accept the notion that it is sufficient to remit these appellees to the vagaries of the political process which, contrary to the majority's suggestion, has proved singularly unsuited to the task of providing a remedy for this discrimination. I, for one, am unsatisfied with the hope of an ultimate "political" solution sometime in the indefinite future while, in the meantime, countless children unjustifiably receive inferior educations that "may affect their hearts and minds in a way unlikely ever to be undone." *Brown v. Board of Education*, 347 U.S. 483 … (1954). I must therefore respectfully dissent.

…It seems to me inescapably clear that this Court has consistently adjusted the care with which it will review state discrimination in light of the constitutional significance of the interests affected and the invidiousness of the particular classification. In the context of economic interests, we find that discriminatory state action is almost always sustained, for such interests are generally far removed from constitutional guarantees. Moreover, "[t]he extremes to which the Court has gone in dreaming up rational bases for state regulation in that area may in many instances be ascribed to a healthy revulsion from the Court's earlier excesses in using the Constitution to protect interests that have more than enough power to protect themselves in the legislative halls." *Dandridge v. Williams*, 397 U.S., at 520 (dissenting opinion). But the situation differs markedly when discrimination against important individual interests with constitutional implications and against particularly disadvantaged or powerless classes is involved. The majority suggests, however, that a variable standard of review would give this Court the appearance of a "superlegislature…." I cannot agree. Such an approach seems to me a part of the guarantees of our Constitution and of the historic experiences with oppression of and discrimination against discrete, powerless minorities which underlie that document. In truth, the Court itself will be open to the criticism raised by the majority so long as it continues on its present course of effectively selecting in private which cases will be afforded special consideration without acknowledging the true basis of its action.

…The majority today attempts to force this case into the same category for purposes of equal protection analysis as decisions involving discrimination affecting commercial interests. By so doing, the majority singles this case out for analytic treatment at odds with what seems to me to be the clear trend of recent decisions in this Court, and thereby ignores the constitutional importance of the interest at stake and the invidiousness of the particular classification, factors that call for far more than the lenient scrutiny of the Texas financing scheme which the majority pursues. Yet if the discrimination inherent in the Texas scheme is scrutinized with the care demanded by the interest and classification present in this case, the unconstitutionality of that scheme is unmistakable.

…The Court now suggests that only interests guaranteed by the Constitution are fundamental for purposes of equal protection analysis, and since it rejects the contention that public education is fundamental, it follows that the Court concludes that public education is not constitutionally guaranteed. It is true that this Court has never deemed the provision of free public education to be required by the Constitution. Indeed, it has on occasion suggested that state-supported education is a privilege bestowed by a State on its citizens. See *Missouri ex rel. Gaines v. Canada*, 305.U.S. at 349. Nevertheless, the fundamental importance of education is amply indicated by the prior decisions of this Court, by the unique status accorded public education and some of our most basic constitutional values….

We are told that this case requires us "to condemn the State's judgment in conferring on political subdivisions the power to tax local property to supply revenues for local interests...." Yet no one in the course of this entire litigation has ever questioned the constitutionality of the local property tax as a device for raising educational funds. The District Court's decision, at most, restricts the power of the State to make educational funding dependent exclusively upon local property taxation so long as there exist interdistrict disparities in taxable property wealth. But it hardly eliminates the local property tax as a source of educational funding or as a means of providing local fiscal control.

The Court seeks solace for its action today in the possibility of legislative reform. The Court's suggestions of legislative redress and experimentation will doubtless be of great comfort to the schoolchildren of Texas' disadvantaged districts, but considering the vested interests of the wealthy school districts in the preservation of the status quo, they are worth little more. The possibility of legislative action is, in all events, no answer to this Court's duty under the Constitution to eliminate unjustified state discrimination. In this case we have been presented with an instance of such discrimination, in a particularly invidious form, against an individual interest of large constitutional and practical importance. To support the demonstrated discrimination in the provision of educational opportunity, the State has offered a justification which, on analysis, takes on at best an ephemeral character. Thus, I believe that the wide disparities in taxable district property wealth inherent in the local property tax element of the Texas financing scheme render that scheme violative of the Equal Protection Clause.

I would therefore affirm the judgment of the District Court.

MILLIKEN *v.* BRADLEY
418 U.S. 717; 94 S.Ct. 3112; 41 L.Ed. 2d 1069 (1974)

Bradley and others contended that the Detroit public school system was racially segregated as a result of the official policies and actions of Michigan and Detroit officials. They sought implementation of a plan to eliminate the segregation and establish a unitary non-racial school system. The District Court ordered the Board of Education to submit Detroit-only desegregation plans. It also ordered state officials, including Governor Milliken, to submit desegregation plans encompassing the three-county metropolitan area, even though the 85 outlying school districts in these counties were not charged with having violated constitutional rights. After the Court of Appeals sustained the judgment the case was brought to the Supreme Court by writ of certiorari.

MR. CHIEF JUSTICE BURGER delivered the opinion of the Court.

We granted certiorari in these consolidated cases to determine whether a federal court may impose a multi-district, area-wide remedy to a single-district *de jure* segregation problem absent any finding that the other included school districts have failed to operate unitary school systems within their districts, absent any claim or finding that the boundary lines of any affected school district were established with the purpose of fostering racial segregation in public schools, absent any finding that the included districts committed acts which effected segregation within the other districts, and absent a meaningful opportunity for the included neighboring school districts to present evidence or be heard on the propriety of a multidistrict remedy or on the question of constitutional violations by those neighboring districts.

I

The action was commenced in August, 1970, by the respondents, the Detroit Branch of the National Association for the Advancement of Colored People and individual parents and students, on behalf of a class later defined by order of the United States District Court for the Eastern District of Michigan, dated February 16, 1971, to include "all school children in the City of Detroit, Michigan, and all Detroit resident parents who have children of school age."

II

Ever since *Brown v. Board of Education*, 347 U.S. 483 (1954), judicial consideration of school desegregation cases has begun with the standard:

> "[I]in the field of public education the doctrine of 'separate but equal' has no place. Separate educational facilities are inherently unequal...."

This has been reaffirmed time and again as the meaning of the Constitution and the controlling rule of law.

The target of the *Brown* holding was clear and forthright: the elimination of state-mandated or deliberately maintained dual school systems with certain schools for Negro pupils and others for white pupils. This duality and racial segregation were held to violate the Constitution in the cases subsequent to 1954, including particularly *Green v. County School Board of New Kent County*, 391 U.S. 430 (1968); *Monroe v. Board of Comm'rs*, 391 U.S. 450 (1968); *Swann v. Charlotte-Mecklenburg Board of Education*, 402 U.S. 1 (1971); *Wright v. Council of the City of Emporia*, 407 U.S. 451 (1972); *United States v. Scotland Neck Board of Education*, 407 U.S. 484 (1972).

The *Swann* case, of course, dealt

> "with the problem of defining in more precise terms than heretofore the scope of the duty of school authorities and district courts in implementing *Brown* I and the mandate to eliminate dual systems and establish unitary systems at once."

... In *Brown v. Board of Education*, 349 U.S. 294 (1955) (*Brown* II), the Court's first encounter with the problem of remedies in school desegregation cases, the Court noted:

> "In fashioning and effectuating the decrees, the courts will be

> guided by equitable principles. Traditionally, equity has been characterized by a practical flexibility in shaping its remedies and by a facility for adjusting and reconciling public and private needs...."

In further refining the remedial process, *Swann* held, the task is to correct, by a balancing of the individual and collective interests, "the condition that offends the Constitution." A federal remedial power may be exercised "only on the basis of a constitutional violation" and, "[a]s with any equity case, the nature of the violation determines the scope of the remedy."

...It is obvious from the scope of the interdistrict remedy itself that absent a complete restructuring of the laws of Michigan relating to school districts the District Court will become first, a *de facto* "legislative authority" to resolve these complex questions, and then the "school superintendent" for the entire area. This is a task which few, if any, judges are qualified to perform and one which would deprive the people of control of schools through their elected representatives.

Of course, no state law is above the Constitution. School district lines and the present laws with respect to local control, are not sacrosanct and if they conflict with the Fourteenth Amendment, federal courts have a duty to prescribe appropriate remedies.... *Wright v. Council of the City of Emporia*, 407 U.S. 451 (1972); *United States v. Scotland Neck Board of Education*, 407, U.S. 484 (1972), (state or local officials prevented from carving out a new school district from an existing district that was in process of dismantling a dual school system); cf., *Haney v. County Board of Education of Sevier County*, 429 F. 2d 364 (CA8 1970), (State contributed to separation of races by drawing of school district lines); *United States v. Texas*, 321 F. Supp. 1043 (ED Tex. 1970), aff'd, 447 F. 2d 441 (CA5 1971), *Edgar v. United States*, 404 U.S. 1016 (1972), (one or more school districts created and maintained for one race). But our prior holdings have been confined to violations and remedies within a single school district. We therefore turn to address, for the first time, the validity of a remedy mandating cross-district or interdistrict consolidation to remedy a condition of segregation found to exist in only one district.

The controlling principle consistently expounded in our holdings is that the scope of the remedy is determined by the nature and extent of the constitutional violation.... Before the boundaries of separate and autonomous school districts may be set aside by consolidating the separate units for remedial purposes or by imposing a cross-district remedy, it must first be shown that there has been a constitutional violation within one district that produces a significant segregative effect in another district. Specifically, it must be shown that racially discriminatory acts of the state or local school districts, or of a single school district have been a substantial cause of interdistrict segregation. Thus an interdistrict remedy might be in order where the racially discriminatory acts of one or more school districts caused racial segregation in an adjacent district, or where district lines have been deliberately drawn on the basis of race. In such circumstances an interdistrict remedy would be appropriate to eliminate the interdistrict segregation directly caused by the constitutional violation. Conversely, without an interdistrict violation and interdistrict effect, there is no constitutional wrong calling for an interdistrict remedy.

The record before us, voluminous as it is, contains evidence of *de jure* segregated conditions only in the Detroit Schools; indeed, that was the theory on which the litigation was initially based and on which the District Court took evidence.... With no showing of significant violation by the 53 outlying school districts and no evidence of any interdistrict violation or effect, the court went beyond the original theory of the case as framed by the pleadings and mandated a metropolitan area remedy. To approve the remedy ordered by the court would impose on the outlying districts, not shown to have committed any constitutional violation, a wholly impermissible remedy based on a standard not hinted at in *Brown* I and II or any holding of this Court....

III

We recognize that the six-volume record presently under consideration contains language and some specific incidental findings thought by the District Court to afford a basis for interdistrict relief. However, these comparatively isolated findings and brief comments concern only one possible interdistrict violation and are found in the context of a proceeding that, as the District Court conceded, included no proof of segregation practiced by any of the 85 suburban school districts surrounding Detroit.

...It does not follow that an interdistrict remedy is constitutionally justified or required. With a single exception, discussed later, there has been no showing that either the State or any of the 85 outlying districts engaged in activity that had a cross–district effect. The boundaries of the Detroit School District, which are coterminous with the boundaries of the city of Detroit, were established over a century ago by neutral legislation when the city was incorporated; there is no evidence in the record, nor is there any suggestion by the respondents, that either the original boundaries of the Detroit School District, or any other school district in Michigan, were established for the purpose of creating, maintaining, or perpetuating segregation of races. There is no claim and there is no evidence hinting that petitioner outlying school districts and their predecessors, or the 30-odd other school districts in the tricounty area – but outside the District Court's "desegregation area" – have ever maintained or operated anything but unitary school systems. Unitary school systems have been required for more than a century by the Michigan Constitution as implemented by state law. Where the schools of only one district have been affected, there is no constitutional power in the courts to decree relief balancing the racial composition of that district's schools with those of the surrounding districts.

...Neither the Court of Appeals nor the District Court offered any indication in the record or in their opinions as to how, if at all, the availability of state-financed aid for some Michigan students outside Detroit, but not for those within Detroit, might have affected the racial character of any of the State's school districts. Furthermore, as the respondents recognize, the application of our recent ruling in *San Antonio School District v. Rodriguez*, 411 U.S. 1 (1973), to this state education financing system is questionable, and this issue was not addressed by either the Court of Appeals or the District Court. This, again, underscores the crucial fact that the theory upon which the case proceeded related solely to the establishment of Detroit city violations as a basis for desegregating Detroit schools and that, at the time of trial, neither the parties nor the trial judge was concerned with a foundation for interdistrict relief.

IV

Petitioners have urged that they were denied due process by the manner in which the District Court limited their participation after intervention was allowed, thus precluding adequate opportunity to present evidence that they had committed no acts having a segregative effect in Detroit. In light of our holding that, absent an interdistrict violation, there is no basis for an interdistrict remedy, we need not reach these claims. It is clear, however, that the District Court, with the approval of the Court of Appeals, has provided an interdistrict remedy in the face of a record which shows no constitutional violations that would call for equitable relief except within the city of Detroit. In these circumstances there was no occasion for the parties to address, or for the District Court to consider whether there were racially discriminatory acts for which any of the 53 outlying districts were responsible and which had a direct and significant segregative effect on schools of more than one district.

We conclude that the relief ordered by the District Court and affirmed by the Court of Appeals was based upon an erroneous standard and was unsupported by record evidence that acts of the outlying districts effected the discrimination found to exist in the schools of Detroit. Accordingly, the judgment of the Court of Appeals is reversed and the case is remanded for further proceedings consistent with this opinion leading to prompt formulation of a decree directed to eliminating the segregation found to exist in Detroit city schools, a remedy which has been delayed since 1970.

Reversed and remanded.

MR. JUSTICE STEWART concurred.

MR. JUSTICE WHITE, with whom MR. JUSTICES DOUGLAS, BRENNAN, and MARSHALL joined, dissented, saying in part:

The District Court and the Court of Appeals found that over a long period of years those in charge of the Michigan public schools engaged in various practices calculated to effect the segregation of the Detroit school system. The Court does not question these findings, nor could it reasonably do so. Neither does it question the obligation of the federal courts to devise a feasible and effective remedy. But it promptly cripples the ability of the judiciary to perform this task, which is of fundamental importance to our constitutional system, by fashioning a strict rule that remedies in school cases must stop at the school district line unless certain other conditions are met. As applied here, the remedy for unquestioned violations of the equal protection rights of Detroit's Negroes by the Detroit School Board and the State of Michigan must be totally confined to the limits of the school district and may not reach into adjoining or surrounding districts unless and until it is proved there has been some sort of "interdistrict violation" – unless unconstitutional actions of the Detroit School Board have had a segregative impact on other districts, or unless the segregated condition of the Detroit schools has itself been influenced by segregative practices in those surrounding districts into which it is proposed to extend the remedy.

Regretfully, and for several reasons, I can join neither the Court's judgment nor its opinion. The core of my disagreement is that deliberate acts of segregation and their consequences will go unremedied, not because a remedy would be infeasible or unreasonable in terms of the usual criteria governing school desegregation cases, but because an effective remedy would cause what the Court considers to be undue administrative inconvenience to the State. The result is that the State of Michigan, the entity at which the Fourteenth Amendment is directed, has successfully insulated itself from its duty to provide effective desegregation remedies by vesting sufficient power over its public schools in its local school districts. If this is the case in Michigan, it will be the case in most States....

The Court draws the remedial line at the Detroit School District boundary, even though the Fourteenth Amendment is addressed to the State and even though the State denies equal protection of the laws when its public agencies, acting in its behalf, invidiously discriminate. The State's default is "the condition that offends the Constitution," *Swann v. Charlotte-Mecklenburg Board of Education*, *supra* ... and state officials may therefore be ordered to take the necessary measures to completely eliminate from the Detroit public schools "all vestiges of state-imposed segregation...." I cannot understand, nor does the majority satisfactorily explain, why a federal court may not order an appropriate interdistrict remedy, if this is necessary or more effective to accomplish this constitutionally mandated task. As the Court unanimously observed in *Swann*: "Once a right and a violation have been shown, the scope of a district court's equitable powers to remedy past wrongs is broad, for breadth and flexibility are inherent in equitable remedies...." In this case, both the right and the State's Fourteenth Amendment violation have concededly been fully established, and there is no acceptable reason for permitting the party responsible for the constitutional violation to contain the remedial powers of the federal court within administrative boundaries over which the transgressor itself has plenary power.

The unwavering decisions of this Court over the past 20 years support the assumption of the Court of Appeals that the District Court's remedial power does not cease at the school district line. The Court's first formulation of the remedial principles to be followed in disestablishing racially discriminatory school systems recognized the variety of problems arising from different local school conditions and the necessity for that "practical flexibility" traditionally associated with courts of equity. *Brown v. Board of Education....* Indeed, the district courts to which the *Brown* cases were remanded for the formulation of remedial decrees were specifically instructed that they might consider, *inter alia*, "revision of school districts and attendance areas into compact units to achieve a system of determining admission to the public schools on a nonracial basis...." The malady addressed in *Brown* II was the statewide policy of requiring or permitting school segregation on the basis of race, while the record here concerns segregated schools only in the city of Detroit. The obligation to rectify the unlawful condition nevertheless rests on the State. The permissible revision of school districts contemplated in *Brown* II rested on the State's responsibility for desegregating its unlawfully segregated schools, not on any segregative effect which the condition of segregation in one school district might have had on the schools of a neighboring district. The same situation obtains here and the same remedial power is available to the District Court.

Later cases reinforced the clearly essential rules that state officials are fully answerable for unlawfully caused conditions of school segregation which can effectively be controlled only by steps beyond the authority of local school districts to take, and that the equity power of the district courts includes the ability to order such measures implemented. When the highest officials of the State of Arkansas impeded a federal court order to desegregate the public schools under the immediate jurisdiction of the Little Rock School Board, this Court refused to accept the local board's assertion of its good faith as a legal excuse for delay in implementing the desegregation order. The Court emphasized that "from the point of view of the Fourteenth Amendment, they [the local school board members] stand in this litigation as the agents of the State." *Cooper v. Aaron*, 358 U.S. 1, 16 (1958)....

Nor does the Court's conclusion follow from the talismanic invocation of the desirability of local control over education. Local autonomy over school affairs, in the sense of the community's participation in the decisions affecting the education of its children, is, of course, an important interest. But presently constituted school district lines do not delimit fixed and unchangeable areas of a local educational community. If restructuring is required to meet constitutional requirements, local authority may simply be redefined in terms of whatever configuration is adopted, with the parents of the children attending schools in the newly demarcated district or attendance zone continuing their participation in the policy management of the schools with which they are concerned most directly. The majority's suggestion that judges should not attempt to grapple with the administrative problems attendant on a reorganization of school attendance patterns is wholly without foundation. It is precisely this sort of task which the district courts have been properly exercising to vindicate the constitutional rights of Negro students since *Brown I* and which the Court has never suggested they lack the capacity to perform. Intradistrict revisions of attendance zones, and pairing and grouping of schools, are techniques unanimously approved in *Swann* which entail the same sensitivity to the interest of parents in the education their children receive as would an interdistrict plan which is likely to employ the very same methods. There is no reason to suppose that the District Court, which has not yet adopted a final plan of desegregation, would not be as capable of giving or as likely to give sufficient weight to the interest in community participation in schools in an interdistrict setting, consistent with the dictates of the Fourteenth

Amendment. The majority's assumption that the District Court would act otherwise is a racial departure from the practical flexibility previously left to the equity powers of the federal judiciary....

MR. JUSTICE MARSHALL, with whom MR. JUSTICES DOUGLAS, BRENNAN, and WHITE joined, dissented....

FRONTIERO *v.* RICHARDSON
93 S.Ct. 1764; 411 U.S. 677; 36 L.Ed.2d 583 (1973)

The facts in this case are contained in the opinion below.

Mr. Justice BRENNAN announced the judgment of the Court in an opinion in which Mr. Justice DOUGLAS, Mr. Justice WHITE, and Mr. Justice MARSHALL join.

The question before us concerns the right of a female member of the uniformed services to claim her spouse as a 'dependent' for the purposes of obtaining increased quarters allowances and medical and dental benefits under 37 U.S.C. §§ 401, 403, and 10 U.S.C. §§ 1072, 1076, on an equal footing with male members. Under these statutes, a serviceman may claim his wife as a 'dependent' without regard to whether she is in fact dependent upon him for any part of her support.... A servicewoman, on the other hand, may not claim her husband as a 'dependent' under these programs unless he is in fact dependent upon her for over one-half of his support.... Thus, the question for decision is whether this difference in treatment constitutes an unconstitutional discrimination against servicewomen in violation of the Due Process Clause of the Fifth Amendment. A three-judge District Court for the Middle District of Alabama, one judge dissenting, rejected this contention and sustained the constitutionality of the provisions of the statutes making this distinction.... We noted probable jurisdiction.... We reverse.

I

In an effort to attract career personnel through reenlistment, Congress established ... a scheme for the provision of fringe benefits to members of the uniformed services on a competitive basis with business and industry. Thus, under 37 U.S.C. § 403, a member of the uniformed services with dependents is entitled to an increased 'basic allowence for quarters' and, under 10 U.S.C. § 1076, a member's dependents are provided comprehensive medical and dental care.

Appellant Sharron Frontiero, a lieutenant in the United States Air Force, sought increased quarters allowances, and housing and medical benefits for her husband, appellant Joseph Frontiero, on the ground that he was her 'dependent.' Although such benefits would automatically have been granted with respect to the wife of a male member of the uniformed services, appellant's application was denied because she failed to demonstrate that her husband was dependent on her for more than one-half of his support. Appellants then commenced this suit, contending that, by making this distinction, the statutes unreasonably discriminate on the basis of sex in violation of the Due Process Clause of the Fifth Amendment. In essence, appellants asserted that the discriminatory impact of the statutes is twofold: first, as a procedural matter, a female member is required to demonstrate her spouse's dependency, while no such burden is imposed upon male members; and, second, as a substantive matter, a male member who does not provide more than one-half of his wife's support receives benefits, while a similarly situated female member is denied such benefits. Appellants therefore sought a permanent injunction against the continued enforcement of these statutes and an order directing the appellees to provide Lieutenant Frontiero with the same housing and medical benefits that a similarly situated male member would receive.

Although the legislative history of these statutes sheds virtually no light on the purposes underlying the differential treatment accorded male and female members, a majority of the three-judge District Court surmised that Congress might reasonably have concluded that, since the husband in our society is generally the 'breadwinner' in the family-and the wife typically the 'dependent' partner – it would be more economical to require married female members claiming husbands to prove actual dependency than to extend the presumption of dependency to such members.' Indeed, given the fact that approximately 99% of all members of the uniformed services are male, the District Court speculated that such differential treatment might conceivably lead to a 'considerable saving of administrative expense and manpower.'

II

At the outset, appellants contend that classifications based upon sex, like classifications based upon race, alienage, and national origin, are inherently suspect and must therefore be subjected to close judicial scrutiny. We agree and, indeed, find at least implicit support for such an approach in our unanimous decision only last Term in *Reed v. Reed*,...

In *Reed*, the Court considered the constitutionality of an Idaho statute providing that, when two individuals are otherwise equally entitled to appointment as administrator of an estate, the male applicant must be preferred to the female. Appellant, the mother of the deceased, and appellee, the father, filed competing petitions for appointment as administrator of their son's estate. Since the parties, as parents of the deceased, were members of the same entitlement class the statutory preference was invoked and the father's petition was therefore granted. Appellant claimed that this statute, by giving a mandatory preference to males over females without regard to their individual qualifications, violated the Equal Protection Clause of the Fourteenth Amendment.

The Court noted that the Idaho statute 'provides that different treatment be accorded to the applicants on the basis of their sex; it thus establishes a classification subject to scrutiny under the Equal Protection Clause....' Under 'traditional' equal protection analysis, a legislative classification must be sustained unless it is 'patently arbitrary' and bears no rational relationship to a legitimate governmental interest....

In an effort to meet this standard, appellee contended that the statutory scheme was a reasonable measure designed to reduce the workload on probate courts by eliminating one class of contests. Moreover, appellee argued that the mandatory preference for male applicants was in itself reasonable since 'men (are) as a rule more conversant with business affairs than ... women.' Indeed, appellee maintained that 'it is a matter of common knowledge, that women still are not engaged in politics, the professions, business or industry to the extent that men are.' And the Idaho Supreme Court, in upholding the constitutionality of this statute, suggested that the Idaho Legislature might reasonably have 'concluded that in general men are better qualified to act as an administrator than are women.'

Despite these contentions, however, the Court held the statutory preference for male applicants unconstitutional. In reaching this result, the Court implicitly rejected appellee's apparently rational explanation of the statutory scheme, and concluded that, by ignoring the individual qualifications of particular applicants, the challenged statute provide 'dissimilar treatment for men and women who are ... similarly situated....' The Court therefore held that, even though the State's interest in achieving administrative efficiency 'is not without some legitimacy,' '(t)o give a mandatory preference to members of either sex over members of the other, merely to accomplish the elimination of hearings on the merits, is to make the very kind of arbitrary legislative choice forbidden by the (Constitution)....' This departure from 'traditional' rational-basis analysis with respect to sex-based classifications is clearly justified.

There can be no doubt that our Nation has had a long and unfortunate history of sex discrimination. Traditionally, such discrimination was rationalized by an attitude of 'romantic paternalism' which, in practical effect, put women, not on a pedestal, but in a cage. Indeed, this paternalistic attitude became so firmly rooted in our national consciousness that, 100 years ago, a distinguished Member of this Court was able to proclaim:

> 'Man is, or should be, women's protector and defender. The natural and proper timidity and delicacy which belongs to the female sex evidently unfits it for many of the occupations of civil life. The constitution of the family organization, which is founded in the divine ordinance, as well as in the nature of things, indicates the domestic sphere as that which properly belongs to the domain and functions of womanhood. The harmony, not to say identity, of interests and views which belong, or should belong, to the family institution is repugnant to the idea of a woman adopting a distinct and independent career from that of her husband... .
>
> '... The paramount destiny and mission of woman are to fulfil the noble and benign offices of wife and mother. This is the law of the Creator.' *Bradwell v. State of Illinois....*'

As a result of notions such as these, our statute books gradually became laden with gross, stereotyped distinctions between the sexes and, indeed, throughout much of the 19th century the position of women in our society was, in many respects, comparable to that of blacks under the pre-Civil War slave codes. Neither slaves nor women could hold office, serve on juries, or bring suit in their own names, and married women traditionally were denied the legal capacity to hold or convey property or to serve as legal guardians of their own children.... And although blacks were guaranteed the right to vote in 1870, women were denied even that right – which is itself 'preservative of other basic civil and political rights' – until adoption of the Nineteenth Amendment half a century later.

It is true, of course, that the position of women in America has improved markedly in recent decades. Nevertheless, it can hardly be doubted that, in part because of the high visibility of the sex characteristic, women still face pervasive, although at times more subtle, discrimination in our educational institutions, in the job market and, perhaps most conspicuously, in the political arena....

Moreover, since sex, like race and national origin, is an immutable characteristic determined solely by the accident of birth, the imposition of special disabilities upon the members of a particular sex because of their sex would seem to violate 'the basic concept of our system that legal burdens should bear some relationship to individual responsibility....' *Weber v. Aetna Casualty & Surety Co*.... And what differentiates sex from such non-suspect statuses as intelligence or physical disability, and aligns it with the recognized suspect criteria, is that the sex characteristic frequently bears no relation to ability to perform or contribute to society. As a result, statutory distinctions between the sexes often have the effect of invidiously relegating the entire class of females to inferior legal status without regard to the actual capabilities of its individual members.

We might also note that, over the past decade, Congress has itself manifested an increasing sensitivity to sex-based classifications. In Tit. VII of the Civil Rights Act of 1964, for example, Congress expressly declared that no employer, labor union, or other organization subject to the provisions of the Act shall discriminate against any individual on the basis of 'race, color, religion, sex, or national origin.' Similarly, the Equal Pay Act of 1963 provides that no employer covered by the Act 'shall discriminate ... between employees on the basis of sex.' And § 1 of the Equal Rights Amendment, passed by Congress on March 22, 1972, and submitted to the legislatures of the States for ratification, declares that '(e)quality of rights under the law shall not be denied or abridged by the United States or by any State on account of sex.' Thus, Congress itself has concluded that classifications based upon sex are inherently invidious, and this conclusion of a coequal branch of Government is not without significance to the question presently under consideration....

With these considerations in mind, we can only conclude that classifications based upon sex, like classifications based upon race, alienage, or national origin, are inherently suspect, and must therefore be subjected to strict judicial scrutiny. Applying the analysis mandated by that stricter standard of review, it is clear that the statutory scheme now before us is constitutionally invalid.

III

The sole basis of the classification established in the challenged statutes is the sex of the individuals involved. Thus, under 37 U.S.C. §§ 401, 403, and 10 U.S.C. §§ 2072, 2076, a female member of the uniformed services seeking to obtain housing and medical benefits for her spouse must prove his dependency in fact, whereas no such burden is imposed upon male members. In addition, the statutes operate so as to deny benefits to a female member, such as appellant Sharron Frontiero, who provides less than one-half of her spouse's support, while at the same time granting such benefits to a male member who likewise provides less than one-half of his spouse's support. Thus, to this extent at least, it may fairly be said that these statutes command 'dissimilar treatment for men and women who are ... similarly situated.' *Reed v. Reed....*

Moreover, the Government concedes that the differential treatment accorded men and women under these statutes serves no purpose other than mere 'administrative convenience.' In essence, the Government maintains that, as an empirical matter, wives in our society frequently are dependent upon their husbands, while husbands rarely are dependent upon their wives. Thus, the Government argues that Congress might reasonably have concluded that it would be both cheaper and easier simply conclusively to presume that wives of male members are financially dependent upon their husbands, while burdening female members with the task of establishing dependency in fact.

The Government offers no concrete evidence, however, tending to support its view that such differential treatment in fact saves the Government any money. In order to satisfy the demands of strict judicial scrutiny, the Government must demonstrate, for example, that it is actually cheaper to grant increased benefits with respect to all male members, than it is to determine which male members are in fact entitled to such benefits and to grant increased benefits only to those members whose wives actually meet the dependency requirement. Here, however, there is substantial evidence that, if put to the test, many of the wives of male members would fail to qualify for benefits. And in light of the fact that the dependency determination with respect to the husbands of female members is presently made solely on the basis of affidavits rather than through the more costly hearing process, the Government's explanation of the statutory scheme is, to say the least, questionable.

In any case, our prior decisions make clear that, although efficacious administration of governmental programs is not without some importance, 'the Constitution recognizes higher values than speed and efficiency.' *Stanley v. Illinois....* And when we enter the realm of 'strict judicial scrutiny,' there can be no doubt that 'administrative convenience' is not a shibboleth, the mere recitation of which dictates constitutionality. See *Shapiro v. Thompson,... Carrington v. Rash....* On the contrary, any statutory scheme which draws a sharp line between the sexes, Solely for the purpose of achieving administrative convenience, necessarily commands 'dissimilar treatment for men and women who are ...

similarly situated,' and therefore involves the 'very kind of arbitrary legislative choice forbidden by the (Constitution) ....' *Reed v. Reed*.... We therefore conclude that, by according differential treatment to male and female members of the uniformed services for the sole purpose of achieving administrative convenience, the challenged statutes violate the Due Process Clause of the Fifth Amendment insofar as they require a female member to prove the dependency of her husband.

Reversed.

Mr. Justice STEWART concurs in the judgment, agreeing that the statutes before us work an invidious discrimination in violation of the Constitution. *Reed v. Reed*....

Mr. Justice REHNQUIST dissents for the reasons stated by Judge Rives in his opinion for the District Court, *Frontiero v. Laird*....

Mr. Justice POWELL, with whom THE CHIEF JUSTICE and Mr. Justice BLACKMUN join, concurring in the judgment.

I agree that the challenged statutes constitute an unconstitutional discrimination against servicewomen in violation of the Due Process Clause of the Fifth Amendment, but I cannot join the opinion of Mr. Justice BRENNAN, which would hold that all classifications based upon sex, 'like classifications based upon race, alienage, and national origin,' are 'inherently suspect and must therefore be subjected to close judicial scrutiny.' It is unnecessary for the Court in this case to characterize sex as a suspect classification, with all of the far-reaching implications of such a holding. *Reed v. Reed* which abundantly supports our decision today, did not add sex to the narrowly limited group of classifications which are inherently suspect. In my view, we can and should decide this case on the authority of *Reed* and reserve for the future any expansion of its rationale.

There is another, and I find compelling, reason for deferring a general categorizing of sex classifications as invoking the strictest test of judicial scrutiny. The Equal Rights Amendment, which if adopted will resolve the substance of this precise question, has been approved by the Congress and submitted for ratification by the States. If this Amendment is duly adopted, it will represent the will of the people accomplished in the manner prescribed by the Constitution. By acting prematurely and unnecessarily, as I view it, the Court has assumed a decisional responsibility at the very time when state legislatures, functioning within the traditional democractic process, are debating the proposed Amendment. It seems to me that this reaching out to pre-empt by judicial action a major political decision which is currently in process of resolution does not reflect appropriate respect for duly prescribed legislative processes.

There are times when this Court, under our system, cannot avoid a constitutional decision on issues which normally should be resolved by the elected representatives of the people. But democratic institutions are weakened, and confidence in the restraint of the Court is impaired, when we appear unnecessarily to decide sensitive issues of broad social and political importance at the very time they are under consideration within the prescribed constitutional processes.

CRAIG v. BOREN
97 S.Ct. 451; 429 U.S. 190; 50 L.Ed. 2d 397 (1976)

The facts in this case are contained in the opinion below.

Mr. Justice BRENNAN delivered the opinion of the Court.

The interaction of two sections of an Oklahoma statute ... prohibits the sale of "nonintoxicating" 3.2% beer to males under the age of 21 and to females under the age of 18. The question to be decided is whether such a gender-based differential constitutes a denial to males 18- 20 years of age of the equal protection of the laws in violation of the Fourteenth Amendment....

II

A

Before 1972, Oklahoma defined the commencement of civil majority at age 18 for females and age 21 for males.... In contrast, females were held criminally responsible as adults at age 18 and males at age 16.... After the Court of Appeals for the Tenth Circuit held in 1972, on the authority of *Reed v. Reed*,... that the age distinction was unconstitutional for purposes of establishing criminal responsibility as adults, *Lamb v. Brown*,... the Oklahoma Legislature fixed age 18 as applicable to both males and females.... In 1972, 18 also was established as the age of majority for males and females in civil matters,... except that §§ 241 and 245 of the 3.2% beer statute were simultaneously codified to create an exception to the gender-free rule.

Analysis may appropriately begin with the reminder that *Reed* emphasized that statutory classifications that distinguish between males and females are "subject to scrutiny under the Equal Protection Clause...." To withstand constitutional challenge, previous cases establish that classifications by gender must serve important governmental objectives and must be substantially related to achievement of those objectives. Thus, in *Reed*, the objectives of "reducing the workload on probate courts,"... and "avoiding intrafamily controversy,"... were deemed of insufficient importance to sustain use of an overt gender criterion in the appointment of administrators of intestate decedents' estates. Decisions following *Reed* similarly have rejected administrative ease and convenience as sufficiently important objectives to justify gender-based classifications.... And only two Terms ago, *Stanton v. Stanton*,... expressly stating that *Reed v. Reed* was "controlling,"... held that *Reed* required invalidation of a Utah differential age-of-majority statute, notwithstanding the statute's coincidence with and furtherance of the State's purpose of fostering "old notions" of role typing and preparing boys for their expected performance in the economic and political worlds....

Reed v. Reed has also provided the underpinning for decisions that have invalidated statutes employing gender as an inaccurate proxy for other, more germane bases of classification. Hence, "archaic and overbroad" generalizations, *Schlesinger v. Ballard*,... concerning the financial position of servicewomen, *Frontiero v. Richardson*,... and working women, *Weinberger v. Wiesenfeld*,... could not justify use of a gender line in determining eligibility for certain governmental entitlements. Similarly, increasingly outdated misconceptions concerning the role of females in the home rather than in the "marketplace and world of ideas" were rejected as loose-fitting characterizations incapable of supporting state statutory schemes that were premised upon their accuracy. *Stanton v. Stanton*, *Taylor v. Louisiana*.... In light of the weak congruence between gender and the characteristic or trait that gender purported to represent, it was necessary that the legislatures choose either to realign their substantive laws in a gender-neutral fashion, or to adopt procedures for identifying those instances where the sex-centered generalization actually comported with fact....

In this case, too, "*Reed*, we feel is controlling...." We turn then to the question whether, under *Reed*, the difference between males and females with respect to the purchase of 3.2% beer warrants the differential in age drawn by the Oklahoma statute. We conclude that it does not.

B

The District Court recognized that *Reed v. Reed* was controlling. In applying the teachings of that case, the court found the requisite important governmental objective in the traffic-safety goal proffered by the Oklahoma Attorney General. It then concluded that the statistics introduced by the appellees established that the gender-based distinction was substantially related to achievement of that goal.

C

We accept for purposes of discussion the District Court's identification of the objective underlying §§ 241 and 245 as the enhancement of traffic safety. Clearly, the protection of public health and safety represents an important function of state and local governments. However, appellees' statistics in our view cannot support the conclusion that the gender-based distinction closely serves to achieve that objective and therefore the distinction cannot under *Reed* withstand equal protection challenge.

The appellees introduced a variety of statistical surveys. First, an analysis of arrest statistics for 1973 demonstrated that 18-20-year-old male arrests for "driving under the influence" and "drunkenness" substantially exceeded female arrests for that same age period. Similarly, youths aged 17-21 were found to be overrepresented among those killed or injured in traffic accidents, with males again numerically exceeding females in this regard. Third, a random roadside survey in Oklahoma City revealed that young males were more inclined to drive and drink beer than were their female counterparts. Fourth, Federal Bureau of Investigation nationwide statistics exhibited a notable increase in arrests for "driving under the influence." Finally, statistical evidence gathered in other jurisdictions, particularly Minnesota and Michigan, was offered to corroborate Oklahoma's experience by indicating the pervasiveness of youthful participation in motor vehicle accidents following the imbibing of alcohol. Conceding that "the case is not free from doubt," the District Court nonetheless concluded that this statistical showing substantiated "a rational basis for the legislative judgment underlying the challenged classification."

Even were this statistical evidence accepted as accurate, it nevertheless offers only a weak answer to the equal protection question presented here. The most focused and relevant of the statistical surveys, arrests of 18-20-year-olds for alcohol-related driving offenses, exemplifies the ultimate unpersuasiveness of this evidentiary record. Viewed in terms of the correlation between sex and the actual activity that Oklahoma seeks to regulate driving while under the influence of alcohol the statistics broadly establish that .18% of females and 2% of males in that age group were arrested for that offense. While such a disparity is not trivial in a statistical sense, it hardly can form the basis for employment of a gender line as a classifying device. Certainly if maleness is to serve as a proxy for drinking and driving, a correlation of 2% must be considered an unduly tenuous "fit." Indeed, prior cases have consistently rejected the use of sex as a decisionmaking factor even though the statutes in question certainly rested on far more predictive empirical relationships than this.

Moreover, the statistics exhibit a variety of other shortcomings that seriously impugn their value to equal protection analysis. Setting aside the obvious methodological problems, the surveys do not adequately justify the salient features of Oklahoma's gender-based traffic-safety law. None purports to measure the use and dangerousness of 3.2% beer as opposed to alcohol generally, a detail that is of particular importance since, in light of its low alcohol level, Oklahoma apparently considers the 3.2% beverage to be "nonintoxicating...." Moreover, many of the studies, while graphically documenting the unfortunate increase in driving while under the influence of alcohol, make no effort to relate their findings to age-sex differentials as involved here. Indeed, the only survey that explicitly centered its attention upon young drivers and their use of beer albeit apparently not of the diluted 3.2% variety reached results that hardly can be viewed as impressive in justifying either a gender or age classification.

There is no reason to belabor this line of analysis. It is unrealistic to expect either members of the judiciary or state officials to be well versed in the rigors of experimental or statistical technique. But this merely illustrates that proving broad sociological propositions by statistics is a dubious business, and one that inevitably is in tension with the normative philosophy that underlies the Equal Protection Clause. Suffice to say that the showing offered by the appellees does not satisfy us that sex represents a legitimate, accurate proxy for the regulation of drinking and driving. In fact, when it is further recognized that Oklahoma's statute prohibits only the selling of 3.2% beer to young males and not their drinking the beverage once acquired (even after purchase by their 18-20-year-old female companions), the relationship between gender and traffic safety becomes far too tenuous to satisfy *Reed's* requirement that the gender-based difference be substantially related to achievement of the statutory objective.

We hold, therefore, that under *Reed*, Oklahoma's 3.2% beer statute invidiously discriminates against males 18-20 years of age....

We conclude that the gender-based differential contained in Okla.Stat ., Tit. 37, § 245 (1976 Supp.) constitutes a denial of the equal protection of the laws to males aged 18-20 and reverse the judgment of the District Court.

It is so ordered.

Mr. Justice POWELL, concurring.

I join the opinion of the Court as I am in general agreement with it. I do have reservations as to some of the discussion concerning the appropriate standard for equal protection analysis and the relevance of the statistical evidence. Accordingly, I add this concurring statement.

With respect to the equal protection standard, I agree that *Reed v. Reed*, is the most relevant precedent. But I find it unnecessary, in deciding this case, to read that decision as broadly as some of the Court's language may imply. *Reed* and subsequent cases involving gender-based classifications make clear that the Court subjects such classifications to a more critical examination than is normally applied when "fundamental" constitutional rights and "suspect classes" are not present.

I view this as a relatively easy case. No one questions the legitimacy or importance of the asserted governmental objective: the promotion of highway safety. The decision of the case turns on whether the state legislature, by the classification it has chosen, had adopted a means that bears a "'fair and substantial relation'" to this objective....

It seems to me that the statistics offered by appellees and relied upon by the District Court do tend generally to support the view that young men drive more, possibly are inclined to drink more, and for various reasons are involved in more accidents than young women. Even so, I am not persuaded that these facts and the inferences fairly drawn from them justify this classification based on a three-year age differential between the sexes, and especially one that it so easily circumvented as to be virtually meaningless. Putting it differently, this gender-based classification does not bear a fair and substantial relation to the object of the legislation.

Mr. Justice STEVENS, concurring.

There is only one Equal Protection Clause. It requires every State to govern impartially. It does not direct the courts to apply one standard of review in some cases and a different standard in other cases. Whatever criticism may be leveled at a judicial opinion implying that there are at least three such standards applies with the same force to a double standard.

I am inclined to believe that what has become known as the two-tiered analysis of equal protection claims does not describe a completely logical method of deciding cases, but rather is a method the Court has employed to explain decisions that actually apply a single standard in a reasonably consistent fashion. I also suspect that a careful explanation of the reasons motivating particular decisions may contribute more to an identification of that standard than an attempt to articulate it in all-encompassing terms. It may therefore be appropriate for me to state the principal reasons which persuaded me to join the Court's opinion.

In this case, the classification is not as obnoxious as some the Court has condemned, nor as inoffensive as some the Court has accepted. It is objectionable because it is based on an accident of birth, because it is a mere remnant of the now almost universally rejected tradition of discriminating against males in this age bracket, and because, to the extent it reflects any physical difference between males and females, it is actually perverse. The question then is whether the traffic safety justification put forward by the State is sufficient to make an otherwise offensive classification acceptable.

The classification is not totally irrational. For the evidence does indicate that there are more males than females in this age bracket who drive and also more who drink. Nevertheless, there are several reasons why I regard the justification as unacceptable. It is difficult to believe that the statute was actually intended to cope with the problem of traffic safety, since it has only a minimal effect on access to a not very intoxicating beverage and does not prohibit its consumption. Moreover, the empirical data submitted by the State accentuate the unfairness of treating all 18-21-year-old males as inferior to their female counterparts. The legislation imposes a restraint on 100% of the males in the class allegedly because about 2% of them have probably violated one or more laws relating to the consumption of alcoholic beverages. It is unlikely that this law will have a significant deterrent effect either on that 2% or on the law-abiding 98%. But even assuming some such slight benefit, it does not seem to me that an insult to all of the young men of the State can be justified by visiting the sins of the 2% on the 98%.

Mr. Justice BLACKMUN, concurring in part....

Mr. Justice STEWART, concurring in the judgment....

Mr. Chief Justice BURGER, dissenting.

I am in general agreement with Mr. Justice REHNQUIST's dissent, but even at the risk of compounding the obvious confusion created by those voting to reverse the District Court, I will add a few words....

On the merits, we have only recently recognized that our duty is not "to create substantive constitutional rights in the name of guaranteeing equal protection of the laws." *San Antonio School Dist. v. Rodriguez....* Thus, even interests of such importance in our society as public education and housing do not qualify as "fundamental rights" for equal protection purposes because they have no textually independent constitutional status.... Though today's decision does not go so far as to make gender-based classifications "suspect," it makes gender a disfavored classification. Without an independent constitutional basis supporting the right asserted or disfavoring the classification adopted, I can justify no substantive constitutional protection other than the normal *McGowan v. Maryland,...* protection afforded by the Equal Protection Clause.

The means employed by the Oklahoma Legislature to achieve the objectives sought may not be agreeable to some judges, but since eight Members of the Court think the means not irrational, I see no basis for striking down the statute as violative of the Constitution simply because we find it unwise, unneeded, or possibly even a bit foolish.

With Mr. Justice REHNQUIST, I would affirm the judgment of the District Court.

Mr. Justice REHNQUIST, dissenting.

The Court's disposition of this case is objectionable on two grounds. First is its conclusion that men challenging a gender-based statute which treats them less favorably than women may invoke a more stringent standard of judicial review than pertains to most other types of classifications. Second is the Court's enunciation of this standard, without citation to any source, as being that "classifications by gender must serve important governmental objectives and must be substantially related to achievement of those objectives." The only redeeming feature of the Court's opinion, to my mind, is that it apparently signals a retreat by those who joined the plurality opinion in *Frontiero v. Richardson* ... from their view that sex is a "suspect" classification for purposes of equal protection analysis. I think the Oklahoma statute challenged here need pass only the "rational basis" equal protection analysis expounded in cases such as *McGowan v. Maryland*,... and *Williamson v. Lee Optical Co.*,... and I believe that it is constitutional under that analysis.

I

In *Frontiero v. Richardson*, the opinion for the plurality sets forth the reasons of four Justices for concluding that sex should be regarded as a suspect classification for purposes of equal protection analysis. These reasons center on our Nation's "long and unfortunate history of sex discrimination,..." which has been reflected in a whole range of restrictions on the legal rights of women, not the least of which have concerned the ownership of property and participation in the electoral process. Noting that the pervasive and persistent nature of the discrimination experienced by women is in part the result of their ready identifiability, the plurality rested its invocation of strict scrutiny largely upon the fact that "statutory distinctions between the sexes often have the effect of invidiously relegating the entire class of females to inferior legal status without regard to the actual capabilities of its individual members...."

Subsequent to *Frontiero*, the Court has declined to hold that sex is a suspect class, *Stanton v. Stanton*,... and no such holding is imported by the Court's resolution of this case. However, the Court's application here of an elevated or "intermediate" level scrutiny, like that invoked in cases dealing with discrimination against females, raises the question of why the statute here should be treated any differently from countless legislative classifications unrelated to sex which have been upheld under a minimum rationality standard....

Most obviously unavailable to support any kind of special scrutiny in this case, is a history or pattern of past discrimination, such as was relied on by the plurality in *Frontiero* to support its invocation of strict scrutiny. There is no suggestion in the Court's opinion that males in this age group are in any way peculiarly disadvantaged, subject to systematic discriminatory treatment, or otherwise in need of special solicitude from the courts.

The Court does not discuss the nature of the right involved, and there is no reason to believe that it sees the purchase of 3.2% beer as implicating any important interest, let alone one that is "fundamental" in the constitutional sense of invoking strict scrutiny. Indeed, the Court's accurate observation that the statute affects the selling but not the drinking of 3.2% beer further emphasizes the limited effect that it has on even those persons in the age group involved. There is, in sum, nothing about the statutory classification involved here to suggest that it affects an interest, or works against a group, which can claim under the Equal Protection Clause that it is entitled to special judicial protection.

It is true that a number of our opinions contain broadly phrased dicta implying that the same test should be applied to all classifications based on sex, whether affecting females or males. e.g., *Frontiero v. Richardson,... Reed v. Reed....* However, before today, no decision of this Court has applied an elevated level of scrutiny to invalidate a statutory discrimination harmful to males, except where the statute impaired an important personal interest protected by the Constitution. There being no such interest here, and there being no plausible argument that this is a discrimination against females, the Court's reliance on our previous sex-discrimination cases is ill-founded. It treats gender classification as a talisman which without regard to the rights involved or the persons affected calls into effect a heavier burden of judicial review.

The Court's conclusion that a law which treats males less favorably than females "must serve important governmental objectives and must be substantially related to achievement of those objectives" apparently comes out of thin air. The Equal Protection Clause contains no such language, and none of our previous cases adopt that standard. I would think we have had enough difficulty with the two standards of review which our cases have recognized the norm of "rational basis," and the "compelling state interest" required where a "suspect classification" is involved so as to counsel weightily against the insertion of still another "standard" between those two. How is this Court to divine what objectives are important? How is it to determine whether a particular law is "substantially" related to the achievement of such objective, rather than related in some other way to its achievement? Both of the phrases used are so diaphanous and elastic as to invite subjective judicial preferences or prejudices relating to particular types of legislation, masquerading as judgments whether such legislation is directed at "important" objectives or, whether the relationship to those objectives is "substantial" enough.

I would have thought that if this Court were to leave anything to decision by the popularly elected branches of the Government, where no constitutional claim other than that of equal protection is invoked, it would be the decision as to what governmental objectives to be achieved by law are "important," and which are not. As for the second part of the Court's new test, the Judicial Branch is probably in no worse position than the Legislative or Executive Branches to determine if there is any rational relationship between a classification and the purpose which it might be thought to serve. But the introduction of the adverb "substantially" requires courts to make subjective judgments as to operational effects, for which neither their expertise nor their access to data fits them. And even if we manage to avoid both confusion and the mirroring of our own preferences in the development of this new doctrine, the thousands of judges in other courts who must interpret the Equal Protection Clause may not be so fortunate.

II

The applicable rational-basis test is one which

> "permits the States a wide scope of discretion in enacting laws which affect some groups of citizens differently than others. The constitutional safeguard is offended only if the classification rests on grounds wholly irrelevant to the achievement of the State's objective. State legislatures are presumed to have acted within their constitutional power despite the fact that, in practice, their laws result in some inequality. A statutory discrimination will not be set aside if any state of facts reasonably may be conceived to justify it." *McGowan v. Maryland*....

Our decisions indicate that application of the Equal Protection Clause in a context not justifying an elevated level of scrutiny does nor demand "mathematical nicety" or the elimination of all inequality. Those cases recognize that the practical problems of government may require rough accommodations of interests, and hold that such accommodations should be respected unless no reasonable basis can be found to support them. *Dandridge v. Williams*.... Whether the same ends might have been better or more precisely served by a different approach is no part of the judicial inquiry under the traditional minimum rationality approach. *Richardson v. Belcher*....

The Court "accept(s) for purposes of discussion" the District Court's finding that the purpose of the provisions in question was traffic safety, and proceeds to examine the statistical evidence in the record in order to decide if "the gender-based distinction closely serves to achieve that objective...." (Whether there is a difference between laws which "closely serv(e)" objectives and those which are only "substantially related" to their achievement, we are not told.) I believe that a more traditional type of scrutiny is appropriate in this case, and I think that the Court would have done well here to heed its own warning that "[i]t is unrealistic to expect ... members of the judiciary ... to be well versed in the rigors of experimental or statistical technique...." One need not immerse oneself in the fine points of statistical analysis, however, in order to see the weaknesses in the Court's attempted denigration of the evidence at hand.

One survey of arrest statistics assembled in 1973 indicated that males in the 18-20 age group were arrested for "driving under the influence" almost 18 times as often as their female counterparts, and for " drunkenness" in a ratio of almost 10 to 1.3. Accepting, as the Court does, appellants' comparison of the total figures with 1973 Oklahoma census data, this survey indicates a 2% arrest rate among males in the age group, as compared to a .18% rate among females.

Other surveys indicated (1) that over the five-year period from 1967 to 1972, nationwide arrests among those under 18 for drunken driving increased 138%, and that 93% of all persons arrested for drunken driving were male; (2) that youths in the 17-21 age group were overrepresented among those killed or injured in Oklahoma traffic accidents, that male casualties substantially exceeded female, and that deaths in this age group continued to rise while overall traffic deaths declined; (3) that over three-fourths of the drivers under 20 in the Oklahoma City area are males, and that each of them, on average, drives half again as many miles per year as their female counterparts; (4) that four-fifths of male drivers under 20 in the Oklahoma City area state a drink preference for beer, while about three-fifths of female drivers of that age state the same preference; and (5) that the percentage of male drivers under 20 admitting to drinking within two hours of driving was half again larger than the percentage for females, and that the percentage of male drivers of that age group with a blood alcohol content greater than .01% was almost half again larger than for female drivers.

The Court's criticism of the statistics relied on by the District Court conveys the impression that a legislature in enacting a new law is to be subjected to the judicial equivalent of a doctoral examination in statistics. Legislatures are not held to any rules of evidence such as those which may govern courts or other administrative bodies, and are entitled to draw factual conclusions on the basis of the determination of probable cause which an arrest by a police officer normally represents. In this situation, they could reasonably infer that the incidence of drunk driving is a good deal higher than the incidence of arrest.

And while, as the Court observes, relying on a report to a Presidential Commission which it cites in a footnote, such statistics may be distorted as a result of stereotyping, the legislature is not required to prove before a court that its statistics are perfect. In any event, if stereotypes are as pervasive as the Court suggests, they may in turn influence the conduct of the men and women in question, and cause the young men to conform to the wild and reckless image which is their stereotype.

The Court also complains of insufficient integration of the various surveys on several counts that the injury and death figures are in no way directly correlated with intoxication, that the national arrest figures for drunk driving contain no breakdown for the 18 to 21-year-old group, and that the arrest records for intoxication are not tied to the consumption of 3.2% beer.... But the State of Oklahoma and certainly this Court for purposes of equal protection review can surely take notice of the fact that drunkenness is a significant cause of traffic casualties, and that youthful offenders have participated in the increase of the drunk-driving problem. On this latter point, the survey data indicating increased driving casualties among 18-21-year-olds, while overall casualties dropped, are not irrelevant.

Nor is it unreasonable to conclude from the expressed preference for beer by four-fifths of the age-group males that that beverage was a predominant source of their intoxication-related arrests. Taking that as the predicate, the State could reasonably bar those males from any purchases of alcoholic beer, including that of the 3.2% variety. This Court lacks the expertise or the data to evaluate the intoxicating properties of that beverage, and in that posture our only appropriate course is to defer to the reasonable inference supporting the statute that taken in sufficient quantity this beer has the same effect as any alcoholic beverage.

Quite apart from these alleged methodological deficiencies in the statistical evidence, the Court appears to hold that that evidence, on its face, fails to support the distinction drawn in the statute. The Court notes that only 2% of males (as against .18% of females) in the age group were arrested for drunk driving, and that this very low figure establishes " an unduly tenuous 'fit'" between maleness and drunk driving in the 18 to 20-year-old group. On this point the Court misconceives the nature of the equal protection inquiry.

The rationality of a statutory classification for equal protection purposes does not depend upon the statistical "fit" between the class and the trait sought to be singled out. It turns on whether there may be a sufficiently higher incidence of the trait within the included class than in the excluded class to justify different treatment. Therefore the present equal protection challenge to this gender-based discrimination poses only the question whether the incidence of drunk driving among young men is sufficiently greater than among young women to justify differential treatment. Notwithstanding the Court's critique of the statistical evidence, that evidence suggests clear differences between the drinking and driving habits of young men and women. Those differences are grounds enough for the State reasonably to conclude that young males pose by far the greater drunk-driving hazard, both in terms of sheer numbers and in terms of hazard on a per-driver basis. The gender-based difference in treatment in this case is therefore not irrational.

The Court's argument that a 2% correlation between maleness and drunk driving is constitutionally insufficient therefore does not pose an equal protection issue concerning discrimination between males and females. The clearest demonstration of this is the fact that the precise argument made by the Court would be equally applicable to a flat bar on such purchases by anyone, male or female, in the 18-20 age group; in fact it would apply *a fortiori* in that case given the even more "tenuous 'fit'" between drunk- driving arrests and femaleness. The statistics indicate that about 1% of the age group population as a whole is arrested. What the Court's argument is relevant to is not equal protection, but due process whether there are enough persons in the category who drive while drunk to justify a bar against purchases by all members of the group.

Cast in those terms, the argument carries little weight, in light of our decisions indicating that such questions call for a balance of the State's interest against the harm resulting from any overinclusiveness or underinclusiveness.

Vlandis v. Kline.... The personal interest harmed here is very minor; the present legislation implicates only the right to purchase 3.2% beer, certainly a far cry from the important personal interests which have on occasion supported this Court's invalidation of statutes on similar reasoning. *Cleveland Board of Education v. LaFleur, Stanley v. Illinois....* And the state interest involved is significant the prevention of injury and death on the highways.

This is not a case where the classification can only be justified on grounds of administrative convenience. *Vlandis v. Kline,...Stanley v. Illinois....* There being no apparent way to single out persons likely to drink and drive, it seems plain that the legislature was faced here with the not atypical legislative problem of legislating in terms of broad categories with regard to the purchase and consumption of alcohol. I trust, especially in light of the Twenty-first Amendment, that there would be no due process violation if no one in this age group were allowed to purchase 3.2% beer. Since males drink and drive at a higher rate than the age group as a whole, I fail to see how a statutory bar with regard only to them can create any due process problem.

The Oklahoma Legislature could have believed that 18-20-year-old males drive substantially more, and tend more often to be intoxicated than their female counterparts; that they prefer beer and admit to drinking and driving at a higher rate than females; and that they suffer traffic injuries out of proportion to the part they make up of the population. Under the appropriate rational-basis test for equal protection, it is neither irrational nor arbitrary to bar them from making purchases of 3.2% beer, which purchases might in many cases be made by a young man who immediately returns to his vehicle with the beverage in his possession. The record does not give any good indication of the true proportion of males in the age group who drink and drive (except that it is no doubt greater than the 2% who are arrested), but whatever it may be I cannot see that the mere purchase right involved could conceivably raise a due process question. There being no violation of either equal protection or due process, the statute should accordingly be upheld.

ROMER *v.* EVANS
116 S.Ct. 1620 (1996)

The facts in this case are contained in the opinion below.

Justice Kennedy delivered the opinion of the Court.

One century ago, the first Justice Harlan admonished this Court that the Constitution "neither knows nor tolerates classes among citizens." *Plessy v. Ferguson* ... (dissenting opinion). Unheeded then, those words now are understood to state a commitment to the law's neutrality where the rights of persons are at stake. The Equal Protection Clause enforces this principle and today requires us to hold invalid a provision of Colorado's Constitution.

I

The enactment challenged in this case is an amendment to the Constitution of the State of Colorado, adopted in a 1992 statewide referendum. The parties and the state courts refer to it as "Amendment 2," its designation when submitted to the voters. The impetus for the amendment and the contentious campaign that preceded its adoption came in large part from ordinances that had been passed in various Colorado municipalities. For example, the cities of Aspen and Boulder and the City and County of Denver each had enacted ordinances which banned discrimination in many transactions and activities, including housing, employment, education, public accommodations, and health and welfare services.... What gave rise to the statewide controversy was the protection the ordinances afforded to persons discriminated against by reason of their sexual orientation.... Amendment 2 repeals these ordinances to the extent they prohibit discrimination on the basis of "homosexual, lesbian or bisexual orientation, conduct, practices or relationships."

Yet Amendment 2, in explicit terms, does more than repeal or rescind these provisions. It prohibits all legislative, executive or judicial action at any level of state or local government designed to protect the named class, a class we shall refer to as homosexual persons or gays and lesbians. The amendment reads:

> "No Protected Status Based on Homosexual, Lesbian, or Bisexual Orientation. Neither the State of Colorado, through any of its branches or departments, nor any of its agencies, political subdivisions, municipalities or school districts, shall enact, adopt or enforce any statute, regulation, ordinance or policy whereby homosexual, lesbian or bisexual orientation, conduct, practices or relationships shall constitute or otherwise be the basis of or entitle any person or class of persons to have or claim any minority status, quota preferences, protected status or claim of discrimination. This Section of the Constitution shall be in all respects self-executing."

Soon after Amendment 2 was adopted, this litigation to declare its invalidity and enjoin its enforcement was commenced in the District Court for the City and County of Denver. Among the plaintiffs (respondents here) were homosexual persons, some of them government employees. They alleged that enforcement of Amendment 2 would subject them to immediate and substantial risk of discrimination on the basis of their sexual orientation. Other plaintiffs (also respondents here) included the three municipalities whose ordinances we have cited and certain other governmental entities which had acted earlier to protect homosexuals from discrimination but would be prevented by Amendment 2 from continuing to do so. Although Governor Romer had been on record opposing the adoption of Amendment 2, he was named in his official capacity as a defendant, together with the Colorado Attorney General and the State of Colorado.

The trial court granted a preliminary injunction to stay enforcement of Amendment 2, and an appeal was taken to the Supreme Court of Colorado. Sustaining the interim injunction and remanding the case for further proceedings, the State Supreme Court held that Amendment 2 was subject to strict scrutiny under the Fourteenth Amendment because it infringed the fundamental right of gays and lesbians to participate in the political process.... To reach this conclusion, the state court relied on our voting rights cases,... and on our precedents involving discriminatory restructuring of governmental decision-making.... On remand, the State advanced various arguments in an effort to show that Amendment 2 was narrowly tailored to serve compelling interests, but the trial court found none sufficient. It enjoined enforcement of Amendment 2, and the Supreme Court of Colorado, in a second opinion, affirmed the ruling.... We granted certiorari and now affirm the judgment, but on a rationale different from that adopted by the State Supreme Court.

II

The State's principal argument in defense of Amendment 2 is that it puts gays and lesbians in the same position as all other persons. So, the State says, the measure does no more than deny homosexuals special rights. This reading of the amendment's language is implausible. We rely not upon our own interpretation of the amendment but upon the authoritative construction of Colorado's Supreme Court. The state court, deeming it unnecessary to determine the full extent of the amendment's reach, found it invalid even on a modest reading of its implications. The critical discussion of the amendment ... is as follows:

> "The immediate objective of Amendment 2 is, at a minimum, to repeal existing statutes, regulations, ordinances, and policies of state and local entities that barred discrimination based on sexual orientation. See Aspen, Colo., Mun. Code Section(s) 13-98 (1977) (prohibiting discrimination in employment, housing and public accommodations on the basis of sexual orientation); Boulder, Colo., Rev. Code Section(s) 12-1-2 to -4 (1987) (same); Denver, Colo., Rev. Mun. Code art. IV, Section(s) 28-91 to -116 (1991) (same); Executive Order No. D0035 (December 10, 1990) (prohibiting employment discrimination for 'all state employees, classified and exempt' on the basis of sexual orientation); Colorado Insurance Code, Section(s) 10-3-1104, 4A C. R. S. (1992 Supp.) (forbidding health insurance providers from determining insurability and premiums based on an applicant's, a beneficiary's, or an insured's sexual orientation); and various provisions prohibiting discrimination based on sexual orientation at state colleges."
>
> "Metropolitan State College of Denver prohibits college sponsored social clubs from discriminating in membership on the basis of sexual orientation and Colorado State University has an antidiscrimination policy which encompasses sexual orientation."

> "The 'ultimate effect' of Amendment 2 is to prohibit any governmental entity from adopting similar, or more protective statutes, regulations, ordinances, or policies in the future unless the state constitution is first amended to permit such measures."

Sweeping and comprehensive is the change in legal status effected by this law. So much is evident from the ordinances that the Colorado Supreme Court declared would be void by operation of Amendment 2. Homosexuals, by state decree, are put in a solitary class with respect to transactions and relations in both the private and governmental spheres. The amendment withdraws from homosexuals, but no others, specific legal protection from the injuries caused by discrimination, and it forbids reinstatement of these laws and policies.

The change that Amendment 2 works in the legal status of gays and lesbians in the private sphere is far-reaching, both on its own terms and when considered in light of the structure and operation of modern anti-discrimination laws. That structure is well illustrated by contemporary statutes and ordinances prohibiting discrimination by providers of public accommodations. "At common law, innkeepers, smiths, and others who 'made profession of a public employment,' were prohibited from refusing, without good reason, to serve a customer." *Hurley v. Irish-American Gay, Lesbian and Bisexual Group of Boston, Inc.*,... (1995). The duty was a general one and did not specify protection for particular groups. The common law rules, however, proved insufficient in many instances, and it was settled early that the Fourteenth Amendment did not give Congress a general power to prohibit discrimination in public accommodations, *Civil Rights Cases*,... (1883). In consequence, most States have chosen to counter discrimination by enacting detailed statutory schemes....

Colorado's state and municipal laws typify this emerging tradition of statutory protection and follow a consistent pattern. The laws first enumerate the persons or entities subject to a duty not to discriminate. The list goes well beyond the entities covered by the common law. The Boulder ordinance, for example, has a comprehensive definition of entities deemed places of "public accommodation." They include "any place of business engaged in any sales to the general public and any place that offers services, facilities, privileges, or advantages to the general public or that receives financial support through solicitation of the general public or through governmental subsidy of any kind...." The Denver ordinance is of similar breadth, applying, for example, to hotels, restaurants, hospitals, dental clinics, theaters, banks, common carriers, travel and insurance agencies, and "shops and stores dealing with goods or services of any kind...."

These statutes and ordinances also depart from the common law by enumerating the groups or persons within their ambit of protection. Enumeration is the essential device used to make the duty not to discriminate concrete and to provide guidance for those who must comply. In following this approach, Colorado's state and local governments have not limited anti-discrimination laws to groups that have so far been given the protection of heightened equal protection scrutiny under our cases.... Rather, they set forth an extensive catalogue of traits which cannot be the basis for discrimination, including age, military status, marital status, pregnancy, parenthood, custody of a minor child, political affiliation, physical or mental disability of an individual or of his or her associates – and, in recent times, sexual orientation....

Amendment 2 bars homosexuals from securing protection against the injuries that these public-accommodations laws address. That in itself is a severe consequence, but there is more. Amendment 2, in addition, nullifies specific legal protections for this targeted class in all transactions in housing, sale of real estate, insurance, health and welfare services, private education, and employment....

Not confined to the private sphere, Amendment 2 also operates to repeal and forbid all laws or policies providing specific protection for gays or lesbians from discrimination by every level of Colorado government. The State Supreme Court cited two examples of protections in the governmental sphere that are now rescinded and may not be reintroduced. The first is Colorado Executive Order D0035 (1990), which forbids employment discrimination against "'all state employees, classified and exempt' on the basis of sexual orientation.... Also repealed, and now forbidden, are "various provisions prohibiting discrimination based on sexual orientation at state colleges." The repeal of these measures and the prohibition against their future reenactment demonstrates that Amendment 2 has the same force and effect in Colorado's governmental sector as it does elsewhere and that it applies to policies as well as ordinary legislation.

Amendment 2's reach may not be limited to specific laws passed for the benefit of gays and lesbians. It is a fair, if not necessary, inference from the broad language of the amendment that it deprives gays and lesbians even of the protection of general laws and policies that prohibit arbitrary discrimination in governmental and private settings. See, e.g., Colo. Rev. Stat. Section(s) 24-4-106(7) (1988) (agency action subject to judicial review under arbitrary and capricious standard); Section(s) 18-8-405 (making it a criminal offense for a public servant knowingly, arbitrarily or capriciously to refrain from performing a duty imposed on him by law); Section(s) 10-3-1104(1)(f) (prohibiting "unfair discrimination" in insurance); 4 Colo. Code of Regulations 801-1, Policy 11-1 (1983) (prohibiting discrimination in state employment on grounds of specified traits or "other non-merit factor"). At some point in the systematic administration of these laws, an official must determine whether homosexuality is an arbitrary and thus forbidden basis for decision. Yet a decision to that effect would itself amount to a policy prohibiting discrimination on the basis of homosexuality, and so would appear to be no more valid under Amendment 2 than the specific prohibitions against discrimination the state court held invalid.

If this consequence follows from Amendment 2, as its broad language suggests, it would compound the constitutional difficulties the law creates. The state court did not decide whether the amendment has this effect, however, and neither need we. In the course of rejecting the argument that Amendment 2 is intended to conserve resources to fight discrimination against suspect classes, the Colorado Supreme Court made the limited observation that the amendment is not intended to affect many anti-discrimination laws protecting non-suspect classes....

In our view that does not resolve the issue. In any event, even if, as we doubt, homosexuals could find some safe harbor in laws of general application, we cannot accept the view that Amendment 2's prohibition on specific legal protections does no more than deprive homosexuals of special rights. To the contrary, the amendment imposes a special disability upon those persons alone. Homosexuals are forbidden the safeguards that others enjoy or may seek without constraint. They can obtain specific protection against discrimination only by enlisting the citizenry of Colorado to amend the state constitution or perhaps, on the State's view, by trying to pass helpful laws of general applicability. This is so no matter how local or discrete the harm, no matter how public and widespread the injury. We find nothing special in the protections Amendment 2 withholds. These are protections taken for granted by most people either because they already have them or do not need them; these are protections against exclusion from an almost limitless number of transactions and endeavors that constitute ordinary civic life in a free society.

III

The Fourteenth Amendment's promise that no person shall be denied the equal protection of the laws must co-exist with the practical necessity that most legislation classifies for one purpose or another, with resulting disadvantage to various groups or persons.... We have attempted to reconcile the principle with the reality by stating that, if a law neither burdens a fundamental right nor targets a suspect class, we will uphold the legislative classification so long as it bears a rational relation to some legitimate end....

Amendment 2 fails, indeed defies, even this conventional inquiry. First, the amendment has the peculiar property of imposing a broad and undifferentiated disability on a single named group, an exceptional and, as we shall explain, invalid form of legislation. Second, its sheer breadth is so discontinuous with the reasons offered for it that the amendment seems inexplicable by anything but animus toward the class that it affects; it lacks a rational relationship to legitimate state interests.

Taking the first point, even in the ordinary equal protection case calling for the most deferential of standards, we insist on knowing the relation between the classification adopted and the object to be attained. The search for the link between classification and objective gives substance to the Equal Protection Clause; it provides guidance and discipline for the legislature, which is entitled to know what sorts of laws it can pass; and it marks the limits of our own authority. In the ordinary case, a law will be sustained if it can be said to advance a legitimate government interest, even if the law seems unwise or works to the disadvantage of a particular group, or if the rationale for it seems tenuous. See *New Orleans v. Dukes*,...(1976) (tourism benefits justified classification favoring pushcart vendors of certain longevity); *Williamson v. Lee Optical of Okla., Inc.*,...(1955) (assumed health concerns justified law favoring optometrists over opticians); *Railway Express Agency, Inc. v. New York*,...(1949) (potential traffic hazards justified exemption of vehicles advertising the owner's products from general advertising ban); *Kotch v. Board of River Port Pilot Comm'rs for Port of*

New Orleans,...(1947) (licensing scheme that disfavored persons unrelated to current river boat pilots justified by possible efficiency and safety benefits of a closely knit pilotage system). The laws challenged in the cases just cited were narrow enough in scope and grounded in a sufficient factual context for us to ascertain that there existed some relation between the classification and the purpose it served. By requiring that the classification bear a rational relationship to an independent and legitimate legislative end, we ensure that classifications are not drawn for the purpose of disadvantaging the group burdened by the law....

Amendment 2 confounds this normal process of judicial review. It is at once too narrow and too broad. It identifies persons by a single trait and then denies them protection across the board. The resulting disqualification of a class of persons from the right to seek specific protection from the law is unprecedented in our jurisprudence. The absence of precedent for Amendment 2 is itself instructive; "[d]iscriminations of an unusual character especially suggest careful consideration to determine whether they are obnoxious to the constitutional provision." *Louisville Gas & Elec. Co. v. Coleman*,... (1928).

It is not within our constitutional tradition to enact laws of this sort. Central both to the idea of the rule of law and to our own Constitution's guarantee of equal protection is the principle that government and each of its parts remain open on impartial terms to all who seek its assistance. "'Equal protection of the laws is not achieved through indiscriminate imposition of inequalities.'" *Sweatt v. Painter*,...(1950) (quoting *Shelley v. Kraemer*,... (1948)). Respect for this principle explains why laws singling out a certain class of citizens for disfavored legal status or general hardships are rare. A law declaring that in general it shall be more difficult for one group of citizens than for all others to seek aid from the government is itself a denial of equal protection of the laws in the most literal sense....

Davis v. Beason,... (1890), not cited by the parties but relied upon by the dissent, is not evidence that Amendment 2 is within our constitutional tradition, and any reliance upon it as authority for sustaining the amendment is misplaced. In *Davis*, the Court approved an Idaho territorial statute denying Mormons, polygamists, and advocates of polygamy the right to vote and to hold office because, as the Court construed the statute, it "simply excludes from the privilege of voting, or of holding any office of honor, trust or profit, those who have been convicted of certain offenses, and those who advocate a practical resistance to the laws of the Territory and justify and approve the commission of crimes forbidden by it." To the extent *Davis* held that persons advocating a certain practice may be denied the right to vote, it is no longer good law. *Brandenburg v. Ohio*,... (1969) (*per curiam*). To the extent it held that the groups designated in the statute may be deprived of the right to vote because of their status, its ruling could not stand without surviving strict scrutiny, a most doubtful outcome. *Dunn v. Blumstein*,... (1972); cf. *United States v. Brown*,... (1965); *United States v. Robel*,... (1967). To the extent *Davis* held that a convicted felon may be denied the right to vote, its holding is not implicated by our decision and is unexceptionable. See *Richardson v. Ramirez*,... (1974).

A second and related point is that laws of the kind now before us raise the inevitable inference that the disadvantage imposed is born of animosity toward the class of persons affected. "[I]f the constitutional conception of 'equal protection of the laws' means anything, it must at the very least mean that a bare ... desire to harm a politically unpopular group cannot constitute a legitimate governmental interest." *Department of Agriculture v. Moreno,...* (1973). Even laws enacted for broad and ambitious purposes often can be explained by reference to legitimate public policies which justify the incidental disadvantages they impose on certain persons. Amendment 2, however, in making a general announcement that gays and lesbians shall not have any particular protections from the law, inflicts on them immediate, continuing, and real injuries that outrun and belie any legitimate justifications that may be claimed for it. We conclude that, in addition to the far-reaching deficiencies of Amendment 2 that we have noted, the principles it offends, in another sense, are conventional and venerable; a law must bear a rational relationship to a legitimate governmental purpose, *Kadrmas v. Dickinson Public Schools,...* (1988), and Amendment 2 does not.

The primary rationale the State offers for Amendment 2 is respect for other citizens' freedom of association, and in particular the liberties of landlords or employers who have personal or religious objections to homosexuality. Colorado also cites its interest in conserving resources to fight discrimination against other groups. The breadth of the Amendment is so far removed from these particular justifications that we find it impossible to credit them. We cannot say that Amendment 2 is directed to any identifiable legitimate purpose or discrete objective. It is a status-based enactment divorced from any factual context from which we could discern a relationship to legitimate state interests; it is a classification of persons undertaken for its own sake, something the Equal Protection Clause does not permit. "[C]lass legislation ... [is] obnoxious to the prohibitions of the Fourteenth Amendment...." *Civil Rights Cases....*

We must conclude that Amendment 2 classifies homosexuals not to further a proper legislative end but to make them unequal to everyone else. This Colorado cannot do. A State cannot so deem a class of persons a stranger to its laws. Amendment 2 violates the Equal Protection Clause, and the judgment of the Supreme Court of Colorado is affirmed.

It is so ordered.

Justice SCALIA, with whom THE CHIEF JUSTICE and Justice THOMAS join, dissenting.

The Court has mistaken a Kulturkampf for a fit of spite. The constitutional amendment before us here is not the manifestation of a "'bare ... desire to harm'" homosexuals, but is rather a modest attempt by seemingly tolerant Coloradans to preserve traditional sexual mores against the efforts of a politically powerful minority to revise those mores through use of the laws. That objective, and the means chosen to achieve it, are not only unimpeachable under any constitutional doctrine hitherto pronounced (hence the opinion's heavy reliance upon principles of righteousness rather than judicial holdings); they have been specifically approved by the Congress of the United States and by this Court.

In holding that homosexuality cannot be singled out for disfavorable treatment, the Court contradicts a decision, unchallenged here, pronounced only 10 years ago, see *Bowers v. Hardwick*,... (1986), and places the prestige of this institution behind the proposition that opposition to homosexuality is as reprehensible as racial or religious bias. Whether it is or not is precisely the cultural debate that gave rise to the Colorado constitutional amendment (and to the preferential laws against which the amendment was directed). Since the Constitution of the United States says nothing about this subject, it is left to be resolved by normal democratic means, including the democratic adoption of provisions in state constitutions. This Court has no business imposing upon all Americans the resolution favored by the elite class from which the Members of this institution are selected, pronouncing that "animosity" toward homosexuality, is evil. I vigorously dissent.

I

Let me first discuss Part II of the Court's opinion, its longest section, which is devoted to rejecting the State's arguments that Amendment 2 "puts gays and lesbians in the same position as all other persons," and "does no more than deny homosexuals special rights...." The Court concludes that this reading of Amendment 2's language is "implausible" under the "authoritative construction" given Amendment 2 by the Supreme Court of Colorado.

In reaching this conclusion, the Court considers it unnecessary to decide the validity of the State's argument that Amendment 2 does not deprive homosexuals of the "protection [afforded by] general laws and policies that prohibit arbitrary discrimination in governmental and private settings." I agree that we need not resolve that dispute, because the Supreme Court of Colorado has resolved it for us. In *Evans v. Romer*,... (1994), the Colorado court stated:

> "[I]t is significant to note that Colorado law currently proscribes discrimination against persons who are not suspect classes, including discrimination based on age...; marital or family status...; veterans' ...; and for any legal, off-duty conduct such as smoking .... *Of course Amendment 2 is not intended to have any effect on this legislation, but seeks only to prevent the adoption of anti-discrimination laws intended to protect gays, lesbians, and bisexuals...."* (emphasis added).

The Court utterly fails to distinguish this portion of the Colorado court's opinion. Colorado Rev. Stat. Section(s) 24-34-402.5 (Supp. 1995), which this passage authoritatively declares not to be affected by Amendment 2, was respondents' primary example of a generally applicable law whose protections would be unavailable to homosexuals under Amendment 2.... The clear import of the Colorado court's conclusion that it is not affected is that "general laws and policies that prohibit arbitrary discrimination" would continue to prohibit discrimination on the basis of homosexual conduct as well. This analysis, which is fully in accord with (indeed, follows inescapably from) the text of the constitutional provision, lays to rest such horribles, raised in the course of oral argument, as the prospect that assaults upon homosexuals could not be prosecuted. The amendment prohibits special treatment of homosexuals, and nothing more. It would not affect, for example, a requirement of state law that pensions be paid to all retiring state employees with a certain length of service; homosexual employees, as well as others, would be entitled to that benefit. But it would prevent the State or any municipality from making death-benefit payments to the "life partner" of a homosexual when it does not make such payments to the long-time roommate of a nonhomosexual employee. Or again, it does not affect the requirement of the State's general insurance laws that customers be afforded coverage without discrimination unrelated to anticipated risk. Thus, homosexuals could not be denied coverage, or charged a greater premium, with respect to auto collision insurance; but neither the State nor any municipality could require that distinctive health insurance risks associated with homosexuality (if there are any) be ignored.

Despite all of its hand-wringing about the potential effect of Amendment 2 on general antidiscrimination laws, the Court's opinion ultimately does not dispute all this, but assumes it to be true. The only denial of equal treatment it contends homosexuals have suffered is this: They may not obtain *preferential* treatment without amending the state constitution. That is to say, the principle underlying the Court's opinion is that one who is accorded equal treatment under the laws, but cannot as readily as others obtain *preferential* treatment under the laws, has been denied equal protection of the laws. If merely stating this alleged "equal protection" violation does not suffice to refute it, our constitutional jurisprudence has achieved terminal silliness.

The central thesis of the Court's reasoning is that any group is denied equal protection when, to obtain advantage (or, presumably, to avoid disadvantage), it must have recourse to a more general and hence more difficult level of political decisionmaking than others. The world has never heard of such a principle, which is why the Court's opinion is so long on emotive utterance and so short on relevant legal citation. And it seems to me most unlikely that any multilevel democracy can function under such a principle. For *whenever* a disadvantage is imposed, or conferral of a benefit is prohibited, at one of the higher levels of democratic decisionmaking (i.e., by the state legislature rather than local government, or by the people at large in the state constitution rather than the legislature), the affected group has (under this theory) been denied equal protection. To take the simplest of examples, consider a state law prohibiting the award of municipal contracts to relatives of mayors or city councilmen. Once such a law is passed, the group composed of such relatives must, in order to get the benefit of city contracts, persuade the state legislature-unlike all other citizens, who need only persuade the municipality. It is ridiculous to consider this a denial of equal protection, which is why the Court's theory is unheard-of.

The Court might reply that the example I have given is not a denial of equal protection only because the same "rational basis" (avoidance of corruption) which renders constitutional the *substantive discrimination* against relatives (i.e., the fact that they alone cannot obtain city contracts) also automatically suffices to sustain what might be called the *electoral-procedural discrimination* against them (i.e., the fact that they must go to the state level to get this changed). This is of course a perfectly reasonable response, and would explain why "electoral-procedural discrimination" has not hitherto been heard of: a law that is valid in its substance is automatically valid in its level of enactment. But the Court cannot afford to make this argument, for as I shall discuss next, there is no doubt of a rational basis for the substance of the prohibition at issue here. The Court's entire novel theory rests upon the proposition that there is something special-something that cannot be justified by normal "rational basis" analysis-in making a disadvantaged group (or a nonpreferred group) resort to a higher decisionmaking level. That proposition finds no support in law or logic.

II

I turn next to whether there was a legitimate rational basis for the substance of the constitutional amendment-for the prohibition of special protection for homosexuals. It is unsurprising that the Court avoids discussion of this question, since the answer is so obviously yes. The case most relevant to the issue before us today is not even mentioned in the Court's opinion: In *Bowers v. Hardwick*... (1986), we held that the Constitution does not prohibit what virtually all States had done from the founding of the Republic until very recent years-making homosexual conduct a crime. That holding is unassailable, except by those who think that the Constitution changes to suit current fashions. But in any event it is a given in the present case: Respondents' briefs did not urge overruling *Bowers*, and at oral argument respondents' counsel expressly disavowed any intent to seek such overruling.... If it is constitutionally permissible for a State to make homosexual conduct criminal, surely it is constitutionally permissible for a State to enact other laws merely *disfavoring* homosexual conduct. (As the Court of Appeals for the District of Columbia Circuit has aptly put it: "If the Court [in *Bowers*] was unwilling to object to state laws that criminalize the behavior that defines the class, it is hardly open ... to conclude that state sponsored discrimination against the class is invidious. After all, there can hardly be more palpable discrimination against a class than making the conduct that defines the class criminal." *Padula v. Webster*,... (1987).) And *a fortiori* it is constitutionally permissible for a State to adopt a provision not even disfavoring homosexual conduct, but merely prohibiting all levels of state government from bestowing special protections upon homosexual conduct. Respondents (who, unlike the Court, cannot afford the luxury of ignoring inconvenient precedent) counter *Bowers* with the argument that a greater-includes-the-lesser rationale cannot justify Amendment 2's application to individuals who do not engage in homosexual acts, but are merely of homosexual "orientation." Some courts of appeals have concluded that, with respect to laws of this sort at least, that is a distinction without a difference. See *Equality Foundation of Greater Cincinnati,*

Inc. v. Cincinnati,... ("[F]or purposes of these proceedings, it is virtually impossible to distinguish or separate individuals of a particular orientation which predisposes them toward a particular sexual conduct from those who actually engage in that particular type of sexual conduct"); *Steffan v. Perry*, 41 F. 3d 677.... The Supreme Court of Colorado itself appears to be of this view....

But assuming that, in Amendment 2, a person of homosexual "orientation" is someone who does not engage in homosexual conduct but merely has a tendency or desire to do so, *Bowers* still suffices to establish a rational basis for the provision. If it is rational to criminalize the conduct, surely it is rational to deny special favor and protection to those with a self-avowed tendency or desire to engage in the conduct. Indeed, where criminal sanctions are not involved, homosexual "orientation" is an acceptable stand-in for homosexual conduct . A State "does not violate the Equal Protection Clause merely because the classifications made by its laws are imperfect," *Dandridge v. Williams*,... (1970). Just as a policy barring the hiring of methadone users as transit employees does not violate equal protection simply because some methadone users pose no threat to passenger safety, see *New York City Transit Authority v. Beazer*,... (1979), and just as a mandatory retirement age of 50 for police officers does not violate equal protection even though it prematurely ends the careers of many policemen over 50 who still have the capacity to do the job, see *Massachusetts Bd. of Retirement v. Murgia*,... (1976) *(per curiam)*, Amendment 2 is not constitutionally invalid simply because it could have been drawn more precisely so as to withdraw special antidiscrimination protections only from those of homosexual "orientation" who actually engage in homosexual conduct. As Justice Kennedy wrote, when he was on the Court of Appeals, in a case involving discharge of homosexuals from the Navy: "Nearly any statute which classifies people may be irrational as applied in particular cases. Discharge of the particular plaintiffs before us would be rational, under minimal scrutiny, not because their particular cases present the dangers which justify Navy policy, but instead because the general policy of discharging all homosexuals is rational." *Beller v . Middendorf*....

Moreover, even if the provision regarding homosexual "orientation" were invalid, respondents' challenge to Amendment 2-which is a facial challenge-must fail. "A facial challenge to a legislative Act is, of course, the most difficult challenge to mount successfully, since the challenger must establish that no set of circumstances exists under which the Act would be valid." *United States v. Salerno*,... (1987). It would not be enough for respondents to establish (if they could) that Amendment 2 is unconstitutional as applied to those of homosexual "orientation;" since, under *Bowers*, Amendment 2 is unquestionably constitutional as applied to those who engage in homosexual conduct, the facial challenge cannot succeed. Some individuals of homosexual "orientation" who do not engage in homosexual acts might successfully bring an as-applied challenge to Amendment 2, but so far as the record indicates, none of the respondents is such a person. See App. 4-5 (complaint describing each of the individual respondents as either "a gay man" or "a lesbian").

III

The foregoing suffices to establish what the Court's failure to cite any case remotely in point would lead one to suspect: No principle set forth in the Constitution, nor even any imagined by this Court in the past 200 years, prohibits what Colorado has done here. But the case for Colorado is much stronger than that. What it has done is not only unprohibited, but eminently reasonable, with close, congressionally approved precedent in earlier constitutional practice.

First, as to its eminent reasonableness. The Court's opinion contains grim, disapproving hints that Coloradans have been guilty of "animus" or "animosity" toward homosexuality, as though that has been established as Unamerican. Of course it is our moral heritage that one should not hate any human being or class of human beings. But I had thought that one could consider certain conduct reprehensible – murder, for example, or polygamy, or cruelty to animals – and could exhibit even " animus" toward such conduct. Surely that is the only sort of "animus" at issue here: moral disapproval of homosexual conduct, the same sort of moral disapproval that produced the centuries-old criminal laws that we held constitutional in *Bowers*. The Colorado amendment does not, to speak entirely precisely, prohibit giving favored status to people who are *homosexuals*; they can be favored for many reasons – for example, because they are senior citizens or members of racial minorities. But it prohibits giving them favored status *because of their homosexual conduct* – that is, it prohibits favored status *for homosexuality*.

But though Coloradans are, as I say, entitled to be hostile toward homosexual conduct, the fact is that the degree of hostility reflected by Amendment 2 is the smallest conceivable. The Court's portrayal of Coloradans as a society fallen victim to pointless, hate-filled "gay-bashing" is so false as to be comical. Colorado not only is one of the 25 States that have repealed their antisodomy laws, but was among the first to do so.... But the society that eliminates criminal punishment for homosexual acts does not necessarily abandon the view that homosexuality is morally wrong and socially harmful; often, abolition simply reflects the view that enforcement of such criminal laws involves unseemly intrusion into the intimate lives of citizens....

There is a problem, however, which arises when criminal sanction of homosexuality is eliminated but moral and social disapprobation of homosexuality is meant to be retained. The Court cannot be unaware of that problem; it is evident in many cities of the country, and occasionally bubbles to the surface of the news, in heated political disputes over such matters as the introduction into local schools of books teaching that homosexuality is an optional and fully acceptable "alternate life style." The problem (a problem, that is, for those who wish to retain social disapprobation of homosexuality) is that, because those who engage in homosexual conduct tend to reside in disproportionate numbers in certain communities,... and of course care about homosexual-rights issues much more ardently than the public at large, they possess political power much greater than their numbers, both locally and statewide. Quite understandably, they devote this political power to achieving not merely a grudging social toleration, but full social acceptance, of homosexuality. See, e.g., Jacobs, The Rhetorical Construction of Rights: The Case of the Gay Rights Movement, 1969-1991, 72 Neb. L. Rev. 723, 724 (1993) ("[T]he task of gay rights proponents is to move the center of public discourse along a continuum from the rhetoric of disapprobation, to rhetoric of tolerance, and finally to affirmation").

By the time Coloradans were asked to vote on Amendment 2, their exposure to homosexuals' quest for social endorsement was not limited to newspaper accounts of happenings in places such as New York, Los Angeles, San Francisco, and Key West. Three Colorado cities – Aspen, Boulder, and Denver – had enacted ordinances that listed "sexual orientation" as an impermissible ground for discrimination, equating the moral disapproval of homosexual conduct with racial and religious bigotry.... The phenomenon had even appeared statewide: the Governor of Colorado had signed an executive order pronouncing that "in the State of Colorado we recognize the diversity in our pluralistic society and strive to bring an end to discrimination in any form," and directing state agency-heads to "ensure non-discrimination" in hiring and promotion based on, among other things, "sexual orientation...." I do not mean to be critical of these legislative successes; homosexuals are as entitled to use the legal system for reinforcement of their moral sentiments as are the rest of society. But they are subject to being countered by lawful, democratic countermeasures as well.

That is where Amendment 2 came in. It sought to counter both the geographic concentration and the disproportionate political power of homosexuals by (1) resolving the controversy at the statewide level, and (2) making the election a single-issue contest for both sides. It put directly, to all the citizens of the State, the question: Should homosexuality be given special protection? They answered no. The Court today asserts that this most democratic of procedures is unconstitutional . Lacking any cases to establish that facially absurd proposition, it simply asserts that it *must* be unconstitutional, because it has never happened before.

> "[Amendment 2] identifies persons by a single trait and then denies them protection across the board. The resulting disqualification of a class of persons from the right to seek specific protection from the law is unprecedented in our jurisprudence. The absence of precedent for Amendment 2 is itself instructive ...."

> "It is not within our constitutional tradition to enact laws of this sort. Central both to the idea of the rule of law and to our own Constitution's guarantee of equal protection is the principle that government and each of its parts remain open on impartial terms to all who seek its assistance."

As I have noted above, this is proved false every time a state law prohibiting or disfavoring certain conduct is passed, because such a law prevents the adversely affected group-whether drug addicts, or smokers, or gun owners, or motorcyclists-from changing the policy thus established in "each of [the] parts" of the State. What the Court says is even demonstrably false at the constitutional level. The Eighteenth Amendment to the Federal Constitution, for example, deprived those who drank alcohol not only of the power to alter the policy of prohibition *locally* or through *state legislation*, but even of the power to alter it through *state constitutional amendment* or *federal legislation*. The Establishment Clause of the First Amendment prevents theocrats from having their way by converting their fellow citizens at the local, state, or federal statutory level; as does the Republican Form of Government Clause prevent monarchists.

But there is a much closer analogy, one that involves precisely the effort by the majority of citizens to preserve its view of sexual morality statewide, against the efforts of a geographically concentrated and politically powerful minority to undermine it. The constitutions of the States of Arizona, Idaho, New Mexico, Oklahoma, and Utah to this day contain provisions stating that polygamy is "forever prohibited…." Polygamists, and those who have a polygamous "orientation," have been "singled out" by these provisions for much more severe treatment than merely denial of favored status; and that treatment can only be changed by achieving amendment of the state constitutions. The Court's disposition today suggests that these provisions are unconstitutional, and that polygamy must be permitted in these States on a state-legislated, or perhaps even local-option, basis – unless, of course, polygamists for some reason have fewer constitutional rights than homosexuals.

The United States Congress, by the way, *required* the inclusion of these antipolygamy provisions in the constitutions of Arizona, New Mexico, Oklahoma, and Utah, as a condition of their admission to statehood. (For Arizona, New Mexico, and Utah, moreover, the Enabling Acts required that the antipolygamy provisions be "irrevocable without the consent of the United States and the people of said State" – so that not only were "each of [the] parts" of these States not "open on impartial terms" to polygamists, but even the States as a whole were not; polygamists would have to persuade the whole country to their way of thinking.) Idaho adopted the constitutional provision on its own, but the 51st Congress, which admitted Idaho into the Union, found its constitution to be "republican in form and … in conformity with the Constitution of the United States…." Thus, this "singling out" of the sexual practices of a single group for statewide, democratic vote – so utterly alien to our constitutional system, the Court would have us believe – has not only happened, but has received the explicit approval of the United States Congress.

I cannot say that this Court has explicitly approved any of these state constitutional provisions; but it has approved a territorial statutory provision that went even further, depriving polygamists of the ability even to achieve a constitutional amendment, by depriving them of the power to vote. In *Davis v. Beason*,… (1890), Justice Field wrote for a unanimous Court:

> "In our judgment, Section(s) 501 of the Revised Statutes of Idaho Territory, which provides that 'no person ... who is a bigamist or polygamist or who teaches, advises, counsels, or encourages any person or persons to become bigamists or polygamists, or to commit any other crime defined by law, or to enter into what is known as plural or celestial marriage, or who is a member of any order, organization or association which teaches, advises, counsels, or encourages its members or devotees or any other persons to commit the crime of bigamy or polygamy, or any other crime defined by law ... is permitted to vote at any election, or to hold any position or office of honor, trust, or profit within this Territory,' is not open to any constitutional or legal objection."

To the extent, if any, that this opinion permits the imposition of adverse consequences upon mere abstract advocacy of polygamy, it has of course been overruled by later cases. See *Brandenburg v. Ohio*,... (1969) (per curiam). But the proposition that polygamy can be criminalized, and those engaging in that crime deprived of the vote, remains good law. See *Richardson v. Ramirez*,... (1974). *Beason* rejected the argument that "such discrimination is a denial of the equal protection of the laws...." Among the Justices joining in that rejection were the two whose views in other cases the Court today treats as equal-protection lodestars – Justice Harlan, who was to proclaim in *Plessy v. Ferguson*,... (1896) (dissenting opinion), that the Constitution "neither knows nor tolerates classes among citizens," and Justice Bradley, who had earlier declared that "class legislation ... [is] obnoxious to the prohibitions of the Fourteenth Amendment," *Civil Rights Cases*,... (1883)....

This Court cited *Beason* with approval as recently as 1993, in an opinion authored by the same Justice who writes for the Court today. That opinion said: "[A]dverse impact will not always lead to a finding of impermissible targeting. For example, a social harm may have been a legitimate concern of government for reasons quite apart from discrimination.... It remains to be explained how Section(s) 501 of the Idaho Revised Statutes was not an "impermissible targeting" of polygamists, but (the much more mild) Amendment 2 is an "impermissible targeting" of homosexuals. Has the Court concluded that the perceived social harm of polygamy is a "legitimate concern of government," and the perceived social harm of homosexuality is not?

IV

I strongly suspect that the answer to the last question is yes, which leads me to the last point I wish to make: The Court today, announcing that Amendment 2 "defies ... conventional [constitutional] inquiry," and "confounds [the] normal process of judicial review," employs a constitutional theory heretofore unknown to frustrate Colorado's reasonable effort to preserve traditional American moral values. The Court's stern disapproval of "animosity" towards homosexuality might be compared with what an earlier Court (including the revered Justices Harlan and Bradley) said in *Murphy v. Ramsey*,... (1885), rejecting a constitutional challenge to a United States statute that denied the franchise in federal territories to those who engaged in polygamous cohabitation:

> "[C]ertainly no legislation can be supposed more wholesome and necessary in the founding of a free, self-governing commonwealth, fit to take rank as one of the co-ordinate States of the Union, than that which seeks to establish it on the basis of the idea of the family, as consisting in and springing from the union for life of one man and one woman in the holy estate of matrimony; the sure foundation of all that is stable and noble in our civilization; the best guaranty of that reverent morality which is the source of all beneficent progress in social and political improvement."

I would not myself indulge in such official praise for heterosexual monogamy, because I think it no business of the courts (as opposed to the political branches) to take sides in this culture war.

But the Court today has done so, not only by inventing a novel and extravagant constitutional doctrine to take the victory away from traditional forces, but even by verbally disparaging as bigotry adherence to traditional attitudes. To suggest, for example, that this constitutional amendment springs from nothing more than "'a bare ... desire to harm a politically unpopular group,'" quoting *Department of Agriculture v. Moreno*,... (1973), is nothing short of insulting. (It is also nothing short of preposterous to call "politically unpopular" a group which enjoys enormous influence in American media and politics, and which, as the trial court here noted, though composing no more than 4% of the population had the support of 46% of the voters on Amendment 2, see App. to Pet. for Cert. C-18.)

When the Court takes sides in the culture wars, it tends to be with the knights rather than the villeins – and more specifically with the Templars, reflecting the views and values of the lawyer class from which the Court's Members are drawn. How that class feels about homosexuality will be evident to anyone who wishes to interview job applicants at virtually any of the Nation's law schools. The interviewer may refuse to offer a job because the applicant is a Republican; because he is an adulterer; because he went to the wrong prep school or belongs to the wrong country club; because he eats snails; because he is a womanizer; because she wears real-animal fur; or even because he hates the Chicago Cubs. But if the interviewer should wish not to be an associate or partner of an applicant because he disapproves of the applicant's homosexuality, then he will have violated the pledge which the Association of American Law Schools requires all its member-schools to exact from job interviewers: "assurance of the employer's willingness" to hire homosexuals. Bylaws of the Association of American Law Schools, Inc. Section(s) 6-4(b); Executive Committee Regulations of the Association of American Law Schools Section(s) 6.19, in 1995 Handbook, Association of American Law Schools. This law-school view of what "prejudices" must be stamped out may be contrasted with the more plebeian attitudes that apparently still prevail in the United States Congress, which has been unresponsive to repeated attempts to extend to homosexuals the protections of federal civil rights laws, see, e.g., Employment Non-Discrimination Act of 1994, S. 2238, 103d Cong., 2d Sess. (1994); Civil Rights Amendments of 1975, H. R. 5452, 94th Cong., 1st Sess. (1975), and which took the pains to exclude them specifically from the Americans With Disabilities Act of 1990, see 42 U. S. C. Section(s) 12211(a) (1988 ed., Supp. V).

Today's opinion has no foundation in American constitutional law, and barely pretends to. The people of Colorado have adopted an entirely reasonable provision which does not even disfavor homosexuals in any substantive sense, but merely denies them preferential treatment. Amendment 2 is designed to prevent piecemeal deterioration of the sexual morality favored by a majority of Coloradans, and is not only an appropriate means to that legitimate end, but a means that Americans have employed before. Striking it down is an act, not of judicial judgment, but of political will. I dissent.

VACCO v. QUILL
117 S. Ct. 2293 (1997)

The facts in this case are contained in the opinion below.

Chief Justice REHNQUIST delivered the opinion of the Court.

In New York, as in most States, it is a crime to aid another to commit or attempt suicide, but patients may refuse even lifesaving medical treatment. The question presented by this case is whether New York's prohibition on assisting suicide therefore violates the Equal Protection Clause of the Fourteenth Amendment. We hold that it does not.

Petitioners are various New York public officials. Respondents Timothy E. Quill, Samuel C. Klagsbrun, and Howard A. Grossman are physicians who practice in New York. They assert that although it would be "consistent with the standards of [their] medical practice[s]" to prescribe lethal medication for "mentally competent, terminally ill patients" who are suffering great pain and desire a doctor's help in taking their own lives, they are deterred from doing so by New York's ban on assisting suicide. Respondents, and three gravely ill patients who have since died, sued the State's Attorney General in the United States District Court. They urged that because New York permits a competent person to refuse life-sustaining medical treatment, and because the refusal of such treatment is "essentially the same thing" as physician-assisted suicide, New York's assisted-suicide ban violates the Equal Protection Clause....

The District Court disagreed: "[I]t is hardly unreasonable or irrational for the State to recognize a difference between allowing nature to take its course, even in the most severe situations, and intentionally using an artificial death-producing device." The court noted New York's "obvious legitimate interests in preserving life, and in protecting vulnerable persons," and concluded that "[u]nder the United States Constitution and the federal system it establishes, the resolution of this issue is left to the normal democratic processes within the State."

The Court of Appeals for the Second Circuit reversed.... The court determined that, despite the assisted-suicide ban's apparent general applicability, "New York law does not treat equally all competent persons who are in the final stages of fatal illness and wish to hasten their deaths," because "those in the final stages of terminal illness who are on life-support systems are allowed to hasten their deaths by directing the removal of such systems; but those who are similarly situated, except for the previous attachment of life-sustaining equipment, are not allowed to hasten death by self-administering prescribed drugs." In the court's view, "[t]he ending of life by [the withdrawal of life-support systems] is *nothing more nor less than assisted suicide*." (emphasis added). The Court of Appeals then examined whether this supposed unequal treatment was rationally related to any legitimate state interests, and concluded that "to the extent that [New York's statutes] prohibit a physician from prescribing medications to be self-administered by a mentally competent, terminally-ill person in the final stages of his terminal illness, they are not rationally related to any legitimate state interest." We granted certiorari,... and now reverse.

The Equal Protection Clause commands that no State shall "deny to any person within its jurisdiction the equal protection of the laws." This provision creates no substantive rights. *San Antonio Independent School Dist. v. Rodriguez....* Instead, it embodies a general rule that States must treat like cases alike but may treat unlike cases accordingly. *Plyler v. Doe....* If a legislative classification or distinction "neither burdens a fundamental right nor targets a suspect class, we will uphold [it] so long as it bears a rational relation to some legitimate end." *Romer v. Evans....*

New York's statutes outlawing assisting suicide affect and address matters of profound significance to all New Yorkers alike. They neither infringe fundamental rights nor involve suspect classifications. *Washington v. Glucksberg,... San Antonio School Dist....* These laws are therefore entitled to a "strong presumption of validity." *Heller v. Doe....*

On their faces, neither New York's ban on assisting suicide nor its statutes permitting patients to refuse medical treatment treat anyone differently than anyone else or draw any distinctions between persons. Everyone, regardless of physical condition, is entitled, if competent, to refuse unwanted lifesaving medical treatment; no one is permitted to assist a suicide. Generally speaking, laws that apply evenhandedly to all "unquestionably comply" with the Equal Protection Clause....

The Court of Appeals, however, concluded that some terminally ill people, those who are on life-support systems, are treated differently than those who are not, in that the former may "hasten death" by ending treatment, but the latter may not "hasten death" through physician-assisted suicide. This conclusion depends on the submission that ending or refusing lifesaving medical treatment "is nothing more nor less than assisted suicide." Unlike the Court of Appeals, we think the distinction between assisting suicide and withdrawing life-sustaining treatment, a distinction widely recognized and endorsed in the medical profession and in our legal traditions, is both important and logical; it is certainly rational....

The distinction comports with fundamental legal principles of causation and intent. First, when a patient refuses life-sustaining medical treatment, he dies from an underlying fatal disease or pathology; but if a patient ingests lethal medication prescribed by a physician, he is killed by that medication....

Furthermore, a physician who withdraws, or honors a patient's refusal to begin, life-sustaining medical treatment purposefully intends, or may so intend, only to respect his patient's wishes and "to cease doing useless and futile or degrading things to the patient when [the patient] no longer stands to benefit from them." The same is true when a doctor provides aggressive palliative care; in some cases, painkilling drugs may hasten a patient's death, but the physician's purpose and intent is, or may be, only to ease his patient's pain. A doctor who assists a suicide, however, "must, necessarily and indubitably, intend primarily that the patient be made dead." Similarly, a patient who commits suicide with a doctor's aid necessarily has the specific intent to end his or her own life, while a patient who refuses or discontinues treatment might not....

The law has long used actors' intent or purpose to distinguish between two acts that may have the same result.... Put differently, the law distinguishes actions taken "because of" a given end from actions taken "in spite of" their unintended but foreseen consequences....

Given these general principles, it is not surprising that many courts, including New York courts, have carefully distinguished refusing life-sustaining treatment from suicide.... In fact, the first state-court decision explicitly to authorize withdrawing lifesaving treatment noted the "real distinction between the self-infliction of deadly harm and a self-determination against artificial life support." *In re Quinlan,... Garger v. New Jersey....* And recently, the Michigan Supreme Court also rejected the argument that the distinction "between acts that artificially sustain life and acts that artificially curtail life" is merely a "distinction without constitutional significance a meaningless exercise in semantic gymnastics," insisting that "the *Cruzan* majority disagreed and so do we." *Kevorkian,* 447 Mich., at 471....

Similarly, the overwhelming majority of state legislatures have drawn a clear line between assisting suicide and withdrawing or permitting the refusal of unwanted lifesaving medical treatment by prohibiting the former and permitting the latter. *Glucksberg....* And "nearly all states expressly disapprove of suicide and assisted suicide either in statutes dealing with durable powers of attorney in health-care situations, or in "living will' statutes. " *Kevorkian....*Thus, even as the States move to protect and promote patients' dignity at the end of life, they remain opposed to physician-assisted suicide.

New York is a case in point. The State enacted its current assisted-suicide statutes in 1965. Since then, New York has acted several times to protect patients' common-law right to refuse treatment.... In so doing, however, the State has neither endorsed a general right to "hasten death" nor approved physician-assisted suicide. Quite the opposite: The State has reaffirmed the line between "killing" and "letting die...." More recently, the New York State Task Force on Life and the Law studied assisted suicide and euthanasia and, in 1994, unanimously recommended against legalization.... In the Task Force's view, "allowing decisions to forego life-sustaining treatment and allowing assisted suicide or euthanasia have radically different consequences and meanings for public policy."

This Court has also recognized, at least implicitly, the distinction between letting a patient die and making that patient die. In *Cruzan v. Director, Mo. Dept. of Health*,... we concluded that "[t]he principle that a competent person has a constitutionally protected liberty interest in refusing unwanted medical treatment may be inferred from our prior decisions," and we assumed the existence of such a right for purposes of that case. But our assumption of a right to refuse treatment was grounded not, as the Court of Appeals supposed, on the proposition that patients have a general and abstract "right to hasten death," but on well established, traditional rights to bodily integrity and freedom from unwanted touching.... In fact, we observed that "the majority of States in this country have laws imposing criminal penalties on one who assists another to commit suicide." *Cruzan* therefore provides no support for the notion that refusing life-sustaining medical treatment is "nothing more nor less than suicide."

For all these reasons, we disagree with respondents' claim that the distinction between refusing lifesaving medical treatment and assisted suicide is "arbitrary" and "irrational...." Granted, in some cases, the line between the two may not be clear, but certainty is not required, even were it possible. Logic and contemporary practice support New York's judgment that the two acts are different, and New York may therefore, consistent with the Constitution, treat them differently. By permitting everyone to refuse unwanted medical treatment while prohibiting anyone from assisting a suicide, New York law follows a longstanding and rational distinction.

New York's reasons for recognizing and acting on this distinction including prohibiting intentional killing and preserving life; preventing suicide; maintaining physicians' role as their patients' healers; protecting vulnerable people from indifference, prejudice, and psychological and financial pressure to end their lives; and avoiding a possible slide towards euthanasia are discussed in greater detail in our opinion in *Glucksberg*.... These valid and important public interests easily satisfy the constitutional requirement that a legislative classification bear a rational relation to some legitimate end.

The judgment of the Court of Appeals is reversed.

It is so ordered.

Justice SOUTER, concurring in the judgment.

Even though I do not conclude that assisted suicide is a fundamental right entitled to recognition at this time, I accord the claims raised by the patients and physicians in this case and *Washington v. Glucksberg* a high degree of importance, requiring a commensurate justification.... The reasons that lead me to conclude in *Glucksberg* that the prohibition on assisted suicide is not arbitrary under the due process standard also support the distinction between assistance to suicide, which is banned, and practices such as termination of artificial life support and death-hastening pain medication, which are permitted. I accordingly concur in the judgment of the Court.

GLOSSARY

Acquittal. A decision of innocence by the trial court.

Adjudicate. To invoke judicial authority for the final determination of a question.

Advisory opinion. A non-binding opinion or response to an agency of the government seeking advice on the constitutionality of a measure.

Affidavit. A sworn statement in lieu of one's appearance in court; normally limited to civil not criminal cases.

Amicus curiae. ("friend of the court") Term commonly used to designate an individual or group who, while not a party to the case, has a vested interest in the outcome and who files a brief on behalf of one party or the other to the controversy.

Appellate jurisdiction. The authority to review cases already determined by inferior courts.

Arraignment. A pre-trial process of charging an accused, before a magistrate, of a specific crime.

Bellum. War.

Bill of Attainder. A law that inflicts punishment without judicial process.

Collegial. More than one; a collection.

Common law. Law developed through judicial decisions, in contrast to statutory law created by legislatures. Judge-made law enhanced by the use of precedent.

Concurrent jurisdiction. Jurisdiction possessed by a number of courts, each authorized to examine the subject matter.

Concurring opinion. An opinion in a case in which the author(s) agree with the decision of the court but not necessarily the reasoning used to reach that decision.

Consent decree. A court order recognizing the mutual agreement of the parties.

Declaratory judgment. A decision in which the court *declares* the rights of the parties involved without ordering that a particular action be done.

De facto. In fact or in reality as opposed to a legal requirement.

Dissenting opinion. An opinion in a case in which the author(s) disagree with the opinion of the court; the minority opinion.

Docket. A list of the litigation pending before a court, either for the first time (original) or from a lower court (appellate).

Equity. Usually refers to attempts (sometimes by specialized "equity courts") to achieve decisions which are "fair" or "equitable" as determined by the "spirit" of the law even though they do not follow the "letter" of the law. Natural right or impartial justice.

Ex officio. Powers inherent in the office but not specifically conferred.

Ex parte. Action on the part of one party only.

Ex post facto. ("after the fact") A retroactive criminal statute; an act punishing behavior not criminal when done.

Ex relatione. On the relation or the information.

Habeas corpus. ("you have the body") A writ employed to release a person from unlawful imprisonment.

In camera. In chambers or the judicial office.

Injunction. A court decree issued at the request of a complainant to compel another party to do or not to do a particular thing.

In re. In relation to; in the matter of; concerning; regarding.

Judicial notice. The court recognizes, without comment, some common fact known to all.

Jus sanguinis. ("the law of blood") A person's citizenship is determined by the parents' nationality.

Jus soli. ("the law of soil or place") Citizenship is determined by the place of birth.

Justicable. A proper matter for judicial decision.

Moot. No controversy exists or it is no longer relevant.

Obiter dictum or ***dictum*** ("words said in passing") A remark or an opinion expressed by a judge which bears little relation to the decision of the case and is not a binding precedent.

Original jurisdiction. The authority to adjudicate a cause at its inception.

Per curiam. A court opinion or decision without signed authorization; a decision without lengthy opinion.

Posse comitatus. Those persons, representing the power of the county, who are called to assist the sheriff in certain cases.

Remand. To send the case back to a lower court.

***Res judicata*.** Once the process of litigation has been completed, the decision in the case is final and of binding effect.

Sovereign. The ultimate power to govern a nation and to alter its supreme law.

Standing. The requirement of a justiciable controversy that in order to bring suit challenging the validity of governmental action one must have sustained or be in immediate danger of sustaining a direct injury to his legal rights.

Stare decisis. ("let the decision stand") The rule of precedent under which the court perceives that it is bound by earlier rulings.

Supra. ("above") Usually refers to an earlier statement or quote.

Talesman or venireman. A person summoned to serve on a jury.

Trover. A court created solution or remedy for an illegal interference or disruption of another party's property.

Vacate. To eliminate or negate; to nullify.

***Vel non*.** Whether or not; usually negative.

Writ of Certiorari. ("to be informed of') A writ or order to an interior court to send the record of the case to the high court for the purpose of review.

Writ of Mandamus. ("we command") A writ issued by a court of proper jurisdiction directing a party to perform the act specified therein.

THE CONSTITUTION OF THE UNITED STATES

We the People of the United States, in Order to form a more perfect Union, establish Justice, insure domestic Tranquillity, provide for the common defence, promote the general Welfare, and secure the Blessings of Liberty to ourselves and our Posterity, do ordain and establish this Constitution for the United States of America.

ARTICLE I

Section 1. All legislative Powers herein granted shall be vested in a Congress of the United States, which shall consist of a Senate and House of Representatives.

Section 2. The House of Representatives shall be composed of Members chosen every second Year by the People of the several States, and the Electors in each State shall have the Qualifications requisite for Electors of the most numerous Branch of the State Legislature.

No Person shall be a Representative who shall not have attained to the age of twenty five Years, and been seven Years a Citizen of the United States, and who shall not, when elected, be an Inhabitant of that State in which he shall be chosen.

Representatives and direct Taxes shall be apportioned among the several States which may be included within this Union, according to their respective Numbers, which shall be determined by adding to the whole Number of free Persons, including those bound to Service for a Term of Years, and excluding Indians not taxed, three fifths of all other Persons. The actual Enumeration shall be made within three Years after the first Meeting of the Congress of the United States, and within every subsequent Term of ten Years, in such Manner as they shall by Law direct. The Number of Representatives shall not exceed one for every thirty Thousand, but each State shall have at Least one Representative; and until such enumeration shall be made, the State of New Hampshire shall be entitled to chuse three, Massachusetts eight, Rhode-Island and Providence Plantations one, Connecticut five, New-York six, New Jersey four, Pennsylvania eight, Delaware one, Maryland six, Virginia ten, North Carolina five, South Carolina five, and Georgia three.

When vacancies happen in the Representation from any State, the Executive Authority thereof shall issue Writs of Election to fill such Vacancies.

The House of Representatives shall chuse their Speaker and other Officers; and shall have the sole Power of Impeachment.

Section 3. The Senate of the United States shall be composed of two Senators from each State, chosen by the Legislature thereof, for six Years; and each Senator shall have one Vote.

Immediately after they shall be assembled in Consequence of the first Election, they shall be divided as equally as may be into three Classes. The Seats of the Senators of the first Class shall be vacated at the Expiration of the second Year, of the second Class at the Expiration of the fourth Year, and of the third Class at the Expiration of the sixth Year, so that one third may be chosen every second Year; and if Vacancies happen by Resignation, or otherwise, during the Recess of the Legislature of any State, the Executive thereof may make temporary Appointments until the next Meeting of the Legislature, which shall then fill such Vacancies.

No Person shall be a Senator who shall not have attained to the Age of thirty Years, and been nine Years a Citizen of the United States, and who shall not, when elected, be an Inhabitant of that State for which he shall be chosen.

The Vice President of the United States shall be President of the Senate, but shall have no Vote, unless they be equally divided.

The Senate shall chuse their other Officers, and also a President pro tempore, in the Absence of the Vice President, or when he shall exercise the Office of President of the United States.

The Senate shall have the sole Power to try all Impeachments. When sitting for that Purpose, they shall be on Oath or Affirmation. When the President of the United States is tried, the Chief Justice shall preside: And no Person shall be convicted without the Concurrence of two thirds of the Members present.

Judgment in Cases of Impeachment shall not extend further than to removal from Office, and disqualification to hold and enjoy any Office of honor, Trust or Profit under the United States: but the Party convicted shall nevertheless be liable and subject to Indictment, Trial, Judgment and Punishment, according to Law.

Section 4. The Times, Places and Manner of holding Elections for Senators and Representatives, shall be prescribed in each State by the Legislature thereof; but the Congress may at any time by Law make or alter such Regulations, except as to the Places of chusing Senators.

The Congress shall assemble at least once in every Year, and such Meeting shall be on the first Monday in December, unless they shall by Law appoint a different Day.

Section 5. Each House shall be the Judge of the Elections, Returns and Qualifications of its own Members, and a Majority of each shall constitute a Quorum to do Business; but a smaller Number may adjourn from day to day, and may be authorized to compel the Attendance of absent Members, in such Manner, and under such Penalties as each House may provide.

Each House may determine the Rules of its Proceedings, punish its Members for disorderly Behavior, and, with the Concurrence of two thirds, expel a Member.

Each House shall keep a Journal of its Proceedings, and from time to time publish the same, excepting such Parts as may in their Judgment require Secrecy; and the Yeas and Nays of the Members of either House on any question shall, at the Desire of one fifth of those Present, be entered on the Journal.

Neither House, during the Session of Congress, shall, without the Consent of the other, adjourn for more than three days, nor to any other Place than that in which the two Houses shall be sitting.

Section 6. The Senators and Representatives shall receive a Compensation for their Services, to be ascertained by Law, and paid out of the Treasury of the United States. They shall in all Cases, except Treason, Felony and Breach of the Peace, be privileged from Arrest during their Attendance at the Session of their respective Houses, and in going to and returning from the same; and for any Speech or Debate in either House, they shall not be questioned in any other Place.

No Senator or Representative shall, during the Time for which he was elected, be appointed to any civil Office under the Authority of the United States, which shall have been created, or the Emoluments whereof shall have been encreased during such time; and no Person holding any Office under the United States, shall be a Member of either House during his Continuance in Office.

Section 7. All Bills for raising Revenue shall originate in the House of Representatives; but the Senate may propose or concur with Amendments as on other Bills.

Every Bill which shall have passed the House of Representatives and the Senate, shall, before it become a Law, be presented to the President of the United States; If he approve he shall sign it, but if not he shall return it, with his Objections to that House in which it shall have originated, who shall enter the Objections at large on their Journal, and proceed to reconsider it. If after such Reconsideration two thirds of that House shall agree to pass the Bill, it shall be sent, together with the Objections, to the other House, by which it shall likewise be reconsidered, and if approved by two thirds of that House, it shall become a Law. But in all such Cases the Votes of both Houses shall be determined by yeas and Nays, and the Names of the Persons voting for and against the Bill shall be entered on the Journal of each House respectively. If any Bill shall not be returned by the President within ten Days (Sundays excepted) after it shall have been presented to him, the Same shall be a Law, in like Manner as if he had signed it, unless the Congress by their Adjournment prevent its Return, in which Case it shall not be a Law.

Every Order, Resolution, or Vote to which the Concurrence of the Senate and House of Representatives may be necessary (except on a question of Adjournment) shall be presented to the President of the United States; and before the Same shall take Effect, shall be approved by him, or being disapproved by him, shall be repassed by two thirds of the Senate and House of Representatives, according to the Rules and Limitations prescribed in the Case of a Bill.

Section 8. The Congress shall have Power To lay and collect Taxes, Duties, Imposts and Excises, to pay the Debts and provide for the common Defence and general Welfare of the United States; but all Duties, Imposts and Excises shall be uniform throughout the United States;

To borrow Money on the credit of the United States;

To regulate Commerce with foreign Nations, and among the several States, and with the Indian Tribes;

To establish an uniform Rule of Naturalization, and uniform Laws on the subject of Bankruptcies throughout the United States;

To coin Money, regulate the Value thereof, and of foreign Coin, and fix the Standard of Weights and Measures;

To provide for the Punishment of counterfeiting the Securities and current Coin of the United States;

To establish Post Offices and post Roads;

To promote the Progress of Science and useful Arts, by securing for limited Times to Authors and Inventors the exclusive Right to their respective Writings and Discoveries;

To constitute Tribunals inferior to the supreme Court;

To define and punish Piracies and Felonies committed on the high Seas, and Offences against the Law of Nations;

To declare War, grant Letters of Marque and Reprisal, and make Rules concerning Captures on Land and Water;

To raise and support Armies, but no Appropriation of Money to that Use shall be for a longer Term than two Years;

To provide and maintain a Navy;

To make Rules for the Government and Regulation of the land and naval Forces;

To provide for calling forth the Militia to execute the Laws of the Union, suppress Insurrections and repel Invasions;

To provide for organizing, arming, and disciplining, the Militia, and for governing such Part of them as may be employed in the Service of the United States, reserving to the States respectively, the Appointment of the Officers, and the Authority of training the Militia according to the discipline prescribed by Congress;

To exercise exclusive Legislation in all Cases whatsoever, over such District (not exceeding ten Miles square) as may, by Cession of particular States, and the Acceptance of Congress, become the Seat of the Government of the United States, and to exercise like Authority over all Places purchased by the Consent of the Legislature of the State in which the Same shall be, for the Erection of Forts, Magazines, Arsenals, dock-Yards, and other needful Buildings; –And

To make all Laws which shall be necessary and proper for carrying into Execution the foregoing Powers, and all other Powers vested by this Constitution in the Government of the United States, or in any Department or Officer thereof.

Section 9. The Migration or Importation of such Persons as any of the States now existing shall think proper to admit, shall not be prohibited by the Congress prior to the Year one thousand eight hundred and eight, but a Tax or duty may be imposed on such Importation, not exceeding ten dollars for each Person.

The Privilege of the Writ of Habeas Corpus shall not be suspended, unless when in Cases of Rebellion or Invasion the public Safety may require it.

No Bill of Attainder or ex post facto Law shall be passed.

No capitation, or other direct, Tax shall be laid, unless in Proportion to the Census or Enumeration hereinbefore directed to be taken.

No Tax or Duty shall be laid on Articles exported from any State.

No Preference shall be given by any Regulation of Commerce or Revenue to the Ports of one State over those of another: nor shall Vessels bound to, or from, one State, be obliged to enter, clear or pay Duties in another.

No Money shall be drawn from the Treasury, but in Consequence of Appropriations made by Law; and a regular Statement and Account of the Receipts and Expenditures of all public Money shall be published from time to time.

No Title of Nobility shall be granted by the United States: And no Person holding any Office of Profit or Trust under them, shall, without the Consent of the Congress, accept of any present, Emolument, Office, or Title, of any kind whatever, from any King, Prince, or foreign State.

Section 10. No State shall enter into any Treaty, Alliance, or Confederation; grant Letters of Marque and Reprisal; coin Money; emit Bills of Credit; make any Thing but gold and silver Coin a Tender in Payment of Debts; pass any Bill of Attainder, ex post facto Law, or Law impairing the Obligation of Contracts, or grant any Title of Nobility.

No State shall, without the Consent of the Congress, lay any Imposts or Duties on Imports or Exports, except what may be absolutely necessary for executing it's inspection Laws: and the net Produce of all Duties and Imposts, laid by any State on Imports or Exports, shall be for the Use of the Treasury of the United States; and all such Laws shall be subject to the Revision and Controul of the Congress.

No State shall, without the Consent of Congress, lay any Duty of Tonnage, keep Troops, or Ships of War in time of Peace, enter into any Agreement or Compact with another State, or with a foreign Power, or engage in War, unless actually invaded, or in such imminent Danger as will not admit of delay.

ARTICLE II

Section 1. The executive Power shall be vested in a President of the United States of America. He shall hold his Office during the Term of four Years, and, together with the Vice President, chosen for the same Term, be elected, as follows

Each State shall appoint, in such Manner as the Legislature thereof may direct, a Number of Electors, equal to the whole Number of Senators and Representatives to which the State may be entitled in the Congress: but no Senator or Representative, or Person holding an Office of Trust or Profit under the United States, shall be appointed an Elector.

The Electors shall meet in their respective States, and vote by Ballot for two Persons, of whom one at least shall not be an Inhabitant of the same State with themselves. And they shall make a List of all the Persons voted for, and of the Number of Votes for each; which List they shall sign and certify, and transmit sealed to the Seat of the Government of the United States, directed to the President of the Senate. The President of the Senate shall, in the Presence of the Senate and House of Representatives, open all the Certificates, and the Votes shall then be counted. The Person having the greatest Number of Votes shall be the President, if such Number be a Majority of the whole Number of Electors appointed; and if there be more than one who have such Majority, and have an equal Number of Votes, then the House of Representatives shall immediately chuse by Ballot one of them for President; and if no Person have a Majority, then from the five highest on the List the said House shall in like Manner chuse the President. But in chusing the President, the Votes shall be taken by States, the Representation from each State having one Vote; A quorum for this Purpose shall consist of a Member or Members from two thirds of the States, and a Majority of all the States shall be necessary to a Choice. In every Case, after the Choice of the President, the Person having the greatest Number of Votes of the Electors shall be the Vice President. But if there should remain two or more who have equal Votes, the Senate shall chuse from them by Ballot the Vice President.

The Congress may determine the Time of chusing the Electors, and the Day on which they shall give their Votes; which Day shall be the same throughout the United States.

No Person except a natural born Citizen, or a Citizen of the United States, at the time of the Adoption of this Constitution, shall be eligible to the Office of President; neither shall any Person be eligible to that Office who shall not have attained to the Age of thirty five Years, and been fourteen Years a Resident within the United States.

In Case of the Removal of the President from Office, or of his Death, Resignation, or Inability to discharge the Powers and Duties of said Office, the Same shall devolve on the Vice President, and the Congress may by Law provide for the Case of Removal, Death, Resignation or Inability, both of the President and Vice President, declaring what Officer shall then act as President, and such Officer shall act accordingly, until the Disability be removed, or a President shall be elected.

The President shall, at stated Times, receive for his Services, a Compensation, which shall neither be encreased nor diminished during the Period for which he shall have been elected, and he shall not receive within that Period any other Emolument from the United States, or any of them.

Before he enter on the Execution of his Office, he shall take the following Oath or Affirmation:– "I do solemnly swear (or affirm) that I will faithfully execute the Office of President of the United States, and will to the best of my Ability, preserve, protect and defend the Constitution of the United States."

Section 2. The President shall be Commander in Chief of the Army and Navy of the United States, and of the Militia of the several States, when called into the actual Service of the United States; he may require the Opinion, in writing, of the principal Officer in each of the executive Departments, upon any Subject relating to the Duties of their respective Offices, and he shall have Power to grant Reprieves and Pardons for Offences against the United States, except in Cases of Impeachment.

He shall have Power, by and with the Advice and Consent of the Senate, to make Treaties, provided two thirds of the Senators present concur; and he shall nominate, and by and with the Advice and Consent of the Senate, shall appoint Ambassadors, other public Ministers and Consuls, Judges of the supreme Court, and all other Officers of the United States, whose Appointments are not herein otherwise provided for, and which shall be established by Law; but the Congress may by Law vest the Appointment of such inferior Officers, as they think proper, in the President alone, in the Courts of Law, or in the Heads of Departments.

The President shall have Power to fill up all Vacancies that may happen during the Recess of the Senate, by granting Commissions which shall expire at the End of their next Session.

Section 3. He shall from time to time give to the Congress Information of the State of the Union, and recommend to their Consideration such Measures as he shall judge necessary and expedient; he may, on extraordinary Occasions, convene both Houses, or either of them, and in Case of Disagreement between them, with Respect to the Time of Adjournment, he may adjourn them to such Time as he shall think proper; he shall receive Ambassadors and other public Ministers; he shall take Care that the Laws be faithfully executed, and shall Commission all the Officers of the United States.

Section 4. The President, Vice President and all civil Officers of the United States, shall be removed from Office on Impeachment for, and Conviction of, treason, bribery, or other high Crimes and Misdemeanors.

ARTICLE III

Section 1. The judicial Power of the United States, shall be vested in one supreme Court, and in such inferior Courts as the Congress may from time to time ordain and establish. The Judges, both of the supreme and inferior Courts, shall hold their Offices during good Behaviour, and shall, at stated Times, receive for their Services, a Compensation, which shall not be diminished during their Continuance in Office.

Section 2. The judicial Power shall extend to all Cases, in Law and Equity, arising under this Constitution, the Laws of the United States, and Treaties made, or which shall be made, under their Authority;–to all Cases affecting Ambassadors, other public Ministers and Consuls;–to all Cases of admiralty and maritime Jurisdiction;–to Controversies to which the United States shall be a Party;–to Controversies between two or more States;–between a State and Citizens of another State;–between Citizens of different States;–between Citizens of the same State claiming Lands under Grants of different States, and between a State, or the Citizens thereof, and foreign States, Citizens or Subjects.

In all Cases affecting Ambassadors, other public Ministers and Consuls, and those in which a State shall be Party, the supreme Court shall have original Jurisdiction. In all the other Cases before mentioned, the supreme Court shall have appellate Jurisdiction, both as to Law and Fact, with such Exceptions, and under such Regulations as the Congress shall make.

The Trial of all Crimes, except in Cases of Impeachment, shall be by Jury; and such Trial shall be held in the State where the said Crimes shall have been committed; but when not committed within any State, the Trial shall be at such Place or Places as the Congress may by Law have directed.

Section 3. Treason; definition, proof and punishment. Treason against the United States, shall consist only in levying War against them, or in adhering to their Enemies, giving them Aid and Comfort. No Person shall be convicted of Treason unless on the Testimony of two Witnesses to the same overt Act, or on Confession in open Court.

The Congress shall have Power to declare the Punishment of Treason, but no Attainder of Treason shall work Corruption of Blood, or Forfeiture except during the Life of the Person attainted.

ARTICLE IV

Section 1. Full Faith and Credit shall be given in each State to the public Acts, Records, and judicial Proceedings of every other State. And the Congress may by general Laws prescribe the Manner in which such Acts, Records and Proceedings shall be proved, and the Effect thereof.

Section 2. The Citizens of each State shall be entitled to all Privileges and Immunities of Citizens in the several States.

A Person charged in any State with Treason, Felony, or other Crime, who shall flee from Justice, and be found in another State, shall on Demand of the executive Authority of the State from which he fled, be delivered up, to be removed to the State having Jurisdiction of the Crime.

No Person held to Service or Labour in one State, under the Laws thereof, escaping into another, shall, in Consequence of any Law or Regulation therein, be discharged from such Service or Labour, but shall be delivered up on Claim of the Party to whom such Service or Labour may be due.

Section 3. New States may be admitted by the Congress into this Union; but no new State shall be formed or erected within the Jurisdiction of any other State; nor any State be formed by the Junction of two or more States, or Parts of States, without the Consent of the Legislatures of the States concerned as well as of the Congress.

The Congress shall have Power to dispose of and make all needful Rules and Regulations respecting the Territory or other Property belonging to the United States; and nothing in this Constitution shall be so construed as to Prejudice any Claims of the United States, or of any particular State.

Section 4. The United States shall guarantee to every State in this Union a Republican Form of Government, and shall protect each of them against Invasion; and on Application of the Legislature, or of the Executive (when the Legislature cannot be convened) against domestic Violence.

ARTICLE V

The Congress, whenever two thirds of both Houses shall deem it necessary, shall propose Amendments to this Constitution, or, on the Application of the Legislatures of two thirds of the several States, shall call a Convention for proposing Amendments, which, in either Case, shall be valid to all Intents and Purposes, as Part of this Constitution, when ratified by the Legislatures of three fourths of the several States, or by Conventions in three fourths thereof, as the one or the other Mode of Ratification may be proposed by the Congress; Provided that no Amendment which may be made prior to the Year One thousand eight hundred and eight shall in any Manner affect the first and fourth Clauses in the Ninth Section of the first Article; and that no State, without its Consent, shall be deprived of it's equal Suffrage in the senate.

ARTICLE VI

All Debts contracted and Engagements entered into, before the Adoption of this Constitution, shall be as valid against the United States under this Constitution, as under the Confederation.

This Constitution, and the Laws of the United States which shall be made in Pursuance thereof; and all Treaties made, or which shall be made, under the Authority of the United States, shall be the supreme Law of the Land; and the Judges in every State shall be bound thereby, any Thing in the Constitution or Laws of any State to the Contrary notwithstanding.

The Senators and Representatives before mentioned, and the Members of the several State Legislatures, and all executive and judicial Officers, both of the United States and of the several States, shall be bound by Oath or Affirmation, to support this Constitution; but no religious Test shall ever be required as a Qualification to any Office or public Trust under the United States.

ARTICLE VII

The Ratification of the Conventions of nine States, shall be sufficient for the Establishment of this Constitution between the States so ratifying the Same

done in Convention by the Unanimous Consent of the States present the Seventeenth Day of September in the Year of our Lord one thousand seven hundred and Eighty-seven and of the Independence of the United States of America the Twelfth. In Witness whereof We have hereunto subscribed our Names. [names omitted]

AMENDMENT I

[Proposed by Congress Sept. 25, 1789; ratified December 15, 1791.]

Congress shall make no law respecting an establishment of religion, or prohibiting the free exercise thereof; or abridging the freedom of speech, or of the press; or the right of the people peaceably to assemble, and to petition the Government for a redress of grievances.

AMENDMENT II

[Proposed by Congress Sept. 25, 1789; ratified December 15, 1791.]

A well regulated Militia, being necessary to the security of a free State, the right of the people to keep and bear Arms, shall not be infringed.

AMENDMENT III

[Proposed by Congress Sept. 25, 1789; ratified December 15, 1791.]

No Soldier shall, in time of peace be quartered in any house, without the consent of the Owner, nor in time of war, but in a manner to be prescribed by law.

AMENDMENT IV

[Proposed by Congress Sept. 25, 1789; ratified December 15, 1791.]

The right of the people to be secure in their persons, houses, papers, and effects, against unreasonable searches and seizures, shall not be violated, and no Warrants shall issue, but upon probable cause, supported by Oath or affirmation, and particularly describing the place to be searched, and the persons or things to be seized.

AMENDMENT V

[Proposed by Congress Sept. 25, 1789; ratified December 15, 1791.]

No person shall be held to answer for a capital, or otherwise infamous crime, unless on a presentment or indictment of a Grand Jury, except in cases arising in the land or naval forces, or in the Militia, when in actual service in time of War or public danger; nor shall any person be subject for the same offence to be twice put in jeopardy of life or limb; nor shall be compelled in any criminal case to be a witness against himself, nor be deprived of life, liberty, or property, without due process of law; nor shall private property be taken for public use, without just compensation.

AMENDMENT VI

[Proposed by Congress Sept. 25, 1789; ratified December 15, 1791.]

In all criminal prosecutions, the accused shall enjoy the right to a speedy and public trial, by an impartial jury of the State and district wherein the crime shall have been committed, which district shall have been previously ascertained by law, and to be informed of the nature and cause of the accusation; to be confronted with the witnesses against him; to have compulsory process for obtaining witnesses in his favor, and to have the Assistance of Counsel for his defence.

AMENDMENT VII

[Proposed by Congress Sept. 25, 1789; ratified December 15, 1791.]

In Suits at common law, where the value in controversy shall exceed twenty dollars, the right of trial by jury shall be preserved, and no fact tried by a jury, shall be otherwise re- examined in any Court of the United States, than according to the rules of the common law.

AMENDMENT VIII
[Proposed by Congress Sept. 25, 1789; ratified December 15, 1791.]

Excessive bail shall not be required, nor excessive fines imposed, nor cruel and unusual punishments inflicted.

AMENDMENT IX
[Proposed by Congress Sept. 25, 1789; ratified December 15, 1791.]

The enumeration in the Constitution, of certain rights, shall not be construed to deny or disparage others retained by the people.

AMENDMENT X
[Proposed by Congress Sept. 25, 1789; ratified December 15, 1791.]

The powers not delegated to the United States by the Constitution, nor prohibited by it to the States, are reserved to the States respectively, or to the people.

AMENDMENT XI
[Proposed by Congress March 5, 1794; ratified January 8, 1798.]

The Judicial power of the United States shall not be construed to extend to any suit in law or equity, commenced or prosecuted against one of the United States by Citizens of another State, or by Citizens or Subjects of any Foreign State.

AMENDMENT XII
[Proposed by Congress December 12, 1803; ratified January 8, 1804.]

The Electors shall meet in their respective states and vote by ballot for President and Vice- President, one of whom, at least, shall not be an inhabitant of the same state with themselves; they shall name in their ballots the person voted for as President, and in distinct ballots the person voted for as Vice- President, and they shall make distinct lists of all persons voted for as President, and of all persons voted for as Vice-President, and of the number of votes for each, which lists they shall sign and certify, and transmit sealed to the seat of the government of the United States, directed to the President of the Senate;–The President of the Senate shall, in the presence of the Senate and House of Representatives, open all the certificates and the votes shall then be counted;–The person having the greatest number of votes for President, shall be the President, if such number be a majority of the whole number of Electors appointed; and if no person have such majority, then from the persons having the highest numbers not exceeding three on the list of those voted for as President, the House of Representatives shall choose immediately, by ballot, the President. But in choosing the President, the votes shall be taken by states, the representation from each state having one vote; a quorum for this purpose shall consist of a member or members from two- thirds of the states, and a majority of all the states shall be necessary to a choice. And if the House of Representatives shall not choose a President whenever the right of choice shall devolve upon them, before the fourth day of March next following, then the Vice-President shall act as President, as in the case of the death or other constitutional disability of the President.–The person having the greatest number of votes as Vice- President, shall be the Vice-President, if such number be a majority of the whole number of Electors appointed, and if no person have a majority, then from the two highest numbers on the list, the Senate shall choose the Vice-President; a quorum for the purpose shall consist of two-thirds of the whole number of Senators, and a majority of the whole number shall be necessary to a choice. But no person constitutionally ineligible to the office of President shall be eligible to that of Vice-President of the United States.

AMENDMENT XIII

[Proposed by Congress February 1, 1865; ratified December 18, 1865.]

Section 1. Neither slavery nor involuntary servitude, except as a punishment for crime whereof the party shall have been duly convicted, shall exist within the United States, or any place subject to their jurisdiction.

Section 2. Congress shall have power to enforce this article by appropriate legislation.

AMENDMENT XIV

[Proposed by Congress June 16, 1866; ratified July 23, 1868.]

Section 1. All persons born or naturalized in the United States, and subject to the jurisdiction thereof, are citizens of the United States and of the State wherein they reside. No State shall make or enforce any law which shall abridge the privileges or immunities of citizens of the United States; nor shall any State deprive any person of life, liberty, or property, without due process of law; nor deny to any person within its jurisdiction the equal protection of the laws.

Section 2. Representatives shall be apportioned among the several States according to their respective numbers, counting the whole number of persons in each State, excluding Indians not taxed. But when the right to vote at any election for the choice of electors for President and Vice President of the United States, Representatives in Congress, the Executive and Judicial officers of a State, or the members of the Legislature thereof, is denied to any of the male inhabitants of such State, being twenty-one years of age, and citizens of the United States, or in any way abridged, except for participation in rebellion, or other crime, the basis of representation therein shall be reduced in the proportion which the number of such male citizens shall bear to the whole number of male citizens twenty-one years of age in such State.

Section 3. No person shall be a Senator or Representative in Congress, or elector of President and Vice President, or hold any office, civil or military, under the United States, or under any State, who, having previously taken an oath, as a member of Congress, or as an officer of the United States, or as a member of any State legislature, or as an executive or judicial officer of any State, to support the Constitution of the United States, shall have engaged in insurrection or rebellion against the same, or given aid or comfort to the enemies thereof. But Congress may by a vote of two-thirds of each House, remove such disability.

Section 4. The validity of the public debt of the United States, authorized by law, including debts incurred for payment of pensions and bounties for services in suppressing insurrection or rebellion, shall not be questioned. But neither the United States nor any State shall assume or pay any debt or obligation incurred in aid of insurrection or rebellion against the United States, or any claim for the loss or emancipation of any slave; but all such debts, obligations and claims shall be held illegal and void.

Section 5. The Congress shall have power to enforce, by appropriate legislation, the provisions of this article.

AMENDMENT XV

[Proposed by Congress February 27, 1869; ratified March 30, 1870.]

Section 1. The right of citizens of the United States to vote shall not be denied or abridged by the United States or by any State on account of race, color, or previous condition of servitude.

Section 2. The Congress shall have power to enforce this article by appropriate legislation.

AMENDMENT XVI

[Proposed by Congress July 12, 1909; ratified February 25, 1913.]

The Congress shall have power to lay and collect taxes on incomes, from whatever source derived, without apportionment among the several States, and without regard to any census or enumeration.

AMENDMENT XVII

[Proposed by Congress May 16, 1912; ratified May 31, 1913.]

The Senate of the United States shall be composed of two Senators from each State, elected by the people thereof, for six years; and each Senator shall have one vote. The electors in each State shall have the qualifications requisite for electors of the most numerous branch of the State legislatures.

When vacancies happen in the representation of any State in the Senate, the executive authority of such State shall issue writs of election to fill such vacancies: Provided, That the legislature of any State may empower the executive thereof to make temporary appointments until the people fill the vacancies by election as the legislature may direct.

This amendment shall not be so construed as to affect the election or term of any Senator chosen before it becomes valid as part of the Constitution.

AMENDMENT XVIII

[Proposed by Congress Decmber 17, 1917; ratified January 29, 1918.]

Section 1. After one year from the ratification of this article the manufacture, sale, or transportation of intoxicating liquors within, the importation thereof into, or the exportation thereof from the United States and all territory subject to the jurisdiction thereof for beverage purposes is hereby prohibited.

Section 2. The Congress and the several States shall have concurrent power to enforce this article by appropriate legislation.

Section 3. This article shall be inoperative unless it shall have been ratified as an amendment to the Constitution by the legislatures of the several States, as provided in the Constitution, within seven years from the date of the submission hereof to the States by the Congress.

AMENDMENT XIX

[Proposed by Congress June 5, 1919; ratified August 26, 1920.]

The right of citizens of the United States to vote shall not be denied or abridged by the United States or by any State on account of sex.

Congress shall have power to enforce this article by appropriate legislation.

AMENDMENT XX

[Proposed by Congress March 3, 1932; ratified January 23, 1933.]

Section 1. The terms of the President and Vice President shall end at noon on the 20th day of January, and the terms of Senators and Representatives at noon on the 3d day of January, of the years in which such terms would have ended if this article had not been ratified; and the terms of their successors shall then begin.

Section 2. The Congress shall assemble at least once in every year, and such meeting shall begin at noon on the 3d day of January, unless they shall by law appoint a different day.

Section 3. If, at the time fixed for the beginning of the term of the President, the President elect shall have died, the Vice President elect shall become President. If a President shall not have been chosen before the time fixed for the beginning of his term, or if the President elect shall have failed to qualify, then the Vice President elect shall act as President until a President shall have qualified; and the Congress may by law provide for the case wherein neither a President elect nor a Vice President elect shall have qualified, declaring who shall then act as President, or the manner in which one who is to act shall be selected, and such person shall act accordingly until a President or Vice President shall have qualified.

Section 4. The Congress may by law provide for the case of the death of any of the persons from whom the House of Representatives may choose a President whenever the right of choice shall have devolved upon them, and for the case of the death of any of the persons from whom the Senate may choose a Vice President whenever the right of choice shall have devolved upon them.

Section 5. Sections 1 and 2 shall take effect on the 15th day of October following the ratification of this article.

Section 6. This article shall be inoperative unless it shall have been ratified as an amendment to the Constitution by the legislatures of three-fourths of the several States within seven years from the date of its submission.

AMENDMENT XXI

[Proposed by Congress February 20, 1933; ratified December 5, 1933.]

Section 1. The eighteenth article of amendment to the Constitution of the United States is hereby repealed.

Section 2. The transportation or importation into any State, Territory, or possession of the United States for delivery or use therein of intoxicating liquors, in violation of the laws thereof, is hereby prohibited.

Section 3. This article shall be inoperative unless it shall have been ratified as an amendment to the Constitution by conventions in the several States, as provided in the Constitution, within seven years from the date of the submission hereof to the States by the Congress.

AMENDMENT XXII

[Proposed by Congress March 24, 1947; ratified February 26, 1951.]

Section 1. No person shall be elected to the office of the president more than twice, and no person who has held the office of president, or acted as president, for more than two years of a term to which some other person was elected president shall be elected to the office of the president more than once. But this article shall not apply to any person holding the office of president when this article was proposed by the congress, and shall not prevent any person who may be holding the office of president, or acting as president, during the term within which this article becomes operative from holding the office of president or acting as president during the remainder of such term.

Section 2. This article shall be inoperative unless it shall have been ratified as an amendment to the constitution by the legislatures of three-fourths of the several states within seven years from the date of its submission to the states by the congress.

AMENDMENT XXIII

[Proposed by Congress June 16, 1960; ratified March 29, 1961.]

Section 1. The District constituting the seat of Government of the United States shall appoint in such manner as the Congress may direct:

A number of electors of President and Vice President equal to the whole number of Senators and Representatives in Congress to which the District would be entitled if it were a State, but in no event more than the least populous State; they shall be in addition to those appointed by the States, but they shall be considered, for the purposes of the election of President and Vice President, to be electors appointed by a State; and they shall meet in the District and perform such duties as provided by the twelfth article of amendment.

Section 2. The Congress shall have power to enforce this article by appropriate legislation.

AMENDMENT XXIV

[Proposed by Congress August 27, 1962; ratified January 23, 1964.]

Section 1. The right of citizens of the United States to vote in any primary or other election for President or Vice President, for electors for President or Vice President, or for Senator or Representative in Congress, shall not be denied or abridged by the United States or any State by reason of failure to pay any poll tax or other tax.

Section 2. The Congress shall have power to enforce this article by appropriate legislation.

AMENDMENT XXV

[Proposed by Congress July 6, 1965; ratified February 10, 1967.]

Section 1. In case of the removal of the President from office or of his death or resignation, the Vice President shall become President.

Section 2. Whenever there is a vacancy in the office of the Vice President, the President shall nominate a Vice President who shall take office upon confirmation by a majority vote of both Houses of Congress.

Section 3. Whenever the President transmits to the President pro tempore of the Senate and the Speaker of the House of Representatives his written declaration that he is unable to discharge the powers and duties of his office, and until he transmits to them a written declaration to the contrary, such powers and duties shall be discharged by the Vice President as Acting President.

Section 4. Whenever the Vice President and a majority of either the principal officers of the executive departments or of such other body as Congress may by law provide, transmit to the President pro tempore of the Senate and the Speaker of the House of Representatives their written declaration that the President is unable to discharge the powers and duties of his office, the Vice President shall immediately assume the powers and duties of the office as Acting President.

Thereafter, when the President transmits to the President pro tempore of the Senate and the Speaker of the House of Representatives his written declaration that no inability exists, he shall resume the powers and duties of his office unless the Vice President and a majority of either the principal officers of the executive department or of such other body as Congress may by law provide, transmit within four days to the President pro tempore of the Senate and the Speaker of the House of Representatives their written declaration that the President is unable to discharge the powers and duties of his office. Thereupon Congress shall decide the issue, assembling within forty-eight hours for that purpose if not in session. If the Congress, within twenty-one days after receipt of the latter written declaration, or, if Congress is not in session, within twenty-one days after Congress is required to assemble, determines by two-thirds vote of both Houses that the President is unable to discharge the powers and duties of his office, the Vice President shall continue to discharge the same as Acting President; otherwise, the President shall resume the powers and duties of his office.

AMENDMENT XXVI

[Proposed by Congress March 23, 1971; ratified June 30, 1971.]

Section 1. The right of citizens of the United States, who are eighteen years of age or older, to vote shall not be denied or abridged by the United States or by any State on account of age.

Section 2. The Congress shall have power to enforce this article by appropriate legislation.

AMENDMENT XXVII

[Proposed by Congress 1790; ratified May 7, 1992]

No law varying the compensation for the services of Senators and Representatives shall take effect until an election of Representatives shall have intervened.

INDEX OF CASES

A

B

C

G

H

I

J

K

T

U

V

W

NOTES TO CHAPTER I

[1] see Cicero, *Paradox and De Officiis*. Wolfgang W. Friedmann, *Legal Theory*. 5th ed., (New York: Columbia University Press.1967).

[2] Jerome Frank. *Law and the Modern Mind* (New York: Brentano's, Inc., 1930), p. 32. Emphasis added.

[3] Roscoe Pound. *Sources and Forms of Law* (Notre Dame. Indiana: University of Notre Dame Press, 1946), p. 30; Harry H. Wellington. *Interpreting the Constitution: The Supreme Court and the Process of Adjudication* (New Haven: Yale University Press,1990), pp. 77-80.

[4] Roscoe Pound. *The Spirit of the Common Law* (Boston: Marshall Jones Company, 1921).

[5] Ibid., p. 7.

[6] Henry J. Abraham. *Justices & Presidents.- A Political History of Appointments to the Supreme Court* (New York: Oxford University Press, 1992), pp. 3-9.

NOTES TO CHAPTER II

[1] For a detailed description see the *United States Government Organization Manual* 1991-1992 (Washington, D.C.: U.S. Government Printing Office), pp. 43-56.

[2] *Marbury v. Madison*, 1 Cranch 137 (1803). To examine the history and the establishing concepts since the adoption of the Constitution of the United States and the structure created therefrom, examine the following sources: Kermit Hall, William M. Wiecek, and Paul Finkelman. *American Legal History* (New York: Oxford University Press, 1991); Robert H. Horwitz (ed.) *The Moral Foundations of the American Republic*, 2nd edition, (Charlottesville, VA: The University Press of Virginia, 1979).; Peter F. Nandulli (ed.) *The Constitution and American Political Development* (Urbana, IL: The University of Illinois Press, 1992); and Mark Silverstein. *Constitutional Faiths: Felix Frankfurter and Hugo Black*. Ithica, NY: Cornell University Press, 1984).

[3] Spaeth. *An Introduction to Supreme Court Decision Making* (Scranton: Chandler Publishing Company, 1965). p.2; Lawrence Baum. *The Supreme Court* (D.C: Congressional Quarterly Press, 1992) 4th edition, pp. 8-12.

NOTES TO CHAPTER III

[1] See Robert J. Steamer. *Chief Justice: Leadership and the Supreme Court* (Columbia, S.C.: University of South Carolina Press, 1990), pp. 9-12.

[2] Speech made on November 2, 1968, as cited in Congressional Quarterly, *Weekly Report*. May 23, 1969, p. 98. A fine study of the relationship between the Executive and Judicial Branches is provided by Henry J. Abraham in his *Justices and Presidents: A Political History of Appointments to the Supreme Court*, 3rd edition, (New York: Oxford University Press, 1992).

[3] For an excellent analysis of the Bork hearings see Professor Philip Bobbitt's *Constitutional Interpretation* (Oxford, UK: Blackwell Press, 1991) chap.4, pp.83-108. For Judge Bork's own view, see Robert Bork, *The Tempting of America: The Political Seduction of the Law* (New York: Free Press, 1990).

[4] See, for example, Stephen L. Carter. "Foreword" in Lani Guinier. *The Tyranny of the Majority*. (New York: The Free Press, 1994).

[5] Felix Frankfurter. "Some Observations on the Nature of the Judicial Process of Supreme Court Litigation," 98 *Proceedings of the American Philosophical Society* 233 (1954).

[6] *The Roosevelt Court., A Study in Judicial Politics and Values*. 1937-1947 (New York: The Macmillan Company, 1948).

[7] Some of the classic works of the behavioralist school include: Glendon A. Schubert, *Constitutional Politics: The Political Behavior of Supreme Court Justices and the Constitutional Policies That They Make* (New York: Hold, Rinehart and Winston, Inc., 1960); Walter F. Murphy and C.H. Pritchett, *Courts, Judges, and Politics* (New York: Random House, 1961); and John D. Sprague, *Voting Patterns of the United States Supreme Court: Cases in Federalism 1589-1959* (Indianapolis: The Bobbs-Merrill Company, Inc., 1968).

[8] See "Constitutional Interpretation" in the *Encyclopedia of the American Judicial System* (New York: Charles Scribner's Sons, 1987) pp. 972-986.

[9] "Our 'Legislative' Courts." *The Southwestern Social Science Quarterly*, 46, 1 (June, 1965), p. 11; also see, Christopher Wolfe. *The Rise of Modern Judicial Review* (New York: Basic Books, 1986); and Robert Bork. *The Tempting of America* (New York: Free Press, 1990).

[10] *Ibid.*; also, Sylvia Snowiss. *Judicial Review and the Law of the Constitution* (New Haven: Yale University Press, 1990).

[11] *Ibid.*, p. 12; also see, Raoul Berger. *Government by the Judiciary: The Transformation of the Fourteenth Amendment,* 2nd edition (Indianapolis: Liberty Fund, 1997).

[12] "Rejoinder to 'Our Legislative Courts' ." *The Southwestern Social Science Quarterly*. 46. 1 (June 1965), p. 16; also see, Ronald Dworkin, *Law's Empire* (Cambridge, MA: Belknop Press, 1986).

[13] *Ibid.*, p. 18; see, Albert P. Melone and George Mace. *Judicial Review and American Democracy* (Ames, IA: Iowa State Press, 1988).

[14] *Ibid.*, pp. 18-19; also see *Judicial Review and the National Political Process* (Chicago: The University of Chicago Press, 1980) by Professor Jesse H. Choper.

[15] 'The Role of Oral Argument." Alan F. Westin (ed.) *The Supreme Court: Views from Inside.* (New York: W.W. Norton & Company. Inc.. 1961). p. 57; Lawrence Baum. *American Courts: Process & Policy,* 2nd edition (Boston: Houghton Mifflin Co., 1990), pp. 65-69.

[16] *Ibid.*, pp. 59.60.

[17] In 1965. the Court refused to review a lower court's decision which, in effect, invalidated the practice of voluntary prayers, such as moments of silence. or children's prayers each morning in public school classrooms. *Stein v. Oshinsky*, 382 U.S. 957; in *Wallace v. Jaffree* (1985), the Court invalidated an Alabama law requiring a "moment of Silence" in public school classrooms for the purpose of allowing "willing" students to pray to "Almighty God:" and, in 1992 it reaffirmed the Vitale decision in *Lee v. Weisman* with respect to a public prayer at a high school graduation.

[18] See Randall W. Bland, *Private Pressure on Public Law* (D.C.: University Press of America, 1992), Revised Edition, pp. 180-184.

NOTES TO CHAPTER IV

[1] See George W. Carey. The Federalist.- Design for a Constitutional Republic (Urbana: University of Illinois Press. 1989), p. 133-134.

[2] It should be noted at this point that the decision of the Court was beclouded by the fact that Justices Reed and Burton concurred in the opinion of Justice Frankfurter, that reapportionment was nonjusticiable: while Justice Rutledge felt that it was justiciable but concurred in the result of the dismissal in this case. The

three dissenting Justices Black, Douglas and Murphy, were in agreement that it was a matter subject to review by the Conn. Refer to Alexander M Bickel. The Least Dangerous Branch: The Supreme Court at the Bar of Politics, 2nd Edition (New Haven: Yale University Press, 1986), pp. 189-196.

NOTES TO CHAPTER V

[1] Thomas J. Norton. *The Constitution of the United States: Its Sources and its Application*, (New York: Committee for Constitutional Government, Inc., 1965) p. 226: For the philosophical foundations of federal relations between the national and state governments, see the superb analysis by Professor George W. Carey of Georgetown University in *The Federalist: Design for a Constitutional Republic* (Urbana & Chicago: University of Illinois Press, 1989), pp. 107-125.

[2] Randall W. Bland. *The Black Robe and The Bald Eagle*. Vol. 1. (San Francisco and London: Austin and Winfield, 1996) p. 13.

NOTES TO CHAPTER VI

[1] For an acute constitutional dissection and analysis of the terms directed at the Presidential office, refer to Edward S. Corwin. *The President: Office and Powers*, Fifth revised edition by Randall W. Bland, *et. al.* (New York: The New York University Press, 1984).

[2] This truly significant question is *difficult* to answer since the drafters of Articles I and II gave certain powers to *each* political branch in formulating foreign policy for the United States. Consequently, there has been a great deal of misunderstanding on the part of, not only citizens, but Presidents and members of Congress as well. For a comprehensive treatment see, Randall Bland and David Adler, *The Supreme Court and the Foreign Policy of the United States Since 1789.* (Lawrence, KS: The University Press of Kansas, 1993).

[3] 0ther significant recent studies of the constitutional relationship between Congress and the President on dealing with external affairs include: Cecil V. Crabb. Jr. and Pat M. Holt. invitation to Struggle. *Congress, the President, and Foreign Policy.* 4th Edition (Washington, D. C.: Congressional Quarterly, Inc. 1992); Louis Henkin. *Constitutionalism, Democracy, and Foreign Affairs* (New York: Columbia University Press, 1990); Abram D. Sofaer. *War, Foreign Affairs, and Constitutional Power* (Cambridge, MA: Ballinger, 1976); and Robert F. Turner. *Repealing the War Power Resolution: Restoring the Rule of Law in U.S. Foreign Policy.* (Washington, D.C: Brassey's Plublishing, 1991).

NOTES TO CHAPTER VII

[1] See *Black's Law Dictionary*, 6th edition (St. Paul, Minnesota: West Publishiing Company, 1990) p. 322.

[2] At the Constitutional Convention in Philadelphia, Rufus King led a one-man crusade for the adoption of this clause for the protection of American property. On September 14, 1787, when King's prohibition came to the floor for a vote, Clinton Rossiter noted that, the members "accepted [lit] without a murmur, pausing only to tighten it slightly." (emphasis added). See *1787: The Grand Convention* (New York: W.W. Norton & Company. 1987) p. 230.

NOTES TO CHAPTER VIII

[1] In the dreadful decision of *Plessy v. Ferguson* (1896), the Supreme Court upheld a Louisiana law requiring "separate but equal" accommodations for all white and colored railroad passengers as not violative of either the Thirteenth or the Fourteenth Amendments. Viewing this as a social, rather than political problem, the court cited the dual school system in the District of Columbia as a proper example justifying their decision. See Richard Kluger *Simple Justice: The History of Brown v. Board of Education and Black America's Struggle for Equality* (New York, 1976), pp, 173-174.

[2] For a full examination of this transitional period and an analysis of the various factors involved, see Bland. *Private Pressure on Public Law.* (1973), pp, 37-44. also, Vincent Gordon Harding, "Wrestling toward the Dawn." in David Thelen (ed.) *The Constitution and American Life* (Itliaca, NY: Cornell University Press, 1988), pp. 58-79.

NOTES TO CHAPTER IX

[1] Thomas J. Norton. *The Constitution of the United States: Its Sources and Its Application*. (New York: Committee for Constitutional Government, Inc., 1965) p. 226.

[2] As a matter of fact, the Court, while elevating the importance of "substantive due process," began to retreat in a series of cases from its protection of procedural rights; see *Hurtado v. California* (1884), *Maxwell v. Dow* (1900), and *Twining v. New Jersey* (1908).

[3] As cited in Bland, et al. *Practicing Political Science: An Introduction to the Study of Politics*. (Sarasota, Florida: Omni Press, Inc. 1975) p. 30.

[4] There were some notable occasions during the period on which the Court upheld the state regulation. In *Muller v. Oregon* (1908) the Court was noticeably savaged by the arguments and brief submitted by Louis D. Brandeis, who defended the Oregon law limiting the employment of women to ten hours a day. Known today as the "Brandeis Brief," the written document relied almost solely on sociological and economic data, rather than legal or historical arguments, to show the harmful effects of excessive physical work on women; also see *Bunting v. Oregon* (1917) and *Stettler v. OHara* (1917).

NOTES TO CHAPTER X

[1] *Ex post facto* laws are retroactive *criminal* statutes; there is no similar prohibition on retroactive civil laws. *Bills of Attainder* are legislative enactments which punish persons without providing for judicial process.

[2] It should also be mentioned that Justice Felix Frankfurter, the author of the first flag-salute decision, *Minersville School District v. Gobitis* (1940), wrote a stinging dissenting opinion which could serve as a model for his position on judicial restraint; see Silverstein, *Constitutional Faith.* (Ithaca: Cornell Press, 1984) pp. 148, 191.

NOTES TO CHAPTER XI

[1] For excellent discussions of the abortion decisions (1973-1992) see the following studies: David Thelen (ed.) *The Constitution and American Life* (Ithaca: Cornell University Press, 1988); Randy Barnett (ed.) *The Right Retained by the People: The Historv and Meaning of the Ninth Amendment* (Fairfort. VA: George Mason University Press. 1989). and Mary C. Segers, "Murray, American Pluralism and the Abortion Controversy" in Robert P. Hunt and Kenneth L. Grasso (eds.) *John Courtney Murray and The American Civil Conversation.* (Grand Rapids: Eandsnians Publishing, 1992).

NOTES TO CHAPTER XII

[1] Nor is such illegally seized evidence barred from federal civil cases. See United States v. janis, 428 U.S. 433 (1976).

[2] 401 U.S. 222 (1971). Compare the decision in *Nix v. Whiteside*, 475 U.S. 157.

[3] See the Guide to Patterson's The American Presidency (New York: McGraw Hill Publishing Company, 1990), "The President, the Supreme Court and Foreign Policy Leadership," p. 123.

NOTES TO CHAPTER XIII

[1] For an in-depth explanation of *Brown* and the other school desegregation cases see Richard Kluger, *Simple Justice: The History of Brown* v. *Board of Education and Black America's Struggle for Equality* (New York: Alfred A. Knopf, 1976); for the earlier "seedtime" for the education cases, examine Randall Bland, "The Collective Central Struggle for Negro Rights: 1915-1940", North Carolina Law Journal, Spring 1970, pp. 81-98.

[2] For a collective effort at painting Thurgood Marshal's "judicial portrait" refer to Roger Goldman with David Gallen (Eds.) *Thurgood Marshall: Justice for All* (New York: Carroll & Graf Publishers, Inc., 1992); also refer to Randall Bland, "Justice Thurgood Marshall: An Analysis of His First Years on the Court," North Carolina Central Law Journal, Spring 1973, pp. 183-202; and Private Pressure on Public Law, p. 83.

www.ingramcontent.com/pod-product-compliance
Ingram Content Group UK Ltd.
Pitfield, Milton Keynes, MK11 3LW, UK
UKHW021035150926
475561UK00003B/118

9 781572 920910